P.O. Box 7150
Austin, Texas 78713
www.greenbeltpress.com

Print ISBN: 978-1-953359-00-1
E-book ISBN: 978-1-953359-02-5

Manufactured in Austin, Texas, USA

Business Law

17th Edition

John R. Allison
Robert A. Prentice

CONTENTS

PART I
THE LEGAL ENVIRONMENT OF BUSINESS

CHAPTER 1

NATURE AND SOURCES OF LAW

- The Necessity of Law and Ethics
- Law and Business Strategy
- Law As a Subject of Study
- What Is the Law?
- Requisites of a Legal System
- Some Classifications of Law
- Law, Justice, and Ethics
- Law, Globalization, and Science & Technology

A.P. Herbert once wrote: "The general mass, if they consider the law at all, regard it as they regard some monster in the zoo. It is odd, it is extraordinary; but there it is, they have known it all their lives, they suppose that there must be some good reason for it, and accept it as inevitable and natural." (UNCOMMON LAW (1936)).

THE NECESSITY OF LAW AND ETHICS

Benjamin Rush wrote that "where there is no law, there is no liberty," and even a short thought experiment about living in a lawless society should make it obvious that this is true. Additionally, law provide a crucial predicate to economic growth. Even as strong an opponent of government regulation as economist Friedrich Hayek remarked that under no economic system that could be imagined would a functioning legal system not be a critical component. In his book THE MYSTERY OF CAPITAL (2000), Hernando de Soto argued that perhaps the most important advantage that developed economies enjoy over developing economies is a functioning legal system that can with relative efficiency enforce a body of laws that produce order and facilitate economic exchange. More recently, Robert Cooter and Hans-Berndt Schafer in SOLOMON'S KNOT (2012) noted the importance of innovation to economic development and gave several recent examples of "countries surg[ing] ahead where improved laws effectively supported innovative business ventures, and countries lag[ing] where law failed to provide this support." According to Cooter and Schafer, "[t]he types of law needed to protect the makers of wealth include property, contracts, crimes, finance, corporations, regulation, antitrust, labor law, taxation, and torts." In this text, we will study all those types of law, except for taxation, as well as many more.

Ethics evolved for the same purpose that law evolved—to enable people to live together in groups. In societies where people tend to act ethically, that is, in accordance with general societal standards for right and wrong behavior, there is trust. For obvious reasons, the level of trust in a society is strongly and positively correlated with economic growth. Ethical societies tend to be prosperous and safe. Societies where ethical rules are observed mainly in the breach tend to be poor, chaotic, and unsafe. (Note that in this book we will, to the consternation of some, use the words "ethics" and "morals" interchangeably for when people do the right thing, it is common to say both that they acted ethically and that they acted morally.)

WHAT IS THE LAW?

Ever since the law began to take form, scholars have spent impressive amounts of time and thought analyzing its purposes and defining what it is and what it ought to be—in short, fitting it into a philosophic scheme of one form or another. Although space does not permit inclusion of even the major essays in which these philosophers defend their respective views, their conclusions provide us with useful observations about the nature of law. Consider, for example, the following:

> We have been told by Plato that law is a form of social control, an instrument of the good life, the way to the discovery of reality, the true reality of the social structure; by Aristotle that it is a rule of conduct, a contract, an ideal of reason, a rule of decision, a form of order; by Cicero that it is the agreement of reason and nature, the distinction between the just and the unjust, a command or prohibition; by Aquinas that it is an ordinance of reason for the common good, made by him who has care of the community, and promulgated [thereby]; by Bacon that certainty is the prime necessity of law; by Hobbes that law is the command of the sovereign; by Spinoza that it is a plan of life; by

Leibniz that its character is determined by the structure of society; by Locke that it is a norm established by the commonwealth; by Hume that it is a body of precepts; by Kant that it is a harmonizing of wills by means of universal rules in the interests of freedom; by Fichte that it is a relation between human beings; by Hegel that it is an unfolding or realizing of the idea of right. (Huntington Cairns, Legal Philosophy from Plato to Hegel (1949)).

Although these early writers substantially agree as to the general purpose of law—the ensuring of orderliness to all human activity—their definitions of the term vary considerably. Today there is still no definition of law that has universal approval, even in legal circles—a fact that is no doubt attributable to its inherent breadth. One can understand how very broad the law is by considering just these few widely varying matters with which the law must deal: (1) the standards of care required of an engineer designing a self-driving car, (2) the determination of whether a worker in the modern "gig economy" is an employee entitled to various benefits or an independent contractor who is not so entitled, and (3) the determination of the circumstances under which a company is liable for bullying that occurs in the workplace.

A brief comment about sources of law is in order at this early point. In our legal system (and in most others throughout the world), there are primary and secondary sources. Primary sources, which contain legally binding rules and procedures, include federal and state constitutions, statutes (legislative enactments), administrative agency regulations, and court decisions; also included are federal treaties and city ordinances. Secondary sources summarize and explain the law, and sometimes criticize and suggest changes in it. Such sources are not legally binding, but are frequently referred to and used by courts, administrative agencies, legislative staff members, and practicing attorneys as aids in determining what the law is or should be. Secondary sources include research articles in academic legal periodicals, restatements (which consist of summaries of and commentary on specific subject areas of law by experts in those areas), legal texts and encyclopedias, and others.

REQUISITES OF A LEGAL SYSTEM

For a legal system to function properly, particularly within a democratic government such as ours, it must command the respect of the great majority of people governed by it. To do so, the legal rules that compose it must, as a practical matter, possess certain characteristics. They must be (1) relatively certain, (2) relatively flexible, (3) known or knowable, and (4) apparently reasonable.

In the following chapters we consider these requirements more fully and determine the extent to which our legal system satisfies them. For the moment, we give brief descriptions of each of the four.

Certainty

One essential element of a stable society is reasonable certainty about its laws, not only at a given moment but over long periods of time. Many of our activities, particularly business activities, are based on the assumption that legal principles will remain stable into the foreseeable future. If this were not so, chaos would result. For example, no television network would enter into a contract with a professional football league, under which it is to pay millions of dollars for the right to televise league games, if it were not reasonably sure that the law would compel the league to live up to its contractual obligations or to pay damages if it did not. And no lawyer would advise a client on a contemplated course of action without similar assurances.

Because of these considerations, the courts (and to a lesser extent the legislatures) are generally reluctant to overturn principles that have been part of the law for any appreciable length of time. This is not to say, of course, that the law is static. Many areas of American law are dramatically different than they were 50 or even 25 years ago. However, most of these changes resulted from a series of modifications of existing principles based on experience rather than from an abrupt reversal of them.

Flexibility

In any nation, particularly a highly industrialized one such as the United States, societal changes occur with accelerating (almost dismaying) rapidity. Each change presents new legal problems that must be resolved without undue delay. This necessity was recognized by Justice Cardozo when he wrote that "the law, like the traveler, must be ready for the morrow." (Benjamin N. Cardozo, THE GROWTH OF THE LAW (1924)).

Some problems are simply the result of scientific and technological advances. Before Orville and Wilbur Wright's day, for example, it was a well-established principle that landowners had unlimited rights to the airspace above their property, any invasion of which constituted a *trespass*—a wrongful entry. But when the courts became convinced that the flying machine was here to stay, the utter impracticality of this view became apparent and owners' rights were subsequently limited to a "reasonable use" of their airspace. Creation of the Internet required a rethinking of vast bodies of law.

Other novel problems result from changing methods of doing business or from shifting attitudes and ethical views. Recent examples of the former are the proliferating use of the business franchise and of the general credit card. Attitudinal changes involve such questions as the proper ends of government, the propriety of gay marriage, and the circumstances in which abortions should be permitted.

Some of these problems, of course, require solutions that are more political than legal in nature. This is particularly true where large numbers of the citizenry are faced with a common problem, such as the many difficulties faced by disabled persons in overcoming stereotypical attitudes and physical barriers, and where the alleviation of the problem may well be thought to constitute a legitimate function of either the state or federal government. The passage by Congress of the Americans with Disabilities Act of 1990 is an example of an attempted solution at the federal level of this particular problem.

Regardless of political considerations, however, many problems (particularly those involving disputes between individuals and companies) can be settled only through the judicial process—that is, by one of the parties instituting legal action against the other. The duty to arrive at a final solution in all such cases falls squarely on the courts, no matter how novel or varied the issues. Although we are very fortunate in the U.S. to be able to resort to courts to enforce legal rights, court actions should always be viewed as a last resort. Negotiated settlements, mediation, arbitration, and other non-judicial dispute resolution techniques also play an important role in our society.

Knowability

© **2020 John R. Allison & Robert A. Prentice**

One of the basic assumptions underlying a democracy—and, in fact, almost every form of government—is that the great majority of its citizens are going to obey its laws voluntarily. It hardly need be said that obedience requires some knowledge of the rules, or at least a reasonable means of acquiring this knowledge, on the part of the governed. No one, not even a lawyer, "knows" all the law or all the rules that make up a single branch of law; that could never be required. But it is necessary for persons who need legal advice to have access to experts on the rules—lawyers. It is equally necessary that the law be in such form that lawyers can determine their clients' positions with reasonable certainty to recommend the most advantageous courses of action.

Reasonableness

Most citizens abide by the law. Many do so even when they are not in sympathy with a particular rule, out of a sense of responsibility, a feeling that it is their civic duty, like it or not; others, no doubt, do so simply through fear of getting caught if they do not. But by and large the rules have to appear reasonable to the great majority of the people if they are going to be obeyed for long. The so-called Prohibition Amendment, which met with such wholesale violation that it was repealed in 1933, is the classic example of a rule lacking widespread acceptance. Closely allied with the idea of reasonableness is the requirement that the rules reflect, and adapt to, changing views of morality and justice.

SOME CLASSIFICATIONS OF LAW

Although the lawmaking and adjudicatory processes are the major concern in Part I, the products that result from the lawmaking process—the rules themselves and the bodies of law that they makeup—must not be overlooked. At the outset, particularly, it is useful to recognize some of the more important *classifications of law*.

Subject Matter

One way of classifying all the law in the United States is on the basis of the subject matter to which it relates. Fifteen or twenty branches or subjects are of particular importance, among them:

- Administrative law
- Agency law
- Constitutional law
- Contracts
- Corporation law
- Criminal law
- Domestic relations
- Evidence
- Partnerships
- Intellectual property
- Personal property
- Real property
- Sales
- Torts
- Wills and estates

Federal and State Law

Another way of categorizing all law in this country is on the basis of the governmental unit from which it arises. On this basis, all law may be said to be either *federal law* or *state law.* Although there are some very important areas of federal law, as we shall see later, the great bulk of our law is state (or "local") law. Virtually all the subjects in the preceding list, for example, are within the jurisdiction of the individual states. Thus, it is correct to say that there are 50 bodies of contract law in the United States, 50 bodies of corporation law, and so on. But this is not as bewildering as it appears, because the rules that constitute a given branch of law in each state substantially parallel those that exist in the other states—particularly in regard to common law subjects.

Common Law (Case Law) and Statutory Law

The term *common law* has several different meanings. It sometimes is used to refer only to the judge-made rules in effect in England at an early time—the "ancient unwritten law of England." It sometimes is also used to refer only to those judge-made rules of England that were subsequently adopted by the states in this country. In this text, however, we define the term more broadly to mean *all the rules and principles currently existing in any state, regardless of their historical origin, that result from judicial decisions in those areas of law where legislatures have not enacted statutes establishing definitive rules.* This type of law, examined further in Chapter 4, is frequently referred to as case law or judge-made law. Also, the term common law is sometimes used to refer to an entire legal system, the English Common Law, a system that prevails in countries having had an early English presence. The subjects of contracts, torts, and agency are dominated by common law rules.

The term *statutory law,* by contrast, is generally used to refer to the state and federal statutes in effect at a given time—that is, rules that have been formally adopted by legislative bodies rather than by the courts. Statutory law is comprised of state and federal constitutions, city ordinances, and even treaties. Local governments such as cities have authority to enact laws only to the extent authorized by state legislation. As we will see in Chapter 4, courts are normally expected to apply statutory law only according to the exact wording of the statutes. The precise meaning of particular statutory language can sometimes be determined and applied to particular facts, however, can only accomplished through interpretation of that language by a court. Corporation law, criminal law, tax law, and a few other areas are primarily statutory, subject, of course, to judicial interpretation when absolutely necessary for specific application of the law.

Civil and Criminal Law

Civil Law

The most common types of controversies are civil actions—that is, actions in which the parties bringing the suits (the *plaintiffs*) are seeking to enforce private obligations or duties against the other parties (the *defendants*). *Civil laws,* then, are all those laws that spell out the rights and duties existing among individuals, business firms, and sometimes even government agencies. Contract law, tort law, and sales law all fall within the civil category.

The usual remedy that the plaintiff is seeking in a civil suit is *damages*—a sum of money roughly equivalent to the loss they suffered as a result of the defendant's wrong. Another civil remedy is the *injunction*—a court decree ordering the defendant to do or not to do some particular thing. The term civil law is also sometimes used in a broader sense to refer to an entire legal system, the Roman Civil Law, which is based originally on Roman law and more recently on France's Napoleonic Code from the early 1800s. This system is used in countries that do not base their law on either the English Common Law or on Islamic law.

Criminal Law

Criminal law, in contrast to civil law, comprises those statutes by which a state or the federal government prohibits specified kinds of conduct and which additionally provide for the imposition of *fines or imprisonment* on persons convicted of violating them. Criminal cases are always brought by the government whose law has allegedly been violated. In enacting criminal statutes, a legislature is saying that certain activities are so inherently inimical to the public good that they constitute wrongs against organized society as a whole.

In addition to the nature of the liability imposed, criminal prosecutions also differ from civil lawsuits in another significant respect: In a criminal action it is necessary that the government's case be proved "beyond a reasonable doubt," whereas in civil actions the plaintiff—the person bringing the suit—need prove his or her allegations only by "a preponderance of the evidence." *Beyond a reasonable doubt* means exactly what it says. *Preponderance of the evidence* means *more likely than not*.

Crimes are either felonies or misdemeanors, depending on the severity of the penalty that the statute prescribes. A *felony*, the more serious of the two, is usually defined as a crime for which the legislature has provided a maximum penalty of either imprisonment for more than one year or death. Examples of felonies are murder, arson, rape, fraud involving substantial loss to victims, and so on. *Misdemeanors* are all crimes carrying lesser penalties, such as most traffic offenses, very minor theft that does not involve violence, and so on.

Finally, it should be noted that some wrongful acts are of a dual nature, subjecting the wrongdoer, at least potentially, to both criminal and civil penalties. For example, if X steals Y's car, the state could bring a criminal action against X, and Y could also bring a civil action to recover damages arising from the theft.

Public and Private Law

Some branches of law deal more directly with the relationship between the government and the individual than do others. On the basis of the degree to which this relationship is involved, law is occasionally classified as *public law* or *private law*.

When an area of law is directly concerned with the government-individual (or government-business) relationship, it falls within the public law designation. Subjects that are most clearly of this nature are criminal law, constitutional law, and administrative law. Because criminal laws deal with acts that are prohibited by a government itself, the violation of which is a ''wrong against the state,'' such laws more directly affect the government-individual relationship than do any of the other laws. To the extent that our federal Constitution contains provisions substantially guaranteeing that certain rights of the individual or business cannot be invaded by federal and state government activities, the subject of constitutional law falls within the same category. Administrative law—comprising the principles that govern the procedures and activities of government boards and commissions—is of similar nature, in that such agencies are also concerned with the enforcement of certain state and federal statutes (and regulations promulgated thereunder) against individual citizens and businesses.

Many other areas of law, which are primarily concerned with the creation and enforcement of the rights of one individual against another, fall within the private law category. Although a state is indeed concerned that all its laws be properly enforced, even when individuals' or business firms' rights alone are being adjudicated, the concern in these areas is distinctly secondary to the interests of the parties themselves. There also are many areas of law that are of a mixed public-private nature; examples include state or federal statutes that regulate business activities and also create rights and obligations that individuals and businesses themselves may enforce.

It should be obvious that these many different ways of classifying law are often overlapping. As in most other situations, classifications serve only as aids to assist understanding of a subject, and nothing more.

LAW AND BUSINESS STRATEGY

The successful manager considers all aspects of the firm's competitive environment. Just as the pricing practices of competitors must be taken into account in formulating long- and short-term strategies, for example, so must the legal environment of business be considered. The successful manager's toolbox includes a facility for factoring legal and regulatory matters into strategic plans. As Michael Porter noted in his landmark book COMPETITIVE STRATEGY (1998), "no structural analysis is complete without a diagnosis how present and future government policy, at all levels, will affect structural conditions."

For example, in considering whether to enter a foreign market, a manager must determine whether contracts entered into in that nation can be enforced, whether intellectual property such as trade secrets, trademarks, and patents can be protected, and whether taxation and the threat of expropriation present intolerable risks.

Michigan professor George Siedel has pointed out in his book USING THE LAW FOR COMPETITIVE ADVANTAGE (2002) that "because law is an untapped source of competitive advantage that will continue to be misunderstood by many managers, selected companies should be able to leverage their legal resources into a source of competitive advantage that is sustainable over the long term." In the modern business world, it is critical that managers be "legally astute," as Professor Connie Bagley of the Yale School of Management pointed out in her book WINNING LEGALLY (2005).

In their article *Finding the Right Corporate Legal Strategy,* MIT SLOAN MANAGEMENT REVIEW, Fall 2014, professors Bird and Orozco place business legal strategies into five categories.

Avoidance

Sometimes, especially when managers have only a rudimentary understanding of legal and regulatory dynamics, they simply view the law as a costly and somewhat random barrier to business. They either comply with the law if that is cheap and feasible, or look to avoid it if not. For example, when the City of El Paso passed an ordinance that put a cap on interest rates that firms could charge when they made car loans, TitleMax simply required their El Paso customers to drive to nearby Canutillo, TX, where TitleMax could make loans unencumbered by such an ordinance.

Another example of an avoidance strategy underlies the modest beginnings of one of

America's most successful airlines. In 1967, Herb Kelleher and Rollin King incorporated a tiny airline in Texas with a business model based on legal and regulatory considerations. By limiting their flights to Texas, they could escape federal regulation with its attendant costs and thereby become the lowest cost carrier in the state. Thus was born Southwest Airlines.

The TitleMax and Southwest Airlines cases are legal examples of regulatory arbitrage. But consider Volkswagen. When it could not meet existing environmental emissions standards with its diesel engines, it simply programmed in a "defeat device" that could detect when engines were undergoing government testing and change engine performance to pass the tests even though the engines spewed out up to 40 times as much pollution when out on the highway. This was an illegal, unethical, and ultimately quite costly avoidance strategy.

Or think about Uber. According to one of its former attorneys, its strategy was often to move into a city, "[g]et super popular, ignore the laws, and if you try to enforce them, we'll use the power of the bully pulpit." This was a high-risk avoidance strategy that was not exactly ethically admirable and produced decidedly mixed practical results.

Compliance

When managers understand the important role that law and regulation can play in helping our society and economy work effectively, they often focus on complying with the law that they view as a necessary constraint on their managerial actions.

Consider that in the 1990s, Microsoft dominated its markets and found itself constantly in court in both the U.S. and Europe spending hundreds of millions of dollars defending (sometimes unsuccessfully) antitrust lawsuits. Another extremely successful tech company, Intel, also dominated its markets at the time, but avoided those antitrust litigation expenditures by carefully trainings its employees regarding how to avoid violating antitrust laws. Later, Intel seemed to have lost focus and got into antitrust trouble itself. More recently, Google has been forced to pay billions of dollars in fines to antitrust regulators in the European Union; it, Amazon, and other dominant companies are also being looked at more closely by antitrust enforcers in the U.S. because of the way they are using their dominant market power.

As another example, clothing store Forever 21's business model is aimed copying rivals' successful designs as close as possible *without* violating their copyrights. Occasionally the firm might stray too close to the line and lose a lawsuit, but its strategic goal has been to play the game as close to the line as possible without violating any intellectual property rights of other parties. Moreover, if a company goes too close to a legal line and is sued, the expense of defending against a lawsuit can be huge and damaging to the company's reputation even if it wins the case.

Given the massive and costly compliance requirements of modern laws such as Sarbanes-Oxley and Dodd-Frank, compliance simply must be a priority for all public companies and a thoughtful strategic approach to optimizing compliance should be of critical concern.

Prevention

With a deep level of functional area-specific legal knowledge, managers may use the law to preempt future discrete business-related risks. Companies doing business abroad can foresee that in many markets they may be asked to pay bribes and their managers can easily calculate the overwhelming fines—sometimes in the billions of dollars— that can result from getting caught making such payments. Careful training of employees can help prevent such losses.

Ethics and compliance training in other areas can also position a company to avoid the worst impact of criminal punishments should some employees stray from the straight-and-narrow. The U.S. Sentencing Guidelines for corporations can reduce fines by 95% for companies that have formulated and implemented good-faith compliance programs for their employees.

Value

When managers fully understand the big-picture impact that legal and regulatory constraints have in their industry, they can creatively use the law to produce identifiable value. In their book, EDISON IN THE BOARDROOM REVISITED (2011), Julie Davis and Suzanne Harrison point out that many managers are not educated to manage the intellectual property that their companies produce. Yet some companies earn more than a billion dollars a year by licensing revenue from their patents, trade secrets, and other forms of intellectual property. Increasingly, companies are realizing the huge strategic advantage they can gain from obtaining, maintaining, and exploiting their intellectual capital.

Here are three more quick examples:

- Over the years, Disney has consistently and aggressively used copyright and trademark law to profit from its creative intellectual property and has lobbied vigorously to extend legal protections for that creative content.
- In 2012, Google paid $12.5 billion to acquire Motorola Mobility. The primary driver of the acquisition was legal in nature. By acquiring Motorola Mobility's patent portfolio, Google was in a much stronger legal position to protect its role as a player in the smart phone market.
- In her book FACTORY MAN (2014), Beth Macy tells the story of how a furniture maker in Virginia invoked international law to avoid being plowed under by unfair economic competition on the part of Chinese competitors.

Transformation

When managers have a sophisticated and broad knowledge of legal and regulatory matters that cuts across functional domains, they are positioned to take advantage of opportunities to transform aspects of their business in beneficial ways.

For example, according to Bird and Orozco, once upon a time a significant part of Qualcomm's business was manufacturing handsets, but Qualcomm could tell that the future probably lay in its code-division multiple access (CDMA) wireless technology:

> So the company decided to bet its future on CDMA and a business model that combined legal expertise related to patent standards with a shrewd approach to contact licensing....
> Qualcomm's new business model hinged on the following strategy: contribute CDMA wireless technology patents to develop an industry standard, and encourage key stakeholders, such as the wireless equipment vendors and network operators, to adopt that

standard. The company achieved those seemingly conflicting objectives—diffusing technology while retaining some control—by implementing a sophisticated legal strategy. To encourage technology diffusion, Qualcomm inverted the idea of patent exclusivity in the wireless industry by offering anyone the opportunity to license its proprietary technology while it retained the rights to key technology know-how. In negotiating those licenses, Qualcomm offered specific terms to speed up the adoption of its technology and reduce the risks of an unproven technology…These terms were exchanged for ongoing royalties and up-front fees that locked in those customers and provided Qualcomm with much-needed cash for additional research and development. Licensing income continues to be an important source of revenue for Qualcomm; licensing generated about 30% of the company's revenue in fiscal 2013.

These five categories of legal strategy suggested by Bird and Orozco likely overlap and certainly do not exhaust the possibilities. But they do give us a rudimentary framework for considering the importance and potential value of legal strategy for business.

LAW, JUSTICE, AND ETHICS

Law and Justice

There is a close relationship between law and justice, but the terms are not equivalent. Most results of the application of legal rules are "just"—fair and reasonable. Where this is not so to any degree, the rules are usually changed. Yet it must be recognized that results occasionally "are not fair." Without attempting to defend the law in all such instances, some cautions should nevertheless be voiced.

First, there is never complete agreement as to what is just; there are always some decisions that seem just to some people but not to others. And even if there were unanimity of opinion—a perfect justice, so to speak—the facts in many cases are such that it is simply impossible to attain this end.

In some situations, for example, a legal controversy may arise between two honest persons who dealt with each other in good faith, as sometimes occurs in the area of "mutual mistake." Take this case: P contracts to sell land to G for $40,000, both parties mistakenly believing that a General Motors plant will be built on adjoining land. When G learns that the plant will not be built, she refuses to go through with the deal. If a court rules that the mistake frees G of his contractual obligations, the result might be quite unjust as far as P is concerned. And if it rules otherwise, the decision might seem quite unfair to G. Yet a decision must be made, one way or the other.

Second, in some instances it is fairly clear who is right and who is wrong, but the situation has progressed to the point where it is impossible, either physically or legally, to put the "good" person back into the original position. These "bad check" cases will illustrate: A buys a television from Z, giving Z her personal check in payment. If the check bounces, it is clear that Z should be allowed to recover the set. But what if the television has been destroyed by fire while in A's hands? Here the most the law can do is give Z a *judgment* against A—an order requiring A to pay a sum of money to Z equal to the amount of the check, which A may or may not be financially able to do. Or suppose that A had resold the television to X before Z learned that the check had bounced. Would it not be unfair to permit Z to retake the set from X, an innocent third party? In such cases the law must simply do the best it can to achieve a fair result, hopefully taking into account not only the immediate effect of a decision but also long-term effects on the behavior of others in the future.

In his influential book, *A Theory of Justice,* philosopher John Rawls articulated that a society fashioning principles to guide behavior should do so through a "veil of ignorance," that is, it should do so with no knowledge of how such principles would affect any particular individuals, thus increasing the likelihood that the rules will be fair and reasonable to all affected by them. Given that this ideal is, to say the least, quite difficult to achieve in practice, many believe the use of fair procedures when both making and applying principles and rules provides the best way to come as close to the ideal as possible. This belief is reflected in the procedural rules employed in civil litigation and criminal prosecutions, discussed in Chapters 2 (Court Systems, Jurisdiction, & Functions) and 3 (Litigation & Alternative Dispute Resolution), the requirement of procedural due process discussed in Chapter 5 (Constitutional Law and Business), the rules required by the federal Administrative Procedure Act and analogous state laws for the making and application of rules by administrative agencies discussed in Chapter 6 (Lawmaking by Administrative Agencies), and elsewhere in our legal system.

Law and Ethics

Although the terms *law* and *ethics* are not synonymous, legal standards and ethical standards parallel one another more closely than many people believe. For example, criminal statutes prohibit certain kinds of conduct that are clearly ''ethically wrong''—murder, theft, arson, and the like. And other rules of law impose civil liability for similar kinds of conduct that, although not crimes, are also generally felt to be wrongful in nature—such as negligence, breach of contract, and fraud. To illustrate: S, in negotiating the sale of a race horse to B, tells B that the horse has run an eighth of a mile in 15 seconds on several occasions within the past month. In fact, the animal has never been clocked under 18 seconds, and S knows this. B, believing the statement to be true, purchases the horse. In such a case, S's intentional misstatement constitutes the tort of *fraud*, and B—assuming they can prove these facts in a legal action brought against S—has the right to set aside the transaction, returning the horse and recovering the price they have paid.

Why, then, are the terms *law* and *ethics* not precisely synonymous? First, in some situations ethical standards are higher than those imposed by law. For example, a person who has promised to keep an offer open for a stated period of time generally has the legal right to withdraw the offer before the given time has elapsed (for reasons appearing in a later chapter). Yet many persons who make such offers feel ethically compelled to keep their offers open as promised, even though the law does not require this. Second, sometimes the law imposes higher standards than do our ethical standards.

For example, no religions or philosophies feature a 65-mile-per-hour speed limit as a major tenet, yet it is often illegal to drive faster. Third, many rules of law and court decisions are based on statutory or practical requirements that have little or no relationship to ethical considerations. For example, in the area of minors' contracts, we will see later that most courts feel, on balance, that it is sound public policy to permit minors to disaffirm (cancel) their contracts until they reach the age of majority, even though the contracts were otherwise perfectly valid and even though the persons with whom the minors dealt did not overreach or take advantage of them in any way. These observations notwithstanding, a society's ethical standards will always heavily influence its legal standards. The relationship between legal standards and ethical standards, as well as many related questions, is explored thoroughly in this text's chapters on business ethics.

The interplay between law and ethics is illustrated in the following case, which addresses the critical question of what duties citizens should owe each other in our society. Legal and ethical duties are for practical reasons not completely coextensive, but they will tend to be similar because of how significantly our ethical beliefs influence our legal reasoning and legal policy.

Because the study of law involves to a very great extent the ability to reason from cases, students must have some familiarity with court procedures and jurisdiction. For this reason, major emphasis on cases will begin in the following chapter. The case below is our first, and therefore requires a few prefatory comments:

1. This is a *wrongful death* action authorized by state statute to allow close relatives of deceased persons to sue those whose wrongful acts have contributed to a death. Every state has a wrongful death statute. Without such statutes, we could be held liable for carelessly or intentionally injuring others but could escape civil liability if we killed them. Under a state wrongful death statute, the *wrongful* act must be a *tort*, such as negligence or assault and battery, for which the deceased could have filed suit if only injury and not death had occurred. The subject of torts is discussed in substantial detail in later chapters.

2. In a civil case, the jury is normally the "*judge of the facts*," that is, it determines from the evidence presented in court what the facts are. In its complaint, the plaintiff alleged that certain events occurred, facts which, if proved, will establish a legally recognized claim against the defendant. The plaintiff must then produce evidence showing that these events really did occur, and it is the task of the jury to decide whether the evidence is sufficient to so prove its asserted facts. In making this decision about the evidence and the facts, the jury must assess whether the plaintiff's evidence meets its *burden of proof*, a concept more fully discussed in Chapter 3. On the other hand, the trial judge decides the *law*. A judge can grant a summary judgment, terminating the case before it ever goes to trial. Summary judgment is appropriately granted if the evidence in the case so clearly indicates that factually one side or the other is entitled to prevail that a trial would be a waste of time. Only if the judge can conclude that there is "no genuine issue of material fact" should a summary judgment be granted on this ground. Because the only function of a jury is to resolve disputed issues of fact, there is no job for a jury to perform if there is no disputed factual issue. A determination about whether the evidence is even sufficient to create a genuine issue of disputed fact is treated as a question of law for the trial judge to resolve. The following case involves a situation in which the trial judge had granted a summary judgment for the defendant.

3. If a trial court does grant a summary judgment motion, the losing party can always seek review in an appellate court. If the appellate court finds that the ruling was in error, the case will be returned to the trial court with instructions to hold a trial on the issue.

4. This wrongful death lawsuit was a *civil lawsuit* seeking monetary damages for the alleged negligence of the defendants. In virtually every state, an automobile driver involved in an accident is legally required to remain at the scene of an accident

and render to victims aid that is reasonable under the circumstances. However, "failure to stop and render aid" violates a duty under *criminal law*. Thus, in the following case, the driver (Mairs) could have been criminally prosecuted for fleeing the scene of the accident. There is a high probability that Mairs was criminally prosecuted, although the outcome of any such prosecution is unknown to the authors. The decision whether to prosecute someone for a crime rests with one or more prosecuting attorneys; in a case like this one involving state law (rather than federal law), the prosecutors are employed at the county level. If the criminal conduct is also a tort, as in this case, there can be two separate legal proceedings, one civil and one criminal.

PODIAS V. MAIRS
926 A.2d 859 (N.J.App. 2007)

Defendants Swanson and Newell were asleep in their friend Mairs' car. Mairs was driving and all three had been drinking beer. Around 2:00 a.m., Mairs lost control of the car and struck a motorcycle driven by Antonios Podias. All three exited the car and "huddled" around it. Swanson saw Podias lying in the roadway and because he saw no movement and heard no sound, told Mairs and Newell that he thought Mairs had killed the cyclist. At that time, there were no other cars on the road.

Even though all three had cell phones, no one called for assistance. Instead they argued about whether the car had collided with the motorcycle. And, within minutes of the accident, Mairs called his girlfriend on Newell's cell phone since his was lost when he got out of the car. Swanson made 17 calls and Newell 26 calls over the next many minutes, though not one was an emergency assistance call. As Swanson later explained: "I didn't feel responsible to call the police." And Newell just "didn't want to get in trouble."

After about five or ten minutes, the trio all decided to get back in the car and leave the scene. Swanson instructed Mairs "not to bring up his name or involve him in what occurred" and "don't get us [Swanson and Newell] involved, we weren't there." The three then drove south for a short distance until Mairs' car broke down. Mairs pulled over and waited in the bushes for his girlfriend to arrive, while Swanson and Newell ran off into the woods. Before they deserted him, Swanson again reminded Mairs that "there was no need to get [Swanson and Newell] in trouble." Mairs thought Swanson was "just scared" and that both defendants were concerned about Mairs "drinking and driving." Meanwhile, another car ran over Podias in the dark and he died as a result of injuries sustained in these accidents.

When State Police located Mairs hours after the accident, he said that he was alone in the car at the time of the accident, but several months later admitted that Swanson and Newell were passengers in the car at the time of the accident and that he had lied to the police because his friends had asked him to.

Plaintiff Sevasti Podias, individually and on behalf of decedent's estate, sued several defendants for negligence. All of the defendants except for Swanson and Newel, either settled or were found liable after a jury trial. Prior to trial, the trial judge granted Swanson and Newell's motion for summary judgment, finding that they had no legal duty to volunteer emergency assistance to one whose injury they neither caused nor substantially assisted another in bringing about. Plaintiff appealed.

Parillo, Judge:

A. Traditional tort theory emphasizes individual liability, which is to say that each particular defendant who is to be charged with responsibility must be proceeding negligently. Ordinarily, then, mere presence at the commission of the wrong, or failure to object to it, is not enough to charge one with responsibility inasmuch as there is no duty to take affirmative steps to interfere. See W. Page Keeton, et al., Prosser and Keeton on the Law of Torts (Prosser) § 46, at 323-24 (5th ed. 1984).

Because of this reluctance to countenance "inaction" as a basis of liability, the common law "has persistently refused to impose on a stranger the moral obligation of common humanity to go to the aid of another human being who is in danger, even if the other is in danger of losing his life." *Id.* Thus, the common law rule imposes "no independent duty of rescue at all" and relieves a bystander from any obligation to provide affirmative aid or emergency assistance, even if the bystander has the ability to help. *Praet v. Borough of Sayreville*, 527 A.2d 486 (N.J. App. Div. 1987). The underlying rationale for what has come to be known as the "innocent bystander rule" seems to be that by "passive inaction," defendant has made the injured party's situation no worse, and has merely failed to benefit him by interfering in his affairs.

Of course, exceptions are as longstanding as the rule. For instance, if one already has a pre-existing legal duty to render assistance, who either by statute or "public calling" has undertaken a duty to give service, then it is that duty which impels him to act, for which omission he may be liable. *Praet, supra*, 527 A.2d 486. So too, at common law, those under no pre-existing duty may nevertheless be liable if they choose to volunteer emergency assistance for another but do so negligently.

Over the years, liability for inaction has been gradually extended still further to a "limited group of relations, in which custom, public sentiment, and views of social policy have led courts to find a duty of affirmative action." Prosser, supra, § 56 at 373-74. Thus, a duty to render assistance may either be "contractual, relational or transactional." *Praet, supra*. In New Jersey, courts have recognized that the existence of a relationship between the victim and one in a position to provide aid may create a duty to render assistance. In *Szabo v. Pennsylvania R.R. Co.*, 40 A.2d 562 (E. & A. 1945), for instance, the Court held that if the employee, while engaged in the work of his or her employer, sustains an injury rendering them helpless to provide for their own care, the employer must secure medical care for the employee. According to the Court, "[t]his duty arises out of strict necessity and urgent exigency." *Ibid.*

To establish liability, however, such relationships need not be limited to those where a pre-existing duty exists, or involving economic ties, or dependent on the actor's status as, for instance, a landowner or business owner. Rather, it may only be necessary "to find some definite relation between the parties of such a character that social policy justifies the imposition of a duty to act." Prosser, *supra*, § 56 at 374. So, for instance, the general duty which arises in many relations to take reasonable precautions for the safety of others may include the obligation to exercise control over the conduct of third persons with dangerous propensities. *J.S. v. R.T.H.*, 714 A.2d 924 (1998); 1965 Restatement §§ 315 and 319. In *J.S. v. R.T.H.*, the Court held that when a spouse has actual knowledge or special reason to know of the likelihood of her spouse engaging in sexually abusive behavior against a particular person, the spouse has a duty of care to take reasonable steps to prevent or warn of the harm, and breach of such a duty constitutes a proximate cause of the resultant injury.

So too, even though the defendant may be under no obligation to render assistance himself, he is at least required to take reasonable care that he does not prevent others from giving it. *Soldano v. O'Daniels*, 90 Cal. Rptr. 310 (Ct. App. 1983). In other words, there may be liability for interfering with the plaintiff's opportunity of obtaining assistance. And even where the original danger was created by innocent conduct, involving no fault on the part of the defendant, there may be a duty to make a reasonable effort to give assistance and avoid further harm where the prior innocent conduct has created an unreasonable risk of harm to the plaintiff. Indeed, one commentator has suggested that "the mere knowledge of serious peril, threatening death or great bodily harm to another, which an identified defendant might avoid with little inconvenience, creates a sufficient relation to impose a duty of action." Prosser, *supra*, § 56 at 377.

Actually, the extension of liability based on these and other "relational" features mirrors evolving notions of duty, which are no longer tethered to rigid formalisms or static historical classifications. This progression is not surprising. The assessment of duty necessarily includes an examination of the relationships between and among the parties. The fundamental question is "whether the plaintiff's interests are entitled to legal protection against the defendant's conduct." *Weinberg v. Dinger*, 524 A.2d 366 (N.J. 1987)). In this regard, the determination of the existence of duty is ultimately a question of fairness and public policy, *Olivo v. Owens-Illinois, Inc.*, 895 A.2d 1143 (N.J. 2006), which in turn draws upon "notions of fairness, common sense, and morality." *Hopkins v. Fox & Lazo Realtors*, 625 A.2d 1110 (N.J. 1993).

The duty determination, which is a judicial one, involves a complex analysis that weighs and balances several related factors, including:

> The nature of the underlying risk of harm, that is, its foreseeability and severity, the opportunity and ability to exercise care to prevent the harm, the comparative interests of, and the relationships between or among the parties, and, ultimately, based on considerations of public policy and fairness, the societal interest in the proposed solution. *J.S. v. R.T.H., supra.*

Specifically, "[f]oreseeability of the risk of harm is the foundational element in the determination of whether a duty exists." *J.S. v. R.T.H.* Foreseeability, in turn, is based on the defendant's knowledge of the risk of injury. A corresponding consideration is the practicality of preventing it. Also included in the analysis is "an assessment of the defendant's 'responsibility for conditions creating the risk of harm' and an analysis of whether the defendant had sufficient control, opportunity, and ability to have avoided the risk of harm." *Id.* And ultimately, there is public policy, which "must be determined in the context of contemporary circumstances and considerations." *Id.* (noting that in a society growing increasingly intolerant of drunken driving, the imposition of a duty on social hosts "seems both fair and fully in accord with the State's policy").

Governed by these principles, we are satisfied that a reasonable jury could find defendants breached a duty which proximately caused the victim's death. In the first place, the risk of harm, even death, to the injured victim lying helpless in the middle of a roadway, from the failure of defendants to summon help or take other precautionary measures was readily and clearly foreseeable. Not only were defendants aware of the risk of harm created by their own inaction, but were in a unique position to know of the risk of harm posed by Mairs' own omission in that regard, as well as Mairs' earlier precipatory conduct in driving after having consumed alcohol. Even absent any encouragement on their part, defendants had special reason to know that Mairs would not himself summon help, but instead illegally depart the scene of a hit-and-run accident, N.J.S.A. 39:4-129, either intentionally or because of an inability to fulfill a duty directly owed the victim, thereby further endangering the decedent's safety.

Juxtaposed against the obvious foreseeability of harm is the relative ease with which it could have been prevented. All three individuals had cell phones and in fact used them immediately before and after the accident for their own purposes, rather than to call for emergency assistance for another in need. The ultimate consequence wrought by the harm in this case--death--came at the expense of failing to take simple precautions at little if any cost or inconvenience to defendants. Indeed, in contrast to Mairs' questionable ability to appreciate the seriousness of the situation, defendants appeared lucid enough to comprehend the severity of the risk and sufficiently in control to help avoid further harm to the victim. In other words, defendants had both the opportunity and ability to help prevent an obviously foreseeable risk of severe and potentially fatal consequence.

In our view, given the circumstances, the imposition of a duty upon defendants does not offend notions of fairness and common decency and is in accord with public policy. As evidenced by the grant of legislative immunity to volunteers afforded by the Good Samaritan Act, N.J.S.A. 2A:62A-1, public policy encourages gratuitous assistance by those who have no legal obligation to render it. *Praet, supra*. Simply and obviously, defendants here were far more than innocent bystanders or strangers to the event. On the contrary, the instrumentality of injury in this case was operated for a common purpose and the mutual benefit of defendants, and driven by someone they knew to be exhibiting signs of intoxication. Although Mairs clearly created the initial risk, at the very least the evidence reasonably suggests defendants acquiesced in the conditions that may have helped create it and subsequently in those conditions that further endangered the victim's safety. Defendants therefore bear some relationship not only to the primary wrongdoer but to the incident itself. It is this nexus which distinguishes this case from those defined by mere presence on the scene without more, and therefore implicates policy considerations simply not pertinent to the latter.

B. [The court then examined the facts and determined that there was sufficient evidence for a jury to find defendants liable for negligence because they had aided and abetted Mairs' wrongful post-accident conduct by not acting reasonably under the circumstances to assist Podias, such as calling 911.]

Reversed and remanded.

LAW, GLOBALIZATION, AND SCIENCE & TECHNOLOGY

The law is always evolving in response to philosophical, practical, social, and other influences. Currently, three forces shaping the law are of overarching importance. One is the interaction of law and morality highlighted in the preceding section. The two other forces dramatically impacting all areas of the law are globalization and science & technology.

Law and Globalization

As business goes global, so does its regulation. This requires cooperation and coordination on an unprecedented scale. Companies that develop intellectual property in our information age often wish to protect that property and exploit it economically, not only in their home country but throughout the world. This necessitates international conventions to establish global rules for patents, copyrights and other forms of intellectual property. It also requires international organizations to enforce those rules. These are explored in this text's chapter on intellectual property law.

As another example, consider the Enron scandal which rocked confidence in American business. Congress responded by passing the Sarbanes-Oxley Act of 2002, which imposed new rules for corporate disclosure, corporate governance, and audit firm practice (among other changes). These will be discussed in some detail in our chapters on business ethics and securities regulation. Sarbanes-Oxley's provisions were written to govern not only American companies, but also foreign companies that list their shares on American stock exchanges or otherwise access our capital markets and foreign accounting firms that audit those companies. European companies and accounting firms are especially concerned that Sarbanes-Oxley has serious implications for their corporate governance and audit practices. They resent the export of American law. Indeed, the Foreign Corrupt Practices Act, discussed in the international law chapter, is alleged by some to inappropriately export American moral norms to the developing world.

On the other hand, European Union antitrust laws are stricter than American laws. General Electric was unable to acquire Honeywell because of EU rules, even though both are American companies and U.S. antitrust officials had approved the deal. Japanese rules can make it difficult for American companies to enter certain industries in Japan. Every company hoping to do business abroad, and some that don't, must be concerned with the international legal environment as well as their own domestic rules.

Law and Technology

Technological innovations, such as creation of the Internet, have many implications for how business is done and how it is regulated. In some areas, old principles simply needed to be adapted and reapplied to the new technological reality. In many other areas, the law has been substantially rewritten. As you peruse this text, you will see many examples of these changes. And you will see more as legal regimes adapt to the latest advances in drones, 3D printers, DNA testing, data mining, cloud computing and the like. Advances in technology and new scientific discoveries affect the law directly and also may reshape the societal norms that underlie many legal rules.

CHAPTER 2

COURT SYSTEMS, JURISDICTION, AND FUNCTIONS

- Court Systems

- Problems of Jurisdiction

- Law, Equity, and Remedies

Legal rules and principles take on vitality and meaning only when they are applied to real-life controversies between real persons, when the rules are applied to facts—when, for example, a particular plaintiff is successful or unsuccessful in his or her attempt to recover a specific piece of land from a particular defendant, or where one company is successful or unsuccessful in recovering damages from another company as a result of an alleged breach of contract on the latter company's part. Adjudication, the fitting of rules to facts required for settling legal controversies, is primarily performed by state and federal courts, although state and federal administrative agencies also conduct adjudicative types of proceedings.

The primary reason for looking at the courts and the work that they do is to gain an overall awareness of this important legal process. There is, however, another reason for doing so. In the following chapters many actual cases are presented. The reader is given the basic facts of a particular controversy, the judgment entered by the trial court on the basis of those facts, and excerpts of the appellate court's decision in affirming or reversing the trial court's judgment. Obviously, some familiarity with court systems and the judicial process will facilitate one's understanding of the legal significance of each step in these proceedings.

In this chapter, then, we take a brief look at the state and federal court systems and at some problems of jurisdiction arising in those systems. We also examine some additional matters, such as venue, conflict of laws, and the law-equity distinction. In Chapter 3, we will study the litigation process more closely.

COURT SYSTEMS

As a result of our federal system of government, we live under two distinct, and essentially separate, sovereign types of government—the state governments and the federal government. Each has its own laws and its own court system. For this reason, it is necessary to study both systems to acquire an adequate knowledge of the court structures within which controversies are settled.

The Typical State System

Although court systems vary somewhat from state to state, most state courts fall into three general categories. In ascending order, they are (1) courts of limited jurisdiction, (2) general trial courts, and (3) appellate courts (which frequently exist at two levels).

Courts of Limited Jurisdiction

Every state has trial courts that are limited as to the kinds of cases they can hear and are thus called *courts of limited jurisdiction*. Examples include justice of the peace courts, municipal courts, traffic courts, probate courts (hearing matters of wills and decedents' estates), and domestic relations courts (handling divorce, custody, and child support cases). Numerically speaking, these courts hear most cases that come to trial. However, they need not be discussed in detail here because many of the matters they hear are relatively minor in nature (such as traffic violations) and others involve very specialized subject matter (such as a dispute over a deceased person's estate).

General Trial Courts

The most important cases involving state law begin in the *general trial courts*. These are courts of *general jurisdiction*; they are empowered to hear all cases except those expressly assigned by statute to specialized trial courts, which are courts of *limited jurisdiction*. Virtually all important cases involving contract law, criminal law, and corporation law, for example, originate in the general trial courts. In many states these courts are called *district courts,* in others *common pleas courts*, and in still others *superior courts*. Whatever the specific name, one or more such courts normally exist in every county of every state. Throughout the remainder of the text, we will sometimes refer to these general trial courts simply as state trial courts to distinguish them from federal trial courts. When this is done, we are referring to the state trial courts of general jurisdiction rather than to those of limited jurisdiction.

Appellate Courts

All states have one or more *appellate courts*, which hear appeals from judgments entered by the courts below. Until not long ago, several of the less populous states had only one such court, usually but not always called the *supreme court*—the so-called "court of last resort" in that state. In more populous states there has for many years been a layer of one or more intermediate appellate courts between the trial courts and the supreme court. Appellate courts decide legal questions; they do not hear testimony of witnesses or otherwise entertain new evidence. Today, larger populations and amounts of litigation have led all states to create at least one intermediate-level court of appeals.

The Federal Court System

Article III, Section 1 of the U.S. Constitution provides that "the judicial power of the United States shall be vested in one Supreme Court, and in such inferior courts as the Congress may from time to time ordain and establish." The numerous federal courts that exist today by virtue of this section can, at the risk of oversimplification, be placed into three main categories similar to those of the state courts: (1) specialized trial courts, (2) U.S. district courts, and (3) appellate courts—the courts of appeal and the Supreme Court.

Specialized U.S. Courts

Some federal courts have very specialized subject matter jurisdiction. Examples include the U.S. Tax Court, which hears only federal tax cases, and the U.S. Claims Court, which hears only claims against the U.S. government. These and other specialized federal courts are somewhat analogous to the courts of limited jurisdiction in state court systems.

U.S. District Courts

The basic trial courts within the federal system are the U.S. district courts, sometimes called *federal district courts.* Most federal cases originate in these courts. Congress has created 94 judicial districts, each of which covers all or part of a state or a U.S. territory. Federal districts are defined by state lines, with each state having at least one district. More populous states have two, three, or four U.S. districts. U.S. territories such as Puerto Rico, Guam, and the Virgin Islands each have one federal district court. Within each federal district, there usually are several *divisions* in different cities, with one or more federal district judges in each division. Each federal district also includes a federal criminal prosecutor's office and a federal marshal's office.

Although the federal district courts are the most important courts in the federal system, they are not really courts of general jurisdiction in the same sense as are state trial courts with the general jurisdiction. State courts of general jurisdiction are essentially a repository of general judicial power; if no other court has jurisdiction over a particular type of case, then a state court of general jurisdiction has power to hear the case. Federal courts, however, are part of the federal government, and the federal government is a government of limited powers under our Constitution. Thus, as we will see shortly, even our most important federal trial courts—the U.S. district courts—have power to hear only those cases that have been specifically placed within their jurisdiction by the Constitution and federal statutory enactments.

Appellate Courts

There are 13 U.S. courts of appeal. Eleven of these, located in "circuits" across the country, have jurisdiction to hear appeals from the district courts located in the states within their respective boundaries. Each of these 11 appellate courts also hears appeals from the rulings of federal administrative agencies. The jurisdiction of the remaining two appellate courts is somewhat different from that of the others. The U.S. Court of Appeals for the District of Columbia hears appeals from the federal district court located in the District, as well as appeals from rulings of federal administrative agencies. The other appellate court is the U.S. Court of Appeals for the Federal Circuit, which hears all appeals from patent applicants whose applications were rejected by the U.S. Patent & Trademark Office, all appeals from patent infringement cases from all U.S. District Courts, as well as appeals from the International Trade Commission (which includes ITC decisions on whether to ban imports because of infringement of U.S. patents, copyrights, or trademarks) and the federal Merit Systems Protection Board (Board decisions regarding the discharge or discipline of federal agency employees protected as civil servants under federal law).

Appeals from judgments of the U.S. courts of appeal can be taken to the U.S. Supreme Court. Cases decided by state supreme courts can also be taken to the U.S. Supreme Court if the case involves a question of federal law. In an appeal to the U.S. Supreme Court from either a U.S. Court of Appeals or the highest court in a state, however, appeals are not a matter of right. Rather, the parties who seek review must petition the Supreme Court for a *writ of certiorari,* and the Court has absolute discretion in deciding which of these cases are sufficiently important to warrant the granting of certiorari. (A writ of certiorari is an order of a higher court requiring a lower court to send to it the documentary record of the trial.) In a typical year the Court hears only about 80-100 of the several thousand appeals that are made. The typical state court system and the federal system are shown in Figure 2.1.

Figure 2.1 Federal and State Court Systems

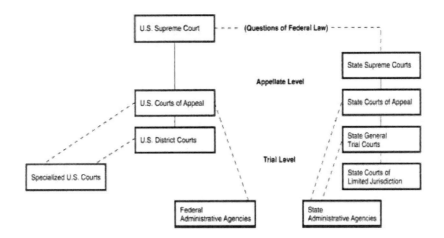

Several general comments can be made about this diagram. There are two primary types of courts in both the state and federal systems—trial courts and appellate courts. Trial courts must settle questions of both *fact and law*, whereas appellate courts rule on questions of law only. Questions of fact are "what happened" questions: for instance, did the defendant corporations expressly or implicitly agree not to sell goods to the plaintiff? Questions of law, by contrast, are "what is the rule applicable to the facts?"

Once a case is initiated within a given court system, it will normally stay within that system until a final judgment is reached. Thus, if a case is properly commenced in a state court of general jurisdiction, any appeal from the trial court's judgment must be made to the next higher state court rather than to a federal appellate court. Should a case reach the highest court in the state, that court's judgment is usually final. In other words, on matters of state law, state supreme courts are indeed supreme. However, should a state supreme court rule on a case that turns on interpretation of a federal statute or a provision of the U.S. Constitution, an appeal could be taken to the U.S. Supreme Court, which has the final word on matters of *federal law.* Again, however, the U.S. Supreme Court has discretion whether to hear an appeal, whether it is from a U.S. Court of Appeals or from a decision on federal law made by the highest court in a state court system.

With regard to the title of an appealed case, the state and federal courts follow somewhat different rules. In most state courts, the original plaintiff's name appears first—just as it did in the trial court. Suppose, for example, that Pink (plaintiff) sues Doe (defendant) in a state trial court, where the case is obviously *Pink v. Doe.* If the judgment of the trial court is appealed, the rule followed by most state courts is that the title of the case remains *Pink v. Doe* in the appellate courts, no matter which party is the appellant (the one bringing the appeal). In the federal courts and in some states, however, the appellant's name appears first. Under this rule, if Doe (defendant) loses in a U.S. district court and appeals to a U.S. court of appeals, the title of the case will be *Doe v. Pink* in the higher court. For this reason, when one sees a case in a federal appellate court so entitled, one cannot assume that Doe was the party who originated the action in the trial court. That determination must be made by referring to the facts of the case as set forth in the decision of the appellate court. In addition, when there are multiple plaintiffs and/or multiple defendants, the title of the case typically is abbreviated so that only the first listed plaintiff and first listed defendant are named.

COURT JURISDICTION

In a general sense, the term *jurisdiction* refers to the legal power of a governmental body or official to take some type of action. With respect to courts, jurisdiction means the power to adjudicate, that is, to hear and decide a case and render a judgment that is legally binding on the parties. A court normally has such power only if it has both *subject matter jurisdiction* and *personal jurisdiction.*

Subject Matter Jurisdiction

Subject matter jurisdiction consists of the power to hear a particular kind of case. In each of our states, provisions in the state constitution specify which types of cases are within the subject matter jurisdiction of which types of courts. State legislative enactments (statutes) then provide more detail on the subject matter jurisdiction of particular state courts, whether general or specialized courts. In the federal system, the U.S. Constitution specifies in general terms the kinds of cases that are within the subject matter jurisdiction of the federal courts, and federal statutes provide more detail. The federal courts themselves have also added more detail to the jurisdictional rules through their interpretations of the relevant constitutional and statutory provisions.

Subject Matter Jurisdiction of the Federal Courts

As we have already seen, the federal courts have subject matter jurisdiction over only those kinds of cases specified by the U.S. Constitution.

Criminal Cases

Federal courts have jurisdiction over criminal cases in which a violation of a federal criminal statute is alleged. There is a large body of federal criminal law, including statutes making it a crime to smuggle drugs into the United States, hijack an airplane, commit securities fraud, threaten the president, cross state lines after having committed a state law crime, and so on. Some federal statutes, such as the securities and antitrust laws, include both civil liability and criminal penalty provisions. Congress has power to pass criminal laws, like civil ones, only if there is some basis in the Constitution authorizing it to do so. Many federal criminal laws are based on the constitutional provision that empowers Congress to pass laws regulating interstate commerce (commerce between states or between a state and a foreign country), but some are enacted under the power granted by other constitutional provisions. For example, congressional power to criminalize fraud in securities transactions derives from its authority to regulate interstate commerce, and its power to criminalize counterfeiting derives from the authority to "coin money."

Civil Cases

We are primarily concerned about the jurisdiction and functions of courts in civil cases. Most of the time it will be obvious whether a particular civil case can be heard by a federal court, but sometimes there are difficult questions. These questions may arise when a plaintiff's attorney thinks it would be in the client's best interest to have the case decided by a federal rather than a state court, but where some of the facts relating to the jurisdictional question are not clear.

Federal Question Cases. Federal courts have subject matter jurisdiction over any civil case in which the plaintiff's claim arises from the U.S. Constitution or a federal statute. For example, if a group of environmentally concerned citizens sues a corporation alleging that it was polluting a stream in violation of the federal Clean Water Act, there would be a *federal question*. The plaintiff's claim must directly raise a question of federal law; if the plaintiff's claim does not raise a federal question, the defendant cannot create federal subject matter jurisdiction by raising a federal question in a defense or counterclaim.

It is common for a plaintiff to assert two or more legal claims based on the same set of factual circumstances. If one of these claims raises a federal question and thereby creates federal subject matter jurisdiction, the federal court also has subject matter jurisdiction over any other claim arising out of the same facts, even if the other claim is based on state law rather than federal law. This type of federal subject matter jurisdiction is called "pendent" (or "ancillary") jurisdiction and represents a pragmatic attempt to avoid multiple lawsuits. In such a case, the federal court would apply the relevant state law to resolve the state-law claim. Decisions about what the relevant facts are would be applied to both the federal and state claims.

Federal jurisdiction based on a federal question may be either *exclusive* or *concurrent*. A claim arising under the U.S. Constitution creates concurrent federal-state jurisdiction, which means that it can be heard by either a federal or state court. A claim arising under a federal statute creates concurrent federal-state jurisdiction unless the statute itself states that only a federal court can decide cases under the statute. This is *exclusive* federal court jurisdiction. A number of federal statutes, such as patent, copyright, antitrust, and securities laws, provide for exclusive federal court jurisdiction.

If a federal question case is taken to a federal court, it is normally done at the outset, in one of the federal district courts. However, if (1) a particular federal question case is characterized by concurrent federal-state jurisdiction, (2) the plaintiff chooses to file the case in a state court, and (3) the case proceeds through the state court system until all avenues of appeal in that system are exhausted, either party may ask the U.S. Supreme Court to review the case because of the presence of the federal question. In this situation, as in others, the U.S. Supreme Court has discretion to hear or not hear the case.

Diversity of Citizenship Cases. Diversity of citizenship creates federal subject matter jurisdiction only if the amount in controversy is greater than $75,000. When federal jurisdiction exists because of *diversity of citizenship*, it is always concurrent federal-state jurisdiction, and the plaintiff has a choice of filing in a federal court. If the plaintiff chooses to file in a state court and the case is heard in the state court system, there can be no appeal to the U.S. Supreme Court or any other federal court. (Thus, the situation is different with a diversity case filed in state court than with a federal question case filed in state court.) In the case of an individual, citizenship in a state for federal jurisdiction purposes means U.S. citizenship plus residency in that state. The phrase diversity of citizenship encompasses several different situations. By far the most important situation included within the phrase is one in which the plaintiff and defendant are citizens of different states. Diversity of citizenship also exists when one party is a citizen of a state in the United States and the other is a citizen of another nation.

In several ways, federal courts have interpreted the diversity of citizenship concept rather narrowly to exclude some kinds of cases that logically might have been included. For example, if a case involves multiple plaintiffs and/or multiple defendants, diversity of citizenship exists only if there is *no common state citizenship on opposite sides of the case*. Thus if P1, a citizen of Nebraska, and P2, a citizen of Kansas, join in a suit against D1, a citizen of New York, and D2, a citizen of Kansas, there is no diversity of citizenship.

If a corporation is a plaintiff or defendant, it is considered to be a citizen of the state where it was *incorporated*; in addition, if it has its *principal place of business* in another state, it is viewed as a citizen of that state as well. Thus, for the purpose of determining whether a federal court has jurisdiction on the basis of diversity of citizenship, it is possible for a corporation to be a citizen of two states. Neither Congress nor the U.S. Supreme Court has defined the term principal place of business. Lower federal courts, however, have held that the state where a company has its headquarters is its principal place of business. Suppose that P, a citizen of New York, sues D Corporation, which was incorporated in Delaware and has its headquarters in New York. Because there is common state citizenship on opposite sides of the case (New York), a federal court would not have subject matter jurisdiction on the basis of diversity of citizenship.

The original reason for permitting diversity of citizenship cases to be heard by federal courts was to guard against "hometown verdicts"—decisions by juries or judges that are biased against an out-of-state party. If this ever was a problem, there is little if any evidence that it is still a problem. In any event, if there is such a problem, it is unclear how placing these cases in a federal trial court can solve it. Juries in federal courts are taken from the local population just as they are in state courts, and federal judges are almost always from the state where they serve. For these reasons, and also because diversity of citizenship cases involve questions of state law, several bills to eliminate diversity of citizenship as a basis for federal subject matter jurisdiction have been introduced in Congress over the years. No such bill has passed, however.

What did pass, in early 2005, was the Class Action Fairness Act that, among other things, eliminated the requirement of *complete diversity of citizenship* for most class action lawsuits where the matter in controversy exceeds $5 million. The purpose of the act was to eliminate perceived forum shopping (choosing to file in states or even counties perceived to be friendly to plaintiffs) by plaintiffs' attorneys in large class action and other mass litigation suits. The law vests subject matter jurisdiction for most such suits in the federal district courts. So, if such a lawsuit is filed in a county in Illinois or Mississippi which has a reputation for handing out huge damage awards, defendants can remove the case to federal court.

Removal from State to Federal Court

When concurrent federal-state jurisdiction exists, the plaintiff has the initial choice of filing in state or federal court. If the plaintiff chooses state court, however, the defendant may have a *right of removal*. This means that, within a short time after the plaintiff files the case in state court, the defendant may have the case moved to a federal district court in the same geographic area. The defendant has a right of removal in any federal question case, so that if a defendant chooses, they can always have a federal court rule on claims against them that are based on federal law. The right also exists in diversity of citizenship cases, except in the situation where the plaintiff filed the suit in the state where the defendant is a citizen.

Personal Jurisdiction

In the great majority of cases, a court must have *personal jurisdiction* in addition to subject matter jurisdiction. Personal jurisdiction is the court's jurisdiction over the parties to the case. In a civil lawsuit, the plaintiff submits to the court's personal jurisdiction by filing the case; thus, any question about personal jurisdiction relates to the defendant. Personal jurisdiction over the defendant is a requirement in so-called *in personam* cases, in which the plaintiff seeks a judgment that will be legally binding against the defendant (whether an individual, corporation, government agency, or other entity). The judgment might be an award of money damages that the defendant has to pay or some other remedy such as an injunction requiring the defendant to take or refrain from taking some particular action. Most cases are of the *in personam* variety. The other type of case is an *in rem* action, which will be discussed after this section on personal jurisdiction.

In our legal system, personal jurisdiction is a concept that arises only in civil cases, not in criminal ones, because in a criminal case the defendant must be arrested and bodily brought before the court before they can be tried. Unlike some countries, in the U.S. a defendant in a criminal case cannot be tried *in absentia*, in other words, tried for a crime without actually being present. This is one of the main reasons why, in the U.S., a state must grant *extradition* and turn over a criminal defendant within its borders if asked by the state where that defendant is charged with a crime *and* if the crime charged is a felony.

The rules for a court's acquisition of personal jurisdiction over a defendant all have the same objective: compliance with the U.S. constitutional requirement of *procedural due process*. What is required by procedural due process is (1) adequate notice, (2) a meaningful opportunity to be heard (that is, a hearing), (3) an impartial decision maker (one who does not have a personal stake in the outcome), and (4) in court actions, some substantial contact between the defendant and the *forum state* (the state where the lawsuit has been filed).

Appearance

As we will see, some of the methods for obtaining personal jurisdiction differ depending on whether the defendant is a *resident* of the forum state or a *non-resident*. However, regardless of the residency of the defendant, the defendant automatically submits to the court's personal jurisdiction if they make an *appearance*. In this context, the word *appearance* is a term of art. It does not refer to an actual physical presence in court; instead the term refers to the taking of any formal steps to defend the case. Thus if the defendant, normally acting through an attorney, files a motion to dismiss on the basis that the plaintiff's complaint does not allege facts that establish a legally recognized claim even if proved, an answer to the plaintiff's complaint, or almost any other court papers aimed at defending against the claim, the defendant has made an appearance. Once this has happened the trial court has personal jurisdiction and the defendant cannot thereafter challenge the existence of such jurisdiction. Therefore, if the defendant wishes to contest the court's personal jurisdiction, this must be completed before taking any other action that would constitute an appearance.

The major exception to this rule is the *special appearance*—a motion or other formal action taken by the defendant solely for the purpose of challenging the court's personal jurisdiction. If the only action the defendant takes is to challenge the court's personal jurisdiction, this action does not give the court personal jurisdiction. If the defendant properly makes the special appearance before taking any other formal action in the case but the trial court denies the challenge to its personal jurisdiction, the defendant can then defend the case on its merits without losing the right later to have an appellate court rule on the personal jurisdiction question.

Service of Summons

If the defendant has not made an appearance, the plaintiff must see to it that the court acquires personal jurisdiction. Whether the defendant is a resident or nonresident, the preferred method is *personal service of summons.* The summons is the formal notice of the lawsuit. (Although summons is the most commonly used term, courts in a few states call it "process" or "citation.") A copy of the plaintiff's complaint is usually attached to the summons. *Personal service* means delivery to the defendant in person while the defendant is physically within the forum state. Traditionally, an officer such as a sheriff, marshal, deputy sheriff or marshal, or constable was always used to deliver the summons. In recent years, however, the rules in many places have been changed to permit other persons, such as the plaintiff's attorney, to deliver a summons. In the federal district courts, for example, the rules were changed in the past few years to place responsibility on the plaintiff's attorney for seeing that the summons is served; the actual delivery of the summons to the defendant can be performed by any person at least 18 years old who is not a party to the lawsuit (such as a clerk in the office of the plaintiff's attorney). Whoever attempts to deliver a summons must make a sworn statement to the court that the attempt was either successful or unsuccessful.

In the case of a resident defendant, there are several alternatives to personal service of summons, including (1) permitting the authorized summons server to leave the summons at the defendant's residence with someone older than a specified age (such as 16 or 18 years), (2) permitting the server to leave the summons at the defendant's regular place of business, or (3) permitting the server or the court clerk to mail the summons to the defendant's residence or business. In the latter case, registered or certified mail is required in some places, but only first class mail is required in others. In some states, it is required that personal service first be attempted before one of these alternatives can be used; in other places this is not required. A few courts in the U.S. have allowed service via e-mail as a last resort, though this remains relatively unusual.

Corporate Defendants

Although many of the rules for acquiring personal jurisdiction over a corporation are the same as for an individual, some are a bit different because of the nature of a corporate entity. The rules regarding the making of an appearance are the same for a corporation as for an individual.

If there is no appearance, there are several possible means for serving summons on a corporation. First, if the corporation has a *registered agent* in the forum state, service on that agent is sufficient. This service may be by personal delivery or by some alternative method permitted in that particular court system. A corporation is supposed to have a registered agent for receiving summonses and other legal notices in the state where it is incorporated and in any other state where it does business, but many companies do not actually do this. In this regard, *doing business* usually means having some physical presence in the state, not just advertising or receiving mail or telephone orders. In most places, service of summons also may be accomplished by delivering it to an *officer* of the corporation if one is located within the forum state.

Long-arm Statutes and Due Process

As a general rule, a summons is effective to give a court personal jurisdiction only if it is served on the defendant within the forum state. Thus if P files a suit for breach of contract against D in a state or federal court in Michigan, a summons issued normally must be served on D within Michigan to give the court personal jurisdiction. This requirement presents little problem if D is a resident of Michigan. Not only will it usually be possible personally to deliver the summons to a resident defendant but, as we have already seen, various alternatives are available for accomplishing service of summons to someone who is a resident of the forum state. Also, if a corporate defendant has either its headquarters or a registered agent in the forum state, the requirement is not difficult to meet.

However, if an individual defendant is a resident of some other state or nation or if the out-of-state corporation has no registered agent in the forum state, serving a summons becomes more difficult. The defendant in such a case is not likely to "hang around" in the forum state so that a summons can be served. If personal jurisdiction cannot be obtained, the plaintiff is faced with the prospect of filing suit in a state (or nation) where personal jurisdiction can be obtained; unless the claim is quite large, the substantial extra expense could mean that pursuing the claim is not economically feasible.

There are certain circumstances in which it is possible for a court to gain personal jurisdiction over a defendant even though that defendant has not made an appearance and has not been served with a summons within the forum state. The *procedural due process* guarantee in the Constitution is essentially aimed at ensuring basic procedural fairness when a court or other government entity engages in an adjudicative activity. In 1945, the U.S. Supreme Court decided that the due process requirement of basic fairness is satisfied if a nonresident defendant has had substantial prior contact with the forum state. (The Court used the term "minimal" contact, but "substantial" better describes the concept as it has been applied over the years.) In addition to the substantial contact requirement, the Supreme Court said that a particular state had to have a statutory procedure for making sure that a summons was actually forwarded to the nonresident defendant at its out-of-state address.

In response to this Supreme Court decision, every state has adopted a so-called long-arm statute specifying such a procedure. In many states, the *long-arm statute* specifies that personal jurisdiction can be acquired over a nonresident defendant who has "done business" or committed a "tort" (that is, wrongful conduct for which civil liability can be imposed) within the forum state. In other states, the statute simply provides that jurisdiction can be acquired in any circumstances in which the defendant's prior contact with the state is sufficient to comply with the fairness requirement of due process. Regardless of the exact language of the state long-arm statute, however, the ultimate question is whether the nonresident defendant had substantial contact with the forum state because this is the constitutional requirement.

Long-arm statutes provide that, when the evidence shows that the defendant has had sufficient contact with the forum state, the summons is to be sent to a central office in the forum state. In most states, this is the secretary of state's office. The official in charge of that office then has the responsibility to send the summons to the defendant at its out-of-state address. When the nonresident defendant receives the summons, the defendant either has to respond to the merits of the complaint or, if the defendant believes that it has not had substantial contact with the forum state, it will have an attorney make a *special appearance* in the court. A special appearance is simply a motion filed with the court in the forum state asking that the case be dismissed for the sole reason that the defendant has not had substantial contact with the forum state and that there is thus no basis for the court to exercise personal jurisdiction. The defendant must do this before taking any other action to defend itself. If the court in the forum state decides that it does have personal jurisdiction, and the defendant must defend against the plaintiff's complaint, the nonresident defendant has preserved its right to appeal the ruling on personal jurisdiction because it challenged the court's personal jurisdiction before doing anything else in court.

The courts have divided the due process requirement of significant contacts into two categories. The first is usually referred to as *general personal jurisdiction.* This occurs when the nonresident has had "substantial continuing contacts" with the forum state. In other words, the nonresident has either maintained a physical presence in the forum state or has continually targeted activities at the forum state over a substantial period of time. In such a case, a state or federal court can acquire personal jurisdiction over the nonresident defendant regardless of the nature of the dispute and regardless of whether the dispute arose from one of the specific contacts the defendant had with the forum state.

The second type is usually referred to as *specific personal jurisdiction.* Assuming that there is an insufficient basis for general personal jurisdiction, the court may still be able to obtain specific personal jurisdiction over the nonresident defendant. If the nonresident defendant has intentionally engaged in a specific act in the forum state (such as going into the state and committing a tort or making a contract with someone in the forum state) or targeted the forum state in some manner, and if the dispute arises out of that specific contact, there is a basis for specific personal jurisdiction.

The bottom line is that there are two types of situations in which the nonresident may be said to have had sufficient contact with the forum state to enable a state or federal court there to acquire personal jurisdiction over the nonresident defendant. Again, the reason for the requirement of substantial contacts is to comply with due process under the Constitution, which seeks to ensure fundamental procedural fairness.

The Internet and Substantial Contacts with the Forum State

The Internet has given rise to a new set of considerations regarding personal jurisdiction, and courts are still sorting them out. At one extreme, state or federal courts usually will *not* find that personal jurisdiction of any type exists in, say, California, just because a California computer user can access a passive web site on a server in New York to read or view photos or videos. At the other extreme, if a specific transaction is made over the Internet between the California computer user and New York web site operator, such as a contract for the sale of merchandise, and the California resident sues the New York resident in California for breach of contract, a California court can acquire *specific personal jurisdiction* over the New York resident *in a dispute over that particular web transaction.*

In a different situation, if the New York-based web site generates substantial revenue from California computer users, perhaps by taking orders and shipping goods to purchasers in California, then courts likely will conclude that *general personal jurisdiction* exists in New York such that a court in California can acquire personal jurisdiction over the New York web site operator in *any dispute* with a California resident.

Various other fact patterns have arisen and will continue to arise in Internet-related litigation, and courts have so far struggled to develop consistently applicable rules. Suppose, for instance, that the above-mentioned New York-based web-site operator posts content on its site (on the NY web server) that allegedly amounts to either (a) infringement of the California residents trademark or (b) defamation of the Calfornia resident's character (i.e., the tort of defamation—libel or slander, discussed in Chapter 8). Assume that the New York operator's web site is accessible in California (naturally, it is), but that the web operator has not done substantial business in California or done anything else to give a California court specific or general personal jurisdiction over the New York web-site owner. Some courts have concluded that a California court in this situation can obtain specific personal jurisdiction over the New York party because the specific wrongful act of trademark infringement or defamation has been committed in California. There is not universal agreement on this proposition, however, and court decisions have tended to be confusing.

Personal Jurisdiction in Federal Courts

As noted, federal courts generally use the same standards as state courts to determine personal jurisdiction. After all, if it is unfair to make a defendant in Maine go to Oregon to defend a claim in state court there, it is probably also unfair to make that defendant go to Oregon to defend a claim in federal court. Personal jurisdiction is in many ways a geographic concept, so federal courts typically apply the long-arm statutes of the states in which they sit.

Two other rules are worth knowing. There is the 100-mile "bulge provision" that allows a federal court to exercise personal jurisdiction over certain parties who have been joined to a case if those parties are within 100-miles of the court even if they are located in another state and state courts in the state in which the federal court sits would not have personal jurisdiction over them.

There is also Rule 4(k)(2) of the Federal Rules of Civil Procedure, which allows a federal court in a case in which subject matter jurisdiction is based on a question of federal law (not in a diversity of citizenship case without a federal question) to exercise personal jurisdiction over a foreign defendant that has enough contacts with the U.S. as a whole to establish personal jurisdiction. This exception is rarely employed, however.

The following U.S. Supreme Court case explains the consequences of the difference between general and specific personal jurisdiction, and deals with the personal jurisdiction problems associated with an attempt by a large number of plaintiffs from several states to sue a defendant that is both incorporated and headquartered in a different state. The Court's decision and explanation apply to both state and federal courts.

BRISTOL-MYERS SQUIBB CO. v. SUPERIOR COURT
U.S. Supreme Court, 2017 U.S. LEXIS 3873 (2017)

More than 600 plaintiffs, most of whom are not California residents, filed this civil action in a California state court against Bristol-Myers Squibb Company (BMS), asserting a variety of state-law claims based on injuries allegedly caused by a BMS drug called Plavix. Plavix is a blood thinner that helps prevent blood clots after a heart attack or stroke. BMS, a large pharmaceutical company, is incorporated in Delaware and headquartered in New York, and more than half of its U.S. workforce is employed in New York and New Jersey. Five BMS research and laboratory facilities, which employ a total of around 160 employees, are located in California. BMS also employs about 250 sales representatives in California and maintains a small state-government advocacy office in Sacramento.

BMS did not develop Plavix in California, did not create a marketing strategy for Plavix in California, and did not manufacture, label, package, or work on the regulatory approval of the product in California. BMS instead engaged in all of these activities in either New York or New Jersey. However, between 2006 and 2012, BMS sold almost 187 million Plavix pills in California, earning more than $900 million, a little over one percent of the company's nationwide sales revenue.

BMS moved to dismiss this lawsuit for lack of personal jurisdiction. After much litigation in the California state court system, the California Supreme Court held that although California courts did not have general personal jurisdiction over BMS in this case, they could exercise specific personal jurisdiction. BMS appealed.

Alito, Justice:

It has long been established that the Fourteenth Amendment limits the personal jurisdiction of state courts. *See Daimler AG v. Bauman,* 134 S.Ct. 746 (2014); *World-Wide Volkswagen Corp. v. Woodson,* 444 U.S. 286 (1980); *International Shoe Co. v. Washington,* 326 U.S. 310 (1945). Because "[a] state court's assertion of jurisdiction exposes defendants to the State's coercive power," it is "subject to review for compatibility with the Fourteenth Amendment's Due Process Clause," *Goodyear Dunlop Tires Operations v. Brown,* 564 U.S. 915 (2011), which "limits the power of a state court to render a valid personal judgment against a nonresident defendant," *World-Wide Volkswagen.* The primary focus of our personal jurisdiction inquiry is the defendant's relationship to the forum state. *See Walden v. Fiore,* 134 S.Ct. 1115 (2014); *Phillips Petroleum v. Shutts,* 472 U.S. 797 (1985).

Since our seminal decision in *International Shoe,* our decisions have recognized two types of personal jurisdiction: "general" (sometimes called "all-purpose") jurisdiction and "specific" (sometimes called "case-linked") jurisdiction. "For an individual, the paradigm forum for the exercise of general jurisdiction is the individual's domicile; for a corporation, it is an equivalent place, one in which the corporation is fairly regarded as at home." *Goodyear* at 924. A court with general jurisdiction may hear any claim against that defendant, even if all the incidents underlying the claim occurred in a different State. But "only a limited set of affiliations with a forum will render a defendant amenable to" general jurisdiction in that State. *Daimler.*

Specific [personal] jurisdiction is very different. In order for a state court to exercise specific jurisdiction, "the suit" must "aris[e] out of or relat[e] to the defendant's contacts with the forum." *Daimler.* In other words, there must be "an affiliation between the forum and the underlying controversy, principally, [an] activity or an occurrence that takes place in the forum State and is therefore subject to the State's regulation." *Goodyear* at 919. For this reason, "specific jurisdiction is confined to adjudication of issues deriving from, or connected with, the very controversy that establishes jurisdiction." *Id.*

In determining whether personal jurisdiction is present, a court must consider a variety of interests. These include "the interests of the forum State and of the plaintiff in proceeding with the cause in the plaintiff's forum of choice." *Kulko v. Superior Court of Cal.,* 436 U.S. 84 (1978). But the "primary concern" is "the burden on the defendant." *World-Wide Volkswagen* at 292. Assessing this burden obviously requires a court to consider the practical problems resulting from litigating in the forum, but it also encompasses the more abstract matter of submitting to the coercive power of a State that may have little legitimate interest in the claims in question. As we have put it, restrictions on personal jurisdiction "are more than a guarantee of immunity from inconvenient or distant litigation. They are a consequence of territorial limitations on the power of the respective States." *Hanson v. Denckla,* 357 U.S. 235 (1958). "[T]he States retain many essential attributes of sovereignty, including, in particular, the sovereign power to try causes in their courts. The sovereignty of each State . . . implies a limitation on the sovereignty of all its sister States." *World-Wide Volkswagen,* at 293. And at times, this federalism interest may be decisive. . . .

Our settled principles regarding specific jurisdiction control this case. In order for a court to exercise specific jurisdiction over a claim, there must be an "affiliation between the forum and the underlying controversy, principally, [an] activity or an occurrence that takes place in the forum State." *Goodyear,* at 919.

For this reason, the California Supreme Court's "sliding scale approach" is difficult to square with our precedents. Under the California approach, the strength of the requisite connection between the forum and the specific claims at issue is relaxed if the defendant has extensive forum contacts that are unrelated to those claims. Our cases provide no support for this approach, which resembles a loose and spurious form of general jurisdiction. For specific jurisdiction, a defendant's general connections with the forum are not enough. As we have said, "[a] corporation's 'continuous activity of some sorts within a state . . . is not enough to support the demand that the corporation be amenable to suits unrelated to that activity.'" *Goodyear,* at 927.

This case illustrates the danger of the California approach. The State Supreme Court found that specific jurisdiction was present without identifying any adequate link between the State and the nonresidents' claims. As noted, the nonresidents were not prescribed Plavix in California, did not purchase Plavix in California, did not ingest Plavix in California, and were not injured by Plavix in California. The mere fact that other plaintiffs were prescribed, obtained, and ingested Plavix in California—and allegedly sustained the same injuries as did the nonresidents—does not allow the State to assert specific jurisdiction over the nonresidents' claims.

As we have explained, "a defendant's relationship with a . . . third party, standing alone, is an insufficient basis for jurisdiction." *Walden.* This remains true even when third parties (here, the plaintiffs who reside in California) can bring claims similar to those brought by the nonresidents. Nor is it sufficient—or even relevant—that BMS conducted research in California on matters unrelated to Plavix. What is needed—and what is missing here—is a connection between the forum and the specific claims at issue.

Our decision in *Walden* illustrates this requirement. In that case, Nevada plaintiffs sued an out-of-state defendant for conducting an allegedly unlawful search of the plaintiffs while they were in Georgia preparing to board a plane bound for Nevada. We held that the Nevada courts lacked specific jurisdiction even though the plaintiffs were Nevada residents and "suffered foreseeable harm in Nevada." Because the "relevant conduct occurred entirely in Georgia . . . the mere fact that [this] conduct affected plaintiffs with connections to the forum State did not suffice to authorize jurisdiction."

In today's case, the connection between the nonresidents' claims and the forum is even weaker. The relevant plaintiffs are not California residents and do not claim to have suffered harm in that State. In addition, as in *Walden,* all the conduct giving rise to the nonresidents' claims occurred elsewhere. It follows that the California courts cannot claim specific jurisdiction. *See World-Wide Volkswagen* (finding no personal jurisdiction in Oklahoma because the defendant "carried on no activity whatsoever in Oklahoma" and dismissing "the fortuitous circumstance that a single Audi automobile, sold [by defendants] in New York to New York residents, happened to suffer an accident while passing through Oklahoma" as an "isolated occurrence").

Our straightforward application in this case of settled principles of personal jurisdiction will not result in the parade of horribles that respondents conjure up. Our decision does not prevent the California and out-of-state plaintiffs from joining together in a consolidated action in the States that have general jurisdiction over BMS. BMS concedes that such suits could be brought in either New York or Delaware. Alternatively, the plaintiffs who are residents of a particular State—for example, the 92 plaintiffs from Texas and the 71 from Ohio—could probably sue together in their home States. Reversed.

In Rem Cases

As mentioned earlier, a court usually must have personal jurisdiction over a defendant because most lawsuits are of the in *personam* variety, in which the plaintiff is seeking a judgment for damages or an equitable remedy against the defendant. However, if the plaintiff's case is characterized as *in rem*, rather than in personam, the court is not required to have personal jurisdiction over a particular party. (It still must have subject matter jurisdiction, however.) State and federal courts inherently have *in rem* jurisdiction over any item of property located in the forum state, whether the property is real estate or an item of tangible or intangible personal property. If a notice of the lawsuit is published in a newspaper of general circulation in the area where the property is located, the court has power to render a judgment affecting the status of title to the property even without having personal jurisdiction over the owner of the property.

Suppose, for example, that D borrowed money from Bank B and executed a document giving B a mortgage on a home or other piece of real estate. The mortgage makes the real estate collateral for the loan and gives B a right to take ownership and possession of the property if D fails to repay the loan on its agreed terms. If D defaults, B will exercise its right by filing a *mortgage foreclosure* action in court. The object of the action is not D, but instead is the acquisition of the title to the property. This is an *in rem* case, and it is not required that the court have personal jurisdiction over D. B can simply have a notice published in a local newspaper, which is not sufficient notice for personal jurisdiction but is sufficient for an *in rem* case to proceed. As a practical matter, if it is possible to get personal jurisdiction over D, B will usually see to it that the court obtains personal jurisdiction, so that B can also get an in *personam* "deficiency judgment" against D. This is a judgment for any amount of the loan that may remain unpaid if the proceeds from the sale of the property are inadequate.

Other examples of in rem cases include court actions to establish ownership to lost or abandoned property or to give the government title over property that has been forfeited because it was used in connection with certain crimes such as drug dealing.

In addition, the federal law prohibiting one from registering a domain name—a web address, or "url"—that is the same as or confusingly similar to someone else's preexisting trademark and allows the trademark owner to not only sue for damages, but also to ask a federal court to transfer ownership of the domain name to it. In such a case, the federal "anticybersquatting" law provides that if the trademark owner files its lawsuit in a federal court in the state where the computer server that stores the domain name is located, the court can exercise *in rem* jurisdiction over the domain name as an item of intangible property and transfer it to its rightful owner even if no personal jurisdiction has been obtained over the wrongdoer.

Related Matters

If a court has both subject matter and personal jurisdiction, there still may be other preliminary matters to consider, such as venue, *forum non conveniens,* and conflict of laws.

Venue

If a state district court in Texas has subject matter and personal jurisdiction in a case filed by P, *every* district court in Texas has such jurisdiction. The question of where within the state the lawsuit should be heard is a question of *venue*. Every state has statutes that specify which counties are appropriate venues. Typically, venue is appropriate in either the county where the defendant resides or where the accident or transaction took place. Sometimes venue may be proper in other places; if the case involves real estate, an appropriate venue may be the county where the land is located. If there are two or more permissible venues, the plaintiff normally may choose among them when filing the lawsuit. In the federal court system, federal statutes specify which federal districts are appropriate venues.

Rules about venue have some of the same ultimate objectives as rules pertaining to personal jurisdiction, the main one of which is fairness, and a secondary one is efficiency.

Forum Non Conveniens

A court with both subject matter and personal jurisdiction may decline to exercise them if another court, more conveniently connected to the suit, also has both types of jurisdiction. Under the doctrine of *forum non conveniens*, the court may choose to transfer the suit or even dismiss it, forcing the plaintiff to file in the more convenient court.

For example, in one case arising out of a defendant's agent carelessly causing a fire in the plaintiff's warehouse in Virginia, the plaintiff sued 400 miles away in New York City where the state court had subject matter jurisdiction over the simple tort case and personal jurisdiction because of the defendant corporation's many business contacts in New York. However, the New York court declined to exercise its jurisdiction on grounds that the suit was more conveniently brought in Virginia where the plaintiff and all witnesses were located and where the accident had occurred. The only justification the plaintiff gave for filing in New York—that a New York jury was likely to give a bigger verdict—was inadequate.

In determining the most convenient forum, courts will consider private interest factors such as ease of access to sources of proof, costs of obtaining witnesses' attendance, the possibility of a view of the site of the accident, and the convenience of the parties. Public factors to be considered include the imposition of jury service on residents of the community, the congestion of court dockets, and the interest in having local controversies decided at home.

The *forum non conveniens* doctrine can also be applied internationally. For example, a U.S. court of appeals affirmed a decision of the U.S. district court in New York City that used the doctrine as a basis for transferring a case from that federal court in New York to a court in India. The case involved claims against Union Carbide Corporation arising from the tragic leak of toxic gases from a chemical factory that killed more than 2000 people in Bhopal, India. The federal trial judge took this action only after being convinced that Indian law and procedure were designed to handle such claims and provide substantial justice and that an Indian court would take jurisdiction over the claims. The court also conditioned its dismissal in favor of the Indian courts on Union Carbide's consent to the jurisdiction of the Indian courts and its waiver of any statute of limitations defense, i.e, not asserting that time for filing the claim had expired. (*In re Union Carbide Corp. Gas Plant Disaster,* 809 F.2d 195 (2d. Cir. 1987). It can be seen that the doctrine of *forum non conveniens* is actually a very specialized type of venue question.

Conflict of Laws

Assume D Corporation, formed in Delaware with its principal place of business in Colorado, hires P from California to do subcontracting work on D's condominiums in New Mexico. The contract is negotiated in California, Colorado, and New Mexico before being signed in Colorado. When New Mexico officials ordered P to stop work because she did not have a license to do such work in New Mexico, D fired her. P sued in Colorado to recover for the work she had performed before being stopped from completing the project. Several states' laws are potentially applicable to this case. If they all lead to the same result, it does not matter which state's rules are applied. However, in this case, New Mexico law bars P from recovery because she had no license. Colorado and California law would allow her to recover despite the lack of a license. Thus, there is a *conflict of laws.* To determine which state's laws to apply, we must resort to *choice of law* rules, which are designed to prevent a plaintiff with multiple jurisdictions from which to choose (because all have subject matter and personal jurisdiction) from "forum shopping" for the jurisdiction with the laws most favorable to them. Each state has a set of choice of law rules for determining which state's or nation's law should be used to resolve the case.

Conflict of laws questions also can arise in international disputes. Recall for a moment the example of the case against Union Carbide that was transferred from a federal court in New York to a court in India under the doctrine of *forum non conveniens*. The federal court could have retained jurisdiction and decided the case. If so, it probably would have applied the law of India to decide the case; to do so, the court obviously would have to call on experts in Indian law.

Contract Cases. If the parties stipulate in the contract that, for example, "California law will govern any disputes arising out of this contract," the courts will normally respect that choice if it was fairly bargained and California has at least a passing connection to the parties or the transaction. It is especially desirable for the parties to an international transaction to negotiate and include a clause in their contract specifying which nation's law should be applied to any dispute arising from the deal.

Absent a choice by the parties, the traditional view was to apply the law of the state in which the contract was made to any litigation about the validity of the contract and to apply the law of the state in which the contract was to be performed to any litigation about the performance of the contract.

The strong modern trend, however, is to use an *interest analysis*. Using an interest analysis to determine which state's law to apply, courts would consider such factors as the relevant policies of the forum and of other interested states, the protection of justified expectations (that is, which state's laws did the parties assume would apply), certainty, predictability, ease of determination of the law to be applied, and uniformity of result.

In contract cases specifically, most modern courts attempt to determine the state with the "most significant relationship" to the parties and the transaction, considering such factors as (1) the place of contracting; (2) the place of negotiation; (3) the place of performance; (4) the location of the subject matter of the contract; and (5) the domicile, residence, nationality, place of incorporation, and place of business of the parties.

In the factual situation outlined previously, the Colorado Supreme Court applied New Mexico's law, reasoning that New Mexico's interest in protecting its citizens from substandard construction by unlicensed subcontractors outweighed Colorado's interest in validating agreements and protecting parties' expectations. (*Wood Bros. Homes, Inc. v. Walker Adjustment Bureau*, 601 P.2d 1369 (Colo. 1979)).

Tort Cases. Assume that a husband and wife from New Mexico are killed when a plane the husband is piloting crashes in Texas. The parties intended to return to New Mexico and had no other contacts with Texas. The estate of the wife filed suit against the husband's estate in state court in Texas. Texas's doctrine of interspousal immunity would not allow the suit. New Mexico has no such doctrine; its law would allow the suit. Which state's law should apply? The traditional view is to apply the law of the place of the tort—Texas. But why would Texas courts care whether a New Mexico wife's estate can recover from a New Mexico husband's estate? Again, the strong modern trend is to move away from an automatic choice of the law of the place of the tort to an interest analysis. Today, most courts use the following factors in deciding which state has the most significant relationship to the occurrence and the parties: (1) the place where the injury occurred; (2) the place where the conduct causing the injury occurred; (3) the domicile, residence, nationality, place of incorporation, and place of business of the parties; and (4) the place where the relationship, if any, between the parties is centered. In this case, New Mexico law was applied. (*Robertson v. McKnight*, 609 S.W.2d 534 (Tex. 1980)).

LAW, EQUITY, AND REMEDIES

In the next chapter we will examine the major steps in the process of adjudication, paying particular attention to the roles played by the trial and appellate courts in that process. We will see that in all legal controversies the plaintiff is asking for a **remedy**—an order addressed to the defendant, requiring that person either to pay money or to do (or not to do) a particular act. A remedy, then, is "the means by which a plaintiff's right is enforced or the violation of a right is prevented, redressed, or compensated." (BLACK'S LAW DICTIONARY (1979).) All remedies are either "legal" or "equitable" in nature, a fact that can be explained only by a brief glimpse at the development of the early court systems in England.

Courts of Law

Nearly 1,000 years ago, the first Norman kings of England established a system of courts by designating individuals throughout the country to be their personal representatives in the settling of certain kinds of legal disputes. These representatives could grant only very limited types of relief: (1) money damages to compensate for harm caused, (2) possession of real estate, or (3) possession of personal property.

In settling disputes, the courts made up their own rules as they went along, based largely on the customs and moral standards then prevailing, plus their own ideas of "justice" in particular situations. The formulation of rules in this manner, a process that continues today in some branches of law, gave birth to the *common law* (which we will study in more detail in Chapter 4). The royal courts ultimately became known as *courts of law*, and the remedies that they granted were *remedies at law*.

Courts of Equity

When plaintiffs needed relief other than what the courts of law could grant, they often petitioned the king. Such petitions were frequently decided by the king's chancellor, who granted relief when he thought the claim was a fair one. Out of the rulings of successive chancellors arose a new body of "chancery" rules and remedies for cases outside the jurisdiction of the courts of law. This developed eventually into a system of *courts of equity*, as distinct from the courts of law.

A plaintiff who wanted a legal remedy, such as money damages, would bring an *action at law* in a court of law. A plaintiff wanting some other relief, such as an *injunction* or a *decree of specific performance* brought an *action in equity* in an equity court. Examples of the almost countless situations in which a plaintiff might seek and have a good chance of receiving an injunction include a request for an order forcing defendant to stop grazing cattle on land belonging to plaintiff; a request that the court order defendant to cease its copying of plaintiff's copyrighted musical composition, story, or screenplay; or a request that the court prohibit the defendant from continuing to dam up a creek that supplies water to the plaintiff's downstream property. A *decree of specific performance* is similar to an injunction, and orders a defendant to comply with the terms of a contract it made with the plaintiff and which it breached. An example would be a request by the plaintiff that the court order the defendant to transfer title to a unique item of property that the plaintiff had agreed to buy from the defendant. All parcels of land ("real property," or "real estate") are considered unique for this purpose because the disappointed buyer (plaintiff) cannot take an award of monetary damages and buy the same tract of land from someone else. Unique items of *personal property* (property other than real estate) include things like shares of stock in a "closely held corporation," where the shares are not traded on a public market, a portrait or other work of art, or a rare piece of furniture.

Other common equitable actions, in addition to those asking for injunctions and decrees of specific performance, include (1) divorce actions, (2) mortgage foreclosure suits, (3) actions for an *accounting*, brought by one party seeking a share of the profits from a business partnership, a share of revenues from the use of a patent or copyright, and similar situations, and (4) the probate, or administration, of a deceased person's estate, and (5) the supervision by a court of a trustee who is administering a trust for the benefit of the trust's beneficiaries.

The Present Scene

Although the distinction between legal and equitable remedies persists today, there has been a fusion of law and equity courts in virtually all states. This means that separate courts of law and equity, as such, have been eliminated. Instead, the basic trial and appeals courts in the state and federal systems are empowered to hear both legal and equitable actions.

Today, the basic distinctions between the two kinds of actions are these:

1. Whether an action is one at law or in equity depends solely on the *nature of the remedy* that the plaintiff is seeking. Most lawsuits involve requests for monetary damages and thus are *actions at law*.

2. Equitable remedies are considered to be *exceptional*. A plaintiff can obtain an injunction or other equitable remedy only if it can prove that it has *no adequate remedy at law*. This means that no equitable remedy is available if the court concludes that the plaintiff can be fairly and adequately compensated for its loss by receiving monetary damages. Equitable remedies are exceptional in other ways, as well, because a court takes into account factors that would not be relevant in the typical money damages case. A court will not grant plaintiff an equitable remedy if (a) the plaintiff does not have "clean hands"—that is, has been guilty of unfair conduct in his or her dealings with the defendant; or (b) The granting of an equitable remedy might harm the public or interfere substantially with the rights of some third party who is not involved in the case.

3. There is *no jury* in an equitable action. Questions of both fact and law are decided by the court, that is, the trial judge. In a case in which a plaintiff is seeking both a legal and an equitable remedy, such as both monetary damages and an injunction, a jury can be impaneled to determine whether the plaintiff has proved its claim and what damages should be awarded, but the decision whether to grant the injunction (or other equitable remedy) is decided solely by the judge. A trial judge usually has discretion to have a jury impaneled to hear evidence and render a nonbinding *advisory verdict* on the facts related to an equitable remedy, but this is an uncommon occurrence.

3. Proceedings in equitable actions are *less formal* than those at law, particularly in regard to the order in which witnesses' testimony can be presented and the determination of admissibility of evidence. The reason is that there is no jury, the trial judge serving as the fact finder, and a judge is presumed to have sufficient training and experience to ignore improper evidence that might affect lay jurors, to be able to sort things out even when witnesses' testimony is heard in an /illogical order, and to otherwise be unaffected by factors that might interfere with jurors' ability to make a fair and impartial decision about the facts.

CHAPTER 3

LITIGATION AND ALTERNATIVE METHODS OF DISPUTE RESOLUTION

- The Adversarial System
- Litigation: Pretrial Proceedings
- Litigation: Trial Proceedings
- Litigation: The Appellate Courts
- Note on Performance of Judges
- Alternative Dispute Resolution

Many American novels, movies, and television programs feature courtroom scenes to produce dramatic tension for readers and viewers. This is appropriate, because courtroom battles can produce high drama. Nothing quite matches the tension that litigants and attorneys feel when a jury verdict is about to be announced in open court. Most of these dramatic presentations attempt, always very imperfectly, to show what happens in criminal trials. Some of these books, movies, and TV shows are partly accurate, but every one of them takes a great deal of literary license for dramatic effect—they never are truly accurate representations of what actually occurs in real trial proceedings because their goal is to entertain, not to inform.

As noted earlier, this text focuses almost exclusively on civil law and civil litigation, because it is far more relevant to our students' professional careers. This chapter will look at the litigation process in *civil lawsuits*, where an individual, company, or government agency sues another one of these types of parties. And, of course, vice-versa. We will examine such a proceeding from the initiation of a civil suit through the trial process and all the way to final appeal. We hope to help you to understand that litigation can be extremely complicated, expensive, and time-consuming. Indeed, litigation is usually something to be avoided unless it is the only resort after other methods of dispute settlement have failed. But when you cannot avoid litigation, it pays to understand the process.

Although many of the procedures in civil lawsuits and criminal prosecutions are the same, there also are a number of important differences. Some of these differences are noted in the chapter on criminal law and business.

Because of the time and expense of civil and criminal legal proceedings, those that are filed are often settled by agreement at an early stage. A formal legal proceeding hanging over the parties, and the natural uncertainty about the ultimate outcome that usually exists, about 95% of all civil cases and criminal prosecutions are settled before trial. Understanding the process in such a proceeding is extremely important, however, because everything that happens—every action of a trial judge on even the seemingly smallest issue during each stage of the process—alters the bargaining position of both parties by changing the actual or perceived probability of the ultimate outcome.

The filing of a lawsuit plus subsequent procedural developments tend to make both parties more serious about the merits of their own claims and the merits of their opponents' claims. These changes increase the likelihood that the parties will reach a negotiated settlement to avoid uncertainty. Negotiated outcomes also are often fairer than all-or-nothing outcomes imposed by a court, too. But of course, not always. The settlement of a civil lawsuit produces a contract between the parties, with the advice of their attorneys. The same is also true in a criminal prosecution, where an outcome agreed to by the government prosecutor and the defendant and defendant's attorney is often referred to as a "plea bargain."

After we have studied the civil litigation process, we will explore some other ways of resolving disputes, especially those that arise in business. These other methods, which are sometimes grouped together under the name *alternative dispute resolution*, include arbitration, mediation, and other techniques. Such methods are being used with greater frequency today in an effort to resolve disputes more quickly, less expensively, and without destroying valuable relationships.

THE ADVERSARIAL SYSTEM

Before studying the process of civil litigation, it is important to note that both civil and criminal proceedings in the United States are based on the so-called *adversarial system.* This approach to litigation is one of the key features of the common-law system that it inherited from England.

The term *adversarial* has a very specialized meaning in this context. Even in a nation that do/es not use the adversarial system, the parties to a lawsuit or a criminal prosecution obviously are *adversaries.* However, when we use the term *adversarial* to describe the English/American approach to litigation, we are referring primarily to the amount of control that the parties and their attorneys have over the procedure.

Under the adversarial system, the parties themselves (acting through their attorneys) research the law and find and develop the evidence. They decide which issues are going to be presented, which legal arguments are going to be made, which evidence should be gathered and presented, and how the evidence is to be introduced in court. The trial judge does not make these decisions; indeed, the judge normally takes no action unless a party specifically requests it. For example, if one party's attorney attempts to introduce testimony or physical evidence that is not legally admissible, the judge usually will not exclude the evidence unless the other party's attorney makes an objection to the inclusion of that evidence, citing a specific legal reason. If an attorney overlooks a relevant legal argument and fails to make it, the judge normally will not take the initiative to include that argument in the legal analysis of the case.

Although the parties and their attorneys have primary control over the issues and evidence, the trial judge obviously has the duty to exercise ultimate supervisory authority over the entire process. There are, naturally, some differences in the details of how the adversarial system is used in the various countries that employ it. For example, state and federal courts in the U.S. employ lay juries as fact-finders in more types of cases than do courts in other common-law countries such as the UK, Canada, Australia, New Zealand, and India.

The adversarial system can be contrasted with the so-called *inquisitorial system* of litigation used in European nations and, indeed, in most other parts of the world that did not inherit the English legal system. In general, the trial judge (or, sometimes, a panel of trial judges) in the inquisitorial system has much more control over the process, and the parties have much less than in the adversarial system. The judge often will have the authority to decide which issues will be addressed, although the parties certainly will provide important input. The judges are usually in charge of the investigation and gathering of evidence; they do not do this personally but have investigators who answer directly to them. Judges make rulings and take various other actions on their own initiative rather than merely responding to the parties' requests for action. It should be noted that there is significant variation in procedural details among the many countries that use the inquisitorial system, just as there is variation within the adversarial system.

There are good and bad points about both of these systems. The adversarial system requires fewer judges and more lawyers than the inquisitorial system. The inquisitorial system requires that more of the time and energy devoted to a case be expended by public officials (judges and investigators) than by the parties and attorneys. Thus, the adversarial system shifts more of the cost to the private sector, whereas the inquisitorial system places more of the cost in the public sector. The adversarial system also puts primary responsibility for developing the facts in the hands of those (parties and their attorneys) who have a natural incentive to do a more thorough job. However, putting this responsibility in the hands of the parties and their attorneys also means that the fact-gathering process may be aimed more at seeking strategic advantage than finding the truth.

A Note on Attorneys' Fees

Many, perhaps most, other countries follow a "loser pays" system in which the party losing at trial (if there is a clear win and loss) to pay a reasonable attorney fee to the winning party, regardless of whether the plaintiff or defendant wins. This is often called the "English Rule." There are differences among other social policies in different nations, however, that cause the "English" loser pay system to work better than it would in the U.S. In the U.S., even though many observers argue in favor of a "loser pays" system to prevent winning defendants from having to pay so much money to attorneys just for defending them even when they end up winning the case, such a rule would also have the effect of preventing many parties (especially individuals) from pursuing legitimate claims against a defendant because they simply could not afford to risk an adverse ruling.

In some countries with loser pay systems, unlike the U.S., better publicly funded legal aid programs are available to people involved in lawsuits, trade unions sometimes cover legal costs for their members (even if the case does not involve the union); and, trade unions in many nations represent a much larger percentage of the workforce than they do in the U.S. In the end, however, in any complex system every rule or decision involves unavoidable tradeoffs.

Recognizing the difficulties and injustices that can be created by the use of a pure version of either the American system in which each party usually pays all of its own attorney fees and the loser pay system in which the losing party pays both its own and the other party's attorney fees, a number of countries have mixed systems in which trial judges have an enormous amount of discretion to allocate attorney fees as justice demands. A 2013 research paper—Eisenberg, Fisher, & Rosen-Zvi, *When Courts Determine Fees in a System with a Loser Pays Norm: Fee Award Denials to Winning Plaintiffs and Defendants,* 60 UCLA L. Rev. 1452 (2013)—reported the results of an empirical study of how trial judges award attorney fees in Israel. Israel has a primarily loser pay system, but the study found many deviations from the pure loser pay rule to avoid unjust results. For example, the system is almost purely loser pay when two companies of basically the same size are the parties to the lawsuit, but court decisions vary widely on the award of attorney fees when a large company is one part and an individual or small company is the other. There are many other examples of variations from the loser pay rule revealed in this study.

There have always been inequalities in life because some people have a lot more money than others. This fact can sometimes plague legal systems, too, and becomes a particular problem in court actions when the resources of plaintiff and defendant are very unequal. Good attorneys cost money. Pretrial discovery in the American system of litigation can be quite expense. Thus, there is a danger that a much wealthier individual or a large corporation can win a "war of attrition" with small business or with an individual who is not wealthy.

This is not just a problem in the U.S., but in many other nations, as well. For example, the *Irish Independent*, a leading newspaper in Ireland, reported recently that a judge on the nation's High Court had publicly stated that "only paupers and millionaires" can afford to go to court in the country. The judge's assertion was based on the fact that financial assistance is available to those in court proceedings who are very poor, and the "millionaires," of course, have money to pay for excellent attorneys, thus leaving those with middle incomes at a great disadvantage. The judge went on to urge the nation's lawmakers to impose caps on attorney fees to bring down litigation costs so that unequal economic playing fields do not make such a difference in court.

It should be noted that, in the U.S., the degree to which there is public financial assistance is available for low-income litigants in civil cases varies greatly by state. Naturally, members of the middle class are still disadvantaged in states with economic assistance that is limited to relatively poor litigants. Unlike civil lawsuits, in criminal cases in the U.S. there is a constitutional requirement that the state pay for an attorney to represent an indigent criminal defendant. Many other countries do likewise for indigent criminal defendants.

LITIGATION: PRETRIAL PROCEEDINGS

Pretrial proceedings consist of two stages, *the pleading stage* and the *discovery stage*. We will look at each of these steps briefly.

The Pleading Stage

The typical suit is commenced by the plaintiff, through an attorney, filing a *complaint* (or petition) with the court having jurisdiction of the case. At the same time, the plaintiff asks the court to issue a summons to the defendant.

After being served with the summons, the defendant has a prescribed period of time in which to file a response, normally an *answer* to the complaint. After that has been completed, the plaintiff can file a *reply* to the answer if the answer raised new issues. The complaint, answer, and reply make up the pleadings of a case, the main purpose of which is to permit the court and the parties to ascertain the actual points in issue.

The Complaint

The *complaint* sets forth the plaintiff's version of the facts and ends with a "prayer" (request) for a certain remedy based on these facts. The plaintiff alleges those facts that, if ultimately proved by the evidence, will establish a legally recognized claim against the defendant. Suppose, for example, that the plaintiff bought a boat from the defendant, a dealer. The plaintiff claims that the boat leaks badly. After the two parties are unable to resolve their differences, the plaintiff institutes a lawsuit by filing a complaint. The complaint may allege that the parties made an agreement for the sale of the boat on a particular date for a particular price, the price was paid and the boat delivered, the plaintiff used the boat and found that it leaked, the defective condition of the boat is in violation of a warranty made by the dealer, and the plaintiff has suffered economic harm because the boat is worth far less in its defective condition than it would have been worth if not defective. If these facts are ultimately proved, the plaintiff has a good claim against the defendant for breach of warranty. However, the plaintiff might also allege that the defendant intentionally lied about the condition of the boat, thus committing the tort of fraud or perhaps violating a state deceptive trade practice statute.

In most complaints, the remedy requested by the plaintiff is an award of money damages to be paid by the defendant to compensate the plaintiff for his or her loss. If the plaintiff seeks some other remedy, such as an injunction, it will be requested in the complaint. Sometimes the plaintiff's complaint may request multiple remedies, such as damages for past harm and an injunction to prevent future harm. In the boat example, the plaintiff might request money damages for breach of warranty or perhaps fraud. This is not the type of case in which the plaintiff would seek an injunction. The plaintiff might, however, request the equitable remedy of rescission, an order of the court canceling the contract, along with *restitution*, a return of the purchase price.

Motion to Dismiss

Before filing an answer to the plaintiff's complaint, the defendant can file a *motion to dismiss*, which is sometimes called a *motion for judgment on the pleadings*. (An older term for this motion, which is still used in a few states, is the *demurrer*.) The defendant files such a motion if they believe that the plaintiff has no claim even if all the allegations in the complaint are true. In this motion, the defendant asserts that the plaintiff has not even stated a "cause of action"—that is, that even if the plaintiff's allegations are true (which the defendant is not admitting), the law does not recognize such a claim. The motion does not refer to any evidence but merely takes aim at the allegations made in the plaintiff's complaint. Suppose, for example, that Ralph, the owner of a retail store in Milwaukee, is upset about some of the business practices of a competing retailer in town. In a private conversation between Ralph and George, the president of the other retailer, Ralph says, "You and your people are liars and cutthroats; you screw your customers whenever you think you can get away with it; you have the morals of a gutter rat." The conversation is not overheard by anyone else, and Ralph does not repeat any of it to anyone. If George sues Ralph for the tort of defamation, alleging these facts, Ralph will probably file a motion to dismiss and the court will grant it. Even if what Ralph said about George and his company was false, the tort of defamation (slander or libel) can occur only if false defamatory statements about someone are *communicated* to a third party. Thus, George and his company have no claim against Ralph even if events were exactly as George described in his complaint.

If the court grants the motion to dismiss, sometimes the plaintiff will be given an opportunity to amend the complaint. This opportunity is only helpful if the plaintiff's attorney simply forgot to include something. If the problem cannot be corrected by an amendment to the complaint, the court will dismiss the plaintiff's case. However, if the court denies the defendant's motion to dismiss, the defendant will then file an answer.

Like other actions of a trial judge, a ruling on a motion to dismiss can be appealed to a higher court. The plaintiff can begin such an appeal immediately if the trial court grants the motion to dismiss, because this results in a final determination of the case at that level. However, if the trial judge denies the motion to dismiss, the defendant must wait until the case ends at the trial level before appealing; in this situation, the trial judge's ruling on the motion to dismiss probably will be only one of several grounds for the appeal.

The motion to dismiss is the first of several types of motions that give the trial judge an opportunity to end the litigation early when they are convinced that there is no doubt about the outcome and thus no reason to continue.

How Detailed Does the Complaint Have to be to Survive a Motion to Dismiss?

The question of how much detail the plaintiff must include in the complaint to survive the defendant's motion to dismiss is an extremely important one. The reason is that, if little detail is required, the defendant must spend a lot of money going through pretrial discovery before knowing exactly what the allegations are against it. If too much detail is required, on the other hand, a great many plaintiffs with good claims will be denied access to the courts because it is very common for most of the relevant evidence to be in the hands of the defendant. Thus, the decision about how much detail a plaintiff must provide in its complaint is a dollars and cents issue—it determines how much each side must invest at the beginning of a case to move it forward. The decision whether to pursue a legal claim, and the decision by a defendant about how hard to fight it instead of just settling it with the plaintiff despite believing it to be of no merit, is a business decision. The size of the necessary up-front investment is a critical part of every business decision.

Federal Rule of Civil Procedure 8 allowed a plaintiff to file a proper complaint simply by "a short and plain statement of the claim." In its first definitive interpretation of Rule 8, in *Conley v. Gibson*, 355 U.S. 41 (1957), the U.S. Supreme Court ruled that a complaint should not be dismissed for "failure to state a claim" (failure to allege sufficient facts which, if proved, would establish a legally recognized claim against the defendant) "unless it appears *beyond doubt* that the plaintiff can prove no set of facts in support of his claim which would entitle him to relief." (Emphasis added.)

The *Conley* decision guided lower federal courts, and most state courts, for fifty years until the Court overruled it in *Bell Atlantic Corp. v. Twombly,* 550 U.S. 544 (2007). In *Twombly*, the Court held the rule in Conley placed too great a burden on defendants by requiring them to defend against a complaint unless the trial judge is convinced without any doubt that there is no possible way that the plaintiff can ever prove its factual allegations. A complaint might still be sufficient even though the trial judge believes the plaintiff's allegations to be improbable, the *Twombly* Court held, but the standard established by the Court in *Conley* simply went too far and placed an unfairly heavy burden on defendants.

Then, two years after *Twombly*, the Court's five-member majority in *Ashcroft v. Iqbal,* 556 U.S. 662 (2009) moved even farther away from the *Conley* decision than it had in *Twombly*. In *Iqbal*, the Court held that a plaintiff's complaint must state its allegations in such detail that a trial judge finds them to be a "plausble" (believable) contention that the defendant has committed a specific wrong against the plaintiff.

The *Iqbal* case has been widely criticized, including in dissenting opinions filed by four of the nine justices. Federal procedural rules such as the one at issue in *Conley*, *Twombly*, and *Iqbal*, are not legally binding on state courts, although most state supreme courts had voluntarily followed the 1957 ruling in *Conley*. A large number of state courts have expressly refused to follow the 2009 decision in the *Iqbal* case, deciding instead to continue with the approach taken by the Court in *Conley*. Given the complexity and great expense of modern civil litigation, the old *Conley* rule may very well go too far in plaintiffs' direction. But according to many observers and many state courts, *Iqbal* appears to go too far in defendants' direction. As is often the case in legal and public policy debates, a middle ground is often the most desirable but can be exceedingly difficult to achieve.

One of the criticisms leveled at the majority's decision in *Iqbal* is that it requires a trial judge to determine whether the allegations of fact in a plaintiff's complaint are "plausible." Plausibility, or believability, is in its essence a factual issue, and factual issues are never decided at such an early stage of a case. Moreover, no evidence has been introduced at this point in a case, and thus there is nothing on which to base a decision about what the facts are. Observers have noted the almost inevitable inconsistency and unpredictability that will result from having hundreds of federal district judges each make determinations about whether the plaintiffs' allegations are "plausible" when no evidence has yet been produced. Federal district judges have indeed been struggling to find a principled and consistent basis for determining "plausibility."

The Answer

If there is no motion to dismiss, or if one is filed but denied, the defendant responds to the complaint by filing an answer. One thing it usually contains is a *denial* of the plaintiff's allegations. In some places, the defendant is permitted to make a *general denial*, which simply denies all the plaintiff's allegations together. In other court systems, the rules require a defendant to deny each allegation individually; any allegation not denied is deemed to be admitted. The rules in some systems permit a general denial in most cases, but require specific denials of certain types of allegations. Regardless of the form, a denial is essentially a formality that places the plaintiff's allegations in issue and places the burden on the plaintiff to prove the assertions they have made.

It must be remembered that the plaintiff in a civil lawsuit (and the prosecution in a criminal case) bears the overall burden of proof. In other words, if the plaintiff does not ultimately produce evidence that convinces the jury (or judge if there is no jury) of the correctness of the allegations in the complaint, the plaintiff loses. Although the defendant must respond with an answer, they are not obligated to prove anything. Nevertheless, if a defendant believes that the facts create a legally recognized *defense* (sometimes called an *affirmative defense*) against the plaintiff's claim, they will assert the defense in the answer after the denial.

A defense defeats the plaintiff's claim *even if the plaintiff is able to prove those facts that establish all the elements of his or her claim*. Asserting a defense consists of alleging those facts that, if ultimately proved by the defendant, will establish a legally recognized defense against the plaintiff's claim. For virtually every type of civil claim, the law recognizes one or more defenses. In the boat example, the defendant might allege as a defense to the breach of warranty claim that there was a *disclaimer* in the sale contract stating clearly and conspicuously that the boat was a reconditioned one and was being sold on an "as is" basis. If proved, this allegation would defeat the plaintiff's breach of warranty claim. Such a defense would not defeat a fraud claim, however. (In criminal cases, there are also legally recognized defenses against virtually all types of criminal charges.)

When asserting a defense, the defendant does not make a claim or request a remedy but simply tries to defeat the plaintiff's claim. Sometimes, however, the defendant may wish to assert a claim against the plaintiff in the form of a *counterclaim*. The defendant will allege facts that, if proved by the defendant, will establish a legally recognized claim against the plaintiff, and the defendant will ask for money damages or some other remedy. Either party alone might prevail on its claim, or both may prevail; in the latter event, the amount of the smaller judgment will be subtracted from the amount of the larger judgment.

Most counterclaims arise from the same set of circumstances that led to the plaintiff's claim (a so-called *compulsory* counterclaim). In such a case, the rules in most court systems require that the defendant assert the claim in this case as a counterclaim if it is to be asserted at all; they cannot keep quiet about it now and later sue the plaintiff (with their roles and names obviously reversed) on the claim. However, if the defendant's claim against the plaintiff arises from an unrelated set of circumstances, it is a so-called *permissive* counterclaim, and the defendant has a choice of asserting a counterclaim in the present case or suing separately.

In the boat example, the defendant might assert a counterclaim alleging that the plaintiff had not paid all the boat's purchase price, in violation of the sale contract, and request damages in the amount of the unpaid portion. It is not a rare occurrence for a plaintiff to have the tables turned by a counterclaim and to regret that they ever filed a lawsuit.

The Reply

If the defendant raises new matter—additional facts—in the answer, the plaintiff must file a reply. In this pleading, the plaintiff will either deny or admit the new facts alleged in the answer. The most obvious situation in which this occurs is when the defendant asserts a defense and/or counterclaim in the answer.

Defendant's Failure to Respond

Assuming that the court has jurisdiction, the defendant must respond within a specified time period by filing either a motion to dismiss or an answer. This time period is 20 days in the federal district courts and about the same amount of time in most state courts. The clock starts ticking when the defendant receives the summons and complaint. If the defendant does not respond during this period, the court may grant a *default judgment* against the defendant. By failing to respond, the defendant has given up the right to contest liability. The only issue to be determined is the amount of money damages to which the plaintiff is entitled, or the appropriateness of some other remedy the plaintiff may be seeking. The court will conduct a hearing at which the plaintiff presents evidence on the question of damages or other requested remedy.

The Pretrial Discovery Stage

In early years, cases moved directly from the pleading stage to the trial stage. This meant that each party, going into the trial, had little information as to the specific evidence that the other party would rely on in presenting his or her case. Trial proceedings, as a result, often became what was commonly described as a "cat and mouse" game, with the parties often bringing in evidence that surprised their opponents. This situation was a natural outgrowth of the control parties have over evidence gathering and presentation in the adversarial system.

The undesirability of these proceedings was long perceived by lawyers and judges, with the result that, in 1938 in the Federal Rules of Civil Procedure, Congress provided means (called *discovery proceedings*) by which much of the evidence that each party was going to rely on in proving his or her version of the facts would be fully disclosed to the other party before the case came to trial. The most common discovery tools recognized by these federal rules, which have now been essentially adopted by the states, are *depositions, interrogatories, and requests for production of documents.*

A deposition is testimony of a witness that is taken outside of court. Such testimony is given under oath, and both parties to the case must be notified so that they can be present when the testimony is given and thus have the opportunity to cross-examine the witness. Depositions are taken for these reasons (1) to learn what the key witnesses know about the case, (2) to gain leads that will help obtain additional information, (3) to preserve the testimony of witnesses who might die or disappear, and (4) to establish a foundation for cross-examination of witnesses who might later change their stories.

Interrogatories are written questions submitted by one party to the other, which must be answered under oath. Use of this device is a primary way by which the questioning party may gain access to evidence that otherwise would be solely in the possession of his or her adversary.

A demand for documents permits a party to gain access to those kinds of evidence—such as business records, letters, and hospital bills—that are in the possession of the other party. Under modern rules of civil procedure, the party seeking the documents has the right to obtain them for purposes of inspection and copying.

A party must make a good faith effort to comply with the other party's legitimate discovery request. The court can impose various sanctions on parties and attorneys who do not make such an effort. These penalties may include the assessment of discovery costs, attorney's fees, or monetary penalties. In cases of flagrant disregard of legitimate discovery requests, the court can even dismiss a claim or defense or grant a default judgment against the offending party.

Soon after 1938, state legislatures began adopting pre-trial discovery procedures for state courts patterned after the Federal Rules, and for many years all states have had them.

Electronic Discovery

Not that long ago, document discovery was about exchanging reams of paper, drawers of paperwork, or warehouses full of documents, depending on how complicated the case was. But today, more than 90% of corporate documents are created electronically. Furthermore, corporate employees send billions of e-mails and texts per day. These electronic documents are frequently the keys to proving cases. In an important antitrust case, Microsoft CEO Bill Gates was surprised during cross-examination by an e-mail in which he had asked "How much do we need to pay you to screw Netscape?" Wall Street investment banking firms paid hundreds of millions of dollars of settlements in 2002 and 2003 after disclosure of e-mails indicating that in order to get investment banking business, securities analysts had recommended stocks that they knew were overvalued. Accounting giant Arthur Andersen's demise is largely traceable to an attorney's instructions to follow document retention policies that prosecutors read as an order to destroy Enron-related documents. The LIBOR price-fixing scandal of 2012, which cost companies billions of dollars to settle, was uncovered because of incriminating texts and e-mails.

Electronic documents often incriminate corporations. Sometimes they do the opposite and exculpate them. Destruction of them can create liability, especially for securities firms and health-care companies that are required to keep them for a certain time. Attorneys now recommend to their corporate clients that they have document retention, management, and destruction policies, but many companies do not have their IT act sufficiently together to be able to smoothly and efficiently store documents or access them when courts require their production.

E-mails and other electronic documents have become so important in most business litigation that the Federal Rules of Civil Procedure were amended in late 2006 providing companies with guidelines about storing, destroying, and retaining such documents. Although companies are not required to keep all of their electronic documents forever, they must have in place a system to ensure that such documents are available for any legal dispute that could reasonably be expected to arise. This includes keeping so-called "meta-data," that is, data about data, such as the author's name, the date the document was created, and any comments or annotations that were added by users along the way.

Intentional hiding or destroying paper or electronic documents relevant to existing or contemplated litigation is called *spoliation*. In some jurisdictions it is recognized as a tort and in others it violates criminal law.

Because electronic discovery is so expensive, either side could conceivably use it as a tactical weapon. The Federal Rules of Civil Procedure grant to courts discretion to allocate costs in such a way as to preserve fairness. The court in *Zubulake v. UBS Warburg PLC*, 216 F.R.D. 280 (S.D.N.Y. 2003) applied a seven-factor analysis in determining the extent to which a plaintiff seeking documents, rather than the defendant, should bear the cost of production: (a) The extent to which the request is specifically tailored to discover relevant information; (b) The availability of such information from other sources; (c) The total cost of production, compared to the amount in controversy; (d) The total cost of production, compared to the resources available to each party; (e) The relative ability of each party to control costs and its incentive to do so; (f) The importance of the issues at stake in the litigation; and (g) The relative benefits to the parties of obtaining the information.

Compliance with discovery requests from the other party is usually performed voluntarily, because an attorney understands that the trial judge can order compliance when necessary. Making unreasonable requests in which one side asks for far too much evidence that may or may not be relevant, or in which the demand is vague, simply to impose greater costs on the other, will be brought to the attention of the trial judge. The judge will order the requestor to make the request more reasonable, and if it is not, the judge will not require the recipient to comply with it. Failure to comply can bring monetary penalties, or if severe enough, a judge can even dismiss a plaintiff's case or grant a judgment against a defendant.

A common failure to comply with discovery rules is for the recipient of a request for depositions, documents, or other evidence to try to evade it—to not comply, to offer excuses for not complying, and to otherwise stall for time. The requesting party will likewise bring this type of noncompliance to the attention of the judge. The judge will order compliance if the request is found to have been reasonable. Continued noncompliance can bring harsh penalties, including fines, payment of all associated costs, and even the grant by the judge of a default judgment in the case against the offending party regardless of what the evidence might show.

For example, in 2016, Jessica Hernandez, an attorney at a Chicago law firm specializing in immigration law, informed the firm's senior partner, Michael Katz, that she was pregnant and sought a short maternity leave. According to Ms. Hernandez, Katz suggested that rather than return to her full-time position as an associate after giving birth, Hernandez should switch to a contract position and reapply for a full-time job after maternity leave. Hernandez, wishing to stay on as a full-time, salaried associate, told Katz that arrangement was not acceptable. When they were not able to reach agreement, Katz fired Hernandez. She sued for pregnancy discrimination in violation of Title VII of the 1964 Civil Rights Act. Her lawyer asked Katz for several relevant depositions and documents, and during the next three years Katz failed to comply over and over. Finally, in 2019, the federal district court judge granted default judgment to Hernandez for over $229,000. In a case like this, a party's willful noncompliance with discovery usually means that the requested evidence would have been highly unfavorable to their side of the case. In other words, Katz almost certainly knew that his compliance would result in the production of evidence that would cause him to lose the case. This is the inference that a judge will make, in any event.

Another recent example of a trial judge coming down hard on the flagrant refusal to comply with pretrial discovery is *Klipsch Group, Inc. v. ePRO E-Commerce Limited*, 880 F.3d 620 (2nd Cir. 2018), the federal appeals court agreed with the district court that a defendant sued for selling counterfeit headphones (knock-offs) in violation of federal trademark law had engaged in "persistent discovery misconduct." The court concluded that the defendant had apparently destroyed many electronic documents, among other violations, and required the defendant to pay $5 million in penalties to account for the other party's costs in the process.

Summary Judgment

At or near the end of discovery, plaintiff, defendant, or both may file a motion for *summary judgment* as to one or more of the issues in the lawsuit. In filing such a motion a party is arguing to the judge, in essence, that the evidence produced during discovery makes it so clear that the moving party is legally entitled to prevail that a trial would be a waste of time. A judge should grant such a motion only if a thorough review of the evidence obtained through discovery indicates that there is "no genuine issue as to any material fact"—that is, from the perspective of a reasonable person, that there is no real question as to any important factual matter.

Although summary judgment can be granted against either party, the fact that the plaintiff has the burden of proof means that summary judgments for the defendant are more common than for the plaintiff. Thus, if a *defendant* files a motion for summary judgment, it will be granted unless the plaintiff has presented at least enough evidence during discovery to create a genuine issue on all the required elements of its claim. If the plaintiff has failed to produce enough evidence to create a genuine fact issue on even one of the elements of its claim, the defendant is entitled to a summary judgment.

However, if a *plaintiff files* the motion, the court will grant it only if (1) the plaintiff has produced evidence so strong that it proves *all* of the elements of its claim so clearly that there is no genuine fact issue on any of these elements, (2) the defendant has failed to present evidence that creates doubt about any of these elements, and (3) the defendant also has failed to present evidence sufficient to create a genuine issue on an affirmative defense.

LITIGATION: TRIAL PROCEEDINGS

The Trial Stage

Unless a lawsuit is settled out of court or disposed of by the granting of a motion to dismiss or motion for summary judgment, it will eventually come up for trial. In the *trial stage* a jury may be impaneled, evidence presented, a verdict returned, and a judgment entered in favor of one of the parties.

Trial by Jury

In most civil lawsuits in which the plaintiff is seeking a so-called remedy at law, there is a constitutional right to jury trial. Because most lawsuits involve claims for money damages. In federal courts, the Seventh Amendment to the U.S. Constitution grants the right to a jury trial for money damage claims of $20 or more. For federal criminal cases, the right to jury trial is found in the Sixth Amendment, and has been found by the Supreme Court to apply to all criminal cases in which the maximum possible punishment is more than six months in jail. The Supreme Court has also held that the Constitution's guarantee of a right to jury trial in criminal (but not civil) cases applies to the states through the vehicle of the Fourteenth Amendment's Due Process Clause. Almost all states provide similar guarantees in their state constitutions for both civil and criminal cases tried in state courts. When it is not guaranteed in a state constitution, it is a right protected by state legislation.

In *Duncan v. Louisiana*, 391 U.S. 145, 156 (1968), the U.S. Supreme Court stated that the primary purpose of requiring jury trials in criminal cases when requested is to "prevent oppression by the Government" by "Providing an accused with the right to be tried by a jury of his peers gave him an inestimable safeguard against the corrupt or overzealous prosecutor and against the compliant, biased, or eccentric judge."

Moreover, in a 2020 case, *Ramos v. Louisiana*, __ U.S. __, 2020 WL 1906545, the U.S. Supreme Court overruled its own 1972 precedent to hold that the Sixth Amendment, through the Due Process Clause, requires a *unanimous verdict* in state courts to convict a criminal defendant of a crime carrying a possible penalty of more than six months in prison. The Court had earlier required unanimous verdicts in such cases in federal courts. The rationale for the holding in *Ramos* was that less-than-unanimous verdicts in criminal cases had been allowed in states for the purpose of reducing the influence of African-American jurors. It was often the case that only a small number of blacks would be on juries in the courts of some states, and racist majorities in the legislatures of those states had used the measure to dilute whatever effect black jurors might have.

When there is a right to jury trial, a jury will be impaneled if either party formally requests one. Failure to demand a jury trial constitutes a waiver of the right to one. The jury is a fact-finding body; its function is to consider all of the evidence and determine to the best of its ability what really happened. The jury determines whether particular testimony or other evidence is credible and how much strength it seems to have as proof of the alleged facts.

The jury is required to follow the judge's instructions as to the applicable legal principles. If neither party requests a jury, the trial judge performs the fact-finding role in addition to the judicial function. When there is no jury, the trial judge usually is required to prepare formal written "Findings of Fact" and "Conclusions of Law" after hearing the case. Although it is increasingly common today for both parties to waive a jury trial, especially in business disputes, there are still a great many jury trials. Most of the discussion in the remainder of this chapter assumes that there is a jury.

The use of juries drawn randomly from the local population is another unique feature of litigation inherited from the English system. The jury system is sometimes criticized as being inefficient and unpredictable. Critics offer several arguments to support the claim that the jury system is an inferior method for resolving civil disputes, including the following:

1. Jurors do not have to meet any particular educational requirements.
2. Jurors do not have the experience or training to sift through substantial amounts of evidence, weigh it, and make carefully reasoned decisions.
3. Untrained and inexperienced decision makers are likely to be influenced too easily by irrelevant sympathies or by the rhetoric of a highly skilled attorney.
4. Many of the rules of procedure and evidence that lengthen and complicate lawsuits exist only to accommodate an untrained and inexperienced fact-finding body.

5. There are some types of cases, such as patent infringement suits, that are simply too complex factually and legally for most jurors to understand.

Supporters of the jury system in civil cases counter with a number of their own arguments, such as the following:

1. General experience in "living" is more important for deciding the average case than is any kind of specialized training or experience.
2. Juries serve as a limited but valuable check on the power of the judicial branch of government.
3. Juries provide a means for direct, continuous input of community values into the legal system.
4. In the case of factually and legally complex cases, the use of juries forces attorneys to simplify the case.

Impaneling a Jury

When a jury is to be impaneled, names of prospective jurors are drawn from a list of those who have been randomly selected from public records (such as voter registration or driver license) for possible duty during the term. Each prospective juror is questioned in an effort to make sure that the jury will be as impartial as possible. This questioning is conducted by the plaintiff's and defendant's attorneys, by a judge, or by all three, depending on the practice in the particular court system. This preliminary questioning of prospective jurors is called the *voir dire* examination. (*Voir dire*, from the French, means "to speak the truth.")

If questioning indicates that a particular person probably would not be capable of making an impartial decision, the judge will excuse the person by granting a *challenge for cause* made by one of the attorneys. A challenge for cause may be granted, for example, if it is shown that a prospective juror has a close friendship, family relationship, or business association with one of the parties or attorneys, a financial interest in the case, or a clear bias resulting from any other aspect of the action.

The attorney for each party also has a limited number of *peremptory challenges* (or *strikes*). Such challenges permit the attorney to have a prospective juror removed without giving any reason for doing so. The U.S. Supreme Court has ruled, however, that attorneys in civil or criminal cases, or government prosecutors in criminal cases, violate the *Due Process Clause* and *Equal Protection Clause* of the U.S. Constitution if they exclude jurors because of their race. Proving this, of course, can be quite difficult.

Once the number of prospective jurors who have survived both kinds of challenges reaches the number required by law to hear the case, they are sworn in and the case proceeds. Traditionally the number of jurors has been 12, but in recent years courts in quite a few states and in the federal system have reduced the number of jurors in civil cases, with eight or nine being a common number.

However, the U.S. Supreme Court held, in *Ballew v. Georgia*, 435 U.S. 223 (1978), that when there is a right to a jury trial in a *criminal case* (more than six months in prison at stake), having a jury of fewer than 6 members violates the right to a jury that represents a "fair cross-section of the population" that is guaranteed by the 6th and 14th amendments in state and federal courts.

Function of the Jury

We said that the sole function of a jury in both civil and criminal cases is to serve as a fact-finder—a judge of the facts that decides as a group what happened when particular facts are in dispute. An essential part of this right is that a jury must decide the facts based *solely on the evidence* presented during the trial. The following case decided by a U.S. Court of Appeals demonstrates the importance of this principle and how it is applied in one of myriad circumstances that can arise.

United States v. Brown
U.S Court of Appeals for the Eleventh Circuit, 947 F.3d 655 (2020)

Corrine Brown, a member of Congress from Florida, was indicted by a federal grand jury for wire fraud, mail fraud, conspiracy to commit wire and mail fraud, and theft of government funds. The charges related to One Door for Education—Amy Anderson Scholarship Fund ("One Door for Education"), an organization that purported to be a charity that raised funds for, among other things, scholarship assistance for disadvantaged students and the purchase of computers to be donated to schools. According to the indictment, Brown and her alleged co-conspirators used Brown's official position as a member of Congress to solicit contributions to One Door for Education and to induce individuals and entities to make donations to that organization for the stated charitable purposes.

But upon receipt of the contributions, the indictment alleged, Brown and her co-conspirators distributed a total of only $1,200 for scholarships from the more than $800,000 collected for that stated purpose. The indictment further asserted that Brown and her co-conspirators used the vast majority of the remaining monies for their own personal and professional benefit. In particular, the indictment charged that they used the funds to pay for a variety of personal expenses such as luxury vacations, and to pay for events hosted by Brown or held in her honor, including spending the monies for the use of luxury boxes at sporting and concert events.

In Brown's trial on these alleged crimes in federal district court, "Juror 13," so designated because that was his number in the original pool of prospective jurors, was selected to serve on the jury. All jurors swore an oath to pay careful attention to the evidence presented, to deliberate together in private, and render a verdict based solely on the evidence presented. During the jury's deliberations, Juror 13 stated to the group that he had been told by the "Holy Spirit" that Brown was innocent of all charges. Another juror sent a note to the judge, stating: "Your Honor, With all due respect, I'm a little concerned about a statement made by Juror #13 when we began deliberation. He said 'A Higher Being told me Corrine Brown was Not Guilty on all charges.' He later went on to say he 'trusted the Holy Ghost.' We all asked that he base his verdict on the evidence provided, the testimony of the witnesses and the laws of the United States. Other members of the Jury share my concern."

The judge temporarily suspended deliberations and questioned Juror 13 at length about what he had said, and what he meant by it. The judge was concerned about whether this juror had meant merely that he would seek god's guidance in interpreting the evidence, which would not be a violation of the judge's instructions, or whether the juror meant that he would vote on guilt or innocence based on his perceived divine revelation. The latter would violate the judge's legally correct instruction that jurors must base their votes only on the evidence presented during trial.

After lengthy questioning, the judge concluded that the juror was very honest and sincere and had meant the latter, that he would vote on guilt or innocence based on the divine dictate he had perceived. The judge removed the juror, who was then replaced by an alternate juror who had also been in the jury box throughout the trial and had seen and heard all of the evidence. The jury ultimately convicted the defendant Brown. Brown was sentenced to a lengthy prison term. Brown appealed to the U.S. Court of Appeals for the 11th Circuit.

Rosenbaum, Circuit Judge:

To put into perspective the questions we must consider, we begin our inquiry with a brief review of our jury system. The jury is a central foundation of our justice system and our democracy. For centuries, it has been an inspired, trusted, and effective instrument for resolving factual disputes and determining ultimate questions of guilt or innocence in criminal cases. Though the jury system is not without its flaws, juries reach fair and impartial verdicts by undertaking "deliberations that are honest, candid, robust, and based on common sense. That process engenders the community to accept jury verdicts, "an acceptance essential to respect for the rule of law.

Bedrock to that trusted system, a juror's deliberations and verdict must be based upon the evidence developed at the trial. That requirement goes to the fundamental integrity of all that is embraced in the constitutional concept of trial by jury. Due process also requires a jury capable and willing to decide the case *solely* on the evidence before it, and a trial judge ever watchful to prevent prejudicial occurrences and to determine the effect of such occurrences when they happen.

In other words, if a juror bases his decision on some improper consideration, that deprives the parties of due process and shatters the Sixth Amendment's promise that a jury's verdict will be based on the evidence. As we have noted, the entire premise of a trial and all the precautions underlying the admission and exclusion of evidence exist for the purpose of ensuring that verdicts are determined based on the relevant and reliable evidence presented at trial. So conduct or beliefs that cause a juror's verdict to be rooted in something other than the evidence undermine the jury and trial system as a whole. For these reasons, if our jury system is to be viewed as legitimately convicting or acquitting individuals—a circumstance necessary to the continued vitality of the rule of law in our country—jurors' decisions must be based on the evidence presented at trial. . . .

If the constitutional right to a jury trial means anything, it means a right to a verdict based on the evidence. Indeed, the entirety of our procedural mechanisms is geared to achieve this result: we have trials so we can ensure all jurors consider the same universe of evidence; we have an entire body of rules—the Federal Rules of Evidence—devoted to controlling the information on which jurors can rely in reaching their decision; and we expressly instruct the jurors that they must determine their verdict based on the evidence. Then, if a defendant loses at trial, on appeal, we review the record to be certain that sufficient evidence supports the verdict.

We do these things to try to ensure that only those proven guilty based on admissible evidence will be convicted and to try to prevent convictions that arise from prejudice or even ostensibly noble reasons—such as a juror's belief that God has told him to convict, irrespective of the evidence. The consistent application of these practices underpins the public's faith in the jury system and delivers due process of law, an ideal in which our system of justice is grounded.

So we must steadfastly insist that a deliberating juror who is incapable of reaching a verdict based on the evidence be dismissed, regardless of whether that juror intends to convict or acquit a defendant. If we do not, we guarantee that, under at least some circumstances, a juror who is unable to arrive at a verdict rooted in the evidence will nonetheless be allowed to convict a defendant. That is unacceptable.

Here, the district court became aware that during deliberations, Juror 13 in Defendant-Appellant Corrine Brown's trial made remarks suggesting he might not base his verdict on the evidence adduced at trial. Specifically, Juror 13 informed the other jurors at the outset of deliberations that "[t]he Holy Spirit told [him]" that Brown was not guilty on all counts.

The district court questioned Juror 13 for a while, in the presence of the defendant and the prosecuting and defense attorneys. The record of this questioning revealed that, in questioning the juror, the judge was careful, polite, and respectful. The judge slowly sought to ascertain whether Juror 13 meant that he had prayed to the Holy Spirit for guidance and wisdom in reaching a verdict based on the evidence—which would not run afoul of the court's instructions to return a verdict based on the evidence—or whether he meant instead that he believed the Holy Spirit had "told" him to return a certain verdict irrespective of what the evidence showed—which would violate the court's instructions. Among many other things, Juror 13 said to the judge that he had received information from his "Father in Heaven" as to what he was told to do in relation to what he heard here . . . this past two weeks"—specifically to find Brown not guilty of all 24 charges.

The trial judge observed that "a district court should excuse a juror during deliberations only when no substantial possibility exists that they're basing their decision on the sufficiency of the evidence." Based on Juror 13's responses and physical demeanor, the district court concluded that Juror 13 was not capable of rendering a verdict rooted in the evidence presented at trial but that, despite his best intentions, Juror 13 would instead arrive at a verdict based on his perceived divine revelation, uninformed by the actual evidence. For this reason, the district court dismissed Juror 13 from the jury. . . .

There is certainly nothing wrong with jurors choosing to pray for wisdom and guidance in adjudging the evidence. But in our system, ultimately, jurors must root their verdicts in the evidence and the court's instructions on the law. Because the district court permissibly found that Juror 13 was unable to comply with that cardinal precept, it did not abuse its discretion by excusing Juror 13 based upon that finding. . .

We find no clear error in the district court's factual findings. And for that reason, the district court certainly did not abuse its discretion in dismissing Juror 13 from the jury. To hold otherwise would undermine our system of justice by allowing jurors to return verdicts based not on the evidence or law, but instead on a juror's perceived divine revelation, irrespective of the evidence. Though here, the juror's perceived divine revelation might have worked in the criminal defendant's favor had the district court not learned of it mid-deliberations, a contrary holding would allow criminal defendants to be *convicted* based on a divine revelation divorced from the evidence, rather than the evidence presented at trial—a troubling result, to say the least. And regardless of whether it works in favor of or against the defendant, a rule that would allow a juror to base his verdict on something other than the evidence would be antithetical to the rule of law and is contradicted by decades of precedent.

. . . . The district court did not dismiss Juror 13 because of Juror 13's religion. Rather, it dismissed him because it found him incapable of rendering a verdict rooted in the evidence. So long as the district court's ruling in that respect was not clearly erroneous, it makes no difference why Juror 13 was incapable of arriving at a verdict based on the evidence. . . . For the reasons we have explained, we affirm the judgment of the district court.

Presentation of Evidence

After the attorneys for both sides have made opening statements outlining their cases, the plaintiff begins to present its case. As we have seen, the plaintiff has the *burden of proof*—the duty to prove the facts alleged in the complaint. In a normal civil case, the plaintiff must convince the fact-finder of the truth of the allegations by a *preponderance of the evidence*—in other words, the plaintiff has to convince the fact-finder that it is *more likely than not* that each of its allegations is true. The plaintiff attempts to meet this burden by presenting evidence to support his or her version of the facts. This evidence may consist of the sworn testimony of witnesses, as well as physical evidence such as documents, photographs, and so on. When an item of physical evidence is introduced in court, it is usually required that a witness with personal knowledge about the item give sworn testimony about its authenticity. A witness who gives false testimony while under oath may be convicted of the crime of *perjury*.

The testimony of a witness is normally elicited by questions from an attorney. When a witness is called to testify in court by the plaintiff's attorney, that attorney questions the witness first. This is called the direct examination. As a general rule, an attorney cannot ask leading questions during the *direct examination*. The attorney for the other side must object, however, before the judge will order the attorney to stop asking leading questions. A leading question is one that suggests its own answer, that is, it "puts words into the witness's mouth." "You saw the defendant's car smash into the plaintiff's car while the defendant was going at a high rate of speed, didn't you?" is a leading question.

If the attorney calls an *adverse witness*, however, the rule against leading questions does not apply. An adverse witness is either the opposing party to the case or some other witness for the other side. After each of the plaintiff's witnesses testifies, the defendant's attorney has an opportunity to conduct a *cross-examination* of that witness. The attorney is permitted to ask leading questions in cross-examination. The purpose of cross-examination is to discredit or cast doubt on the witness's testimony. For example, a cross-examination might divulge that (1) pertinent facts in the direct examination were omitted, (2) a witness's powers of observation were poor, (3) the witness made a statement in the past (such as in a deposition) that is inconsistent with his or her present testimony, thus creating doubt about his or her credibility, or (4) the witness is not completely disinterested because they stand to gain or lose something from the outcome of the case.

At the judge's discretion, the plaintiff's attorney may then have a chance to conduct a *redirect examination* to deal with any new matters that might have developed during cross-examination. The judge similarly has discretion to permit another cross-examination after the redirect, but this is unusual.

After all the plaintiff's evidence has been presented, the defendant then has the same opportunity. The defendant's purpose will be to offer evidence tending to show that the plaintiff's allegations are not correct. If the defendant has asserted a defense or counterclaim, they also will offer evidence to meet the burden of proof on those allegations. The procedures and rules are the same when the defendant presents evidence as when the plaintiff was doing so, except that the roles obviously are reversed on direct, cross-, and redirect examination.

Rules of Evidence

Before going on, a brief mention of the *rules of evidence* is necessary. These rules attempt to ensure that the evidence presented in a court of law is relevant to the issues and is as accurate and reliable as possible.

The rules of evidence apply whether there is a jury performing the fact-finding role or whether the trial judge is doing so. The rules are more important, however, and are often applied more strictly in a trial before a jury than in one before a judge. As mentioned earlier, even if evidence is inadmissible under the rules of evidence, it will be excluded only if the attorney for the other side objects. Such an objection is made during the trial when an attempt is made to introduce the evidence. Before trial, however, if an attorney can identify inadmissible evidence that the other side probably will try to present in court and can convince the judge that the other side may be able to "sneak in" some of this evidence before the attorney has a chance to object, the judge may grant a motion ordering the other side not to make the attempt.

Although the rules of evidence are so numerous and complex that a complete treatment is impossible here, we can provide a flavor of them by discussing three kinds of evidence that are commonly excluded by the rules.

Irrelevant Evidence. If witness is asked a question that has no logical relationship to any of the disputed issues of fact, the opposing attorney may object on the basis that the answer would constitute *irrelevant evidence*. In a negligence suit arising from an auto accident, for example, such matters as the defendant's religious beliefs or the fact that they were convicted of a charge of reckless driving several years earlier would have no bearing on the present case. Objections to such evidence would be sustained by the court. Documents or other physical evidence can also be excluded on grounds of irrelevancy.

Hearsay. In our common experience, we all know that second-hand information is usually not as reliable as first-hand information. The law takes this fact into account by holding that, in general, *hearsay evidence* is not admissible in court. Hearsay evidence may take the form of oral testimony by a witness, or it may consist of a statement in a written document that is offered as evidence. Oral or written evidence is hearsay if (1) it consists of a statement made by some person who is not testifying personally in court and (2) the evidence is offered in court for the purpose of proving the truth of that statement.

Thus if an issue in a particular case is whether a trucker delivered a shipment of goods to the X Company on a certain day, witness W (a jogger in the vicinity at the time) could testify that she saw packages being unloaded from a truck on the day in question. But neither W nor any other witness would normally be allowed to testify that she *was told by a third party*, Z, that Z saw goods being unloaded on the day in question. In the latter situation, W's testimony would be inadmissible hearsay because it related a statement of Z, who is not testifying in person, and the evidence is being offered for the purpose of proving that what Z said is true.

There are many situations in which second-hand statements can be placed into evidence because they are not offered for the purpose of proving the truth of the statements. In a breach of contract case, for example, the plaintiff or some other witness may testify in court that the defendant (D) said "I will sell you my car for $10,000." This would not be hearsay, because the witness's testimony is not being offered for the purpose of proving that the internal content of D's statement is true. Indeed, D's statement cannot be characterized as true or false; there may be a question about whether D actually said it, but there can be no issue about the truth or falsity of the statement's content. Sometimes such a statement is called a *verbal act*. Another example would be, in a defamation case brought by P against D, the statement allegedly made by D that "P is a thief, a liar, and a cheat." A witness's testimony in court that D said this would be offered for the purpose of proving that D actually said such a thing and not for the purpose of proving the content of D's statement as a factual matter.

Even if evidence constitutes hearsay, sometimes it is nevertheless admissible under an exception to the hearsay rule. Exceptions exist for situations in which, despite being within the definition of hearsay, particular kinds of evidence are likely to possess a relatively high degree of reliability. For example, a ledger or other business record includes "statements" of the person who made the entry in the record; these statements relate to the factual details of particular actions or business transactions. If the person who made the entry is not testifying personally about his or her recollection of a certain transaction, but instead the business record is offered to prove particular facts about the transaction, the business record is hearsay. There is, however, a well-established exception for business records. Such records are usually made with care because the business firm relies on them for many important purposes. The exception usually applies if a witness in custody of the records can testify under oath that the record was made "in the usual course of business" and was made at or near the time of the act or transaction being recorded. The exception can apply to the regularly kept records of non-business organizations, as well.

Opinion. Sometimes a witness is asked for or volunteers information that they believe to be true but that is not based on the witness's personal knowledge. As a general rule, such *opinion evidence*, whether in oral or written form, is not legally admissible. For example, in an auto accident case, a witness properly could testify that they had observed the defendant's car weaving back and forth on a highway shortly before the accident. On the basis of this observation, however, the witness could not testify that the defendant was "obviously drunk." Evidence normally is supposed to take the form of information based on direct observation; the drawing of inferences, the forming of opinions, and the reaching of conclusions are tasks for the jury (or the judge if there is no jury).

Opinion evidence is not always excluded. On technical matters that lie outside the knowledge of ordinary jurors, it is frequently necessary that qualified experts be permitted to state their opinions as an aid to the jury's or judge's determination of what facts probably occurred. Thus a physician may give an opinion as to cause of death or as to whether a particular course of medical treatment is generally accepted within the medical community. Similarly, a civil engineer may give an opinion as to the likely cause of a bridge collapsing.

An expert must, however, testify as to the *factual basis* for the opinion—what evidence led the expert to form the particular opinion, and the reasoning employed in forming it. Unless the attorney for one party *stipulates* (agrees) that a particular witness called by the other party is qualified to testify as an expert, the judge must make a ruling on whether the witness is so qualified. In the average situation, a person called as an expert witness is stipulated as such by the other side. Normally, someone who is to be an expert witness in a case must prepare a detailed written report laying out not only the expert's opinions but also the evidence that supports these opinions, the report being provided to the attorney for the other side and to the trial judge.

Motion for Directed Verdict/Judgment as a Matter of Law

After all the plaintiff's evidence has been presented, the defendant's attorney often makes a motion for *directed verdict*. In the federal courts, this is now called a motion for *judgment as a matter of law* (JMOL). This motion makes the same assertion as the earlier motion for summary judgment, except that the motion for directed verdict is based on more evidence, including the personal testimony of witnesses in court. The motion asserts that the plaintiff's evidence on one or more of the required elements of its case is either nonexistent or so weak that there is no genuine issue of disputed fact. Thus, "reasonable minds could not differ" on the factual question, and the judge should decide the case "as a matter of law" instead of sending it to the jury. Sometimes it is said that the motion raises the issue of whether there is a "jury question."

If the defendant's motion for directed verdict is denied, the defendant then presents its case as discussed earlier. At the close of the defendant's case, the plaintiff can make a motion for directed verdict. The motion contends that the plaintiff's evidence on the required elements of its claim is so overwhelming and the defendant's rebuttal evidence is so weak that reasonable minds could not differ in the conclusion that the plaintiff has met its burden of proof. Again, the motion asks the judge to decide the case as a matter of law and not send it to the jury. The defendant can also make a motion for directed verdict at this time, regardless of whether they had earlier made one after presentation of the plaintiff's case. Motions for directed verdict are denied in most cases, because once a case has progressed this far there usually are genuine issues of fact that must be resolved.

Instructions to the Jury

When a case is submitted to the jury, the judge provides instructions to guide the jury in its deliberations. These instructions are often read aloud to the jury in open court, and in most states, a written copy of these instructions is then given to the jury before they begin their deliberations. The instructions typically contain several parts, including (1) general rules of conduct, such as requirements that the jurors refrain from discussing the case with anyone except other jurors in formal deliberations until the case is over and not speculate about the effect that insurance coverage or attorney fees might have on the ultimate judgment; (2) definitions of certain relevant legal terms; and (3) the court's charge to the jury.

The *charge* is the core of the instructions and gives the jury a legal framework for performing its job. A charge may be *general or special* or a combination of the two types, depending on the court system. In the same system, different types of charges may be used in different types of cases; in a particular state, for instance, a special charge might be used in civil cases and a general charge in criminal ones. Although the *general charge* is most common, mixed special and general charges are increasing in usage. A general charge outlines and explains the relevant legal principles for the jury; it then asks them to decide the relevant facts and reach a verdict either for the plaintiff or for the defendant. (In a criminal case, the charge would ask for a verdict of guilty or acquittal.) A *special charge* is a series of questions to the jury; each question relates to a disputed fact and asks for a yes or no answer. Regardless of the type of charge used, in a typical case in which the plaintiff is seeking an award of money damages, there will be a question at the end of the charge that asks the jury to determine the amount of damages, assuming that the jury has ruled for the plaintiff (in a general charge) or has answered all questions favorably to the plaintiff (in a special charge).

The following case illustrates the critical importance of the judge's instructions to the jury.

RILEY v. WILLIS
Florida Court of Appeals, 585 So. 2d 1024 (1991)

Juanita Willis, a minor, and her sister were walking along the side of Highway 50 in Brooksville with their dog between them. The dog was not on a leash. Juanita walked closest to the road. Joseph Riley was driving on Highway 50, which he used every day to travel to and from work. Just as Riley's truck pulled even with the girls, the dog darted toward the road. Juanita leaned into the road and was struck by the front of Riley's truck. Juanita, plaintiff, filed suit against Riley, defendant, alleging that Riley's negligence was the cause of her injuries. Riley raised the defense of contributory negligence. Under Florida law, as in most states today, if the jury finds that both the plaintiff and the defendant are negligent, the plaintiff's damages are reduced by the percentage that his or her negligence contributed to the occurrence. However, if the plaintiff's negligence contributed more to the occurrence than did the defendant's, the plaintiff cannot receive any money damages.

In the trial, Riley testified that he saw the two girls and slowed from 45 mph to about 35 mph as he approached but did not sound his horn or move to the left of his lane. He also stated that after his truck pulled alongside the girls, he lost sight of them and did not see the dog bolt or Juanita bend into the road.

At the close of the evidence, the trial judge gave the jury instructions about what a plaintiff has to prove to establish a claim of negligence against the defendant and what a defendant has to prove to establish a defense of contributory negligence. In addition, the court included an instruction setting forth a Florida statute detailing the special duty of a motorist to avoid "obstructions" in the roadway by moving to the left of the center of the highway. This instruction had been requested by Juanita's attorney. However, the judge refused to include an instruction, requested by Riley's attorney, concerning a county ordinance that required people to keep their dogs on a leash. The jury found that the plaintiff's negligence contributed 40 percent to the incident and the defendant's 60 percent. The trial judge entered judgment requiring defendant to pay 60 percent of the amount of damages found by the jury to have been suffered by the plaintiff.

Riley appealed on the following grounds: (1) The trial judge should not have included the jury instruction about a motorist's special duty to avoid obstructions. (2) The trial judge should have included the jury instruction about the county ordinance requiring an owner to keep his or her dog on a leash, because Juanita's dog was not on a leash and this contributed substantially to the accident.

Goshorn, Judge:

Riley asserts that an instruction governing a motorist's duty to avoid an obstacle was improperly given. The instruction contained section 316.081 (l) (b), Florida Statutes (1987), which provides in relevant part: "(1) Upon all roadways of sufficient width, a vehicle shall be driven upon the right half of the roadway, except as follows: (b) When an obstruction exists making it necessary to drive to the left of the center of the highway; provided any person so doing shall yield the right-of-way to vehicles traveling in the proper direction upon the unobstructed portion of the highway within such distance as to constitute an immediate hazard...."

The controversy surrounding the instruction concerns the word "obstruction" and whether evidence of an obstruction hindering Riley was presented at trial. The term "obstruction" is not defined by Chapter 316. Black's Law Dictionary 972 (rev. 5th ed. 1979) defines "obstruction" as "a hindrance, obstacle or barrier." The evidence presented at trial is unrefuted that at the time of the accident Riley's view was unobstructed and the road was clear. It is also unrefuted that Juanita did not bend into the path of Riley's oncoming truck until the truck was practically upon her. Prior to that moment, Juanita and Ebony [her sister] were walking along the side of the road. The obvious inference from the instruction is that Juanita herself was an obstacle that Riley was statutorily obligated to avoid. Yet no testimony or other evidence was presented that Juanita posed an obstacle to the oncoming truck, making it necessary for Riley to drive to the left of the center of the highway.

Jury instructions must be supported by facts in evidence, and an instruction not founded upon evidence adduced at trial constitutes error. Whether that error requires reversal depends on whether the appeals court believes that the improper instruction probably had an effect on the jury's affected the jury's deliberations by misleading or confusing it. The instruction at issue in [this case] quite likely confused and misled the jury by creating the erroneous impression that Riley was obligated to somehow avoid Juanita when she reached out into the road and became an "obstacle" simultaneously with Riley's passing. The giving of the improper instruction requires reversal.

Riley also appeals the trial court's refusal to instruct the jury on Hernando County Ordinance 86-2, section 6-5, the local leash law: "The owner, harborer, keeper or person having custody or care of an animal shall ensure that: (1) All dogs, except police dogs on active duty, shall be kept under physical restraint by a responsible person at all times while off the premises of the owner, harborer or keeper." The trial court refused to grant the instruction because no evidence was presented that Juanita owned the dog. However, the ordinance is also applicable to a person who is a "harborer, keeper or person having custody or care of an animal." The record is undisputed that the dog was walking unleashed between Juanita and Ebony until it darted toward the road and Juanita tried to grab it....

A party is entitled to have the jury instructed upon its theory of the case when there is evidence to support the theory. In *Orange County v. Piper,* 523 So. 2d 196 (Fla. 5th DCA) this court set forth three elements that must be met in order to establish that failure to give a requested jury instruction constitutes reversible error: (1) The requested instruction accurately states the applicable law, (2) The facts in the case support giving the instruction, and (3) The instruction was necessary to allow the jury to properly resolve all issues in the case.

[The requested instruction met these requirements.] Riley's theory of the case attempted to show that, but for the girls' failure to walk the dog on a leash, the dog would not have darted toward the road and Juanita would not have lunged into Riley's oncoming truck. Riley's requested instruction sought to bolster his claim that Juanita's own negligence resulted in the accident; her failure to comply with the local leash law was a direct and proximate cause of her accident. Indeed, violation of a municipal ordinance is prima facie evidence of negligence [i.e., negligence "per se]. The failure to give the requested instruction was reversible error. [Reversed and remanded for a new trial.]

The Jury's Verdict

We saw that the traditional practice drawn from English law was that juries always consisted of 12 members, and that this number has been reduced in some states and in federal district courts. Traditional English practice also required that a jury must reach a unanimous verdict or else there was no jury verdict at all. When a jury is not able to reach a verdict with the required degree of agreement, it is a "hung jury."

The requirement of a unanimous vote in one direction or another was also a traditional requirement of the English common law in both civil and criminal cases. In civil cases, because neither a person's freedom nor their life are at stake, verdicts have been allowed in state and federal courts in recent years by less than unanimous votes, such as 9-3 or 10-2 (or, similar proportions when juries consist of fewer than 12 members).

After the Verdict

After the jury has reached its verdict, the court usually enters a judgment in conformity with it. Occasionally this does not happen, however, because the losing party still has an opportunity to make two additional types of motions. One is the *motion for judgment notwithstanding the verdict* (*or motion for judgment* N. O. V, an abbreviation for the Latin equivalent, *non obstante veredicto*). In the federal system, this motion is now called a renewed motion for judgment as a matter of law (JMOL) and must be filed within 10 days of the verdict.

This motion makes the same contention earlier made in the motion for directed verdict (and even earlier in the motion for summary judgment); it essentially asserts that the judge earlier should have granted a directed verdict in favor of the movant and should not have let the case go to the jury because the evidence was so one-sided in the movant's favor.

Although a judge rarely grants this motion, it does provide the judge with something of a "safety valve" if a jury goes completely against the evidence. The other post-verdict motion that may be filed by the party who suffered an adverse jury verdict is the *motion for new trial*. This motion alleges that the trial judge committed one or more errors in the trial that probably affected the outcome. The errors alleged in such a motion may include erroneous rulings on objections to evidence, erroneous wording of the instructions that misstated the applicable law, granting a judgment based on insufficient evidence, and so on.

The following case illustrates what happens when a party attempts to appeal without having filed one of these post-verdict motions in the trial court.

MAGEE v. BEA CONSTRUCTION CORP.

U.S. Court of Appeals for the First Circuit
797 F.3d 88 (2015)

Zoraida Magee and her husband Robert, the plaintiffs, are citizens of New Jersey. Having retired, they wished to build a vacation home in Vieques, Puerto Rico. To that end, they entered into an oral contract with BEA Construction Corp. in December of 2008 for the assembly of a prefabricated house on a lot that they owned in Vieques. The plaintiffs gave BEA an $80,000 down payment in return for BEA's promise to complete the project within 16 months. Work commenced shortly thereafter, but after one year little work had been done and the business relationship between BEA and the Magees began to sour. At that time, the parties agreed that BEA would stop work and reimburse the unspent portion ($74,406) of the down payment, and that the Magees would not take legal action. Ultimately, however, BEA repaid only $1,000 to the plaintiffs. The parties then entered into a second oral agreement for the assembly of a smaller and cheaper home. This new project was to be completed within four months and the plaintiffs were to receive credit against the contract price for any monies owed to them with respect to the original project. BEA began receiving materials in May of 2011 but by July of 2012 it had managed to do nothing more than dig a square hole and place rebar steel rods for concrete reinforcement in the ground. , and the filed suit against BEA for breach of contract in federal district court (federal subject matter jurisdiction being based on diversity of citizenship and the required amount in controversy).

The jury found that BEA breached a valid contract with the Magees and that the total amount of monetary damages incurred by the Magees was $150,000. The trial judge entered judgment ordering BEA to pay this amount to the Magees. BEA appealed to the U.S. Court of Appeals for the First Circuit.

SELYA, Circuit Judge:

Though BEA's appellate brief is not a model of clarity, we construe it liberally and tease from its heated rhetoric three lines of argument. These lines of argument can be summarized as follows: that the jury (i) erroneously found BEA in breach of its contractual obligations; (ii) compounded this error by incorrectly finding that the plaintiffs were not in breach; and (iii) arbitrarily failed to credit pivotal testimony. A common thread links the three components of this asseverational array: whether viewed singly or in the ensemble, all of BEA's arguments boil down to an attack on the sufficiency of the evidence. That attack stumbles at the threshold. It is an elementary principle that a party who wishes to challenge the sufficiency of the evidence on appeal must first have sought appropriate relief in the trial court. BEA flouted this elementary principle, however, and there is a price to pay.

We need not tarry. BEA could have moved for the entry of judgment as a matter of law at various points during and after the trial, see Fed. R. Civ. P. 50(a)-(b), but it never deigned to file such a motion at the close of the plaintiffs' case, at the close of all the evidence, or even after the verdict. By the same token, BEA could have moved for a new trial following the verdict, see Fed. R. Civ. P. 59, but it did not deign to do so. BEA's decision to forgo any and all of these anodynes precludes it from challenging the legal sufficiency of the evidence for the first time on appeal. We need go no further. The lesson of this case is that "courts are most frequently moved to help those who help themselves." Paterson-Leitch Co. v. Mass. Mun. Wholesale Elec. Co., 840 F.2d 985, 989 (1st Cir. 1988). BEA did little to help itself, and . . . the judgment is affirmed.

LITIGATION: THE APPELLATE COURTS

Nature and Role of Appellate Courts

If a party is dissatisfied with the outcome in the trial court, and his or her attorney believes that legally material errors may have been committed in the trial, the party may wish to appeal the trial court's decision to a higher court.

The function of an appellate court is very different from that of a trial court. An appellate court does not hear evidence or make any factual determinations; instead the court seeks to determine whether material errors were committed by the trial court. A material error is one that probably affected the outcome. If a case is appealed to the highest court in a particular system after having been heard by an intermediate level appellate court, the high court essentially "reviews the review" of the intermediate appellate court.

In most appellate courts, the party who is appealing is usually referred to as the *appellant*; the other party is the *appellee*. Sometimes different terms are used, such as *petitioner and respondent*, which are the terms used by the US Supreme Court. When an appellate court writes its opinion in a case, it normally uses either of these sets of terms to refer to the parties. Occasionally, however, the court's opinion will refer to the parties by their original trial court designations—plaintiff and defendant.

An appellate court always includes at least 3 judges, and often more. When the court has more than 3 members, it sometimes expands its capacity for work by dividing into panels of 3 judges for each case. When this is done, the entire membership of the court has the authority to review the decision of the 3-judge panel, although it usually does not do so. For example, the various U. S. Courts of Appeal, many of which have more than 10 judges, usually divide into 3-member panels to hear cases, and only rarely does the entire membership of one of these courts review a panel decision. The U.S. Supreme Court, however, does not divide into panels; all nine justices participate in deciding each case.

The Process of Appeal

The Record

The appellant's attorney begins the appeal by filing a notice of appeal and by requesting that the clerk of the trial court prepare the record of the case and send it to the appellate court. There is a fee for preparation of the record. The most important part of the record is the *transcript* of the trial. During the trial, an official court reporter was recording every word of the proceedings, including all the attorneys' questions, witnesses' answers, attorneys' objections, and the judge's rulings. The transcript is a printed copy of this verbatim account. Copies of the pleadings, motions, jury instructions, and other official papers in the case also are included in the record if they are relevant to some point being raised on appeal. In addition, the record may include items of physical evidence that were introduced and considered in the trial court; such items might include a written contract, business records, or a map or photograph.

Written Briefs

The appellant's attorney prepares an *appellant's brief* and files it with the appellate court. The brief sets forth errors that the appellant claims were made by the trial judge. These alleged errors usually relate to the trial judge's actions in (1) ruling on motions, (2) ruling on objections to evidence, or (3) stating the relevant law in the jury instructions. The remainder of the brief then presents arguments, based on applicable legal principles, that the cited actions of the trial judge amounted to material errors. The appellee's attorney then responds with the *appellee's brief (or reply brief)*, in which it is argued that under applicable law the trial judge's actions were correct (or even if erroneous, the errors did not affect the outcome and were ''harmless'').

Oral Arguments

Appellate courts usually schedule several periods of time during the year in which the parties to appeals are permitted to make *oral arguments.* During one two-week period, for example, an appellate court might hear oral arguments in 50 or so cases. In each case, the attorney for each side will have a brief period (typically from 30 to 60 minutes) to clarify and emphasize the most important points in the written briefs and to give the appellate court judges an opportunity to ask questions.

Appellate Court's Decision

As was mentioned earlier, an appellate court serves a very different role from that of a trial court. The court studies the record, considers the legal points made in the briefs and oral arguments, does legal research, and decides whether one or more material errors occurred in the trial.

Review of Trial Court's Factual Determinations

Some of the points raised by the appellant may require the appellate court to study the evidence that appears in the record, such as the transcript of witnesses' testimony and physical evidence that has been included in the record. For example, if the appellant claims that the trial judge erred in ruling on a motion for summary judgment, directed verdict, or judgment N.O.V., the appellate court must determine whether the evidence in the record created a genuine fact issue or whether it was overwhelming in the other direction. The court does not, however, decide what the facts are; fact-finding is a trial court function.

Indeed, even if the judges on the appellate court believe that they might have reached a different conclusion had they been performing the fact-finding task in the trial court, they normally will not overturn the trial court's (jury's or trial judge's) factual determinations so long as there is any substantial evidence in the record to support those conclusions. Appellate court judges recognize that the jury or judge that performed the fact-finding role was in a better position to assess the evidence, especially when key evidence took the form of testimony from witnesses who testified and were cross-examined in person. Moreover, in any multilevel decision-making system, it makes very little sense to redo everything at successive levels.

Review of Trial Court's Legal Determinations

Much of the appellate court's attention is focused on pure legal questions, that is, reviewing the trial judge's rulings on legal questions. For example, when trial judges rule on a motion to dismiss or decide how to frame the instructions to the jury, they make decisions as to what the applicable legal principles are. In some cases, especially when there is no jury, the trial judge makes formal written *conclusions of law.* These legal principles may derive from precedents (prior decisions in other cases), federal or state statutes, administrative agency regulations, or constitutional provisions. In response to the appellant's contentions on appeal, the appellate court decides whether the trial court's interpretations and applications of these legal principles were correct. An appellate court is not so reluctant to overturn the trial court's legal determinations as it is to reverse factual determinations. Appeals courts typically say that they conduct a "de novo" review of a trial court's legal determinations, meaning that the appeals court feels free to start with a blank slate and decide legal questions without regard to what the trial court decided on such questions.

Decision Making

The appellate court judges deliberate individually on a case and consult with each other. They decide the case by majority vote. If the majority concludes that no material errors occurred, it *affirms* the lower court's decision, usually sending the case back to the trial court for appropriate action to enforce the judgment. If the court decides that some material error was committed, it *reverses* the lower court's decision. (Sometimes the terms *vacate* or set *aside* are used instead of reverse.) Occasionally, an appellate court may reverse the decision outright and order a contrary judgment. In most cases of reversal, however, the appellate court *remands* the case to the lower court, where some type of further proceeding will be conducted in accordance with the appellate court's opinion. The further proceeding in the lower court may be of a very limited nature, such as merely requiring the trial judge to reconsider some portion of the decision by applying a slightly different legal standard to the already-established facts. Sometimes, though, the additional proceeding necessary to correct the error after remand may be a completely new trial.

Appellate Court's Opinion

One of the judges is assigned the primary responsibility for writing the court's formal opinion; however, the key language of the opinion is the product of agreement among the judges in the majority. If another judge does not agree with some of the reasoning or language of the opinion but still agrees with the overall result, they may wish to write a separate concurring opinion setting forth areas of disagreement.

If the decision is not unanimous, a judge who disagrees with the decision and result reached by the majority has the opportunity to write a dissenting opinion setting forth their views. Although a dissenting opinion has no effect on the outcome of that case, a persuasive dissent on a close and controversial issue may provide "ammunition" for continuing debate on the question in future cases (or in future legislative debates).

As we have already mentioned, an appellate court usually upholds a jury's or a trial judge's factual findings but is not so reluctant to reverse on the basis of errors of law committed by the trial judge. The case below involves review of a legal question—whether the trial court was correct in deciding a case as a matter of law in the defendant's favor after the jury's verdict for the plaintiff, or whether the jury's verdict against the defendant should have been allowed to stand because there was a genuine fact issue.

At the heart of the case is whether certain evidence about an unusual chain of events was sufficient for a jury to infer that the unknown contents of several phone calls was the "tipping" of "material nonpublic information" about upcoming corporate acquisitions that constituted illegal insider trading. The concepts in this case are very important because in all decision-making contexts, including the legal one, facts are simply inferences drawn from

---

SEC v. GINSBURG

U.S. Court of Appeals, 11th Circuit, 362 F.3d 1292 (2004)

Scott Ginsburg ("Ginsburg") was chairman and CEO of Evergreen Media Corporation. On Friday, July 12, 1996, Ginsburg met with EZ Corporation's CEO about an acquisition of EZ. On Sunday evening, July 14, Ginsburg called his brother Mark and they spoke for 26 minutes. The next day, Mark bought 3800 shares of EZ. Mark spoke with Jordan Ginsburg (his and Scott's father) over the next few days and they admit they talked about buying EZ shares. Over the next week or so, there were more developments in the acquisition, more phone calls from Ginsburg to his brother and father and more purchases of EZ stock by them.

In early 1997, Evergreen was in the process of merging with Chancellor Broadcasting. On March 20, 1997, Ginsburg attended a meeting with senior executives of Katz Media Group and Hicks, Muse, Tate & Furst, an investment firm that owned a majority interest in Chancellor. A potential acquisition of Katz by Chancellor was discussed and a due diligence team headed by Ginsburg was appointed. A confidentiality agreement was signed. On June 16, 1997, a Katz executive met with Ginsburg and urged him to call Katz's chairman to discuss the purchase. He said Ginsburg should act quickly because Katz was having discussions with other companies. That same evening, a call was placed from a cell phone registered to Ginsburg to a phone registered to his brother Mark. The next day, Mark bought 150,000 shares of Katz.

After Mark and Jordan profited substantially by selling EZ and Katz shares once deals were publicly announced, the Securities and Exchange Commission brought civil insider trading charges against Ginsburg, alleging that he had communicated material nonpublic information to his brother and father. A jury found for the SEC, concluding that Ginsburg had violated Section 10b-5's rules against insider trading. However, the district judge entered a judgment as a matter of law [called a judgment notwithstanding the verdict in most state courts] for Ginsburg, concluding that the evidence was insufficient to permit a reasonable jury to find that he had tipped off his brother or father about inside information. The SEC appealed.

Carnes, Circuit Judge:

The nature of a judgment as a matter of law and our review of it is such that we take the evidence at trial in the light most favorable to the party who won before the jury only to have its victory taken away by the court. We draw from the evidence all reasonable inferences in support of the verdict, because the jury could have done so.

We review a decision to grant a motion for judgment as a matter of law de novo, applying the same standards used by the district court. A judgment as a matter of law is warranted only "if during a trial by jury a party has been fully heard on an issue and there is no legally sufficient evidentiary basis for a reasonable jury to find for that party on that issue." Fed. R. Civ. P. 50(a)(1). That means, as we have already said, that we review the evidence, and the inferences arising therefrom, in the light most favorable to the non-moving party. We "may not weigh the evidence or decide the credibility of witnesses." Adler. However, the nonmoving party "must provide more than a mere scintilla of evidence to survive a motion for judgment as a matter of law." *Isenbergh v. Knight-Ridder Newspaper*

Sales, Inc., 97 F.3d 436 (11th Cir. 1996).

The parties disagree about which body of precedent controls the sufficiency of the evidence issue upon which the district court granted judgment as a matter of law. The sufficiency issue in general involves the circumstances in which it will be inferred from A's act following a conversation with B, who knew a given fact, that A had been informed of that fact when he acted. As it arises in insider trading cases, the more specific issue is when it may be inferred from a trade in stock by A, following a conversation with insider B, that B disclosed inside information to A who acted upon it. The SEC argues, logically, that the sufficiency of the evidence and the permissibility of inferences that may be drawn from the evidence in this insider trading case are governed by our insider trading decisions, especially Adler, which is the closest of those cases to the facts we have here. Ginsburg argues, and the district court concluded, that the decision should be controlled by an employment retaliation decision, *Burrell v. Bd. of Trustees of Georgia Military College*, 970 F.2d 785 (11th Cir. 1992).

This is what we are talking about. Decision maker A comes into contact with information possessor B and soon thereafter engages in conduct C. When will that factual scenario support an inference that, despite their denials, A was told the information by B and on that basis A did C? More to the point, does an earlier decision of this Court concluding that scenario would not support an inference the information was communicated and acted upon in an employment retaliation case, compel us to conclude that the same scenario would not support an inference of communicated information and action based upon it in insider trading cases?

We think the earlier employment retaliation decision in *Burrell* does not control this case, because insider trading cases are different from employment retaliation cases. The context in which the facts arise and the strength of the competing inferences can differ. As a result, evidence that may appear to be materially identical for purposes of determining whether a decision maker knew a particular fact can actually have different probative force in an insider trading case than in an employment retaliation case. ["Probative" means "tends to prove."] There are many sound, non-retaliatory business reasons to take some job action that is challenged as retaliatory. That multitude of potential reasons dilutes the strength of any inference that because a decision maker took an action against an employee he must have been told of a fact which could have led him to take the action for a prohibited reason.

[Authors note: In the earlier Eleventh Circuit decision in *Burrell*, the fired employee had claimed that her having written a letter to the editor of the local newspaper complaining about what she believe was racial discrimination at a state-operated military prep school in the small city was the reason for her later dismissal as the vice-president of a local financial institution. The evidence in that case showed, however, that it was at least as likely that she was fired for other reasons, most notably that she had serious conflicts with the newly hired CEO at the financial institution where she had worked, conflicts that ultimately had to be taken before the firm's board of directors. Because of this and other plausible reasons for the plaintiff's firing, there had been an insufficient basis for making the logical leap from her having written the letter to the newspaper and her firing several months later, and a jury could not be allowed the freedom to draw the inference.]

By contrast, people do not make large stock trades for as many reasons as businesses take job actions. Although there are exceptions, people generally buy when they believe the price of a stock is going up and sell when they believe it is going down (either absolutely or relative to the expected performance of other stock). The fact finder in an insider trading case need only infer the most likely source of that belief. The temporal proximity of a phone conversation between the trader and one with insider knowledge provides a reasonable basis for inferring that the basis of the trader's belief was the inside information.

The larger and more profitable the trades, and the closer in time the trader's exposure to the insider, the stronger the inference that the trader was acting on the basis of inside information. The magnitude of the incentive to trade on insider information is illustrated by the trades that were made in this case. In less than a month Jordan made $412,875 by trading EZ stock in the direction someone with knowledge of the insider information his son possessed would have, and Mark made a total of $1,393,022 by trading EZ and Katz stock as someone privy to the insider information of his brother would have.

It is not at all clear that the same considerations apply with equal force in job discrimination cases. The inference that a job action was based on a retaliatory motive which arose from imparted information may well be weaker than the comparable inferences in insider trading cases for several reasons. For one thing, the incentive to tip and to act on tipped information is usually a great deal stronger than the incentive to impart and act upon information about an employee engaging in legally protected conduct. We expect that most people would rather make $412,875 or $1,393,022 in a short period trading stocks than they would like to see an employee be punished for something the employee had a legal right to do.

Because it is far from clear that employment retaliation cases are interchangeable with insider trading cases, the district court should have looked to the more specifically applicable precedent instead of regarding it as wrongly decided in light of decisions that had nothing to do with insider trading. [The *Adler* insider trading case involved similar trading following similar phone calls and the Court set aside a judgment as a matter of law for the defendant.]

Ginsburg offered evidence of public information about the companies as motivation for Mark's trading, argued that the trades were consistent with prior trading history, and put forward innocent explanations for the calls. The district court commented that "it is plausible that the investments . . . were driven not by tips but rather by public knowledge." It is also plausible that they were driven by insider information. And it was up to the jury to choose between those competing plausible theories of fact.

The jury was free to disbelieve Ginsburg's evidence just as the *Adler* jury was free to disbelieve what we characterized as the "strong" evidence of a preexisting stock trade plan in *Adler*. Evidence of the innocent explanations for the calls between the parties in this case and of Mark's trading habits is not enough to justify overturning the jury's verdict. If it were otherwise, family members who regularly traded in a particular stock or type of stock could trade based on insider information with impunity.

The district court stated that "the phone records are insufficient to compel an inference that Scott Ginsburg conveyed material, non-public information to Mark," but that is not the issue. The SEC did not have the burden of putting in evidence that *compelled* the inference Ginsburg conveyed nonpublic information to Mark. All it was required to do was put in evidence that reasonably *permitted* that inference, [that is, enough evidence to *allow*, or *permit*, a fact finder to draw such an inference]. It did that. The call/trade pattern occurrences coupled with the jury's right to disbelieve the innocent explanations of the calls and trades are enough to support the verdict. Reversed.

Enforcement of Judgments

If a judgment for the plaintiff survives the appellate process (or if no appeal was ever made), the plaintiff may still have to worry about enforcing the judgment. In the relatively unusual case in which the court's judgment grants an injunction or other equitable remedy, the court will enforce the judgment by fining or jailing the defendant for contempt of court if the defendant fails to comply. In the typical case, however, the judgment awards an amount of money damages to the plaintiff. If the defendant is financially well-off, is well-insured for this type of claim, or is a corporation with adequate assets, enforcement of a money judgment will probably present no major obstacles. It can be very difficult, however, to collect a judgment from some people. Indeed, the probable collectability of any judgment is one of the things a party often must take into account in deciding whether to file a lawsuit in the first place.

If the defendant refuses to pay a valid judgment, the plaintiff will ask the court to issue a *writ of execution.* This writ empowers a law enforcement official to seize defendant's nonexempt property and sell it at auction until enough money is raised to satisfy the judgment. Another procedure is a *writ of garnishment*, which orders a third party holding property belonging to the defendant to deliver the property to the custody of the court. In most cases, the third party is a bank, stock broker, or other entity holding funds or securities belonging to the defendant.

A writ of garnishment can also be issued against a third party who owes a debt to the defendant, ordering the third party to pay the debt to the plaintiff instead of the defendant. If the writ of garnishment targets some type of property other than money, a law enforcement officer will sell the property at auction and the proceeds will be applied to pay the judgment. Many (but not all) states even allow garnishment of wages—a court order to the defendant's employer to pay a specified percentage of the defendant's wages or salary to the plaintiff every week or month until the judgment is fully paid. Federal law places a limit on the portion of a person's wages that can be taken by garnishment.

In speaking of *nonexempt* assets, we are referring to the fact that all states have *exemption laws* specifying that certain types of property cannot be seized for the purpose of satisfying a court judgment. The laws vary quite a bit among the states, some states having very liberal statutes exempting much valuable property and others having extremely limited statutes exempting very little. The most common type of property protected by exemption laws is an individual's *homestead,* or residence; however, many states provide for such an exemption only up to a limited dollar amount.

If a defendant has no nonexempt assets in the forum state, the plaintiff can have the judgment enforced by execution or garnishment in any other state where the defendant has such assets. As long as the court that issued the judgment had subject matter and personal jurisdiction, the authorities in other states are required by the U.S. Constitution's *Full Faith and Credit Clause* to enforce the judgment. Although it is more difficult to enforce a judgment by trying to seize assets located in another nation, it sometimes can be performed if such assets can be identified. The United States is a party to treaties with many countries that obligate each nation to honor the valid court judgments of the other country or countries that have signed the treaty. However, a court in one country will not enforce the judgment of a court in another country if such enforcement would contravene an important public policy of the nation in which enforcement is sought.

Regardless of whether a plaintiff can collect a judgment—in fact, regardless of whether the plaintiff wins or loses the lawsuit once a case is finally concluded, the plaintiff is finished. The doctrine of *res judicata* ("the thing has been adjudicated") specifies that a plaintiff cannot start over by filing another claim against the defendant based on the same general facts. The plaintiff is barred from reasserting not only the same claim, but also any other claim that they reasonably could have asserted the first time around. If the later claim arises from the same general events as the earlier claim, the doctrine of res judicata applies even if the plaintiff has come up with new evidence.

ALTERNATIVE DISPUTE RESOLUTION

We have already noted some of the criticisms directed at the American legal system, as well as some of the responses from the supporters of the system. There can be no question that in the United States, there is an enormous amount of litigation that consumes tremendous resources. Many people, particularly in the business community, argue that Americans are too eager to sue, there are too many lawsuits of questionable merit, and these lawsuits take too much time and cost far too much money. They also commonly assert that there are too many lawyers with too much influence.

Others contend that there is much value in the way we traditionally have resolved many controversies in the United States. One can argue, for instance, that we tend to use formal litigation more than people in most other countries for several legitimate reasons:

(1) We are the most heterogeneous, diffuse, and open society the world has ever known. These characteristics tend to produce more use of formal adjudication than in more homogeneous, static societies. (2) We place great value on the rule of law," rather than the "rule of individuals," another factor that tends to cause people to look to courts for the interpretation and enforcement of rules. (3) We are not, nor would we want to be, a passive people who accept wrongs with fatalistic resignation as is the custom in some societies. (4) One of the strong legal traditions we inherited from England is the attitude that the courts have authority to formulate legal principles when there is no legislation applicable to a case. Because courts in our system have this limited type of lawmaking power, we naturally use them to set norms of behavior for society to a greater extent than people do in nations with a different system. (5) Our legal profession is much better educated than in most nations, with attorneys being more independent and more readily available to people who feel that their rights have been violated. In some parts of the world, the scarcity of lawyers leads people to obtain help from organized crime syndicates in making and collecting claims.

It also bears mentioning that most of the increase in litigation rates in recent years is not the result of greedy individuals trying to "make a killing" by filing claims against businesses, but instead is attributable to greatly increased filings of cases (1) by corporations against other corporations as a strategic business maneuver and (2) by and against government agencies.

Although there is much disagreement about whether there really are too many lawsuits in the United States, most knowledgeable observers agree that the litigation process is not nearly as efficient as it should be—lawsuits commonly take far too much time and money. In addition, in the case of disputes between business firms, lawsuits tend to decrease the chances that they will be able to maintain a valuable commercial relationship with each other. Although litigation is sometimes necessary and courts will always play a central role in dispute resolution in this country, recent times have witnessed widespread efforts to use other methods.

These other methods are frequently referred to as *alternative dispute resolution* (ADR) techniques. Although these methods do not always work and certainly are not a cure-all for society's problems, they often enable the parties to a dispute to lessen the "sharpness" of the adversarial system, replacing it with an increased emphasis on trust, respect, and win-win solutions.

Negotiated Settlement

Before we address specific methods of ADR, it is important first to point out that most disputes never get to the courtroom. Sometimes a person or business will just "lump it," that is, take a loss rather than pursue a claim. A corporation may do this to keep a valued customer or supplier, perhaps thinking that this particular problem is a one-time occurrence. Also, people sometimes do not pursue claims because they decide that it is not worth it; the perceived likelihood of winning or the size of the claim may lead to a conclusion that pressing a claim will be more trouble and expense than it is worth. Sometimes, instead of lumping it, a party may be able to reach a compromise with the other without ever going to court.

Even when lawsuits are filed, approximately 95 percent of them are resolved without a trial. Some of these are disposed of by some pretrial action of the judge, such as the granting of summary judgment. A large percentage of claims filed in court are resolved by a negotiated out-of-court settlement, with part of the agreement being the dropping of all claims and counterclaims.

The problem with the traditional practice of filing suit and then ultimately settling it out of court is that it usually has been performed very inefficiently. Parties and their attorneys generally have not started thinking seriously about settlement talks until the trial date is very near, thousands of dollars and many months (or years) having already been spent on pretrial discovery and strategic maneuvering. It seems that parties and their attorneys often have felt that they just were not "ready" to talk settlement until just before trial. Thus, enormous time and money traditionally have been spent preparing for an event (the trial) that usually does not happen. In addition, spending so much time, money, and energy battling each other during a lengthy pretrial process tends to make the parties harden their positions, escalating the intensity of the conflict.

Arbitration

Arbitration is a very old method for resolving disputes that in recent years has become increasingly popular. In arbitration, the parties select an arbitrator (or a panel of three arbitrators), submit very brief pleadings, and present evidence and arguments to the arbitrator. The arbitrator makes a decision, usually called an *award*, which is legally enforceable like a court judgment if the parties had agreed beforehand that it would be binding. Thus, arbitration resembles litigation in that there is actually an adjudication by a third party whose decision is binding.

Despite this superficial resemblance to litigation, arbitration is quite different in many ways. Most of these differences translate into cheaper, faster, and less painful dispute resolution. These differences also increase the chances that the parties can walk away from the process with a commercial relationship still intact. The parties have the ability to control the entire process. They select the decision maker, who may be an expert in the subject matter of the dispute. They also can decide what rules and procedures to use. Unlike litigation, the proceeding can be kept entirely private, which often may be very important to the disputants. There is no required pretrial discovery, although the parties do frequently agree to exchange documents before the arbitration hearing. The parties can decide whether the arbitrator is required to strictly follow particular rules evidence; most of the time, arbitrators do follow at least the general spirit of the rules of evidence even if they do not follow them strictly. The parties can also agree whether arbitrators are required to follow particular rules of law; most of the time arbitrators do follow the law relatively closely.

However, there is essentially no appeal from an arbitrator's award. A court will not review the arbitrator's factual or legal determinations. A court normally will set aside an arbitration award and require a new arbitration hearing only if the evidence shows that the award was affected by fraud or collusion or if there was some serious procedural error such as lack of notice to one of the parties. Although arbitration has a number of advantages over litigation, one can readily see that there are also some important tradeoffs that the parties should know about before agreeing to arbitrate.

Arbitration is generally categorized as either *labor arbitration or commercial arbitration.* Labor arbitration involves the resolving of disputes within the labor-management context, usually when the particular group of employees is represented by a union. The relationship between the company and unionized employees is based primarily on a collective bargaining agreement. Almost all collective bargaining agreements include a multistage process for resolving workplace disputes, with legally binding arbitration as the last step. Most of these disputes involve claims by employees that they have been fired or otherwise disciplined without the adequate justification the contract requires. The federal Taft-Hartley Act makes collective bargaining agreements, including arbitration provisions, legally binding.

The term *commercial arbitration* is usually used to describe almost all other forms of arbitration. It includes the use of arbitration to resolve disputes arising from almost any kind of business transaction, including construction contracts, agreements for the sale of goods (such as supplies or equipment), insurance arrangements, joint ventures, and many others. In the United States, the Federal Arbitration Act (FAA) makes written commercial arbitration agreements and arbitrator awards legally enforceable if the underlying business transaction affected interstate commerce. If there is no significant effect on interstate commerce, state arbitration statutes in every state usually make the arbitration agreement and award enforceable.

In addition, most of the world's significant trading nations are parties to one or more multilateral treaties under which they agree to enforce arbitration agreements and awards in international commercial transactions involving citizens of other nations that signed the particular treaty. The most important of these treaties is the 1958 United Nations Convention on the Enforcement of Arbitral Awards.

Most commercial arbitration agreements (domestic or international) are of the pre-dispute (or *future dispute*) variety; this is a clause in a commercial contract in which the parties agree that if there is any future dispute arising from the transaction, they will submit that dispute to legally binding arbitration. It is also possible for parties to make an agreement to arbitrate after a dispute has already occurred, but this is not usually what happens.

Although the parties to an arbitration agreement can agree as they wish, they usually specify that the arbitration will be coordinated and supervised by an established arbitration organization. In domestic commercial arbitration, the oldest and most frequently used organization is the American Arbitration Association (AAA), which handles about 200,000 commercial arbitration cases per year. In international commercial arbitration, there are several important sponsoring organizations, including the AAA, the International Chamber of Commerce in Paris, and the London Court of Arbitration (which is not a court despite its name).

Although most arbitration is voluntary (i.e, created by contract), the trial courts in many states and in many federal districts have adopted *court-annexed arbitration.* These programs generally apply to cases involving money damage claims below certain amounts, which range from a few thousand dollars to $150,000 (and a few state programs have no limits). In this form of arbitration, shortly after the lawsuit is filed, the trial judge refers the case to arbitration, with a panel of local attorneys serving as arbitrators. The parties must participate in the arbitration, but the award is not legally binding if either party formally demands a regular trial within a short time after the award (usually 30 days).

In recent years, "voluntary" commercial arbitration has become very popular with business as a means of controlling litigation expenses. It is becoming increasingly difficult to buy stock, to open bank accounts, to buy products, to license software, or to get a job without agreeing to arbitrate all disputes that might arise from the transaction or relationship. Although arbitration works better and is fairer when used by businesses in disputes with each other, companies actually do not even use it very often to resolve disputes with other firms.

Instead, arbitration clauses are more commonly inserted by firms into contracts with employees and consumers where the latter typically have very little bargaining power and little or no choice in the matter. Courts have made it increasingly difficult for parties with weaker bargaining power, such as employees and consumers, to challenge the enforceability of arbitration agreements in such "adhesion" contracts (i.e., "take-it-or-leave-it" deals between parties of very unequal bargaining power such as in most consumer and employment contracts.)

For example, in *American Express Co. v. Italian Colors Restaurant,* 570 U.S. 228 (2013), American Express had a contract with merchants who accept American Express cards that contained a provision stating that there "shall be no right or authority for any Claims to be arbitrated on a class action basis." Nonetheless, some merchants filed a class action antitrust lawsuit against American Express, which moved to compel individual arbitration under the FAA. The Court of Appeals held that because the cost of expert witness testimony that would be required to prove an antitrust claim would greatly exceed the maximum potential recovery for any individual plaintiff, the class-action waiver was unenforceable and arbitration could not proceed. The Supreme Court reversed, noting that the "overarching principle" of the FAA is that arbitration is a matter of contract and that parties' agreements to arbitrate should be "rigorously enforced." Furthermore, the Court said, "the antitrust laws do not guarantee an affordable procedural path to the vindication of every claim."

Because pre-dispute arbitration clauses have become so common in "adhesion" contracts between companies and either consumers or employees, such clauses are often referred to as "mandatory" or "compulsory." They are indeed mandatory after the contract has been agreed to, but the absence of any real opportunity for consumers and employees to negotiate these contracts, use of a term like "mandatory" carries a lot of truth.

A 2019 study by Professors Amit Seru of the Stanford Graduate School of Business, Mark Egan of Harvard Business School, and Gregor Matvos of the University of Texas McCombs School of Business used data from the Financial Industry Regulatory Authority from thousands of arbitration proceedings involving customer disputes with stockbrokers and investment advisors. They found that financial industry professionals are in a position to have far more information about potential arbitrators than securities customers. The data also revealed that some arbitrators are much friendlier to industry professionals than to customers. Professor Seru stated: "This is not like having judges, who get paid the same no matter what happens. Here, you only get paid if you're selected as an arbitrator. They have incentives to slant toward the business side, because they know that those who don't do so won't get picked. Everyone knows what's happening."

The following case points out just how limited is a court review of an arbitration decision.

OXFORD HEALTH CARE PLANS LLC v. SUTTER
U.S. Supreme Court, 2013 U.S. 4358 (2013)

Respondent Sutter, a pediatrician, agreed to provide medical care to members of petitioner Oxford's network of patients. Sutter sued in state court in New Jersey on behalf of himself and a proposed class of other New Jersey physicians under contract with Oxford, alleging that Oxford had failed to make full and prompt payment to the doctors in violation of their contracts and various state laws.

*Oxford moved to compel arbitration of Sutter's claims, relying on an arbitration clause in the parties' contract that read: "No civil action concerning any dispute arising under this Agreement shall be instituted before any court, and all such disputes shall be submitted to final and binding **arbitration** in New Jersey, pursuant to the rules of the American **Arbitration** Association with one arbitrator."*

The state court dismissed the suit, referring it to arbitration. The parties agreed that the arbitrator should decide whether their contract authorized class arbitration, and he determined that it did after construing the arbitration provision. Oxford did not wish to face the claims of all the physicians with which it had contracted in New Jersey, so it filed a motion in federal court to vacate the arbitrator's decision on grounds that he had "exceeded [his] powers" under §10(a)(4) of the Federal Arbitration Act (FAA). The trial court denied the motion and the court of appeals affirmed.

While the arbitration proceeded, a new Supreme Court decision, Stolt-Nielsen, SA v. Animal Feeds, Int'l Corp., 559 U.S. 662 (2010), bolstered Oxford's argument, so it asked the arbitrator to reconsider his decision. He did not change his mind. Oxford then returned to federal court, renewing its effort to vacate the arbitrator's decision under §10(a)(4). Once again, the lower courts ruled against Oxford. The Court of Appeals underscored the limited scope of judicial review that §10(a)(4) allows: So long as an arbitrator "makes a good faith attempt" to interpret a contract, "even serious errors of law or fact will not subject his award to vacatur." Oxford could not prevail under that standard, the court held, because the arbitrator had "endeavored to give effect to the parties' intent" and "articulate[d] a contractual basis for his decision." Oxford's objections to the ruling were "simply dressed-up arguments that the arbitrator interpreted its agreement erroneously." The Supreme Court granted certiorari.

Kagan, Justice:

Under the FAA, courts may vacate an arbitrator's decision "only in very unusual circumstances." *First Options of Chicago, Inc. v. Kaplan*, 514 U. S. 938 (1995). That limited judicial review, we have explained, "maintain[s] arbitration's essential virtue of resolving disputes straightaway." *Hall Street Associates, L. L. C. v. Mattel, Inc.*, 552 U. S. 576 (2008). If parties could take "full-bore legal and evidentiary appeals," arbitration would become "merely a prelude to a more cumbersome and time-consuming judicial review process." *Ibid.*

Here, Oxford invokes §10(a)(4) of the FAA, which authorizes a federal court to set aside an arbitral award "where the arbitrator[] exceeded [his] powers." A party seeking relief under that provision bears a heavy burden. "It is not enough . . . to show that the [arbitrator] committed an error — or even a serious error." *Stolt-Nielsen*. Because the parties "bargained for the arbitrator's construction of their agreement," an arbitral decision "even arguably construing or applying the contract" must stand, regardless of a court's view of its (de)merits. *Eastern Associated Coal Corp. v. Mine Workers*, 531 U. S. 57 (2000). Only if "the arbitrator act[s] outside the scope of his contractually delegated authority" — issuing an award that "simply reflect[s] [his] own notions of [economic] justice" rather than "draw[ing] its essence from the contract" — may a court overturn his determination. *Id.* So the sole question for us is whether the arbitrator (even arguably) interpreted the parties' contract, not whether he got its meaning right or wrong.

[The arbitrator's decisions] are, through and through, interpretations of the parties' agreement. The arbitrator's first ruling recited the "question of construction" the parties had submitted to him: "whether [their] Agreement allows for class action arbitration." To resolve that matter, the arbitrator focused on the arbitration clause's text, analyzing (whether correctly or not makes no difference) the scope of both what it barred from court and what it sent to arbitration. The arbitrator concluded, based on that textual exegesis, that the clause "on its face . . . expresses the parties' intent that class action arbitration can be maintained." When Oxford requested reconsideration in light of *Stolt-Nielsen*, the arbitrator explained that his prior decision was "concerned solely with the parties' intent as evidenced by the words of the arbitration clause itself." He then ran through his textual analysis again, and reiterated his conclusion: "The text of the clause itself authorizes" class arbitration. Twice, then, the arbitrator did what the parties had asked: He considered their contract and decided whether it reflected an agreement to permit class proceedings. That suffices to show that the arbitrator did not "exceed his powers." §10(a)(4).

Oxford's contrary view relies principally on *Stolt-Nielsen*. As noted earlier, we found there that an arbitration panel exceeded its powers under §10(a)(4) when it ordered a party to submit to class arbitration. Oxford takes that decision to mean that "even the 'high hurdle' of Section 10(a)(4) review is overcome when an arbitrator imposes class arbitration without a sufficient contractual basis." Under *Stolt-Nielsen*, Oxford asserts, a court may thus vacate "as ultra vires" [i.e. without authority] an arbitral decision like this one for misconstruing a contract to approve class proceedings.

But Oxford misreads *Stolt-Nielsen*: We overturned the arbitral decision there because it lacked any contractual basis for ordering class procedures, not because it lacked, in Oxford's terminology, a "sufficient" one. The parties in *Stolt-Nielsen* had entered into an unusual stipulation that they had never reached an agreement on class arbitration. In that circumstance, we noted, the panel's decision was not—indeed, could not have been—"based on a determination regarding the parties' intent."

The contrast with this case is stark. In *Stolt-Nielsen*, the arbitrators did not construe the parties' contract, and did not identify any agreement authorizing class proceedings. So in setting aside the arbitrators' decision, we found not that they had misinterpreted the contract, but that they had abandoned their interpretive role. Here, the arbitrator did construe the contract (focusing, per usual, on its language), and did find an agreement to permit class arbitration. So to overturn his decision, we would have to rely on a finding that he misapprehended the parties' intent. But §10(a)(4) bars that course: It permits courts to vacate an arbitral decision only when the arbitrator strayed from his delegated task of interpreting a contract, not when he performed that task poorly. *Stolt-Nielsen* and this case thus fall on opposite sides of the line that §10(a)(4) draws to delimit judicial review of arbitral decisions.

The remainder of Oxford's argument addresses merely the merits: The arbitrator, Oxford contends at length, badly misunderstood the contract's arbitration clause. … We reject this argument because, and only because, it is not properly addressed to a court. Nothing we say in this opinion should be taken to reflect any agreement with the arbitrator's contract interpretation, or any quarrel with Oxford's contrary reading. All we say is that convincing a court of an arbitrator's error — even his grave error— is not enough. So long as the arbitrator was "arguably construing" the contract — which this one was — a court may not correct his mistakes under §10(a)(4). The potential for those mistakes is the price of agreeing to arbitration. The arbitrator's construction holds, however good, bad, or ugly.

In sum, Oxford chose arbitration, and it must now live with that choice. Oxford agreed with Sutter that an arbitrator should determine what their contract meant, including whether its terms approved class arbitration. The arbitrator did what the parties requested: He provided an interpretation of the contract resolving that disputed issue. His interpretation went against Oxford, maybe mistakenly so. But still, Oxford does not get to rerun the matter in a court. Under §10(a)(4), the question for a judge is not whether the arbitrator construed the parties' contract correctly, but whether he construed it at all. Because he did, and did not "exceed his powers," we cannot give Oxford the relief it wants. We accordingly affirm.

For a number of years, television shows have presented the resolution of disputes by so-called "judges." There have been, and continue to be, several of them. One of the most popular and longstanding is "Judge Judy." Judy and these other "judges" are arbitrators, though some of them may have been lower-level trial judges in their pre-television lives. Participants agree in advance to be legally bound by the outcome, and the law treats the decision of the TV judge as an arbitration award subject to the rules of either state arbitration laws or the Federal Arbitration Act.

Mediation

Other forms of ADR differ from arbitration in that they do not produce a decision that is legally binding on the parties. Instead, these methods are aimed at facilitating agreed settlements by (1) creating a structure that encourages the parties to get together and seriously negotiate much earlier, before they have hardened their positions and spent so much time and money, (2) building trust and respect between the parties, (3) making the parties more realistic about the weaknesses of their positions and the strengths of the other side's positions before the dispute has escalated very far, and (4) creating an environment in which the parties are more likely to think of creative solutions that can benefit both sides rather than thinking about the dispute only in legalistic and dollar terms.

The most important version of this type of ADR is *mediation*. Like ADR generally, most mediation is entirely voluntary; it is created and controlled by the parties. The *mediator* does not impose a solution but tries to help the parties themselves achieve one. Various approaches are used in mediation, depending on the wishes of the parties, the nature of the dispute, and the skill and personality of the mediator. The mediator may do as little as persuade the parties to talk to each other. Going further, they might help the parties agree on an agenda for a meeting and provide a suitable environment for negotiation. The mediator might point out that particular proposals are unrealistic, help the parties formulate their own proposals, and even make proposals for them to consider. In some situations, the mediator may try very hard to persuade them to accept a settlement they believe to be reasonable.

Mediation has facilitated resolution of a wide range of disputes, such as many kinds of business disputes, labor disputes, landlord-tenant disagreements, and multi-party controversies over environmental protection. It also can be very useful in combination with some other form of ADR, such as arbitration. It is common to find a clause in a contract specifying that in the event of a future dispute between the parties, they are required to submit the dispute to mediation and that if mediation fails to lead to a settlement agreement, they further agree that the dispute will then be submitted to bind arbitration.

Although most mediation is voluntary, a number of states and a few federal districts are using court-annexed mediation, in which a trial judge refers the parties to mediation shortly after the case is filed. Although participation in this type of mediation is required, the mediator still does not impose an outcome on the parties.

CHAPTER 4

COMMON AND STATUTORY LAW

- Origin of Common Law
- Common Law—The Doctrine of Stare Decisis
- Profile of Our Federal and State Statutory Law
- Statutory Law—The Rationale
- Limitations on Legislative Bodies
- Statutory Law and Common Law—A Contrast
- Statutory Interpretation
- Uniform State Statutes

There are several basic processes by which law is made: (1) the formulation of rules by the courts—the judges—in deciding cases coming before them in those areas of law in which no statutes apply; (2) the enactment and interpretation of statutes; (3) the interpretation and application of constitutional provisions; and (4) the promulgation of rules and regulations by administrative agencies. In this chapter we look at the first and second of these lawmaking processes. First we show how common law (or case law) is formed by the courts. Then we turn our attention to the enactment and interpretation of statutory law.

ORIGIN OF COMMON LAW

As we described in Chapter 2, the early king's courts in England largely made up the law on a case-by-case basis. If, for example, a plaintiff asked for damages for breach of contract in a situation in which the defendant denied that a contract ever existed, the court had to spell out the nature of a contract—that is, specify the minimum elements that the court felt must exist for it to impose contractual liability on the defendant. Similarly, if a defendant admitted making the contract in question but sought to escape liability for reasons of illness or military service, the court had to decide what kinds of defenses ought to be legally recognizable—defenses that should free the defendant from his or her contractual obligations.

Over a period of time, as more and more cases were settled, a rudimentary body of contract law came into being. Thereafter, when other cases arose involving contractual matters, the courts quite naturally looked to the earlier cases to see what principles of law had been established. The same procedure was followed in many other branches of law, and the legal rules that arose in this manner constituted the common law, or case law, of England.

The common-law rules that had developed in England became the law of our early colonies. When those colonies achieved statehood, they adopted those rules as a major part of their respective bodies of law. As the territories became states, they followed suit so that at one time the major portion of the law of all states was common law. There is one exception—Louisiana continues to be governed by the civil law (rather than common law) system adopted in most European countries. In a civil law system, virtually all law is codified.

The Current Scene

Gradually, the state legislatures began to pass increasing numbers of statutes, with the result that today most branches of the law are statutory in nature. For example, all states now have comprehensive statutes governing the areas of corporation law, criminal law, tax law, municipal corporations, and commercial law. Some of these statutes have been based largely on the common-law principles that were in effect earlier. Others, however, have been passed to create bodies of rules that did not exist previously or that expressly overrule common-law principles.

Despite the ever-increasing amount of statutory law in this country (which we examine in some detail later in this chapter), several branches of law today are still essentially common law in nature in 49 states—particularly the subjects of contracts, torts, and agency. In these areas, in which the legislatures have not seen fit to enact comprehensive statutes, the courts still settle controversies on the basis of judge-made or case law—the rules formulated by the courts in deciding earlier cases over the years, as illustrated in Figure 4.1.

In deciding each case, judges bear the twin burden of attempting to provide ''justice'' for the case at hand while at the same time setting a precedent that will serve the greater interests of society when applied in future cases. The common-law rules, like legislative statutes, must serve public policy interests—the ''community common sense and common conscience.'' Therefore, courts have laid great stress on the customs, morals, and forms of conduct that are generally prevailing in the community at the time of decision. There is no doubt that occasionally the judge's personal feelings as to what kinds of conduct are just and fair, what rule would best serve societal interests, and simply what is "right" or "wrong" enter the picture.

Figure 4.1 Common Law

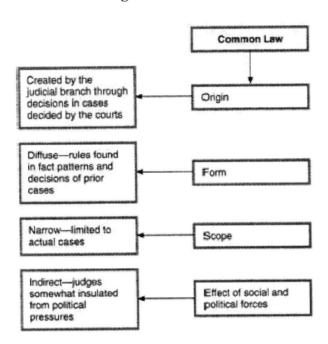

Role of the Judge

Famous jurist Benjamin Cardozo in his book THE NATURE OF THE JUDICIAL PROCESS, contended that four "directive forces" shaped the law, and especially the common law, as follows: (1) philosophy (logic), (2) history, (3) custom, and (4) social welfare (or sociology).

In a lecture on the role of philosophy in the law, Cardozo briefly commented on the special tasks of the judge in interpreting statutes and constitutions, and then continued:

> We reach the land of mystery when constitution and statute are silent, and the judge must look to the common law for the rule that fits the case. . . . The first thing he does is to compare the case before him with the precedents, whether stored in his mind or hidden in the books. . . . Back of precedents are the basic juridical conceptions which are the postulates of judicial reasoning, and farther back are the habits of life, the institutions of society, in which those conceptions had their origin, and which, by a process of interaction, they have modified in turn. . . . If [precedents] are plain and to the point, there may be need of nothing more. Stare decisis (''to stand by decisions'') is at least the everyday working rule of the law.

Early in that same lecture, however, Cardozo cautioned that the finding of precedent was only part of the judge's job and indicated how the law must grow beyond the early precedents:

> The rules and principles of case law have never been treated as final truths, but as working hypotheses, continually retested in those great laboratories of the law, the courts of justice. . . . In [the] perpetual flux [of the law,] the problem which confronts the judge is in reality a twofold one: he first must extract from the precedents the underlying principle, the ratio decidendi [the ground of decision]; he must then determine the path or direction along which the principle is to move and develop, if it is not to wither and die.. . .
>
> The directive force of a principle may be exerted along the line of logical progression; this I will call the rule of analogy or the method of philosophy, along the line of historical development; this I will call the method of evolution; along the line of the customs of the community; this I will call the method of tradition; along the lines of justice, morals and social welfare, the mores of the day; and this I will call the method of sociology.. . .

COMMON LAW—THE DOCTRINE OF STARE DECISIS

The heart of the common-law process lies in the inclination of the courts generally to follow precedent—to stand by existing decisions. This policy, as we were told by Cardozo, is referred to as the doctrine of *stare decisis*. Under this approach, when the fact pattern of a particular controversy is established, the attorneys for both parties search for earlier cases involving similar fact patterns in an effort to determine whether applicable principles of law have been established. If this research produces a number of similar cases (or even one) within the state where a rule has been applied by the appellate courts, the trial court will ordinarily feel constrained to follow the same rule in settling the current controversy.

Types of Precedent

Authority originating in courts above the trial court in the appellate chain is called mandatory authority. The judge must follow it. Thus, a state trial judge in Ohio will follow the rulings of the Ohio Supreme Court if there are any precedents from this court; if not, the judge will follow the prior decisions of Ohio's intermediate appellate courts. The intermediate appellate courts will do the same thing, and the Ohio Supreme Court will follow its own precedents. In matters of federal law, the Ohio Supreme Court will follow the holdings of the U.S. Supreme Court. A judge who does not follow mandatory authority is not impeached or shot at dawn but certainly runs a strong risk of reversal.

What if a trial judge searches the law books and discovers that there is no precedent in the state on the legal question presented? In such a case, the judge may examine the decisions of courts of other states. For example, assume a state trial judge in Oregon is faced with the question of whether a landlord who did not attempt to lease an apartment after a tenant moved out in the middle of a lease should be barred from suing the tenant for damages. No Oregon cases address the issue, and the only case "on point" was rendered by the Alabama Supreme Court. Must the Oregon judge follow the Alabama precedent? No. Because the Oregon judge's decision cannot be appealed to the Alabama Supreme Court, the latter's rulings are not mandatory authority.

The Alabama decision would constitute persuasive authority. That is, the Oregon judge can study the Alabama decision and, on finding it persuasive, may choose to follow it. However, if the judge finds the decision not to be persuasive, the judge need not apply its rationale in Oregon.

What if there are two existing precedents, that of the Alabama Supreme Court and one from the North Dakota Supreme Court, that reach diametrically opposed results on the same issue? Again, they are both only persuasive authority for the Oregon judge who can study them and follow the one that seems more reasonable. Of course, the judge can also reject both persuasive precedents and create yet a third approach to the issue. Despite the importance of stability to the law, the majesty of the common law lies in its flexibility and adaptability. Although judges revere stability, they will change a rule when they become convinced that it was wrongly established and never served society's interests or that, although it was a good rule when established, changing social, moral, economic, or technological factors have rendered it outmoded. If no valid reason supports a common-law rule, no matter how long it has been established, the judges should and usually will change it.

Sometimes common-law rules change slowly. Exceptions or qualifications to a rule will slowly appear in the case law. Most of the history of the common law is of a slow evolution as the law keeps pace with a changing society. Sometimes the law will change dramatically, as when modern judges decide an established rule no longer serves society and must be scrapped.

So strong is the hold of mandatory authority that judges will usually follow it even though they violently disagree with its reasoning and result. The following case illustrates this fact. The decision is by a Michigan intermediate appellate court, sitting between the trial court and the Michigan Supreme Court in the appellate chain.

EDWARDS v. CLINTON VALLEY CENTER

Court of Appeals of Michigan, 360 N.W. 2d 606 (1984)

The plaintiff is the estate of Jean Edwards, who was fatally stabbed by a former mental patient. The defendant is a government mental hospital that refused to admit the killer after she was brought to the facility by police when she threatened to "kill someone." The plaintiff alleges that the defendant's refusal to admit the killer was negligent. The trial judge dismissed the suit on a purely legal ground—governmental immunity. The plaintiff appealed.

Bronson, Presiding Judge:

Under the rule of *stare decisis,* this Court is bound to follow decisions of the Michigan Supreme Court, even if we disagree with them. The rule of *stare decisis,* founded on considerations of expediency and sound principles of public policy, operates to preserve harmony, certainty, and stability in the law. However, the rule "was never intended to perpetuate error or to prevent the consideration of rules of law to be applied to the ever-changing business, economic, and political life of a community." *Parker v. Port Huron Hospital,* 105 N.W.2d 1 (1960).

In *Perry v. Kalamazoo* State Hospital, 273 N.W.2d 421 (1978), the majority of the Supreme Court held that governmental immunity for tort liability extends to the day-to-day care public mental hospitals provide. An attempt to distinguish the instant case from Perry could not possibly withstand logical or honest analysis. As a member of the Court of Appeals, I am obligated to follow the decisions of our higher court. For that reason, and that reason alone, the order of summary judgment is affirmed.

I feel compelled, however, to register my fundamental disagreement with the result

© **2020 John R. Allison & Robert A. Prentice**

adopted by the Perry majority. I am much more inclined to follow the narrow interpretation of governmental immunity advanced by the dissenters, because the operation of a mental hospital is not an activity which can be done only by the government, it is not a governmental function within the meaning of [the Michigan statutes establishing governmental immunity], and, therefore, a mental hospital should not be immune from liability for its torts.

If ever a factual situation invited reconsideration of the wisdom of a broad interpretation of what is, in the first place, an archaic doctrine, it is presented in the instant case. The Pontiac police bring Wilma Gilmore to the state-operated Clinton Valley Center. Gilmore threatens to kill someone. Gilmore had been previously institutionalized at the center. The center refuses to admit Gilmore.

Four days later, Gilmore once again goes to the police and repeats her homicidal threats. She is told to leave. Two days later, Gilmore enters the apartment of Jean Edwards and fatally stabs her in the arms, throat, and abdomen. Of note is that nowhere in the record does the center offer a reason for its refusal to admit Gilmore.

I fail to see how summarily relieving the hospital of responsibility for such obvious gross negligence, without requiring of it even the slightest explanation, serves any viable public interest or protects the people of our state. Instead, it harshly imposes the entire risk of the center's negligence on Jean Edwards and her family. The time has come for either the Legislature or our Supreme Court to preserve and promote justice by modifying the doctrine of governmental immunity. Affirmed.

PROFILE OF OUR FEDERAL AND STATE STATUTORY LAW

Although a significant portion of our law is still common law in nature, most of our federal and state law today results from the enactment of statutes by legislative bodies. These are the formally adopted rules that constitute our *statutory law*, the second of the major sources of law. All states, for example, have comprehensive statutes governing such subjects as banking law, criminal law, education, consumer sales, and motor vehicle law.

Similarly, at the federal level, sweeping statutes in the areas of antitrust law, labor law, food and drug regulation, and securities law have long been in effect. Newer statutes are added every year, such as the Federal Trademark Dilution Act of 1995, the Digital Millennium Copyright Act of 1998, the Sarbanes-Oxley Act of 2002, and the Dodd-Frank Act of 2010.

In this section our initial objectives are to look at the reasons for the existence of statutory law, to become acquainted with the basic rules that delineate the jurisdictions of the federal and state governments, and to note the contrasts between statutory and common law. We then turn our attention to the closely related area of statutory interpretation—the process by which the courts try to determine the precise meaning of legislation that is applicable to particular cases—and conclude with a summary of selected state statutes that are of special significance to the business community. As a backdrop for a better understanding of the issues that are addressed in this chapter, however, a brief description of the vast scope of our statutory law is first in order. Some important information about statutory law is contained in Figure 4.2.

Figure 4.2 Statutory Law

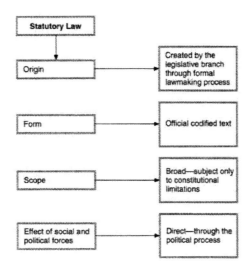

STATUTORY LAW—THE RATIONALE

There are many reasons for the existence of statutory law, three of which deserve special mention.

1. One of the primary functions of any legislative body is to adopt measures having to do with the structure and day-to-day operation of the government of which it is a part. Thus many federal statutes are of the "nuts and bolts" variety, relating to such matters as the operation of the federal court system, the Internal Revenue Service, and the administration and employment rules of the U.S. Civil Service Commission. In a similar vein, many state statutes relate to such matters as the property tax laws, the operation of school systems, and the setting forth of powers of municipalities within their borders.

2. Many activities are of such a nature that they can hardly be regulated by common-law principles and the judicial processes. In the area of criminal law, for example, it is absolutely essential for the general populace to know what acts are punishable by fine and imprisonment; the only sure way to set forth the elements of specific crimes is through the enactment of federal and state criminal statutes.

Similarly, the activities of corporations are so complex and so varied that they do not lend themselves to judicial regulation. Few judges, for example, have either the expertise to deal with such questions as the conditions under which the payment of corporate dividends should be permitted or the time to deal with the spelling out of such conditions on a case-by-case basis. Thus the only practical way to deal with these and other problems is by the drafting of detailed statutes, which, in total, make up the comprehensive corporation laws of the states.

3. A third function of a legislature is to change expressly (or even overrule) common-law rules when it believes such modifications are necessary, and—even more commonly—to enact statutes to *remedy new problems* to which common-law rules do not apply. Thus a state legislature might pass a statute making nonprofit corporations (such as hospitals) liable for the wrongs of their employees to the same extent as are profit-making corporations, thereby reversing the early common-law rule of nonliability for such employers. Or a legislature, aware of increasing purchases of its farmlands by foreign citizens—a situation not covered by common-law rules— might react to this perceived evil by passing a statute placing limits on the number of acres aliens may own or inherit.

LIMITATIONS ON LEGISLATIVE BODIES

Procedural Requirements

All state constitutions (and, to a lesser extent, the federal Constitution) contain provisions about the manner in which statutes shall be enacted. As a general rule, acts that do not conform to these requirements are void. For example, virtually all state constitutions provide that revenue bills "shall originate in the House of Representatives," a requirement that also appears in the federal Constitution. Typical state constitutions also contain provisions (1) restricting the enactment of "special" or "local" laws that affect only a portion of the citizenry, (2) requiring that the subject of every act be set forth in its title, and (3) prohibiting a statute from embracing more than one subject. Additionally, all constitutions prescribe certain formalities in regard to the enactment processes themselves, such as specific limitations on the time and place of the introduction of bills, limitations on the amendment of bills, and the requirement that bills have three separate readings before final passage.

These kinds of provisions, although appearing to be unduly technical, actually serve meritorious purposes. For example, although legislatures normally strive to pass statutes of general application, it is necessary that some laws operate only on certain classes of persons or in certain localities of a state. Such special or local laws are valid only if the basis of their classification is reasonable; two of the purposes of the constitutional provisions just mentioned are to ensure such reasonableness and to guarantee that the classes of persons covered be given notice of the consideration of the bill before its passage. Similarly, the purpose of requiring that the subject of an act be expressed in its title is to ensure that legislators voting on a bill are fully apprised as to its subject, thereby guarding against the enactment of "surprise" legislation. And the purpose of the requirement that a bill contain one subject is to prevent the passage of omnibus bills (those that bring together entirely unrelated, or incongruous, matters).

Requirement of Certainty

All statutes are subject to the general principle of constitutional law that they be "reasonably definite and certain." Although the Constitution itself does not expressly contain such a provision, the courts have long taken the view that if the wording of a statute is such that persons of ordinary intelligence cannot understand its meaning, the statute violates the due process clause of the Constitution and is thus invalid. In such instances, it is said that the statute is "unconstitutionally vague."

As a practical matter, most statutes that are challenged on the ground of vagueness or uncertainty are upheld by the courts. This is because most statutes are understandable if studied carefully, and because the courts are extremely reluctant to declare a statute unconstitutional if they can avoid doing so. Thus, if the wording of a statute is subject to two possible but conflicting interpretations, one of which satisfies constitutional requirements and the other of which does not, the former interpretation will be accepted by the courts if they can reasonably do so.

An application of the vagueness analysis in a criminal case occurred in *Kolender v. Lawson*, 461 U.S. 352 (1983), in which the U.S. Supreme Court struck down, on the ground of vagueness, a California statute that required persons who loitered or wandered on the streets to provide "credible and reliable" identification and to account for their presence when requested to do so by a peace officer. The court said, "It is clear that the full discretion accorded to the police to determine whether the suspect has provided a 'credible and reliable' identification necessarily entrusts lawmaking to the moment-to-moment judgment of the policeman on his beat," and "furnishes a convenient tool for harsh and discriminatory enforcement by local prosecuting officials against particular groups deemed to merit their displeasure." In addition to criminal cases, courts typically require more certainty in the language of legislation that affects a fundamental right such as free speech than in other legislation not imposing criminal penalties and not affecting fundamental rights.

In a case involving regulation of business, rather than criminal charges or legislation affecting a fundamental right such as free speech, the courts will not be as demanding in applying the vagueness test. A less stringent standard is applied to civil statutes that regulate economic activity. An economic regulation is invalidated "only if it commands compliance in terms 'so vague and indefinite as really to be no rule or standard at all' . . . or if it is 'substantially incomprehensible.'" *U.S. v. Clinical Leasing Service, Inc.*, 925 F.2d 120 (5th Cir. 1991).

STATUTORY LAW AND COMMON LAW—A CONTRAST

Statutory law and common law differ in several significant respects. The most obvious of these are the *processes* by which each comes into being and the form of each after it becomes operative.

Processes and Form

Legislative acts become law only after passing through certain formal steps in both houses of the state legislatures (or of Congress) and, normally, by subsequent approval of the governor (or the president). The usual steps are (1) introduction of a bill in the house or senate by one or more members of that body; (2) referral of the bill to the appropriate legislative committee, where hearings are held; (3) approval of the bill by that committee and perhaps others; (4) approval of the bill by the house and senate after full debate; and (5) signing of the bill by the executive (or legislative vote overriding an executive veto). At each of these stages the opponents of the bill are given considerable opportunity to raise objections, with the result that the bill may be voted down or may pass only after being substantially amended. *Common-law rules*, by contrast, are creatures of the judicial branch of government; they are adopted by the courts for settling controversies involving points of law on which the legislature has not spoken.

In addition to these obvious contrasts between the two types of law, others are equally significant. We note these briefly as follows.

Social and Political Forces

The social and political forces within a state have a greater and more evident impact on statutory law than on common law. The steps required in the enactment of statutes enable representatives of vocal special interest groups (who are frequently at odds with one another) to attract considerable publicity to their causes. And, of course, the raw political power that each is able to exert on the legislators plays a significant, although not always controlling, part in the final disposition of a bill.

In addition to the political and financial pressures that have always been wielded by lobbyists, the past 25 years have seen an enormous increase in the activities of political action committees (PACs). Whereas lobbyists' activities are intended to sway the votes of lawmakers, PACs direct their efforts to raising funds for the election of candidates who will support their particular causes. Recent scandals involving Jack Abramoff, Tom DeLay, and many others indicate to many that campaign reform is seriously needed. As governments grow more powerful, more and more is at stake, meaning that huge amounts of money enter the processes.

Money creates opportunity for abuse, yet the First Amendment means that there are Constitutional limitations on the reform that can be undertaken. Over the years the Supreme Court has frequently addressed the difficult issues that arise in the collision between values in this area. In *McConnell v. Federal Election Commission*, 540 U.S. 93 (2003), for example, the Court upheld sweeping limitations on campaign donations, but in most other decisions the Court has ruled in favor of the right to make donations as an expression of free speech. An example is *Citizens United v. Federal Election Commission*, 558 U.S. 310 (2010), which held that corporations are "persons" for purposes of political speech and that the First Amendment's free speech clause prohibited the government from restricting their political expenditures.

Although courts are somewhat more insulated from such pressures than are legislatures, the idea that judges decide cases in some sort of cocoon unaffected by politics is obviously wrong. Judges are human beings with their own individual political and moral views that they cannot entirely shake as they deliberate individual cases. Furthermore, judges at the state level are often chosen in fiercely partisan elections featuring the same funding and political issues as any other election. The fact that the future makeup of the Supreme Court seems to always play a major role in presidential campaigns further highlights the political role of the courts.

Legislative Scope

Subject only to the relatively few constitutional limitations placed on it, the legislative power to act is very broad. Thus legislatures are not only free to enact statutes when case law is nonexistent, but they also can pass statutes that expressly overrule common-law principles. Examples of the latter are those statutes involving the legality of married women's contracts. Under English and early American common law, it was firmly established that married women lacked the capacity—the legal ability—to contract, and thus any agreements they entered into while married had no effect. Today, all states have enacted statutes that give married women the same rights to contract as those enjoyed by other citizens.

As for jurisdictional scope, legislatures have the power to pass broad statutes encompassing all aspects of a given subject, whereas the courts can ''make law'' only in deciding the cases that come before them. Every state, for example, has comprehensive corporation acts, in which virtually all aspects of corporate activities, from incorporation procedures to dissolution procedures, are specified in detail. Similarly, every state has an all-encompassing criminal code, within which the criminal offenses in the state are defined.

STATUTORY INTERPRETATION

We have seen that legislative bodies make law whenever they enact statutes. By doing so, they formally state what kinds of conduct they are requiring or prohibiting in specified situations and what results they expect from the passage of these laws on the rights and duties of affected parties.

But the true scope and meaning of a particular statute is never known with precision until it is formally construed by the courts in settling actual disputes arising under it. This search for legislative intent, which usually necessitates a *statutory interpretation*, is thus another major source of our law. Interpretation is the process by which a court determines the precise legal meaning of a statute as it applies to a particular controversy.

Interpretation: a Necessary Evil?

Like all human language, that used in legislation may sometimes be susceptible to two or more reasonable meanings and consequently require interpretation by a court before the statute may be applied to a given case.

Consider the following situation. X flies a stolen airplane from one state to another and is convicted under a U.S. statute that makes the interstate movement of stolen motor vehicles a federal crime. In this statute, a motor vehicle is defined as "an automobile, automobile truck, automobile wagon, motorcycle, or any other self-propelled vehicle not designed for running on rails." Is an airplane a "motor vehicle" under this law? The problem is that the words of the statute are broad enough to embrace aircraft if they are given a literal interpretation; yet it is at least arguable that Congress did not really intend such a result. The U.S. Supreme Court answered no to the question in *McBoyle v. U.S.*, 283 U.S. 25 (1931), holding that the term vehicle is "commonly understood as something that moves or runs on land, not something which flies in the air"—although it admitted that "etymologically the term might be considered broad enough to cover a conveyance propelled in the air."

Plain Meaning Rule

The primary source of legislative intent is, of course, the language that makes up the statute itself. In the relatively rare case when a court feels that the wording of an act is so clear as to dictate but one result and that the result is not "patently absurd," the consideration of other factors is unnecessary. If, for example, a state statute provides that "every applicant for examination and registration as a pharmacist shall be a citizen of the United States," a state pharmacy board would have to refuse to process the application of an alien even though they may have *applied for* U.S. citizenship as of the date of the pharmaceutical examination (*State v. Dame*, 249 P.2d 156 (Wyo. 1952)). In cases of this sort (and occasionally in others in which the language is somewhat less precise), the courts say that the statute possesses a plain meaning and that interpretation is thus unnecessary.

Aids to Interpretation

Many statutes, however, do not easily lend themselves to the plain meaning rule. There are several reasons why courts frequently must interpret statutes before applying them, including the following: (1) Legislatures sometimes draft statutes with an element of "deliberate imprecision," intentionally giving courts a degree of latitude in applying the statute. They may do this because they legitimately recognize the difficulty of defining certain concepts in the abstract or because they want to avoid making a specific decision on a controversial political issue. (2) Even if a legislature tries to define all the key elements of a statute with great precision, the effort sometimes fails because some concepts are extremely difficult to define without reference to a specific set of facts. (3) The complex process of amendment and deletion as a bill goes through the legislature sometimes leads to a product that is less clear than the originally introduced bill. (4) The choice of particular language may have been the result of compromise among factions in the legislature, which sometimes leads to a lack of clarity. (5) At its best, language is imperfect, and few words are susceptible to but one meaning.

Therefore, in many cases a court must interpret a statute before using it as a basis for deciding a case. Even when a court asserts that a statute has a plain meaning, it often bolsters its conclusion by resorting to various interpretive aids. The aids or devices used by a court to ascertain the legislative intent may be grouped into several categories:

(1) A court sometimes refers to a dictionary or other standard reference source. It is presumed that legislative bodies use words in their common, ordinary sense, and a standard dictionary may be the best starting point to determine common English usage. General rules of grammar and punctuation are also usually followed unless there is a clear indication that the legislature intended otherwise. (2) The court will always examine the law's *textual context*, which involves reading the statute as a whole rather than concentrating solely on the language in question. (3) Sometimes a court will refer to the *legislative history* of a particular statue. The main sources of legislative history for federal statutes are committee reports by committees in the House or Senate with jurisdiction to conduct hearings on proposed legislation; verbatim, sworn testimony by witnesses testifying before these committees is often considered as well when available. Statements by individual members of Congress in the Congressional Record are also sometimes referred to, though they are typically less helpful. Legislative history for state legislative enactments is usually harder to come by. (4) The statute's *circumstantial context* may be taken into account by a court seeking to discern the meaning of legislative language. This term simply describes evidence showing the conditions or social problem that led the legislature to act. (5) A court will consider *precedent* when interpreting a statute. Thus, prior judicial interpretations of the same statute, or of similar language in another statute, may be taken into account.

Anytime interpretation of a statute's language is called for, the court's job is not to improve on what the legislature said or to make the statute mean what the court thinks it *should mean*, but only to do its best to ascertain what the legislature *did mean*. Even though determining what the legislature meant can be an elusive goal, the courts must do the best they can.

The following U.S. Supreme Court case from June 2020 provides an important example of the interpretation of the prohibition against sex discrimination in employment in Title VII of the 1964 Civil Rights Act. The 6-3 majority opinion illustrates an approach that places primacy on the exact text of a statute, the words used by Congress above all else. The original 166-page opinion is, naturally, heavily edited, and there were stinging dissents by Justices Alito, Thomas, and Kavanaugh.

BOSTOCK v. CLAYTON COUNTY
U.S. Supreme Court, 2020 U.S. LEXIS 3252 (June 15, 2020)

Gorsuch, Justice:

Today, we must decide whether an employer can fire someone simply for being homosexual or transgender. …Few facts are needed to appreciate the legal question we face. Each of the three cases before us started the same way: An employer fired a long-time employee shortly after the employee revealed that he or she is homosexual or transgender—and allegedly for no reason other than the employee's homosexuality or transgender status.

This Court normally interprets a statute in accord with the ordinary public meaning of its terms at the time of its enactment. After all, only the words on the page constitute the law adopted by Congress and approved by the President. If judges could add to, remodel, update, or detract from old statutory terms inspired only by extratextual sources and our own imaginations, we would risk amending statutes outside the legislative process reserved for the people's representatives. And we would deny the people the right to continue relying on the original meaning of the law they have counted on to settle their rights and obligations.

Our task is clear. We must determine the ordinary public meaning of Title VII [of the 1964 Civil Rights Act]'s command that it is "unlawful . . . for an employer to fail or refuse to hire or to discharge any individual, or otherwise to discriminate against any individual with respect to his compensation, terms, conditions, or privileges of employment, because of such individual's race, color, religion, sex, or national origin." To do so, we orient ourselves to the time of the statute's adoption, here 1964, and begin by examining the key statutory terms in turn before assessing their impact on the cases at hand and then confirming our work against this Court's precedents.

Appealing to roughly contemporaneous dictionaries, the employers say that, as used here, the term "sex" in 1964 referred to "status as either male or female [as] determined by reproductive biology." ... Still, that's just a starting point. The question isn't just what "sex" meant, but what Title VII says about it. Most notably, the statute prohibits employers from taking certain actions "because of " sex.... Title VII's "because of " test incorporates the "simple" and "traditional" standard of but-for causation. That form of causation is established whenever a particular outcome would not have happened "but for" the purported cause.

[The Court then examined the dictionary definition in 1964 of "discriminate" and concluded that,] taken together, an employer who intentionally treats a person worse because of sex—such as by firing the person for actions or attributes it would tolerate in an individual of another sex—discriminates against that person in violation of Title VII.

At first glance, another interpretation might seem possible. Discrimination sometimes involves "the act, practice, or an instance of discriminating categorically rather than individually." So how can we tell which sense, individual or group, "discriminate" carries in Title VII? The statute answers that question directly. It tells us three times—including immediately after the words "discriminate against"—that our focus should be on *individuals*, not groups: Employers may not "fail or refuse to hire or . . . discharge any *individual*, or otherwise … discriminate against any individual with respect to his compensation, terms, conditions, or privileges of employment, because of such *individual's* . . . sex."

The consequences of the law's focus on individuals rather than groups are anything but academic. Suppose an employer fires a woman for refusing his sexual advances. It's no defense for the employer to note that, while he treated that individual woman worse than he would have treated a man, he gives preferential treatment to female employees overall. The employer is liable for treating this woman worse in part because of her sex. Nor is it a defense for an employer to say it discriminates against both men and women because of sex. This statute works to protect individuals of both sexes from discrimination, and does so equally. So an employer who fires a woman, Hannah, because she is insufficiently feminine and also fires a man, Bob, for being insufficiently masculine may treat men and women as groups more or less equally. But in both cases the employer fires an individual in part because of sex. Instead of avoiding Title VII exposure, this employer doubles it.

From the ordinary public meaning of the statute's language at the time of the law's adoption, a straightforward rule emerges: An employer violates Title VII when it intentionally fires an individual employee based in part on sex. It doesn't matter if other factors besides the plaintiff's sex contributed to the decision. And it doesn't matter if the employer treated women as a group the same when compared to men as a group. If the employer intentionally relies in part on an individual employee's sex when deciding to discharge the employee—put differently, if changing the employee's sex would have yielded a different choice by the employer—a statutory violation has occurred. Title VII's message is "simple but momentous": An individual employee's sex is "not relevant to the selection, evaluation, or compensation of employees." *Price Waterhouse v. Hopkins*, 490 U.S. 228 (1989).

The statute's message for our cases is equally simple and momentous: An individual's homosexuality or transgender status is not relevant to employment decisions. That's because it is impossible to discriminate against a person for being homosexual or transgender without discriminating against that individual based on sex. Consider, for example, an employer with two employees, both of whom are attracted to men. The two individuals are, to the employer's mind, materially identical in all respects, except that one is a man and the other a woman. If the employer fires the male employee for no reason other than the fact he is attracted to men, the employer discriminates against him for traits or actions it tolerates in his female colleague. Put differently, the employer intentionally singles out an employee to fire based in part on the employee's sex, and the affected employee's sex is a but-for cause of his discharge. Or take an employer who fires a transgender person who was identified as a male at birth but who now identifies as a female. If the employer retains an otherwise identical employee who was identified as female at birth, the employer intentionally penalizes a person identified as male at birth for traits or actions that it tolerates in an employee identified as female at birth. Again, the individual employee's sex plays an unmistakable and impermissible role in the discharge decision.

That distinguishes these cases from countless others where Title VII has nothing to say. Take an employer who fires a female employee for tardiness or incompetence or simply supporting the wrong sports team. Assuming the employer would not have tolerated the same trait in a man, Title VII stands silent. But unlike any of these other traits or actions, homosexuality and transgender status are inextricably bound up with sex. Not because homosexuality or transgender status are related to sex in some vague sense or because discrimination on these bases has some disparate impact on one sex or another, but because to discriminate on these grounds requires an employer to intentionally treat individual employees differently because of their sex.

Nor does it matter that, when an employer treats one employee worse because of that individual's sex, other factors may contribute to the decision. Consider an employer with a policy of firing any woman he discovers to be a Yankees fan. Carrying out that rule because an employee is a woman and a fan of the Yankees is a firing "because of sex" if the employer would have tolerated the same allegiance in a male employee. Likewise here. When an employer fires an employee because she is homosexual or transgender, two causal factors may be in play—both the individual's sex and something else (the sex to which the individual is attracted or with which the individual identifies). But Title VII doesn't care. If an employer would not have discharged an employee but for that individual's sex, the statute's causation standard is met, and liability may attach.

There is simply no escaping the role intent plays here: Just as sex is necessarily a but-for cause when an employer discriminates against homosexual or transgender employees, an employer who discriminates on these grounds inescapably intends to rely on sex in its decisionmaking. Imagine an employer who has a policy of firing any employee known to be homosexual. The employer hosts an office holiday party and invites employees to bring their spouses. A model employee arrives and introduces a manager to Susan, the employee's wife. Will that employee be fired? If the policy works as the employer intends, the answer depends entirely on whether the model employee is a man or a woman. To be sure, that employer's ultimate goal might be to discriminate on the basis of sexual orientation. But to achieve that purpose the employer must, along the way, intentionally treat an employee worse based in part on that individual's sex.

An employer musters no better a defense by responding that it is equally happy to fire male and female employees who are homosexual or transgender. Title VII liability is not limited to employers who, through the sum of all of their employment actions, treat the class of men differently than the class of women. Instead, the law makes each instance of discriminating against an individual employee because of that individual's sex an independent violation of Title VII. So just as an employer who fires both Hannah and Bob for failing to fulfill traditional sex stereotypes doubles rather than eliminates Title VII liability, an employer who fires both Hannah and Bob for being gay or transgender does the same.

All that the statute's plain terms suggest, this Court's cases have already confirmed. Consider three of our leading precedents. In *Phillips v. Martin Marietta Corp.*, 400 U.S. 542 (1971), a company allegedly refused to hire women with young children, but did hire men with children the same age. Because its discrimination depended not only on the employee's sex as a female but also on the presence of another criterion—namely, being a parent of young children—the company contended it hadn't engaged in discrimination "because of" sex. The company maintained, too, that it hadn't violated the law because, as a whole, it tended to favor hiring women over men. Unsurprisingly by now, these submissions did not sway the Court. That an employer discriminates intentionally against an individual only in part because of sex supplies no defense to Title VII. Nor does the fact an employer may happen to favor women as a class.

In *Los Angeles Dept. of Water and Power v. Manhart*, 435 U.S. 702 (1978), an employer required women to make larger pension fund contributions than men. The employer sought to justify its disparate treatment on the ground that women tend to live longer than men, and thus are likely to receive more from the pension fund over time. Even so, the Court recognized, a rule that appears evenhanded at the group level can prove discriminatory at the level of individuals. True, women as a class may live longer than men as a class. But "[t]he statute's focus on the individual is unambiguous," and any individual woman might make the larger pension contributions and still die as early as a man. The employer violated Title VII because, when its policy worked exactly as planned, it could not "pass the simple test" asking whether an individual female employee would have been treated the same regardless of her sex.

In *Oncale v. Sundowner Offshore Services, Inc.,* 523 U.S. 75 (1998), a male plaintiff alleged that he was singled out by his male co-workers for sexual harassment. The Court held it was immaterial that members of the same sex as the victim committed the alleged discrimination. Nor did the Court concern itself with whether men as a group were subject to discrimination or whether something in addition to sex contributed to the discrimination, like the plaintiff's conduct or personal attributes. "[A]ssuredly," the case didn't involve "the principal evil Congress was concerned with when it enacted Title VII." But, the Court unanimously explained, it is "the provisions of our laws rather than the principal concerns of our legislators by which we are governed." Because the plaintiff alleged that the harassment would not have taken place but for his sex—that is, the plaintiff would not have suffered similar treatment if he were female—a triable Title VII claim existed.

The lessons these cases hold for ours are by now familiar. First, it's irrelevant what an employer might call its discriminatory practice, how others might label it, or what else might motivate it. In *Phillips*, the employer could have accurately spoken of its policy as one based on "motherhood." In much the same way, today's employers might describe their actions as motivated by their employees' homosexuality or transgender status. But [w]hen an employer fires an employee for being homosexual or transgender, it necessarily and intentionally discriminates against that individual in part because of sex. And that is all Title VII has ever demanded to establish liability.

Second, the plaintiff's sex need not be the sole or primary cause of the employer's adverse action. In *Phillips*, *Manhart*, and *Oncale*, the defendant easily could have pointed to some other, nonprotected trait and insisted it was the more important factor in the adverse employment outcome. So, too, it has no significance here if another factor—such as the sex the plaintiff is attracted to or presents as—might also be at work, or even play a more important role in the employer's decision.

Finally, an employer cannot escape liability by demonstrating that it treats males and females comparably as groups. As *Manhart* teaches, an employer is liable for intentionally requiring an individual female employee to pay more into a pension plan than a male counterpart even if the scheme promotes equality at the group level. Likewise, an employer who intentionally fires an individual homosexual or transgender employee in part because of that individual's sex violates the law even if the employer is willing to subject all male and female homosexual or transgender employees to the same rule. …

The employers turn to Title VII's list of protected characteristics—race, color, religion, sex, and national origin. Because homosexuality and transgender status can't be found on that list and because they are conceptually distinct from sex, the employers reason, they are implicitly excluded from Title VII's reach. …But that much does not follow. We agree that homosexuality and transgender status are distinct concepts from sex. But, as we've seen, discrimination based on homosexuality or transgender status necessarily entails discrimination based on sex; the first cannot happen without the second. Nor is there any such thing as a "canon of donut holes," in which Congress's failure to speak directly to a specific case that falls within a more general statutory rule creates a tacit exception. Instead, rwhen Congress chooses not to include any exceptions to a broad rule, courts apply the broad rule. And that is exactly how this Court has always approached Title VII. "Sexual harassment" is conceptually distinct from sex discrimination, but it can fall within Title VII's sweep. *Oncale*. Same with "motherhood discrimination." *Phillips*. Would the employers have us reverse those cases on the theory that Congress could have spoken to those problems more specifically? Of course not. As enacted, Title VII prohibits all forms of discrimination because of sex, however they may manifest themselves or whatever other labels might attach to them.

The employers try the same point another way. Since 1964, they observe, Congress has considered several proposals to add sexual orientation to Title VII's list of protected characteristics, but no such amendment has become law. Meanwhile, Congress has enacted other statutes addressing other topics that do discuss sexual orientation. This post-enactment legislative history, they urge, should tell us something.

But what? There's no authoritative evidence explaining why later Congresses adopted other laws referencing sexual orientation but didn't amend this one. Maybe some in the later legislatures understood the impact Title VII's broad language already promised for cases like ours and didn't think a revision needed. Maybe others knew about its impact but hoped no one else would notice. Maybe still others, occupied by other concerns, didn't consider the issue at all. All we can know for certain is that speculation about why a later Congress declined to adopt new legislation offers a "particularly dangerous" basis on which to rest an interpretation of an existing law a different and earlier Congress did adopt. *PBGC v. LTV Corp.*, 496 U.S. 633 (1990); see also *Sullivan v. Finkelstein*, 496 U.S. 617 (1990) (Scalia, J., concurring) ("Arguments based on subsequent legislative history…should not be taken seriously, not even in a footnote.").

Ultimately, the employers are forced to abandon the statutory text and precedent altogether and appeal to assumptions and policy. Most pointedly, they contend that few in 1964 would have expected Title VII to apply to discrimination against homosexual and transgender persons. And whatever the text and our precedent indicate, they say, shouldn't this fact cause us to pause before recognizing liability?

It might be tempting to reject this argument out of hand. This Court has explained many times over many years that, when the meaning of the statute's terms is plain, our job is at an end. The people are entitled to rely on the law as written, without fearing that courts might disregard its plain terms based on some extratextual consideration. Of course, some Members of this Court have consulted legislative history when interpreting ambiguous statutory language. But that has no bearing here. "Legislative history, for those who take it into account, is meant to clear up ambiguity, not create it." *Milner v. Department of Navy*, 562 U.S. 562 (2011). And as we have seen, no ambiguity exists about how Title VII's terms apply to the facts before us. To be sure, the statute's application in these cases reaches "beyond the principal evil" legislators may have intended or expected to address. *Oncale*. But "'the fact that [a statute] has been applied in situations not expressly anticipated by Congress" does not demonstrate ambiguity; instead, it simply "demonstrates [the] breadth" of a legislative command. *Sedima S.P.RlL. v. Imrex Co.*, 473 U.S. 479 (1985). And "it is ultimately the provisions of" those legislative commands "rather than the principal concerns of our legislators by which we are governed." *Oncale*; see also A. Scalia & B. Garner, Reading Law: The Interpretation of Legal Texts 101 (2012) (noting that unexpected applications of broad language reflect /only Congress's "presumed point [to] produce general coverage—not to leave room for courts to recognize ad hoc exceptions").

Ours is a society of written laws. Judges are not free to overlook plain statutory commands on the strength of nothing more than suppositions about intentions or guesswork about expectations. In Title VII, Congress adopted broad language making it illegal for an employer to rely on an employee's sex when deciding to fire that employee. We do not hesitate to recognize today a necessary consequence of that legislative choice: An employer who fires an individual merely for being gay or transgender defies the law.

CHAPTER 5
CONSTITUTIONAL LAW

- Organization of the Federal Government

- Authority of Federal and State Governments

- Protecting Basic Rights

The most important single document in the United States is the U.S. Constitution. This document is the foundation of our democratic system of government and the basis of our many freedoms. Although drafted in a simpler time, the Constitution has evolved over the past 200 years to keep pace with changes in American society. Partly through amendment, but more importantly through flexible Supreme Court interpretations, the Constitution has remained as vital and timely as it was when originally written.

Few areas of the law can be studied without reference to the Constitution. For example, Chapter 2 discussed the structure of the federal court system, which is established in the Constitution, as well as the exercise of personal jurisdiction by state and federal courts, which is constrained by the Constitution's due process provisions. The Constitution governs the ability of the government to intervene in business activities; for example, Chapter 6 points out that the government's power to conduct inspections and searches of business firms is limited by the Fourth Amendment of the Constitution. The Constitution contains several protections for defendants charged with crimes, as discussed in Chapter 7. The Constitutional right to freedom of speech affects the principles of defamation law discussed in Chapter 8 and the rules of trademark and copyright law discussed in Chapter 9. Although not everyone realizes this fact, the Constitution has at least as much relevance to the operation of business enterprises as it does to the personal affairs of individuals. Our discussion of constitutional law in this chapter is fairly broad, but it will emphasize the role the Constitution plays in both empowering the government to regulate business and placing limits on the exercise of these regulatory powers.

Before turning to a discussion of the U.S. Constitution, it bears mentioning that every state in this country also has a constitution. These documents include many provisions similar to those found in the federal Constitution, such as those separating state governments into three branches and protecting fundamental liberties. Most state constitutions are much more detailed than the U.S. Constitution. A state constitutional provision is the supreme law within that state, unless it conflicts with the U.S. Constitution or some other federal law.

The U.S. Constitution contains three general categories of provision:

- It prescribes the basic organization of the federal government into legislative, executive, and judicial branches.
- It delineates the authority of the federal government, in contrast with the states, by granting specific powers to the three branches of the federal government.
- It protects certain basic rights of individuals and businesses by placing limitations on federal and state governmental power.

ORGANIZATION OF THE FEDERAL GOVERNMENT

One major function of the Constitution is to establish the basic organization of the federal government into legislative, executive, and judicial branches. The essential function of the legislative branch, Congress, is to make laws, as well as to collect revenue and appropriate funds for carrying out those laws.

The main function of the executive branch is to enforce these laws; however, the executive branch also plays the primary role in conducting foreign relations and directing our military forces. The basic task of the judicial branch is to decide how particular laws should be applied to actual disputed cases.

Separation of Powers

As a general proposition, each branch of the federal government is supposed to exercise only those types of powers expressly given to it by the Constitution. Stated somewhat differently, one branch generally is not supposed to encroach on the powers of another branch. The doctrine of *separation of powers* is, however, a flexible one that is subject to various exceptions based on practicality.

Checks and Balances

The Constitution expressly provides for a number of *checks and balances* to insure against any single branch of government developing an excessive degree of power. Examples include the requirement that the president sign legislation passed by Congress (the executive veto power) and the ability of Congress to override a presidential veto by a two-thirds vote in both houses.

Judicial Review

Another type of permissible interplay among the three branches of government is *judicial review*. Although this could be characterized as another form of check and balance, the concept of judicial review is not expressed in the Constitution. During the early days of the Republic, the question of which branch had ultimate authority to determine constitutional issues was unsettled. In *Marbury v. Madison, 5* U.S. 137(1803), the U.S. Supreme Court assumed this power for the judicial branch of government. Because of the practicality and logic of placing this task in the hands of the federal courts and because of the stature of Chief Justice John Marshall, the author of the opinion in *Marbury*, the doctrine of judicial review has been generally accepted. Under the principle of judicial review, the federal courts have the final say in deciding whether the Constitution has been violated by a congressional law or executive action. It has been said that ''the Constitution means what the Supreme Court says it means.'' This is only a slight exaggeration, and emphasizes that Congress cannot enact a law that changes the Supreme Court's interpretations of the Constitution, something that can be done only by a constitutional amendment or by a later decision of the Supreme Court itself, both of which are very unusual. It is very difficult to amend the U.S. Constitution, and the Supreme Court has always been extremely reluctant to overrule its own prior decisions.

Federal courts also have the power to determine whether actions of *state* courts, legislatures, and executive officials violate the U.S. Constitution. Similarly, state courts have the power to invalidate state legislative and executive actions under their particular state's constitution.

Delegation of Powers

The final category of exception to the separation of powers doctrine is found in the principle that Congress may expressly delegate legislative powers to the other two branches. Congress often delegates rulemaking powers, for example, to federal administrative agencies that are outside the legislative branch. For example, in the Securities Exchange Act of 1934, Congress prohibited fraudulent and deceptive practices in connection with the sale of securities and delegated to the Securities and Exchange Commission the power to make rules specifying in more detail the types of conduct that would violate this prohibition. Congress also has delegated certain rule-making powers to the federal courts, namely, the limited power to prescribe rules of procedure and evidence. Express delegations of legislative power are normally valid so long as Congress (1) indicates the basic policy objectives it is seeking to achieve and (2) provides some degree of guidance as to how the power is to be exercised. (At the state government level, the same general principles typically are applied to the separation of powers doctrine and its exceptions.)

Authority of Federal and State Governments

A second major function of the U.S. Constitution is to delineate the authority of the federal government vis-a-vis that of the states. In our dual system of sovereignty, there are 51 primary governments—the federal government and the 50 state governments. When the original 13 colonies ratified the Constitution, they agreed to cede certain important sovereign powers to the federal government; as other states were added they similarly agreed. Under our system of federalism, the federal government has those powers that are specifically given to it in the Constitution—the so-called *delegated powers* (or *enumerated powers*). Those powers not granted to the federal government continue to reside with the states—the so-called *reserved powers*.

Our discussion of federal authority will focus on the power of Congress and primarily on the power of that federal legislative body to regulate business activities. Article I, section 8 of the Constitution spells out the powers of the U.S. Congress, the most important of which include the power:

> To lay and collect Taxes, Dues, Imposts and Excises, to pay the Debts and provide for the common
> Defense and general Welfare of the United States; . . .
> To borrow Money on the Credit of the United States;
> To regulate Commerce with foreign Nations, and among the several States, and with the Indian Tribes;
> To establish an uniform rule of Naturalization, and uniform Laws on the subject of Bankruptcies throughout the United States;
> To coin Money, regulate the Value thereof, and of foreign Coin, and fix the Standard of Weights and Measures;
> To establish Post Offices and post Roads;
> To promote the Progress of Science and useful Arts, by securing for limited Times to Authors and Inventors the exclusive right to their respective Writings and Discoveries;
> To constitute Tribunals inferior to the Supreme Court;
> To declare War, grant Letters of Marque and Reprisal, and make Rules concerning Captures on Land and Water;
> To raise and support Armies, but no Appropriation of Money to that Use shall be for a longer Term than two Years;
> To provide and maintain a Navy;
> To make Rules for the Government and Regulation of the land and naval forces;
> To provide for calling forth the Militia to execute the Laws of the Union, suppress Insurrections and repel Invasions;
> To provide for organizing, arming, and disciplining the Militia, and . . .
> To make all Laws which shall be necessary and proper for carrying into Execution the

foregoing Powers, and all other Powers vested by this Constitution in the Government of the United States, or in any Department or Officer thereof.

State Police Power

In most circumstances, the lines of demarcation between the authority of the federal and state governments are quite clear. Most of the legislative powers delegated to the federal government under article I, section 8—such as the power to operate post offices and to maintain the various armed forces—involve such obviously federal powers that no state reasonably could claim to possess any regulatory authority over them.

By the same token, the powers reserved to the states are also relatively clear and well established. Virtually all the powers of a particular state derive from the *state police power*—a term referring to the inherent governmental power to regulate the health, safety, morality, and general welfare of its people. Statutes relating to the operation of motor vehicles, the manufacture and sale of alcoholic beverages, and the regulation of crime obviously fall within the police power, because they are directly involved with matters of health, safety, and morals. Typical state laws based on the "general welfare" component of the police power are those that regulate such matters as marriage and divorce, the inheritance of property, and landlord-tenant relationships. The power to enact zoning laws specifying restrictions on the use of real estate also falls within the state police power, but state legislatures normally delegate this power to their cities; thus, most zoning regulations are actually found in city ordinances or the regulations of city zoning commissions. Amendment 10 in the Constitution's Bill of Rights reserves all powers not granted to the federal government to "the states, or to the people."

State legislatures may delegate any part of the police power to local political subdivisions such as cities or counties. They also sometimes delegate very limited police powers to specialized political subdivisions of the state, such as port authorities, flood control districts, school districts, water supply and conservation districts, hospital districts, and so forth. Later, when we discuss limits that the U.S. Constitution places on state governmental powers, it should be understood that these limits are the same whether the state power is exercised directly by the state or is delegated to a local government entity.

Federal Power—The Commerce Clause

In examining the authority of the federal government, we are primarily concerned with the power to regulate business. Although in many areas there is a clear delineation between the powers of the federal government on one hand and the state governments on the other, one area presents difficult problems—regulation of commercial activities. Despite the fact that the federal power to regulate commerce is very broad, the states also have a substantial amount of regulatory power over commerce. The dual nature of the power to regulate commerce has created many instances of state-federal friction.

Federal Regulation of Interstate Commerce

Article I, section 8 of the U.S. Constitution grants to Congress the power "to regulate Commerce with foreign Nations, and among the several States." Many provisions of the Constitution were aimed at preventing various kinds of provincialism and thus at making the United States truly "united." By giving Congress the primary authority to regulate interstate commerce, the *Commerce Clause* was intended to make the United States a common market, with the many economic advantages of trade that is unhindered by state boundaries. Before the adoption of the Constitution, economic Balkanization had plagued trade relations among the Colonies under the Articles of Confederation because the Colonies had erected various barriers to free trade among themselves.

By giving Congress the power to regulate trade with foreign nations, the framers of the Constitution recognized that the nation could not join the international trading community unless it could speak with one voice in maintaining international trade relations.

Until the late 1930s, the Supreme Court interpreted Congress's authority under the commerce clause fairly narrowly, holding that it could primarily regulate commerce that (a) actually crossed state lines, or (b) involved instrumentalities of interstate commerce such as rivers or railroads. Beginning in the 1930s, the Court added a third and extremely broad category, holding that Congress could regulate commerce occurring entirely within the border of a single state so long as the commercial activity had "any appreciable effect" on interstate or foreign commerce.

So, for example, in *Wickard v. Filburn,* 317 U.S. 111 (1942), Congress was attempting to help farmers by keeping wheat prices from falling too far. Congress chose to do so by limiting production. Farmer Filburn was told that he could not grow as many acres of wheat as he desired. Since he was not located near a state line and intended to grow the wheat only for his own use, he argued that Congress could not tell him what to do. But the Supreme Court held that if an exception was made for farmer Filburn, then exceptions would have to be made for other farmers and the *aggregate effect* on interstate commerce could be appreciable.

Even though Filburn was a very small farmer, to grant him an exception would undermine the regulatory scheme that Congress had in place. Therefore, Filburn would just have to go buy the rest of the wheat he needed somewhere else. Congress had the authority under the Commerce Clause to pass that law because markets for wheat are interstate in nature, and the cumulative effect of allowing farmers to grow wheat in excess of the number of acres allowed by federal regulations intended to stabilize prices during the Depression would have a substantial effect on interstate wheat markets. The wheat they grew for home consumption was wheat that they would not buy in the marketplace.

Much legislation passed by Congress since the 1930s has been grounded in its power to regulate commerce. Congress often uses the Commerce Clause as a constitutional foundation for enacting legislation even when its primary goal is not an economic one. Examples of this include laws aimed at protecting the environment and prohibiting employment discrimination. "Commerce" includes almost anything remotely related to an economic activity, including manufacturing, advertising, contracting, sales and sales financing, transportation, capital-raising, and so on. Because the federal regulatory power encompasses intrastate commercial activity that affects *interstate* or foreign commerce, few local businesses can escape the reach of the federal government.

In *McLain v. Real Estate Board of New Orleans*, 444 U.S. 232 (1980), a question arose whether a number of New Orleans real estate firms and trade associations had violated the federal antitrust laws by entering into several price-fixing contracts. The lower courts dismissed the action, ruling that the defendants' actions, which involved sales of land in New Orleans, were "purely local" in nature and thus not subject to federal law. The Supreme Court reversed, finding that the indirect effects of the defendants' activities were sufficiently related to interstate commerce to justify application of federal law. This finding of sufficient effect—a "not insubstantial effect"—was based primarily on the fact that (1) significant amounts of money lent by local banks to finance real estate purchases came from out-of-state banks, and (2) most of the mortgages taken by the local banks were "physically traded" by them to financial institutions in other states.

In two recent cases, laws were struck down as not within the authority of Congress under the Commerce clause, but neither truly involved the regulation of commerce or affected it in any substantial way. One law attempted to punish violence against women (*U.S. v. Morrison*, 529 U.S. 598 (2000)), and the other limited the carrying of guns on high school campuses (*U.S. v. Lopez*, 514 U.S. 549 (1995). The Court held that neither law regulated economic activity in even an indirect way, so they could not be grounded in the Commerce Clause. In addition, these two acts of Congress were criminal laws, which removed them even farther from the realm of economic regulation, and the laws also proscribed conduct that had long been viewed by the law as within the sole province of state and local governments.

The following case provides a good example of how federal courts, here the US Supreme Court, analyze whether Congress has acted within the scope of its constitutionally granted legislative power.

GONZALES v. RAICH
U.S. Supreme Court, 545 U.S. 1 (2005)

California authorizes the use of marijuana for medicinal purposes. The question presented in this case is whether the power vested in Congress by the Commerce Clause includes the power to prohibit the local cultivation and use of marijuana in compliance with California law. Respondents Raich and Monson are California residents who suffer from a variety of serious medical conditions and have sought to avail themselves of medical marijuana pursuant to the terms of California's Compassionate Use Act. They are being treated by licensed, board-certified family practitioners, who have concluded, after prescribing a host of conventional medicines to treat respondents' conditions and to alleviate their associated symptoms, that marijuana is the only drug available that provides effective treatment. Both women have been using marijuana as a medication for several years pursuant to their doctors' recommendation, and both rely heavily on cannabis to function on a daily basis. Indeed, Raich's physician believes that forgoing cannabis treatments would certainly cause her excruciating pain and could very well prove fatal. Respondent Monson cultivates her own marijuana, but Raich is unable to cultivate her own, and thus relies on two caregivers to provide her with locally grown marijuana at no charge. After federal agents raided Monson's house and destroyed her plants, respondents sued the U.S. Attorney General Gonzales and the head of the DEA seeking injunctive and declaratory relief prohibiting the enforcement of the federal Controlled Substances Act (CSA), to the extent it prevents them from possessing, obtaining, or manufacturing cannabis for their personal medical use. The district court ruled against respondents and the Ninth Circuit reversed. Attorney General Gonzales appealed.

Stevens, Justice:
The case is made difficult by respondents' strong arguments that they will suffer

irreparable harm because, despite a congressional finding to the contrary, marijuana does have valid therapeutic purposes. The question before us, however, is not whether it is wise to enforce the statute in these circumstances; rather, it is whether Congress' power to regulate interstate markets for medicinal substances encompasses the portions of those markets that are supplied with drugs produced and consumed locally.

[The Court first reviewed the lengthy history of Congressional efforts to regulate the selling of illicit drugs, including marijuana.] To effectuate these goals, Congress devised a closed regulatory system making it unlawful to manufacture, distribute, dispense, or possess any controlled substance except in a manner authorized by the CSA. Respondents in this case do not dispute that passage of the CSA was well within Congress' commerce power. Rather, they argue that the CSA's categorical prohibition of the manufacture and possession of marijuana as applied to the intrastate manufacture and possession of marijuana for medical purposes pursuant to California law exceeds Congress' authority under the Commerce Clause.

In assessing the validity of congressional regulation, none of our Commerce Clause cases can be viewed in isolation. Our understanding of the reach of the Commerce Clause, as well as Congress' assertion of authority thereunder, has evolved over time. The Commerce Clause emerged as the Framers' response to the central problem giving rise to the Constitution itself: the absence of any federal commerce power under the Articles of Confederation. For the first century of our history, the primary use of the Clause was to preclude the kind of discriminatory state legislation that had once been permissible. Then, in response to rapid industrial development and an increasingly interdependent national economy, Congress ushered in a new era of federal regulation under the commerce power, beginning with the enactment of the Interstate Commerce Act in 1887, and the Sherman Antitrust Act in 1890.

Cases decided during that "new era," which now spans more than a century, have identified three general categories of regulation in which Congress is authorized to engage under its commerce power. First, Congress can regulate the channels of interstate commerce. Second, Congress has authority to regulate and protect the instrumentalities of interstate commerce, and persons or things in interstate commerce. Third, Congress has the power to regulate activities that substantially affect interstate commerce. Only the third category is implicated in the case at hand.

Our case law firmly establishes Congress' power to regulate purely local activities that are part of an economic "class of activities" that have a substantial effect on interstate commerce. As we stated in *Wickard v. Filburn,* 317 U.S. 111 (1942), "even if appellee's activity be local and though it may not be regarded as commerce, it may still, whatever its nature, be reached by Congress if it exerts a substantial economic effect on interstate commerce." We have never required Congress to legislate with scientific exactitude. When Congress decides that the "'total incidence'" of a practice poses a threat to a national market, it may regulate the entire class. In this vein, we have reiterated that when "'a general regulatory statute bears a substantial relation to commerce, the de minimis character of individual instances arising under that statute is of no consequence.'"

In *Wickard,* we upheld the application of regulations promulgated under the Agricultural Adjustment Act of 1938, which were designed to control the volume of wheat moving in interstate and foreign commerce in order to avoid surpluses and consequent abnormally low prices. The regulations established an allotment of 11.1 acres for Filburn's

1941 wheat crop, but he sowed 23 acres, intending to use the excess by consuming it on his own farm. Filburn argued that even though we had sustained Congress' power to regulate the production of goods for commerce, that power did not authorize "federal regulation of production not intended in any part for commerce but wholly for consumption on the farm." [The Court rejected this argument, noting]: "The effect of the statute before us is to restrict the amount which may be produced for market and the extent as well to which one may forestall resort to the market by producing to meet his own needs. That appellee's own contribution to the demand for wheat may be trivial by itself is not enough to remove him from the scope of federal regulation where, as here, his contribution, taken together with that of many others similarly situated, is far from trivial."

Wickard thus establishes that Congress can regulate purely intrastate activity that is not itself "commercial," in that it is not produced for sale, if it concludes that failure to regulate that class of activity would undercut the regulation of the interstate market in that commodity. The similarities between this case and *Wickard* are striking. Like the farmer in *Wickard*, respondents are cultivating, for home consumption, a fungible commodity for which there is an established, albeit illegal, interstate market. Just as the Agricultural Adjustment Act was designed "to control the volume of wheat moving in interstate and foreign commerce in order to avoid surpluses . . ." and consequently control the market price, a primary purpose of the CSA is to control the supply and demand of controlled substances in both lawful and unlawful drug markets.

In *Wickard*, we had no difficulty concluding that Congress had a rational basis for believing that, when viewed in the aggregate, leaving home-consumed wheat outside the regulatory scheme would have a substantial influence on price and market conditions. Here too, Congress had a rational basis for concluding that leaving home-consumed marijuana outside federal control would similarly affect price and market conditions. Even respondents acknowledge the existence of an illicit market in marijuana; indeed, Raich has personally participated in that market, and Monson expresses a willingness to do so in the future.

More concretely, one concern prompting inclusion of wheat grown for home consumption in the 1938 Act was that rising market prices could draw such wheat into the interstate market, resulting in lower market prices. The parallel concern making it appropriate to include marijuana grown for home consumption in the CSA is the likelihood that the high demand in the interstate market will draw such marijuana into that market. While the diversion of homegrown wheat tended to frustrate the federal interest in stabilizing prices by regulating the volume of commercial transactions in the interstate market, the diversion of homegrown marijuana tends to frustrate the federal interest in eliminating commercial transactions in the interstate market in their entirety. In both cases, the regulation is squarely within Congress' commerce power because production of the commodity meant for home consumption, be it wheat or marijuana, has a substantial effect on supply and demand in the national market for that commodity.

In assessing the scope of Congress' authority under the Commerce Clause, we stress that the task before us is a modest one. We need not determine whether respondents' activities, taken in the aggregate, substantially affect interstate commerce in fact, but only whether a "rational basis" exists for so concluding. Given the enforcement difficulties that attend distinguishing between marijuana cultivated locally and marijuana grown elsewhere, and concerns about diversion into illicit channels, we have no difficulty concluding that Congress had a rational basis for believing that failure to regulate the intrastate manufacture and possession of marijuana would leave a gaping hole in the CSA. Thus, as in *Wickard*, when it enacted comprehensive legislation to regulate the interstate market in a fungible commodity, Congress was acting well within its authority to "make all Laws which shall be necessary and proper" to "regulate Commerce . . . among the several States." That the regulation ensnares some purely intrastate activity is of no moment. As we have done many times before, we refuse to excise individual components of that larger scheme.

We acknowledge that evidence proffered by respondents in this case regarding the effective medical uses for marijuana, if found credible after trial, would cast serious doubt on the accuracy of the findings that require marijuana to be listed [as a prohibited substance]. But the possibility that the drug may be reclassified in the future has no relevance to the question whether Congress now has the power to regulate its production and distribution. Respondents' submission, if accepted, would place all homegrown medical substances beyond the reach of Congress' regulatory jurisdiction. The Ninth Circuit's decision is vacated and remanded.

Comment: The Court relied on *Wickard v. Filburn* as a precedent to be followed in *Gonzales v. Raisch*. Do you think that this is correct, or do you see sufficient differences between the facts in *Wickard* and those in *Gonzales* that might justify a conclusion that the former is not a precedent for the latter?

In a controversial ruling, the Supreme Court in 2012 addressed the constitutionality of the "individual mandate" provision of the Affordable Care Act ("Obamacare"). *Nat'l Federation of Indep. Business v. Sebelius*, 132 S.Ct. 2566 (2012). The mandate required most Americans to buy health insurance (or make a "shared responsibility payment"), whether they wanted to or not, as part of the statutory plan to help fund a system that would provide health insurance for everyone. In the opinion of the Court's majority, Chief Justice Roberts upheld the mandate as part of Congress's taxation power, which is broader than its power under the Commerce Clause. However, he also wrote that the Commerce Clause did *not* provide a basis for validating the individual mandate. Roberts wrote, in part, that although Congressional power to regulate commerce is broad and that *Wickard v. Filburn* properly held that individual actions could be aggregated in order to determine that activity had "affected" interstate commerce and thereby justified federal regulation, that the:

> …individual mandate, however, does not regulate existing commercial activity. It instead compels individuals to *become* active in commerce by purchasing a product, on the ground that their failure to do so affects interstate commerce. Construing the Commerce Clause to permit Congress to regulate individuals precisely *because* they are doing nothing would open a new and potentially vast domain to congressional authority. Every day individuals do not do an infinite number of things. In some cases they decide not to do something; in others they simply fail to do it. Allowing Congress to justify federal regulation by pointing to the effect of inaction on commerce would bring countless decisions an individual could *potentially* make within the scope of federal regulation, and--under the Government's theory-- empower Congress to make those decisions for him.

The implications of this holding for the scope of Congress's power under the Commerce Clause going forward are not clear. The distinction drawn by the Chief Justice's majority opinion between the power of Congress to regulate "action" under the Commerce Clause, but not "inaction," is likely to be very difficult to apply because so many "actions" can also be viewed as "inactions," and vice-versa. For example, if you are ticketed for running a red light, is your offense the action of driving through the intersection when the light is red, or is it the inaction of failing to stop when the light is red? Also, there is debate about whether the Chief Justice's statements concerning the power of Congress under the Commerce Clause are "dicta" that will not be binding precedent for lower federal courts or for the Supreme Court in future decisions, because the court majority upheld the insurance mandate under Congress's taxing power, and the statements about congressional power under the Commerce Clause were therefore not necessary to the decision in the case.

An important update to the situation involved in the Supreme Court's 2012 decision on the constitutionality of Affordable Care Act is that Congress later repealed the individual mandate requiring individuals to pay something for health care insurance. Thus, that part of the ACA that the Supreme Court relied upon to uphold the act under the taxing power of Congress no longer exists. Because of this, a federal district court in Texas held that the entire ACA is unconstitutional. That court has been ordered by the Supreme Court to hold further hearings on whether the entire act is unconstitutional as the district court held, or whether parts of it are okay because they are within the power of Congress. The latter include the law's requirements that insurance companies allow people to remain on their parents' health insurance policies until the age of 26 and the requirement that insurance companies cannot deny health insurance coverage because of a "preexisting condition."

State Regulation of Commerce

Despite the dominant federal role, the states retain substantial authority to regulate commercial activities. A state's police power permits it to protect the health, safety, and general welfare of its citizens. This power includes the authority to regulate commercial activities within the state, even if those activities have a substantial effect on interstate or foreign commerce and even if they originated outside the state. To give effect to the primary power of the federal government in these areas, however, the courts have developed several principles that limit the power of the states. These include preemption, discrimination against interstate commerce, and unduly burdening interstate commerce. Although different, all these concepts are closely related, and more than one of them may sometimes be at issue in the same case. (These principles also apply to state laws that affect foreign commerce—that is, international trade. Unless indicated otherwise in this discussion, international commerce will be included within the term *interstate commerce*.)

Federal Preemption. The concept of *federal preemption* is a general principle of constitutional law that applies to any state-federal conflict. The doctrine of preemption is relevant regardless of whether a particular federal power comes from the Commerce Clause or from some other provision of the Constitution. However, we discuss the preemption doctrine in the context of the federal Commerce Clause power because it is in this context that most of the issues arise.

If a particular governmental power is exclusively federal, we say that there is federal preemption of this field of government activity. Federal preemption may be either express or implied, or it may result from a direct conflict between state and federal law. As we mentioned in the previous section, some federal powers in the Constitution are obviously of an exclusively federal nature, such as conducting foreign affairs, maintaining an army, and establishing a monetary system. The state governments have no power to act in such matters. In the case of other powers granted to the federal government, however, it may not be so obvious that the power is exclusively federal. When the Constitution gives the federal government a certain type of authority and a state attempts to exercise a similar or related power, the courts may have to determine whether there actually is federal preemption.

Express Preemption. When a preemption question arises, we begin with one basic proposition: the *Supremacy Clause* found in article VI, section 1 of the Constitution makes federal law the "supreme law of the land." The Supremacy Clause applies regardless of the specific source of the state or local law and regardless of the specific source of the federal law. The Supremacy Clause means, among other things, that if the Constitution gives a power to the federal government, the federal government also has the authority to prohibit the states from exercising a similar power. For example, the Constitution specifically gives Congress the power to enact copyright laws that protect the creative work of writers, painters, photographers, film makers, and others. When using this power to pass copyright legislation, Congress engaged in *express preemption* by specifying in the legislation that the states have no power to adopt laws granting copyright protection or anything closely resembling copyright protect to works of creative expression.

Another example of express federal preemption is found in the Airline Deregulation Act of 1978, a law that generally removed federal regulation of airline routes and fares and opened them to competition. Desiring to also forestall the possibility of state or local government regulation of the economics of air travel, Congress included a provision stating that "a state, political subdivision of a state, or political authority of at least two states may not enact or enforce a law, regulation, or other provision having the force and effect of law related to a price, route, or service of an air carrier."

Applying this provision, courts have concluded that state consumer protection laws usually cannot be used against airline business practices such as the conduct of their frequent flyer programs. Some tort law claims against airlines have held to not be preempted, and consumers may also assert claims against airlines based on breach of contract. Airlines typically do not find it difficult, however, to use language in policies such as those pertaining to frequent flyer programs that prevents the creation of airline contractual obligations.

Although Congress has this power of express preemption, it does not always use it. Congress has sometimes engaged in express preemption, it has sometimes said nothing about the issue at all, and in some statutes it has stated expressly that states do have the power to adopt similar or related laws so long as those laws do not conflict with or hinder the objectives of the federal law.

Implied Preemption. When Congress has chosen to regulate some activity but has said nothing about whether the states do or do not have power to pass related laws, a question of *implied preemption* may arise. For example, Congress has extensively regulated labor-management relations, as discussed in Chapter 30. Federal law establishes a framework within which groups of employees may fairly and democratically decide whether they want to form a union and, if so, which labor organization they wish to represent them in negotiating with the employer about wages, hours, and working conditions. The conduct of both employers and unions is closely regulated during this process. Once a group of employees decides to be represented by a particular union and the union is officially certified, the employer is under a legal obligation to bargain with the union in good faith.

The objective of the regulated negotiation process is to achieve a collective bargaining agreement governing the rights and responsibilities of the employer and employees during the term of the contract. Suppose that, in State X, there has been a history of labor strife in a particular industry that is important to the state's economy. Strikes by employees and lockouts by employers have sometimes resulted, causing economic harm to the state. In response, State X's legislature passes a statute authorizing the state governor to issue an executive order ending a strike or lockout in that industry after a stated time period if the governor finds that serious harm is being done to the state's economy. Assume that, when the governor later exercises this power, a union or employer challenges the validity of the state law under which the governor acted. Because the federal labor-management relations laws say nothing about state authority to engage in similar regulation, a challenge to the state law is likely to be based on a claim of implied preemption. (The employer or union might also claim that the law places an undue burden on interstate commerce—this concept will be discussed shortly.)

When a claim of implied preemption is made, the party challenging the state law is asking the court to draw an inference about the intent of Congress—in other words, that party tries to prove that Congress implicitly intended to preempt the regulation of this general area. The challenger usually must prove two conditions before a court will conclude that implied preemption exists. First, it must be shown that the federal regulation is relatively *comprehensive*. In other words, the court must be convinced that Congress attempted to impose a fairly complete regulatory structure on this type of activity. Otherwise, it makes no sense to infer a preemptive intent on the part of Congress. This first condition is clearly met in the case of federal labor-management relations laws.

Second, it also must be shown that there is a very strong need for a uniform national regulatory policy in this area, so that individual state laws of this type are likely to interfere with the objectives of the federal regulatory effort. Most unions represent employees in several states, and many of the employers that negotiate with unions also operate in more than one state. Moreover, a group of employers may negotiate with one large union, and sometimes one large employer must negotiate with several unions. In other words, relationships between companies and unions generally transcend state boundaries, but the objective of a particular negotiation is a single contract. If these often-sensitive negotiations had to be conducted within a framework of several different sets of state regulations, it would be extremely difficult for the parties ever to achieve a collective bargaining agreement, and the collective bargaining agreement is the cornerstone of federal regulation in this area. Thus, the second condition for implied preemption also exists. Because both conditions are met, the Supreme Court has concluded that the states are preempted from adopting laws dealing with the company-union relationship.

Even in a situation in which there is implied federal preemption, states still may protect important state interests by passing laws that are only peripherally related to the federally regulated area and that are not likely to interfere with the federal regulatory objectives. For example, despite implied preemption, an employee may be punished under state criminal or tort law for assault and battery or property destruction even though the wrongful conduct occurred during the course of a union-sponsored strike.

Direct Conflict. A much narrower form of preemption occurs when a specific state law is in *direct conflict* with a specific provision of federal law. In the labor-management relations setting, recall that there is no express federal preemption. There is implied preemption, however. But for the sake of illustrating a direct conflict between state and federal law, now let us also assume that one (or both) of the requirements for implied preemption were not met. This would mean that there is no implied federal preemption of this general field of regulatory activity, and the states could enact laws regulating company-union relations. However, if a particular state provision comes into direct conflict with a federal law, the state law is void to the extent of the conflict. Suppose that, even if there is no express or implied federal preemption, there is a specific federal statute that empowers the U.S. president to seek a federal court injunction ending a strike or lockout under certain carefully prescribed conditions. In such a case, the law in State X authorizing its governor to halt strikes or lockouts might very well be void because of a direct conflict with the federal law.

A state law is not void because of direct conflict just because the state provision deals with the same type of activity. Moreover, the mere fact that a state law is more stringent than a similar federal law does not make the state law void. For example, the fact that California law places stricter pollution control standards on automobiles does not mean that this state law is in conflict with federal auto emission control regulations. In addition, there is no direct conflict just because a state permits something that federal law prohibits, or vice-versa. There are many instances in which there is no federal law prohibiting a particular action, but there is a law in a state that does prohibit that activity. And the same is true in reverse.

A state law is void because of direct conflict in only two situations. First, there is a direct conflict if it is impossible to comply with both the state and federal laws. For example, suppose that a state law were to *require* wholesalers to grant quantity discounts to retailers in the state even in circumstances in which the discounts are not justified by lower costs of selling in larger quantities. This law would require conduct that violates the federal Robinson-Patman Act's prohibition of price discrimination (discussed in the chapter on Antitrust Law).

Second, even if it is literally possible to comply with both laws, there nevertheless is a direct conflict if the state law substantially interferes with the purpose of the federal law. For example, suppose that when Congress passed the law giving the president authority to stop strikes or lockouts in certain carefully defined situations, it clearly indicated the intent to permit government interference in company-union confrontations only when national defense is threatened or when a national economic emergency exists. In such a case, the hypothetical law giving the governor of State X the power to stop strikes when economic injury to the state is threatened might be void for direct conflict because it interferes with objectives of the federal law.

It should be reemphasized that either type of direct conflict is really just a narrower form of implied preemption applying only to a specific state law and a specific federal law rather than to an entire field of regulated activity. A recent example of this type of federal preemption, in June 2013, occurred in *Arizona v. Inter-Tribal Council of Arizona, Inc.*, __ US __ (2013), in which the US Supreme Court invalidated provisions of Arizona's "voter ID" legislation that required voters to present evidence of US citizenship that would be very difficult for illegal immigrants to obtain, such as a driver's license, birth certificate, naturalization papers, or a passport. This state law would necessarily apply to both state and federal elections when they occur simultaneously, and federal law allows voters to simply swear under penalty of perjury that they are citizens of the United States by checking either a "yes" or "no" box on a federal form, accompanied by their signature. The Supreme Court ruled that the Arizona law interfered with the paramount authority of Congress to determine eligibility to vote in federal elections. A number of other states have recently enacted laws requiring various forms of identification in addition to the voter registration cards that have been traditionally required, purportedly to make voting fraud more difficult to perpetrate, despite the fact that there has been little if any evidence of actual voting fraud. Lower federal courts have invalidated various state laws requiring photo identification and other restrictions on voting as violations of the federal Voting Rights Act based on findings that these laws had an unreasonable effect on the ability of some ethnic minorities to vote, and even that some state legislatures seemed to have been specifically targeting these minorities for political gain. Part of the courts' analyses in these cases also focused on the almost complete lack of evidence that voter fraud had been a problem.

Discrimination Against Interstate Commerce. Even when there is no preemption of any kind, a state cannot pass a law that discriminates against interstate commerce (or international commerce). Such discrimination interferes with the primary authority of Congress over interstate and foreign commerce, and thus violates the Supremacy Clause. States may not, for example, shelter their own industries from competition emanating from other states or nations. (Although it may not be wise to do so, Congress does have the power to shelter American companies from foreign competition.)

Although states may act to preserve their own natural resources, they cannot do so by discriminating against out-of-state buyers. They also cannot require that business operations that could be conducted more efficiently elsewhere take place within the state. For example, a state could not require that shellfish caught off its shores be processed in-state before being shipped elsewhere for sale.

A state's intent to discriminate might be explicit or it might be inferred from surrounding circumstances. For example, in *Philadelphia v. New Jersey,* 437 U.S. 617 (1978), the state legislature of New Jersey explicitly prohibited garbage from being imported into the state. Operators of several landfills in New Jersey, as well as several cities from other states that had agreements with these landfill operators for waste disposal, challenged the law. The Supreme Court held that the law unconstitutionally discriminated against interstate commerce; even a desire on the part of New Jersey to conserve landfill space was not a strong enough state interest to justify an explicit discrimination against the interstate transportation of solid waste. In its opinion the Court also distinguished the so-called quarantine cases, in which state quarantine laws had been upheld. The Court said that these laws, which forbade the transportation of diseased livestock or plants, had been held to be constitutional because they were aimed primarily at the act of moving the livestock or plants from one place to another, whether the movement was totally within the state or into it from another state.

Sometimes the circumstances may lead a court to conclude that a state intended to discriminate against interstate commerce even though the intent was not made explicit. As with any question of intent in the law, the court attempts to draw the most logical inference from surrounding circumstances. An example is *Hunt v. Washington State Apple Advertising Commission*, 432 U.S. 333(1977), which involved a North Carolina law, unique in the 50 states, that required all apples sold in the state to have only the applicable grade under U.S. Department of Agriculture grading standards stamped on the crates; state grades were expressly prohibited. For many years all apples shipped from the state of Washington had been stamped with grades under that state's grading system. In all cases, Washington state grades were superior to the comparable federal ones. The state of Washington and its apple industry had spent decades developing the quality and national reputation of its apples. If they still wanted to sell apples in North Carolina, Washington apple growers would have to segregate apples intended for shipment there and package them differently, in addition to losing the competitive advantage of being able to use their well-known grading standards. North Carolina asserted that the law was adopted to protect consumers in the state from deception and confusion caused by multiple grading systems.

The evidence was very convincing, however, that North Carolina was really engaging in economic protectionism by placing Washington apples at a disadvantage in the North Carolina market. The factors indicating an intent to discriminate against interstate commerce included (1) the complete lack of evidence that any consumers in North Carolina had ever been confused or deceived by multiple apple grading standards, (2) the fact that customers do not normally buy apples in the crates on which grades are stamped, and (3) the fact that the local North Carolina apple industry would clearly benefit from the Washington apple industry's increased costs of selling in North Carolina and its inability to use its highly reputed grading system. The law was found unconstitutional. However, the Supreme Court chose not to rule that the North Carolina legislature intentionally discriminated against out-of-state apple growers despite there being so much evidence to support this conclusion, but instead chose to invalidate the North Carolina law based on its actual impact—it constituted an undue burden on the free flow of interstate commerce by imposed unnecessary inefficiencies and costs on out-of-state apple growers who want to ship apples into the state.

When a court concludes that a state has intentionally discriminated against interstate commerce, the state action is almost always void. It would be a rare case indeed in which a state could prove a sufficiently important state interest to justify such discrimination, because the interest could almost always be promoted by less restrictive means that do not discriminate in this way.

Not only state statutes and state administrative actions, but also state court decisions, can violate the Commerce Clause because they interfere with the primary authority of Congress to regulate interstate and foreign commercial activities. For example, in *Alamo Recycling, LLC v. Anheuser Busch Inbev Worldwide, Inc.*, 239 Cal.App.4th 983 (Cal.App.4th Dist. 2015), the California court held that a plaintiff's complaint had to be dismissed because it asked for an injunction that, if granted, would prohibit alcohol and soft drink beverage manufacturers from engaging in activity occurring outside the state of California. The activity by companies such as Anheuser Busch (Budweiser, etc.) consisted of marking beverage containers with words indicating that those possessing used beverage containers could redeem them for cash at California recycling centers. The California container recycling law, however, only applied to containers made in California, and the out-of-state beverage manufactures like Anheuser were arguably violating the California law. The California court nevertheless held that it had no power to issue an injunction against such companies that prohibited activity (marking the containers) occurring completely outside of California.

Two common examples of state actions that may superficially appear to be unconstitutional discriminations against interstate commerce that are actually valid are: (a) First, it has been found to be constitutional for a state to charge higher tuition and fees to non-residents to attend a state university in the state because students and their families from outside the state have not been paying taxes to the state where the university is located as in-state residents have been paying. (b) Second, if a state government itself is a seller or buyer of goods or services, the state is constitutionally allowed to treat in-state parties more favorably than out-of-state parties that do business with the state. Where the state itself is a market participant, the normal rules concerning discrimination against interstate commerce do not apply.

As one of many examples of state legislation crossing an impermissible boundary in the regulation of modern online commerce, in 2005 the Supreme Court held in *Granholm v. Heald*, 544 U.S. 460 (2005), that the states of Michigan and New York violated the Commerce Clause by adopting legislation that required out-of-state wineries making sales online to residents of those states to have a three-level distribution system within the state, when in-state wineries could make online sales to the state's residents without having that type of structure. The legislation in both states was found to be an unconstitutional discrimination against interstate commerce.

Unduly Burdening Interstate Commerce. Another restriction on the power of the states to regulate commercial activities is that they may not unduly burden the free flow of interstate or international commerce. The concept we just discussed, discrimination against interstate commerce, involves a question of intent, whereas the concept of unduly burdening involves a question of impact. The two concepts are closely related, often both being raised by a challenger in the same case. Some of the same information will often be relevant to both types of claims. Despite their close relationship, however, the two concepts provide separate grounds for invalidating a state regulatory measure.

If a state law challenged on this basis is shown to hinder the free flow of interstate commerce in some way, the court uses a balancing analysis to determine whether the law is constitutional. The analysis is very similar to the balancing of competing interests that takes place throughout constitutional law and, indeed, throughout the law generally. To determine whether there is an undue burdening of interstate commerce, the court balances the local interest being furthered by the state law against the degree of burden it places on interstate commerce. In general, the stronger the state interest, the greater will be the burden that can be tolerated under the Constitution. Purely economic interests of a state are certainly legitimate, but such interests typically do not weigh as heavily as a state's interest in protecting the safety and health of its citizens or protecting them against fraudulent or other wrongful practices. In addition, some economic interests are stronger than others; thus, a state law aimed at preventing the spread of a citrus fruit disease that could wipe out a major industry in the state could permissibly burden interstate commerce to a greater extent than one aimed at protecting an economic interest of less magnitude.

The *Hunt* case discussed in the previous section illustrates the undue burdening concept. There, the local interest did not weigh very heavily in the balancing process because there was no evidence to indicate that consumers actually had been deceived or confused by multiple apple grading standards, and the regulation would not have solved such a problem if there had been one. On the other side, the evidence demonstrated that the North Carolina law would impose substantial economic inefficiency on the selling of Washington apples in

North Carolina. The Washington apple industry had developed substantial economies of scale in packaging, storing, and shipping its apples, and compliance with the North Carolina law would destroy much of these scale economies. As noted, in the *Hunt* case, the Supreme Court ultimately struck down the statute because it unduly burdened interstate commerce. Even though there was ample evidence to infer intentional discrimination against interstate commerce, the Court said that it was not necessary to make a ruling on that separate contention.

Finally, many of the cases involving the undue burdening concept have challenged various state and local taxes on property items used in interstate commerce. Examples include state road use taxes on trucks used in interstate transportation, and state or local property taxes on items such as railroad cars, airplanes, barges on inland waterways, and shipping containers. For example, in *Xerox Corp. v. Harris County*, 459 U.S. 145 (1982), a local property tax on stored goods was found unconstitutional because it was preempted by a federal law that set up a system of customs bonded warehouses for goods in international transit in which the goods, which were held only temporarily in the warehouses while awaiting shipment elsewhere, were federally exempted from taxation. The local property tax was unconstitutional, however, only when applied to goods stored in these customs-bonded warehouses. Usually, however, there is no federal regulatory scheme that preempts state or local taxes on the instrumentalities of interstate commerce. In most cases, state and local government entities do have the right to tax such items located or used within their jurisdiction. It usually is only fair that the owners should pay some type of tax to contribute to the cost of police and fire protection and other services they receive within the taxing jurisdiction.

Such a tax must be carefully designed, however, to avoid being invalidated by the courts. First, it is obvious that the tax must not discriminate against interstate commerce by being higher for items used in interstate commerce than for items used only within the state. Assuming that the tax is nondiscriminatory, the Supreme Court has held that such a tax must meet three additional requirements to avoid being invalid under the undue burdening theory. The tax (1) can only be applied to property or activities that have a substantial ''nexus'' (that is, connection) with the taxing jurisdiction, (2) must be reasonably related to the services provided by the taxing jurisdiction, and (3) must be ''apportioned'' so that the item is not subjected to multiple taxation in the various places in which it is used or located. This last condition, the requirement of apportionment, has been an issue in a great many cases. It basically requires a formula that bases the tax only on the degree of connection the item has with the particular taxing jurisdiction. For example, a state might apportion a property tax on railroad cars by taxing only a fraction of the value of the cars that corresponds to the average fraction of a tax year the cars are located in the state.

The case that follows, decided by the U.S. Supreme Court in 2018, applies the Commerce Clause concepts discussed above to the extraordinarily important issue of a state's ability to require out-of-state online sellers to charge and remit to a state sales taxes when the seller does not have any sort of physical presence within the taxing state. In the process of reaching a conclusion, the Court also had to grapple with thorny issues involving stare decisis, because longstanding Supreme Court precedent from the days before the internet required that an out-of-state seller have a physical presence within a state before the state could demand the collection and payment of sales taxes.

SOUTH DAKOTA V. WAYFAIR, INC.
United States Supreme Court, 138 S.Ct. 2080 (2018)

When a consumer purchases goods or services, the consumer's state often imposes a sales tax. This case requires the Court to determine when an out-of-state seller can be required to collect and remit that tax. All concede that taxing the sales in question here is lawful. The question is whether the out-of-state seller can be held responsible for its payment, and this turns on a proper interpretation of the Commerce Clause of the U.S. Constitution.

Like most states, South Dakota has a sales tax. It taxes the retail sales of goods and services in the state. Sellers are generally required to collect and remit this tax to the state Department of Revenue. If for some reason the sales tax is not remitted by the seller, then in-state consumers are separately responsible for paying a use tax at the same rate. Many states employ this kind of complementary sales and use tax regime.

Under this Court's decisions in *Bellas Hess* and *Quill*, [before the internet, when the issue was mail order sales with delivery by the U.S. Postal Service or other public delivery service] South Dakota may not require a business to collect its sales tax if the business lacks a physical presence in the state. Without that physical presence, South Dakota instead must rely on its residents to pay the use tax owed on their purchases from out-of-state sellers. The impracticability of this collection from the multitude of individual purchasers is obvious. And consumer compliance rates are notoriously low. See, *e.g.,* GAO, Report to Congressional Requesters: Sales Taxes, States Could Gain Revenue from Expanded Authority, but Businesses Are Likely to Experience Compliance Costs 5 (GAO-18-114, Nov. 2017) (Sales Taxes Report); California State Bd. of Equalization, Revenue Estimate: Electronic Commerce and Mail Order Sales 7 (2013) (Table 3) (estimating a 4 percent collection rate).

It is estimated that *Bellas Hess* and *Quill* cause the states to lose between $8 and $33 billion every year. In South Dakota alone, the Department of Revenue estimates revenue loss at $48 to $58 million annually. Particularly because South Dakota has no state income tax, it must put substantial reliance on its sales and use taxes for the revenue necessary to fund essential services. Those taxes account for over 60 percent of its general fund.

In 2016, South Dakota confronted the serious inequity *Quill* imposes by enacting S. 106--"An Act to provide for the collection of sales taxes from certain remote sellers, to establish certain Legislative findings, and to declare an emergency." The legislature found that the inability to collect sales tax from remote sellers was "seriously eroding the sales tax base" and "causing revenue losses and imminent harm . . . through the loss of critical funding for state and local services." The legislature also declared an emergency: "Whereas, this Act is necessary for the support of the state government and its existing public institutions, an emergency is hereby declared to exist."

To that end, the Act requires out-of-state sellers to collect and remit sales tax "as if the seller had a physical presence in the state." Respondents Wayfair, Inc., Overstock.com, Inc., and Newegg, Inc., are merchants with no employees or real estate in South Dakota. Wayfair, Inc., is a leading online retailer of home goods and furniture and had net revenues of over $4.7 billion last year. Overstock.com, Inc., is one of the top online retailers in the United States, selling a wide variety of products from home goods and furniture to clothing and jewelry; and it had net revenues of over $1.7 billion last year. Newegg, Inc., is a major online retailer of consumer electronics in the United States. Each of these three companies ships its goods directly to purchasers throughout the United States, including South Dakota. Each easily meets the minimum sales or transactions requirement of the Act, but none collects South Dakota sales tax.

South Dakota filed a declaratory judgment action against respondents in state court, seeking a declaration that the requirements of the Act are valid and applicable to respondents and an injunction requiring respondents to register for licenses to collect and remit sales tax. Respondents moved for summary judgment, arguing that the Act is unconstitutional. South Dakota conceded that the Act cannot survive under *Bellas Hess* and *Quill* but asserted the importance, indeed the necessity, of asking this Court to review those earlier decisions in light of current economic realities. The trial court granted summary judgment to respondents.

The South Dakota Supreme Court affirmed. It stated: "However persuasive the state's arguments on the merits of revisiting the issue, *Quill* has not been overruled and remains the controlling precedent on the issue of Commerce Clause limitations on interstate collection of sales and use taxes." South Dakota appealed to the U.S. Supreme Court, which agreed to hear the case.

Kennedy, Justice:

The Constitution grants Congress the power "To regulate Commerce . . . among the several States." The Commerce Clause reflects a central concern of the Framers that was an immediate reason for calling the Constitutional Convention: the conviction that in order to succeed, the new Union would have to avoid the tendencies toward economic Balkanization that had plagued relations among the Colonies and later among the states under the Articles of Confederation. Although the Commerce Clause is written as an affirmative grant of authority to Congress, this Court has long held that in some instances it imposes limitations on the states absent congressional action. Of course, when Congress exercises its power to regulate commerce by enacting legislation, the legislation controls. But this Court has observed that, in general, Congress has left it to the courts to formulate the rules to preserve the free flow of interstate commerce. . . .

From early in its history, a central function of this Court has been to adjudicate disputes that require interpretation of the Commerce Clause in order to determine its meaning, its reach, and the extent to which it limits state regulations of commerce. *Gibbons* v. *Ogden*, 9 Wheat. 1 (1824), began setting the course by defining the meaning of commerce. Chief Justice Marshall explained that commerce included both "the interchange of commodities" and "commercial intercourse." A concurring opinion further stated that Congress had the exclusive power to regulate commerce. Had that latter submission prevailed and states been denied the power of concurrent regulation, history might have seen sweeping federal regulations at an early date that foreclosed the states from experimentation with laws and policies of their own, or, on the other hand, proposals to reexamine *Gibbons'* broad definition of commerce to accommodate the necessity of allowing states the power to enact laws to implement the political will of their people. . . .

This Court's doctrine has developed further with time. Modern precedents rest upon two primary principles that mark the boundaries of a state's authority to regulate interstate commerce. First, state regulations may not discriminate against interstate commerce; and second, states may not impose undue burdens on interstate commerce. State laws that discriminate against interstate commerce face "a virtually *per se* rule of invalidity." *Granholm* v. *Heald*, 544 U. S. 460, 476 (2005). State laws that "regulate even-handedly to effectuate a legitimate local public interest . . . will be upheld unless the burden imposed on such commerce is clearly excessive in relation to the putative local benefits." These two principles guide the courts in adjudicating cases challenging state laws under the Commerce Clause.

The Court explained the now-accepted framework for state taxation in *Complete Auto Transit, Inc.* v. *Brady*, 430 U. S. 274 (1977). The Court held that a state "may tax exclusively interstate commerce so long as the tax does not create any effect forbidden by the Commerce Clause. After all, interstate commerce may be required to pay its fair share of state taxes. The Court will sustain a tax so long as it (1) applies to an activity with a substantial nexus with [connection or contact with] the taxing state, (2) is fairly apportioned, (3) does not discriminate against interstate commerce, and (4) is fairly related to the services the state provides. . . .

In 1992, the Court reexamined the physical presence rule in *Quill*. That case presented a challenge to North Dakota's attempt to require an out-of-state mail-order house that has neither outlets nor sales representatives in the state to collect and pay a use tax on goods purchased for use within the state. . . . [This Court upheld the physical-presence requirement.]

The physical presence rule has been the target of criticism over many years from many quarters. *Quill*, it has been said, was premised on assumptions that are unfounded and riddled with internal inconsistencies. [According to some observers,] *Quill* created an inefficient online sales tax loophole that gives out-of-state businesses an advantage. And while nexus rules are clearly necessary, the Court should focus on rules that are appropriate to the twenty-first century, not the nineteenth. Each year, the physical presence rule becomes further removed from economic reality and results in significant revenue losses to the states. These critiques underscore that the physical presence rule, both as first formulated and as applied today, is an incorrect interpretation of the Commerce Clause.

Quill is flawed on its own terms. First, the physical presence rule is not a necessary interpretation of the requirement that a state tax must be applied to an activity with a substantial nexus with the taxing state. Second, *Quill* creates rather than resolves market distortions. And third, *Quill* imposes the sort of arbitrary, formalistic distinction that the Court's modern Commerce Clause precedents disavow.

It has long been settled that the sale of goods or services has a sufficient nexus to the state in which the sale is consummated to be treated as a local transaction taxable by that state. . . . Generally speaking, a sale is attributable to its destination.

The central dispute is whether South Dakota may require remote sellers to collect and remit the tax without some additional connection to the state. The Court has previously stated that the imposition on the seller of the duty to insure collection of the tax from the purchaser does not violate the Commerce Clause. It is a familiar and sanctioned device. There just must be a substantial nexus with the taxing state. It is an inescapable fact of modern commercial life that a substantial amount of business is transacted with no need for physical presence within a state in which business is conducted. . . .

The *Quill* majority expressed concern that without the physical presence rule a state tax might unduly burden interstate commerce by subjecting retailers to tax-collection obligations in thousands of different taxing jurisdictions. But the administrative costs of compliance, especially in the modern economy with its internet technology, are largely unrelated to whether a company happens to have a physical presence in a state.

For example, a business with one salesperson in each state must collect sales taxes in every jurisdiction in which goods are delivered; but a business with 500 salespersons in one central location and a website accessible in every state need not collect sales taxes on otherwise identical nationwide sales. In other words, under *Quill*, a small company with diverse physical presence might be equally or more burdened by compliance costs than a large remote seller. The physical presence rule is a poor proxy for the compliance costs faced by companies that do business in multiple states. Other aspects of the Court's doctrine can better and more accurately address any potential burdens on interstate commerce, whether or not *Quill*'s physical presence rule is satisfied.

The Court has consistently explained that the Commerce Clause was designed to prevent states from engaging in economic discrimination so they would not divide into isolated, separable units. But it is not the purpose of the Commerce Clause to relieve those engaged in interstate commerce from their just share of state tax burden. And it is certainly not the purpose of the Commerce Clause to permit the judiciary to create market distortions. If the Commerce Clause was intended to put businesses on an even playing field, the physical presence rule is hardly a way to achieve that goal.

Quill puts both local businesses and many interstate businesses with physical presence at a competitive disadvantage relative to remote sellers. Remote sellers can avoid the regulatory burdens of tax collection and can offer *de facto* lower prices caused by the widespread failure of consumers to pay the tax on their own. This guarantees a competitive benefit to certain firms simply because of the organizational form they choose while the rest of the Court's jurisprudence is all about preventing discrimination between firms. In effect, *Quill* has come to serve as a judicially created tax shelter for businesses that decide to limit their physical presence and still sell their goods and services to a state's consumers—something that has become easier and more prevalent as technology has advanced.

Worse still, the rule produces an incentive to avoid physical presence in multiple states. Distortions caused by the desire of businesses to avoid tax collection mean that the market may currently lack storefronts, distribution points, and employment centers that otherwise would be efficient or desirable. The Commerce Clause must not prefer interstate commerce only to the point where a merchant physically crosses state borders. Rejecting the physical presence rule is necessary to ensure that artificial competitive advantages are not created by this Court's precedents. This Court should not prevent states from collecting lawful taxes through a physical presence rule that can be satisfied only if there is an employee or a building in the state. . . .

Consider, for example, two businesses that sell furniture online. The first stocks a few items of inventory in a small warehouse in North Sioux City, South Dakota. The second uses a major warehouse just across the border in South Sioux City, Nebraska, and maintains a sophisticated website with a virtual showroom accessible in every state, including South Dakota. By reason of its physical presence, the first business must collect and remit a tax on all of its sales to customers from South Dakota, even those sales that have nothing to do with the warehouse. But, under *Quill*, the second, hypothetical seller cannot be subject to the same tax for the sales of the same items made through a pervasive

Internet presence. This distinction simply makes no sense. . . . The basic principles of the Court's Commerce Clause jurisprudence are grounded in functional, marketplace dynamics; and states can and should consider those realities in enacting and enforcing their tax laws. . . .

The dramatic technological and social changes of our increasingly interconnected economy mean that buyers are closer to most major retailers than ever before—regardless of how close or far the nearest storefront. Between targeted advertising and instant access to most consumers via any internet-enabled device, a business may be present in a state in a meaningful way without that presence being physical in the traditional sense of the term. A virtual showroom can show far more inventory, in far more detail, and with greater opportunities for consumer and seller interaction than might be possible for local stores. Yet the continuous and pervasive virtual presence of retailers today is, under *Quill*, simply irrelevant. This Court should not maintain a rule that ignores these substantial virtual connections to the state.

The physical presence rule as defined and enforced in *Bellas Hess* and *Quill* is not just a technical legal problem--it is an extraordinary imposition by the judiciary on states' authority to collect taxes and perform critical public functions. Forty-one states, two territories, and the District of Columbia now ask this Court to reject the test formulated in *Quill*. *Quill*'s physical presence rule intrudes on states' reasonable choices in enacting their tax systems. And that it allows remote sellers to escape an obligation to remit a lawful state tax is unfair and unjust. It is unfair and unjust to those competitors, both local and out of state, who must remit the tax; to the consumers who pay the tax; and to the states that seek fair enforcement of the sales tax, a tax many states for many years have considered an indispensable source for raising revenue.

The *Quill* Court did not have before it the present realities of the interstate marketplace. In 1992, less than 2 percent of Americans had Internet access. Today that number is about 89 percent. When it decided *Quill*, the Court could not have envisioned a world in which the world's largest retailer would be a remote seller.

For these reasons, the Court concludes that the physical presence rule of *Quill* is unsound and incorrect. The Court's decisions in *Quill Corp.* v. *North Dakota*, 504 U. S. 298 (1992), and *National Bellas Hess, Inc.* v. *Department of Revenue of Ill.*, 386 U. S. 753 (1967), should be, and now are, overruled. [A state may collect sales taxes from an online seller regardless of whether that seller has a physical presence in the taxing state.]

[The dissenting justices argued primarily that, even though they agreed that the old rules requiring a seller to have a physical presence in the state were seriously out of date, the principle of stare decisis required the Court to follow precedent and leave the issue for Congress to resolve by passing legislation delegating to states the power to tax internet sales.]

Other State Limitations

At this point, two other constitutional limitations on the discretion of states are appropriately mentioned—the full faith and credit clause, and the contract clause.

Article IV, section 1 of the Constitution provides in part that "full faith and credit shall be given in each State to the public acts, records, and judicial proceedings of every other State," The import of the *Full Faith and Credit Clause* is quite clear: The courts of one state must recognize court judgments and other public actions of its sister states. Thus a business firm that obtains a valid judgment against a debtor in one state may enforce that judgment in the courts of any other state in which that debtor's property may be located. The requirement is, however, subject to two important limitations.

First, if the court that entered the judgment originally did not have jurisdiction, the courts of other states are not obligated to (and will not) recognize the judgment. Second, if the judgment violates the public policy of the state where enforcement is sought, the courts of that state will not enforce it. For example, if a court in State A awards damages for breach of a loan contract that included a rate of interest that was valid in State A and the creditor then tries to enforce the judgment against the debtor's property in State B, where that interest rate is higher than allowed by State B's law, the courts of State B may well refuse to enforce the judgment on public policy grounds.

Our Constitution's Full Faith and Credit Clause obviously has no applicability to the enforcement of American state or federal court judgments in other nations or to the enforcement in this country of court judgments from other nations. Similar principles are generally applied, however. Under customary international law, the doctrine of *comity* generally calls for the enforcement of another nation's court judgments subject to two exceptions. First, if a court in one country did not have complete jurisdiction in a case in which it rendered a judgment, a court in another country will not enforce that judgment. This doctrine and its exceptions have also been embodied in a number of bilateral and multilateral treaties to which the United States is a party.

Article I, section 10 of the Constitution provides that "no State shall . . . pass any . . . Law impairing the Obligation of Contracts. . . ." The *Contract Clause,* which applies only to the states and not to the federal government, is intended to prevent states from changing the terms of existing contracts by passage of subsequent legislation.

When a state passes a statute that might affect contractual obligations, it normally includes a "grandfather clause" specifying that the new law applies only to transactions entered into after the effective date of the law. This not only ensures compliance with the Contract Clause, but also makes the state statute fairer. However, even if a state law does have an effect on preexisting contractual rights and obligations, it does not violate the contract clause if the law promotes an important state government interest and interferes with contracts only to an extent that is reasonably necessary to further the state interest.

PROTECTING BASIC RIGHTS

The Constitution contains numerous provisions aimed at protecting individuals and businesses by limiting the powers of the federal and state governments to regulate our affairs. Many of our basic rights are guaranteed in the Bill of Rights—the first 10 amendments to the Constitution. Other protective provisions are found in the body of the original Constitution itself and in subsequent amendments.

Before we look at several of the most important rights-protecting provisions of the Constitution, two preliminary observations are necessary. First, by its express terms, the Bill of Rights applies only to the *federal* government and not to state or local governments. Nothing in the Constitution specifically prohibits the states from infringing freedom of speech, for example. However, the U.S. Supreme Court has used the Fourteenth Amendment's due process clause as a vehicle for applying almost everything in the Bill of Rights to state and local governments. The Fourteenth Amendment, which was passed in

1868 shortly after the Civil War, includes several provisions that expressly limit the powers of the states.

As we will see later, one of these provisions—the due process clause—directly guarantees certain important rights. In addition, under the *doctrine of incorporation,* the Supreme Court has concluded that the concept of due process includes many other basic rights. Thus, the Fourteenth Amendment's due process clause implicitly incorporates almost all the protections in the Bill of Rights and applies them to state and local governments. Among the many guarantees applied to the states in this way are freedom of speech, freedom of the press, freedom of religion, right to an attorney, privilege against self-incrimination in criminal cases, and freedom from unreasonable searches and seizures. (The only two important guarantees in the Bill of Rights that the Supreme Court has held inapplicable to the states are (1) the right to jury trial in *civil cases* and (2) the requirement that a person be indicted by a grand jury before being tried for a criminal offense. However, the states are free to devise their own rules regarding these two matters; in fact, state constitutional and statutory provisions guarantee these rights in most circumstances.) Although the doctrine of incorporation has always been very controversial among constitutional scholars, it is now so firmly embedded in our law as to be beyond question.

Second, it must be emphasized that the protective provisions of the Constitution are limitations on government; thus, these provisions apply only to governmental actions and not to actions by individuals or business firms. Thus, the Constitution's free speech and assembly provisions do not prevent a private employer from restricting the speech of its employees or a private university from banning a political rally on its campus. However, Constitutional protections apply when a governmental body either compels the private action or substantially participates in it or when governmental power is used to enforce the private action against others. This includes state universities.

For example, there is a violation of the equal protection clause of the Fourteenth Amendment when a private attorney in a criminal or civil case intentionally excludes potential jurors on the basis of race. The reason for the Constitution's applicability is that jury selection is such an integral part of a governmental process that the government is essentially a co-participant with the private attorney.

Another example is found in the rule that a court—an arm of the government—will not enforce a private deed restriction that excludes those of a particular race from purchasing property in a subdivision on the basis of their race; to do so would violate the equal protection clause. However, the mere fact that a particular business or industry is subject to substantial government regulation does not turn the actions of the regulated business firms into governmental actions. For example, public utilities such as telephone and electric companies are very closely regulated by the states, but their actions are not subject to the Constitution unless the government in a particular situation has actually compelled, substantially participated in, or enforced those actions.

Even though the Constitution does not prohibit private actions, a federal or state statute might. For example, racial discrimination by a private employer or restaurant does not violate the equal protection clause, but it does violate a federal statute—the Civil Rights Act of 1964. We will now turn to a discussion of several important Constitutional guarantees.

Privileges and Immunities

Article IV, section 2 of the Constitution states, in part, that "the citizens of each State shall be entitled to all privileges and immunities of the several states." The basic aim of the Privileges and Immunities Clause (PIC) is to prohibit states from discriminating against residents of other states merely because of their residency. Thus a state cannot prohibit travel by nonresidents within its borders, nor can it deny nonresident plaintiffs access to its court system. The PIC is yet another provision of the Constitution intended to prevent states from erecting barriers around their borders. The fundamental individual right (and also the national interest) that the clause protects from state infringement is that of moving freely among the states without being unreasonably disadvantaged because of the state of residency.

Like other constitutional guarantees, the PIC is not an absolute limitation on governmental power. A state law may treat residents of other states differently if the law protects a legitimate "local" (state) interest and does not discriminate more than is necessary. For example, because state universities are substantially assisted by the taxes that state residents pay, the charging of higher tuition for nonresident students does not violate the PIC. The PIC is one of the few constitutional protections that applies only to individuals and not to corporations.

In *Hicklin v. Orbeck,* 437 U.S. 518 (1978), the Supreme Court struck down a statute known as "Alaska Hire" as violative of the Privileges & Immunities Clause. The Alaska statute required all employers engaged in specific lines of work relating to construction of the TransAlaska pipeline to hire qualified Alaska residents in preference to nonresidents. The Supreme Court held that such discrimination could be viable only if nonresidents were a "peculiar source of the evil" the state legislature was trying to cure, which was not the case.

In *McBurney v. Young,* 133 S.Ct. 1709 (2013), the Court held that Virginia's failure to give non-citizens the same right afforded citizens to access state documents via a state "freedom of information act" did *not* violate the PIC. The PIC, the Court held, is aimed at constituting the citizens of the U.S. as one people by placing the citizens of each State on the same footing with those of other states, so far as the advantages of citizenship are concerned. However, this does not mean that a state may never distinguish among persons on the basis of state citizenship or residence or offer all services to citizens and noncitizens alike. PIC protects only those privileges and immunities that are "fundamental," such as the right to pursue a common calling and to take, hold, and/or transfer property.

Freedom of Religion

The First Amendment contains two clauses protecting freedom of religion. It provides that "Congress shall make no law (1) respecting an establishment of religion, or (2) prohibiting the free exercise thereof." Although the Establishment and Free Exercise clauses overlap (and sometimes even conflict), they clearly create two separate guarantees. Both guarantees provide that the government's role is to be one of "benevolent neutrality," neither advancing nor inhibiting religion.

Businesses do not typically get too involved in freedom of religion issues, but it can happen. For example, in Chapter 30, we will learn that because Congress has outlawed discrimination on grounds of religion in employment, companies cannot refuse to hire job applicants just because they must make "reasonable accommodations" for the religious practices of their employees. They cannot refuse to hire someone because they are Jewish or Muslim, for example. On the other hand, in *Hosanna-Tabor Evangelical Lutheran Church v. EEOC,* 132 S.Ct. 694 (2012), the Supreme Court held that a church did not have to abide by the rules of the Americans with Disabilities Act (ADA) because the employee in question was intimately involved in delivering the church's religious message and therefore came within a "ministerial exception" to the law.

In *Burwell v. Hobby Lobby*, 134 S.Ct. 2751 (2014), the U.S. Supreme Court held that a closely held corporation (one with a very small number of shareholders, often but not always members of the same family, and with shares not traded on the public market) can claim a religious freedom exemption from being required by the 2011 Affordable Care Act to provide contraception to employees as part of its health insurance benefits program. The case involved an interpretation of the language of the federal Religious Freedom Restoration Act, however, and not the First Amendment's freedom of religion clause, though the Court's decision clearly would apply to a claim based on the constitution's religious freedom guarantee.

Issues similar to the one in *Burwell* continue to arise regularly in lower federal courts. And, after the Supreme Court recognized that same-sex couples enjoyed the same constitutional right to marriage as a man and a woman in *Obergefell v. Hodges*, 576 U.S. 644 (2015). The issues are typically similar to that in *Burwell*, where a business denies equal treatment to same-sex couples and claims that its actions are protected by the freedom of religion guarantee. Two examples follow:

Phillips, a baker in Colorado, refused to create a wedding cake for a same-sex couple in 2012. Phillips told the couple he would make a custom cake for them for other purposes, but not for their wedding because of his Christian religious opposition to same-sex marriage. The couple, Craig and Mullins, filed a complaint with the human rights agency in Colorado that supervises compliance with the state's civil rights law. The agency ruled against the baker, and a Colorado appeals court agreed. The Colorado Supreme Court did not hear the case, and the U.S. Supreme Court agreed to do so. In *Masterpiece Cakeshop v. Colorado Civil Rights Commission* 138 S.Ct. 1719 (2018), the Supreme Court sided with the baker, but did not rule on the constitutional issue under the First Amendment. Instead, it held that the Colorado Civil Rights Commission violated the baker's freedom of expression (not religion) by expressing hostility toward the baker's views of same-sex marriage.

Young, who runs a bed and breakfast lodging in Honolulu, Hawaii, refused to rent a room to a lesbian couple, Cervilli and Bufford. The owner of the B&B said that, although her lodging was open to the general public, she would only rent a room to a male-female married couple. Hawaii is one of 21 states whose civil rights laws protect people on the basis of sexual orientation. A state agency and the Hawaii Supreme Court held that freedom of religion does not give a business owner the right to discriminate against people on the basis of sexual orientation In *Aloha Bed & Breakfast v. Dianne Cervelli*, 139 S.Ct. 1319 (2019), the U.S. Supreme Court refused to hear the case, thus allowing the state supreme court decision to stand. Obviously, much remains to be decided on this issue.

Freedom of Speech

No right of Americans receives greater protection than freedom of speech. As with most other constitutional guarantees, the First Amendment's *Free Speech Clause* has been expanded to limit not only the actions of the federal government but also the actions of state and local governments. Unlike citizens in so many other countries, we may freely criticize public officials and the laws of our government.

All methods of expression are within the scope of the Free Speech Clause, including oral and written communications, and those recorded on tape, film, and so on. Moreover, *symbolic expression* is also protected. In other words, expression by nonverbal means such as wearing black arm bands or picketing is protected from government suppression. The giving of money to political candidates, charitable organizations, or various other entities is even treated as a form of protected expression.

However, a government limitation of symbolic expression is somewhat more likely to be upheld than a limitation on verbal expression, simply because the conduct that constitutes symbolic expression is somewhat more likely to interfere substantially with some important public interest. If symbolic expression does not substantially interfere with an important public interest, however, it is fully protected.

The right of association is also viewed as a component of free speech. The groups and organizations we join often provide us with one of our most effective means of expressing our beliefs and opinions. Thus, a government limitation on our ability to associate with groups of our choice is a limitation on free speech.

Not only does free speech include the right to express oneself, but it also includes the right to avoid expressing opinions that we do not agree with. For example, in *Pacific Gas & Electric Co. v. Public Utilities Commission of California,* 475 U.S. 1 (1986), the Supreme Court overturned on free speech grounds an order of the California utility regulatory agency that had required an investor-owned utility to include in its billing envelopes a leaflet expressing the views of a consumer group with which the utility disagreed. The Court held that the agency's order unconstitutionally burdened the utility's freedom not to speak, a right that is protected because all speech inherently involves choices of what to say and what to leave unsaid.

Corporate Speech

In addition to protecting the speech of individuals, the First Amendment has also been interpreted to protect the expressions of corporations. This proposition was evident in the above reference to the *Pacific Gas & Electric* case. Corporate speech, like individual speech, has informational value—it contributes to the public debate on important issues. Thus, in *First National Bank of Boston v. Bellotti,* 435 U.S. 765 (1978), the Supreme Court struck down a state statute that prohibited expenditures by business corporations for the purpose of influencing the vote on state referendum proposals, unless a particular proposal "materially affected" the business or property of the corporation. The law was passed to silence the voice of corporations in the public debate over an upcoming referendum concerning a personal income tax. Because the referendum did not deal with a corporate income tax, it did not materially affect the business or property of corporations; thus the statute prohibited corporations from issuing press releases, publishing advocacy advertisements, or otherwise speaking out on the personal income tax issue. The First National Bank of Boston wished to speak out because it felt that a personal income tax would harm the overall economic climate of the state. In overturning the law, the Supreme Court noted that "the inherent worth of the speech in terms of its capacity for informing the public does not depend upon the identity of its source, whether corporation, association, union, or individual."

Political Speech

The *Bellotti* case raises the issue of political speech and this is a Constitutional hot potato whether the speaker is an individual, a corporation, or some other group. In a very controversial decision, the Supreme Court overruled 30 years of case law in *Citizens United v. FEC,* 130 S.Ct. 876 (2010) in largely exempting political speech from government regulation. The Court followed earlier precedents in holding that money can be speech and stressed that campaign donations did not lose their free speech attributes just because they were made by corporations.

Unprotected Speech

Although almost all expression is constitutionally protected, a few categories are not. If a particular type of expression is unprotected, this simply means that the government may limit or prohibit it without violating the First Amendment.

The first category of unprotected speech is obscenity. So companies that sell pornography cannot expect significant First Amendment free speech exception.

A second category of unprotected speech is *defamation*. Companies that publish (communicate) slanders or libels are potentially liable in damages to the person whose reputation is injured.

The third category of unprotected speech is a rather amorphous one commonly referred to as *fighting words:* threats, epithets, profanity, false alarms, and the like, which by their nature are likely to lead to violence.

Commercial Speech.

The First Amendment was adopted to protect political speech, and speech relating to causes and/or candidates receives substantial First Amendment protection. But what about *commercial speech,* which is speech intended primarily to propose a commercial transaction? Advertising is the most obvious form of commercial speech. Until the mid-1970s, the general assumption was that commercial expression was not protected. However, the Supreme Court extended free speech protection to advertising in *Virginia Board of Pharmacy v. Virginia Citizens Consumers Council,* 425 U.S. 748 (1976); in that case, the Court struck down a state law that banned the advertising of prices for prescription drugs.

According to the Supreme Court, commercial speech is protectable primarily because of its informational value. Prescription drug consumers in the *Virginia Pharmacy* case could not learn, before the advertising ban was struck down, that price variations of up to 600 percent existed among competing pharmacies.

Commercial speech is only protected if it relates to a lawful activity and if it is not misleading. Thus, commercial speech that either relates to an unlawful activity or is misleading could be listed as another category of unprotected speech. Although most commercial speech is protected by the First Amendment, it receives a lower level of protection than noncommercial speech. A restriction on commercial speech will be valid if the government can show that it is necessary to further a substantial governmental interest, does further that governmental interest, and does not restrict commercial speech to any greater degree than is necessary to advance the governmental interest.

A state statute in California prohibited businesses from explicitly adding a "surcharge," an additional charge on the bill, for use of a credit card by customers. The legislation did, however, allow businesses to assess a charge and then deduct a "discount" for using cash if the customer did not use a credit card. Businesses pay large amounts of money each year in fees to credit card companies, and they must either increase all of their prices to account for these fees or seek some other way to cover these costs. The reasons why the California legislature passed this legislation restricting the way in which businesses passed along these fees to customers was not clear.

Several California businesses challenged the constitutionality of the California legislation as a violation of free speech. The businesses argued that they wanted to apply surcharges to credit card users, but did not because of the legislation. They argued that they wanted to use surcharges instead of simply raising the price of all of their products or giving discounts to cash customers for the purpose of better communicating to customers the true costs of credit card use. The case, finally decided by the U.S. Court of Appeals for the Ninth Circuit in 2018, is presented below.

ITALIAN COLORS RESTAURANT, et al. v. BECERRA, CA. ATTY. GENERAL
U.S. Court of Appeals, Ninth Circuit, 878 F.3d 1165 (2018)

In 1974, Congress amended the federal Truth-in-Lending Act to add a provision that prohibited lenders from imposing an extra charge on customers who use a credit card, apparently to encourage the use of credit cards at a time when most transactions were made with cash. The law allowed companies to deduct a discount, however, which amounted to exactly the same thing mathematically. This law expired in 1984, and several states soon passed state laws specifying the same thing. California was one of the states that adopted such legislation.

Five California businesses, Italian Colors Restaurant, Laurelwood Cleaners, Family Graphics, Stonecrest Gas & Wash, and Leon's Transmission Service, filed a lawsuit in 2014 in federal district court in California against the California Attorney General challenging the constitutionality of this state statue, contending that it violated plaintiffs' rights of free speech.

Plaintiffs pay thousands of dollars every year in credit card fees, which are typically 2–3% of the cost of each transaction. With the exception of Stonecrest, each plaintiff charges a single price for goods, with prices slightly higher than they would be otherwise to compensate for the credit card fees. Stonecrest currently offers discounts to customers who use cash or debit cards.

Each plaintiff asserts that it would impose a credit card surcharge if it were legal to do so. Stonecrest, which already offers different prices for cash customers and credit card customers, would describe this difference as a surcharge rather than a discount. Italian Colors would also charge different prices and label the difference as a surcharge. Laurelwood would charge different prices and express the price difference as an additional percentage fee, or surcharge, that customers will pay if they decide to use credit. Likewise, Family Graphics would have two different prices, and would express that difference as a percentage fee that is incurred for using a credit card. And Leon's Transmission would charge a fee for credit-card transactions, *i.e.*, offer a base price and impose an additional surcharge for using a credit card. They have not imposed credit card surcharges for fear of violating the California statute.

The district court granted summary judgment in favor of plaintiffs, declared the statute an unconstitutional restriction of commercial speech, and permanently enjoined its enforcement. The state of California appealed to the U.S. Court of Appeals for the Ninth Circuit.

VANCE, Judge:

Plaintiffs put forth several reasons why they desire to impose credit card surcharges rather than offer cash discounts. First, they contend that credit card surcharges are a more effective way of conveying to customers the high cost of credit card fees. Second, plaintiffs state that their current practice forces them to raise their prices slightly to compensate for the credit card fees, making their goods and services appear more expensive than they would be otherwise.

Third, plaintiffs believe that imposing a credit card surcharge would be more effective than offering a cash discount in encouraging buyers to use cash. Scholars [in cognitive psychology and behavioral economics] have posited that credit card companies prefer cash discounts over credit card surcharges for precisely this reason. *See* Amos Tversky & Daniel Kahneman, *Rational Choice and the Framing of Decisions*, 59 J. Bus. S251, S261 (1986). Although mathematically equivalent, surcharges may be more effective than discounts because "the frame within which information is presented can significantly alter one's perception of that information, especially when one can perceive the information as a gain or a loss." Jon D. Hanson & Douglas A. Kysar, *Taking Behavioralism Seriously: Some Evidence of Market Manipulation*, 112 Harv. L. Rev. 1420 (1999). Indeed, research has shown that economic actors are more likely to change their behavior if they are presented with a potential loss than with a potential gain. Plaintiffs point to one study in which 74% of consumers reacted negatively to a credit card surcharge, while only 22% reacted positively to cash discounts. *See* Adam J. Levitin, *The Antitrust Super Bowl: America's Payment Systems, No-Surcharge Rules, and the Hidden Costs of Credit*, 3 Berkeley Bus. L.J. 265 (2005).

[In other words, the way information and choices are presented alters the behavior of many people who make decisions based on that information. This is called "framing." How information and choices are "framed" often has a real effect on the choices and decisions that are then made. Because consumers so often view surcharges in a more negative way than discounts, information provided about the costs of credit card purchases as a surcharge, rather than a discount, will cause more buyers to use cash or its equivalent, and thus reduce the costs of transactions. The issue in this case is one of how commercial information is conveyed.]

The district court held that is a content-based restriction on commercial speech rather than an economic regulation. Applying intermediate scrutiny, he district court found that the surcharges plaintiffs desire to post are neither misleading nor related to unlawful activity; that the state's asserted interest in preventing consumer deception, though substantial, is not advanced by the statute, and that there is no reasonable fit between that state interest and the scope of the statute. Thus, the district court struck down the statute as violating the First Amendment.

The parties also dispute whether the statute even regulates speech. The Attorney General argues that it restricts conduct—namely, the practice of imposing a surcharge for credit card users. In *Expressions Hair Designs v. Schneinerman*, 137 S.Ct. 1144 (2017), the U.S. Supreme Court held that New York's ban on credit card surcharges regulates the communication of prices rather than prices themselves, and thus was a regulation of communicated information—commercial speech—and not just the regulation of the conduct of setting prices. The Supreme Court first noted that this statute "Tells merchants nothing about the amount they are allowed to collect from a cash or credit card payer. What the law does regulate is how sellers may communicate their prices."

Like the plaintiffs in *Expressions*, plaintiffs in this case want to post a single sticker price and charge an extra fee for credit card use. [The California statute] prohibits plaintiffs from expressing their prices in this way, but it does allow retailers to post a single sticker price and offer discounts to customers paying with cash—despite the mathematical equivalency between surcharges and discounts. Thus, the California statute, like New York's surcharge ban, regulates commercial speech. . . .

It is obvious that the activity to which plaintiffs' desired speech is directed—charging credit card users more than cash users—is not unlawful. After all, California law permits cash discounts. [Moreover, what the California merchants propose to do, present the price difference as a surcharge rather than a discount or some kind of disguised charge, is not misleading or false.]

The California statute does *not* promote the accuracy of information in plaintiffs' places of business. The law has the effect of allowing retailers to charge credit card users more for the same goods, but only if this price differential is expressed as a discount to cash users, rather than a surcharge for credit card users. But the higher cost is a result of credit card fees, and referring to the price differential as a discount prevents retailers from accurately conveying that causal relationship. In other words, the statute prevents retailers like plaintiffs "from communicating with their customers in an effective and informative manner about the cost of credit card usage and why credit card customers are charged more than cash users. . . .

There is no reasonable fit between the broad scope of [the statute's restrictions and any asserted state interest.] California has other, more narrowly tailored, means of preventing consumer deception. For example, the state could simply ban deceptive or misleading surcharges. Alternatively, California could require retailers to disclose their surcharges both before and at the point of sale, as Minnesota does. These alternatives would restrict less speech and would more directly advance California's asserted interest in preventing consumer deception.

In sum, the California statute restricts plaintiffs' non-misleading commercial speech. This restriction does not directly advance the Attorney General's asserted state interest in preventing consumer deception, nor is it narrowly drawn to achieving that interest. For these reasons, we agree with the district court that the California statute violates the First Amendment. We affirm the district court's grant of summary judgment for plaintiffs on the First Amendment claim. [The California statute cannot be enforced.]

Equal Protection

The Fourteenth Amendment was passed in 1868, shortly after the Civil War. It states, in part, that "no State shall . . . deny to any person within its jurisdiction the equal protection of the laws." Although no provision of the Constitution explicitly mentions equal protection in connection with the federal government, the concept has been found to be implicit in the Fifth Amendment's due process clause, which does apply to the *federal* government. Thus, the guarantee of equal protection acts as a limitation on all levels of government—federal, state, and local.

The fundamental thrust of the *Equal Protection Clause* is to prohibit the government from making arbitrary and unreasonable distinctions among persons. Because virtually every law and regulation involves distinctions and classifications—for example, applying to some industries but not to others, applying to larger companies but not to smaller ones, giving benefits to older people but not to younger ones—legal questions involving the Equal Protection Clause arise frequently. Unfortunately, the Supreme Court's interpretations of the clause have not been clear or consistent. The Court has definitely identified two different levels of protection under the clause and has probably identified a third. For our purposes, we will characterize the Equal Protection Clause as providing three different levels of protection against unreasonable distinctions. We will first examine those aspects of the law under the Equal Protection Clause that are relatively certain and then look briefly at those that are less clear.

Economic and Social Regulation

One area that is reasonably clear is the application of the Equal Protection Clause to economic and social regulation. The Supreme Court realizes that legislatures must make distinctions in passing such legislation. Only the poor need welfare; the rich do not. Some industries cause pollution; others do not. Some jobs imperil the safety of workers; others do not. Therefore, the Supreme Court uses a lax standard for economic and social legislation when equal protection challenges are raised. This standard is often referred to as the *rational basis test*. The distinction or classification merely has to have a rational basis; in other words, there merely has to be a legitimate government interest (not even a strong one), and the distinction must have some rational relationship with that interest. If a state legislature, for example, has identified a problem and has made a good faith effort to solve it, the test is normally met. Only if the court can conceive of no reasonable set of facts that would justify the distinction and it is clearly a display of arbitrary power and not a matter of judgment will the distinction be invalidated on equal protection grounds.

To decide that the rational basis test applies to economic or social regulation is almost to decide the case. There is such a strong presumption of reasonableness that discrimination in such regulations is almost always upheld. Distinctions need not be drawn with mathematical nicety, nor must a legislature attack all aspects of a problem at once. Thus, *North Dixie Theatre, Inc. v. McCullion,* 613 F. Supp. 1339 (S.D. Ohio 1985) involved a law requiring operators of flea markets who leased space to persons wishing to sell automobiles to have a type of license not required of persons who leased land to regular car dealers. The court held that the law constituted permissible discrimination because the state has a legitimate interest in preventing fraud, and it is rational to presume that fraud will be a bigger problem in a flea market than in a stationary car dealership that will probably still be there when a defrauded customer goes back to complain.

Strict Scrutiny

Another relatively clear area of law under the equal protection clause today involves governmental distinctions based on race or national origin, or that affect fundamental rights. The highest level of protection applies in such cases. If a law or other government action discriminates against someone because of the person's ethnic group or ancestral origin, the courts apply what they refer to as *strict scrutiny*. The test is essentially the same one that courts apply to content-based restrictions on noncommercial speech. The government must demonstrate that the distinction is necessary to protect a compelling interest and that the distinction is narrowly tailored to discriminate no more than is absolutely necessary. A governmental body can almost never meet this test, and a distinction based on race or national origin will almost always be void.

The courts have also applied the strict scrutiny standard to government distinctions and classifications that interfere with fundamental rights such as free speech, right to privacy, and right to travel interstate. The Equal Protection Clause has no independent significance when applied to such matters, however, because these fundamental rights are protected by other constitutional provisions.

The courts apply the strict scrutiny test primarily to intentional racial or national origin distinctions by the government. If a distinction or classification is neutral on its face but happens to have a disproportionate impact on a particular ethnic group, strict scrutiny does not apply. In such a case of *de facto* discrimination, the courts apply the rational basis test. Examples include public school districts that follow a ''neighborhood school'' concept, which may result in particular schools having predominantly white or predominantly black enrollments solely because of housing patterns and not because of any discriminatory act by the school district. There is no violation of the equal protection clause. (A word of caution is in order, however: If government *employment* practices are challenged for being discriminatory, de facto discrimination might be illegal under Title VII of the 1964 Civil Rights Act. Although the equal protection clause of the Constitution would not apply, de facto employment discrimination can be illegal under this federal statute whether a government or private employer is involved. Employment discrimination is discussed in Chapter 30.)

Thus far, the only form of racially based distinction that has been upheld is *affirmative action*. Sometimes referred to as "benign" or "reverse" discrimination, affirmative action programs grant limited preferences to racial and ethnic minorities. Affirmative action in the employment setting, by either government or private employers, is governed by Title VII of the 1964 Civil Rights Act, our most important employment discrimination law. Affirmative action occurs in several other contexts, as well; in any nonemployment situation in which an affirmative action program is instituted by a governmental body, the equal protection clause applies. Examples include programs that give limited preferences to minorities in admission to state universities or in the awarding of government contracts for the purchase of goods or services. The purposes of such programs include increasing diversity in state-supported higher education, helping minority-owned businesses become established by enabling them to break into government contract work, and assisting minorities in overcoming the effects of past discrimination in various endeavors.

Although affirmative action has proved to be the only situation in which racial or national origin distinctions have been permitted under the equal protection clause, the government must meet stringent requirements to justify them. For example, in *Richmond v. J. A. Croson Co.,* 488 U.S. 469 (1989), the Supreme Court struck down the minority business enterprise (MBE) set-aside program for awarding city government contracts in Richmond, Virginia. Under this program the City of Richmond required that 30 percent of the dollar volume of all city construction contracts be awarded to businesses that were owned and controlled by blacks, Hispanics, Asians, or Native Alaskans. The percentage could be met by a white-owned general contractor subcontracting work to MBEs. The MBE program was challenged by a white-owned construction company that lost a small contract to install guard rails on a highway, even though its bid was slightly lower than the successful bid of the MBE.

The Supreme Court in *Crosson* held that the city did have compelling interests in both remedying the effects of past discrimination and making sure that city tax money was not spent to support an industry that engaged in discriminatory practices (that is, discriminatory subcontracting). However, the Court held that for an MBE program to be valid, the city had to produce evidence demonstrating (1) that discrimination against MBEs in the awarding of city contracts and subcontracts had occurred in the past, (2) a reasonable estimate of the extent of that discrimination, and (3) that it had narrowly tailored the program to take race into account to the least extent possible to serve the city's compelling interest. The city had not fulfilled these requirements. In light of this decision, Richmond let its MBE program expire; thereafter, the amount of MBE participation in city construction contracts dropped to almost zero in Richmond. This result has been repeated in a number of other places. However, many other state and local government agencies are attempting to satisfy the requirements of the *Croson case.*

Intermediate Scrutiny

We know that the rational basis test applies to classifications in economic regulations and most social legislation, and we also know that the strict scrutiny test applies to government distinctions based on race or national origin. There are a number of other types of distinctions, however, about which the law is not very clear. There appears to be a "middle tier" of protection that applies to distinctions based on important personal characteristics other than race or national origin. Sometimes courts refer to an "intermediate" level of scrutiny. It is fairly clear that this middle tier of protection applies to gender-based distinctions; in such a case, the government must prove that the classification *substantially* advances an *important* government interest. This test is stricter than the rational basis test but not as stringent as the strict scrutiny test.

When such a test is applied, however, most gender-based distinctions will violate the equal protection clause. For example, in *Arizona v. Norris,* 463 U.S. 1073 (1983), the Supreme Court struck down an Arizona state employees' retirement plan that paid women smaller monthly benefits than men because actuarial tables predicted that the average woman would live longer than the average man. The plan was deemed unfair to the plaintiff, who could not count on living as long as the "average" woman. (If this same type of sex-discriminatory employee benefit plan is used by a private employer, the equal protection clause obviously does not apply. However, such a benefit plan in private employment will violate the prohibition against sex discrimination in Title VII of the 1964 Civil Rights Act.)

Several other kinds of distinctions may also fall within this middle tier of protection, including those based on "alienage" (whether a person is a U. S. citizen or merely a legal resident), age, a child's legitimacy or illegitimacy, and a few others involving important personal characteristics. The Supreme Court has not given clear guidance on these distinctions, however.

Due Process of Law

Among other clauses in the Fifth Amendment, the Due Process Clause states that "no person shall . . . be deprived of life, liberty, or property without due process of law." The provision applies to actions of the federal government. Among the several provisions of the Fourteenth Amendment, there is also a due process clause that applies to actions of state and local governments. The two clauses are identical, both in their language and in the way they have been interpreted by the courts; thus, there is no reason for distinguishing between the two and people usually refer to the Due Process Clause as a single provision that applies to all levels of government. The courts have interpreted the due process clause as limiting government action in two different ways: the first kind of limitation is referred to as *substantive due process*; the second is called *procedural due process*. Today, procedural due process is much more important than substantive due process.

Substantive Due Process

The substantive component of due process prohibits statutes, regulations, and other kinds of government action that are arbitrary and irrational. Until the late 1930s, the Supreme Court used substantive due process as a basis for invalidating many economic regulations; basically, if the Court disagreed with the law's underlying rationale, it found the law to be arbitrary and irrational. For example, a law limiting the number of hours that bakers could work was found violative of substantive due process because it unreasonably interfered with "the freedom of master and employee to contract in relation to their employment." Since the late 1930s, the Supreme Court has taken a dramatically different view of substantive due process. Under the modern interpretation, the Court refuses to "sit as a super-legislature second-guessing the wisdom of legislation."

The standard the Court applies today is essentially the same ''rational basis'' test that is applied to economic classifications under the equal protection clause. Although most courts have been very reluctant to find that legislative actions have no rational basis, they occasionally will do so. One recent example is in *Brantley v. Kuntz*, 2015 WL 75244 (W.D. TX 2015), in which the U.S. district court for the western district of Texas in Austin found that a Texas state regulation of African hair braiders made so little sense, with no basis in reality, that it violated substantive due process. The state regulation imposed on these hair braiders requirements that they have a complete hair salon setup, with a certain number of sinks, chairs, and on and on. The judge said there was no relationship at all between the requirements of the regulation and any plausible state interest such as health and safety.

State regulation of barbershops and hair salons in some states like Texas is far in excess of what is needed for public health and safety. The same is true of the state regulation of quite a few other occupations, but in most cases the regulations are not so incredibly stupid that they violate substantive due process. They just waste money and make it harder for small businesses to operate.

Procedural Due Process

The other type or protection found in the due process clause as interpreted by courts is the *procedural*. When procedural due process applies, it essentially guarantees that the government will follow fair procedures before taking certain actions against individuals or companies. Procedural due process is a constitutional requirement when the local, state, or federal government action is *adjudicative*—that is, when a court or other government agency applies rules to the conduct of a specific person or company. Although procedural due process is not a constitutional requirement for *legislative* government actions—those in which a legislature or other government agency makes rules for prospective application to persons or companies—in most situations there are legislative requirements that fair procedures be followed.

One important example of the latter is the federal Administrative Procedures Act (APA), in which the federal APA specifies the types of procedures that federal agencies must follow when they are engaging in legislative-type rule making. The APA also specifies rules of fair procedure for federal agencies to follow when applying rules to the particular conduct of individuals and companies. When legislation such as the APA requires fair procedures for these adjudicative government actions, the legislation usually just adds more detail to the procedures that already are required by the constitutional requirement of procedural due process.

Deprivation of Life, Liberty, or Property. The Due Process Clause applies only if particular government action ''deprives'' a person of "life, liberty, or property." This prerequisite exists whether substantive or procedural due process is at issue; however, most of the problems in determining whether this requirement has been met arise in the procedural due process context. Due process questions almost never involve governmental deprivation of "life," the obvious exception being a criminal prosecution in which the death penalty is a possibility. Thus, the question normally is whether particular government action constitutes a deprivation of "liberty" or "property." These terms are interpreted rather broadly. The term *deprivation of liberty* includes virtually any substantial restriction on the freedom of an individual or company, and the term *deprivation of property* includes virtually any substantial negative effect on any type of property interest.

It can be seen from this statement that the term deprivation really just means a substantial adverse impact; there does not have to be total destruction of a liberty or property interest to constitute a deprivation. One example of the breadth of the term *property* is that a person can even be viewed as having a property interest in a job with a local, state, or federal government agency. If there is a statutory provision or an agency regulation that gives the employee some type of legally enforceable job security, the person has a property interest in the job and must be given procedural due process before the job can be terminated. The statute or regulation might, for example, provide that the employee can be terminated only for "good cause" or only in other described conditions. Such a guarantee creates a property interest. There are many other examples of situations in which individuals or corporations have legal rights that rise to the level of property interests.

Basic Procedural Requirements. When procedural due process applies to government action, the government must provide the affected party with (1) advance notice of the proposed action, (2) an "opportunity to be heard," that is, a hearing of some type, and (3) an impartial decision maker. If this same type of sex-discriminatory employee benefit plan is used by a private employer, the equal protection clause obviously does not apply. However, such a benefit plan in private employment will violate the prohibition against sex discrimination in Title VII of the 1964 Civil Rights Act.

These requirements are very flexible. The type of notice that will be sufficient may vary with the circumstances. The general rule is simply that the timing and content of the notice must be such that the affected party is reasonably apprised of the nature of the proposed action and has an adequate opportunity to prepare a response.

The requirement of a hearing is also very flexible; the fact that procedural due process applies does not mean that there has to be a full-blown court-like hearing. The hearing must be "meaningful under the circumstances" and might range from a very informal face-to-face meeting between the affected party and the decision maker all the way to a very formal trial-type hearing. The kind of hearing required in a particular case depends on how important the affected party's interest is, how important the government's interest is, and what seems to be the best way to optimize those conflicting interests under the circumstances.

The requirement of an impartial decision maker usually means only that a person having the responsibility for making the decision (either alone or as a member of a decision-making group) should not have prejudged the case and should not have a substantial monetary or emotional stake in the outcome of the decision. The mere fact that a decision maker has a particular ideology or has very strong views about the general subject of the decision does not disqualify them.

There are several reasons for requiring fair procedures in any decision-making process, including those in government. The most important reason is that fair procedures generally tend to produce better decisions because these procedures improve the chances that all relevant issues will be identified, all important positions will be presented and considered, and relevant information will be adequately screened and tested.

Another important reason for fair procedures is making people feel as if their views count for something, thus increasing their acceptance of decisions even when those decisions go against them. It is much easier to get the compliance and cooperation necessary to carry out decisions when people accept those decisions as being legitimate.

Takings Clause

The final constitutional provision we will examine is the *Takings Clause* of the Fifth Amendment. It applies explicitly to the federal government and, through the doctrine of incorporation, also applies to state and local governments. The Takings Clause states that private property shall not "be taken for public use without just compensation." The clause recognizes the ancient principle that a sovereign may take private property for public purposes. This long recognized governmental power is referred to as the power of *eminent domain*. The Takings Clause, however, also places limitations on this power. Private property can be taken only for a public purpose, but this requirement is interpreted so broadly that almost any governmental objective will suffice. The most important limitation is that the government must pay "just compensation"—the fair market value—of the property it takes.

The concept of property is very broad under the Takings Clause. It obviously includes land, as well as the many different types of interests in land such as subsurface mineral rights, easements, and "air rights" (the right to use the air space above land). It also includes any other tangible property, such as a boat or piece of equipment, and intangible property rights such as those that exist in a company's trade secret information.

The government is required to pay the owner when there has been a "taking." Remember that procedural due process applies to any government action that has a significant negative effect on a property interest. However, to be a taking for which compensation must be paid, there must be much more than just a significant negative effect on the property interest. All or most of the property's value and utility must have been appropriated by the government's action. When the government physically appropriates the ownership of property, as when it builds a highway on your land, there obviously is a taking. If you do not agree to sell the land, the government must take legal action to condemn the property and have a court determine its fair value.

Difficult questions can arise, however, when the government does something that has a substantial negative effect on the utility and value of a property interest, without actually appropriating the property. When the government engages in some physical act that greatly diminishes the utility and value of someone's property, courts sometimes view the action as a taking. For example, the government might extend an airport runway so that takeoffs and landings are now very low over an adjoining tract of land.

If the government has not bought the adjoining land, either through negotiated purchase or condemnation, the property owner is likely to file suit claiming a de facto, taking of his or her property. If the court concludes that the government's actions substantially destroyed the owner's ability to make productive use of his or her property, the court usually decides that there has been a taking for which compensation is due. Although the government's action can constitute a taking without totally destroying all possible uses of the property, one of the factors a court will consider in determining whether there has been a sufficiently large destruction of value is whether there are other comparably productive uses for the property.

The issue of whether there has been a taking can also arise when some law or regulation affects the value of property. Most of the time, a regulation that limits the uses an owner can make of his or her property or that otherwise affects its value will not constitute a taking. Courts usually view these regulations as one of the burdens a person or company must bear in return for the many benefits of living in an organized society.

The most obvious example is a city zoning law that permits only single-family homes in certain areas, multifamily dwellings in other areas, retail stores elsewhere, and various categories of industry in yet other sections. Despite occasional claims by property owners that they are deprived of the greater financial return they could receive by putting their property to some other use, zoning laws almost never constitute takings. Among other reasons for this conclusion, zoning usually benefits property values on the whole because of the predictability it creates.

The Supreme Court's many cases involving application of the Takings Clause to regulations have not provided very clear guidance. Unfortunately, the cases in this area are of a rather ad hoc nature. Generally speaking, a regulation that limits use will only constitute a taking in circumstances in which a particular property owner is forced to bear an unusual financial burden that is totally out of proportion with the benefits to be received by either the property owner or the community.

For example, in *Nollan v. California Coastal Commission,* 483 U.S. 825 (1987), the Supreme Court held that a state agency had committed a taking when it required a landowner to grant public access across a section of the owner's private beach; the requirement was imposed as a condition before the agency would permit the landowner to demolish an old structure and replace it with a house on the property. The Court found a taking because of a combination of factors: (1) the landowner was singled out for a special burden not imposed on a general community of landowners; (2) the restriction on the owner's ability to demolish and build was not really related to the condition of granting public access; and (3) the granting of access to the public resembled the actual appropriation of an easement by the government (an easement—the right to do something on someone else's land—is a property interest).

The following case is a recent, important takings case by the U.S. Supreme Court.

HORNE V. DEPARTMENT OF AGRICULTURE
576 U.S. 350 (2015)

The Agricultural Marketing Agreement Act of 1937 authorizes the Secretary of Agriculture to promulgate "marketing orders" to help maintain stable markets for various agricultural products. The marketing order for raisins requires growers in certain years to give a percentage of their crop to the Government, free of charge. The required allocation is determined by the Raisin Administrative Committee, a Government entity composed largely of growers and others in the raisin business appointed by the Secretary. In 2002-2003, this Committee ordered raisin growers to turn over 47 percent of their crop. In 2003-2004, 30 percent.

The Raisin Committee acquires title to the reserve raisins that have been set aside, and decides how to dispose of them in its discretion. It sells them in noncompetitive markets; donates them to charitable causes; releases them to growers who agree to reduce their raisin production; or disposes of them by "any other means" consistent with the purposes of the raisin program. Proceeds from Committee sales are principally used to subsidize handlers who sell raisins for export. Raisin growers retain an interest in any net proceeds from sales the Raisin Committee makes, after deductions for the export subsidies and the Committee's administrative expenses. In the years at issue in this case, those proceeds were less than the cost of producing the crop one year, and nothing at all the next.

The Hornes are both raisin growers and handlers. In 2002, they refused to set aside any raisins and turned away the Government trucks that came to pick up the raisins. The Government then assessed against the Hornes a fine equal to the market value of the missing raisins—some $480,000—as well as an additional civil penalty of just over $200,000. The Hornes filed this lawsuit to challenge the fine, arguing that the reserve requirement was an unconstitutional taking of their property under the Fifth Amendment.

After much litigation, the Ninth Circuit agreed with the Hornes that the validity of the fine rose or fell with the constitutionality of the reserve requirement, but held that the case did not involve a per se taking, reasoning that "the Takings Clause affords less protection to personal than to real property," and concluding that the Hornes "are not completely divested of their property rights," because growers retain an interest in the proceeds from any sale of reserve raisins by the Raisin Committee. The Hornes appealed.

Roberts, Chief Justice:

The petition for certiorari poses three questions, which we answer in turn. The first question presented asks "Whether the government's 'categorical duty' under the Fifth Amendment to pay just compensation when it physically takes possession of an interest in property, applies only to real property and not to personal property." The answer is no.

There is no dispute that the "classic taking [is one] in which the government directly appropriates private property for its own use." *Tahoe-Sierra Preservation Council, Inc. v.*

Tahoe Regional Planning Agency, 535 U.S. 302 (2002). Nor is there any dispute that, in the case of real property, such an appropriation is a per se taking that requires just compensation. See *Loretto v. Teleprompter Manhattan CATV Corp.*, 458 U.S. 419 (1982).

Nothing in the text or history of the Takings Clause, or our precedents, suggests that the rule is any different when it comes to appropriation of personal property. The Government has a categorical duty to pay just compensation when it takes your car, just as when it takes your home. The Takings Clause provides: "[N]or shall private property be taken for public use, without just compensation." It protects "private property" without any distinction between different types. The principle reflected in the Clause goes back at least 800 years to Magna Carta, which specifically protected agricultural crops from uncompensated takings. Clause 28 of that charter forbade any "constable or other bailiff" from taking "corn or other provisions from any one without immediately tendering money therefor, unless he can have postponement thereof by permission of the seller." Cl. 28 (1215).

The colonists brought the principles of Magna Carta to the New World, including that charter's protection against uncompensated takings of personal property. [The Court quoted early state statutes from Massachusetts, Virginia, and South Carolina.] … Nothing in this history suggests that personal property was any less protected against physical appropriation than real property.

Prior to this Court's decision in *Pennsylvania Coal Co. v. Mahon*, 260 U.S. 393 (1922), the Takings Clause was understood to provide protection only against a direct appropriation of property—personal or real. *Pennsylvania Coal* expanded the protection of the Takings Clause, holding that compensation was also required for a "regulatory taking"— a restriction on the use of property that went "too far." And in *Penn Central Transp. Co. v. New York City*, 438 U.S. 104 (1978), the Court clarified that the test for how far was "too far" required an "ad hoc" factual inquiry. That inquiry required considering factors such as the economic impact of the regulation, its interference with reasonable investment-backed expectations, and the character of the government action.

Four years after *Penn Central*, however, the Court reaffirmed the rule that a physical appropriation of property gave rise to a per se taking, without regard to other factors. In *Loretto*, the Court held that requiring an owner of an apartment building to allow installation of a cable box on her rooftop was a physical taking of real property, for which compensation was required. That was true without regard to the claimed public benefit or the economic impact on the owner. The Court explained that such protection was justified not only by history, but also because "[s]uch an appropriation is perhaps the most serious form of invasion of an owner's property interests," depriving the owner of "the rights to possess, use and dispose of" the property. That reasoning—both with respect to history and logic—is equally applicable to a physical appropriation of personal property.

The reserve requirement imposed by the Raisin Committee is a clear physical taking. Actual raisins are transferred from the growers to the Government. Title to the raisins passes to the Raisin Committee. The Committee's raisins must be physically segregated from [other] raisins. Raisin growers subject to the reserve requirement thus lose the entire "bundle" of property rights in the appropriated raisins—"the rights to possess, use and dispose of" them, *Loretto*, 458 U.S., at 435, with the exception of the speculative hope that some residual proceeds may be left when the Government is done with the raisins and has deducted the expenses of implementing all aspects of the marketing order. The

Government's "actual taking of possession and control" of the reserve raisins gives rise to a taking as clearly "as if the Government held full title and ownership," as it essentially does. The Government's formal demand that the Hornes turn over a percentage of their raisin crop without charge, for the Government's control and use, is "of such a unique character that it is a taking without regard to other factors that a court might ordinarily examine."

The second question presented asks "Whether the government may avoid the categorical duty to pay just compensation for a physical taking of property by reserving to the property owner a contingent interest in a portion of the value of the property, set at the government's discretion." The answer is no. . . .

[W]hen there has been a physical appropriation, "we do not ask . . . whether it deprives the owner of all economically valuable use" of the item taken. ("When the government physically takes possession of an interest in property for some public purpose, it has a categorical duty to compensate the former owner, regardless of whether the interest that is taken constitutes an entire parcel or merely a part thereof." For example, in *Loretto*, we held that the installation of a cable box on a small corner of Loretto's rooftop was a per se taking, even though she could of course still sell and economically benefit from the property. The fact that the growers retain a contingent interest of indeterminate value does not mean there has been no physical taking, particularly since the value of the interest depends on the discretion of the taker, and may be worthless, as it was for one of the two years at issue here.

The third question presented asks "Whether a governmental mandate to relinquish specific, identifiable property as a 'condition' on permission to engage in commerce effects a per se taking." The answer, at least in this case, is yes.

The Government contends that the reserve requirement is not a taking because raisin growers voluntarily choose to participate in the raisin market. According to the Government, if raisin growers don't like it, they can "plant different crops," or "sell their raisin-variety grapes as table grapes or for use in juice or wine." "Let them sell wine" is probably not much more comforting to the raisin growers than similar retorts have been to others throughout history. In any event, the Government is wrong as a matter of law. In *Loretto*, we rejected the argument that the New York law was not a taking because a landlord could avoid the requirement by ceasing to be a landlord. We held instead that "a landlord's ability to rent his property may not be conditioned on his forfeiting the right to compensation for a physical occupation." As the Court explained, the contrary argument "proves too much":

> "For example, it would allow the government to require a landlord to devote a substantial portion of his building to vending and washing machines, with all profits to be retained by the owners of these services and with no compensation for the deprivation of space. It would even allow the government to requisition a certain number of apartments as permanent government offices."

As the Court concluded, property rights "cannot be so easily manipulated." The decision of the Court of Appeals for the Ninth Circuit is reversed.

CHAPTER 6

LAWMAKING BY ADMINISTRATIVE AGENCIES

- Rise of the Administrative Agency
- The Agency—An Overview
- Legislative Delegation of Lawmaking Power
- Functions and Powers
- Other Developments

In the preceding chapters we have studied the major processes by which law is made—the formulation of common-law rules by the courts, the enactment of statutes by the legislative bodies, and the interpretation of statutes by the courts. But this examination does not present the total lawmaking picture.

Administrative agencies—the hundreds of boards and commissions existing at all levels of government—also "make law" by their continual promulgation of rules and regulations. The number of administrative agencies has grown so rapidly in the past century that the practical impact of local, state, and federal agencies on the day-to-day activities of individuals and businesses is today probably at least as great as that of legislatures and courts. Every day, boards and commissions across the country engage in such traditional functions as assessing properties for tax purposes, granting licenses and business permits, and regulating rates charged in the transportation and public utility industries—actions that affect millions of Americans. And major federal agencies such as the Environmental Protection Agency (EPA) and Occupational Safety and Health Administration (OSHA) have issued regulations having a broad impact on the nation's businesses. Justice Jackson was right when he wrote in *FTC v. Ruberoid Co.,* 343 U.S. 470 (1952):

> The rise of administrative bodies probably has been the most significant legal trend of the last century and perhaps more values today are affected by their decisions than by those of all the courts. . . . They also have begun to have important consequences on personal rights. . . . They have become a veritable fourth branch of the Government, which has deranged our three-branch legal theories as much as the concept of a fourth dimension unsettles our three-dimensional thinking.

As the political winds shift back and forth over the years, the impact of agencies often waxes and wanes. President Trump's practice of placing fierce critics of federal agencies in charge of those very agencies has certainly lessened agency impact—both good and bad—in recent years.

RISE OF THE ADMINISTRATIVE AGENCY

At the risk of oversimplification, we can say that two major factors are responsible for the dramatic growth of the administrative agency over the years. First was a change in attitude toward government regulation of business. Until about 1880, the basic attitude of the state and federal governments toward business firms was a hands-off philosophy frequently characterized by the *laissez-faire* label. The theory was that trade and commerce could best thrive in an environment free of government controls. By the end of the nineteenth century, however, various monopolistic practices had begun to surface. The passage of the Sherman Act in 1890 reflected the growing idea that a certain amount of government regulation of business was necessary to preserve minimum levels of competition.

A second, and perhaps even more powerful, reason for the emergence of the modern administrative agency is that as our nation grew and became more industrialized, many complex problems sprang up that did not easily lend themselves to traditional types of regulation. Some were posed by technological advances such as the greatly increased generation and distribution of electrical power, and the rapid growth of the airline industry. Today, the development of the Internet poses similar complications.

Others problems resulted from changes in social and economic conditions, particularly the rise of the giant manufacturers and the new methods by which they marketed their products on a national basis. The solution of these problems required expertise and enormous amounts of time for continuous regulation, which the courts and the legislatures simply did not possess. Faced with this situation, the legislative bodies sought new ways to regulate business (and to implement nonbusiness government programs, such as Social Security) that would be more workable.

Today, Americans rely more than ever upon administrative agencies to collect taxes, distribute food stamps, build highways, supervise schools, ensure worker safety, preserve the environment, and on and on, although to some, the major role played by administrative agencies is just another example of the hated "big government."

THE AGENCY—AN OVERVIEW

To understand the basic workings of administrative agencies and the nature of the legal problems we will discuss later, it will be helpful to see how the typical agency is created and how it receives its powers. For this purpose, the Federal Trade Commission provides a good example.

By 1900 or so, it was apparent that some firms in interstate commerce were engaging in practices that, although not violating the Sherman Act, were nonetheless felt to be undesirable. Although persons who were injured by these practices were sometimes able to obtain relief in the courts, the relief was sporadic, and there was no single body that could maintain surveillance of these practices on a continuing basis.

Accordingly, in 1914 Congress passed the Federal Trade Commission Act, which created the *Federal Trade Commission (FTC)* and authorized it (among other things) to determine what constituted "unfair methods of competition" in interstate commerce. Not only could the commission issue regulations defining and prohibiting such practices, but additionally, it could take action against companies that it believed to be violating such regulations.

Several federal agencies are considered to be part of the executive branch, such as the Small Business Administration (SBA), OSHA, and the Federal Aviation Administration (FAA). Others are structurally independent of the executive branch; once the president's appointment of agency heads and members is confirmed by the Senate, the president has no direct control over the appointee and cannot remove him or her from office. Examples of *independent regulatory agencies* include the FTC, the Securities and Exchange Commission (SEC), the National Labor Relations Board (NLRB), and the Federal Reserve Board (FRB).

LEGISLATIVE DELEGATION OF LAWMAKING POWER

The administrative agency sits somewhat uncomfortably in our tripartite (legislative-executive-judicial) system of government. An agency that is technically part of the executive branch or perhaps an independent regulatory agency may exert powers that entail adjudication and rulemaking as well as traditional executive functions such as investigation and enforcement. A constitutional problem arises because the Constitution in article I, section 1, clearly vests all legislative powers in the Congress and does not provide for delegation of those powers. Therefore, rules and regulations that have been promulgated by agencies and that have the force and effect of law have been challenged as resulting from an unconstitutional delegation of legislative power. Only in a couple of cases decided during the 1930s, in which the Supreme Court found "delegation running riot," have such challenges succeeded.

The courts are well aware of the very practical need for administrative agencies that was described earlier in this chapter. Therefore, they will uphold any agency ruling, regulation, or act that is within standards set forth in an enabling act if that act lays down an "intelligible principle" to guide the agency and its agents. The Supreme Court has noted that its "jurisprudence has been driven by a practical understanding that in our increasingly complex society, replete with ever changing and more technical problems, Congress simply cannot do its job absent an ability to delegate power under broad directives." (*Mistretta v. U.S.,* 488 U.S. 1 (1989)).

FUNCTIONS AND POWERS

Ministerial and Discretionary Powers

Before addressing the legal problems that are presented when agencies' rules or orders are appealed to the courts, we will briefly look at the nature of agency activities. The activities of these government boards and commissions vary widely. The functions and powers of some agencies are only *ministerial*—concerned with routinely carrying out duties imposed by law. Boards that issue and renew drivers' licenses fall within this category, as do the many Social Security offices that give information or advice to persons filing for Social Security benefits.

But most agencies also possess broad *discretionary powers*—powers that require the exercise of judgment and discretion in carrying out their duties. Again, there is variety in the specific powers of these agencies. Some agencies' discretionary power is largely *investigative* in nature. Two examples are the authority granted to the Internal Revenue Service to inquire into the legality of deductions on taxpayers' returns and the authority of some commissions to make investigations for the purpose of recommending needed statutes to legislatures. Other agencies have largely *rule-making powers,* with perhaps some investigative but little *adjudicative power* (rule-enforcement power).

"Full-fledged" federal agencies, such as the FTC and the NLRB, possess all three types of discretionary power—investigative, rule-making, and adjudicative. Thus, typically a board will conduct investigations to determine if conditions warrant the issuance of rules to require (or prohibit) certain kinds of conduct; then it will draw up the regulations and thereafter take action against individuals or firms showing evidence of violating them. In drawing up the rules the board acts quasi-legislatively, and in enforcing them it acts quasi-judicially.

Investigative Power

Agencies frequently hold hearings before drafting regulations, and the investigative powers they possess in connection with such hearings are largely determined by the statutes by which they are created. Normally, agencies can order the production of accounts and records relative to the problem being studied and can *subpoena* witnesses and examine them under oath. More disruptive to businesses are the powers most major agencies have to investigate whether statutes they are charged with enforcing and rules they have promulgated are being violated. The two most intrusive forms of investigative power are the subpoena and the physical search and seizure.

Subpoena Power

In the exercise of its adjudicative powers, which are soon to be discussed, agencies may issue subpoenas compelling witnesses to appear and give testimony at an agency hearing. In any sort of investigation, agencies also may issue *subpoenas duces tecum*, which order the production of books, papers, records, and documents. Agency authority is construed very broadly in this area. According to *United States v. Powell,* 379 U.S. 48 (1964), an agency must demonstrate that (1) the investigation will be conducted for a legitimate purpose, (2) the inquiry is relevant to the purpose, (3) the information sought is not already possessed by the agency, and (4) the administrative steps required by law have been followed. The agency does not, however, have to prove that there is "probable cause" to believe that a violation of the law has occurred, as is usually required in criminal investigations by the police. Once the agency has established an apparently valid purpose for the investigation, the burden shifts to the company or individual being investigated to show that the purpose is illegitimate (for example, undertaken for harassment).

Search and Seizure

Many agencies carry out on-site inspections or searches when investigating matters under their jurisdiction. From city health inspectors checking a restaurant's kitchen to OSHA personnel investigating trenches at a construction site to federal mine safety inspectors probing underground coal mines, such investigations are a frequent and, for the investigated company, troublesome occurrence.

These searches have constitutional implications, because the warrant clause of the Fourth Amendment protects commercial buildings as well as private homes. As the Supreme Court pointed out in *Marshall v. Barlow's, Inc.,* 436 U.S. 307 (1978), the searching of businesses by the British immediately preceding the American Revolution was particularly offensive to the colonists and provided part of the rationale for the warrant requirement.

However, we are not accorded as great an expectation of privacy for our businesses as for our homes. For example, several types of businesses, including gun dealers, stone quarries, day care centers, and fishing vessels, have been held to be so "pervasively regulated" that they can have little or no reasonable expectation of privacy. The following case addresses this clash between legitimate law enforcement concerns and business privacy rights.

CITY OF LOS ANGELES v. PATEL
135 S. Ct. 2443 (2015)

Respondent hotel owners challenged on Fourth Amendment grounds a provision of the Los Angeles Municipal Code that compels "[e]very operator of a hotel to keep a record" containing specified information concerning guests and to make this record "available to any officer of the Los Angeles Police Department for inspection" on demand. The trial court upheld the provision. The Ninth Circuit reversed, ruling that the provision constituted a warrantless search that violated the Fourth Amendment. The City of Los Angeles appealed to the Supreme Court.

Sotomayor, Justice:

Los Angeles Municipal Code (LAMC) §41.49 requires hotel operators to record information about their guests, including: the guest's name and address; the number of people in each guest's party; the make, model, and license plate number of any guest's vehicle parked on hotel property; the guest's date and time of arrival and scheduled departure date; the room number assigned to the guest; the rate charged and amount collected for the room; and the method of payment. [This and additional information] must be "kept on the hotel premises in the guest reception or guest check-in area or in an office adjacent" thereto for a period of 90 days. §41.49(3)(a).

Section 41.49(3)(a) — the only provision at issue here—states, in pertinent part, that hotel guest records "shall be made available to any officer of the Los Angeles Police Department for inspection," provided that "[w]henever possible, the inspection shall be conducted at a time and in a manner that minimizes any interference with the operation of the business." A hotel operator's failure to make guest records available for police inspection is a misdemeanor punishable by up to six months in jail and a $1,000 fine.

We hold that §41.49(3)(a) is facially unconstitutional because it fails to provide hotel operators with an opportunity for precompliance review. The Fourth Amendment protects "[t]he right of the people to be secure in their persons, houses, papers, and effects, against unreasonable searches and seizures." It further provides that "no Warrants shall issue, but upon probable cause." Based on this constitutional text, the Court has repeatedly held that "searches conducted outside the judicial process, without prior approval by [a] judge or [a] magistrate [judge], are per se unreasonable . . . subject only to a few specifically established and well-delineated exceptions." *Arizona v. Gant*, 556 U. S. 332 (2009).

Search regimes where no warrant is ever required may be reasonable where "special needs . . . make the warrant and probable-cause requirement impracticable," *Griffin v. Wisconsin*, 483 U.S. 868 (1987), and where the "primary purpose" of the searches is "[d]istinguishable from the general interest in crime control," *Indianapolis v. Edmond*, 531 U.S. 32 (2000). Here, we assume that the searches authorized by §41.49 serve a "special need" other than conducting criminal investigations: They ensure compliance with the recordkeeping requirement, which in turn deters criminals from operating on the hotels' premises. The Court has referred to this kind of search as an "administrative searc[h]." *Camara v. Municipal Court*, 387 U.S. 523 (1967). Thus, we consider whether §41.49 falls within the administrative search exception to the warrant requirement.

The Court has held that absent consent, exigent circumstances, or the like, in order for an administrative search to be constitutional, the subject of the search must be afforded an opportunity to obtain precompliance review before a neutral decisionmaker. And, we see no reason why this minimal requirement is inapplicable here. While the Court has never attempted to prescribe the exact form an opportunity for precompliance review must take, the City does not even attempt to argue that §41.49(3)(a) affords hotel operators any opportunity whatsoever. Section 41.49(3)(a) is, therefore, facially invalid.

A hotel owner who refuses to give an officer access to the registry can be arrested on the spot. The Court has held that business owners cannot reasonably be put to this kind of choice. Absent an opportunity for precompliance review, the ordinance creates an intolerable risk that searches authorized by it will exceed statutory limits, or be used as a pretext to harass hotel operators and their guests. Even if a hotel has been searched 10 times a day, every day, for three months, without any violation being found, the operator can only refuse to comply with an officer's demand to turn over the registry at his or her own peril.

To be clear, we hold only that a hotel owner must be afforded an opportunity to have a neutral decision maker review an officer's demand to search the registry before he or she faces penalties for failing to comply. Actual review need only occur in those rare instances where a hotel operator objects to turning over the registry. Moreover, this opportunity can be provided without imposing onerous burdens on those charged with an administrative scheme's enforcement. For instance, respondents accept that the searches authorized by §41.49(3)(a) would be constitutional if they were performed pursuant to an administrative subpoena. These subpoenas, which are typically a simple form, can be issued by the individual seeking the record — here, officers in the field — without probable cause that a regulation is being infringed. Indeed, the City has cited no evidence suggesting that without an ordinance authorizing on-demand searches, hotel operators would regularly refuse to cooperate with the police.

Rather than arguing that §41.49(3)(a) is constitutional under the general administrative search doctrine, the City and Justice Scalia in dissent, contend that hotels are "closely regulated," and that the ordinance is facially valid under the more relaxed standard that applies to searches of this category of businesses. Over the past 45 years, the Court has identified only four industries that "have such a history of government oversight that no reasonable expectation of privacy . . . could exist for a proprietor over the stock of such an enterprise," *Marshall v. Barlow's, Inc.*, 436 U. S. 313. Simply listing these industries refutes petitioner's argument that hotels should be counted among them. Unlike liquor sales, firearms dealing, mining, or running an automobile junkyard, *New York v. Burger,* 482 U.S. 691 (1987), nothing inherent in the operation of hotels poses a clear and significant risk to the public welfare. Moreover, "[t]he clear import of our cases is that the closely regulated industry . . . is the exception." *Barlows, Inc.* To classify hotels as pervasively regulated would permit what has always been a narrow exception to swallow the rule. Affirmed.

Rule Making

Much of the legislative-type activity of federal agencies is carried out through their rule-making function. Sometimes Congress spells out the procedures for rule-making by a particular agency in that agency's enabling statute. Sometimes the agency is left to follow the Administrative Procedure Act (APA), which the more specific statutes normally follow anyway. The APA provides a comprehensive set of procedural guidelines for a variety of agency activities. In the rule-making area, the APA provides for two basic types—*informal* and *formal*. A third type, called *hybrid rule-making*, has also developed.

Informal Rule Making

Sometimes Congress will authorize informal rule making. To properly promulgate a rule under these procedures, the agency usually publishes a notice of the proposed rule in the *Federal Register*. There follows a comment period, typically of 30 days, in which any interested citizen or company may send written comments to the agency regarding the rule. Such comments might argue that the rule is unnecessary, is unduly burdensome to business, does not go far enough to remedy the problem, goes too far, and the like. The agency is then supposed to digest and react to the comments, perhaps by altering or even scrapping the proposed rule. Normally the rule is modestly altered, and then published in final form in the *Federal Register.* At that point, it becomes effective. Ultimately it will be codified in the *Code of Federal Regulations* along with the rules of all other federal administrative agencies.

Formal Rule Making

Formal rule making also involves "notice and comment," but it supplements these with formal hearings at which witnesses testify and are cross-examined by interested parties. Transcripts of the testimony are preserved and become part of the public record. Formal rule making can be very expensive and time-consuming but theoretically leads to especially well-considered results.

Hybrid Rule Making

Hybrid rule making closely resembles formal rule making, except that there is no right to cross-examine the agency's expert witnesses, and, as we shall soon see, a different standard of review is applied by the courts if the rule-making procedure is challenged.

Judicial Review of Rule Making

Naturally some parties are likely to be aggrieved by promulgation of rules that affect them adversely. Few important rules are issued without a subsequent court challenge. Courts will invalidate rules issued pursuant to an unconstitutional delegation of legislative power (as noted above, an extremely rare occurrence) and rules that are unconstitutional (perhaps because they discriminate on the basis of race in violation of equal protection principles).

Courts will also invalidate rules not issued in accordance with applicable procedural standards. For example, if an agency engaged in informal rule making fails to publish a proposed version of the rule in the Federal Register so that comments may be received, the rule will likely be invalidated if challenged. The courts will permit minor deviations from APA procedures, but major ones are risky.

Standards of Review: Questions of Law. Courts are often asked to review agency decisions in issuing and applying rules. Often these reviews involve *questions of law*. Courts are experts on the law. Therefore, they have the authority to substitute their interpretations for those made by the agency. Nonetheless, the Supreme Court held in *Chevron U.S.A., Inc. v. Natural Resources Defense Council,* 467 U.S. 837 (1984), that it makes sense to give deference to an agency's decisions when it interprets *statutes* that Congress put it in charge of administering. And in *Auer v. Robbins,* 519 U.S. 452 (1997), the Court held that Courts should also, in proper circumstances, give deference to agencies' interpretations of *their own regulation.* "*Chevron* deference" and "*Auer* deference" are very important concepts, and also quite controversial. Both are unpopular with conservatives who are suspicious of administrative power and regularly introduce bills in Congress to prohibit courts from deferring to agency interpretations of statutes and their own regulations. Here is the Supreme Court's most recent decision in the area.

KISOR v. WILKIE
U.S. Supreme Court, 139 S. Ct. 2400 (2019)

Kisor is a Vietnam War veteran whose 1982 application for disability benefits from the Department of Veterans Affairs (VA) was denied on grounds that he did not have PTSD as he claimed. In 2006, Kisor moved to reopen his case and, based on a new psychiatric report, the VA agreed that Kisor suffered from PTSD, but it granted him benefits only from

2006 rather than from 1982. Kisor appealed, but a single administrative law judge, acting as the Board of Veterans' Appeals, a part of the VA, affirmed the timing decision based on its interpretation of a VA regulation that allowed retroactive benefits if it found there were "relevant official service department records" that it had not considered in its original denial. Although Kisor had provided new department records showing his participation in combat, the Board deemed them not "relevant" because the original denial was not on grounds that Kisor had not participated in combat.

Kisor appealed the refusal to grant retroactive benefits. The Court of Appeals for Veterans Claims affirmed for the same reason given by the Board. The Federal Circuit affirmed based on deference to the Board's interpretation of the VA rule. Kisor had argued that to count as "relevant," a service record need not counter the basis for the prior denial but could instead relate to some other criterion for obtaining disability benefits. The Federal Circuit found the regulation "ambiguous" between the two views and then applied Auer *deference, holding that the VA's construction of its own regulation should govern unless "plainly erroneous or inconsistent with the VA's regulatory framework." Kisor appealed to the Supreme Court.*

Kagan, Justice:

This Court has often deferred to agencies' reasonable readings of genuinely ambiguous regulations. [The only issue in this case is whether the Court should discard *Auer* deference.] We answer that question no. *Auer* deference retains an important role in construing agency regulations. But even as we uphold it, we reinforce its limits.

Begin with a familiar problem in administrative law: For various reasons, regulations may be genuinely ambiguous. They may not directly or clearly address every issue; when applied to some fact patterns, they may prove susceptible to more than one reasonable reading. Sometimes, this sort of ambiguity arises from careless drafting—the use of a dangling modifier, an awkward word, an opaque construction. But often, ambiguity reflects the well-known limits of expression or knowledge. The subject matter of a rule "may be so specialized and varying in nature as to be impossible"—or at any rate, impracticable—to capture in its every detail. *SEC v. Chenery Corp.*, 332 U.S. 194 (1947) . Or a "problem [ ] may arise" that the agency, when drafting the rule, "could not [have] reasonably foresee[n]." *Id.* Whichever the case, the result is to create real uncertainties about a regulation's meaning.

We have explained *Auer* deference as rooted in a presumption about congressional intent—a presumption that Congress would generally want the agency to play the primary role in resolving regulatory ambiguities. *See Martin v. OSHA,* 499 U.S. 144 (1991). Congress, we have pointed out, routinely delegates to agencies the power to implement statutes by issuing rules. In doing so, Congress knows (how could it not?) that regulations will sometimes contain ambiguities. But Congress almost never explicitly assigns responsibility to deal with that problem, either to agencies or to courts. Hence the need to presume, one way or the other, what Congress would want. And as between those two choices, agencies have gotten the nod. We have adopted the presumption—though it is always rebuttable—that "the power authoritatively to interpret its own regulations is a component of the agency's delegated lawmaking powers." *Martin.* Or otherwise said, we have thought that when granting rulemaking power to agencies Congress usually intends to give them, too, considerable latitude to interpret the ambiguous rules they issue.

In part, that is because the agency that promulgated a rule is in the "better position [to] reconstruct" its original meaning. *Martin*. Consider that if you don't know what some text (say, a memo or an e-mail) means, you would probably want to ask the person who wrote it. And for the same reasons, we have thought, Congress would too (though the person is here a collective actor). The agency that "wrote the regulation" will often have direct insight into what that rule was intended to mean.

In still greater measure, the presumption that Congress intended *Auer* deference stems from the awareness that resolving genuine regulatory ambiguities often "entail[s] the exercise of judgment grounded in policy concerns." *Thomas Jefferson University v. Shalala*, 512 U.S. 504 (1994). … If you are a judge, you probably have no idea what [an agency's] rule means, or whether its policy is implicated when a previously approved moiety is connected to lysine through a non-ester covalent bond. And Congress, we have thought, knows just that: It is attuned to the comparative advantages of agencies over courts in making such policy judgments. Agencies (unlike courts) have "unique expertise," often of a scientific or technical nature, relevant to applying a regulation "to complex or changing circumstances." It is because of those features that Congress, when first enacting a statute, assigns rulemaking power to an agency and thus authorizes it to fill out the statutory scheme. And so too, when new issues demanding new policy calls come up within that scheme, Congress presumably wants the same agency, rather than any court, to take the laboring oar.

Finally, the presumption we use reflects the well-known benefits of uniformity in interpreting genuinely ambiguous rules. We have noted Congress's frequent "preference for resolving interpretive issues by uniform administrative decision, rather than piecemeal by litigation." *Ford Motor Credit Co. v. Milhollin*, 444 U.S. 555 (1980). That preference may be strongest when the interpretive issue arises in the context of a "complex and highly technical regulatory program." *Thomas Jefferson University*. After all, judges are most likely to come to divergent conclusions when they are least likely to know what they are doing. … *Auer* deference thus serves to ensure consistency in federal regulatory law, for everyone who needs to know what it requires.

But all that said, *Auer* deference is not the answer to every question of interpreting an agency's rules. Far from it. The possibility of deference can arise only if a regulation is genuinely ambiguous. And when we use that term, we mean it—genuinely ambiguous, even after a court has resorted to all the standard tools of interpretation. Still more, not all reasonable agency constructions of those truly ambiguous rules are entitled to deference. We presume that Congress intended for courts to defer to agencies when they interpret their own ambiguous rules. But when the reasons for that presumption do not apply, or countervailing reasons outweigh them, courts should not give deference to an agency's reading, except to the extent it has the "power to persuade."

The upshot of all this goes something as follows. When it applies, *Auer* deference gives an agency significant leeway to say what its own rules mean. In so doing, the doctrine enables the agency to fill out the regulatory scheme Congress has placed under its supervision. But that phrase "when it applies" is important—because it often doesn't. This Court has cabined *Auer's* scope in varied and critical ways—and in exactly that measure, has maintained a strong judicial role in interpreting rules. What emerges is a deference doctrine not quite so tame as some might hope, but not nearly so menacing as they might fear.

That brings us to the lone question presented here—whether we should abandon the longstanding doctrine just described. [The Court first rejected Kisor's arguments that *Auer* deference is inconsistent with various technical provisions of the Administrative Procedures Act.] To supplement his two APA arguments, Kisor turns to policy, leaning on a familiar claim about the incentives *Auer* creates. According to Kisor, *Auer* encourages agencies to issue vague and open-ended regulations, confident that they can later impose whatever interpretation of those rules they prefer. But the claim has notable weaknesses, empirical and theoretical alike. First, it does not survive an encounter with experience. No real evidence— indeed, scarcely an anecdote—backs up the assertion. And even the argument's theoretical allure dissipates upon reflection. For strong (almost surely stronger) incentives and pressures cut in the opposite direction. "[R]egulators want their regulations to be effective, and clarity promotes compliance." Brief for Administrative Law Scholars as Amici Curiae. Too, regulated parties often push for precision from an agency, so that they know what they can and cannot do. And ambiguities in rules pose risks to the long-run survival of agency policy. Vagueness increases the chance of adverse judicial rulings. And it enables future administrations, with different views, to reinterpret the rules to their own liking. Add all of that up and Kisor's ungrounded theory of incentives contributes nothing to the case against *Auer*.

Finally, Kisor goes big, asserting (though fleetingly) that *Auer* deference violates "separation-of-powers principles." In his view, those principles prohibit "vest[ing] in a single branch the law-making and law-interpreting functions." If that objection is to agencies' usurping the interpretive role of courts, this opinion has already met it head-on. Properly understood and applied, *Auer* does no such thing. Courts retain a firm grip on the interpretive function. If Kisor's objection is instead to the supposed commingling of functions (that is, the legislative and judicial) within an agency, this Court has answered it often before. That sort of mixing is endemic in agencies, and has been "since the beginning of the Republic." It does not violate the separation of powers, we have explained, because even when agency "activities take 'legislative' and 'judicial' forms," they continue to be "exercises of[ ] the 'executive Power'"—or otherwise said, ways of executing a statutory plan. *Id.* So Kisor's last argument to dispatch Auer deference fails as roundly as the rest.

If all that were not enough, stare decisis cuts strongly against Kisor's position. "Overruling precedent is never a small matter." *Kimble v. Marvel Entertainment,* 135 S.Ct. 2401 (2015). Adherence to precedent is "a foundation stone of the rule of law." *Michigan v. Bay Mills Indian* Community, 572 U.S. 782 (2014). And that is even more than usually so in the circumstances here. First, Kisor asks us to overrule not a single case, but a "long line of precedents"—each one reaffirming the rest and going back 75 years or more. Second, because that is so, abandoning *Auer* deference would cast doubt on many settled constructions of rules.

With that, we can finally return to Kisor's own case. Applying the principles outlined in this opinion, we hold that a redo is necessary for two reasons. First, the Federal Circuit jumped the gun in declaring the regulation ambiguous. We have insisted that a court bring all its interpretive tools to bear before finding that to be so. It is not enough to casually remark, as the court did here, that "[b]oth parties insist that the plain regulatory language supports their case, and neither party's position strikes us as unreasonable." Rather, the court must make a conscientious effort to determine, based on indicia like text, structure, history, and purpose, whether the regulation really has more than one reasonable meaning. The

Solicitor General argued in this Court that the Board's reading is the only reasonable one. Perhaps Kisor will make the converse claim below. Before even considering deference, the court must seriously think through those positions.

And second, the Federal Circuit assumed too fast that *Auer* deference should apply in the event of genuine ambiguity. That is not always true. A court must assess whether the interpretation is of the sort that Congress would want to receive deference. The Solicitor General suggested at oral argument that the answer in this case might be no. He explained that all 100 or so members of the VA Board act individually (rather than in panels) and that their roughly 80,000 annual decisions have no "precedential value." He thus questioned whether a Board member's ruling "reflects the considered judgment of the agency as a whole." The questions the Solicitor General raised are exactly the kind the court must consider in deciding whether to award Auer deference to the Board's interpretation.

We accordingly vacate the judgment below and remand the case for further proceedings. It is so ordered.

Standards of Review: Questions of Fact and Policy. An agency issuing rules must also make decisions as to facts and policy. Two tests predominate in the review of these types of decisions. The *arbitrary and capricious test* assumes the correctness of an agency's decision, placing the burden on any challenger to prove that the decision was not simply erroneous but so far off the mark as to be arbitrary and capricious. The *substantial evidence test* requires that an agency's decision be based not just on a scintilla of evidence, but on such relevant evidence as a reasonable mind might accept as adequate to support a conclusion.

The arbitrary and capricious test is usually used to judge any policy decision by an agency. Findings of fact made pursuant to formal rule making are judged by the substantial evidence test. Factual determinations made in informal rule making are gauged by the arbitrary and capricious test unless an agency's authorizing act calls for use of the substantial evidence test. Many courts have noted that there is little practical difference in how the two tests are usually applied. Both require court deference to agency decision making, though that deference is not unlimited.

Adjudication

Most major federal agencies also exercise substantial powers of adjudication. That is, they not only issue rules and investigate to uncover violations, they may also charge alleged violators and try them to determine whether a violation has actually occurred.

Because the agency is acting as legislator, police officer, prosecutor, *and* judge and jury, care must be taken to avoid abuse. For that reason, the APA and the courts demand that formal procedural requirements be followed. Although procedural due process under the Constitution applies to agency adjudications, these statutorily prescribed procedures typically provide more specific detail than the general procedural requirements of the Constitution. Over the years, procedures have evolved such that a person or company brought before an administrative agency for adjudication of a charged violation will usually have the right to notice, the right to counsel, the right to present evidence, and the right to confront and cross-examine adverse witnesses.

A jury trial is not allowed, but the case is heard by an administrative law judge (ALJ), who is the finder of fact in the first instance. Although the thousands of ALJs in the federal system are employees of the agencies whose cases they hear, they cannot be disciplined except for good cause as determined by the federal Merit System Protection Board. Thus, the ALJs exercise substantial autonomy and are seldom puppets of the agency employing them.

Under the APA, all ALJ decisions are reviewable by the employing agency. The agency reviews the record developed in the hearing that was conducted by the ALJ, and reviews the ALJ's fact-findings and legal conclusions. Although the agency usually conducts a limited appellate-type review of the ALJ's findings and conclusions, it does have the power to substitute its own findings and conclusions for those of the ALJ. If the agency does so, however, it still must base its decision on the evidence that appears in the ALJ-hearing record—it cannot disregard this record.

Adjudication is a very influential process. Not only are findings of fact required (for example, did the employer consult the union before deciding to move the plant?), but the ALJ and the agency must also interpret the applicable law (for example, is the employer required to consult the union before deciding to move the plant?). During the Reagan administration, the NLRB largely rewrote American labor policy through the process of adjudication. Although this was done piecemeal through several decisions involving unfair labor practice charges, the change in the law was as complete as if major rule making had been undertaken.

The quasi-judicial powers of major federal agencies are so significant that such decisions are normally reviewed directly by the circuit courts of appeal. Other types of decisions—such as the decision to issue a subpoena or to promulgate a new rule—are normally reviewed in the first instance by federal district courts. Figure 6.1 helps illustrate the adjudicatory process of a federal agency.

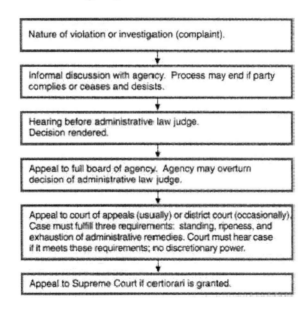

Figure 6.1 Administrative Law Process

Many different kinds of agency action obviously can have an effect on the liberty or property of individuals and companies. As we saw in the previous chapter, procedural due process requires that many of these actions be preceded by notice and a hearing of some type.

OTHER DEVELOPMENTS

To make federal agencies more open to public view and more responsive to the needs of constituents and to fiscal and economic concerns, many changes have been made over the years.

Freedom of Information Act

The Freedom of Information Act of 1967 (FOIA), with significant amendments in 1974, is codified as section 552 of the Administrative Procedure Act. Before its enactment it was extremely difficult for a private citizen to obtain and examine government-held documents. The agency from which the information was requested could deny the applicant on the grounds that he or she was not properly and directly concerned or that the requested information should not be disclosed because to do so would not be in the public interest. Under the FOIA, any person may reasonably describe what information is sought, and the burden of proof for withholding information is on the agency. A response is required of the agency within 10 working days after receipt of a request, and denial by the agency may be appealed by means of an expedited federal district court action. There are, of course, exemptions—nine specific areas to which the disclosure requirements do not apply. That is, if the information concerns certain matters, the agency is not required to comply with the request. The nine exemptions apply to matters that are:

1. Secret in the interest of national defense or foreign policy;
2. Related solely to internal personnel rules and practices of an agency;
3. Exempted from disclosure by statute;
4. Trade secrets and commercial or financial information obtained from a person and privileged or confidential;
5. Interagency or intra-agency memoranda or letters;
6. Personnel and medical files, the disclosure of which would constitute an invasion of personal privacy;
7. Certain investigatory records compiled for law enforcement purposes;
8. Related to the regulation or supervision of financial institutions;
9. Geologic and geophysical information and data, including maps concerning wells.

In general, these exemptions are interpreted narrowly. This can be worrisome for businesses, as well as political agencies, especially given the 800,000+ FOIA requests every year. To protect businesses under Exemption 4 (trade secrets, etc.), they are given an opportunity to object to a request for disclosure. Agencies are required to explain in writing if they choose to override such an objection. In 1974, a lower court required companies seeking to invoke Exemption 4 to establish that "substantial competitive harm would likely result" from disclosure. However, recently the Supreme Court created a more pro-business standard. In *Food Marketing Institute v. Argus Leader Media*, 139 S.Ct. 2356 (2019), the court held that companies need show only that they have treated the information as private and, possibly, that the government has assured them that the information will be kept confidential when submitted.

Privacy Act

The Federal Privacy Act of 1974 seeks to protect individuals from unnecessary disclosures of facts about them from files held by federal agencies. Although the need of federal agencies for information is recognized through a large series of exceptions and qualifications, the general thrust of the Privacy Act is to prohibit federal agencies from disclosing information from their files about an individual without that individual's written consent. Federal agencies are specifically forbidden from selling or renting an individual's name and address, unless authorized by another law.

Government in the Sunshine Act

A further effort to open up the government is provided by the 1976 Government in the Sunshine Act, codified as section 552b of the Administrative Procedure Act. The purpose of the Act is to assure that "every portion of every meeting of an agency shall be open to public observation." There are, however, exceptions to the open meeting requirement. If the meeting qualifies for one of ten specified exemptions and the agency by majority vote decides to do so, the meeting may be closed to the public. The exemptions of the Act are similar to the nine provided for in the FOIA but are not identical.

Most states have passed some form of open meetings laws. There is considerable diversity, but the common purpose is to permit the public to view the decision-making process at all stages.

Regulatory Flexibility Act

We are all presumed to know the law and when final versions of federal rules are published in the *Federal Register,* legally speaking, we are all put on notice of their existence. Congress realized, however, that as a practical matter many persons, especially small businesses, do not closely follow proposed and final rules printed in the *Federal Register*. Therefore, Congress passed the Regulatory Flexibility Act (RFA) in 1980. Among other provisions, the RFA requires most federal agencies to transmit to the Small Business Administration, on a semiannual basis, agendas briefly describing areas in which they may propose rules having a substantial impact on small entities (including small businesses, small governmental units, and nonprofit organizations). In this way the small businesses may be on the lookout for potential changes. Also, when any rule is promulgated that will have a significant economic impact on a substantial number of small entities, the agency proposing the rule must give notice not only through the *Federal Register* but also through publications of general notice likely to be obtained by small entities, such as trade journals.

The RFA initially provided little help to small business because it allowed agencies to avoid a cost-benefit analysis by certifying (with very little supporting data) that their regulation would not have a disparate impact on small entities. Congress then added the Small Business Regulatory Enforcement Fairness Act of 1996 (SBREFA), which contained a judicial review provision giving individuals or entities the power to sue federal agencies if they do not adequately take into account the disparate impact their proposed regulations will have on small businesses. In subsequent litigation, small businesses have often prevailed where there was a gross violation of federal rulemaking procedures by an agency, but have usually lost in cases where the agency made some effort to comply with the procedural requirements.

CHAPTER 7

CRIMINAL LAW AND BUSINESS

- Nature of Criminal Law
- Constitutional Protections
- General Elements of Criminal Responsibility
- General Criminal Defenses
- State Crimes Affecting Business
- Federal Crimes Affecting Business
- Computer Crime
- White Collar Crime

Businesses are the victims of crime. Businesses commit crimes. This sad reality necessitates a general overview of the role of criminal law in the legal environment of business. Armed robberies, bad checks, employee pilfering, computer hacking, and other criminal acts cost businesses billions of dollars annually. Consumers suffer as well, because these losses are manifested either in the form of higher prices or, worse, failed businesses. Plus, there are the costs to taxpayers of maintaining police forces, court systems, and prisons. The General Accountability Office recently noted that estimates of the annual costs of crime range from $690 billion to $3.41 trillion.

The strong interrelationship between criminal law and the vital interests of business is highlighted by frequent references to criminal acts in other chapters of this text. For example, there is discussion of contracts calling for criminal acts in Chapter 13, of trade secret theft in Chapter 9, of insider trading in Chapter 28, of illegal competitive acts in Chapter 29, and of criminal environmental violations in Chapter 31.

NATURE OF CRIMINAL LAW

A crime is a wrong committed against society. Indeed, that wrong is also defined by society, because the criminal law is one of a civilized society's primary tools for conforming the behavior of its citizens to societal norms. Even in a society with as many freedoms as America's, limits must be placed on individual and corporate actions. Today's drug epidemic is a vivid reminder of the damage that certain types of individual activity can inflict on society as a whole. Criminalizing activity is often far from the best way to address the causes of that activity or to solve the problems that arise from it. Nonetheless, criminal law is one of society's most important mechanisms for controlling individual behavior, and that will not change anytime soon.

Civil and Criminal Law Contrasted

Most of this text discusses civil law matters. While there are many similarities between criminal law and civil law, there are also important distinctions. The civil law adjusts rights between or among individuals. The basis of the controversy may be a broken commercial promise, an injury caused by someone's careless driving, or infringement of a patent or trademark. The focus is on adjusting the rights of the parties to the transaction. The criminal law, on the other hand, focuses on the individual's relationship to society. In enacting criminal statutes, a government is saying that there are certain activities so inherently contrary to the public good that they must be flatly prohibited in the *best interests of society.*

A civil lawsuit is brought by one individual or company (the plaintiff) against another (the defendant). A criminal action, on the other hand, is always brought by an agent of the government (the prosecutor or district attorney) against the alleged wrongdoer. The essence of the civil suit is an injury that the defendant's wrongful act caused to the individual plaintiff. The essence of a criminal prosecution is the injury that the defendant's wrongful act caused society. Of course, there are usually individual victims of criminal acts. The suffering of those victims is not ignored by the criminal law, but more emphasis is placed on the impact that such conduct has upon society at large.

A plaintiff in a civil suit usually requests money damages as compensation for injuries sustained by the defendant's wrongful conduct. In a criminal action, however, even a successful prosecution will not usually produce a dime for the plaintiff. Rather, the remedy sought by the prosecutor typically is punishment for the defendant, such as a fine (which usually goes to the state), imprisonment, or both. Of course, many types of acts (such as battery) constitute both criminal wrongs and actionable torts. As illustrated in Figure 7.1, the same activity might be the subject of both a civil suit by the victim and a criminal action by the state.

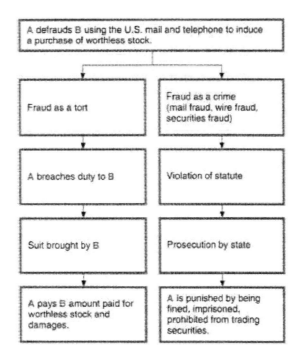

Figure 7.1 A Single Act as Both Tort and Crime

A critical difference between civil and criminal actions lies in the burden of proof. A plaintiff in a civil action must prove the elements of recovery by only "a preponderance of the evidence." Because the consequences of a criminal conviction are generally considered much more severe, a higher standard of proof must be met by prosecutors. Jurors must be convinced of the defendant's guilt "beyond a reasonable doubt" before the guilty verdict is appropriate. Figure 7.2 outlines major differences between civil and criminal law.

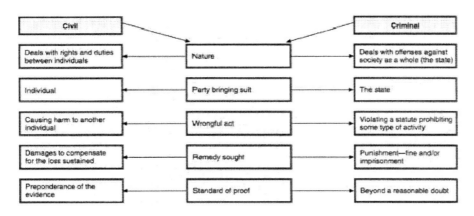

Figure 7.2 Major Differences Between Civil and Criminal Law

Classification of Crimes

Degree of Seriousness

Except for the most serious crime of treason, crimes are either *felonies* or *misdemeanors*, depending on the severity of the penalty that the statute provides. The definition of felony varies from state to state, but it is usually defined as any crime in which the punishment is either death or imprisonment for more than one year in a state penitentiary, as in the cases of murder, robbery, or rape. *Misdemeanors* are all crimes carrying lesser penalties (such as fines or confinement in county jails)—for example, petit larceny and disorderly conduct. In the federal system, felonies are crimes for which the designated penalty is more than one year in prison; misdemeanors are crimes with lesser designated penalties. Yet another category used in some states is *petty offenses,* covering such infractions as traffic and building code violations.

The distinction between felonies and misdemeanors can be important because of various penalties often imposed on persons convicted of the former, such as loss of the right to vote, to hold public office, or to pursue various careers.

Degree of Moral Turpitude

Crimes such as murder, rape, arson, or robbery are evil in and of themselves. Such acts are called *malum in se*, meaning that they are criminal because they are inherently wicked. Other acts, such as jaywalking or speeding, are *malum prohibitum*, meaning that they are crimes merely because the legislature has said that they are wrongful. Typically, greater punishments attach to crimes that involve moral turpitude.

Jurisdiction

As has already been noted, in America a federal criminal justice system is superimposed over state and local systems. These systems generally address different concerns. Murder is usually a concern only of the state in which it occurred unless, for example, it occurred on federal property, the victim was a federal official, or it occurred as part of an interstate kidnapping. Still, there are several areas of overlap and actions that might well violate both federal and state laws. For example, during the wave of bank robberies during the 1930s Depression, a federal law against bank robberies was passed so that the Federal Bureau of Investigation and federal prosecutors could supplement the efforts of state police and judicial systems. In recent years, Congress has often enacted criminal laws that intruded into areas traditionally relegated to the states.

Purpose of Punishment

Perhaps the most salient feature of the criminal justice system is the punishment that it imposes on wrongdoers. As noted earlier, the punishment is not imposed to compensate the victim. That is the province of the civil tort system. Rather, there are four primary purposes of criminal punishment. First, there is *rehabilitation* or reformation. Although published rates of recidivism (relapse into crime) indicate that this is the most difficult of the punishment goals to attain, it is important that our system at least attempt to reform wrongdoers.

A second, less ambitious, purpose of punishment is simply *restraint* or incapacitation, on the theory that a robber cannot rob and a rapist cannot rape while they are locked up. A third purpose of punishment, and a somewhat controversial one, is that of *retribution*. The concept of retribution predates the Bible's admonition of "an eye for an eye," and society's infliction of retribution on criminals still has strong popular support.

A final purpose of punishment is *deterrence*. The law seeks to persuade the wrongdoer being punished not to err again and, at the same time, to provide an example that might generally deter other potential lawbreakers. The effectiveness of various types of criminal sanctions in deterring crime is not clear. One very controversial subject is the death penalty. Although the evidence regarding whether a state will reduce its murder rate by adopting the death penalty is mixed, advocates justify the ultimate punishment on restraint and retribution grounds.

CONSTITUTIONAL PROTECTIONS

Once arrested, criminal defendants have the considerable power and resources of the government lined up against them. The potential for abuse of that power is considerable, and one need not be a student of history to discover blatant examples of such abuses. Because our system operates on the theory that it is better that a guilty man or woman go free than that an innocent man or woman should suffer unjust punishment, we provide manifold protections for criminal defendants. Many of these protections are set forth in the Bill of Rights. Through the controversial process of "incorporation," most of these rights have been applied to the states as well. Additionally, many state constitutions contain parallel protections. The following discussion will help complete the examination of constitutional law begun in Chapter 5.

Fourth Amendment

The Fourth Amendment protects people (and, as we saw in Chapter 6, businesses) against "unreasonable searches and seizures," requiring that search warrants generally not be issued absent "probable cause." A search warrant will be issued by a judge if the police have produced evidence that would lead a reasonably prudent person to believe there is a substantial likelihood that the defendant is guilty of the offense the police charge. The Fourth Amendment requires that the warrant "particularly describe" the place to be searched and the persons or things to be seized. A controversial question regards enforcement of this prohibition. What happens to evidence that the police seize without a valid warrant? In *Mapp v. Ohio,* 367 U.S. 643 (1961), the Supreme Court held that "all evidence obtained by searches and seizures in violation of the Constitution is . . . inadmissible in a state court." This holding was very controversial, opponents arguing that "the crook should not go free just because the constable has erred." In recent years, the increasingly conservative Supreme Court has fashioned a number of exceptions to this "exclusionary rule," weakening its impact substantially. For example, in *United States v. Leon,* 468 U.S. 189 (1984), the Court created a "good faith" exception for situations in which the police searched pursuant to an apparently valid search warrant that was later determined to have been improperly issued. The Court reasoned, in part, that the exclusionary rule was meant to deter police abuses rather than to correct errors by judges.

In 2018 in *Carpenter v. U.S.,* 138 S.Ct. 2206 (2018), the Court held that a warrant is required for police to access cell site location information from a suspect's cell phone company. The Court noted that for many Americans cell phones hold "the privacies of life" and citizens do not give up their expectation of privacy just because they know their companies will have this data.

Fifth Amendment

The Fifth Amendment contains a number of provisions that protect criminal defendants from government abuse. For example, individuals cannot be held to answer for major federal criminal charges unless they have been indicted by a *grand jury*. A grand jury typically consists of 23 members of the community who hear evidence presented by the prosecution. If a majority concludes that there is probable cause to believe that the defendant has committed a crime alleged, the grand jury issues a true bill. The right to indictment by grand jury is one of the few protections in the Bill of Rights that the Supreme Court has not applied to the states. However, many state constitutions have similar provisions.

The Fifth Amendment also protects defendants from *double jeopardy,* which is being tried twice for the same offense. This means that when a jury finds a defendant "not guilty," the government cannot simply re-indict the defendant for the same crime and try again to convict. However, it does not mean that defendants acquitted of criminal assault and battery could not be sued civilly by their alleged victim. Because of the different burden of proof, the same body of evidence that did not convince a criminal jury beyond a reasonable doubt might convince a civil jury applying a preponderance of evidence standard. Thus, O.J. Simpson was acquitted of criminal charges, but later successfully sued by relatives of the murder victims. The fact that a state prosecution will not bar a subsequent federal prosecution and vice versa constitutes another major exception to the double jeopardy prohibition.

The Fifth Amendment mandates that no person be deprived of life, liberty, or property without *due process* of law. We know quite a bit about due process from previous chapters. One aspect of due process, for example, is that no one should be convicted of violating a statute that is unduly vague, so that well-intentioned people could not conform their conduct to comply with the law. In *Kolender v. Lawson*, 461 U.S. 352 (1981), for example, a California criminal statute requiring persons on the street to provide "credible and reliable" identification and to account for their presence when requested to do so by a police officer was held to be unduly vague.

As another example, it would be a due process violation for a prosecutor intentionally to suppress material evidence favorable to the accused. *Brady v. Maryland,* 373 U.S. 83 (1963). But the Supreme Court held that the government's accidental destruction of evidence that might have supported the defendant's innocence did not violate due process. Nor was due process violated by the government's innocent failure to use the most modern, sophisticated scientific methods of examining evidence. *Arizona v. Youngblood,* 488 U.S. 51 (1988).

The most controversial part of the Fifth Amendment, as interpreted by the Supreme Court, is its protection against self-incrimination. No person "shall be compelled in any criminal case to be a witness against himself." This can include matters of document production as well as of oral testimony. The right is not available to corporations and is individual to the person charged. In a case of interest to all businesspersons, *United States v. Doe*, 465 U.S. 605 (1984), the court held that the sole owner of a corporation could not claim the privilege against self-incrimination to avoid producing records that belong to *the corporation*. Had the business been a sole proprietorship, the owner could have claimed the privilege because the records would have been the owner's, not a separate entity's.

The most famous self-incrimination case is *Miranda v. Arizona*, 384 U.S. 436 (1966), which excluded from evidence any incriminating statements made by a defendant (and evidence to which those statements led police, called "fruit of the poisonous tree") who had not been fully warned of his constitutional right against self-incrimination (and his right to counsel). Thus, the famous "Miranda warning" was born.

The Supreme Court has riddled *Miranda* with exceptions over the years. Although it has noted that "*Miranda* has become embedded in routine police practice to the point where the warnings have become part of our national culture," the Court in *Berghuis v. Thompkins*, 560 U.S. 370 (2010), held that a criminal suspect who was aware of his rights but chose not to "unambiguously" invoke them did in fact waive those rights so that his subsequent voluntary statements were admissible.

Technological advances have raised questions such as: If the police forced you to use your thumbprint to open your cell phone, would that be self-incrimination?

Sixth Amendment

The Sixth Amendment contains a litany of constitutional protections for criminal defendants, including the important right to counsel that was mentioned in the previous discussion of the *Miranda* case. Generally speaking, all individuals facing potential incarceration have the right to consult an attorney and to have one provided if they cannot afford one. The right to counsel is made more meaningful by defendants' Sixth Amendment rights to be informed of the nature of the accusation, to confront witnesses against them, and to call witnesses on their own behalf.

There is also the right to a "speedy and public trial." Court backlogs have threatened to make a mockery of the right to a "speedy" trial, but the federal government and most states have now passed "speedy trial" acts that place time limits on the government and give criminal cases priority over civil cases on crowded court dockets.

Importantly, there is also a right to trial by an impartial jury that applies in cases involving "serious" criminal charges. Juries, serving as the "conscience of the community," are a critical safeguard against the heavy hand of the government.

Eighth Amendment

The Eighth Amendment contains important protections for criminal defendants. It states that "excessive bail" shall not be required. Thus, when a judge sets bail before trial, the aim should be not to punish the defendant who is presumed innocent, but simply to guarantee the defendant's appearance at trial. In recent years, Congress has increased the courts' authority to deny bail in situations in which defendants pose special harm to the public.

The Eighth Amendment also bans "excessive fines" and "cruel and unusual punishment." The Supreme Court has held that the Eight Amendment bars the death penalty for minors and the mentally retarded, but not for the mentally ill.

GENERAL ELEMENTS OF CRIMINAL RESPONSIBILITY

As a general rule, the prosecutor in a criminal case must do three things to obtain a valid conviction: (1) show that the defendant's actions violated an existing criminal statute, (2) prove beyond a reasonable doubt that the defendant did do the acts alleged, and (3) prove that the defendant had the requisite intent to violate the law. The first element is important because although many of our crimes have strong common-law roots, today almost all crimes are statutory in nature. The other two elements of act and intent deserve separate consideration.

Guilty Act

A basic element of a criminal conviction is the *actus reus*, a Latin term meaning "guilty act." This is a critical part of a criminal conviction because our legal system generally does not punish persons for their thoughts. Evil thoughts alone normally do not injure society and therefore do not justify bringing to bear the full power of the government's criminal justice system. This does not mean that a defendant must always successfully complete a criminal act to be guilty. Generally, any act that clearly is a step in the commission of a crime will be sufficient for a conviction for *attempted* larceny, murder, and so on, if the intent requirement is also present.

The guilty act must be voluntary and generally must be an act of commission rather than mere omission. However, there are exceptions. Failure to perform a legally imposed duty will constitute a sufficient *actus reus*. An example is failure to fulfill the legally required duty to file an income tax return.

Guilty Mind

Generally, defendants are not guilty unless their guilty act is coupled with a guilty mind, that is, unless the defendants had *mens rea*, an intent to do wrong. A murder conviction, for example, requires the act of killing the victim plus the evil intent to take a life.

Because a person's actual intent can rarely be known with absolute certainty, juries may often presume a criminal intent on the part of the defendant based on the established facts. Thus, a jury may presume that an armed prowler apprehended at night entered the house "with the intention of committing a felony," one of the usual statutory elements of the crime of burglary. Intent is often a difficult element to prove beyond a reasonable doubt, but as Justice Oliver Wendell Holmes once stated, "even a dog distinguishes between being stumbled over and being kicked."

Many crimes are called *specific intent* crimes, in that conviction is appropriate only if the defendant had the intent to commit the exact forbidden act charged. For other crimes, *general intent* will suffice, meaning that the defendant had the general intent to commit a wrongful act even though he or she did not intend to bring about the specific result. First degree murder is typically a specific intent crime; to be guilty the defendant must have intended to take a human life. However, if a defendant became very drunk and went on a rampage, killing a man with a gun, he may be found guilty of second-degree murder even though he was so drunk he did not know he had a gun. This is an example of general intent.

There are a few crimes for which negligence will suffice and no intent need be proven. Negligent vehicular homicide is an example. There are even some *strict liability* crimes, in which defendants can be found guilty absent intent or even careless behavior. These are typically misdemeanors. Examples include selling liquor to minors, violating traffic rules, and violating pure food and drug laws.

GENERAL CRIMINAL DEFENSES

Defenses Negating Intent

Many defenses raised in a criminal case are aimed at negating the *mens rea* element by showing that the defendant did not intend to commit a crime. Several such defenses exist. We will learn in the chapter on voidable contracts that many of these concepts also provide grounds for escaping contractual obligations.

Insanity

There are several approaches, none satisfactory, to handling defendants who "plead insanity." Some states use the *M'Naghten* test, which excuses defendants whose mental defects renders them incapable of appreciating the difference between right and wrong. Others excuse defendants who may appreciate the difference between right and wrong but who suffer a mental defect causing an "irresistible impulse" to commit the crime. The District of Columbia courts developed the *Durham* rule, which simply asks whether the defendant was insane at the time of the crime and, if so, whether the crime was a product of that insanity. Finally, the Model Penal Code provides that a defendant "is not responsible for criminal conduct if at the time of such conduct as a result of a mental disease or defect he lacks substantial capacity either to appreciate the wrongfulness of his conduct or to conform his conduct to the requirements of the law." In whatever form, the insanity defense seldom succeeds.

Intoxication

If a person *voluntarily* becomes intoxicated (or "high" on drugs), the general rule is that this may negate specific intent but will not negate general intent, as discussed above. Voluntary intoxication is generally no defense to crimes requiring mere negligence or recklessness.

Involuntary intoxication, however, is generally treated as equivalent to insanity. Thus, if a defendant unforeseeably became intoxicated because of an unusual reaction to prescribed medication, courts would be reluctant to hold that person responsible for crimes committed under the influence of that medication.

Mistake

Because ignorance of the law is no excuse, a *mistake of law* is generally no defense to a criminal charge. Thus, a defendant who has intentionally performed a specific act cannot usually defend by saying: "I didn't know that it was illegal," or even "My attorney told me that it was okay." The courts' refusal to hold an attorney's advice to be a valid defense discourages "attorney shopping." However, many courts will find that a mistake of law negates the intent element if (1) the law was not reasonably made known to the public, or (2) the defendant reasonably relied on an erroneous but official statement of the law (such as in a judicial opinion or administrative order).

A defense based on *mistake of fact* is more likely to succeed. Thus, a defendant charged with stealing a blue 12-speed bicycle might successfully defend by showing that he owned an identical blue 12-speed bicycle parked at the next rack and mistakenly rode off on the wrong one.

Other Defenses

Entrapment

Police undercover work is often aimed at catching criminals "in the act." If the police not only create an opportunity for a criminal act but also persuade the defendants to commit a crime that they would not otherwise have committed, the defendants may have a good *entrapment* defense. The entrapment defense presents difficult factual questions, for the court must draw the line between an unwary innocent and an unwary criminal. The key issue is whether the defendant was *predisposed* to commit the crime. That is, the criminal idea must originate with the defendant, not with the police officer. The Supreme Court has held that entrapment results "[w]hen the criminal design originates with the [police who] implant in the mind of an innocent person the disposition to commit the alleged offense and induce its commission in order that they may prosecute." *Sorrells v. United States,* 287 U.S. 435 (1932). The entrapment defense seldom succeeds, but occasionally it does.

Self-Defense

Self-defense and defense of others may justify acts of violence that otherwise would be criminal. Although the courts do not require "detached reflection in the presence of an uplifted knife," *Brown v. United States,* 256 U.S. 335 (1921), the general rule permits only that degree of force reasonable under the circumstances. Deadly force can be used if the defendant has a reasonable belief that imminent death or grievous bodily injury will otherwise result. The law does not allow one to shoot an assailant in the back once that assailant is clearly fleeing and poses no further threat. In some cases, retreat might even be required as preferable to deadly force. Non-deadly force can be used in the degree reasonably believed necessary to protect persons or property from criminal acts, although obviously, a lesser degree of force will be viewed as "reasonable" in defense of property.

Immunity

Through the process of *plea bargaining,* defendants often agree to testify against other criminals in return for consideration at time of sentencing and perhaps *immunity* from prosecution of certain potential charges. It is often said that such persons are "turning state's evidence" to help the prosecutor's case.

STATE CRIMES AFFECTING BUSINESS

So many crimes against persons and property are contained in state criminal codes that it would be impossible to list them all. Furthermore, there is such variation from state to state that it is difficult to generalize about criminal law. Nonetheless, this section briefly describes a few of the more common crimes against businesses.

Theft

Many state statutes criminalize the unlawful taking of another's property under a general statute that often terms the crime "theft." Such statutes consolidate a variety of related crimes that developed separately at the common law, such as larceny, burglary, false pretenses, and embezzlement.

Larceny

At common law, *larceny* was the trespassory taking away of the personal property of another with wrongful intent permanently to deprive that person of the use of the property. Larceny is viewed as an injury to the owner's interest in possessing the goods. Shoplifting is a good example. Promising to sell someone your car, taking the money, and then refusing to turn over the car is not larceny, because there is no wrongful taking. The concept of personal property generally does not include trees or personal services but would include computer programs and trade secrets.

Burglary

At common law, *burglary* was the trespassory breaking and entering of the dwelling house of another during the nighttime with intent to commit a felony. Over time, many of the technical requirements have been dropped. Now, most statutes would find burglary even though the building broken into was not a dwelling house and even though it occurred during the day. Burglary with use of a weapon is called aggravated burglary.

False Pretenses

Obtaining goods by *false pretenses* was defined by the common law as obtaining title to someone else's property by knowingly or recklessly making a false representation of existing material fact that is intended to and does defraud victims into parting with their property. Technically, false pretenses is an injury to title, not mere possession. Title passes to the thief, quite unlike larceny. Examples of such conduct are the filing of false claims with insurance companies and the taking of buyers' money for goods or services with no intent of delivering such goods or services.

Embezzlement

A wholly statutory offense, *embezzlement* is the fraudulent conversion of the property of another by one who has lawful possession of it. This crime somewhat overlaps with larceny, but the original possession by the wrongdoer is lawful. An example is an attorney who receives funds from a client for payment of a settlement but later decides to spend the money on herself or himself instead.

Specialized Statutes

The common-law classifications and general theft statutes have been supplemented by a variety of more specific laws aimed at the same types of conduct. Most states have separate statutes relating to a number of special offenses, such as the setting back of automobile odometers with the intent to defraud and the knowing delivery of "short weights"—the charging of buyers for quantities of goods that are greater than the quantities that were actually delivered.

Robbery

Robbery is stealing from people or in their presence by use of force or threat of force. It is, essentially, a form of larceny but the extra element of force makes it a more serious offense. Removing someone's earring by stealth would be larceny; ripping it from the victim's earlobe would be robbery. Use of a weapon escalates the crime to aggravated robbery.

Forgery

Forgery is the false making or altering of a legally significant instrument (such as a check, credit card, deed, passport, mortgage, or security) with the intent to defraud. Writing an *insufficient funds check* is not forgery, although it may constitute false pretenses or violate a state bad check law. But changing the true payee's name as written on a check to your own and cashing the check is certainly forgery.

Forgery is a crime with roots deep in the common law, but changing technologies can challenge traditional rules, as the following case illustrates.

PEOPLE v. AVILA
Colorado Court of Appeals, 770 P.2d 1330 (1988)

For fees of between $1500 and $3000, Avila, a lawyer, altered the driver records of two of his clients whose driver's licenses were under revocation for alcohol-related offenses. Avila would instruct his contact in the Motor Vehicle Division (MVD) Office, who had access to the data base where the driving records were maintained on computer disk, to delete the clients' records. The client would later apply for a driver's license, stating that he had no previous driver's license, which the altered computer records would verify. Avila was convicted of two counts of second-degree forgery. He appealed.

Van Cise, Judge:

Initially, we note that much of Avila's argument relies on the assertion that forgery cannot be committed on a computer. We reject that contention.

A forgery can be made by any number of artificial means. Indeed, "whether [the forgery] is made with the pen, with a brush[,] . . . with any other instrument, or by any other device whatever; whether it is in characters which stand for words or in characters which stand for ideas . . . is quite immaterial . . ." *Benson v. McMahon*, 127 U.S. 457 (1888).

Avila also contends, in essence, that there was insufficient evidence to sustain his convictions. We disagree. The elements of second degree forgery pertinent to this case are that (1) the defendant, (2) with intent to defraud, (3) falsely alters, (4) a written instrument, (5) which is or purported to be, or which is calculated to become or to represent if completed, a "written instrument officially issued or created by a public office, public servant, or government agency." Section 18-5-103(1)(c).

Avila contends that there was no written instrument in this case so the forgery conviction cannot stand. We disagree. Section 18-5-101(9) defines "written instrument" as follows:

> "Written instrument" means any paper, document, or other instrument containing written or printed matter or the equivalent thereof, used for purposes of reciting, embodying, conveying, or recording information . . . which is capable of being used to the advantage or disadvantage of some person.

A fair reading of the statute indicates that a computer disc is included in the definition of a "written instrument."

Next, Avila contends that, since the driving records were deleted, the evidence at trial does not support the finding that he falsely altered a written instrument. He argues that "alter" means to change, while "delete" means to cause to vanish completely. Therefore, he claims he committed no forgery. We are not persuaded. Section 18-5-101(2) states:

> To "falsely alter" a written instrument means to change a written instrument without the authority of anyone entitled to grant such authority, whether it be in complete or incomplete form, by means of erasure, obliteration, deletion, insertion of new matter, transposition of matter, or any other means, so that such instrument in its thus altered form falsely appears or purports to be in all respects an authentic creation of or fully authorized by its ostensible maker.

The record shows that the driving records of two of Avila's clients were deleted so that instead of containing their history of driving violations, the computer found no driving records and thus would display the message "no record found." Under the plain language of the statute, Avila's actions constituted a false alteration within the meaning of 18-5-101(2).

Next, Avila asserts that there is a distinction between a document falsely made and a genuine document that contains false information. Based on this distinction, he contends that the written instruments were not false but rather were genuine MVD documents which contained false information and, as such, they cannot form the basis for a forgery conviction. We disagree. In *DeRose v. People,* 64 Colo. 332, 171 P. 359 (1918), the court held that a false statement of fact in an instrument which is genuine is not forgery. It stated: "This writing is what it purports to be—a true and genuine instrument, although it contains false statements. It is not a false paper, and the execution of such a document does not constitute forgery."

In *DeRose,* defendant was a railroad foreman whose job was to draft and submit the time rolls for his men. He was charged with forgery because he credited one of his men with more days than the man had worked. Because the defendant was authorized to draft and submit the time roll, the court found that the document was not "falsely made." It was a genuine railroad time roll prepared by one authorized to do so, but which contained false information. In *DeRose* the defendant had the authority to perform the general act that led to the production of the document containing the false information. In contrast, in the instant case, testimony showed that Avila's confederate at the MVD had no authority to delete driver histories. Therefore, under *DeRose,* the documents were forged. [Affirmed.]

Arson

At common law, *arson* was the malicious burning of the dwelling house of another. Today, the building burned need not be a dwelling house. And as all too commonly occurs, people who burn their own house (or other building or personal property) for purposes of defrauding an insurance company are almost certainly violating a state criminal statute prohibiting such fraud.

FEDERAL CRIMES AFFECTING BUSINESS

As with state crimes, there are so many federal criminal statutes that it would be impossible to list them all. Many have been passed in response to perceived crises. In the era of the giant trusts in the late 1800s, Congress passed many antitrust laws, including some carrying criminal penalties (discussed in Chapter 29). In the wake of the Watergate scandal in the early 1970s, investigation disclosed widespread bribery of foreign officials by U.S. companies, leading to enactment of the Foreign Corrupt Practices Act (discussed in Chapter 32). After the Enron scandal, Congress made wholesale changes in the criminal penalties for securities law violations. Rather than list all such federal criminal statutes, we will briefly address a few of the more general ones.

Mail and Wire Fraud

Two very general federal statutes punish *mail fraud* (use of the mails to defraud or swindle) and *wire fraud* (similar use of telephone, telegraph, radio, or television). The typical mail or wire fraud case would involve use of the mails or telephones to make false representations to sell products or securities. For example, the mail fraud law has been used to punish fraudulent representations in the use of the mails to advertise such articles as hair-growing products that proved to be worthless, retrofit carburetors that totally failed to improve automobile fuel economy, and false identification cards that the sellers knew were ordered by purchasers for the purpose of deceiving third parties. Similarly, schemes for the operation of "mail-order" schools, where degrees or diplomas are awarded "without requiring evidence of education or experience entitled thereto," and where the operators know such documents are likely to be used by purchasers to misrepresent their qualifications to prospective employers, violate these sections of the law. However, the statutes have been construed to cover a wide variety of factual situations, including insider trading

In the following case the Supreme Court dealt with a difficult mail fraud issue.

SCHMUCK v. UNITED STATES
U.S. Supreme Court, 489 U.S. 705 (1989)

Petitioner Schmuck, a used-car distributor, purchased used cars, rolled back their odometers, and then sold the automobiles to Wisconsin retail dealers for prices artificially inflated because of the low mileage readings. These unwitting car dealers, relying on the altered odometer figures, then resold the cars to customers, who in turn paid prices reflecting Schmuck's fraud. To complete the resale of each car, the dealer who bought it from Schmuck would submit a title-application form to the Wisconsin Department of Transportation on behalf of the retail customer. The receipt of a Wisconsin title was a legal prerequisite for transferring title and obtaining car tags.

Schmuck was convicted on 12 counts of mail fraud. He appealed, alleging that the mailings that were the crux of the indictment—the submissions of the title-application forms by the auto dealers—were not in furtherance of the fraudulent scheme and, thus, did not satisfy the mailing element of the crime of mail fraud. The circuit court rejected Schmuck's claim but reversed on other grounds. The Supreme Court granted certiorari to resolve both issues. (The following excerpt addresses only the mail fraud issue.)

Blackmun, Justice:
"The federal mail fraud statute does not purport to reach all frauds, but only those limited instances in which the use of the mails is a part of the execution of the fraud, leaving all other cases to be dealt with by appropriate state law." *Kann v. United States,* 323 U.S. 88, 95 (1944). To be part of the execution of the fraud, however, the use of the mails need not be an essential element of the scheme. *Pereira v. United States,* 347 U.S. 1, 8 (1954). It

is sufficient for the mailing to be "incident to an essential part of the scheme," or "a step in [the] plot." *Badders v. United States,* 240 U.S. 391, 394 (1916).

Schmuck argues that mail fraud can be predicated only on a mailing that affirmatively assists the perpetrator in carrying out his fraudulent scheme. The mailing element of the offense, he contends, cannot be satisfied by a mailing, such as those at issue here, that is routine and innocent in and of itself, and that, far from furthering the execution of the fraud, occurs after the fraud has come to fruition, is merely tangentially related to the fraud, and is counterproductive in that it creates a "paper trail" from which the fraud may be discovered. We disagree both with this characterization of the mailings in the present case and with this description of the applicable law.

We begin by considering the scope of Schmuck's fraudulent scheme. Schmuck was charged with devising and executing a scheme to defraud Wisconsin retail automobile customers who based their decisions to purchase certain automobiles at least in part on the low-mileage readings provided by the tampered odometers. This was a fairly large-scale operation. Evidence at trial indicated that Schmuck had employed a man known only as "Fred" to turn back the odometers on about 150 different cars. Schmuck then marketed these cars to a number of dealers, several of whom he dealt with on a consistent basis over a period of about 15 years. Thus, Schmuck's was not a "one-shot" operation in which he sold a single car to an isolated dealer. His was an ongoing fraudulent venture. A rational jury could have concluded that the success of Schmuck's venture depended upon his continued harmonious relations with and good reputation among retail dealers, which in turn required the smooth flow of cars from the dealers to their Wisconsin customers.

Under these circumstances, we believe that a rational jury could have found that the title-registration mailings were part of the execution of the fraudulent scheme, a scheme which did not reach fruition until the retail dealers resold the cars and effected transfers of title. Schmuck's scheme would have come to an abrupt halt if the dealers either had lost faith in Schmuck or had not been able to resell the cars obtained from him. These resales and Schmuck's relationships with the retail dealers naturally depended on the successful passage of title among the various parties. Thus, although the registration-form mailings may not have contributed directly to the duping of either the retail dealers or the customers, they were necessary to the passage of title, which in turn was essential to the perpetuation of Schmuck's scheme. As noted earlier, a mailing that is "incident to an essential part of the scheme," *Pereira*, 347 U.S., at 8, satisfies the mailing element of the mail fraud offense. The mailings here fit this description. See, e.g., *United States v. Locklear,* 829 F.2d 1314, 1318-1319 (CA4 1987) (retail customers obtaining title documents through the mail furthers execution of wholesaler's odometer tampering scheme).

We also reject Schmuck's contention that mailings that someday may contribute to the uncovering of a fraudulent scheme cannot supply the mailing element of the mail fraud offense. The relevant question at all times is whether the mailing is part of the execution of the scheme as conceived by the perpetrator at the time, regardless of whether the mailing later, through hindsight, may prove to have been counterproductive and return to haunt the perpetrator of the fraud. The mail fraud statute includes no guarantee that the use of the mails for the purpose of executing a fraudulent scheme will be risk free. Those who use the mails to defraud proceed at their peril.

For these reasons, we agree with the Court of Appeals that the mailings in this case satisfy the mailing element of the mail fraud offenses.

Travel Act

Section 1952 of Title 18 of the *United States Code* is called the Travel Act. It punishes anyone who travels in interstate or foreign commerce or uses any facility in such commerce to (1) distribute the proceeds of illegal activity, (2) commit any crime of violence or further any unlawful activity, or (3) promote, manage, establish, carry on, or facilitate any unlawful activity. Obviously, this is a very broad act that federalizes all sorts of traditionally state crimes. The "interstate commerce" element can be met by simply mailing a letter or using a telephone, for these are instrumentalities of interstate commerce. The Act has been used, for example, to convict a city electrical inspector who took bribes from private electrical contractors to overlook code violations and to facilitate departmental paperwork even though all the letters mailed by the defendant stayed in one state. The mail is a facility of interstate commerce because it can be used to send letters from state to state. A merchandising executive for apparel retailer Aeropostale, Inc. who gave business to a t-shirt supplier in exchange for bribes was convicted under the Travel Act, as well as the mail and wire fraud statutes. *U.S. v. Finazzo*, 850 F.3d 94 (2d Cir. 2017).

Hobbs Act

The Hobbs Act, 18 U.S.C. Sec. 951, punishes anyone who "in any way or degree obstructs, delays, or affects commerce or the movement of any article or commodity in commerce, by robbery or extortion . . ." This law punishes extortion (obtaining money or something else of value by use of violence or threat of violence) but not merely accepting bribes. The distinction between the two can be difficult to draw but has been characterized as the difference between "pay me and be assisted" (commercial bribery) and "pay me or be precluded" (extortion).

As an indication of how broad this statute is, in *Taylor v. U.S.,* 136 S.Ct. 2074 (2016), the Supreme Court held that because Congress had authority to regulate the national market for marijuana, including intrastate activities that had an aggregate effect on interstate commerce, it could also, through the Hobbs Act, punish a defendant who robbed a drug dealer of drugs or drug proceeds because "[b]y targeting a drug dealer in this way, a robber necessarily affects or attempts to affect commerce over which the United States has jurisdiction."

Racketeer Influenced and Corrupt Organizations Act

In 1970 Congress passed the Racketeer Influenced and Corrupt Organizations Act (RICO) to attack organized crime, especially its infiltration into legitimate business. RICO is an unusual criminal statute in that it expressly contains parallel civil provisions. In other words, it provides for both criminal penalties and private civil suits for damages. However, RICO neither included a definition of "organized crime" nor expressly required a link between a defendant's activities and organized crime. Therefore, about nine-tenths of the civil suits and many of the criminal prosecutions brought under RICO have had no connection with professional criminals (as thought of in the common sense) but have, instead, named as defendants accounting firms, banks, law firms, manufacturing corporations, anti-abortion protestors, and a wide variety of others.

Fortunately, most of the criminal prosecutions brought under RICO have attacked the more traditional manifestations of organized crime. Prosecutors have secured RICO criminal convictions in cases involving marijuana smuggling, kickbacks to judges, extortion of "protection money" by police officers, loan sharking, gambling, and the like. However, even in criminal prosecutions the government has occasionally pushed RICO to its limits by prosecuting actions in circumstances it is difficult to believe Congress had in mind when passing RICO.

False Claims Act

Also known as "The Lincoln Law," the False Claims Act (FCA) (31 U.S.C. §3729) was enacted during the Civil War to punish contractors who defrauded the federal government when selling supplies for the war. The basic elements of an FCA offense are: (a) D made a claim or statement in order to induce the government to pay money; (b) the claim was "material"; (c) the claim was false; and (d) defendant knew that the claim or statement was false.

Common examples of FCA violations include a government contractor that makes a claim for payment for goods it did not deliver, or certifies that goods it delivered met government standards when they did not, or claims that it meets federal eligibility requirements for a grant or payment when it does not. Criminal penalties under the FCA include up to five years in jail and a fine for each offense.

Importantly, the FCA also has a civil side whereby the government, sometimes through whistleblowers called "relators," who bring the government's attention to a fraud. This is done secretly so the government can decide whether or not it wishes to bring a lawsuit. If it does, the relator may be rewarded 15-25% of the recovery should the government succeed. If it does not, the relators may pursue the lawsuit in their own names and be rewarded 25-30% of the recovery if successful. This is called the *qui tam* provision. Between 1986 and 2019, the government recovered $44 billion under the FCA; 80% of the recoveries were initiated by whistleblowers.

The following case is a civil FCA action. Its principle holding would apply equally in a criminal action.

UNIVERSAL HEALTH SERVS. v. U.S. ex rel. ESCOBAR
U.S. Supreme Court, 136 S. Ct. 1989 (2016)

Yarushka, a teenager, suffered from bipolar disorder. Her parents sent her to one of defendant UHS's facilities where she was given a medication that worsened her condition and then caused seizures that killed her. Her parents, the plaintiffs, learned that in violation of federal requirements, few employees at the facility were actually licensed to provide mental health counseling or to prescribe medications. Nonetheless, UHS was billing the government under the Medicaid program for the services it provided to Yarushka as if the facility complied with federal rules.

Plaintiffs filed a qui tam action against UHS on the "implied false certification theory of liability," which treats a payment request to the government as a claimant's implied certification of compliance with relevant statutes, regulations, or contract requirements that are material conditions of payment and treats a failure to disclose noncompliance as a misrepresentation that renders the claim false or fraudulent. UHS disputed the validity of the implied false certification theory, arguing that plaintiffs must point to a specific lie UHS told to the government in order to win. The District Court rejected the implied false certification theory and dismissed the complaint. Plaintiffs appealed and the Circuit Court reversed, accepting the theory. UHS appealed.

Thomas, Justice:

The False Claims Act, 31 U. S. C. §3729 et seq., imposes significant penalties on those who defraud the Government. This case concerns a theory of False Claims Act liability commonly referred to as "implied false certification." According to this theory, when a defendant submits a claim, it impliedly certifies compliance with all conditions of payment. But if that claim fails to disclose the defendant's violation of a material statutory, regulatory, or contractual requirement, so the theory goes, the defendant has made a misrepresentation that renders the claim "false or fraudulent" under §3729(a)(1)(A). This case requires us to consider this theory of liability and to clarify some of the circumstances in which the False Claims Act imposes liability.

We first hold that, at least in certain circumstances, the implied false certification theory can be a basis for liability. Specifically, liability can attach when the defendant submits a claim for payment that makes specific representations about the goods or services provided, but knowingly fails to disclose the defendant's noncompliance with a statutory, regulatory, or contractual requirement. In these circumstances, liability may attach if the omission renders those representations misleading.

We further hold that False Claims Act liability for failing to disclose violations of legal requirements does not turn upon whether those requirements were expressly designated as conditions of payment. Defendants can be liable for violating requirements even if they were not expressly designated as conditions of payment. Conversely, even when a requirement is expressly designated a condition of payment, not every violation of such a requirement gives rise to liability. What matters is not the label the Government attaches to a requirement, but whether the defendant knowingly violated a requirement that the defendant knows is material to the Government's payment decision.

A misrepresentation about compliance with a statutory, regulatory, or contractual requirement must be material to the Government's payment decision in order to be actionable under the False Claims Act. ... Section 3729(b)(4) defines materiality using language that we have employed to define materiality in other federal fraud statutes: "[T]he term 'material' means having a natural tendency to influence, or be capable of influencing, the payment or receipt of money or property." *Neder v. U.S.*, 527 U.S. 1, 16 (1999).

When evaluating materiality under the False Claims Act, the Government's decision to expressly identify a provision as a condition of payment is relevant, but not automatically dispositive. Likewise, proof of materiality can include, but is not necessarily limited to, evidence that the defendant knows that the Government consistently refuses to pay claims in the mine run of cases based on noncompliance with the particular statutory, regulatory, or contractual requirement. Conversely, if the Government pays a particular claim in full despite its actual knowledge that certain requirements were violated, that is very strong evidence that those requirements are not material. Or, if the Government regularly pays a particular type of claim in full despite actual knowledge that certain requirements were violated, and has signaled no change in position, that is strong evidence that the requirements are not material.

Because both opinions below assessed respondents' complaint based on interpretations of §3729(a)(1)(A) that differ from ours, we vacate the First Circuit's judgment and remand the case for reconsideration of whether respondents have sufficiently pleaded a False Claims Act violation. It is so ordered.

Computer Crime

The explosive growth of the use of computers in the business world in the past few years has brought with it a corresponding increase in computer misuse. The *Avila* forgery case mentioned earlier in this chapter is a good example. Burgeoning computer crime and corresponding government responses justify separate discussion of the area of computer crime. Traditional (pre-computer) state and federal laws applicable to such crimes as larceny are not necessarily appropriate for prosecution of cases of computer fraud and computer theft. For example, some cases held that an employee's unauthorized use of his employer's computer facilities in private ventures could not support a theft conviction because the employer had not been deprived of any part of value or use of the computer. Other cases have held that use of a computer is not "property" within traditional theft statutes.

Computer crimes fall mainly into three broad categories: unauthorized access, theft of information, and theft of funds. Among schemes that have been subject to prosecution are (1) stealing a competitor's computer program, (2) paying an accomplice to delete adverse information and insert favorable false information into the defendant's credit file, (3) a bank president's having her account computer coded so that her checks would be removed and held rather than posted so she could later remove the actual checks without their being debited, (4) a disgruntled ex-employee's inserting a virus into his former employer's computer to destroy its records, and (5) three computer hackers' foray into the forbidden recesses of computers that ran a large telecommunications company's phone network.

Computer crime costs business in the U.S. as much as estimated $400 billion per year (including thefts of funds, losses of computer programs and data, losses of trade secrets, and damage to computer hardware). Furthermore, a substantial amount of computer crime is never discovered, and a high percentage of that which is discovered is never reported because (1) companies do not want publicity about the inadequacy of their computer controls and (2) financial institutions such as banks and savings and loans fear that reports of large losses of funds, even when insured, are likely to cause customers to withdraw their deposits.

Whatever the actual loss caused by computer misuse, both Congress and the state legislators have passed statutes to deal specifically with computer crime.

Federal Laws

Although there have been convictions for computer crimes under general federal statutes—such as those dealing with wire fraud, theft, and misappropriation, Congress has enacted laws aiming specifically at criminal activity involving computers. For example, the Comprehensive Crime Control Act of 1984 contained a section on the use of computers in credit card fraud and established penalties for violation. The Electronic Communications Privacy Act of 1986 updated federal rules against intercepting wire and electronic communications (formerly known as "wiretapping") to cover e-mails, encrypted satellite-transmitted television broadcasts, cable television signals, and other electronic communications. The Child Pornography Prevention Act of 1996 criminalized the production and distribution of computer-generated, sexual images of children.

The most important federal statute in this area may be the Access Device and

Computer Fraud and Abuse Act of 1984, which has been amended several times (most importantly by the National Information Infrastructure Protection Act of 1996). This act protects any computer attached to the Internet (even if all the computers involved are located in the same state). The current version of the law makes it a crime to (a) access computer files without authority and subsequently to transmit classified government information; (b) access without authority information from financial institutions, the U.S. government, or private sector computers used in interstate commerce; (c) intentionally access a U.S. department or agency nonpublic computer without authorization in such a way as to affect the government's use of the computer; (d) access a protected computer, without or beyond authorization, with the intent to defraud and obtain something of value; (e) cause damage in one of several forms (e.g., sending damaging viruses) by computer hacking; (f) knowingly and with intent to defraud traffic in passwords which would permit unauthorized access to a government computer or affect interstate or foreign commerce; and (g) transmit in interstate or foreign commerce any threat to cause damage to a protected computer with intent to extort something of value.

The Computer Fraud and Abuse Act has been used to punish (i) hackers who sent out worm viruses to crash computers, (ii) hackers who broke into company data bases and deleted information, and (c) a spammer who inundated a company with thousands of e-mail messages, forcing it to shut down its computers.

UNITED STATES v. NOSAL
828 F.3d 865 (9th Cir. 2016)

Nosal worked at executive search firm Korn/Ferry International when he decided to launch a competing firm along with a group of co-workers. When Nosal left Korn/Ferry, the company revoked his computer access credentials, even though he remained for a time as a contractor. His accomplices Becky Christian and Mark Jacobson used their access to Korn/Ferry's data base to steal information for use at the contemplated new firm. After Christian and Jacobson left Korn/Ferry and had their access credentials revoked, they nonetheless continued to access the database using the credentials of Nosal's former executive assistant, Jacqueline Froehlich-L'Heureaux ("FH"), who remained at Korn/Ferry at Nosal's request.

Nosal was charged with a violation of the Computer Fraud and Abuse Act, 18 U.S.C. § 1030. After one appeal to the Ninth Circuit ("Nosal I"), a jury convicted Nosal of conspiracy to violate the "without authorization" provision of the Computer Fraud and Abuse Act. Nosal appealed.

McKeown, Circuit Judge:
This is the second time we consider the scope of the CFAA, which imposes criminal penalties on whoever "knowingly and with intent to defraud, accesses a protected computer without authorization, or exceeds authorized access, and by means of such conduct furthers the intended fraud and obtains anything of value . . . ." Id. § 1030(a)(4).

Only the first prong of the section is before us in this appeal: knowingly and with intent to defraud accessing a computer "without authorization." Embracing our earlier precedent and joining our sister circuits, we conclude that "without authorization" is an unambiguous, non-technical term that, given its plain and ordinary meaning, means accessing a protected computer without permission. This definition has a simple corollary: once authorization to access a computer has been affirmatively revoked, the user cannot sidestep the statute by going through the back door and accessing the computer through a third party. Unequivocal revocation of computer access closes both the front door and the back door.

In 2012, we addressed [in *Nosal I*] whether [Nosal's co-workers] "exceed[ed] authorized access" with intent to defraud under the CFAA. Distinguishing between access restrictions and use restrictions, we concluded that the "exceeds authorized access" prong of § 1030(a)(4) of the CFAA "does not extend to violations of [a company's] use restrictions.". We affirmed the district court's dismissal of the five CFAA counts related to Nosal's aiding and abetting misuse of data accessed by his co-workers with their own passwords.

The remaining counts relate to statutory provisions that were not at issue in *Nosal I*: access to a protected computer "without authorization" under the CFAA and trade secret theft under the Economic Espionage Act ("EEA"), 18 U.S.C. § 1831 et seq. When Nosal left Korn/Ferry, the company revoked his computer access credentials, even though he remained for a time as a contractor. The company took the same precaution upon the departure of his accomplices, Becky Christian and Mark Jacobson. Nonetheless, they continued to access the database using the credentials of Nosal's former executive assistant, Jacqueline Froehlich-L'Heureaux ("FH"), who remained at Korn/Ferry at Nosal's request. The question we consider is whether the jury properly convicted Nosal of conspiracy to violate the "without authorization" provision of the CFAA for unauthorized access to, and downloads from, his former employer's database called Searcher. Put simply, we are asked to decide whether the "without authorization" prohibition of the CFAA extends to a former employee whose computer access credentials have been rescinded but who, disregarding the revocation, accesses the computer by other means.

We directly answered this question in *LVRC Holdings LLC v. Brekka*, 581 F.3d 1127 (9th Cir. 2009), and reiterate our holding here: "A] person uses a computer 'without authorization' under [the CFAA] . . . when the employer has rescinded permission to access the computer and the defendant uses the computer anyway." This straightforward principle embodies the common sense, ordinary meaning of the "without authorization" prohibition.

Nosal ... spin[s] hypotheticals about the dire consequences of criminalizing password sharing. But these warnings miss the mark in this case. This appeal is not about password sharing. Nor is it about violating a company's internal computer-use policies. The conduct at issue is that of Nosal and his co-conspirators, which is covered by the plain language of the statute. Nosal is charged with conspiring with former Korn/Ferry employees whose user accounts had been terminated, but who nonetheless accessed trade secrets in a proprietary database through the back door when the front door had been firmly closed. Nosal knowingly and with intent to defraud Korn/Ferry blatantly circumvented the affirmative revocation of his computer system access. This access falls squarely within the CFAA's prohibition on access "without authorization," and thus we affirm Nosal's conviction for violations of § 1030(a)(4) of the CFAA.

The dissent mistakenly focuses on FH's authority, sidestepping the authorization question for Christian and Jacobson. To begin, FH had no authority from Korn/Ferry to provide her password to former employees whose computer access had been revoked. Also, in collapsing the distinction between FH's authorization and that of Christian and Jacobson, the dissent would render meaningless the concept of authorization. And, pertinent here, it would remove from the scope of the CFAA any hacking conspiracy with an inside person. That surely was not Congress's intent. We also affirm Nosal's convictions under the EEA for downloading, receiving and possessing trade secrets. Affirmed.

State Laws

Almost all states have passed laws dealing with computer crime. Most of the statutes comprehensively address the problem, outlawing (1) computer trespass (unauthorized access), (2) damage to computers or software (for example, use of viruses), (3) theft or misappropriation of computer services, and (4) obtaining or disseminating information by computer in an unauthorized manner.

WHITE COLLAR CRIME

The term *white collar crime* generally encompasses nonviolent acts by individuals or corporations to obtain a personal or business advantage in a commercial context. Many of the crimes discussed earlier in this chapter are examples of white collar crime. White collar crime has become an extremely controversial subject in recent years for at least two reasons. First, there is evidence that the economic losses caused by white collar crime are at a staggering level (often estimated at more than $100 billion annually) and growing rapidly. Second, there is a perception, based on substantial fact, that criminal penalties for white collar crimes costing the public millions of dollars are often much less severe than criminal penalties imposed on the average street hood who steals a $75 pair of shoes.

Traditional criminal law did not punish corporations for crimes, reasoning that because a corporation is an artificial entity, it could not form the intent required to supply *mens rea*, and it could not be punished by incarceration. Also, American law was slow to punish corporate officials who committed crimes. One reason is illustrated by the oft-quoted sentiment of a federal judge who said that he would not "penalize a businessman trying to make a living when there are felons out on the street."

In recent years, however, the traditional views have changed rather dramatically. Potential criminal liability must now be a significant concern for both corporations and their officials.

Criminal Liability of Corporations

Today, most criminal statutes include corporations in their definition of "persons" who may violate the statute. The traditional reluctance to impose criminal sanctions on corporations has been overcome by modern reasoning that suggests (1) that the *mens rea* necessary to convict a corporation can be supplied by imputing the intent of the corporation's agents who physically commit the crimes to the corporation (as has long been done in the area of tort law), and (2) that corporations can be punished by fines and by innovative punishments that might, for example, require a corporation that has been caught polluting to fund an environmental education course at a local high school.

The general rule today is that corporations can be held criminally liable for any acts performed by employees if those employees are acting within the scope of their authority for the purpose of benefiting the corporation. The basic idea is that the corporation receives the benefit when the agent acts properly and must bear the responsibility when the agent errs. This is simply an application of the *respondeat superior* doctrine (let the master answer for the wrongs of the agent) that is discussed in more detail in Chapter 23. The corporation can even be held liable when the agent is violating company policy or disobeying a specific order from a superior. Some jurisdictions refuse to hold the corporation criminally liable for crimes committed by lower-level employees, but many states find the corporation responsible no matter how far down the ladder the actual wrongdoer is.

Corporations have been indicted for homicide and a wide variety of lesser offenses, including health and safety violations arising out of toxic waste disposal, failure to remove asbestos from buildings, and construction-site accidents.

Federal sentencing guidelines contain provisions that apply specifically to corporate defendants. A sentencing judge now has the prerogative to place a corporation on probation in order to supervise it for a time to ensure that criminal activity is eradicated.

Fortunately for corporations, the suggested punishment structure is mitigated substantially if the defendant company has in place an "effective program to prevent and detect violations of law." The purpose of this mitigation factor is to induce corporations to "police their own" by establishing standards of conduct for employees and using various means to enforce those standards.

Criminal Liability of Corporate Officials

The increase in prosecutions of corporations has been matched by an increase in prosecutions of corporate officers as well. Corporate officers will definitely be held liable for criminal acts that they participate in or authorize. In addition, they will be held liable for acts that they aid and abet through any significant assistance or encouragement. Some courts find sufficient encouragement in mere acquiescence of a superior (which a subordinate may read as tacit approval) and even in failure to stop criminal activity that the official knows is occurring. In rare instances involving *strict liability* statutes, corporate officers have been held criminally liable because they failed to control the criminal acts of subordinates (even where they had no knowledge of the acts or had been assured that the acts had stopped). *United States v. Park,* 421 U.S. 658 (1975).

Indicative of the trend toward increased criminal liability are some recent cases in which corporate officials have been tried for *murder* in the deaths of employees exposed to hazardous conditions in the workplace. Additionally, federal laws have recently been enacted or beefed up to encourage criminal actions against individuals who engage in insider trading, environmental pollution, Medicare fraud, defrauding of the Defense Department, and a host of other activities that have been in the news recently.

Sarbanes-Oxley Act of 2002

As an illustration of federal actions to stop white collar crime, consider that after the wave of corporate scandals involving Enron, Global Crossing, WorldCom, Adelphia, Tyco, HealthSouth, and other companies occurred in late 2001 and early 2002, Congress responded by passing the Sarbanes-Oxley Act (SOX). SOX had many non-criminal components: creation of the Public Company Accounting Oversight Board (PCAOB) to regulate public auditing firms, creation of new rules for auditor independence and corporate governance, and institution of new rules to minimize conflicts of interest in Wall Street investment banking firms. SOX also included several provisions that either created new white-collar crimes or stiffened penalties for old ones, including requiring CEOs and CFOs to certify their belief in the accuracy of their companies' quarterly and annual financial statements as well as the effectiveness of their companies' internal controls and punishing them criminally if they lie.

White collar crime remains controversial as many decry the "overcriminalization" of "regular business activity" while others complain that notwithstanding SOX, almost no one went to jail in the wake of the mortgage scandal that nearly wrecked the world's economy beginning in 2007.

CHAPTER 8:

THE LAW OF TORTS

- A Preface
- Scope and Complexity of Tort Law
- Negligence
- Major Intentional Torts
- Other Intentional Torts
- Special Problems
- Business Torts
- Unfair Competition

A PREFACE

Two areas of law, criminal law and contract law, developed at an early time in England. Although both were intended to eliminate, insofar as possible, various kinds of wrongful conduct, each was concerned with markedly different wrongs. The major purposes of criminal law were to define wrongs against the state—types of conduct so inherently undesirable that they were flatly prohibited—and to permit the state to punish those who committed such acts by the imposition of fines or imprisonment. The major purposes of contract law, however, were (1) to spell out the nature of the rights and duties springing from *private agreements between individuals* and (2) in the event that one party failed to live up to these duties, to compensate the innocent party for the loss resulting from the other's breach of contract.

When criminal law and contract law were still in their initial stages of development, it became apparent that neither one afforded protection to the large numbers of persons who suffered losses resulting from other kinds of conduct equally unjustifiable from a social standpoint—acts of carelessness, deception, and the like. Faced with this situation, the courts at an early time began to recognize and define other "legal wrongs" besides crimes and breaches of contract—and began to permit persons who were injured thereby to bring civil actions to recover damages against those who committed them. Acts that came to be recognized as wrongs under these rules, which were formulated by judges over the years on a case-by-case basis, acquired the name of "torts" (the French word for *wrongs*).

Because tort law applies to such a wide range of activities, any introductory definition of tort must necessarily be framed in general terms—as, for example, "any wrong excluding breaches of contract and crimes," or "any noncontractual civil wrong committed upon the person or property of another." Although such definitions are of little aid in illustrating the specific kinds of torts that are recognized, they do, at least, reflect the historic lines of demarcation between breaches of contract, crimes, and torts.

SCOPE AND COMPLEXITY OF TORT LAW

As human society has become increasingly complex, the legal duties owed by one member of society to others have become considerably more numerous and varied. As a result, tort law encompasses such a wide range of human and organizational conduct that the breaches of some duties have little in common with others. For example, some actions are considered tortious (wrongful) only when the actor intended to cause an injury, whereas in other actions—especially those involving negligence—the actor's intentions are immaterial. Similarly, in some tort actions the plaintiff is required to show physical injury to his person or property as a result of the defendant's misconduct, whereas in other actions such a showing is not required. In the latter situations other kinds of legal injury are recognized, such as damage to reputation or mental suffering.

A somewhat clearer picture of the broad sweep of tort law can be gained from the realization that the rules making up this area of law must deal with such diverse matters as the care required of a surgeon in the operating room, the circumstances in which a contracting party has a legal obligation to inform the other party of facts that she knows that the other party does not possess, and the determination of the kinds of business information (trade secrets) that are entitled to protection against theft by competitors.

Courts clearly engage in some degree of social engineering as they shape the common law of torts. The same may be said of legislatures passing statutes that shape and supplement the common law of torts. Common to all successful tort actions are the twin concepts of *interest* and *duty*. Each time a court allows a plaintiff to receive damages for a tort committed by a defendant, it is saying that the plaintiff has an interest (for example, in bodily integrity, in enjoying the benefits of private property, in a good reputation, etc.) sufficiently important for the law to furnish protection and that, correspondingly, in a civilized society the defendant has a duty (for example, not to strike the plaintiff, not to steal the plaintiff's property, not to falsely injure the plaintiff's reputation, etc.) that was breached. As society evolves technologically, morally, philosophically, and otherwise, tort law evolves also. For example, 125 years ago, Americans had very little privacy. However, as increased wealth has allowed us to purchase and enjoy privacy, most of us have come to value privacy very much. In recent years, most jurisdictions have come to recognize privacy as an interest worth protecting and, as we shall see, have imposed a duty on others not to invade our privacy.

The present chapter focuses primarily on the law of negligence and on selected intentional torts. At the end of the chapter, however, we also discuss two examples of so-called "business torts"—torts that arise directly from competitive rivalry. The law of torts is so broad and pervasive that it cannot be covered in a single chapter. For example, lawsuits arising out of the sale of defective products are also primarily tort-related; they are discussed in Chapter 20. In addition, Chapter 9 discusses intellectual property—trademarks, trade secrets, patents, and copyrights. Infringement of another's intellectual property is also a tort, and Chapter 9 is devoted to this area of the law.

NEGLIGENCE

Negligence, to oversimplify, is carelessness. The courts long ago decided that our interests in economic well-being and personal safety are sufficiently important to be protected from the careless acts of others. Correspondingly, each of us has a duty as we live our lives and carry on our professions to exercise care not to injure others. Even though we may not intend to injure, the harm is just as real to the victim who is struck by the careless driver, struck by the autonomous vehicle that was carelessly designed, burned by the carelessly designed product, disabled by the careless surgeon, or ruined financially by embezzlement that an auditor carelessly failed to detect.

The negligence cause of action is the most important method of redress existing today for persons injured accidentally. The newspapers are filled with accounts of negligence actions involving asbestos exposure, tobacco warnings, marketing of handguns, defective tires, and the like. Whether a plaintiff was injured by a careless driver, a careless product designer, a careless surgeon, or a careless accountant, the same basic elements must be proved to establish a right of recovery: (1) that the defendant owed the plaintiff a duty of due care, (2) that the defendant breached that duty of due care, (3) that the defendant's breach proximately caused the injury, and (4) that the plaintiff suffered injury.

Duty

Few concepts are more fraught with difficulty than that of *duty* in the negligence cause of action. As a general rule, it may be said that we each owe a duty to every person whom we can *reasonably foresee* might be injured by our carelessness. If we drive down the street carelessly, pedestrians and other drivers are within the class of foreseeable plaintiffs we might injure. That we do not know the exact names of our prospective victims is unimportant.

To illustrate quickly, in *Burke v. Pan American World Airways, Inc.,* 484 F.Supp. 850 (S.D.N.Y. 1980), the plaintiff sued the defendants allegedly responsible for a terrible plane collision in the Canary Islands, claiming that she, although in California at the time, felt as though she were being "split in two" and felt an emptiness "like a black hole" at the exact instant of the crash. The plaintiff claimed that in that instant she knew that something terrible had happened to her identical twin sister, who was, in fact, killed in the collision. The plaintiff was prepared to document the phenomenon of "extrasensory empathy" between some pairs of identical twins. Even assuming the plaintiff could establish the point, the court dismissed the suit. When a plane crashes because of an airline's negligence, its passengers are certainly foreseeable victims, as are any persons on the ground hit by falling wreckage. However, Burke's injuries were too bizarre to be reasonably foreseeable, even if she did sustain them. The defendants owed no legal duty to the plaintiff.

The following case is just one illustration of a court's struggle to meld foreseeability and public policy factors to produce a proper scope of duty.

OTIS ENGINEERING CORP. v. CLARK
Texas Supreme Court, 668 S.W.2d 307 (1983)

Matheson, an employee of defendant Otis Engineering Corporation, had a history of being intoxicated on the job. One night he was particularly intoxicated, and his fellow employees believed he should be removed from the machines. Roy, Matheson's supervisor, suggested that Matheson go home, escorted him to the company parking lot, and asked him if he could make it home. Matheson answered that he could, but 30 minutes later and some three miles away he caused an accident killing the wives of plaintiffs Larry and Clifford Clark.

The Clarks sued Otis in a wrongful death action, but the trial court dismissed the suit, holding that Otis could not be liable because Matheson was not acting within the scope of his employment at the time of the accident. The intermediate court of appeals reversed, and Otis appealed to the Texas Supreme Court.

Kilgarlin, Justice:

The Clarks contend that under the facts in this case Otis sent home, in the middle of his shift, an employee whom it knew to be intoxicated. They aver this was an affirmative act which imposed a duty on Otis to act in a non-negligent manner.

In order to establish tort liability, a plaintiff must initially prove the existence and breach of a duty owed to him by the defendant. As a general rule, one person is under no duty to control the conduct of another, *Restatement (Second) of Torts* §315 (1965), even if he has the practical ability to exercise such control. Yet, certain relationships do impose, as a matter of law, certain duties upon parties. For instance, the master-servant relationship may give rise to a duty on the part of the master to control the conduct of his servants outside the scope of employment. This duty, however, is a narrow one.

Though the decisional law of this State has yet to address the precise issues presented by this case, factors which should be considered in determining whether the law should impose a duty are the risk, foreseeability, and likelihood of injury weighed against the social utility of the actor's conduct, the magnitude of the burden of guarding against the injury and consequences of placing that burden on the employer.

While a person is generally under no legal duty to come to the aid of another in distress, he is under a duty to avoid any affirmative action which might worsen the situation. One who voluntarily enters an affirmative course of action affecting the interests of another is regarded as assuming a duty to act and must do so with reasonable care.

Otis contends that, at worst, its conduct amounted to nonfeasance and under established law it owed no duty to the Clarks' respective wives. Traditional tort analysis has long drawn a distinction between action and inaction in defining the scope of duty. However, although courts have been slow to recognize liability for nonfeasance, "[d]uring the last century, liability for 'nonfeasance' has been extended still further to a limited group of relations, in which custom, public sentiment and views of social policy have led the courts to find a duty of affirmative action." W. Prosser, *The Law of Torts* at 339. Be that as it may, we do not view this as a case of employer nonfeasance.

What we must decide is if changing social standards and increasing complexities of human relationships in today's society justify imposing a duty upon an employer to act reasonably when he exercises control over his servants. Even though courts have been reluctant to hold an employer liable for the off-duty torts of an employee, "[a]s between an entirely innocent plaintiff and a defendant who admittedly has departed from the social standard of conduct, if only toward one individual, who should bear the loss?" W. Prosser, *supra,* at 257. Dean Prosser additionally observed that "[t]here is nothing sacred about 'duty,' which is nothing more than a word, and a very indefinite one with which we state our conclusion."

During this year, we have taken a step toward changing our concept of duty in premises cases. In *Corbin v. Safeway Stores Inc. ,* 648 S.W.2d 292 (Tex. 1983), we held that a store owner has a duty to guard against slips and falls if he has actual or constructive knowledge of a dangerous condition and it is foreseeable a fall would occur. Following *Corbin*, why should we be reluctant to impose a duty on Otis? As Dean Prosser has observed, "[c]hanging social conditions lead constantly to the recognition of new duties. No better general statement can be made than the courts will find a duty where in general, reasonable men would recognize and agree that it exists."

Therefore, the standard of duty that we now adopt for this and all other cases currently in the judicial process, is: when, because of an employee's incapacity, an employer exercises control over the employee, the employer has a duty to take such action as a reasonably prudent employer under the same or similar circumstances would take to prevent the employee from causing an unreasonable risk of harm to others. The duty of the employer is not an absolute duty to insure safety, but requires only reasonable care.

Therefore, the trier of fact in this case should be left free to decide whether Otis acted as a reasonable and prudent employer considering the following factors: the availability of the nurses' aid station [on the plant premises], a possible phone call to Mrs. Matheson, having another employee drive Matheson home, and the foreseeable consequences of Matheson's driving upon a public street in his stuporous condition.

[Affirm judgment of court of appeals and remand to trial court.]

Duty of Landowners

Courts have long encountered difficulty in determining the extent of the duty owed by owners or occupiers (such as tenants) of land toward those who come upon the property they control. How much of a duty they owe to visitors to their property in most jurisdictions turns on whether the visitor is a *trespasser* (one who enters the land with no right to do so), a *licensee* (one who has a right to come onto the property for self-benefit, such as a door-to-door sales representative or a neighbor dropping in uninvited), or an *invitee* (one invited by the owner or occupier or who enters for the benefit of the owner or occupier, such as a customer at a store). Under this traditional approach, trespassers may sue only for intentional torts, licensees may also sue for hidden dangers that the landowner knew about, and invitees may sue under the ordinary rules of negligence.

Breach of Duty

To be liable for negligence, a defendant must *breach* (violate) an existing duty. A breach occurs when the defendant fails to exercise the same care as a "reasonable person under similar circumstances" would have exercised. This hypothetical "reasonable person" (some old cases say "reasonable man") standard can be fairly strict in practice because of a jury's tendency, confronted with a seriously injured plaintiff, to use 20-20 hindsight. Many people, including those who serve on juries, believe themselves to be reasonable persons who would not have done whatever the defendant did. They are, of course, supposed to cast their minds back in time to just before the incident, focus only on what the defendant knew or should have known at that time, and look forward from that point. Such an exercise can be quite difficult for many people.

All the Circumstances

Whether or not a defendant's conduct met the "reasonable person" standard of care should be examined in light of all the circumstances that existed at the time of the incident that forms the basis for the lawsuit. Emergency conditions, for example, may be considered. Normally it would be a clear breach of due care to abandon a moving vehicle, but if a cab driver does so because a robber in the back seat has pulled a gun, a jury might determine that, under all the circumstances, there was no breach of due care to render the cab company liable to a pedestrian who was struck by the driverless cab. An unexpected bee sting might cause a bus driver to unavoidably lose control of a bus, though she was a very careful driver.

The established customs of others in the community or of other companies in the industry may also shed light on the proper standard of due care. If the defendant has acted in the same manner as most others in the same situation, it is difficult to conclude that a reasonable person duty was breached. However, custom is not always binding. In one famous case, barges were lost at sea because the tugs towing them had no radio sets to listen to weather reports that would have warned them to take shelter from an approaching storm. That few tug companies used the radio set was not proof that the "reasonable person" standard was met, because "a whole calling may have unduly lagged in the adoption of new and available devices." *The T.J.Hooper*, 60 F.2d 737 (2d Cir. 1932).

Conduct of Others

Traditionally, the courts allowed people to assume that other members of society would act carefully and lawfully. In other words, people had no duty to anticipate the negligent or criminal acts of others nor to exercise reasonable care to prevent harm from such conduct. Consequently, Person A could not be liable to Person B who was harmed by the negligent or intentional wrongdoing of Person C. In the past several decades, however, judges and juries have occasionally ruled that such wrongful actions by third parties can and must be anticipated in some circumstances. Thus, the operator of a hotel located in a high crime area that has itself been the scene of criminal acts in the past may be held to have breached a duty of due care by not providing adequate security for guests who are victimized by crime. Though some courts refuse to impose a duty in such circumstances, providing adequate security is increasingly a concern for hotel owners, apartment owners or managers, common carriers, store owners, concert promoters, and even universities.

Courts in most states now apply general rules of foreseeability to harm caused by a third party to someone on the premises of such businesses and in other circumstances. Under all the circumstances, was this general type of harm a reasonably foreseeable consequence of something that the proprietor or manager did or failed to do? If so, should a property owner have taken steps that were reasonable under the circumstances to reduce the risk of harm to customers, tenants, and so on? As in other cases of alleged negligence, were there risk-reducing measures (more lighting, guards, better locks, security cameras, fire sprinklers, etc.) that were feasible under the circumstances and that a reasonable proprietor or manager should have known about? Also, like other negligence cases, courts will balance the various direct and indirect costs of taking risk-reducing measures against the reduction in risk that will probably occur—a rough, *qualitative* cost-benefit (or risk-utility) analysis.

Proximate Cause

After proving the existence and breach of a duty of due care, the plaintiff in a negligence action must demonstrate that the defendant's breach of duty—that is, its failure to use reasonable care—was a *proximate cause* of the plaintiff's harm. A plaintiff must prove two elements to establish proximate cause.

First, the plaintiff must prove *causation in fact*. This is simply an actual cause-and-effect relationship, and is often called "but-for causation," that is, *but for* the defendant's negligent act or failure to act, the plaintiff's harm would not have occurred. For example, assume that Jill is driving her car at 40 miles per hour on a street where the speed limit is 30 miles per hour when a small child darts into the street from between two cars and is hit by Jill's car. Assume further that the child was so close to Jill's car when he darted into the street that even had Jill been driving 30 miles per hour, or even 20, she could not have avoided striking the child. In such a case we cannot say that "but for" Jill's speeding the accident would not have happened. Jill's careless speeding was not a proximate cause of the accident, and Jill would not be liable.

For defendant's negligence to have been a proximate cause of defendant's harm, the plaintiff does not have to prove that the defendant's negligence was the only cause, but it must have been at least a *substantial contributing cause* to defendant's harm.

Second, for a plaintiff to prove proximate cause, she must also prove that defendant's harm was a *reasonably foreseeable* result of defendant's negligence. An excellent example of how this concept works in practice is found in the famous case, *Palsgraf v. Long Island R.R.,* 163 N.E. 99 (N.Y. 1928). A ticketed passenger was running on a train platform and trying to board a train that had just begun to move. A guard on the train, and another railroad company employee on the platform tried to assist the passenger, the guard grabbing his hand and the other employee giving him a push. This caused a package the passenger was holding to fall under the train wheels. This conduct by the Long Island Railroad Co. was obviously careless—the employees were not using reasonable care—and if they could be held liable, so could their employer because they were unquestionably acting within the scope of their employment. As it turned out, the passenger's package contained powerful fireworks that exploded beneath the wheels of the train.

The force of the explosion shook the platform and tipped over a scale for weighing cargo that sat at the far end of the train platform. Mrs. Palsgraf, who stood near the scale as she waited for a train, was injured when the scale fell on her as a result of the exploding fireworks. The railway company, acting through its employees, owed a duty to use reasonable care in dealing with the boarding passenger, and injury to him and his property was a foreseeable result of the employees' negligence.

The case focused not on the boarding passenger's injury, but on Mrs. Palsgraf's. She lost a negligence case against the railroad because the court concluded that her harm was not a reasonably foreseeable consequence of the employees' negligence. The main factors leading to the court's conclusion of no reasonable foreseeability were: (a) There were a number links in the chain of causal events between the negligence and the harm (i.e., multiple causes in succession), (b) the nature of her harm and its most direct cause (scales falling) were extremely different from the nature of the negligent conduct by the employees, and (c) relatedly, there was no logical connection between two railroad employees' helping a passenger board a moving train and Mrs. Palgraf then being injured by a falling cargo scale. There certainly can be cases in which reasonable foreseeability is found even though the plaintiff's harm occurred at the end of a chain of multiple events, but in the *Palsgraf* case, the fact that the harm was of such a different character than any reasonable person would ever expect to result from what the railroad employees did played a large role in the outcome.

You will recall that reasonable foreseeability was also a major factor in the initial determination of whether the defendant owed the plaintiff a duty of reasonable care in the first place. It may seem odd that courts sometimes entertain the concept of reasonable foreseeability at the initial duty stage, and sometimes at the later analytical stage where the court decides whether defendant's negligence was a *proximate cause* of defendant's harm. The reason it seems odd is that it *is* odd. One should not be confused by this fact, however, because the concept of reasonable foreseeability, the factors included in its determination, and the method of analysis used are identical, regardless of the stage at which a court makes the foreseeability determination.

The reason that an allegedly negligent party's liability is limited by what is reasonably foreseeable is that, in general, people and companies in our legal system are not held legally responsible for consequences over which they have no control. When we act carelessly, there can be many ripple effects and unpredictable consequences. And many incidents have several causes. Suppose, for instance, that Toshika negligently failed to stop her car at a stop sign, causing her to hit the driver's side of another car traveling on a perpendicular road. An ambulance took the driver of the other car to the hospital. At the hospital, the ambulance driver, Earl, met an emergency room nurse, Adrianna, who was initiating care for the injured driver. Earl and Adrianna fell in love, married, and later had a child, Ajax. Twenty years later, Ajax, who developed a serious alcohol problem, murdered

Fred in a bar fight. "But for" Toshika's negligence in running the stop sign, Earl and Adrianna would not have met and had a child who later murdered Fred. Should Fred's family be able to hold Toshika liable for negligence in Fred's death? Of course not, and you should be able to see why. There must be some sort of limiting principle on a person's liability for negligence. Fred's murder was not a reasonably foreseeable consequence of Toshika's careless driving.

Public Policy Concerns

In determining whether there is a duty to use reasonable care toward someone, or whether defendant's negligence was a proximate cause of plaintiff's harm, courts sometimes take public policy concerns into account in addition to reasonable foreseeability. In other words, a court may consider the likely long-term, cumulative effects on society of either imposing or not imposing liability on the defendant. In the *Otis Engineering* case on the question of duty, for instance, one of the factors the court considered was the policy question of whether one who has a degree of authority and control over another should generally be responsible for exercising that control and authority with reasonable care. The court said "Yes," as most other courts have concluded. Because of his position, the supervisor working for Otis had substantial authority over his subordinates, including the inebriated Matheson, and this authority gave him a meaningful degree of control over what Matheson did under the circumstances. It is arguably in the long-term best interest of society as a whole for a person having such authority to be required to use it reasonably under all the circumstances. Many other public policy concerns can be relevant in other cases.

Plaintiff Does *Not* Have to Prove that Defendant's *Exact Harm* was Foreseeable

It is important to emphasize that plaintiff is *not required* to prove that defendant should have foreseen the exact type or severity of harm that plaintiff ended up suffering, but only that defendant should have foreseen that its conduct was likely to lead to the *general kind of harm* that plaintiff incurred. For example, assume that defendant negligently allowed the fire in an outdoor wood or charcoal cooking grill to escape and spread across dry grass and other foliage to the adjoining landowner's property. If the fire burns down the neighbor's home, the victim of the fire who sues for negligence does not have to prove that it was reasonably foreseeable for valuable old letters in her home between her famous author-grandfather and his literary agent to be destroyed. It is reasonably foreseeable that a neighbor's home might be burned, and it is reasonably foreseeable that the neighbor could have *something* valuable in her home.

You "Take Your Victims as You Find Them"

Sometimes the concept of reasonable foreseeability is interpreted rather broadly. For example, if you carelessly injure a person who turns out to be a hemophiliac and who then bleeds to death when most people would not have, you may still liable for the death. Many courts say that we must "take our victims as we find them." Although it may not be reasonably foreseeable to us that our victim would be a hemophiliac, it is reasonably foreseeable that if we negligently cause harm, any particular victim might have any number of conditions making them more vulnerable than the average person. For example, the victim might be a young child, an elderly person, or a person whose immune system has been compromised by chemotherapy treatments. There are a lot of people in society, including those who legally drive cars, who have any one of a countless number of individual vulnerabilities. In a similar vein, we often are liable for harm to the victim of our negligence if our negligence resulted in greater harm because we placed that victim into a hazardous situation (such as our negligent driving not only causing direct damage but also placing the victims in a situation in which they are more vulnerable to other common road hazards, such as being hit by another car).

Independent Intervening Cause

When reasonable foreseeability is the issue, the concept of independent intervening cause can be very important. Such a cause is one that emanates from a third party or source to disrupt the causal connection between the defendant's careless act and the plaintiff's injury. It is neither reasonably foreseeable nor under the defendant's control. Assume that Sue is driving down the street when she comes to an intersection that is blocked by an accident caused by Joe's having run a stop sign. Sue turns her car around and while driving away is hit by a tree that is blown down by a strong wind. Sue can argue that "but for" Joe's carelessness the intersection would not have been blocked and she would have been several miles away from the tree at the time it fell over. But should we hold Joe liable for Sue's injury? No, because the tree's falling is an *unforeseeable* "independent, intervening cause" that breaks up the causal chain between Joe's careless driving and Sue's injury. The key, again, is foreseeability. An intervening cause that was itself reasonably foreseeable will not break the causal chain and the defendant may well be liable for the additional harm caused by the independent intervening event.

The following case provides an excellent example of the factors courts view as important in determining whether an ultimate harm occurring after a series of events was a reasonably foreseeable consequence of a negligent act by defendant that kicked off the chain of events.

BROWN v. PHILADELPHIA COLLEGE OF OSTEOPATHIC MEDICINE
Superior Court of Pennsylvania, 760 A.2d 863 (2000)

Yvette Brown delivered a child at Philadelphia College of Osteopathic Medicine (PCOM) on August 29, 1991. Soon after her delivery, the child was given a blood test to detect congenital syphilis. A PCOM physician told Mrs. Brown that the test results revealed her daughter had been born with syphilis, and that the baby only could have contracted the disease from her. When her husband arrived at the hospital, Mrs. Brown confronted him with the diagnosis and questioned whether he had been faithful to her. Although Mr. Brown initially denied infidelity, he subsequently admitted to having begun an affair with a co-worker during the last trimester of his wife's pregnancy, an affair that did not terminate until after the birth of the child.

Sometime after the baby was released from the hospital, the Browns requested that she be tested again for syphilis. They learned in October 1991 that the child, in fact, did not have syphilis. In addition, results of a test performed on Mr. Brown, which were received by the Browns in December 1991, revealed that Mr. Brown did not have syphilis.

The Browns filed a negligence suit against PCOM. Mrs. Brown testified that after the diagnosis the couple experienced "a lot of arguing, a lot of accusations, distrust" which they had not previously experienced in their marriage. Eventually, Mr. Brown became physically abusive to his wife. Central to the Browns' damage claims in this litigation was an episode of abuse in November 1991 that began when Mrs. Brown received a telephone call at her home from her male partner on the police force. According to Mrs. Brown, upon hearing a man's voice on the line, Mr. Brown became suspicious and "snatched the phone out of the wall and hit me, and he hit me several times." Mrs. Brown then retrieved her service revolver and while bleeding and wearing only her underwear pursued Mr. Brown out of the house. She fired several shots at him, hitting his car. As a result of this incident, both of the Browns were arrested and Mrs. Brown obtained a restraining order against her husband. Subsequently, Mrs. Brown was discharged from the Philadelphia police force for conduct unbecoming an officer. The Browns lived separately thereafter.

A jury returned a verdict in favor of $510,000 in favor of the Browns. PCOM appealed.

Todd, Justice:

In this negligence action, we are called upon to determine whether an erroneous syphilis diagnosis was the proximate cause of the breakdown of a marriage, physical violence and loss of employment. The element of causation lies at the heart of this matter. For purposes of this appeal, we assume that PCOM owed a duty to the Browns and that in delivering the erroneous test results it breached that duty. In addition, we accept, as found by the jury, that PCOM's conduct was an actual cause of the eventual harm suffered by the Browns.

It is not sufficient, however, that a negligent act may be viewed, in retrospect, to have been one of the happenings in the series of events leading up to an injury. Even if the requirement of actual causation has been satisfied, there remains the issue of proximate or legal cause. ...While actual and proximate causation are "often hopelessly confused", a finding of proximate cause turns upon: "whether the policy of the law will extend the responsibility for the [negligent] conduct to the consequences which have in fact occurred....The term 'proximate cause' is applied by the courts to those more or less undefined considerations which limit liability even where the fact of causation is clearly established." *Bell v. Irace*, 619 A.2d 365 (Pa. Super. 1993) (*quoting* W.P. Keeton, Prosser & Keeton, THE LAW OF TORTS (5th ed.1984)).

Proximate cause "is primarily a problem of law." As a threshold issue, therefore, the trial judge must determine whether the alleged tortfeasor's conduct could have been the proximate, or legal, cause of the complainant's injury before sending the case to the jury. In the present case, the learned trial judge made no such threshold determination at any of the appropriate junctures for him to have done so. Instead, the trial court denied PCOM's motions for a nonsuit, a directed verdict and judgment notwithstanding the verdict. This was an error of law that controlled the outcome of the present case and on this basis we are constrained to reverse.

The law of this Commonwealth will not support a finding of proximate cause if, as in the present case, "the negligence was so remote that as a matter of law, [the actor] cannot be held legally responsible for [the] harm which subsequently occurred." *Reilly v. Tiergarten*, 633 A.2d 208 (Pa.Super. 1993). *Accord Bell*, 619 A.2d at 367 ("At the point in the causal chain when the consequence of the negligent act is no longer reasonably foreseeable, 'the passage of time and the span of distance mandate a cut-off point for liability.'")

To determine proximate cause, the Supreme Court of Pennsylvania has stated that "the question is whether the defendant's conduct was a 'substantial factor' in producing the injury." *Vattimo v. Lower Bucks Hosp., Inc.*, 502 Pa. 241, 246, 465 A.2d 1231, 1233 (1983). To determine whether an actor's conduct constitutes a proximate cause of an injury, the courts of the Commonwealth have adopted and relied upon the factors set forth in §433 of the Restatement (Second) of Torts. This section provides:

> The following considerations are in themselves or in combination with one another important in determining whether the actor's conduct is a substantial factor in bringing harm to another: the number of other factors which contribute in producing the harm and the extent of the effect which they have in producing it; whether the actor's conduct has created a force or series of forces which are in continuous and active operation up to the time of the harm, or has created a situation harmless unless acted upon by other forces for which the actor is not responsible; lapse of time.

Applying these factors to the present case, it is abundantly clear that factors other than the negligence of PCOM had a far greater effect in producing the harm complained of by the Browns. Mr. Brown conducted an extramarital affair and confessed this to his wife at a time when the affair was still ongoing. It is this affair and his confession to it, together with Mr. Brown's suspicions that his wife was having an affair herself, not the false diagnosis of syphilis, that had the greatest effect in bringing about the marital discord and eventual breakdown for which the couple seeks compensation. Under the first of the Restatement factors, therefore, the actions of PCOM are not a substantial factor in bringing about these alleged damages.

Even the allegations of the Brown's Complaint show that forces other than the negligence of PCOM were the proximate cause of their damages. The Complaint alleges that:

> As a direct and proximate result of the negligence of PCOM, wife Plaintiff suffered serious and severe physical and psychological damages as a consequence. Because of the nature of the disease and its communicability, wife Plaintiff accused husband Plaintiff of infecting her with a venereal disease, which husband Plaintiff denied. These accusations took place over several days in the course of which, husband Plaintiff admitted to an extramarital affair. As a consequence of this admission, that marital relationship became extremely strained and at one point, resulted in physical violence. In self-defense, wife Plaintiff was caused to discharge a firearm in the direction of husband Plaintiff on the public streets of Philadelphia. As a consequence of this action, wife Plaintiff was terminated from her employment as a Philadelphia Police officer.

Under the second factor, it is clear that PCOM's conduct did not create "a force or series of forces which [were] in continuous and active operation up to the time of the harm." Instead, Mr. Brown confessed his adultery shortly after Mrs. Brown received the erroneous test results, before any retesting or verification of the results could be accomplished.

The third factor is lapse of time. In the present case, the child was born August 29, 1991 and was tested for syphilis shortly thereafter. The erroneous test results were delivered to the Browns, and Mr. Brown confessed his adultery while Mrs. Brown was still hospitalized recovering from the birth. By some time in October, they had learned that the diagnosis had been made in error. The primary physical altercation between the couple that resulted in Mrs. Brown's physical injury, the arrest of both parties, the filing of a protection from abuse order against Mr. Brown and the couple's separation, occurred more than two months after the receipt of the erroneous diagnosis and in the month after they learned that the diagnosis had been in error. Thus, the lapse of more than two months between the erroneous diagnosis and the initial break up of their marriage points to a finding that PCOM's negligence was not a substantial factor in bringing about this harm. Accordingly, under all three factors set forth in the Restatement analysis, PCOM's negligence was not a substantial factor in bringing about the breakdown of the Browns' marriage and, thus, was not a proximate cause of this harm.

Even more clearly, the erroneous test results were not the proximate cause of Mrs. Brown's alleged loss of income and earning capacity during the more than six years between the erroneous test and the trial. Instead, her independent act of discharging her service revolver in the direction of her husband on a public street (the month after she learned that the syphilis test results were erroneous) and the subsequent determination of the Philadelphia Police Department that such an action constituted conduct unbecoming an officer were the proximate causes of the termination of her employment as a police officer. This, combined with her difficulties in finding adequate child care that would permit her to pursue full-time employment, are the proximate causes of her alleged reduction in income and earning capacity.

Our decision that the damages alleged to have been suffered by the Browns are so remote from the actions of PCOM that PCOM cannot be held legally responsible for the harm is dictated by our prior jurisprudence on this issue wherein this Court has rejected similar attempts by plaintiffs to link damages to acts well beyond the point of reasonable foreseeability.

Reversed, judgment vacated, and remanded for entry of judgment notwithstanding the verdict in favor of Appellant.

Injury

As the final element of a negligence cause of action, the plaintiff must prove injury. Negligence recovery is allowed primarily for injury to person or property. Recovery for economic loss not related to personal injury or property damage is generally not allowed, although there are several exceptions for special situations.

Courts historically have been reluctant to allow recovery for emotional distress in negligence cases on the grounds that such injuries are too intangible and too easily faked. During recent years, however, some courts have changed their views on this issue because psychiatric testimony regarding the actual existence of emotional distress has become more dependable. Thus, there are some cases in which the victim of negligence that caused bodily injury or property damage is also allowed to recover damages for resulting emotional distress.

Another issue related to the concept of injury in the law of negligence is "bystander recovery." Thus, a parent who sees or hears an accident killing the parent's child may be allowed to recover for emotional distress although the parent was not within the "zone of danger." Three factors to be weighed in deciding whether to allow bystander recovery are: (1) whether the plaintiff was located near the scene of the accident; (2) whether the emotional shock resulted from a contemporaneous perception of the accident, as opposed to hearing about it later; and (3) whether the plaintiff and the victim were closely related. Some courts have, however, completely rejected bystander recovery, which obviously entails an extension of the concept of duty.

Punitive damages, also known as *exemplary damages*, are *not* recoverable in mere negligence cases. These are monetary damages, over and above the sums necessary to compensate for the plaintiff's injuries, that are assessed against the defendant to punish the wrongdoing and deter others from engaging in similar conduct in the future by holding the defendant up as an example. A defendant in a negligence action is guilty of mere carelessness, so punitive damages are viewed as inappropriate. However, punitive damages are generally available to plaintiffs injured by the intentional torts that we will discuss later in the chapter.

Defenses

Even if the plaintiff establishes all four elements of a negligence cause of action, the defendant may avert or reduce recovery by establishing certain defenses.

Comparative Fault

If the plaintiff is guilty of fault that contributed to the accident, a defense may exist. Under the old system of *contributory negligence*, a plaintiff who was guilty of carelessness that contributed in any material way to the accident was barred from recovery altogether. Even if the jury concluded that the plaintiff was 1 percent at fault and the defendant 99 percent, the plaintiff could recover nothing, no matter how serious the injuries were.

Because of the harshness of the contributory negligence system, almost all states have replaced it with a system of "comparative negligence" (or "comparative fault"). Some states use a system of "pure" comparative negligence, in which the plaintiff recovers the percentage of his damages that were caused by the defendant, even if plaintiff's negligence accounts for a greater portion of his harm than did the defendant's negligence. Thus, if the plaintiff proves that defendant was negligent, the jury concludes that plaintiff's own negligence contributed 70% to his harm, and that plaintiff's monetary damages amounted to $100,000, plaintiff can recover $30,000. However, *most* states have adopted "modified" comparative negligence, which disallows the plaintiff from recovering any damages if her percentage contribution to her harm passes a certain point. Most of these states bar a plaintiff from recovering any damages at all if his own negligence is found to have contributed *more than 50%* to his harm. In the scenario above, if a jury concludes that the plaintiff's own negligence contributed 51% to his harm, he receives no compensation. A few states place the trigger at exactly 50%; that is, if the plaintiff contributes *50% or more* to his harm, he receives nothing.

Statute of Limitations

In negligence, as in other types of private claims, every state has a *statute of limitations* within which the suit must be filed or forever barred. A typical tort statute of limitations is two years. Thus, a plaintiff injured by a defendant's negligence must file suit within two years of the occurrence. Occasionally a plaintiff may not even know of the injury until more than two years after the occurrence; for example, sometimes the side effects of carelessly designed drugs will not show up until a few years after the drugs were taken. Most states have applied "tolling" devices that provide that in such a case the statute of limitations is tolled or suspended; that is, it will not begin to run until the plaintiff knows or should know of the injury. In response to an increase in medical malpractice and products liability lawsuits, several states have passed statutes of "repose" that bar certain actions after, for example, 15 years, whether the injuries sustained were discoverable or not during that period.

No-Fault Systems

Negligence has been eliminated as a basis for lawsuits in at least two contexts that should be mentioned here. Every state has a *workers' compensation* system that allows injured employees to recover benefits from their employers when injured on the job. The employee can recover regardless of the presence of employer fault but forfeits the right to sue the employer even if the employer has been careless. Most jurisdictions, however, allow employees covered by workers' compensation to sue their employer in tort if injured by the employer's gross negligence (for example, if the employer has allowed several employees to be injured by the same defective machine without replacing it) or intentional tort. Workers' compensation is discussed in more detail in the employment law chapter.

Several states have enacted "no fault" automobile statutes. The thrust of these statutes is to reduce litigation by allowing persons who suffer only minor injuries in car accidents to recover only from their own insurance company. Although these laws vary widely from jurisdiction to jurisdiction, in most the plaintiffs' losses must exceed a certain statutory threshold before resort to litigation is allowed.

INTENTIONAL TORTS

Assault and Battery

Assault and battery are similar torts that may be treated together. Although modern courts and statutes frequently use the two terms interchangeably, technically a *battery* is a rude, inordinate contact with the person of another. An *assault*, basically, is any act that creates an apprehension of an imminent battery. That we can sue for assault and battery protects our personal dignity from intrusions of the mind (assault) and body (battery). The courts long ago concluded that we have a legitimate interest in being protected from offensive bodily contacts and from fear of them. Indeed, assault and battery also constitute crimes.

Elements

To establish an assault and battery case, plaintiff must prove (1) the defendant's affirmative conduct, (2) intent, and (3) the plaintiff's injury.

Affirmative Conduct. If Sue is carefully driving down the street and is hit by a car that runs a red light, and as a result Sue's car is pushed into a pedestrian, Sue has not committed assault or battery. Although the pedestrian has sustained both apprehension (assuming she saw the accident as it happened) and rude contact, Sue committed no affirmative act that caused the injuries. The driver of the car that ran the red light did commit an affirmative act that was tortious, but that act was negligence, not assault or battery. However, if, while driving down the street, Sue spotted an enemy and deliberately ran down that person in a crosswalk, she would have committed an assault and battery.

Intent. The intent required for both assault and battery is the intent either to create an offensive contact to the plaintiff's body or the apprehension of it in the plaintiff's mind. Furthermore, people are presumed to intend the natural consequences of their actions. Thus, if A points an unloaded gun at B and utters threats to use it, an assault occurs if B does not know the gun is unloaded even if A's intent is simply to play a harmless prank. The natural consequences of A's act of pointing the gun is to create an apprehension in B.

Under the *doctrine of transferred intent*, if Sam shoots at Bill, but Bill ducks and the bullet hits Carlos, Carlos has an assault (assuming he saw the incident happening) and battery claim against Sam even if he is Sam's best friend and Sam would not intentionally hurt him for the world. The law transfers the intent Sam had to injure Bill to Carlos.

Injury. If a plaintiff seeks to establish an assault, the injury sustained must be in the nature of an apprehension of imminent bodily contact of an offensive nature. A threat of future contact or a threat by a defendant far away is insufficient. Threats or even attempts at violence that the intended victim does not know about until much later do not create the requisite apprehension, as where D shoots and misses P from so far away that P never realizes the shot was fired. Usually the plaintiff's reactions are judged by what would have caused apprehension in a reasonable person, but if the defendant knows that the plaintiff is an unusually sensitive person and threatens contact that the plaintiff finds offensive although most persons would not, an assault occurs.

If the plaintiff sues for battery, the injury that must be demonstrated is an offensive contact. Being struck with a fist, a knife, or a bullet obviously satisfies the requirement. So does being groped, spat on, or poisoned.

The following battery case raises some important workers' compensation issues.

COLE v. STATE OF LOUISIANA, DEPT. OF PUBLIC SAFETY AND CORRECTIONS
Louisiana Supreme Court, 825 So. 2d 1134 (2002)

Bradley Cole was a correctional officer, where he was a member of a tactical unit trained to take charge of inmate riots or disturbances. Cole participated in training exercises to prepare him for the challenges of his job. In one group training exercise involving tactical units from around the state named the "angry crowd exercise," Cole and his officer unit played the role of inmates, and another unit played the role of guards. Cole testified that prior to this date, his tactical unit had never participated in training exercises with other institutions and that during previous exercises with his unit, when batons were used, they were wrapped in Styrofoam and officers wore protective pads. However, during this angry crowd exercise, unpadded batons were used, and officers only wore helmets for protection. Cole testifies that he was grabbed and hit at full force, and that even when he shouted the code word to end the activity, he continued to be beaten. Cole suffered injuries as a result of this activity.

Cole sued for battery, and the trial court rendered judgment in favor of Cole, awarding general damages, future medical damages, and lost wages. The court of appeal affirmed the judgment of the trial court, stating that although the acts of the employees were not vicious, they were nonetheless harmful and done with intent.

Johnson, Justice:

Generally, any action by a worker against his employer for injuries suffered during the course and scope of employment would be exclusively through the Worker's Compensation Act, *La. R.S. 23:1032*, which provides immunity from civil liability in favor of an employer. It is well settled that under this law a worker is ordinarily limited to recovering workers' compensation benefits rather than tort damages for these injuries. However, §1032(B) provides an exception to this exclusivity when a worker is injured as a result of an employer's intentional act. When a plaintiff sustains damages as a result of an intentional battery committed by a co-employee during the course and scope of employment, the exclusivity provisions of the Louisiana Workers' Compensation Act do not apply.

The meaning of "intent" in this context is that actor who either (1) consciously desires the physical result of his act, whatever the likelihood of that result happening from his conduct; or (2) knows that the result is substantially certain to follow from his conduct, whatever his desire may be as to that result.

[T]he intention need not be malicious nor need it be an intention to inflict actual damage, but it is sufficient if the actor intends to inflict either a harmful or offensive contact without the other's consent….[T]he defendant may be liable although intending nothing more than a good-natured practical joke, or honestly believing that the act would not injure the plaintiff, or even though seeking the plaintiff's own good.

Applying the above precepts to the facts of the instant case, we find that the lower courts did not err in finding Cole's injuries were the result of the intentional tort of battery as the evidence supports such a finding. There indeed exists a reasonable factual basis for the trial court's finding that plaintiff met his burden of proof on the elements of battery, since striking a person with a baton is at the very least a "harmful or offensive contact." Further, although the officer(s) who stuck Cole with the unpadded batons may not have had malice nor intended to inflict the actual damages Cole suffered, the striking with the batons was an intentional act. Striking someone at full force with an unpadded baton is indeed a harmful or offensive contact intending that person to suffer such a contact. Accordingly, we find that the elements of the intentional tort of battery are met in this case.

[Affirmed in part, reversed in part.]

Defenses

In addition to the statute of limitations, which typically is two years in such cases, the two primary defenses to assault and battery are consent and self-defense. A plaintiff who has consented to offensive contacts and the threat of them cannot sue for assault and battery. Thus, a boxer who steps into the boxing ring or the quarterback who steps onto the football field consents to the normal contacts that go with the rules of the game. However, a football player who rips off another player's helmet and hits him with it after the play is over commits an assault and battery because the victim's consent does not extend to this contact outside the rules of the game any more than it would extend to being shot by an opponent.

Consent cannot be procured by fraud, nor can it be ill-informed. Thus, if M procures F's consent to sexual intercourse by hiding the fact that he has a venereal disease, her consent to intercourse does not constitute consent to the harmful contact with the disease. She may sue for battery. Doctors performing surgery must be very careful to fully inform their patients regarding the contacts that will take place during the surgery to avoid liability for battery.

Consent to an appendectomy does not extend to the removal of some of the reproductive organs even though it may be the doctor's best medical judgment that they should be removed.

Self-defense creates a well-recognized privilege to assault and battery. Generally, the courts restrict one to that degree of defensive force considered reasonable under all the circumstances.

Defamation

Long ago the courts decided that people have a legitimate interest in preserving their good reputations in the community. Those who damage our reputation by spreading falsehoods commit the tort of defamation and may be liable in damages. Although defamation has historic common-law roots, its development in recent years has been strongly influenced by a series of Supreme Court decisions that have molded the tort in accordance with First Amendment principles.

Libel versus Slander

Defamation takes two basic forms. *Libel* is defamation that is in writing or some other fixed form; *slander* is oral. Television and radio broadcasts, e-mails, and internet postings have generally been categorized as libel. The distinction is important because, traditionally, libel, perhaps because of its more permanent form, was considered more damaging than slander. At common law, a person who proved libel was able to recover damages without any proof of special damages; that is, the very proof that something potentially damaging to the reputation was circulated in public led the court to presume injury. The jury could assess damages without evidence of any specific loss.

Slander, however, required proof of special damages. Generally, a plaintiff had to prove some sort of economic loss stemming from the damage to reputation. Once that was proved, the plaintiff could recover for all sorts of injuries, including humiliation, loss of friendship, and the like. However, in four special categories known as slander per se, no special damages needed to be proved. These categories were imputation of serious crime, of loathsome disease, of incompetence in the plaintiff's profession, and of sexual misconduct.

However, as we shall see, over time Supreme Court's First Amendment decisions have in some ways altered this traditional legal landscape.

Elements

In a defamation case (either libel or slander), the plaintiff must generally establish five elements to prevail: (1) defendant made a statement about the plaintiff as though it were a fact (rather than an opinion), (2) the statement about plaintiff was defamatory, (3) the statement was false, (4) the statement was communicated (sometimes the courts say "published") by the defendant to at least one other person, and (5) the plaintiff's reputation was harmed. Questions of the defendant's fault as we shall see, also arise.

Fact vs. Opinion. Under the First Amendment, there is no such thing as a false idea. We are all entitled to our opinions. Thus, "I think Joe is a jerk" is not actionable. Neither is "I just don't trust Joe; he looks sneaky to me." However, when an editorial writer stated that a plaintiff had lied under oath, the Supreme Court rejected a defense of opinion because the statement was "sufficiently factual to be susceptible of being proved true or false." *Milkovich v. Lorain Journal Co.,* 497 U.S. 1 (1990). *Verifiability* is the key to distinguishing fact from opinion.

Defamatory. To be defamatory, a statement must be of such a nature as to tend to lower the plaintiff's esteem in the eyes of others, that is, to damage plaintiff's reputation. An infinite variety of statements have been held defamatory, but if the defendant falsely tells others that the plaintiff is a thief, a bankrupt, or a Nazi, it is likely that the plaintiff's esteem in the eyes of others will be lowered. Although most defamation actions are brought by individuals, they can also be brought by corporations and other organizations. It is obvious that what is viewed as defamatory can depend on the era, geographic location, and the cultural and social norms of the relevant community.

The defamatory statement must be one that the readers or hearers will associate with the plaintiff. Although not mentioned by name, a person who is obviously referred to in a disparaging way in a "novel" that is closely based on reality may have a claim against the author. So may a member of a small group when the defendant defames the entire group (for example, "All the male clerks at this store have AIDS") although the plaintiff is not mentioned by name. Courts will not hold the defendant liable when larger groups are referred to (such as "All Democrats are communists"). The theory is that the injury dissipates as it spreads over a large group of targets.

The defamatory statement not only must tend to lower the plaintiff's esteem in the eyes of others, but also must be false. The most defamatory statement in the world does not constitute the tort of defamation if it is true. The key question is often: Who has the burden of proving truthfulness or falsity? The common law presumed that everyone was a good person. Therefore, if plaintiffs proved that statements tending to defame them had been published by the defendant, the burden of proof was on the defendant to prove the truthfulness of the statement. Truth, in other words, was an absolute defense to a defamation claim.

The Supreme Court redistributed this burden of proof, at least in some cases, on First Amendment grounds. In *Philadelphia Newspaper, Inc. v. Hepps,* 475 U.S. 767 (1986), the Court held that if the plaintiff is a public figure (such as a famous actress or athlete), a public official (such as a governor), or a "limited" public figure (e.g., a private citizen involuntarily caught up in a high-profile crime), free speech concerns require that the plaintiff have the burden of proof to demonstrate falsity. In the modern era, the common-law presumption that defamatory speech is false has also been rejected when the defendant is a member of the news or entertainment media, regardless of whether the plaintiff is a public figure or limited public figure.

Communication. To be defamatory, a statement must be "published" or communicated by the defendant—that is, overheard or read by a third party. If Joe and Kim are standing alone in a field, miles from anyone else, Joe can say all the nasty things he wants to Kim without committing defamation. Kim's reputation in the community cannot be hurt if no one else hears the statements. If Kim goes back into town and repeats the statements for others, it is Kim doing the communicating, not Joe. If only one person overhears a defamatory statement, it is actionable although obviously the damage to plaintiff is not as severe as where many more people heard or read the statement.

Injury. As noted earlier, the traditional common-law rule presumed damages in libel and the four special types of slander. If a false statement tending to lower the plaintiff's esteem in the eyes of others appeared in a local newspaper, it was sensible to presume that persons read it and that their impressions of the plaintiff were adversely affected. Injury was presumed, and it made no difference that the defendant did not intend to injure the plaintiff. Because injury is typically presumed in a case of libel or slander per se, the court (jury, if there is one) may award substantial damages to the plaintiff even if the plaintiff has not produced evidence of actual harm to his reputation. Even if not required, however, it will always be in the plaintiff's best interest to produce evidence of actual reputational harm (and evidence of any economic loss resulting from the damage to his reputation) if such evidence exists.

The Supreme Court has indicated that this presumption of injury is inconsistent with the First Amendment, at least when the media are reporting about public officials, public figures, or private figures involved in public controversies. In these cases, at least, plaintiffs must introduce some evidence to show that the defamatory publication injured their reputations.

Defenses

Statute of Limitations. In most jurisdictions, the statute of limitations for defamation cases is one year, only half the two-year statute of limitations typically found for other types of tort claims.

Absolute Privilege. To encourage certain types of activity, the courts have created an absolute privilege for the potential defendant in several contexts. That is, even if the plaintiff could prove all the elements of defamation just discussed, no liability would attach even if the defendant acted in bad faith. The two most important of these are the privileges for judicial and legislative proceedings. To encourage judges to judge, witnesses to testify, lawyers to advocate, and legislators to debate the issues aggressively, all are protected absolutely when involved in their respective activities. Note, however, that the absolute privilege is narrow in scope. An attorney who wrote a book about a case after the trial was over or a legislator making statements not while debating a bill but while campaigning would not be protected.

Qualified Privileges. There are also several qualified privileges when the defendant will be protected if he or she acted *in good faith*; that is, malice must be proved in addition to the other elements of the defamation claim. The primary example of this occurs when the media report on public officials, other public figures (such as celebrities), and newsworthy events. A second example is where the defamatory statements are made under circumstances in which both the transmitter and recipient(s) of the information have a legitimate interest in the contents of the communication, such as an employment reference sent by a former employer to a prospective new employer. Some states have legislation creating a qualified privilege for employment references, credit reports, and other commercially useful information, but they typically provide only what the common law would provide, anyway—requiring that malice be proved to overcome the qualified privilege. Some states also have legislation stating that there is a qualified privilege for communications to those who can act in the public interest (for example, complaints to a school board about a teacher). Again, however, the general common law rules of defamation would normally provide for a qualified privilege in this type of case even if there was no special legislation. To overcome a qualified privilege by proving malice, the plaintiff must prove that the one making the false defamatory statement either (1) knew that the statement was false, or (2) acted with a reckless disregard for whether the statement was true or false.

Injurious Falsehood

Closely related to defamation (and perhaps equally as closely connected to the business torts discussed at the end of this chapter) is the tort of *injurious falsehood,* also known as disparagement of goods, slander of goods, and trade libel. The elements are generally the same as for traditional defamation, but the subject matter relates not to an individual's reputation, but to the plaintiff's title to property or to the quality or conduct of the plaintiff's business. The tort is aimed at protecting economic interests and would allow suit against a defendant who, for example, falsely stated that the plaintiff's business was no longer in existence. One major difference between this tort and defamation is that a plaintiff in an injurious falsehood case cannot receive any damages unless the plaintiff proves actual economic loss.

Defamation and Anti-SLAPP Statutes

A *strategic lawsuit against public participation* (SLAPP) is a lawsuit filed by a plaintiff that is intended to intimidate and silence someone else. Those filing such lawsuits normally do not intend to actually win the case, but to stop the defendant from criticizing the plaintiff by imposing large litigation defense costs. In addition to defense costs, the lawsuit may take a lot of the defendant's time and emotional energy. Although such lawsuits may allege several different types of claims against a defendant, a claim of defamation is the most common assertion by the plaintiff in a SLAPP suit. Essentially, a SLAPP lawsuit seeks to prevent defendants from exercising their free speech rights.

Many states in the U.S. and a number of other countries have passed so-called *anti-SLAPP statutes.* Such legislation allows a court to dismiss a lawsuit at an early stage if the defendant convinces the judge that the plaintiff's lawsuit is without merit and that it is primarily intended to silence defendant's criticisms of plaintiff. Anti-SLAPP statutes typically also allow the court to assess a monetary penalty against the plaintiff and reimburse the defendant for attorney fees and other legal costs.

False Imprisonment

The privilege to come and go as we please is important in our society. The courts protect that interest by recognizing the right to sue for the tort of *false imprisonment* when persons are unlawfully confined or restrained without their consent. If the defendant purports to arrest the plaintiff as well, the nearly identical claim of *false arrest* is applicable.

Elements

To prove a false imprisonment claim, the plaintiff must usually prove that the defendant (1) intentionally confined or restrained the plaintiff, (2) without the plaintiff's consent, (3) without lawful authority or in an unreasonable manner, and (4) "injured" the plaintiff.

Intentional Confinement. False imprisonment can occur when the defendant confines the plaintiff in a room, a building, a car, or even a boat. It can even occur in wide-open spaces if the plaintiff is held in one spot against her will by force or threat. If the defendant blocks one exit to a room but another is available to the plaintiff, no confinement occurs.

Regarding the plaintiff's intent, if someone accidentally locks another in a room, perhaps negligence is involved, but not false imprisonment. False imprisonment requires a wrongful intent on the defendant's part. If the defendant stands outside the plaintiff's house with a gun, issuing threats of bodily injury should the plaintiff emerge, the intent requirement is met. Although the defendant would like nothing better than for the plaintiff to come out of the house, the natural consequence of the defendant's intentional actions is to force the plaintiff to remain in the house.

Without Consent. The same force and threats of force that create an assault may force a person to remain in one place against his will. A large man could easily intimidate a small person into staying involuntarily in one place. However, if the plaintiff stays in one place as an accommodation or to clear up an accusation with police, there is no involuntary confinement. Assume that a store clerk tells a customer only: "We believe you have stolen from the cash register and have called the police." If the customer voluntarily stays in the store to give her side of the story, there is no false imprisonment. Both consent and lack of consent can be express or implied—implicit, that is, inferred from all of the surrounding circumstances—unless a statute specifies that either must be express.

Without Lawful Authority or in an Unreasonable Manner. If the defendant has lawful authority for detaining the plaintiff, such as a police officer who has probable cause for an arrest, there is no false imprisonment. In some instances, an ordinary citizen who is not a police officer can make a lawful arrest. An example occurs when someone who owns property or has authority from the owner of the property (such as a security guard or other employee or contractor hired to guard property) seeks to prevent property damage or loss. Such a person may lawfully detain someone else if the guard has probable cause—a reasonable, individualized suspicion—that the other person either has or is about to steal or damage any of the property.

Even if the detention occurs within the scope of the arresting person's lawful authority, the method, means, and duration of the confinement must be reasonable. This is essentially a limitation on lawful authority. What is reasonable, as always, depends on the totality of the circumstances. Physical contact or physical force is not reasonable unless required to accomplish a lawful detention, and no more force can be legally used than is truly necessary to accomplish the detention. Intentionally causing public humiliation or invading the detainee's privacy in a way not required for accomplishing the detention is not reasonable. Finally, the detention can be for only a reasonable time—no longer than is reasonably necessary to investigate and either determine that the arrest was mistaken or to verify the suspicions leading to the detention, contact law enforcement authorities, and wait for such authorities to arrive.

Injury. To win any type of claim in a civil lawsuit, you must prove "injury," but the term is used very broadly to describe various kinds of harm. In the case of false imprisonment, there is injury in the form of wrongfully depriving a person of his liberty-- that deprivation of freedom of movement is an injury in the legal sense. The injury necessary for a valid false imprisonment claim arises automatically from the confinement, even if it is brief. A restraint of hours or days is not required for the necessary injury to occur. However, because the injury is essentially psychological in nature, it will not occur if the plaintiff is unaware of the confinement. Thus, if the plaintiff sleeps through a confinement, there would be no legal injury. But if the plaintiff knows of the confinement, monetary damages are available.

Defenses

Many false imprisonment claims involve merchants. Shoplifting, unfortunately, is a serious problem in the United States. When a shopkeeper detains a suspected shoplifter and presses charges, any number of things can prevent a conviction from being obtained, including prosecutorial or police error, or the failure of a witness to appear. At common law, even a well-founded belief by a shopkeeper that a theft had occurred frequently would not prevent the success of a later false imprisonment claim if, for whatever reason, no criminal conviction was obtained. However, all state legislatures have acted to protect shopkeepers with legislation ("shopkeepers' statutes") that prevents recovery for false imprisonment when shopkeepers have probable cause for suspecting shoplifting and conduct the detention in a reasonable manner even if they were mistaken.

WAL-MART STORES, INC. v. COCKRELL
Texas Court of Appeals, 61 S.W.3d 774 (2001)

Karl Cockrell and his parents went to the layaway department at a Wal-Mart store. Karl decided to leave the store. As he was walking through the front door, a loss-prevention officer stopped him and requested that Karl accompany him to the manager's office. Once in the office, the officer instructed Karl to pull down his pants. The officer shook the pants to remove any stolen property. Nothing fell out. The loss-prevention officer then instructed Karl to remove his shirt. Karl had a large surgical wound on the right side of his abdomen that was covered by a bandage. Karl was told to remove the bandage, despite his explanation that the bandage maintained a sterile environment around his wound. The officer insisted the bandage be removed, and Karl took off the bandage. No merchandise was found. The loss-prevention officer apologized and let Karl go.

Karl sued for false imprisonment. The trial court found in favor of Cockrell. Wal-Mart appealed.

Dorsey, Justice:

The elements of false imprisonment are: (1) a willful detention; (2) performed without consent; and (3) without the authority of law. A person may falsely imprison another by acts alone or by words alone, or by both, operating on the person's will. In a false-imprisonment case, if the alleged detention was performed with the authority of law then no false imprisonment occurred. The plaintiff must prove the absence of authority in order to establish the third element of a false-imprisonment cause of action.

Here Ray Navarro, the loss-prevention officer, testified that Cockrell was in his custody at the point when he escorted him to the office. When Cockrell's counsel asked Navarro, "Was it your decision as to when he [Cockrell] could leave?" he replied, "I guess." Navarro testified that he probably would have let Cockrell leave after seeing that he did not have anything under his shirt.

Cockrell testified that he was not free to leave when Navarro stopped him, and that

Navarro was not going to let him go. He also testified that Navarro and two other Wal-Mart employees accompanied him to the office. When counsel asked Cockrell why he did not leave the office, he replied, "Because the impression I was getting from him, I wasn't going no place."

We conclude that these facts are sufficient to support the jury's finding that Cockrell was willfully detained without his consent.

The court instructed the jury on the "shopkeeper's privilege." This instruction stated: "when a person reasonably believes that another has stolen or is attempting to steal property, that person has legal justification to detain the other in a reasonable manner and for a reasonable time to investigate ownership of the property."

Neither Raymond Navarro nor any other store employee saw Cockrell steal merchandise. However, Navarro claimed he had two reasons to suspect Cockrell of shoplifting. First, he said that Cockrell was acting suspiciously, because he saw him in the women's department standing very close to a rack of clothes and looking around. Later he saw Cockrell looking around and walking slowly by the cigarette aisle and then "pass out of the store." Second, he saw a little "bulge" under Cockrell's shirt.

Cockrell testified that he had done "nothing" and that there was "no way" a person could see anything under his shirt. We conclude that a rational jury could have found that Navarro did not "reasonably believe" a theft had occurred and therefore lacked authority to detain Cockrell.

The extent to which Wal-Mart searched Cockrell compels us to address the reasonable manner of the detention. The "shopkeeper's privilege" expressly grants an employee the authority of law to detain a customer to investigate the ownership of property in a *reasonable manner*.

At least one appellate court has stated that when a store employee has probable cause to arrest a person for shoplifting, the employee may do so and make a "contemporaneous search" of the person and the objects within that person's control. We therefore hold that when a store employee has probable cause to arrest a person for shoplifting, the employee may do so and make a contemporaneous search of the person and objects within that person's immediate control. The contemporaneous search is limited to instances in which a search of the body is reasonably necessary to investigate ownership of property believed stolen. Accordingly, Navarro's contemporaneous search was unreasonable in scope, because he had no probable cause to believe that Cockrell had hidden any merchandise under the bandage.

[Affirmed.]

Trespass

When others infringe on our right to use real property—land and those things attached to it, such as houses—the tort of trespass to real property is committed. The tort has a convoluted common-law history that protects property owners from innocent as well as mean-spirited invasions of the right to use real property.

Elements

Generally speaking, to prevail in a trespass case the plaintiff must establish the following elements: (1) affirmative conduct by the defendant, (2) with intent to enter onto realty in the possession of another, and (3) resulting in actual entry.

Affirmative Conduct. If Joe is driving down the street when Alan runs a stop sign with his car, smashes into Joe, and pushes Joe up onto Ed's lawn, no trespass has been committed by Joe. He invaded Ed's real property but not through any affirmative act of his own.

Intent. The intent element of a trespass cause of action requires the plaintiff to demonstrate only that the defendant intended to enter the place and that the place belonged to the plaintiff. No intent to do harm is required. Thus, if Cindy walks across Ann's land believing that she is walking across her own or across land belonging to her friend Sally who has given her permission to cross it, Cindy commits a trespass actionable by Ann. Cindy's good faith is no defense. However, if Mark has a heart attack and dies instantly while driving down the street, and his car runs onto Ed's lawn, the affirmative conduct element is arguably not met and certainly the intent element is missing. The same may be said of a person who, driving too fast on slick streets, loses control of the car and winds up on someone's lawn. The intent element is missing.

Actual Entry. Entry is required for completion of the tort, but *usually* no real injury. Damage is presumed from the fact of entry, even if the only injury is trampled blades of grass. A judgment in the form of nominal damages of a dollar or so would still be warranted. According to most courts, the invasion need be only slight, including throwing a rock onto the plaintiff's property, shooting a bullet over it, or tunneling under it. Some courts refuse to recognize injury where the invasion is truly minor, such as where A's tree limb grows so far that it extends over B's property line.

The court must sometimes balance competing interests. For example, *in Bradley v. American Smelting and Refining Co.,* 709 P.2d 782 (Wash. 1985), the defendant operated a copper smelter that emitted particulate matter, including arsenic, cadmium, and other metals. Although undetectable by human senses and not harmful to health, this matter did sometimes settle on the plaintiff's property. The court felt constrained to create an exception to the general rule that *any* entry constitutes an injury, stating:

> When [airborne] particles or substance accumulates on the land and does not pass away, then a trespass has occurred. While at common law any trespass entitled a landowner to recover nominal and punitive damages for the invasion of his property, such a rule is not appropriate under the circumstances before us. No useful purpose would be served by sanctioning actions in trespass by every landowner within a hundred miles of a manufacturing plant. Manufacturers would be harassed and the litigious few would cause the escalation of costs to the detriment of the many. The plaintiff who cannot show actual and substantial damages should be subject to dismissal.

A claim of trespass is normally recognized as belonging to the lawful possessor of the land even if he is not the owner. Thus, if T were renting a farm from L, and X trespassed on the farm, T would normally have the right to sue for any injury to current enjoyment of the farm and L would have the right to sue for any permanent damage to the farm.

Defenses

In addition to the typical two-year statute of limitations (which is extended if the trespass is a continuing one, as when the trespasser has erected a small building on the plaintiff's property), the main defenses to a trespass cause of action are consent and legal right. Thus, a tenant has the landlord's consent, pursuant to a lease, to remain on the landlord's property. However, if the tenant stays beyond the term of the lease and refuses to leave, a trespass is committed because consent has expired.

A legal right might arise from, for example, an easement, which is a right to use someone's property for a limited purpose. Thus, if M's land is between N's land and a major highway, N might negotiate an easement from M, paying M a sum of money in exchange for the limited right to travel over M's land going to and from the highway.

The following is an interesting trespass case that also briefly discusses the notion of adverse possession.

VILLARREAL v. CHESAPEAKE ZAPATA, L.P.
2009 Tex. App. LEXIS 5180 (Tex.App. 2009)

In 2004 and 2005, Chesapeake Zapata (Chesapeake) drilled two gas wells on a 67-acre tract of property in Zapata County, Texas, known by the parties as the "Rectangle." Chesapeake leased the Rectangle from the Ramirez Mineral Trust, the entity that Chesapeake believed owned it. The Villarreals subsequently sued Chesapeake for trespass, among other claims, asserting that they were the real owners of the Rectangle.

The trial judge granted summary judgment to Chesapeake on grounds, among others, that (a) the Villareals had not produced a scintilla of evidence regarding their ownership of the Rectangle, (b) that the Ramirez Mineral Trust had acquired ownership of the Rectangle via adverse possession, and (c) there was no evidence of trespass by Chesapeake in light of the lease it signed with the Ramirez Mineral Trust. The Villareals appealed.

Speedlin, Judge:

Before the trial court, the Villareals presented a title opinion and the deposition testimony of their expert, Cornelius Hayes, in which Mr. Hayes details the documentation he reviewed to support his conclusion that the Villarreals owned record title to the Rectangle. Although Chesapeake also presented expert testimony in which their expert reached the conclusion that the Ramirezes owned record title, the conflict in these expert opinions raised a genuine issue of material fact with regard to record title. As a result, if the summary judgment was granted on the basis of record title, it was erroneous.

To support a claim for adverse possession, a claimant must prove: (1) actual possession of the disputed property; (2) under a claim of right; and (3) that is adverse or hostile to the claim of another person and that it was consistently and continuously so for the duration of the statutory period. [The court then examined at length the testimony in the case and summarized evidence that the Ramirez possession of the Rectangle was with the permission of the Villareals and therefore did not meet the "adverse or hostile" element of adverse possession.]

Viewing this testimony in the light most favorable to the Villarreals as required by the applicable standard of review, the foregoing testimony was sufficient to raise a genuine issue of material fact as to whether the Ramirezes' possession of the Rectangle was by permission. Accordingly, a genuine issue of material fact was raised regarding the hostile element of the adverse possession claim, and the trial court erred in granting summary judgment on that claim.

Trespass to real property occurs when a person enters another's land without consent. To recover damages, a plaintiff must prove that: (1) the plaintiff owns or has a lawful right to possess real property; (2) the defendant entered the plaintiff's land and the entry was physical, intentional, and voluntary; and (3) the defendant's trespass caused injury to the plaintiff. We previously discussed the evidence raising a genuine issue of material fact with regard to the Villarreals' ownership of the Rectangle. It is undisputed that Chesapeake intentionally entered and drilled wells on the Rectangle. Finally, Chesapeake's senior account manager, April Smith, testified that Chesapeake had produced 6,363,340 MCF of oil, gas, condensate or other minerals from the wells located on the Rectangle valued at $40,046,955.34. Accordingly, the Villarreals produced more than a scintilla of evidence on each of the elements of their trespass to real property claim.

[The summary judgment granted in favor of Chesapeake was reversed and the case was returned to the trial court for further proceedings.]

Invasion of Privacy

Slowly over the past 75 years or so, the courts have increasingly recognized privacy as an interest worthy of legal protection. Today, many jurisdictions have recognized one or more of the following four varieties of tort that come under the umbrella of *invasion of privacy*.

Intrusion

Intrusion occurs whenever a defendant intrudes into an area where a plaintiff has a reasonable expectation of privacy. The invasion must be highly offensive to a reasonable person to be actionable. Secretly placing a microphone under the plaintiff's bed to overhear the goings-on would be actionable. So might an employer's secretly searching an employee's locker (where the employee provided his own lock and therefore had a justifiable expectation of privacy) without reasonable grounds for doing so.

Disclosure of Embarrassing Private Facts

Where no justification exists, it may be actionable to disclose to the public facts that the plaintiff finds embarrassing or offensive. Because they are "true," the disclosures do not constitute defamation; they may be more akin to blackmail. However, a newsworthiness defense exists, at least for the media. In one case, a woman sued for the embarrassment she was caused by a newspaper's disclosing that her husband was killed in a fire in a motel while accompanied by another woman. The court held that fires are newsworthy events, and the newspaper could not be liable for accurately reporting the names of the victims. (Fry *v. Ionia Sentinel Standard*, 300 N.W.2d 867 (Mich.App. 1980)).

Several employer-employee disputes have involved claims of invasion of privacy, In *Young v. Jackson*, 572 So.2d 378 (Miss. 1992), for example, a woman passed out while wearing protective gear and working in an area of a nuclear power plant contaminated with radioactivity. She was taken to the hospital. Although her fainting was due to complications from a partial hysterectomy, rumors spread throughout the plant regarding its safety and management announced the true cause of the woman's problem in order to assure the other workers that there was no safety issue with radioactivity. The woman had been so embarrassed about her operation that she had not even told her husband. She was humiliated by the announcement and sued her employer. The court quoted the Restatement (Second) of Torts: "One who gives publicity to a matter concerning the private life of another is subject to liability to the other for invasions of his privacy, if the matter publicized is of a kind that (a) would be highly offensive to a reasonable person, and (b) is not of legitimate concern to the public." The court held that plaintiff was understandably upset about the disclosure of these private facts about her health. However, it also held that the employer had a good faith defense for the disclosure in that the information was of legitimate concern to the other employees who were worried about their own health. Because of this "qualified privilege," borrowed from defamation law, the plaintiff could recover damages only if she could prove that the managers had acted with malice toward her. She was not able to prove this.

False Light

Very similar to the tort of defamation, the action for "false-light" privacy renders liable a defendant who makes statements or does acts that place the plaintiff in a false light in the public eye. Although usually these statements or actions would injure the plaintiff's reputation and also be actionable as defamation, occasionally they might involve false statements that the plaintiff had performed many wonderful deeds. Rather than suing for injury to reputation in a defamation suit, a false-light plaintiff seeks compensation for shame, embarrassment, mental anguish, or humiliation.

Appropriation of Name or Likeness (The "Right of Publicity")

A final type of privacy tort protects the economic interests that persons have in the potential exploitation of their names and faces. Thus, if a company uses the name or picture of a famous actress in its advertising campaign without her permission, it has appropriated her name or likeness to her economic detriment. The company should have acquired her consent and paid her for such use. After singer Bette Midler refused to sing for a company's television commercial, it hired one of her back-up singers and asked her to sound as much like Midler as possible. Many listeners thought they were hearing the real Bette Midler, which formed the basis for a successful appropriation suit by Midler *(Midler v. Ford Motor Co., 849 F.2d 460 (9th Cir. 1988)).*

Intentional Infliction of Mental Distress

As noted earlier, because emotional injuries are difficult to prove and to value, courts have traditionally been reluctant to allow recovery for them. But just as such recovery is now allowed in suitable cases of negligence, it is also allowed when emotional distress is intentionally caused. The turning point may have been cases such as *Wilkinson v. Downtin,* 2 Q.B.D. 57 (1897), in which, as a practical joke, the defendant called the plaintiff, a woman whose mental state was somewhat suspect anyway, and falsely told her that her husband had been in a serious accident. This so upset the plaintiff that she had to be hospitalized. Recovery for her emotional distress was allowed.

The requisite elements for proof for the tort of *intentional infliction of mental distress* are generally formulated as follows. First, defendants must act intentionally or recklessly. Defendants will be presumed to intend the natural consequences of their actions. And defendants who are aware of a particular plaintiff's susceptibilities to mental distress will be judged accordingly. Second, the defendants' conduct must be extreme and outrageous. Mere insults are usually insufficient, as are profanity and other abuses of a relatively minor nature. Third, defendants' actions must be the cause of plaintiff's emotional distress. Finally, plaintiff's emotional distress must be severe. Physical consequences are not required, but their presence does assist in establishing proof of severe emotional anguish.

In *Turman v. Central Billing*, Inc., 568 P.2d 1382 (1977), a collection agency was held liable to Turman, who was blind, when it badgered her in trying to collect a small debt assigned to it for collection, even after it knew that she and the creditor had come to a satisfactory settlement. This harassment, which resulted in the plaintiff's hospitalization for anxiety and severe stress, was carried out by repeated phone calls—sometimes twice a day—in which the defendant's agent shouted at her, used profanity, told her several times that her husband would lose his job and the house if she did not pay, and called her "scum" and a "deadbeat." (Such egregious acts also violate the Federal Debt Collection Practices Act.)

This tort cannot be used to evade First Amendment restrictions on recovery for defamation. When the late Reverend Jerry Falwell sued *Hustler* magazine over an extremely rude parody, showing that it had caused him emotional distress, the Supreme Court held that freedom of expression considerations barred recovery. *Hustler Magazine v. Falwell*, 485 U.S. 46 (1988).

Fraud

The essence of the tort of *fraud* is the intentional misleading of one person by another, which results in a loss to the deceived party. Because many kinds of fraudulent conduct occur when the sole purpose of the wrongdoer is to cause the innocent party to enter a contract that the person otherwise would not make, additional consideration of this subject will be undertaken in the chapter relating to reality of consent in contract law.

Conversion and Trespass to Personal Property

The tort of *conversion* renders actionable certain invasions of personal property interests, just as trespass protects real property interests. An example would be where defendant stole plaintiff's automobile.

A tort that generally covers more minor invasions of personal property rights is frequently called *trespass to personal property* (or "trespass to chattels"). This tort would remedy, for example, the defendant's minor vandalism of the plaintiff's car. Recently, the tort of trespass to personal property has arisen in situations in which the defendant has "hacked" into plaintiff's computer system (which is also a crime). In addition, someone who intentionally transmits a software virus, or who floods plaintiff's e-mail system with unsolicited e-mail to such an extent that it either causes problems with the plaintiff's e-mail server or interferes with the ability of plaintiff's employees to do their jobs, has committed the tort of trespass to personal property.

Nuisance

Like trespass to real property, the tort of *nuisance* protects the enjoyment of such property. Frequently nuisance is used to compensate an intangible disruption of the enjoyment of property, as when the plaintiff is injured by the defendant's near-by activities that invade plaintiff's property via light (erection of tall light poles), noise (rock concerts), vibrations (blasting with dynamite), or smells (pig farming). The courts will consider such factors as the type of neighborhood, the nature of the wrong, its proximity to the plaintiff, its frequency or continuity, and the nature and extent of the injury in deciding whether an actionable nuisance exists.

Employer Liability

Ordinarily, the application of the principles of tort law results in the imposition of liability on the wrongdoer alone. There is one major exception, however, which springs from the principles comprising our master-servant law and our law of agency.

Under these principles, an employer is uniformly held liable for the torts of employees if the employees are acting "within the scope of their employment" at the time of the injury. Thus, if Doe, a truck driver employed by the ABC Furniture Company, negligently injures Smith while delivering a piece of furniture to a customer's home, Smith has a cause of action against both Doe and ABC Company, as illustrated in Figure 8.1.

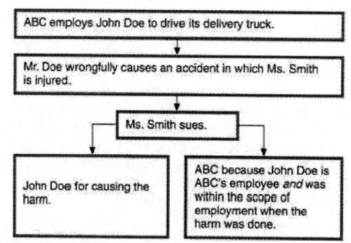

Figure 8.1 Employer's Liability for Employee's Tort

Ordinarily, in such a case, plaintiff brings just one action against both defendants; if she is successful in proving the facts as alleged, she obtains a "joint and several" judgment against Doe and ABC. This means that if she is awarded a judgment of $40,000, she can enforce the judgment against the assets of either party, or of both, until that sum is recovered. (The "scope of employment" issue is covered further in the chapters on agency law.)

Joint and Several Liability

When two defendants' actions together contribute to a plaintiff's injury, they are frequently held jointly and severally liable. The "joint" portion of this liability means that each defendant may be held responsible for the entire loss caused to the plaintiff. Thus, theoretically one defendant who is only 10 percent at fault might have to pay also for the 90 percent fault of another defendant, especially if the latter defendant is judgment-proof (lacking assets or insurance to pay). The relatively harsh result that this can have for "deep pocket" defendants is a major cause of criticism of our present tort system. Most states have abolished or enacted limits on joint and several liability in many types of cases.

BUSINESS TORTS

As we have seen in our discussion of negligence and intentional torts, all of tort law has applicability to businesses. Certain kinds of torts, however, are often referred to as "business torts" because they arise directly from the competitive rivalry between businesses. We now discuss two primary examples. The first is *intentional interference with business relationships*. This tort is sometimes referred to as "tortious interference." It has been developed by courts as part of the law of intentional torts. The second is *unfair competition*, which is quite a bit broader and actually encompasses several closely related torts. The law of unfair competition has many sources, including state court decisions (common law) and both state and federal statutes. Finally, the subject of the next chapter, Chapter 9—Intellectual Property Law—is very closely related. This area of law—misappropriation of trade secrets and infringement of patents, copyrights, and trademarks—also encompasses allegedly wrongful conduct arising from competitive rivalry. As with all areas of law, categorization can be difficult and imprecise.

Intentional Interference with Business Relationships

Beginning with an old English case, *Lumley v. Gye, 118 Eng.Rep.* 749 (Q.B. 1853), in which an opera singer was induced by the defendant theater owner to breach her contract to sing at the plaintiff's theater and appear at the defendant's instead, courts have recognized the general principle that a third party who wrongfully interferes with an existing contract has committed a tort. Most courts have even stretched the concept to hold defendants liable for intentionally interfering with contracts that do not yet exist but are reasonably certain to be entered into, and with certain other kinds of prospective business relationships that have not yet attained the status of binding contracts.

Elements of the Tort

The law in this area varies quite a bit among jurisdictions. Even the name of the tort—variously tortious interference with contract, tortious interference with business relationships, tortious interference with prospective economic advantage—varies from jurisdiction to jurisdiction.

The basic elements of the tort, however, are similar in most states. The factual scenario in such cases typically involves a plaintiff and defendant who are competitors, the plaintiff has a contractual relationship with a third party, and plaintiff contends that the defendant intentionally took actions that led the third party to breach its contract with the plaintiff. In the case of an existing contract, a common formulation of the elements of the tort would be that plaintiff must prove: (a) the existence of a binding contract subject to interference; (b) an intentional act of interference; (c) proximate cause; and (d) actual damage or loss occurred. The intent involved need not be malicious. The simple fact that defendant knew such a contract existed and proceeded to interfere suffices. Defendants cannot interfere with contracts that they are a party to; only outsiders may commit tortious interference.

Texaco, Inc. v. Pennzoil Co., 729 S.W.2d 768 (Tex.App. 1987), involved a situation in which the court found that the defendant had knowingly interfered with an existing contract. Pennzoil sued Texaco for intentional interference with contract rights when Texaco bought a controlling interest in the stock of Getty Oil Co. after, according to Pennzoil, it had already made a contract to acquire Getty. Agreeing with Pennzoil, a jury awarded a huge verdict to Pennzoil.

But what if there is no binding contract, but simply the prospect that plaintiff might have entered into a binding contract or a beneficial economic relationship with the third party? In this setting, a common formulation of the elements of a cause of action requires: (a) a reasonable probability that the parties would have entered into a contractual relationship; (b) an intentional *and malicious* act by defendant that prevented the relationship from occurring, with the purpose of harming plaintiff; (c) defendant lacked privilege or justification to do the act; and (d) actual damage or loss occurred. Because no binding contract exists, it is fair for defendant to compete with plaintiff for the third party's business. Therefore, defendant will not be liable in this setting unless it acted with "malice." Indeed, many courts require more than a vague showing of "malice"; they require that defendant committed an independent tort or violation of law.

One case illustrating the tort of intentional interference with a business relationship that had not yet ripened into a legally enforceable contract involved the following situation. A real estate salesman followed customers away from his former employer's business premises and convinced them to rescind their contracts with that business and to purchase less expensive real estate from him. Although the customers had the right under the federal Truth-in-Lending Act (these were credit sales) to rescind their contracts with the former employer within three days, the salesman was found liable to his former employer for committing this tort. Although there was arguably no interference with a binding contract, there was interference with prospective advantage flowing from an advantageous business relationship. One can see that the relationship came very close to becoming (?) a legally enforceable contract, however.

Other examples of circumstances in which most courts would hold the defendant liable for interference with a business relationship that was not a valid contract include situations in which there was a contract between the plaintiff and a third party, but the contract was not legally enforceable because it was required to be in writing under the Statute of Frauds (discussed in Chapter 15), or was not a valid contract because the plaintiff or the third party had committed fraud in the creation of the contract (or was not valid for similar reasons discussed in Chapter 14).

Because this is an intentional tort, plaintiffs often recover punitive damages as well as compensatory damages.

Privilege of Competition

As noted earlier, the courts in a majority of states do not require the plaintiff to prove that the defendant acted with malice when the defendant knowingly induced someone to breach an existing contract with the plaintiff. A larger number of courts do require proof of (at least) malice, however, when the relationship that the defendant interfered with was not yet a legally enforceable contract or when the contract is terminable at will and therefore either party may withdraw without breach.

In such cases, the defendant is protected by the *privilege of competition*—the right to compete—as long as the defendant did not use clearly improper means to achieve its purpose. Assume that P Co. has an at-will contract to supply ABC Co. with widgets. D Co. is entitled to go to ABC to offer a better price or better quality in order to win ABC's business away from P Co. However, D Co. may not lie about the quality of P's products or its own or defame P's owners in an attempt to win away ABC's business.

Note, however, that if P Co. has a two-year term contract to supply ABC with widgets, D Co. cannot invoke the competition privilege in order to induce ABC to breach its contract with P Co. P Co.'s right to see its contract with ABC enforced outweighs D's right to compete. But D Co. is entitled to induce ABC to switch away from P's products to its own as soon as the existing two-year contract expires.

SPEAKERS OF SPORT, INC. v. PROSERV, INC.
U.S. Court of Appeals, 7th Circuit, 178 F.3d 862 (1999)

Ivan Rodriguez, a highly successful major league catcher, in 1991 signed the first of several one-year contracts making plaintiff Speakers of Sport his agent. Defendant ProServ wanted to expand its representation of baseball players and to this end invited Rodriguez to its office in Washington and there promised that it would get him between $2 and $4 million in endorsements if he signed with ProServ--which he did, terminating his contract (which was terminable at will) with Speakers. This was in 1995. ProServ failed to obtain significant endorsement for Rodriguez and after just one year he switched to another agent who the following year landed him a five-year $42 million contract with the Texas Rangers. Speakers brought this suit a few months later, charging that the promise of endorsements that ProServ had made to Rodriguez tortiously induced him to terminate his contract with Speakers.

The district court ruled against plaintiff Speakers, and Speakers appealed.

Posner, Chief Judge:

Speakers could not sue Rodriguez for breach of contract, because he had not broken their contract, which was terminable at will. Nor, therefore, could it accuse ProServ of inducing a breach of contract. But Speakers did have a contract with Rodriguez, and inducing the termination of a contract, even when the termination is not a breach because the contract is terminable at will, can still be actionable under the tort law of Illinois as an interference with prospective economic advantage.

There is in general nothing wrong with one sports agent trying to take a client from another if this can be done without precipitating a breach of contract. That is the process known as competition, which though painful, fierce, frequently ruthless, sometimes Darwinian in its pitilessness, is the cornerstone of our highly successful economic system. Competition is not a tort, but on the contrary provides a defense (the "competitor's privilege") to the tort of improper interference. It does not privilege inducing a breach of [a term] contract, but it does privilege inducing the lawful termination of a contract that is terminable at will. Sellers do not "own" their customers, at least not without a contract with them that is not terminable at will.

There would be few more effective inhibitors of the competitive process than making it a tort for an agent to promise the client of another agent to do better by him--which is pretty much what this case comes down to. It is true that Speakers argues only that the competitor may not make a promise that he knows he cannot fulfill, may not, that is, compete by fraud. Because the competitor's privilege does not include a right to get business from a competitor by means of fraud, it is hard to quarrel with this position in the abstract, but the practicalities are different. If the argument were accepted and the new agent made a promise that was not fulfilled, the old agent would have a shot at convincing a jury that the new agent had known from the start that he couldn't deliver on the promise. Once a case gets to the jury, all bets are off. The practical consequence of Speakers' approach, therefore, would be that a sports agent who lured away the client of another agent with a promise to do better by him would be running a grave legal risk.

The promise of endorsements was puffing not in the most common sense of a cascade of extravagant adjectives but in the equally valid sense of a sales pitch that is intended, and that a reasonable person in the position of the "promisee" would understand, to be aspirational rather than enforceable—an expression of hope rather than a commitment. So understood, the "promise" was not a promise at all. But even if it was a promise (or a warranty), it cannot be the basis for a finding of fraud because it was not part of a scheme to defraud evidenced by more than the allegedly fraudulent promise itself [which must be shown to establish promissory fraud under Illinois law].

It can be argued, however, that competition can be tortious even if it does not involve an actionable fraud or other independently tortious act, such as defamation, or trademark or patent infringement, or a theft of a trade secret; that competitors should not be allowed to use "unfair" tactics; and that a promise known by the promisor when made to be unfulfillable is such a tactic, especially when used on a relatively unsophisticated, albeit very well to do, baseball player. Considerable support for this view can be found in the case law. But the Illinois courts have not as yet embraced the doctrine, and we are not alone in thinking it pernicious. The doctrine's conception of wrongful competition is vague-- "wrongful by reason of . . . an established standard of a trade or profession" or "a violation of recognized ethical rules or established customs or practices in the business community." Worse, the established standards of a trade or profession in regard to competition, and its ideas of unethical competitive conduct, are likely to reflect a desire to limit competition for reasons related to the self-interest of the trade or profession rather than to the welfare of its customers or clients. The tort of interference with business relationships should be confined to cases in which the defendant employed unlawful means to stiff a competitor. Affirmed.

Justification Defense

Malice also would not be found if the defendant's actions are legally justifiable. *Justification* for a defendant's interference may be found if it is aimed at protecting a third person's legitimate interests (such as when an independent construction inspector hired by a city recommended that the city terminate the plaintiff's construction contract for substandard work), or at protecting the public interest in general.

Furthermore, the defendant can claim justification for interference to protect its own existing legitimate contractual or property interests. For example, assume that X gets a new car franchise from D, an auto manufacturer. Later X makes a contract with P, a motorcycle wholesaler, under the terms of which P is permitted to sell motorcycles in a limited area in X's showroom. D subsequently causes X to break the contract with P because of complaints from new car buyers about dirt and noise associated with P's operation. D's interest in the proper conduct of the new car dealership would likely justify its actions, providing a defense to any tortious interference claim P might bring. Thus, P's only recourse would be a breach of contract action against X.

Manager's Privilege

When a corporation breaches a contract, the other party will frequently sue not only the corporation for breach of contract but also will assert a tortious interference claim against any corporate manager who participated in the decision to breach the contract. Corporate officers or other managers are usually protected from liability by a doctrine called the *manager's privilege* if their decision to have the corporation breach the contract was based solely or essentially on the best interests of the corporation. Such would be the case when it would be far more advisable for a corporation to pay damages resulting from a breach of contract than to live up to a contract that might be financially disastrous. However, if officers are acting primarily to further their own personal interests, this defense is unavailing. If a consultant recommends in good faith that a client breach its contract with ABC Computer and begin buying XYZ's computers, an analogous "consultant's privilege" will protect the consultant from liability if ABC sued it for tortious interference with contract.

Unfair Competition

The term *unfair competition* is an imprecise one. In its broadest sense, it covers all torts arising from competitive rivalry. In its most common usage, however, the term refers only to those business practices that are based on deception. It includes a number of common-law torts, such as (1) falsely causing consumers to believe a product is endorsed by another, and (2) "palming off"—palming off refers to any word or deed causing purchasers to be misled into thinking that defendant's product was produced by someone else for the purpose of taking a free ride on the plaintiff's brand name and reputation. Both (1) and (2) are a form of intentional trademark infringement that constituted a tort long before the development of modern federal trademark law.

State Deceptive Trade Practices Acts

A consumer who is misled by false advertising or other deceptive practices may have the right to sue under a common-law fraud theory or perhaps a breach of express warranty theory if the advertising involved a product. These theories are discussed in other chapters. However, additional consumer protection legislation, passed at both the state and federal levels, also addresses such activity.

Misleading advertising is often prohibited by *state deceptive trade practices* acts. In states having such statutes, the wrongs are thus statutory rather than common law torts. Other types of unfair competition that are usually prohibited by such statutes are the advertising of goods or services with the intent not to sell them on the advertised terms, representing goods as new when they are used or second-hand, and disparagement—making false statements of fact about competitors' goods or services.

For example, in 2015 Anheuser-Busch Co. settled a class action brought against it under the Florida state deceptive trade practices act based on allegations that Anheuser had misled customers by placing on labels of "Beck's" premium brand beer the statement that the beer "originated in" Germany. Plaintiffs contended that they and many thousands of other consumers of Beck's beer paid more for the beer than they otherwise would have because they thought that the beer was imported from Germany, when in fact it was made in the U.S. After two years of litigation, Anheuser agreed to give refunds to customers and to change labels on Beck's to make it clear that the beer is made in the U.S.

Lanham Act

The federal government has also passed various acts that prohibit unfair competition, such as misleading advertising. In this chapter, our focus is on §43(a) of the Lanham Act, which outlaws "any false description or representation." Although this section is frequently used to allow trademark owners to sue competitors for trademark infringement, it has also created a general federal law of unfair competition, which is frequently applied to deceptive advertising. Designed largely to protect consumers, the cause of action is given primarily to the deceptive advertisers' competitors.

Illegal Acts under §43(a)

Section 43(a) of the Lanham Act has supported suits against companies that (1) used pictures of the plaintiff's product to advertise their own inferior brand; (2) used a confusingly similar color and shape of drug capsule that could mislead consumers into thinking that they were buying the plaintiff's nontrademarked brand; (3) printed "$2.99 as advertised on TV" when only the plaintiff had run such ads; (4) claimed that their pain reliever worked faster than the plaintiff's when it did not; and (5) displayed a rock star's picture on an album creating the impression that the star was a featured performer when, in fact, she was not.

As in all advertising, some "puffing" is permitted by the Lanham Act. Puffing in advertising consists of statements that are too general or vague to be viewed as statements of fact that reasonable consumers should rely upon. For example, when a computerized chess game was advertised as "like having Karpov [a famous Russian chess master] as your opponent," mere puffing was found. *Data Cash Systems v. JS&A Group, Inc.,* 223 U.S.P.Q. 865 (N.D.Ill. 1984). The same result was reached in a case involving a claim that defendant sold "America's favorite pasta." *American Italian Pasta Co. v. New World Pasta Co.,* 371 F.3d 397 (8th Cir. 2004).

Commercial Defamation

Through passage of the Trademark Revision Act of 1988, Congress established a cause of action for commercial defamation, thereby increasing the volume of this type of litigation. The Lanham Act now bans false descriptions or representations about the "nature, characteristics [or] qualities of any person's goods, services or commercial activities." Therefore, if Company A runs an ad comparing its products to those of Company B, and in so doing misleadingly describes the characteristics of Company B's products, Company B will be able to recover damages, perhaps including treble damages. For First Amendment reasons, the Act contains express protection for two broad types of activities: (1) political speech, consumer or editorial comment, and satire, and (2) "innocent infringement" (thereby insulating news media that innocently disseminate false advertising).

CHAPTER 9

INTELLECTUAL PROPERTY

- Trade Secrets
- Patents
- Copyrights
- Trademarks

The law of intellectual property—trade secrets, patents, copyrights, and trademarks—has always been important, but has become far more important in modern times because the value of these types of intangible assets has increased tremendously in comparison with the value of tradition capital assets. Individuals and companies today spend far more money and time than just a few years ago in creating and protecting intellectual property. The modern economy is based much more on knowledge, in contrast with tangible assets, than it once was. The natural result of the evolutionary economic process is that knowledge-based assets are simply worth more than they used to be, and now have a total value domestically and internationally that substantially exceeds the value of physical assets.

Intellectual property law is based on several fundamental concepts. First, intellectual property law protects certain types of knowledge, ideas, and expressions by granting exclusive rights to creators. These exclusive rights are a type of intangible property right.

Second, when someone else violates these rights, the violator is actually engaging in a form of competition. It is a type of competition that has been declared unlawful, but it is competition nonetheless. In general, of course, competition is necessary for markets to function properly, and is viewed as being very desirable for consumers. Experience has taught us, however, that some conduct that is competitive in the short run may actually harm competition in the long run.

Suppose, for example, that X (or the company he works for) invests time, energy, and money in coming up with a new invention that provides a benefit to society. Using the knowledge that X developed, Y then begins making and selling a new product that is the same as X's invention. If X has no way to protect his investment in inventing, he is less likely to make these kinds of investments in the future. If we have patent laws, if his invention meets the requirements for obtaining a patent, and if he is able to successfully sue Y for patent infringement, X is more likely to continue investing in the inventive process in the future. In many sectors of the economy, the most important type of competition is the competitive rivalry to innovate.

The same can be said for investing time and money in creative efforts such as writing books, music, and software. Here, copyright law creates certain exclusive rights that are intended to encourage people to continue engaging in these socially desirable creative activities. Thus, intellectual property laws essentially prohibit certain kinds of conduct (such as infringing on someone else's patent, copyright, trade secret, or trademark) that are competitive in the short run, with the objective of creating greater incentives for people and companies to engage in innovative and creative activities that tend to promote competition and also benefit society in other ways (such as the cultural value of creativity) in the long run.

Third, even though there is a general consensus that intellectual property laws benefit society in the long run, such laws can go too far. If, for example, very many patents are granted on inventions that really don't deserve such protection, society pays the short-term price of less competition but does not receive the long-term benefits from genuine innovation. Likewise, if copyright law protects too much or protects it for too long (which many knowledgeable observers believe to be the case today), society pays more for access to creative works in the short run without receiving properly corresponding benefits in the long run.

An ideal system provides protection to intellectual property that is no greater than is necessary to create and maintain the desired incentives to innovate and create over time. No system is ideal. No nation's intellectual property laws, including those of the U.S., are ideal. Most experts continue to believe, however, that societies are better off with these laws than without them, and most of the debate is not concerned with whether there should be protection for intellectual property, but rather with how much protection these laws should provide.

Moreover, a country cannot fully participate in today's global economy without a full slate of intellectual property laws and effective means for enforcing them. This is one of the fundamental obligations of all nations that are members of the World Trade Organization (WTO). Currently, 164 countries representing 98% of all world trade are members. The WTO was created by the Uruguay Round of Negotiations on GATT (General Agreement on Trade & Tariffs), which concluded in 1994. One of the main agreements resulting from the Uruguay Round was TRIPS (Trade-Related Intellectual Property Rights), which set a number of minimum requirements for intellectual property protection in all member nations. Member nations must have laws in place for adequate legal protection of trademarks, trade secrets, patents, and copyrights, and they must effectively enforce those laws. Participating countries also must not discriminate against citizens of other member nations in the application of their intellectual property laws. A failure to comply with these requirements constitutes an unfair international trade practice.

TRADE SECRETS

It is an information age, and nothing is more important to most businesses than information. By means of economic espionage and the hiring of competitors' employees, companies annually acquire from competitors billions of dollars' worth of confidential information. A *trade secret* is any type of knowledge that is not generally known and is not readily available through legal means, if the knowledge gives its owner a competitive advantage over rivals who do not have the knowledge.

A few examples of knowledge that is eligible for trade secret protection include detailed customer information that is not easily available to others, manufacturing processes, chemical formulas, operating and pricing policies, marketing strategies, raw materials sources, and the functional ideas in computer software (i.e., what the software does).

Sources of Trade Secret Law

Common-Law Principles and the UTSA: Trade secrets traditionally were protected by common-law principles (as embodied in the Restatement of Torts), but in recent years 48 states and the District of Columbia have adopted the Uniform Trade Secrets Act (UTSA). Whether a given state has enacted the UTSA or still relies on common-law principles usually does not affect the outcome of a particular case because the principles are practically the same. Thus, the UTSA is essentially the law in American states, but courts in all states often rely on court precedents established earlier when only common-law principles applied.

Economic Espionage Act: Although trade secret law still is primarily state law, in 1996 Congress passed the Economic Espionage Act (EEA) that makes it a federal crime to steal trade secrets. The primary concern of Congress was trade secret theft by agents of foreign companies or governments, but the law applies to everyone, including U.S. nationals. The EEA contains a broad definition of trade secrets and an even broader definition of misappropriation in an attempt to punish every form of unauthorized misappropriation.

Just as importantly, the EEA adopts the traditional view that a trade secret loses its protected status if its owner does not take reasonable measures to protect it from disclosure. Prosecutors must prove not only that the purloined information was a trade secret, but also (a) that the defendant knew the information was a trade secret, (b) that the defendant intended to provide an economic benefit to a person other than the rightful owner, and (c) that the defendant intended to injure the owner of the trade secret. Domestic corporate espionage can be punished by fines of up to $500,000 for individuals and up to $5 million for organizations. Individual defendants also face prison terms of up to ten years. If the trade secret theft is meant to benefit foreign entities, the penalties are even stiffer. Furthermore, any proceeds derived from the violation may be ordered forfeited.

In one of the earliest EEA cases, a maintenance supervisor at PPG-Industries offered to sell trade secrets to a competitor, Owens-Corning. Owens-Corning notified the FBI, which set up a sting operation. After being arrested trying to sell trade secrets to an undercover agent, the PPG employee pled guilty and received a 15-month prison sentence.

Defend Trade Secrets Act: In 2016, Congress enacted the Defend Trade Secrets Act (DTSA), which amended the Economic Espionage Act to add civil liability provisions to the criminal ones of the EEA. The DTSA created a new civil cause of action for trade secret misappropriation that can be enforced in federal court. The law thus creates federal subject matter jurisdiction so that a trade secret case may be filed in federal district court even without diversity of citizenship. The DTSA is patterned very closely on state laws in the great majority of states where legislatures have passed the Uniform Trade Secrets Act. The DTSA does not preempt state secret law, and the same conduct will often violate both state law and the DTSA.

Something new in the DTSA, however, adds to state laws by protecting employees who act as whistleblowers who report trade secret theft in their companies—under certain circumstance, an employee who reports suspected trade secret theft cannot be sued by their company even if they disclosed confidential information in good faith as part of reporting the theft. Very recently, a federal district court in Illinois ruled in *Motorola Solutions, Inc. v. Hytera Communications Corp. Ltd.*, 2020 WL 967944 (N.D. Ill. 2020), that the DTSA can be used to sue a foreign national when the defendant "used" the stolen trade secret information within the United States. "Use" includes selling or even just advertising within the U.S. a product that incorporates unlawfully acquired trade secret information.

Elements of Trade Secret Misappropriation

Although both trade secret and patent law can be used to protect knowledge, the definition of what kind of knowledge can be protected is much broader in trade secret law. In situations where a company has knowledge (in the form of an ''invention'' such as a new process or product) that can potentially be protected either by trade secret or patent law, the company cannot protect the same thing as both a trade secret and as a patented invention. The public disclosure required for a patent destroys secrecy, and the company must choose which form of protection it wants.

To successfully bring a trade secret misappropriation case, a plaintiff must prove (1) the information actually was a trade secret; (2) the plaintiff had maintained measures to protect secrecy that were at least reasonable under the circumstances; and (3) the defendant committed an act that is defined as "misappropriation."

Existence of a Trade Secret

First, a trade secret is information, or knowledge, that has value to its owner because possessing it confers a competitive advantage. That is, information is defined as a trade secret only if it give its owner some advantage over competitors who do not know it. The advantage can be an advantage in the form of lower production or sales costs, greater efficiency, greater customer appeal, better product quality, launching a new product or making a market entry before competitors can, and so forth. *Second*, information *cannot* be a trade secret if it is either (1) general knowledge within an industry or is (2) "readily (easily) ascertainable through legal means."

To win a trade secret misappropriation case, the trade secret owner must prove that (1) it owned information that qualified as a trade secret; (2) it maintained reasonable security measures to protect the trade secret that were at least reasonable under the circumstances; (3) the defendant committed an act that amounts to "misappropriation."

Courts have concluded that a combination of things can be a trade secret, even if none of the individual elements qualifies as a trade secret. For example, in *Metallurgical Industries, Inc. v. Fourtek, Inc.*, 790 F.2d 1195(5th Cir. 1986), the court concluded that a company's combination of improvements to a furnace using a zinc recovery method for separating and recycling expensive carbide from scrap metal was a trade secret even though each individual improvement was not. In a furnace using this process, molten zinc interacts with carbide in the scrap metal, causing the carbide to separate and become brittle so that it can then be ground into a powder and used as a substitute for virgin carbide. Metallurgical had ordered a furnace from a manufacturer, but the furnace that was delivered did not work properly because of several design problems. After experimentation and trial-and-error, Metallurgical modified the furnace by (1) inserting chill plates in one part of the furnace to create a better temperature differential for distilling the zinc, (2) replacing the one large crucible with several smaller ones to prevent the zinc from dispersing in the furnace, (3) replacing segmented heating elements that had caused undesired electric arching with unitary graphite heating elements, and (4) installing a filter in the furnace's vacuum-pumps where clogging of zinc particles had been a serious problem. There was nothing new about any single modification, but the combination was new and not readily known or available. This concept is just common sense, because almost everything is a combination of elements. As we will see in patent law, a patentable invention may also consist of a new combination of previously known elements.

A final observation regarding the existence of a trade secret is worth noting. When a trade secret consists of the solution to some problem, it is not just the final results of a knowledge-development effort that are protectable. In many such cases, most of the time, money, and effort are expended in running into blind-alleys; in other words, a lot of the knowledge gained is in the form of figuring out what does not work. Often referred to as "negative know-how," such knowledge is also protectable as a trade secret if other requirements for protection are satisfied.

Reasonable Security Measures: A prototypical trade secret is the formula for Coca-Cola. With regard to how the company protects the secrecy of the formula, a Coca-Cola company executive testified by affidavit in *Coca-Cola Bottling Co. v. Coca-Cola Co.*, 227

U.S.P.Q. 18 (D.Del. 1985) that "[t]he written version of the secret formula is kept in a security vault at the Trust Company Bank in Atlanta, and that vault can only be opened by a resolution from the company's Board of Directors. It is the company's policy that only two persons in the company shall know the formula at any one time, and that only those persons may oversee the actual preparation of [the product]. The Company refuses to allow the identity of those persons to be disclosed or to allow those persons to fly on the same airplane at the same time."

Although a company often will not be required to use the extreme measures adopted by Coca-Cola, you get the idea. A trade secret owner is not required to keep the information absolutely secret, usually an impossibility, but does have to employ protective measures that are reasonable under the circumstances. The requirement of reasonable security measures closely resembles a requirement that the owner not be negligent in protecting this intangible property. The extent to which the law expects a trade secret owner to go in protecting the secret depends on a variety of factors: (1) How valuable is the information? (2) How much would additional protective measures cost? (3) How much would additional security efforts interfere with employees' ability to do their jobs? (4) How much additional protection would extra security measures actually provide? One can see from these factors that courts often use a rough "cost-benefit" analysis to determine whether the trade secret owner used adequate protective measures. That is, the court weighs the relative costs and benefits of additional protection.

Although the exact type of security required depends on the type of information being protected, typical measures might include providing access to the trade secret information only in restricted areas, keeping doors and gates locked, requiring ID's and good computer password policies, using surveillance cameras or other appropriate devices such as motion detectors, having fences that outsiders can't see through, only allowing access to the information to employees who must know it to do their jobs (access on a "need-to-know" basis), disclosing information to outsiders (such as another company that must be relied on to do the manufacturing) only when it is necessary for the owner to do so in order to use it for commercial benefit and only when confidentiality obligations are imposed on the outsider. Also, even though the courts in all states impose an implied obligation of confidentiality on employees in almost all circumstances, requiring employees to sign written confidentiality, nondisclosure agreements (CNDA's) is a very good idea for several reasons, including the fact that it will contribute to a conclusion that the employer maintained reasonable security measures when there is a close question on that issue.

A good example of the way in which courts balance the relative costs and benefits of additional security measures when deciding whether the owner should have made more protective efforts is *E.I. du Pont de Nemours & Co. v. Christopher*, 431 F.2d 1012 (5th Circ. 1970). There, DuPont was constructing a large petrochemical refining plant that included facilities designed to enable DuPont to use its new, secret process for producing methanol. Apparently, someone who knows a great deal about such refining processes could figure out how DuPont's new process worked by seeing and studying the facility under construction.

The type of security that one would reasonably expect in a case like this would include things like a tall privacy fence around the construction site, restricted access by having locked gates and requiring I.D.'s, using guards who patrolled the perimeter, and so on. In a small airplane, the defendants flew over the construction site and took aerial photographs. The court held that the requirement of reasonable protective efforts did not mean that DuPont was required to build a dome over the construction site. This would have been an extraordinary step, and an exceptionally expensive one, and would be necessary only to protect against an intentional effort to spy. The defendants were found to have misappropriated DuPont's trade secret.

If the events in *Dupont* case were to take place today, the company would have to contend with much more sophisticated methods that thieves might use to study the details of Dupont's secret process from above, such as satellite photos. What should a company like Dupont do in modern times?

Proof of reasonable security measures is a separate requirement for proving trade secret misappropriation. In addition, however, the extent to which the company has maintained security is also closely related to the initial question of whether there is a trade secret at all. The reason is simple: if a court is faced with a close factual question whether a trade secret exists, the fact that the owner took substantial measures to protect the knowledge strongly tends to show that there was a trade secret, and vice-versa. Secrecy measures are expensive to establish, monitor, review, and enforce. Rational company managers are not likely to devote substantial time and money to protecting something that is not valuable and confidential.

Misappropriation: After Manville Corporation spent $9 million over seven years to develop a new method of insulation, one of its competitors hired six key Manville employees and was able to enter the market in less than two years. Manville later prevailed in a lawsuit against the competitor. This is just one of countless examples of improper disclosure (by former employees), acquisition, or use of trade secret information.

Conduct obviously will amount to misappropriation if it is independently illegal, such as bribery, burglary, trespassing, tapping telephones or other electronic message interception, or fraudulent misrepresentations (e.g., as a spy probably would have to make). However, conduct may be ''improper,'' and thus constitute misappropriation, even though it is not illegal by itself. The best known example is found in the *DuPont* case, discussed above, in which the court held that the aerial photography was not illegal and was not a tort, but was nevertheless an act of misappropriation because its only purpose was to intentionally overcome the reasonable security measures that DuPont had put into place. A third category of conduct that constitutes misappropriation, and the most common one, is the breach of a duty of confidentiality.

An obligation to keep information confidential, to not disclose it to others, and to not use it for any purpose than to benefit the owner can be express or implied. The most common example of an implied confidentiality obligation exists in the employment context. As noted earlier, courts treat employees as having an implied obligation of confidentiality to their employers in almost all cases. An implied confidentiality obligation is the result of an implied agreement, one that is inferred from the circumstances. If a company clearly treats information as confidential, and an employee or other person (such as a consultant) works in that environment of confidentiality, a court will usually draw an inference that the employee or other person implicitly agreed to confidentiality. Whether the duty is implied or express in a given case, an employee who acquires trade secret knowledge as a result of the employment relationship commits an act of misappropriation if she intentionally uses the information for her own benefit or discloses it to someone outside the employment relationship either while still an employee or afterwards. If the employee goes to work for another company and discloses or uses the information in her subsequent job, the new employer also will be liable for misappropriation if a manager or supervisor knows about it or as a reasonable person should know about it.

There are two methods of acquiring trade secrets that are not misappropriation: *independent development* and *reverse engineering*. First, if someone else develops the same knowledge on its own, such *independent development* of the knowledge is no misappropriation. Second, there is no misappropriation if (1) the information is found in a product, and (2) someone else *lawfully acquires* the product and *reverse engineers* (disassembles and works backwards) to discover the trade secret. If the technology is *patented*, however, using it is patent infringement no matter how the knowledge is acquired.

In *Smith v. Snap-On Tools Corp.,* 833 F.2d 578 (5th Cir. 1987), the inventor of a new ratchet (plaintiff) neither patented it nor kept it confidential. Instead, he voluntarily offered it to a tool company (defendant), stating that it would be compensation enough if some day he saw defendant sell his invention. Defendant began selling plaintiff's invention and making a lot of money. Plaintiff sued for trade secret misappropriation, but lost because he had voluntarily conveyed the information to defendant without demanding or even requesting confidentiality. No misappropriation by defendant was involved, so no liability for trade secret theft arose. Also, no implied contract to keep the idea confidential or pay compensation if it was used could be inferred from the circumstances.

It is important to emphasize that when someone commits trade secret information and then discloses the information to someone else (such as when an employee changes jobs), both the one who originally misappropriated the trade secret and the one who receives it (such as a new employer) may be liable for misappropriation. The company, such as the new employer, that receives or makes use of the trade secret is liable if a manager at the recipient company *knows* or reasonably *should* know that the information is someone else's (such as the individual's previous employer) confidential information.

Examples of both civil and criminal trade secret cases arise in the U.S. on an almost daily basis. In 2018, Uber agreed to pay $245 million to Waymo, a unit of Google, because evidence revealed, Anthony Levandowski, a former engineer at Waymo (Google) had taken Waymo's trade secret knowledge about advances in self-driving vehicle technology with him when he went to work at Uber, where it was then used.

In 2019, Robert O'Rourke, a 30-year salesman for cast iron products manufacturer Dura Bar, went on trial and was convicted in federal court in Chicago for stealing Dura trade secrets before leaving to work for a Chinese competitor. O'Rourke was a highly respected salesman at Dura until he became disgruntled with Dura management and decided to leave Dura for a Chinese competitor. Over a two-year period, O'Rourke met with the Chinese competitor (the identity of the Chinese company has not been disclosed) and eventually accepted employment with the competitor. Before resigning from Dura, O'Rourke downloaded 1,900 files that contained Dura trade secrets and subsequently attempted to board a flight to China with the trade secrets in hand. O'Rourke was stopped at the gate by the FBI and subsequently charged and convicted of 13 counts of trade secret theft in violation of both state and federal law.

In 2019, the U.S. District Court for the Northern District of California issued a felony criminal indictment accusing Xiaoqing Zheng, a former senior engineer for steam turbine design at GE, plus Zhaoxi Zhang, a Chinese businessman, of conspiring to steal GE's design data and models, engineering drawings, material specifications, configuration files, and other proprietary trade secret information related to GE's turbine technology. The indictment described the sophisticated means that the two defendants used to bypass GE's security measures and to hide the theft. For example, from around June through October of 2017, Zheng allegedly:

- Used a technique called steganography to hide GE's trade secret information in a seemingly innocuous image of a sunset named "New Year.jpg" and sent that file to his personal Hotmail account.
- Used steganography to hide encrypted GE design schematics in images of turbine blades.
- Used his personal Hotmail email account to send encrypted files, using generic zip file names (e.g. "overview-zip.zip" and "test-zip.zip") that included GE's trade secret information regarding manufacturing methods, design schematics, and models.
- Used encrypted text messages and audio messages to discuss the use of GE's trade secrets with his co-defendant, Zhang.

The indictment also described the security measures that GE had employed:

- Maintained perimeter security and restricted access to company property.
- Required visitors to register with security, wear badges, and be escorted by approved personnel.
- Limited access to company computer systems and monitored the same.
- Limited authorization to access systems containing GE proprietary information.
- Required employees to sign proprietary information agreements.
- Advised employees that their inventions and innovations created while employed with GE were the property of GE.
- Required employees to disclose inventions deriving from work at GE.
- Informed employees of GE's trade secret and proprietary information requirements through trainings, handbooks, oral warnings, and signs and banners posted in the workplace.
- Prohibited the use of USB drives.

The criminal case is ongoing as this is being written. And, in 2020, a federal judge sentenced a North Carolina man, Craig German, to 70 months in federal prison after the man pleaded guilty to a conspiracy in which Mr. German and two other men worked together to steal trade secrets, including aircraft wing schematics and anti-ice testing documents from aircraft companies. The men were attempting to develop anti-ice aircraft technology for another company and stole trade secrets to speed the new product to market. Mr. German emailed documents to his co-conspirators.

The following case illustrates how the requirement that a trade secret owner take reasonable security measures occupies a central place in trade secret law.

Abrasic 90 Inc. v. Weldcote Metals, Inc.
U.S. District Court, N.D. Illinois, 364 F.Supp.3d 888 (2019)

Abrasic 90, Inc., doing business as Camel Grinding Wheels, U.S.A. ("CGW") is a manufacturer of grinding and sanding discs. CGW is a company based in Niles, Illinois, that manufactures and sells over 5,000 abrasive products. During the period relevant to this lawsuit, CGW was owned by Gamal, an Israeli corporation.

CGW purchases materials from about 45 suppliers and sells its finished abrasive products through its internal sales force and a cadre of independent sales agents to roughly 4,000 distributors. About half of CGW's distributors receive prices from CGW that are discounted against CGW's "Mix & Match" catalogue, which is CGW's product-by-product starting point for pricing that is distributed to thousands of recipients. A software program tracks CGW's many thousands of pieces of transactional data and exports that data into various Excel spreadsheets. CGW stored its business and financial information—which included these Excel spreadsheets, the Mix & Match catalogue, sales reports containing information such as CGW's profitability by customer and by item, and other information such as shipping packaging weights—on CGW's shared drive. CGW's employees could access and work on the information on the shared drive as desired, and CGW sent some of the information, such as the sales reports, to its independent sales representatives.

From 2000 to January 29, 2018, Joseph O'Mera was CGW's President. O'Mera was also a director of CGW beginning at least as early as 2005. At CGW, O'Mera developed and oversaw various aspects of CGW's operations, identified at least 40 of CGW's 45 suppliers, and played the primary role in negotiating costs with suppliers. O'Mera also set CGW's prices for its entire product line and approved all pricing discounts. During O'Mera's tenure, CGW's annual sales increased from $ 2.8 million to $ 33 million.

O'Mera had an employment agreement with CGW from 2002 through 2007 that included a nine-month non-compete provision and confidentiality requirements. The term of the agreement *may* have been extended to 2012, but there is no evidence that the agreement extended past 2012.

The employment agreement required O'Mera to keep CGW information confidential during the term of his employment and to return the exclusive property of CGW when the agreement or his term of employment ended. Although CGW's parent company in Israel presented O'Mera with another employment agreement in 2013, that agreement was never executed because the parties could not agree on a long-term compensation plan.

So far as the record reflects, no other CGW officer or employee has ever been subject to a non-compete or confidentiality provision in an employment contract. CGW's employee handbook, which O'Mera approved in 2010, provides that employees may not "reveal or discuss information about CGW, its customers or its employees when outside of the company," but it does not impose any obligations on employees after their employment at CGW ends. CGW's independent sales representatives signed agreements informing them that "customer information, pricing, strategies and sales analysis records" were considered confidential and requiring them to return CGW property when their relationships with CGW ended, but nothing in the record suggests that others with access to the information at issue— such as CGW's own employees—entered into similar agreements or were likewise instructed regarding the confidentiality of certain categories of information. CGW also did not generally require others who had access to some of the information at issue, such as CGW's suppliers and distributors, to sign confidentiality or non-disclosure agreements.

Defendant Colleen Cervencik began working at CGW in 1998. She served as CGW's IT Manager from 2012 until approximately April 2018 when she was effectively demoted to a position as a "Special Projects Manager." During her tenure as the IT Manager, Cervencik maintained the shared drive where the information at issue was stored. She generally granted "office personnel" access to the shared drive if they asked for it (there is no evidence that any employee who sought access to the shared drive was denied such access), and about 39 of 108 CGW employees were given access. If an employee was given access to the shared drive, no inquiry was made as to whether the employee needed access to any particular subset of the information at issue, and there were no restrictions as to which folders within the shared drive that the employee could access; that employee had access to the entire shared drive. Nor were any restrictions imposed on what could be saved to the shared drive. None of the folders or files were password protected or encrypted.

There were also no restrictions placed on the employee's ability to download the files, save them to his or her hard drive or an external storage device, print them, or email them. Until April 2018, all employees were instructed to use the same password so that another employee could log in using the other employee's login credentials if necessary. CGW only labeled certain research and development files as "proprietary information." None of the sales and financial information at issue in this case was marked confidential or proprietary. It is undisputed that the shared drive included information that even CGW acknowledges was distributed publicly, such as the widely available Mix & Match pricing catalogue and shipping packaging weights.

In February 2017, CGW hired Ana Maria Gheciu, who holds a degree in network and telecommunications management, to work for Cervencik. Around April 2018, Gheciu replaced Cervencik as IT Manager. Gheciu suggested that CGW implement additional security measures, including limiting employees' access to certain files within the shared drive and implementing an "Acceptable Device Use Policy" requiring that employees remove company data from their personal devices at the time of their separation. CGW did not implement those measures. Indeed, notwithstanding her recommendation to limit the dissemination of company materials via personal devices, Gheciu sent some of the information at issue to O'Mera's personal email account.

In 2017, O'Mera began engaging in business talks with Zika Group Ltd. ("Zika") about Zika's plans to start an abrasives business that would compete with CGW. Those talks ultimately culminated in plans for Zika to acquire and expand the business of Weldcote, historically a manufacturer of welding products, to sell abrasives and safety products to welders. O'Mera accepted Zika's offer to work as CEO of Weldcote on January 28, 2018. But while O'Mera was still President of CGW, in April 2017, O'Mera sent an email to a Zika executive informing the Zika executive that O'Mera had obtained from VSM, a CGW supplier, a commitment to "work [with him] under the same exact pricing terms on their entire product line."

Other emails in the same thread suggest that O'Mera was engaging in similar discussions with CGW's major China vendor, Ningbo. O'Mera told Zika that O'Mera generally had "all the suppliers lined up." O'Mera also wrote in the thread that he had "spent an enormous amount of time on new product testing," and that it would be best if he left CGW before CGW could benefit from his work. O'Mera denies ever having conducted due diligence for Zika with respect to its acquisition of Weldcote, but he at least provided advice about the focus of some of Zika's due diligence work and met with Zika in North Carolina, where the Weldcote facility was then located, to discuss matters related to that potential acquisition.

O'Mera resigned from CGW on the afternoon of January 29, 2018, to join Weldcote as its President. Shortly before resigning, O'Mera gathered his CGW laptop and other equipment from his home and turned it in to CGW. O'Mera kept, however, a flash drive storage device containing both personal files and some of the information at issue. Included among the files O'Mera kept was CGW's "All Items File," which contained a comprehensive summary of CGW's transactional information, including sales data, prices, and costs for its products and the identities of suppliers and distributors. When O'Mera left CGW, neither Cervencik nor Gheciu nor anyone else at CGW asked or instructed him to delete company information that had been emailed to his personal email address or that he had otherwise copied or stored on or in personal devices and accounts.

Jay Hickman worked in sales at CGW from 2005 until February 20, 2018. When Hickman joined CGW, he brought with him the business of 30 to 50 of the more than 200 distributors with whom he had previously worked. Fritz Klug worked in sales at CGW from 2000 until February 20, 2018. When Klug joined CGW, approximately 25% of his prior customers followed him to CGW. Both Hickman and Klug joined O'Mera at Weldcote a few days after resigning from CGW. When Klug resigned from CGW, he told a CGW human resources employee that he was dropping "everything" off, but he retained a memory stick that contained some of the information at issue.

A few months later, O'Mera offered Cervencik a position at Weldcote as its Purchasing manager. On June 16, 2018, Cervencik accepted O'Mera's offer. Over the following week, O'Mera and Hickman asked Cervencik to obtain some of the information at issue from the CGW shared drive. O'Mera asked Cervencik to supply CGW data regarding "VSM roll ordering," information regarding a price increase given to CGW by Inter Abrasives, and data regarding CGW's consumption of flap disc rolls. Hickman also asked Cervencik to obtain some of the information at issue, explaining that he could use her help "with sales from western sales areas that I cover now, and had not for the last 5 years." Cervencik obtained the information O'Mera and Hickman requested before she resigned from CGW on June 22. O'Mera, however, placed the order for which the VSM roll ordering data he requested from Cervencik was relevant before Cervencik had an opportunity to provide him with that data. Cervencik also took with her when she resigned from CGW three thumb drives containing information at issue because she believed it might be helpful to her at Weldcote. When O'Mera, Klug, and Cervencik separated from CGW, no one asked them whether they had any confidential CGW information in their possession or demanded they return it.

Soon after Cervencik resigned, CGW employed a computer forensics company that discovered all of the data that had been taken by O'Mera and Cervencik. Weldcote filed suit in federal court against these individuals and Weldcote for trade secret misappropriation in violation of Illinois state law and the federal Defend Trade Secrets Act. After pretrial discovery, CGW sought a preliminary injunction that would prohibit Weldcote from entering the abrasives market. It presented evidence that Weldcote made significant use of the information taken from CGW.

Tharp, Jr., U.S. District Judge:

A party seeking a preliminary injunction must satisfy three requirements. It must show that: (1) absent a preliminary injunction, it will suffer irreparable harm in the interim period prior to final resolution of its claims; (2) traditional legal remedies would be inadequate; and (3) its claim has some likelihood of succeeding on the merits.

A party moving for preliminary injunctive relief must show that his chances to succeed on his claims are better than negligible. Despite this low bar, the Court concludes that CGW is unlikely to succeed on a theory that the defendants misappropriated CGW's trade secret. Although some of the information at issue may have been ***protectable*** as a trade secret, CGW did not adequately ***protect*** it for it to qualify as a trade secret.

It cannot be reasonably disputed that the defendants copied information from CGW and used it in setting up Weldcote's business. The relevant question is whether the CGW information at issue was truly secret.

Although courts have identified many factors that can be relevant to an assessment of whether information qualifies as a trade secret, there are two basic elements to the analysis. For the information at issue to be considered a trade secret, it must have been sufficiently secret to impart economic value because of its relative secrecy and CGW must have made reasonable efforts to maintain the secrecy of its information. The manner in which the information shared with suppliers and distributors was compiled could, in theory, transform the bits of information that on their own are not trade secrets into trade secrets in their compiled format. Accordingly, the Court has no difficulty concluding that some of the CGW information at issue was *protectable* as a trade secret. The problem for CGW, however, is that it did virtually nothing to protect that information to preserve its status as a trade secret.

CGW took almost no measures to safeguard the information that it now maintains was invaluable to its competitors. The company's almost total failure to adopt even fundamental and routine safeguards for the information at issue belies its claim that the information has economic value to its competitors and makes it quite unlikely that CGW will ultimately prevail on its trade secret claim.

CGW's data security was so lacking that it is difficult to identify the most significant shortcoming, but the company's failure to require those with access to its supposed trade secrets to enter into non-disclosure and confidentiality agreements has to be counted among the most fundamental omissions by the company. Failure to enter into nondisclosure or confidentiality agreements often dooms trade secret claims.

Of course, even if CGW had used non-disclosure or confidentiality agreements, such an agreement, without more, is not enough. The failure to use confidentiality agreements is symptomatic of the non-existence of any CGW policy concerning the confidentiality of its business information. So far as the record reflects, there was no policy at CGW regarding confidentiality beyond a vague, generalized admonition about not discussing CGW business outside of work. That admonition did not define, delineate, or specify which information was considered confidential. The confidentiality language in the employee handbook stating that employees are "not to reveal or discuss information about CGW, its customers or its employees when outside of the company" is too broad and vague to confer meaningful protection over the information at issue.

In the absence of an articulated and developed confidentiality policy, it is not surprising to find that CGW did nothing to train or instruct employees as to their obligation to keep certain categories of information confidential. Those employed by or doing business with CGW who had access to the information at issue in its compiled or uncompiled format were not required to agree not to disclose it. CGW did not have exclusive relationships with its suppliers or distributors, yet, according to the testimony of multiple witnesses, CGW's suppliers and distributors were not generally required to keep the information confidential or enter non-disclosure agreements. Nor did CGW insist that its own employees with access to the information sign non-disclosure agreements or otherwise agree not to disclose it.

Moreover, CGW seems to have employed a policy of benign neglect when employees left the company. Although employees were instructed to return CGW property when they separated from CGW, they were not asked whether they possessed any of the information at issue or instructed to return or delete such information. Requiring that departing employees or contractors return company property when their relationship with the company ends is a routine, normal business practice, but precautions must go beyond normal business practices for the information to qualify for trade secret protection. The motion for a preliminary injunction is denied.

Doctrine of Inevitable Disclosure

The *doctrine of inevitable disclosure* may prevent an employee who has left Company A from working for Company B if the employee's new job duties will inevitably cause the employee to rely upon knowledge of the former employer's trade secrets. Thus, rather than waiting until there is evidence that Company B is using Company A's trade secret and suing for trade secret misappropriation, Company A may ask a court to prevent its former employee from working for Company B.

State and federal courts in about twenty states have addressed the doctrine of inevitable disclosure, almost half of them refusing to recognize it and requiring proof that actual misappropriation had occurred. Among the slight majority that have accepted it, courts commonly require a plaintiff such as Company A to establish three elements: (1) the former and new employer are competitors; (2) the employee possesses trade secret information belonging to Company A; and (3) the employee's new job is at least very similar to his old job so that the trade secrets would "inevitably" be used in his new job.

The doctrine stems from *PepsiCo, Inc. v. Redmond,* 54 F.3d 1262 (7th Cir. 1995), where a court prevented a former PepsiCo employee from assuming a new job at Quaker. The employee, Raymond, had learned PepsiCo trade secrets while working in its sports drink department, was moving to Quaker's sports drink department, and was to have duties very similar to those he had had at PepsiCo.

A more recent case in which a U.S. Court of Appeals applying Pennsylvania state law recognized the doctrine, involved the trade secret recipe for creating the unusual texture ("nooks and crannies," in the company's terminology) of Thomas' English Muffins applied the inevitable disclosure doctrine in granting an injunction against a high-ranking marketing executive from taking essentially the same job with a direct competitor. *Bimbo Bakeries USA, Inc. v. Botticella,* 613 F.3d 102 (3rd Cir. 2010). The employee, Botticella, also had engaged in questionable conduct such as downloading computer files containing confidential information during the last three months in which he worked for Bimbo Bakeries and while he was pursuing a job offer from the competitor. This information had not yet been used, and thus there had not yet been any misappropriation, but when the competitor who had made the lucrative job offer to Botticella found out about his behavior, it withdrew the job offer because Botticella was obviously not the kind of person they wanted to hire. Thus, Botticella didn't get to make muffins anymore.

PATENT LAW

To encourage creation and disclosure of inventions, the U.S. Constitution authorizes the federal government to grant patents to inventors. The first U.S. patent law was adopted by Congress in 1790, and the Patent Act of 1952 plus its many later amendments governed patent law in this country until President Obama signed the American Invents Act (AIA) on September 16, 2011. Both the provisions of the 1952 and the federal case law interpreting it will be applicable for many years to come, however. Most of the AIA's important provisions apply only to patents resulting from applications filed on or after March 16, 2013. Given that the term of a patent is 20 years, counting from the date of the original application, the old rules will apply to large numbers of patents until around 2030, and one must understand both the old and the new rules for a long time. Fortunately, much of the case law, especially as applied to "prior art," remains unchanged by the AIA.

In exchange for disclosing the invention in detail, the inventor patentee receives a 20-year exclusive right to make, use, sell, or offer to sell the patented invention within the U.S., or to import it into the U.S. Anyone else doing any of these things without permission (a "license") is guilty of patent infringement and can be required to pay the patent owner for lost profits or reasonable royalties and be ordered by a court to stop all infringing activities. The 20-year patent is nonrenewable; after expiration of the period the item goes into the public domain and may be made, used, or sold by anyone. Until 1995 the term of patent protection was 17 years from the date the patent was issued, but Congress changed it to 20 years from the date the patent application was first filed. This had already been the term for patent protection in most other countries for many years. Congress made this and several other changes in order to implement the provisions of the international agreements that created the WTO.

Applying for a Patent

An application for a U.S. patent must be filed with the U.S. Patent & Trademark Office (PTO). The application specifies the names of the inventor or inventors and who owns the patent if the owner is someone other than the inventors. Much more often than not, there will be an "assignee-at-issue," which is usually a corporation that employed the inventors. The application must contain a thorough and concise description of the invention and drawings. The description and drawings together must meet the enablement requirement, which means that they must describe the invention with sufficient thoroughness and conciseness to enable a hypothetical "person having ordinary skill in the art (PHOSITA)" ("art" refers to the relevant field of technology) to make the invention and put it into practice without undue experimentation. We refer to the hypothetical PHOSITA, which is a necessary legal construct as is the hypothetical "reasonable person" in the law of negligence or in contract law, but actual experts in the relevant field of technology will often be hired to make sworn statements that are filed with the PTO by a patent applicant, and to present expert reports and testimony in patent infringement litigation.

A patent application must be filed in the name of one or more inventors, even if another entity like an employer actually owns the invention as an "assignee." In recent years, Artificial Intelligence (AI) software, primarily using "machine learning," has advanced to the point of being able to create inventions without human intervention after the software has gone to work. In 2020, the PTO ruled that AI cannot be a named inventor, and that, unless Congress changes the law, only a human can be named as an inventor. Some observers have asked whether an AI-created invention thus has no inventor at all.

The applicant is not required to have actually made the invention physically, and many patents are granted even though the applicant has not created a physical embodiment of the invention. However, physically making the invention is a practical necessity in some situations in order for the inventor to know that the invention works and to be able to write an "enabling" description of the invention. Examples include some fields of chemistry and in biotechnology because the results of experimentation in those fields are highly unpredictable and actual experimentation often has to be undertaken and completed to know whether the invention will work as intended.

After the written description and drawings, the patent includes "claims," which precisely delineate the intangible property right the applicant is asking the PTO to grant. To determine exactly what the invention is, one must look at the precisely drafted claims. When a patent owner sues for patent infringement, the owner is actually suing for infringement of one or more claims within the patent. In the discussion of proving infringement, we discuss claims in more detail and provide an example.

In addition to a regular application, since 1995 U.S. law has permitted a "provisional application," which can be especially advantageous for individuals, small businesses, and nonprofits like universities because it allows for the deferral of many patenting costs for up to a year—this gives the applicant an all-important filing date but provides extra time to do things like seek additional funding and further explore market potential. A provisional application can be filed without including any claims, and the PTO takes no action on it. If the applicant files a regular application within one year (including claims) and does not make any material change in the description or drawings, any resulting patent traces its filing date back to the filing of the provisional. Having as early a filing date as possible is important for many reasons, but the primary reason today is that it cuts off "prior art." This means that, once an inventor has a firm filing date, later-developed evidence of the same or a similar invention by someone else cannot be used to deny a patent to the first filer.

When it is thought that a new invention is likely to find markets outside the owner's home country, it is common for patent applicants in the U.S. and in other nations to apply for patent protection in several countries because a patent granted in any country provides exclusive rights in that particular nation. This can be quite expensive, though. There are international treaties that make the process of filing patent applications on the same invention in multiple countries easier, but an applicant should be convinced that major foreign markets exist before filing outside its home country.

Requirements for Patentability

Not only must the patent application contain an "enabling" written description of the invention, the application must be filed within one year after the inventor engaged in certain activity that created "prior art" (discussed below), for a patent to be valid, the invention itself must be (1) a patentable subject matter, (2) useful, (3) novel, (4) "nonobvious" (that is, someone skilled in this area of technology could not have made a simple, easy mental leap from what the prior art revealed to this later invention), and (5) an "enabling" written description of the invention in the patent that allows a reasonably skilled expert in the technology to make and use the invention merely by studying the description and drawings without having to do a lot of additional experimentation.

Patentable Subject Matter

Inventions that may be patented include (1) machines, (2) manufactures (that is, products), (3) compositions of matter (for example, new compositions of elements in a metal alloy), (4) processes, and (5) any improvement on the first four categories that itself meets all of these requirements. Patents also may be granted on certain new plant varieties. Regular patents are sometimes referred to as "utility" patents. Patent law also recognizes so-called "design patents" for non-functional ornamental design elements in a functional product. We will not discuss design patents. One cannot patent naturally occurring substances or abstract ideas such as formulas or scientific principles. Particular applications of formulas or principles, however, are eligible for patent protection.

For a number of years, there was legal debate about whether patent law can protect biotechnology processes and products. This debate was resolved in the affirmative by the Supreme Court in *Diamond v. Chakrabarty*, 447 U.S. 303 (1980), in which the Court upheld the validity of a patent on new bacteria created by genetic engineering that would "eat" crude oil in an oil spill. The court observed that Congress had intended to provide protection to "anything under the sun made by man" if it meets other patentability requirements. Since then, many patents have been granted by the PTO on things like genetically altered mice and rabbits (for applications in medical research). The dividing line, federal courts have held, is between *discovery* and *invention*.

The *Chakrabarty* decision led to a widespread belief in the patent community, including the PTO, that isolating a human gene so that it could be synthesized in a laboratory for medical research purposes constituted an "invention," and not just a discovery of something in nature. The belief was that, because a gene (which consists of DNA) cannot exist in an isolated state within the human body, isolating it through the use of genetic engineering techniques amounted to enough human intervention to make the isolated gene an invention. In 2013, however, the U.S. Supreme Court's held, in *Association for Molecular Pathology v. Myriad Genetics*, 569 U.S. 576, that an isolated gene in the laboratory is essentially identical to its unisolated counterpart within the human body. Thus, the Court ruled, such a gene is just a discovery of something in its natural state and is not eligible for patent protection. For several scientific reasons, this decision has not had a meaningful impact on research in genetics.

Relatively recent decisions by federal courts and the PTO have made it increasingly difficult to obtain patents on *medical diagnostic techniques*. The reason is that these techniques typically claim methods for diagnosing diseases using correlations between certain conditions in the body and a particular disease. Courts and the PTO have concluded in a number of cases that a statistical correlation is something that just exists in nature, and is not invented by human beings. Thus, they are usually not eligible for patent protection. Similarly, some claims in patents seeking protection for diagnostic methods involving *analyzing* data are have been found ineligible for patent protection when the claimed analysis depends on a naturally existing statistical correlation.

Software Patents. Whether computer software is patentable subject matter also was debated hotly for some time. Copyright law protects the expressive elements in software, mainly the source code, object code, and the screen display if the display shows original expression. But what about the functional ideas in software (what the software does) that can cause the software to be viewed as an "invention"? The question arose because software consists of a large number of algorithms (formulas for solving problems). After many confusing decisions by both the Supreme Court and the Court of Appeals for the Federal Circuit (the intermediate appeals court that hears all patent cases), it now is firmly settled that a computer software program can be a patentable invention as long as it meets the other requirements of patentability, and as long as the patent attorney is very careful to draft the "claims" (discussed later) in the patent application to include language showing that physical parts of a computer are an essential part of the invention. (This is always true, of course, but patent attorneys must be very cautious in drafting the patent application to make it read more like a traditional physical machine.) Algorithms in the abstract cannot be patented, but their specific applications to accomplish certain results can be. In other words, what the software does and how it does it is eligible for patent protection. (In the alternative, the owner of software can often rely on trade secret protection for protecting the functioning of software.)

In recent times, however, it has become clear that someone cannot get a patent on an innovation, even if novel and nonobvious, that just takes some normal human activity or some mental process and shows how it can be done better with computer software. It now must be demonstrated that the invention actually improves computer technology itself in some significant way. This brings U.S. law to a point that is very similar to patent law in Europe, the UK, Japan, and other nations on the patentability of computer software.

Utility

The requirement that an invention be useful is typically referred to as the "utility" requirement. This requirement merely means that the invention must be operable and achieve a useful result. "Operable" and "useful result" essentially mean that it actually does something, and does not defy the laws of physics (like a perpetual motion machine). It does not have to be commercially successful; as earlier mentioned, it is not even required that the inventor has actually made a working version as long as thorough details are disclosed in the patent application. In recent years, the PTO finally rejected a patent application on a process for supposedly achieving "cold fusion" because the experimental results (which were highly questionable and rejected by others in the scientific community) could never be replicated by anyone. Other scientists concluded that the patent applicant had achieved only a chemical reaction rather than an atomic reaction.

One can see that the utility requirement has a very low threshold and will almost always be fulfilled. In a few areas of technology, however, such as biotechnology and some areas of organic chemistry, the inventor must go significantly farther in order to demonstrate operability and a useful result because experimentation in these areas is prone to highly unpredictable results.

The Nature and Importance of "Prior Art"

Before further discussion of the requirements of patentability, it is necessary to explain the concept of "prior art" in patent law, which is evidence of what others have previously done in the relevant technology field. To be patentable, an invention must be novel and nonobvious when compared with the prior art. With some simplification, prior art consists of either of the following: (1) A prior patent anywhere in the world; (2) A prior printed publication anywhere in the world; (3) Evidence of a prior "public use" of the invention; or (4) Evidence that the invention was placed "on sale." The AIA also states that prior art may be created by information that is "otherwise publicly accessible," but no one knows what this might mean. An important qualification must be made about evidence showing a prior *public use* or that the same invention had previously been placed *on sale*. Under the 1952 Patent Act, which still applies to patents granted from applications filed before March 16, 2012, evidence of a public use or that the invention has been placed on sale is prior art only if these events occurred *within the United States*. For inventions granted from applications that were filed on or after March 16, 2013, however, the AIA mandates that these events are prior art if they occurred *anywhere in the world.*

None of these four categories of evidence can be prior art if the invention revealed in that evidence was still experimental at the time. In patent law, "experimental" means that the inventor(s) did not know for certain whether the invention would work as intended from a scientific or engineering perspective. The fact that more research needs to be done to determine the best commercial versions of an invention, or for other marketing purposes, does not mean that the invention is still experimental as long as the inventor(s) are apparently certain that its scientific and engineering objectives have been met. To be prior art, these types of evidence must have revealed "inventions." Whether for the purpose of obtaining a patent, deciding whether an item of evidence constitutes prior art, or for any other purpose in patent law, something does not fall within the definition of "invention" if it is still experimental.

(1) By definition, a *patent* actually granted in any country is publicly available.

(2) A document (either in traditional hard copy or in any other tangible form such as a web page or other electronic document) is treated as a *printed publication* when it is accessible to anyone who is interested and willing to take the time to find it.

(3) *Public use* is an elusive concept, but essentially means either that the invention was (a) used by someone other than the inventor who was not under an express or implied duty of confidentiality to the inventor or to the inventor's employer, (b) used by the inventor or anyone else out in the open so that it could be seen by one or more others who did not owe a confidentiality obligation to the inventor or the inventor's employer, or (c) demonstrated to one or more persons who did not owe a confidentiality obligation to the inventor or the inventor's employer.

(4) An invention is placed *on sale* if it is either sold, subject to a contract of sale, or offered for sale. Unlike a public use, a sale, contract to sell, or offer to sell an invention is prior art even if the transaction was completely confidential. This is the only instance when prior art can be created in secret. The justification for treating confidential sales and offers or contracts to sell as prior art is discussed after the *Helsinn* case that is presented later in the patent law discussion.

A patent or a printed publication is treated as prior art only if it was "enabling"—that is, only if it revealed all of the elements of the later invention that is now in question, with sufficient detail so that a hypothetical ordinarily skilled practitioner in this technology area could have made the invention by studying these revealed details.

A prior public use of an invention that is the same as the current one can be prior art even if the use did not reveal enough detail to have been enabling.

With respect to the fourth type of prior art, an invention the same as this one having been placed on sale, the actions involved in making the sale or offer are also not required to have been enabling (although, as a practical matter, such actions often do reveal enough to be enabling). And, importantly, an invention does not have to have been made physically to be placed on sale.

Also, a public use is the only one of the four types of prior art that can come into existence only if a physical embodiment of the invention has been created—an invention must have been *made* before it can be *used*. In patent law terminology, a working physical embodiment of an invention that is no longer experimental is called an "actual reduction to practice." The practical importance of these concepts is discussed further in the section on the requirements of novelty and timely application filing.

Novelty and Delayed Filing

In the 1952 Patent Act there are two related provisions dealing with the requirement of novelty, and with the requirement that an inventor file a patent application within one year after a piece of prior art came into existence. The first section, § 102(a), states that an inventor should not receive a patent if someone else (other than this inventor) had a patent issued, created a printed publication, made a public use, or put an invention on sale *before this inventor invented*, where the previous invention contained all of the same functional elements as the current one.

The new rules established by the AIA no longer determine novelty based on the inventor's date of invention. Instead, an inventor will not be entitled to a valid patent if someone else had created prior art showing an identical invention even one day before the current inventor filed her patent application. This is but one ramification of the AIA's change from a "first-to-invent" (FTI) to a "first-to-file" (FTF) priority system. In other countries, which have used the FTF system for many years, this rule is absolute. However, there is a very important exception to this rule in the new U.S. system. In this new system in the U.S., if the invention is publicly disclosed by the inventor or by someone who got the invention ideas from the inventor (whether with authorization or dishonestly), the inventor still has one year from the date of this disclosure to file a patent application.

Disclosure creates a "placeholder" for the inventor, and the inventor has this one year within which to file (sometimes called a one-year "grace period") even if someone else then files a patent application covering an identical invention before this inventor does. Thus, it is more descriptive to call the new U.S. system a "first to file or disclose" system, in contrast with the pure FTF systems of other countries. For the sake of brevity, however, we will simply call the new U.S. system an FTF system. There is some question, which the courts will have to resolve, about what constitutes a "disclosure" of the invention by the inventor sufficient to trigger the one-year grace period for filing, but the most likely meaning is that it is triggered if the inventor creates any of the four types of prior art.

Suppose, for example, that Inventor X has invented a new device for improving automobile fuel efficiency. When X applies for a patent, the patent examiner in the PTO will search for and study relevant prior art. Obviously, X should have done a prior art search before filing, to determine whether his invention probably is patentable (but this can be a very difficult determination). Although X should have done this, in reality the quality of applicant prior art searches varies greatly. If it is found that, before X invented, Y had received a patent on an invention that included all of the elements of X's invention, then X's invention does not meet the requirement of novelty. The same would be true if it is found that Y had created one of the other types of prior art before X invented. Although novel means "new," it is possible for X to receive a valid patent on an invention even if someone else had created the same invention first. If, for instance, Y had invented before X did, but Y kept its invention secret (did not get a patent, did not disclose the invention in a prior printed publication, and did not create one of the other types of prior art before X invented), then X's invention is still treated as being novel.

The second section in the 1952 Patent Act, § 102(b), specifies that, if either Inventor

X or someone else created one of these pieces of prior art more than one year before X filed her patent application, X is not entitled to a patent. In the example above, suppose that Y had received a patent or created one of the other pieces of prior art more than one year before X filed his patent application. This provides another reason for denying X a patent. Suppose that the evidence did not establish when X actually invented—inventors should keep good records of their activities leading to an invention, but often they do not. In such a case, even if we don't know whether Y's prior art came into existence before X invented, this prior art destroys X's ability to get a patent if it came into existence more than one year before X filed his patent application. If we know when X invented, and Y's prior art is both before X invented and more than one year before X filed his patent application, there are two alternative reasons for denying X's patent.

Although the rule requiring X to file a patent application within one year after certain events can be applied to something someone else has done, as we have just seen, another common application of this filing-within-one-year rule is to things that Inventor X has done himself. Assume again, for example, that Inventor X invents the new fuel efficiency device, and has not yet filed an application for a patent. X makes a public use of the invention, places it on sale, or makes a written disclosure of the invention's details to someone who does not owe him a confidentiality obligation. X must file an application within one year after doing one of these things or he loses the right to obtain a patent. This is often referred to as the one-year "grace period," and allows X to engage in some preliminary efforts to seek financing or gauge the market even before. At the present time, other countries do not have this grace period and in those countries a patent cannot be obtained if any of these activities occurred any time before the application is filed in such a country. Thus, X may be able to get a U.S. patent if he files an application within a year after a public use, etc., but he cannot get a patent on the same invention in another country.

Quite clearly, the AIA changes the rules of § 102(b) substantially. As previously discussed, if someone other than the inventor has created any of the four types of prior art even one day before the current inventor files her patent application (or one day before the current inventor "discloses" her invention by herself creating prior art), the current inventor is barred from obtaining a valid patent.

It is relatively common for the PTO to miss a relevant piece of prior art. One can easily see that the PTO is much more likely to discover a relevant prior patent or printed publication than it is to discover evidence of a prior public use or a sale or offer to sell. Even prior printed publications can be easy to miss, given that something like a web page or posted boards at an academic conference presentation can be printed publications. However, the PTO can sometimes overlook a prior patent. And, even if the patent examining agency doesn't miss an item of prior art, it can, understandably, misinterpret what a document revealed. When a patent owner sues someone for infringement, the accused infringer will always file an answer that not only includes defenses, but also includes a counterclaim seeking a declaratory judgment of noninfringement and/or invalidity. Statistical research by one of the text's authors reveals that the most common reason for a court decision that invalidates an issued patent is prior art that the PTO had not considered, but that was later discovered by the defendant (that is, attorneys or a prior art search firm hired by the defendant) in a patent infringement lawsuit..

An example helps illustrate all of the above principles. In the recently discovered East Texas oil fields during the mid-1930s, a group of Gulf oil employees developed and used a new technique for oil and gas exploration. The employees owed a confidentiality obligation to Gulf, and use of the newly developed process solely by them was not a public use. However, they used the new process out in the open, without any fences or other barriers to prevent someone else from coming to see what they were doing. Although there was no evidence that someone who was not a Gulf employee had actually observed what they were doing, such a person could have done so. Because the use could have been viewed by someone who did not owe a confidentiality obligation to Gulf, this was treated as a public use.

A man named Rosaire was also developing new exploration techniques somewhere else. About a year after the public use by Gulf, Rosaire independently invented the same new process. Rosaire obtained a patent on the process and later sued two companies for infringing it. The defendants produced evidence of the Gulf public use and the court held Rosaire's patent to be invalid because his invention lacked novelty. Although the validity of Gulf's own patent was not an issue in the case, the evidence revealed that Gulf itself had not applied for a patent until about four years after it made the public use; thus Gulf exceeded the grace-period and was not entitled to a patent on its invention. This means that no one had a patent on the new exploration process and it could be used freely by anyone. If Gulf had kept its use secret, as by using the process only within a fenced area with locked gates, restricted access, guards, and so forth, Gulf's use would not have been prior art that destroyed the patentability of Rosaire's later identical invention, and would not have triggered the one-year clock for Gulf itself.

The foregoing example naturally raises the question of how we sort out patent rights when two inventors independently invent the same thing and try to patent it within a closely contemporaneous time period. Perhaps surprisingly, this is not a rare occurrence. Under the 1952 Patent Act, and indeed throughout the history of U.S. patent law, the U.S. first-to-invent (FTI) system provided that an inventor who was not the first one to file an application still had the opportunity to prove that he invented first. If he proved that he was the first inventor, *and* also that (before the first filer invented) he had either (1) actually made the invention, or (2) continually used reasonable diligences to make the invention (even if he ended up making it after the first filer invented), *or* (3) engaged in one of the activities that created prior art, he was entitled to the patent.

In other words, the first-to-invent but second-to-file inventor would be entitled to the patent if he could prove not only that he invented before the first filer, but also that he actually did something with the invention (one of the above three things) before the first filer had invented. If these three things are different from the "invention," one may wonder what the word "invention" means. For all purposes in U.S. patent law, an "invention" occurs when the inventor or inventors have achieved a "complete mental conception" of an operable invention—an invention that the inventors know will work as intended and is no longer experimental from a scientific or engineering perspective.

For all patents resulting from applications filed on or after March 16, 2013, the rules under the new FTF system implemented by the AIA are far simpler. When there is a contest between a first filer and another inventor who claims to have invented first, the first filer will win, period. This is the system almost all other countries have used for a long time. There can still be a question about whether alleged inventors actually were independent inventors at all, or derived their ideas from someone else, but there will be no contest about the *date* of invention.

Going back to the question of whether the application was filed in time after one of the four types of prior art came into existence, the following case illustrates a situation in which an inventor makes a public use and then waits too long to file. The court not only discusses what constitutes a public use, but also discusses the so-called "experimental use" exception to the one-year rule. If the inventor's use was public, but was being done for genuine experimental purposes to ascertain whether the invention works as intended, the one-year clock is postponed for a reasonable time to allow for this experimentation.

LOUGH v. BRUNSWICK CORP.
U.S. Court of Appeals, Federal Circuit, 86 F.3d 1113 (1996)

Stern drives are marine propulsion devices for boats in which the engine is located inside the boat and is coupled to an outdrive, which includes a propeller located outside the boat ("inboard/outboard boat"). In 1986, Steven Lough worked as a repairman for a boat dealership and marina in Sarasota, Florida.

While repairing Brunswick inboard/outboard boats, he noticed that the upper seal assembly in the stern drives often failed due to corrosion.

Lough determined that the corrosion in the upper seal assembly occurred due to contact between the annular seal and the bell housing aperture. He designed a new upper seal assembly that isolated the annular seal from the aluminum bell housing in order to prevent such corrosion. After some trial and error with his grandfather's metal lathe, he made six usable prototypes in the spring of 1986. He installed one prototype in his own boat at home. Three months later, he gave a second prototype to a friend who installed it in his boat. He also installed prototypes in the boat of the owner of the marina where he worked and in the boat of a marina customer. He gave the remaining prototypes to longtime friends who were employees at another marina in Sarasota. Lough did not charge anyone for the prototypes. For over a year following the installation of these prototypes, Lough neither asked for nor received any comments about the operability of the prototypes. During this time, Lough did not attempt to sell any seal assemblies.

On June 6, 1988, Lough filed a patent application entitled "Liquid Seal for Marine Stern Drive Gear Shift Shafts," which issued as U.S. Patent 4,848,775 (the '775 patent) on July 18, 1989. After learning of Lough's invention, Brunswick designed its own improved upper seal assembly. Lough sued Brunswick on June 12, 1993, alleging infringement of the '775 patent. Brunswick counterclaimed for a declaratory judgment of non-infringement and invalidity. A jury found that Brunswick failed to prove that Lough's invention was in public use before the critical date on June 6, 1987, one year prior to the filing date of the '775 patent. The jury also found that Brunswick infringed of the '775 patent. Based on its infringement finding, the jury awarded Lough $1,500,000 in lost profits. After trial, Brunswick filed a Motion for Judgment as a Matter of Law [same thing as N.O.V.] in which it argued that the claimed invention was invalid because it had been in public use before the critical date. The district court denied Brunswick's motion, and Brunswick appealed.

Lourie, Circuit Judge:
Brunswick challenges that the court's denial of its motion for JMOL on the issue of public use. Brunswick argues that the district court erred in denying its motion for JMOL because the uses of Lough's prototypes prior to the critical date were not experimental. Brunswick asserts that Lough did not control the uses of his prototypes by third parties before

the critical date, failed to keep records of the alleged experiments, and did not place the parties to whom the seals were given under any obligation of secrecy. Based on this objective evidence, Brunswick argues that the uses of Lough's prototypes before the critical date were not "experimental." Thus, Brunswick contends that the jury's verdict was incorrect as a matter of law and that the court erred in denying its JMOL motion.

Lough counters that the tests performed with the six prototypes were necessary experiments conducted in the course of completing his invention. He argues that when the totality of circumstances is properly viewed, the evidence supports the jury's conclusion that those uses were experimental. Lough maintains that a number of factors support the jury's experimental use conclusion, including evidence that he received no compensation for the prototypes, he did not place the seal assemblies on sale until after he filed his patent application, and he gave the prototypes only to his friends and personal acquaintances who used them in such a manner that they were unlikely to be seen by the public. He further argues that, to verify operability of the seal assemblies, prototypes had to be installed by mechanics of various levels of skill in boats that were exposed to different conditions. Thus, he asserts that the court did not err in denying Brunswick's JMOL motion. We disagree with Lough.

One is entitled to a patent unless, [among other things], the invention was . . . in public use . . . in this country, more than one year prior to the date of the application for patent in the United States. We have defined public use as including "any use of [the claimed] invention by a person other than the inventor who is under no limitation, restriction or obligation of secrecy to the inventor." An evaluation of a question of public use depends on "how the totality of the circumstances of the case comports with the policies underlying the public use bar."

These policies include: (1) discouraging the removal, from the public domain, of inventions that the public reasonably has come to believe are freely available; (2) favoring the prompt and widespread disclosure of inventions; (3) allowing the inventor a reasonable amount of time following sales activity to determine the potential economic value of a patent; and (4) prohibiting the inventor from commercially exploiting the invention for a period greater than the statutorily prescribed time.

A patentee may negate a showing of public use by coming forward with evidence that its use of the invention was experimental. Neither party disputes that Lough's prototypes were in use before the critical date. Thus, both parties agree that the issue presented on appeal is whether the jury properly decided that the use of Lough's prototypes in 1986, prior to the critical date, constituted experimental use so as to negate the conclusion of public use.

The law requires that an inventor must file a patent application within one year after his invention is publicly used. Public use means any use of Mr. Lough's invention by any person other than Mr. Lough who was not limited or restricted in their activities regarding the invention, or not obligated to secrecy by Mr. Lough. Such use, however, does not invalidate Lough's patent if the use was primarily for...experimental purposes. . .

The parties do not dispute that the five seal assemblies were used by others before June 6, 1987. The only dispute is whether these uses qualify as experimental uses. Whether an invention was in public use prior to the critical date within the meaning of § 102(b) is a question of law. "The use of an invention by the inventor himself, or of any other person under his direction, by way of experiment, and in order to bring the invention to perfection, has never been regarded as [a public] use." *City of Elizabeth v. American Nicholson*

Pavement Co., 97 U.S. 126, 134 (1877). This doctrine is based on the underlying policy of providing an inventor time to determine if the invention is suitable for its intended purpose, in effect, to reduce the invention to practice.

To determine whether a use is "experimental," a question of law, the totality of the circumstances must be considered, including various objective indicia of experimentation surrounding the use, such as the number of prototypes and duration of testing, whether records or progress reports were made concerning the testing, whether the patentee received compensation for the use of the invention, and the extent of control the inventor maintained over the testing. The last factor of control is critically important, because, if the inventor has no control over the alleged experiments, he is not experimenting. If he does not inquire about the testing or receive reports concerning the results, similarly, he is not experimenting. In order to justify a determination that legally sufficient experimentation has occurred, there must be present certain minimal indicia. The framework might be quite formal, as may be expected when large corporations conduct experiments, governed by contracts and explicit written obligations.

When individual inventors or small business units are involved, however, less formal and seemingly casual experiments can be expected. Such less formal experiments may be deemed legally sufficient to avoid the public use bar, but only if they show the same basic elements that are required to validate any experimental program. Our case law sets out these elements. The question in this appeal is whether Lough's alleged experiments lacked enough of these required indicia so that his efforts cannot, as a matter of law, be recognized as experimental.

Here, Lough either admits or does not dispute the following facts. In the spring of 1986, he noted that the upper seal assembly in Brunswick inboard/outboard boats was failing due to galvanic corrosion between the annular seal and the aperture provided for the upper seal assembly in the aluminum bell housing. He solved this problem by isolating the annular seal from the aluminum bell housing in order to prevent corrosion. After some trial and error, Lough made six prototypes. He installed the first prototype in his own boat. Lough testified at trial that after the first prototype had been in his boat for three months and he determined that it worked, he provided the other prototypes to friends and acquaintances in order to find out if the upper seal assemblies would work as well in their boats as it had worked in his boat. Lough installed one prototype in the boat of his friend, Tom Nikla. A prototype was also installed in the boat of Jim Yow, co-owner of the dealership where Lough worked. Lough installed a fourth prototype in one of the dealership's customers who had considerable problems with corrosion in his stern drive unit. The final two prototypes were given to friends who were employed at a different marina in Florida. These friends installed one prototype in the boat of Mark Liberman, a local charter guide. They installed the other prototype in a demonstration boat at their marina. Subsequently, this boat was sold. Neither Lough nor his friends knew what happened with either the prototype or the demonstration boat after the boat was sold. After providing the five prototypes to these third parties, Lough neither asked for nor received any comments concerning the operability of these prototypes.

It is true that Lough did not receive any compensation for the use of the prototypes. He did not place the seal assembly on sale before applying for a patent. Lough's lack of commercialization, however, is not dispositive of the public use question in view of his failure to present objective evidence of experimentation. Lough kept no records of the alleged testing. Nor did he inspect the seal assemblies after they had been installed by other mechanics. He provided the seal assemblies to friends and acquaintances, but without any provision for follow-up involvement by him in assessment of the events occurring during the alleged experiments, and at least one seal was installed in a boat that was later sold to strangers. Thus, Lough did not maintain any supervision and control over the seals during the alleged testing.

Lough argues that other evidence supports a finding that his uses were experimental, including his own testimony that the prototypes were installed for experimental purposes and the fact that the prototypes were used in such a manner that they were unlikely to be seen by the public. However, the expression by an inventor of his subjective intent to experiment, particularly after institution of litigation, is generally of minimal value. In addition, the fact that the prototypes were unlikely to be seen by the public does not support Lough's position. As the Supreme Court stated in *Egbert v. Lippman*: "[S]ome inventions are by their very character only capable of being used where they cannot be seen or observed by the public eye. An invention may consist of a lever or spring, hidden in the running gear of a watch, or of a ratchet, shaft, or cog-wheel covered from view in the recesses of a machine for spinning or weaving. Nevertheless, if its inventor [publicly uses] a machine of which his invention forms a part, and allows it to be used without restriction of any kind, the use is a public one."

We do not dispute that it may have been desirable in this case for Lough to have had his prototypes installed by mechanics of various levels of skill in boats that were exposed to different conditions. Moreover, Lough was free to test his invention in boats of friends and acquaintances to further verify that his invention worked for its intended purpose; however, Lough was required to maintain some degree of control and feedback over those uses of the prototypes if those tests were to negate public use. Lough's failure to monitor the use of his prototypes by his acquaintances, in addition to the lack of records or reports from those acquaintances concerning the operability of the devices, compel the conclusion that, as a matter of law, he did not engage in experimental use. Lough in effect provided the prototype seal assemblies to members of the public for their free and unrestricted use. The law does not waive statutory requirements for inventors of lesser sophistication. When one distributes his invention to members of the public under circumstances that evidence a near total disregard for supervision and control concerning its use, the absence of these minimal indicia of experimentation require a conclusion that the invention was in public use.

We conclude that the jury's determination that Lough's use of the invention was experimental so as to defeat the assertion of public use was incorrect as a matter of law. The court thus erred in denying Brunswick's JMOL motion on the validity of claims 1-4 of the '775 patent under §102(b). REVERSED.

Below is a major decision by the U.S. Supreme Court on another type of prior art—the "on-sale" bar, which in some ways is similar to a public use, but also is very different in some critical respects. They are similar in that evidence of either of them does not constitute prior art if the invention in question was experimental at the time in question. They are different, though, in that there can be a "public use" only if the invention had actually been *made physically* at the time of the alleged use. The reason for the differences is primarily that the courts have followed the literal language of the patent statute, which is what courts are usually expected to do. Something must have been *made* before it can be *used*. In the case of the on-sale type of prior art, the language of the statute states that an invention was

---

HELSINN HEALTHCARE S.A. v. TEVA PHARMACEUTICALS USA
U.S. Supreme Court, 139 S.Ct. 628 (2019)

Helsinn Healthcare S.A. invented a treatment for nausea and vomiting caused by chemotherapy treatment for cancer. The treated uses the chemical palonosetron. While Helsinn was developing its palonosetron product, it entered into two agreements with another company granting that company the right to distribute, promote, market, and sell a 0.25 mg dose of palonosetron in the United States. The agreements required that the company keep confidential any proprietary information received under the agreements. Nearly two years later, in January 2003, Helsinn filed a provisional patent application covering a 0.25 mg dose of palonosetron. Over the next 10 years, Helsinn filed four patent applications that claimed priority to the January 2003 date. Its last patent application was filed in 2013 after the effective date of the America Invents Act (AIA). This patent resulted in U.S. Patent #8,598,219 (the '219 patent) covering a 0.25 mg dose of the drug.

In 2011, Teva Pharmaceutical Industries, Ltd., sought approval to market a generic version of the 0.25 mg dosage of the drug that was covered by Helsinn's '219 patent under procedures established by the 1984 Hatch-Waxman Act for resolving patent disputes between owners of patented drugs and generic drug manufacturers. Helsinn sued Teva for infringing its patents, including the '219 patent. Teva argued that the '219 patent was invalid under the "on sale" provision of the AIA—which precludes a person from obtaining a patent on an invention that was "in public use, on sale, or otherwise available to the public before the effective filing date of the claimed invention," because the 0.25 mg dose was "on sale" more than one year before Helsinn filed the provisional patent application in 2003. The District Court held that the AIA's "on sale" provision did not apply because the public disclosure of the agreements did not disclose the 0.25 mg dose. The Federal Circuit reversed, holding that the sale was publicly disclosed, regardless of whether the details of the invention were publicly disclosed in the terms of the sale agreements.

Thomas, Justice:

The Leahy–Smith America Invents Act (AIA) bars a person from receiving a patent on an invention that was "in public use, on sale, or otherwise available to the public before the effective filing date of the claimed invention." This case requires us to decide whether the sale of an invention to a third party who is contractually obligated to keep the invention confidential places the invention "on sale" within the meaning of § 102(a).

More than 20 years ago, this Court determined that an invention was "on sale" within the meaning of an earlier version of §102(a) when it was "the subject of a commercial offer for sale" and "ready for patenting." *Pfaff v. Wells Electronics, Inc.*, 525 U.S. 55, 67 (1998). We did not further require that the sale make the details of the invention available to the public. In light of this earlier construction, we determine that the reenactment of the phrase "on sale" in the AIA did not alter this meaning. Accordingly, a commercial sale to a third party who is required to keep the invention confidential may place the invention "on sale" under the AIA.

Petitioner Helsinn Healthcare S.A. (Helsinn) is a Swiss pharmaceutical company that makes Aloxi, a drug that treats chemotherapy-induced nausea and vomiting. Helsinn acquired the right to develop palonosetron, the active ingredient in Aloxi, in 1998. In early

2000, it submitted protocols for Phase III clinical trials to the Food and Drug Administration (FDA), proposing to study a 0.25 mg and a 0.75 mg dose of palonosetron. In September 2000, Helsinn announced that it was beginning Phase III clinical trials and was seeking marketing partners for its palonosetron product.

Helsinn found its marketing partner in MGI Pharma, Inc. (MGI), a Minnesota pharmaceutical company that markets and distributes drugs in the United States. Helsinn and MGI entered into two agreements: a license agreement and a supply and purchase agreement. The license agreement granted MGI the right to distribute, promote, market, and sell the 0.25 mg and 0.75 mg doses of palonosetron in the United States. In return, MGI agreed to make upfront payments to Helsinn and to pay future royalties on distribution of those doses. Under the supply and purchase agreement, MGI agreed to purchase exclusively from Helsinn any palonosetron product approved by the FDA. Helsinn in turn agreed to supply MGI however much of the approved doses it required. Both agreements included dosage information and required MGI to keep confidential any proprietary information received under the agreements.

Helsinn and MGI announced the agreements in a joint press release, and MGI also reported the agreements in its Form 8–K filing with the Securities and Exchange Commission. Although the 8–K filing included redacted copies of the agreements, neither the 8–K filing nor the press releases disclosed the specific dosage formulations covered by the agreements.

On January 30, 2003, nearly two years after Helsinn and MGI entered into the agreements, Helsinn filed a provisional patent application covering the 0.25 mg and 0.75 mg doses of palonosetron. Over the next 10 years, Helsinn filed four patent applications that claimed priority to the January 30, 2003, date of the provisional application. Helsinn filed its fourth patent application—the one relevant here—in May 2013, and it issued as U.S. Patent No. 8,598,219 ('219 patent). The '219 patent covers a fixed dose of 0.25 mg of palonosetron in a 5 ml solution. By virtue of its effective date, the '219 patent is governed by the AIA.

Teva Pharmaceutical Industries, Ltd., and Teva Pharmaceuticals USA, Inc. (Teva), are, respectively, an Israeli company that manufactures generic drugs and its American affiliate. In 2011, Teva sought approval from the FDA to market a generic 0.25 mg palonosetron product. Helsinn then sued Teva for infringing its patents, including the '219 patent. In defense, Teva asserted that the '219 patent was invalid because the 0.25 mg dose was "on sale" more than one year before Helsinn filed the provisional patent application covering that dose in January 2003.

The AIA precludes a person from obtaining a patent on an invention that was "on sale" before the effective filing date of the patent application:

"A person shall be entitled to a patent unless ... the claimed invention was patented, described in a printed publication, or in public use, *on sale,* or otherwise available to the public before the effective filing date of the claimed invention." 35 U.S.C. § 102(a)(1) (emphasis added).

Disclosures described in § 102(a)(1) are often referred to as "prior art."

The patent statute in effect before the passage of the AIA included a similar proscription, known as the "on-sale bar":

"A person shall be entitled to a patent unless—

"(a) the invention was known or used by others in this country, or patented or

250 © 2020 John R. Allison & Robert A. Prentice

described in a printed publication in this or a foreign country, before the invention thereof by the applicant for patent, or

"(b) the invention was patented or described in a printed publication in this or a foreign country or in public use or *on sale* in this country, more than one year prior to the date of the application for patent in the United States." 35 U.S.C. §§ 102(a)-(b) (2006 ed.) (emphasis added).

The District Court determined that the "on sale" provision did not apply. It concluded that, under the AIA, an invention is not "on sale" unless the sale or offer in question made the claimed invention available to the public. Because the companies' public disclosure of the agreements between Helsinn and MGI did not disclose the 0.25 mg dose, the court determined that the invention was not "on sale" before the critical date.

The Court of Appeals for the Federal Circuit reversed. It concluded that "if the existence of the sale is public, the details of the invention need not be publicly disclosed in the terms of sale" to fall within the AIA's on-sale bar. Because the sale between Helsinn and MGI was publicly disclosed, it held that the on-sale bar applied.

We granted certiorari to determine whether, under the AIA, an inventor's sale of an invention to a third party who is obligated to keep the invention confidential qualifies as prior art for purposes of determining the patentability of the invention. We conclude that such a sale can qualify as prior art.

The United States Constitution authorizes Congress "[t]o promote the Progress of Science and useful Arts, by securing for limited Times to Authors and Inventors the exclusive Right to their respective Writings and Discoveries." Art. 1, § 8, cl. 8. Under this grant of authority, Congress has crafted a federal patent system that encourages the creation and disclosure of new, useful, and nonobvious advances in technology and design by granting inventors the exclusive right to practice the invention for a period of years.

To further the goal of motivating innovation and enlightenment while also avoiding monopolies that unnecessarily stifle competition. Congress has imposed several conditions on the limited opportunity to obtain a property right in an idea. One such condition is the on-sale bar, which reflects Congress' reluctance to allow an inventor to remove existing knowledge from public use by obtaining a patent covering that knowledge.

. . . . Every patent statute since 1836 has included an on-sale bar. The patent statute in force immediately before the AIA prevented a person from receiving a patent if, "more than one year prior to the date of the application for patent in the United States," "the invention was ... on sale" in the United States. The AIA, as relevant here, retained the on-sale bar and added the catchall phrase "or otherwise available to the public." "A person shall be entitled to a patent unless" the "claimed invention was ... in public use, on sale, or otherwise available to the public ...."). We must decide whether these changes altered the meaning of the "on sale" bar. We hold that they did not.

Congress enacted the AIA in 2011 against the backdrop of a substantial body of law interpreting § 102's on-sale bar. In 1998, we determined that the pre-AIA on-sale bar applies "when two conditions are satisfied" more than a year before an inventor files a patent application. *Pfaff,* 525 U.S., at 67, 119 S.Ct. 304. "First, the product must be the subject of a commercial offer for sale." "Second, the invention must be ready for patenting," which we explained could be shown by proof of "reduction to practice" [actually making the invention and knowing that it would work as intended—not still experimental] or "drawings or other descriptions of the invention that were sufficiently specific to enable a person skilled in the art to practice the invention." [That is, "enabling detail."]

Although this Court has never addressed the precise question presented in this case, our precedents suggest that a sale or offer of sale need not make an invention available to the public. For instance, we held in *Pfaff* that an offer for sale could cause an inventor to lose the right to patent, without regard to whether the offer discloses each detail of the invention. Other cases focus on whether the invention had been sold, not whether the details of the invention had been made available to the public or whether the sale itself had been publicly disclosed. *E.g., Consolidated Fruit–Jar Co. v. Wright,* 94 U.S. 92, 94 (1877) ("A single instance of sale or of use by the patentee may, under the circumstances, be fatal to the patent ..."); *Smith & Griggs Mfg. Co. v. Sprague,* 123 U.S. 249, 257 (1887) ("A single sale to another ... would certainly have defeated his right to a patent ...").

The Federal Circuit—which has exclusive jurisdiction over patent appeals, has made explicit what was implicit in our precedents. It has long held that "secret sales" can invalidate a patent. *E.g., Special Devices, Inc. v. OEA, Inc.,* 270 F.3d 1353 (2001) (invalidating patent claims based on "sales for the purpose of the commercial stockpiling of an invention" that "took place in secret"); *Woodland Trust v. Flowertree Nursery, Inc.,* 148 F.3d 1368, 1370 (1998) ("Thus an inventor's own prior commercial use, albeit kept secret, may constitute a public use or sale, barring him from obtaining a patent").

In light of this settled pre-AIA precedent on the meaning of "on sale," we presume that when Congress reenacted the same language in the AIA, it adopted the earlier judicial construction of that phrase. See *Shapiro v. United States,* 335 U.S. 1, 16 (1948) ("In adopting the language used in the earlier act, Congress 'must be considered to have adopted also the construction given by this Court to such language, and made it a part of the enactment'"). The new § 102 retained the exact language used in its predecessor statute ("on sale") and, as relevant here, added only a new catchall clause ("or otherwise available to the public"). If "on sale" had a settled meaning before the AIA was adopted, then adding the phrase "or otherwise available to the public" to the statute would be a fairly oblique way of attempting to overturn that settled body of law. The addition of "or otherwise available to the public" is simply not enough of a change for us to conclude that Congress intended to alter the meaning of the reenacted term "on sale."

Helsinn disagrees, arguing that our construction reads "otherwise" out of the statute. Helsinn contends that the associated-words canon requires us to read "otherwise available to the public" to limit the preceding terms in § 102 to disclosures that make the claimed invention available to the public.

As an initial matter, [none of the decisions cited by Teva as precedent] address the reenactment of terms that had acquired a well-settled judicial interpretation. . . . Like other such phrases, "otherwise available to the public" captures material that does not fit neatly into the statute's enumerated categories but is nevertheless meant to be covered. Given that the phrase "on sale" had acquired a well-settled meaning when the AIA was enacted, we decline to read the addition of a broad catchall phrase to upset that body of precedent.

Helsinn does not ask us to revisit our pre-AIA interpretation of the on-sale bar. Nor does it dispute the Federal Circuit's determination that the invention claimed in the '219 patent was "on sale" within the meaning of the pre-AIA statute. Because we determine that Congress did not alter the meaning of "on sale" when it enacted the AIA, we hold that an inventor's sale of an invention to a third party who is obligated to keep the invention confidential can qualify as prior art under § 102(a). We therefore affirm the judgment of the

Comment: The "on-sale bar" involves the only type of evidence that is treated as prior art when it was confidential. A very practical justification for this different treatment is that many transactions between companies are confidential—not publicized. If confidential sales or offers to sell were not treated as prior art, there would be countless commercial transactions in products that are then patented at some later time, which runs contrary to the basic objective of patent law to allow patents only when "new" technology is made available.

Also, the Supreme Court's decision above leaves an important question unanswered: In the *Helsinn* case, Helsinn and its transaction partner made the *fact of the sale* public, but not details such as the 0.25 mg dosage that was later covered by the '219 patent. The question remaining is whether the sale contract would be prior art if the *fact of the transaction* (not just the critical details) had also been kept confidential. Judicial precedent before the AIA became effective in March 2013 as being prior art even if the existence of the sale transaction (offer to sell, contract of sale, or executed sale) was kept secret. From the Court's reasoning in *Helsinn*, it appears logical that this will continue to be counted as prior art when the question is decided. The Court did not decide this question in *Helsinn*, because the facts of the case did not present the issue.

Nonobviousness

Even if there is not a single item of prior art that, by itself, invalidates Inventor X's patent, there is still the chance that X's invention may not meet the requirement of *nonobviousness*. This requirement provides that an inventor is not entitled to a patent on an invention if hypothetical ordinarily skilled practitioner in this art (technology) would have viewed the invention as representing only a trivial, or obvious, advance over the cumulative prior art. Stated differently, to be nonobvious, the differences between the current invention and previous inventions revealed by any of the types of prior art must be more than just obvious, or purely intuitive) to a person having ordinary skill in the field. Under the 1952 Patent Act and earlier legislation, this determination was made based on what the prior art revealed at the time of this invention. Under the AIA, the determination is made based on the prior art existing at the time the patent application was filed, which means that in many cases there may be more prior art available that can be used to show that the invention is obvious.

When a question of nonobviousness arises, either in the PTO or later in court, the first step is to analyze the relevant prior art. Although a single piece of prior art may cause X's invention to be obvious (X's invention is too minor a step beyond what was in the prior art), it is common for the PTO and the courts to combine two or more pieces of prior art in the same or closely related field of technology and say something like "the teachings of this prior patent, when read in the light of the teachings of this other prior printed publication, cause X's invention to be obvious."

The following example may help. Lockwood produced an invention that allowed people to make multiple reservations with airlines, rental car companies, hotels, and so on. His invention was referred to as a "terminal," but it was actually a software invention. He sued American Airlines, claiming that AA's Sabre reservation system infringed on his patent. The court first concluded that AA had not infringed because its Sabre system did not have an audio-visual feature that was an integral part of Lockwood's patented invention. The court then concluded that Lockwood's patent was invalid because his invention was obvious in light of the teachings of two pieces of prior art that were closely enough related that they should be viewed together for this purpose. The first was AA's original reservation system that had been introduced in the early 1960s and used by many thousands of customers, travel agents, and others. The court found that this was prior art because there had been a public use of the system even though the users could not have figured out the details of the software that made the system work (a public use does not have to be enabling). The second was one of Lockwood's own earlier patents. The original AA system included many of the functional ideas in Lockwood's patented invention and the older Lockwood patent disclosed the audio-visual feature. The invention in Lockwood's patent was merely an obvious step beyond the combination of the AA system and the older Lockwood patent.

After studying the relevant prior art, a court sometimes will still be on the fence regarding the nonobviousness question. If there is evidence of so-called "objective factors"—evidence of what actually happened after a patented product or process was marketed—such evidence may help the court resolve the question. Such evidence can take several forms, but it all focuses on the following question: If X's invention was so obvious, then why did this happen? For example, if X's invention was so obvious, then: a) Why was the product so commercially successful? b) Why had there been such a long-felt need for solving the problem that Inventor X solved? c) Why had others tried and failed after substantial efforts to find the solution that Inventor X found? d) Why did one or more competitors start copying X's invention rather than relying on their own solutions?

In addition, if there is evidence to show that X's invention produced a result that was surprising or that was contrary to conventional teachings in this area of technology, this very strongly points toward nonobviousness. Inventor X is certainly not required to show that his invention produces an unexpected result, because most patentable inventions actually produce the results that were theorized, but an unexpected technical result almost compels a conclusion of nonobviousness. For example, Dr. Robert Gore was searching for a better method of stretching Teflon^{TM} into tubing, tape, and other products through a combination of temperature and stretching speed variations. Conventional wisdom taught that, as the temperature was increased, more stretching without breaking could be accomplished by slowing down the stretching speed. Dr. Gore's experiments showed, to the contrary, that increasing the stretching speed increased the amount of stretching without breaking. This evidence helped show that the new process was not obvious.

Ownership of Patent Rights

Although patent law is federal law, questions regarding ownership of patented inventions or rights to use them are determined by state law. An owner can sell or otherwise transfer patent ownership to someone else by executing a written assignment. A patent assignment must be recorded with the PTO. An owner can keep the patent and grant exclusive or nonexclusive licenses that give others the right to make specified uses of the patented technology in return for royalty payments. Licensing of all kinds of intellectual property rights is very common.

If an employee is "hired to invent" (hired to do research and solve this or a similar problem) and invents something on company time while using company resources, the invention and any resulting patent belong to the company without the need for an express assignment to the employer. The company will file the application in the employee's name, but the company will own it (as the "assignee-at-issue"). Even if the employee was not hired for inventive work, if she invents something on company time or using company resources, the company will be granted a nonexclusive license to use the patented invention within its business without payment of a royalty. In this latter case, the employer's implied nonexclusive license is called a "shop right." Of course, many employers have their employees sign "pre-invention assignment agreements" that obligate them to assign title to the employer of all patents generated on company time or using company resources regardless of whether the employees are hired to invent. Under such an obligation, if the inventor-employee later refuses to actually execute the assignment, it will be done for him.

Infringement

As observed earlier, when a patent owner sues for infringement, he is alleging that the defendant infringed one or more of the *claims* in the patent. The invention is actually defined most precisely in the claims. For example, on April 18, 2005, a group of inventors from the state of Illinois and from Canada filed an application for a patent on a newly designed football helmet. The patent, "Sports Helmet," was issued on July 10, 2007. According to the inventors in their written description of the invention (which is found in the patent just before the claims): "The football helmet of the present invention, when compared to previously proposed conventional football helmets, has the advantages of: being designed to attempt to protect a wearer of the helmet from injuries caused upon an impact force striking the helmet; preventing irritation to a player's ear; affording more protection to the jaw of the wearer; and providing for the use of a lighter weight face guard." Of course, the written description contained a great deal more explanation than this about how to make the invention, and was accompanied by a number of drawings to help convey enabling detailed to a person having skill in this field. After the written description and drawings of the invention was the first, broadest claim in the patent:

"What is claimed is:

1. A football helmet comprising:

a. a one-piece shell configured to receive a head of a wearer of the helmet, the shell having an outer surface, a front region, a rear region, and two side regions;

b. an ear flap depending from each side region of the shell wherein the ear flap generally overlies an ear of the wearer, wherein each ear flap has an integral jaw flap that extends forward from the ear flap towards the front region of the shell, the jaw flap having a lower edge, a substantially linear front edge that extends upward from the lower edge and an upper edge that is inclined from the front edge;

c. a chin strap assembly that releasably secures the helmet to the wearer, the chin strap assembly having a central member and at least one flexible strap member extending outwardly from each side of the central member, wherein the strap members releasably connect to the shell; and

d. a pad assembly attached to each ear flap, each pad assembly having an ear flap pad and a jaw pad, the jaw pad having a density of at least 5 pounds per cubic foot and a 25% compression deflection of at least 8 pounds per square inch."

If the defendant's product contains all of these elements, a-d, it literally infringes (even if defendant's product has one or more *additional elements*). If it does not include an element, such as c., it does not infringe. If defendant's product contains one or more elements that are similar but not identical to the corresponding element in the plaintiff's patent claim, there is no literal infringement but there could possibly be infringement under the "doctrine of equivalents" (DOE). For example, if defendant's product contains elements that are identical to a., b., and d., but substitutes something else for element c., the defendant's product may or may not infringe on plaintiff's patent. In such a case, there is no "literal" infringement, and the court will determine whether there is infringement under the DOE by asking whether the element in the defendant's product that is similar (but not identical) to element c. in plaintiff's patent claim "performs substantially the same function in substantially the same way to achieve the same result." If more than one element in the defendant's product is similar but not identical, the analysis will be applied separately to each element.

The same infringement analysis is used for other types of inventions such as processes (where the elements are steps), machines (where the elements are the parts of the structure that perform specific functions), and compositions of matter (where the elements are each chemical, metal, or other part of the composition, in specific proportions). But for there to be either type of infringement, all of the elements in the patent owner's asserted patent claim must be in the defendant's product, machine, process, or composition of matter—all elements must be either identical (literal infringement) or substantially equivalent (DOE infringement).

Remedies

A patent owner who successfully sues for infringement can obtain an injunction and damages. Damage awards in patent cases, which can be in the many millions of dollars, can include lost profits on sales of a patented item that the owner would have made if it hadn't been for the infringement, lost profits on sales of unpatented items that customers would have bought along with the patented items, a reasonable royalty on the defendant's sales that the patent owner probably would not have made for various reasons, plaintiff's losses because it had to drop prices as a result of the illegal competition, and interest on these amounts. If the court concludes that the defendant willfully infringed (knew or should have known it was infringing), the court may multiply the plaintiff's damages by a factor of up to three, and may award attorneys' fees. As in other types of lawsuits, the losing party typically pays court costs.

International Patent Law

As with other types of intellectual property, patent rights are granted under the law of a particular nation. Although there have been many efforts to harmonize the patent laws of various nations, there still is no "international" patent. Even in the European Union (EU), where there is the greatest degree of commonality, and where there is a unified system for filing patent applications, patent rights are still governed by the law of each member nation.

The Paris Convention is the most important international treaty dealing with patent application filing. It provides that, if someone files an application in one member nation, the applicant can file for a patent in another member nation within one year and keep the original filing date. The Paris Convention recently became even more important because all members of the WTO must also be members of the Paris Convention.

The Patent Cooperation Treaty (PCT) is also very important to those who wish to file for patents on an invention in multiple countries. If an inventor files in one member country, then indicates within one year that this is an international application, he may have up to 30 months total (18 months added to the first 12) to file applications in other member countries.

COPYRIGHT LAW

Federal law grants several exclusive rights to the owner of copyrighted works, including the exclusive right to (1) make copies ("reproduction" right), (2) create "derivative works" (such as a new edition of a book, a sequel, a movie from a book, a new version of a software program, an action figure from a fictional movie character, and so on), (3) publicly distribute copies of the work (with an exception called the "first-sale doctrine"), (4) publicly display the work, (5) publicly perform the work, and (6) in the case of a sound recording, to publicly perform the work by digital audio transmission (This sound recording copyright was added to the Copyright Act by Congress in 1972, but it does not apply to traditional analog broadcasting, such as broadcasts over the airwaves by radio stations. However, since 1972, anyone who digitally transmits music, such as streaming digitized music by an Internet radio station or by a service such as Pandora or Spotify, the one doing the streaming must have a license on the sound recording (the recorded performance). This license is in addition to the required license for the copyright on the underlying musical composition. An analog broadcaster such as a traditional AM or FM radio station must have a license only on the musical composition.

With respect to (3), the exclusive right to distribute, an exception is the so-called "first sale doctrine," which allows someone who has purchased or otherwise lawfully acquired a copyrighted work to resell or give away that copy.

Term of Copyright Protection

The first U. S. copyright law was passed by Congress in 1790, and the most recent enactment is the Copyright Act of 1976, which has been amended numerous times since. The term of copyright protection has been extended numerous times, beginning with a term of 14 years (renewable once, for a total of 28 years), then 28 years (renewable once, for a total of 56 years), then life of the author plus 50 years. In 1998, Congress extended the term once more, adding 20 years of protection to not only those expressive works produced in the future but also to any work then still protected. Thus, the term of protection is now life of the author plus 70 years. Many recent changes to copyright law are controversial, and adding 20 years of protection retroactively is one of these. The term of copyright protection is different for a *work-for-hire*. The current term (after the 1998 addition of 20 years) for a work for hire is 95 years from the date of publication or 120 years from the date of creation, whichever is shorter.

Copyright Ownership

Works for Hire: A work created by an *employee while acting in the scope of her employment* is a work-for-hire, with ownership of the copyright automatically and immediately vesting in the employer. In addition, a work created for the employer by an *independent contractor* can be a work-for-hire if: (1) the employer and independent contractor made a written agreement *signed by both parties* <u>before the independent contractor started work,</u> (2) the agreement "specially commissioned the work as a work-for-hire" (expressly using the term work-for-hire), and (3) the work was within one of nine categories—(a) a contribution to a collective work, (b) a part of a motion picture or other audiovisual work, (c) a translation, (d) a supplementary work, (e) a compilation, (f) an instructional text, (g) a test, (h) answer material for a test, or (i) an atlas. If there was no such agreement before work started, or if the work is not one of the specified types, the independent contractor owns the copyright, although in such a case there will be an implied license allowing the employer to make use of the work without paying a royalty. In such a case, the employer also may acquire ownership by means of an assignment if the independent contractor is willing to assign it.

Because these work-for-hire rules are different for independent contractors than for employees, the distinction between the two is very important, as it is in other areas of law such as regulation of the employment relationship, employer liability for torts committed by subordinates, and others. As discussed in more detail in Chapter 23, an independent contractor is hired to do a particular task, with the details of how to accomplish the job are left up to the hired party. On the other hand, when the employer retains the right to control the details of how to accomplish the job, the hired person is an employee.

Assignments: Regarding copyright assignments, whether by an independent contractor to an employer or in any other situation in which a copyright owner transfers ownership of a copyright to an "assignee," the rights of the assignee are less than those of an original owner (whether the original owner is the creator or an employer that gained ownership as a work for hire), because the creator or her heirs can terminate the assignment at any point between 35 and 40 years after the assignment was executed. This is true of any copyright assignment, not just one to an employer. Copyright assignments transferring ownership must be in writing and signed by the assignor (transferor). Thus, it is possible for the parties' conduct to create an *implied license* granting certain rights to use a copyrighted work, but it is impossible to create an implied assignment that transfers ownership because of the writing requirement.

Joint Authorship: It is relatively common for two or more people to be "joint authors," with each of them having all of the rights associated with copyright ownership. A single joint author can exercise these rights of ownership, such as granting licenses to use the copyrighted work, without the consent of the other joint author(s).

Subject Matter

The Copyright Act enumerates several types of protected works:

1. Literary works. The term "literary" is used very broadly, and includes things like books, poems, stories, newspapers, magazines, web pages, computer software, etc.
2. Musical works, including any accompanying words.
3. Dramatic works, including any accompanying music.
4. Pantomimes and choreographic works.

5. Pictorial, graphic, and sculptural works.

6. Motion pictures and other audiovisual works.

7. Sound recordings (protected by a separate copyright since 1972).

8. Architectural works (since 1990, architects have been able to protect not only the blueprints but also the original expression in building designs themselves, although they cannot prevent someone from photographing, painting, or drawing a building from a place commonly accessible to the public).

This list was not intended to be exclusive, however, because the law is meant to protect all "original works of authorship" ("authorship" referring to any creation of original expression).

In copyright law, "original" does not mean the same thing as novel, but it simply means that the expression was original to this particular person. Stated somewhat differently, original expression is expression that was not copied from some other source. It is easier to discuss what is not protected by copyright than it is to discuss what is protected. Following are some examples of things not protected by copyright law; note that some of these are closely related and overlapping.

Facts

In *Feist Publications, Inc. v. Rural Telephone Co.*, 499 U. S. 340 (1991), the U.S. Supreme Court held that facts themselves cannot be copyrighted because the Constitution gives Congress the power to grant copyright protection to "authors" for original expressions. Facts do not have an author, or creator. Some merely discovers facts. The case involved an old-fashioned paper telephone directory listing names alphabetically by last name, plus addresses and phone numbers. Another company used the telephone directory as a source for its own directory that covered a much wider geographic area, making its money through display advertising.

The case has major implications for database compilers. A database collects facts. Although *Feist* involved a paper directory, the same rule applies to electronic databases. The court held, however, that although facts themselves cannot be protected by copyright law, it is possible for a compilation of facts (which is what a database is) to have copyright protection to the extent that the compiler, or creator, of the database used originality or creativity in selecting which facts to include, how to arrange those facts, and how to present them. In the telephone directory, there was simply no room for such originality because there was simply no opportunity for creativity in what to include in the directory or how to present it. Any use of creativity would diminish or destroy the usefulness of the directory.

Most modern electronic databases have "compilation" copyright protection—not for the facts, but for how they were chosen, arranged, and presented. It would not be infringement for someone else to use such a database as a source of a few facts, but the more facts copied, the more likely it is that the copyist has also captured the originality of the compiler in selection, arrangement, or presentation. Database compilers can also use other techniques to add original expression to the database as a whole, whether it's symbols, images, or other things.

Another implication of the rule that facts are not copyrightable is that, if I write a book that includes statements of facts, someone else can copy the facts from my book without being guilty of copyright infringement. I may be able to find original ways to express statements about facts and, if so, my original expressions are protected, but the facts themselves are not.

Ideas

Copyright protects original expressions of ideas, but not the ideas themselves. Someone else may freely take the ideas from my book, article, or other work, but not my original expression of those ideas. Although not infringement, it is, of course, intellectually dishonest *plagiarism* to knowingly use another's ideas without giving them credit. If there is, in fact, copyright infringement because protectable expression was copied, giving credit to the original source is not a defense to the infringement.

Merger Doctrine

An expression of an idea may not be protected by copyright if there is only one way, or only a very small number of ways, to express the idea. Under the "merger doctrine," courts say that in such circumstances the expression ''merges'' with the idea. Protecting the expression would have the practical effect of protecting the idea itself. Protecting ideas is within the purview of trade secret and patent law, not copyright law. For example, the expression contained in a set of rules on the packaging of a consumer product for entering a contest will typically be very simple, and there probably are not very many ways to effectively express the functional ideas on which the contest is based. Here, the expression probably has merged with the ideas and is not protectable by copyright law. Although the merger doctrine can apply to portions of any type of expressive work, it is more commonly encountered in works that are motivated mainly by a desire to achieve effective and efficient functionality. For example, works such as maps, directories, software, and others whose main value is in the functions it performs rather than in its creative expressions, the need to achieve certain functions in a relatively effective and efficient way greatly limits the way that certain ideas can be expressed. These types of works will include original expressions that are protected by copyright, but they usually will include a large number of uncopyrightable elements, including expressions that are treated as unprotectable ideas because of the merger doctrine.

The "merger doctrine" is not really a separate or different concept from the basic requirement that there has to be original expression for there to be copyright protection. The merger doctrine simply applies when the creator of expression has such a small number of different ways to express particular ideas that there is little or no room for the creator to be original in his expression. That is, there is little or no opportunity for the creator to exercise individual choice or judgment when deciding how to express his or her ideas. Stated in yet another way, there is little or no opportunity for the creator be creative in any meaningful way.

It may be helpful to observe that, the simpler the ideas one wishes to express, the fewer different ways there are available to express them. For instance, instructions about how to enter a very simple sweepstakes contest are likely to be uncopyrightable because of the merger doctrine. There are many other examples. Moreover, the merger doctrine is most often found to apply to particular expression when the objective of the work is highly utilitarian, i.e., where it is functionally or factually oriented. In other words, when the primary motivation for creating expression is to achieve functions, the need to achieve these functions effectively, efficiently, or accurately greatly limits the number of different ways available to the creator to express the ideas they wish to express.

Scenes a faire

Very closely related to the lack of protection for ideas is the lack of protection for *scenes a faire*. Scenes a faire are standard techniques necessary to convey particular ideas, such as descriptions of the stereotypical Jewish or Italian mother or the stereotypical Irish father for stories in which these characters are integral to the story being told. If one writes a story in a particular genre, such stock characters are standard and they, along with stereotypical descriptions, mannerisms, and speech are not protected because they are treated as having fallen into the public domain. Likewise, if a scene has to be expressed in a certain way in order to tell a story set in a particular time, place, or culture, the expressions in the scene usually will be uncopyrightable *scenes a faire* because granting copyright protection to such expressions will effectively prevent others from later telling a similar story in a book, movie, or other medium even though all their other expressions are original to them.

In a copyright infringement suit against rapper 50 Cent, a court dismissed the claim, noting that "Any common themes of a young male whose tumultuous upbringing leads him to resort to a life of crime and violence in order to gain power and money are scènes à faire, or standard to any coming of age story of a young man from an inner-city." *Winstead v. Jackson,* 509 Fed.Appx. 139 (3rd Cir. 2013).

The following case explains the requirement that copyright law can only protect *original* expression, why facts cannot meet the originality requirement, and how databases (factual compilations) usually can receive some degree of copyright protection.

Fixation in a Tangible Medium

To be protected by copyright, original expression must be "fixed in a tangible medium." The Copyright Act provides that the fixation is sufficient if the work "can be perceived, reproduced, or otherwise communicated, either directly or with the aid of a machine or device." This simply means that the expression must be recorded on paper, audio tape, video tape, film, a magnetic storage medium such as any of the types of computer disks, carved in stone or other material, or any other medium.

The requirement of fixation can be illustrated by live speeches or lectures, live news or sports broadcasts, and live musical or dance or dramatic performances. If the live expressions have not been previously fixed in a tangible medium (such as choreographic or music notation), the requirement can nevertheless be fulfilled if the author of the expressions simultaneously records them or authorizes someone else to do so. An unauthorized recording is not a fixation and, if the author has not previously fixed the expressions, neither the author nor the unauthorized recorder has a copyright. Although unfixed works are not protected by the 1976 Copyright Act, state law can provide protection; this is the only instance in which state law can play any role in providing copyright protection.

With regard to live musical performances, regardless of whether they have been fixed in a tangible medium, it is a federal crime under a separate provision of the Copyright Act to record them without authorization. Although this provision was added to the Copyright Act in the 1990s, it actually has nothing to do with copyright law itself, and applies regardless of whether infringement is committed at the same time.

Formalities

Registration with the U.S. Copyright Office is not required for copyright protection. Moreover, since 1989 there is no longer any requirement that a copyright notice be placed on a work. For works first published before 1989, each published copy had to contain the word "copyright," the abbreviation "Copr.," or the symbol ©, along with the date of first publication and the name of the copyright owner. Thus, prior to 1989 a person who observed a published work that did not contain a copyright notice could feel assured that the work was in the public domain. For works published after that date, however, this is not the case. Congress abandoned the notice requirement in 1989 because the U.S. became a member of the 100-year-old Berne Convention, an international treaty that provides that copyright protection should be granted in all member nations without the necessity of any formalities.

Although registration and notice are no longer necessary for copyright protection, they are a very good idea. A copyright notice, for example, can serve the practical purpose of emphasizing to others that the work is protected. Registration, which can be accomplished by filling out a form and sending it to the Copyright Office, along with two copies of a published work or one copy of an unpublished work, and a modest fee, has an even more important practical effect. A copyright owner who is a U.S. national cannot file suit in federal court for copyright infringement unless the copyright has been registered.

In addition, a work must be registered within three months after first publication in order for the copyright owner to be able to receive so-called "statutory damages" in an infringement lawsuit—these are damages that the court can award even without proof of actual economic loss within a range between $750 and $30,000 per infringed work. If a U.S.-national owner does not register within the first three months after publication, it can recover statutory damages only for acts of infringement that occur after they actually do register and give notice to the accused infringer. The right to recover statutory damages is accompanied by a right to recover from the infringer an amount determined by the court to be a reasonable attorney fee.

Expressive Designs on Functional Articles

The federal Copyright Act includes a provision stating that a purely ornamental design feature that is on or incorporated into a functional product (a "useful article") can be protected by copyright as a "pictorial, graphic, or sculptural work" if it can be "identified separately from, and is capable of existing independently of, the utilitarian aspects of the article." Under the so-called "useful article doctrine," courts have experienced difficulty with creating and applying a consistent test for determining whether a nonfunctional, expressive design feature of a functional product can be protected by copyright law. Many courts have attempted to use what they call a test of "conceptual separability" that allows copyright protection for the design feature if a non-expert observer can mentally conceptualize the nonfunctional expression separately from the functional aspects of the product. This test has proved to be difficult to put into practice, and courts have reached inconsistent results in applying it.

In one famous U.S. Supreme Court case, *Mazer v. Stein*, 347 U.S. 201 (1954), decided many years before the 1976 Copyright Act included specific provisions on useful articles or on "pictorial, graphic, or sculptural works," the Court held that statuettes—male and female dancing figures made of semivitreous china—used as bases for fully equipped electric lamps were copyrightable, even though the lamp itself was a utilitarian mass-produced item. The Court in *Mazer* did not engage in any meaningful analysis except to say that the statuettes were protectable by copyright regardless of the fact that they had been sold primarily as lamp bases. It appears that the statuettes found protectable in *Mazer* would also be found protectable today under the modern "useful article" doctrine.

Recently, in *Star Athletica, L. L. C. v. Varsity Brands, Inc.*, 580 U.S. __ (2017), the U.S. Supreme Court interpreted the "useful article doctrine" by deciding whether certain designs incorporated into football cheerleaders' uniforms were protectable by copyright as "pictorial, graphic, or sculptural works" (one of the designated types of potentially protectable work specified in the Copyright Act). The court held that a two-prong test was required to make a decision whether these ornamental design elements are eligible for copyright. They are protectable, the Court said, "only if the feature (1) can be perceived as a two-or-three-dimensional work of art separate from the useful article and (2) would qualify as a protectable pictorial, graphic, or sculptural work—either on its own or fixed in some other tangible medium of expression—if it were *imagined separately* [emphasis added] from the useful article into which it is incorporated." This language clearly seems to adopt the concept of "conceptual separability." However, the Court only decided whether expressive design features on uniforms such as these, even if they served the purpose of identifying the apparel as cheerleader uniforms, were potentially protectable. A question remained for the lower court after remand about whether the very simple lines, chevrons, and colorful shapes on the uniforms met the basic requirement of originality for expression to be copyrightable in the first place.

Infringement

To prove copyright infringement, the owner must first prove that the defendant had access to the plaintiff's copyrighted work. Courts presume access, however, in the case of works that have been distributed in a relatively wide fashion. After proving access, in most cases the plaintiff can prove infringement by showing that the defendant's work is "substantially similar" to the plaintiff's work. In some cases, however, the test for infringement is "virtual identity" rather than substantial similarity. The defendant's work must be virtually identical to the plaintiff's in cases where the plaintiff's copyrighted work has only a so-called "thin copyright," such as the copyright in a map or directory or the compiler's copyright in the original selection and arrangement of a database. Thin copyright protection exists in works in which there are relatively few copyrightable elements relative to uncopyrightable elements, which is often the case with a work that is highly functional (utilitarian) in nature, with the main objective being to achieve something in an effective and efficient way. Such a work will often include some protectable original expression, but most of the work typically consists of uncopyrightable pure ideas, facts, *scenes a faire*, expressions from the public domain, and so on. Examples would include instruction manuals, maps, and data bases.

Just as in the case of patent infringement, the plaintiff does not have to prove that a defendant intended to violate copyright law, or even had knowledge that the plaintiff's work was copyrighted. Thus, an innocent infringer can be held liable. The following case provides an excellent illustration of how courts analyze a claim of copyright infringement. Here, it is obvious that the defendants had access to the plaintiffs' copyrighted work, so the only issue is whether the defendants' work (a movie) is substantially similar to the protected expression in the plaintiffs' work (a screenplay).

BENAY v. WARNER BROTHERS ENTERTAINMENT
U. S. Court of Appeals, Ninth Circuit, 607 F.3d 620 (2010)

Plaintiffs are two brothers, Aaron and Matthew Benay, who wrote a screenplay, The Last Samurai ("the Screenplay"). The Benays contend that the creators of the film The Last Samurai ("the Film") copied from the Screenplay without permission. They sued Warner Brothers Entertainment, Inc., Radar Pictures, Inc., Bedford Falls Productions, Inc., Edward Zwick, Marshall Herskovitz, and John Logan (collectively "Defendants"), who wrote, produced, marketed, and/or distributed the Film.

The Benays wrote their Screenplay between 1997 and 1999. They registered it with the Writers Guild of America in 1999 and with the federal copyright office in 2001. The Benays' agent, David Phillips, "pitched" the Screenplay to the president of production at Bedford Falls, Richard Solomon, on the telephone sometime between May 9, 2000, and May 12, 2000. Phillips provided a copy of the Screenplay to Solomon on May 16, 2000. According to Phillips, he provided the Screenplay with the implicit understanding that if Bedford Falls used it to produce a film, the Benays would be appropriately compensated. Solomon informed Phillips after receiving the Screenplay that Bedford Falls had decided to "pass" because it already had a similar project in development. The Film appeared in theaters in 2003, and the Benays sued for copyright infringement in 2005. The district court granted summary judgment for Defendants, and plaintiffs appealed.

W. FLETCHER, Circuit Judge:

The issue before us on appeal is whether there is substantial similarity between protected elements of the Screenplay and comparable elements of the Film. The Benays point to circumstantial evidence that, in their view, indicates that important aspects of the Film were copied from the Screenplay. Defendants contend that the Film was developed independently of the Screenplay.

The protagonist in the Screenplay is James Gamble, a successful West Point professor with a beautiful wife and a five-year-old son. Gamble travels to Japan at the request of President Grant. Gamble owes a debt to the President because then-General Grant saved Gamble's career after he accidentally killed eight of his own men during the Civil War. Gamble is initially successful in training and leading the Japanese Imperial Army, which is victorious in its first battle against the samurai. However, that battle turns out to be a strategic blunder because it incites a full samurai rebellion led by a treacherous samurai named Saigo. Gamble's five-year-old son is killed during Saigo's attack on a Christian church service. The death of his son leads Gamble to launch an attack against Saigo, which results in a devastating loss for the Imperial Army. Gamble falls into an opium-aided stupor, in which he is haunted by his failure, his mistake during the Civil War, and the death of his son. Gamble eventually is pulled out of this crisis by his wife and by Masako, a female samurai warrior who has double-crossed Saigo. The remainder of the Screenplay consists of Gamble's campaign to exact revenge. A series of battles unfolds between the Imperial Army, led by Gamble, and the samurai rebels. The conflict eventually ends with Gamble killing Saigo in a sword fight with the help of Masako, who dies in the fight. Gamble returns to the United States, where he lives in a Japanese-style house with his wife and a newborn child named Masako.

The protagonist in the Film is Nathan Algren, an unmarried alcoholic. He is haunted by his role in an attack on an innocent tribe during the Indian Campaigns. He has just been fired from his dead-end job hawking Winchester rifles when he is recruited by his former commander to train the Japanese Imperial Army in modern warfare. He travels to Japan as a mercenary. After Algren is captured by the samurai at the end of a disastrous first battle, he is exposed to traditional samurai culture. Algren bonds with Katsumoto, the honorable leader of the samurai rebellion, and falls in love with Taka, the widow of a samurai Algren killed while fighting for the Imperial Army. Algren assimilates into a samurai village, eventually joining the samurai in a final futile battle against the modernized Imperial Army. After the samurai army is devastated, Algren confronts the young Emperor and teaches him the value of traditional samurai culture before returning to live with Taka in the samurai village.

The Ninth Circuit employs a two-part test for determining whether one work is substantially similar to another. To prevail in their infringement case, the Benays must prove substantial similarity under *both* the "extrinsic test" and the "intrinsic test." The "extrinsic test" is an objective comparison of specific expressive elements. The "intrinsic test" is a subjective comparison that focuses on whether the ordinary, reasonable audience would find the works substantially similar in the "total concept and feel of the works." On a motion for summary judgment, we apply only the extrinsic test. The intrinsic test is left to the fact-finder. If the Benays fail to satisfy the extrinsic test, they cannot survive a motion for summary judgment.

The extrinsic test is an objective test based on specific expressive elements: the test focuses on articulable similarities between the plot, themes, dialogue, mood, setting, pace, characters, and sequence of events in two works. A court must take care to inquire only whether the protectable elements, standing alone, are substantially similar. Copyright law only protects expression of ideas, not the ideas themselves. Familiar stock scenes and themes that are staples of literature are not protected. Scenes-a-faire, or situations and incidents that flow necessarily or naturally from a basic plot premise, cannot sustain a finding of infringement. Historical facts are also unprotected by copyright law.

The Benays point to a number of similarities between the Screenplay and the Film. Both have identical titles; both share the historically unfounded premise of an American war veteran going to Japan to help the Imperial Army by training it in the methods of modern Western warfare for its fight against a samurai uprising; both have protagonists who are authors of non-fiction studies on war and who have flashbacks to battles in America; both include meetings with the Emperor and numerous battle scenes; both are reverential toward Japanese culture; and both feature the leader of the samurai rebellion as an important foil to the protagonist. Finally, in both works the American protagonist is spiritually transformed by his experience in Japan.

We agree with the district court that "[w]hile on cursory review, these similarities may appear substantial, a closer examination of the protectable elements, including plot, themes, dialogue, mood, setting, pace, characters, and sequence of events, exposes many more differences than similarities between Plaintiffs' Screenplay and Defendants' film." The most important similarities involve unprotectable elements. They are shared historical facts, familiar stock scenes, and characteristics that flow naturally from the works' shared basic plot premise. Stripped of these unprotected elements, the works are not sufficiently similar to satisfy the extrinsic test.

In applying the extrinsic test, we look beyond the vague, abstracted idea of a general plot. Though the Screenplay and the Film share the same basic plot premise, a closer inspection reveals that they tell very different stories.

In both the Screenplay and the Film, an American war veteran travels to Japan in the 1870s to train the Imperial Army in modern Western warfare in order to combat a samurai uprising. Not surprisingly, the stories share similar elements as a result of their shared premise. In both, the protagonist starts in America and travels to Japan where he meets the Emperor, who is struggling to modernize Japan. Both protagonists introduce modern warfare to the Imperial Army, using contemporary Western weaponry and tactics. Both works feature a Japanese foil in the form of the leader of the samurai rebellion. And in both works the protagonist suffers a personal crisis and is transformed as a result of his interaction with the samurai.

Despite these similarities, the two narratives are strikingly different. We agree with the district court's characterization:

> Plaintiffs' protagonist, Gamble, emerges from domestic security, to despair at the loss of his son, to revenge and triumph when he defeats his ruthless antagonist, Saigo. In contrast, the protagonist in Defendants' film moves from isolation and self-destructive behavior, to the discovery of traditional values and a way of life that he later comes to embrace. Thus, unlike Plaintiffs' Screenplay, which is largely a revenge story, Defendants' film is more a captivity narrative reminiscent in some respects to *Dances with Wolves.*

While the works share a common premise, that premise contains unprotectable elements. For example, there actually was a samurai uprising in the 1870s, the Satsuma Rebellion, led by Saigo Takamori, who is sometimes referred to as "The Last Samurai." *See* Charles L. Yates, *Saigo Takamori in the Emergence of Meiji Japan,* 28 Mod. Asian Stud. 449, 449 (1994); Kenneth G. Henshall, A History of Japan: From Stone Age to Superpower 78 (Palgrave Macmillan 2d ed.2004) (1999). While there is no clear historical analogue to the American protagonist who travels to Japan to help fight the samurai rebellion, it is not surprising that a Hollywood film about the rebellion would insert an American character.

This case is similar to *Funky Films,* in which the two works at issue told the story of a small funeral home operated by two brothers after the sudden death of their father. The works shared numerous similarities: in both works the older brother moved home from a distant city, was creative in contrast to his conservative younger brother, and initially had no interest in becoming involved in the family business; in both the business was financially fragile; in both a rival funeral home attempted to take over the home but failed; and in both the younger brother changed his church affiliation in order to increase their client base. However, closer examination of the works revealed one to be essentially a murder mystery and the other to be a study of the way the characters struggle with life in the wake of the cataclysmic death of their father. We therefore held that the plots developed "quite differently" and rejected the plaintiffs' copyright claim. Similarly, the Screenplay and Film in the case now before us tell fundamentally different stories, though they share the same premise and a number of elements that follow naturally from that premise.

The Benays point to similarities between various characters in the two works, most notably the American protagonists. But on close inspection there are only a few similarities that have significance under copyright law. Most of the similarities are either derived from historical facts or are traits that flow naturally from the works' shared premises. Only distinctive characters are protectable, not characters that merely embody unprotected ideas.

The most similar characters in the two works are the American protagonists, but the differences between them at least equal the similarities. The Benays' protagonist, Gamble, begins the Screenplay as a happily married and successful West Point professor, while the Defendants' protagonist, Algren, begins the Film as an unmarried loner, a drunk, and a failure, with a meaningless job selling Winchester rifles; Gamble's flashbacks are to his accidental killing of eight of his own men during a Civil War battle, while Algren's are to his role in a brutal attack on an innocent Indian tribe; and Gamble gains an appreciation of Japanese culture and honor but returns to America at the end of the Screenplay, while Algren fully assimilates into the samurai way of life by the end of the Film.

Although both works include the leader of the samurai rebellion as a central character, he is based on a historical figure, Saigo Takamori, and is therefore unprotected for copyright purposes. Moreover, the Screenplay's Saigo is a treacherous and ruthless warlord who deceives the Emperor, attacks a church service resulting in the death of Gamble's son, and is killed by Gamble at the end of the Screenplay. By contrast, the Film's Katsumoto is an honorable and spiritual samurai who respects the Emperor, fights only to preserve the honor of the samurai way of life, and becomes a friend and mentor to Algren by the end of the Film.

The two works present the Japanese Emperor in starkly different ways. The Emperor in both works seeks to modernize Japan. The Screenplay's Emperor is confident, wise, and forward-looking. The Film's Emperor, on the other hand, is young and tentative, torn between modernization and traditional Japanese culture, and is bullied by his advisors.

There are a number of important characters in the Film and the Screenplay who have no obvious parallel in the other work. In the Screenplay, Gamble's wife Britany and his son Trevor play an important role in the development of the plot. Trevor's death is the catalyst for Gamble's opium-aided breakdown and is the motivation for his revenge against Saigo. Gamble's relationship with his wife Britany is tested throughout the movie. The Screenplay also includes a character named Masako, a beautiful samurai warrior who betrays Saigo to help Gamble. In the Film, Algren is childless. He falls in love with Taka, the widow of a samurai warrior. But Taka plays a very different role in the Film from the roles played by Britany and Masako in the Screenplay. Taka helps Algren assimilate into samurai culture and shares few character traits with Britany. Taka is graceful and giving, while Britany is fiery and strong-willed. Unlike Masako, Taka is not a warrior. In the Screenplay, Britany's father plays an important role in getting Gamble to Japan and is the central figure in a side-plot in which he attempts to break up Gamble's marriage. There is no parallel character or side-plot in the Film. Finally, the Film includes Algren's former commander during the Indian Campaigns, whom Algren despises. There is no parallel character in the Screenplay.

The district court noted that "both works explore general themes of the embittered war veteran, the 'fish-out-of water,' and the clash between modernization and traditions." But to the extent the works share themes, those themes arise naturally from the premise of an American war vet who goes to Japan to fight the samurai, and the works develop those themes in very different ways. The Screenplay exalts the Americanized modernization of Japan, expressed by Gamble triumphantly raising the American flag over Iwo Jima after killing Saigo. It characterizes samurai as part of an ugly class system from Japan's feudal past, and is largely positive about the role of westerners in modernizing Japan. By contrast, the Film is ambivalent toward modernization and is nostalgic for disappearing Japanese traditions. The Film treats the samurai tradition as an honorable way of life, sadly left behind by modernization, and treats westerners as self-interested and exploitative.

Given that both works involve an American war veteran who travels to Japan to help the Emperor fight a samurai rebellion, it is not surprising that they share certain settings: a scene of the protagonist sailing into Japan, scenes in the Imperial Palace, scenes on the Imperial Army's training grounds, and battle scenes in various places in Japan. These are all scenes-a-faire that flow naturally from the works' shared unprotected premise and are therefore disregarded for purposes of the extrinsic test. This setting naturally and necessarily flows from the basic plot premise and therefore constitutes scenes-a-faire and cannot support a finding of substantial similarity.

Some of the settings are strikingly dissimilar. As the district court noted, the "American settings of the two works are drastically different." The Screenplay opens at West Point with a classroom scene, a snowball fight, and a scene in Gamble's comfortable home. The Film, on the other hand, opens at a San Francisco convention hall where the drunk Algren is hawking Winchester rifles. In Japan, the Screenplay includes scenes in samurai castles and in an opium den where Gamble has a spiritual crisis, none of which is in the Film. The Film includes extended scenes in a samurai village. No such village appears in the Screenplay.

Both works contain violent action scenes. But we agree with the district court that the Screenplay "has a triumphant mood" and "is a fast-paced adventure/intrigue story," while the Film "is more nostalgic and reflective in mood" and employs "leisurely sequences" in addition to its battle scenes. The two works have opposing perspectives on the modernization of Japan and the end of samurai culture. Further, the pacing of the two works is substantially different. The Screenplay jumps from battle scene to battle scene, while the Film has a long period of relative calm in which Algren is held in captivity in the samurai village.

There are limited similarities in dialogue between the two works. The Benays point to both works' use of the term "gaijin." But this word, which means "foreigner" or "stranger" in Japanese, naturally flows from the narrative of an American military advisor in Japan. The Benays also point to the use of voice-overs by the protagonists in the two works. But the use of voice-overs is a common cinematic technique. A significant difference between the dialogues is that the Screenplay is written almost entirely in English (except for occasional words like "gaijin"), whereas the Film contains substantial exchanges entirely in Japanese.

A title standing alone cannot be copyrighted, but the copying of a title may have copyright significance as one factor in establishing an infringement claim. The Benays make much of the fact that the two works share the title "The Last Samurai." The Defendants respond that the identity of titles is not significant because Saigo Takamori, the historical figure on which much of the Film is based, is sometimes referred to as "The Last Samurai." *See* Charles L. Yates, *supra,* at 449. The limited copyright significance of the shared title in this case is insufficient to overcome the overall lack of similarities between protected elements of the works. [We affirm the district court's grant of summary judgment to the Defendants.]

Although the law on copyright infringement is the same for musical compositions and recordings is the same as that for other expressive works, the law has proved to be especially difficult to apply in the context of music. Part of the problem is probably traceable to a decision in the 1940s by the U.S. Court of Appeals for the Second Circuit, a federal appeals court whose decisions have always been especially important to the development of copyright law because of the Court's location in New York where the music industry has long been centered (in addition to, at a later time Los Angeles). That decision held that, after the fact of copying had been proved (or admitted), the final determination on infringement should be left up to lay juries without assistance from experts. The test was to be the impression on "the ears of lay people." Such an approach has been exceptionally difficult to apply, and has led to much inconsistency in results.

In 2015, a jury in federal district court in Los Angeles found that the 2013 hit "Blurred Lines" by Robin Thicke infringed on the late-1970s hit "Got to Give it Up" by Marvin Gaye, because of similarities in a combination of some elements of the Gaye song. The district judge let the verdict stand. Many infringement cases against popular musicians followed, creating much anxiety in the music industry. Many observers were concerned, with apparent justification, that the combination of a few chords and other common elements in much popular music could lead to infringement liability.

In 2014, Skidmore filed a copyright infringement suit against the rock band Led Zeppelin, and its remaining three members, Jimmy Page, Robert Plant, and John Paul Jones. Skidmore, trustee for the estate of Wolfe, who had written the 1960s rock song "Taurus" and performed and recorded it with his band Spirit, claimed that the famous electric guitar riff in the 1971 Led Zeppelin song, "Stairway to Heaven," infringed on a guitar sequence in "Taurus." Because the facts of the case arose before 1972, there was no copyright protection for the sound recording of "Taurus." Thus, the case involved the copyright on only the underlying "Taurus" musical composition.

In the federal district court, a jury found that there was not enough originality in the combination of musical elements in a guitar sequence in plaintiff's song to be infringed by the guitar sequence in Led Zeppelin's song. The district judge upheld the verdict, and the plaintiff appealed. Then, a three-judge panel of the U.S. Court of Appeals for the Ninth Circuit in San Francisco reversed and held that the trial judge should have instructed the jury that, although individual elements of a song do not qualify for copyright protection, a combination of those elements, such as "chromatic scales, arpeggios, or short sequences of notes" may be sufficiently original to be protected.

But, in *Skidmore v. Zeppelin*, 2020 WL 1128808 (9th Cir. 2020), the entire 11 judges on the U.S. Court of Appeals for the Ninth Circuit (e.g., the court *en banc*) overturned the panel decision and held that such simple sequences of common musical elements could have only "thin" copyright protection if there was any protection at all. Thus, such simple sequences in "Taurus" could be infringed by those in "Stairway to Heaven" only if they were essentially identical. The en banc Ninth Circuit held that they were not, and there was no infringement. The court did not mention the merger doctrine, but if the sequences of chords and notes in a song like "Taurus" are sufficiently simple, the merger doctrine might prevent the musical elements from having any copyright protection at all.

Another important portion of the *Skidmore* case involved the interplay between the infringement requirements of access and similarity. The three-judge panel of the appeals court had held that here should be a sliding scale of "access" and "substantial similarity," so that very clear proof by the copyright owner that the defendant had access to the plaintiff's copyrighted work would mean that less proof of similarity should be required to prove infringement. The *en banc* Ninth Circuit rejected this approach, holding that a high degree of proof of access to the plaintiff's work does not diminish the degree of similarity required to prove infringement, which is in agreement with previous decisions of other federal courts of appeal.

Separately, it may be a surprise to some people that forwarding an email containing copyrighted material, or "retweeting" a message containing such material, makes a new copy on a server. This can be copyright infringement unless done with the express or implied consent of the copyright owner or unless protected by a defense.

Secondary Infringement

In addition to liability for direct infringement against the party who actually engages in the infringing activity, there also can be *secondary* (or indirect) infringement by a person or company that provides the means to the actual (direct) infringer to commit the infringement or actively induces (encourages) the direct infringer to commit infringement. There are three types of secondary infringement liability: contributory, vicarious, and inducement infringement. The differences among the three types can sometimes be important, but those differences can also be very subtle and extremely difficult to understand and apply. Although this can be an important area of copyright law, it is too complicated for an introductory treatment and thus is beyond the scope of this book.

Defenses

The Copyright Act provides for several defenses to copyright infringement. For example, a nonprofit library may make a copy of a work for archival purposes. Also, an owner of a lawful copy of computer software may make a copy that is necessary for the software to be used (such as copying from a CD or downloading copyright content to the computer's hard drive when the user has consent to do so), as well as one backup copy. It is *not* legal to make copies of a software program, movies, or the like for friends and family unless the fair-use defense applies.

Fair Use Defense

Section 107 of the Copyright Act of 1976 states:

[T]he fair use of a copyrighted work, including such use by reproduction in copies or phonorecords or by any other means . . . for purposes such as criticism, comment, news reporting, teaching (including multiple copies for classroom use), scholarship, or research, is not an infringement of copyright. In determining whether the use made of a work in any particular case is a fair use the factors to be considered shall include— 1. the purpose and character of the use, including whether such use is of a commercial nature or is for nonprofit educational purposes; 2. the nature of the copyrighted work; 3. the amount and substantiality of the portion used in relation to the copyrighted work as a whole; and 4. the effect of the use upon the potential market for or value of the copyrighted work.

Although copying significant portions of a copyrighted work for the purpose of literary criticism, news commentary, classroom teaching, academic research, or parody are more likely to constitute fair use than other forms of copying, this is not an exhaustive list of copying that can be fair use. Moreover, the fact that the purpose of copying is for criticism, news commentary, teaching, or research does not automatically mean that it is fair use. For example, in 2020, a federal district court in New York held that Cox Media Group, a large company that owns many radio and television stations across the U.S. committed copyright infringement by publishing a photograph taken by a man in New York City. The man, Cruz, was on a sidewalk when he witnessed the police arrest of a terrorist suspect. Cruz shared the photo with one friend, who told him that the photo was quite original and might be worth something. Cruz subsequently sold licenses to publish the photo to the TV networks NBC and CNN. Cox Media acquired a copy of the picture and published it without Cruz's permission. The district court granted a summary judgment of infringement to Cruz, and against Cox on its fair use defense, primarily because Cox used the photo for the same purpose as Cruz was using it in licensing to other news organizations, and Cox was potentially usurping existing licensing markets for the photo.

One particular form of criticism or commentary, the parody, is especially likely to be fair use not only because parodies enjoy a high level of First Amendment free speech protection, but also usually hold up very well when the four-factor analysis is employed. A parody is a type of satire that holds up the original to contempt, ridicule, or scorn. For example, in *Campbell v. Acuff-Rose Music, Inc.*, 510 U.S. 569 (1994), the Supreme Court concluded that the rap group 2 Live Crew had engaged in a legally justified fair use in the 1980s when it composed and recorded its rap version of the 1960s pop song "Oh, Pretty Woman." The 1980s rap version used the same very distinctive bass riff several times as had been used in the original, and also used the identical one-line chorus multiple times. The remainder of the lyrics were quite different, though. The lyrics of the original had presented the sanitized fantasies of a young man trying to pick up a girl in a city, whereas the later rap version used bawdy lyrics showing the harsh realities of such a relationship in a big city late at night. The mere fact that 2 Live Crew made a rap version of the original did not prove fair use, but the Court's conclusion that the rap version made fun of the boy's unrealistic fantasy in the original did lead to a finding of fair use. The following case illustrates how the fair-use analysis is employed in the case of a critical commentary on another copyrighted work.

HUGHES v. BENJAMIN a/k/a Sargon of Akkad, et al.
United States District Court, Southern District of New York, 2020 WL 528704 (2020)

Plaintiff Akilah Hughes brings this action against Defendant Carl Benjamin for copyright infringement principally alleging that Benjamin's YouTube video, SJW Levels of Awareness, unlawfully copied Hughes's YouTube video about the 2016 presidential election, "We Thought She Would Win." Now before the Court is Benjamin's motion to dismiss the complaint for failure to allege a cause of action.

Hughes is a popular content creator and filmmaker who maintains the YouTube channel "Akilah Obviously." Her work "covers a broad range of topics, including comedy, race, social commentary, feminism, beauty, and fashion."

On November 8, 2016, the night of the 2016 presidential election, Hughes filmed Hillary Clinton's campaign party at the Jacob Javitz Convention Center in Manhattan. Ten days later, Hughes posted a nine-minute-and-fifty-second video titled "We Thought She Would Win" to her YouTube channel. The video contained her campaign party footage, as well as her thoughts on the night's events (both during the night and after the night was over), including commentary on the implications of Secretary Clinton's defeat by now-President Donald Trump. The video begins with Hughes at the Javitz Center, early in the night, stating that she is "really excited to be ... a woman in the year 2016 after having ... a black president for eight years and now we have Hillary who could potentially be our next president." The video then cuts to Hughes reflecting back on election night after Secretary Clinton's loss, noting that "no one thought she wasn't going to win, so it started out as a very exciting evening and like full of hope" before the mood "just like crept down, until forever." The final five minutes of the video consist of wide-ranging commentary, including Hughes urging her audience to "stand up" before violence is committed against minorities, her negative feelings toward the year 2016, and her gratitude for being "surrounded by like-minded people" in New York City. Hughes alleges that she is the sole owner of the video, and that it is registered with the United States Copyright Office.

Benjamin, like Hughes, is a content creator and filmmaker who maintains the YouTube channels "Sargon of Akkad" and "The Thinkery," where he publishes "anti-ideological and anti-identitarian" content focusing on "the left, racism, feminism, Black Lives Matter, and Islam." Benjamin is "publicly known for his provocative style and strongly-held beliefs against liberal social and political stances." To say the least, Hughes and Benjamin are at opposite ends of the political spectrum.

The day after publishing "We Thought She Would Win," Hughes discovered that Benjamin had posted the video "SJW Levels of Awareness," comprised entirely of six clips of "We Thought She Would Win" totaling one minute and fifty-eight seconds, to one of his YouTube Channels. According to the Complaint, "SJW" is an acronym for "social justice warrior," a term "routinely used by Benjamin in a demeaning context to belittle proponents of perceived liberal social policies and stances. "SJW Levels of Awareness" begins with Hughes expressing her excitement over the potential election of a female president, followed by a clip depicting her subsequent disappointment over Secretary Clinton's loss. SJW Levels of Awareness then cuts to footage of Hughes stating that Trump supporters mean to divide the country, urging people to speak out against bigotry, and observing that 2016 is the worst year of her life. The video concludes with Hughes declaring her appreciation for "living with like-minded people in New York City." "SJW Levels of Awareness" includes no commentary or video recorded by Benjamin himself.

After discovering Benjamin's video, Hughes submitted a "takedown notice" to YouTube pursuant to the 1998 Digital Millennium Act, 17 U.S.C. § 512. YouTube then disabled public access to Benjamin's video. On November 19, 2016, Benjamin sent Hughes an email requesting that she withdraw the takedown notice. On November 22, 2016, after Hughes declined to withdraw her takedown notice, Benjamin sent YouTube a DMCA counter notification claiming that SJW Levels of Awareness was "entirely transformative ... and intended for parody." Hughes alleges that YouTube relied upon Benjamin's counter notification "to reinstate certain features of their service, including allowing for the continued public display of 'SJW Levels of Awareness,'" though she does not specify when YouTube reinstated access to Benjamin's video. On the same day, Benjamin also posted "SJW Levels of Awareness" to his Twitter account, where it remained publicly accessible until his account was suspended.

Hughes initiated this action for damages and injunctive relief. She asserts that Benjamin infringed on her copyright on "We Thought She Would Win" through his public posting of "SJW Levels of Awareness" on YouTube and Twitter. Benjamin then filed a motion to dismiss Hughes's complaint on the ground that it failed to state a claim upon which relief can be granted. Hughes filed an opposition on May 18, 2018, and Benjamin filed a reply on May 30, 2018.

Sullivan, Circuit Judge:

In reviewing a motion to dismiss, a court must accept as true all factual allegations in the complaint and draw all reasonable inferences in favor of the plaintiff. However, that tenet "is inapplicable to legal conclusions." Thus, a pleading that offers only labels and conclusions or a formulaic recitation of the elements of a cause of action will not do. If the plaintiff has not nudged its claims across the line from conceivable to plausible, its complaint must be dismissed."

To establish a prima facie case of copyright infringement, a plaintiff must demonstrate (1) ownership of a valid copyright, and (2) copying of constituent elements of the work that are original. A defendant is deemed to have copied constituent elements of the plaintiff's work where (1) the defendant has actually copied the plaintiff's work; *and* (2) the copying is illegal because a substantial similarity exists between the defendant's work and the protectible elements of plaintiff's. The defendant can defeat a prima facie showing of infringement," however, by proving that the doctrine of fair use permits his or her "employment of the plaintiff's work."

Although fair use is an affirmative defense, and thus the defendant bears the burden of proving it, fair use can nevertheless be adjudicated on a motion to dismiss. At this stage of the litigation, the Court's task is to determine whether "the facts necessary to establish the defense are evident on the face of the complaint," including any materials properly incorporated into the complaint.

In undertaking a fair use analysis, the Court considers the following non-exhaustive list of factors set forth in 17 U.S.C. § 107:

(1) the purpose and character of the use, including whether such use is of a commercial nature or is for nonprofit educational purposes;

(2) the nature of the copyrighted work;

(3) the amount and substantiality of the portion used in relation to the copyrighted work as a whole; and

(4) the effect of the use upon the potential market for or value of the copyrighted work.

The four listed statutory factors in §107 guide but do not control the fair use analysis and are to be explored, and the results weighed together, in light of the purposes of copyright. The ultimate question is whether the copyright law's constitutionally mandated goal of promoting the Progress of Science and useful Arts would be better served by allowing the use than by preventing it. The Court will consider each of the above statutory factors.

1. Purpose and Character of Use: The first factor, the heart of the fair use inquiry, concerns the purpose and character of the allegedly infringing use. In the preamble to § 107, Congress identified "criticism, comment, news reporting, teaching, scholarship, and research" as illustrative purposes of a fair use. Additionally, the commercial use of the new work may weigh against a finding of fair use, which favors non-profit educational purposes. But because nearly all of the illustrative uses listed in the preamble paragraph of

§ 107 are generally conducted for profit in this country, courts do not give much weight to the fact that the secondary use was for commercial gain. Instead, the critical question when applying the first fair use factor is whether the new work is "transformative." Like the overall fair use determination, whether a work is transformative is an open-ended and context-sensitive inquiry, based on how the work in question appears to the reasonable observer. The critical inquiry is whether the new work uses the copyrighted material itself for a purpose, or imbues it with a character, different from that for which it was created.

Most relevant here, a new work may be transformative even where it consists entirely of portions of the original work, or indeed even where it is an "exact replication" of the original work. A secondary work can be transformative in function or purpose without altering or actually adding to the original work. In *Baraban v. Time Warner, Inc.*, for example, the court found that the first statutory fair use factor weighed heavily in favor of fair use where the defendant had copied the plaintiff's photo outright in order to comment on it and on the advertising campaign in which the photo played an integral part. The court noted that the defendant's use of the photo was not exactly parody or satire as those terms have been defined in the case law, but that the defendant's use of the photo in context–as part of a book containing critical commentary–nevertheless clearly fell within the permissible use categories of "comment" and "criticism."

Here, it is clear from the face of Hughes's complaint that Benjamin copied portions of "We Thought She Would Win" for the transformative purposes of criticism and commentary. Beginning with the title of Benjamin's work, "SJW Levels of Awareness," Hughes herself acknowledges that "SJW" or "social justice warrior" is a term routinely used by Benjamin in a demeaning context to belittle proponents of perceived liberal social policies and stances. Although Hughes contends that her own subjective awareness of the term's meaning does not establish that a "reasonable observer" would interpret the term "SJW" in a pejorative manner, the Court concludes that "SJW" or "Social Justice Warrior" has sufficiently entered the modern lexicon such that there can be no serious dispute as to its pejorative meaning in this context. *See, e.g.*, Oxford Univ. Press, *social justice warrior*, Lexico, https://www.lexico.com/definition/social_justice_warrior (last updated 2019) (defining "social justice warrior" as a "derogatory" term for "[a] person who expresses or promotes socially progressive views"); Abby Ohlheiser, *Why 'Social Justice Warrior,' a Gamergate Insult, Is Now a Dictionary Entry*, Wash. Post (Oct. 7, 2015), https://www.washingtonpost.com/news/the-intersect/wp/2015/10/07/why-social-justice-warrior-a-gamergate-insult-is-now-a-dictionary-entry. And "levels of awareness" is plainly used in a sarcastic manner when combined with "SJW," implying a lack of awareness concerning social or political matters.

The Court takes judicial notice of the news articles (which report on the Lexico dictionary entry) for the "fact of their publication," since the articles predate Benjamin's posting of *SJW Levels of Awareness* and thus show that *SJW* was in a dictionary as a derogatory term at that time.

Moreover, the critical nature of *SJW Levels of Awareness* is apparent from the broader context of Benjamin's YouTube channel, where it was posted. As Hughes' complaint alleges, Benjamin "routinely engages and criticizes viewpoints on various social and political issues" on his YouTube channels, specifically targeting topics such as feminism, "the left," and Black Lives Matter. Thus, whether "SJW Levels of Awareness" is accessed by searching for "SJW"-related content on YouTube or by going directly to

Benjamin's YouTube channel, a reasonable observer who came across the video would quickly grasp its critical purpose.

Furthermore, although courts have found transformative uses even in cases involving exact copying, the Court notes that "SJW Levels of Awareness" is *not* an exact copy of "We Thought She Would Win." Rather, Benjamin excerpted "We Thought She Would Win" to depict the specific moments he felt exemplified Hughes's political identity and lack of awareness. For example, Benjamin included Hughes's prediction and hope that Secretary Clinton would win the election, while omitting footage that did not support his message, like Hughes's statement that Secretary Clinton won the popular vote with "record numbers." And he excluded content unrelated to his criticism, like Hughes's commentary on the societal benefits of YouTube. In this way, Benjamin excerpted "We Thought She Would Win" to maximize his criticism of Hughes's liberal viewpoint.[5]

To the extent that Benjamin's selective excerpting was not "fair" to Hughes in the colloquial sense of accurately conveying her level of awareness, courts will not, except in rare circumstances, reject a fair use defense based on the inaccuracy of a critical work. . . .

Because a reasonable observer would plainly infer from the title of Benjamin's video, the context in which it was posted, and its selective copying, that it was intended to criticize Hughes and comment on her perceived lack of awareness, the first fair use factor favors Benjamin.

2. The Nature of the Copyrighted Work: The second fair use factor, the nature of the copyrighted work, calls for recognition that some works are closer to the core of intended copyright protection than others, like works intended for "creative expression for public dissemination. Applying this factor, courts consider (1) whether the copyrighted work is expressive or creative, with a greater leeway being allowed to a claim of fair use where the work is factual or informational, and (2) whether the work is published or unpublished, with the scope for fair use involving unpublished works being considerably narrower. The second fair use factor, however, may be of limited usefulness where the creative work of art is being used for a transformative purpose. The nature of the copyrighted work is not much help in separating the fair use sheep from the infringing goats in a parody case, since parodies almost invariably copy publicly known, expressive works.

Here, the second fair use factor is essentially neutral and of little import. Hughes's work is "factual or informational" in that it provides a first-hand account of a newsworthy event, but it also has "expressive or creative" value in both its commentary and production. Also, "We Thought She Would Win" is a published work, and thus the scope of fair use in this context is not "considerably narrower" than it would be if it had been unpublished. Given these countervailing considerations, and the fact that *SJW Levels of Awareness* is plainly transformative, the second fair use factor has little impact here.

3. Amount and Substantiality of the Portion Used: The third statutory fair use factor turns on whether the amount and substantiality of the portion used in relation to the copyrighted work as a whole is reasonable in relation to the purpose of the copying." In assessing this factor, the Court considers "not only the quantity of the materials used, but also their quality and importance. The crux of the inquiry is whether no more content was taken than necessary, given the purpose and character of the allegedly infringing use. The inquiry must take into account that the extent of permissible copying varies with the purpose and character of the use. Thus, the third factor may favor the defendant even

where the defendant copies an entire work, provided that such copying was reasonably necessary in relation to the work's transformative purpose.

Here, "SJW Levels of Awareness" copied 20% of "We Thought She Would Win," a percentage which, while greater than that found unreasonable in some cases in this Circuit, was still far less than the entire video. In addition, although the selected excerpts were important to Hughes's video (at least as important as any other part of her video), they were also linked to the critical purpose of "SJW Levels of Awareness." As noted above, Benjamin did not copy parts of Hughes's video that undermined or were unrelated to the critical purpose of "SJW Levels of Awareness" Notably, Benjamin also did not copy every part of "We Thought She Would Win" that evinced Hughes's progressive views. Rather, Benjamin copied as much of "We Thought She Would Win" as was deemed reasonably necessary for him to convey his critical message. In these circumstances, the third factor tips in favor of Benjamin.

4. The Effect on the Potential Market for the Copyrighted Work: The fourth fair use factor concerns whether the secondary use usurps the market of the original work. A defendant usurps the original work's market when the infringer's target audience and the nature of the infringing content is the same as the original. Thus, the more transformative the secondary use, the less the likelihood that the secondary use substitutes for the original.

Here, there is no danger that "SJW Levels of Awareness" will usurp the market of progressive commentaries such as "We Thought She Would Win." Benjamin's target audience, which is generally political conservatives and libertarians, is obviously not the same as Hughes's target audience, which is generally political liberals. Moreover, although "SJW Levels of Awareness" is comprised entirely of portions of "We Thought She Would Win," there is no reason to think that Hughes's audience will abandon her progressive YouTube channel to watch the derisively-titled" SJW Levels of Awareness" on a conservative YouTube channel simply because it contains parts of her work. Thus, the fourth fair use factor, like the first and third factors, favors Benjamin.

Because three of the four statutory fair use factors favor Benjamin, including the most important factor (purpose and character of use), and the least important factor (nature of the copyrighted work) is neutral, the Court concludes that the fair use defense clearly applies based on the face of Hughes's Complaint and a review of the videos themselves. Accordingly, Hughes has failed to state a claim of copyright infringement, and Benjamin's motion to dismiss is granted.

A Note on Derivative Works

One of the copyright owner's exclusive rights is to creative derivative works. A derivative work is one that derives from the original. In other words, a derivative work copies at least some substantial amount of original expression from the original copyrighted work, and adds a substantial amount of new expression to make a new creative work. A derivative work may target a different type of audience, be in a different medium, or tap demand in a different market. It does not have to do these things in order to be characterized as a derivative work, but it is often the case that it does so. Examples include toy action figures or fictional movie characters copied from a cartoon character, a new version of a software program, a new edition of a book, a movie or play taken from a novel, and so on. There are almost countless examples of derivative works, and the ability of a copyright owner in an original to exclusively tap demand in a different market or a different medium, or license the right to do so to someone else, is often very profitable.

The point of introducing the concept of derivative works at this juncture is that defendants sued for infringing on a copyright owner's right to make derivative works often claim that their derivative work is protected by the fair use defense. Most unauthorized derivative works are not, in fact, protected by the fair use defense, but quite a few cases throughout history in which a defendant has been successful in asserting the fair use defense did involve unauthorized derivative works. For example, the 1980s 2 Live Crew rap version of the 1960s pop song *Oh, Pretty Woman* was a derivative work that was found to be protected by the fair use defense because the Court found it to be a true parody of the original, meaning both that there was no infringement, and that the new original expression in the parody was protected by copyright. Again, though, most unauthorized derivative works are not fair use.

Moreover, the creator of an unauthorized derivative work can receive no copyright protection for his or her new original expression that was added to create the derivative work. However, if the unauthorized derivative work is found to be protected by the fair-use defense, it is treated as though it were authorized and is thus entitled to its own copyright protection (in addition to not being an infringement of the work from which it derives). However, if the unauthorized derivative work is found to be protected by the fair use defense, it *does* have copyright protection for its new original expression.

Also important is the fact that the owner of a copyright in the original can authorize the creation of a derivative work by granting a license, express or implied. A recent example of this Blizzard, a video game designer and maker, was responsible for the wildly successful game, "Wizard 3," among other video games. Blizzard had allowed users to freely create custom additions to Wizard 3, such as including new maps. Recently, Blizzard introduced a remastered version of the game titled "Wizard 3 Reforged."

With the introduction of Wizard 3 Reforged, Blizzard adopted a new user policy. In this policy, Blizzard stated that it would own the copyright on all custom additions by users. Many fans were understandably unhappy about Blizzard's assertion of ownership. Legally, however, it appears that the company has the right to do this. The reason is that Blizzard authorized users to add their own creative embellishments to the game. Thus, user additions are "authorized derivative works." Such works are copyrighted, but creating derivative works is one of the exclusive rights of the creator of the original copyrighted work, and by authorizing derivative works, Blizzard is granting a license. Blizzard has the legal right to specify the terms of any license it grants, including ownership of copyright in the derivative work. Here, there is no basis for a claim of fair use by game users.

Remedies

A successful plaintiff in a copyright infringement action usually receives actual damages plus the defendant's profits to the extent they were not calculated into the damage award. If the plaintiffs have registered their copyright within three months after publication, they may elect between proving actual damages or receiving "statutory damages" of $750 to $30,000 per copyrighted work infringed by a particular defendant. The amount can be up to $150,000 per copyrighted work for willful infringement. Copyright infringement can also constitute a federal crime which, depending on various circumstances, can be punishable by fines or imprisonment of up to 5 years for a first offense and 10 years for second and later offenses.

Digital Millennium Copyright Act

In 1998 Congress passed the Digital Millennium Copyright Act (DMCA). The most far-reaching and controversial aspect of the DMCA are its so-called "anti-circumvention" provisions, which were enacted mainly in response to heavy lobbying from the movie and recording industries. They apply when an owner of copyrighted material in digital form uses a technological measure (such as encryption, initialization codes, etc.) to effectively limit access to its work or protect the work from being copied. If someone else circumvents this protective measure, such as decrypting the encryption or copying the initialization (start-up) code, there is a violation of the DMCA. This is analogous to picking the lock on the door to a room that contains copyrighted material.

Most people outside the movie, music, and software industries have criticized this provision of the DMCA because it sweeps so broadly. There can be a DMCA violation, for example, even if the one who circumvented the access control intends to use the protected material in a completely legitimate way once gaining access to it. There is no fair use defense to the DMCA and, thus, there can be a violation even if the one gaining access through circumvention makes a fair use of the copyrighted material.

Not only is it illegal to engage in circumvention, but it also is illegal to "traffic in" anti-circumvention measures by making such measures available to others. For example, a teenager in Norway developed a program he called DeCSS that decrypted the encrypted code that prevented copying of DVDs. The encryption protecting the DVDs was called CSS for "content scrambling system." Although he was outside the reach of the DMCA in Norway, a magazine in the US ("2600 Magazine") was found by US courts to have violated the DMCA by posting the DeCSS source code on its web site and also providing a hypertext link in to a place where readers could download the DeCSS program. This program was a circumvention measure and the magazine made it available to others. Thus, there was a DMCA violation.

TRADEMARKS

A *trademark* is any distinctive word, phrase, symbol, or design adopted for the purpose of identifying the origin of goods being offered for sale. A trademark benefits consumers by acting as a symbol enabling them to identify goods or services that have been satisfactory in the past and to reject those that have been unsatisfactory. A trademark also motivates businesses to maintain or improve the quality of their goods or services over time to reap the benefits of a well-earned public trust in a mark. Trademark infringement occurs, therefore, when a competitor of the trademark owner uses a mark so similar to the owned trademark that purchasers of the competitor's goods are likely to be misled as to the origin of the goods that they are purchasing. In other words, a deception is accomplished that permits the competitor (typically a manufacturer or other seller) to take a "free ride" on the reputation and goodwill of the trademark owner (who is, typically, another manufacturer or seller). Although a deception is accomplished, trademark infringement can occur even if the defendant did not intend it (or even if the defendant didn't know about the plaintiff's mark).

Trademark law also governs service marks, used to identify the origin of services such as car rental, video rental, computer repair, insurance, and so on. The legal principles are the same for both trademarks and service marks and, thus, most people simply use the word trademark to refer to either.

A company's name—its business name (or "trade name")—may or may not be protected as a trademark. If the company uses its name, such as Microsoft or IBM, to serve trademark (branding) purposes, the name is protectable as a trademark or service mark.

Trademark law also protects "trade dress"—very distinctive packaging or nonfunctional product design itself—if it serves the same purpose as a trademark. For example, the U.S. Supreme Court held in *Two Pesos, Inc. v. Taco Cabana, Inc.*, 505 U.S. 763 (1992), that the distinctive design of a restaurant's exterior and interior décor were protected as trade dress. The Supreme Court has held, for a distinctive nonfunctional product design feature to be protected as trade dress, the owner must prove that the design feature has acquired "secondary meaning" (i.e., has come to be viewed as a brand by a substantial portion of the relevant consuming public) through its use over time. However, the Court held that the owner of very distinctive packing does not have to prove that it has acquired secondary meaning over time because such is presumed.

Early trademark law was developed by courts as part of the common law of torts. Later, federal statutes were passed that embodied these early principles and modified them in a number of ways. The most recent federal trademark statute is the Lanham Act, passed by Congress in 1946 and amended several times since then. This is, of course, the same pattern we have seen in many other areas of law. The Lanham Act governs marks that are used in connection with the sale of goods and services in interstate commerce. Each state also has a trademark statute that deals with marks that are used within that state. State trademark statutes are essentially identical to the Lanham Act.

Protectability of Marks

For a mark (trademark or service mark) to be legally protectable, it must serve as a "source identifier." This means that, when a substantial number of buyers see or hear the mark, they associate it with a particular source—a particular seller, even if most buyers cannot recall the name of the seller. In trademark law, several different phrases are often used to describe the same concept. Courts often say that a mark must have *secondary meaning*. This means that, although a term may have some original meaning of its own, when a lot of customers see or hear it they mentally associate it with a particular seller; thus, the term "secondary meaning" describes the same idea as "source identifier." If we get rid of the legalese, what both phrases mean in common English is that, for a mark to be protectable, it must serve a branding function. When suing for trademark infringement or when applying for federal registration of a mark with the U.S. Patent & Trademark Office (PTO), the owner must first establish that it has a protectable mark.

Courts have developed four categories of trademarks to assist them in determining whether marks are protectable. A potential trademark may be classified as (1) generic, (2) descriptive, (3) suggestive, or (4) arbitrary or fanciful. These categories, like the tones in a spectrum, tend to blur at the edges.

A *generic* term is a word or phrase used to describe an entire class of goods or services rather than a particular seller's version of a good or service. Generic terms like car, wood, paper, and other nouns can never become protectable marks when used in their generic sense. (As noted below, however, when a generic term is used in connection with a product or service totally unrelated to its original meaning and does serve a branding purpose, it can be a protectable mark.)

A *descriptive* term merely identifies a characteristic or quality of a product or service, such as its color, odor, function, dimensions, or ingredients. A seller of goods or services cannot protect a descriptive term as a trademark unless that seller can produce evidence (such as consumer surveys) proving that the term has acquired secondary meaning (that is, has come to serve a branding purpose) because a substantial portion of the relevant population of consumers have come to treat the term as the seller's particular brand. An example of a descriptive mark is "Vision Center" for a business offering optical goods and services.

In *Zatarains, Inc., v. Oak Grove Smokehouse, Inc.*, 698 F.2d 786 (1983), the main question was whether Zatarains' use of the term "FISH FRI" for its packaged batter for frying fish was so descriptive of batters generally that it could not be protected against the use of the term "FISH FRY" for frying batters by the defendant Oak Grove. The court held that the term "FISH FRI" was indeed a descriptive mark, but that Zatarains' consumer surveys and evidence of substantial advertising and sales over many years proved that the term had acquired secondary meaning as its own brand of batter mix in the New Orleans area. However, the court also concluded that Oak Grove had not committed trademark infringement because Oak Grove had not used the term "FISH FRY" in a trademark sense but instead had merely used it to help describe its own product. Oak Grove had, consequently, made a "fair use" of a term that was almost identical to Zatarain's trademark. It should be emphasized that the "fair use" in trademark law does not mean the same thing that it does in copyright law. In trademark law it refers only to the use by a defendant of a term that is identical or very similar to the plaintiff's descriptive mark (but protectable because of acquired secondary meaning) to help it describe its own product or service.

In *Louboutin v. Yves Saint. Laurent Am. Holding, Inc.*, 103 U.S.P.Q.2d 1937 (2012), the court held that the red sole that Louboutin featured on all its shoes should be treated as a descriptive mark and was protectable because it had become a distinctive symbol, the primary significance of which was to identify the source of the product rather than the product itself or any function that the shoe performed. In other words, the red sole had acquired secondary meaning through use over time—in the minds of a great many shoe customers, the red sole had come to be a brand, which is what a trademark is.

If a mark consists primarily of a geographic designation ("West Coast Video" for a chain of video rental/sale stores), or if it consists primarily of someone's last name (Dell Computers, or much farther back in time, Ford Motor Company), the law treats it in the same way as a descriptive mark, and secondary meaning must be proved.

A very important question that has not been answered definitively is whether a generic term can be descriptive, and thus protectable if acquired secondary meaning is proved, when it is combined with ".com" in a url—a web site address. As this revision is being written, the U.S. Supreme Court has just listened to oral arguments by telephone (because of the coronavirus pandemic) in a case involving "Booking.com," a very popular internet business enabling users to book reservations at any of very large number of hotels and other kinds of lodging. Although not involved in this case, its competitor "Hotels.com" will clearly be affected by the case when it is decided.

A *suggestive* term suggests, rather than describes, some particular characteristic of the goods or services to which it applies and requires the consumer to exercise the imagination in order to draw a conclusion as to the nature of the goods and services. "Coppertone" has been held suggestive in regard to sun tanning products, as has "Roach

Motel" for a roach bait device, "Sleekcraft" for a motor boat, and "Vericheck" for a check verification service.

Sometimes there is a very close factual question about whether a mark is suggestive or merely descriptive, as in the case of "Hog Sandwich," which a court found to be descriptive, but for which an equally good argument can be made that it is suggestive. After all, people usually don't call the meat from this animal "hog," but instead call it "pork." "Hog" suggests a pork sandwich and also suggests that it is a very large sandwich. The term doesn't seem to just describe the sandwich as the court said that it did. A suggestive term can be a protectable mark even without actual proof of acquired secondary meaning because courts view suggestive terms as being "inherently distinctive." In the case involving the "hog sandwich," the court found that the descriptive mark had become distinctive through use over time—consumers came to view the term as a brand that identified only a particular seller's sandwiches, so the producer of the "hog sandwich" did have a protectable mark, but the court's holding that the term was merely descriptive caused the producer to have to invest considerable resources to pay its attorneys to gather and offer evidence in court to prove "acquired secondary meaning" (acquired distinctiveness through consumer usage over time). Not only is substantial cost involved when this has to be proved, but there also is always the risk that a trademark owner will not be able to convince a judge or jury that the mark is suggestive.

Arbitrary or *fanciful* terms bear no relationship to the products or services to which they are applied. Like suggestive terms, these marks are protectable without proof of secondary meaning. "Coined" words that were created to serve as trademarks, such as Kodak, Xerox, and Exxon are fanciful marks. Terms that were generic or descriptive in their original meaning, but that are used as marks in connection with the sale of products or services totally unrelated to that original meaning, are arbitrary marks. Examples include Ivory for soap or Apple for computers. Trademark law treats arbitrary or fanciful marks in the same way—they are so inherently distinctive that they are necessarily protectable, and indeed are the strongest type of marks.

The following case provides an example of the type of analysis a court employs to distinguish between a descriptive and a suggestive trademark, which represents the most important dividing line between categories of marks.

Engineered Tax Services, Inc. v. Scarpello Consulting, Inc.
United States Court of Appeals, Eleventh Circuit, 2020 WL 2478863 (2020)

Engineered Tax Services (ETS) and Scarpello Consulting are both in the business of providing highly specialized tax services. These services are (1) cost segregation and (2) Internal Revenue Code §179D and §45L energy studies. Cost segregation is a tax-planning method by which an owner of real property breaks down a piece of real estate into constituent pieces of personal property for accounting purposes so as to allow for faster depreciation. The accelerated accounting of losses results in a lower tax burden. Cost segregation is often, but not always, performed by, or with the involvement of, licensed engineers. §179D and §45L energy studies calculate tax deductions or credits for building energy-efficient buildings. These energy studies must be conducted by (or with the involvement of) licensed engineers or contractors.

ETS and Scarpello had negotiated for ETS to acquire Scarpello, but no agreement was reached. Soon, Scarpello began a Google AdWords marketing campaign using "engineered tax services" as a keyword. In an AdWords campaign, an advertiser pays Google to display its website as the first result when a user performs a search using one of the advertiser's handpicked keywords. During Scarpello's campaign, therefore, searching on Google for "engineered tax services" returned Scarpello's website as the first result. ETS's site—an unsponsored search result—appeared second.

Scarpello also provided Google marketing copy bearing the title "Engineered Tax Services." As a result, that phrase not only served as a keyword—to bump Scarpello's website to the top of the list—but also appeared as the text of a hyperlink to Scarpello's site.

Not long thereafter, ETS filed for and received from the U.S. Patent & Trademark Office (PTO) a trademark registration for "Engineered Tax Services," which it had been using continuously since 2006 as both its business name and as a trademark.

Within the next year after ETS registered its mark, it discovered that Scarpello had been using the mark in the AdWords campaign, and filed a lawsuit against Scarpello for trademark infringement. The district court granted summary judgment against ETS on the ground that no reasonable jury could have found Engineered Tax Services to be distinctive, either inherently or by virtue of having acquired a distinctive secondary meaning. ETS appealed.

NEWSOM, Circuit Judge:

To be valid, a trademark must be "distinctive"—that is, it must "serve the purpose of identifying the *source* of ... goods or services," not just the goods and services themselves. A mark can be distinctive in one of two ways: It can be inherently distinctive, or it can acquire distinctiveness over time. Whether a mark has either inherent or acquired distinctiveness is a question of fact.

Distinctiveness is a function of what we have called a mark's "strength." We have classified marks into four categories, in descending order of strength: (1) fanciful or arbitrary, (2) suggestive, (3) descriptive, and (4) generic. Fanciful marks (think "Verizon" telecommunications—the name is a made-up word), arbitrary marks (think "Apple" computers—the name is a real word that has nothing to do with the product) and suggestive marks (think "Igloo" coolers—the name is a real word that bears only an oblique relationship to the product" are all inherently distinctive. A descriptive mark (for example, an eyeglasses store called "Vision Center')," by contrast, is *not* inherently distinctive and can become protectable only if it acquires distinctiveness by obtaining a secondary meaning as an identifier of a product's source in the minds of the public. Generic marks (a book-selling company called "Books") can never become protectable.

The dispute here arises at the hazy border between suggestive and descriptive marks. There is little doubt that ETS's mark falls into one of these two categories; ETS insists that its mark is suggestive, while Scarpello argues that the mark is merely descriptive. Because, as just explained, the line separating suggestive from descriptive marks is also the line separating marks with inherent distinctiveness from those without, that line—and determining on which side "Engineered Tax Services" falls—makes all the difference to this appeal. . . .

Scarpello—as the summary judgment movant here and the party challenging the registered mark's validity—bears the burden to *disprove* inherent distinctiveness . . . . As already explained, when ETS registered "Engineered Tax Services," it wasn't required by the PTO to, and didn't, provide evidence of any acquired secondary meaning. [Because of the registration, and because the PTO did not required evidence of acquired distinctiveness and thus must have deemed the mark to be inherently distinctive], the mark is presumed to be inherently distinctive and thus at least suggestive. . . . Scarpello had the burden to prove otherwise.

Two legal tests—we'll call them the "imagination" test and the "third-party-use" test—work in tandem to distinguish suggestive from descriptive marks. We will consider them—and the district court's application of them—in turn.

A mark is merely descriptive, rather than suggestive—and thus is *not* inherently distinctive—if the customer who observes the term can readily perceive the nature of plaintiff's services, *without having to exercise his imagination*. Applying the imagination test, the district court here concluded that, because it is commonly understood that the utilization of a licensed engineer is a well-accepted approach to cost segregation and tax energy studies, and the mark describes that aspect of the services, the mark is merely descriptive. The district court supported its decision primarily with dictionary definitions of the mark's constituent terms. The court's analysis missed the mark for two reasons. First, the court focused too narrowly on the individual meanings of individual words—and in particular, the verb form of the word "engineer"—to the exclusion of the mark as a whole. Second, the court considered only one sense of the word "engineer," to the exclusion of other relevant meanings.

The district court focused its distinctiveness analysis almost exclusively on the verb form of the word "engineer"—considering the phrase "tax services" only briefly—and never addressed the effect of combining the terms "engineered" and "tax services." But as we have explained elsewhere, the whole can indeed be greater than the sum of its parts—ordinary words can be combined in a novel or unique way and thereby achieve a degree of protection denied to the words when used separately. Here, the fact that the undeniably descriptive term "tax services" was modified by the adjective "engineered" is particularly significant because tax services aren't the sort of thing that ordinarily calls for engineering. Inferring the nature of ETS's services from its mark, therefore, is more likely to require imagination than would a more natural pairing of words. Consider two hypothetical alternatives: an accounting firm that performs cost segregation and calls itself "Skillful Tax Services" and a biotech startup that cultures genetically modified [commonly called "engineered in that business] bacteria and calls itself "Engineered Genes." There, the connections between product and mark are easy to draw because the combinations are natural—unlike, we think, "Engineered Tax Services," the meaning of which is not (or is certainly less) immediately apparent.

The district court's failure to analyze the mark holistically likely compounded (and was compounded by) its second error—an unjustifiably narrow focus on a single dictionary definition of the verb "engineer." Citing the *Random House College Dictionary* and *Webster's II New Riverside Dictionary*, the district court considered only one definition—and not even of the verbal adjective "engineered," but of the verb "engineer." That term, the court said, meant "to plan and manage as an engineer." In light of this definition—and because ETS employs some actual engineers—the district court determined that the phrase "Engineered Tax Services" simply described tax services performed by engineers.

ETS contends—and we agree—that there's more to it than that. The verbal-adjective "engineered" can, of course, denote something created or produced by (or with the involvement of) actual engineers—but it can also mean, as ETS's definitions show, "skillfully and deliberately arranged rather than arising naturally or spontaneously," or "designed and built using scientific principles." The district court failed to consider the possibility that the term "engineered" can be understood, in the context of the mark "Engineered Tax Services," both to indicate the involvement of actual engineers and to communicate precision and technical skill.

Considering the mark "Engineered Tax Services" as a whole, and properly accounting for the range of meanings that the term "engineered" can convey, we think it clear that ETS's mark requires the necessary imaginative leap—or, at the very least, that a reasonable jury could so conclude.[10] Indeed, what makes ETS's mark at least plausibly imaginative—and thus suggestive, and thus inherently distinctive—is that the term "engineered" can be understood two ways, and that when combined with the phrase "tax services" to form the mark, "Engineered Tax Services" entails a clever double meaning, referring to tax services that are performed *both* (1) skillfully and scientifically *and* (2) by actual engineers. A potential customer could—without any imagination—understand the mark to communicate *either* the involvement of actual engineers *or* a skillful and scientific approach to providing tax services. But to grasp both simultaneously requires (or so a reasonable jury could conclude) at least a measure of imagination. Only a small imaginative leap is necessary.

ETS cites to an illustrative list of marks, compiled by a respected trademark scholar, that courts have held to be suggestive. 2 *McCarthy on Trademarks and Unfair Competition* § 11:72 (5th ed.). The examples are telling. To highlight just a few, hardly any imagination is required to infer the service provided by "Dial-A-Mattress," or the function of the product marked "Spray 'n Vac." In another illuminating example, we have held that a jury could reasonably have found LaserSpecialist.com to be suggestive—rather than merely descriptive—of oculoplastic surgery.

That a double meaning can render a mark suggestive, and thus inherently distinctive, is hardly a new idea. Both federal courts and the PTO's Trademark Trial and Appeals Board have long recognized as much. *See Blisscraft of Hollywood v. United Plastics Co.*, 294 F.2d 694 (2d Cir. 1961), holding that the mark "Poly Pitcher" was inherently distinctive because it referred both to the product's polyethylene material and to Molly Pitcher, a semi-mythological figure of the American Revolution; *In Re Nat'l Tea Co.*, 144 U.S.P.Q. 1965), which held that the mark "NO BONES ABOUT IT" was not merely descriptive of a boneless ham.

. . . [W]e hold that a reasonable jury could find (1) that ETS's mark carries a double meaning, (2) that an imaginative leap is necessary to grasp that double meaning, and (3) accordingly, that the mark is suggestive, and thus inherently distinctive.

Alongside the "imagination" test, courts considering whether a mark is truly suggestive—or instead, merely descriptive—ask whether competitors would be likely to *need* the terms used in the trademark in describing their products. If a competitor "needs" the mark to describe its own product, the reasoning goes, it must not be distinctive of the mark holder's product.

But the evidence of third-party use here—or more accurately, third party "need"—isn't very compelling. Scarpello provided only two examples in which other entities have made descriptive use of the exact phrase "engineered tax services," and neither unambiguously refers to cost segregation. The first is a printout of online marketing copy describing an energy-efficient heating system. In it, the seller advertises that its "Total Heat System" can help customers qualify for tax deductions—presumably under "with the involvement of an independent engineered tax services firm." Although the copy uses the phrase "engineered tax services" to describe services that ETS provides, the fact that the purveyor of the "Total Heat System" clearly isn't one of ETS's competitors undermines the evidence's probative value. The second example is also marketing copy taken from the internet, but the evidence in the record before us doesn't clearly reveal what the copy is attempting to describe by using ETS's mark. In a couple of sparse paragraphs, a firm called "RB Engineering" boasts a range of services—"structural engineering, forensic engineering and engineered tax services"—but without any meaningful explanation of what those services entail. Scarpello's remaining examples don't even contain the entire registered phrase. Two firms used the term "engineered cost segregation." Another uses "engineering tax services," and another "engineered tax programs"—both describing services including cost segregation. A final example boasts an "engineering approach" to "cost segregation studies."

[T]his evidence . . . doesn't demonstrate, as Scarpello must, that competitors would be likely to *need* the terms used in ETS's trademark in describing their products. Scarpello didn't put into evidence a single example in which the entire phrase "engineered tax services" is used unambiguously to refer to a product or service in ETS's main line of business. . . .

In fact, the variety of phrases that third parties use to describe cost segregation and related services cuts against Scarpello. Scarpello's own handpicked examples demonstrate the many ways to describe cost segregation and energy studies *without* using the precise phrase "engineered tax services." Furthermore, they demonstrate that "cost segregation" is by far the most common way to describe services like ETS's; that phrase occurs more often in Scarpello's examples than all variations of "engineered tax services." With such a well-established alternative available, ETS's mark can hardly be "needed" for competitors in that field. . . . All told, this evidence doesn't even convince us that third parties need to make descriptive use of the words that constitute ETS's mark—let alone convince us that no reasonable jury could find the evidence wanting.

Neither the imagination test nor the third-party-use test can justify summary judgment here, especially considering the presumption of inherent distinctiveness that ETS's mark enjoys by virtue of its registration. We therefore reverse the district court's holding that ETS's mark lacked distinctiveness as a matter of law . . . and remand for proceedings consistent with this decision.

Geography, Priority, and Registration

Trademark law in the U.S. is a hybrid system that provides protection based on the geographic area in which a mark has been used in connection with the sale of goods or services, and then provides expanded protection when the mark is registered with the trademark branch of the PTO. In almost all other countries, protection for a trademark is established by registration. In some of these countries, this is all that is required, but in others there is a requirement that the mark actually be used in connection with the sale of goods or services within a designated time after registration.

Suppose that X Co. begins to make a *substantial* use (use as part of the company's regular, ongoing business) the mark "Morpheus" for its computer services business in northern California. Assume that X is the first one to use this or a similar mark for the same or similar goods or services. X's mark is protected in that geographic area plus a surrounding zone to account for reasonably expected future expansion. If another company, Y, subsequently starts using the same or similar mark in connection with the sale of the same or closely related services, Y does not infringe on X's mark if Y uses it in a *different geographic area* and doesn't otherwise compete for the same customers as X. We call X the "senior user" and Y the "junior user."

In the same scenario, suppose that X Corp. expands its business and the use of its mark to other states such as Oregon and Washington. X's mark is now protected in this wider geographic area (plus a future expansion zone). Moreover, once X has made a substantial use of the mark in interstate commerce (in more than one state), X can seek federal registration for its mark. X's mark obviously cannot be registered if it is generic. Also, if the mark is descriptive (or primarily geographic or primarily someone's last name), X must prove "acquired secondary meaning" to obtain registration. Assuming that these principles provide no obstacle, X can obtain federal registration for its "Morpheus" mark IF there is not another mark registered either with the PTO or with a state trademark registration authority that is the same or confusingly similar for the same or related goods or services.

If X was both the first to use the mark and the first to register it, X has nationwide exclusive rights. Suppose, however, that X did not register before Y began using the same or a similar mark in connection with the same or related goods or services in New York. If Y, the junior user, makes a substantial interstate use of the mark, it becomes eligible for federal registration. Y can obtain federal registration if there is no evidence showing that Y had actual knowledge of X's mark when Y began using the mark and if X had not registered its trademark with a state trademark office. If Y obtains a federal registration, it has nationwide rights with the exception of the geographic area in which X had protection at the time Y filed its registration application. X's area of use is frozen as of the time that Y applied for federal registration.

Intent-to-Use Registration Applications

In a very important development, Congress amended the Lanham Act in 1995 to permit "Intent-to-Use" (ITU) registration applications for those who have not yet made a *substantial* interstate use of a mark but intend to do so in the reasonably near future. In an ITU application, the owner of the mark must declare that it has "good faith intent" ("bona fide intent") to make a substantial use of the mark in interstate commerce at a future date. This is true whether the company has not yet made even a local use of the mark, or has already made a substantial use of it within a single state so as to have protection in that state within the area of use. Assuming that there is no other obstacle to registration, the owner may then file for and obtain a regular registration if there is a substantial interstate use of the mark within six months, a period which can be automatically extended to one year. There can be a further extension to two years upon proof of continuing good faith efforts to make a substantial interstate use, and even to three years upon such proof that the genuine, good faith effort is continuing. If the owner of the mark then makes a substantial *interstate* use within the designated time (6 months to 3 years), it may file a regular registration application, which will then be examined by the Patent & Trademark Office's trademark branch. The important thing about an ITU application is that, if the owner ultimately receives a federal registration and there is a contest over who was first to register, the "priority" date is the date on which the ITU was originally filed rather than the date on which the regular application was filed. If there was no previous ITU, but only a regular application, the priority date is the date on which the regular application was filed. Whichever way registration is achieved, the term of registration is ten years from the time the mark was actually registered, but may thereafter be renewed in ten-year increments by registrants who show that they are still making a substantial use of the mark in interstate commerce.

Disparaging and Scandalous Marks

The Lanham Act contains a provision allowing the trademark branch of the U.S. Patent & Trademark office to refuse an application for federal registration of a mark that the trademark examiner deems to be *disparaging* of a person or group of people. However, in *Matal v. Tam*, 137 S.Ct. 1744 (2017), the U.S. Supreme Court held that allowing the trademark office to deny an important right because the government representative believes the applicant's mark to be disparaging constitutes impermissible viewpoint discrimination in violation of the Constitution's guarantee of free speech. Thus, the trademark office no longer has the authority to decline registration applications for this reason.

The *Matal* case involved a band of Asian-American musicians who performed under the name "The Slants." The term "slants" is short for "slanty eyed," a racial slur used to refer to Asians. Simon Tam was the "front man" for the band.

The Lanham Act also includes a similar provision that was not at issue in this case, one that allows the trademark office to deny federal registration for a mark it views as "immoral" or "scandalous." Two years later, the Supreme Court ruled on the constitutionality of the parallel section of the Lanham Act that allows the Patent & Trademark office to deny a federal registration of a mark that is "immoral or scandalous." Eric Brunetti, producer of clothing items under the brand name FUCT, applied for a federal registration of the mark. A trademark examiner in in the PTO denied the registration application for the reason that the mark was "totally vulgar," and thus was "immoral or scandalous within the meaning of the Lanham Act. Brunetti appealed, a U.S. Court of Appeals reversed on free speech grounds, and in *Iancu v. Brunetti*, 139 S.Ct. 2294 (2019), the Supreme Court affirmed the court of appeals. The Court held that, just like the Lanham Act's denial of federal registration for scandalous trademarks at issue two years earlier in *Matal*, the provision on immoral and scandalous trademarks enabled the government employee to refuse a registration because of the idea expressed in a word or phrase. Even though such marks could be protectable under state common-law rules, federal registration is a valuable government benefit.

Likelihood of Confusion

In most infringement actions, the plaintiff mark owner has the burden of proving that the defendant's mark is so similar to the plaintiff's that the defendant's use will produce a *likelihood of confusion* in buyers' minds as to the true origin of the goods or services. Even if the evidence does not prove that the defendant's use of the same or a confusingly similar mark is likely to cause customer confusion as to actual source, there may still be trademark infringement if the evidence shows that consumers are likely to be confused about affiliation, sponsorship, or endorsement—that is, they are likely to be misled into believing that the plaintiff is associated with defendant or sponsors what the defendant is doing.

Whether such likelihood exists is a question of fact in any particular case and is determined by such factors as similarity of design of the marks, similarity of product, proof of confusion among actual buyers, and marketing surveys of prospective purchasers showing an appreciable misassociation of the defendant's mark with the plaintiff's product. On the basis of these factors, for example, Rotary DeRooting was held to be a mark so similar to Roto-Rooter that the owner of Roto-Rooter was successful in recovering damages from the owner of Rotary DeRooting. *Roto-Rooter Corp. v. O'Neal,* 513 F.2d 44 (5th Cir. 1975).

If the products are dissimilar and unrelated, however, even identical marks may not cause confusion. Thus, where a clothing manufacturer had purchased the right to use the mark "Here's Johnny," a court held that the use of that mark by a manufacturer of portable toilets was not likely to cause purchasers of the toilets to associate them with the producer of "Here's Johnny" men's suits. *Carson v. Here's Johnny Portable Toilets, Inc.*, 698 F.2d 831 (6th Cir. 1983).

Countless other examples exist. In 2019, the U.S. International Trade Commission found that the "Segway" trademark on the revolutionary two-wheel "personal transport devices" was infringed by the mark "Swagway" for hoverboards, and banned imports of the hoverboards using the Swagway brand because it was likely to cause consumers to believe that Segway produced them or that there was some affiliation between the two companies.

Likelihood of confusion is discussed at length in *University of Texas v. KST Electronic, Ltd.*, presented later in this chapter.

Genericide

In addition to the fact that a generic term cannot be protected in the first place, a formerly protectable mark can become generic through usage over time. This concept is discussed later. Terms such as aspirin, cellophane, and escalator, which were at one time protected trademarks, have been held to have become generic through usage and therefore unprotectable. Many people use the term *genericide* to refer a mark's loss of protection by becoming generic. In most cases in which this has happened, the owner of the mark was simply complacent and took few if any steps to make sure that consumers understood that the mark was the owner's brand rather than identifying an entire class of goods or services. In most cases, this complacency occurred because the owner of the mark had a leading position in the market, either because of patent protection or simply because the owner was the first to be extremely successful in the particular market and was able to hold on to its head-start for a long period of time.

Although a number of trademarks have lost their protection through genericide, such an occurrence has now become uncommon because companies in recent years have better recognized the danger and have been proactive in preventing genericide. Companies with valuable brand names have taken a variety of preventive measures such as emphasizing in advertising and packaging that the mark is a brand name, that there is another term that is generic, and that the two should not be confused. For example, in Kimberly-Clark Corp.'s advertising and packaging of its market-leading "Kleenex" tissues, it no longer just uses the term Kleenex by itself, but instead identifies the product as "Kleenex Brand Tissues." Xerox Corp. devotes substantial advertising to the purpose of reminding consumers that "Xerox" is a brand name and should not be used as a noun (for a photocopy or photocopy machine) or as a verb (for making a photocopy). Coca-Cola Corp. spends large amounts of money paying employees to watch TV, listen to radio, go through magazines, etc. to find improper generic uses of its "Coca-Cola," "Coke," "Diet Coke," and other trademarks. Improper uses typically result in letters from Coke's trademark lawyers. Sometimes it also been known to send employees to places that sell or serve soft drinks and ask for a "Coke." If the Coca-Cola representative is served another brand, Coca-Cola's trademark lawyers are again likely to be heard from.

Remedies

Where likelihood of confusion is established, the plaintiff's usual remedies under the Lanham Act or common-law principles are an injunction and damages. The injunction is an order prohibiting or placing limitations on the defendant's further use of the mark, and damages is a recovery of money to compensate the plaintiff for the economic loss (if any) sustained as a result of the infringement. In addition, the trademark owner may recover the amount of the infringer's profits from selling the goods or services in connection with the infringing mark.

Because of a tremendous increase in the trafficking of counterfeit designer goods, Congress passed the Trademark Counterfeiting Act of 1984, which provides escalating criminal penalties for multiple offenders. For example, a second offender, if an individual, can be fined up to $1 million, imprisoned for up to 15 years, or both.

Anti-Dilution Statutes

Approximately half the states have extended trademark protection beyond situations where a "likelihood of confusion" exists by enacting *anti-dilution* statutes. Anti-dilution laws prohibit uses of some marks even where the goods or services are not similar and there is no likelihood of confusion. In 1995, Congress passed the Federal Trademark Dilution Act (FTDA), which became effective in 1996. Like the state statutes, the FTDA does not protect all marks, but only those that a court determines to be "famous." A famous mark is one that is more than just distinctive. In the FTDA, Congress itemized eight factors that tend to show that a mark is famous: (1) The degree of inherent or acquired distinctiveness of the mark; (2) The duration and extent of use of the mark in connection with the goods or services with which the mark is used; (3) The duration and extent of advertising and publicity of the mark; (4) The geographical extent of the trading area in which the mark is used; (5) The channels of trade for the goods or services with which the mark is used; (6) The degree of recognition of the mark in the trading areas and channels of trade used by the marks' owner and the person against whom the injunction is sought; (7) The nature and extent of use of the same or similar marks by third parties; and (8) Whether the mark was registered. If a mark is famous, someone else cannot use that mark or a confusingly similar one even when there is no evidence of a likelihood of consumer confusion.

One example of the application of an anti-dilution case law is *Tiffany v. Boston Club*, 231 F. Supp. 836 (D. Mass. 1964). This case, which was decided according to a state anti-dilution law but which would be decided the same way under the FTDA, involved the old and very well-known "Tiffany" trademark for jewelry, fine glassware, and related products. Over time, the mark has come to be associated with luxury and excellence. The defendant used the "Tiffany" name for a bar. The public is certainly not likely to believe that the owners of the "Tiffany" trademark were also responsible for the bar, and thus there would be no likelihood of confusion. However, use of the name "Tiffany" on the bar may injure the holder of the "Tiffany" trademark in two ways: (1) Such use weakens the mark by diminishing (diluting) its distinctiveness. Moreover, if the bar is allowed to use the mark, others also would be able to use it for unrelated goods or services, thus having a cumulative effect of further dilution over time. This type of harm is usually called *blurring*. (2) This type of use may also undermine the positive image of the mark if it is no longer restricted to luxury-type products. Such harm is usually called *tarnishment*. Tarnishment could also be proved by evidence showing that defendant's use of a mark identical or confusingly similar to the plaintiff's famous mark casts the mark in an unsavory light, such as using the famous "Barbie" trademark for dolls in connection with a pornographic web site. Anti-dilution laws protect against either type of harm.

Since 2006, when Congress passed legislation amending the federal trademark dilution statute to clarify several uncertainties in the law, the owner of a famous mark needs to prove only a *likelihood* of blurring or tarnishment, not *actual* blurring or tarnishment, because trademark owners had found the latter impossible to prove. In addition, the legislation cleared up some lower court conflicts by stating that a mark is famous only if it is very widely known by the general American consuming public, and not just widely known within a local geographic area or a niche market. Furthermore, the amendment stated that a mark can be "famous" based on "acquired distinctiveness" over time, even if it was not inherently distinctive originally. The following case involves allegations of both traditional trademark infringement (and "likelihood of confusion") and dilution.

University of Texas v. KST Electric, Ltd.
U. S. District Court, Western District of Texas, 550 F.Supp.2d 657 (2008)

KST was started by Kenneth and Suanna Tumlinson in 1994. They are avid fans of University of Texas athletics and have had season tickets to the football games for many years. They used the "discontinued" Longhorn Logo shown below, and there is a dispute between UT and KST as to whether KST has totally discontinued use of that mark. However, in 1998 KST designed and began to use the so-called Longhorn Lightening (sic) Bolt Logo (or "LLB Logo") shown below. The logo's design consists of a longhorn silhouette with a "K" on the left cheek area of the longhorn, an "S" on the right cheek area, a "lightning bolt T" (spelled "lightening" by KST) in the face of the silhouette, and the words "ELECTRIC, LTD." in the space between the horns.

The University of Texas's Longhorn Silhouette Logo:

The Challenged Marks:

KST's Longhorn Lightening Bolt Logo
(as displayed on website)

KST's Longhorn Lightening Bolt Logo
(as displayed on sign at office)

KST's Discontinued Longhorn Logo

In March 2002, when UT learned of the LLB Logo, UT asked KST to cease using that logo. KST refused. Eventually, in December 2006, UT filed suit. KST filed a motion for summary judgment in its favor. Below is the district court's opinion and ruling on KST's motion.

Yeakel, District Judge:

In this case the University of Texas ("UT") is suing KST Electric ("KST") for trademark infringement, trademark dilution, and unfair competition under federal law, as well as for several state statutory and common-law claims. [Only the federal claims are discussed below.] UT alleges that several logos developed and used by KST infringe on UT's registered trademark that depicts its mascot, a longhorn steer, in silhouette (referred to by UT as its "longhorn silhouette logo" or LSL).

For both the trademark infringement and unfair competition causes of action, the element in play here is "likelihood of confusion." A "likelihood of confusion" means that confusion is not just possible, but probable. The confusion that both the trademark infringement and unfair competition statutory schemes aim to dissipate is not only as to source, but also as to affiliation, connection, or sponsorship. To frame it another way, the ultimate question is whether relevant consumers are likely to believe that the products or services offered by the parties are affiliated in some way.

It is not necessary that these respective goods and services be identical or even competitive in order to support a finding of likelihood of confusion. Rather, it is sufficient that the goods and services are related in some manner, or that the circumstances surrounding their marketing are such, that they would be likely to be encountered by the same persons in situations that would give rise, because of the marks used thereon, to a mistaken belief that they originate from or are in some way associated with the same source or that there is an association or connection between the sources of the respective goods or services.

In other words, the critical question is whether KST's logos suggest that it is in some way affiliated with or endorsed by UT. In assessing whether use of a mark creates a likelihood of confusion as to affiliation or endorsement, courts consider a list of factors that tend to prove or disprove that consumer confusion is likely. Those factors are: (1) the type of mark allegedly infringed; (2) the similarity between the two marks; (3) the similarity of the products or services; (4) the identity of retail outlets and purchasers; (5) the identity of the advertising media used; (6) the defendant's intent; and (7) any evidence of actual confusion. These factors are a flexible and nonexhaustive list. They do not apply mechanically to every case and should be used only as guides.

(1) Type of mark. The strength of a mark refers to its ability to identify the source of the goods being sold under its aegis. The degree to which a senior user's [like UT] mark is entitled to protection depends partly on whether the mark is classified as generic, descriptive, suggestive or fanciful/arbitrary. The stronger the mark, the greater the protection it receives because the greater the likelihood that consumers will confuse the junior user's use with that of the senior user. The strength of a trademark involves two components: its inherent or intrinsic distinctiveness and the distinctiveness it has acquired in the marketplace, *i.e.,* its commercial strength. Inherent distinctiveness involves a mark's theoretical potential to identify plaintiff's goods or services without regard to whether it has actually done so. Consideration of acquired distinctiveness looks solely to that recognition plaintiff's mark has earned in the marketplace as a designator of plaintiff's goods or services.

UT's longhorn silhouette logo is a fanciful or arbitrary mark. A longhorn silhouette is no way descriptive of UT's educational enterprise [or its athletic enterprises]. These types of marks are generally "strong" marks, and are therefore accorded more protection under trademark law. This factor, then, weighs in favor of confusion in the likelihood of confusion calculus. (Whether it falls into the precise category of fanciful or arbitrary is open to debate, but the relevant point is that both these types of marks are entitled to more protection than descriptive marks.)

(2) Similarity of plaintiff's and defendant's marks. Absolute identity is not necessary for infringement. All that is necessary is enough similarity between the marks to confuse consumers. Moreover, the *greater* the degree of similarity between the two parties' marks, the *lesser* the degree of similarity between their goods or services is required to support a finding of likelihood of confusion.

KST's argument that "[t]here are ... a multitude of differences between the [LLB] and UT's registered longhorn logo," is difficult to swallow. Nevertheless, KST gamely attempts to distinguish the two. The ostensible distinctions include: (1) the tips of the horns on LLB logo are "bent" rather than straight; (2) the nose is rounded off on the LLB logo "as opposed to the indentation" in UT's logo; (3) the ears of the LLB logo are rounded rather than pointed; and (4) there is of course the presence of a "K," an "S," and lightning-bolt infused "T" in the LLB logo. KST's attempt to draw these fine lines to distinguish its logo from UT's ultimately fails. The marks clearly are saliently similar (one might posit that the LLB logo resembles an average artist's attempt to draw UT's mark). A simple viewing of the two marks demonstrates a substantial similarity between them. This factor therefore weighs in favor of a finding of likelihood of confusion.

(3) KST's intent. KST contends that it did not copy the LSL in bad faith. Instead, when it decided to use a longhorn as the basis for its logos, it chose that particular design "to reflect [its owners'] life experience with cattle and longhorns." It further argues that it pulled the template for its longhorn-based logos from a book with barnyard animals and the like. Good faith is not a defense to trademark infringement. The reason for this is clear: if potential purchasers are confused, no amount of good faith can make them less so. Bad faith may, however, prove infringement without more. Because improper motive is rarely, if ever, admitted (and this case provides no exception), the court can only infer bad intent from the facts and circumstances in evidence.

As UT points out, both Kenneth and Suanna Tumlinson testified that they are life-long fans of UT athletics and were therefore aware of the LSL. Further, they operated their business (an electric company that has no obvious connection to cattle or longhorns) for a number of years before they adopted the LLB logo. The Tumlinsons testified that they owned a significant amount of UT apparel with the LSL on it. Thus, prior to adopting their logos, defendants were well aware of the LSL and its appearance. These facts provide circumstantial evidence that the defendants adopted their logo with knowledge of its strong similarity to the LSL. Moreover, setting aside the similarities between the LSL and the LLB logos, the striking similarities between the discontinued Longhorn Logo and the LSL were such that Kenneth Tumlinson putatively ordered those logos removed because they "resembled closer [*sic*] to the UT's logo [*sic*] than we wanted to [*sic*]." Thus, this factor also weighs in favor of likelihood of confusion.

(4) Similarity of the products or services. The only other factor that KST takes up in its brief is the distinct customer bases of KST and UT. This is true. However, as UT points

out, this factor is not as weighty as the others given that direct competition or intrinsic relatedness between the mark holder and the alleged infringer is not required.

UT has established a material fact issue as to the likelihood of confusion element of its federal trademark infringement and unfair competition causes of action that should go to trial. Accordingly, KST's motion for summary judgment on these claims is denied.

KST also argues that it should be granted summary judgment on UT's federal dilution claim because UT has not provided any evidence that the longhorn silhouette logo is *famous* for purposes of the Trademark Dilution Revision Act ("TDRA"). Under the TDRA, which amended the Federal Trademark Dilution Act (FTDA), "the owner of a famous mark ... shall be entitled to an injunction against another person who, at any time after the owner's mark has become famous, commences use of a mark or trade name in commerce that is likely to cause dilution by blurring or dilution by tarnishment of the famous mark, regardless of the presence or absence of actual or likely confusion, of competition, or of actual economic injury."

To state a dilution claim under the TDRA, a plaintiff must show that: (1) the plaintiff owns a famous mark; (2) the defendant has commenced using a mark in commerce that allegedly is diluting the famous mark; (3) a similarity between the defendant's mark and the famous mark gives rise to an association between the marks; and (4) the association is likely to impair the distinctiveness of the famous mark or likely to harm the reputation of the famous mark. The TDRA specifically requires that, to be famous, the mark be *"widely recognized by the general consuming public of the United States* as a designation of source of the goods or services of the mark's owner."

Dilution is a cause of action invented and reserved for a select class of marks—those marks with such powerful consumer associations that even non-confusing uses can impinge on their value. Congress passed the anti-dilution legislation because it sought to protect unauthorized users of famous marks from those "attempting to trade upon the goodwill and established renown of such marks," regardless of whether such use causes a likelihood of confusion about the product's origin. The legislative history speaks of protecting those marks that have an "aura" and explains that the harm from dilution occurs "when the unauthorized use of a famous mark reduces the public's perception that the mark signifies something unique, singular, or particular." Under the TDRA, four nonexclusive factors are relevant when determining whether a mark is sufficiently famous for anti-dilution protection:

(i) The duration, extent, and geographic reach of advertising and publicity of the mark, whether advertised or publicized by the owner or third parties;

(ii) The amount, volume, and geographic extent of sales of goods or services offered under the mark;

(iii) The extent of actual recognition of the mark;

(iv) Whether the mark was registered under the [federal Trademark Acts of 1881 or 1905, or the 1946 Lanham Act].

Last things first. The LSL is registered, and has been for over 20 years. However, one cannot logically infer fame from the fact that a mark is one of the millions on the federal register, but one could logically infer lack of fame from a lack of registration. KST's primary argument goes to the third issue, the actual recognition of the mark, and contends that UT's mark is not sufficiently recognized on a national level to be famous. They base this argument on their expert, Robert Klein, who conducted a national survey that he contends demonstrates that only 5.8% of respondents in the United States "associated the UT registered longhorn logo with UT alone" and that "only 21.1% of respondents in Texas associated the UT registered longhorn logo with UT alone." [The Court then dismissed the validity of the Klein survey favoring KST for several reasons, including the fact that the sample size of 454 was too small for a national survey, the survey instrument included several "leading" questions that suggested the answers called for by the questions, and the Longhorn silhouette logo was not shown to survey respondents in the same context in which it is usually seen—Klein showed respondents the logo in white against white, rather than the common burnt orange against white or white against burnt orange.]

This, however, is not the end of the analysis. Because UT bears the overall burden of proof on the famousness issue, to avoid having summary judgment entered against it UT must submit sufficient evidence to demonstrate that there is at least genuine fact issue that the LSL is "famous."

UT offers evidence of famousness that at first blush appears impressive. Upon closer scrutiny, however, it is apparent that the evidence submitted is evidence of "niche" fame, which is a category of fame to which the TDRA explicitly does not apply. To summarize, UT's response contains evidence that UT football games are regularly nationally televised on ABC and ESPN, and the LSL is prominently featured as UT's logo during these broadcasts. Similarly, the men's college basketball team's games have been televised nationally 97 times in the past five seasons. UT points to the Bowl Championship Series (BCS) Rose Bowl national championship game after the 2005 season, in which UT beat the University of Southern California. That game was, at that point, the highest rated game in the eight-year history of the BCS and was also the highest rated college football game since 1987. Over 35 million people watched it nationwide. Along these same lines, the 2006 Alamo Bowl game between UT and the University of Iowa was the most watched bowl game in ESPN's history, with nearly 9 million viewers. Spanning from 1963-2006, UT football players have been featured solely or as a part of the cover of *Sports Illustrated* ten times (although the logo is not featured prominently or totally visible on all these covers). A writer from SI.com (Sports Illustrated's website) named UT's football helmet as the number 1 non-letter (that is., only bearing the logo) helmet. That same helmet was displayed on two separate Wheaties' boxes: one celebrating UT's national BCS win and the other "commemorating UT's rivalry game with Texas A & M." UT sells "official corporate sponsorships" for $250,000 each (at a minimum) to companies such as Coca-Cola, Dodge, Nike, Pizza Hut, State Farm, and Wells Fargo. The Collegiate Licensing Company (CLC), which licenses the merchandise for many if not most major universities, reported that UT holds the record for most royalties earned in a single year and has been the number one university for licensing royalties for the past two years. Coming in closely behind Notre Dame, *Forbes* recently valued UT's football program as the second most valuable in the country. Finally, retail sales of UT products in stores such as Wal-Mart and Target totaled nearly $400 million in 2005-06.

The central problem for UT is that its circumstantial evidence is largely evidence of niche market fame. Reading through the evidence, it is not at all clear that if one is not a college football fan (or, to a much lesser extent, college baseball or basketball fan) would recognize the LSL as being associated with UT, as all of the evidence relates to the use of the logo in sporting events. The Court is well aware that NCAA college football is a popular sport—the Court counts itself as a more than casual fan of Saturday afternoon football in the Fall—but this hardly equals a presence with the general consuming public (nearly the entire population of the United States). Simply because UT athletics have achieved a level of national prominence does not necessarily mean that the longhorn logo is so ubiquitous and well-known to stand toe-to-toe with Buick or KODAK.

A similar criticism can be leveled at the SI.com article that UT cites. This "evidence" is an opinion column by a staff writer at *Sports Illustrated* and is more intended to start a bar discussion than approach anything definitive.

One of the major purposes of the TDRA was to restrict dilution causes of action to those few truly famous marks like Budweiser beer, Barbie Dolls, and the like. UT has not created a genuine issue of material fact that the longhorn silhouette logo is "a household name." The TDRA is simply not intended to protect trademarks whose fame is at all in doubt." Because UT's evidence fails to demonstrate the extremely high level of recognition necessary to show "fame" under the TDRA, summary judgment is appropriate on this claim. UT's dilution claim is dismissed, but its trademark infringement and unfair competition claims will go to trial.

Anti-Cybersquatting Consumer Protection Act

A *cybersquatter* is someone who registers an Internet domain name (1) that is the same as or confusingly similar to someone else's protected trademark, (2) where there is a bad faith intent to commercially exploit the trademark, and (3) the likely effect is to either cause confusion, or, if the mark is famous, to cause dilution. Because of the widespread prevalence of cybersquatting in recent years, Congress passed the Anti-cybersquatting Consumer Protection Act (ACPA) in 1999.

The ACPA lists several factors for courts to consider in determining whether the defendant has registered a domain name with a bad-faith intent to exploit the plaintiff's trademark. The first four of these factors tend to show good faith, and the next four factors tend to show bad faith. The factors tending to show that defendant acted in *good faith* and is not a cybersquatter are: (1) The defendant itself had preexisting trademark or other intellectual property rights in the words used in the domain name; (2) The domain name consists of the defendant's name; (3) The defendant had made previous use of the word or words in the domain name in connection with the legitimate sale of goods or services; or (4) The defendant is making a genuine noncommercial or fair use of the mark at a web site reached by the domain name.

The factors tending to show that defendant was acting in *bad faith* and thus was an illegal cybersquatter are: (1) the defendant apparently intended to divert consumers from the trademark owner's online location to the defendant's web site in a way that could harm the plaintiff either causing a likelihood of confusion or, if the plaintiff's mark is famous, by causing dilution; (2) the defendant has offered to sell the domain name it registered to someone else without having made a legitimate business use of it (offering goods or services), and without any apparent intent to make a legitimate business use of it; (3) the defendant has given misleading contact information when applying for the registration of the domain name, or has intentionally failed to maintain accurate information for contacting him; or (4) the defendant's prior conduct shows a pattern of registering or acquiring domain names the same as or confusingly similar to the trademarks of others.

Trademark owners may recover statutory damages of up to $100,000 and an injunction where personal jurisdiction over the defendant is acquired. When the court has only *in rem* jurisdiction (discussed in Chapter 2) over the domain name—an item of property located in the jurisdiction where the domain name computer server is—the court can cancel the domain name registration or transfer it to the plaintiff.

International Trademark Concerns

Several years ago, the United States became a signatory to the Madrid Agreement Concerning the International Registration of Marks ("Madrid Agreement"), a multi-lateral treaty sponsored by the World Intellectual Property Association (an agency of the U.N.). In 2003, the U.S. also ratified the "Madrid Protocol," which supplements the Madrid Agreement. In combination, these two treaties allow for one centralized filing of a trademark application in a member country and the payment of a single filing fee. The application is then forwarded to the other member countries designated by the applicant, and no language translation is required. Over 65 countries are now members of both treaties.

PART II
PRINCIPLES OF CONTRACT LAW

CHAPTER 10

NATURE AND CLASSIFICATION OF CONTRACTS

- A Perspective
- Nature of a Contract
- Classification of Contracts
- Contract Law and Sales Law—A Special Relationship

Contract Law—Special Characteristics

Contract law possesses several characteristics that make it the natural starting point for an examination of several other legal subjects. First, there is its pervasiveness in the average person's everyday activities. When a person buys a newspaper, leaves a car at a parking lot, or buys a ticket to a football game, a contract of has been entered into. When someone borrows money, hires someone to paint a house, or insures a car, a contract has again been made. And businesses—whether corner stores or large multinational corporations—must buy or lease office equipment, make agreements with employees, secure heat and light, buy materials from suppliers, and sell their goods and services to customers. All these transactions involve contracts.

Second, the basic principles of contract law are the underpinning of other business-related subjects, including sales of goods, commercial paper, partnership and corporation law, employment law, principal-agent relationships, and other areas.

Third, since the subject of contracts is essentially common-law in nature, the controversies that are presented usually require the courts to examine earlier decisions handed down in cases involving similar fact-patterns. Thus, the doctrine of stare decisis is illuminated; and an allied question—whether today's conditions have so changed as to justify a repudiation of earlier decisions—affords an opportunity to analyze more fully the process of judicial reasoning.

NATURE OF A CONTRACT

A contract is a special sort of agreement—one that the law will enforce in some manner in the event that one party does not perform its promise. As will be seen in the next chapter, some agreements are not enforceable because their terms are too indefinite, or they are entered into in jest, or they involve obligations that are essentially social in nature (such as a date to go to a concert). Even seriously intended, definite business agreements, however, are generally not enforceable unless three additional elements are present—what the courts refer to as consideration, capacity, and legality. These concepts will be explored in later chapters also. Indeed, a comprehensive definition of contract cannot be attempted until these four elements have been examined in some detail. One well-known source defines a contract in the following way: A more technical definition is the following: "A contract is a promise or set of promises for the breach of which the law gives a remedy, or the performance of which the law in some way recognizes as a duty." *Restatement, Contracts 2d*, §1, American Law Institute, 1979. A much simpler definition is that "a contract is an agreement that a court will enforce." "Enforceable" in the context of contract law means that a court will hold a defendant who violated the contract legally responsible by ordering it to pay monetary damages to the plaintiff or, in unusual situations, grant a decree of *specific performance* ordering the defendant to actually perform the terms of the contract.

In our legal system, there are few limits to what can be the subject of a contract. Conracts cover endless types of transactions, and govern countless business and personal relationships. Following is a case in which the contract—a medical school student handbook—governed the relationship between the school and each of its students because a student agrees when accepting an offer to enroll that they will be bound by the handbook's terms. Here, question arising under the contract was the handbook's provision requiring "professionalism."

AMIR AL-DABAGH v. CASE WESTERN RESERVE UNIVERSITY
777 F.3d 355, United States Court of Appeals, Sixth Circuit (2015)

Amir Al-Dabagh enrolled at Case Western's medical school in 2009. He did well academically, as exhibited by recommendation letters praising his "academic excellence" in 2011 and 2013. He even published several articles and won a special award for "Honors with Distinction in Research."

Professionalism was another matter. His troubles began during his first semester. All first-year medical students must participate in discussion sessions and arrive on time to each of them. Al-Dabagh came late to almost thirty percent of the meetings, holding up the class as a result. According to his instructor, he asked not to be marked late each time. According to his own testimony, he asked only once, and only then because the admitted student he was hosting was also running late. But he does not deny the tardiness or its frequency. And in his instructor's judgment, quite reasonably, "[a]sking [a faculty member] to lie about attendance" is "a more serious breach of professionalism than tardiness itself."

The problems did not stop there. In 2013, two female students accused Al-Dabagh of behaving inappropriately at a formal dance called the Hippo Ball—short (we presume) for Hippocrates. One said he propositioned her for sex, "grab[bed her] hand and trie[d] to pull [her] towards the dance floor," and told her that, "[I]f you don't dance with me, I'm gonna embarrass you until you do." The other said she was walking across the room when she "felt someone grab [her] butt." When she turned around, she saw Al-Dabagh—at which point he and her boyfriend nearly came to blows. Later that night, according to a police incident report, Al-Dabagh jumped out of a moving taxi after attempting to stiff its driver out of a twenty-dollar fare. Al-Dabagh recalls the night differently. He never harassed anyone, never tried to welch on the driver, and fell out of the cab when "someone assaulted" him. Whatever happened, the night's events sparked his first run-in with the Committee, which forced him to undergo "an intervention on professionalism" and threatened him with "dismissal" if "further issues" arose.

Further issues arose. Later that year, Al-Dabagh received a stinging evaluation about his performance in an internal medicine internship. Nurses and hospital staffers "consistently complained about his demeanor"; a patient's family once "kicked him out of the room"; and he sometimes gave patient-status presentations without first preparing. Al-Dabagh by contrast asserts that the negative comments stemmed from his "critical . . . attitude" toward one of his supervisors—an account confirmed by another evaluator. But he does not dispute that the Committee "seriously considered" dismissing him in response. It opted for less severe but still drastic measures, requiring him to repeat the internship and enrolling him in "gender specific training." It also added an addendum to his letter of recommendation for residency programs, the existence of which a faculty supporter described as "very permanently . . . damaging" and "too heavy a punishment." The Committee had not written such an addendum in at least twenty-five years. When Al-Dabagh appealed, the Committee reaffirmed its decision, citing "a pattern of unprofessionalism with regard to communication and personal conduct."

Matters came to a head in April 2014, when the university received word that North Carolina had convicted Al-Dabagh for driving while intoxicated. Al-Dabagh insists that he was not in fact drunk. He swerved to miss a deer, he says, and hit a utility pole *instead. The university by this point had already invited Al-Dabagh to graduate. No matter: The Committee convened an emergency session, unanimously refused to certify him for graduation, and dismissed him from the university. After he appealed, the Committee agreed to lighten its punishment, offering to let him withdraw from the university in writing—freeing him to apply to other programs without having to explain a damaging official dismissal.*

Al-Dabagh did not accept the Committee's offer. Instead, he sued the university in federal district court, alleging that it breached its state-law duties of good faith and fair dealing when it declined to award him a degree. The court agreed, ordering the university "to issue a diploma to Al-Dabagh as having satisfied the requirements to become a doctor of medicine and to list him as having graduated in whatever ways are customary for the school." The university appealed.

Sutton, Circuit Judge:

Authority to decide whether a medical student deserves a degree usually rests with the student's school. In this unusual case, that did not happen. A federal district court found that Amir Al-Dabagh had proven himself worthy of a diploma and ordered Case Western Reserve University School of Medicine to give him one—disregarding the university's determination that he lacked the professionalism required to discharge his duties responsibly. Because that lack-of-professionalism finding amounts to an academic judgment to which courts owe considerable deference, we must reverse.

Anyone who has ever been to a doctor's office knows the value of a good bedside manner. That is why Case Western does more than just teach its students facts about the human body. Its curriculum identifies nine "core competencies." First on the list is professionalism. Medical knowledge does not make an appearance until the fifth slot.

The curriculum tells a student to exercise professionalism in four ways:

- Consistently demonstrate ethical, honest, responsible and reliable behavior.
- Identify challenges to professionalism and develop a strategy to maintain professional behaviors when adherence to professional standards is threatened in the clinical and/or research settings.
- Engage in respectful dialogue with peers, faculty, and patients, to enhance learning and resolve differences.
- Recognize personal limitations and biases and find ways to overcome them.

The university's student handbook emphasizes professionalism in several other places. Here: Case Western values "student professionalism . . . as highly as mastery of the basic sciences and clinical skills." And here: A Case Western degree conveys not only "a level of competency as measured by performance on tests" but also "a commitment to professional responsibility." And here: "Medical school education entails the mastery of didactic, theoretical, and technical material, as well as the demonstration of appropriate professional and interpersonal behavior."

The task of figuring out whether a student has mastered these professionalism requirements falls to the university's Committee on Students. Assembled from the university's faculty and administrators, the Committee "conducts detailed reviews" of a student's exam scores, clinical performance, and "professional attitudes and behavior." A student cannot receive a degree without the Committee's approval, good grades notwithstanding. . . .

Ohio treats the relationship between a university and its students as "contractual in nature." *Behrend v. State*, 379 N.E.2d 617, 620 (Ohio Ct. App. 1977). Case Western's student handbook supplies the contract's terms, as the parties agree, and makes clear that the only thing standing between Al-Dabagh and a diploma is the Committee on Students's finding that he lacks professionalism. Unhappily for Al-Dabagh, that is an academic judgment. And we can no more substitute our personal views for the Committee's when it comes to an academic judgment than the Committee can substitute its views for ours when it comes to a judicial decision. Ohio law allows a court to overturn such judgments only if they are "arbitrary and capricious," regardless of "whether the court would have decided . . . matter[s] differently." *Bleicher v. Univ. of Cincinnati Coll. of Med.*, 604 N.E.2d 783, 788 (Ohio Ct. App. 1992). [If, unlike in the present case, the institution is state-run, and the Constitution applies to its decisions,] Federal Due Process law comes to the same end. A court must "show great respect for the faculty's professional judgment" and may not "override" that judgment "unless it is such a substantial departure from accepted academic norms as to demonstrate that the . . . committee responsible did not actually exercise professional judgment." *Regents of Univ. of Mich. v. Ewing*, 474 U.S. 214, 225 (1985).

Al-Dabagh's dismissal on professionalism grounds amounts to a deference-receiving academic judgment for several reasons. The student handbook—the governing contract—says professionalism is part of Case Western's academic curriculum at least four times. Judges are "ill equipped" to second-guess the University's curricular choices. The Ohio Supreme Court indeed has deferred to a similar form of academic judgment by this same institution in the past. In a case with greater equities than this one, the Court approved the medical school's refusal to admit a gifted blind applicant because its goal was not to train "specialized" doctors—she wished to be a psychiatrist—but generalist ones capable of "functioning in a broad variety of clinical situations." *Ohio Civil Rights Comm'n v. Case W. Reserve Univ.*, 666 N.E.2d 1376, 1387 (Ohio 1996).

Nor do we have any reason to doubt the propriety of *this* curricular choice. Professionalism has been a part of the doctor's role since at least ancient Greece. The original Hippocratic Oath required adherents to "refrain . . . from acts of an amorous nature" in "whatsoever house [they] may enter," "whatever may be the rank of those whom it may be [their] duty to cure." 3 *The London Medical Repository* 258 (James Copland ed., 1825). It is entirely reasonable to assess the presence of professionalism early. For once a medical student graduates, we must wait for a violation before we may punish the absence of it. *See Pons v. Ohio State Med. Bd.*, 614 N.E.2d 748 (Ohio 1993) (affirming a medical board's decision to suspend a doctor after he had sex with an emotionally vulnerable patient). Cases defining "academic decisions" in the Due Process context [because the university was state-run] confirm the point. The United States Supreme Court has even deemed "academic" a school's decision to dismiss a student who "lacked a critical concern for personal hygiene." *Horowitz v. Bd. of Curators of Univ. of Mo.*, 435 U.S. 78, 81 (1978).

We repeatedly have emphasized that "academic evaluations" may permissibly extend beyond "raw grades and other objective criteria." Other circuits have come to the same conclusion. Dismissing a medical student for lack of professionalism is "academic," says one. *Halpern v. Wake Forest Univ. Health Scis.*, 669 F.3d 454, 463 (4th Cir. 2012).

Refusing to approve a Ph.D. thesis because its acknowledgement section was unprofessional is "academic," says another. *Brown v. Li*, 308 F.3d 939, 943, 952 (9th Cir. 2002). Dismissing a student for "non-cognitive" problems like "sleeping in" is "academic," says still another. *Richmond v. Fowlkes*, 228 F.3d 854, 856, 858 (8th Cir. 2000). And so on. *See Harris v. Blake*, 798 F.2d 419, 423 (10th Cir. 1986) (dismissing a student for failing to attend practical class sessions is "academic"); *Perez v. Tex. A & M Univ. at Corpus Christi*, No. 14-40081, 2014 WL 5510955, *4 (5th Cir. Nov. 3, 2014) (dismissing a student for tardiness is "academic"). Whether we take our cue from Case Western's curriculum, the student handbook contract between the student and university, the Supreme Court, the Ohio cases, our own cases, or cases from other circuits, the conclusion is the same: The Committee's professionalism determination is an academic judgment. That conclusion all but resolves this case. We may overturn the Committee only if it "substantially departed from accepted academic norms" when it refused to approve Al-Dabagh for graduation. And given Al-Dabagh's track record—one member of the Committee does not recall encountering another student with Al-Dabagh's "repeated professionalism issues" in his quarter century of experience, we cannot see how it did. . . .

Al-Dabagh, last of all, claims that the Committee faulted him for things that didn't happen (for instance, the sexual harassment incidents at the Hippo Ball) and disregarded his explanations for the things that did (for instance, his poor internship performance and his driving-while-intoxicated conviction). He invites us to decide for ourselves whether he behaved in a sufficiently professional way to merit a degree. That, as we have made clear, goes beyond our job description. It was neither arbitrary nor capricious for the Committee to credit other accounts above Al-Dabagh's. And if a dismissal from medical school for poor hygiene and untimeliness falls within the realm of reason, *Horowitz*, 435 U.S. at 91 n.6, it should go without saying that Al-Dabagh's dismissal falls within the realm of reason too.

For these reasons, we reverse. [The university was within its contractual rights to deny a diploma to Al-Dabagh.]

CLASSIFICATION OF CONTRACTS

Contracts have many facets and, consequently, may be categorized in a variety of ways. Different aspects may be important in different contexts. In one case it may be important that the contract is "bilateral" rather than "unilateral." The outcome of another case may turn on whether the contract is "voidable" rather than "void." An important purpose of this chapter is to introduce the various categories of contracts.

Bilateral and Unilateral Contracts

Most contracts consist of the exchange of mutual promises, the actual performance of which is to occur at some later time. When a manufacturer enters into a contract in May with a supplier, calling for the supplier to deliver 10,000 steel wheels in September at a specified price, each party has promised the other to perform one or more acts at a subsequent time. Such contracts, consisting of "a promise for a promise," are bilateral contracts.

The same terminology applies to offers (proposals) that precede the making of a contract. If the terms of an offer indicate that all the offeror wants at the present time from the offeree is a return promise—rather than the immediate performance of an act—then the proposal can be called a *bilateral offer*. The *offeror* is the person making the definite proposal; the *offeree* is the one to whom it is made. Thus, if a professional football team sends a contract to one of its players in June, offering him $800,000 for the coming season, it is clear that all the club presently wants is the player's promise to render his services at a later time. Such an offer is bilateral; and if the player accepts it by signing and returning the contract, a bilateral contract has been formed. Of course, if the player is the first one to make a commitment by making a definite offer to play for the team at a definite salary and on other definite terms, the player is the offeror and the team is the offeree. (Note that, as in the previous example, people often say they are "sending a contract" when what they are really doing is sending an offer for a contract.)

Some offers, called *unilateral offers*, are phrased in such a way that they can be accepted only by the performance of a particular act. An example of such an offer would be the promise by a TV station to pay $5,000 to the first person who brings to its executive offices any piece of a fallen satellite. This offer can only be accepted by the actual physical production of a portion of the designated satellite, at which time a unilateral contract is formed; a mere promise by an offeree that they will bring in the item later does not result in the formation of a contract. The reason is that the *apparent intent* of the offeror was that the offer could only be accepted by the actual performance of the requested act by the offeree. In the previous example of the professional football player, the apparent intent of the offeror was that the offer could be accepted merely by the offeree's clear indication of an intent to accept. As is true with other questions in contract law about intent, a court must infer what a person's intent apparently was from all of the circumstances, including exactly what was said or written, the background (what had previously happened), relevant evidence of prior transactions between the party, the surrounding circumstances at the time of the offer, and any evidence of customs that the parties had established between themselves or of any relevant customs in the industry if both parties are members of a given industry.

Offers for unilateral contracts occur much less frequently than offers for bilateral contracts—most contracts are bilateral. And, in cases where there is doubt as to the type of offer made, the courts generally presume them to be bilateral in nature, which means that the offeree can accept merely by indicating a definite intent to accept. One type of unilateral offer, however, is made frequently in the real world—the promise by a seller of property to pay a real estate agent a commission when the agent finds a buyer for it. The real estate agent performs a brokerage function, bringing together willing buyers and sellers. Brokers in other contexts are also frequently parties to unilateral contracts—typically, one using broker's services makes a unilateral offer of a commission if the broker finds what the party needs, such as financing. The following case presents another example, in which an employment agency offers to provide an employee to a company that is looking for someone. An employment agency is simply a broker in a labor market. The case also shows another consequence of an offer being a unilateral one, namely, if the offeree performs the requested act, he has accepted the offer even if he has verbally expressed reservations.

PRECISION CONCEPTS CORP. v. GENERAL
EMPLOYMENT & TRIAD PERSONNEL SERVICES
Ohio Court of Appeals, 2000 Ohio App. LEXIS 3322 (2000)

General Employment, an employment agency, contacted Precision, a computer company, regarding a job opening at Precision. General Employment sent a potential employee, Tavery Tan, to Precision for an interview. Precision eventually hired Ms. Tan but *refused to pay General Employment its fee for procuring the employee. On September 11, 1998, Precision filed a complaint in the Franklin County Court of Common Pleas against General Employment. The complaint sought a declaration, in part, that there was no contractual relationship between Precision and General Employment. General Employment filed an answer and a counterclaim for breach of contract. The trial court dismissed Precision's complaint and rendered judgment to General Employment on its counterclaim in the sum of $17,624.99. Precision appealed.*

Tyack, Justice:

To prove the existence of a contract, the elements of mutual assent (generally, offer and acceptance) and consideration must be shown. It must also be shown that there was a meeting of the minds and that the contract was definite as to its essential terms. Manifestation of mutual assent requires each party make a promise or begin to render a performance. Such manifestation of assent may be made wholly or partly by written or spoken words, or by other acts or the failure to act. Acceptance of an offer may be expressed by word, sign, writing, or act.

As indicated above, the dispute in the case at bar centers on the fee allegedly owed by appellant (Precision Concepts Corp.) to appellee (General Employment) for procuring Ms. Tan. Appellant asserts it never agreed to pay a fee equaling one-third of Ms. Tan's first-year salary. The facts, construed most strongly in favor of appellant, establish the following. Appellant placed an ad in the newspaper indicating its desire to hire a senior applications developer. Charles E. Anthony, Jr., employed at Precision at the pertinent time, was the professional services manager and was contacted by appellee. Appellee's representative told Mr. Anthony that it had an applicant for the position. Mr. Anthony and the representative discussed the applicant's qualifications, and appellee sent appellant the applicant's resume.

Mr. Anthony testified that appellee informed him that it charged a fee of around thirty-three percent. Mr. Anthony told appellee that appellant did not generally pay that percentage and asked if the fee was negotiable. Appellee's representative responded that the fee was not negotiable.

On July 3, 1998, appellee's representative, Jasbir Sahota, sent a fax to Mr. Anthony informing him that the applicant, Tavery Tan, would be at appellant's office on Monday, July 6, 1998. On that Monday, Ms. Tan interviewed with Mr. Anthony. On that same day, appellant was faxed a fee schedule from appellee setting forth the terms and conditions should appellant hire Ms. Tan. The fee schedule contained a fee of one-third of the successful applicant's first-year salary. Such fee schedule was never signed by a representative of appellant.

After Ms. Tan's interview with Mr. Anthony, he recommended that she be hired. Mr. Anthony told appellant's president and co-owner, Robert W. Molitors, that he would like Ms. Tan to be hired but that he could not recommend hiring her if appellant had to pay the one-third fee. Mr. Anthony testified that he thought Mr. Molitors "was looking to negotiate the fee down and basically he told me to go ahead and proceed with it." Mr. Anthony explained that he then continued the interview process with Ms. Tan and was going to have her "talk" to more people. Ms. Tan was interviewed by another employee of appellant who also recommended she be hired.

Ms. Tan was hired by appellant with an annual salary of $50,000. Mr. Molitors testified that appellant extended an offer to Ms. Tan without negotiating a lower fee "knowing that, hopefully, we could get to an agreement." Mr. Molitors further stated, "we went ahead and made the offer thinking we could work out the negotiations." Upon being asked if appellant ever negotiated a reduced fee, Mr. Anthony responded, "I am not 100 percent sure. I wasn't that involved with it, but I got from the gist of the conversation that we were going to go ahead and proceed with the hire since there was no contract in place and afterward we would negotiate a better fee."

Both Mr. Anthony and Mr. Molitors acknowledged that they were aware appellee charged a one-third fee for its services. However, Mr. Molitors testified that appellant had not signed any agreement and had not agreed verbally to any terms or conditions (relating to the fee). In an affidavit, Mr. Molitors stated that appellant rejected appellee's contract terms.

As a factual matter, the above evidence establishes that Mr. Molitors did not believe appellant had an agreement with appellee regarding the fee amount. However, it does not follow that there was no binding contract. The undisputed facts lead this court to conclude that as a legal matter, a unilateral contract was formed between the parties.

A unilateral contract is one in which the promisor receives no promise as consideration for his or her promise. By the promisor's offer, no obligation is imposed upon the offeree—only a condition, the performance of which is entirely optional with the offeree. As set forth in the *Restatement of the Law 2d, Contracts* (1981), Section 45(1), where an offer invites an offeree to accept by rendering a performance and does not invite a promissory acceptance, an option contract is created when the offeree tenders the invited performance. Such an offer has often been referred to as an offer for a unilateral contract. In such a situation, the contract is not formed until accepted by performance by the offeree. Consideration is not necessary prior to acceptance by performance and after acceptance, the obligation to pay becomes enforceable.

In the case at bar, appellee offered its services to appellant—the procuring of an employee. If appellant hired appellee's applicant, appellee's fee was one-third of the employee's annual salary. Appellant was under no obligation to interview and/or hire Ms. Tan. Appellant was aware of appellee's fee should Ms. Tan be hired. Appellant hired Ms. Tan and in doing so, accepted appellee's offer of procuring an employee for a one-third fee.

The fact that appellant did not like the fee appellee indicated it would charge should appellant hire Ms. Tan does not preclude the finding of a binding contract. Appellant intended and/or desired to negotiate the fee down; however, appellant never did so. Secretly held, unexpressed intent is not relevant to whether a contract is formed. There is evidence that Mr. Anthony initially told appellee that its fee was too high; however, appellee informed Mr. Anthony that such fee was not negotiable. Again, appellant hired Ms. Tan with knowledge of the fee charged by appellee, and it did so without negotiating down such fee. Accordingly, a unilateral contract was formed when appellant hired Ms. Tan, and appellant became obligated to pay appellee a fee equal to one-third of Ms. Tan's first-year salary.

Affirmed.

Express, Implied, and Quasi-Contracts

As has been indicated, the essence of a contract is an agreement (an understanding) that has been arrived at in some fashion. If the intentions of the parties are stated fully and in explicit terms, either orally or in writing, they constitute an *express contract*. The typical real estate lease and construction contract are examples of contracts normally falling within this category.

Express contracts are frequently in writing and of considerable length, but this is not necessarily so. If B orally offers to sell his used car to W for $450 cash, and W answers, "I accept," an express contract has been formed. The communications between B and W, while extremely brief and purely oral, are themselves sufficient to indicate the obligations of each.

An *implied contract* is one in which the promises (intentions) of the parties have to be inferred primarily from their conduct and from the circumstances in which it occurred. It is reasonable to infer, for example, that a person who is getting a haircut in a barbershop actually desires the service and is willing to pay for it. If the patron does not pay voluntarily, a court will have no hesitation in saying that by his conduct the patron had made an implied promise to pay a reasonable price, and will hold him liable on this obligation.

The words and conduct test is a good starting point in distinguishing between the two kinds of agreement, but it is also an oversimplification. This is primarily so because some agreements are reached through the use of words and conduct both—especially in the case where one person requests a service from another without specifying a price that they are willing to pay for it. For example, if T asks J to keep his lawn mowed during the two months that T will be in Europe, and if J performs the requested service, T's request for the service carries with it in the eyes of the law an implied promise that he will pay J the "reasonable value" of his services. Thus the contract that has been formed upon J's completion of the work is an implied contract, even though T requested the service expressly.

A *quasi-contract*, in contrast to express and implied contracts, exists only in those exceptional circumstances where a court feels compelled to impose an obligation upon one person regardless of whether they had any intention of making a contract. The technical name for implied contracts is *contracts implied in fact*, and for quasi-contracts *contracts implied in law*. For simplicity, we use the less formal terms "implied" and "quasi".

One situation in which a quasi-contract obligation will be imposed is where it is necessary to promote an important public policy such as the performance of emergency medical care: The classic illustration is that of a doctor who renders first aid to an unconscious man and later sends a bill for his services. It is perfectly obvious that the patient neither expressly nor impliedly promised to pay for the services when they were rendered; yet to permit him to escape liability entirely on the grounds that a contract was not formed would be to let him get something for nothing—a result the law generally abhors. To solve this dilemma, the courts pretend that a contract was formed and impose a quasi-contractual obligation on the person receiving the service.

The other main situation in which a quasi-contractual obligation will often be imposed is where one party conferred a benefit on the other because of an honestly mistaken belief that they were under a legal or moral obligation to do so. In the *Deskovick v. Porzio* case, below, we see a situation in which a quasi-contractual obligation was imposed because money was paid as the result of an honestly mistaken belief that there was a strong moral obligation to do so.

A quasi-contractual obligation is imposed only in circumstances where the failure to impose such an obligation would result in one party receiving an "unjust enrichment"—a benefit which, on the grounds of fairness alone, they ought to pay for. Suppose, for example, that A plants and cultivates crops on land belonging to B, without B's knowledge. In such a case, B, upon learning the facts, is entitled to bring a *quantum meruit* action to recover from A the reasonable value of the benefit (the profit which A made as a result of the use of the land), for otherwise A would be unjustly enriched. *Quantum meruit* means, literally, "as much as is deserved."

Three limitations on the quasi-contractual principle should be noted.

1. It cannot be invoked by one who has conferred a benefit unnecessarily or as a result of negligence or other misconduct. Thus, suppose that the X Company contracts to blacktop Y's driveway at 540 Fox Lane for $1,900, and the company's employees instead mistakenly blacktop the driveway of Y's neighbor, Z, at 546 Fox Lane, in Z's absence. In such a situation Z has no liability to the X Company, since his retention of the blacktop, while a benefit to him, is not an unjust benefit or an unjust retention under the circumstances.

2. Quasi-contracts are contracts in fiction only, since they are not based upon an agreement between the parties. They are not "true" contracts. However, quasi-contractual remedies are often granted in contractual contexts. For example, suppose that A and B make a contract, but that it turns out to be unenforceable because the terms of the agreement are too vague, the contract was required to be in writing but was not, or one party was induced by fraud or mistake to make the contract.

In such a case, when one party, thinking that there was a contract and that he had an obligation to fulfill, confers a valuable benefit on the other by providing services, money, or goods, the recipient is under a quasi-contractual obligation to compensate the other for the reasonable value of the benefit. These situations provide examples of a court's imposition of a quasi-contractual obligation on a recipient of something of value because the other conferred a benefit on the recipient as the result of an honestly mistaken belief that there was a legal obligation to do what was done.

3. A plaintiff generally will not be allowed quasi-contractual recovery from one person if he originally looked to another for compensation. Assume that C sells a house to B, and B hires A to plant shrubs around the house. A does so, but before he is paid, B dies and C generously allows B's widow to rescind the sales contract. If A sues C on quasi-contractual grounds, claiming that C was unjustly enriched by the planting of the shrubs, recovery will probably be denied because A originally looked to B for compensation and may still proceed against B's estate.

In the first of the following two cases, a state court sets forth the general rules as to the nature and legal effects of implied contracts. The second presents a situation where a recovery of money by the plaintiffs under the quasi-contract doctrine is justified.

CARROLL v. LEE
Supreme Court of Arizona, 712 P.2d 923 (1986).

Judy Carroll lived with Paul Lee for fourteen years. Ultimately they settled in Ajo, Arizona where Paul operated an automobile repair shop. Although Judy used the name Lee during this time, the couple did not marry or ever seriously consider marriage. In 1982 they "went their separate ways."

Prior to the relationship little personal property was owned by either party, and neither owned any real property (i.e., land). During the course of the relationship the couple jointly acquired three parcels of land, several antique or restored automobiles, a mobile home, and various other items of personal property. The real property was titled to the couple in one of three ways. Title was held either (1) as joint tenants with the right of survivorship, (2) as husband and wife, or (3) as husband and wife as joint tenants with the right of survivorship. (The mobile home and some of the automobiles were titled to Paul T. Lee and Judy Lee, with other automobiles titled to Paul T. Lee alone.)

During the time the couple lived together, Paul supplied virtually all of the money used to pay their living expenses, while Judy "kept the house" by cleaning, cooking, doing laundry, and working in the yard. After the couple split up Judy filed this partition action claiming a one-half interest in the jointly titled property listed above. (The fact that the properties were titled to both parties did not, in and of itself, convey a one-half interest to Judy. This was because Paul proved that the money used in purchasing them came from the operation of the repair shop, which he owned personally. In such a case, the rule in Arizona—and in most states—is that "where property is paid for by one party and title is taken in the name of that party and a second party who are not husband and wife, it is presumed that the property was taken for the benefit of the one paying for the property." Thus it was necessary for Judy to prove an agreement existed between them that they be co-owners, in order to rebut this presumption.)

The trial court ruled in favor of Judy, finding that an implied contract existed under which it was agreed that Paul and she would be co-owners of the property. (This finding was based on a 1984 case, Cook v. Cook, *691 P.2d 664, in which the Supreme Court of Arizona upheld an implied contract between an unmarried couple in circumstances similar to those presented by this case.) Paul appealed, and the court of appeals reversed the judgment (for reasons appearing below). Judy petitioned the Supreme Court of Arizona for review.*

Gordon, Vice Chief Justice:

In *Cook v. Cook, supra,* [this court approved] an agreement between unmarried cohabitants to pool income, acquire assets, and share in the accumulations. We compiled basic concepts of contract law:

> The sine qua non [essential element] of any contract is the exchange of promises. From this exchange flows the obligation of one party to another. Although it is most apparent that two parties have exchanged promises when their words express a spoken or written statement of promissory intention, mutual promises need not be express in order to create an enforceable contract. *Restatement (Second) of Contracts* 54. Indeed, a promise 'may be inferred wholly or partly from conduct,' id, and there is no distinction in the effect of the promise whether it is expressed in writing, or orally, or in acts, or partly in one of these ways and partly in others.' *Id.* §19. Thus, two parties may by their course of conduct express their agreement, though no words are ever spoken. From their conduct alone the trier of fact can determine the existence of an agreement. *Id.* §4.

The court of appeals [ruled that our decision in *Cook* was not applicable to the instant case because] "no evidence, in words or conduct, suggests mutual promises to contribute funds to a pool...." [In other words, the court of appeals refused to apply the *Cook* rule because in that case both parties were earning income, while in the instant case Paul was the sole income producer. The Supreme Court disagreed with the court of appeals decision, and continued:]

In Arizona we recognize implied contracts, and there is no difference in legal effect between an express contract and an implied contract. An implied contract is one not created or evidenced by explicit agreement, but inferred by the law as a matter of reason and justice from the acts and conduct of the parties and circumstances surrounding their transaction. Furthermore, in this state monetary consideration is not always required as consideration.... Clearly a promise for a promise constitutes adequate consideration....

We believe Judy proved the property requested to be partitioned was acquired through joint common effort and for a common purpose. It is not necessary for her to prove that she produced by her labor a part of the very money used to purchase the property. The parties had an implied partnership or joint enterprise agreement at the very least, based on the facts and circumstances presented. Recovery for Judy should be allowed in accordance with these implied expectations. [The court here reviewed testimony by Paul in which he stated that it was his "preference" that Judy stay at home, cook meals, do washing and yard work, and that she did, in fact, perform these services. This testimony ended with the following:]

> Q. Did you ever intend that she be an owner with you at that time, at the time that you were acquiring these properties, that she be an owner of those properties at that time?
> A. You mean a co-owner? Q. Yes.
> A. I suppose at the time I had it planned that way....
> [Judy's relevant testimony is as follows:]
> Q. All right. What type of an arrangement, if any, did you and Paul discuss about what he expected from your relationship in terms of contribution?
> A. We didn't really discuss it. It just was there. He went to work. I stayed home and kept the house and, mostly because that's what he wanted me to do.

There was evidence from which the trial court could find the existence of an agreement for property to be acquired and owned jointly, as such was the method in which Paul took title in both the real and personal property.... Since Judy was a co-owner of the property under a contract theory, she had the right [under Arizona law] to seek partition and divide the jointly owned assets....

We therefore vacate the opinion of the court of appeals and remand the case to the trial court for a redistribution of property not inconsistent with this opinion.

Comment. This case has been edited to emphasize the implied contract question. An additional question of equal importance was also presented: whether a finding that an implied contract existed even though the plaintiff's services were entirely of a "homemaking" nature was contrary to public policy, on the ground that enforcement of such a contract might discourage marriage. The court of appeals, by refusing to apply the *Cook* rule, felt that the enforcement of such a contract would have that effect. The higher court, in a part of its decision omitted here, set forth reasons why enforcement of an implied contract in the circumstances presented here was not contrary to the public policy of the state.

DESKOVICK ET AL. v. PORZIO
Superior Court of New Jersey, 187 A.2d 610 (1963)

Plaintiffs in this action are brothers, Michael and Peter Deskovick, Jr. Their father, Peter Deskovick, Sr., was hospitalized in 1958 until his death in 1959. During this period Michael paid the hospital and medical bills as they came in, under the impression that the father was financially unable to do so. (This impression was based on statements made by the senior Deskovick in which he indicated an apparently genuine fear that he would not be able to pay the expenses of the hospitalization.) After the father's death it was discovered that, in fact, his estate was adequate to cover all of the payments made by Michael. The plaintiffs thereupon brought this action against the executor of their father's estate, Porzio, to recover the amounts paid out.

In the trial court, plaintiffs proceeded on the theory that an implied contract existed between them and their father in the foregoing fact-pattern. (No mention of quasi-contractual liability was made.) While the evidence was somewhat conflicting as to whether Michael intended to be repaid out of his father's estate at the time he made the payments, the trial judge ruled as a matter of law that no such intention was present, and, for that reason, no implied contract had been formed. Accordingly, the court directed a verdict for the defendant. On appeal, plaintiffs contended for the first time that the estate should be liable on the theory of quasi-contract. (As a general rule, the parties cannot raise new issues on appeal. It does not appear why this was permitted in this case.)

Conford, Justice:

... If the question whether plaintiffs intended to be repaid at the time they advanced the monies in question were the sole material issue, we would conclude the trial court erred in taking the case out of the jury's hands [because of the conflicting evidence on that point]. However, their intent to be repaid was immaterial in the factual situation presented, for the following reasons.

It is elementary that the assertion of a contract implied in fact [an "implied contract"] calls for the establishment of a consensual understanding as to compensation or reimbursement inferable from the circumstances under which one furnishes services or property and another accepts such advances. Here an essential for such a mutual understanding was absent *in that the decedent, on behalf of whom these advances were being made, was totally ignorant of the fact.* [Emphasis added.]

[After thus concluding that the proper reason why no implied contract was formed was that the father could not give his implied consent to his sons' actions when he was not aware of them, the appellate court turned to the question of whether recovery might be allowed under the quasi-contract theory, as follows:]

It is elementary that one who pays the debt of another as a volunteer, having no obligation or liability to pay nor any interest menaced by the continued existence of the debt, cannot recover therefor from the beneficiary. Nor can such a volunteer claim the benefit of the law of subrogation. If plaintiffs were mere volunteers, therefore, they would not, within these principles, be entitled to be subrogated to the creditor position of the hospitals and physicians whose bills they paid.

Notwithstanding the foregoing principles, however, we perceive in the evidence adduced at the trial, particularly in the version of the facts reflected in the deposition of Michael, adduced by defendant, a quasi-contractual basis of recovery which in our judgment ought to be submitted to a jury at a retrial of the case in the interests of substantial justice.

It is said that a "quasi-contractual obligation is one that is created by the law for reasons of justice, without any expression of assent.... 1 *Corbin on Contracts* (1950), §19, p. 38; 1 *Williston, Contracts* (1957), §3A, p. 13. This concept rests "on the equitable principle that a person shall not be allowed to enrich himself unjustly at the expense of another, and on the principle that whatsoever it is certain that a man ought to do, that the law supposes him to have promised to do." *The Restatement of Restitution* (1937) undertakes to formulate a number of rules growing out of recognized principles of quasi-contract. *Id.*, at p. 5 et seq. Section 26 (p. 116), entitled "Mistake in Making Gifts," reads: "(1) A person is entitled to restitution from another to whom gratuitously and induced thereto by a mistake of fact he has given money if the mistake (a) was caused by fraud or material misrepresentation...." An innocent misrepresentation by the donee is within the rule. *Id.*, comment, at p. 117. A "mistaken belief in the existence of facts which would create a moral obligation upon the donor to make a gift would ordinarily be a basic error" justifying restitution. *Id.*, at p. 118....

We think the foregoing authorities would apply in favor of sons, who, during their father's mortal illness, believing him without means of meeting medical and hospital bills as a result of what he had previously told them, and wishing to spare him the discomfort of concern over such expenses at such a time, themselves assumed and paid the obligations. The leaving by the father of an estate far more than sufficient to have met the expenditures would, in such circumstances, and absent others affecting the basic equitable situation presented, properly invoke the concept of a *quasi-contractual obligation* of reimbursement of the sons by the estate. [Emphasis added.] Such circumstances would take the payors out of the category of voluntary intermeddlers as to whom the policy of the law is to deny restitution or reimbursement.... Judgment reversed and remanded.

Valid, Voidable, and Void Contracts

A valid contract is one in which all of the required elements are present. As a result, it is enforceable against both parties.

In some circumstances, one of the parties to a contract has the legal right to withdraw from it at a later time without liability. Such contracts are referred to as *voidable contracts*. Contracts in which fraud is present fall within this category, because the law permits the one who has been defrauded to set aside the contract. Minors' contracts are another common example of voidable contracts. (Because of their importance, voidable contracts are considered separately in Chapter 14.)

Courts occasionally designate a third type of contract as being void. Such contracts are those which, so far as the law is concerned, never existed at all. Contracts are usually void for either of two reasons: (1) one of the parties is wholly incompetent at the time of contracting (such as a person who has been legally declared insane) or (2) the purpose of the contract is totally illegal (such as an agreement calling for the commission of a crime). The designation *void contract* is admittedly self-contradictory—an improper combination of terms. Nevertheless, this label is used by the courts to distinguish such contracts from those which are merely voidable; and in that sense it is a useful term.

Another type of contract is referred to as being "unenforceable." An *unenforceable contract* was valid at the time it was made but was subsequently rendered unenforceable because of the application of some special rule of law. For example, if a debtor goes through bankruptcy proceedings, the debtor's nonexempt assets are distributed among creditors and the debtor ultimately receives a discharge in bankruptcy. Under bankruptcy law, this discharge prevents a creditor who was not paid in full from bringing legal action to recover the balance of the debt; thus the contract that created the indebtedness was rendered unenforceable by virtue of the discharge. Other examples of unenforceable contracts include those sued upon after the statute of limitations has expired, oral contracts that should have been in writing under the statute of frauds (see Chapter 15), and those calling for performance of personal services by a person who died after the agreement was made.

Negotiated Contracts and Contracts of Adhesion

The terms of many contracts are agreed upon only after a certain amount of bargaining, or "dickering," takes place between the parties. After one party makes an offer to the other, for example, the latter—the offeree—may indicate that they will accept only if a specified change is made in the terms of the offer. Or the offeree may respond with a counteroffer, a different proposal from that of the original offer. Contracts that result from these kinds of exchanges are "negotiated contracts."

Contracts of adhesion, by contrast, are formed where one party—usually having greatly superior bargaining power than the other—prepares the terms of a proposed contract and presents it to the other party on a *take-it-or-leave*-it basis. Examples of such "standard form" contracts are apartment leases, hospital admission forms, and sales contracts of new car dealers. While the terms of contracts of adhesion usually favor the parties who have prepared them, such contracts are generally enforceable unless the terms are so shockingly one-sided as to be, in the opinion of the courts, "unconscionable" in nature. (Unconscionable contracts are considered further in Chapter 13.)

Executory and Executed Contracts

Once a contract is formed, it is an *executory contract* until both parties have fully performed their obligations. When performance has taken place, the contract is said to be an executed contract. If one party has fully performed his or her part of the bargain but the other party has not, the contract is executed as to the former and executory as to the latter.

CONTRACT LAW AND SALES LAW—A SPECIAL RELATIONSHIP

Contracts for the sale of goods—tangible articles of "personal property" (anything tangible other than real estate) such as automobiles, computers, machine tools, grain, and items of clothing—are governed by both the general rules of contract law and provisions in Article 2 of the Uniform Commercial Code (UCC). Article 2 of the UCC covers sale of goods contracts in all states except Louisiana.

So-called ''sales law'' is simply a branch of contract law. The general rules of contract law apply unless there is a provision in Article 2 of the UCC that applies a different rule. On many questions, such as what constitutes an offer, the UCC is silent, and general rules of contract law apply. Also, some provisions of the UCC simply restate the general rules. However, for sale of goods contracts, Article 2 of the UCC does sometimes prescribe a different rule that the general common law rules would. In these chapters on contract law, we focus mainly on the general common law rules that apply to all types of contracts, but we also discuss special rules applying to sale of goods contracts when they are meaningfully different than the general rules.

CHAPTER 11

THE AGREEMENT

- Intention of the Parties
- Requirements of the Offer
- Termination of the Offer
- The Acceptance

The first and foremost element of any contract is an agreement—a reasonably definite commitment between two or more persons to do something or not do something. It is for this reason that the liability or obligation resulting from the making of a contract (as distinguished from that imposed by the law of torts or the criminal law) is sometimes described as being "consensual" in nature. The usual view taken by the law today is that if two or more persons, expressly or by implication, have reached a reasonably clear agreement as to what each party is to do, then that agreement will be enforceable by the courts. This means that if either party refuses to perform his or her part of the agreement without a lawful excuse, the other party is entitled to recover damages in a breach of contract action. On the other hand, if it is found that a legally sufficient agreement has not been formed, neither party has contractual liability to the other.

Because the word "agreement" encompasses a broad spectrum of situations where some kind of understanding has been reached (ranging from the extremely concise to the hopelessly vague), the courts are faced with the problem of deciding just what kinds of agreements are sufficiently definite to warrant judicial relief if they are breached. The best approach to this problem is to break the agreement down into two parts—the offer and the acceptance. The inquiries then become whether either party made an offer to the other, and, if so, whether the offer was followed by an acceptance. Before considering the legal definitions of these terms, we will briefly mention the rules used by the courts to ascertain the intentions of the parties—with emphasis upon the applicability of these rules to the offer and acceptance.

INTENTION OF THE PARTIES

In cases where the parties disagree as to whether their communications constituted an offer and an acceptance, the court will frequently emphasize the principle that the intention of the parties is controlling. If the court finds that their intentions were the same (that there was a "meeting of minds," as it is sometimes phrased), then there is a contract.

One caution about this principle, however, should be noted. When the courts view the parties' communications for the purpose of determining whether their intentions were one and the same, it is the parties' manifested (or apparent) intentions that control, rather than their actual subjective intentions. A person's manifested or apparent intent is frequently referred to by the courts as "objective" intent, while actual or secret intent is called "subjective" intent. Thus the test used by the courts that is described here is referred to as the "objective test." For example, if X writes a letter to Y containing a proposal which meets the legal requirements of an offer, and if Y promptly accepts the offer in a return letter, there is a contract—even if X later claims to have had some mental reservations about the proposal, or says that he really did not intend his letter to be an offer. Thus, when it is said that there must be a meeting of minds to have a contract, this usually means that there must only be a legal, or apparent, meeting of minds.

There are two compelling reasons for the frequent use of this objective view:

1. It is virtually impossible for a judge or jury to determine what a person's actual intent was at a prior time, or even at the present time.

2. It would be unfair to allow someone to indicate a particular intention to another person and then to come into court and claim that they did not mean what was apparently meant—

reliable contractual relationships maintained.

REQUIREMENTS OF THE OFFER

Inherent in the many definitions of the word *offer* is the idea that it is a proposal made by one person, called the offeror, to another, the offeree, indicating what the offeror will give in return for a specified promise or act on the part of the offeree. That is, the offeror must manifest a definite, present willingness to enter into a contractual relationship with the other party. Sometimes the manifestation is referred to as a *conditional statement* of what the offeror will do for the offeree. Used in this manner, the term "statement" is broad enough to include both words and conduct by which the offeror indicates a willingness to contract. Thus, if a person in a drugstore shows a magazine to the cashier and deposits $4.50 (the stated price) on the counter, it is perfectly clear that they made an offer to purchase the item without speaking a word. Similarly, when a company delivers an unordered article of merchandise under circumstances which indicate to the recipient that a charge will be made for the article if it is accepted, the company's act constitutes an offer to sell the product at the stated price. Of course, the recipient of such unsolicited merchandise does not incur a duty to pay for it unless they actually use it or otherwise indicates acceptance of the sender's offer. If the unsolicited goods are sent by *mail,* ordinarily no duty to pay arises even if the recipient uses the goods. The federal Postal Reorganization Act of 1970 provides that, except for "merchandise mailed by a charitable organization soliciting contributions," the mailing of any unsolicited merchandise "may be treated as a gift by the recipient, who shall have the right to retain, use, discard, or dispose of it in any manner he sees fit without any obligations whatsoever to the sender."

In order for a particular communication (or act) to achieve the legal status of an offer. These requirements are (1) a manifestation of an intent to contract; (2) a reasonably definite indication of what the offeror and the offeree are to do; and (3) a communication of the proposal to the intended offeree.

The Intent to Contract

Preliminary Negotiations

Some language is so tentative or exploratory in nature that it should be apparent that an immediate contract is not contemplated. Such communications do not constitute offers; they are designated preliminary negotiations, or "dickering." For example, the statement "I'd like to get $4,000 for this car" would normally fall into this category, as would a letter indicating "I will not sell my home for less than $56,000." If the addressee in either of these instances were to reply, "I accept your offer," a contract would not result since no offer was made in either case. Along similar lines, it is usually held that requests for information—called inquiries—do not manifest a genuine intent to contract, and consequently such questions do not constitute offers in most circumstances. Thus, if A writes B, "Would you rent your summer home for the month of June for $900?" and B replies, "Yes, I accept your offer," there is no contract. (The most that can be said in this situation is that B has now made an offer to A, and it will ripen into a contract only if A subsequently accepts it.)

Difficult questions sometimes arise when there are multiple offerees. Suppose that A writes to B: "I hereby offer to sell my farm to you for $720,000." The letter informs B that

A is simultaneously making the same offer to several other potential purchasers. B should know that although the language appears to be an offer, this letter is merely preliminary negotiation because A does not intend to be bound to sell the farm to several different persons. On the other hand, if the letter does not disclose that the offer is being made to others, B can make an effective acceptance. (If another offeree, not knowing of the offer to B, also effectively accepts, A faces certain liability in a breach of contract action.)

The decision in the well-known case below helps show how the courts try to draw the lines between preliminary negotiations and offers in several common situations.

RICHARDS v. FLOWERS ET AL.
California Court of Appeal, 14 Cal. Rptr. 228 (1961)

Mrs. Richards, plaintiff, wrote defendant Flowers on January 15, 1959, as follows: "We would be interested in buying your lot on Gravatt Drive in Oakland, California, if we can deal with you directly and not run through a realtor. If you are interested, please advise us by return mail the cash price you would expect to receive."

On January 19, 1959, Flowers replied: "Thank you for your inquiry regarding my lot on Gravatt Drive. As long as your offer would be in cash I see no reason why we could not deal directly on this matter. Considering what I paid for the lot, and the taxes which I have paid I expect to receive $4,500 for this property. Please let me know what you decide."

On January 25, 1959, Mrs. Richards sent the following telegram to Flowers: "Have agreed to buy your lot on your terms will handle transactions through local title company who will contact you would greatly appreciate your sending us a copy of the contour map you referred to in your letter as we are desirous of building at once...."

On February 5, 1959, Flowers entered into an agreement to sell the property to a third party, Mr. and Mrs. Sutton. Mrs. Richards, after learning of the Sutton transaction, called upon defendant to deliver his deed to her, claiming the above correspondence constituted a contract between the two of them. Flowers refused to do so, denying that his letter of January 19 constituted an offer to sell, whereupon Mr. and Mrs. Richards brought suit, asking for specific performance of the alleged contract. (The Suttons intervened in this action to protect their interest by supporting Flowers' contention that a contract was not formed between Flowers and plaintiffs.)

The trial court ruled that defendant's letter of January 19 did constitute an offer to sell, but it further ruled that plaintiff's telegram of January 25 was not a valid acceptance under a particular section of the California Code known as the "statute of frauds" (the provisions of which are not necessary to our consideration of this case). Accordingly the court entered judgment for the defendant. The Richardses appealed.

Shoemaker, Justice:

. . . Under the factual situation in the instant case, the interpretation of the series of communications between the parties is a matter of law and an appellate court is not bound by the trial court's determination. Respondent Flowers argues that the letter of January 19th merely invited an offer from appellants for the purchase of the property and that under no reasonable interpretation can this letter be construed as an offer. We agree with the respondent. Careful consideration of the letter does not convince us that the language therein used can reasonably be interpreted as a definite offer to sell the property to appellants. As pointed out in *Restatement of the Law, Contracts*, Section 25, comment a: "It is often difficult to draw an exact line between offers and negotiations preliminary thereto. It is common for one who wishes to make a bargain to try to induce the other party to the intended transaction to make the definite offer, he himself suggesting with more or less definiteness the nature of the contract he is willing to enter into...." Under this approach our letter seems rather clearly to fall within the category of mere preliminary negotiations. Particularly is this true in view of the fact that the letter was written directly in response to appellants' letter inquiring if they could deal directly with respondent and requesting him to suggest a sum at which he might be willing to sell. From the record, we do not accept the argument that respondent Flowers made a binding offer to sell the property merely because he chose to answer certain inquiries by the appellants. Further, the letter appears to us inconsistent with any intent on his part to make an offer to sell. In response to appellants' question, respondent stated that he would be willing to deal directly with them rather than through a realtor as long as their "offer would be in cash." We take this language to indicate that respondent anticipated a future offer from appellants but was making no offer himself.

Appellants refer to the phrase that he would "expect to receive" $4,500 and contend this constitutes an offer to sell to them at this price. However, respondent was only expressing an indication of the lowest price which he was presently willing to consider. Particularly is this true inasmuch as respondent wrote only in response to an inquiry in which this wording was used. We conclude that respondent by his communication confined himself to answering the inquiries raised by appellants, but did not extend himself further and did not make an express offer to sell the property. We have before us a case involving a mere quotation of price and not an offer to sell at that price.

The cause, therefore, comes within the rule announced in such authorities as *Nebraska Seed Co. v. Harsh*, 1915, 152 N.W. 310, wherein the seller had written the buyer, enclosing a sample of millet seed and saying, "I want $2.25 per cwt. for this seed f.o.b. Lowell." The buyer telegraphed his acceptance. The court, in reversing a judgment for plaintiff buyer, stated: "In our opinion the letter of defendant cannot be fairly construed into an offer to sell to the plaintiff. After describing the seed, the writer says, 'I want $2.25 per cwt. for this seed f.o.b. Lowell.' He does not say, 'I offer to sell to you.' The language used is general, . . . and is not an offer by which he may be bound, if accepted, by any or all of the persons addressed", and *Owen v. Tunison*, 1932, 158 A. 926, wherein the buyer had written the seller inquiring whether he would be willing to sell certain store property for $6,000. The seller replied: "Because of improvements which have been added and an expenditure of several thousand dollars it would not be possible for me to sell it unless I was to receive $16,000.00 cash...." The court, in holding that the seller's reply did not constitute an offer, stated: "Defendant's letter . . . may have been written with the intent to open negotiations that might lead to a sale. It was not a proposal to sell." It would thus seem clear that respondent's quotation of the price which he would "expect to receive" cannot be viewed as an offer capable of acceptance.

Since there was never an offer, hence never a contract between respondent Flowers and appellants, the judgment must be affirmed, and it becomes unnecessary to determine whether an appellant's purported acceptance complied with the statute of frauds or whether appellants failed to qualify for specific performance in any other regard. Judgment affirmed.

Other Evidence on the Question of Intent

Up to this point, we have seen that the courts lay great stress on the actual language of a particular communication in determining whether it evidences an intent to contract. In addition, courts will take into account relevant evidence from several other sources if it sheds light on what reasonable people in the circumstances probably would have intended, such as: (1) Evidence of a well-established custom in the industry in which the parties are members, assuming that the parties have not stated otherwise in this transaction; (2) Evidence of a custom that these parties may have established between themselves in a series of previous similar transactions, assuming that the parties have not stated otherwise in this transaction; (3) Evidence from the conduct of the parties both before and after the alleged agreement was made.

Regarding evidence of the parties' conduct before the alleged agreement was made, courts almost always consider any relevant evidence about the factual background—the surrounding circumstances in which the communication was made. Examination of the background sometimes makes it quite clear that an intent to contract was not present, even though the language taken by itself meets the requirements of an offer, as where a statement is apparently made in jest, excitement, or anger. In *Higgins v. Lessig*, 49 Ill.App. 459 (1893), for example, a man who learned that his $15 harness had been stolen became so angry that he launched into a tirade in which he stated that he would "give $100 to any man who will find out who the thief is." The court held that this was not an enforceable offer, but merely the "extravagant exclamation of an excited man."

Higgins is consistent with the "objective theory" of contracts mentioned above, because a reasonable person hearing the owner's statement would have realized that once he calmed down he would not seriously wish to pay $100 for the return of a $15 harness. However, under this view parties are not required to read each other's minds. In *Lucy v. Zehmer*, 84 S.E.2d 516 (Va. 1954), for example, a man who claimed that he was only jesting when he offered to sell his farm to his neighbors was held to the bargain because the buyers reasonably believed that he was serious. Although the parties were drinking, they twice reduced their agreement to writing and its terms were reasonable.

This does not mean, however, that parties' intentions are always gauged totally objectively. Suppose, for example, that A promises to pay B $1,000,000 for his ranch. A stranger overhearing the promise might well believe that it was a serious offer because it outwardly appeared to be such. However, if B *knows* that A is a practical joker and nearly flat broke then B also knows that the statement is not a serious offer. If B attempted to accept the offer, no contract would result because of B's subjective knowledge. A's apparently serious offer does not bind him if B knows or reasonably should know that A is jesting.

KOLODZIEJ v. MASON
2014 U.S. App. LEXIS 23816 (11th Cir. 2014)

Defendant Mason, an attorney, was representing criminal defendant Serrano in a murder trial. NBC news interviewed Mason, who argued that Serrano had an alibi--on the day of the murders, Serrano claimed to be on a business trip several hundred miles away. Hotel surveillance video confirmed that Serrano was at a La Quinta Inn in Atlanta, Georgia, several hours before and after the murders occurred in Bartow, Florida. The prosecution argued that after being recorded by the hotel security camera in the early afternoon, Serrano slipped out of the hotel and, traveling under several aliases, flew from Atlanta to Orlando, where he rented a car, drove to Bartow, Florida, and committed the murders. From there,

Serrano allegedly drove to the Tampa International Airport, flew back to Atlanta, and drove from the Atlanta International Airport to the La Quinta, to make an appearance on the hotel's security footage once again that evening.

Mason argued that it was impossible for his client to have committed the murders in accordance with this timeline, focusing particularly on the claim that Serrano had made it from the Atlanta airport to the La Quinta in 28 minutes or less. Mason said to the reporter: "I challenge anybody to show me, and guess what? Did they bring in any evidence to say that somebody made that route, did so? State's burden of proof. If they can do it, I'll challenge 'em. I'll pay them a million dollars if they can do it."

NBC did not broadcast Mason's original interview during the trial, which ended in a guilty verdict. Thereafter, NBC featured an edited version of Mason's interview in its "Dateline" television program. The edited version removed much of the surrounding commentary, including Mason's references to the State's burden of proof, and Mason's statement aired as, "I challenge anybody to show me—I'll pay them a million dollars if they can do it."

Plaintiff Kolodziej, then a law student at the South Texas College of Law, saw the edited version of Mason's interview and understood the statement as a serious challenge, open to anyone, to "make it off the plane and back to the hotel within [twenty-eight] minutes"—that is, in the prosecution's timeline—in return for one million dollars. Kolodziej then traveled the alleged route within 28 minutes. He sent Mason a recording of his journey and demanded $1 million. Mason refused to pay, denying that he had made a serious offer. Kolodziej sued for breach of contract, even after seeing an unedited version of the original interview.

The trial court granted summary judgment to defendant Mason; Kolodziej appealed.

Wilson, Circuit Judge:

The case before us involves the potential creation of an oral, unilateral contract. A valid contract—premised on the parties' requisite willingness to contract—may be "manifested through written or spoken words, or inferred in whole or in part from the parties' conduct." *L & H Constr. Co. v. Circle Redmont, Inc.*, 55 So.2d 30 (Fla.App. 2011). We use "an objective test . . . to determine whether a contract is enforceable." See *Leonard v. Pepsico*, 88 F.Supp.2d at 128 (noting that the determination of whether a party made an offer to enter into a contract requires "the [c]ourt to determine how a reasonable, objective person would have understood" the potential offeror's communication).

We do not find that Mason's statements were such that a reasonable, objective person would have understood them to be an invitation to contract, regardless of whether we look to the unedited interview or the edited television broadcast seen by Kolodziej. Neither the content of Mason's statements, nor the circumstances in which he made them, nor the conduct of the parties reflects the assent necessary to establish an actionable offer—which is, of course, essential to the creation of a contract.

As a threshold matter, the "spoken words" of Mason's purported challenge do not indicate a willingness to enter into a contract. Even removed from its surrounding context, the edited sentence that Kolodziej claims creates Mason's obligation to pay (that is, "I challenge anybody to show me—I'll pay them a million dollars if they can do it") appears colloquial. The exaggerated amount of "a million dollars"—the common choice of movie villains and schoolyard wagerers alike—indicates that this was hyperbole. As the district court noted, "courts have viewed such indicia of jest or hyperbole as providing a reason for an individual to doubt that an 'offer' was serious." Thus, the very content of Mason's spoken words "would have given any reasonable person pause, considering all of the attendant circumstances in this case."

Those attendant circumstances are further notable when we place Mason's statements in context. As Judge Learned Hand once noted, "the circumstances in which the words are used is always relevant and usually indispensable." *N.Y. Trust Co. v. Island Oil & Transp. Corp.,* 34 F.2d 655 (2d Cir. 1929). Here, Mason made the comments in the course of representing a criminal defendant accused of quadruple homicide and did so during an interview solely related to that representation. Such circumstances would lead a reasonable person to question whether the requisite assent and actionable offer giving rise to contractual liability existed. Certainly, Mason's statements—made as a defense attorney in response to the prosecution's theory against his client—were far more likely to be a descriptive illustration of what that attorney saw as serious holes in the prosecution's theory instead of a serious offer to enter into a contract.

Nor can a valid contract be "inferred in whole or in part from the parties' conduct" in this case. *See L&H Constr. Co.* By way of comparison, consider *Lucy v. Zehmer,* 84 S.E.2d 516 (Va. 1954), the classic case describing and applying what we now know as the objective standard of assent. That court held that statements allegedly made "in jest" could result in an offer binding the parties to a contract, since "the law imputes to a person an intention corresponding to the reasonable meaning of his words and acts." Therefore, "a person cannot set up that he was merely jesting when his conduct and words would warrant a reasonable person in believing that he intended a real agreement."

Applying the objective standard here leads us to the real million-dollar question: "What did the party say and do?" Here, it is what both parties did not say and did not do that clearly distinguishes this case from those cases where an enforceable contract was formed. Mason did not engage in any discussion regarding his statements to NBC with Kolodziej, and, prior to Kolodziej demanding payment, there was no contact or communication between the parties. Mason neither confirmed that he made an offer nor asserted that the offer was serious. [Unlike in other cases where an offer has been found,] Mason did not have the payment set aside in escrow; nor had he ever declared that he had money set aside in case someone proved him wrong. Mason had not made his career out of the contention that the prosecution's case was implausible; nor did he make the statements in a commercial context for the "obvious purpose of advertising or promoting [his] goods or business." He did not create or promote the video that included his statement, nor did he increase the amount at issue. He did not, nor did the show include, any information to contact Mason about the challenge. Simply put, Mason's conduct lacks any indicia of assent to contract.

In fact, none of Mason's surrounding commentary—either in the unedited original interview or in the edited television broadcast—gave the slightest indication that his statement was anything other than a figure of speech. In the course of representing his client, Mason merely used a rhetorical expression to raise questions as to the prosecution's case. We could just as easily substitute a comparable idiom such as "I'll eat my hat" or "I'll be a monkey's uncle" into Mason's interview in the place of "I'll pay them a million dollars," and the outcome would be the same. We would not be inclined to make him either consume his headwear or assume a simian relationship were he to be proven wrong; nor will we make him pay one million dollars here.

In further illustration of the lack of assent to contract in this case, we question whether even Kolodziej's conduct—his "acceptance"—manifested assent to any perceived offer. Under the objective standard of assent, we do not look into the subjective minds of the parties; the law imputes an intention that corresponds with the reasonable meaning of a party's words and acts. We thus find it troublesome that, in all this time—ordering the transcript, studying it, purchasing tickets, recording himself making the trip—Kolodziej never made any effort to contact Mason to confirm the existence of an offer, to ensure any such offer was still valid after Serrano's conviction, or to address the details and terms of the challenge. However, we will not attribute bad intent when inexperience may suffice. Kolodziej may have learned in his contracts class that acceptance by performance results in an immediate, binding contract and that notice may not be necessary, but he apparently did not consider the absolute necessity of first having a specific, definite offer and the basic requirement of mutual assent. We simply are driven to ask, as Mason did in his response letter: "Why did you not just call?" Perhaps a judge's interpretation of an old aphorism provides the answer: "If, as Alexander Pope wrote, 'a little learning is a dangerous thing,' then a little learning in law is particularly perilous."

Just as people are free to contract, they are also free from contract, and we find it neither prudent nor permissible to impose contractual liability for offhand remarks or grandstanding. Nor would it be advisable to scrutinize a defense attorney's hyperbolic commentary for a hidden contractual agenda, particularly when that commentary concerns the substantial protections in place for criminal defendants. Having considered the content of Mason's statements, the context in which they were made, and the conduct of the parties, we do not find it reasonable to conclude that Mason assented to enter into a contract with anyone for one million dollars. Affirmed.

Advertisements

Advertisements are usually considered to be preliminary negotiations, rather than offers to sell. The general rule is that a store advertisement that merely names the company, describes the article to be sold, and gives the price of the article "constitutes nothing more than an invitation to patronize the store." And this is usually true even if the terms "offer" or "special offer" appear in the advertisement.

The historic rationale for this rule is based (1) on the fact that most advertisements are silent on other material matters, such as the available quantity and credit terms, (2) on the traditional principle that sellers of goods have the right to choose the parties with whom they deal and do not intend to commit themselves to sell to the potentially unlimited numbers of persons who might read advertisements, and (3) on the fact that a merchandiser cannot exactly predict the volume of responses from customers and would therefore not usually intend to be legally committed whenever a customer responds that she wants the advertised item. The rule also applies to catalogs, price quotations, and even articles displayed on a shelf with a price tag; these also are generally treated as not being offers to sell the merchandise.

Thus, when a customer goes to the advertiser's store and tenders the advertised price, a contract is normally not formed. Rather, the customer is making an offer to purchase, which the store can accept or reject.

Exceptions can arise in a few circumstances, however, in which advertisements can be offers. An advertisement may be an offer in several related types of situations in which the quantity is clearly limited, or the number of possible persons who can accept is clearly limited, and other language is used indicating that the seller is making a promise to sell to the first ones who respond in the way called for in the advertisement. For example, many courts probably would treat the following advertisement as being an offer to sell: "Three 2007 Mazda MX-5 Miata convertibles with R305 trim package at $22,395.00 each, on sale Saturday only while they last!" Thus, the first three buyers who show up the following Saturday ready, willing, and able to pay the advertised price are accepting the offer and creating an enforceable contract. A similar example, from *Lefkowitz v. Great Minneapolis Surplus Store*, 86 N.W.2d 689 (Minnesota 1957), involved an advertisement stating: "1 Black Lapin Stole, Beautiful, Worth $139.50 . . . $1.00, Saturday 8 a.m., First-Come, First-Served." The court found that this was a definite offer, and when the first customer showed up after the store opened at 8 a.m. ready and able to buy the fur stole, there was an acceptance creating a contract. Yet another example would be: "Any person entering our store on Christmas Day wearing a bathing suit can buy an XYZ CD Player for only $220." Likewise, an ad (or instructions on a product package) that instructs customers to send in a "proof-of-purchase" from a product package, in return for which the seller will provide a rebate or something else to the customer, will typically be an offer. An advertisement or product package providing a coupon that a customer is instructed to send or bring, with some benefit being promised in return, will typically be an offer.

In a similar vein, advertisements of rewards are usually treated by the courts as being offers. For example, an advertised reward for the return of a missing dog would be an enforceable offer if it is clear and definite, since realistically there can be only one person accepting (or, say, two people who act together and share the reward), and because it calls for specific action that will constitute acceptance—returning the dog.

Likewise, advertisements promising rewards for information leading to the apprehension of criminals are usually held to constitute offers. Even though several people might be in a position to accept by providing the information, the number will normally be very small, and reward offers clearly call for specific action by the responder. Obviously, the evidence must show that the person returning the dog, providing the information about the criminal, and so on, must have known of the offer before taking the action. If there was no such knowledge, the person returning the dog or providing the information was not an offeree of the offer. One can see that advertisements found by the courts to constitute offers are either offers for a unilateral contract or otherwise make it clear that something is being definitely promised in return for specific conduct on the part of the person or persons responding.

Consumer Protection

The general rule on advertising creates the potential for abuse by unscrupulous merchants who might place advertisements, never intending to live up to their terms. Virtually all states have enacted consumer protection statutes that generally impose civil and/or criminal liability upon businesses who unfairly refuse to sell goods or services in conformity with the terms of their offer. For example, statutes in many states list deceptive trade practices, among which is the "advertising of goods or services with the intent not to sell them as advertised." Other states have special "bait and switch" advertising statutes which typically impose liability upon advertisers who lure readers into the store by offering fabulous deals on products, but then either have an insufficient quantity for an expected reasonable demand or focus all their sales efforts at convincing the shoppers to buy more expensive items that were not advertised.

Auctions

If conducted openly and fairly, auctions are an efficient way of determining a reasonable price in transactions between willing sellers and buyers. The UCC auction provision, Sec. 2-328, is generally consistent with common-law auction rules. In the typical "with reserve" auction, the act of putting a particular item up for auction indicates only a willingness to consider offers to purchase. A bidder's ensuing bid is treated as an offer which may be accepted when the auctioneer (the seller's agent) announces "sold" either verbally or through the fall of the hammer or some other customary means. Because no contract is formed until the hammer falls, the bidders are free to withdraw their bids prior to that event and, more importantly, the seller is free to withdraw the item from sale if no bids are as high as the seller desires.

Auctions are presumed to be with reserve unless they are explicitly represented as being "without reserve." The act of putting an article up for sale in a without reserve auction is treated as a definite offer. The first bid creates a contract binding on the seller, unless a higher bid is made. The seller can no longer withdraw the item (although, somewhat illogically, bidders may withdraw their bids until the hammer falls). The highest bidder has a contract for sale that he can enforce.

Reasonable Definiteness

The requirement that the offer be reasonably definite is largely a practical one. The terms of an agreement have to be definite enough that a court can determine whether both parties lived up to their promises, in the event that a question of breach of contract arises. If the offer is too indefinite, the court is unable to do this.

As a general rule, then, a communication must cover all major matters affecting the proposed transaction in order to constitute an offer. If one or more of these is missing, the communication is merely a preliminary negotiation. Thus if S makes a written proposal to sell his farm Blackacre to B upon specified terms and conditions, "at a mutually agreeable price," and if B promptly sends an acceptance, there is no contract for the reason that S's proposal was not an offer. In a similar case, a company told an injured employee that it would "take care of him" and offer him "light work" when his doctor certified that he was capable of doing such a job. The company later refused to rehire him, and he sued to recover damages, alleging that this was a breach of contract. In ruling against the employee, the court said that since no specific position was mentioned, and there was no discussion of rates of pay or hours of employment, it had no way of determining the amount of the employee's loss. The statement of the company, in other words, was held to be too indefinite to constitute an offer. *Laseter v. Pet Dairy Products Company*, 246 F.2d 747 (1957). Similarly, if X writes Y, "I will sell you my car for $1,000, credit terms to be arranged," and Y replies, "I accept," there is no contract. X's statement does not constitute an offer, since there is no way of knowing what credit terms would be acceptable to her or whether any credit terms will ever be agreed on.

Despite the foregoing, the requirement of "reasonable definiteness" is, as the term itself indicates, relative rather than absolute. Thus it is not necessary that every detail be set forth in a contract, so long as there is agreement on major points. Where there is such agreement, missing terms about routine or mechanical matters may be supplied by the courts to "save" the contract; they may say in regard to such matters that there was implied agreement. For example, if X agrees to do certain clean-up work around a construction site for Y for $1,000, neither party can successfully contend that the agreement was too vague simply because no time of performance was specified. In this situation, it is implied that X will have a reasonable time in which to perform.

It also is important to note that, when courts believe that the parties intended to commit themselves to a contract, but some terms are either missing or ambiguous, they will examine other relevant evidence of what reasonable people probably would have intended the particular terms to be. Because this is another question of intent, courts will consider relevant evidence of the same kinds mentioned earlier in connection with determining the initial question of whether there was any intent to make a contractual commitment in the first place. Courts will not engage in guesswork, however, but must have actual evidence from which reasonable conclusions may be drawn. For example, in *MPG Petroleum, Inc. v. CrossTex CCNG Marketing, Ltd,*, 2006 WL 2831018 (Tex.App. 2007), one company agreed to buy gas delivered by the other at to-be-agreed-upon "points of interconnection" between their two sets of facilities. The parties signed a "letter of agreement," but never did agree upon where the "points of interconnection" should be. The court held that this was an essential term of the contract and the failure to agree upon it prevented the "letter of agreement" from constituting a binding contract.

Definiteness of the Agreement: Sales Law

Among the most significant modifications of the common law achieved by the UCC is a general relaxation of the degree of definiteness required in the agreement. Several provisions indicate that the drafters of the UCC wanted to make the formation of binding contracts somewhat easier than under common law. They recognized that businesspersons frequently intend to enter into enforceable agreements in situations where it is impracticable to make those agreements as definite as required by common law. A prime example of this approach is found in Sec. 2-204(3). This section broadly states that a sales contract is enforceable even if one or more terms are left open, so long as (1) the court feels that the parties intended to make a binding contract and (2) the agreement and the surrounding circumstances give the court a reasonably certain basis for granting an appropriate remedy (such as money damages). Of course, there is a line beyond which the courts will not go. For instance, the larger the number of undecided terms, the less likely it is that a court will find that the parties intended to be legally bound. For this reason, a seller and buyer who wish to make an agreement with one or more terms left for future determination would do well to state specifically whether they intend to be bound in the meantime.

In addition to Sec. 2-204, a number of other sections of the UCC deal with specific omissions or ambiguities often occurring in sales contracts. We will examine the most important of these "gap-fillers" here.

Open Price Provisions. In some circumstances a seller of goods may be primarily concerned with being assured of a market for the goods they are producing. Or perhaps a buyer wants a guaranteed supply of certain needed products. In either case price may be of only secondary importance. Thus buyer and seller might draw up a contract for the sale and purchase of goods at a later date, with the contract providing that the price shall be agreed upon later. Or the contract may say nothing about price at all. (Open price terms may be especially desirable in a market where the going price is subject to daily or weekly fluctuation.)

At common law many courts refused to enforce either type of agreement because of its indefiniteness. Under Sec. 2-305 of the UCC, however, agreements of this nature are now enforceable if the court feels that the parties did intend to be bound by them. (Of course, if the evidence indicates that the agreement was merely tentative and the parties intended to be legally bound only if and when the price was ultimately set, there is no contract until that condition is met. The UCC cannot supply missing contractual intent.)

Whenever a court is called upon to enforce a contract in which the price (for one reason or another) was never actually set, and where it finds that the parties intended to be bound by the open price agreement, the court is faced with the task of providing a price term. Sec. 2-305 establishes a number of principles to guide the court in such a situation.

1. If the parties had expressly left the price for later agreement and then failed to agree, the price set by the court should be a "reasonable price at the time for delivery."

2. If the agreement had said nothing at all about price, and the price was never settled on, the method of determining it should depend on the circumstances. If the price had failed to be set through no fault of either party, the court should fix a "reasonable price at the time for delivery," as in item 1. But if the failure to set a price was caused by the fault of either party, the party not at fault can either treat the contract as cancelled or fix a "reasonable price" himself or herself. This price is binding and the court will uphold it, so long as it is found to be actually reasonable.

3. If the agreement had provided that the price was to be subsequently fixed according to a definite standard set or recorded by a third party, the rules for determining the unresolved price are exactly as they were in item 2. For example, the parties might have agreed that the contract price was to be the market price reported in a certain trade journal on a given date, but no such price was reported in the journal on that date. Or they might have agreed that an impartial third person was to set the price at a future date, but the third party later failed to do so. In either case, the price will be a "reasonable price at the time for delivery." This reasonable price will be set by the court if neither party was at fault; if one party caused the agreed upon method to fail, the other party may set a reasonable price.

4. If the parties had agreed that one of them was to set the price at a later time, the deciding party is obligated to set the price in good faith. Although good faith is defined differently for merchants and nonmerchants, the most compelling evidence of good or bad faith generally is whether the price fixed was a reasonable market price at that time. Good faith is generally defined in Sec. 1- 201(19) of the UCC as "honesty in fact." In the case of a merchant, it is defined in Sec. 2-103 (1) (b) as "honesty in fact and the observance of reasonable commercial standards of fair dealing in the trade." Generally, the merchant definition will apply, since open price terms are rare among nonmerchants. If the party responsible for setting the price fails to do so or if they fix a price in bad faith, the other party can either treat the contract as cancelled or set a reasonable price.

Open Time Provisions. The absence of a time provision does not cause a sales contract to be unenforceable. Sec. 2-309 states that, where a contract calls for some type of action by the seller (such as shipment or delivery) but does not specify the time for such action, a court may infer a "reasonable time" for performance. Of course, a reasonable time in a given case depends on all the circumstances known to the parties. For instance, suppose that the parties did not set a specific time for delivery but that the seller knew the reason for the buyer's purchase and the use to which the buyer intended to put the goods. A reasonable time for delivery would certainly be soon enough for the buyer to put the goods to their intended use.

Open Delivery Provisions. A sale of goods contract may also be enforceable even if certain delivery terms are to be decided at a later time. Another delivery term that might be absent is a provision for the place of delivery. Where the parties have not included this provision in their contract, Sec. 2-308 sets forth the following rules to serve as "gap-fillers."

1. The goods should be delivered to the buyer at the seller's place of business.

2. If the seller has no place of business, they should be delivered to the buyer at the seller's residence.

3. Where the contract refers to specifically identified goods, and both parties knew when making the contract that the goods were located at some other place, that place is where delivery should be made.

The UCC also attempts to account for other omitted details relating to delivery. For example, if the agreement contemplates shipping the goods but does not mention shipping arrangements, the seller has the right under Sec. 2-311 to specify these arrangements. (His or her actions are subject only to the limitation that they be in good faith and within limits set by commercial reasonableness.) Another example is the situation where the contract fails to indicate whether the goods are to be delivered all at once, or in several lots. In such a case Sec. 2-307 obligates the seller to deliver them all at one time. However, there is one exception to this duty. If both parties, when making the contract, know that the circumstances are such that delivery in a single lot is not practicable, then the seller can deliver in several lots. This would apply, for instance, to a situation where the quantity involved is so large that both parties realize that a single shipment is not feasible. In that case, the UCC provides that the seller should deliver in the smallest number of shipments that are reasonably feasible.

Open Payment Provisions. UCC Sec. 2-310 is a "gap-filler" for contracts that are silent as to the time of the buyer's performance—that is, the time of payment. The basic rule is that unless the parties have otherwise agreed, payment is due at the time and place at which the buyer is to receive the goods. The buyer generally has the right to inspect the goods (and reject them if they do not conform to the contractual requirements) before making the payment, unless the contract provides otherwise.

Communication of the Offer

Returning to the common-law principles applicable to the formation of all types of contracts, it is a primary rule that an offer has no effect until it has legally reached the offeree. This requirement of communication is based on the obvious proposition that an offeree cannot agree to a proposal before knowing about it. To illustrate: A city council, via a public advertisement, offers to pay $200 to the person or persons who apprehend an escaped criminal. If X captures the fugitive on his farm, only to learn of the offer later, his act does not constitute an acceptance of the offer and he is not entitled to the reward under the principles of contract law. The relatively few cases that involve this kind of fact pattern generally follow this view. (However, a *few* courts have allowed recovery on noncontract grounds, such as public policy.)

The principle takes on broader scope—and is more difficult to apply—in situations where there has been clear-cut communication of some terms of the agreement but questionable communication of others. The so-called fine print cases illustrate the problem. For example, statements printed on the back of parking lot tickets frequently provide that "the company shall not be liable for loss of, or injury to, the automobile, regardless of cause," or words of similar import. The usual view is that such provisions have not been legally communicated to the owner of the car and that the owner is not bound by them unless they were actually brought to his or her attention when the contract was made.

One should not conclude, however, that an actual communication of all terms is required in all cases. If a court feels that the offeror has made a reasonable effort, under the circumstances, to call the terms of the offer to the offeree's attention, then a legal communication has occurred. A subsequent acceptance of the offer would be binding on the offeree in such a case, even though they might not have been aware of all its terms.

The case of *Green's Executors v. Smith*, 131 S.E. 846 (1926) is particularly instructive. In that case Smith sent a folder to each of his auto storage garage patrons, which indicated on the cover, in large type, that "new storage rates" would be effective at a future date. Inside the folder various rates were set forth, followed by a "note" which provided, in effect, that commencing with the new rates, patrons would also accept liability for injuries to third parties caused by Smith's drivers while taking the cars to and from patrons' homes. Subsequent litigation raised the question whether patrons were bound by the note even if they had not read it.

The court held that they were not. Quoting from an earlier decision, the court said: "When an offer contains various terms, some of which do not appear on the face of the offer, the question whether the offeree is bound by the terms depends on the circumstances. . . . The question arises when a person accepts a railroad or steamboat ticket, bill of lading, warehouse receipt, or other document containing conditions. He is bound by all the conditions whether he reads them or not if he knows that the document contains conditions. But he is not bound by conditions of which he is ignorant . . . unless he knows that the writing contains terms or unless he ought to know that it contains terms, by reason of previous dealings, or by reason of the form, size, or character of the document." The court continued: "There was nothing on the face of the folder, nor in its form or character, to indicate that it contained [a liability change]. The paper only purported to contain a schedule of rates for services at plaintiff's garage, and defendant had no reason, on account of her previous dealings with plaintiff or otherwise, to know that plaintiff proposed . . . a new contract of such unusual terms."

The case below presents the issue of communication of the offer in a web-based transaction. On the issue presented here, there is a split among state and federal courts, and not all of them would reach the same conclusion as in the following case. The case does, however, present an excellent example of how courts try to analyze the question of whether all of the terms of an offer have been effectively communicated.

CULLINANE v. UBER TECHNOLOGIES, INC.
United States Court of Appeals, First Circuit (893 F.3d 53 2018)

Uber provides a ride-hailing service that transports customers throughout some cities, including Boston. Uber licenses the Uber mobile application to the public so that users may request transportation services from independent third party providers in the users' local area. To be able to request and pay for third party transportation services, Uber App users must first register with Uber by creating an account. At the time plaintiffs created their accounts, prospective users could either register through the Uber App or register directly through Uber's website.

All four plaintiffs downloaded the Uber App on iPhones and used it to create Uber accounts. When they used Uber's App to order transportation, they were charged for tolls that they do not believe they were required to pay. They sued for a refund. The case ended up in federal court and the trial judge granted Uber's motion to compel arbitration and dismissed the case. Plaintiffs appealed.

TORRUELLA, Circuit Judge:

All prospective Uber passengers must go through Uber's registration process. When plaintiffs used the Uber App to register, the process included three different screens that asked for user information. The first screen, titled "Create an Account," asked users to enter an e-mail address, a mobile phone number, and a password for the account. Immediately above the phone's keyboard—which occupied half of the phone screen—written in dark gray against a black background, was the text: "We use your email and mobile number to send you ride confirmations and receipts." The second screen, "Create a Profile," required the user to enter a first and last name and a photo. The third and final screen prompted the user to enter the appropriate payment information for Uber's services. The third screen, the "Link Card" screen, looked like this:

As depicted in this screenshot, the screen contained a thick gray bar at the top of the screen with the title "Link Card." To the left of the title was a "CANCEL" button and to the right was a nonworking and barely visible "DONE" button. Below the thick gray title bar was a blank text field where users could enter their credit card information. The blank text field was white, contrasting with the black background, horizontally traversing the screen, and included some light gray numbers to exemplify the type of information required. In addition, at the beginning of the blank text field, and to the left of the light gray numbers, there was an icon representing a credit card. The "Link Card" screen automatically included a number pad covering half of the screen for users to enter credit card information.

The screen also included text, just below the blank text field, that instructed users to "scan your card" and "enter promo code." This text was written in light gray bolded font. The "scan your card" text had a bright blue camera icon to its left, and the "enter promo code" had a bright blue bullet-shaped icon enclosed in a circle. The record is unclear as to whether the "scan your card" and "enter promo code" texts were clickable buttons.

Finally, the "Link Card" or "Link Payment" screen (this changed a little over time) also included dark gray text which read: "By creating an Uber account, you agree to the:" Below this text was the phrase "Terms of Service & Privacy Policy" in bold white text enclosed in a gray rectangle. According to Uber, this rectangular box indicated that this phrase was a "clickable button."

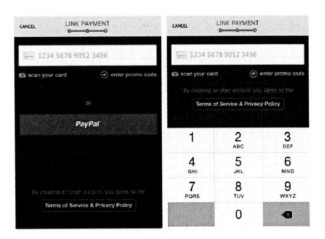

This screen provided payment options for PayPal or a credit card. Below these choices, at the bottom of the screen, appeared "By creating an Uber account you agree to the Terms of Service & Privacy Policy."

If the user selected the blank text field to their credit card information, the user would then "engage the keyboard" and the "Link Payment" screen would resemble the "Link Card" screen. In the alternative, a user choosing the PayPal option would be temporarily sent to the PayPal site to enter PayPal login information and then be returned to the Uber app. All screens included a gray bar at the top. Within this bar the user was presented with the screen title written in capital letters in a dark colored font. Below the title, but within the gray bar, was an illustration of three circles connected by a green line. These circles indicated the user's progress through Uber's registration process.

In addition, on all screens the gray bar incorporated two buttons: one to the left and one to the right of the screen's title. The left button was a "CANCEL" button, written in all capital letters. This button was enabled throughout the registration process, even before the user interacted with the screen. On the first two screens the right button was a "NEXT" button, also written in all capital letters. The "NEXT" button would remain barely visible and inoperative until after the user had entered the required information for each screen. In both versions of the third screen, the "NEXT" button was replaced by a "DONE" button. The "DONE" button was barely visible and inoperable until the user entered the payment information.

Uber's Terms and Conditions (the "Agreement") consisted of an approximately ten-page document that was available to Uber App users during the registration process via a hyperlink. If the user "clicked" on the "Terms of Service & Privacy Policy" button on the third screen, he or she would be taken to another screen that contained two additional clickable buttons entitled "Terms & Conditions" and "Privacy Policy." The Agreement was displayed on the user's screen once the "Terms & Conditions" button was clicked. However, the Uber App did not require prospective users to "click" any of these buttons or access the Agreement before they could complete the registration process. Uber's "Terms of Service & Privacy Policy" button was a hyperlink.

Plaintiffs allege that most Uber users would have accessed this document on a mobile phone converting the document to over thirty-five pages of text on an approximately 4.7-inch iPhone screen. The "Agreement" included, among a great many other sections, a "Dispute Resolution" clause providing that "The user and Uber agree that any dispute, claim or controversy arising out of or relating to this Agreement or the breach, termination, enforcement, interpretation or validity thereof or the use of the Service or Application will be settled by binding arbitration administered by the American Arbitration Association.... **You acknowledge and agree that you and Uber are each waiving the right to a trial by jury or to participate as a plaintiff in any class action or representative proceeding.**"

Under the FAA (Federal Arbitration Act), a written provision in a contract to settle by arbitration a controversy thereafter arising out of such contract is be valid, irrevocable, and enforceable. Nevertheless, the FAA does not require parties to arbitrate when they have not agreed to do so. Therefore, in deciding a motion to compel arbitration, a court must first determine whether there exists a written agreement to arbitrate. When deciding whether the parties agreed to arbitrate a certain matter, courts generally should apply ordinary state-law principles that govern the formation of contracts.

Any provision in a proposed contract, including an arbitration clause, will be enforced if it has been reasonably communicated and accepted. Reasonably conspicuous notice of the existence of contract terms and unambiguous manifestation of assent to those terms by consumers are essential if electronic bargaining is to have integrity and credibility. With this in mind, there is a two-step inquiry for the enforceability of clauses in online agreements. The burden to show that the terms were reasonably communicated and then accepted lies on the party seeking to enforce the term in question.

Uber makes no claim that any of the plaintiffs actually saw the arbitration clause or even clicked on the "Terms of Service & Privacy Policy" button. Rather, it relies solely on a claim that its online presentation was sufficiently conspicuous as to bind the plaintiffs whether or not they chose to click through the relevant terms. Therefore, we must determine whether the terms of the Agreement were reasonably communicated to the plaintiffs. We note that in the context of web-based contracts, clarity and conspicuousness are a function of the design and content of the relevant interface.

"Conspicuous" means that a terms is so written, displayed or presented that a reasonable person against which it is to operate ought to have noticed it. Whether or not a term is conspicuous is for the court to decide. Several non-exhaustive examples of general characteristics that make a term conspicuous include using larger and contrasting font, the use of headings in capitals, or somehow setting off the term from the surrounding text by the use of symbols or other marks. In addition, when the terms of the agreement are only available by following a link, the court must examine the language that was used to notify users that the terms of their arrangement could be found by following the link, how prominently displayed the link was, and any other information that would bear on the reasonableness of communicating the terms.

After reviewing the Uber App registration process, we find that the plaintiffs were not reasonably notified of the terms of the proposed agreement. We note at the outset that

Uber chose not to use a common method of conspicuously informing users of the existence and location of terms and conditions: requiring users to click a box stating that they agree to a set of terms, often provided by hyperlink, before continuing to the next screen. Instead, Uber chose to rely on simply displaying a notice of deemed acquiescence and a link to the terms. In order to determine whether that approach reasonably notified users of the Agreement, we begin our analysis with how this link was displayed.

Uber contends that the gray rectangular box with the language "Terms of Service & Privacy Policy" was reasonably conspicuous, both visually and contextually, because it was displayed in a larger font, in bold, contrasting in color, and highlighted by the box around it. Furthermore, Uber argues that the screen contained a total of twenty-six words, making it difficult for a user to miss it.

While the language and the number of words found on the "Link Card" and "Link Payment" screens could be seen to favor Uber's position, the reading of Uber's "Terms of Service & Privacy Policy" hyperlink must be contextualized. That is, it may not be read in a vacuum. Other similarly displayed terms presented simultaneously to the user in both versions of the third screen diminished the conspicuousness of the "Terms of Service & Privacy Policy" hyperlink.

Uber's "Terms of Service & Privacy Policy" hyperlink did not have the common appearance of a hyperlink. While not all hyperlinks need to have the same characteristics, they are commonly blue and underlined. Here, the "Terms of Service & Privacy Policy" hyperlink was presented in a gray rectangular box in white bold text. Though this does not decided the issue by itself, the characteristics of the hyperlink raise concerns as to whether a reasonable user would have been aware that the gray rectangular box was actually a hyperlink.

Next, the overall content of the "Link Card" and "Link Payment" screens show that the "Terms of Service & Privacy Policy" hyperlink was not a conspicuous term. Along with the "Terms of Service & Privacy Policy" hyperlink, the "Link Card" and "Link Payment" screens contained other terms displayed with similar features. For example, the terms "scan your card" and "enter promo code" were also written in bold and with a similarly sized font as the hyperlink. Both versions of the third screen also included the words "CANCEL" and "DONE"—the latter being barely visible until the user had entered the required payment information—in all capital letters and dark colored font. Meanwhile, the top of the screens featured the terms "Link Card" or "Link Payment" in large capital letters and dark colored font. These had the largest-sized font in both versions of the third screen.

Uber's "Terms of Service & Privacy Policy" hyperlink was even less conspicuous on the "Link Payment" screen. The inclusion of the additional payment option and the placement of a large blue PayPal button in the middle of the screen were more attention-grabbing and displaced the hyperlink to the bottom of the screen.

It is thus the design and content of the "Link Card" and "Link Payment" screens of the Uber App interface that lead us to conclude that Uber's "Terms of Service & Privacy Policy" hyperlink was not conspicuous. Even though the hyperlink did possess some of the characteristics that make a term conspicuous, the presence of other terms on the same screen with a similar or larger size, typeface, and with more noticeable attributes diminished the hyperlink's capability to grab the user's attention. If everything on the screen is written with conspicuous features, then nothing is conspicuous.

Furthermore, when we consider the characteristics of the text used to notify potential users that the creation of an Uber account would bind them to the linked terms, we note that this phrase was even less conspicuous than the "Terms of Service & Privacy Policy" hyperlink. This notice was displayed in a dark gray small-sized non-bolded font against a black background. The notice simply did not have any distinguishable feature that would set it apart from all the other terms surrounding it.

Because both the "Link Card" and "Link Payment" screens were filled with other very noticeable terms that diminished the conspicuousness of the "Terms of Service & Privacy Policy" hyperlink and the notice, we find that the terms of the Agreement were not reasonably communicated to the Plaintiffs. As such, Uber's motion to compel arbitration fails, and the litigation can continue in court.

TERMINATION OF THE OFFER

Because of the rule that an offer can be accepted at any time before it is legally terminated, it becomes necessary to see what events will cause the offer to die. The rules in this area of the law are rather mechanical in their operation, and we need touch upon them but briefly.

Termination by Act of the Parties

Most offers are terminated by the conduct of the parties themselves by (1) revocation, (2) rejection, or (3) lapse of time.

Revocation

A revocation is a withdrawal of the offer by the offeror. Like the offer itself, it is effective only when it has been communicated to the offeree. Thus, in almost all states, a revocation sent my mail, courier service, or other independent intermediary is effective to terminate the offer only when actually received. (However, in one state, California, a revocation is effective when sent by such means.)

The ordinary offer can be revoked at any time—assuming, of course, that it is communicated to the offeree before an acceptance has occurred. This is generally true even if the offeror had promised to keep the offer open a certain length of time. Thus, if X makes an offer to Y, stating that the offer will remain open thirty days, X can revoke it the very next day if he wishes. While this may seem unfair to Y, the reason for this view lies in the fact that Y has not given "consideration" (something of value) in return for X's promise to keep the offer open.

There are two notable exceptions to the general rule that an offer may be revoked at any time prior to its acceptance.

Option. In an *option* (or option contract, as it is frequently called) the offeree—either at the request of the offeror or acting on his or her own initiative—does give the offeror some consideration (usually a sum of money, but it can take other forms) in return for the offeror's promise to keep the offer open. Once the consideration is accepted by the offeror, the offer cannot be revoked during the specified period of time.

Thus, assume that X says to Y: "I offer to sell my farm to you for $100,000, this offer to remain open for 30 days." Y knows the general rule is that X may revoke this offer at any time before acceptance, yet Y truly wishes to buy the farm and needs time to line up his financing. Y may offer to pay X $50 in exchange for X's promise to keep the offer open for 30 days. If X accepts, an option contract is formed and X must keep the offer open. The amount paid for the option need not be a large sum, and a counteroffer will not terminate the offer.

Sales Law—The Firm Offer. The general rule and exception noted above apply with equal force to sales transactions. However, for sale of goods transactions, the UCC has added a second exception to the general rule by creating another type of irrevocable offer, referred to in Sec. 2-205 as a *firm offer*.

The following requirements must exist for an offer to be irrevocable under this section:

1. It must be an offer to buy or sell goods.

2. It must be made *by* a merchant.

3. It must be written and signed by the offeror.

4. It must give assurance that it will be held open.

If all these requirements are met, the offer is irrevocable even if the offeree gives no consideration for the assurance that it will remain open.

The period of time during which the offeror cannot revoke the offer is the time stated in the offer so long as it does not exceed three months. If the offer contains an assurance that it will be held open but mentions no time period, it will be irrevocable for a reasonable time, again not exceeding three months. (The three-month limitation applies only where the offeree is relying on Sec. 2-205 to make the offer irrevocable. If they give consideration for the offeror's assurance that the offer will remain open, an option exists, and the three-month limitation does not apply. Likewise, the other conditions necessary for Sec. 2-205 do not apply if an option has been created.)

Rejection

A rejection occurs when the offeree notifies the offeror that they do not intend to accept. Like the offer and the revocation, it takes effect only when it has been communicated (in this case, to the offeror). Thus, if an offeree mails a letter of rejection but changes his or her mind and telephones an acceptance before the letter arrives, there is a contract. One form of rejection is the counteroffer—a proposal made by the offeree to the offeror that differs in any material respect from the terms of the original offer. Thus, if the price stated in an offer is $500, and the offeree replies, "I'll pay $400," the original offer is ended forever. A recent case, *Thurmond v. Weiser*, 699 S.W.2d 680 (Tex. 1985), provides a further illustration. There the owner of a small Texas farm offered to sell it for $260,000. The buyer made a counter-offer of $250,000, which was rejected by the seller. Several negotiations ensued, which ended with the buyer sending a written ''acceptance'' of the $260,000 offer. The owner refused to convey the land, and in subsequent litigation it was held that there was no contract. The court ruled (1) that the original offer to sell for $260,000 was terminated by the buyer's counteroffer of $250,000, and (2) that because the seller did not renew her offer of $260,000 during the negotiations following the counteroffer, there was no outstanding offer capable of being accepted by the buyer.

A response in which the offeree deletes a term from, or adds a term to, the terms of the offer also constitutes a counteroffer. In the preceding case, for example, if the buyer had replied to the original offer, "Accept offer of $260,000; assume highway commission's proposed plan to relocate road on north side will be abandoned," the offer is again terminated.

Lapse of Time

If revocation and rejection were the only recognized means of terminating offers, many offers would remain open forever. To prevent such an unworkable result, a third method of termination is recognized—termination by the mere passage of a reasonable length of time. If not otherwise terminated, and if not accepted, an offer will terminate after the passage of a time stated in the offer as being its duration. If the offer does not state a time when it will expire, it will termination upon the passage of a reasonable period of time. What is reasonable depends on the circumstances of each case; thus it is virtually impossible to formulate general rules in this area of law.

What we will do instead is list the circumstances or factors that the courts consider in reaching an answer in a given case.

1. A circumstance of particular importance is the language used in the offer. Obviously, if an offeror states, "I must hear from you very soon," the time within which the offeree must accept is somewhat shorter than if such language were not used.

2. Another important circumstance is the means of communication used by the offeror. Sending the offer by overnight express (express mail or courier service) normally implies an urgency that the use of regular mail does not.

3. Yet another factor of special importance is based upon prevailing market conditions. If the price of a commodity is fluctuating rapidly, for example, a reasonable time might elapse within hours or even minutes from the time the offer is received.

4. A final factor to be taken into consideration is the method by which the parties have done business in the past.

An offer in some circumstances may thus lapse soon after it has been made, while in other circumstances it may remain open weeks or even months. While there are surprisingly few cases in this area of law, *Ward v. Board of Education*, 173 N.E. 634 (1930) is one of them. In that case Ward received an offer of employment for the following school year on June 18, and she mailed her acceptance on July 5. In subsequent litigation, the higher court stated the applicable rule as follows: "It is a primary rule that a party contracting by mail, as she did, when no time limit is made for the acceptance of the contract, shall have a reasonable time, acting with due diligence, within which to accept." Applying that rule, where Ms. Ward had no explanation for her delay other than the fact that she was hoping to hear from another school board, the court held that the offer had lapsed prior to July 5 and there was, therefore, no contract. The fact that the new school year would start fairly soon had an effect on what would be considered a reasonable time.

Termination by Operation of Law

The rule that a revocation must be communicated to the offeree in order for it to take effect is based on the grounds of both fairness and logic. In ordinary circumstances, it seems reasonable that the offeree ought to be legally able to accept any offer until they have been put on notice that the offer has been terminated.

Certain exceptional events, however, will terminate an offer automatically—without notice to the offeree. These events fall into three categories: (1) death or adjudication of insanity of either party, (2) destruction of the subject matter of the contract, and (3) intervening illegality. The termination of an offer by any of these events is said to occur by operation of law.

To illustrate: On September 10, B offers a specific TV set to W for $525. On September 13, B dies. If W mails a letter of acceptance on September 14, there is no contract even if W is unaware of B's death. In the same example the result would be identical if, instead of B's death on September 13, the TV set were destroyed that day through no fault of B's. As another example, X offers to loan $1,000 to Y for one year with interest at the rate of 20 percent. Before the offer is accepted, a state statute takes effect which limits the rate of interest on that particular type of loan to 14 percent. The offer is terminated automatically.

The various events that automatically terminate unaccepted offers generally do not terminate existing contracts (except those calling for the rendering of personal services, which we will discuss in Chapter 17). Thus, in the first example, if B's offer of September 10 had been accepted by W before B's death on September 13, B's estate would remain bound by the obligation to deliver the TV set.

Similarly, the various terminations by operation of law do not generally apply to options because they are actually contracts themselves. Thus, if B had promised on September 10 to keep his offer open for ten days, and if W had given B a sum of money in return for this promise, B's death on September 13 would not terminate the offer.

Figure 11.1 summarizes the various ways by which an offer may terminate.

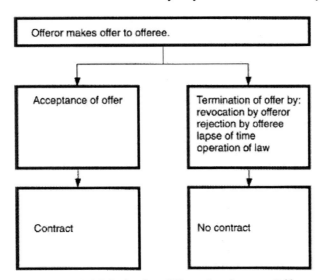

Figure 11.1 Methods of Terminating an Offer

THE ACCEPTANCE

An offer ripens into a contract if, and only if, it is accepted by the offeree. Remember that a bilateral offer is accepted by the offeree's making the return promise that the offeror has requested, while a unilateral offer is accepted only by the actual performance of the requested act.

In the average situation, the offeree's response to the offer is so clearly an acceptance or so clearly is not an acceptance that there are no misunderstandings between the parties. Sometimes, however, legal difficulties do crop up—as, for example, where the offeree "accepts" the offer but then adds new terms to it or where the offeree's response is vague or indecisive. Another difficulty is the determination of the precise moment at which the acceptance becomes effective—specifically, whether the acceptance has to be actually communicated to the offeror before it becomes legally effective.

In the following discussion, emphasis is given to the acceptance of offers for bilateral contracts—those in which the offeror merely wants a return promise on the part of the offeree. Special problems raised by the acceptance of unilateral offers are considered later in the chapter.

Requirements of the Acceptance

An acceptance is an expression on the part of the offeree by which they indicate a definite intent to be bound by the terms of the offer. Under general contract law, the acceptance must be a "mirror image" of the offer. Thus if a purported (intended) acceptance varies from the terms of the offer in any way—sometimes called a conditional acceptance—it ordinarily constitutes a counteroffer rather than an acceptance, as illustrated in Figure 11.2.

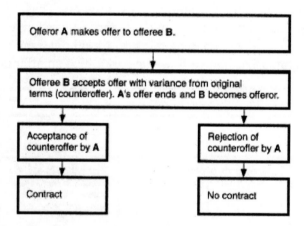

Figure 11.2 Legal Ramifications of the Counteroffer

While an offeree usually states expressly that they are accepting the offer, it is not necessary that this particular term be used. Any language showing that the offeree is definitely assenting to the proposal is sufficient. Regardless of the particular words used by the offeree in his or her response to the offer, the response must meet certain requirements in order to constitute an acceptance. An acceptance (1) must demonstrate a definite, present intent to accept the offer, (2) must be unconditional and not add any terms that are additional to or different from those of the offer, and (3) must be legally communicated to the offeror or to the offeror's agent.

Requirement of a Definite Indication of Intent to Accept

An acceptance is an expression on the part of the offeree by which they indicate a definite intent to be bound by the terms of the offer. Here, the same rules apply and the same types of evidence are considered as when the question was whether the alleged offeror had actually made an offer. Both parties must manifest a definite intent to be legally bound to a contract on reasonably definite terms.

To illustrate: X, in response to an advertisement placed by Y, sends a bid to Y offering to perform the described landscaping work for $23,000. Y replies by telegram: "offer satisfies all requirements; will give it my prompt attention." Subsequently, Y hires another landscaper to do the job, and, when X sues Y to recover damages for breach of contract, Y contends that his response did not constitute an acceptance of the offer. Applying the general rule to this case, Y's reply is too indefinite and tentative to satisfy the requirement that there be a definite manifestation of intent to accept. Thus Y is correct in his contention that a contract was not formed. On the other hand, each case has to be decided on its own merits, including consideration of the circumstances surrounding the communications. Thus a different result might be reached in the foregoing example if the evidence indicated that X and Y had in the past considered such language to be binding.

Silence. As a general rule, there is no duty on the offeree to reply to an offer. Silence on the part of the offeree, therefore, does not usually constitute an acceptance. This is true even when the offer states, "If you do not reply within ten days, I shall conclude that you have accepted," or contains language of similar import. The reasons underlying this view are fairly obvious: (1) the view is consistent with the basic idea that any willingness to contract must be manifested in some fashion, and (2) it substantially prevents an offeree from being forced into a contract against his or her will.

In exceptional circumstances, however, the courts may find that the general rule is unfair to the offeror—that under the facts of the particular case, the offeree owed the offeror a duty to reject if they did not wish to be bound. In such cases, silence on the part of the offeree does constitute an acceptance. While it is difficult to generalize about these exceptional situations, two types of case present little controversy.

If an offeree initially indicates that silence on his or her part can be taken as acceptance, there is no reason why that person should not be bound by the statement. For example: "If you do not hear from me by March 1, you can conclude that we have a contract."

If a series of past dealings between the parties indicates that the parties consider silence to be an acceptance, it can be assumed by the offeror that this understanding continues until it is expressly changed. For example: a retail jewelry store has, over the years, received periodic shipments of both ordered and unordered jewelry from a large supplier; during this time, the retailer-buyer has always paid for any unordered goods not returned within two weeks. A failure by the retailer to reject a particular shipment, or to give notice of such rejection, within two weeks would very likely operate as an acceptance under the circumstances.

In both the preceding kinds of cases, the courts are likely to say that the offeror "had reason to understand" that silence on the part of the offeree was to be taken as a manifestation of assent, and that the offeree should have been well aware of this fact.

Requirement that an Acceptance be Unconditional and Not Add To or Change the Terms of the Offer

We have already seen that when an attempted acceptance changes the terms of the offer, it becomes a counteroffer and a rejection rather than an acceptance. The same is true when the attempted acceptance adds new terms or conditions to those of the offer.

Thus, if S writes to B: "I hereby offer to sell my farm to you for $50,000," no acceptance would result if B responded: "I accept, if I can pay $2,000 for each of the next 25 years" or "I accept if you promise to repaint the barn before sale." The general common law rule is that the acceptance must be a "mirror image" of the offer in order for a contract to result.

The following case presents an intriguing situation in which both parties originally assumed, quite understandably, that an agreement had clearly been reached—until the sharp-eyed bus driver began to compare the language of the school board's "acceptance" with the language of his offer. At that point, the fun began.

LUCIER v. TOWN OF NORFOLK
Supreme Court of Errors of Connecticut, 122 A. 711 (1923)

Lucier, plaintiff, operated a school bus for the defendant town for the school years of 1915, 1916, 1918, and 1919. In the summer of 1920 plaintiff and defendant began negotiating a contract for the coming year.

After several communications between the parties, plaintiff was asked by the Norfolk Town School Committee to submit a bid covering the transportation of students for the 1920-1921 school year. On August 12, plaintiff submitted his bid, offering to provide transportation at $175 per week each school week for that year.

On August 17 the board passed the following resolution: "Voted to award the contract for transporting children to and from Gilbert school and to and from various points in town to Mr. E.A. Lucier for the sum of $35 per day." The next day, a member of the committee, one Stevens, told plaintiff that the board "had voted to award him the contract" and requested plaintiff to have his buses ready.

On the first day of school, September 7, plaintiff transported the students as agreed. On the evening of September 7 the board presented plaintiff with a formal contract for him to sign, the contract embodying the wording of the August 17 resolution. Plaintiff refused to sign the contract, on the ground that it was not in accordance with his bid for compensation at the rate of $175 per week, but at the rate of $35 per day instead. Thereupon defendant refused to employ plaintiff and awarded the transportation contract to a third party.

Plaintiff brought action to recover damages for breach of contract, alleging that a contract was formed on his terms and was breached by defendant. (Specifically, plaintiff's argument was that his bid was accepted on August 18 when Stevens told him that the board "had voted to award him the contract.") Defendant contended that a contract was formed on its terms and that plaintiff was guilty of the breach. The trial court ruled that no contract was formed in this situation (but did award plaintiff $35 dollars, the reasonable value of his services performed on September 7). Plaintiff appealed.

Keeler, Justice:

. . . Summarily stated, the contentions of the plaintiff are: that the negotiations between him and the school board [resulted] in a contract express or implied, and the minds of the negotiating parties met; that Stevens, by reason of his position, had authority to make a contract binding the town; and that [plaintiff's bid, followed by Stevens' actions] resulted in a contract being formed....

[Other] than as to the price to be fixed for the service, there is no dispute between the parties as to the terms submitted in the notice to bidders, and the plaintiff bid with reference to them, his offer conforming to these terms, the price for the service being the only open item in the transaction. The dispute turns upon the question of a rate per week as contrasted with a rate per day. The committee received from the plaintiff a bid of $175 per week; this undoubtedly meant to it the same as $35 per day, a result arrived at by a simple act of division of the larger number by five, the number of school days in the ordinary school week. It would seem that the committee [members] were justified in reaching this conclusion, in that the plaintiff's pay in the contract for the year just past had been at a sum per day, and the notice for bids had called for a bid by the day.... When, therefore, the committee received a bid by the week they very naturally in their vote awarding the contract to the plaintiff substituted what they deemed an equivalent sum by the day, to accord with the requirement of the notice. This also was evidently the understanding of Stevens, when he afterward informed the plaintiff that the contract had been awarded to the latter. Subsequent events showed that this construction of his bid was not intended by the plaintiff, and that he intended to insist on the distinction between pay by the day and pay by the week, in that the latter afforded him compensation for work which would not in fact be required, when in any week a school day came upon a holiday.

In the pleadings, each side claimed the equivalence in fact and in effect of the expressions in the bid with those in the vote, each resolving the question of intent favorably to the contention by each, and each consequently claimed a contract which had been broken by the other party. Both are wrong. It clearly appears from the facts found that the trial judge correctly found that there was no meeting of minds, and hence no contract. The plaintiff had the burden of establishing his construction of the claimed contract and has failed.

But the plaintiff further insists that he was in effect informed by Stevens that his bid had been accepted by the committee, that the latter was bound by Stevens' statement, and that he [the plaintiff] acted in accordance with the information conveyed to him. Further, that Stevens was the agent of the committee, and had authority to bind it, and that the committee was so bound when Stevens told him that the contract had been awarded to him, which information was in his mind equivalent to a statement that his bid had been accepted in the form tendered.... So he says that whatever the committee really intended in the matter, it was bound by Stevens' statement that the contract had been awarded to him on the terms of his bid, even though the vote stated the price of the service at a sum differing therefrom. [The court rejected this contention of plaintiff, ruling that Stevens was simply informing plaintiff of the board's action so that he could get his equipment in readiness, and that Stevens did not intend—nor did he have the authority—to bind the board to anything other than the specific resolution as passed.] Judgment affirmed.

A Note of Caution. In some situations the offeree's response does constitute an acceptance even though it contains one or more terms that were not set forth in the offer itself. This is true where a reasonable person, standing in the place of the offeree, would justifiably believe that the "new" terms were within the contemplation of, and were agreeable to, the offeror despite the failure to include them in the offer. Following are two illustrations.

For several years X has been performing maintenance work upon Y Company's assembly line equipment, and has always granted Y Company 90 days in which to pay for the work. If X writes to Y, offering to perform preventive maintenance on various equipment for $1,000, and Y responds, we accept on condition that we will have 90 days in which to pay,'' Y's response very likely constitutes an acceptance. Under the circumstances—the manner in which they had been doing business in the past—Y could assume that it was implied that X would grant the usual credit. (Custom in the industry could give rise to a similar implication, if clearly proved by Y.)

F offers to sell certain land to D for $55,000 cash. D replies by telegram, ''I accept, assuming you will convey good title.'' This is an acceptance, even though F did not mention the quality of his title, because it is implied (under real property law) that a seller of land guarantees good or marketable title unless they indicate a contrary intention.

The purpose of the foregoing is simply to warn the student that it is possible for a term or condition to be literally new without necessarily being new in the legal sense. Thus, while the responses of the offerees in the preceding examples appear at first glance to constitute counteroffers, in the eyes of the law they add nothing new and therefore constitute valid acceptances.

Additional or Different Terms in Sale of Goods Contracts. Under the UCC's provisions for sale of goods contracts, an acceptance may be effective even though it contains terms that conflict with, or add to, the terms of the offer. A major reason for rejection of the mirror-image rule by the drafters of the Code lies in the manner in which many sales contracts are entered into. Generally, such contracts are not fully negotiated. For example, commercial buyers often use their own printed forms in ordering goods from manufacturers or wholesalers, and the latter companies frequently use their own forms in notifying buyers of their acceptance. Naturally, the terms and conditions of the two forms are rarely identical, because the order forms used by buyers contain buyer-oriented terms, while forms used by sellers to invite, acknowledge, or accept orders contain seller-oriented terms.

In the vast majority of situations, the parties do not pay much attention to the other's forms. The seller provides the goods, the buyer pays for them, and the forms are filed away and forgotten. However, in the occasional situation where problems result and one side or the other wishes to sue for breach of contract, strict adherence to the mirror-image rule would always allow the potential defendant to claim that there was no binding contract because of differences in the forms.

To illustrate: Suppose that on its purchase order form buyer B ordered a quantity of goods at a certain price from seller S, and that seller S sent a purchase acknowledgment form to B indicating that the goods would be shipped. S's form, however, contained a clause stating that interest would be charged on late payments. Later B notified S that he did not want the goods and would not go through with the deal, whereupon S sued B to recover damages for breach of contract. Both parties look at the forms for the first time. In such a case the common law presumes that by responding with the varying term on interest rates, S intended to make a counteroffer, which B has not accepted. Thus no contract was ever formed, with the result that B has no liability to S.

In the modern era where so much commercial activity occurs through ''form swapping,'' the mirror image rule provides a haven for welshers such as B in the foregoing example. The drafters of the UCC sought to eliminate such results in situations where the parties truly intended to contract. Section 2-207, which is often called the ''Battle of the

Forms'' provision, addresses this problem. As our analysis will show, Sec. 2-207 reverses the common-law assumption, and presumes instead that an offeree who responds with varying terms intends to contract, unless he clearly indicates that he intends a counteroffer instead. Unfortunately, Sec. 2-207 is one of the most complicated, controversial, and inconsistently applied provisions of the entire Code.

Text of Section 2-207. This section reads, in material part, as follows (emphasis added):

1. A definite and seasonable expression of acceptance or a written confirmation which is sent within a reasonable time *operates as an acceptance* even though it states terms *additional to or different from* those offered or agreed upon unless acceptance is expressly made conditional on assent to the additional or different terms.

2. The additional terms are to be construed as proposals for addition to the contract.

   Between merchants, such terms become part of the contract unless:

   a. the offer expressly limits acceptance to the terms of the offer;

   b. they materially alter it; or

   c. notification of objection to them . . . is given within a reasonable time after notice of them is received.

3. Conduct by both parties which recognizes the existence of a contract is sufficient to establish a contract for sale although the writings of the parties do not otherwise establish a contract . . . [T]he terms of the particular contract consist of those terms on which the writings of the parties agree [together with terms provided by UCC "gap-filler" rules].

Subsection 1—Is There a Contract? The primary import of this provision is that, in a sale of goods transaction, an offeree's response that clearly indicates a definite intent to accept constitutes an acceptance even if it contains one or more terms additional to or different from those found in the offer. Thus Sec. 2- 207 clearly rejects the mirror-image rule.

Assume that Buyer B orders 2,000 A-20 widgets from seller S for $9,000, the price appearing in S's catalog. S sends his acknowledgment form as follows: ''Accept your sales order #1379; 2,000 A-20 widgets/$9,000''; but on the back of the form is the new term ''seller makes no warranties, express or implied, as to goods sold.'' *A contract now exists,* despite the new term in S's response. In other words, under subsection 1, S's acknowledgment constitutes an acceptance rather than a counteroffer, resulting in a binding contract. If S did not wish to be bound unless the buyer accepted the warranty exclusion, S should have made the matter a subject of negotiation by clearly conditioning the acceptance upon B's approval of the exclusion. If S does not make this condition clear, and if it appears that S's response is intended primarily as an acceptance, a contract results.

In situations where the offeree's form agrees with the offeror's as to key terms, such as price, quantity, and date of delivery, differing only as to non-bargained ancillary terms, courts are likely to hold that the offeree's primary purpose was to form a contract. On the other hand, if the offeror's form orders 100,000 pounds of plastic at $2.00 per pound and the offeree's form confirms the order of 100,000 pounds of plastic at $2.25 per pound, the second document is not an acceptance.

Subsection 2—Is the New Term Included in the Agreement? If subsection 1 analysis leads to the conclusion that a contract has been formed, the remaining question is whether the warranty exclusion has become part of it.

If B notices the clause and agrees to it, then it is, of course, included. If B notices the clause and objects to it, then it does not become part of the contract. But what about the usual case where B does not notice the clause, or, if he does notice it, simply ignores it? In this situation, a distinction is made between terms that are ''different from'' those of the offer, and those which are "additional to" those of the offer.

Different Terms. If the term in the acceptance is different from (i.e., conflicts with) a term of the offer, the term does not become a part of the contract unless the offeror expressly agrees to it. Thus, in the above example, if B's order form had contained a clause setting forth certain warranties that were to be made by the seller (e.g., ''seller warrants the widgets to be in conformity with U.S. Department of Defense specification #497 dated 6-15-90''), S's warranty exclusion clause would clearly not be part of the contract.

Additional Terms. As to any term in the acceptance that is an additional term (i.e., regarding a matter not addressed in the offer), Sec. 2-207(2) provides that, *if both parties are merchants*, the term becomes a part of the contract without any further assent on the part of the offeror, *unless* (a) the offer stated that acceptance is limited to the terms of the offer itself; or (b) the term "materially alters" the contract; or (c) the offeror objects to the new term within a reasonable time after receiving the offeree's acceptance. Thus, in our example involving the widget purchase, if both B and S were merchants, and if B's order form made no reference to warranties, S's warranty-exclusion clause would automatically become part of the contract, unless barred by a, b, or c. (Therefore, in determining whether there is a contract (under subsection 1), it is not necessary that the parties be merchants. But their status as merchants is important in determining whether the additional term becomes part of the contract under subsection (2).) The reason for this is that the drafters of the UCC felt that additional terms should be included in the contract without express agreement only where the transaction is between two professionals.

In this case, most courts would hold that a warranty exclusion clause does materially alter an offer and therefore does not become part of the contract. Thus, the goods would be covered by any warranties implied by the law—because the seller was a merchant, and the seller's attempted disclaimer was not part of the contract, the UCC would imply a warranty that the goods are fit for the ordinary purposes for which such goods are used (the ''implied warranty of merchantability''). The courts decide whether or not there was a material alteration on a case-by-case basis. The basic thrust of subsection 2(b) is that the offeree is not allowed to slip anything really important past the offeror by simply including it in the acceptance form. Rather, the offeree should call the matter to the offeror's attention and make it a subject of negotiation.

Written Confirmation of Informal Agreement. A second situation in which UCC Section 2-207 is important occurs when (1) a seller and buyer have made an informal agreement of sale, such as a purely oral agreement (say, over the telephone) or an agreement formed by various "pieces" of informal notes, memos, messages, and so on (or a combination of oral statements and informal writings); (2) either (a) one of the parties subsequently prepares and sends a formal written confirmation of the agreement to the other party, or (b) the two parties subsequently exchange forms; and (3) the subsequent written confirmation or the subsequently exchanged forms add to or change the terms that were first agreed upon informally. If the evidence proves that the parties had truly made a contract informally, then there is a contract based on that informal understanding. Thus, the first part of 2-207 dealing with the question of whether there was a contract is irrelevant. The second part of 2-207 is then applied to determine whether the additional or different terms are part of the contract. In other words, the additional or different terms are treated as proposals for adding to or changing the informal contract, and the rules of 2-207(2) determine whether they are included.

Agreement Implied from Conduct. A third situation in which UCC Section 2-207 is important occurs when the parties do not have a prior informal agreement and, their exchanged forms did not create a contract for one reason or another—such as when the offeree does not definitely indicate an intent to accept, or when the offeree does indicate an intent to accept but its attempted acceptance specifically states that it should not be considered an acceptance unless the offeror expressly consents to the new or different terms. In such a case the documents do not produce a contract, yet sellers often ship goods and buyers often pay for them in such instances. Here, subsection 3 of 2-207 implies a contract from the conduct of the parties under the same circumstances that common-law rules of contract law find implied contracts to exist. The terms of the contract consist of those matters that the two forms do agree upon, supplemented by any evidence from their conduct showing what they intended particular terms to be, and also supplemented as necessary by the "gap-filler" provisions of the UCC.

For example, in one case a buyer and seller exchanged a series of purchase orders, acknowledgments and letters regarding a purchase of aluminum. At no time did the buyer's forms and the seller's forms agree as to a date of delivery. Buyer committed itself to purchase on September 1 and demanded delivery within seven weeks. Seller immediately acknowledged the order, but set a delivery date of nine weeks, later changed to eleven. Buyer stated that this was not acceptable. Seller told buyer either to accept it or obtain the aluminum elsewhere. Nonetheless, seller delivered the aluminum after eleven weeks and buyer accepted and partially paid for the aluminum. Certain defects were found and litigation resulted. The court held that the parties' correspondence did not create a contract. Seller's response materially altered the buyer's offer. In short, the communications indicated that the parties "dickered" over a key term, but never reached agreement. Nonetheless, the conduct of the parties (the seller's shipping the goods and the buyer's partially paying for them) did establish formation of a contract under subsection 3 of 2-207 (as under common-law rules pertaining to implied contracts). The court then used the UCC "gap-fillers" to establish a reasonable time of delivery in order to determine whether seller had breached. *Alliance Wall Corp. v. Ampat Midwest Corp.*, 477 N.E.2d 1206 (Ohio App. 1984).

And in *Review Video LLC v. Enlighten Technology*, 2005 U.S. Dist. LEXIS 442 (N.D. Iowa 2005), defendant buyer sent seven orders for goods to defendant for items totaling over $150,000. Plaintiff seller issued purchasers orders for the goods and defendant agreed to the specified prices. When defendant did not pay for the goods, plaintiff sued. Defendant admitted that it owed the purchase price but denied that it owed interest charges of 1.5% per month on past due amounts because it never signed a document indicating that it would pay interest.

Because the parties were merchants and defendant's original order did not mention interest but plaintiff seller's response did, the court determined that UCC 2.207(2) applied:

Section 2-207 determines whether an additional term, as opposed to a different term, contained in a written confirmation but not expressly negotiated, is appropriately considered to be part of a contract. According to that provision, an additional term, in this case the monthly interest charge, is to be construed as a proposal for addition to the contract. 2-207(2):

The mere acceptance of goods, even if done repeatedly, does not by itself constitute a valid acceptance of newly proposed contract terms. Between merchants, such as the plaintiff and the defendant, the additional term becomes part of the contract unless:

a. the offer expressly limits acceptance to the terms of the offer;

b. [the additional term] materially alter[s] [the contract]; or

c. notification of objection to [the additional term] has already been given or is given within a reasonable time after notice of them is received.

The defendant does not contend that it limited acceptance of its offer to the terms of the offer. Further, the defendant does not contend that it notified the plaintiff of any objection to the additional monthly interest charge term within a reasonable time after receiving notice of the term. Accordingly, the court must determine whether the additional monthly interest charge term is a term that materially alters the contract, and therefore should not be considered part of the contract.

The court further held that, because payment of interest on overdue accounts is usually required in commercial transactions, it therefore did not "materially alter" the agreement. Therefore, the court ordered defendant to pay the interest.

Special Problems with Software Licenses and Online Transactions.

Many disputes arising from modern transactions, especially those involving businesses and consumers, focus on whether the consumer is legally bound by particular terms that the company sought to impose and enforce. This was the problem, as we saw, in the *Cullinane v. Uber* case above in which several customers believed they were not bound by an arbitration clause in the agreement with Uber for ride-sharing services.

These sorts of disputes occur in many different contexts, but courts have had particular problems with situations involving the purchase of software. All or practically all courts have treated software transactions as involving a sale of goods that is governed by Article 2 of the UCC, which is sometimes a logical thing to do and sometimes is not, because the customer actually buys only a CD or other storage medium plus one copy of the software's intangible object code (the 1's and 0's), and is merely a licensee of the right to use the software subject to certain restrictions. Moreover, in the case of software ''purchased'' by downloading it from the Internet, nothing tangible at all is purchased. On the other hand, when someone buys a computer with software preloaded on the computer's hard drive, the predominant part of the transaction is the purchase of a tangible commodity, and it does make logical sense to treat the transaction as a sale of goods governed by Article 2 of the UCC.

Regardless of the sometimes questionable logic of treating software as a good, the courts do so and apply Article 2 of the UCC with respect to deciding whether there is a contract, what are the terms of the contract, and other matters such as warranties. It should also be recalled, however, that many of the traditional common-law rules of contract law continue to apply to sale of goods transactions, such as the rules for determining whether there is a definite expression of intent to make an offer or a definite expression of intent to make an acceptance. Thus, in software transactions, common-law rules apply unless altered by Article 2 of the UCC.

On the other hand, many consumers in more recent times are able to acquire only a subscription to a particular software program—here, the user is also paying a fee periodically for a license to use the software, but does not acquire ownership of an electronic copy that they can keep. In such an instance, the transaction probably will be treated by the law as a purchase of services, not goods, and not governed by the UCC, but the law on this point is not settled.

With respect to the determination of what the terms of an agreement are, who is treated as the offeror and who is the offeree in software and other online transactions can make a big difference. Under traditional contract law rules, the customer would be treated as the initial offeror, and a seller who simply made goods or services available for sale would be the offeree. If this approach is taken, a customer-offeror who at the time of making a purchase offer is not made reasonably aware of terms the seller wants to impose, the customer's offer does not include these terms. Then, if the seller purports to accept and adds terms, these are treated as terms that are additional to or different from the offer.

Although some courts have employed this traditional contract law approach to software transactions, not all of them have. Indeed, a majority of state and federal courts (federal courts applying state law) have reversed the traditional rules and treated the seller as the offeror, so that when the customer-offeree accepts, they accept all of the offeror's terms.

In either case, whether the seller or customer is treated as the offeror, the issue of communication is often critical. That is, did the seller provide the customer a reasonable opportunity to see the proposed terms before making a commitment to the transaction? To confuse things even further, however, several courts have held that customers are legally bound by the seller's proposed terms even if the customer has a chance to see these terms only after making a purchase.

To put the matter simply, courts have caused the law in this area to be a big mess, and very difficult to understand.

Requirement that an Acceptance be Unequivocal

Returning to common law principles, an acceptance is an expression on the part of the offeree by which they indicate an intent to be bound by the terms of the offer. The courts require the expression be reasonably definite and unequivocal, and be manifested by some overt word or act. These requirements were developed, as a practical matter, to deal with the many situations where—from the language used by the offeree—his or her real intent is not at all clear; that is, the offeree's response is neither a clear-cut acceptance nor a flat rejection of the offer. At best, such responses cause initial delay and uncertainty between the parties as to whether a contract exists; at worst, litigation may ensue, with interpretation left to the courts.

To illustrate: X, in response to an advertisement placed by Y, sends a bid to Y offering to perform the described landscaping work for $23,000. Y replies by telegram: "Offer satisfies all requirements; will give it my prompt attention." Subsequently Y hires another landscaper to do the job, and, when X sues Y to recover damages for breach of contract, Y contends that his response did not constitute an acceptance of the offer. Applying the general rule to this case, Y's reply is too indefinite and tentative to satisfy the "unequivocal" requirement. Thus Y is correct in his contention that a contract was not formed. On the other hand, each case has to be decided on its own merits, including consideration of the circumstances surrounding the communications. Thus, a different result might be reached in the foregoing example if the evidence indicated that X and Y had in the past considered such language to be binding.

In *Cedar Rapids Lumber Co. v. Fisher*, 105 N.W. 595 (Iowa 1905), a school board advertised for bids for the construction of a school building. After fourteen bids were received, the board wired one contractor: "You are low bidder. Come on morning train." The board and the contractor were subsequently unable to agree to a formal contract, and litigation ensured. The Iowa Supreme Court ruled that the board's telegram did not of itself constitute an acceptance of the contractor's bid, saying that it indicated no more than a willingness on the part of the board to enter into contractual negotiations.

When Does Acceptance Take Effect? Reasonable Medium or Mailbox Rule

Offers, revocations, and rejections are effective when received. Acceptances are also effective upon receipt, but they often are effective even sooner than that. That is, under the "mailbox rule" or "reasonable medium rule," an acceptance may be effective as soon as it is sent if the medium chosen is reasonable. The "mailbox rule" originally applied only when the offeree used the U.S. mail for sending the acceptance, and this term is often still used even though it has been generally expanded by the courts to apply to any means of communication that is reasonable under the circumstances. Although there is variation from state to state in this area of the law, courts typically deem a chosen medium to be reasonable if (1) it is the same one used by the offeror; (2) it is one customarily used in prior dealings between the parties; (3) it is customarily used within the trade or industry in which the parties are doing business; or (4) it is one which is impliedly authorized by the language of the offer (for example, an acceptance by mail is probably reasonable in response to an offer by telegram if the offer indicated that there was no urgency about reaching an agreement).

If the offeree uses a medium that is not reasonable, the acceptance will be effective only when received. However, if the medium chosen by the offeree is reasonable, the acceptance will be effective when dispatched (out of the possession of the offeree or offeree's agent). Assume that A mails an offer to B. If B mails an acceptance, there is a contract the minute the acceptance is dispatched even if the post office delays the acceptance or even loses it altogether. (Of course, if the acceptance is lost, the offeree will bear the burden of proving by other evidence that it was, in fact, mailed.) If A calls B to revoke the offer after B has mailed the acceptance, it is too late for the revocation to be effective. The offer, already accepted, has ripened into a binding contract.

Exceptions

There are at least three situations where the reasonable medium rule is not applicable. First, and most important, the offeror may specifically state in the offer that an acceptance will be effective only when actually received by the offeror. This is simply part of the general rule that the offeror is the "master of the offer," and can put any terms or conditions they want in the offer. The offeree can take them or leave them. It is an excellent idea for any offeror to do this, because it removes the possibility that the offeror will be legally bound by a contract for a period of time (while the message of acceptance is in transit) without knowing about it.

Second, also because of the rule that the offeror is the master of his or her offer, the offeror may require that an acceptance be made by a particular medium. If a particular means of communication is clearly specified as a requirement, then an acceptance sent by any other medium will not result in a contract being formed upon dispatch, but only upon receipt by the offeror. Note that there can be a factual question of what the offeror actually intended when they merely stated that the offeree "may" use a particular medium for accepting. Unless there is other evidence showing that the offeror actually meant the suggestion to be a requirement, "may" or other merely suggestive language will not be treated as requiring that the offer use that method of accepting.

Third, if an offeree sends a rejection first, and later changes his mind and sends an acceptance, the acceptance is not effective until received. Therefore, an offeror who receives the rejection first may assume that it is effective. In other words, in such a situation, the first message to be received by the offeror (rejection or acceptance) will be the effective one.

Also, courts have generally not applied the mailbox rule to e-mails. They have held instead that an acceptance is effective not when sent but when it arrives at the recipient's e-mail server (even if it has not yet been read by the offeror).

When Acceptance Takes Effect: UCC Changes for Sale of Goods Transactions

The Uniform Commercial Code generally adopts the reasonable medium rule of the common law, UCC Sec. 2- 206(1)(a), providing that an offer may be accepted by "any medium reasonable in the circumstances." However, whereas the common law holds that if an unreasonable method of acceptance is utilized, it is not effective until received, UCC Sec. 1-201(38) provides that such an acceptance will be deemed effective as of the time it is sent, *if* it is received within the time that a seasonably dispatched acceptance using a reasonable medium would normally arrive.

Acceptance of Unilateral Offers

Offers for unilateral contracts pose two unique problems insofar as offer and acceptance principles are concerned: (1) whether it is necessary for the offeree, having performed the requested act, to notify the offeror of that fact, and (2) whether the offeror has the right to revoke the offer after the offeree has commenced to perform but before the performance is completed.

Is Notice Required?

The general rule is that a unilateral offer is accepted the moment the offeree performs the requested act; giving notice that the act has taken place is usually not required. This rule does not apply, obviously, to offers that expressly request notification. In such offers, a contract is not formed until the requisite notice is given. Another type of case requiring notice involves those exceptional situations where the act is of such a nature that the offeror "has no adequate means of ascertaining with reasonable promptness and certainty" that the act has taken place. The typical cases in this category are contracts of guaranty—those in which one person guarantees a loan made to another. For example: A, in Columbus, asks B, in Miami, to lend $1,000 to C, a Miami resident, A promising to pay the debt if C fails to do so. In this situation, most courts take the view that while a contract is formed between A and B the moment that B makes the loan, A's resulting obligation is discharged (terminated) if B fails to notify him within a reasonable time that the loan has been made.

When Can Revocation Be Made?

Where the requested act will take a period of time for completion, the traditional rule has been that the offeror can revoke the offer at any time before full performance has taken place, even if the offeree has started to do the job. In such a case a contract is never formed. (However, under the quasi-contract theory, the offeree is ordinarily entitled to recover the reasonable value of his or her performance prior to the revocation. In the event that this partial performance is of no value to the offeror, the offeree will, of course, recover nothing.)

In recent years a growing number of courts have felt that the traditional view is unfair to the offeree in many circumstances, and they have abandoned it in favor of several other approaches. The most widely accepted of the newer views is that where the act is one that of necessity will take a period of time to complete, the right of revocation is suspended once the offeree starts to perform and remains suspended until the offeree has had a reasonable time to complete the act. This view is consistent with the traditional view to the extent that no contract is formed until the act has been completed, but it affords an interim protection to the offeree that the traditional view does not. Thus we have yet another illustration of the courts' freedom, within the framework of the common law, to modify those earlier principles whose application has brought about results of questionable merit.

"Prompt Shipment" Offers: Sales of Goods and the Unilateral-Bilateral Distinction

Prior to adoption of the UCC, if a buyer ordered goods using such terms as "prompt shipment," "for current shipment," or "ship at once," the offer was usually construed as being an offer for a unilateral contract. Under this common-law view, actual shipment was the only way in which the offer could be accepted; a promise to ship would not cause a contract to come into existence (a result that sometimes came as a surprise to one or both of the parties). Sec. 2-206 (1) of the UCC rejects that view by providing that an offer containing such language shall be construed as inviting acceptance either by prompt shipment or by a prompt promise to ship. Therefore, an offeree's sending of a return promise to ship forms a bilateral contract in such circumstances (although prompt shipment must follow or the contract will be breached). The buyer can still require acceptance of the offer only by the act of shipment itself, but they now must explicitly state this in the offer. Sec. 2-206 thus blurs the common-law distinction between bilateral and unilateral offers by permitting the offeree, in this limited instance, a choice as to how his or her acceptance shall be made.

CHAPTER 12

CONSIDERATION

An elusive concept called *consideration* is the second element ordinarily required in a contract. Generally, if an agreement lacks consideration, neither party can enforce it, even if it is in writing. As a practical matter, consideration is present in most agreements; but since this is not always the case, we need a basic understanding of the doctrine of consideration in order to determine when an agreement is legally binding.

HISTORICAL NOTE

Courts have long struggled with the question of what agreements ought to be enforced. No system of law has ever enforced all promises, nor could this feasibly be done. Present-day concepts of consideration have resulted from a mixture of logic and historical accident. At one time, contracts had to be "sealed" in order to be enforced. A *sealed contract* had to have a bit of wax affixed to it, on which the initials or other distinctive marks of each of the parties were imprinted. Today, sealed contracts are virtually unknown, though a few jurisdictions will enforce such a contract even in the absence of consideration. Most jurisdictions, however, will enforce no contract, sealed or unsealed, in the absence of consideration.

The present-day requirements of consideration center in part on the notion that one party to an agreement should not be bound by it if the other party is not similarly bound. A's promise to give a present to B should not be binding on A because B is not bound to do anything. Promises to make gifts are generally unenforceable. Another important aspect of consideration is that it can help prevent one contracting party from exploiting the other, as shall be illustrated later in this chapter in connection with a discussion of the preexisting obligation rule.

THE BASIC CONCEPT OF CONSIDERATION

Courts agree substantially about the kinds of promises or acts constituting consideration in most situations. Although several definitions of and tests for consideration have been formulated over the years, most lead to the same conclusion when applied to agreements where the existence of consideration is questioned. Our discussion focuses on a popular approach that emphasizes the "bargain" element of a transaction, which helps distinguish a promise of a mere gift (which may not be enforced) from an enforceable commercial promise to do something that the other party has bargained for.

Assume that Company A promised to deliver 5,000 tires to Company B on July 1 in exchange for Company B's promise to pay $300,000. Assume further that Company B breached the promise; Company A sued for breach of contract; and Company B raised the defense that no consideration existed to support its promise. How would B's contention be analyzed?

The *first* determination is whether the promisee (Company A, the party that received the promise that was not performed) suffered a *legal detriment,* defined as (a) doing (or promising to do) something that it was not obligated to do, or (b) refraining from doing (or promising to refrain from doing) something that it had a right to do. Unless Company A had a preexisting legal or contractual obligation to deliver the 5,000 tires, it is clear that Company A did suffer a legal detriment in this transaction. It promised to do something it did not otherwise have to do—to deliver 5,000 tires.

The *second element* of consideration is that there must have been a *bargained-for exchange*. This simply means that, when the parties reached an agreement, they must have bargained, or agreed, that each was giving something up in return for what the other party was giving up.

Sometimes the requirement of a bargained-for exchange is broken into two parts. The *first part* is that the detriment (A's promise to deliver the 5,000 tires) must *induce* the promise that was not performed (B's promise to pay $300,000). Unless there is some other explanation for why Company B promised to pay $300,000 to Company A, it is clear that the detriment did induce the promise in this case. The *second part* of the bargained-for exchange requirement is that the promise (B's promise to pay $300,000) must *induce* the detriment (A's promise to deliver the 5,000 tires). Again, unless some other reason appears to explain why A promised to deliver the 5,000 tires, it seems clear that it was in order to earn the $300,000 promised by B.

Viewing it as a cross-inducement is just another way of saying *bargained-for exchange*. In this example, both a legal detriment and a bargained-for exchange are present, so the contract is enforceable.

Viewed in this light, consideration at a general level is easy to understand and, obviously, is present in most cases. Companies and individuals promise to deliver goods and services because they want the money that other companies and individuals are willing to pay for those goods and services.

Consider another example. Assume that X promises to install a home air-conditioning unit for Y, and Y promises to pay X $1,100 for the job. Consideration will become important if one of the parties, let us say X, breaches the promise, is sued by Y, and claims lack of consideration as a defense. A court will quickly find: (1) The promisee (Y) has suffered a legal detriment (promising to do something he did not have to do—pay $1,100). (2) The detriment (Y's promise to pay $1,100) induced the promise (X's promise to install the air-conditioning unit). Obviously X bargained for Y's promise of payment; that is how X makes his living. (3) The promise (X's promise to install the air-conditioning unit) induced the detriment (why else would Y have promised to pay $1,100?). Try to analyze the following cases using the three basic elements of consideration.

HAMER v. SIDWAY
Court of Appeals of New York, 27 N.E. 256 (1891)

William E. Story, Sr., promised to pay his nephew, William E. Story, II, $5,000 if he would refrain from drinking, using tobacco, swearing, and playing cards or billiards for money until he became twenty-one years of age. The nephew refrained from all the specified activities as he was requested to do, and on his twenty-first birthday he wrote his uncle a letter asking him for the money.

The uncle, in reply, assured the nephew, "You shall have the $5,000 as I promised you." The uncle went on, however, to explain that he had worked very hard to accumulate that sum of money and would pay it "when you are capable of taking care of it, and the sooner that time comes the better it will suit me."

Two years later the uncle died, without having made payment. The administrator of the uncle's estate, Sidway, refused to pay the $5,000, and suit was brought to recover that sum. (The plaintiff is Hamer, rather than the nephew, for the reason that at some time before *litigation was begun the nephew had assigned—that is, sold—his rights against the estate to Hamer. Thus Hamer's right to recover is entirely dependent upon whether the nephew had a valid contractual claim against his uncle.)*

The trial court ruled that the uncle's promise to pay the $5,000 was not supported by consideration on the part of the nephew (the promisee) and entered judgment for the defendant. The plaintiff appealed.

Parker, Justice:

The defendant contends that the contract was without consideration to support it, and therefore invalid. He asserts that the promisee, by refraining from the use of liquor and tobacco, was not harmed, but benefited; that that which he did was best for him to do, . . . and insists that it follows that, unless the promisor was benefited, the contract was without consideration—a contention which, if well founded, would [inject into the law, in many cases, an element so difficult to measure that needless uncertainty would result]. Such a rule could not be tolerated, and is without foundation in the law....

Pollock, in his work on Contracts, page 166, says: "'Consideration' means not so much that one party is profiting as that the other abandons some legal right . . . as an inducement for the promise of the first." Now, applying this rule to the facts before us, the promisee used tobacco, occasionally drank liquor, and he had a legal right to do so. That right he abandoned for a period of years upon the strength of the promise of the [uncle] that for such forbearance he would give him $5,000. We need not speculate on the effort which may have been required to give up the use of those stimulants. *It is sufficient that he restricted his lawful freedom of action within certain prescribed limits upon the faith of his uncle's agreement, and now, having fully performed the conditions imposed, it is of no moment whether such performance actually proved a benefit to the promisor, and the court will not inquire into it;* . . . [Emphasis added.] Few cases have been found which may be said to be precisely in point, but such as have been, support the position we have taken.... Judgment reversed.

Comment. Two consideration principles are underscored here, as a result of the higher court's rejection of the defenses raised by the uncle's estate. First, if a *promisee* incurs a detriment by giving up a legal right, the promisee has given consideration even though they may have received a benefit at the same time. Thus, the nephew gave consideration by giving up certain rights—such as the right to smoke—even though he may have also been physically benefited by this forbearance. Second, even though the promisor typically receives some benefit from what the promisee gave up in return for the promisor's promise, it is not a requirement that the promisor has received any such benefit, and the courts normally do not make any inquiry into whether the promisor received a benefit.

Although consideration is usually present in contracts, and indeed is typically proved by the same evidence that proved that there was an agreement, obviously it is not always present. Consider the following three examples.

(1) Company A to Company B: "Because you are having such tough times, we will charge you 20 percent less for custodial services than our contract with you calls for." In most jurisdictions, a court would not hold A to this promise. It is basically a gift, since *B suffered no legal detriment.*

(2) Company A to Company B: "We have an old metal press that we are no longer using. If you would like to come over some time and pick it up, you may have it." If A reneges on this promise,

it will not be deemed enforceable. Even if we assumed that B suffered a detriment in the transaction (making the effort to pick up the press), *that detriment did not induce A's promise.* A was not "bargaining for" that act. Rather, this is basically a promise to make a gift and is unenforceable.

(3) Wife attacks her husband (D) with an ax, knocking him down. As she is about to decapitate him, P intervenes, catching the ax on its downward flight. P's hand is badly mutilated. D jumps up and promises to pay P $1,000 for saving his life. P has clearly suffered a detriment, and it is exactly what D bargained for. However, the *promise did not induce the detriment.* That is, because D made his promise after P acted, we cannot say that his promise caused her to do what she did. Thus, most courts would not enforce this promise. See *Harrington v. Taylor,* 36 S.E.2d 227 (N.C. 1945).

Performance of Preexisting Obligations

As a general rule, a promisee does not incur a detriment by performing, or promising to perform, an act that they were under a preexisting duty to perform. One can be under a *preexisting obligation* because of the general law of a state or the federal government, or because a prior contract has not yet been carried out.

Obligations Imposed by Law

The following is a simple illustration of an obligation imposed by law. X's store has been burglarized, and X promises a local policeman $75 if he uncovers, and turns over to the authorities, evidence establishing the identity of the culprit. If the policeman furnishes the requested information, he is not entitled to the reward. Under city ordinances and department regulations he already has a duty to do this; therefore it does not constitute a detriment to him.

Contractual Obligations

Greater difficulty is presented in situations where the preexisting obligation exists (or may exist) as the result of a prior contract between the parties. While such situations involve varying fact-patterns, the starting point can be illustrated as follows. Assume that D contracts to drill a seventy-foot well for G for $200. After he commences work, D complains that he is going to lose money on the job and may not finish it unless he gets more money. G then says: "All right. Finish up and I'll pay you $100 extra." D then completes the job, but G refuses to pay the additional $100. D brings suit to hold G to his promise. In this situation most courts would rule that D's act of completing the well was simply the performance of his original obligation—that he incurred no detriment thereby, and cannot enforce G's promise to pay the additional money. Thus, as a general rule, a *modification contract*—a contract that alters the terms of an existing contract—requires some new consideration in order to be enforceable. (Consideration would have been present in the above case, for example, had the modification contract required something extra of D—such as drilling the well to a depth of eighty feet.)

The primary rationale for the rule that performance of one's preexisting obligations does not constitute consideration is the prevention of coerced modification contracts. In other words, referring to the original example, the purpose is to prevent D—by threatening to stop work, or by actually stopping it—from enforcing the new promise made by G to pay more, in these circumstances.

Application of the preexisting obligation rule in most instances makes sense and brings about reasonable results. The following case is typical of those in which the rule prevents the enforceability of the modification contract. Following this case, a number of exceptions to the rule (and the reasoning underlying them) will be noted.

QUARTURE v. ALLEGHENY COUNTY
Superior Court of Pennsylvania, 14 A.2d 575 (1940)

Quarture, plaintiff, owned land in Pennsylvania. A portion of it was taken when the defendant county relocated and widened a state highway. Plaintiff needed legal help to recover damages from the county, and he employed a lawyer, Sniderman, to represent him in this effort.

A written contract was entered into, under the terms of which Sniderman was to "institute, conduct, superintend or prosecute to final determination, if necessary, a suit or suits, action or claim against the County of Allegheny on account of taking, injuring, and affecting (my, our) property in the relocation, widening, and opening of the State Highway known as Route No. 545." The contract further provided that Sniderman was to receive, as a fee for his services, "10 percent of all that might be recovered."

Sniderman represented plaintiff before the Board of Viewers of Allegheny County, and the board awarded plaintiff $1,650 damages. Plaintiff was dissatisfied with this amount and wished to appeal that award. Subsequently, a new agreement was entered into between plaintiff and Sniderman. This agreement provided that Sniderman would appeal the case to the court of common pleas and that Quarture would pay him a fee of 33 percent of whatever recovery might be obtained on appeal.

Plaintiff, represented by Sniderman, then brought this action in the court of common pleas, appealing the award of the Board of Viewers, and the court awarded him a judgment of $2,961. At this point Sniderman filed a petition with the court, asking it to distribute to him 33 percent of the judgment—$987. Quarture objected, contending that his promise to pay the larger percentage was not supported by consideration and that Sniderman was thus bound by his original contract (a fee of 10 percent). The court rejected this contention and awarded Sniderman $987. Plaintiff appealed.

Stadtfeld, Justice:
. . . Our first duty is to construe the original [contract]. What is meant by the terms "final determination?" . . . In the case of *Ex parte Russell*, 20 L.Ed. 632, it was said: "The final determination of a suit is the end of litigation therein. This cannot be said to have arrived as long as an appeal is pending."

The proceedings before the Board of Viewers cannot be considered as a "final determination," as their award is subject to appeal by either the owner of the property or by the municipality. If it were intended to provide for additional compensation in case of appeal from the award of viewers, it would have been a simple matter to have so provided in the contract. We cannot rewrite the contract; we must construe it as the parties have written it....

The general principle is stated in 13 C.J. 351, as follows: "A promise to do what the promisor is already bound to do cannot be a consideration, for if a person gets nothing in return for his promise but that to which he is already legally entitled, the consideration is unreal." Likewise, at p. 353. "The promise of a person to carry out a subsisting contract with the promisee or the performance of such contractual duty is clearly no consideration, as he is doing no more than he was already obliged to do, and hence has sustained no detriment, nor has the other party to the contract obtained any benefit. Thus a promise to pay additional compensation for the performance by the promisee of a contract which the promisee is already under obligation to the promisor to perform is without consideration."

There are many cases in which this rule of law is laid down or adhered to, but one that clearly sets out the reason for the rule is *Lingenfelder v. Wainwright Brewing Co.,* 15 S.W. 844. In that case, plaintiff, an architect engaged in erecting a brewery for defendant, refused to proceed with his contract upon discovering that a business rival had secured one of the subcontracts. The company, being in great haste for the building, agreed to pay plaintiff additional compensation as an inducement to resume work. It was held that the new promise was void for want of consideration, the court saying:

> It is urged upon us by plaintiff that this was a new contract. New in what? Plaintiff was bound by his contract to design and supervise this building. Under the new promise he was not to do any more or anything different. What benefit was to accrue to defendant? He was to receive the same service from plaintiff under the new [contract] that plaintiff was bound to render under the original contract. What loss, trouble, or inconvenience could result to plaintiff that he had not already assumed? No amount of metaphysical reasoning can change the plain fact that plaintiff took advantage of defendant's necessities, and extorted the promise of 5 percent on the refrigerator plant as the condition of his complying with his contract already entered into.... What we hold is that, when a party merely does what he has already obligated himself to do, he cannot demand an additional compensation therefor, and although by taking advantage of the necessities of his adversary he obtains a promise for more, the law will regard it as *nudum pactum,* and will not lend its process to aid in the wrong....

While we do not question the value of the services rendered by Mr. Sniderman, we are nevertheless constrained by reason of our interpretation of the [first] agreement, *to limit the right of recovery to the amount stipulated therein [in view of the fact that the carrying on of the appeal was nothing more than what the first agreement required of him].* [Emphasis added.] It is unfortunate that [the] agreement did not stipulate additional compensation in case of an appeal. Judgment reversed.

Modification Contracts: Contracts for the Sale of Goods. The drafters of the UCC made several modifications of the common law aimed at preventing technical rules from impeding enforcement of the parties' factual bargain. As an example, the drafters believed that if the parties to a sales contract subsequently modified it voluntarily, that modification should be enforceable whether or not supported by consideration. Accordingly, UCC Sec. 2-209(1) rejects the general common-law rule by providing that "an agreement modifying a contract [for the sale of goods] needs no consideration to be binding." To illustrate: S and B have agreed that S will sell a certain quantity of goods (such as 10,000 gallons of fuel oil) to B at a certain price. S later finds that he is not going to be able to deliver by the agreed-upon date. He contacts B, who agrees to an extension of the time for delivery. B subsequently has a change of heart and demands the goods on the original date. Under the UCC, B is bound by the agreed-upon modification even though S gave no additional consideration for the extension of time. (The reasoning behind Sec. 2-209 has prompted several states, including California, New York, and Michigan, to adopt a similar rule for common-law contracts.)

Although the modification agreement need not be supported by new consideration, it must still meet two requirements that the UCC imposes on all contracts falling within its scope. First, the modification must be made in good faith—that is, it must not be a coerced modification. And, second, the contract must not be "unconscionable"—i.e., shockingly one-sided. The concepts of coercion [duress] and unconscionability are discussed in later chapters.

To avoid difficulties caused by claims of subsequent modifications, many parties place in their written contracts clauses stating that subsequent modifications not evidenced by a writing shall have no effect. Such NOM ("no oral modification") clauses are expressly made enforceable by Sec. 2-209(2).

Adequacy of Consideration

Whenever the enforceability of a promise is at issue, a finding that the promisee incurred a legally recognized detriment results in the promisor being bound by the contract. This is usually true even if the actual values of the promise and the detriment are unequal—as is reflected in the oft-repeated statement that "the law is not concerned with the adequacy of consideration."

To illustrate: X contracts to sell an acreage in Montana to Y for $60,000. Y later discovers that the actual value of the land is under $30,000. Y is liable on his promise to pay $60,000, even though what he received was worth much less. Under the usual test, X incurred a detriment when he promised to convey the land—the surrender of his right to retain the property. The presence of this detriment constituted a consideration sufficient to support Y's promise to pay; and Y's claim of inadequacy is therefore of no relevance. The legal sufficiency of an act or promise, rather than its adequacy, is controlling.

Mutuality of Obligation

The requirement of mutuality of obligation dictates that there must be consideration on the part of both parties to the contract. As we have indicated, in the typical bilateral contract each party's promise is supported by the promise of the other, and the requirement is met. If, however, in a particular case there is no mutuality because consideration is lacking on the part of one of the parties, neither party is bound by the agreement. Such an agreement is called an *illusory contract*. For example, A and B enter into a written agreement under the terms of which A promises to employ B as his foreman for one year at a salary of $22,000 and B promises to work in that capacity for the specified time. The last paragraph of the agreement provides that "A reserves the right to cancel this contract at any time." Because A has thus not absolutely bound himself to employ B for the year, A has incurred no detriment (no unconditional obligation) by such a promise, with the result that B's promise to work for the year is not binding upon him. Thus, he can quit work at any time without liability to A. In such a case the requirement of mutuality of obligation has not been met, since A is said to have a "free way out" of the contract, and his promise is therefore "illusory."

Requirements and Output Contracts

Buyers and sellers of goods will sometimes enter into contracts where the quantity of the goods being sold—such as gasoline or coal—is not specified; rather, the quantity is to be determined by subsequent events. In some instances, the language of the contract is such that the buyer clearly has a "free way out"; that is, under the terms of the contract the buyer does not absolutely promise to buy any specific amount of goods. For example, S and B enter into a contract under the terms of which B promises to buy from S all the coal that he "might wish" over the next six months at a specified price per ton, with S promising to sell such quantity. Because of the language used, either intentionally or accidentally, B has not bound himself to buy any quantity of coal at all; thus the contract is illusory, since B has incurred no detriment. Because mutuality of obligation is lacking, the result is that if B later desires some coal, he is free to buy it from whomever he chooses. Conversely, if B orders coal from S, S has no duty to supply it.

However, if a buyer and seller agree that buyer will definitely purchase its requirements for a certain good during a specific period of time, courts will normally enforce the parties' agreement. Thus, if an ice company contracts to sell to an ice cream manufacturer "all the ice you will need in your business for the next two years" at a specified price per ton, the agreement will be a legally enforceable *requirements contract* despite the possibility that the buyer may ultimately turn out to have no requirements at all.

In a similar vein, courts will enforce a so-called *output contract*, if the seller and buyer definitely agree that the buyer will purchase all of the seller's production—it's *output*—during a specified period of time.

Settlement of Debts

After a debt becomes due, sometimes the creditor and debtor enter into a *settlement agreement.* This occurs when the creditor, either on his or her own initiative or that of the debtor, promises to release the debtor of all further liability if the debtor pays a specified sum of money. If, after the specified sum is paid, the creditor seeks to recover the balance of the debt on the ground that the agreement lacked consideration on the part of the debtor, the success of the suit usually depends on whether the original debt was "unliquidated" or "liquidated."

Unliquidated Debts

An *unliquidated debt* is one where a genuine dispute exists between the debtor and creditor as to the existence or amount of the indebtedness. Compromise agreements as to such debts are usually binding. The amount of a claim in a tort case is always subject to doubt, and thus the debt of the one who committed the tort is always an unliquidated debt. There can also be unliquidated debts in many other situations. For example, suppose that B buys a boat from S, and promises to pay $40,000 for it. B makes a down payment of $20,000, and they agree that the balance is due in 60 days. After taking possession of the boat, B determines that there is a defect in the boat's motor. B then refuses to pay the full balance of $20,000. This is an unliquidated debt because there is a genuine dispute about whether the seller has breached the contract by selling a defective boat or whether the buyer has breached the contract by not paying the full balance. Therefore, a settlement agreement between the parties for, say, $17,000, will be legally enforceable. In the case of an unliquidated debt, the debtor gives up the right to claim in good faith that he owes less, and the creditor gives up the right to claim in good faith that he is entitled to more. Each side has given consideration. Such a settlement agreement is sometimes called an *accord and satisfaction*.

Liquidated Debts

In the case of *liquidated debts,* those in which there is no genuine basis for a good faith dispute as to the existence or the amount of the indebtedness, compromise agreements are less frequently binding. For example: A agrees to lend $10,000 to B, and B agrees to repay the debt on a specific date along with 6% interest on the total amount. On or after the date for repayment, B says that he is unable to repay the full amount, and they agree that A will accept $9,000 in full settlement of the debt. B pays that amount, but A later seeks to recover the additional amount (another $1,000 plus the interest).

The common-law rule here is that A's promise to release B from the remainder of the debt is not binding, and he can therefore recover the unpaid balance. The reasoning is that, because there was no basis for a genuine, good faith dispute about the existence or amount of the debt, the payment of $9,000 by B did not constitute a detriment to him, since it was less than what he was already obligated to pay under the loan contract. He was simply performing a ''pre-existing duty.'' This rule is followed by the courts of most states even where the promise to release is in writing.

Payment by Check

What if a debtor pays only part of a debt by check, but conspicuously marks the check "Payment in full," or uses similar words such as "In full satisfaction." This is an offer to settle the debt. When the creditor receives the check and either cashes or deposits it, this is an acceptance of the offer. Does the resulting agreement settle the debt for an amount less than what was owed? Here, the same rules apply. The answer will be No in the case of a liquidated debt and is probably Yes in the case of an unliquidated one. A provision in the UCC dealing with checks (UCC 3-311) makes it clear that the common-law rules continue to apply to part-payment checks.

In relatively large businesses that process large numbers of payments by check, there is a good chance that the "Payment in full" or similar designation on a check will be overlooked. As a result, a number of courts have held that accepting and processing a check in such circumstances does not support an inference that the creditor agreed to the compromise. UCC Article 3-311 helps resolve this problem by allowing corporate payees to notify customers that instruments that are "in full satisfaction" must be sent to a designated office. If the customer does not comply by sending the instrument to the designated office, the claim is not discharged by the creditor's cashing of the check even if the debt is an unliquidated one.

Use of Credit Cards and Modern Electronic Payment Systems

In recent years, fewer people are writing checks and those who do write them are writing them much less frequently. Thus, the rules for settlement of debts by check do not have the same degree of importance as they once did, though these rules still apply when checks are used. Many, perhaps most, payments these days are made by credit card, debit card, direct payments from a bank account, and payment apps such as PayPal, Apple Pay, and so on. In these situations, there is little opportunity for a debtor to signify an intention to settle a debt with a less-than-full payment. If the debtor does find a way to indicate such an intent when making the payment the common law rules will apply, but UCC 3-311 applies only to checks and not to these other payment methods.

Special Statutes in Several States on Debt Settlements

In a growing number of states (*but still a minority*), legislation has been adopted that rejects the common law rule on settlement of debts by providing that all settlement agreements, if in writing, are binding upon the creditor even though consideration is absent. Typical of such statutes is Sec. 1541 of the California Civil Code, which reads as follows: "An obligation is extinguished by a release therefrom given to the debtor by the creditor upon a new consideration, or in writing, with or without new consideration." These statutes mirror the provision in Article 2 of the UCC that removed the requirement of consideration for modifications of sale of goods contracts.

PROMISSORY ESTOPPEL

While it is well established that a promise to make a gift is generally unenforceable by the promisee even where they have performed some act in reliance upon the promise, unusual circumstances exist where the application of this view brings about results that are grossly unfair to the promisee. In such circumstances, the courts occasionally will invoke the doctrine of *promissory estoppel* (or "justifiable reliance" theory, as it is often called) to enforce the promise.

The basic idea underlying this doctrine is that if the promisor makes a promise under circumstances in which they should realize that the promisee is almost certainly going to rely on the promise in a particular way, and if the promisee does so rely, thereby causing a substantial change in his or her position, the promisor is bound by the promise even though consideration is lacking on the part of the promisee. To illustrate: Tenant T leases a building from Landlord L from January 1, 1985, to December 31, 1986. In early December 1986, T indicates that he is thinking of remodeling the premises and wants a renewal of the lease for another two years. L replies, "We'll get to work on a new lease soon. I don't know about two years, but you can count on one year for sure." T then spends $500 over the next few weeks in having the first-floor rooms painted, but the parties never execute a new lease. If L seeks to evict T in March 1987 on the ground that his promise to renew was not supported by consideration, he will probably be unsuccessful—that is, he will be held to his promise regarding the year 1987. In this case, where L should have realized the likelihood of T's conduct in consequence of his promise, L is said to be "estopped by his promise"; that is, he is barred by his promise from contending that the lack of consideration on T's part caused his promise to be unenforceable.

To illustrate further: "A has been employed by B for forty years. B promises to pay A a pension of $200 per month when A retires. A retires and forbears to work elsewhere for several years while B pays the pension. B's promise is binding." *Restatement, Contracts 2d,* The American Law Institute, Section 90, 1973.

Applications of Promissory Estoppel

Promissory estoppel is a doctrine of increasing importance and broadening application. We discuss promissory estoppel in this chapter because it is most commonly thought of as a method of enforcing a variety of promises that lack consideration. However, many courts invoke promissory estoppel in a variety of situations where they believe that contractual formalities are unnecessarily blocking attainment of the reasonable intentions and expectations of the parties. Consideration is one such formality; the requirement that some contracts be in writing in order to be enforceable is another. When the writing requirement is discussed in Chapter 15, we will see how promissory estoppel often provides an alternative means of enforcing oral promises that the parties intended to be enforceable, but did not put in writing.

Promissory estoppel doctrine is not completely consistent from jurisdiction to jurisdiction, but typical examples of the wide variety of uses of promissory estoppel include:

(1) X worries about floods and asks his insurance company whether his current policy protects his house from flood damage, indicating that he will procure a different policy if it does not. The company assures X that his current policy does cover flood damage. After X's house is damaged by a flood, examination of the policy clearly indicates that flood damage is excluded. The insurance company refuses to pay. Many courts would allow X to enforce the company's promise on grounds of promissory estoppel. *Travelers Indemnity Co. v. Holman*, 330 F.2d 142 (5th Cir. 1964).

(2) P interviews for a job with D Co., telling D that he has a good job with X Co. but would quit there if D offered him a job. D offers P a job, realizing that he will now resign his job with X. When P reports for work, D tells him that it no longer needs him and points out that his employment was ''at-will'' anyway (so that D is within its rights to terminate P at any time). Many courts would allow P to recover from D on promissory estoppel grounds. *Roberts v. Geosource Drilling Co., 757* S.W.2d 48 (Tex. App. 1988).

(3) Just before L, a general contractor, submits a bid on a construction project, M, a paving subcontractor, calls L and submits an $8,000 bid for the paving work. This is the lowest paving bid, so L reduces his overall bid, submits the bid, and is awarded the contract. Before L can inform M of the bid's success, M calls L to revoke its $8,000 offer, refusing to do the work for less than $15,000. M argues that it revoked its offer before L accepted it and that as of the time of revocation there was nothing to indicate to M that it had a contract it could enforce against L. Many courts would bind M to its promise through the doctrine of promissory estoppel. *Drennan v. Star Paving Co.*, 333 P.2d 757 (Cal. 1958).

GARWOOD PACKAGING, PNC. v. ALLEN & CO.
U.S. Court of Appeals, 7th Circuit, 378 F.3d 698 (2004)

Plaintiff Garwood Packaging, Inc. (GPI) had flopped in its food-packaging system and by 1993 had run up debts of $3 million and was broke. It engaged Martin to help find investors. Martin told GPI that Allen & Co., an investment company for whom he worked, would consider investing $2 million of its own money if another investor could be found to make a comparable investment. Allen also decided to reduce its risk exposure by finding other investors to put in half of the promised $2 million.

Martin located Hobart Corporation that was prepared to manufacture $2 million worth of GPI packaging machines in return for equity in the company. As a precondition, Hobart demanded releases from other GPI creditors, as did the other investors that Allen was bringing into the deal.

Martin told Garwood and McNamara, GPI's principals, that he would see that the deal went through "come hell or high water." Based on several statements of that nature, Garwood and McNamara moved from Indiana to Ohio to be near Hobart's plant where they expected their equipment to be made. They also forgave their personal loans to GPI and incurred other costs. And GPI did not explore other funding opportunities.

Eventually, however, the investors Allen was bringing in to pay half of its promised $2 million got cold feet, so Allen decided not to invest. The deal collapsed and GPI took bankruptcy. When Allen withdrew, no contract had been signed and no agreement had been reached as to how much stock either Allen or Hobart would receive in exchange for their promised contributions to GPI. Nor had releases been obtained from the creditors.

GPI sued Allen on a promissory estoppel theory. The trial judge granted summary judgment to Allen, and GPI appealed.

Posner, Circuit Judge:

GPI claims that Martin's unequivocal promise to see the deal through to completion bound Allen by the doctrine of promissory estoppel, which makes a promise that induces reasonable reliance legally enforceable. Restatement (Second) of Contracts Sec. 90(1). If noncontractual promises were never enforced, reliance on their being enforceable would never be reasonable, so let us consider why the law might want to allow people to rely on promises that do not create actual contracts and whether the answer can help GPI.

The simplest answer to the "why" question is that the doctrine merely allows reliance to be substituted for consideration as the basis for making a promise enforceable. On this view promissory estoppel is really just a doctrine of contract law. The most persuasive reason for the requirement of consideration in the law of contracts is that in a system in which oral contracts are enforceable—and by juries, to boot—the requirement provides some evidence that there really was a promise that was intended to be relied on as a real commitment. Actual reliance, in the sense of a costly change of position that cannot be recouped if the reliance turns out to have been misplaced, is substitute evidence that there may well have been such a promise. The inference is especially plausible in a commercial setting, because most businesspeople would be reluctant to incur costs in reliance on a promise that they believed the promisor didn't consider himself legally bound to perform.

In other words, reasonable reliance is seen as nearly as good a reason for thinking there really was a promise as bargained-for reliance is. In many such cases, it is true, no promise was intended, or intended to be legally enforceable; in those cases the application of the doctrine penalizes the defendant for inducing the plaintiff to incur costs of reliance. The penalty is withheld if the reliance was unreasonable; for then the plaintiff's wound was self-inflicted—he should have known better than to rely.

A relevant though puzzling difference between breach of contract and promissory estoppel as grounds for legal relief is that while the promise relied on to trigger an estoppel must be definite in the sense of being clearly a promise and not just a statement of intentions, its terms need not be as clear as a contractual promise would have to be in order to be enforceable. The reason for this difference between breach of contract and promissory estoppel is unclear.

But even though the court is not precluded from finding a promise by its vagueness, the vaguer the alleged promise the less likely it is to be found to be a promise. And if it is really vague, the promisee would be imprudent to rely on it -- he wouldn't know whether reliance was worthwhile. The broader principle, which the requirement that the promise be definite and at least minimally clear instantiates, is that the promisee's reliance must be reasonable; if it is not, then not only is he the gratuitous author of his own disappointment, but probably there wasn't really a promise, or at least a promise intended or likely to induce reliance. The "promise" would have been in the nature of a hope or possibly a prediction rather than a commitment to do something within the "promisor's power to do ("I promise it will rain tomorrow"); and the "promisee" would, if sensible, understand this. He would rely or not as he chose but he would know that he would have to bear the cost of any disappointment.

We note, returning to the facts of this case, that there was costly reliance by GPI, and by Garwood and McNamara. The reliance was on statements by Martin, of which "come hell or high water" was the high water mark but is by no means an isolated example. Martin repeatedly confirmed to GPI that the deal would go through, that Allen's commitment to invest $2 million was unconditional, that the funding would be forthcoming, and so on; and these statements induced the plaintiffs to incur costs they would otherwise not have done.

But were these real promises, and likely to be understood as such? Those are two different questions. A person may say something that he intends as merely a prediction, or as a signal of his hopes or intentions, but that is reasonably understood as a promise, and if so, as we know (this is the penal or deterrent function of promissory estoppel), he is bound. But what is a reasonable, and indeed actual, understanding will often depend on the knowledge that the promisee brings to the table. McNamara, with whom Martin primarily dealt, is a former investment banker, not a rube. He knew that in putting together a deal to salvage a failing company there is many a slip 'twixt cup and lips. Unless blinded by optimism or desperation he had to know that Martin could not mean literally that the deal would go through "come hell or high water," since if Satan or a tsunami obliterated Ohio that would kill the deal. Even if Allen had dug into its pockets for the full $2 million after the investors who it had hoped would put up half the amount defected, the deal might well not have gone through because of Hobart's demands and because of the creditors. GPI acknowledges that the Internal Revenue Service, one of its largest creditors, wouldn't give a release until paid in full. Some of GPI's other creditors also intended to fight rather than to accept a pittance in exchange for a release. Nothing is more common than for a deal to rescue a failing company to fall apart because all the creditors' consent to the deal cannot be obtained--that is one of the reasons for bankruptcy law. Again these were things of which McNamara was perfectly aware.

The problem, thus, is not that Martin's promises were indefinite, but that they could not have been reasonably understood by the persons to whom they were addressed (mainly McNamara, the financial partner in GPI) to be promises rather than expressions of optimism and determination. To move to Ohio, to forgive personal loans, to forgo other searches for possible investors, and so forth were in the nature of gambles on the part of GPI and its principals. They may have been reasonable gambles, in the sense that the prospects for a successful salvage operation were good enough that taking immediate, even if irrevocable, steps to facilitate and take advantage of the expected happy outcome was prudent. But we often reasonably rely on things that are not promises. A farmer plants his crops in the spring in reasonable reliance that spring will be followed by summer rather than by winter. There can be reasonable reliance on statements as well as on the regularities of nature, but if the statements are not reasonably understood as legally enforceable promises there can be no action for promissory estoppel.

Suppose McNamara thought that there was a 50 percent chance that the deal would go through and believed that reliance on that prospect would cost him $100,000, but also believed that by relying he could expect either to increase the likelihood that the deal would go through or to make more money if it did by being able to start production sooner and that in either event the expected benefit of reliance would exceed $100,000. Then his reliance would be reasonable even if not induced by enforceable promises. The numbers are arbitrary but the example apt. GPI and its principals relied, and may have relied reasonably, but they didn't rely on Martin's "promises" because those were not promises reasonably understood as such by so financially sophisticated a businessman as McNamara. So we see now that the essence of the doctrine of promissory estoppel is not that the plaintiff has reasonably relied on the defendant's promise, but that he has reasonably relied on its being a promise in the sense of a legal commitment, and not a mere prediction or aspiration or bit of puffery. Affirmed.

FORMAL PROMISES TO CHARITABLE INSTITUTIONS

The law generally looks favorably upon charitable institutions, such as churches, hospitals, and colleges. One result of this policy is that many courts enforce formal promises (e.g., charitable subscriptions) to make gifts to such institutions, even though technically there is no conventional consideration. Among the approaches that courts use to enforce promises to make such gifts are (1) invention of consideration, by finding that each donor's promise is made in consideration of the promises of the other donors (i.e., a donor's promise is supported by the detriment incurred by other donors who made similar promises); (2) promissory estoppel, by finding that donors should foresee that the donee institution will rely on the promised gift, for example, by drawing up plans and beginning construction; and (3) where all else fails, many courts will simply enforce the promise on grounds of public policy because these organizations cannot survive otherwise.

PROMISES MADE SUBSEQUENT TO THE RUNNING OF A STATUTE OF LIMITATIONS

All states have *statutes of limitations* limiting the time a creditor has in which to bring suit against the debtor after the debt becomes due. These periods of time vary widely among the states, and there is no typical statute. If the specified period of time elapses without the initiation of legal proceedings by the creditor, the statute is said to have "run." While the running of a statute does not extinguish the debt, it does cause the contract to be unenforceable—that is, it prevents the creditor from successfully maintaining an action in court to collect the debt.

To what extent is the situation altered if the debtor, after the statute of limitations has run, makes a new promise to pay the debt? One might conclude that such a promise is unenforceable, since there is clearly no consideration given by the creditor in return. This, however, is not the case.

In all states, either by statute or by judicial decision, such a promise, if in writing, is enforceable despite the absence of consideration. In such a case, the debt is said to have been "revived," and the creditor now has a new statutory period in which to bring suit. (If the new promise was to pay only a portion of the original indebtedness, such as $200 of a $450 debt, the promise is binding only to the extent of that portion—in this case, $200.)

The debt is also revived if a part payment is made by the debtor after the statute has run. If, for example, a five-year statute had run on a $1,000 debt, and the debtor thereafter mailed a check for $50 to the creditor, the creditor now has an additional five years in which to commence legal action for the balance. A mere acknowledgment by the debtor that the debt exists will also revive the obligation to pay.

Imposition of liability in the above instances is based on the theory that the debtor has, by making the part payment or acknowledgment, impliedly promised to pay the remaining indebtedness. The debtor can escape the operation of this rule by advising the creditor, when making the payment or acknowledgment, that they are not making any promise as to payment of the balance.

It bears mentioning that these rules regarding the reviving of a debt by part payment or acknowledgement after the statute of limitations has expired *do not apply* to debts that have been *discharged* in bankruptcy. A debt that has been discharged in bankruptcy is not revived by part payment or acknowledgement.

CHAPTER 13

ILLEGALITY

- Contracts Contrary to Statute
- Contracts Contrary to Public Policy
- Effect of Illegal Contracts

In the case of *Everet v. Williams,* 9 Law. Quart. Rev. 197 [England], a lawsuit was filed by one partner against another, alleging that they had gone into business together and that the defendant had kept more than his share of partnership profits. The complaint was rather vague regarding the nature of the business, alleging that the parties "proceeded jointly in [dealing for commodities] with good success on Hounslow Heath, where they dealt with a gentleman for a gold watch"; that in Finchley they "dealt with several gentlemen for divers watches, rings, swords, canes, hats, cloaks, horses, bridles, saddles, and other things"; and that a gentleman of Blackheath had items the defendant thought "might be had for little or no money in case they could prevail on the said gentleman to part with the said things." It is told that when it dawned on the court that the partners were highwaymen (the English equivalent of American stagecoach robbers), the solicitors (attorneys) for both parties were jailed and the plaintiff and defendant were both hanged. This possibly apocryphal case vividly makes the point that courts do not generally enforce illegal contracts. Indeed, the third element of an enforceable contract is legality of purpose—the attainment of an objective that is not prohibited by state or federal law.

In this chapter we will examine some of the most common kinds of contracts that are ordinarily illegal under state law. Within a given state, a contract is illegal because it is either (1) contrary to that state's statutes (including the regulations of its administrative agencies) or (2) contrary to the public policy of that state, as defined by its courts.

All states have criminal statutes. Such statutes not only prohibit certain acts but, additionally, provide for the imposition of fines or imprisonment on persons who violate them. Any contract calling for the commission of a crime is clearly illegal. Many other statutes simply prohibit the performance of specified acts without imposing criminal penalties for violations. Contracts that call for the performance of these acts are also illegal. (An example of the latter is lending money under an agreement that obligates the borrower to pay interest at a rate in excess of that permitted by statute.)

Still other contracts are illegal simply because they call for the performance of an act that the courts feel has an adverse effect on the general public. (Examples of contracts contrary to public policy are those under which a person promises never to get married or never to engage in a certain profession.) As a general rule, contracts that are illegal on either statutory or public policy grounds are void. This means that (1) in cases where the contract is entirely executory, neither party is bound by the agreement, and (2) in cases where one of the parties has performed his or her part of the bargain, such party cannot recover the consideration, or the value of the consideration, that has passed to the other party. (Exceptions to this general rule will be discussed later in the chapter.) Furthermore, courts will not allow even quasi-contractual recovery where illegal action is involved. By denying recovery to the parties to an illegal transaction, courts reason that they will deter illegal activity.

CONTRACTS CONTRARY TO STATUTE

Wagering Agreements

All states have statutes relating to *wagering agreements*, or gambling contracts. Under the general language of most of these statutes, making bets and operating games of chance are prohibited. Any obligations arising from these activities are void (nonexistent) in the eyes of the law, and thus completely unenforceable by the winner.

Bets and Lotteries

In most instances wagering agreements are easily recognized. Simple bets on the outcome of athletic events and lotteries such as bingo (when played for money) are the most common of them. On the other hand, merchants holding promotional schemes such as supermarket drawings sometimes have difficulty determining if they are holding an illegal lottery, especially because definitions vary widely from state to state. Courts tend to rule that a scheme that does not require a purchase of goods by the participant is not a lottery because consideration (which most courts view as an essential part of a lottery) is lacking. That is why so many contests state "no purchase necessary."

In recent years a growing number of state statutes have been liberalized to permit wagering and lottery activities within narrow limits. For example, so-called "friendly bets"—those defined as not producing substantial sources of income—are frequently exempted from the basic wagering statutes, as are some lotteries operated by religious or charitable organizations. Additionally, many states have sanctioned state-operated lotteries by special statutes.

Many contracts whose performance is dependent upon an element of chance are clearly not wagers. This is particularly true of *risk-shifting contracts* (as distinguished from *risk-creating contracts*). An insurance policy is a risk-shifting contract. If a person insures his or her home against loss by fire, for example, the contract is perfectly legal even though it is not known at the time the policy is issued whether the insurer will have liability under it. The contract is legal despite this uncertainty because the owner had an "insurable interest" in the home prior to taking out the policy—that is, a financial loss would have resulted if a fire had occurred. Thus an insurance policy is simply a contract by which an existing risk is shifted to an insurance company for a consideration paid by the owner. By contrast, an insurance policy on a building which the insured does not own and in which they have no other financial interest is clearly a wager (risk-creating contract) and is unenforceable.

Persons have insurable interests in the lives of, and thus can take out a life insurance policy on, themselves, their spouses, and their children. Companies have insurable interests in the lives of their top executives.

Licensing Statutes

All states have *licensing statutes*, requiring that persons who engage in certain professions, trades, or businesses be licensed. Lawyers, physicians, real estate brokers, contractors, electricians, and vendors of milk and liquor are but a few examples of persons commonly subject to a wide variety of such statutes. In many instances, particularly those involving the professions, passing a comprehensive examination (along with proof of good moral character) is a condition of obtaining a license. In others, only proof of good moral character may be required.

To find out whether an unlicensed person can recover for services rendered under a contract, one must check the particular statute involved. Some licensing statutes expressly provide that recovery by unlicensed persons shall not be allowed (no matter how competent their work). Others, however, are silent on the matter, in which case their underlying purposes must be determined. Most courts take the view in such instances that if the statute is *regulatory*—its purpose being the protection of the general public against unqualified persons—then the contract is illegal and recovery is denied. On the other hand, if the statute is felt to be merely *revenue raising* and not clearly designed for public protection, recovery is allowed.

The reasoning behind this distinction, of course, is that allowing recovery of a fee or commission by an unlicensed person in the first category would adversely affect public health and safety, while the enforcement of contracts in the second category does not have this result. Thus an unlicensed milk vendor who has sold and delivered a quantity of milk will ordinarily not be permitted to recover the purchase price from the buyer. Similarly, an unlicensed physician, real estate agent, or attorney will be denied his or her fee. On the other hand, a corporation that has merely failed to obtain a license to do business in a particular city is still permitted to enforce its contracts, because city licensing ordinances applicable to corporations are normally enacted for revenue raising purposes.

By congressional enactment, the federal government requires licenses for engaging in some activities, such as acting as a securities broker or an investment advisor. In *Matter of Living Benefits Asset Management, LLC*, 916 F.3d 528 (5th Cir. 2019), a company (Living Benefits, LLC) provided advisory and consulting services to a business that sought to purchase "life settlement contracts" to use as collateral for obtaining debt financing. These contracts involved those who had purchased life insurance policies and subsequently sold the rights to collect on the policies at death to an entity that paid more than the policies' cash value (what the life insurance carrier would pay to the policy owner if the policy was canceled), but less than the benefit that would be paid to a beneficiary in the event of the insured's death. These contracts provide a way for those having life insurance to acquire needed cash while living in a larger amount than if they "cashed in" the policy.

The amount of a possible death benefit, and thus the return to the entity that bought the contract, declines as further premiums are paid. Thus, the purchaser of a life settlement contract is taking a risk on how long the insured person will live, and also a risk that the insured will stop paying premiums and forfeit the policy. The client of Living Benefits, LLC, Kestrel Aircraft Co. contracted to pay Living Benefits over $900,000 for its advice about purchasing life settlement contracts, regardless of whether Kestrel actually invested in any of these contracts. Ultimately, Kestrel did not buy any, and it refused to pay the agreed fee to Living Benefits. Living Benefits sued Kestrel for breach of contract. Both the federal district court and the U.S. Court of Appeals for the Fifth Circuit held that Living Benefits could not recover its fee because these life settlement contracts fell within the definition of securities as "investment contracts," and that Living Benefits had not met the legal requirement of registering under the federal Investment Advisers Act. Failure to register caused the contract to provide advisory services for a fee to be void.

Usury

In large part because of the practical hardships resulting from high interest rates charged desperate borrowers, all states have statutes establishing the maximum rate of interest that can be charged on ordinary loans. Charging interest in excess of the permitted rate constitutes *usury*.

The interest ceilings that are imposed by the usury statutes vary from state to state. Traditionally the basic statutes have varied from 6 percent to 12 percent per annum. However, as a result of inflationary pressures over the years, the basic statutes now generally range from 10 percent to 16 percent per annum.

More important, many kinds of loans are not governed by the basic state statutes. For

© **2020 John R. Allison & Robert A. Prentice**

example, most states put no limit on the rate of interest that can be charged on loans made to corporations. And, under federal regulations, national banks are permitted to charge interest rates that are usually in excess of those permitted by the state usury laws.

Additionally, all states in recent years—again, partly because of inflationary pressures—have adopted special statutes permitting higher rates of interest on other specified kinds of loans. For example, most state laws today provide that interest rates charged by issuers of bank credit cards (such as Visa and MasterCard), and by department stores on their revolving credit accounts, can be at an annual percentage rate of 18 percent. Similarly, home purchase and construction loans, car loans, and loans by credit unions may generally carry annual interest rates ranging from 18 to 25 percent. It should also be noted that most states have adopted special statues that expressly permit small loan companies, such as "personal loan companies," to charge rates of interest that are considerably higher than those of the general interest statutes. For example, a loan company that qualifies under such statutes may be allowed to charge interest at the rate of 3 percent *per month* on the first $150 of a loan, 2 percent per month on the amount from $151 to $300, and 1 percent on the balance. These statutes usually provide that if interest is charged in excess of the specified rates, the loan is void. In such a case, neither principal nor interest can be recovered.

The basic statutes also vary widely insofar as the effect of usury is concerned. Many states permit the usurious lender to recover the principal and interest at the lawful rate, but not the excess interest. In such states the lender suffers no penalty. In others, the lender is permitted to recover the principal only, forfeiting all interest. And in three or four states, the lender forfeits both interest and principal.

It is thus clear that no determination can be made as to the legality or effect of a given loan without inspecting the statutes of the state in which the transaction took place.

CONTRACTS CONTRARY TO PUBLIC POLICY

Contracts in Restraint of Trade

Many contracts that unreasonably restrain trade or competition in interstate commerce are in violation of one or more federal antitrust statutes, such as the Sherman and Clayton acts. Long before the enactment of these statutes, however, many other contracts in restraint of trade were illegal under the common law of the various states, and this continues to be the case today. Thus a contract that is not subject to the Sherman or Clayton acts may still result in such restraint of trade that courts will set it aside under common law principles. These principles are briefly summarized here.

Contracts that contain *covenants not to compete* (or "noncompetition agreements," or sometimes just "noncompetes")—agreements in which one party promises not to compete with another—compose one group of contracts that are in restraint of trade. However, such promises are not necessarily illegal. Generally, covenants not to compete are lawful if certain conditions are met: (1) The agreement must be of an "ancillary" nature. (2) The promisee must have a legitimate business interest that warrants temporary protection from competition. (3) The agreement must be reasonable in its scope so that it does not limit competition more than is reasonably necessary to protect the promisee's legitimate interest.

The Ancillary Requirement

An *ancillary covenant* is one that is a subsidiary or auxiliary part of a larger agreement. A common example of an ancillary covenant is that found in a contract calling for the *sale of a business,* where the contract contains a promise by the seller of the business not to engage in the same type of business within a prescribed geographical area for a certain length of time after the sale. Similarly, agreements not to compete are relatively common in partnership agreements, obligating a partner who leaves the business to not enter into competition with the partnership in a described market for a stated period of time. Equally common are non-competition covenants in *employment contracts,* under which the employee promises not to compete with the business of his or her employer for a specified period of time after the employment is terminated. Nonancillary covenants, on the other hand, stand alone; they do not protect any existing, legally recognized interest such as that in the prior examples. These covenants—such as a promise by a father to pay $10,000 for the son's promise not to engage in medical practice—are generally considered to be an unreasonable restraint of trade in all circumstances, and are thus illegal and unenforceable on public policy grounds.)

Reasonableness—Sale of Business Contracts. When a business is being sold, the interest to be protected relates to the goodwill of the business. A restrictive covenant on the part of the seller, in a particular case, is thus enforceable if its space and time limitations are no broader than are reasonably necessary to afford such protection. For example, a promise by the seller of a retail grocery in Kalispell, Montana, that he will not engage in the retail grocery business ''within the City of Kalispell for the period of one year after the sale'' is probably reasonable and thus lawful. Similarly, in *Gann v.* Morris, 596 P.2d 43 (1979), a promise by the seller of a silk-screening business in Tucson, Arizona, that he would not operate a competing business within a hundred-mile radius of Tucson for a specified period of time was held to be reasonable in view of the fact that at least one of the business's customers was located that distance away.

Thus, in the above instances, if the seller should violate his or her promise, the purchaser of the business is entitled to an injunction against them. (On the other hand, if the restraint is found to be excessive—as would be the case if the seller of the grocery in Kalispell was prohibited from engaging in the grocery business "anywhere within the state of Montana" for one year—the restraint is illegal, and thus unenforceable by the buyer.) In a noncompetition agreement in this or any other ancillary context, a reasonable geographic restriction on the effectiveness of the obligation not to compete cannot exceed the market area of the business being protected—that is, the geographic scope cannot be greater than the area within which one making the promise can inflict competitive harm on the other. A reasonable geographic area might be relatively small, such as the city of Chicago, or it might be nationwide.

Reasonableness—Employment Contracts. Restrictive covenants in employment contracts are reasonable (1) if the restriction is reasonably necessary to protect the employer, and (2) if the restriction is ''not unreasonably excessive'' as to the employee. Because of this second requirement, geographical restraints in employment contracts are more likely to be set aside by the courts than those in contracts where businesses are being sold. Courts will also be stricter with time restraints in employment contracts than in sale of business contracts. In one recent case, a one-year covenant was held to be unreasonably long, the court commenting that one year could be several generations in the fast-moving high-tech industry in which defendant employee worked. *Earthweb, Inc. v. Schlack,* 71

F.Supp.2d 299 (S.D.N.Y. 1999). In markets that are not as rapidly changing, longer periods of time may be reasonable; however, it is rare for a court to uphold as reasonable a time period of longer than two years in the employment context.

A non-competition clause in an employment agreement also must be reasonably limited as to the geographic area within which the employee is forbidden to compete, or as to the customers that the employee may serve after leaving this employer (if the employee is one who dealt with customers during her employment). As stated earlier, an agreement not to compete in an employment contract must not extend beyond the employer's market area, that is, it may not extend beyond an area within which the employee will be capable of causing competitive harm to the employer after leaving the company. Depending on the circumstances, this might be a local area such as the Houston, TX metropolitan area, a regional area such as several southeastern states in the U.S., or even the entire U.S. Of course, some markets are global in nature, but U.S. law cannot operate to limit competition outside the U.S.

If the employee in question deals with customers as part of her job, the non-competition agreement can be reasonably limited by the customers whom the employee can serve after leaving the company instead of being limited by geographic area. Courts in some states will enforce such an agreement only with respect to customers that this employee actually dealt with while working for the employer. However, the courts in most states do not apply such a rigid rule and apply a general test of reasonableness to the scope of the customer limitation. For example, a court might conclude in a particular case that a covenant not to compete is reasonable when it prohibits an employee, after leaving the company, from soliciting customers. And keep in mind that a noncompetition agreement must be reasonable *both* as to its time limitation and its geographic or customer scope.

SYSTEMS AND SOFTWARE, INC. v. BARNES
Supreme Court of Vermont, 886 A.2d 762 (2005)

Systems & Software, Inc. (SSI), plaintiff, is engaged in the business of designing, developing, selling, and servicing software that allows utility providers to organize data regarding customer information, billing, work management, asset management, and finance and accounting. In August 2002, SSI hired Barnes as an at-will employee to become a regional vice-president of sales. At the time he began work for SSI, Barnes signed a noncompetition agreement that, among other things, prohibited him—during his employment and for six months thereafter—from becoming associated with any business that competes with SSI. In April 2004, Barnes voluntarily left his position with SSI and started a partnership with his wife called Spirit Technologies Consulting Group. Spirit Technologies' only customer was Utility Solutions, Inc., which, like SSI, provides customer-information-systems software and service to municipalities and utilities nationwide.

On April 27, 2004, SSI sued Barnes and requested an injunction to enforce the parties' noncompetition agreement. The trial court held for SSI and granted an injunction that prohibited Barnes from working as a consultant or otherwise with Utility Solutions or any other direct competitor of SSI. Barnes appealed.

Reiber, Chief Justice:

Like many other courts, this Court has adopted a position with respect to enforcement of noncompetition agreements similar to that set forth in § 188(1) of the Restatement

(Second) of Contracts (1981), which provides that a restrictive covenant "is unreasonably in restraint of trade if (a) the restraint is greater than is needed to protect the promisee's legitimate interest, or (b) the promisee's need is outweighed by the hardship to the promisor and the likely injury to the public." A court will enforce a restrictive covenant in an employment agreement to the extent that enforcement is reasonably tailored to protect a legitimate interest of the employer. We have stated that "we will proceed with caution" when asked to enforce covenants against competitive employment because such restraints run counter to public policy favoring the right of individuals to engage in the commercial activity of their choice. Nonetheless, we will enforce such agreements unless the agreement is found to be contrary to public policy, unnecessary for protection of the employer, or unnecessarily restrictive of the rights of the employee, with due regard being given to the subject matter of the contract and the circumstances and conditions under which it is to be performed.

Here, in arguing that the trial court erred by enforcing the parties' agreement, Barnes first asserts that the agreement does not safeguard a legitimate interest of the employer because it was not needed to protect trade secrets or confidential customer information. This argument fails because it is based on a faulty premise—that noncompetition agreements may be enforced to protect *only* trade secrets or confidential customer information. Most states do not limit the scope of noncompetition agreements [only to situations in which the employee has access to trade secrets or confidential customer information]. ... Employers may use noncompetition agreements to protect the goodwill of a business in addition to trade secrets and other confidential information.... Noncompetition agreements may protect legitimate employer interests such as customer relationships and employee-specific goodwill that are significantly broader than proprietary information such as trade secrets and confidential customer information.... [The law] sometimes allows an employer contractually to prevent all competition by a former employee, even competition that does not make use of the employer's proprietary information.

It is not necessary in this case to identify the complete range of employer interests, beyond trade secrets and confidential customer information, that may be protected through noncompetition agreements. Here, the trial court found that SSI had a legitimate protectable interest, and the evidence supports the court's finding. The trial court found that during his employment with SSI, Barnes had acquired inside knowledge about the strengths and weaknesses of SSI's products—knowledge that he could use to compete against SSI. As the court pointed out, both SSI and United Solutions, Barnes's only client, served a small market of customers; thus, the loss of even a single contract could deprive SSI of revenue for many years, especially considering the need for service and software updates. Given these circumstances, we find no basis for overturning the trial court's conclusion that SSI had a legitimate protectable interest.

Barnes argues, however, that even assuming the parties' agreement protects a legitimate interest, the agreement is more restrictive than necessary to protect that interest. He contends that less drastic solutions were available to the trial court to fashion a more reasonable restraint on his employment. For example, he suggests that the court could have simply prohibited him from soliciting SSI's current customers, or, at a minimum, prohibited him from dealing with noncooperative [i.e. not electricity "co-ops"] utilities, given that SSI has not dealt with cooperatives for nearly twenty years. According to Barnes, a complete ban on competition is not only unduly restrictive, but it effectively prevents him from working in his field of expertise for six months, thereby imposing a hardship that far outweighs any potential harm to SSI.

We do not find these arguments persuasive, particularly in the context of this case, which does not present any of the hallmarks of an unequal bargaining relationship between employer and employee. Barnes is a sophisticated consultant, who accepted employment with SSI after working for one of SSI's competitors. At the time he was hired, SSI informed Barnes that a condition of his employment was that he sign a covenant not to compete. Barnes signed the agreement, which explicitly prohibited him from competing with SSI for a six-month period following the parties' separation, would not prevent Barnes from earning a living. Barnes now claims hardship based on nothing more than a bald statement that he will be unable to work for six months if the agreement is enforced. We find no error in the court's decision not to invalidate the contract based on this unsupported claim.

Nor do we find error based on the superior court's refusal to rewrite the agreement to make it more favorable to Barnes. Although a restraint on competition is easier to justify if the restraint is limited to the taking of his former employer's customers as contrasted with competition in general, employers may seek to protect the good will of the business with either a general covenant not to compete or with a specific prohibition on contact with customers.

Determining which restraints are reasonable has not been an exact science. The reasonableness of the restrictions will vary by industry and will depend highly on the nature of the interest justifying the restrictive covenant. Generally, courts will uphold a contractual ban on an employee's post-employment competition if it would be difficult for an employer to determine when an employee is soliciting its customers. Because it is essentially impossible to monitor an employee's "use" of goodwill, this interest will support a complete ban on competition as long as it is reasonably limited temporally and geographically.

Here, the evidence demonstrates that SSI provided Barnes access not only to existing customers but also to information concerning the strengths and weaknesses of SSI's products, the individual needs of the customers he served, and the prices paid by those customers for SSI's products and services. The trial court found that in the course of his employment with SSI, Barnes acquired knowledge of SSI's software designs, customer base, marketing strategy, business practices, and other sensitive information revealing the strengths and weaknesses of SSI's software products. Because of the nature of SSI's business, which often involves customers initiating competitive bidding for contracts, it would be extremely difficult to monitor whether Barnes was using the goodwill and knowledge he acquired while working for SSI to gain a competitive edge against SSI.

Barnes also claims that he has not competed with SSI or violated the covenant not to compete, but the evidence supports the court's findings to the contrary. The only customer of Barnes's consulting firm was Utility Solutions, which directly competed against SSI for at least two different contracts. Further, shortly after Barnes left SSI's employ, he represented Utility Solutions at a trade fair in a booth near SSI's booth and identified himself as Utility Solution's sales director. Moreover, the trial court found "not credible" Barnes's claim that he was hired by Utility Solutions exclusively to market a new software product for two of the company's existing cooperative clients [i.e. electricity "co-ops"]. Under these circumstances, the trial court's injunction was reasonable.

We find unavailing Barnes's reliance on *Concord Orthopaedics Professional Ass'n v. Forbes,* 142 N.H. 440, 702 A.2d 1273 (1997), for the proposition that the trial court was required to narrow the parties' agreement to restrict Barnes from soliciting only SSI's current customers. In *Forbes,* a doctor left the employ of a physician's group and then sued his former employer, claiming that a covenant banning him from competing with the group within a twenty-five-mile radius of its business was unenforceable. The court upheld the agreement with respect to patients the doctor had treated while working for the group, but determined that the group lacked any legitimate interest in preventing the doctor from competing for new patients in the area. The present case is distinguishable because, while working for SSI, Barnes acquired specific information concerning SSI's customers, products, and services that could allow him to gain an advantage in competing against SSI for new clients. That was not the situation in *Forbes.*

Thus, the evidence supports the trial court's findings and conclusions, which, in turn, support its decision to enforce the agreement to the extent that Barnes is prohibited for a six-month period from working for Utility Solutions or any other direct competitor of SSI. According to the employment agreement, the six-month period begins only after issuance of a final unappealable judgment. Affirmed.

Blue-Pencil Rule: Will the Courts Rewrite the Non-Compete Clause?

Some courts find that an unreasonably broad time, geography, or activity restriction renders a restrictive covenant completely unenforceable. Today, courts in a majority of states apply the so-called "blue pencil" rule. The term derives from the time when editors of paper manuscripts used a blue pencil to mark changes and suggestions for the writer. Under this approach, courts finding that a contract's restrictions on competition serve an employer's legitimate interests but are unreasonably broad (either in terms of geography or time), hear evidence on what would be reasonable under the circumstances and then rewrite the covenant so that the restrictions are reasonable in scope and then will enforce them to that extent. Thus, a promise not to compete in the entire state of New York for three years might be rewritten to cover only a few counties in New York (e.g., where the promisor had worked) for one year. Many observers argue that the blue-pencil rule removes an incentive for employers to draft reasonable restrictions in the first place.

Exculpatory Clauses

The law of torts imposes certain duties on all persons, one of which is to carry out one's activities in a reasonably careful manner. If a person violates this duty by performing an act carelessly, they are guilty of the tort of negligence and is answerable in damages to anyone who was injured thereby.

Businesses and others often try to avoid this potential liability through the use of *exculpatory clauses* that purport to excuse them from liability resulting from their own negligence. Such clauses are generally—though not always—held to be contrary to public policy, and thus unenforceable against the injured party.

The Public Interest Inquiry

In general, an exculpatory clause will not be enforceable to relieve one of liability for negligence if the contract involves a matter that "substantially affects the public interest"—in other words, in contracts involving goods or services that are essential to daily life.

An early landmark case, *Little Rock & Fort Smith Ry Co. v. Eubanks,* 3 S.W. 808 (1886), is instructive on the public policy aspects of exculpatory clauses. This case was decided before states passed workers compensation legislation that provides benefits to employees for on-the-job injuries on a no-fault basis, but its reasoning applies today to any situation in which the matter affects a matter of public concern. A brakeman was hired by a railroad only after he promised not to sue the company for any injuries that resulted from the company's negligence. When the company raised the clause as a defense in a negligence suit filed by the brakeman's family after his death in an accident caused by a defective switch, the court stated that parties' contracts are normally enforceable as written. However, parties to contracts are not allowed to make agreements that violate express provisions of the law or injuriously affect public policy. If such clauses as that signed in this case were enforced, the court stated:

> [t]he consequence would be that every railroad company, and every owner of a factory, mill, or mine, would make it a condition precedent to the employment of labor, that the laborer should release all right for injuries sustained in the course of the service, whether by the employer's negligence or otherwise. The natural tendency of this would be to relax the employer's carefulness in those matters of which he has the ordering and control, such as the supplying of machinery and materials, and thus increase the perils of occupations which are hazardous even when well managed. And the final outcome would be to fill the country with disabled men and paupers whose support would become a charge upon the counties or upon public charity.

Most courts will give effect to exculpatory clauses where they involve only recreational activities, such as where people go rafting, sky-diving, or horseback riding, or other activities that are completely optional on the part of the participant and thus do not affect the public interest. On the other hand, such clauses typically are not effective to bar a negligence claim in situations where the party in whose favor the clause operates is providing services or goods that are essential to everyday life, such as lodging (as in a residential apartment lease), medical services, utility services, legal services, and so on.

In a situation in which an exculpatory clause is potentially effective because it does not involve a matter affecting the public interest, it will be effective to bar a negligence suit only if the clause is (1) either very conspicuous or specifically called to the attention of the potential plaintiff, and (2) written in a way that clearly informs the potential plaintiff that the drafter of the clause seeks to be relieved from liability for its negligence or the negligence of its employees. An exculpatory clause buried in the fine print of a lengthy standard-form contract will not be given effect. Finally, keep in mind that exculpatory clauses can only relieve defendants of liability for simple negligence. Clauses that attempt to avoid liability for acts of intentional wrongdoing or even gross negligence are not effective.

SEIGNEUR v. NATIONAL FITNESS INSTITUTE, INC.
Maryland Court of Special Appeals, 752 A.2d 631(2000)

Defendant NFI operates an exercise and fitness facility which plaintiff Seigneur chose to help her on a weight loss and fitness program because (a) her chiropractor recommended NFI, (b) NFI advertised that it employed "degreed, certified fitness, clinical exercise and health specialists," and (c) NFI promised to "provide advice based upon scientific evidence." To apply for membership, plaintiff had to sign a contract containing a clause that provided in emphasized print: "Important Information: I, the undersigned applicant, agree and understand that I must report any and all injuries immediately to NFI, Inc. staff. It is further agreed that all exercises shall be undertaken by me at my sole risk and that NFI, Inc. shall not be liable to me for any claims, demands, injuries, damages, actions, or courses of action whatsoever, to my person or property arising out of or connecting with the use of the services and facilities of NFI, Inc., by me, or to the premises of NFI, Inc. Further, I do expressly hereby forever release and discharge NFI, Inc. from all claims, demands, injuries, damages, actions, or causes of action, and from all acts of active or passive negligence on the part of NFI, Inc., its servants, agents or employees."

Josties, defendant's employee, performed an initial evaluation of plaintiff. She asked plaintiff to use an upper torso machine and placed a 90-pound weight on it, despite her knowledge that plaintiff had a history of lower back problems, a herniated disk, and was in poor physical condition. While attempting to lift the load as instructed, plaintiff felt a tearing sensation in her right shoulder. She informed Josties, who ignored the complaint and completed the evaluation. Since the incident, plaintiff has had pain and difficulty using her shoulder. A doctor attributes plaintiff's difficulties to the injury on the upper torso machine. Plaintiff filed a negligence lawsuit against NFI, which moved for summary judgment on grounds of the exculpatory clause quoted above. The trial court granted the motion and plaintiff appealed.

Salmon, Judge:

To decide this case, we must first determine whether the exculpatory clause quoted at the beginning of this opinion unambiguously excused NFI's negligence. In construing the Participation Agreement, we are required to give legal effect to all of its unambiguous provisions. Our primary concern when interpreting a contract is to effectuate the parties' intentions. Not all attempts to limit liability by way of exculpatory clauses are successful. For instance, in *Calarco v. YMCA of Greater Metropolitan Chicago*, 501 N.E.2d 268 (Ill.App. 1986), the court considered a contract purporting to exculpate the YMCA from liability to a plaintiff who was injured when a weight machine fell on her hand while she was exercising. In *Calarco*, the clause in question read:

> In consideration of my participation in the activities of the Young Men's Christian Association of Metropolitan Chicago, I do hereby agree to hold free from any and all liability the YMCA of Metropolitan Chicago and its respective officers, employees and members and do hereby for myself, my heirs, executors and administrators, waive, release and forever discharge any and all rights and claims for damages which I may have or which may hereafter accrue to me arising out of or connected with my participation in any of the activities of the YMCA of Metropolitan Chicago. I hereby do declare myself to be physically sound, having medical approval to participate in the activities of the YMCA.

The *Calarco* court concluded that the above-quoted clause did not contain a clear and adequate description of covered activities, such as "use of the said gymnasium or the facilities and equipment thereof," to clearly indicate that injuries resulting from negligence in maintaining the facilities or equipment would be covered by the release. "Participation in any of the activities of the YMCA" could be read to mean that the exculpatory clause from liability only pertains to participating in the activities at the YMCA, but not to liability from use of the equipment at the YMCA. Pertinent to this case, plaintiff at the time of the occurrence was not even using the equipment herself, but was assisting someone else who was using a universal machine which was apparently stuck. It is unclear whether this was "participation" in an "activity" under the meaning of the clause. Thus, the court held that "the language of the clause here is not sufficiently clear, explicit and unequivocal to show an intention to protect the YMCA from liability arising from the use of its equipment" at the YMCA.

Powell v. American Health Fitness Center of Ft. Wayne, 694 N.E.2d 757 (Ind. App. 1998) is another case in which the Court found that the exculpatory clause in question was too ambiguous to be enforced. In *Powell,* a health club member was injured while using a fitness club's whirlpool. Referring to the exculpatory clause contained in the club's agreement with the injured member, the court stated:

> Nowhere does the clause specifically or explicitly refer to the negligence of American Health. As a matter of law, the exculpatory clause did not release American Health from liability resulting from injuries she sustained while on its premises that were caused by its alleged negligence. Therefore, the exculpatory clause is void to the extent it purported to release American Health from liability caused by its own negligence.

In the foregoing cases where the clause was held to be ambiguous, the common thread was that the clause did not clearly indicate that the injured party was releasing the health clubs from liability for the clubs' own negligence. Without this clear expression of intent, the courts in those cases felt compelled to invalidate the exculpatory clauses in question. Nevertheless, given the judiciary's reluctance to interfere with the right of parties to contract, courts are almost universal in holding that health clubs, in their membership agreements, may limit their liability for future negligence if they do so unambiguously.

In Maryland, for an exculpatory clause to be valid, it "need not contain or use the word 'negligence' or any other 'magic words.'" *Adloo v. H.T. Brown Real Estate, Inc* ., 686 A.2d 298 (1996). An exculpatory clause "is sufficient to insulate the party from his or her own negligence 'as long as [its] language . . . clearly and specifically indicates the intent to release the defendant from liability for personal injury caused by the defendant's negligence . . . .'" In the instant case, there is no suggestion that the agreement between NFI and Ms. Seigneur was the product of fraud, mistake, undue influence, overreaching, or the like. The exculpatory clause unambiguously provides that Ms. Seigneur "expressly hereby forever releases and discharges NFI, Inc. from all claims, demands, injuries, damages, actions, or courses of action, and from all acts of active or passive negligence on the part of NFI, Inc., its servants, agents or employees." Under these circumstances, we hold that this contract provision expresses a clear intention by the parties to release NFI from liability for all acts of negligence.

More than one hundred years ago, it was noted that "the right of parties to contract as they please is restricted only by a few well defined and well settled rules, and it must be a very plain case to justify a court in holding a contract to be against public policy. This legal principle continues to hold true today.

Three exceptions have been identified where the public interest will render an exculpatory clause unenforceable. They are: (1) when the party protected by the clause intentionally causes harm or engages in acts of reckless, wanton, or gross negligence; (2) when the bargaining power of one party to the contract is so grossly unequal so as to put that party at the mercy of the other's negligence; and (3) when the transaction involves the public interest.

© **2020 John R. Allison & Robert A. Prentice**

Ms. Seigneur has not alleged that NFI's agents intentionally caused her harm, or engaged in reckless, wanton, or gross acts of negligence. She does assert, however, that the second and third exceptions are applicable.

Appellants argue that NFI "possesses a decisive advantage in bargaining strength against members of the public who seek to use its services." She also claims that she was presented with a contract of adhesion and that this is additional evidence of NFI's grossly disproportionate "bargaining power."

It is true that the contract presented to Ms. Seigneur was a contract of adhesion. But that fact alone does not demonstrate that NFI had grossly disparate bargaining power. There were numerous other competitors providing the same non-essential services as NFI. The exculpatory clause was prominently displayed in the Participation Agreement and Ms. Seigneur makes no claim that she was unaware of this provision prior to her injury.

To possess a decisive bargaining advantage over a customer, the service offered must usually be deemed essential in nature. "As [teaching the art of parachute jumping] is not of an essential nature, Parachutes Are Fun, Inc. had no decisive advantage of bargaining strength against any member of the public seeking to participate." *Winterstein v. Wilcom,* 293 A.2d 821 (1972). In *Shields v. Sta-Fit, Inc.,* 903 P.2d 525 (Wash. App. 1995), the Court pointed out that: "Health clubs are a good idea and no doubt contribute to the health of the individual participants and the community at large. But ultimately, they are not essential to the state or its citizens. And any analogy to schools, hospitals, housing (public or private) and public utilities therefore fails. Health clubs do not provide essential services."

As it relates to exculpatory clauses, unless the clause is patently offensive, Maryland [courts will it]. Here, the clause passes the not-patently-offensive test. Affirmed.

Bailment Contracts

Bailment contracts are similar to real estate leases and employment contracts in that they, too, are so widely used as to substantially affect the public interest. Accordingly, the status of exculpatory clauses in such contracts is essentially the same as those in leases and employment contracts—that is, highly suspect in the eyes of the law.

A *bailment* occurs when the owner of an article of personal property temporarily relinquishes the possession and control of it to another. The owner who has parted with the possession is the *bailor,* and the one receiving it is the *bailee.* Typical bailments result from checking a coat at a nightclub, leaving a car at a garage for repairs, and storing goods at a warehouse. Similarly, the consumer is a bailee when renting a car, equipment, and so on.

The existence of a bailment creates a duty on the part of the bailee to use reasonable care in taking care of the property in his possession and, thus, the bailee is liable to the bailor for loss of or damage to the property resulting from the bailee's negligence. In most states, when there is loss of or damage to the property while in the bailee's possession, negligence is presumed and the burden is on the bailee to explain how this happened without negligence.

Commercial bailees such as auto repair shops frequently attempt to escape this liability by the use of an exculpatory clause in the bailment contract. These are typically not effective to bar the owner of the property, such as a car, from suing for negligence if the property is stolen or damaged. The customer must, of course, prove negligence.

When a person leaves a car at a parking lot, it may or may not be a bailment transaction. There is a bailment only if the parking lot operator has control of the car by having an attendant on duty and keeping the car keys. If there is no bailment, there typically is not duty to exercise reasonable care in taking care of the car, and the exculpatory clause is irrelevant. When the parking lot owner has such control and a bailment exists, an exculpatory clause seeking to relieve the lot owner from liability for negligence in the event the car is stolen or damaged typically will only be effective if it is *very conspicuous and clearly states* that the bailee will not be liable for negligence, although courts in a majority of states do not require that the word "negligence" be used. Regarding the requirement of conspicuousness, an exculpatory clause printed on the back of an identification ticket or receipt, for example, is not sufficiently conspicuous. These same rules generally apply to clauses seeking to limit the liability to a certain amount

Additionally, some bailees are expressly permitted by statute to limit their liability by contract. Under federal law, for example, common carriers in interstate commerce such as railroads, airlines, and trucking companies are permitted to do so within certain limits: thus the limitations on the amount of liability commonly found in bills of lading and other transportation contracts are generally enforceable.

Unconscionable Contracts

As a general rule, the courts are not concerned with the fairness or unfairness of a particular contract. In other words, where competent parties have struck an agreement it will normally be enforced even if it proves much more advantageous to one party than to the other. However, occasionally the freedom to contract is abused so that the terms of a particular contract are so extremely unfair to one of the parties in light of common mores and business practices that they "shock one's conscience." Courts will not enforce such an *unconscionable contract* against the abused party.

A case vividly illustrating the common law approach to unconscionability is *Williams v. Walker-Thomas Furniture Co.*, 350 F.2d 445 (D.D.C. 1965). There, a Mrs. Williams purchased some furniture on credit under a contract which contained the standard provision that the company would retain title to the goods until all monthly payments were made, and that the company could repossess in event of default. The contract also contained a clause that if Mrs. Williams purchased additional goods on credit, the company had the right to credit pro rata her monthly payments against all such goods. She did, in fact, buy a number of additional items between 1957 and 1962, and the company, as permitted by the pro rata clause, during that time had applied her payments so that a small balance remained due on all items, even those purchased in 1957 and 1958. In 1962, by which time Mrs. Williams had made payments of over $1,400, she was unable to make additional payments. When the company then sought to repossess all of the goods in her hands, the court refused repossession as to the first items that she had purchased, noting:

> When a party of little bargaining power, and hence little real choice, signs a commercially unreasonable contract with little or no knowledge of its terms, it is hardly likely that his consent, or even an objective manifestation of consent, was ever given to all the terms. In such a case the usual rule that the terms of the agreement are not to be questioned should be abandoned, and the court should consider whether the terms of the contract are so unfair that enforcement should be withheld.

The common law of unconscionability was introduced to the sale of goods through UCC Sec. 2-302, which allows a court finding a sales contract or any clause of the contract to be unconscionable to: (1) refuse to enforce the contract, or (2) enforce the remainder of the contract without the unconscionable clause, or (3) limit the application of any unconscionable clause so as to avoid any unreasonable result. Although the doctrine of unconscionability originated in the common law, its specific codification by the drafters of the UCC has since led more courts to apply it to transactions not governed by the UCC.

Courts generally will refuse to enforce the contract because of unconscionability only if the party seeking to avoid the contract proves both procedural and substantive unconscionability. *Procedural unconscionability* exists when there is a lack of meaningful choice on the part of one of the parties. Courts must analyze the contract formation process, including such matters as the inability of one of the parties to bargain because of immaturity or old age, lack of sophistication, mental disability, inability to speak English, lack of education or business acumen, and the like; relative bargaining power; whether the party in the strongest economic position simply offered a printed form or boilerplate contract on a take-it-or-leave-it basis to the weaker party (adhesion contracts); whether the terms were explained to the weaker party; whether there were alternative sources for the goods or services; whether high-pressure or deceptive sales tactics were used; and whether important clauses were hidden in the fine print. Contracts entered into in a commercial context are generally presumed not to be unconscionable; businesspersons should be able to protect themselves. Courts are much more likely to find unconscionability in order to aid a consumer than to aid a business.

In order to ascertain *substantive unconscionability*, the courts examine the terms of the contract itself to determine whether they are oppressive, perhaps because they involve unfair disclaimers of warranty, inflated prices, denial of basic rights and remedies to consumers, penalty clauses, and the like. The courts will decide whether or not a particular contract is unconscionable on a case-by-case basis in light of the overall commercial context in which it was made and as of the time it was made. Just because a bargain has turned out poorly for one party does not mean that the contract was unconscionable when made.

Courts will not use the concept to reallocate the risks taken by the parties when they entered into the contract. For example, in *Doughty v. Idaho Frozen Foods Corp.*, 736 P.2d 460 (Idaho App. 1987), a potato farmer contracted to supply a portion of the coming season's anticipated potato crop to a food processing company. If the delivery contained a larger portion of potatoes that weighed at least 10 ounces each, the agreed base price increased, and vice-versa; the contract allowed the buyer to refuse delivery if less than 10% of the potatoes weighed less than 10 ounces. The growing season turned out to be unfavorable because of the weather, and, because the farmer would not receive a very good price under the contract, he breached the contract by refusing to deliver any potatoes at all to the buyer, and chose instead to sell them in another market at a better price. The farmer filed a court action seeking a declaratory judgment that he had not breached the contract because it was unconscionable and thus unenforceable. The court held that the contract was not procedurally unconscionable because it was not a contract of adhesion between parties of greatly unequal bargaining power—the parties used a contract created by a large cooperative group of 1,200 potato growers with large collective economic power. The court held that it was not substantively unconscionable because the two parties knowingly agreed to bargain on the risk that the potato crop that year would contain many large potatoes many small ones.

The circumstances in the following care are much different than in the *Doughty* case.

Gonzalez v. A-1 Self Storage, Inc.
Superior Court of New Jersey, 795 A.2d 885 (2000)

On May 17, 1999, plaintiff Lisa Gonzalez rented an eight by ten foot space for short-term storage of her personal belongings from defendant A–1 Storage, Inc. in Jersey City, New Jersey. Gonzalez, the plaintiff and A-1, the defendant, signed defendant's rental agreement and plaintiff paid defendant $196.90, representing rent of $126 per month, a prorated amount of $60.90, and a $10 charge for the purchase of a lock.

On July 3, 1999, plaintiff returned to the storage facility to retrieve the stored items and discovered that all of the possessions had been either destroyed or damaged by the entry of water into the storage space from the top of the unit. The defendant denied responsibility, and plaintiff filed suit. Plaintiff represented herself in the case, and alleged that her damages included the loss of several items with priceless sentimental value. She submitted to the court a list of her lost and damaged possessions:

Two television sets, a VCR, a sofa bed, other furniture, clothing and numerous personal items which were irreplaceable including a video of her child with her deceased grandmother, handmade bedding, clothing, linens and other valuables, some of which had been handed down through two generations of family members.

Plaintiff testified as to the damages and offered 39 pictures into evidence that clearly demonstrated substantial water, mildew, and rust damage. In her complaint, the plaintiff alleged negligence in the maintenance of the storage space, and sought recovery of $5,000 damages plus court costs and fees. Defendant's operator admitted that there was water damage and that he had tried unsuccessfully to clean certain items, primarily clothing, without first asking plaintiff's permission. Efforts to remove rust from the TVS and other electronic appliances were also without success.

Curran, Judge:

The relationship between the parties here may be characterized as a "bailment for hire," in which the "bailor" places personal property in the custody of a "bailee" and compensates the bailee for keeping the property. Once a bailee accepts responsibility for the goods delivered, the bailee has the burden of producing evidence as to the fate of those goods. To hold otherwise would place an impossible burden on a plaintiff-bailor, [who cannot possibly know why the damage occurred in most cases].

In the present case, defendant/bailee accepted a contractual responsibility for the goods delivered to it by plaintiff/bailor. Defendant then failed to provide for the safekeeping of the things entrusted to the custody of the bailee. At trial, plaintiff charged that defendant was negligent in that the top of the storage unit was only a fence-like grate through which substantial water had cascaded to drench the items within the unit. Defendant denied any negligence and made no assertions that reasonable efforts were made by it to provide a safe, suitable space for plaintiff's belongings, but simply . . . asserted that the provisions of the rental agreement completely shielded it from liability.

Defendant asserts that it should not be held liable for the damage to plaintiff's property because of the presence of two provisions in its contract:

10. NON–LIABILITY OF THE OWNER AND INSURANCE OBLIGATIONS OF OCCUPANT. Occupant, at occupant's expense, shall maintain a policy of fire and extended coverage insurance with burglary, vandalism and malicious mischief

endorsement for at least 100% of actual cash value of such stored property. Occupant expressly agrees that the carrier of such insurance shall not be subrogated to any claim of occupant against owner, owner's agents or employees. The Owner shall not be liable for personal injury or property damage . . . . The Occupant hereby agrees to indemnify and hold the owner harmless from and against any and all claims for damages to property or personal injury, including attorney's fees or costs. . . .

11. RELEASE OF OWNER'S LIABILITY. Any and all personal property stored within or on the leased premises by Occupant shall be at Occupant's sole risk and no bailment is created hereunder. Owner shall have no liability for loss or damage to any property of Occupant stored in the space, or otherwise, arising from any cause whatsoever. . . . Owner shall not be liable to Occupant for any loss or damage that may be occasioned by or through Owner's acts, omissions to act, or negligence, or by acts of negligence of Owner's or other Occupants on the premises .... The Occupant does hereby waive and release any rights of recovery against Owner that it may have hereunder. Owner's liability shall not exceed the sum of $50.00 and Occupant's sole remedy at law or in equity shall be the right to recover a sum within such limit.

Defendant argues that plaintiff was on notice to obtain insurance and that her failure to do so, coupled with the abundant contractual disclaimers of liability, render the issue of defendant's negligence moot. The issue this court is concerned with, however, is not whether the text of these two paragraphs form a barrier insulating the defendant here from liability. Instead, the issue before the court is whether these paragraphs, together with the rest of the contract, so pervert the ideals of good faith and fair dealing that the contract as a whole is rendered unconscionable. The Court finds that, as a matter of law, they do.

In recent years, unconscionability has frequently been considered in the context of the sale of goods under the Uniform Commercial Code (U.C.C.). However, neither historically nor today is that concept limited to such contracts. The principle of denying equitable relief under unconscionable circumstances has long been used by New Jersey courts of equity. Moreover, some decisions of the law courts before the enactment of the U.C.C.'s section 2–302, though applying other concepts on the surface, may actually represent an invocation of the doctrine of unconscionability. Accordingly, this court does not hesitate to draw upon the U.C.C., its comments, and relevant New Jersey decisions, even though the transaction herein may not have been a sale of goods in the traditional sense.

Like the concepts of "public policy" or "proximate causation," the doctrine of unconscionability has understandably eluded a stringent definition . . . . In *Kugler v. Romain,* 279 *A.*2d 640 (N.J. 1971), the Court described unconscionability as "an amorphous concept obviously designed to establish a broad business ethic." The Court further stated that "the standard of conduct contemplated by the unconscionability doctrine is good faith, honesty in fact and observance of fair dealing." The Uniform Commercial Code provides that it is up to the court to find as a matter of law that the contract or any clause or any clause of the contract was unconscionable at the time it was made.

The basic test of unconscionability is whether, in the light of the general commercial background and the commercial needs of the particular trade or case, the clauses involved are so one-sided as to be unconscionable under the circumstances existing at the time of the making of the contract. . . .

In the case at bar, the clauses of defendant's boilerplate contract are so one-sided as to be unconscionable under the circumstances. Paragraph 10 of the contract requires plaintiff to procure insurance coverage while simultaneously depriving any potential insurer of its right to sue defendant even where [read in conjunction with paragraph 11] damage is caused by defendant's own negligence. The clause goes on to require plaintiff to indemnify defendant and pay all of defendant's related attorney's fees and costs.

Paragraph 11 of the contract declares that there is no "bailment created hereunder" and attempts to circumvent any sort of conceivable liability that could otherwise arise between the parties. Adding insult to injury, the clause then stipulates that defendant's liability "shall not exceed $50 and that plaintiff's only remedy at law or in equity" is the recovery of the $50. . . . It is clear to this court that a limited liability sum of $50 is unconscionable.

Additionally, defendant attempts in paragraph 11 to strip plaintiff of any rights of recovery against defendant by stating that "Occupant does hereby waive and release any rights of recovery against Owner."

Paragraphs 23 and 30 of this contract listed below further tip the scales in favor of defendant by requiring plaintiff to defend defendant against any and all related claims brought against defendant and by excluding all warranties that might otherwise offer plaintiff a fair measure of protection against an unsafe storage facility. . . .

Last, the present scenario does not involve a relationship between two business entities, both experienced in the storage industry and accustomed to dealing with one another. Instead, what we have here is a lone consumer, inexperienced and pressed for time, dealing with an experienced merchant in the merchant's industry. There is no evidence whatsoever that the terms of the contract were ever negotiated. Indeed, quite the opposite is true. The contract is clearly a boilerplate form, prepared by defendant with preprinted charges of $15.00 for late payments and $25.00 for returned checks, and with room for modification in only the size, cost, and rental date.

In sum . . . the contract viewed in its entirety . . . is outrageous. The contract attempts to: (1) avoid liability for all of defendant's actions, including defendant's own negligence; (2) require plaintiff to obtain insurance while denying a potential third party insurance company its right to sue defendant; (3) require plaintiff to indemnify and defend defendant against all related claims if defendant is sued; (4) limit all liability of defendant to a sum of only $50; (5) deny the formation and obligations of a bailment; (6) require plaintiff to waive and release any rights of recovery; and (7) require plaintiff to pay all attorney's fees and costs for any related legal action.

The total "one-sidedness" of the terms here, together with the absence of any evidence even remotely suggesting that the parties engaged in a good faith negotiation, requires this Court to find that the standard of "good faith, honesty in fact, and observance of fair dealing" has not been met and that . . . the entire contract must be rendered void and unenforceable. Accordingly, judgment is for plaintiff, Lisa Gonzalez, in the amount of $5,000 for defendant's negligence.

EFFECT OF ILLEGAL CONTRACTS

As noted early in the chapter, illegal contracts are generally void and unenforceable. This means that neither party to such a contract will be assisted by the courts in any way, regardless of the consequences to the parties involved. Thus, if S brings suit to recover the purchase price of a quantity of liquor that he has sold and delivered to B in violation of law, his action will be dismissed. Conversely, if B had paid the purchase price when the contract was made and S subsequently failed to deliver the liquor, any action brought by B to recover the price will also be unavailing.

Courts feel that such a hands-off policy is, in most cases, the best way to discourage the making of illegal contracts. There are exceptional situations, however, in which the courts feel that the results obtained under such a policy are so questionable as to warrant some measure of judicial relief. We will examine three of these situations.

Rights of Protected Parties

Some statutes have as their clear purpose the protection of a certain class of persons. Any contract made in violation of such a statute is enforceable by persons within that class, despite its illegality. For example: a Nebraska insurance company, not licensed to sell insurance in Colorado, issues a fire insurance policy on K's home in Denver. The home is destroyed by fire, and the company refuses to pay on the ground that the contract was illegal. The company is liable on its policy. It would be a ludicrous result if K, a person for whose benefit the licensing statutes were enacted, were to be denied recovery on the ground of illegality.

Parties Not Equally at Fault

In most illegal contracts the parties are equally at fault (or substantially equally at fault). In such instances when an action is brought to enforce the contract, the defendant may successfully assert the defense of *in pari delicto* (literally, "at equal fault").

In some situations, however, the plaintiff may convince the court that they were not equally at fault with the defendant—*i.e.*, that his or her guilt was substantially less than the defendant's. In such a case the plaintiff's action may be maintained. The exception applies particularly—but not exclusively—where the plaintiff was ignorant of essential facts when the contract was made, through no fault of his or her own. For example: X forges a warehouse receipt, which makes it appear that he is the owner of certain goods stored at a warehouse. X takes the receipt to a trucking company and employs it to pick up the goods at the warehouse and to deliver them to his place of business. The trucking company does so, not knowing that X is not the owner of the goods. The company is entitled to receive its transportation charge from X, even though it was a participant in an illegal transaction.

Severable Contracts

Sometimes a single contract turns out on analysis to be two separate agreements. This can be illustrated by a contract under which a retiring restaurant owner agrees to sell to a former competitor his "ten pinball machines for $50 and one electric broiler for $75." In such a contract, called a severable contract, the fact that one of the agreements may be illegal does not prevent the other from being enforced. Thus, if the sale of the pinball machines is prohibited by law, the seller is still under an obligation to deliver the broiler. However, most contracts that contain several promises on the part of both parties are not severable. The promises of the two parties usually are so interdependent that the court must rule that they resulted in the creation of a single, indivisible contract. In such cases, if any part of the contract is illegal, the entire agreement is unenforceable.

CHAPTER 14

VOIDABLE CONTRACTS

- Capacity
- Reality of Consent
- Fraud
- Innocent Misrepresentation
- Mistake
- Duress
- Undue Influence
- Home Solicitation Statutes

A *voidable* contract is a contract that, despite meeting all other legal requirements, can be canceled by one of the parties. Several different terms are used interchangeably for the cancellation of a contract under certain circumstances, including avoidance, disaffirmance, and rescission. In this chapter we will examine the most common grounds for the rescission of a contract: *lack of reality of consent* and *lack of legal capacity.*

REALITY OF CONSENT

A contract that has been entered into between two persons having full capacity to contract, and which appears to be valid in all other respects, may still be voidable if it turns out that the apparent consent of one or both of the parties was, in fact, not genuine. Contracts that are tainted with *fraud, innocent misrepresentation, mistake, duress,* or *undue influence* can ordinarily be voided, or *rescinded,* by the innocent parties. In such instances the courts will allow rescission on the ground that there was "no reality of consent." That is, although it *appears* from the form of the contract alone that the consent of both parties was genuine (or "real"), in fact it was not.

FRAUD

Leaving aside, for the moment, any attempt to define the term, the essence of *fraud* is deception—the intentional misleading of one person by another. Perhaps the most common type of fraud occurs when one person simply lies to another about a material fact, as a result of which a contract is made. Thus, if S, the owner of a current model car, tells B that he purchased it new six months ago, S knowing that it was in fact "second-hand" when he acquired it, S is guilty of fraud if B, believing this statement to be true, subsequently purchases the car. In this case, B—after learning the true facts—ordinarily can either rescind the contract and recover the purchase price or keep the car and recover damages from S.

Elements of Fraud

One person can mislead another in so many ways that the courts have been reluctant to fashion a hard and fast definition of fraud; any precise definition almost certainly could be circumvented by person's intent on getting around it. Instead, the courts generally recognize that the various forms of deception they wish to forestall usually contain common elements. When a court is called upon to decide in a given case whether the conduct of one of the parties was fraudulent, its usual approach is to see if the required elements are present. If so, fraud has been established and the victim will be afforded relief.

To be successful in a fraud action, the plaintiff is required to show all of the following:

1. That defendant made a misrepresentation of a material fact.

2. That the statement was made with the *intent to deceive* (i.e., defendant *knew* or *should have known* that the statement was false).

3. That plaintiff *reasonably relied* on the misrepresentation.

4. That plaintiff suffered an *injury* as a result.

Misrepresentation of a Material Fact

Misrepresentation of a material fact (or misstatement) is broadly interpreted to include any word or conduct that causes the innocent person to reach an erroneous conclusion of fact. Thus a seller of apples who selects the best ones in a basket and puts them on top of others of inferior quality has, in the eyes of the law, made a "statement" to a prospective buyer that all the apples are of the same quality as those which are visible.

In order for a misstatement to be fraudulent, it must be a *statement of fact*—an actual event, circumstance, or occurrence. Statements about the age of a horse, the number of acres in a tract of land, and the net profit made by a business during a given year are all statements of fact—that is, statements about a fact. And, the misstatement must be material (important). A statement that a 640-acre tract of land holds 642 acres would be false, but probably not materially so; a statement that it contained 670 acres probably would be materially false. If the innocent person can prove that a particular statement made to them was false in a material way, the first element of fraud has been established.

Predictions. Statements as to what will happen in the future are clearly not statements of fact and therefore are not fraudulent even if they turn out to be in error. Thus, if a seller of stock tells a buyer that the stock is "bound to double in value within six months," the buyer is not entitled to relief in the event the increase in value does not come about. The same is true when the seller of a motel states that "it will certainly net $14,000 in the coming year." The reason for the view that such statements do not constitute fraud, of course, is that no one can predict what will happen in the future, and a reasonable person would not put faith in such statements.

One important type of statement about a present or future event or condition does impose a legal obligation on the one making it if it proves to be false: statements that are "warranties"—guarantees as to existing fact or assurances about future performance of a product by the seller. For example: A manufacturer of house paint states on the cans that "this paint, when applied according to the manufacturer's instructions above, will not crack, fade, or peel within two years of its application." If the statement proves to be false, a buyer who has purchased the paint in reliance on the statement can recover damages. The recovery in such a case would be on breach of warranty rather than on fraud, except in the rare situation where the buyer can prove that the seller knew the representation to be false when they made it. However, statements that are clearly matters of opinion do not create warranties. Most warranties on goods are governed by provisions in Article 2 of the UCC, including sections 2-312, 313, 314, 315, and 316. It is important to note that damages for breach of warranty will almost always be much lower than damages for fraud; moreover, punitive damages are available in fraud cases and not in warranty cases.

Opinion. Statements of *opinion*, like predictions, are also distinguished from statements of fact. Contracts cannot be set aside on the ground of fraud simply because one of the parties, prior to making the contract, expressed an opinion that later turned out to be incorrect.

Most statements of opinion, in which the declarant is merely expressing personal feelings or judgments on a matter about which reasonable persons might have contrary views, are usually easy to recognize. For example, statements that "this is an excellent neighborhood in which to raise children" or that "this painting will harmonize beautifully with the colors of your living room" involve conclusions with which others might disagree; thus they cannot be the basis of an action of fraud brought by one who relied upon them.

Other statements, however, are not so easily placed in the "opinion" or "fact" categories. A statement by the seller of a boat that it is "perfectly safe" or a statement by a home owner that "the foundation is sound" are closer to being statements of fact than the previous representations about the neighborhood and the painting. But there are varying degrees of safety and soundness, so these statements too can be held in given situations to constitute only expressions of opinion—particularly if the declarant and the innocent party were on a relatively equal basis insofar as their experience and general knowledge of the subject matter were concerned. (On the other hand, if the declarant is considerably more knowledgeable than the other party, such statements are likely to be viewed as statements of *fact*, and thus fraudulent if false. For example, in the case of *Groening v. Opsata*, 34 N.W.2d 560 (1948), it was held that a false statement by the seller of a summer home located on an eroding cliff on the shore of Lake Michigan that "it isn't too close [to the lake]" and that "there is nothing to fear, everything is all right" constituted fraud, in view of the fact that the seller was a builder of homes in the area.)

Value. Statements about an article's *value* have also caused difficulties. Nevertheless, the courts today adhere to the traditional view (in most circumstances) that the value of an article or piece of property is a matter of opinion rather than fact. Two practical reasons are the basis for this view: (1) an awareness that many types of property are prized by some people but are considered of little value by others, and (2) a recognition of the fact that sellers generally overvalue the things they are attempting to sell, and prospective buyers must accordingly place little or no reliance upon such statements. Consequently, if a seller states that "this apartment building is easily worth $80,000," the buyer normally cannot rescind the contract on the ground of fraud, even though they relied on the statement and can prove later that the actual market value of the building at the time of sale was nowhere near the stated figure and that the seller knew this at the time.

Again, the general rule is not followed when the declarant's experience and knowledge of the particular subject matter are *markedly superior* to those of the other party—especially if they are so great that the declarant is considered an "expert" in the eyes of the law. In order to prevent such a person from taking grossly unfair advantage of those who are clearly less knowledgeable, his or her intentional misrepresentations *are* held to be fraudulent. Thus, a "certified gemologist" who told a lay person that a gemstone was, "in his opinion, not very valuable at all," could be liable for fraud if he said it while knowing that this was a lie.

Law. Under the early common-law rule of this country, *statements of law* made by lay persons were clearly held not to constitute statements of fact and thus could not be the basis for actions of fraud. If the seller of a vacant lot that carries a C-1 zoning classification assures the buyer that "this classification permits the erection of duplex rental units," a statement that the seller knows is not true, the buyer who purchases the property in reliance on the statement ordinarily cannot maintain an action for damages. The rule was based on two grounds: (1) the generally reasonable feeling that a statement made by a nonlawyer about a point of law should not be relied upon by the one to whom it is made, and (2) the somewhat more questionable maxim that "everyone is presumed to know the law."

While this is still the rule applied to most cases, it is subject to an increasing number of exceptions. One major exception comprises statements of law made by persons who—because of their professional or occupational status—can reasonably be expected to know the law relating to their specialty, even though they are not attorneys. Thus intentional misrepresentations of law by persons such as real estate brokers and bank cashiers as to legal matters within their particular specialties are frequently held to be fraudulent.

Silence. The traditional common-law rule was *caveat emptor* (let the buyer beware). Under this rule, buyers had the responsibility to look out for themselves in making a purchase. Thus, assume that a seller knew that a car had been involved in an accident that bent the car's frame. If the seller told the buyer: "This car has never been in an accident," a clear misstatement of material fact would have occurred. When the buyer learned the truth, he could rescind due to fraud. But what if the seller did not make such a statement, but simply kept silent about the accident? The traditional rule stated that mere silence (failure to disclose a material fact) does not constitute fraud. The reasoning was that in most instances the parties are dealing at arm's length, possessing roughly the same amount of experience and knowledge relating to the subject matter of the contract. Parties are said to deal at "arm's length" when their relationship is such that neither part owes a duty to divulge information to the other party, as distinguished from such fiduciary relationships such as attorney-client, guardian-ward, employer-employee, principal-agent, and business partner relationships. And, in many instances, the facts not disclosed could have been ascertained by the buyer with reasonable inspection or inquiry.

Today, however, *caveat emptor* has been subjected to many exceptions. Court rulings and state consumer protection statutes have created a number of situations in which sellers must volunteer adverse information or be charged with fraud.

The courts have found several types of situations where the withholding of information is so manifestly unfair that silence should be held to constitute fraud. To prevent unfairness of this degree, the courts say that, in such situations, a "duty to speak" exists. It is difficult to summarize the duty-to-speak categories with precision, because the silence cases involve such a wide variety of fact-patterns, and because the rules of the various states applicable to duty to speak situations are often couched in general terms (to give the courts substantial discretion in their application). Additionally, the law is continuing to evolve in this area, as the courts seek to raise moral standards in the marketplace by applying the rules to situations that were earlier outside their scope.

Despite these factors, several fairly well-defined situations do exist in which the courts generally agree that a duty to speak exists.

(1) The *first* of these instances is the sale of property that contains a *latent defect* (or *hidden defect*)—one that a normal inspection by the average prospective purchaser would not reveal. Common examples are a cracked motor block in an automobile and a termite infestation in a house. A property owner who has knowledge of such conditions is guilty of fraud if they do not apprise the prospective purchaser of them—assuming, of course, that the innocent purchaser subsequently enters into a contract to buy the property.

While the latent defect rule, abstractly stated, is highly commendable, the practical protection it affords is less than one might hope for. Frequently it is difficult for the buyer to prove that the defect actually existed at the time of purchase—particularly if a long period of time has elapsed before its discovery. And even if this hurdle is cleared, the buyer has to establish that the seller knew, or should have known, of the defect when the sale occurred. The seller's contention that they were honestly unaware of the defective condition is frequently accepted by a jury.

Normally the rule on hidden defects does not work in reverse. Thus, if the buyer possesses information about the property that causes its value to be higher than the seller believes it to be, the buyer does not have a duty to divulge this information to the seller—*unless* the buyer is an expert in the field by reason of training or experience.

(2) A *second* duty to speak situation occurs where a *fiduciary relationship* exists—that is, where one of the parties occupies a position of "trust and confidence" relative to the other. This differs from the ordinary situation, where the parties are dealing "at arm's length." For example, when a partnership is considering a land purchase, a partner who is part owner of the land under consideration has a duty to divulge his or her interest to the co-partner before the purchase is made. Similarly, a corporate officer who is purchasing stock from a shareholder has a duty to disclose any special facts of which they have knowledge, by virtue of that position, which would affect the value of the stock.

(3) The *third* category comprises situations in which one party has *superior knowledge* about the subject matter of the contract as a result of his or her experience, training, or special relationship with the subject matter. In this type of circumstance the rule has obvious application where the silent party—the one possessing the superior knowledge—is an expert in the area, but it often applies to other parties as well. The rule commonly applied is that if one party has superior knowledge, or knowledge that is not within the reasonable reach of the other party, and which the other party could not discover by the exercise of means available to both parties, there is a duty on the party possessing the knowledge to disclose it. Under this rule, for example, a buyer of Oklahoma land who, by virtue of his employment with an oil company, learns of an oil "strike" on an adjacent ranch would be guilty of fraud if he did not disclose this information to the seller, a rancher. On the other hand, if the buyer was simply another ranch owner in the area, his or her nondisclosure of this information would probably not be fraudulent.

Outside of these situations, most courts take the view that neither party has a duty to volunteer information to the other, even though it might bear materially on the other's decision of whether to contract. Thus, the seller of a trash collection business probably has no duty to tell a prospective purchaser of indications that the city is going to institute a collection service of its own, if this information is as available to the buyer as it is to the seller.

Intent to Deceive

The second element of fraud is *knowledge of falsity* (or, as it is sometimes called, "scienter"). Thus the innocent party must ordinarily prove that the person making the statement knew, or should have known, that it was false at the time it was made. However, the knowledge of falsity requirement is also met if a person makes a statement "with a reckless disregard for the truth," even if the declarant did not actually know it was false. Thus, if the seller of a used car has no idea as to its mileage but nevertheless states that "it has not been driven more than 30,000 miles," the statement constitutes fraud if it is later proven that the true mileage materially exceeded that figure.

Reliance

The victim of a misrepresentation must show that they reasonably relied on the misstatement at the time of contracting. Sometimes this is not difficult to establish. The innocent party does not have to prove that the fact in regard to which the misrepresentation was made was the primary factor in inducing them to make the contract. It is sufficient that the misrepresentation involved a matter tending to influence the decision.

Reliance does not exist, of course, if the one accused of fraud can prove that the other party actually knew the true facts before making the contract. Also, a charge of fraud will fail if the victim's reliance was not reasonable under the circumstances. While the old rule of *caveat emptor* is much less significant than formerly, a buyer still cannot blindly accept everything they are told. For example, a buyer given an opportunity to view the property is presumed to observe any patent (obvious) defects that might exist. To illustrate—the seller of a used television set tells the buyer it "produces an excellent picture on all channels." If the buyer viewed the set in operation prior to the sale and complained of reception on one channel, that person could hardly contend after the sale that he had reasonably relied on the seller's representation.

Injury

The last element of a successful fraud action is a showing by the innocent party that they suffered an injury (or "harm," or "damage"), usually an economic loss, as a result of the misrepresentation. In most cases proof of injury is the easiest of the fraud elements to prove. For example, in a typical case involving the sale of property, the buyer is able to show that the value of the property they received is substantially less than it would have been if the seller's representations had been true.

Remedies for Fraud

Once fraud is established, the defrauded party always has the right to rescind the contract. When such a person chooses the remedy of *rescission*, they must ordinarily return the consideration, if any, that was received from the other party. Rescission, then, is designed to restore the parties to their original positions.

In some instances the defrauded party may wish to keep the consideration (for example, a parcel of land), even though it had been misrepresented by the seller. In such a case the buyer may keep the consideration (i.e., "affirm the contract") and bring suit for *damages*—which in the usual situation is, at the minimum, the difference between the actual value of the property the buyer received, and the value it would have had if the representations had been true. Additionally, because fraud is an intentional tort that involves malice by the defendant, the innocent party may be awarded punitive damages as well.

As a general rule, the defrauded party must elect either to rescind the contract or to recover damages. However, when the fraud involves the making of a sales contract, such an election need not be made. Sec. 2-721 of the UCC provides, in part, that where fraud is established, "Neither rescission nor a claim for rescission of the contract . . . shall bar or be . . . inconsistent with a claim for damages or other remedy. Thus in circumstances where a buyer or seller seeking rescission can show that they will suffer a loss notwithstanding the rescission, damages may also be recovered."

The fraud case below presents several of the issues we have just discussed.

LIBHART v. COPELAND
949 S.W.2d 783 (Texas App. 1997)

Walter Libhart became pastor of Tabernacle Baptist Church in 1973. Early in his pastorate, the church's membership increased to 166, but over the years, membership declined to between ten and twenty members. In January 1992 the church members *decided to sell the sanctuary. Five months later, another church offered to buy it for $90,000. The church met on July 12 to discuss this offer. As pastor, Libhart presided over the meeting. The Copelands did not attend this meeting. After some discussion, the members voted to accept the offer, sell the sanctuary, and dissolve the church. The congregation voted to loan Libhart the proceeds remaining after payment of the church's debts on the condition that he sell the parsonage which the church gave him in 1987. Libhart would repay the loan with the proceeds from this sale. According to Libhart, Edna Stone ("Stone") moved that the congregation give him the church van. Those present voted unanimously in favor of this motion.*

The Copelands later learned about the decisions made in the July 12 meeting. Michael Copeland ("Michael") served as chairman of deacons and as a trustee for the church. Because of his position, he solicited the opinion of an attorney about the appropriate disposition of church assets upon dissolution. Because of the advice he received, and because he was concerned that the members who voted in the July 12 meeting were misinformed, he wrote a letter to Libhart detailing his concerns. Upon receipt of the letter, Libhart scheduled another meeting for July 26.

Claudell Copeland ("Claudell") secretly taped the July 26 meeting. During this meeting, the members voted to divide the church's remaining funds after payment of debts among Reverend Marvin Weido, Arlington Baptist College, and other charitable organizations. Stone asked what would be done with the van. Libhart responded, "Whatever you want to do with it, sister." The congregation also voted to forgive the July 12 loan in exchange for Libhart's promise that he would distribute the proceeds from the sale of the parsonage to worthy causes. Libhart assured those present that he would prepare a financial statement detailing the final distribution of the church's assets by August 1.

No church funds were distributed to any of the charitable organizations mentioned in the July 26 meeting. Libhart sold the van in 1993 for $5,000. He sold the parsonage to Tracey and David Reynolds, his daughter and son-in-law, on June 2, 1994, for $10. Libhart did not prepare the promised financial statement until April of 1993. The statement reflects that $73,233.63 in net proceeds remained after the sale of the sanctuary. . . .

The parties do not dispute that Libhart and his wife, Carolyn Johnson, used $55,000 of the $59,022.60 "gift" to pay for their new home near Penelope in Hill County.

Plaintiffs Claudell Copeland, Michael Copeland, and Edna Stone (collectively "Plaintiffs") are former members of Tabernacle Baptist Church who filed suit against defendants Libhart and Johnson, alleging fraud, constructive fraud, and conversion in connection with the disposition of the church's assets after its dissolution in July 1992. The court used the term "constructive fraud" to describe (1) making a promise without having any intent to keep the promise, and (2) failing to disclose material facts when there is a legal duty to do so. A jury found in Plaintiffs' favor on all causes of action and awarded actual damages of $126,000 against Libhart and Johnson jointly and severally. The jury also assessed punitive damages of $50,000 each against Libhart individually and Johnson individually. The trial judge entered judgment based on this verdict. Defendants appealed

DAVIS, Chief Justice:

[First, the appeals court concluded that (1) the individual plaintiffs had legal standing to sue for themselves and other church members, and (2) the First Amendment's prohibition of government entanglement with religion does not prevent courts from hearing civil legal disputes among church members or between members and clergy.]

Generally a court should not intervene in church disputes. However, when church proceedings are tainted by fraud, judicial review is appropriate. Plaintiffs brought this suit on behalf of the former church and its members, including themselves. They alleged that Libhart and Johnson fraudulently misrepresented "material facts regarding the sale proceeds of the church facilities"; that they converted the church van; that the church has "been deprived of the proper disposition of church assets due to their misrepresentations; and that Libhart and Johnson have been unjustly enriched by being allowed to retain the property which was purchased with the assets wrongfully diverted from Tabernacle Baptist Church.

Plaintiffs' alleged that Libhart and Johnson fraudulently obtained and converted for their own use the proceeds from the sale of the sanctuary. When Libhart sold the parsonage to David and Tracey, his son-in-law and daughter, in 1994, he had an attorney prepare a warranty deed from Tabernacle Baptist Church to them. Libhart signed the deed on behalf of the church as pastor, David signed as chairman of the board, and Johnson signed as secretary.

The trial court made an additional finding of fact that Libhart and Johnson fraudulently obtained the parsonage from the church.

To prove fraud, a plaintiff must show:

(1) the defendant made a material representation;

(2) which was false;

(3) the defendant made the representation knowing it to be false or made it recklessly as a positive assertion without any knowledge of its truth;

(4) the defendant intended that the plaintiff act upon the representation;

(5) the plaintiff acted in reliance upon the representation; and

(6) suffered injury as a result.

A claim of fraud can be based on a promise to perform a future action made with a present intent not to perform. And a misrepresentation may consist of the concealment of a material fact when there is a duty to speak. The duty to speak or to disclose arises when one party knows that the other party is relying on the concealed fact, provided that he knows the relying party is ignorant of the facts and does not have an equal opportunity to discover the truth. . . .

The members of the church unanimously voted on July 12 to loan a portion of the sanctuary proceeds to Libhart on the condition subsequent that he repay the loan with proceeds from the sale of the parsonage. The members voted two weeks later to absolve the loan in exchange for Libhart's promise that he would donate the proceeds from the sale of the parsonage to worthy causes. From this we conclude that some probative evidence exists to support a finding that the members of the church relied upon representations by Libhart which proved to be false. Thus, the evidence is legally sufficient to support the jury's finding on the issue of reliance on Libhart's representations.

Plaintiffs also alleged that the members of the church also relied upon Johnson's representations regarding the disposition of the proceeds from the sale of the sanctuary and the parsonage, because of the confidential relationship established during her years of service to the church. The judge's charge instructed the jurors that they could find Johnson liable for fraud if they found that she had failed to disclose a material fact, intended to induce the members to take some action by withholding that fact, and the members were injured because they acted without knowledge of the undisclosed fact. Thus, we must determine whether any probative evidence supports a finding that the members of the church acted without knowledge of a material fact which Johnson failed to disclose.

Libhart and Johnson served the church for nineteen years. In addition, Johnson served as an officer of the church. Claudell testified that she looked up to Libhart and Johnson very much because of their respective positions as pastor and pastor's wife. Libhart testified that Johnson and he had a special duty of confidence and trust to the congregation. Claudell recalled that Michael and she went on a trip with Libhart and Johnson to Gun Barrel City in December 1991. As they drove along the highway, Libhart and Johnson noted "every piece of property" that was for sale and wrote down the phone numbers displayed in order to later check on the property.

Libhart testified that Johnson and he had been looking for a home in the country before the church decided to sell the sanctuary. They had selected their new home in Penelope and knew its price before the church met on July 12. Libhart agreed that he could not have repaid the loan based on his income in 1992. From these facts we find probative evidence that would allow the jury to infer that Johnson and Libhart had decided to purchase their new home with the sanctuary proceeds before the church voted concerning the disposition of the proceeds. The record also contains probative evidence that Johnson and Libhart did not intend to repay the loan as they promised, particularly in light of the fact that they were financially unable to do so at the time the church voted to loan them the money.

The church voted to loan them the money based on Libhart's affirmative representations that they would repay it with the parsonage proceeds. Johnson was present and did not refute these representations. From this we conclude that some probative evidence exists to support a finding that the church relied upon Johnson's failure to disclose material facts. Thus, the evidence is legally sufficient to support the jury's finding on the issue of reliance on Johnson's failure to disclose.

The church parsonage rightfully belongs to Tabernacle Baptist Church. In addition, the money (over $66,000) which Defendants diverted from the sales proceeds of the church facilities rightfully belongs to Tabernacle Baptist Church. The parties do not dispute that Libhart and Johnson received $66,277.60 of the sanctuary proceeds for themselves. Libhart testified that he attempted to sell the parsonage for $55,000 and agreed that it was worth that much. He later sold it to David and Tracey for $10. The church voted to loan the sanctuary proceeds to Libhart in exchange for his promise that he would repay the loan with the parsonage proceeds. Two weeks later, Libhart persuaded the members to forgive his loan in exchange for his promise that he would donate the parsonage proceeds to certain charities. Johnson, though present, did not refute these representations.

Because Libhart failed to sell the parsonage and donate its proceeds to charity, the vote to absolve his loan is tainted by fraud. Thus, the loan of the sanctuary proceeds was not absolved and remained conditioned on its subsequent repayment out of the proceeds from the sale of the parsonage. Libhart failed to repay the loan. Therefore, the church suffered pecuniary loss as a result of Johnson's and his misrepresentations. From this we conclude that some probative evidence exists to support a finding that Libhart's and

Johnson's misrepresentations caused injury to the church. Thus, the evidence is legally sufficient to support the jury's finding of injury.

The jury is the sole judge of the witnesses' credibility and the weight to be accorded their testimony. The jurors may also derive inferences from the evidence and decide between conflicting inferences. A jury finding based on conflicting evidence and inferences is generally conclusive. We will not substitute our judgment for the jury's. We cannot say that the jury's findings that the church relied upon Libhart's and Johnson's misrepresentations and its damages findings are so contrary to the overwhelming weight of the evidence as to be clearly wrong and unjust. Thus, the evidence is factually sufficient to support the jury's findings of reliance and injury.

A fraud plaintiff cannot recover exemplary damages absent a finding that the plaintiff sustained actual damages as a result of the fraud alleged. We have already found the evidence sufficient to support the jury's award of actual damages. Because the church suffered actual damages, exemplary damages can also be awarded for fraud. The trial court's judgment against the defendants Libhart and Johnson for actual and punitive damages is affirmed.

INNOCENT MISREPRESENTATION

If all the elements of fraud are present in a particular case, except that the person making the misstatement honestly (and reasonably) believed the statement to be true, that person is guilty of innocent misrepresentation rather than fraud. Under the rule of most states, the victim can rescind the contract on that ground, but is not given the alternative remedy of damages because innocent misrepresentation is not a tort and fraud is not only an intentional tort, but also necessarily involves malice. Innocent misrepresentation and fraud are contrasted in Figure 14.1.

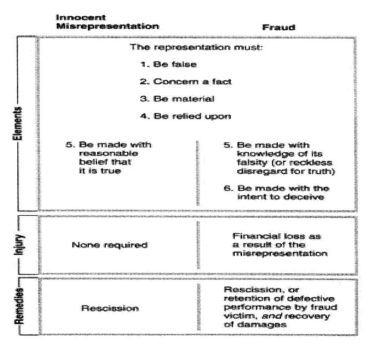

Figure 14.1 Fraud and Innocent Misrepresentation

MISTAKE

Cases are continually arising where one of the parties to a contract attempts to have it set aside by the court on the ground that they were mistaken in some respect at the time the contract was made. Often the mistake involves opinion or judgment rather than fact, in which case no relief will be granted. For example, a person contracts to buy land for $30,000 thinking this is its true value. If its actual value proves to be much less, they have shown bad judgment and will not be permitted to rescind the contract. Similarly, if a person purchases stock in the belief that it will greatly increase in value in a short time, they obviously cannot have the contract set aside in the event that it does not perform as hoped. If rescission were permitted on grounds such as these, the basic value of all contracts would be destroyed.

However, in certain limited situations a plea of mistake will afford grounds for rescission of a contract, if the mistake was one of fact. The general rule is that if both parties were mistaken as to a material fact at the time of contracting, either party can rescind the agreement. On the other hand, if only one of the parties was mistaken, rescission will not be granted unless that person can show that the other party knew, or should have known, of the mistake at the time the contract was made. When both parties are mistaken, the mistake is a *mutual (or "bilateral") mistake*; when only one is mistaken, it is a *unilateral mistake*.

Mutual Mistake

The following examples illustrate the general principle that a contract can be set aside if there is a mutual mistake as to the *existence,* the *identity,* or the *character* of the subject matter of the contract.

1. B purchases S's summer home on April 10. Subsequently, B learns that, unknown to either party, the home was destroyed by fire on April 1. Since both parties entered into the contract under the mistaken assumption that the subject matter of the contract actually existed at that time, B can have the contract set aside.
2. P owns two properties outside Woodsfield, Ohio. G, after viewing both acreages, makes P a written offer to purchase one for $18,000. P accepts the offer. It later develops that G had one property in mind while P, after reading the description contained in G's offer, honestly and reasonably believed that G was referring to the other property. Either party can rescind the agreement, because there was a mutual mistake about the identity of the contract's subject matter.
3. C purchases a gemstone from D for $25. At the time of contracting, both parties believe the stone is a topaz. In fact, it turns out to be an uncut diamond worth $700. Since both parties were mistaken about the true character of the contract's subject matter, D can have the contract rescinded, thereby recovering the stone.

The principle is not applicable to situations where both parties realize that they are *in doubt* as to a particular matter, but enter into a contract nonetheless. Thus, in example 3 above, if neither C nor D had any idea what the stone was when they made the contract, D could not rescind the contract when the E stone proved to be an uncut diamond (nor could C have rescinded had the stone turned out to be a worthless one). In such an instance both parties had, by contract, "assumed the risk" as to the stone's value. With these general rules of law in mind let us examine the problem presented by the following case.

WILKIN v. 1ST SOURCE BANK
548 N.E.2d 170 (Ind. App. 1990)

Olga Mestrovic died on August 31, 1984. Her last will and testament was admitted to probate on September 6, 1984, and 1ˢᵗ Source Bank was appointed personal representative ("executor" or "administrator") of the estate. At the time of her death, Olga Mestrovic was the owner of a large number of works of art created by her husband, Ivan Mestrovic, an internationally-known sculptor and artist. By the terms of Olga's will, all the works of art created by her husband and not specifically devised were to be sold and the proceeds distributed to members of the Mestrovic family.

Also included in the estate of Olga Mestrovic was certain real property. In March of 1985, the Bank entered into an agreement to sell the real estate to the Mr. and Mrs. Wilkins. The agreement of purchase and sale made no mention of any works of art, although it did provide for the sale to the Wilkinses of such personal property as the stove, refrigerator, dishwasher, drapes, curtains, sconces and French doors in the attic.

Immediately after closing on the real estate, the Wilkinses complained that the premises were left in a cluttered condition and would require substantial cleaning effort. The Bank, through its trust officer, proposed two options: the Bank could retain a rubbish removal service to clean the property or the Wilkinses could clean the premises and keep any items of personal property they wanted. The Wilkinses opted to clean the property themselves. At the time arrangements were made concerning the cluttered condition of the real property, neither the Bank nor the Wilkinses suspected that any works of art remained on the premises.

During their clean-up efforts, the Wilkinses found eight drawings apparently created by Ivan Mestrovic. They also found a plaster sculpture of the figure of Christ with three small children. The Wilkinses claimed ownership of the works of art, based upon their agreement with the Bank that if they cleaned the real property then they could keep such personal property as they desired.

The probate court ruled that there was no agreement for the purchase, sale or other disposition of the eight drawings and plaster sculpture. According to the lower court, there was no meeting of the minds, because neither party knew of the existence of the works of art. The Wilkinses appealed.

HOFFMAN, Judge:

On appeal, the Wilkins [sic] contend that the court's conclusions of law were erroneous. When the error charged is the trial court's application of the law, then this Court must correctly apply the law to the trial court's findings of fact. . . .

The necessity of mutual assent, or "meeting of the minds" [which is absent when the parties to a contract were both mistaken about the identity of something that is the subject of the contract, or mistaken about some other fundamental assumption they both made when making the contract], is illustrated in the classic case of *Sherwood v. Walker* (1887), 66 Mich. 568, 33 N.W. 919. The owners of a blooded cow indicated to the purchaser that the cow was barren. The purchaser also appeared to believe that the cow was barren. Consequently, a bargain was made to sell at a price per pound at which the cow would have brought approximately $80.00. Before delivery, it was discovered that the cow was with calf and that she was, therefore, worth from $750.00 to $1,000.00. The court ruled that the transaction was voidable:

[T]he mistake was not of the mere quality of the animal, but went to the very nature of the thing. A barren cow is substantially a different creature than a breeding one. There is as much difference between them ... as there is between an ox and a cow....

Like the parties in *Sherwood,* the parties in the instant case shared a common presupposition as to the existence of certain facts which proved false. The Bank and the Wilkins considered the real estate which the Wilkins had purchased to be cluttered with items of personal property variously characterized as "junk," "stuff" or "trash." Neither party suspected that works of art created by Ivan Mestrovic remained on the premises.

As in *Sherwood,* one party experienced an unexpected, unbargained-for gain while the other party experienced an unexpected, unbargained-for loss. Because the Bank and the Wilkins did not know that the eight drawings and the plaster sculpture were included in the items of personal propertythat cluttered the real property, the discovery of those works of art by the Wilkins was unexpected. The resultant gain to the Wilkins and loss to the Bank were not contemplated by the parties when the Bank agreed that the Wilkins could clean the premises and keep such personal property as they wished.

The following commentary on *Sherwood* is equally applicable to the case at bar: "Here the buyer sought to retain a gain that was produced, not by a subsequent change in circumstances, nor by the favorable resolution of known uncertainties when the contract was made, but by the presence of facts quite different from those on which the parties based their bargain." Palmer, Mistake and Unjust Enrichment 16–17 (1962), *quoted in* J. Calamari & J. Perillo, The Law of Contracts § 9–26 (1987).

The probate court properly concluded that there was no valid agreement for the purchase, sale or other disposition of the eight drawings and plaster sculpture, because [the parties were mistaken about the fundamental assumption that only "junk" and "rubbish" were contained in the attic, and not valuable works of art.] The judgment of the St. Joseph Probate Court is affirmed.

Unilateral Mistake

Where only one party to a contract is mistaken about a material fact, rescission is ordinarily not allowed unless the mistake was (or should have been) apparent to the other party. Two examples follow.

(1) B purchases a painting from S for $300; B believes it was painted by a well-known artist. B does not, however, disclose this belief to S. In fact, the painting is the work of an amateur and consequently worth no more than $50. Since only B was mistaken as to the identity of the artist, the mistake is unilateral and the contract cannot be rescinded. On the other hand, B would have been permitted to rescind if S had been aware of B's mistake and had not corrected it.

(2) X furnishes three contractors with specifications for a building project and asks them to submit construction bids. C submits a bid for $48,000 and D submits one for $46,500. E's bid, because of an error in addition, is $27,000 rather than the intended $47,000. If X accepts E's bid, E can have the contract set aside if the jury finds (as is likely to be the case) either that X actually knew of the mistake when he accepted the bid or that he should have been aware of the mistake because of the wide discrepancy in the bids.

Cautions

The "mutual-unilateral mistake" rule of thumb, while widely followed, by no means settles all cases that arise in the general area of mistake. In the first place, there is some disagreement as to what constitutes a bilateral mistake.

First, many courts take the view that such a mistake exists only where the parties have arrived at their erroneous conclusions independently of one another, rather than one party simply relying on information supplied by the other. The latter case would often be one of innocent misrepresentation, however, which would be a separate basis for rescission.

Second, a few states have statutes relating to contracts entered into under mistake of fact that sometimes permit rescission where common-law principles would not.

Third, the court will sometimes settle cases purely on "equitable principles"—the basis of overall fairness in particular situations—thereby giving little or no weight to the bilateral-unilateral factor. Many unilateral mistake cases arise in construction contracts when erroneous bids are made.

A common approach allows rescission if three factors are present: (1) The mistake was one of mere negligence—for example, the misreading of plans or the erroneous adding of a column of figures due to exhaustion or haste. (2) Rescission would cause no injury to the non-mistaken party other than loss of the erroneous bargain—for example, if the mistake is discovered and called to the attention of the non-mistaken party before the contract is awarded or soon thereafter (i.e., before construction commences while the lowest non-mistaken bid could still be accepted). (3) Holding the mistaken party to his or her bid would be "unconscionable." Thus, a mistaken bidder in a school construction contract was allowed to rescind on the basis of unilateral mistake where the day after the contract was awarded he called the school district's attention to a simple error in addition that had led to a bid of $534,175 rather than the intended $634,175. *Taylor v. Arlington ISD*, 335 S.W.2d 371(Tex. 1960).

Additional Types of Mistake

Occasionally, a mistake involves the provisions of the contract itself rather than the contract's subject matter. For example, an offeree might accept an offer that they misread, only to learn later that the offer was in fact substantially different than it seemed. This is a unilateral mistake, and the offeree is bound by the resulting contract (unless the acceptance itself discloses the mistake to the offeror).

Mutual mistakes as to the value of an article being sold generally are held to constitute mistakes of opinion rather than fact, and rescission is not permitted in such cases. Thus, if B buys a painting from S for $10,000, both parties correctly believing that the artist was Andrew Wyeth, B obviously cannot have the contract set aside simply because he later learns that the painting's true value is only $5,000. A mistake only about value is different than a mistake about the *identity or some fundamental attribute* of the item that happened to affect its value.

There is somewhat greater uncertainty insofar as mistakes of law are concerned. The courts at one time refused to permit rescission of contracts where a *mistake of law* existed, either bilateral or unilateral, on the theory that such a mistake was not a mistake of fact. (This idea was consistent with the view that a *misstatement of law* does not constitute a misstatement of fact, under the law of fraud.) Today, however, most courts treat *mistakes of law* and *fact* the same—that is, they will set aside contracts which both parties entered into under a mistake of law as well as those in which the mistake of one party was apparent to the other.

DURESS

Occasionally a person will seek to escape liability under a contract on the ground that they were forced to enter into it. Often the courts find that the "force" is insignificant in the eyes of the law, and the complaining party is held to the contract. For example, if a person enters into a contract simply because they know that failure to do so will incur the wrath of some third person, such as his or her employer or spouse, relief will not be granted. If, on the other hand, the degree of compulsion is so great as to totally rob the person of free will, *duress* exists, and the contract can be rescinded.

One early definition of duress that still remains authoritative is the following:

> (1) Any wrongful act of one person that compels a manifestation of apparent assent by another to a transaction without his volition, or (2) any wrongful threat of one person by words or other conduct that induces another to enter into a transaction under the influence of such fear as precludes him from exercising free will and judgment, if the threat was intended or should reasonably have been expected to operate as an inducement. *Restatement, Contracts.* §492.

A necessary element of duress is fear—a genuine and reasonable fear on the part of the victim that they will be subjected to an injurious, unlawful act by not acceding to the other party's demands. Thus, if a person signs a contract at gunpoint or after being physically beaten, duress exists, and the victim can escape liability on that ground. Duress also exists when a person makes a contract as a consequence of another person's threat of harm (for instance, kidnapping a child) if the contract is refused.

Generally, the innocent party must show that the act actually committed or threatened was a wrongful one. For instance, a contract entered into between a striking union and an employer cannot be set aside by the latter on the ground of duress if the strike was a lawful one—as, for example, if the strike occurred after an existing "no-strike" contract between union and employer had expired.

The threat of a criminal suit is generally held to constitute duress. For example: X proposes a contract to Y and tells him that if he refuses to sign the agreement, X will turn over evidence to the prosecuting attorney's office tending to prove that Y had embezzled money from his employer six weeks earlier. To prevent this, Y signs the contract. Y can have the contract rescinded on the ground of duress, because a threat to use the criminal machinery of the state for such a purpose is clearly wrongful—regardless of whether or not Y had actually committed the crime in question. Threat of a civil suit, on the other hand, usually does not constitute duress.

While a contract cannot be set aside simply because there is a disparity of bargaining power between the parties, the courts are beginning to accept the idea that *economic duress* (or business compulsion) can be grounds for the rescission of a contract in exceptional situations, as when there is a threat to do economic harm unless the party with weaker economic power agrees to a contract, and the threatened party has little or no realistic choice but to agree. The decision in the next case sets forth three requirements that ordinarily must be met in order for a plaintiff to be successful in a suit asking rescission because of economic duress.

TOTEM MARINE TUG & BARGE v. ALYESKA PIPELINE
Supreme Court of Alaska, 584 P.2d 15 (1978)

Totem Marine Tug and Barge, Inc., entered into a contract with Alyeska Pipeline Services under which Totem was to transport large quantities of pipeline construction materials from Houston, Texas, to Alaska. After Totem began its performance, many problems arose. One major difficulty was the fact that the tonnages to be shipped were six times greater than Alyeska had indicated. Additionally, long delays occurred in getting Totem's vessels through the Panama Canal, which resulted from Alyeska's failure to furnish promised documents to Totem by specified dates. After these and other problems, Alyeska cancelled the contract without cause.

At the time of the wrongful termination, Alyeska owed Totem about $300, 000. Officers of Alyeska at first promised that it would pay Totem invoices promptly, but later they told Totem that it would have its money "in six to eight months." (Totem alleged that the delay in payment occurred after Alyeska learned through negotiations with Totem lawyers that Totem's creditors were pressing it for their payments, and that without immediate cash it would go into bankruptcy—allegations that Alyeska did not deny.)

After further negotiations, a settlement agreement was made in 1975 under which Alyeska paid Totem $97,000 in return for surrender of all claims against it. In early 1976 Totem brought this action to rescind the settlement agreement on the ground of economic duress, and to recover the balance allegedly due under the original contract. The trial court ruled as a matter of law that the circumstances under which the settlement occurred did not constitute duress, and dismissed the complaint. Totem appealed.

Burke, Justice:

. . . This court has not yet decided a case involving a claim of economic duress, or what is also called business compulsion.... [In recent cases] this concept has been broadened to include myriad forms of economic coercion which force a person to involuntarily enter into a particular transaction....

There are various statements of what constitutes economic duress, but as noted by one commentator, "The history of generalization in the field offers no great encouragement for those who seek to summarize results in any single formula." Dawson, *Economic Duress,* 43 Mich. L. Rev. (1947).... [However, many states adopt the view that] duress exists where: (l) one party involuntarily accepted the terms of another, (2) circumstances permitted no other [realistic] alternative, and (3) such circumstances were the result of coercive acts of the other party....

One essential element of economic duress is that the plaintiff show that the other party, by wrongful acts or threats, intentionally caused him to enter into a particular transaction.... This requirement may be satisfied where the alleged wrongdoer's conduct is criminal or tortious, but an act or threat may also be wrongful if it is wrongful in the moral sense....

Economic duress does not exist, however, merely because a person has been the victim of a wrongful act; in addition, the victim must have no choice but to agree to the other person's terms or face serious financial hardship. Thus, in order to avoid a contract, a party must also show that he had no reasonable alternative to agreeing to the other party's terms, or as it is often stated, that he had no adequate remedy if the threat were carried out....

Turning to the instant case, we believe that Totem's allegations, if proved, would support a finding that it executed a release of its contract claims against Alyeska under economic duress. Totem has alleged that Alyeska deliberately withheld payment of an acknowledged debt, knowing that Totem had no choice but to accept an inadequate sum in settlement of that debt; that Totem was faced with impending bankruptcy; that Totem was unable to meet its pressing debts other than by accepting the immediate cash payment offered by Alyeska; and that through necessity, Totem thus involuntarily accepted an inadequate settlement offer from Alyeska and executed a release of all claims under the contract. If the release was in fact executed under these circumstances, we think that . . . this would constitute the type of wrongful conduct and lack of alternatives that would render the release voidable by Totem on the ground of economic duress....

Reversed, and case remanded.

UNDUE INFLUENCE

There are some circumstances in which a person can escape contractual liability by proving that his or her consent was brought about by the *undue influence* of the other party to the contract. While many kinds of influence are perfectly lawful, influence is undue (excessive) where one party so dominates the will of the other that the latter's volition actually is destroyed. A common example occurs where one person, as the result of advanced age and physical deterioration, begins to rely more and more upon a younger, more energetic acquaintance or relative for advice until the point is reached where the older person's willpower and judgment are almost totally controlled by the dominant party. If the older, weaker person can show (1) that they were induced to enter into a particular contract by virtue of the dominant party's power and influence, rather than as the result of exercising his or her own volition, and (2) that the dominant party used this power to take advantage of them, undue influence is established and they are freed of liability on this ground.

The same general rules for undue influence in the making of contracts also apply to the making of wills. Therefore, it may be helpful to read the *Casper v. McDowell* case in Chapter 35, which addresses an undue influence claim regarding a will.

HOME SOLICITATION STATUTES

Several states have enacted *home solicitation statutes* which protect persons who are subjected to high-pressure sales tactics by salespersons who come to their homes. These statutes supplement the common-law concepts discussed above. The general rule is that a buyer has an automatic three-day period in which to cancel a contract where: (1) the contract is for land, goods or services worth over $25; (2) the sale was initiated by the seller; and (3) the contract was completed at a place other than the seller's place of business (usually the buyer's home). The buyer need not show fraud, undue influence, or mistake. The three-day right to rescind is automatic. The federal Truth-in-Lending Act also provides for a three-day right to rescind in the case of credit transactions affecting interstate commerce, such as a mortgage transaction in connection with the purchase of a home.

LEGAL CAPACITY

The term capacity means the legal ability—the ability or "competence" in the eyes of the law—to perform a particular act, such as making a valid contract.

Contracts Made by Minors

A person must have legal capacity to make a completely valid contract, and a contract made without such capacity is typically voidable by the party without capacity. It is not void, and will have full effect if the one without capacity raises no objection. According to the English common-law rules adopted by all of our states, a contract made between a minor and an adult can be *disaffirmed* by the minor (but not by the adult) at any time before they become an adult or within a reasonable time after reaching adulthood. *Disaffirmance* may be accomplished by a clear indication of an intent to not be bound by the contract, or, if the minor simply does not perform her obligations under the contract and is sued for breach by the adult, the minor may assert her lack of legal capacity as a defense to any liability for breaching the contract.

If a contract between a minor and an adult is fully *executed*, that is, has been fully performed by both parties, the question is whether the minor can still disaffirm the contract and get back whatever they gave up when performing the contract. The general rule is that the minor can do so. For example, if a minor buys a car from a dealer, the minor can return the car and get his money back while still a minor. The law in a minority of states would require the minor to account for any damage or depreciation to the car, but in a majority of states the minor is entitled to the full amount they paid without any deduction for damage or depreciation.

The law on contracts of minors was once more important than it is today, because the traditional common-law rule was that a person did not become an adult until age twenty-one. In the last one-third of the twentieth century, however, all states have lowered the age at which one reaches adulthood and can make contracts, own property, and make a will specifying how his property will be disposed of at his death at age eighteen. Thus, a lot fewer significant contracts are made by minors in the modern era. Also, the ages at which a person may legally do other things, such as drink alcohol or get married are set by separate state laws.

Exceptions

The old common-law term in contract law for necessities of life was "necessaries." According to the law of all states, minors are fully obligated on contracts for necessaries such as food, lodging, clothing, and medicine so that others will be willing to sell such essentials to them. Whether other goods or services constitute necessaries will be a question of fact determined by all of the circumstances.

Another exception to the general rule that a minor may get out of a contract occurs in the case of entities such as "common carriers" (airlines, trains, buses, ferries, etc.) that have a legal duty to deal with everyone who requests (and is able to pay for) their services. Disaffirmance against such entities is generally not permitted once the contract has been fully executed. Thus, a 17-year-old who purchases and uses an airline ticket is not permitted to recover his or her fare, but can surrender the ticket *before* the flight and receive a refund.

In addition, a minor cannot disaffirm a marriage contract if they were above the age set by legislation in the particular state for marriage by minors (such as 16 or 17). A minor also may not get out of a military enlistment contract, and legislation in all states prevents minors from disaffirming contracts with banks or insurance companies.

In most states, minors who *misrepresent their age* as being that of an adult, the minor can still disaffirm the contract as if there had been no misstatement, as long as the contract has not yet been performed. When the other party has already performed its part of the contract, however, the courts in most states will allow the minor to disaffirm only if the other party will not incur any kind of loss as the result of allowing the minor to cancel the contract.

Mentally Impaired and Intoxicated Persons

Persons with impaired mental capacity are, like minors, given substantial protection by the law insofar as their contractual obligations are concerned. Those with substantial mental impairments include those who are mentally retarded, brain-damaged, severely senile, or mentally ill. Some mentally impaired persons are formally declared to be incompetent by a court after hearings and examination by psychologists or psychiatrists. After a person has been *adjudicated insane*, a guardian is appointed. Thereafter, any contract made by the insane person rather than by the guardian is absolutely void—that is, creates no liability whatever, even if it is never disaffirmed by the incompetent person or the guardian.

Many mentally impaired persons have never been the subject of incompetency proceedings, but are nonetheless *insane in fact*. If at the time the contract was made, the person was so impaired that she was *incapable of understanding the nature and effect of the particular agreement,* then the contract is voidable. A person may be senile, delusional, or otherwise impaired in some aspects of life, but if he nevertheless has a good grasp of business decisions (especially simple ones), a contract he makes may be completely valid—the critical question is always whether the person apparently understood the nature and consequences of the particular contract in question. A contract made by someone who is *insane in fact* is treated in the same way as a contract made by a minor.

In the case of contracts made by a person who is either adjudicated insane or merely insane in fact, liability to pay for *necessities* furnished by others would exist under the quasi-contract principle.

People occasionally seek to escape liability under a contract on the ground that they were *intoxicated* when it was made. Success in doing so depends primarily on the degree of intoxication found to exist at that time. Disaffirmance is allowed only if a person can establish that they were so intoxicated as not to understand the nature and effect of the agreement—the same test used in the case of those who claim that they were *insane in fact.* Thus a question of fact is presented, for a lesser degree of intoxication is not grounds for disaffirmance. The right of a person who was intoxicated to the point of not having understood the nature and effect of a contract has essentially the same right to disaffirm the contract after regaining sobriety as a minor would have, with one exception: a previously insane person must return the full amount or value of anything she received under the contract while intoxicated.

CHAPTER 15

Written Documentation: The Statute of Frauds and Parol Evidence Rule

- The Statute of Frauds

- Contracts that Must Be in Writing

- Contracts Calling for Sale of Goods

- When Is the Writing Sufficient?

- The Parol Evidence Rule

Many people think that contracts are never enforceable unless they are in writing; thus we hear movie magnate Sam Goldwyn's famous aphorism, "Oral contracts aren't worth the paper they're written on." Insofar as the law is concerned, however, most oral contracts are just as enforceable as written contracts *if their terms can be established in court.* In this chapter we will examine the relatively few kinds of contracts that are required by law to be in writing; then we will consider general problems relating to written contracts. In a situation where the law requires a contract to be in writing, any contract that does not meet that requirement—i.e., one that is entirely oral in nature, or that is written but ambiguous or incomplete—is an "unenforceable" contract, rather than a "void" or "voidable" one. Thus, as the term indicates, neither party is bound by such a contract—with limited exceptions noted later. Note, however, that although many types of contracts are enforceable even if there is little or no written documentation, many lawsuits based on oral contracts that are otherwise valid are dismissed by the courts because their terms cannot be sufficiently established. If a contract is important, it is always wise to document it in writing even if the law does not require this. Also, even if a contract is required to be in writing, if both parties have fully performed the contract, a court will not "undo" the contract simply because it was supposed to be in writing but was not.

THE STATUTE OF FRAUDS

In England, prior to the latter part of the seventeenth century, all oral contracts were enforceable as long as their existence and terms could be established. Under this approach, it became apparent that many unscrupulous plaintiffs were obtaining judgments against innocent defendants by the use of *perjured testimony*—false testimony given under oath. To illustrate: P claimed that D had breached a particular oral contract, a contract that D denied having ever made. If P could induce his witnesses (usually by the payment of money) to falsely testify that they heard D agree to the alleged contract, and if D could neither refute such testimony by witnesses of his own nor otherwise prove that P's witnesses were lying, a judgment would be granted in favor of P. D's situation was particularly difficult because, at the time of which we are speaking, the parties to a civil suit were not permitted to testify in their own behalf; thus the testimony of other witnesses was even more important than it is today. To reduce the possibility that this could happen, in 1677 Parliament passed "An Act for the Prevention of Frauds and Perjuries"—or, as it is commonly called, the *statute of frauds.*

The statute of frauds required certain types of contracts to be in writing in order to be enforceable. Virtually every American state has its own statute of frauds patterned after the original English version, which required the following types of contracts or promises to be in writing (or evidenced by a written memorandum):

(1) A contract calling for the sale of an interest in land.

(2) A contract that cannot be performed within one year of its making.

(3) A promise by one person to pay the debt of another.

(4) A promise made in consideration of marriage.

(5) A promise by the administrator or executor of an estate to pay a debt of the estate out of his or her own funds.

Modern Rationale

Obviously, a continuing rationale for the statute of frauds is the hope that written agreements will diminish the chances that a plaintiff will simply fabricate the existence of a contract and sue. It also represents a policy judgment that written evidence is more reliable than fading memories and sometimes unreliable eyewitness oral testimony. Additionally, the requirement of a writing serves the cautionary function of reminding the parties of the significance of their acts and increasing the chances that they would express their intent more precisely.

On the other hand, the statute of frauds also allows some parties to evade obligations that they have willingly undertaken. Indeed, it appears that it is used more often today for enabling a defendant to escape a legitimate contractual obligation than for defeating a plaintiff's fabricated lawsuit. This concern has led England, where the statute of frauds originated, to virtually discard it. Indeed, most nations do not have a requirement that contracts be in writing, and the Convention on Contracts for the International Sale of Goods (CISG) provides that "a contract for sale need not be concluded in or evidence by writing and is not subject to any other requirements as to form."

Furthermore, state courts in the U.S. have attempted to balance the opposing policing interests regarding written documentation for contracts by developing various exceptions to the writing requirement when other evidence makes it clear that a contract really did exist. These exceptions will be addressed as this chapter proceeds. All of this does not diminish the practical importance of putting our contracts in writing, and making them as definite and precise as possible. Doing so often prevents many future problems.

CONTRACTS THAT MUST BE IN WRITING

Contracts for the Sale of Land

As a practical matter, the most important contracts required by the statute to be in writing are those calling for the sale of an interest in land—real estate (or as it is often called in legal circles, "real property"). With an exception to be noted later, contracts for the transfer of an interest in real property that are either oral or in writing but vague or incomplete are absolutely unenforceable. Thus, if X orally agrees to sell a farm to Y for a specified price, neither can enforce the contract in court even if it can be proved.

In most cases it is easy to determine whether a contract does or does not involve the sale of land. Real property consists of the earth's surface and the soil, rocks, and minerals beneath the surface; the right to use the area in the air above the surface up to a reasonable height; vegetation; buildings, and other structures permanently attached to the land in a relatively permanent fashion. Growing crops and timber, being physically attached to the ground, are also generally considered to be real property when sold in conjunction with the land (but not when sold separately from the land). Thus, if S, by a written agreement, contracts to sell his farm to B for $450,000, B is entitled to receive any crops, trees, and other vegetation then growing on it, as well as the land itself. Of course, the parties can always agree to specify in the sale contract that seller is not transferring ownership of anything that would normally be treated as real property. On the other hand, if S contracts merely to sell a crop or timber to B, the crop or timber is considered *personal property*. A contract for the sale of *tangible* personal property (i.e., "goods") only has to be in writing if it is for a price of $500 or more, a requirement found in Article 2 of the Uniform Commercial Code.

The total ownership of a parcel of real property, whether it be a residential home and lot, a commercial building, a shopping center, a farm or ranch, or any other real estate, can be divided into various sub-interests. Any sub-interest is treated as an *interest in land*, and a contract for the sale or other transfer of it must be in writing. *Interests in land* include the right to use only the surface of the land, or separate ownership of the mineral rights. Mineral rights include such things as the right to extract coal, oil and gas, gravel, and any of various metals and minerals. Transfer of an undivided fractional interest in either the whole or any part of the total interest in land, such as the 50% fractional interest in real property owned by a husband or wife under the law of many states, must be in writing. Or, for example, if the owner of a 100% interest in a parcel of real estate agrees to sell to someone else a 30% undivided interest (that is, not a specific, identifiable portion of the land, but just an interest in the whole), the contract must be in writing.

Real estate mortgages and easements are also interests in land. A real estate *mortgage* is a conveyance (transfer) of an interest in land by a debtor to a creditor as security for the debt, and is an interest that is contingent upon the debtor's default. An *easement* is the right of one person to do something on someone else's land. Examples of easements include the landowner's giving permission to another to run a power line over the property, a pipeline or cable beneath the property, and road or trail for driving a vehicle or herding sheep across a portion of the property, and so on. Easements can be created in two ways—expressly or by implication. If created in an express manner, an agreement to grant an easement must be evidenced by a complete written document. An easement created by implication, on the other hand, need not be evidenced by a writing. One example of such an easement is an "implied easement of necessity." This is created when a landowner transfers ownership of part of his or her property to another, the portion sold or otherwise transferred being situated in such a way that the buyer has no access to it except by going across the seller's remaining land.

While real estate *leases* also convey interests in land and thus normally fall within the Statute of Frauds, most states have enacted special statutes providing that oral leases of one year's duration or less are valid. But leases for a term of more than one year must be written.

In addition to the requirement that a contract for the sale of any interest in real property be in writing, the actual transfer of ownership must itself be evidenced by a written *deed* that clearly states that the seller is "conveying," "granting," or "selling" the real property; provides an adequate *legal description* of the property; and is signed by the *grantor* (such as a seller). A *gift* of an interest in land also must be accomplished by a written deed.

Effect of Part Performance—Estoppel

As noted earlier, in some circumstances the courts have felt that oral contracts ought to be enforceable even though they are not in writing. Accordingly, they have recognized limited exceptions to the rules embodied in the statute of frauds. In the case of any type of contracts that are required to be in writing, courts have applied a so-called "part performance" exception, which provides that when one party to the contract performs all or a substantial part of his part of the contract, and when that performance clearly was made to fulfill the agreement that the parties made, that party can enforce the contract against the other even though the Statute of Frauds applied and the requirement of written documentation had not been satisfied. This is just another application of "promissory estoppel," which was discussed in Chapter 12 on Consideration—promissory estoppel came into existence as a substitute for the requirement of consideration when there had been reasonable, foreseeable, and substantial reliance on the promise of the other, even though there had been no agreement at the time of the promise that the promise would do something in return. Over time, however, promissory estoppel has come to serve other purposes, including the creation of an exception to the Statute of Frauds requirement of written documentation.

The part performance, or promissory estoppel, that can create an exception to the written documentation requirement for contracts for the sale of real property must, however, take a very specific form. For this exception to apply to real estate contracts so that a buyer can enforce the contract against the seller without adequate documentation, the buyer, in reliance upon the oral contract, must have (1) paid all or part of the consideration for the interest in real estate, (2) taken possession of it, and (3) made valuable (substantial) improvements to it.

If the interest in real property that is agreed to be transferred is not a type that involves the grantee actually living on the land, such as a right to drill for oil and gas or explore for other minerals, the requirements for the promissory estoppel exception are modified to fit the circumstances. In such a case, an oral contract to transfer this type of interest would be enforceable if the grantee paid all of part of the consideration and engaged in other conduct showing an exercise of *dominion*, or control, over the particular type of interest. An example would be the grantee of an oil and gas drilling right moving its drilling equipment to the property, digging a pond for wastewater from the drilling process, and beginning to drill.

In these circumstances the courts will permit the buyer to enforce the contract if the buyer's actions in paying consideration, possessing, and improving the property are clearly "referable" to the oral contract that the buyer claims to have been created. Stated differently, the buyer's actions must be good evidence that an oral contract has actually been made. Thus, the buyer's actions must be of such a nature that a reasonable person would take only if they legitimately expected to become the owner of the particular interest in real property. The following case illustrates application of the promissory estoppel exception to the requirement of written documentation for a transfer of real estate.

CASTILLO v. RIOS
Texas Court of Appeals, 2001 Tex. App. LEXIS 2552 (2001)

In 1992, Castillo and his wife moved into a house at 8905 Quinn in Dallas. They signed a two-year lease/purchase agreement to pay a rental payment each month and an additional amount to be credited to the down payment once the lease expired and the Castillos bought the property. As the end of the lease term neared, Castillo was about to be arrested and his marriage was ending; thus, he could not afford to purchase the home. In April 1994, Castillo asked Rios, his employer, if he wanted to buy the house from him. According to Rios, he and Castillo reached an oral agreement by which Rios gave Castillo a Ford Taurus, $1,000 for the down payment, and an additional $500 in exchange for the house. Thereafter, Castillo closed on the house.

In reliance on the oral agreement, Rios testified he completely remodeled the house, installing sheetrock, new cabinets, flooring, and carpeting. According to Rios, Castillo and other members of his work crew were paid to perform the labor on these improvements. Rios valued the improvements at $35,000, but no receipts were offered into evidence. After making *the improvements, he moved into the home and made the mortgage payments each month. However, Castillo refused to transfer title to the property and provide Rios with a deed.*

Four years later, Castillo sued to evict Rios. Rios then brought this action to establish his right to title. At the time of trial, Rios had been in possession of the house for five-and-one-half years. The trial court overruled Castillo's statute of frauds defense and ordered him to convey the property to Rios by general warranty deed. Castillo appealed.

Roach, Justice:

In *Hooks v. Bridgewater*, 229 S.W. 1114 (Tex. 1921), the Texas Supreme Court established a three-prong test that must be met to exempt an oral contract for the sale of real estate from the statute of frauds. Pursuant to Hooks, an oral contract for the purchase of real property is enforceable if the purchaser: (1) pays the consideration, whether it be in money or services; (2) takes possession of the property; and (3) makes permanent and valuable improvements on the property with the consent of the seller or, without such improvements, other facts are shown that would make the transaction a fraud upon the purchaser if the oral contract was not enforced. These steps are seen as sufficient evidence of the agreement because they provide affirmative corroboration of the agreement by both parties to the agreement.

In this case, the evidence on the second prong (possession) was undisputed: Rios took possession of the property in 1994 and continued to reside there at the time of trial. Further, at all times, he made the required mortgage payment.

With respect to the first prong, i.e., payment of consideration, [the trial court believed Rios' testimony that] he gave Castillo a car, $1,000 for the down payment, and an additional $500 in exchange for the house.

With respect to the third prong, i.e., the making of valuable and permanent improvements with Castillo's consent, Rios testified that he replaced the sheetrock and installed new cabinets and flooring in the house. Rios, who was a building contractor, valued these improvements at $35,000. [The trial judge believed Rios' testimony that] Castillo knew about the improvements because Castillo helped with the labor on them. In addition, Rios also put in a concrete driveway.

We conclude there was more than a scintilla of evidence from which the trial judge could reasonably conclude that Rios paid the consideration, took possession of the house, and made valuable and permanent improvements to the property with Castillo's consent. [Affirmed.]

Comment: Contrary to the court's statement in the *Castillo* case, in most states it is *not* necessary that the seller *knew of and consented to* the improvements that the buyer made to the real estate in order to fulfill the improvements requirement.

Contracts Not Performable Within One Year

The section of the statute requiring that *agreements not to be performed within one year of the making thereof* be in writing is based on the fact that disputes over the terms of long-term oral contracts are particularly likely to occur; witnesses die, the parties' memories become hazy, and so on. Despite the logic underlying this provision, it has posed numerous problems in practice.

In deciding whether a particular agreement falls within this section, the usual (but not the only) approach taken by the courts is to determine whether it was *reasonably possible*, under its own terms, for the contract in question to have been performed within one year from the time it was made. If so, the contract is "outside" the statute and need not be in writing. The fact that performance *actually* may have taken more than one year is immaterial. These examples illustrate some common interpretations of this provision.

(1) A, on June 1, 2020, orally agrees to work for B as a personal secretary at a salary of $3,000 per month ''as long as this arrangement is satisfactory to both parties.'' This is known as an ''at-will'' employment contract. It gives either party the right to terminate it at any time. It does not have to be in writing to be enforceable, because it can be fully performed *by its own terms* in less than a year. Assume that A worked for B for two years, and in the third year, B refused to pay wages for work A had performed. If A sued, most courts would hold that B could not successfully assert a statute of frauds defense. Even though performance actually took longer, the contract could have been fully performed in less than one year. A minority of courts, rejecting the "reasonably possible" test, would hold that if performance longer than one year was *within the contemplation of the parties*, the contract would have to be in writing.

(2) On June 1, 2020, A promises to work for B "as long as you [B] shall live." Most courts, but not all, would hold that this contract also need *not* be in writing to be enforceable. B might die in less than a year. If he did, the contract would have been fully performed in less than a year. Again, it is irrelevant if B actually did live longer than a year.

(3) A promises on June 1, 2020, to work for B "for the next two years." This contract must be in writing to be enforceable, because it is not possible to work for two years in less than one year. True, it is again possible that B might die in less than a year, but the contract will not have been fully performed as written. (Instead, B's death would have excused performance under the doctrine of impossibility discussed later in Chapter 17.)

(4) A promises on June 1, 2020, to sing a two-hour concert at XYZ University on August 12, 2021. This contract must be in writing to be enforceable. Even though the performance itself will take only two hours, by the contract's terms that performance must occur more than one year after the contract was made.

Promise to Pay the Debt of Another

If A has received a benefit from B, then B's claim that A has made a promise to B is more plausible than if A has received no such benefit. To avoid perjury, the Statute of Frauds requires that if A has not received such a benefit, A's ''promise to answer for the debt, default or miscarriage of another'' must be in writing to be enforceable. The classic example is a "guaranty contract" in which A promises B that he will pay C's debt to B *if* C does not. Because A received no benefit in this transaction, the law is suspicious and demands that B provide written evidence of A's promise.

There are three standard elements of a guaranty contract. First, the guarantor promises to pay the debtor's obligation *if* the debtor does not. In other words, guaranty contracts occur in situations of "secondary liability." The creditor is to look primarily to the debtor for repayment, and only if the debtor does not pay is the creditor to look to the guarantor. If, on the other hand, A tells B: "Send C's bills to me," A is the primary debtor to whom B is to look first for payment. A is making the debt his own, not promising to pay the debt of another. Such a promise is not a guaranty and therefore need not be in writing to be enforceable.

Second, a guaranty promise is made for the benefit of the debtor. If the guarantor's *main purpose* in making the promise is to benefit himself, it is not a guaranty contract and need not be in writing to be enforceable. An aunt who, out of pity, promises a landlord that she will pay her niece's rent if the niece does not pay is making a guaranty promise that must be in writing to be enforceable. On the other hand, assume that Guarantor Company has a government contract to build a wind tunnel to test airplanes. Guarantor hires Joe Debtor to do the concrete work. Because Joe does not pay his bills, Creditor Concrete Supply stops delivering concrete, halting construction and endangering Guarantor's contract with the government. If an official of Guarantor called Creditor on the phone and said: "Please keep delivering concrete to Joe Debtor, and we'll pay the bills if he doesn't," the promise would be enforceable though never put in writing because Guarantor's main purpose in making the promise is obviously to benefit itself. Therefore, this is not a guaranty promise and need not be in writing to be enforceable.

Third, a guaranty promise is made to the creditor, not to the debtor. If in the previous example, Guarantor Company had told Joe Debtor: "Keep ordering concrete, and we'll pay the bill if you don't," such a promise is not a guaranty and need not be in writing in order to be enforceable.

Other Contracts Required to be in Writing

Two other relatively insignificant categories of contracts—*promises made in consideration of marriage and executors' contracts*—fall within the statute. Thus, if A promises to pay B $5,000 when and if B marries C, A is liable only if his promise is in writing. The same is true in regard to prenuptial agreements, in which parties about to be married to each other expressly spell out their interests in the other's properties. Indeed, some states have passed statutes requiring that ''palimony'' contracts—agreements for support or division of property between cohabiting lovers who are not married—be in writing to be enforceable.

Likewise, if the administrator or executor of an estate promises personally to pay a debt of the deceased, the creditor can hold the promisor liable only if the promise is in writing.

In addition, many borrowers have recently sued banks claiming some form of breach of an oral promise to lend, to refinance an existing loan, or to refrain from enforcing remedies contained in a written loan agreement. In one case, for example, a jury awarded $28 million for breach of an alleged oral promise to extend an existing line of credit. In another, a jury awarded $69 million for breach of an alleged oral promise to make a loan. To protect banks and other lending institutions from such liability, many states have recently passed laws barring the enforcement of oral lending agreements without a signed contract.

THE UCC STATUTE OF FRAUDS—CONTRACTS FOR THE SALE OF GOODS

Section 2-201 of the Uniform Commercial Code, known as the *UCC statute of frauds*, states that a contract for the *sale of goods* for a price of $500 or more must be in writing to be enforceable, with some exceptions. As is true of the other statute of frauds provisions applicable to non-goods transactions, the requirement of § 2-201(1) can be satisfied either (1) by having the contract itself in writing, or (2) by having a subsequent written memorandum that confirms the earlier oral agreement and its terms. In either situation, *the writing must be signed by the party against whom enforcement is sought.*

The UCC Subsequent Confirmation Rule

The language of § 2-201(1) regarding enforceability of oral sales contracts parallels that of the basic statute of frauds. That is, if an oral sales contract is followed by a writing signed by only one of the parties, the signer is bound by the contract but the non-signer is not. To eliminate this one-sidedness in certain circumstances, subsection 2 of § 2-201 provides a third method of satisfying the writing requirement of subsection 1.

Suppose that two parties have orally agreed on a sale of goods. One of the parties then sends a signed letter or other written communication to the other party, saying: "This is to confirm that on June 20 we entered into an agreement for the sale of 175 men's suits on the following terms [the terms being stated in the letter]." If this is the only writing the parties make, the question is whether it can be used to satisfy the requirements of Sec. 2-201(1). If the sender of the written confirmation breaches the contract, the letter can be used in a lawsuit by the letter's recipient against the sender because the sender signed it. But if it is the recipient who breaches the contract, can the sender use the letter in his lawsuit to recover damages from the recipient, the non-signer? In transactions not governed by the UCC, as we have seen, the answer is No. But as to sales of goods, however, as in the above example, the answer sometimes is Yes.

Under § 2-201(2), a confirmation such as the one described above can be used by the sender against a non-signing recipient if the following requirements are met:

(1) The writing must be "sufficient against the sender." In other words, the *sender* must have *signed* the confirmation, and its contents must meet the relatively lenient sufficiency requirements discussed later in the chapter.

(2) Both parties must be *merchants.*

(3) The recipient must have had reason to know of the contents of the confirmation but *had not objected to it in writing within ten days after receiving it.*

UCC Exceptions

Section 2-201(3) defines three situations in which an oral contract for the sale of goods at a price of $500 or more, if the agreement and its terms are proved, will be enforceable despite the absence of adequate written documentation. The first exception can be used only by a seller; the other two can be used by either a seller or a buyer.

(1) If the oral contract is for goods to be *specifically manufactured for the particular buyer*, it is enforceable against the buyer if two requirements are met:

a. The goods must be of a type not suitable for sale to others in the ordinary course of the seller's business. For example: Suppose that C is an importer of small, foreign-made pickup trucks, and D is a manufacturer of campers that are mounted on pickups. C orally orders from D a number of campers made to fit the pickups imported by C (that is, they will fit no other pickups on the market). If C repudiates the bargain after the campers are made, D will be hard-pressed to sell them elsewhere. He might eventually be able to do so, but considerable effort would probably be required. Thus the goods cannot be sold in the ordinary course of his business.

b. The seller must either have substantially started the manufacture of the goods, or have made commitments for procuring them, before they learned of the buyer's repudiation of the agreement.

(2) If the defendant "admits in his pleading, testimony or otherwise *in court* that a contract for sale

415 © 2020 John R. Allison & Robert A. Prentice

was made," it will be enforceable even though oral. The common-law court decisions (transactions not covered by the UCC) on this point are conflicting, most courts holding that such an admission does *not* remove the requirement of a writing. Thus the UCC exception represents a significant innovation in this regard. Note that not just any admission will suffice; the admission by the defendant must become part of official court records.

(3) An oral agreement will be enforced to the extent that payment has been made and accepted or that the goods have been received and accepted. Suppose, for example, that X and Y have made an oral contract for Y to sell X twenty-five television sets at a price of $300 each. Before any of the sets are delivered, X makes a prepayment of $1,800, which Y accepts. Y then refuses to honor the contract. Even if Y were not bound by the contract, X could of course get her money back under the *unjust enrichment* (i.e., quasi contract) theory (see Chapter 10). But under the UCC, her part payment will make the contract partially enforceable, and she will be able to maintain a suit for breach of a contract obligation to deliver six of the twenty-five television sets.

Similarly, if X has made no payment but Y has made a partial shipment which X has accepted, the oral contract is again partially enforceable. That is, if Y delivers and X accepts six television sets, and X then repudiates the agreement, Y can maintain a suit for breach of a contract obligation to pay $1,800. Prior to enactment of the UCC, part performance of this type made the *entire contract* enforceable. Also, the statutory language in this exception does not address the situation in which the buyer has made a partial prepayment that cannot be allocated to a certain number of individual units of goods. For example, what if buyer makes and seller accepts a $5,000 down payment on a single $20,000 automobile? In the few cases involving this question since enactment of the UCC, most courts have applied the common-law rule and have held the entire contract to be enforceable despite the absence of a sufficient written document.

Compliance with the statute of frauds under UCC 2-201 is summarized in Figure 15.1.

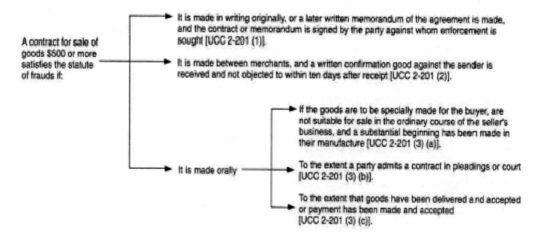

Figure 15.1 Compliance with the Statute of Frauds in
Contracts for the Sale of Goods, UCC § 2-201.

Modification Contracts

Under § 2-209 of the UCC, agreements that modify existing sale of goods contracts must be in writing in order to be enforceable in two situations:

(1) The modification must be in writing if the original agreement had provided that it could be modified only by a writing. Section 2-209(2) has an additional provision applicable to those sales

contracts entered into between a merchant and a non-merchant. In such a case, if the contract results from use of the *merchant's form* (with that form containing the requirement that any later modification had to be in writing), that requirement must itself be ''separately signed'' by the non-merchant in order to be binding upon them.

(2) The modification must be in writing if the whole contract, *as modified,* is required to be in writing under the UCC statute of frauds (Sec. 2-201, discussed above).

Other Statutes Requiring Written Documentation

In addition to the basic statute of frauds and § 2-201 and § 2-209 of the UCC for *sale of goods transactions*, § 9-203 of the UCC imposes the same requirement for *security agreements* governed by Article 9. A security agreement creates a *security interest* in an item of either tangible or intangible personal property by making the personal property collateral to secure payment of a debt, such as a debt for the purchase price of a car or boat. Intangible personal property such as a patent or a right to receive performance under a contract (such as the right to receive money in payment of an "account receivable" is commonly made subject to a security agreement as a means for the owner of the property to obtain credit. A security agreement is security analogous to a mortgage on real estate.

Section 2A-201 of the UCC requires that a *lease of goods* for a price of $1,000 or more must be written. All states have additional statutes—usually narrow in scope—that require still other kinds of contracts to be in writing. For example, most states require *real estate listing contracts* that promise to pay a commission to a realtor who finds a ready, willing, and able buyer to be in writing for the property owner's promise to the realtor to be enforceable. Also, state laws usually require *insurance contracts* ("insurance policies") to be in writing. And, a *contract for the sale of securities* (corporate stocks or bonds and other kinds of contracts for investments) is required to be in writing under § 8-219 of the UCC.

WHEN IS THE WRITING SUFFICIENT—GENERAL CONTRACT LAW?

The original statute of frauds began: "No action shall be brought [upon the following kinds of contracts] unless the agreement upon which such action shall be brought, or some memorandum or note thereof, shall be in writing and signed by the party sought to be charged therewith or some other person thereunto by him lawfully authorized." Thus, even if the full contract is not in writing, a *sufficient written memorandum* may satisfy the statute of fraud's requirements. In such situations, the courts generally require that the writing include at least the following: (1) names of both parties, (2) the subject matter of the contract, (3) the consideration to be paid, and (4) any other terms that the court feels are material under the circumstances. Under this fairly strict approach, if any basic term is missing, the contract continues to be unenforceable.

This does not mean, however, that the writing must be in any particular form, or be complete in every detail. And because of the provision that a memorandum or note of the contract may satisfy the statute of frauds, it is entirely possible that an oral contract can be validated by the production in court of a confirming telegram, sales slip, check, invoice, or some other writing—assuming, of course, that it contains all the material terms of the agreement.

Additionally, it frequently happens that the contract is evidenced by two or more separate writings, none of which alone is sufficiently complete. In such cases the writings may be construed together, thus satisfying the memorandum requirement, if the writings *clearly refer to one another*, if they are *physically attached to one another*, or if they all *clearly relate to the same transaction*.

The requirement that the contract or written memorandum be signed by the party against whom the agreement is to be enforced (or that party's authorized agent) can be fulfilled in several ways, because a "signature" is any mark that the writer intends to be her signature. It may be satisfied by a longhand signature, by initials, by the letterhead on a sheet of paper, a company's trademark appearing on the paper, or a name on an email, as long as the individual or company representative apparently intended it to be a signature, that is, an individualized mark of approval of the document.

SHATTUCK v. KLOTZBACH
Massachusetts Superior Court, 2001 Mass. Super. LEXIS 642 (2001)

In April 2001, the plaintiff and the defendants began discussions concerning the sale of a property at 5 Main Street, Marion, MA. On April 9, 2001, the plaintiff sent an e-mail to the defendants which contained an offer for the property. Defendant responded and noted that e-mail was the "preferred" manner of communication during their negotiations.

The parties ultimately entered into a purchase and sale agreement, but prior to closing it was terminated because defendants could not procure a "wharf license" as the contract required. Nevertheless, commencing in July 2001, the parties again began communicating via e-mail concerning the sale of the same property. In an e-mail sent July 24, 2001, the plaintiff wrote to the defendant that he was increasing his offer to $1.825 million. Multiple e-mails were exchanged during the summer, and finally, on September 10, 2001, the plaintiff sent the defendant an e-mail which stated that the plaintiff's attorney had told him there were no complications and the attorney would draft a very standard purchase and sale agreement for $1,825,000 "with no usual contingencies." The defendant responded the same day by e-mail stating "once we sign the P&S we'd like to close ASAP. You may have your attorney send the P&S and deposit check for 10% of purchase price ($182,500) to my attorney." The e-mail concluded by stating that "I'm looking forward to closing and seeing you as the owner of '5 Main Street,' the prettiest spot in Marion village." All e-mails detailed above contained a salutation at the end which consisted of the type written name of the respective sender. Defendant later refused to perform and plaintiff sued for specific performance. Defendant raised a statute of frauds defense. Plaintiff admitted that a real estate contract must be in writing to be enforceable, but argued that the statute was satisfied by the e-mails.

Murphy, Justice:

Where the defendant pleads the statute of frauds, the burden is on the plaintiff to prove the existence of a memorandum complying with the statute's requirements. "A memorandum is signed in accordance with the statute of frauds if it is signed by the person to be charged in his own name, or by his initials, or by his Christian name alone, or by a printed, stamped or typewritten signature, if signing in any of these methods he intended to authenticate the paper as his act." *Irving v. Goodimate Co.*, 70 N.E.2d 414 (1946). Here, all e-mail correspondences between the parties contained a typewritten signature at the end. Taken as a whole, a reasonable trier of fact could conclude that the e-mails sent by the defendant were "signed" with the intent to authenticate the information contained therein as his act.

Moreover, courts have held that a telegram may be a signed writing sufficient to satisfy the statute of frauds. This court believes that the typed name at the end of an e-mail is more indicative of a party's intent to authenticate than that of a telegram as the sender of an e-mail types and sends the message on his own accord and types his own name as he so chooses. In the case at bar, the defendant sent e-mails regarding the sale of the property and intentionally and deliberately typed his name at the end of all such e-mails. A reasonable trier of fact could conclude that the e-mails sent by the defendant regarding the terms of the sale of the property were intended to be authenticated by the defendant's deliberate choice to type his name at the conclusion of all e-mails.

The defendant finally contends that the e-mails, even if sufficiently authenticated, do not contain the essential terms. A memorandum sufficient to satisfy the statute of frauds need not be a formal document intended to serve as a memorandum of the oral contract, but must contain the essential terms of the contract agreed upon: in the case of an interest in real estate, the parties, the locus, the nature of the transaction, and the purchase price. Multiple writings relating to the subject matter may be read together in order to satisfy the memorandum requirement so long as the writings, when considered as a single instrument, contain all the material terms of the contract and are authenticated by the signature of the party to be charged. The writings may, but need not, incorporate each other by reference. *Tzitzon Realty Co. v. Mustonen*, 227 N.E.2d 493 (1967).

In this case, the e-mails contain terms for the sale of 5 Main Street, Marion Village, Marion, MA. The e-mails further refer to a purchase price of $1,825,000 and the defendant explicitly asked the plaintiff to send a "deposit check for 10% of [the] purchase price ($182,500) . . ." Finally, the multiple e-mails reveal the parties to the sale--the plaintiff and defendant. Thus, a reasonable trier of fact could conclude that the parties had formed an agreement as to the essential terms of a land sale contract; the parties, the locus, the nature of the transaction, and the purchase price. Defendant's motion to dismiss is denied.

Comment: The Uniform Electronic Transaction Act (UETA), now enacted as state law by 47 states and the District of Columbia, provides in § 7 that a sign or mark "attached to or logically associated with a record and executed or adopted by a person with the intent to sign the record" is a signature. This means that an email with the sender's name on it in a logical place is a signed document. Although a few courts have held that if a name at the bottom of an e-mail is automatically generated by the e-mail system rather than typed by the sender, it does not constitute an intentional signing for statute of frauds purposes, most courts do not make this distinction because the sender had made a choice in setting up her email program preferences to have her name placed at the end of the message (and can change those preferences at any time), and after an email is printed out for use in a court, it likely will be impossible to determine whether the sender's name was included as part of the email program preferences or whether it was specifically added to just this message. Note that only New York, Washington State, and Illinois have not yet enacted the UETA.

WHEN IS THE WRITING SUFFICIENT?—SALE OF GOODS CONTRACTS

Contracts calling for the sale of goods are often made in the business world under circumstances where, because of time constraints or other factors, the parties put only the barest essentials of the agreement in writing. Recognizing this reality, § 2-201 of the UCC (requiring a contract for the sale of goods for a price of $500 or more to be in writing) has greatly relaxed the requirements of the sufficiency of the writing. For sales of goods, that section provides that the writing (whether the contract itself, or memorandum, or subsequent confirmation) merely has to be "sufficient to indicate that a contract for sale has been made between the parties."

The only terms that must be included in the writing are the parties' names, an indication that an agreement has been made, and the quantity. Other terms that are orally agreed upon, even the price, can be proved in court by oral testimony. Terms that are not agreed upon at all may sometimes be supplied by evidence of relevant industry custom, custom between the parties, the conduct of the parties, or by the so-called "gap filler" provisions in UCC Article 2.

DIGITAL SIGNATURES

In order to facilitate the rise of the Internet and e-commerce, governments at every level have enacted laws meant to ensure the validity of digital signatures. Numerous states enacted a patchwork of individual state laws that were well-intended but created confusion that inhibited e-commerce. To create some uniformity, the federal government passed the Electronic Signatures in Global and National Commerce Act of 2000 (E-Sign) giving presumptive validity to digital signatures (as well as digital contracts and records) and preempting statutes in states that had not yet acted to adopt the Uniform Electronic Transactions Act (UETA), promulgated by the National Conference of Commissioners on Uniform State Laws (NCCUSL). The fundamental premise of E-Sign was that the medium in which a record, signature or contract is created, presented or retained does not affect its legal significance. Form is irrelevant, so it does not matter whether information is set forth in an electronic rather than paper format. E-Sign was meant to bolster e-commerce until the states could widely adopt UETA, which has a similar philosophy. Most states have now done so, automatically preempting E-Sign. As observed in the previous comment after the *Shattuck v. Klotzbach* case, above, 47 states have now enacted the UETA.

Although E-Sign and UETA both bolster e-commerce, they do not mandate that all documents be digital. Indeed, under UETA most UCC documents, wills, codicils, testamentary trusts, and certain legal notices must all continue to be in paper form. Over time, that will likely change.

On an international level, many nations have passed digital signature laws and the United Nations Commission on International Trade Law (UNCITRAL) promulgated a Model Law on Electronic Commerce. Matters of authentication of signatures (and choice of technology for authentication) will continue to cause problems for some time.

THE PAROL EVIDENCE RULE

Whenever a contract (or a memorandum thereof) is reduced to writing, the writing ought to contain *all* the material terms of the agreement. This is true not only for contracts that fall within the statute of frauds, but also, as a practical matter, for all other contracts for which a writing is created even if they aren't required to be written. Whether or not the statute of frauds requires a particular contract to be in writing, an additional and very important reason for creating a complete document containing all important terms that were agreed to is the *parol evidence rule*. This rule provides, in general, that when any contract has been reduced to writing and shows that the parties apparently intended the written document to be the "final word" as to the terms the parties agreed on, neither party can introduce "parol" (outside the document) evidence in court for the purpose of adding to or changing the terms of that document. More specifically, the rule prohibits a party to a written contract from unilaterally introducing either oral or written statements or agreements made at or prior to the time the written contract was made if those statements or agreements either conflict with, or add to, the clear, unambiguous terms of the written contract.

Among the policy reasons for the existence of the parol evidence rule are: (1) Because a written contract is more reliable than oral testimony, the rule helps prevent perjury or fraud. (2) The rule encourages the parties to put their important agreements in writing, thus increasing the reliability of commercial transactions. (3) The rule emphasizes a longstanding rule of contract interpretation to the effect that final expressions of intent should prevail over earlier tentative expressions of intent.

As to sales contracts, the UCC's parol evidence rule in Sec. 2-202 is essentially the same as the common-law parol evidence rule.

The Parties' "Final Word" as to the terms of the Contract

As just observed, the parol evidence rule applies only if a court is convinced that the parties apparently intended the written document to be the last word on what terms they agreed to. In this regard, the most important requirement is that the document appears to be *complete*. The document does not have to include every conceivable term that anyone could ever think of including in a contract like this, but it does have to include all or most of those terms that parties to a transaction like this one would normally be expected to agree upon.

Many written contracts include a *merger clause*, in which the parties specifically state that they intend the document to be the final word as to the terms on which they have agreed. Various terminology can be used to express this intention. For instance, a clause in the document might say something like "We intend that this written document be the complete memorialization of the agreed terms." However it is phrased, a merger clause makes it easier for a judge to conclude that the document was intended to be the parties' final word in situations in which there otherwise would be a close question. However, a merger clause cannot cause the parol evidence rule to apply to a document that is clearly incomplete.

Exceptions

The courts feel that the parol evidence rule brings about clearly undesirable results in some circumstances; accordingly, they have recognized a number of exceptions to it. (In general, these exceptions apply both to cases governed by common-law principles and those governed by sales law.) Following are the most important situations in which a party to a written contract is permitted to introduce parol evidence in subsequent legal proceedings:

(1) The written contract is ambiguous, and the parol evidence tends to clear up the ambiguity. Such evidence does not "contradict or add to" the writing.

(2) The written contract contains an obvious mistake, such as a typographical or clerical error, and the parol evidence tends to correct the error.

(3) The parol evidence shows that the contract was not a valid one, as, for example, that it was

induced by fraud, innocent misrepresentation, or duress on the part of the other party, or was formed under mutual mistake of fact.

(4) The evidence shows that the contract was subject to a condition precedent, i.e., that the parties had agreed that a specified event had to occur before the contract would be effective, and that the event had not occurred.

(5) The evidence tends to prove that the parties made either an oral or written agreement that modified the written contract *after* the written document had been created. Parties to written contracts often change their minds and later alter the agreements. Use of such evidence does not contradict the basic reasoning behind the parol evidence rule which is that preliminary contract terms, which may vary substantially as the contract is negotiated, become merged into the final written contract.

(6) For the *sale of goods only*, under the UCC, a sixth exception allows evidence about the course of prior dealings of the parties or custom of the trade in which the parties are engaged to explain or supplement a writing, even when the evidence appears to contradict its unambiguous terms. This is a major relaxation of the parol evidence rule for sale of goods contracts.

CHAPTER 16

RIGHTS OF THIRD PARTIES

- Third-Party Beneficiaries
- Assignments
- Delegation of Duties

As a general rule, the rights created by the formation of a contract can be enforced only by the original parties to the agreement. A contract is essentially a private agreement affecting only the contracting parties themselves; both legal and practical difficulties would arise if a stranger to the contract (a *third party*) were permitted to enforce it. Suppose, for example, that X employed B to paint her house and that B subsequently refused to do the job. If Y, one of X's neighbors, were to bring suit against B to recover damages for breach of contract, it would be ludicrous if he were permitted to get a judgment. Since Y was not a party to the contract, he clearly has "no standing to sue," and his suit would be dismissed.

However, in certain exceptional circumstances a third party is permitted to enforce a contract made by others, particularly (1) where it appears, expressly or by necessary implication, that at the time the contract was made the parties to the contract intended that that person receive the benefit of the contract, or (2) where one of the parties, after making the contract, assigned (transferred) his or her rights to a third party. In the former situation the third party is called a *third-party beneficiary*, and in the latter they are designated as an *assignee* of the contract.

THIRD-PARTY BENEFICIARIES

The law recognizes three kinds of beneficiaries—creditor, donee, and incidental. Generally, creditor and donee beneficiaries (also known as "intended" beneficiaries) can enforce contracts made by others, while incidental beneficiaries cannot.

Creditor Beneficiaries

When a contract is made between two parties for the express benefit of a third person, the latter is said to be a *creditor beneficiary* if they earlier furnished consideration to one of the contracting parties. To illustrate: A owes X $500. A later sells a piano to B, on the understanding that B, in return, is to pay off A's indebtedness to X. In this situation, X is a creditor beneficiary of the contract between A and B, inasmuch as she originally gave consideration to A, which created the debt in her (X's) favor. Once A has delivered the piano, X is entitled to recover the $500 from B—by suit, if necessary. If A refused to deliver the piano to B, should B be required to pay X? Obviously, the answer is "no." The promisor (B) can raise the same defenses against an intended beneficiary (X) as they can raise against the promisee (A). In this case, the defense is A's failure to perform. Defenses such as lack of consideration, incapacity, fraud, mistake, or statute of frauds would also be effective. If B raises an effective defense to avoid paying X, clearly X could sue A on the original $500 debt.

Assumption of Mortgage

One typical situation involving a creditor beneficiary arises when mortgaged real estate is sold, with the purchaser agreeing to pay off the existing mortgage. For example: assume that S owns a home subject to a $15,000 mortgage held by the Y Bank. S finds a buyer for the home, Z, who is willing to assume the mortgage. S and Z then enter into a contract, under the terms of which S agrees to convey the property to Z, and Z promises to pay S's existing indebtedness to the bank. The Y Bank now has become a creditor beneficiary of the contract between S and Z, since it originally gave consideration to S by making the loan, and it can hold Z liable on his promise to pay the indebtedness. (The assumption of the mortgage by Z does not by itself free S of his liability. Thus the bank can look to either party for payment in case Z defaults—unless it has expressly released S from his obligation.) However, in most mortgages today, Z, even if willing, would not be allowed to assume the mortgages. "Due on sale clauses" (provisions in the mortgage which make the entire balance owed by S due immediately upon sale of the property) would render the loan "non-assumable."

Donee Beneficiaries

Where a contract is made for the benefit of a third person who has not given consideration to either contracting party, that person is designated a *donee beneficiary* of the contract. To illustrate: P, an attorney, agrees to perform certain legal services for Q, with the understanding that Q will pay the $200 legal fee to R, P's son-in-law. Here P has made a gift of $200 to R, and R—the donee beneficiary of the contract—can enforce it against Q if Q refuses to pay him voluntarily.

Life Insurance Contracts

The most common type of contract involving donee beneficiaries is that of the ordinary life insurance policy. If A insures his life with the B Insurance Co. and the policy expressly designates C as the beneficiary of the proceeds of that policy, C—the donee beneficiary—can enforce the contract against the company. The fact that C has not furnished consideration to the company is immaterial; it is sufficient that A, the insured, has done so by making his premium payments. If A did not pay the premiums that the contract required, obviously B Insurance Co. would not have to pay C the proceeds of the policy, again illustrating that claims of intended beneficiaries against the promisor are subject to the same defenses that could be raised against the promisee.

Incidental Beneficiaries

An *incidental beneficiary* is a person whom the contracting parties did not intend to benefit by making the contract, but who nevertheless will benefit in some way if the contract is performed. Such a beneficiary, unlike a donee beneficiary, has no rights under the contract and thus is not entitled to enforce it. For example, a retail merchant in a college town would benefit from a contract between a construction firm and the university calling for the construction of a four-level parking facility on campus property just across the street from his (or her) store. However, if the builder breaches the contract with the university by refusing to go ahead with the project, the merchant cannot recover damages from the builder.

In determining whether a beneficiary is a donee beneficiary or an incidental beneficiary, the usual test is whether the contract was made primarily for his or her benefit. If so, the beneficiary is a donee beneficiary; if not, they are merely an incidental beneficiary. Strong evidence that a beneficiary is intended arises where the contract expressly designates the third party as such or where the promisor's performance is to be rendered directly to the third party. Consider these illustrations:

1. A hires B Co. to construct a building. Soon after construction begins, A breaches the contract; as a result, B Co. lays off employee X. If X sued A for breach of contract, he would lose. His employment was an incidental benefit of the contract, but clearly A and B Co. did not make the contract for the purpose of benefiting X.

2. A promises to build an office building for B. The plans and specifications call for use of electrical wiring made by L Company. A uses wiring made by M Company instead. L could not sue A for

breach of contract because the purpose of this requirement was not to provide business for L.

3. City hires ABC Water Co. to provide water for its citizens' needs at an agreed rate. If ABC charged more than the agreed rate, the citizens would probably be allowed to sue as intended beneficiaries for breach of contract. ABC's performance, after all, was to be directed to the citizens. However, assume that citizen X's warehouse burns down, in part because ABC did not provide adequate water pressure for the fire fighters. Although the same reasoning would appear to apply, most courts would deny recovery by X against ABC on *public policy* grounds. For fear that allowing recovery in the latter instance would impose crushing financial burdens on entities with government contracts, such as public utilities, most courts would characterize X as a mere incidental beneficiary. *H. R. Moch Co. v. Rensselaer Water Co.,* 159 N.E. 896, N.Y. 1928.

The following case involves an alleged creditor beneficiary.

U. S. v. STATE FARM MUTUAL AUTOMOBILE INS. CO.
U.S. Court of Appeals, 5th Circuit, 936 F.2d 206 (1991)

Defendant State Farm issued to various armed services members standard boating and automobile accident insurance policies. Twenty-four of these army personnel were injured in accidents that entitled them to recover medical and hospital expenses under the policies. The United States treated these people free of any personal expense at government medical institutions as it is required to do by federal statute 10 U.S.C. § 1074 and § 1076. The government then brought this action seeking reimbursement as a third-party beneficiary to the insurance policies for the value of the medical services provided. The trial court granted summary judgment to the government, and State Farm appealed.

Higginbotham, Circuit Judge:

Under Mississippi law, in order for a stranger to a contract to sue to enforce its term, "the contract between the original parties must have been entered into for his benefit, or at least such benefit must be the direct result of the performance within the contemplation of the parties." *Burns v. Washington Savings,* 171 So.2d 322 (Miss.1965). The third party need not be expressly identified in the contract; it is enough that the beneficiary is a member of a class intended to be benefited. At the same time, the right of the third party beneficiary to maintain an action on the contract must "spring" from the terms of the contract itself.

The State Farm policies at issue here contained the following emphasized provisions:

Persons for Whom Medical Expenses are Payable.
We will pay medical expenses for bodily injury sustained by:
    a. The firm person named in the declarations;
    b. his or her spouse; and
    c. her relatives.
Payment of Medical Expenses.
We may pay the injured person or any person or organization performing the services.

We have read similar policy language to support third party claims by medical care providers. State Farm urges that it is obligated only for medical expenses actually incurred by the insured. No such limitation is imposed by the terms of the policies. State Farm is obligated to pay the costs of reasonable medical services, whether such costs were borne personally by the insured or, as here, directly by the medical care provider. We also cannot accept State Farm's contention that the policies' facility of payment clause—which provides, "We may pay the injured person or any person or organization performing the service"—makes the government an optional payee or incidental beneficiary. [Affirmed.]

ASSIGNMENTS OF RIGHTS

All contracts create certain rights and duties. With exceptions to be noted later, the *rights* a person has acquired under a contract can be transferred, or *assigned*, by that person to a third party. A right to receive another's performance under a valid contract is a property right—an item of intangible personal property, ownership of which can often be transferred. It can also serve as collateral for a debt in a so-called *secured transaction* governed by Article 9 of the Uniform Commercial Code. Also, as with other kinds of property, a contract right can be given away—consideration is normally received, but receipt of consideration in return for a transfer of ownership of any kind of property interest is not legally required. An ownership transfer is quite different from an executory contract. In addition, a contract right can be seized by a government for nonpayment of taxes, and can be seized to help satisfy a civil court judgment, just as can other types of property.

Suppose, for example, that A agrees to add a family room to B's home for $13,500 and that A performs the required work. A thereafter assigns his right to collect the $13,500 to C, in which case A is the assignor and C the *assignee*. C can now recover the $13,500 from B, just as A could have done had there been no assignment. The relationship among the parties to an assignment is set forth in Figure 16.1. While a person's duties under a contract can also be transferred to a third party in some circumstances, such a transfer is a delegation rather than an assignment. The delegation of duties is discussed later in the chapter.

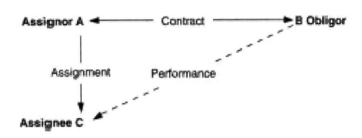

Figure 16.1 Assignment of Rights

Status of the Assignee

Whenever an assignment takes place, just as when ownership of real estate or goods occurs, the assignee acquires no greater rights than those possessed by the assignor. Putting it another way, the obligor (the person with a duty to perform) can assert the same defenses (if any) against the assignee they had against the assignor. This can be easily illustrated by referring again to Figure 16.1. If B refuses to pay C and C brings suit against him on the contract, B can escape liability if he can prove that A breached his contract in some material way—by failing to complete the job, for example, or by using materials inferior to those required by the contract. In such a case C's only redress is the right to recover from A any consideration he had given to A in payment for the assignment.

427 © **2020 John R. Allison & Robert A. Prentice**

What Rights Can Be Assigned?

Occasionally, when an assignee requests the obligor to perform his or her part of the bargain, the obligor refuses to do so on the ground that the assigned right was of such a nature that it could not be legally transferred without his or her consent. Usually, this contention is not accepted by the courts; most contractual rights can be assigned without the obligor's consent. This is especially true where the assigned right was that of *collecting a debt*. The reasoning is that it is ordinarily no more difficult for a debtor (obligor) to pay the assignee than to pay the assignor (the original creditor); hence the obligor has no cause to complain.

Some rights, however, cannot be assigned without the obligor's consent. Following are the most common of these situations:

1. The terms of the contract expressly prohibit assignment by one or both parties. (Such clauses are narrowly construed, however, often being interpreted to impose a duty on the assignor not to assign, but not to render invalid an assignment that does occur.)

2. The contract is ''personal'' in nature; specifically, the right in question involves a substantial personal relationship between the original parties to the contract. If X, for example, agrees to be Y's secretary for one year, any assignment by Y of the right to X's services would be invalid unless X consented to it. In fact, many (perhaps most) employment contracts fall within this category.

3. The assignment would materially alter the duties of the obligor. For example: S, of Columbus, Ohio, agrees to sell certain goods to B, also of Columbus, with the contract providing that "S will deliver the goods to the buyer's place of business." If B assigned this contract to the X Company of Cheyenne, Wyoming, S's obligation would be drastically increased and he would not be bound by the assignment unless he consented to it.

Additionally, the assignment of some rights is prohibited by statute. For example, a federal law (31 U.S.C.A. § 3727) generally prohibits assignment of claims against the federal government, and some state statutes prohibit the assignment of future wages by wage earners. When the assignment of rights is prohibited by statute, such rights cannot be assigned even with the obligor's consent.

SCHUPACH v. MCDONALD'S SYSTEM, INC.
Supreme Court of Nebraska, 264 N.W.2d 827 (1978)

McDonald's, defendant, is the corporation that grants all McDonald's fast food restaurant franchises. In 1959, defendant granted a franchise to a Mr. Copeland, giving him the right to own and operate McDonald's first store in the Omaha Council Bluffs area. A few days later, in conformity with the negotiations leading up to the granting of the franchise, McDonald's sent a letter to Copeland giving him a "Right of First Refusal"—the right to be given first chance at owning any new stores that might subsequently be established in the area. In the next few years Copeland exercised this right and opened five additional stores in Omaha. In 1964, Copeland sold and assigned all of his franchises to Schupach, plaintiff, with McDonald's consent.

When McDonald's granted a franchise in the Omaha-Council Bluffs area in 1974 to a third party without first offering it to Schupach, he brought this action for damages resulting from establishment of the new franchise, claiming that the assignment of the franchises to him also included the right of first refusal.

Defendant contended, among other things, that the right it gave to Copeland was personal in nature, and thus was not transferable without its consent. Plaintiff alleged, on the other hand, that the right was not personal in nature, or, in the alternative, that its transfer was, in fact, agreed to by defendant. On these issues the trial court ruled that the right was personal in nature. It also ruled, however, after analyzing voluminous correspondence between the parties, that defendant had consented to the transfer. It entered judgment for plaintiff, and defendant appealed.

White, Justice:

McDonald's was founded in 1954 by Mr. Ray Kroc. Kroc licensed and later purchased the name of McDonald's [and all other rights relating thereto] from two brothers named McDonald, who were operating a hamburger restaurant in San Bernardino, California. In 1955 Kroc embarked on a plan to create a nationwide standardized system of fast-food restaurants.

At the trial, Kroc testified about the image he sought to create with McDonald's. He wanted to create "an image people would have confidence in. An image of cleanliness. An image where the parents would be glad to have the children come and/or have them work there."

Kroc testified that careful selection of franchisees was to be the key to success for McDonald's and the establishment of this image.... People were selected "who had a great deal of pride, and had an aptitude for serving the public, and had dedication."

Fred Turner, the current president of McDonald's, testified [in a similar vein].... He stated that by 1957 it became apparent that McDonald's could only achieve its goal by careful selection of persons who would adhere to the company's high standards. He stated that an individual's managerial skills and abilities were a matter of prime importance in the selection process....

Summarizing, the evidence is overwhelming, [and establishes the conclusion that] the Right of First Refusal was intended to be personal in nature, and was separately a grant independent of the terms of the franchise contract itself. [It also establishes the fact that] the grant depended upon the personal confidence that McDonald's placed in the grantee, and that to permit the assignability by the grantee without permission of McDonald s would serve to destroy the basic policy of control of the quality and confidence in performance in the event any new franchises were to be granted in the locality....

[The court also held, contrary to the court below, that McDonald's had not given its permission to the transfer of the right, and reversed.]

Form of the Assignment

As a general rule, any words or conduct indicating an intention on the part of the assignor to transfer his or her contractual rights are normally sufficient. Some assignments, however, are required by statute to be in writing. For example, the assignment of a contract that falls within the statute of frauds must be evidenced by a writing; similarly, under the statutes of most states, the assignment of one's rights to collect wages from an employer must also be in writing. Likewise, the federal Copyright Act requires that assignment of a copyright be in writing and signed by the grantor.

Notice of Assignment

A valid assignment takes effect the moment it is made, regardless of whether the obligor is aware that the assignment has occurred. However, the assignee should give *immediate notice* to the obligor whenever an assignment is made in order to protect the rights received under it.

A primary reason for giving notice is that an obligor who does not have notice of an assignment is free to go ahead and render performance to the assignor, thereby discharging his or her contractual duties. Suppose, for example, that X is owed $500 by Y and that X assigns the right to collect the debt to Z. If Y, not knowing of the assignment, pays the debt to X (assignor), Z has lost her right to collect the indebtedness from Y. Any other result would be patently unfair to Y. Z's only redress in such a case is to recover payment from X, who clearly has no right to retain the money. On the other hand, if Y did pay the $500 to X *after* being informed of the assignment, Z could still collect from Y.

Notice of assignment can also be important in a case where successive assignments occur. To illustrate: R owes money to S. S assigns his right to collect the debt to A on June 10, then assigns the same right to B on June 15, B not knowing of the prior assignment. Suppose that the first assignee, A, does not give notice of assignment to until June 25, while the second assignee, B, gives notice on June 20. In such a situation, a number of courts—though not a majority—would rule that B is entitled to payment of the debt, rather than A; in other words, the assignee who first gives notice prevails. (In states adopting this minority view, A's only redress is to recover the consideration, if any, that he gave to S in exchange for the assignment.) The majority view is that A, the first assignee, collects, even if he did not give notice first.

Sale of Goods Contracts

The Uniform Commercial Code's provisions on assignments, primarily § 2-210, are generally similar to the common-law rules discussed above, rendering ineffective only assignments that would (1) materially change the obligor's duties; (2) increase materially the burden or risk imposed on the obligor by contract, or (3) impair materially the obligor's chance of obtaining return performance. The Code is perhaps even more "pro-assignment" than the common law. For example, it contains numerous restrictions on anti-assignment clauses that are not present in the common law. Most important, perhaps, several types of assignments come within the scope of Article 9's provisions relating to secured transactions. Although this text does not discuss these rules in great detail, we emphasize that Article 9 does alter several of the common law's rules on assignments where secured transactions occur. For example, it may give priority to a second assignee over a first assignee if the second assignee was the first to file a proper financing statement covering the assignment.

DELEGATION OF DUTIES

Our discussion so far has been directed to those cases in which contractual rights alone have been transferred, or assigned—in other words, to those common situations in which it is reasonably clear that the parties understood that the assignor alone would be the party who would perform the contract, as they originally contracted to do. In many circumstances, however, a *delegation of duties*—the transfer of one party's contractual duties to another—is intended as part of the assignment of rights, and in other circumstances a delegation of duties may occur without an assignment of rights. Note that, when X has a duty to perform a contract for Y, Y has a contract right. We will briefly examine these situations.

Delegation in Conjunction with an Assignment

If an assignment occurs in which the assigning party also delegates his or her contractual duties to the assignee, that party is the *delegator* (or assignor-delegator), and the party to whom the duties are transferred is the *delegatee* (or assignee-delegatee). The remaining party—the party to the original contract to whom the performance is owed—is the *obligee*. When a delegation occurs in conjunction with an assignment, the delegatee usually (but not necessarily) expressly or impliedly promises they will perform the delegator's duties under the contract. Assuming such a promise, the relationships are diagrammed in Figure 16.2. This discussion is based upon the assumption of a valid delegation—i.e., one in which the obligee has consented to the delegation, or in which the duty is of such nature that it can be delegated without the obligee's consent. (Non-delegable duties—those that cannot be assigned without the obligee's consent—will be examined later.)

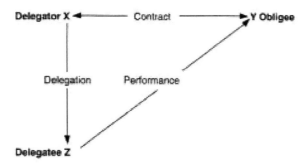

Figure 16.2 Delegation of Duties

Obligations of the Parties

Where a delegation occurs, and where the delegatee expressly or impliedly promises to perform the delegator's duties, the delegatee assumes the primary responsibility for performance of those duties. The delegator, however, remains secondarily liable for performance of those duties. To illustrate: X contracts to put in a driveway for Y, and X then delegates the duty to Z. If Z fails to do the job, X must either perform the job or be liable to Y, the obligee, for damages for breach of contract. Thus, where the contract is never performed, the obligee has causes of action against both the delegatee and delegator. In other words, a delegation of duties—even when consented to by the obligee—does not in and of itself free the delegator of liability. (Thus, although a delegation is generally defined as a "transfer" of duties, this term is not entirely accurate in view of the retention of secondary liability by the delegator.)

The above discussion has assumed that the delegatee has promised, expressly or by clear implication, to perform the delegator's duties. In some situations, however, it is unclear whether the delegatee has made an implied promise to perform. Going back to the driveway illustration, for example, the assignment document might state that X hereby assigns to Z "all of my rights and obligations under my contract with Y," or it may simply say that X hereby assigns to Z the "entire contract" that he (X) has with Y. In either case, if Z accepts the assignment of rights but neither expressly promises to perform the contract nor commences performance, are they liable to Y if the driveway is never built? While there is disagreement on this point, the trend among the courts of most states is to find an implied assumption of duties by Z in both cases—with Z thus incurring liability in case they fail to perform.

Novation

If the party to whom a contractual duty is owed specifically releases the original party with whom it had contracted (the delegator), and agrees that the delagatee will be substituted for the delegator as the only one who owes the obligation, the delegator is no longer obligated on the contract. Such a consensual substitution of parties is called a *novation*.

Delegation in Absence of Assignment—Subcontracts

A delegation of duties may be made without an assignment of the delegator's rights under his or her contract with the obligee. In such cases, where the delegatee by contract promises to perform the delegator's duties, the general rule is that the delegatee's only obligation is to the delegator. In the real world, a delegation of duties in the absence of an assignment most often involves a partial delegation of duties. To illustrate: X, a builder, contracts to build a home for Y for $92,000. X then subcontracts the electrical work to the Z Company, an electrical firm. If the Z Company fails to do the work, or does it in an unacceptable manner, it is liable to X but not to Y. (Similarly, note that if the Z Company does perform, it may look only to X, the delegator, for payment. In other words, in the usual situation, the subcontractor is neither an intended beneficiary nor an assignee of the contract between the prime contractor-delegator and the obligee.)

What Duties Are Delegable?

In exceptional circumstances the obligee, upon learning of the delegation, will notify the parties that they will not accept performance by the delegatee. The general rule applicable to such a controversy is that any contractual duty may be delegated without the obligee's consent except (1) duties arising out of contracts which expressly prohibit delegation, and (2) contracts in which the obligee has a "substantial interest" in having the obligor-delegator perform personally.

Under the latter rule, contracts calling for the performance of *personal services*—such as those of a teacher, physician, or lawyer—are clearly non-delegable without the obligee's consent (even if the delegatee is as professionally competent as the delegator). Most other contracts call for the performance of duties that are described as essentially routine in nature, such as the repair of a building, the sale of goods, or the overhaul of machinery, and these duties are generally held to be delegable. (This result is not as unfair to the objecting obligee as it might appear, because, as we noted earlier, they may hold the delegator liable if the delegatee's performance is defective.) The UCC's rules on delegation are virtually identical to those of the common law.

Chapter 17

DISCHARGE OF CONTRACTS

- Discharge By Operation of Conditions
- Discharge By Performance
- Discharge By Breach
- Discharge By Legal Impossibility
- Discharge By Commercial Impracticability
- Discharge By Frustration of Purpose
- Discharge By Parties' Agreement
- Discharge By Operation of Law

Sooner or later all contractual obligations come to an end. When this occurs in a particular case, the contract is said to be *discharged*. What is meant by this is that the *duties* of the contracting parties have been discharged.

There are many ways in which a discharge, or termination, can come about. Most of these result from the conduct of the parties themselves, while others involve events completely outside the control of either party. Some sources recognize at least twenty separate and distinct ways in which a person's contractual obligations can be discharged. The most important of these are discharge by (1) operation of conditions; (2) performance; (3) breach by the other party; (4) circumstances excusing performance (impossibility, impracticability, and frustration); (5) agreement of the parties; and (6) operation of law.

DISCHARGE BY OPERATION OF CONDITIONS

Conditions, Generally

In many contracts the parties simply exchange mutual promises to perform specified duties, with neither promise being conditioned or qualified in any way. In some situations, however, the performance of the contemplated contract is beneficial to one or both of the parties only if a certain event occurs in the future. And in other situations a contract may be mutually beneficial to the parties when entered into, but would be of little benefit if some event should occur before the stated time of performance arrives.

In these situations the parties can achieve substantial protection by the use of conditions in their contract. The term *condition*, in its broadest sense, can be defined as an express or implied provision in a contract which, upon the occurrence or nonoccurrence of a specified event, either creates, suspends, or terminates the rights and duties of the contracting parties. While this definition refers to a provision or clause in a contract creating the condition, the terms may also be used to refer to the event itself that is designated in such provision.

The law recognizes three kinds of conditions—*conditions precedent, conditions subsequent, and conditions concurrent*. Each type of condition can be further classified as *express or implied.* Our discussion initially will focus on the nature of express conditions, with consideration of implied conditions precedent and implied conditions subsequent being delayed until we reach the subjects of performance and impossibility, respectively.

Conditions Precedent

A *condition precedent* is a clause in a contract which indicates that the promises made therein are not to be operative until a specified event occurs. For example, X makes this offer to Y: "If the city rezones your property at 540 Fox Lane from C-3 to C-1 within thirty days, I will pay you $418,000 cash for it." Y accepts the offer. While a contract has now been formed, it is clear that the specified event must occur before either party incurs "a duty of immediate performance." The act of rezoning, therefore, is a condition precedent. And, because the condition resulted from the language of the contract, rather than by implication, the rezoning constitutes an express condition precedent. Conditions precedent can usually be identified by clauses containing the words if, in the event, or when. Thus the following language creates a condition precedent: "If X is able to obtain a building permit from the city within sixty days, it is agreed that Y will construct a swimming pool for her, according to the attached specifications, for $49,000."

Where a contract clearly creates a condition precedent, no duty of performance arises until the specified event occurs. In the above case, then, should the rezoning not occur within the specified time, the condition is said to have ''failed'' and both parties are accordingly discharged of their obligations. In other words, the parties' duties under the contract are terminated.

Conditions Subsequent

Occasionally both parties to a contract are willing to incur a duty of immediate performance, but want to be freed of their obligations if a particular circumstance arises before the performance date. The parties can achieve this protection by use of an express *condition subsequent*—a clause in a contract providing that upon the happening of a specified event, the contract shall be inoperative (or void). Thus, the essential difference in legal effect between the two basic kinds of conditions is that the occurrence of a condition precedent imposes a duty of immediate performance, while the occurrence of a condition subsequent removes such a duty. True conditions subsequent are rare, but consider this example: An insurance policy states "If written notice is given to the Company of Mr. A's death within 30 days of its occurrence, the Company will pay $100,000 to the beneficiaries. If the Company refuses to pay, and the beneficiaries do not file suit within one year of the death, any obligation of the Company under this contract shall be discharged."

In the above example, the death and the giving of written notice are conditions precedent which give rise to the Company's duty of immediate performance. However, that duty may be extinguished by the occurrence of a condition subsequent—the failure to file suit within one year. Conditions precedent and subsequent are contrasted in Figure 17.1.

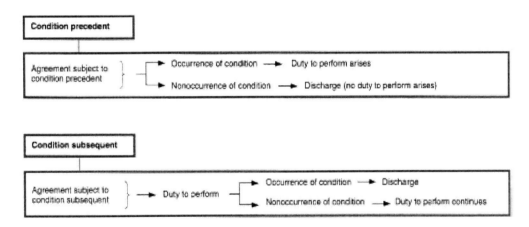

Figure 17.1 Conditions Precedent and Conditions Subsequent

Most conditions subsequent (as is true of conditions generally) are express rather than implied. They can ordinarily be recognized by language providing that the contract is to be void, inoperative, or canceled if a certain event occurs in the future. The relatively few situations in which implied conditions subsequent exist will be discussed later in the chapter.

Conditions Concurrent

Conditions concurrent exist when a contract expressly provides (or if one can reasonably infer from its terms) that the performances of the parties are to occur at the same time. A common example is a land sale contract which provides that the seller is to deliver the deed on payment of the purchase price. The duty of each party is thus conditioned on performance by the other. The seller has no duty to deliver the deed until the buyer pays (or tenders) the purchase price, and the buyer has no duty to pay until the seller delivers (or tenders) the deed. (A tender is an offer to perform one's obligation.)

The legal consequences that result from the use of express conditions precedent and subsequent are clear, once either condition is proven to exist. It is, however, often a more difficult question whether the parties conditioned their obligations at all, and, if so, whether the condition in the particular case fell in the precedent or subsequent category. The following case highlights the impact that such a determination might have on the outcome of a particular controversy.

RINCONES v. WINDBERG
Texas Court of Appeals, 705 S.W.2d 846 (1986)

Rincones and Mena, plaintiffs, entered into a contract with Windberg, defendant, under which they were to "compile, research and edit material for academic and student services for a migrant program handbook." The contract was termed a "Consultant Agreement," and under it each plaintiff was to write specified chapters, for which Windberg would pay each $1,250 per chapter for their respective chapters.

The handbook was ultimately to be used by California authorities, and the parties were aware that the funds to pay plaintiffs would ultimately come from the State of California. The consultant agreement, however, made no mention of Windberg's obligation to pay being contingent upon his receipt of funding by California. Plaintiffs submitted the drafts of their respective chapters to Windberg, but he refused to pay for them because "the publication was not accepted by California," and no funding from that state, therefore, was available for the project.

Plaintiffs then brought this action to recover the monies promised them. The primary question was whether Windberg's receipt of funding from California was a condition precedent to his obligations under the contract, as Windberg contended. The trial court found (1) that the contract was partly written and partly oral; (2) that, under the oral agreement and the circumstances surrounding it, the parties had agreed that the contract was contingent upon California's funding of the project; and (3) that California refused to fund the project. The court concluded that a "condition precedent" existed; that proof of the condition was not barred by the parol evidence rule; that the condition precedent had not been met; that the contract was of no further force and effect, and that Windberg thus had no liability under it. The plaintiffs appealed.

Shannon, Chief Justice:

. . . The meaning of "condition precedent" in Texas jurisprudence is less than clear. For purposes of the parol evidence rule, however, we think that the definition from [a previous case] correctly states that a condition precedent is a condition "which postpones the effective date of the instrument until the happening of a contingency." *Baker v. Baker,* 183 S.W.2d 724 (Tex. 1943). By way of contrast, a condition subsequent "is a condition referring to a future event, upon the happening of which the obligation is no longer binding upon the other party, if he chooses to avail himself of the condition." *Id.* [The court here noted that parol evidence of a condition *precedent* is admissible to vary or contradict a complete written contract, while parol evidence of a condition *subsequent* is not admissible to vary or contradict such a written contract. The reason is that the parol evidence rule, discussed in Chapter 15, allows parol evidence to be introduced for the purpose of showing that there was never a valid contract in the first place.]

We now examine the record in an effort to determine whether the evidence supports the court's conclusion that funding from California was a condition precedent to the contract, or whether, to the contrary, the evidence shows an already effective and binding contract subject to a condition subsequent. The admissibility of the parol evidence turns on whether the contract was binding and effective from its inception, or whether it would become binding and effective only upon the occurrence of the contingency.

The evidence shows that all parties devoted substantial amounts of time and money attempting to perform their obligations under the Consultant Agreement. Appellants (plaintiffs) prepared and submitted a first draft of their manuscript, which Hardy [an associate of Windberg] took to California for revisions and recommendations. Thereafter, appellants worked on revisions and submitted a second draft for approval. Hardy, meanwhile, made several trips to California and spent $4,000 of her own money attempting to gain approval and receive funding from the state. All parties initially thought approval and funding for the project was certain, and performed under the contract accordingly. Only after several months had passed did they learn that political changes in California had placed their funding in jeopardy.

In our opinion the evidence shows that the parties understood that they had a binding and effective contract, and performed accordingly. The evidence is not [consistent] with a determination that the parties had agreed to postpone the effective date of the contract until the condition, funding from California, occurred.... [We conclude] that the parol payment condition [is a condition subsequent rather than a condition precedent].

As such, [the parol evidence rule causes any evidence from outside the written contract that shows Windberg's payment obligation to have been conditional on his receipt of funding from California inadmissible. Thus, Windberg's obligation was not so conditioned.] The judgment is reversed and the case is remanded to the trial court for new trial consistent with this opinion.

DISCHARGE BY PERFORMANCE

Most contracts are discharged by performance—by each party completely fulfilling his or her promises. In such cases, obviously, no legal problems exist. Nevertheless, the subject of performance merits special attention for several reasons.

In the first place, many cases arise in which the actual performance of a promisor is, to some extent, defective. Sometimes the performance falls far short of what was promised; other times, it deviates from the terms of the contract in only minor respects. As one might expect, the legal consequences of a major breach of contract are more severe and far-reaching than those resulting from a minor breach.

Second, in some cases the courts must determine whether the defective performance constituted a breach of a condition or a mere breach of a promise. A breach of a condition, no matter how slight, usually frees the non-defaulting party, while a breach of a promise generally does not unless it is a material one.

Promises: Degree of Performance Required

Many agreements consist simply of the exchange of mutual promises, with neither party's obligations expressly conditioned in any way. In most of these contracts, however, it is usually apparent from their nature that one of the parties is to perform his or her part of the bargain before the other is obligated to do so. For example: If X contracts to landscape Y's new home for $1,500, it can reasonably be inferred that the work is to be done by X before he can demand payment of Y. In this regard, it is sometimes said that the actual performance of one's promises constitutes an implied condition precedent that must be met by that person.

Thus, in general, when a promisor seeks to recover the contract price, they must show that they have *fully* performed the promise in some cases or *substantially performed* it in others—depending on the nature of the obligation involved. If it is determined that this performance has met the applicable minimum standard, the promisor is entitled to recover the contract price minus damages (if any) suffered by the promisee. However, if the performance falls short of this minimum, the promisor's obligation has not been discharged, and they will recover little or nothing. (The rules determining the extent of recovery in each of these situations will be discussed immediately after the next case in the chapter.)

Total Performance

Some promises are of such a nature that they can be discharged only by complete performance. If a promisor's performance falls short of that called for under such a contract, even though the breach is minor, his or her obligation is not discharged. Suppose, for example, that B contracts in May to buy a car from S for $2,000—the contract providing that the price is to be paid in full by B on June 1, at which time S is to assign the car title to her. If, on June 1, B tenders S a check for $1,950, S has no obligation to transfer the title. A contract under which a seller of land is obligated to convey "merchantable title" falls into the same category; delivery of a deed conveying any interest or title less than that specified will not discharge the seller's obligation.

Substantial Performance

Many obligations are of such a nature that it is unlikely (indeed, not even to be expected, given the frailties of mankind) that a 100 percent performance will actually occur. The typical example involves a construction contract under which a builder agrees to build a home according to detailed plans and specifications. It is quite possible that the finished building will deviate from the specifications in one or more respects no matter how conscientious and able the builder is. In contracts of this sort, if the promisee-owner seeks to escape liability on the ground of nonperformance of the promisor-builder, it is ordinarily held that the promisor has sufficiently fulfilled the obligation if his or her performance, though imperfect, conformed to the terms of the contract in all major respects. This rule is known as the doctrine of *substantial performance*.

In order for the doctrine to be applicable, two requirements must ordinarily be met:

1. Performance must be "substantial"—that is, the omissions and deviations must be so slight in nature that they do not materially affect the usefulness of the building for the purposes for which it was intended.

2. The omissions or deviations must not have been occasioned by bad faith on the part of the builder.

This is ordinarily interpreted to mean that the omissions or deviations must not have been made knowingly by the builder.

Using the illustration involving the construction of a house, let us examine three cases where the builder is bringing suit against the owner to recover the last payment of $5,000 called for under the contract and where the owner is refusing to pay on the ground of inadequate performance.

1. The owner proves that the following defects exist: (a) the plaster in all rooms is considerably softer than expected, because the builder used one bag of adamant for each hod of mortar instead of the two bags called for by the contract, and (b) water seepage in the basement is so great as to make the game room virtually unusable, as a result of the builder's failure to put a required sealant on the exterior of the basement walls. Here the defects are so material, and so affect the enjoyment and value of the home, that the builder has not substantially performed his obligations. Thus recovery will be denied, even if the breaches on the part of the builder are shown to be accidental rather than intentional.

2. The owner proves that the following defects exist: (a) the detached garage was given but one coat of paint rather than the two required; (b) the water pipes in the walls were made by the Cohoes Company rather than the Reading Company as was specified (though otherwise the two types of pipe are virtually identical); and (c) the wallboard installed in the attic is 1/8 inch sheeting instead of the 1/4 inch that was called for. Here the defects are so slight in nature, even when taken in total, that the builder has substantially performed the contract and can thus probably recover under the doctrine.

3. Same facts as case 2, but, in addition, the owner can show that one or more of the deviations were intentional; for example, he produces evidence tending to prove that the builder ordered the installation of the substitute pipe and wallboard knowing that they were not in conformity with the contract. Here the deviations are willful (rather than the result of simple negligence); therefore the builder is guilty of bad faith and the doctrine is not applicable.

Obviously, the requirement that performance be "substantial" is a somewhat elastic one, and necessitates a comparison of the promisor's actual performance with that which the terms of the contract really required of him. The following case is typical of those presenting substantial performance problems.

LANE WILSON COMPANY v. GREGORY
Louisiana Court of Appeals, 322 So.2d 369 (1975)

Lane Wilson Company, plaintiff, contracted to build a swimming pool for Gregory, defendant, at Gregory's KOA Campground outside Monroe, Louisiana, for $12,000. Under the written agreement, the pool was to be thirty by sixty feet, with a depth varying from three feet to six feet. Later the parties orally modified their contract by agreeing that plaintiff would add a diving board and increase the depth of the pool to accommodate persons using the diving board. It was also orally agreed that a walkway around the pool would be enlarged and a longer fence built than was originally contemplated. The cost of these modifications raised the contract price to $13,643.

During construction, defendant paid $8,400 on the contract. After the job was completed, however, he refused to pay the balance due because of various defects in the pool's construction (the most important of which are described in the appellate court's decision following). Plaintiff then brought this action to recover the balance allegedly due. The trial court held that plaintiff had substantially performed the contract, and that plaintiff *was thus entitled to the balance of the contract price minus a credit of $300 to remedy one of the defects (the installation of a chlorinator). Defendant appealed.*

Burgess, Judge:

. . . Defendant alleged [in his answer] that plaintiff had not constructed the pool according to the terms of the contract.... This appeal presents two issues. First, has plaintiff substantially performed the contract, thereby enabling him to recover the balance due on the contract price? Second, if plaintiff has substantially performed, are there any defects in the construction which entitle defendant to damages in an amount sufficient to remedy the faulty performance?

In *Airco Refrigeration Service, Inc., v. Fink,* 134 So.2d 880 (1961), the Supreme Court considered . . . the meaning of "substantial performance." The Court stated:

> The principal question presented in this case is whether or not there has been substantial performance so as to permit recovery on the contract. This is a question of fact. Among the factors to be considered are the extent of the defect or non-performance; the degree to which the purpose of the contract is defeated; the ease of correction, and the use or benefit to the defendant of the work performed.

In light of the factors enumerated above, we cannot say the trial court was manifestly erroneous in finding that plaintiff substantially performed the contract. Defendant contracted for a 30 by 60 foot swimming pool deep enough to accommodate persons using a diving board. The defects alleged by defendant are not such that defeat the purpose of the contract or prevent defendant from using the pool. In addition, the defects for which plaintiff may be held accountable are easily remedied.

[The court here examined all of the defects in the job in order to determine whether or not plaintiff had substantially performed the contract. The most important of these defects were described as follows:]

(a) Rather than measuring 30 by 60 feet as called for by the contract, the pool's measurements fluctuate from 59 feet six inches to 59 feet three and one half inches in length, and from 29 feet one-half inch to 29 feet three and one-half inches in width.

(b) The walls of the pool are not vertical, but slope severely to form a bowl-shaped pool.

(c) Plaintiff installed only six water inlets as opposed to twelve water inlets called for by the contract; this deficiency coupled with the poor placement of the inlets results in insufficient water circulation in the pool.

(d) The pool is not ten feet deep as the parties allegedly agreed.

[The court here expressed its opinion as to the materiality of these defects as follows:]

(a) In the instant case we find the deviations in dimensions, which could be discovered only by measuring the pool, in no way defeat the purpose of the contract. Plaintiff also testified the method of constructing the pool made it impossible to achieve perfect compliance with the exact measurements called for by the contract. Therefore, we find the slight deviation in measurements did not constitute a breach of the contract.

(b) Defendant made no complaint about the shape of the pool walls until after suit was filed. The defect, if it be one at all, was apparent and defendant is held to have accepted same since he made no objection to the walls until suit was filed.

(c) The number of water inlets was changed at the suggestion of the supplier of the equipment because twelve water inlets would have lowered the water pressure and caused improper circulation in the pool. Defendant agreed to the change in plumbing and cannot now claim that change as a defect.

(d) Defendant failed to prove that the parties agreed to a ten-foot depth for the pool. We find the pool, as constructed, is deep enough to accommodate a diving board and, therefore, there is no defect in regard to the depth of the pool.

[On the basis of this analysis, the court agreed with the trial court that plaintiff had substantially performed the contract. The court then turned to the question of defendant's damages. On this point the court ruled that, in addition to the $300 damages (credit) allowed by the trial court, additional damages should have been allowed to compensate defendant for his removal of incorrect depth markers and the installation of new markers; for his removal of waste cement and cement forms; and to compensate defendant for 200 feet of pipe owned by him that plaintiff used in building the pool. The court summarized these adjustments as follows:]

Totaling the amounts listed above, we find defendant is entitled to $331.02 as damages to correct defects in plaintiff's performance, in addition to the $300 allowed by the trial court for the cost of an additional chlorinator which plaintiff admitted the pool needed.

For the reasons assigned the judgment in favor of plaintiff is amended to reduce the award from $4,943.36 to the sum of $4,612.34, and as amended is affirmed.

Substantial Performance—Amount of Recovery

As noted earlier, if the rule of substantial performance is applicable to a particular case, the promisor-plaintiff is entitled to recover *the contract price* minus damages (that is, the promisor may recover the amount that the promisee agreed to pay under the contract, minus damages—if any—which the promisee sustained as a result of the deviations). Since the damages are typically inconsequential, the promisor usually recovers a high percentage of the contract price. By contrast, where the doctrine is not applicable, the recovery may be little or nothing. The general rules for such situations can be summarized as follows:

1. Where the performance falls short of being substantial and the breach is intentional, the promisor receives nothing. The rationale, of course, is that an intentional wrongdoer should not be rewarded—particularly where the promisee has not received the performance they were entitled to. (The rule of non-recovery also has an affirmative aspect—it strongly "persuades" the promisor to actually finish the job, since they will receive nothing otherwise.)

2. In the somewhat rarer case where the performance is not substantial but the breach is unintentional, recovery is allowed on the basis of quasi-contract. For example, if the promisor is permanently injured when only halfway through the job, they are entitled to receive the reasonable value of the benefit received by the promisee as a result of the partial performance.

3. If the performance is clearly substantial but the breach is willful, there are conflicting views. Some courts deny any recovery, regardless of other circumstances, embracing the principle that aid should never be given the intentional wrongdoer. Most courts, while endorsing this principle in the abstract, in practice allow the promisor to recover "'the reasonable value of the benefit resulting from the performance, minus damages" (as distinguished from the "contract price, minus damages" recovery allowed in situations where the substantial performance requirements are met). Such a recovery is especially common where a failure to allow the promisor anything would result in the promisee being unjustly enriched—a result most likely to occur in cases where the performance is of such a nature that it cannot be returned by the promisee.

PERSONAL SATISFACTION CONTRACTS

Under the ordinary contract, someone who undertook to perform a job impliedly warrants only that they will perform in a "workmanlike manner," i.e., the performance will be free of material defect and of a quality ordinarily accepted in that line of work. If the performance meets this standard, they are entitled to recover the contract price even if the person for whom the work was done is not satisfied with it.

Some contracts, however, provide that "satisfaction is guaranteed," or contain other language of similar nature. In such cases, it is usually held that such satisfaction is a condition precedent that must be met in order for the promisor to recover under the contract; workmanlike performance alone will not suffice. In determining whether the condition has been met, the courts distinguish between two kinds of contracts: (1) those in which matters of personal taste, esthetics, or comfort are dominant considerations, and (2) those that entail work of mere "mechanical utility."

For contracts in the first category, the condition is fulfilled only if the *promisee is actually satisfied* with the performance that was rendered—no matter how peculiar or unreasonable that person's tastes may be. For example: X, an artist, contracts to paint a portrait of Y for $500 "that will meet with Y's complete satisfaction." When the portrait is completed, Y refuses to pay on the ground that he simply does not like it. If X brings suit to recover the $500, a question of fact is presented: Is Y's claim of dissatisfaction genuine? If the jury so finds, the condition has not been met and X is denied recovery. (Of course, if the jury finds that Y's claim of dissatisfaction is false—that is, he is actually satisfied and is simply using this claim as a ground to escape an otherwise valid contract—then the condition has been met and recovery is allowed.)

For contracts in the second category, where the performance involves work of mere mechanical fitness (or mechanical utility), an objective test is used. For example: M agrees to overhaul the diesel engine in T's tractor-trailer for $200, guaranteeing that T will be "fully satisfied" with the job. In this case, the condition precedent is met if the jury finds that a *reasonable person would have been satisfied* with M's job, even though T himself is dissatisfied.

PERFORMANCE BY AN AGREED TIME

If a contract does not provide a time by which performance is to be completed, the general rule is that each party has a reasonable time within which to perform his or her obligations. Whether the performance of a promisor in a given case took place within such a time is ordinarily a question for the jury. In practice this rule poses few problems and seems to produce acceptable results.

A more troublesome situation is presented by contracts that do contain a stated time of performance. For example: A printer agrees to print up 15,000 letterheads for a customer, with the contract specifying "delivery by April 10." If delivery is not made until April 14, and the customer refuses to accept the goods because of the late performance, the question for the jury is whether the stated time of performance legally constituted a condition precedent. If it did, the condition has obviously not been met and the customer has no obligation to accept the shipment.

The general rule is that such a provision, of and by itself, *does not create a condition precedent.* Under this view, it is sufficient if the performance occurs within a reasonable time after the date specified. Thus, in the preceding illustration, the customer is very likely obligated to accept the letterheads where delivery was only four days late. The customer may recover any damages caused by the delay in accordance with rules of recovery discussed in the next chapter.

Time-of-the-Essence Clauses

In some situations, however, the parties clearly intend that performance must actually take place by the specified time in order for the promisor to recover from the other party. In such situations, performance by the agreed upon time does constitute a condition precedent. The intention can be manifested in two ways: (1) by the express wording of the agreement itself and (2) by implication (reasonable inference from the nature and subject matter of the contract alone). Two examples may be helpful.

1. P agrees to print up and deliver 15,000 letterheads to Q by April 10, the contract further providing that *time is of the essence.* By this clause, the parties have made the stated time of performance an express condition precedent. Thus, if P fails to deliver the letterheads until April 11, Q can refuse to accept the belated performance. P's failure to meet the condition frees Q of her obligations under the contract. Additionally, Q can recover damages from P in a breach of contract suit. (An alternative open to Q is to accept the late performance and ''reserve her rights'' against P—in which case she is entitled to an allowance against the purchase price to the extent that she has suffered damages as a result of the late performance.)

2. A chamber of commerce purchases fireworks, for a Fourth of July celebration it is sponsoring, with the contract providing that ''delivery is to be made prior to July 4th.'' The fireworks arrive too late on July 4th to be used. From the nature of the *subject matter alone* it can be inferred that the stated time is a condition precedent, and the late delivery obviously did not meet that condition. In such a case it is said that time was made a condition ''by operation of law'' (that is, without regard to other factors). The courts are reluctant to rule from the subject matter of the contract or from the nature of the contract alone that time is of the essence. Limited instances in which such a ruling *may* be made, however (in addition to the rare case typified in example 2), are option contracts where, for example, a seller of land contracts to keep an offer open ninety days and contracts in which the value of the subject matter is fluctuating rapidly.

At one time, many courts ruled that time was presumed to be of the essence in sale of goods contracts. Today, however, this is not the general rule. Thus, in most states, a late delivery does not free the buyer unless they can clearly prove that delivery by the date contained in the contract was material and that the seller knew or should have been aware of the materiality.

Moreover, a number of states have adopted legislation in modern times specifying that a time-is-of-the-essence condition cannot be implied, and that time is never of the essence unless the contract expressly indicates that it is. Thus, one must check the law of a particular state to be certain.

DISCHARGE BY BREACH

Actual Breach

It would be contrary to common sense if a person who had materially breached a contract were nevertheless able to hold the other party liable on it, and the law does not tolerate such a result. As the preceding section on performance indicates, an *actual breach*— failure of the promisor to render performance that meets the minimum required by law (full performance in some cases and substantial performance in others)—ordinarily results in the other party's obligations being discharged. In such cases, the promisor's *material* (not trivial) breach operates as "an excuse for nonperformance" insofar as the other's obligation is concerned.

This principle has found its way into the law of sales. Thus, if Seller S on May 1 contracts to deliver a thousand gallons of crude oil to Buyer B on August 15, and on that date S delivers only two hundred gallons with no indication that the balance will be delivered shortly thereafter, B can cancel the entire contract, returning the oil already delivered (see Secs. 2-610 and 2-711 of the UCC).

Anticipatory Breach

If one contracting party indicates to the other, before the time of performance arrives, that they are not going to perform his or her part of the bargain, an *anticipatory breach* has occurred; in most cases this has the same effect as an actual breach. For example: In March, X contracts to put in a sewer line for a city, with the contract providing that the work will be commenced by June 1. On April 10, X tells the city that he will not do the job. The city can immediately hire a new contractor to do the work and can institute a suit for damages against X as soon as the damages can be ascertained, without waiting until June to do so. (Such action is not mandatory; the city may ignore the repudiation in the hope that X will have a change of heart and actually commence the work on schedule.)

The doctrine of anticipatory breach does not apply to promises to pay money debts, such as those found in promissory notes and bonds. To illustrate: S borrows $500 from T on February 1, giving T a promissory note in that amount due September 1. If S tells T on August 6 that he will not pay the debt, T must nevertheless wait until September 2 before bringing suit to recover the $500.

DISCHARGE BY LEGAL IMPOSSIBILITY

Between the time of contracting and the time of performance, some event may occur that will make the performance of the contract—for one party, at least—considerably more difficult or costly than originally expected. When this happens, a promisor may contend that the occurrence legally discharged his or her obligations under the contract—that is, it created a *legal impossibility*. (A related subject, the doctrine of *commercial impracticability*, will be discussed subsequently.) For example: A, an accountant for a large corporation who "moonlights" in his spare time, contracts in May to perform certain auditing services for B during the first three weeks of August, A's regularly scheduled vacation. In June, A is transferred to a city five hundred miles away; as a result, he does not perform the promised services. If B were to seek damages for breach of contract, the issue presented would be whether A's transfer discharged his obligations under the contract.

In such a case, the courts resort to a two-step process. The first question to be decided is whether one of the parties had assumed the risk in some manner. For example, in the case above, a court might conclude—from a reading of the entire contract, or from testimony regarding the negotiations leading up to the contract—that B had, in fact, agreed that A need not perform if he were relocated. If so, B had assumed the risk, and A need not perform.

If no assumption of risk is apparent (as is often the case), the court must proceed to the second question: whether it can rule, on the basis of the circumstances under which the contract was made, that the contract necessarily contained an implied condition subsequent. In other words, in the case above, A would be excused from performing the contract only if he could convince the court that he and B agreed by implication that the contract would be voided if he were transferred before the date of performance.

In most cases of this sort, the promisor's contention that an implied condition subsequent existed is rejected by the courts. The usual view is that such possibilities should have been guarded against by an express condition in the contract. Thus, when a corporation promises to manufacture engines by a certain date under a contract containing no express conditions, the fact that it is unable to do so because of a strike at one of its plants is no legal excuse for its nonperformance of the contract. And when a contractor agrees to construct a building by a certain date, with a monetary penalty imposed for late completion, the law normally does not excuse late performance simply because unexpectedly bad weather delayed the work. Nor will a court normally free a builder from his obligations, in the absence of an express condition, merely because unexpectedly high labor or materials costs will cause him to suffer a loss if he is held to the contract.

Notwithstanding these generalizations, there are limited situations in which the defense of legal impossibility is accepted by the courts. We will discuss them briefly.

True Impossibility

Essentially, a contract is rendered impossible of performance only where the supervening event—the event occurring between the making of the contract and the time of performance—was unforeseeable at the time of contracting and creates an objective impossibility. An objective impossibility results in a situation where, as a result of the unanticipated occurrence, no one can perform the contract—that is, performance is physically impossible. By contrast, an occurrence that makes performance by the promisor, only, impossible (but does not make performance by others impossible) does not discharge the promisor's obligations. For example, the inability of a buyer of a condominium to make a cash payment of $10,000 at the time of closing, as required by the contract, is not excused because his or her business suffered a catastrophic loss just prior to that time. (The difference between the two types of impossibility is often summarized thus: where a promisor is claiming objective impossibility, he is saying "No one can perform," while in the subjective impossibility situation he is simply saying "I cannot perform.")

Up until recent years, implied conditions subsequent—i.e., conditions resulting in legal (objective) impossibility—have been recognized by the courts in only three situations: (1) in contracts calling for personal services, (2) where the subject matter of the contract is destroyed without the fault of either party, and (3) where the performance of the contract becomes illegal after the contract is formed.

The view is commonly held among lay persons, and sometimes finds its way into court decisions, that promisors are freed of their obligations by any "act of God," or *force majeure*—i.e., a force of nature of such degree that it could not be guarded against or prevented by any degree of care or diligence (such as an earthquake or unprecedented flood). This generalization is true when the subject matter of a contract is destroyed by such an occurrence, but it is not necessarily true in other cases. For example, the destruction of a partially completed building by a tornado may be accepted by a court as grounds for permitting the contractor additional time in which to complete the job, but as a general rule, it does *not discharge* the contractor from the obligation to rebuild. Because of this rule, and because of uncertainty as to application of the act-of-God defense to other contracts, construction contracts (and many others) typically contain express conditions subsequent excusing delays in performance, or completely excusing performance, in the event of adverse weather conditions, strikes, and so forth. The following clause, in a maritime shipping contract, is typical:

> FORCE MAJEURE: In the event of any strike, fire or other event falling within the term 'Force Majeure' preventing or delaying shipment or delaying reception of the goods by the buyer, then the contract period of shipment or delivery shall be extended by 30 days on telex request made within seven days of its occurrence. Should shipment or delivery of the goods continue to be prevented beyond 30 days, the unaffected party may cancel the fulfilled balance of the contract. Should the contract thus be cancelled and/or performance be prevented during any extension to the shipment or delivery period *neither party shall have any claim against the other*. [Emphasis added.]

Personal Services

In contracts calling for the rendering of *personal services*, such as the ordinary employment contract, the death or incapacity of the promisor (employee) terminates the agreement. The same is true of contracts that contemplate a *personal relationship* between the promisor and the other party. In such cases the courts will accept the argument that the performer's promise was *subject to the implied condition* that his or her death prior to the time of performance (or illness at the time of performance) rendered the contract null and void.

Note, however, that many obligations are not personal in nature. For example: If B contracts to sell his land to W for $30,000, and B thereafter dies, the agreement is not terminated. The reason is that B's estate, acting through the executor, is just as capable of delivering a deed to W as was B, had he lived. Nor would the contract be terminated if W, rather than B, had died. W's estate is just as capable of paying the $30,000 as W would have been, had he lived.

Destruction of the Subject Matter

The principle is well established that destruction of the subject matter of a contract without the fault of either party, before the time for performance, terminates the contract. Where such a situation occurs, the courts will accept the argument that the destruction *constituted an implied condition subsequent* and will rule, as in the personal service contracts, that a legal impossibility has occurred. For example: If C contracted in January to move D's house in March, the contract would be discharged if the house were destroyed by flood in February. In this regard, it can be said that the destruction of the subject matter of a contract by an act of God creates a legal impossibility. It should be noted, however, that it is the fact of destruction that discharges, rather than the cause of destruction (as long as the destruction is not attributable to neglect or misconduct of the parties). To illustrate: X contracts with an investors' syndicate to drive its race car at the next Indianapolis 500, and the night before the race the car is destroyed by a fire set by an arsonist. Both parties are discharged from their obligations, although the arsonist's act is not an act of God.

Beyond cases such as the above, it is often difficult to determine what is meant by the "subject matter" of a contract; the term is often used by the courts to include not only the precise subject matter involved, but any other "thing" or property that performance of the contract necessarily depends on. For example, the X Company in January agrees to manufacture and deliver five hundred widgets to the Y Company in March. In February the

X Company's only plant is destroyed by fire, with the result that the widgets cannot be manufactured. In this case the courts will ordinarily rule that the existence of the plant is so necessary to the fulfillment of the contract that its destruction excuses the X Company from its obligations. (Such a ruling would not be made, however, if the X Company operated several plants and if there was no indication in the contract, expressly or impliedly, that the parties intended for the widgets to come from the particular plant that was destroyed.) Special problems arise in the "destruction" cases involving sales of goods. These "risk of loss" rules for goods are governed by article 2 of the UCC.

The case below raises a "destruction of the subject matter" issue in regard to the performance of a construction contract that contained no express conditions subsequent. (However, as noted earlier, the general subject of impossibility should also be considered with a related view, the "doctrine of commercial impracticability," which is discussed soon after this case.)

LA GASSE POOL CONSTR. CO. v. CITY OF FORT LAUDERDALE
Florida Court of Appeal, 288 So.2d 273 (1974)

The La Gasse Company, plaintiff, made a contract with the City of Fort Lauderdale under which it was to repair and renovate one of the city's swimming pools for a specified price. One night, when the job was almost completed, vandals damaged the pool so badly that most of the work had to be redone.

When the city refused to pay more than the contract price, plaintiff brought this action to recover compensation for the additional work. The primary contention of plaintiff was that the damage to its work constituted a destruction of the subject matter of the contract, and that it was consequently discharged from any obligation to redo the work. Accordingly, plaintiff argued, when it did do the work over again it was entitled to additional compensation for its services. The trial court rejected this contention, holding that plaintiff had the responsibility under the original contract to redo the work, and it entered judgment for defendant. Plaintiff appealed.

Downey, Judge:
. . . The question presented for decision is: Where the work done by a contractor, pursuant to a contract for the repair of an existing structure, is damaged during the course of the repair work, but the existing structure is not destroyed, upon whom does the loss fall where neither contractor nor the owner is at fault?

The general rule is that under an indivisible contract to build an entire structure, loss or damage thereto during construction falls upon the contractor, the theory being that the contractor obligated himself to build an entire structure, and absent a delivery thereof he has not performed his contract. If his work is damaged or destroyed during construction he is still able to perform by rebuilding the damaged or destroyed part; in other words, doing the work over again.

In the case of contracts to repair, renovate, or perform work on existing structures, the general rule is that total destruction of the structure . . . without fault of either the contractor or owner, excuses performance by the contractor and entitles him to recover the value of the work done. The rationale of this rule is that the contract has an implied condition that the structure will remain in existence so the contractor can render performance. Destruction of the structure makes performance impossible, and thereby excuses the contractor's nonperformance.

But where the building or structure to be repaired is not destroyed, [and] the contractor's work is damaged so that it must be redone, performance is still possible, and it is the contractor's responsibility to redo the work so as to complete the undertaking. In other words, absent . . . some other reason for lawful nonperformance, the contractor must perform his contract. Any loss or damage to his work during the process of repairs which can be rectified is his responsibility. The reason for allowing recovery without full performance in the case of total destruction, i.e., impossibility of performance is absent where the structure remains and simply requires duplicating the work.... Thus the judgment for [defendant] is affirmed.

Subsequent Illegality

If, after a contract is made, its performance becomes illegal because of a change in the law (including a promulgation of an administrative agency's regulation), a legal impossibility is created. Thus if B in September contracts to sell fifty pinball machines to G in December, the parties' obligations would be discharged if a state statute prohibiting such a transaction took effect in November.

DISCHARGE BY COMMERCIAL IMPRACTICABILITY

Under the traditional views just discussed, most contracts did not present situations in which legal impossibility was recognized. Thus most contracting parties were not freed from their obligations even in cases where their performance was clearly made more difficult by events that occurred after the contracts were entered into. Today, however, courts are more likely to free contracting parties than was the case earlier, because of increasing recognition of the *doctrine of commercial impracticability*.

The drafters of the UCC felt that sellers of goods should be excused from their obligations not only where the strict conditions of impossibility existed, but also where performance was literally possible but would necessarily be so radically different from that originally contemplated by the parties that it was impracticable.

Commercial Impracticability Under the UCC

Section 2-615 of the UCC reads, in part, as follows: "Delay in delivery or nondelivery in whole or in part by a seller . . . is not a breach of his duty under a contract for sale if performance as agreed has been made impracticable by the occurrence of a contingency the non-occurrence of which was a basic assumption upon which the contract was made."

While a full discussion of the scope and ramifications of the commercial impracticability doctrine cannot be undertaken here, several of its basic characteristics can be noted. These characteristics are best explained in Comment 4 following § 2-615, which reads as follows:

> Increased cost alone does not excuse performance unless the rise is due to some unforeseen contingency which alters the essential nature of the performance. Neither is a rise or a collapse in the market in itself a justification, for that is exactly the type of business risk which business contracts made at fixed prices are intended to cover. But a severe shortage of raw materials or of supplies due to a contingency such as war, embargo, local crop failure,

unforeseen shutdown of major sources of supply or the like, which either causes a *marked increase in cost or altogether prevents the seller* from securing supplies necessary to his performance, is within the contemplation of this section. [Emphasis added.]

Thus this section clearly recognizes certain kinds of contingencies *in addition* to those constituting true impossibilities that may free the seller of his or her obligations under the contract. In that regard, however, under both Comment 1 to § 2-615 and the case law that has developed with respect to this section, the seller must show that the contingency was not within the contemplation of the parties at the time of contracting.

A second change brought about by the impracticability doctrine is its recognition that a "marked increase" in cost will free the seller, if caused by an unforeseen contingency. By contrast, increased cost of performance alone is almost never recognized under the impossibility doctrine as a ground for excusing performance. However, determination of what constitutes a marked increase in cost is left to the courts to decide on a case-by-case basis, and the courts have interpreted this term quite narrowly. That is, under the decisions, the courts have generally taken the view that the seller must prove that the cost of performance, because of the contingency, would at least be double or triple the original cost of performance. Thus the increased cost provision does not afford sellers relief in as many cases as would at first appear.

After adoption of the UCC by states in the 1950s and 1960s, the courts generally recognized commercial impracticability as an excuse for nonperformance in sales contracts only, continuing to require a showing of strict impossibility where other types of contracts were involved. Today, however, there is a growing tendency among the courts to apply the commercial impracticability yardstick to all kinds of contracts.

DISCHARGE BY FRUSTRATION OF PURPOSE

Occasionally, after a contract is entered into, some event or condition will occur that clearly does not fall within the impossibility or commercial impracticability doctrines, yet one of the parties will argue that it so frustrated the purposes of the contract that its occurrence ought to free him nonetheless. (In other words, such a party is contending that the happening of the event caused the contract to become worthless to him.) To illustrate: D, a car dealer embarking on an ambitious expansion program, makes a contract with C, a contractor, under the terms of which he is to pay C $250,000 for the construction of new showroom facilities. Shortly thereafter, because of an unanticipated national defense emergency, the federal government orders a 90 percent reduction in the production of new automobiles. D contends that this action constitutes grounds for canceling its construction contract, since he will obviously have few new cars to sell.

Here the courts are on the horns of a dilemma. On the one hand, they understand that the virtual stoppage of new car production substantially eliminates the purpose for which the contract was made—and may even drive D into bankruptcy if he is held to its terms. On the other hand, the adoption of a general rule to the effect that contracts are discharged whenever the *purposes* of one of the parties cannot be attained as a result of unanticipated future occurrences would cast great uncertainty on the enforceability of almost all contracts.

While it is risky to generalize about the kinds of cases in which the doctrine of frustration may be accepted as grounds for avoiding contractual liability, it can safely be said that the courts—while giving the doctrine due consideration in their decisions—actually find it to be *inapplicable* in the great majority of cases. Thus, in the example above, D's contention that he was freed on the ground of frustration of purpose will probably, though not certainly, be rejected. The following case discusses the entire bundle of doctrines—impossibility, commercial impracticability, and frustration of purpose—tracing their origins and rationale.

NORTHERN IND. PUB. SERV. CO. v. CARBON COUNTY COAL CO.
U.S. Court of Appeals, 7th Circuit, 799 F.2d 265 (1986)

In 1978 Northern Indiana Public Service Company (NIPSCO), an electric utility in Indiana, contracted to buy 1.5 million tons of coal every year for 20 years, at a price of $24 a ton (subject to various provisions for escalation which by 1985 had driven the price up to $44 a ton) from Carbon County Coal Co., which operated a coal mine in Wyoming. NIPSCO's rates are regulated by the Indiana Public Service Commission which, because of complaints from consumers about higher rates, ordered NIPSCO to make a good faith effort to find and purchase electricity from other utilities that could produce it at prices lower than NIPSCO's internal generation. NIPSCO was able to buy substantial amounts of electricity from other utilities at costs below the costs of generating its own electricity using Carbon County's coal. Therefore, NIPSCO stopped accepting coal deliveries from Carbon and brought suit seeking a declaration that it was excused from its obligations under the contract. The trial court ruled against NIPSCO and it appealed.

Posner, Judge:

In the early common law, a contractual undertaking unconditional in terms was not excused merely because something had happened (such as an invasion, the passage of a law, or a natural disaster) that prevented the undertaking. *See Paradine v. Jane,* Aleyn, 26, 82 Eng. Rep. 897 (K.B. 1647). Excuses had to be written into the contract; this is the origin of *force majeure* clauses. Later it came to be recognized that negotiating parties cannot anticipate all the contingencies that may arise in the performance of the contract; a legitimate judicial function in contract cases is to interpolate terms to govern remote contingencies—terms the parties would have agreed on explicitly if they had had the time and foresight to make advance provision for every possible contingency in performance. Later still, it was recognized that physical impossibility was irrelevant, or at least inconclusive; a promisor might want his promise to be unconditional, not because he thought he had superhuman powers but because he could insure against the risk of nonperformance better than the promisee, or obtain a substitute performance more easily than the promisee. Thus the proper question in an "impossibility" case is not whether the promisor could not have performed his undertaking but whether his nonperformance should be excused because the parties, if they had thought about the matter, would have wanted to assign the risk of the contingency that made performance impossible or uneconomical to the promisor or to the promisee; if to the latter, the promisor is excused.

Section 2-615 of the Uniform Commercial Code takes this approach. It provides that "delay in delivery . . . by a seller . . . is not a breach of his duty under a contract for sale if performance as agreed has been made impracticable by the occurrence of a contingency the non-occurrence of which was a basic assumption on which the contract was made...." Performance on schedule need not be impossible, only infeasible—provided that the event which made it infeasible was not a risk that the promisor had assumed. Notice, however, that the only type of promisor referred to is a seller; there is no suggestion that a buyer's performance might be excused by reason of impracticability. The reason is largely semantic. Ordinarily all the buyer has to do in order to perform his side of the bargain is pay, and while one can think of all sorts of reasons why, when the time came to pay, the buyer might not have the money, rarely would the seller have intended to assume the risk that the buyer might, whether through improvidence or bad luck, be unable to pay for the seller's goods or services. To deal with the rare case where the buyer or (more broadly) the paying party might have a good excuse based on some unforeseen change in circumstances, a new rubric was thought necessary, different from "impossibility" (the common law term) or "impracticability," and it received the name "frustration"...

The leading case on frustration remains *Krell v. Henry,* [1903] 2 K.B. 740 (C.A.). Krell rented Henry a suite of rooms for watching the coronation of Edward VII, but Edward came down with appendicitis and the coronation had to be postponed. Henry refused to pay the balance of the rent and the court held that he was excused from doing so because his purpose in renting had been frustrated by the postponement, a contingency outside the knowledge, or power to influence, of either party. The question was, to which party did the contract (implicitly) allocate the risk? Surely Henry had not intended to insure Krell against the possibility of the coronation's being postponed, since Krell could always relet the room, at the premium rental, for the coronation's new date. So Henry was excused....

Since impossibility and related doctrines are devices for shifting risk in accordance with the parties' presumed intentions, which are to minimize the costs of contract performance, one of which is the disutility created by risk, they have no place when the contract explicitly assigns a particular risk to one party or the other.... [A] fixed-price contract is an explicit assignment of the risk of market price increases to the seller and the risk of market price decreases to the buyer, and the assignment of the latter risk to the buyer is even clearer where, as in this case, the contract places a floor under price but allows for escalation. If, as is also the case here, the buyer forecasts the market incorrectly and therefore finds himself locked into a disadvantageous contract, he has only himself to blame and so cannot shift the risk back to the seller by invoking impossibility or related doctrines.... It does not matter that it is an act of government that may have made the contract less advantageous to one party. Government these days is a pervasive factor in the economy and among the risks that a fixed price contract allocates between the parties is that of a price change induced by one of government's manifold interventions in the economy. Since "the very purpose of a fixed-price agreement is to place the risk of increased costs on the promisor (and the risk of decreased costs on the promisee)," the fact that costs decrease steeply (which is in effect what happened here— the cost of generating electricity turned out to be lower than NIPSCO thought when it signed the fixed-price contract with Carbon County) cannot allow the buyer to walk away from the contract. *In re Westinghouse Elec. Corp. Uranium Contracts Lit.,* 517 F.Supp. 440, 452 (E.D.Va. 1981). [Affirmed.]

DISCHARGE BY PARTIES' AGREEMENT—RESCISSION

Once a contract has been formed, it is always possible for the parties to make a new agreement that will discharge or modify the obligations of one or both parties under the original contract. The new agreement can take any of several forms, the most common of which are rescission, novation, and accord and satisfaction.

A contract can always be canceled by mutual agreement. When this agreement occurs, the contract is *rescinded,* and the obligations of both parties are thereby discharged. An oral rescission agreement is generally valid and binding, even where the original contract was in writing—with one major exception. A rescission agreement must be in writing if it involves a retransfer of real property. (Additionally, under Sec. 2-209(2) of the UCC, modification or rescission of a written *sales contract* must be evidenced by a writing if the original contract so provides.)

Accord and Satisfaction

After a contract has been formed, the parties may agree that one of them will accept, and the other will render, a performance different from what was originally called for. Such an agreement is an *accord.* Thus, if B owes W $1,800, and they later agree that B will air-condition W's home in satisfaction of the debt, an accord exists. Reaching an accord does not, of and by itself, terminate the existing obligation. To effect a discharge, a *satisfaction* must take place—the actual performance of the substituted obligation. B's indebtedness is discharged by *accord and satisfaction* when he completes the air-conditioning job.

DISCHARGE BY OPERATION OF LAW

In addition to the types of discharge already discussed, other events or conditions can bring about a *discharge by operation of law.* The most common of these are bankruptcy proceedings, the running of a statute of limitations, and the fraudulent alteration of a contract.

Bankruptcy Proceedings

If an individual has been adjudged bankrupt after proper bankruptcy proceedings have taken place, they receive a *discharge in bankruptcy* from a court which covers most—but not all—of his or her debts. While the discharge technically does not extinguish the debts that are subject to it, it does so as a practical matter by prohibiting creditors from thereafter bringing court action against the debtor to recover any unpaid balance.

Running of Statutes of Limitations

All states have statutes providing that after a certain amount of time has elapsed, a contract claim is barred. The time limits vary widely from one jurisdiction to another. In some states, for example, claimants are given three years in which to bring suit on oral contracts and five years on written ones; in others, the times vary from two to eight years on oral contracts and from three to fifteen years on written ones. In any event, if a contract claimant lets the applicable time elapse without initiating legal proceedings, the statute of limitations has run and subsequent court action by that person is barred. The period of time begins the day after the cause of action accrues.

Alteration

The law generally strives to discourage dishonest conduct. Consistent with this policy is the rule that the fraudulent, material *alteration* of a written contract by one of the parties discharges the other party as a matter of law.

CHAPTER 18

CONTRACT INTERPRETATION
AND
REMEDIES FOR BREACH

- Contract Interpretation
- Remedies for Breach of Contract

This chapter addresses two of the most practically important areas in all of contract law. Often a contract exists, in that all the basic elements of a binding contract (agreement, consideration, capacity, legality) are present, but its meaning is not clear. It expresses the general rights and obligations of the parties, but what it means *exactly* in relation to the events that have occurred since the contract was formed cannot be agreed upon by the parties to the contract. Indeed, questions regarding the meaning of contracts generate more litigation than any other type of contract question. The first portion of this chapter discusses the basic rules which courts apply when resolving disputes as to the meaning of a contract's terms.

If a plaintiff convinces the court that a contract exists, and that the defendant has breached that contract as interpreted by the court, he has gained nothing unless the law provides him a full and appropriate remedy. The second half of this chapter explores the various avenues of remedy available to a party injured by a breach of contract.

CONTRACT INTERPRETATION

It is told that the defenders of the bastion of Sebasta surrendered to Temures, their besieger, after he promised that "no blood would be shed" should they do so. Temures was good to the letter of his word. But, upon being buried alive, the defenders probably wished they had asked their lawyer to check the fine print. Most modern breach-of-contract lawsuits also involve, often among several issues, a dispute as to the meaning of the contract generally or some of its specific terms. It is a rare situation indeed when both parties to a contract agree as to the meaning of all of its provisions. Such difficulties are perhaps inevitable, a combination of the imprecision of human language, inattention to detail by the drafters of the agreement, and the inability of the parties to foresee events as they will eventually transpire. In Chapter 4, we discussed statutory law and learned that legislators face similar limitations in drafting statutes, giving rise to that "necessary evil"—judicial interpretation.

Similarly, courts are often called upon to determine the meaning of contracts and their provisions. Courts do this through the process of *interpretation* (sometimes called "construction"), which focuses on determining the meaning of words used in the contract and the legal effect to be given those words.

Intent of the Parties

The primary role of a court asked to interpret a contract is to determine the intent of the parties at the time the contract was made and to give effect to that intent. The court's job is not to improve the contract or to rewrite it to address matters that the parties should have considered but did not. As with the process of statutory interpretation, the parties' intent is the centerpiece of the process. The court's own evaluation as to how the contract should have been written is irrelevant.

There is disagreement as to the optimum approach to determining contract intent. Most courts speak of an "objective" test that gauges the meaning of a contract's words by how a hypothetical "reasonably intelligent person" would understand them. However, it is not at all rare to see courts strive to determine the common intent of the contracting parties at the time they made the contract.

Contractual interpretation generally raises questions of law to be resolved by the court. However, if a contract's wording is ambiguous, extrinsic evidence may be admitted to determine the parties' intent. Juries often play a role in resolving this question of fact.

While determination of the parties' intent is the overarching goal of contract interpretation, the courts, once they have determined that intent, are constrained by considerations of public policy. In other words, they cannot give effect to a contract where the intent is to produce illegal, unethical, or unconscionable activity.

Plain Meaning Rule

We learned in Chapter 4 that the primary source of legislative intent is the wording of the statute itself. It should not be surprising, then, that in determining the intent of the parties to a contract, courts look first to the language of that contract. The parties' own words are the main evidence of their intentions at the time they made the contract.

Indeed, the words of the contract may be the only evidence of the parties' intentions that a court will consider. As in statutory interpretation, there is a well- recognized *plain meaning rule*. If the language of the contract appears clear and unambiguous, the plain meaning rule requires that the courts determine the intent of the parties solely from the face of the instrument. Absent ambiguity, the courts should not resort to extrinsic evidence (such as the actions of the parties, the testimony of the parties, or even the past practices of the parties) in their search for intent. Any attempt to alter the obvious meaning of the words with outside evidence would likely stray from the parties' intent at the time they made the agreement.

A few courts have rejected the plain meaning rule, concluding that it "asserts a semantic perfection which cannot hope to be achieved." *PG&E v. G. W. Thomas Drayage Rigging* Co., 442 P.2d 641 (Cal. 1968). Even in plain meaning rule jurisdictions, courts often conclude that the language of the parties, though it appears clear, is not in fact "plain and unambiguous." When that happens, courts resort to extrinsic evidence such as all relevant writings and oral statements, other conduct of the parties manifesting their intent, negotiations, prior course of dealing, and other relevant factors.

The following case examines these divergent approaches to the introduction of extrinsic evidence.

ISBRANDTSEN v. NORTH BRANCH CORPORATION
Supreme Court of Vermont, 556 A.2d 81 (1988)

Plaintiff (grantee) bought from defendant (grantor) a townhouse at a ski resort. Defendant operated recreational facilities, ski trails, parking areas, and assorted outbuildings. There were four townhouses and all adjoined a common area known as the "club" which contained a kitchen, restaurant, and sitting room. Defendant operated and maintained all these areas. Defendant's business depended in part upon rental income derived from lessees of owners of the townhouses who did not use them on a year-round basis. The development was designed so that the temporarily unoccupied townhouses could be rented out to paying guests. This benefited the owners, who derived a percentage of income from the rentals, and it assured the defendant the income required to continue providing the maintenance services necessary to all occupants.

The deed through which defendant sold the townhouse to plaintiff contained this clause: "The premises hereby conveyed shall be used only for private, single family residence purposes, except that, under express agreement between Grantor and Grantee, the premises may be rented or used for paying guests in connection with Grantor's operations."

Plaintiff asked the lower court to declare that she could rent her townhouse to paying guests without defendant's knowledge or consent. Defendant claimed that this clause prohibited plaintiff from any such rental except by and with defendant's express consent. The trial judge ruled for the defendant and the plaintiff appealed.

Gibson, Justice:

The question of whether a contract term is ambiguous is a matter of law for the court to decide. A provision in a contract is ambiguous only to the extent that reasonable people could differ as to its interpretation. Here, plaintiff argues that the deed contains internal inconsistencies which render its terms ambiguous and therefore subject to rules of construction that would warrant judgment in her favor. In particular, plaintiff contends that before the restriction on commercial rental can be given effect, there must first be an agreement between the parties, and that since there is no such agreement, plaintiff is free to do as she wishes.

Before extrinsic evidence may be used to aid in the construction of a written instrument, ambiguity must first be found. In determining whether an ambiguity exists, many courts have adopted the traditional "four corners" test or "plain meaning rule," which states that if a writing appears to be plain and unambiguous on its face, its meaning must be determined from the four corners of the instrument without resort to extrinsic evidence of any nature: "If the term in question does not have a plain meaning it follows that the term is ambiguous." J. Calamari & J. Perillo, THE LAW OF CONTRACTS §3-10, at 166-67 (3d ed. 1987).

A number of courts, recognizing that "plain meaning" cannot exist in a vacuum, have allowed the admission of evidence as to the circumstances surrounding the making of the agreement as well as the object, nature and subject matter of the writing. *See, e.g., Pacific Gas & Elec. Co. v. G. W. Thomas Drayage & Rigging Co.*, 442 P.2d 641 (Cal. 1968).

We believe it appropriate, when inquiring into the existence of ambiguity, for a court to consider the circumstances surrounding the making of the agreement. Ambiguity will be found where a writing in and of itself supports a different interpretation from that which appears when it is read in light of the surrounding circumstances, and both interpretations are reasonable.

If ambiguity is found on that basis, the court may then rely on subordinate rules of construction in order to interpret the meaning of the disputed terms. If, however, no ambiguity is found, then the language must be given effect in accordance with its plain, ordinary and popular sense.

In making its determination as to ambiguity in the instant case, the trial court properly considered evidence as to the circumstances under which the conveyance was made. In the late 1960s, plaintiff and her family stayed at North Branch (presumably under a rental agreement as described above) on at least three separate occasions before her husband decided to purchase a townhouse for her. This purchase, which was a gift from Mr. Isbrandtsen to his wife, consisted of one of two new townhouses built in 1969, both of which were joined to the original four buildings. The new townhouses, which had no common "club" areas (having been built after the main buildings), each contained six bedroom units.

At the time defendant conveyed the property to plaintiff, she was asked, like every other owner, to sign a "Business Use Agreement" allowing defendant to rent out the property when she was not in actual occupancy. She declined to do so, advising defendant that she and her family intended to occupy the entire townhouse for their own use. It was uncontested at trial that of the other townhouse owners, all five had executed a "Business Use Agreement."

Plaintiff acknowledges that the restriction to use the property only "for private, single-family residence purposes" limits its use to residential purposes as opposed to business or commercial uses. The clause immediately following that phrase provides one exception to the restriction: the premises may be rented or used for paying guests under express agreement between defendant and the owner. The words "under express agreement" were inserted for a purpose and may not be ignored. The law is clear that an agreement must be viewed in its entirety, with an eye toward giving effect to all material parts in order to form a harmonious whole.

While the language of the restrictive clause is somewhat awkward, that in itself does not render it ambiguous. "If a contract, though inartfully worded or clumsily arranged, fairly admits of but one interpretation, it may not be said to be ambiguous or fatally unclear." *Allstate Ins. Co. v. Goldwater,* 415 N.W.2d 2 (Mich. App. 1987). Likewise, the fact that a dispute has arisen as to proper interpretation does not automatically render the language ambiguous. Such an approach would merely invite court interference any time a litigant alleged a dispute as to a contractual term.

Viewing the language of the deed in light of the surrounding circumstances, we hold that only one reasonable interpretation exists: that absent an express agreement between plaintiff and defendant, plaintiff is prohibited by the deed from renting her property to paying guests. Likewise, absent such an express agreement, defendant may not rent out plaintiff's property in part or in whole. The restriction serves to protect defendant's interest in maintaining and operating its innkeeping business while serving also to protect plaintiff, who may not want her property rented out indiscriminately to transient individuals. Affirmed.

If courts decide to resort to evidence outside the language of the contract, the best evidence of the parties' intent may be their later conduct in carrying it out. For example, in one case both Jewell and Thomas signed a promissory note. Jewell claimed that he had signed only to assist Thomas in getting the loan and that Thomas should therefore repay Jewell for the payments he made to the bank. Thomas claimed that Jewell was the primary obligor on the note. The evidence showed that as soon as the note was signed, Jewell treated the note as his own obligation, taking over complete responsibility for servicing the debt. Thomas never dealt with the bank. The court concluded that the intent of the parties appeared to be as asserted by Thomas. *Jewell & Co. v. Thomas,* 434 N.W.2d 532 (Neb. 1989).

Rules of Interpretation

As in statutory interpretation, various rules of contract interpretation have developed over the years to assist the courts in determining the parties' intent from the words that they used. Courts should not apply the rules so conservatively as to obstruct the parties' true intentions, nor so liberally as to allow one of the parties to escape his obligations. As noted earlier, the courts are not at liberty to rewrite the contract while purporting to interpret it.

The first task in contract interpretation is to determine to the extent possible the parties' *principal* objective in forming the contract. This principal objective is accorded great weight, and all the contract's terms are construed in order to carry out that objective.

The parties' intentions are generally (though not exclusively) judged in an objective fashion from their expressed intent. Secret intentions are deemed irrelevant. Intentions expressed through either words or actions are given effect unless they conflict with law, morals, or public policy.

Contracts often contain conflicting and inconsistent terms. These will be interpreted, insofar as possible, to achieve the intentions of both parties. If possible, a contract will be construed so as to give effect to all of its provisions. The courts disfavor a construction which requires that a portion of the contract be ignored.

The courts also presume that the parties intended their agreement to be legal, reasonable, and effective. If alternative constructions are both plausible, the one that is preferred is the one less likely to render it illegal, unreasonable, or ineffective. Assume that a contract grants a patent licensee "exclusive use in the U.S.A." of the patented product. If the licensee argues that the right is to be perpetual and the licensor argues that it is to last only the life of the patent, the latter interpretation would be favored because the former would be inconsistent with antitrust laws.

Other aids to interpretation include the following:

1. Words and phrases are given their ordinary meaning, unless the parties indicate otherwise. Although the courts are not slaves to dictionaries, they do frequently consult them. Similarly, technical words are presumed to be used in their commonly accepted technical sense.

2. Specific language controls general language. For example, if a contract provided in one clause that a sole shareholder guaranteed payment for electrical service provided to his company, and another clause provided that the sole shareholder guaranteed electrical service provided to his company at a specific address, the court would likely conclude that the sole shareholder was not liable for electrical service provided to the company at other addresses.

3. When a contract is embodied in a printed form, any conflicting provisions added by the parties will prevail. Handwriting will prevail over typewriting. Thus, if a preprinted form contained a provision limiting liability to $1,000, but the figure $2,500 was handwritten into the relevant blank on the form, the latter would set the limit of liability.

4. Ambiguous language is construed against the party who prepares the agreement. This is especially true where the contract is a preprinted adhesion contract where there is little opportunity for negotiation. In *Comprehensive Health Ins. Ass'n v. Dye,* 531 N.E.2d 505 (Ind. App. 1988), for example, an insurance contract prepared by the insurance company contained two different definitions of ''preexisting conditions'' that would not be covered by the policy. One excluded any sickness that had been diagnosed or treated before the policy was issued; the other excluded any sickness for which a reasonable person would have sought diagnosis or treatment. The court chose to apply the first definition because it was narrower and therefore more favorable to the insured.

5. Where numbers are expressed, words prevail over figures where they are in conflict. For instance, if a typed contract indicated in one place that the purchase price was ''eight hundred dollars'' but in another place indicated that it was ''$805,'' the former would prevail.

6. In every contract, courts will imply a duty of good faith, fair dealing, and cooperation on the part of both parties. The law of the jurisdiction at the place and time the contract is made is also generally read into the contract. Courts will not imply any other terms, unless a contract is silent on a particular point. In such an instance, courts may occasionally imply terms. For example, a contract that is silent as to duration will generally be construed to last for a reasonable time. An obligation to pay money is construed to require that the money be paid in legal tender.

These rules of interpretation, when applied to a specific contract, will not always point in the same direction, as the following case illustrates.

INNES v. WEBB

Texas Court of Civil Appeals, 538 S.W.2d 237 (1976)

Appellee Webb wished to buy a house owned by Huller. Appellant Innes, a real estate broker, prepared an earnest money contract between Webb and Huller. Webb gave Innes a check for $2,000 as earnest money; Innes gave the money to Huller. Huller left town and never completed the contract. Webb seeks return of his $2,000, pointing to a provision in the standard preprinted form that was used for the earnest money contract which provided that if the seller did not comply with the contract for any reason, "Purchaser may demand back the earnest money...." In essence, Webb alleged that Innes held the funds as stakeholder subject to Webb's demand for return of the funds should Huller breach. Innes emphasized a provision that was typed onto the form which stated: "$2,000 escrow to be turned over to Seller for initial deposit on materials and administrative costs." The trial court held for Webb in the sum of $2,000 and broker Innes appealed.

Young, Justice:

The contract was prepared by a broker and contains two apparently inconsistent clauses: one, a printed clause, requiring the return by the broker to the purchaser of the earnest money on purchaser's demand if the seller fails to comply with the contract; and the other, a typewritten clause, requiring the broker to turn over the "$2,000.00 escrow" to the seller "for initial deposit for materials and administrative costs." Appellant urges that we should be guided here by the rule of construction which provides that the written or typewritten part of a contract controls in the event of any conflict thereof with the printed portion of the contract. The rationale for this rule is that the written or typed words are the immediate language of the parties themselves whereas the language of the printed form is intended for general use only, without reference to the particular aims and objectives of the parties. *Leslie Lowry & Co. v. KTRM, Inc.*, 239 S.W.2d 898, 900 (Tex.Civ.App.—Beaumont 1951).

On the other hand, appellee contends that our case should be controlled by the rule which requires that an agreement be construed most strictly against the party who drafted it and thus was responsible for the language used.

When we attempt to apply these rules to our case, we find that we apparently have two conflicting rules urged by the parties. The question then arises which rule should prevail here. Our answer to that question is that the rule should be applied which says typed matter controls the printed instead of the rule which says that a contract will be construed against the author. *Universal C.I.T. Credit Corp. v. Daniel*, 150 Tex. 513, 243 S.W.2d 154 (1951); *Leslie Lowry & Co. v. KTRM, Inc., supra;* 17A C.J.S. Contracts § 324, p.217.

The rule of strict construction against the author has been dealt with in those authorities as follows: In *Daniel,* our Supreme Court held that the rule applies only after ordinary rules of interpretation (such as the typed controls the printed) have been applied. In *KTRM,* that Court simply applied the typed controls the printed rule over the authorship rule. In 17A C.J.S., the statement is made that the authorship rule is the last one the courts will apply.

For all of those reasons, we hold that the typewritten clause in the contract determines the responsibility of the appellant for his disposition of the "$2,000.00 escrow"; that he delivered that money to the seller under the clause; that, therefore, he did not breach the contract in so delivering the money. Reversed.

The following case involves a somewhat complex set of facts in which a federal appeals court applying New York law in a diversity of citizenship case interpreted the terms of an executive employee's compensation agreement. In particular, the aspect of the employment agreement at issue was the executive's stock option plan. The employer's board of directors, acting as a committee to apply the terms of the stock option plan, apparently became unhappy with the executive and drastically cut the value of his stock options just before firing him, resulting in a loss to him of over $5 million. Of course, he sued the company. In the decision below, the court also applies *the implied covenant of good faith and fair dealing* that is part of New York contract law. This implied obligation was first recognized by New York state courts in the late nineteenth and early twentieth centuries and has gradually been adopted by courts in a majority of states. The obligation to act fairly and in good faith in contractual relationships is now found in both the *Uniform Commercial Code* for sale of goods contracts and the *Second Restatement of Contracts* for contracts in general. This implied obligation has a variety of applications, including the role it plays in courts' interpretation of terms in a contract.

FISHOFF v. COTY, INC.
U.S. Court of Appeals, 2nd Circuit, 634 F.3d 647 (2011)

Appellee Michael Fishoff (plaintiff in the trial court) was employed by Appellant Coty Inc., a privately held corporation (defendant in the trial court), which describes itself as "a global beauty leader and the world's largest fragrance company." Fishoff served as Coty's Chief Financial Officer from July 2002 until December 2008, when the company severed its employment contract with Fishoff. The facts of this lawsuit arise from efforts by the company, coinciding with the termination of Fishoff's employment, to reduce the value of his stock options.

When Fishoff was hired in 2002, Coty provided him with an employment letter addressing his compensation package, including his eligibility to participate in the company's Long-Term Incentive Plan ("LTIP" or "Plan"). In November 2002, Coty awarded Fishoff a nonqualifiedstock option to purchase up to 50,000 shares of Coty stock at a purchase price of $14 per share. Approximately one year later, Fishoff was awarded another 50,000 nonqualified stock options at a purchase price of $17 per share. In September 2004, he received 50,000 additional options with a purchase price of $23.25. And in September 2005, Fishoff received his final installment of 50,000 options with a purchase price of $25.50 per share. Each of these awards was governed by the terms of Coty's LTIP.

The LTIP states, that "[u]nless otherwise expressly provided in the Plan," Coty's Board of Directors, which operated as the "Committee" charged with administering the LTIP, retains discretion to interpret the terms of the LTIP. Pursuant to this discretion, the Board may "amend any terms of, or alter, suspend, discontinue, cancel or terminate" existing awards "consistent with the latest version of the Plan as in effect from time to time." The Plan further provides "there is no obligation for uniformity of treatment of Employees, Participants, or holders or beneficiaries of Awards," and "[t]he terms and conditions of Awards need not be the same with respect to each recipient." "Award" is defined to include, inter alia, the types of stock options at issue in this case.

Section 6 of the LTIP relates to the Board's discretion with respect to specific awards, providing, among other things, that the Board determines who receives options and how many options each individual receives; what, if any, restrictions there are on when those options can be exercised; and how much the optionee will receive after cashing in, or exercising, the option. Except in circumstances not relevant here, the LTIP provides: "Upon any valid exercise of an Option or any portion thereof . . . the respective Participant shall be entitled to receive only a payment in cash equal to the excess, if any, of the Fair Market Value, as of the Exercise Date, of the Shares underlying the Option or portion thereof so exercised over the aggregate exercise price of such Option or portion thereof." The defined term, "Fair Market Value," means the cash value of the share underlying each option. Pursuant to the terms of the Plan, Fair Market Value was to "be determined" by the Board periodically (the "Valuation Date[s]"), "using a nationally recognized investment bank (or other comparable valuation expert) selected by the [Board]."

In terms of the restrictions on the exercise of the options at issue in this case, the LTIP provides that options "may be exercised only on an Exercise Date," which is defined as "the last day of any month, except the month prior to the month in which a Valuation Date falls." Coty states that Valuation Dates were usually in March and September, but the LTIP does not specify any particular date on which a valuation must take place.

The parties have not provided much color on Fishoff's relationship with Coty, but it clearly reached a low point during his last months at the company. In September 2008, the Board determined that the Fair Market Value of Coty's stock was $58 per share. Approximately two months later, Fishoff decided to exercise all of his 200,000 options and provided the company with notice of the transaction. Because the November Exercise Date (November 30, 2008) fell on a Sunday, Fishoff tendered his notice in person on Monday, December 1, 2008, as he was entitled to do by New York General Construction Law Section 25. The next day, Coty confirmed that Fishoff's notice was effective for the month of November and they provided him with notice of the cash value for his redemption, which totaled $7,612,500.

Three days later, Coty changed course, and the Board convened an official meeting on December 5 to alter the established terms of the LTIP. First, the Board voided all options exercise notices that had been tendered in December, including Fishoff's, on the ground that the notices were late because they were not provided on or before Sunday, November 30, 2008. Second, the Board decided there would be four valuation dates each year instead of two. Third, the Board redefined "Exercise Date" such that an optionee could only exercise options four times a year, on the fifteenth business day after each valuation. Fourth, the Board decided that January 31, 2009, would be the next valuation date, and if anyone wanted to exercise their options, they would have to wait until February 2009.

Four days later, on December 9, 2008, Coty informed Fishoff that his options exercise had been voided, because it was not "submitted prior to the last day of the month." Two days later, Coty notified Fishoff that his employment was being terminated. Fishoff consulted a lawyer about Coty's treatment of his options. That lawyer, apparently concluding that Fishoff had a cause of action against the company, drafted a complaint on Fishoff's behalf, which Fishoff forwarded to Coty's Board. Shortly thereafter, on January 19, 2009, the Board convened again.

As the Board's actions during the January meeting suggest, Coty developed a plan *to avoid paying Fishoff based on the then-applicable Fair Market Value of the shares. First, Coty would agree to honor Fishoff's options exercise as a November exercise, though the company would not pay Fishoff the $58 per share he was entitled to as a November exerciser. Rather, the Board would authorize a special valuation limited exclusively to Fishoff's shares. Thus, while everyone else who exercised options in November received $58 per share, Fishoff would receive some other payment amount. Then, Coty engaged a new bank, Rothschild, Inc., to conduct a valuation that would set the value of Fishoff's shares as of November 30, 2008. On February 19, 2009, more than two months after he exercised his options, the Board notified Fishoff that Rothschild had finally reached a dollar value for his options. Fishoff was to receive $31 per share for a total cash payment of approximately $2.2 million, or $5.4 million less than he would have gotten had he been treated the same as all of the other optionees who exercised options in November.*

Three days after the Board decided to retroactively reduce the value of his options from $7,612,500 to $2,212,500, Fishoff commenced this lawsuit. His complaint alleged, among other things, breach of contract. On July 17, 2009, the district court issued a memorandum opinion and order applying New York General Construction Law Section 25 to hold that Fishoff had timely exercised his options for November 2008, even though he had not filed his notice of intent to exercise until Monday, December 1, 2008. New York General Construction Law Section 25 states that "[w]here a contract by its terms authorizes or requires the payment of money or the performance of a condition on a . . . Sunday, . . . unless the contract expressly or impliedly indicates a different intent, such payment may be made or condition performed on the next succeeding business day." The district court reasoned that "because an option is 'a contract to keep an offer open,' the offeree must do something to accept the offer," and "that required 'something' can reasonably be seen as a 'condition' that must be performed for the offer to be accepted." Applied in the context of the LTIP and Award Agreements, the district court explained, "Coty's main contention is that section 3(a) of the Award Agreements allows for the exercise of an option to be made 'at any time.' Coty ignores that section 3(a) explicitly qualifies its own applicability with the preface, 'subject to the provisions of the LTIP and this Award (including section 3(e)).'" The district court continued,

> *Section 3(e) states explicitly, "notwithstanding the foregoing, the Option may be exercised . . . only . . . as of an Exercise Date." Because the Award Agreements do not define "Exercise Date," one must look to the LTIP, which defines that term as "the last day of any month." Section 6(d)(ii) of the LTIP qualifies these terms further; it states, "any provision of the LTIP or any Award Agreement to the contrary notwithstanding, the provisions of this section shall apply . . . . Options becoming exercisable in accordance with their terms may be exercised only on an Exercise Date."*

The district court thus concluded that, "Section 25 of the GCL extends that date to Monday if the last day of the month is a Sunday. Indeed, in Fishoff's case, because November 30, 2008 was a Sunday, his December 1, 2008 exercise was a condition that was otherwise expected to be performed on a Sunday and therefore was a timely 'November' exercise." Based in part on its finding that Fishoff had filed a timely November options exercise, the district court denied summary judgment to Coty on Fishoff's breach of contract claim.

The district court framed the dispositive issue as "whether the LTIP permits Coty the discretion to apply different Fair Market Values to shares exercised by different Participants *on the same day." Having concluded that "the answer was clear—the LTIP is unambiguous and does not provide for such discretion," the district court explained that the sole remaining issue was whether any other November exercisers were awarded payments of $58 per share minus their respective purchase prices." Coty stipulated that every other LTIP participant who had delivered a timely November exercise received payment based upon the $58 per share price. Accordingly, the district court issued an order awarding Fishoff the difference between Coty's retroactive valuation and the $58 per share rate, which amounted to $5.4 million, plus prejudgment interest on that sum.*

KEARSE, Circuit Judge:

New York General Construction Law Section 25 provides in relevant part that: "Where a contract by its terms authorizes or requires the payment of money or performance of a condition on a Saturday, Sunday or a public holiday . . . unless the contract expressly or impliedly indicates a different intent, such payment may be made or condition performed on the next succeeding business day." Fishoff's options could *only* be exercised on an "Exercise Date," which was defined in Section 2 of the LTIP, in pertinent part, as "the last day of any month." In 2008, November 30 was a Sunday. Accordingly, Fishoff personally delivered his notice of intent to exercise his options on Monday, December 1, 2008, and the district court deemed this a timely exercise pursuant to New York General Construction Law Section 25.

Coty argues that the district court's conclusion was in error because the LTIP does not *require* an optionee to deliver his notice of intent to exercise on an Exercise Date; it only limits the day on which such options can be processed. The plain language of Section 25, however, is not limited to "required" acts; it also reaches acts that are "authorized." Plainly, the LTIP authorized the filing of a notice of intent to exercise on an Exercise Date; Coty does not argue otherwise. Under the terms of the LTIP, the filing of a notice of intent to exercise one's options is a "condition" to the exercise of such options. Because there is no other provision of the LTIP that indicates the intent of the parties different from the norm provided by Section 25 of the New York General Construction Law, impliedly or explicitly, we conclude the district court committed no error in holding that Fishoff gave timely notice for a November exercise.

Under New York law [and the law of most other states], a covenant of good faith and fair dealing is implied in all contracts. This covenant embraces a pledge that neither party shall do anything which will have the effect of destroying or injuring the right of the other party to receive the fruits of the contract. Where the contract contemplates the exercise of discretion, this pledge includes a promise not to act arbitrarily or irrationally in exercising that discretion. Courts have equated the covenant of good faith and fair dealing with an obligation to exercise that discretion "reasonably and with proper motive, not arbitrarily, capriciously, or in a manner inconsistent with the reasonable expectations of the parties." A breach of the duty of good faith and fair dealing is considered a breach of contract.

In this case, Coty does not argue that its decision to cut its share price by almost 50% in order to devalue Fishoff's options is consistent with the implied duty of good faith and fair dealing. Indeed, it is difficult to conceive of a set of facts under which Coty's seemingly arbitrary post hoc valuation, which was applied *only* to Fishoff and only *after* he exercised his options, would not be a clear violation of the duty of good faith and fair dealing; Coty's actions plainly denied Fishoff the fruits of the contract. Rather, Coty urges that the implied duty is of no consequence because the LTIP "expressly provides an unrestricted discretionary right" as codified in Section 3(b) of the LTIP. We disagree with the interpretation of the contract advanced by Coty. Discretion to modify or cancel an incentive will not be implied if there exists no explicit contractual provisions assigning the employer absolute discretion to pay such compensation. While Section 3(b) gives Coty a considerable amount of discretion in making determinations about the "Plan" and "Awards" issued thereunder, it is silent as to Coty's discretion to alter share value after an optionee has validly exercised his options. If nothing else, the fact that Coty initially issued a written confirmation of Fishoff's exercise that included a $58 Fair Market Value for the shares, indicates that Coty at one time also recognized this limitation on its discretion.

Moreover, the terms of the LTIP, Section 6(d)(ii), provide that once an optionee has made a valid exercise, Coty must make payment to the optionee based upon the Fair Market Value of the company's shares that was in place on the date the options exercise was made. "Upon any valid exercise the respective Participant *shall* be entitled to receive . . . a payment in cash . . ." (emphasis added). In this case, that payment was to be in an amount equal to the difference between the "Fair Market Value" of the company's shares "*as of* the Exercise Date" and the purchase price of the options—that is, the difference between the valuation in place on the date Fishoff exercised his options and their respective purchase prices. Once the exercise was processed and that difference was computed, Coty was required to make payment to Fishoff "as promptly as practicable." To the extent that any other part of the LTIP could be read to conflict with these strictures, Section 6(d)(ii) makes clear that it applies with full force and effect "notwithstanding" "any provision of the Plan or any Award Agreement to the contrary." Thus, once Fishoff's exercise was, by operation of law, a valid November exercise, he was entitled to be compensated at the $58 per share rate that all other November exercisers received....

For the foregoing reasons, we AFFIRM the judgment of the district court awarding $5.4 million plus prejudgment interest to Fishoff.

Uniform Commercial Code

The UCC, in § 2-202, permits more liberal use of extrinsic evidence in determining the parties' intent in sale-of-goods contracts than was historically allowed under common-law rules in interpreting various types of contracts. The UCC assumed that the parties considered matters such as (1) course of performance, (2) course of dealing, and (3) usage of trade when making their agreement. Thus, in construing a sales contract courts may resort to this extrinsic evidence without finding that the words of the contract are ambiguous.

A *course of performance*, according to UCC § 2-208, arises out of "repeated occasions for performance by either party with knowledge of the nature of the performance and opportunity for objection to it by the other." Such performance which is accepted and acquiesced in without objection by the other party is a strong indication of what the parties intended.

A *course of dealing*, according to UCC § 1-205, is "a sequence of previous conduct between the parties to a particular transaction which is fairly to be regarded as establishing a common basis of understanding for interpreting their expressions and other conduct." Thus, whereas course of performance arises out of the same contract the court is trying to interpret, course of dealing arises out of earlier transactions between the parties.

Finally, a *usage of trade*, according to UCC § 1-205, is "any practice or method of dealing having such regularity of observance in a place, vocation, or trade as to justify an expectation that it will be observed with respect to the transaction in question."

It certainly makes sense to assume that the parties' conduct in performing the contract evidences their intentions and to assume that their intent at the time of making the contract took into account their prior dealings and the customs of their industry. UCC § 1-205(4) establishes a priority for interpretation. Express terms of the agreement are the primary source for interpretation. Next in line is course of performance which, where conflicting, controls course of dealing. Course of dealing, in turn, prevails over a conflicting usage of trade. Use of this type of extrinsic evidence is, of course, consistent with the UCC's various "gap-filler" provisions that we studied in Chapter 11.

It is important to note, however, that in more recent times most courts have begun to more liberally take into account evidence of course of performance, course of dealing, and usage of trade, and usage of trade as aids in interpreting contracts of all kinds, and not just sale of goods contracts.

REMEDIES FOR BREACH OF CONTRACT

Assuming that a valid contract exists and that one of the parties to that contract has breached its obligations (as those obligations were interpreted by the court), the matter of remedies arises. We have already touched on the concept of remedies in several chapters. For example, in Chapter 14 we learned that rescission is available as a remedy where contracts were induced by fraud. In Chapter 17, we discussed remedies that are available where parties have only partially, but not completely, performed their contracted obligations.) The party who received the promises that were not performed will often look to the judicial system for a remedy (though, as we learned in Chapter 3, remedies may also be provided by alternative means of dispute resolution, such as arbitration). The form, availability, and extent of remedies will play a big part in a party's decision whether to litigate. If the law does not provide a remedy, or provides an inappropriate or inadequate remedy, the wronged party may never sue.

In our legal system, the freedom to contract entails the freedom to breach one's obligations. Our system of remedies aims not at coercing parties into performing their obligations, but at providing adequate remedies for the other party when breaches do occur. The distinction is subtle, but our free enterprise system's main goal is to encourage people to do business with those who make promises by assuring them that adequate remedies will be available to compensate them should the promisors not perform.

Our discussion is divided into two major sections because of the historical distinction (explored in the introductory chapters) between actions at law and actions in equity. Because the law/equity distinction has largely disappeared, virtually every court can grant remedies that traditionally were available in courts of law (i.e., money damages) and those traditionally available in courts of equity (e.g., orders of specific performance and injunction).

As with earlier contract law chapters, we will note areas where the Uniform Commercial Code alters common law rules because of the special needs of sales of goods transactions.

Money Damages

The primary remedy available for breach of contract is money damages. Because this remedy originated in courts at law, a jury trial is available to plaintiffs seeking such damages. The main goal of an award of damages is to compensate the plaintiff for losses caused by the defendant's failure to perform as promised. We will emphasize *compensatory damages* in this discussion, but also explore other types of damages, including nominal damages and liquidated damages.

Compensatory Damages

The amount of money a jury might award depends upon which interest the law is attempting to compensate. There are three such interests that we must address.

1. *Expectation Interest.* The law usually seeks to compensate the plaintiff's expectation interest. That is, the law seeks to put the plaintiff in the position in which he expected to be after the defendant performed his promise. In other words, the law attempts to give the plaintiff the "benefit of his bargain."

2. *Reliance Interest.* In situations where it is not feasible or fair to award the plaintiff expectation damages, the law may seek to return the plaintiff to where he was before the contract was entered into. Because this frequently entails reimbursing the plaintiff for funds he spent (or other detriment incurred) in reliance on the defendant's promise, this is called the *reliance* interest.

3. *Restitution Interest.* Finally, a defendant who fails to perform a promise should not be allowed to keep a benefit conferred by a plaintiff who did perform his promise. Therefore, in a breach-of-contract action, the defendant is often ordered to compensate the plaintiff for such a benefit. This is called making restitution, and the law is compensating the plaintiff's *restitution* interest.

Illustration: Assume that D Company hired Ralph to build a storage shed for D for the sum of $10,000. Soon after the contract was made, D repudiated it. If Ralph sued for breach of contract, proving that he could have built the shed for $7,500, he will likely recover $2,500, the profit that he expected to receive from the transaction. This award gives Ralph the benefit of his bargain by placing him in the position he expected to occupy (a $2,500 profit in his pocket) if D performed its promise.

Assume, on the other hand, that sometime after Ralph began building the shed, D breached the contract, telling Ralph not to finish because D would pay nothing. If Ralph could not prove the profit he would have made had the shed been completed, but could show that he had spent $3,400 on labor and materials before the breach, the law would award Ralph that $3,400 to compensate his reliance interest. Ralph spent that amount in reliance on D's promise. (If Ralph could also establish the $2,500 expected profit, he would recover $5,900, because this is the sum required to place him in as good a position as he expected to be in when D performed.)

Assume, on the other hand, that on the day the contract was made, a corporation, D, paid Ralph $2,000 as an advance. Ralph told D the next day that he would not go through with the job, but was keeping the $2,000. If D sued Ralph, it would recover at least $2,000 in restitution.

The matter of *expectation damages* must be explored more thoroughly. Placing a plaintiff in the position they expected to be in had the defendant performed as promised is a complicated matter. The general term "expectation damages" can be broken down into at least three subcategories: (a) "direct" or "general" damages, including those losses clearly and directly caused by the defendant's breach; (b) "consequential" or "special" damages, including lost profits and injury to persons or property resulting from the defendant's defective performance; and (c) "incidental" damages, including such matters as costs incurred by the plaintiff in arranging for substitute performance.

Assume that D Corporation promised to repair a plastic-molding machine for P Corporation for $15,000 by June 1. D understood that time was of the essence, because P had a big contract to produce plastic cups that called for a June 1 start-up date. On May 20, D informed P that it would not perform its promise. P quickly but thoroughly investigated, and found that X Company was willing to make the repairs for $17,000. Working quickly, X completed the repairs on June 15, but P lost $5,000 in profits because the machine was idled for two weeks. Because it cost P $2,000 more to have the machine repaired than it would have had D performed as promised, P can recover $2,000 in *direct damages*. P will also recover $5,000 in *consequential damages* to compensate for the lost profits. Finally, any costs incurred by P in finding X could be recovered as *incidental damages*.

Although this illustration gives a general idea as to calculation of compensatory damages to redress the expectation interest, remember that there are some very important limitations on the plaintiff's recovery:

1. *Causation*. Plaintiff must prove that the defendant's breach was a "substantial factor" in bringing about his or her injury. Assume that Pam proves that she runs a retail clothing store, that Dan promised to deliver winter coats to Pam by September 1, that the coats were not delivered until October 1, and that Pam's revenues for the month of September were down 40 percent from the previous year. Pam appears to have a strong case, but if evidence adduced at trial discloses that the street leading to Pam's store was under construction during the entire month of September so that it was very difficult for customers even to reach Pam's store, and that other stores in the area also sustained lost revenue, a jury might conclude that Dan's delay was not a "substantial factor" in bringing about the plaintiff's loss.

2. *Reasonable Certainty*. Judges and juries should not have to speculate as to the amount of damages the plaintiff sustained that was due to the defendant's breach. Therefore, the plaintiff must establish losses with "reasonable certainty," a higher standard of proof than is demanded for other issues. This is often a problem in consequential damages, such as lost profits at a sports event.

Assume, for example, that Pete, a candidate for governor in a primary election, contracted to have D Newspaper Co. run one of his ads on the Sunday before election day. The newspaper failed to run the ad, and Pete lost the election. If Pete sued for the salary he would have received as governor, it would be pure speculation to conclude that the missing ad caused Pete to lose the primary election or that Pete would have won the general election had he succeeded in the primary. Therefore, a court probably would deny Pete's claim for these consequential damages.

While the law does not wish to compensate the plaintiff for losses that did not occur, at the same time persons who have breached their promises should not escape liability simply because the plaintiff cannot prove the amount of damages to the penny. For that reason, the law requires reasonable, not absolute, certainty. The UCC reflects the trend in the common law by requiring the plaintiff to prove damages not with mathematical certainty, but with "whatever definiteness and accuracy the facts permit, but no more" (§ 1-106, comment 1).

Courts often are less demanding of a plaintiff's proof where the defendant's breach was willful and in situations where precision of proof is inherently impossible (such as in calculation of loss to "goodwill"). Similarly, where a defendant's wrong has caused the difficulty in proof of damages, many courts hold that the defendant "shall not be heard to complain." In short, where the courts are certain that a breach has occurred and that the plaintiff has suffered a loss, they hesitate to deny recovery on grounds that the plaintiff has failed to establish the amount of damages to a reasonable certainty. On the other hand, where the evidence is not clear that a loss even occurred, the reasonable certainty requirement is more likely to bar recovery. An interesting illustration of these general rules follows.

ERICSON v. PLAYGIRL, INC.
California Court of Appeals, 140 Cal.Rptr. 921 (1977)

Plaintiff John Ericson, in an attempt to boost his career as an actor, agreed that defendant Playgirl, Inc. could publish without compensation as the centerfold of its January 1974 issue of Playgirl *photographs of Ericson posing naked. No immediate career boost to Ericson resulted. In April 1974, defendant wished to use the pictures again for its annual edition entitled* Best of Playgirl, *a publication with half the circulation of* Playgirl *and without the advertising. Ericson agreed to a rerun of his pictures in* Best of Playgirl *on two conditions: that certain of them be cropped to more modest exposure, and that Ericson's photograph occupy a quarter of the front cover, which would contain photographs of five other persons on its remaining three-quarters. Defendant honored the first of these conditions but, due to an editorial mix-up, Ericson's photograph did not appear on the cover of* Best of Playgirl. *Ericson sued for breach of contract, seeking to recover for the loss of publicity he would have received had his picture appeared on the cover as agreed.*

The trial court entered a $12,500 judgment on behalf of Ericson, based in large part on the testimony of an advertising manager for TV Guide who placed the value to an entertainer of an appearance on the cover of a national magazine at $50,000. (1/4 cover x $50,000 = $12,500.) Playgirl appealed.

Fleming, Acting Presiding Justice:

Damages must be clearly ascertainable and reasonably certain, both in their nature and origin. Plaintiff's claim of damages for breach of contract was based entirely on the loss of general publicity he would have received by having his photograph appear, alongside those of five others, on the cover of *Best of Playgirl*. Plaintiff proved that advertising is expensive to buy, that publicity has value for an actor. But what he did not prove was that loss of publicity as the result of his non-appearance on the cover of *Best of Playgirl* did in fact damage him in any substantial way or in any specific amount. Plaintiff's claim sharply contrasts with those few breach of contract cases that have found damages for loss of publicity reasonably certain and reasonably calculable, as in refusals to continue an advertising contract. In such cases the court has assessed damages at the market value of the advertising, less the agreed contract price. Plaintiff's claim for damages more closely resembles those which have been held speculative and conjectural, as in the analogous cases of *Jones v. San Bernardino Real Estate Board*, 336 P.2d 606 (Cal.1959), where the court declined to award purely conjectural damages for loss of commissions, contacts, business associations, and clientele allegedly occasioned by plaintiff's expulsion from a local realty board; and of *Fisher v. Hampton*, 118 Cal.Rptr. 811 (Cal.App. 1975), where the court rejected an award of damages for defendant's failure to drill a $35,000 oil well when geological reports opined that oil would not be found and no evidence whatever established that plaintiff had been damaged.

An examination of the cases allowing recovery of damages for loss of publicity as a result of breach of contract discloses that in each instance the lost publicity grew out of the loss of the artist's exercise of his profession, i.e., loss of the opportunity to act, to broadcast, to sing, to conduct an orchestra, to entertain; or resulted from the loss of credit to the artist for professional services connected with a particular work, i.e., a script, play, musical composition, design, production, and the like. Publicity in both these categories performs a similar function in that it permits patrons and producers to evaluate the artist's merits in connection with the performance of his art. Damages for the loss of such publicity do not present insuperable difficulties in calculation, for the artist's future earnings can be directly correlated to his box office appeal or to his known record of successes.

A yawning gulf exists between the cases that involve loss of professional publicity and the instant case in which plaintiff complains of loss of mere general publicity that bears no relation to the practice of his art. His situation is comparable to that of an actor who hopes to obtain wide publicity by cutting the ribbon for the opening of a new resort-hotel complex, by sponsoring a golf or tennis tournament, by presenting the winning trophy at the national horse show, or by acting as master of ceremonies at a televised political dinner. Each of these activities may generate wide publicity that conceivably could bring the artist to the attention of patrons and producers of his art and thus lead to professional employment. Yet none of it bears any relation to the practice of his art. Plaintiff's argument, in essence, is that for an actor all publicity is valuable, and the loss of any publicity as a result of breach of contract is compensable. Carried to this point, we think his claim for damages becomes wholly speculative. It is possible, as plaintiff suggests, that a television programmer might have seen his photograph on the cover of *Best of Playgirl,* might have scheduled plaintiff for a talk show, and that a motion picture producer viewing the talk show might recall plaintiff's past performances, and decide to offer him a role in his next production. But it is equally plausible to speculate that plaintiff might have been hurt professionally rather than helped by having his picture appear on the cover of *Best of Playgirl,* that a motion picture producer whose attention had been drawn by the cover of the magazine to its contents depicting plaintiff posing naked in Lion Country Safari might dismiss plaintiff from serious consideration for a role in his next production. The speculative and conjectural nature of such possibilities speaks for itself.

Assessment of the value of general publicity unrelated to professional performance takes us on a random walk whose destination is as unpredictable as the lottery and the roulette wheel. When, as at bench, damages to earning capacity and loss of professional publicity in the practice of one's art are not involved, we think recovery of compensable damages for loss of publicity is barred by the [statutory] requirement that damages for breach of contract be clearly foreseeable and clearly ascertainable.

Plaintiff, however, is entitled to recover nominal damages for breach of, contract. We evaluate plaintiff's right to nominal damages by analogy to [a California statute], which provides minimum statutory damages of $300 for knowing commercial use of a person's name or likeness without his consent. The judgment is modified to reduce the amount of damages to $300, and, as so modified, the judgment is affirmed.

Foreseeability. Another important limitation on recovery of compensatory damages is that the loss sustained by the plaintiff should have been reasonably foreseeable to the defendant. Assume that Sam's Repair Shop promised to fix Al's car and deliver it to him on June 1. Sam was a day late, delivering the car on June 2. However, on June 1, Al had been bitten by a rabid dog and his injuries had been exacerbated because he had had no car with which to drive himself to the emergency room. The extra medical injuries (potential consequential damages) could not be compensated because the injury was not reasonably foreseeable to Sam.

The leading case in this area is *Hadley v. Baxendale,* 156 Eng.Rep. 145 (1854), where plaintiff's flour mill suffered a broken gear. Plaintiff hired defendant to transport the gear and its attached drive shaft to the manufacturer for repairs. Plaintiff told defendant that the gear was part of his milling machinery and that defendant should act promptly. Plaintiff did not, however, tell defendant that his entire mill would be shut down until the repairs were made. Defendant breached the contract by performing two days late. Plaintiff sued for the profits lost during this two-day period. The court held that it was not reasonably foreseeable to defendant that plaintiff's entire operation would be shut down for two days; therefore, the lost profits could not be recovered. In so ruling, the English court set forth two important rules. First, it held that a plaintiff can recover direct damages "as may fairly and reasonably be considered ... arising naturally, i.e., according to the usual course of things" from the breach itself. Second, the court held that plaintiff may recover consequential damages "such as may reasonably be supposed to have been in the contemplation of both parties, at the time they made the contract, as the probable result of it." Thus, the court introduced reasonable foreseeability as an important aspect of recovery for consequential damages.

Reliance Measure

If the law cannot compensate the plaintiff's expectation interest, perhaps because the plaintiff cannot establish with reasonable certainty the profit he would make on the transaction, the courts often protect the reliance interest instead.

Other situations where the reliance interest is compensated include cases where a contract is frustrated by impossibility of performance or where there has been partial performance of an oral contract that the statute of frauds required to be in writing.

Plaintiffs suing for the reliance interest are allowed to recover such items as expenses incurred in preparing to perform their part of the contract, expenses incurred in actually performing, and losses incurred due to forgone opportunities that they would have pursued absent the contract with the defendant.

Assume that defendant promises to deliver a model stove to plaintiff at a trade fair. Plaintiff plans to demonstrate the stove and take orders from customers. Defendant fails to deliver the stove in time for the fair. If plaintiff could prove with reasonable certainty the profits he would have made from demonstrating the stove, he can recover them under the expectation interest. However, this is likely to be too speculative to establish with reasonable certainty. Therefore, at the very least, the court can compensate plaintiff's reliance interest by making defendant pay the costs, such as rental of the space at the trade fair and of materials to construct a booth, that plaintiff incurred in reliance on defendant's promise.

Restitution Interest

Assume that in the trade fair case, the plaintiff had made an advance payment to the defendant of $400. Because the defendant did not perform, the plaintiff should recover that amount also. The defendant has received a benefit and the law requires the defendant to make restitution to the plaintiff. The key to restitution is *unjust enrichment*—the defendant should forfeit benefits he received from the plaintiff's performance in cases where the defendant did not do as he promised. The concept of restitution pervades the law of both legal and equitable remedies, and we shall return to it later in this chapter.

Mitigation of Damages

There is no reason for the law to compensate the plaintiff for losses arising from the defendant's breach that the plaintiff could reasonably have avoided. Therefore the mitigation of damages doctrine requires plaintiffs to take reasonable steps to minimize the accumulation of damages.

Once aware of the other party's breach, a potential plaintiff may not continue his activities so as to increase his damages. For example, assume that Deeco, Inc., hires Peeco, Inc., to build a parking garage. After Peeco has spent $10,000 in commencing performance, Deeco unequivocally tells Peeco that it no longer wants the parking garage built and will not pay for it. If Peeco continues to work on the garage, spending another $8,000, it clearly has failed to mitigate its damages. It may recover the first $10,000, but not the subsequent $8,000, which was clearly avoidable.

A party may even be obliged to take positive steps to minimize damages. For example, assume that Juanita has a five-year contract to work for Acme Corporation as a research chemist. After one year, Acme fires Juanita without cause. Juanita should not sit home for the next four years. If she does, passing up several opportunities to obtain comparable jobs at comparable pay, the law will not compensate her for her lost salary. Instead, the law places on Juanita the obligation to make reasonable efforts to find comparable work. She needs not take a job that does not utilize her education, nor need she move across the country in order to find a position. Reasonableness is the key. At the same time, any reasonable expenses Juanita incurs (e.g., hiring an employment agency) in attempting to mitigate her damages are compensable, even if ultimately unsuccessful.

The duty to mitigate is incorporated in Article 2 of the Uniform Commercial Code. When a buyer of goods breaches a contract, the seller is often obliged to make conscientious efforts to find another buyer for those goods. If the second buyer pays less, the seller may recover from the breaching party not only the difference in purchase price but also the incidental expenses incurred in finding a new buyer.

Although almost every party in every situation has a duty to mitigate, a majority of jurisdictions make an exception for landlords where a lease has been executed. They do not require the landlord to search for a new tenant when the current tenant breaches its lease by moving out and refusing to pay rent. Many jurisdictions, on the other hand, do not recognize this exception.

Consider one other wrinkle. Assume that Acme has contracted to rent a truck from We-Haul Leasing, Inc. Acme breaches, but points out to We-Haul that it can mitigate its damages by leasing the truck to the next customer that comes in needing a truck. However, if We-Haul has a different truck that it would have rented to that next customer, then it cannot effectively mitigate its damages. It could have had two rentals if Acme had lived up to its part of the lease. Therefore, We-Haul may recover from Acme.

Nominal Damages

Nominal damages are a form of compensatory damages given in a trivial amount (such as six cents or one dollar). It is appropriate to grant nominal damages, for example, where the plaintiff establishes a breach of contract but cannot prove his or her damages with reasonable certainty. *Ericson v. Playgirl, Inc.* is an example (although a special statute established a minimum recovery of $300). Nominal damages are also appropriate to remedy a technical breach of contract in situations where the plaintiff did not suffer any injury. Assume that P contracts to sell a tract of land to D for $50,000. D breaches, refusing to pay anything, and P sues. Before the suit progresses very far, a new buyer appears and pays P $70,000 for the land. P has not suffered any injury from D's breach. Still, D has breached a promise and the court will, as a matter of principle, allow P to recover nominal damages. In addition to the principle at stake, P is now the prevailing party in the lawsuit, making D responsible for paying court costs (but usually not attorney's fees) in many jurisdictions. (Other jurisdictions do not allow the plaintiff to recover court costs unless a specified minimum amount has been recovered. Such statutes are aimed at discouraging litigation over valid but trivial claims.)

Liquidated Damages

A *liquidated damages* provision is a clause in a contract that stipulates the amount of damages that will be paid in the event of a breach. Such a clause has several purposes. It may avoid a protracted dispute and trial on the issue of damages. This will lower the parties' costs of proof and society's cost of providing a judge and jury. Such a clause may diminish the losses of the defaulting party or, conversely, establish a minimum level of recovery from the non-defaulting party in a case where losses may well be speculative. It allows both parties to better calculate their level of risk in a given transaction.

Courts generally wish to enforce contracts as made by the parties, but they do tend to be leery of liquidated damages clauses, mostly out of a fear that such clauses may be used as a "penalty" to unfairly punish or coerce one of the parties. Typically, courts set forth three criteria for an enforceable liquidated damages clause. First, the injury arising from the breach must be difficult or impossible to estimate accurately. If the amount of damages arising from a breach is easy to determine, a liquidated damages clause does not save trial time and expense and therefore loses much of its justification. Second, the parties must intend for the clause to provide a remedy for the injured party, not a penalty for the defaulting party. This relates back to the notion that part of the freedom of contract is the freedom to breach a contract.

In virtually every case involving the enforceability of a liquidated damages clause, the focus of the court becomes the third criterion—whether the amount established as liquidated damages is a *reasonable* estimate of the actual loss caused by the subsequent breach. The courts will not enforce a clause that sets an amount so far above the true damages sustained that it constitutes a *penalty* imposed on the defendant rather than legitimate compensation for the plaintiff's loss. The reasonableness of the estimate is judged as of the time the contract is entered into, although UCC § 2-718(1) allows amounts that are reasonable considering anticipated or actual harm. (Indeed, even at common law if the estimate turns out to be wildly inaccurate as a gauge of the actual damages, even if it seemed reasonable when the contract was made, the courts are unlikely to enforce it.)

Whether a liquidated damages clause is an unenforceable penalty provision is a matter of law for the judge to decide. The labels used by the parties in the contract do not control. In *U.S. v. Bethlehem Steel Co.*, 205 U.S. 105 (1907), because of a promise for early delivery, the government agreed to buy guns from defendant even though its bid was higher than those of competitors. The contract provided that for each day defendant's delivery was late, a "penalty" of $35 would be imposed. Because this sum represented the average difference in price between defendant's bid and those of the cheaper, but slower, suppliers, it was enforced as a genuine attempt to gauge the government's actual damages.

One form of liquidated damages clause that is almost always enforced is that calling for the breaching party to pay the attorney's fees of the non-defaulting party who is forced to bring a lawsuit.

UNITED AIR LINES, INC. v. AUSTIN TRAVEL CORP.
U.S. Court of Appeals, 2d Circuit, 867 F.2d 737 (1989)

Plaintiff United Air Lines owns and markets to travel agents the Apollo CRS, a computerized reservation system that provides subscribers access to a vast data bank through which they may make airline reservations, issue tickets, and reserve car rentals and hotel rooms. United is paid a monthly subscription fee and charges airlines a booking fee each time a travel agent uses Apollo to book a flight on another airline. United also markets its ABS, a back-office accounting and management system for travel agents.

Defendant Austin is a travel agency that formerly used a different CRS. However, in 1985 it acquired two small travel agencies (Karson and Fantasy) that subscribed to Apollo. Austin assumed their contracts with United and then executed a five-year Apollo contract to cover its Oceanside and Mitchell Field locations. The contract for Oceanside and Mitchell Field provided for liquidated damages consisting of (1) 80 percent of the remaining monthly fees due under the contract, (2) 80 percent of the variable charges accrued by generation of tickets and itineraries for the month preceding termination, multiplied by the number of months remaining on the contract, and (3) 50 percent of the average monthly booking fee revenues, using the first six months of the contract as a basis for calculation, multiplied by the number of months remaining on the contract. The Fantasy contract contained only the first two elements of liquidated damages.

Austin breached the agreement when one of United's rivals offered to indemnify Austin for any damages incurred for breach if it would terminate the Apollo contracts and buy the rival's system. United brought this breach of contract action. The trial judge held for United, ruling, most importantly, that the liquidated damages clauses were valid and enforceable. Austin appealed.

Miner, Circuit Judge:

It is commonplace for contracting parties to determine in advance the amount of compensation due in case of a breach of contract. 5 CORBIN ON CONTRACTS § 1054, at 319 (1964). A liquidated damages clause generally will be upheld by a court, unless the liquidated amount is a penalty because it is plainly or grossly disproportionate to the probable loss anticipated when the contract was executed. Liquidated damages are not penalties if they bear a "reasonable proportion to the probable loss and the amount of actual loss is incapable or difficult of precise estimation." *Leasing Service Corp v. Justice*, 673 F.2d 70, 73 (2d Cir. 1982).

The liquidated damages fixed in the Apollo contracts were, as the district court found, reasonable at the time the contracts were executed. Most of United's costs when providing Apollo service are either fixed or determined in the early stages of the contractual relationship. The few costs that United would avoid by an early termination of an Apollo contract are estimated to be "less than 20 percent of the amount of revenue from the monthly fixed usage fees and variable charges." The Apollo contracts' liquidated damages clauses provide for recovery by United of only 80% of the fixed and variable charges. Austin is thus provided with better than adequate credit for the costs United is able to avoid by the early removal of the Apollo CRSs from Austin premises.

Austin complains that the 20% discount incorporated by the liquidated damages provisions underestimates the savings realized by United in the event of early contract termination. Austin points to testimony by a representative of a competing CRS vendor that United's avoidable costs likely equal forty to fifty percent of United's total costs. The testimony of a competitor about United's costs and savings is inherently suspect, and United presented sufficient evidence to justify the 20% figure. The appropriate analysis is not whether a better quantification of damages could have been drafted by the contracting parties, but whether the amount of liquidated damages actually inserted in the contract is reasonable. We note as well, as the district court did, that CRS contracts of United's competitors often call for 100% of rent due on the unexpired term of the contract; United obligated Austin for only 80%. There is no indication that the estimate of probable loss, identified in the contracts as liquidated damages, is either unfair or unreasonable. Indeed, the liquidated damages provisions edge closer toward over-generousness to Austin than they do toward unreasonableness.

Austin further depicts the liquidated damages clauses as imposing penalties because they provide the same amount of damages for each possible breach of the contract, no matter how insignificant. Austin argues that establishing a single liquidated damages amount for any breach indicates that a fair estimation of probable loss for each breach was not conceived when the contract was drafted and executed.

Austin, however, ignores basic tenets of contract law. "A party may terminate a contract only because of substantial nonperformance by the other party so fundamental 'as to defeat the objects of the parties in making the agreement'." *Maywood Sportservice, Inc. v. Maywood Park Trotting Ass'n, Inc.*, 14 Ill.App.3d 141, 302 N.E.2d 79, 84 (1973). Neither United nor Austin can terminate the contracts because of a non-material breach. Thus, liquidated damages can only be owed to United in the event of a material breach by Austin.

Furthermore, the presumed intent of the parties is that a liquidated damages provision will apply only to material breaches. Additionally, for a non-material breach to allow an aggrieved party to abrogate the contract it must be explicitly stated in the agreement of the parties. We are not persuaded that the liquidated damages outlined in the Apollo contracts were meant to apply to trivial breaches. Article 12 of the Lease Agreement states in unexceptional language that liquidated damages are to be awarded for a failure of "any of the covenants, agreements, terms or conditions." We take this language to refer to material breach. Absent a more explicit demonstration of intent to apply the termination provisions to trivial breaches, the liquidated damages clauses must be enforced. [Affirmed.]

Equitable Remedies

Courts of equity developed in England because the early courts at law could give only one form of remedy—money damages. In other words, they could award a landowner damages caused by a neighbor's trespassing, but could not order the neighbor not to trespass again in the future. Courts of equity developed in large part to provide more flexible forms of remedy in situations where fairness seemed to demand them. Several forms of equitable remedy are available to the party injured by breach of contract. Whereas damages are generally assessed by juries, equitable remedies are within the province of the court and are enforced through the court's authority to hold in contempt persons who violate its orders.

Specific Performance

When a plaintiff asks the court for an order of *specific performance*, they are asking the judge to order the defendant to perform the promise that was made. Obviously there may be many instances where specific performance is a remedy that a plaintiff would prefer. If the judge orders specific performance, the plaintiff receives exactly what was bargained for and need not worry about collecting a money judgment or searching for someone to provide substitute performance.

Nonetheless, the courts presume that an award of money damages is the primary remedy in breach-of-contract cases. Specific performance is reserved for the "extraordinary" cases where money damages are inadequate to fully compensate the plaintiff. Specific performance is most frequently ordered when "unique" property is at stake, so that an award of money damages would not fully compensate the plaintiff who could not take the money anywhere to buy the item originally contracted for. Assume, for example, that plaintiff contracted to buy a secret recipe from defendant. If defendant breached its promise to deliver the recipe, an award of damages to plaintiff would not enable plaintiff to obtain the recipe elsewhere, because it remains defendant's trade secret.

Other items often held to be "unique" include rare books and coins, family heirlooms, priceless works of art, items in extremely short supply, patents, copyrights, and shares of closely held corporations which cannot be bought through any market or stockbroker. For historical reasons, courts view every tract of land as unique (even though it may be the same size and have the same characteristics as a tract adjacent to it). Therefore, contracts to sell real property are always enforceable through orders of specific performance. The same may be said of contracts to sell businesses, for these are also presumed to be unique.

Courts will often specifically enforce contracts against *insolvent* defendants, because an award of money damages against a defendant who cannot pay is certainly not adequate compensation. (Conflicts with the priorities given creditors under the bankruptcy laws must be avoided, however.) Specific performance is often granted in cases where the plaintiff's monetary damages are difficult to measure with reasonable certainty; absent specific performance, the plaintiff might be relegated to mere nominal damages.

Limitations. There are several factors that limit the availability of the specific performance remedy. First and foremost, specific performance is available only within the *discretion* of a court of equity. In attempting to achieve fairness and equity, courts must consider such factors as hardship to the defendant and impact on societal interests.

Additionally, courts consider traditional equitable rules such as the "clean hands" doctrine (no equitable remedy will be granted to a plaintiff who has breached his or her obligations in any material way), the doctrine of unconscionability (the courts will not be a party to enforcing an extremely one-sided bargain), and the doctrine of laches (no remedy for a party who has "slept on his rights" by unduly delaying the bringing of suit). Obviously courts will not order specific performance in contracts that involve illegality, mistake, or fraud.

Specific performance will not be granted in *personal service contracts*. Assume that Sally hires Waldo to paint her portrait because he is the best-known portrait artist in the state and Sally's personal favorite. If Waldo refuses to live up to his obligations the court might allow Sally to recover damages, but would not order specific performance. One reason often given is that it would violate the Thirteenth Amendment's proscription against involuntary servitude to force Waldo to paint against his will. A more plausible policy ground is the *difficulty of supervision* involved. How could a court effectively enforce Waldo's obligation? How could it supervise him to ensure that he did a "good job"? A court can transfer title to land, but it cannot paint for Waldo or sing for a reluctant rock star. For the same reason, courts often refuse to order specific performance in long-term contracts that might require them to undertake years of supervision.

Specific performance and damages are normally thought of as alternative forms of remedies. However, a plaintiff might be able to obtain both in the same case, especially if a court could feasibly order only partial performance by the defendant.

UCC. If there has been any trend in the common law of specific performance in recent years, it has been to soften the "adequacy" of remedy test, thereby increasing the availability of specific performance. That trend is reflected in UCC § 2-716, which authorizes specific performance in sale-of-goods contracts "where the goods are unique or in *other proper circumstances*." [Emphasis added.] Still, even under the UCC, specific performance remains an "extraordinary" remedy.

Injunction

Assume that Chuck, a football coach, has a five-year contract with the Armadillos, an NFL franchise. In the second year of the contract, Chuck is offered a much more lucrative deal by Big State University and announces that he is accepting it. Obviously the Armadillos will wish to force Chuck to live up to his contract. Just as obviously, no court would order Chuck to specifically perform that contract. In addition to the "involuntary servitude" consideration, there is the difficulty of supervision. How could a court ensure that Chuck hired the right assistants, kept the best players, or called the appropriate plays? However, while a court could not feasibly order Chuck to do what he had promised to do (coach the Armadillos), it could order him not to do what he had promised not to do (coach Big State U). By signing a full-time contract with the Armadillos, Chuck had implicitly promised not to take any conflicting obligations. Such an order is called an *injunction.*

As with orders of specific performance, injunctive orders are within the court's equitable discretion. Courts will consider factors of fairness, unconscionability, and the plaintiff's *clean hands* in deciding whether to issue such orders. Injunctions are often used in cases involving sports and entertainment, and in normal employment relationships when a party seeks to enforce a covenant not to compete signed by a former employee. We studied the enforceability of these covenants in Chapter 13.

Reformation

Assume that Sharon and Nick reach an oral agreement that Nick's attorney reduces to writing. After the contract is signed, Sharon realizes that because of the attorney's error, the writing does not accurately reflect the oral agreement. Sharon may ask a court for an order of *reformation*. In effect, Sharon is asking the court to rewrite the contract, but only for the limited purpose of enforcing its true terms. The court is not making a new contract, but simply enforcing the parties' agreement as made. Sharon should have read the contract before she signed it, but if she can prove that an error has caused a discrepancy between the oral agreement and the written contract, her negligence would not bar reformation in most courts.

The parol evidence rule (see Chapter 15), which prevents introduction of oral testimony to vary the terms of a written contract, would not block Sharon's efforts in this case. It applies only when the writing was intended to be the final and complete statement of the parties' agreement. Most courts conclude that such is not the case where an error in reducing the oral agreement to writing has occurred.

However, the statute of frauds (see Chapter 15, again) does pose serious problems. What if the agreement is the type that the statute of frauds requires to be in writing? Is Sharon asking the court to enforce an oral agreement in contravention of the statute of frauds? Some courts think that this is exactly what she is asking, and will refuse reformation. Other courts reason that they are simply correcting the mistaken written agreement, and will grant reformation.

In relatively rare instances, some courts will reform contracts not to enforce the parties' original agreement, but to modify that original agreement to conform to the law. For example, we learned in Chapter 13 that if a covenant not to compete is drawn too broadly, many courts will rewrite it to cover a smaller geographic area or a shorter time span and will then enforce the modified version.

Rescission

An order of *rescission* is a court order terminating the contractual duties of each party. Usually (but not always) such an order will also allow each party to obtain restitution for any performance rendered to the other party. Rescission is granted as a remedy in a wide variety of contracts, including those involving voidable agreements (e.g., fraud, mistake, undue influence, innocent misrepresentation, or parties lacking capacity) and those involving illegal activity.

Restitution

An order of *restitution* seeks to place a party in the position they were in before the contract was entered into. As noted earlier in this chapter, sometimes such an order will take the form of a damages award telling the defendant to pay the plaintiff the monetary value of the benefit the plaintiff conferred on the defendant. But the notion of restitution is very broad. It can also include an equitable order for the defendant to return specific property that the plaintiff transferred to the defendant pursuant to the agreement that the defendant has breached or the court is rescinding (on grounds of mistake, indefiniteness, lack of capacity, statute of frauds violation, etc.).

Assume, for example, that plaintiff transferred a cow to defendant, both parties believing that the cow was barren but having since discovered that the cow was pregnant at the time of the contract (see mistake cases, Chapter 14). Plaintiff will ask the judge for rescission and for an order of specific restitution, requiring defendant to return the cow. Courts are generally willing to grant restitution in mistake cases (unless defendant has already transferred the cow to an innocent third party). However, had this been a breach case where no mistake was made but the defendant simply failed to pay the purchase price, most courts would refuse to issue an order of rescission, reasoning that money damages would adequately compensate the plaintiff.

Restitution, generally speaking, is used not to enforce promises, but to prevent unjust enrichment by returning the parties to their pre-contract positions following rescission or breach.

PART III
SALES, COMMERCIAL TRANSACTIONS, AND BANKRUPTCY

CHAPTER 19

INTRODUCTION TO THE LAW OF SALES

- Scope of Article 2 of the UCC
- Review of Basic Principles of Sales Contracts
- CISG
- Documents of Title

A college student purchases a cell phone. A home owner buys several cans of house paint. A manufacturer of computer chips purchases silicon and other materials and ultimately sells chips to a computer maker. All of the above have at least two things in common. First, they are ordinary transactions of the type occurring countless times a day. Second, they involve sales of *goods*. Thus, we can hardly question the relevance of studying the law of sales.

The principles governing sales of goods do not exist in a vacuum. Indeed, Article 2 of the Uniform Commercial Code (UCC), which provides the legal rules for contracts selling goods, is closely related to the common law which governs other types of contracts. Thus, in explaining contract law (Chapters 10–18), we have already noted pertinent instances where the UCC altered the common law in order to facilitate commercial transactions in goods. (These concepts are briefly recapitulated later in this chapter.) In Chapters 19-20, we will explore in more detail the law governing the sale of goods. In so doing, we will also treat a few closely related matters, such as the law regarding leases of goods and another subject known as *documents of title.*

SCOPE OF ARTICLE 2 OF THE UCC

Article 2 of the UCC deals with the sale of goods. It forms the basis for most of the following discussion of the law of sales.

Sale of Goods Contracts

A sale is defined in §2-106 of the UCC as "the passing of title from the seller to the buyer for a price." Thus, Article 2 does not apply to leases (such as the lease of an automobile) or to other types of bailments (such as the storage of furniture in a warehouse) because only temporary possession of the goods (rather than title) is transferred in these transactions. Article 2 also does not apply to gifts, because no price is paid. A barter transaction *(i.e.,* the trading of goods for other goods or services without the exchange of money) *is*, however, governed by Article 2.

Goods

In the majority of cases there is no problem ascertaining whether the subject matter should be classified as *goods*. Occasionally, however, the term may present problems. Essentially, two requirements must be met before a particular item of property is classified as a good:

1. It must be *tangible.* In other words, it must have a physical existence. Thus, intangible property such as a patent, copyright, trademark, investment security, or contract right would not come within the scope of Article 2.
2. It must be *movable.* This requirement obviously excludes real estate, which is tangible but not movable. (Of course, almost anything, even real estate, is capable of being moved, shovel by shovel, if enough effort is expended. But the word is intended reasonably rather than literally.)

Using these two requirements we can easily envision the wide variety of products that are classified as goods, from airplanes to computers to toothpaste.

Should things that are attached to real estate be considered goods? Because of the movability requirement this question would involve considerable conceptual difficulty were it not for §2-107 of the UCC, which sets forth the following basic rules:

1. A contract for the sale of *minerals or a structure* (such as a building or its materials) is a contract for the sale of goods if they are to be severed from the land by the *seller*. If, however, they are to be severed from the land by the *buyer*, the transaction is a sale of real estate and is governed by the principles of real estate law rather than by the UCC. Two examples may be of some help. First, suppose that S and B agree that S will sell to B a quantity of gravel to be taken from beneath the surface of land owned by S. If their agreement states that S will dig and remove the gravel, the transaction is a sale of goods. If, on the other hand, B is to dig and remove the gravel, the transaction is a sale of real estate. Second, suppose that S and B agree that S will sell to B a storage building (or perhaps the lumber from the building) located on land owned by S. If their agreement indicates that B will remove the building from the land, the transaction is a sale of real estate. If removal is to be by S, it is a sale of goods.

2. A contract for the sale of *growing crops or timber* is a contract for the sale of goods, regardless of who is to sever them from the land.

3. A contract for the sale of *anything else attached to real estate* is a sale of goods if it can be severed *without material harm* to the real estate. For example: X and Y agree that X will sell to Y a window air conditioner that is now attached to X's home. The air conditioner is bolted to a metal shelf supported by braces that are secured to the side of the house by bolts. It is fairly evident that the air conditioner can be removed without material harm to the real estate. Suppose, however, that the subject of the sale is a floor furnace. In this case a gaping hole in the floor would result. This would be a material harm, causing the sale to be treated as a sale of real estate rather than goods.

The rules regarding sales of goods attached to real estate apply to those contracts under which the items are being sold apart from the land. However, if two parties agree that one will sell a tract of land to the other, including a building or some timber located on the land, the sale is treated as a sale of real estate.

The UCC also gives special attention to three other potential problems of classification. It provides that (1) unborn animals are goods; (2) money treated as a commodity, such as a rare coin, is a good (though money used as a medium of exchange is not); and (3) things that are specially manufactured for the buyer are goods. Although item #3 seems clear-cut, the framers of Article 2 felt that such a sale might be seen as predominantly a sale of services rather than goods and therefore stated it definitely.

Sales of services (such as construction and employment contracts) are obviously not within the scope of Article 2. However, as we saw in item 3, goods and services sometimes are so entwined that classification is no easy task. For example, when a hospital supplies blood to a patient, is the hospital selling a good or supplying a service? When a beautician applies hair dye to a customer's hair in a beauty parlor, is it a contract for goods or services? In such contracts involving both goods and services, most courts attempt to determine whether the *predominant factor, thrust, and purpose* of the transaction as a whole is that of selling a good or supplying a service. This determination often turns on the intent of the buyer, as gauged by several factors, including the relative dollar value involved.

For example, in *De Filippo v. Ford Motor Co.*, 516 F.2d 1313 (3d Cir. 1975), the court held that the sale of a car dealership, which included sales of items that were clearly goods (e.g., cars, parts, and accessories) as well as items that clearly were intangible and therefore not goods (e.g., goodwill, notes receivable, and used car warranties), was predominantly a sale of goods because the contract's terms assigned little dollar value to the intangible items. The court refused to split the contract into two parts, applying the UCC to one portion but not to the other.

And in *Grossman v. Aerial Farm Service, Inc.*, 384 N.W.2d 488 (Minn.App. 1986), the court held that a contract for the aerial spraying of a herbicide on a farm was predominantly a contract for services because the farmers could have applied the herbicide through several methods of ground spraying, but chose a method of application that could be performed only by a contractor equipped to handle their specific request. Thus, the farmers' selection of this type of service gave the contract its predominant character.

The UCC provides in §2-314(1) that food sold in restaurants is a sale of goods (at least as far as creation of the implied warranty of merchantability is concerned), although an argument could be made that the predominant reason a person dines out is the service. The following case illustrates how challenging these issues can be.

ROTTNER v. AVG TECHNOLOGIES USA, INC.
U.S. Dist. Court, District of Massachusetts, 2013 U.S. Dist. LEXIS 63595 (2013)

PC TuneUp is software advertised to optimize a computer's performance by scanning the operating system and removing and fixing harmful errors. Defendants, including AVG Technologies, design and sell PC TuneUp. In February of 2012, plaintiff Rottner's computer began malfunctioning. The internet speed also appeared sluggish. Rottner searched for software that would repair the internal problems and boost the computer's overall performance. His search turned up an advertisement for a free trial of PC TuneUp, which, in turn, led to AVG's website. The website claimed that PC TuneUp would boost internet speed, eliminate freezing and crashing, optimize disk space and speeds, extend battery life, protect privacy, monitor hard drive health, and restore the PC to its peak performance.

However, when Rottner downloaded, installed, and ran the trial version of PC TuneUp, his computer's performance became worse rather than better. In following defendants' additional instructions to try to make PC TuneUp work, Rottner lost personal files and had to reformat his hard drive.

Rottner sued defendants for, among other theories, breach of express warranty and of the implied warranty of merchantability. Defendants moved to dismiss, arguing that the software in question was not a "good" within the meaning of the UCC and that, therefore, no implied warranty of merchantability could exist.

Stearns, District Judge:

Defendants contend that the claims for breach of express and implied warranties are inapplicable in this case because those claims are pled under Article 2 of the Uniform Commercial Code (UCC), which covers sales of goods, UCC §2-102, whereas software — the subject of this dispute — is not, according to AVG, a "good" under Delaware law. AVG relies on two cases — *Neilson Bus. Equip. Ctr. v Italo Monteleone*, 524 A.2d 1172 (Del. 1987) and *Wharton Mgmt. Grp. v. Sigma Consultants, Inc.*, 1990 Del. Super. LEXIS 54 (Del. Super. 1990)—for this proposition.

In *Neilson*, the court held that a lease of computer hardware, software, and support services was predominantly a contract for goods, and thus came under Article 2 of the UCC. However, the court left open the question of whether the sale of software alone would be considered a sale of a good under Article 2. In *Wharton*, the court distinguished *Neilson* and found that the sale of customized software was a contract for services, and not goods, under the UCC.

Rottner distinguishes the sale of a software package, as in this case, with cases involving the design of software or the transfer of intellectual property. Although the Delaware courts have not directly addressed this distinction, courts nationally have consistently classified the sale of a software package as the sale of a good for UCC purposes. Rottner's is the more persuasive view of this dispute. Software is not clearly a good or a service in the abstract, and may qualify as either depending on the particular circumstances of the case. *See RRX Indus., Inc. v. Lab-Con, Inc.* 772 F.2d 543 (9th Cir. 1985) ("Because software packages vary depending on the needs of the individual consumer, we apply a case-by-case analysis."). Delaware, like other jurisdictions that have adopted the UCC, applies a "predominance" test to determine whether a contract is for goods or services. *See Neilson.*

The holding of *Neilson* turned on the fact that the contract involved the sale of tangible hardware along with software and services, and thus is readily distinguishable from this case. However, PC TuneUp also bears no resemblance to the custom designed software in *Wharton.* In *Wharton,* the programmer had to "prepare a study of the customer's existing operations, to design, develop, and install computer software which would meet [his] specific needs and objectives." In essence, "it was [the programmer's] knowledge, skill and ability for which Wharton bargained . . . [and] purchased in the main . . . The means of transmission is not the object of the agreement." In contrast, PC TuneUp is a "generally available standardized software." *Olcott Int'l & Co. v. Micro Data Base Sys., Inc.,* 793 N.E.2d 1063 (Ind.App. 2003) (distinguishing "the development of a software program to meet a customer's specific needs" as a contract for services). Thus, the sale of PC TuneUp is more like the sale of a tangible good—it is "movable at the time of identification to the contract for sale." UCC §2-105. Indeed, Rottner was able to download and install the full version of PC TuneUp after a one-stop payment over the internet. Because the sale of PC TuneUp is predominantly like the sale of a good rather than the provision of services, the UCC warranty provisions apply. The motion to dismiss is denied.

Merchants

For the most part, Article 2 applies to all sales contracts, even those in which neither the seller nor the buyer is a merchant. However, a few provisions of Article 2 do require one or both of the parties to be merchants in order for such provisions to be applicable. For this reason, we will now examine the UCC definition of a *merchant.*

Most people who see the word *merchant* probably think of someone engaged in the retail grocery business, the retail clothing business, or similar endeavors. While such people (or corporations) are indeed merchants, the UCC definition includes many others as well, such as manufacturers, wholesalers, and others.

Sec. 2-104 of the UCC details three different ways in which a person or organization can be considered a merchant.

1. One who "deals in goods of the kind" that are involved under the particular contract in question is a merchant; thus, not only retailers but also wholesalers and even manufacturers are merchants. Parties are considered merchants, however, only for the types of goods dealt with regularly in their businesses. That is, a merchant in one type of goods is not a merchant for all purposes. Thus a retail shoe seller is a merchant with respect to transactions involving the purchase or sale of shoes. But if that person buys a new car or sells a secondhand lawn mower, he or she is not a merchant in those transactions.

2. Even if a person does not regularly "deal" in a particular type of goods, he is nevertheless a merchant if he "by his occupation holds himself out as having knowledge or skill peculiar to the practices or goods involved in the transaction." While most persons who fall within this provision are also merchants under the first provision by dealing in the particular goods, there are a few who do not really deal in goods but who are merchants within this second category. For example, if we assume that the word deal means "to buy and sell goods," a building contractor does not actually deal in goods. He buys building materials but does not resell them; instead he uses them in the performance of a service—constructing a building. However, he does, by his occupation, hold himself out as having "knowledge or skill peculiar to the practices or goods" involved in certain transactions and thereby is a merchant by definition. Of course, his status is irrelevant in any agreement to construct a building, because that agreement is essentially for services and not within the scope of Article 2. But his status as a merchant can be important with respect to a dispute arising from the sale contract between him and his materials supplier.

3. If parties are not merchants under either of the first two categories, they may nevertheless be treated as one by *employing a merchant* to act in their behalf in a particular transaction. The UCC states that one is a merchant if one employs "an agent or broker or other intermediary who by his occupation holds himself out" as having knowledge or skill peculiar to the goods or practices involved in the transaction. Suppose, for example, that Smith, who does not regularly deal in grain, hires a professional grain broker to procure a large quantity of feed for Smith's cattle. In this situation Smith is considered a merchant.

The common thread running through all the above categories of merchants is the possession of or access to a degree of commercial expertise not found in a member of the general public. The UCC occasionally treats merchants differently than nonmerchants. For example, it imposes a higher duty of "good faith" on them. Also, some provisions of the UCC apply only to merchants who are deemed such because they deal in goods, while others apply only to merchants who are deemed such because they hold themselves out as having skill peculiar to the practice. In most provisions, both types of merchants are treated in the same manner.

Courts in different states have taken various views as to whether a farmer or rancher is a "merchant" for UCC purposes. The following case represents one point of view.

BROOKS COTTON CO. v. WILLIAMS
Tennessee Court of Appeals, 381 S.W.3d 414 (2012)

Defendant/Appellant Williams is a cotton and soybean farmer with a high school education. According to Plaintiff/Appellee Brooks Cotton Co. Williams orally agreed to sell his entire 2010 cotton production to Brooks Cotton at a specified price. Williams ultimately produced approximately 1206 bales of cotton in 2010, but delivered only a small portion of it to Brooks Cotton.

Because Williams did not live up to the contract, Brooks Cotton sued for breach of the oral agreement. Williams contended that the contract was unenforceable because it was not in writing as required by the UCC's statute of frauds provision. However, Brooks Cotton sent written confirmation of the alleged agreement to Williams within 30 days after the oral agreement. Because Williams did not object or respond to the written confirmation, the oral agreement for sale of goods is enforceable, but only if both parties to the contract are merchants. The trial court held in ruling on a summary judgment motion that Willliams was a merchant. He appealed.

486 © 2020 John R. Allison & Robert A. Prentice

Stafford, Judge:

The term "merchant" is defined by Tennessee law:

"Merchant" means a person who deals in goods of the kind or otherwise by his occupation holds himself out as having knowledge or skill peculiar to the practices or goods involved in the transaction or to whom such knowledge or skill may be attributed by his employment of an agent or broker or other intermediary who by his occupation holds himself out as having such knowledge or skill.

U.C.C. §2-104(1). Accordingly, a contract "'[b]etween merchants' means [] any transaction with respect to which both parties are chargeable with the knowledge or skill of merchants."

The framers of the U.C.C. intended the term merchant to encompass three distinct classes. Accordingly, for individuals to be considered merchants, they must be either:

1. A person who deals in goods of the kind;
2. A person who by his occupation holds himself out as having knowledge or skill peculiar to the practices or goods involved in the transaction; or
3. A person who employs an agent or broker or other intermediary who by his occupation holds himself out as having such knowledge or skill.

While this definition is instructive, it does not end the inquiry into whether a farmer is one who "deals in goods" or who "by his occupation holds himself out as having knowledge or skill peculiar to the practices or goods involved in the transaction." Accordingly, we must look beyond the plain language of the statute in order to determine whether a farmer is a merchant under the UCC Statute of Frauds.

According to *Williston on Contracts*, the question of whether a farmer can be a merchant for purposes of the Statute of Frauds has led to different applications among the states. …In some cases, it has been noted that the duty imposed upon the farmer as a merchant is based on the principle that a farmer is only required to have nonspecialized business knowledge to be considered a merchant. On the other hand, it has been noted that the term "merchant" as defined in Uniform Commercial Code § 2-104(1) has its roots in the law merchant concept of a professional in business, suggesting that farmers do not solely by virtue of their occupation hold themselves out as being professional merchants.

Mr. Williams cites various cases that have applied the above rule and found that a farmer cannot be considered a merchant for purposes of the Statute of Frauds. … However, many of the courts cited by Mr. Williams note that a farmer could be considered a merchant, but that the facts simply were insufficient to conclude that the farmer was a merchant in that particular case.

In contrast, Brooks Cotton cites a number of jurisdictions where the courts have found that a farmer may qualify as a merchant for purposes of the Statute of Frauds. … In *Goldkist, Inc. v. Brownlee,* 355 S.E.2d 773 (Ga.App. 1987), the court held that farmers who were familiar with the practice of oral booking of crops, as was allegedly practiced in this case, could be considered merchants for purposes of the Statute of Frauds:

To allow a farmer who deals in crops of the kind at issue, or who otherwise comes within the definition of "merchant" [for purposes of the Statute of Frauds], to renege on a confirmed oral booking for the sale of crops, would result in a fraud on the buyer. The farmer could abide by the booking if the price thereafter declined but reject it if the price rose; the buyer, on the other hand, would be forced to sell the crop following the booking at its peril, or wait until the farmer decides whether to honor the booking or not.

Defendants' narrow construction of "merchant" would, given the booking procedure used for the sale of farm products, thus guarantee to the farmers the best of both possible worlds (fulfill booking if price goes down after booking and reject it if price improves) and to the buyers the worst of both possible worlds. On the other hand, construing "merchants" [for purposes of the Statute of Frauds] as not excluding as a matter of law farmers such as the ones in this case, protects them equally as well as the buyer. If the market price declines after the booking, they are assured of the higher booking price; the buyer cannot renege, as [the merchant exception to the Statute of Frauds] would apply.

We conclude that the framers of the U.C.C. did not intend to exclude all farmers from the category of merchants, simply because a farmer's primary occupation is the cultivation, rather than the sale, of crops. The sale of crops is as integral to the business of commercial farming as the cultivation. The framers included crops in their definition of goods. Therefore, the framers clearly intended to include those that sell crops commercially in the definition of merchant, so long as that person either "deals in goods of the kind" or who "by his occupation holds himself out as having knowledge or skill peculiar to the practices or goods involved in the transaction." In addition, the definition of merchant is broadly construed for purposes of the Statute of Frauds, encompassing "almost every person in business," including an experienced commercial farmer.

Based on the foregoing, we cannot conclude that the framers intentionally intended to omit experienced commercial farmers from the category of merchants. Accordingly, we adopt the rule that a farmer may be considered a merchant for the purposes of the merchant exception to the Statute of Frauds, when the farmer possesses sufficient expertise in not only the cultivation, but also the sale of crops. ... Trial courts should consider the following, nonexhaustive, criteria in determining whether a particular farmer is a merchant for purposes of the Statute of Frauds:

> (1) The length of time the farmer has been engaged in the practice of selling his product to the marketers of his product; (2) the degree of business acumen shown by the farmer in his dealings with other parties; (3) the farmer's awareness of the operation and existence of farm markets; and (4) the farmer's past experience with or knowledge of the customs and practices which are unique to the particular marketing of the product which he sells.

Colorado-Kansas Grain Co. v. Reifschneider, 817 P.2d 631 (Colo. App. 1991).

Applying the above factors to Mr. Williams ... there are facts in this case both supporting and undermining a conclusion that Mr. Williams is a merchant for purposes of the U.C.C. Statute of Frauds. Therefore, we conclude that the existence of genuine issues involving the inferences to be drawn from the facts in this case should have prevented the trial court from granting summary judgment to either party. Reversed and remanded.

Leases

Thousands of times a day, Americans rent cars, garden equipment, machines to clean rugs, and numerous other goods. Leasing is also quite common in industry. For example, assume that Company A needs to buy 100 new delivery trucks from Company C, but cannot afford them. Company B ("lessor") agrees to buy the 100 trucks and then to lease them to Company A ("lessee"). Every day, innumerable such transactions occur in our economy.

Leases of goods present many of the same legal issues that arise in sales of goods. Indeed, some courts held that Article 2 applied to leases because UCC 2-102 states that it applies to "transactions in goods." Although most courts disagreed, many extended provisions of Article 2 to leases by analogy, reasoning that the rules governing sales could be helpful in resolving lease disputes. This proved unsatisfactory, however, because Article 2 was not designed to address leasing problems.

Therefore, almost all states have adopted Article 2A, which is designed to cover leases of goods in the same manner that Article 2 covers sales. It is intended to apply to virtually every type of lease of tangible personal property.

Article 2A's provisions resemble the common law of bailment for hire. This is the most-litigated pre-Article 2A issue related to the difference between a true lease (governed by bailment law) and a lease intended as security for a loan (subject to UCC Article 9). Return, for example, to the hypothetical example of a lease of 100 trucks. If Company A falls behind in its payments, the rights of Company B vis-a-vis Company A's other creditors will depend on whether the agreement is structured as a true lease or as a security interest.

Although Article 2 receives most of our attention in this chapter and the next, we should highlight a few of Article 2A's provisions.

Lessee's Remedies

Remedies are usually set forth in the lease contract. The parties to the lease generally have the right to set their own terms and to vary any provision of Article 2A. However, when the lease does not establish remedies, Article 2A provides that in event of default by the lessor, the lessee has the right, among others, to cancel the lease, to recover paid-in rents and security deposits to the extent "just under the circumstances," to obtain substitute goods, and to recover damages.

Lessor's Remedies

If the lessee breaches the lease by wrongfully refusing delivery or failing to make payments when due, the remedies available to the lessor include cancellation of the lease, repossession and disposition, and damages. "Reasonable" liquidated damages clauses will be enforced. Mitigation of damages by re-leasing is not required, but if an item is re-leased, the lessor is not entitled to recover double profits.

Warranties

Finance lessors (those who do not select, manufacture, or supply goods out of inventory, but simply serve as a financial conduit so that the lessee may obtain use of goods—such as Company B in the aforementioned truck example) are automatically exempted from implied warranties. For other lessors, Article 2A's warranty provisions generally track those of Article 2, which will be discussed in detail in Chapter 20. Warranties not affecting third parties may be disclaimed by written and conspicuous provisions.

Consumer Leases

A consumer lease is one that a lessor regularly engaged in the business of leasing or selling makes to an individual lessee who takes primarily for a personal, family, or household purpose, providing total payments do not exceed $25,000. Article 2A contains several provisions to protect consumers in such leases, including one allowing a consumer to recover attorney's fees when a court finds a provision in the lessor's form lease to be "unconscionable."

REVIEW OF BASIC PRINCIPLES OF SALES CONTRACTS

In explaining basic contract law, Chapters 10–18 focused on the common law of contracts but highlighted changes that Article 2 makes for sales contracts. The first part of this chapter examined the scope of Article 2's coverage. The next chapters will go into great detail regarding some very important features of Article 2. Before leaving this chapter, however, we will present a quick overview of some basic Article 2 rules on contract formation, enforcement, and interpretation.

Contract Formation

The basic elements needed to form a contract at common law (agreement, consideration, capacity of the parties, legality of purpose) are also essential to formation of a sales contract under Article 2. However, the drafters of the Code meant it to be nontechnical and to operate fairly. For example, the common law says that even if an offeror promises to keep an offer open for a specified period of time, he may revoke the offer at any time before acceptance (unless he has been given consideration to keep it open). As explained in Chapter 11, §2-205's "firm offer rule" provides a fairer rule, holding merchants to their signed promises to keep offers open for a specified time less than three months' duration even in the absence of consideration.

Even more importantly, the Code's rules on formation of an agreement do not turn on whether there existed a detailed offer and a detailed acceptance, each containing all important elements of the contract. Rather, the drafters of the Code realized that parties often, perhaps pursuant to a quick phone conversation, intend to form a contract but fail to agree as to a specific term such as price or date of delivery. Therefore, §2-204 provides that a contract is made if the parties clearly intend one to exist and there is a reasonably certain basis for giving an appropriate remedy. Resort may be had to the "gap-fillers" to provide terms the parties omit. For example, §2-305 will provide the price if that term has been omitted, §2-308 fills in the gap if the parties did not determine the place for delivery, §2-309 fills in the time of delivery, and §2-310 fills in the time of payment.

The common law also generally requires that an acceptance be the "mirror image" of the offer on all important terms before a contract exists. The framers of the UCC realized that this requirement was unduly technical, given the modern commercial world's reliance on form contracts that cannot feasibly be fully negotiated for each transaction. Therefore §UCC 2-207, the "battle of the forms" provision, states that a contract is formed if the offeree's primary intent is to accept an offer even if the offeree's form does not match the offeror's form in all particulars. That section then gives rules to decide the content of that contract. The essence of §2-207 is that no party is allowed to unfairly surprise the other with contract provisions hidden in fine print.

The area of consideration also illustrates the Code's nontechnical approach. As noted in Chapter 12, §2-209 states that, unlike at the common law, an agreement modifying a sales contract *needs no consideration to be binding.* Parties are bound to their promises to modify an existing contract, and another technical defense is eliminated. Somewhat surprisingly, perhaps, the doctrine of promissory estoppel plays almost no role in Article 2.

Contract Enforcement

No body of commercial law can be free of technical rules, of course. Like the common law, Article 2 carries a statute of frauds requirement that certain contracts for the sale of goods—those of $500 or more—must be in writing in order to be enforceable (§2-201). However, consistent with its overall approach, the Code makes several exceptions to this technical defense, providing that oral contracts of $500 or more are enforceable where (1) the seller has already substantially begun producing specially made goods; (2) payment has been made and accepted or goods have been received and accepted; (3) between merchants there has been a confirmatory memorandum sent and the receiving party did not object to its terms in writing within 10 days; or (4) the party against whom the contract is to be enforced admitted in court proceedings that an oral agreement existed. The Code also has its own parol evidence rule, §2-202, which again is more generous than the common law, allowing unambiguous final written agreements to be explained or supplemented by course of dealing, usage of trade, or course of performance.

The Code also grants the parties the right to shape the contract's terms as they please. For example, they can establish their own remedies with very few limitations. However, in the interests of fairness, the Code does impose some limitations. As explained in Chapter 13, a contractual provision that is unconscionable will not be enforced. Under §2-302, a party with superior bargaining power or sophistication will not be allowed to impose unfair terms on another party with far less bargaining power. And, if a seller with far greater bargaining power contractually limits the remedies of the buyer of a defective product so severely that the remedy fails of its essential purpose depriving the buyer of the substantial value of the bargain, the limitation is unenforceable under §UCC 2-719(2).

Contract Interpretation

The Code follows general rules of contract interpretation, but, as noted in Chapter 18, allows more liberal use of extrinsic evidence to determine the parties' intent in sale of goods contracts. The Code assumes that the parties considered three important concepts when they formed their agreement. First is *course of performance*, which arises out of "repeated occasions for performance by either party with knowledge of the nature of the performance and opportunity for objection to it by the other." Second is *course of dealing,* "a sequence of previous conduct between the parties to a particular transaction which is fairly regarded as establishing a common basis of understanding for interpreting their expressions and other conduct." Third is *usage of trade,* defined as "any practice or method of dealing having such regularity of observance in a place, vocation or trade as to justify an expectation that it will be observed with respect to the transaction in question." In essence, this means that in determining the meaning of the contract, the courts may consider, in order of importance, the previous course of performance of this particular contract, the past course of dealing between the parties in other contracts they have had, and, finally, the usage of the trade in general as established by contracts and performance of other persons in the industry.

Duty of Good Faith

Finally, interpretation and enforcement of contracts for the sale of goods are favored not only by Article 2's specific policies against surprise, unfairness, and unconscionability, but also by its "good faith" requirements. UCC §1-203 specifically states that "[e]very contract or duty within this Act imposes an obligation of good faith in its performance or enforcement." Section 2-103(1)(b) goes farther, defining the "good faith" duty of a merchant to mean acting with "honesty in fact and the observance of reasonable commercial standards of fair dealing in the trade." This again highlights that Article 2 is not a collection of dry rules, but an attempt to establish a framework promoting efficient, but also fair, commercial transactions in goods.

CISG

As will be discussed in Chapter 32, the United Nations *Convention on Contracts for the International Sale of Goods* (CISG) is a multilateral treaty drafted in 1980. The United States adopted the treaty in 1988, and more than 90 nations, including most of the world's important trading nations, have adopted the CISG. Its goal is to facilitate international trade by minimizing the adverse impact that differences in the laws of two trading partners might have. In a sale of goods transaction in which the seller and buyer are from different nations, and both nations have adopted the treaty, the CISG is the governing law unless the seller and buyer expressly agree that some other body of law should apply. Even if the seller and buyer do not expressly agree to be bound by some other body of law, they can modify any of the CISG's provisions by agreement.

The ability of the parties to modify the rules of contract law by their agreement is nothing new, of course; the same is true with regard to almost all of the common law of contracts and the rules of our UCC.

Although much of the CISG resembles Article 2 of our UCC, there are some significant differences. For example, the UCC's Article 2 applies to sales of goods to consumers, but the CISG omits transactions for personal, family, or household use. Also, under the UCC a sale of goods contract for $500 or more has to be in writing, but the CISG expressly provides that written documentation is not required so long as other evidence proves the existence and terms of the contract. This difference is more theoretical than real, however, because almost all international sales contracts are actually evidenced by documents that would satisfy the requirements of our UCC.

Another difference between the UCC and CISG relates to an acceptance containing terms that are additional to or different from the terms of the offer. As you have read, the UCC modifies the common-law "mirror-image" rule and consequently makes it easier to form an enforceable sale of goods contract than under common-law rules. The CISG, however, includes a provision that is virtually identical to the common-law mirror image rule: under the CISG, an acceptance containing a term that materially adds to or changes the offer is a counteroffer rather than an acceptance. One other difference relates to the creation of irrevocable offers. The "firm offer" provision of UCC §2-205 makes it somewhat easier to create an irrevocable offer than do traditional common law contract rules; the CISG makes it even easier than the UCC. Under the CISG, an offer for the sale or purchase of goods is irrevocable if it includes language indicating that it is irrevocable or even if it merely states a time for acceptance. Unlike the UCC, the CISG does not require the offer to be written, and does not include a time limit on an offer's irrevocable status.

DOCUMENTS OF TITLE

When goods are shipped by a carrier or stored in a warehouse before sale, a *bailment* often occurs. The owner of the goods is the *bailor*, the warehouseman or carrier is the *bailee.* An owner of goods who sends them through a carrier receives a receipt called a *bill of lading*, which contains instructions to the carrier regarding destination and the like, as well as the terms of the shipping agreement. If goods are stored with a bailee/warehouseman before sale, the owner will receive a warehouse receipt, which will also contain the terms of the storage agreement. Both instructions are sometimes referred to as documents of title, because they provide evidence of title to goods.

Documents of title—such as bills of lading, warehouse receipts, dock warrants, dock receipts, and other orders for delivery of goods which are treated in the regular course of business as adequate evidence that the holder is entitled to receive, hold, and dispose of the goods covered, are governed by Article 7 of the UCC. A *negotiable document of title* is one which by its terms specifies that the goods are to be delivered to "bearer" or to the "order" of a named person. Documents not meeting this requirement are *nonnegotiable documents of title*. A negotiable document of title (e.g., "Deliver to bearer" or "Deliver to order of Dan Owens") entitles whoever is in legal possession of it (as bearer or as Dan Owens's endorsee) to possession of the underlying goods.

A nonnegotiable document of title (e.g., "Delivery to Dan Owens"), on the other hand, is not equivalent to ownership of the goods. Regardless of who presents the document, the bailee is under a duty to deliver the goods only to the party who is supposed to receive them under the bailor's instructions. The difference between a negotiable and a nonnegotiable document is somewhat akin to the difference between a five-dollar bill and a copy of a contract.

CHAPTER 20

SALES: WARRANTIES AND PRODUCT LIABILITY

- Warranty
- Negligence
- Strict Liability
- Federal Consumer Legislation
- Legislative Limitations on the Products Liability Revolution

Products liability is one of the most important and controversial fields of law. Machinery, drugs, and other products often cause injuries to consumers and businesses. The injuries can be bodily, economic, or both. Injured parties often seek compensation from manufacturers, wholesalers, and retailers of the products. Judgments against defendants can range from burdensome to ruinous. As courts have attempted to strike a balance between the interests of injured plaintiffs on the one hand and economically vulnerable defendants on the other, the pendulum has swung back and forth.

At this writing, manufacturers and sellers of opioids are settling products-related lawsuits (many of which involve fraud claims that are not covered in this chapter) for billions of dollars, plaintiffs' attorneys are just beginning to explore the potential liability of sellers of e-cigarettes for both exploding batteries and lung injuries, and controversial lawsuits are being filed against Amazon seeking to hold it liable for injuries caused by products sold over its platform. This entire area is quite controversial and will remain so for the foreseeable future.

Under products liability law and sales law, three primary legal theories may be available to an injured consumer seeking redress: (1) breach of warranty, (2) negligence, and (3) strict liability. The first is primarily a contract theory and is governed by Article Two of the Uniform Commercial Code (UCC); the other two are tort-based theories. The elements of negligence have been discussed in Chapter 8 and are applied here in the context of lawsuits over injuries caused by products. The principles of strict liability derive primarily from §402A of the American Law Institute's Restatement (Second) of Torts. Unlike the UCC, the Restatement is not a statute, but a highly detailed summary by experts of the common law principles created by courts in a wide variety of legal fields. Like the UCC, the strict liability theory applies primarily to transactions involving goods and not to those involving real estate or services.

WARRANTIES

A *warranty* is an assurance or guarantee that goods will conform to certain standards. If the standards are not met, the buyer can recover damages from the seller, under a breach of warranty theory.

Such has not always been the case, for although suits involving warranties date as far back as fourteenth century England, *caveat emptor* ("let the buyer beware") governed in America until the beginning of the twentieth century. The concept of *caveat emptor* allowed the seller to escape liability altogether, in the absence of fraud.

With the growth of business and industry came a clear need to move away from laissez-faire values and to place legal strictures on sales transactions. Chains of distribution widened the distance between manufacturers and ultimate consumers, and increased sophistication in product design made inspection for defects more difficult for consumers. As a result, courts came to recognize the existence of three types of warranties, discussed in the following pages: express warranties, implied warranties, and warranties of title.

Express Warranties

Express warranties are those that originate from the words or actions of the seller. To create an express warranty, the seller does not have to use the word *warranty or guarantee*, and the buyer does not have to show that the seller intended to make a warranty. Under §2-313 of the UCC, a seller can create an express warranty in three different ways: (1) by an affirmation of fact or a promise relating to the goods, (2) by a description of the goods, or (3) by providing a sample or model of the goods. Such representations by the seller create contractual obligations to the extent that they become part of the "basis of the bargain," that is, when they formed a part of the parties' understanding with each other.

Affirmation of Fact or Promise

By making an affirmation of fact or a promise relating to the goods, the seller tacitly guarantees that the goods will conform to the specifics set forth. For example, the seller might claim, "This boat is equipped with a two-year-old, 100-horsepower engine that was overhauled last month." The statement contains several affirmations of fact: (1) the boat is equipped with an engine, (2) the engine is two years old, (3) it generates 100 horsepower, and (4) it was overhauled last month. The seller might further state, "I assure you that this boat will not stall when run in choppy water." The affirmations concern past and present conditions; the promise, by contrast, relates to future events. Both affirmations and promises may create express warranties.

A seller's *commendation or expression of opinion* does not constitute an express warranty; neither does a statement that relates only to the value of the goods. Thus, the seller could claim that his boat was a "first-class vessel, worth $25,000 at retail" without creating a warranty. The law is not so rigid as to disallow "puffing" of products; it assumes that a consumer can distinguish between mere sales talk and fact. Still, at times the distinction between fact and opinion is not easy to make. Statements that are specific and absolute are more readily construed as warranties than indefinite ones. Terms put in writing are more likely to create warranties than those given orally. A warranty is more likely to be found if the statement is objectively *verifiable* (for example, "This machine is one year old."). The nature and seriousness of the defect may also have a bearing on the determination.

Description of Goods

A descriptive word or phrase used in a sale of goods may create an express warranty that the goods will conform to the description. The word *pitted* or *seedless* on a box of prunes or raisins warrants that the fruit will have no seeds. Recognized trade terms may also constitute descriptions. For example, the term Scotchgard, used in connection with furniture upholstery, describes fabric that has been treated to make it water- and stain-resistant. Goods described by trade terms are warranted to possess those characteristics generally associated with the terms in the trade or business involved.

Sample or Model

If the seller provides to the buyer a sample or model of the goods to be sold, a warranty arises that the goods will conform to the sample or model. A sample is a single item taken from the mass to be sold, whereas a model is used to represent the goods. In a sale of wheat, a sample of one bushel might be drawn from the thousand bushels to be sold. But when the item being sold has not yet been manufactured or is too difficult to transport, a model might be used instead.

Basis of the Bargain

Under §2-313, an express warranty is created only if the affirmation or promise, description, model, or sample is part of the "basis of the bargain." Courts have applied this phrase to two types of circumstances. First is the case in which the seller makes a statement about the goods, and circumstances indicate that both parties intended the statement to be a part of the agreement. This would certainly be true if the statement appeared in the sales contract itself and would apply also when it is reasonably clear that the statement played a material part in the buyer's decision to purchase the goods. The second type of case involves statements of fact contained in a brochure, provided to the buyer by the seller. Under pre-Code law, the burden of proof was generally on buyers to show that they had read the statement and relied on it. A buyer who could not prove reliance could not recover on the breach of warranty theory. By contrast, under the "basis of the bargain" language, courts *assume* that the statement became a part of the contract unless the seller can show "good reason" for the contrary (§2-313, comment 8).

In *Community Television Services, Inc. v. Dresser Industries, Inc.*, 586 F.2d 637 (8th Cir. 1978), plaintiff television stations hired defendant to design, manufacture, and construct a 2,000-foot broadcast tower. When the tower collapsed in a storm, they sued defendant for breach of express warranty. Defendant pointed out that the tower met the design specifications established by plaintiffs. However, plaintiffs pointed out that defendant had promised not only to meet the design specifications. Defendant's sales literature stated:

> Properly designed towers will safely withstand the maximum wind velocities and ice loads to which they are likely to be subjected. Dresser-Ideco can make wind and ice load recommendations to you for your area based on U.S. Weather Bureau data.
>
> In the winter, loaded with ice and hammered repeatedly with gale force winds, these towers absorb some of the roughest punishment that towers take anywhere in the country ... yet continue to give dependable, uninterrupted service.

This statement was held to have constituted an affirmation of fact or a promise about the product that was not fulfilled, and plaintiffs won the lawsuit.

What should happen when, *after* a sale has been made, the buyer requests a promise from the seller that the goods meet certain standards? If given, does this promise become "part of the basis of the bargain"? Before the enactment of the UCC, the answer probably would have been *no*; today it is probably *yes*. Under §2-209(1), the seller's post-sale promise is a modification of the contract and becomes an integral part of the agreement, even without additional consideration from the buyer.

A similar problem occurs sometimes in a sales negotiation, during which the seller makes statements that fail to appear in the written contract. Buyers who attempt to base a claim for breach of warranty on a recollection of oral statements are often thwarted by the parol evidence rule of UCC §2-202. Under this rule, if the court finds that the written form was intended as the final expression of the parties' agreement, any oral statement in contradiction of the written terms will not be admissible as evidence.

Implied Warranties: Introduction

An implied warranty is created through the mere act of selling and is imposed on the seller by law. Its purpose is to protect buyers who suffer economic and commercial losses when products fail to serve their needs. Unlike with express warranties, specific representations about a product have not actually been made. The consumers have been guided, instead, by the belief that their purchases are suitable for their intended use. In §2-

314 and §2-315, the UCC creates two types of implied warranties: the implied warranty of merchantability and the implied warranty of fitness for a particular purpose.

Implied Warranty of Merchantability

The law injects into the sales contract a warranty that the goods are "merchantable," if the seller is a *merchant with respect to the type of goods being sold.* (When a student sells his car to a neighbor, no implied warranty of merchantability exists because the student is not a merchant in automobiles.)

Merchantable means essentially that the goods are *fit for the ordinary purpose for which such goods are used.* The warranty of merchantability requires, for example, that shoes have their heels attached well enough that they will not break off under normal use. The warranty does not require, however, that ordinary walking shoes be suitable for mountain climbing. To be merchantable, goods must also serve their ordinary purpose safely. A refrigerator that keeps food cold but that gives an electric shock when the handle is touched is not merchantable. This is not to say that the seller becomes an insurer against accident or malfunction; the purchaser is expected to maintain her goods against the attrition of use.

The *implied warranty of merchantability* also does not guarantee that goods will be of the highest quality available. They are required to be only of *average or medium grade*, in addition to being adequately packaged and labeled.

Jurisdictions differ regarding the application of the implied warranty of merchantability to sales of *used* goods. Most limit the warranty to sale of new goods. In *Man Engines & Components, Inc. v. Shows*, 434 S.W.3d 132 (Tex. 2014), the court held that if a manufacturer sells a product (in this case a yacht) to Buyer A, who later sells it to Buyer B, Buyer B may win a breach of the implied warranty of merchantability lawsuit against the manufacturer, even though B bought a used good, by proving that the yacht was unmerchantable at the time it left the manufacturer's possession.

When applied to food, the implied warranty of merchantability can be related to wholesomeness. A tainted pork chop, for instance, is not merchantable. The UCC explicitly states that the implied warranty of merchantability extends to food sold at service establishments such as restaurants and hotels, whether the food is consumed on or off the premises even though one might reasonably argue that these establishments are primarily selling a service rather than a good.

Many cases alleging a breach of the implied warranty of merchantability involve objects in food that caused harm to the consumer. Exceptional examples range from a mouse in a bottled soft drink to a screw in a slice of bread. In such cases the courts traditionally have distinguished between "foreign" and "natural" objects. They usually find that if the object is foreign to the mass (such as the mouse or screw mentioned above), the warranty of merchantability has been breached. If, however, the object is natural (such as a bone in a piece of fish), no breach of warranty has occurred.

A growing number of courts have rejected this approach and have based their decisions instead on the "reasonable expectation" of the consumer. The controlling factor in this approach is whether a consumer can reasonably expect the object in question to be in the food. A piece of chicken may be expected to contain a bone but not when in a chicken sandwich; an olive may be expected to contain a pit but not when a hole at the end indicates that it has been pitted. Bones and olive pits will not render food unmerchantable under the "foreign-natural object" test *but may do so under the reasonable expectation test*. Thus, the results of a legal suit may vary considerably, depending on which approach is used. A famous case in this area follows.

WEBSTER v. BLUE SHIP TEA ROOM, INC.
Supreme Judicial Court of Massachusetts, 198 N.E.2d 309 (1964)

Plaintiff, Webster, who was born and brought up in New England, ordered a cup of fish chowder while dining at the defendant's "quaint" Boston restaurant. She choked on a fish bone contained in the soup, necessitating two esophagoscopies at the Massachusetts General Hospital. The plaintiff sued for breach of the implied warranty of merchantability. A jury returned a verdict for the plaintiff. The defendant appealed the trial judge's refusal to direct a verdict for the defendant.

Reardon, Justice:

We must decide whether a fish bone lurking in a fish chowder, about the ingredients of which there is no other complaint, constitutes a breach of implied warranty under applicable provisions of the Uniform Commercial Code. As the [trial] judge put it, "Was the fish chowder fit to be eaten and wholesome? Nobody is claiming that the fish itself wasn't wholesome. But the bone of contention here—I don't mean that for a pun—but was this fish bone a foreign substance that made the fish chowder unwholesome or not fit to be eaten?"

The plaintiff has vigorously reminded us of the high standards imposed by this court where the sale of goods is involved.

The defendant asserts that here was a native New Englander eating fish chowder in a "quaint" Boston dining place where she had been before; that "[f]ish chowder, as it is served and enjoyed by New Englanders, is a hearty dish, originally designed to satisfy the appetites of our seamen and fishermen"; that "[t]his court knows well that we are not talking of some insipid broth as is customarily served to convalescents." We are asked to rule in such fashion that no chef is forced "to reduce the pieces of fish in the chowder to miniscule size in an effort to ascertain if they contained any pieces of bone." In so ruling, we are told (in the defendant's brief), "the court will not only uphold its reputation for legal knowledge and acumen, but will, as loyal sons of Massachusetts, save our world-renowned fish chowder from degenerating into an insipid broth containing the mere essence of its former stature as a culinary masterpiece."

Chowder is an ancient fish dish preexisting even "the appetites of our seamen and fishermen." It was perhaps the common ancestor of the "more refined cream soups, purees, and bisques." Berolzheimer, THE AMERICAN WOMAN'S COOK BOOK (Publisher's Guild Inc., NY, 1941) p. 176. The all-embracing Fannie Farmer states in a portion of her recipe, fish chowder is made with a "fish skinned, but head and tail left on. Cut off head and tail and remove fish from backbone. Cut fish in 2-in. pieces and set aside. Put head, tail, and backbone broken in pieces, in stewpan; add 2 cups cold water and bring slowly to boil."

Thus, we consider a dish which for many years, if well made, has been made generally as outlined above. It is not too much to say that a person sitting down in New England to consume a good New England fish chowder embarks on a gustatory adventure which may entail the removal of some fish bones from his bowl as he proceeds. We are not inclined to tamper with age old recipes by any amendment reflecting the plaintiff's view of the effect of the Uniform Commercial Code on them. We are aware of the heavy body of case law involving foreign substances in food, but we sense a strong distinction between them and those relative to unwholesomeness of the food itself, e.g., tainted mackerel, and a fishbone in fish chowder. We consider that the joys of life in New England include the ready availability of fresh fish chowder. We should be prepared to cope with the hazards of fish bones, the occasional presence of which in chowders is, it seems to us, to be anticipated, and which, in the light of a hallowed tradition, do not impair their fitness or merchantability. Judgment for the defendant.

Implied Warranty of Fitness for a Particular Purpose

In §2-315, the UCC provides "Where the seller at the time of contracting has reason to know any particular purpose for which the goods are required and that the buyer is relying on the seller's skill or judgment to furnish suitable goods, there is . . . an implied warranty that the goods shall be fit for such purpose" (hence the name *implied warranty of fitness for a particular purpose*, sometimes referred to as warranty of fitness). Note that the seller is not required to be a merchant, although merchants are defendants in most cases.

Often the liability incurred by the seller under the implied warranty of fitness is greater than that incurred under the implied warranty of merchantability—a difference that can be best illustrated by a simple example. Suppose that a buyer purchases an electric clock and discovers that its hands do not glow in the dark. The packaging carries no reference to visibility of the dial; neither does the instruction card. No breach of the implied warranty of merchantability exists here, for visibility of the dial under all conditions is not within the realm of a clock's "ordinary purpose." Yet, seller may be liable to buyers for breach of the implied warranty of fitness for a particular purpose if they knew that the buyer had a particular reason to need a clock with a lighted dial.

According to one formulation, a consumer may win a breach of the implied warranty of fitness case by proving:

1. The seller had reason to know (at the time of sale) of the buyer's particular purpose;

2. The seller had reason to know that the buyer was relying on the seller's skill or judgment to furnish appropriate goods;

3. The buyer did, in fact, reasonably rely upon the seller's skill or judgment; and

4. The goods were not, in fact, fit for the specific purpose intended by the buyer.

KLEIN V. SEARS ROEBUCK & CO.
U.S. Court of Appeals, Fourth Circuit, 773 F.2d 1421 (1985)

Steven and Claudia Klein (plaintiffs) moved to a new home and his parents decided to buy a riding mower as a gift. Claudia and Steven's parents went to a local Sears store where they consulted with a Sears salesman about the intended purchase. They informed the salesman that they had no experience with lawnmowers and that the property on which the mower was to be used was a ¾-acre tract containing numerous hills. The salesman recommended a Sears Craftsman, eight horsepower electric start rear engine riding mower with a 30-inch cutting deck. The sale, however, was conditioned on an inspection of the Kleins' property, to be conducted at the time of delivery of the mower. A few days later, the Sears salesman delivered the mower to the Kleins' residence. At this time, the salesman conducted an inspection of the property and pronounced the mower suitable for mowing the property, although he warned that it should be driven vertically up and down the hills.

A year or so later, Steven was mowing vertically up a 19 degrees slope on the property when the mower tipped over backwards and his hand came in contact with the rotating mower blade. It was seriously injured. Plaintiffs sued Sears on a breach of the implied warranty of merchantability claim, among others. The jury found for plaintiffs. Sears appealed, arguing that the trial judge should have granted it a directed verdict.

Sprouse, Circuit Judge:

Under Maryland law, recovery for breach of warranty requires proof of three elements: (1) the existence of a warranty, (2) a breach of the warranty, and (3) harm proximately caused by the breach. The implied warranty of fitness for a particular purpose arises "where the seller at the time of contracting has reason to know any particular purpose for which the goods are required and that the buyer is relying on the seller's skill or judgment to select or furnish suitable goods." Md. Com. Law Code Ann. § 2-315(1) (1975).

There was ample evidence presented that Claudia and Steven's parents relied on the Sears salesman to recommend a suitable mower and that the salesman had reason to know of both their reliance and the particular purpose for which the mower was being purchased. This was sufficient to constitute an implied warranty of fitness for a particular purpose.

We also find adequate evidence to support the finding that Sears breached the warranties. Assuming the accuracy of Sears' assertion that it only promised that the mower was fit to cut grass safely when used properly, there was ample evidence that Steven was operating the mower in a manner consistent with the representations made by Sears' salesmen, i.e. vertically on a slope that was pronounced safe.

Likewise, Sears' assertions regarding proximate cause involve factual issues properly resolved by the jury. Throughout the trial, Sears contended that Steven's misuse of the mower was the proximate cause of the accident while the Kleins countered that the mower was unsuitable for its intended use. While there was evidence presented on both sides of this issue, the jury obviously was convinced that the accident was caused by the failure of the machine to conform to the [implied warranty of fitness.]

Affirmed.

Warranties in Leases

Article 2A of the UCC contains warranty provisions for leases of goods. Except for "finance leases," Article 2A's rules regarding imposition and disclaimer of express and implied warranty liability are generally the same as those of Article 2 that we have just discussed.

Warranties of Title

In most sales of goods, a warranty as to the validity of the seller's title automatically exists. Sec. 2-312 of the UCC imposes two basic types of *warranty of title*. The first is a warranty that the *title conveyed shall be good and its transfer rightful*. This warranty is obviously breached if the seller has stolen the goods from some third party and therefore has no title at all. Other breaches, however, are not so obvious. Suppose that A buys goods from B and then is approached by C who claims to be the rightful owner. Inquiries reveal that there is some basis for C's claim and that the matter can be resolved only through a lawsuit.

Will A have to become involved in a lawsuit initiated by C to determine if she bought a good title from B? Or has B breached his warranty of title by conveying a "questionable" title? The answer is that A has the option of returning the goods to B and getting her money back or defending against C's claim. If A takes the latter route and wins the lawsuit, she can recover her legal expenses from B. If A loses the lawsuit, she can recover from B not only her legal expenses, but also the value of the goods lost to C. A breach of the warranty of title exists if C's claim places a "substantial shadow" on the title, even if it ultimately might be proved invalid.

The second type of title warranty is that the goods shall be delivered free from any security interest or other lien or encumbrance of which the buyer at the time of contracting has no knowledge. This warranty will be breached, for instance, if B sells mortgaged goods to A without telling A of the mortgage.

Warranties of title accompany a sale of goods unless the seller indicates by specific language that no such assurances are being made or unless the circumstances indicate as much (for example, in a public sale of goods seized by the sheriff to satisfy a debt, rightful transfers of title are generally not guaranteed).

An additional obligation—not, strictly speaking, a warranty of title—is imposed on some sellers by §2-312: Unless otherwise agreed, a seller who is a merchant in the type of goods involved is deemed to warrant that *the goods sold do not infringe on the patents, copyrights, or trademarks of a third party*. If a claim of infringement is made by a third party against the buyer, the seller is responsible—unless, of course, the goods were manufactured according to the buyer's specifications.

Conflicting and Overlapping Warranties

Two or more warranties sometimes exist in a single sales transaction. For example, a machine might be warranted to perform certain functions and to last for a specified time. In addition to these express warranties, an implied warranty of merchantability or of fitness for a particular purpose, or both, might exist.

When more than one warranty is created in a given transaction, the buyer does not have to choose among them. The warranties are *cumulative*, such that the buyer can take advantage of any or all of them. According to §2-317, courts should interpret the warranties as being consistent whenever such an interpretation is reasonable. In the unusual event that two warranties are in conflict and cannot both be given effect, the court must attempt to determine the intent of the parties as to which warranty should prevail. Several rules offer guidance in determining intention:

1. Exact or technical specifications take precedence over inconsistent samples or models or general language of description.

2. A sample drawn from the goods to be sold takes precedence over inconsistent general language or description.

3. An express warranty, regardless of how it was created, takes precedence over the implied warranty of merchantability if the two are inconsistent. An express warranty does not take precedence over the implied warranty of fitness for a particular purpose, although it is difficult to imagine a situation in which the two would be inconsistent.

These rules are not absolute and can be disregarded by the court if they produce an unreasonable result.

Disclaimers Excluding or Limiting Warranties

As we have seen, a sales transaction can give rise to three types of warranties: express warranties, implied warranties, and warranties of title. But the creation of these warranties is by no means automatic. The UCC allows a seller to disavow the existence of warranties or to limit the circumstances in which liability will apply by including a *disclaimer* in the sales contract. Theoretically, disclaimers can be justified on the grounds that their use advances freedom of contract, permitting parties to bargain over contract terms and to allocate the risk of loss. Yet in reality, the arrangement tends to be one-sided: consumers usually are in no bargaining position and often do not read disclaimers when making a purchase. For this reason, Massachusetts passed a law that prohibits disclaimers of the implied warranties of merchantability and fitness if the purchaser is a consumer, and courts of other states may find a particular disclaimer *unconscionable* under UCC § 2-302.

Disclaimers of Express Warranties

A seller who wishes to avoid liability on an express warranty obviously should not do anything to create a warranty in the first place (perhaps an impractical measure to take in making sales!). An alternative would be to include a disclaimer in the contract. However, if a warranty has actually become part of the contract, an attempt to disclaim liability will usually not be effective. Sec. 2-316(1) states that a disclaimer will be disregarded if it is inconsistent with the words or conduct that created the express warranty. Suppose that an express warranty has been created by a statement of the seller, by the use of a sample, or by a written description of the goods. Liability could not then be disclaimed by specifying: "These goods are sold without warranties." Such a statement would almost always be inconsistent with the words or conduct that created the warranty. In short, it is extremely difficult for a seller to disclaim an express warranty which has become part of the contract.

Disclaimers of Implied Warranties

Because the existence of an implied warranty depends on circumstances rather than on the precise words used by the seller, such a warranty is relatively easy to disclaim. The UCC permits disclaimers of implied warranties through (1) the use of language specified in §2-316 of the Code, (2) the buyer's examination of the goods, or (3) custom and usage.

Disclaimer by Language. In the case of the *warranty of merchantability*, the language used by the seller to disclaim liability does not have to be in writing. If written, however, the disclaimer must be "conspicuous" enough to be noticed by any reasonable person involved in the purchase. (A disclaimer printed in larger type or in a different color than the remainder of the document will probably be considered conspicuous.) In addition, the word *merchantability* must be used, unless the seller uses a phrase such as "with all faults" or "as is"—language that serves to disclaim *both* or *either* of the implied warranties.

In the case of the *warranty of fitness for a particular purpose,* the disclaimer must be in writing and must be conspicuous. Yet the statement itself can be a general one, such as, "There are no warranties extending beyond the description on the face hereof."

Disclaimer by Examination. If before making a contract, the buyer fully examines the goods (or a sample or model of them) or deliberately refuses to examine them at all, no implied warranty exists for *reasonably apparent* defects. Yet if the buyer has no opportunity to examine the goods before contracting, the seller becomes liable for such defects.

When defects are hidden, the seller is always liable, unless it can be proved that the buyer had knowledge of the defects before contracting. When deciding whether a defect is "reasonably apparent" or "hidden," a court will take into account the buyer's knowledge or skill. Such a factor obviously has a bearing on what an examination should have revealed to the buyer. For example, in *Dempsey v. Rosenthal,* Mr. Dunphy's defective condition—the undescended testicle—was not readily observable. A manual manipulation of the scrotal area would have been the only means to verify the condition. The court found that Ms. Dempsey, the buyer, did not know this and should not be charged with knowledge of the fact. The type of examination that would be undertaken by the average buyer of a male puppy would not disclose the defective condition, so recovery was not barred by the inspection provisions of UCC § 2-316.

Disclaimer by Custom or Usage*.* Implied warranties are sometimes excluded or modified by *trade usage* (industry-wide custom) or by a custom that has been established between the contracting parties. An industry-wide custom will have no effect, however, on a buyer who is not a member of the particular industry and is unaware of the custom.

Limitation on Damages*.* In contract cases, punitive damages traditionally have not been available to plaintiffs. For this reason, express and implied warranty suits usually involve two types of damages: basis-of-the-bargain damages (the value of the goods warranted less the value received) and consequential damages (personal and property damages proximately caused by the warranty breach, along with any indirect economic loss foreseeable by the defendant). The buyer injured by a breached warranty also has the option to rescind the contract.

The UCC allows limitations to be placed by the seller on damages that may be recovered by a breach of warranty. For example, recovery may be limited to *liquidated damages*—that is, a specified amount to be paid in the event of a breach. A limitation may also be placed on the type of remedy available, guaranteeing, for example, only the replacement of the product without charge.

However, such limitations will not be given effect if they are *unconscionable.* For example, UCC §2-719(3) provides that "[l]imitation of consequential damages for injury to the person in the case of consumer goods is prima facie unconscionable. . . ." Furthermore, comment 1 to § 2-719 provides that "it is of the very essence of a sales contract that at least minimum adequate remedies be available. . . ." Even a clause that appears not to be unconscionable may be ignored if "because of circumstances [it] fails in its purpose or operates to deprive either party of the substantial value of the bargain."

For example, in *Great Dane Trailer v. Malvern Pulpwood*, 785 S.W.2d 13 (Ark. 1990), plaintiff Malvern Pulpwood bought two large trailers from defendant Great Dane, which issued warranties limited to repair or replacement of defective parts. Remedies were limited by the exclusion of consequential and incidental damages. The trailers exhibited serious defects, as did their replacements, so Malvern sued for breach of the implied warranties of merchantability and fitness. Great Dane defended on the basis of the "repair or replacement" warranty and disclaimer. The court observed:

Under [UCC] § 2-719, parties to an agreement may limit the buyer's remedies to the repair and replacement of nonconforming goods or parts and to make the remedy agreed upon the sole remedy, unless circumstances cause the exclusive or limited remedy to fail of its essential purpose. When there is substantial evidence tending to show that a particular piece of machinery obviously cannot be repaired or its parts replaced so that it is made free of defects, a jury verdict, which implicitly concludes that a limitation of the remedy to the repair and replacement of nonconforming parts deprived the purchaser of the substantial value of the bargain, should be sustained. Such a limited remedy fails whenever the warrantor, given the opportunity to do so, fails to correct the defect within a reasonable period.

The serious defects of the trailers and their replacements indicated to the court that the exclusive remedies "failed of their essential purpose," leading the court to affirm a jury verdict for plaintiff buyer.

Defenses

Privity Defense

Privity is a legal term for the direct relationship between buyer and seller. *Privity of contract* means relationship of contract. Under the early common law, if Manufacturer A sold a tractor to Retailer B who in turn sold it to Consumer C, there was privity of contract between A and B and between B and C, but not between A and C. Because warranties arose from direct contractual relationships, and did not "run with the goods" to subsequent purchasers and users, C could sue B but not A.

Because the manufacturer was often the party most at fault for a defective product, most jurisdictions largely eliminated the privity requirement for suit, and allowed a consumer to sue all "merchants" of the particular defective good—those who made a living selling the product, typically the retailer, the wholesaler, and the manufacturer.

Innocent Bystanders. Because defects in goods often injure persons other than the purchaser, §2-318 of the UCC modified the common law's privity requirement extending warranty protection to such bystanders. Sec. 2-318 offers three alternatives for jurisdictions to adopt. A plurality of jurisdictions has adopted Alternative A, which allows recovery only for personal injuries to guests or members of the buyer's family or household. Alternatives B and C extend coverage to any natural person (Alternative B) or person (Alternative C) who may reasonably be expected to use, consume, or be affected by the goods.

Plaintiff Misconduct Defenses

When a plaintiff's carelessness contributes to a products-related accident, the defendant can use that carelessness as a defense to warranty claims in most jurisdictions. Because the plaintiff's carelessness defenses to warranty claims are generally the same as such defenses to a strict liability claim, which we are about to discuss, we defer discussion of the matter to the strict liability section.

Statute of Limitations and Notice Requirements

Under UCC §2-725, an action for breach of contract for sale of goods must be commenced within four years after the cause of action accrues. A traditional tort statute of limitations begins to run only when the right to sue is or should be discovered (and typically lasts two years). The UCC has a similar rule where a warranty *explicitly* extends to future performance of the goods and discovery of the breach must await the time of such performance. In such cases, the statute of limitations does not begin to run until the breach is or should be discovered.

However, for all other suits under Article 2, the UCC statute of limitations begins to run when the goods are tendered for delivery. Thus, if the defect is not discovered for four years, the suit may well be time-barred before the defect is discovered. Many potential plaintiffs lose the right to sue by allowing the seller to attempt to effect repairs until after the four-year limit has expired. Furthermore, the Code provides that by agreement the parties may reduce the period of limitation to not less than one year but may not extend it. Thus, the statute of limitations often bars warranty suits.

Some warranty actions are barred by a plaintiff's failure to comply with UCC §2-607(3), which imposes on buyers a duty to notify the seller of a breach within a reasonable time after they discover or should discover any breach, or be barred from remedy. The purpose of such a requirement is to minimize litigation by giving the seller a chance to effect repairs or otherwise satisfy the buyer. Courts have generally been reluctant to allow this provision to bar recovery by consumers who suffered personal injuries caused by a breach of warranty. Courts are inclined to construe a "reasonable time" as being a longer period in a personal injury case than in a suit brought for economic loss by a commercial purchaser. The courts are split as to whether a person who bought an item from a retailer must give notice not only to that retailer but also to the manufacturer to be allowed to sue the manufacturer.

NEGLIGENCE

Because the elements of negligence have been discussed at length in Chapter 8, our purpose here is simply to apply them to the area of products liability. Remember that in an action based on negligence, the defendant must have owed a duty to the plaintiff, and this duty must have been breached. Where a sales transaction is involved, the seller's duty to use reasonable care arises from the mere act of placing goods on the market. The economic benefit derived from a sale generates a responsibility to consumers, for the act of selling directly affects the interests of those who have no choice but to rely on the integrity of sellers. Privity of contract is no longer required in the usual negligence suit. The manufacturer's liability for negligence is often predicated on negligent design or manufacture; in addition, *both* manufacturer and seller may be liable for failure to inspect or failure to adequately warn.

If the seller is a retailer, distributor, or wholesaler, it usually has no duty to inspect new goods, barring knowledge of defects. A duty to inspect does exist, however, when the seller is involved in the installation of goods (new or used) or in their preparation for eventual sale. Liability is imposed to the extent that defects are *reasonably apparent*. By the same token, a manufacturer is charged with taking reasonable measures to discover flaws created during the production process.

A *duty to warn* arises when a product's design (or its intended use) subjects the user to hazard or risk of injury. The danger in question need only be reasonably foreseeable—discoverable only within the limits of existing technology. Warnings given must be adequate in their specifics and must extend to all individuals whose harm is reasonably foreseeable. There is no duty to warn of obvious dangers—no duty, for example, to warn about fire on a box of matches.

Negligent manufacture is often cited in cases in which defects are the result of oversight, human or mechanical error, or lack of judgment. For example, production line employees might not be properly trained, or materials selected for construction might not have sufficient strength to resist the stresses of normal use.

In contrast, actions based on charges of *negligent design* hold the manufacturer responsible for more than the exercise of care in production. In addition to warning about risks and hazards inherent in a design, the manufacturer is expected to design a product with optimal safety as the ideal, compromised only when the costs of improving the design exceed the benefits derived therefrom. Under the rule adopted by most states, there is a duty to design products so that accidents are unlikely to occur and so that injuries suffered will be minimal if an accident does occur. To illustrate, say X is driving a car that explodes when struck in the rear by Y, who has negligently maneuvered his truck. X may recover from Y for initial injuries and may possibly recover from the car's manufacturer for additional injuries resulting from the impact if, for example, the gas tank was located vulnerably close to the rear bumper.

Of course, it would be unreasonable to expect cars to be accident-proof in all situations. (If this were the law, some courts have observed, manufacturers would produce nothing but tanks.) In evaluating the adequacy of design standards, courts have considered such factors as the state of existing technology, the expectation of the ordinary consumer, the danger of a product in relation to its social use, and compliance with government safety standards.

To conclude, the negligence theory became viable as an avenue of recovery to injured plaintiffs when the privity requirement was eliminated. This theory offers some advantages over the warranty theory; for example, buyers do not have to prove that a warranty existed, nor do disclaimers in the sales contract usually allow sellers to escape liability resulting from their negligence.

Yet certain disadvantages exist as well. A plaintiff must prove negligent conduct on the part of the manufacturer or seller, and proof of negligence is at times almost impossible to establish. How is the plaintiff to prove what was said and done in the manufacturer's plant as the product was designed and manufactured? Another impediment to recovery under the negligence theory is that any type of plaintiff misconduct, even simple plaintiff carelessness, will reduce or bar recovery. In addition, most jurisdictions hold that the UCC provides the only avenue for product liability recovery for mere *economic* loss (generally defined as all losses other than personal injury and tangible damage to property other than the product itself). For example, the majority rule is that if a piece of equipment contains an electrical defect that causes it to be destroyed in a fire resulting in no other loss, warranty provides the buyer's only avenue for recovery. Suit on a negligence theory (and, as we are about to see, a strict liability theory) is precluded in most states.

STRICT LIABILITY

Warranty and negligence theories do not afford consumers as much protection as they ought, in fairness, to have. Many warranty claims are barred, for example, by disclaimers, the statute of limitations, or failure to give notice of breach within a reasonable time. Negligence suits may fail because plaintiff is unable to prove specific acts of negligence by defendant. Therefore, virtually all jurisdictions have adopted the theory of *strict liability* by which manufacturers and sellers are held liable irrespective of fault. (See Figure 20.1 for a comparison of strict liability with negligence.) Today, strict liability is the most common basis for imposing product liability for personal injuries.

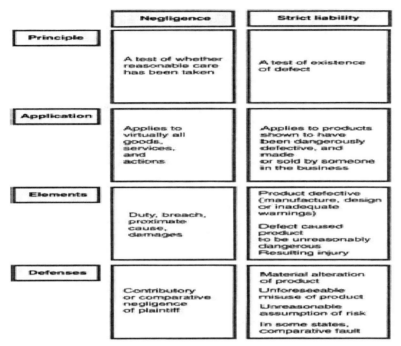

Figure 20.1 Differences between Negligence and Strict Liability

Justification for the strict liability theory lies in the notion that manufacturers and other sellers are better able to bear losses than injured consumers and that, in many cases, losses will be transferred to the buying public in the form of higher prices on products. Thus, society at large assumes the cost of damages suffered by a few—an arrangement that is perhaps more equitable in that it offers relief for those injured by defective products through no fault of their own. Proponents of strict liability argue, in addition, that eliminating the need to prove negligence in a tort action will make manufacturers and sellers more mindful of accident prevention. Finally, there is an economic basis for adopting this liability theory.

Elements of Strict Liability

The elements of strict liability are recorded in section 402 of the American Law Institute's *Restatement (Second) of Torts*, a summary and clarification of American common-law principles. Section 402A reads:

> 1. One who sells any product in a defective condition unreasonably dangerous to the user or consumer or to his property is subject to liability for physical harm thereby caused to the ultimate user or consumer, or to his property, if
>
> a. the seller is engaged in the business of selling such a product, and
>
> b. it is expected to and does reach the user or consumer without substantial change in the condition in which it is sold.
>
> 2. The rule stated in Subsection (1) applies although
>
> a. the seller has exercised all possible care in the preparation and sale of his product, and
>
> b. the user or consumer has not bought the product from or entered into any contractual

relation with the seller.

Two points regarding §402A merit special emphasis. First, subsection (l)(a) limits application of the strict liability theory to those engaged in the business of selling the products in question. Second, subsection (2) makes it clear that negligence and privity are not issues under the strict liability theory.

Thus, in certain respects, strict liability may be viewed as an extension of the implied warranty of merchantability, where the warranty theory was applied to foreign objects in food and drink. Recall our discussion of the "reasonable expectation" and "foreign-natural object" tests. Taken further, strict liability is applied in cases involving virtually all kinds of goods. Although there is, in fact, some overlapping here with the warranty theory, actions based on strict liability are nevertheless considered to be actions in tort rather than under warranty.

The crux of a § 402A action is the sale of a *defective product that is unreasonably dangerous* to the *user or consumer* or to their property. Section 402A covers only sales of products, not services. A product is defective if it is unreasonably dangerous because of a flaw in the product or a weakness in its design or because adequate warning of risks and hazards related to the design has not been given.

A strict liability action differs from a negligence action in that the plaintiff need not prove the defect resulted from the defendant's failure to use reasonable care. Although in failure-to-warn cases the manufacturer will almost always be found negligent, the same cannot be said of resellers. New products packaged with inadequate warnings may be resold without subjecting intermediaries and retailers to liability under the negligence theory; yet these very resellers could be held liable under section 402A because no fault is required under the strict liability theory.

Defective conditions may result not only from flaws or harmful ingredients within the product but also from foreign objects in its composition and defects in its container. In this regard, a product is not defective "when it is safe for normal handling or consumption." For example, beer consumed only occasionally and in moderate amounts is probably not harmful. If an adult drinks too much beer at a party and then becomes ill, the seller is not liable. To be safe, a product should be properly packaged and otherwise treated so that it will not deteriorate or be rendered dangerous within a reasonable period of time under normal conditions.

The question of what constitutes an "unreasonably" dangerous product is taken up in §402A, comments i and k. Presumably, certain products are reasonably dangerous or "unavoidably unsafe"—that is to say, existing technology and scientific knowledge are insufficient to produce a completely safe result. An example often cited is that of the rabies vaccine, which has dangerous side effects, but which is the only existing treatment against a deadly disease. Drugs sold under prescription and experimental treatments also fall within this category. Unavoidably unsafe products must be accompanied by instructions and warnings, so that the user can decide whether to undergo the risks involved. If the harmful consequences of using a product generally exceed the benefits and if safer alternatives are available, a product will be considered unreasonably unsafe. In defining what is meant by "unreasonably unsafe," section 402A also considers the expectations of the ordinary consumer, stating: "The articles sold must be dangerous to an extent beyond that which would be contemplated by the ordinary consumer who purchases it, with the ordinary knowledge common to the community as to its characteristics. . . . Good butter is not unreasonably dangerous merely because, if such be the case, it deposits cholesterol in the arteries and leads to heart attacks; but bad butter, contaminated with poisonous fish oil, is unreasonably dangerous."

Another stipulation in section 402A is that products must be in a defective condition when they leave the seller. The burden of proof lies with the plaintiff to show that the product was defective at the time of sale. Subsequent alteration or further processing may operate to relieve the seller of liability.

In addition, the plaintiff's injury must occur as a result of a defect in the product itself, rather than from conditions surrounding its use or consumption. For example, if an Africanized "killer" bee stings a longshoreman unloading crates of tropical fruit, the fruit company is not liable under section 402A because even if there is proof that the bee was a stowaway in the fruit, there is no defect inherent in the fruit itself.

Among the most problematic strict liability cases are those based on a product's allegedly defective warning. The following case is illustrative.

KNIGHT v. JUST BORN, INC.
U. S. District Court, District of Oregon, 2000 U.S. Dist. LEXIS 9716 (2000)

Mr. Knight regularly ate Hot Tamales candy, manufactured by Just Born, Inc. One day, Knight picked up a small handful of the Hot Tamales, walked into his living room where he turned on the television and "popped a couple of candies in [his] mouth." He described his injury as follows: "And it was the next two I popped in my mouth. I chewed the first one, and I kind of had the second one over in the side of my mouth. And that was the one that when I bit in to [sic] it, instantly I had a sensation of like a fireball inside of my mouth. I knew there was something wrong, because instead of the usual gumdrop, jelly-type consistencies that those candies always had had, this one had inside the shell like a syrupy liquid that I bit in to. And instantaneously, this fire spread through my mouth, is the only way I can describe it."

After the incident, the skin sloughed off the inside of Mr. Knight's mouth. He could not eat anything for several days. He suffered headaches, an inability to swallow or speak, and a tongue "so swollen that it didn't feel like it fit inside [his] mouth." He didn't feel normal again for ten days to two weeks.

Knight sued both Just Born, Inc., the manufacturer, and Costco, the retailer in strict liability. Both plaintiff and defendants moved for summary judgment.

Stewart, Magistrate Judge:

In Oregon, a product liability civil action is: "a civil action brought against a manufacturer, distributor, seller or lessor of a product for damages for personal injury, death or property damage arising out of: (1) Any design, inspection, testing, manufacturing or other defect in a product; (2) Any failure to warn regarding a product; or (3) Any failure to properly instruct in the use of a product." (ORS 30.900.) [The court then quoted the language of 402A.]

> The justification for strict liability has been said to be that the seller, by marketing his product for use and consumption, has undertaken and assumed a special responsibility toward any member of the consuming public who may be injured by it; that the public has the right to and does expect . . . that reputable sellers will stand behind their goods; that public policy demands that the burden of accidental injuries caused by products intended

for consumption be placed upon those who market them, and be treated as a cost of production against which liability insurance can be obtained; and that the consumer of such products is entitled to the maximum of protection at the hands of someone, and the proper persons to afford it are those who market the products.

Liability for unreasonably dangerous defective products normally arises either from manufacturing defects or design defects (including a failure to warn). Mr. Knight does not contend that Hot Tamales are defectively designed. Rather, as described above, his claim is focused on a manufacturing defect and a failure to warn.

All product liability actions are premised on a product that is "in a defective condition unreasonably dangerous to the user." ORS 30.920(1). The standard by which "unreasonably dangerous" is measured is the "consumer contemplation test" set forth in Comment i from RESTATEMENT (SECOND) OF TORTS, §402A. According to Comment i from the RESTATEMENT (SECOND) OF TORTS, §402A, "unreasonably dangerous" means that "the article sold must be dangerous to an extent beyond that which would be contemplated by the ordinary consumer who purchases it, with the ordinary knowledge common to the community as to its characteristics."

A plaintiff proceeding under the consumer expectation test need not produce specific evidence of defect. Instead, this test applies when the plaintiff cannot point to a specific manufacturing flaw. "In some cases the plaintiff can produce direct evidence of a mistake in fabrication," but: "[i]n the type of case in which there is no evidence, direct or circumstantial, available to prove exactly what sort of manufacturing flaw existed . . . the plaintiff may nonetheless be able to establish his right to recover, by proving that the product did not perform in keeping with the reasonable expectations of the user."

If a product fails in an unusual, unexpected fashion, "the inference is that there was some sort of defect, a precise definition of which is unnecessary." Thus, Mr. Knight need not produce direct evidence as to whether and how the Hot Tamale contained a "hot spot" of extra cinnamic aldehyde in order to create a question for the jury. Rather, if he has presented enough evidence to satisfy the consumer expectations test, then a jury will be allowed to infer a defect in the Hot Tamale. This court's function is to determine whether the evidence in this case would allow a jury to make an informed decision as to whether the allegedly defective Hot Tamale "performed as an ordinary consumer would have expected."

In order to satisfy the consumer expectations test, a plaintiff must prove: "(1) what an ordinary consumer would expect from the allegedly defective product, and (2) that the product failed to meet those expectations." By placing a food item into the marketplace, a seller represents to consumers that the product is safe for consumption. That is the one and only purpose for which a food product is intended. Viewing the evidence in the light most favorable to Mr. Knight, the Hot Tamale which he consumed did not live up to either the explicit representation of great taste or the implicit representation of safe to eat. Therefore, given the mix of explicit and implicit representations that Hot Tamales are safe to consume, a jury could reasonably believe that the Hot Tamale at issue did not satisfy a reasonable consumer's expectations.

In sum, Mr. Knight's claim is not foreclosed by the lack of definite and specific direct evidence regarding the alleged defect in the Hot Tamale. Although Mr. Knight is not entitled to summary judgment on this claim, he is nonetheless entitled to present his case to a jury. Therefore, both motions for summary judgment are denied.

Restatement (Third) of Torts: Products Liability

As strict liability law developed, most alleged product defects sorted into three categories: manufacturing defects (as alleged in *Just Born*), design defects (perhaps alleging that a machine should have featured a safety device that its design omitted), and inadequate warnings. Most courts initially used the "consumer expectation" test to determine whether a particular defect rendered a product "unreasonably dangerous." This test worked pretty well for manufacturing defects and warning defects, but the complicated factors often involved in design defect cases led many courts to conclude that the average consumer had no basis upon which to form a reasonable expectation regarding the safety of product designs. Therefore, most courts adopted a "risk/utility" test in cases of claimed design defects. Under this test, plaintiffs are required to demonstrate that the foreseeable risks presented by the product's current design outweigh the design's utility. A lawnmower without a blade would be much safer for consumers to use, but it would not cut much grass. Note that the risk/utility test reintroduces negligence factors into its calculation, arguably inconsistent with overall strict liability theory.

Judicial disagreement on this and other strict liability issues led the American Law Institute to issue in 1997 the Restatement (Third) of Torts focusing specifically on strict liability. The Restatement (Third) explicitly recognizes the three types of strict liability claims. Section 2(a) essentially replicates that traditional §402A approach for manufacturing defects, imposing liability whenever a product "departs from its intended design even though all possible care was exercised."

Section 2(b), on the other hand, replaces strict liability in design cases with an explicit negligence standard, providing that "[a] product . . . is defective in design when the foreseeable risks of harm posed by the product could have been reduced or avoided by the adoption of a *reasonable alternative design* by the seller . . . , and the omission of the alternative design renders the product not reasonably safe." Section 2(b) requires plaintiffs in most cases to demonstrate the availability of a reasonable alternative design and to show that defendant acted unreasonably in not adopting that alternative design. It explicitly rejects the consumer expectation test for design defects.

Restatement (Third) §2(c) similarly imposes a negligence standard in warning defect cases, providing that a product "is defective because of inadequate instructions or warnings when the foreseeable risks of harm posed by the product could have been reduced or avoided by the provision of reasonable instructions or warnings by the seller ... and the omission of the instructions renders the product not reasonably safe."

Many states have, through explicit adoption of the Restatement (Third) or, more commonly, through piecemeal judicial decision making, reintroduced negligence concepts into aspects of strict products liability doctrine, contrary to the original intended approach of §402A. In *Tichner v. Omega Flex, Inc.*, 104 A.3d 328 (Pa. 2014), the Pennsylvania Supreme Court made a lengthy and spirited defense of the original §402A approach.

Defenses and Limitations

The strict liability theory is not an answer to every plaintiff's prayer. Various defenses and limitations operate against plaintiffs, a number of which are effective in some states but not in others.

Privity Defense

Most states abolished the privity requirement for filing strict liability lawsuits, enabling injured consumers to sue retailers, wholesalers, manufacturers, and others, often all at the same time. Manufacturers, as an example, may no longer defend a strict products liability lawsuit by claiming: plaintiff has no contract with me!

Innocent Seller Defense

Because elimination of the privity defense enables injured consumers to sue retailers, wholesalers, and/or manufacturers, a consumer might choose to sue only a retailer. This is burdensome on a retailer, which might have to pay a judgment to a consumer and then seek reimbursement (indemnity) from the wholesaler which might, in turn, seek reimbursement for what it paid to the retailer from the manufacturer. Often, the only fault lies with the manufacturer and other entities are sued simply for selling a defective product made by another. Therefore, about 20 states have enacted so-called "innocent seller" statutes that often prevent injured consumers from suing those retailers, wholesalers, and other entities solely because they are in the chain of distribution. It often requires plaintiffs to sue manufacturers only, because they are usually in the best position to recognize and remedy product defects. There are exceptions, of course.

Consider Texas. Under its innocent seller statute, even innocent sellers may be sued if the manufacturer cannot be successfully sued in Texas because of (a) a lack of personal jurisdiction in the Texas courts, or (b) insolvency of the manufacturer. Otherwise, non-manufacturing sellers such as retailers cannot be sued unless they bear some responsibility for plaintiff's injury in that the plaintiff proves:

(1) that the seller participated in the design of the product;

(2) alteration or modification;

(3) that the seller installed the product, or had the product installed, on another product and the claimant's harm resulted from the product's installation onto the assembled product;

(4) that:

> (A) the seller exercised substantial control over the content of a warning or instruction that accompanied the product;
>
> (B) the warning or instruction was inadequate; and
>
> (C) the plaintiff's harm resulted from the inadequacy of the warning or instruction;

(5) that:

> (A) the seller made an express factual representation about an aspect of the product;
>
> (B) the representation was incorrect;
>
> (C) the plaintiff relied on the representation in obtaining or using the product; and
>
> (D) if the aspect of the product had been as represented, the plaintiff would not have been harmed by the product or would not have suffered the same degree of harm; or

(6) that:

(A) the seller actually knew of a defect to the product at the time the seller supplied the product; and

(B) the plaintiff's harm resulted from the defect.

If plaintiffs do sue innocent sellers, they are immediately entitled to indemnity for their costs and expenses in defending the lawsuit from the manufacturer and need not wait until the end of litigation to demand that right.

Economic Loss Doctrine

When he ate a defective Hot Tamale, Knight suffered personal injuries, which are the primary focus of the strict liability tort. The *economic loss doctrine* has been adopted in many jurisdictions to draw a strong line between tort liability and contract liability and it has important ramifications for products liability law. It generally holds that if a defective product damages only itself, a lawsuit must be brought on a contract-based warranty theory. However, if humans are injured, a negligence or strict liability theory is also appropriate. And if other property is damaged, a tort-based negligence suit may be viable as well.

Both the innocent seller defense and the economic loss doctrine appear in this case.

LOPEZ v. HURON
Texas Court of Appeals, 490 S.W.3d 517 (2016)

Huron makes and sells masa. Lopez agreed to supply Huron with plastic bags suitable for packaging the masa. Lopez ordered the bags from A.J. Plastics, Inc., which made the bags and shipped them directly to Lopez. Many of the bags failed, ruining the masa contained therein. Huron's customers returned the masa they had purchased from Huron, which had to refund their money. Huron sued Lopez and A.J. Plastics and a jury found for Huron against Lopez on implied warranty of merchantability and fitness claims and against A.J. Plastics on a merchantability claim. Lopez appealed, arguing that Texas' version of an "innocent seller" statute (section 82.003) protected him from liability because he was not the manufacturer of the defective bags.

Marion, Judge:

We disagree with Lopez's contention that the application of section 82.003 is not limited to products liability actions. As this court has stated, "Chapter 82 of the Texas Civil Practice and Remedies Code addresses product liability." *Fields v. Klatt Hardware & Lumber, Inc.* 374 S.W.3d 543 (Tex. App. 2012).

The term "product liability" action is statutorily defined as: "any action against a manufacturer or seller for recovery of damages arising out of personal injury, death, or property damage allegedly caused by a defective product whether the action is based in strict tort liability, strict products liability, negligence, misrepresentation, breach of express or implied warranty, or any other theory or combination of theories."

Lopez contends Huron's claim of breach of implied warranty is a products liability action because the statutory definition expressly encompasses breach of implied warranty claims. Huron counters that not every breach of implied warranty claim is encompassed within the definition of a products liability action because a products liability action as defined must seek the recovery of damages "arising out of personal injury, death, or property damage." In essence, Huron argues the phrase "arising out of personal injury, death, or property damages" has acquired a particular meaning as it relates to breach of implied warranty and product liability claims, and that meaning must be applied in determining whether Huron's breach of implied warranty claim falls within the statutory definition of a products liability action. Huron contends his breach of implied warranty claim is not a products liability action because his claims sounds in contract, not tort.

The law recognizes a distinction exists between products liability claims and contractual claims. In Texas, the perimeters between these two types of claims is governed by the economic loss rule. *Sharyland Water Supply Corp. v. City of Alton*, 354 S.W.3d 407 (Tex.2011). "The economic loss rule applies when losses from an occurrence arise from failure of a product and the damage or loss is limited to the product itself." *Equistar Chemicals v. Dresser-Rand Co.*, 354 S.W.3d 864 (Tex. 2007). "In such cases, recovery is generally limited to remedies grounded in contract (contract-based statutory remedies), rather than tort." *Sharyland*. "The rule does not preclude tort recovery if a defective product caused physical harm to the ultimate user or consumer or other property of the user or consumer in addition to causing damage to the product itself." *Eauistar*.

The same rule applies in determining whether an implied warranty claim is a contractual or a tort claim. Acknowledging a breach of implied warranty claim can be either a contract or tort claim, the Texas Supreme Court has held the nature of the claim is determined by examining the alleged damages. *JCW Electronics v. Garza*, 257 S.W.3d 701 (Tex. 2008). "When the damages are purely economic, the claims sounds in contract." *Id.* "But a breach of implied warranty claim alleging damages for death or personal injury sounds in tort." *Id.*

The statutory definition of a "products liability action" recognizes that the "recovery of damages arising out of personal injury, death, or property damage" has a particular meaning in the law which must be applied in construing the statute. By limiting the damages recoverable in a "products liability action" in this manner, the Legislature incorporated the concept of the economic loss rule into the definition.

An implied warranty claim is a contractual claim if the only injury is to the defective product itself. In this case, Lopez contends Huron alleged damage to "other property," namely the masa packaged inside the plastic bags that spoiled. "Texas courts have rejected the argument that damage to a finished product caused by a defective component part constitutes damage to 'other property,' so as to permit tort recovery for damage to the finished product." *Pugh v. Gen. Terrazzo Supplies, Inc.* 243 S.W.3d 84 (Tex. App. 2007).

In this case, Huron used the plastic bags as a component in a final product, namely the packaged masa. In the context of this commercial transaction, damage to the packaged masa could be reasonably contemplated by Huron and Lopez in the event the bags were defective. The only damages Huron alleged were for economic loss relating to the final product. Because the claim is for damage to a finished product caused by a defective component, there is no damage to "other property." Accordingly, because Huron's claim did not seek "damages arising out of personal injury, death, or property damage" under the particular meaning that phrase has acquired, Huron's claim [against Lopez] is not a products liability action [and is therefore not barred by the innocent seller statute]. Affirmed.

Remember that only about 20 states have innocent seller statutes and that in some of those states, unlike in Texas, the statute applies to warranty lawsuits for economic damage as well as tort-based suits for personal injury and injury to "other property."

To give just one more example of the economic loss doctrine in action, in *Red Rose Transit Auth. v. North American Bus Industries,* 2013 U.S. Dist. LEXIS 6969 (E.D. Pa. 2013), a bus with a defect in its electrical system caught fire and burned up, damaging a bus barn in which it was stored and other buses stored therein. Fortunately, no humans were injured in the fire. The court held: "The economic loss doctrine prohibits plaintiffs from recovering in tort economic losses which flow from a breach of contract." Therefore, regarding damage to the defective bus itself (including decreased value, repair costs, and lost profits), plaintiff buyer (a public transit authority) could sue only on breach of warranty grounds. The court held that the buyer could have negotiated stronger warranty provisions had it chosen to do so. However, regarding the damage to the other buses and he bus barn, plaintiff could bring a tort-based claim on a negligence theory and could have brought a strict liability suit to recover for any personal injuries had any occurred.

Plaintiff Misconduct Defenses

In negligence cases, of course, a plaintiff's carelessness is simply compared with the defendant's in most jurisdictions. The plaintiff's own carelessness can reduce or even bar recovery. In strict liability claims (and, in most jurisdictions, express and implied warranty claims), "plaintiff carelessness" is not treated as a single concept. Rather, several types of plaintiff misconduct are recognized, with differing effects on liability.

One category is simple plaintiff carelessness, often described as the *failure to discover or guard against* a defect in a product. Although some jurisdictions compare such plaintiff carelessness with the defendant's fault under a comparative negligence statute, others conclude that consumers are entitled to assume that products are defect-free. Unwilling to impose an obligation on consumers to assume that products they use might be defective, these latter jurisdictions hold that simple plaintiff carelessness is no defense at all to strict liability (or warranty) claims.

Another category of plaintiff misconduct is *product misuse*, which occurs when a plaintiff uses a product for a purpose for which it was not designed. For example, a consumer might use a pop bottle as a hammer or a lawn mower as a hedge trimmer. In some jurisdictions, unforeseeable product misuse indicates that the product is not defective and constitutes a complete defense to strict liability (and warranty) claims; in other jurisdictions, it is merely evidence of plaintiff misconduct to be compared with the defendant's fault. However, when the plaintiff's misuse is foreseeable to the defendant (for example, that the purchaser of a sports car might exceed the speed limit), many jurisdictions impose on the defendant a duty to warn against the misuse, or perhaps even to install safety devices to guard against the misuse. Therefore, foreseeable misuse typically is no defense.

A final category of plaintiff misconduct is *assumption of risk*, which occurs when a plaintiff, having discovered a defect in the product and fully appreciating its danger, voluntarily uses the product anyway. In *Sargia v. Skil Corp.*, 1985 U.S. Dist. LEXIS 12752 (S.D.N.Y), the plaintiff (a professional carpenter) was using the defendant's portable saw when he noticed that the "bumper" for the saw's protective blade guard had fallen off, causing the lower guard to obstruct the front of the blade, preventing it from beginning to cut. Although he had two similar saws on the job site, the plaintiff continued to use the defective one, manually retracting the blade guard before each cut. Six hours later, the plaintiff started the saw and then reached over with his left hand to retract the guard with its lift lever. Unfortunately, he missed the lever and hit the blade, amputating 3/8th of an inch of his finger. This was held to be an assumption of the risk by the plaintiff. In some jurisdictions, assumption of the risk is a complete bar to recovery; in others, it is evidence of the plaintiff's fault to be compared with that of the defendant under a comparative fault statute.

FEDERAL CONSUMER LEGISLATION

Over the years Congress has enacted a number of federal regulatory laws dealing with the safety and quality of goods. For the most part these laws have focused solely on protecting ultimate consumers from physical harm, and until recently, they were enacted piecemeal and were rather narrow in scope. Examples include the Food, Drug and Cosmetic Act (1938), the Flammable Fabrics Act (1953), the Refrigerator Safety Act (1956), the Hazardous Substances Act (1960), and the Poison Prevention Packaging Act (1970).

Consumer Product Safety Act

In 1972 Congress enacted the *Consumer Product Safety Act*—the first law to deal with the safety of consumer products in general—and created a federal agency, the Consumer Product Safety Commission (CPSC), to administer it. Some consumer products are not covered by the Consumer Product Safety Act because they come under the aegis of other federal laws. The most important of these are food, drugs, and cosmetics, which are regulated by the Food and Drug Administration under the Food, Drug, and Cosmetic Act. Automobiles are also excluded because of coverage by the other legislation.

The CPSC possesses broad powers and performs many functions, ranging from safety research and testing to preparing safety rules and standards for more than 10,000 products. It has the power to ban or recall products and to require special labeling in certain circumstances. It can levy civil penalties on those who violate the Act and criminal penalties on those who willfully violate it. Yet despite the extensive range of its power, the CPSC has been criticized for not issuing sufficient standards to ensure the integrity of consumer products. Additionally, the CPSC has been woefully underfunded and understaffed in recent years, making it very difficult for the agency to effectively perform its tasks.

Because the maximum fine the CPSC can impose upon companies for failing to disclose problems with their products is (as of 2018) $110,000 for each violation and $16,075 for any series of violations, some believe that the CPSC lacks the enforcement threat to be effective. When Wal-Mart was caught failing to report safety hazards with fitness machines, the $750,000 fine it was assessed cost the company the equivalent of only 1 minute and 33 seconds worth of company sales. Still, the CPSC often attempts to punish companies through bad publicity, and 17 of 18 penalty settlements from 2015-2017 exceeded $1 million and most exceeded $2 million.

Magnuson-Moss Warranty Act

In 1975 Congress passed the consumer-oriented *Magnuson-Moss Warranty Act* (MMWA). It applies only to purchases by ultimate consumers for personal, family, or household purposes and not to transactions in commercial or industrial settings. The MMW does not regulate the safety or quality of consumer goods. Instead it prevents deceptive warranty practices, makes consumer warranties easier to understand, and provides an effective means of enforcing warranty obligations. The MMWA is limited to consumer transactions, and it modifies the UCC warranty rules in some respects; in non-consumer transactions, the UCC rules govern.

The type of warranty to which the MMWA applies is much more narrowly defined than is an express warranty under the UCC. Specifically, it is (1) any written affirmation of fact made by a supplier to a purchaser relating to the quality or performance of a product and affirming that the product is defect free or that it will meet a specified level of performance over a period of time; or (2) a written undertaking to "refund, repair, replace, or take other action" if a product fails to meet written specifications. Obviously, express warranties that are not in writing, such as those created by verbal description or by sample, will continue to be governed solely by the UCC, even though a consumer transaction is involved.

The MMWA does not require anyone to give a warranty on consumer goods. It applies only if the seller *voluntarily chooses* to make an express written warranty (perhaps in an effort to render a product more competitive). When a written warranty is provided for a product costing $10 or more, it must be labeled as either "full" or "limited." When the cost of goods exceeds $15, the warranty must be contained in a single document, must be written in clear language that includes (1) a description of items covered and those excluded, along with specific service guarantees; (2) instructions on how to proceed in the event of product failure; (3) the identity of those to whom the warranty is extended; and (4) limitations on the warranty period.

Under a full warranty, the warrantor (and no one else in the chain of distribution) must assume certain minimum duties and obligations. For instance, the seller must agree to *repair or replace* any malfunctioning or defective product within a "reasonable" time and without charge. If the warrantor makes a reasonable number of attempts to remedy the defect and is unable to do so, the consumer can choose to receive a *cash refund or replacement* of the product without charge. No *time limitation* can be placed on a full warranty; and consequential damages (such as for personal injury or property damage) can be disclaimed only if the limitation is *conspicuous*.

A written warranty that does not meet the minimum requirements must be designated conspicuously as a *limited warranty*. It may cover, for example, parts but not labor, or it may levy shipping and handling fees. If a time limit (such as 24 months) is all that prevents the warranty from being a full one, it can be designated as a "full 24-month warranty."

Because its purpose is to regulate *written* warranties, the MMWA generally does not cover implied warranties of merchantability and fitness for a particular purpose. These are governed by the UCC, and as we have seen, the UCC allows implied warranties to be disclaimed. However, drafters of the MMWA saw fit to limit the use of disclaimers where written warranties are involved, because of certain abusive practices prevalent at the time: Sellers were providing limited express warranties in bold print and then disclaiming implied warranties, thus leaving the consumer with few rights while appearing to offer substantial protection.

For this reason, the Magnuson-Moss Warranty Act *prohibits a disclaimer of implied warranties* (1) when an express written warranty is given, whether full or limited, or (2) when a service contract is made with the consumer within 90 days after the sale. (Under a service contract the seller agrees to service and repair a product for a set period of time in return for a fixed fee.) If the written warranty specifies a *time* limitation, however, implied warranties may be suspended by a disclaimer effective *after* the written warranty expires.

The MMWA Act is usually enforced by the Federal Trade Commission (FTC), but the Attorney General or an injured consumer can also initiate an action if informal procedures for settling disputes prove ineffective. Sellers are authorized to dictate the informal procedures by which a particular dispute is to be settled. If these procedures follow FTC guidelines, the consumer cannot resort to court action until all established means have been exhausted.

LEGISLATIVE LIMITATIONS ON THE PRODUCTS LIABILITY REVOLUTION

From 1960 until the mid-1980s, the general trend in products liability law was strongly pro-plaintiff. New theories allowed new classes of injured persons to sue defendants that had never previously been vulnerable to suit. Injured consumers have been well served, and it is certainly arguable that products liability litigation has been the most influential factor in bringing about improved product designs and safety practices that have saved thousands of lives.

Recent years, however, have seen a countervailing pressure to reform products liability law in order to roll back the "products liability revolution." Business groups have alleged that damage awards have increased insurance premiums, raised the prices of some products, induced some companies to cease manufacturing certain products, and arguably, caused American business to suffer a competitive disadvantage abroad. The expense of designing eminently safe products, coupled with insurance rates much higher than those in Europe, has added significantly to the costs of production. These developments raised a storm of protest among manufacturers and sellers, leading both individual states and Congress to enact laws making it more difficult for injured consumers to sue successfully.

Among reforms passed in many states are: (a) ceilings on damage awards in product liability suits, (b) caps on punitive damage awards, (c) elimination or modification of joint & several liability, (d) requiring plaintiffs to show the economic and technological feasibility of alternative designs in design defect cases, (e) statutes of repose providing a time period (often from 5 to 15 years) after which the manufacturer is not liable for injuries caused by a product, the statute of limitations notwithstanding, and (f) creation of "state of the art" defenses that prevent defendants' engineering and other decisions from being judged by 20-20 hindsight.

Federal product liability reform has been suggested repeatedly over the years for the twin purposes of reining in the products liability revolution and creating uniformity of standards so that manufacturers and other products liability defendants will not be subjected to varied and conflicting standards as they operate in many states and plaintiffs will not be able to forum shop in filing products liability suits. In the 1990s, President Clinton vetoed a broad federal product liability "reform" act. Nonetheless, over the years Congress has enacted numerous laws limiting product liability, including: (a) the General Aviation Revitalization Act which sets an 18-year statute of repose for small aircraft and aircraft parts, (b) the National Childhood Vaccine Injury Act of 1986 which minimizes potential financial liability of vaccine manufacturers with the goal of creating a stable supply of needed vaccines, (c) the Good Samaritan Food Donation Act of 1996 which protects people or companies from most civil suits that might otherwise arise from food donations; and (d) the Protection of Lawful Commerce in Arms Act which grants substantial protection from liability to gun manufacturers whose products are used by criminal shooters.

CHAPTER 21

BANKRUPTCY

- Overview of Debtor-Creditor Relations
- Bankruptcy Proceedings
- Liquidation Proceedings
- Business Reorganization
- Adjustment of Debts
- International Considerations

Bankruptcy law is critical to the effective functioning of a competitive economy. Not all firms will prosper, especially in difficult financial times. Bankruptcy law can often help firms reorganize as an alternative to going out of business, can balance the competing claims of creditors, and can give individuals a fresh start. Although individuals file most bankruptcy proceedings, businesses of all sizes are liquidated or rehabilitated, often affecting the livelihoods of many employees, the security of suppliers and customers, and even the economies of local communities.

Bankruptcy law balances the interests of debtors and creditors. Repeat players in the game, such as credit card companies and banks, have a lot at stake when bankruptcy law is framed and amended. For example, in 2005 the Bankruptcy Abuse Prevention and Consumer Protection Act (BAPCPA) was enacted after more than a decade of controversy. Opponents of the reform claimed that the banks and credit card companies supporting the reforms were earning record profits while targeting broad groups of people whom they knew with actuarial certainty would get into financial difficulty if given easy credit. Opponents called the new law an attack on the middle class, while supporters termed it a needed return to personal fiscal responsibility. BAPCBA certainly had an impact. In 2005, 2,078,000 bankruptcies were filed, but BAPCBA drove that number down to 827,395 in 2007. In 2018, there were 22,245 business bankruptcy filings and 753,333 non-business filings.

OVERVIEW OF DEBTOR-CREDITOR RELATIONS

The treatment of debtors has varied greatly over the years. During certain early periods, debtors were forced to become servants of their creditors, were thrown into prison, or even had body parts removed for failure to pay a debt. Fortunately, we now have more humane solutions, but still struggle to balance the creditor's rights with the debtor's desire for relief from debts.

Numerous devices have been developed through the years for resolving debtor-creditor disputes. In this chapter we will deal primarily with one such procedure—*bankruptcy* under federal law. However, many of the other methods available under state common-law principles, state statutes, and private agreements may actually be preferable to bankruptcy when it is possible to use them. Bankruptcy has traditionally been viewed as an avenue of last resort. Before we turn to a detailed examination of the federal bankruptcy law, we first will survey some of the alternatives.

Alternatives to Bankruptcy

Although time and space do not permit a detailed analysis of each method of debt resolution, the following methods are frequently used when debtors cannot pay their obligations: (1) foreclosure on a real estate mortgage, (2) enforcement of a secured transaction (Article 9 of the UCC), (3) enforcement of an artisan's lien, (4) enforcement of a mechanic's lien, (5) writ of execution on a judgment, (6) garnishment, (7) attachment, (8) receivership, (9) canceling a fraudulent conveyance, (10) composition of creditors, and (11) assignment for the benefit of creditors.

Foreclosure on a Real Estate Mortgage

Under the terms of a mortgage agreement, the mortgagee (creditor) has the right to declare the entire mortgage debt due and enforce his rights through a remedy called *foreclosure.* In most states the mortgagee is required to sell the mortgaged real estate (even if it is the person's homestead) under the direction of the court, using the proceeds to pay the foreclosure costs and the balance of the debt. If any proceeds are left over, the surplus goes to the mortgagor. If the proceeds are insufficient to cover the costs of foreclosure and the remaining indebtedness, the mortgagor is liable to the mortgagee for the unpaid balance of the debt. However, before the actual foreclosure sale and for a certain period of time thereafter (set by state statute), the mortgagor can redeem the property by full payment of costs, indebtedness, and interest.

Enforcement of a Secured Transaction

Under Article 9 of the UCC, when a debtor defaults on the security agreement made with a secured party (the creditor), the *collateral* (personal property) that is the subject of the security agreement can be used to satisfy the debt. Secured parties can retain possession of the collateral or take it from the debtor, either by court order or without court action if it can be accomplished peaceably. They can then either (1) keep the collateral in satisfaction of the debt by giving proper notice to the debtor of such intention (assuming the debtor does not object), or (2) sell the collateral through a "commercially reasonable" process. The secured party must always sell the collateral if proper objection is made by the debtor to the party keeping it or if the collateral is classified as "consumer goods" and the debtor has paid 60 percent or more of the debt.

If the collateral is kept by the secured party, the debt is discharged. If the collateral is sold and the proceeds are insufficient to pay the debt and the costs of enforcing the security interest, the secured party is usually entitled to seek a deficiency judgment for the balance. The debtor can redeem the collateral at any time until its sale or disposal.

Enforcement of an Artisan's Lien

The *artisan's lien,* a possessory lien given to creditors who perform services on personal property or take care of goods entrusted to them, was developed at common law. If the debtor does not pay for the services, the creditor is permitted to obtain a judgment and/or to foreclose and sell the property in satisfaction of the debt. Any proceeds remaining from the sale of the property after paying the debt and costs of sale must be returned to the debtor. In order to exercise this lien, the creditor must have retained possession of the property and must not have agreed to provide the services on credit. Many states have passed statutes governing the procedures to be followed in enforcing such a lien. If the creditor operates a warehouse and the claim arises from unpaid storage charges, the procedures which must be followed are set forth in Article 7 of the Uniform Commercial Code.

Enforcement of a Mechanic's Lien

Certain other liens have been made available to creditors by state statutes. One of the most common is the *mechanic's lien*—a lien against real estate for labor, services, or materials used in improving the realty. When the labor or materials are furnished, a debt is incurred. To make the real property itself security for the debt, the creditor must file a notice of lien in a manner provided by statute. To be effective, it usually must be filed within a specified period (usually 60 to 120 days) after the last materials or labor were furnished. If the notice is properly filed and the debt is not paid, the creditor can foreclose and sell the real estate in satisfaction of the debt. This is similar to a foreclosure of a real estate mortgage.

More than $5 million in artisan's and mechanic's liens were filed in the wake of completion of the Trump D.C. Hotel in 2017.

Writ of Execution on a Judgment

Once a debt becomes overdue, a creditor can file suit for payment in a court of law and, if successful, be awarded a judgment. If the judgment is not satisfied by the debtor, the creditor has the right to go back to court and obtain a *writ of execution.* The writ, issued by the clerk of the court, directs the sheriff or other officer to levy upon (seize) and sell any of the debtor's nonexempt property within the court's jurisdiction. The judgment is paid from the proceeds of the sale, and any balance is returned to the debtor. One limitation on the writ is that it can be levied only on nonexempt property. That is, exempt property, such as the debtor's homestead, cannot be taken to satisfy the judgment.

Garnishment

Another limitation of the writ of execution is that it usually cannot reach debts owed to the judgment debtor by third parties or the debtor's interests in personal property legally possessed by third parties.

However, the law does permit the creditor (using the proper court procedure) to require these persons to turn over to the court or sheriff money owed or property belonging to the debtor. This method of satisfying a judgment is called *garnishment*; the third party, called the garnishee, is legally bound by the court order. The most common types of "property" garnished are wages and bank accounts. The Federal Consumer Credit Protection Act (CCPA) generally limits garnishment of a debtor's current wages to 25 percent of take-home pay and prohibits the debtor's employer from discharging them because of garnishment for "any one indebtedness." Some state laws place greater restrictions on garnishment of wages.

Attachment

The seizing of a debtor's property under a court order, known as *attachment*, is a statutory remedy and can be exercised only in strict accordance with the provisions of the particular state statutes. Under some statutes, it is available to a creditor even before a judgment has been rendered. Statutory grounds for attachment prior to judgment are limited, usually including situations where the debtor is unavailable to be served with a summons or where there is a reasonable belief that the debtor may conceal or remove property from the jurisdiction of the court before the creditor can obtain a judgment.

To employ attachment as a remedy, the creditor must file with the court an affidavit attesting to the debtor's default and the legal reasons why attachment is sought. Additionally, the creditor must post a bond sufficient to cover at least the value of the debtor's property, the value of the loss of use of the goods suffered by the debtor (if any), and court costs in case the creditor loses the suit. Most states require the opportunity for some form of hearing before a judge. The court then issues a *writ of attachment,* directing the sheriff or other officer to seize nonexempt property sufficient to satisfy the creditor's claim. If the creditor's suit against the *debtor* is successful, the property seized may then be sold to satisfy the judgment.

Receivership

Attachment may prove inadequate to protect creditors while they pursue their claims if the debtor's property requires care (such as crops, livestock, etc.). In such cases, on essentially the same grounds as for attachment, the court may appoint a receiver to care for and preserve the property pending the outcome of the lawsuit in which one or more creditors are seeking to collect unpaid debts. It is then said that the debtor's property is placed in *receivership*. The object of receivership is to prevent a debtor from "wasting" assets while being pursued by creditors. Receivership may also be the appropriate protective device where the debtor has a going business and where creditors can convince the court that it is being grossly mismanaged.

Canceling a Fraudulent Conveyance

Debtors may transfer property to a third party by gift or contract under circumstances in which their creditors are defrauded. If such fraud can be established, creditors can have the conveyance (transfer) set aside and the property made subject to their claims—even if the property is in the hands of a third party.

The fraud necessary to have a conveyance set aside can be either fraud in fact or fraud implied in law. *Fraud in fact* occurs when debtors transfer property with the specific intent of defrauding their creditors. A creditor will usually encounter difficulty in having a conveyance voided on this ground, simply because of the inherent problems in proving fraudulent intent. The creditor's chances of proving this intent will, however, be somewhat greater if the transfer was to the debtor's spouse or other relative. In addition, it is often the case that the debtor actually had no such fraudulent intent, but the creditor is harmed nevertheless.

To assist the creditor, most states have enacted laws (such as the Uniform Voidable Transactions Act or the similar Uniform Voidable Transfers Act) which create a presumption of fraud under certain circumstances. This means that, in some situations, the burden of proof shifts to the debtor. If the debtor fails to prove the absence of fraud, there is *fraud implied in law* and the transfer is voided. Generally speaking, these statutes create a presumption of fraud whenever a debtor transfers property without receiving "fair consideration" in return and the debtor has insufficient assets remaining to satisfy creditors.

Composition of Creditors

Sometimes debtors or their creditors recognize early (before bankruptcy) that the debtor is in financial difficulty. Instead of pursuing remedies under bankruptcy, the debtor and creditors make a contract to resolve the debts. The contract—referred to as a *composition of creditors*—calls for the debtor's immediate payment of a sum less than that owed and for the creditor's immediate discharge of the debt. This payment can be made from any of the debtor's assets, including exempt property. Such contracts are held to be binding by the courts. The advantage of an immediate payment and minimum costs makes the composition attractive to creditors. Whether the composition agreement is binding on nonparticipating creditors depends on state law. At common law the agreement was not binding on these creditors.

Assignment for the Benefit of Creditors

Under common-law principles and, in some states, under statute, an *assignment for the benefit of creditors* is available as an alternative to bankruptcy. In such an arrangement, the debtor voluntarily transfers title to some or all assets to a "trustee" or "assignee" for the creditors' benefit. By such a transfer, the debtor irrevocably gives up any claim to or control over the property. The trustee or assignee liquidates (sells) the property and makes payment to the creditors on a pro rata basis according to the debt amounts.

Creditors can either accept or reject the partial payment. One accepting such a payment may in effect be releasing the balance of the claim. In most states, creditors who do not participate in the assignment cannot reach the assets that have been so assigned. They do, however, have rights to any surplus remaining after participating creditors have been paid, any nonexempt property not assigned, and any nonexempt property acquired after the assignment. Nonparticipating creditors may also be able to force the debtor into bankruptcy.

BANKRUPTCY PROCEEDINGS

History of Bankruptcy Statutes

Bankruptcy as a legal device was initially applied only to commercial business failures. The first Bankruptcy Act in England was adopted in 1542 and applied only to traders or merchants who were unable to pay their debts. It was not until 1861 that bankruptcy was extended to other types of debtors.

The founders of the United States were well acquainted with the problems of debtors. In drafting the U.S. Constitution, they stated in Article I, Section 8, clause 4: "The Congress shall have the power . . . to establish . . . uniform laws on the subject of bankruptcies throughout the United States."

Bankruptcy Proceedings Today

Today's bankruptcy law comes primarily from the 1978 Bankruptcy Reform Act, also known as the Bankruptcy Code, as amended several times (most importantly by the Bankruptcy Abuse Prevention and Consumer Protection Act of 2005) (BAPCPA). Before 1978, federal district courts handled bankruptcy cases, often delegating the responsibility for hearing them to ''bankruptcy referees'' who were not federal judges but who performed many of the same functions. The 1978 Code established a set of bankruptcy courts, with one such court in each federal district. Bankruptcy judges are complemented by U.S. Trustees who, as we shall see, usually select the trustees who administer the debtors' estates.

Bankruptcy courts hear and decide all of the issues directly involving the bankruptcy proceeding itself, but related non-bankruptcy matters, such as a tort claim by or against the debtor, are generally decided by the federal district court. An appeal from a bankruptcy court decision is heard by a federal district court or, under certain conditions, by a bankruptcy appellate panel or even a Court of Appeals.

The Bankruptcy Code provides for three different kinds of proceedings: (1) liquidation; (2) reorganization; and (3) adjustment of the debts of an individual with regular income. These provisions are contained in Chapters 7, 11, and 13 of the Bankruptcy Code. Additionally, Chapter 12 provides a provision primarily available to family farmers. Our discussion will focus primarily on Chapter 7's liquidation proceeding, often referred to as "straight bankruptcy," because it is the most common type. We will, however, devote some attention to the other three types of proceedings at the end of this chapter. It should also be noted that current bankruptcy law contains a special section, Chapter 9, dealing with the rehabilitation of bankrupt municipalities. We will not address Chapter 9 in any detail, but recently it has been used by Detroit, Michigan, San Bernardino County, California, and other towns and counties.

LIQUIDATION PROCEEDINGS

Stated very generally, the object of a *liquidation proceeding* under Chapter 7 of the Bankruptcy Act is to sell the debtor's assets, pay off creditors insofar as it is possible to do so, and legally discharge the debtor from further responsibility. Chapter 7 filings general constitute around 70% of all individual bankruptcy filings.

Commencement of the Proceedings

A liquidation proceeding will be either a *voluntary case*, commenced by the debtor, or an *involuntary case*, commenced by creditors.

Voluntary Case

The filing of a *voluntary case* automatically subjects the debtor and its property to the jurisdiction and supervision of the Bankruptcy Court. Any debtor, whether an individual, a partnership, or a corporation, may file a petition for voluntary bankruptcy, with the following exceptions: (1) banks, (2) savings and loan associations, (3) credit unions, (4) insurance companies, (5) railroads, and (6) governmental bodies. These exempted organizations are covered by special statutes and their liquidation is supervised by particular regulatory agencies.

A debtor does not have to be insolvent in order to file a petition for voluntary bankruptcy, but as a practical matter it is usually insolvency that prompts such a petition. In addition, a husband and wife may file a joint petition, if both spouses consent.

To reduce the number of Chapter 7 voluntary filings by individuals, the BAPCPA required, first, that people undergo credit counseling before filing for bankruptcy. Second, the law requires voluntary filers to undergo a "means test" to determine if they can pay their debts. If they can, the courts should shift them from the liquidation bankruptcy of Chapter 7 to Chapter 13's provisions for adjustment of debts of individuals with regular income where the debtors will be required to make payments to creditors rather than receive a full discharge. The means test is a rough calculation which deems it an abuse of Chapter 7 for a debtor who can make payments to seek discharge of all obligations. These requirements will be discussed in more detail in the section relating to Chapter 13.

Involuntary Case

The types of organizations that are not permitted to file a voluntary liquidation case also cannot be subjected to an involuntary case. In addition to these exemptions, creditors also cannot file an involuntary case against farmers, family farmers, or nonprofit corporations.

If the debtor has twelve or more creditors, at least three must join in filing the case. If there are fewer than twelve creditors, the involuntary case may be filed by one or more of them. Regardless of the number of creditors, those filing the petition must have noncontingent unsecured claims against the debtor totaling in the aggregate at least $16,750 (in 2019). [Note: Most of the dollar values in these statutes are periodically adjusted for inflation.]

The debtor and his property automatically become subject to the jurisdiction and supervision of the bankruptcy court if the involuntary petition is not challenged. However, if the debtor contests the creditors' petition, the creditors must prove either (1) that the debtor has not been paying debts as they became due or (2) that the debtor's property has been placed in a receivership or an assignment for the benefit of creditors within 120 days before the involuntary petition was filed. If the filing creditors prove either of the above, the debtor and his property are then under the supervision of the court. If no such proof is made, the petition is dismissed.

Automatic Stay

As soon as the petition is filed in either a voluntary or involuntary case, an automatic stay is in operation. The automatic stay puts creditors' claims "on hold" until they are dealt with in the bankruptcy proceeding, and prevents creditors from taking any judicial, administrative, or other action against the debtor. A secured creditor, however, may petition the bankruptcy court and receive protection against the loss of its security. The court-ordered protection for *secured creditors* may take the form of cash payments from the debtor, substitute collateral, or an express grant of relief from the automatic stay permitting foreclosure of the security interest. BAPCPA created several exceptions to the automatic stay provision, which no longer stops or postpones (a) evictions by landlords (in cases where a judgment of possession was obtained prior to the bankruptcy filing or the eviction is based on endangerment of the rental property or illegal use of controlled substances), (b) actions to withhold, suspend or restrict a driver's license, (c) actions to withhold, suspend or restrict a professional or occupational license, (d) lawsuits to establish paternity, child custody, or child support, (e) divorce proceedings, or (f) lawsuits involving domestic violence.

The Trustee

After the debtor becomes subject to the bankruptcy proceeding, the U.S. Trustee must appoint an interim trustee to take over the debtor's property or business. A U.S. Trustee is appointed to monitor certain aspects of bankruptcy cases and to appoint and supervise the standing and panel trustees. Within a relatively short time thereafter, a permanent trustee will take over. This trustee may be elected by the creditors, but if they do not do so, the interim trustee receives permanent status.

The trustee is an individual or corporation who, under the court's supervision, administers and represents the debtor's estate. (Which property is included within the debtor's estate is discussed later.) The basic duties of the trustee are to: (1) investigate the financial affairs of the debtor; (2) collect assets and claims owned by the debtor; (3) temporarily operate the debtor's business, if necessary; (4) reduce the debtor's assets to cash; (5) receive and examine the claims of creditors, and challenge in bankruptcy court any claim which the trustee feels to be questionable; (6) oppose the debtor's discharge from his obligations when the trustee feels that there are legal reasons why the debtor should not be discharged; (7) render a detailed accounting to the court of all assets received and the disposition made of them; and (8) make a final report to the court when administration of the debtor's estate is completed. To fulfill these duties as representative of the debtor's estate, the trustee has the power to sue and be sued in that capacity, to use or sell property of the estate, and to employ accountants, attorneys, appraisers, auctioneers, and other professionals with court approval.

If they wish, unsecured creditors may elect a creditors' committee of three to eleven members for the purpose of consulting with the trustee. This committee may make recommendations to the court or U.S. Trustee regarding the latter's duties and may submit questions to the court or U.S. Trustee concerning administration of the debtor's estate.

Creditors' Meetings

Within a reasonable time after commencement of the case, the U.S. Trustee must call and preside at a meeting of unsecured creditors. The debtor will have already supplied the court with a list of creditors, so that they may be notified of the meeting. The judge of the bankruptcy court is not permitted to attend a creditors' meeting.

At the first meeting, creditors may elect the trustee. In order for such election to be possible, at least 20 percent of the total amount of unsecured claims which have been filed and allowed must be represented at the meeting. A trustee is elected by receiving the votes of creditors holding a majority, in amount, of unsecured claims represented at the meeting.

The other major item of business at the first creditors' meeting is an *examination of the debtor*. The debtor, under oath, will be questioned by the creditors and the trustee concerning (1) the debtor's assets, and (2) matters relevant to whether the debtor will be entitled to a discharge.

Duties of the Debtor

The bankruptcy law imposes the following duties on the debtor: (1) within a reasonable time after commencement of the proceedings, file with the court a list of creditors, a schedule of assets and liabilities, a schedule of income and expenditures, and a statement of financial affairs; (2) file with the court a statement of intention with respect to the retention or surrender of any property of the estate which secures consumer debt, specifying that such property shall be claimed as exempt, redeemed, or the debt reaffirmed thereon, and perform these intentions within 45 days after filing the notice; (3) cooperate and respond truthfully during the examination conducted at the first creditors' meeting; (4) surrender to the trustee all property to be included in the debtor's estate, as well as all documents, books, and records pertaining to this property; (5) cooperate with the trustee in whatever way necessary to enable the trustee to perform her duties; and (6) appear at the hearing conducted by the court concerning whether the debtor should be discharged.

A debtor who fails to fulfill any of these duties may be denied a discharge from liabilities.

The Debtor's Estate

Types of Property

The property owned by the debtor that becomes subject to the bankruptcy proceeding, ultimately to be sold by the trustee, is the *debtor's estate.* This includes all tangible and intangible property interests of any kind, unless specifically exempted. For example, the estate could consist of consumer goods, inventory, equipment, any of the various types of interests in real estate, patent rights, trademarks, copyrights, accounts receivable, and various contract rights.

After-Acquired Property. In addition to property owned at the time the bankruptcy petition (either voluntary or involuntary) was filed, the debtor's estate also includes after-acquired property under some circumstances. Specifically, the estate includes any type of property that the debtor acquires, or becomes entitled to acquire, within 180 days after the petition filing date (1) by inheritance, (2) as a beneficiary of a life insurance policy, or (3) as a result of a divorce decree or a property settlement agreement with the debtor's spouse. And, of course, if a particular item of property is part of the estate, any proceeds, income, production, or offspring from it will also be part of the estate. However, the debtor's earnings from his own labor or personal service after the filing date are not included in the estate.

Exemptions

A debtor who is an individual (rather than a partnership or corporation) may claim certain *exemptions*. This means that certain types of property are exempt and are not included in the debtor's estate. The debtor may keep such property and still receive a discharge from liabilities at the close of the proceedings. Every state has exemption statutes setting forth the types of property which are exempt from seizure under a writ of execution. Before passage of the 1978 Bankruptcy Code, the debtor's exempt property in a federal bankruptcy case was determined solely by the exemption statutes of the state where the debtor lived. The 1978 Code, however, included for the first time a list of federal exemptions that are available to the debtor in bankruptcy regardless of the state of domicile.

Under the federal exemption a debtor may claim, among others, the following exemptions (and each spouse may claim them in a joint case): (1) the debtor's interest in a homestead used as a residence, up to a value of $25,150; (2) the debtor's interest in a motor vehicle, up to a value of $4,000; (3) the debtor's interest, up to $625 per item, in household furnishings, household goods, appliances, wearing apparel, animals, crops or musical instruments used primarily for personal, family, or household (nonbusiness) uses, subject to a total of $13,400 for all such items; (4) the debtor's interest in jewelry, up to a total of $1,700 in value, held primarily for personal purposes; (5) the debtor's interest in any kind of property, not to exceed in value $1,325, and any unused portion of the homestead exemption, subject to a limit of $12,575; (6) the debtor's interest in implements, tools, or professional books used in her trade, not to exceed $2,525 in value; (7) any unmatured life insurance policies owned by the debtor (except for credit life policies); (8) the debtor's aggregate interest, not to exceed $13,400 in value, in any accrued dividend or interest under, or loan value of, any unmatured life insurance contract owned by the debtor; (9) professionally prescribed health aids for the debtor or a dependent of the debtor; (10) the debtor's right to receive: a social security benefit, unemployment compensation, or a local public assistance benefit, (b) a veterans' benefit, (c) a disability, illness, or unemployment benefit, (d) alimony, support or separate maintenance, and (e) a payment under a stock bonus, pension, profit sharing, annuity or similar plan or contract on accountant of illness, disability, death, age, or length of service (with some qualifications); (11) the right to receive (a) awards under crime victim's reparation laws, (b) payments on account of wrongful death of a dependent, (c) payments on life insurance contracts due to the death of one upon whom the debtor depended, (d) payments on account of bodily injury not to exceed $25,150, and (e) payment in compensation for loss of future earnings of the debtor or one on whom the debtor was dependent; and (12) retirement funds to the extent that they are in an account that is exempt from taxation under certain sections of the Internal Revenue Code. The amounts in #10 (d)-(e) and #11(b)-(e) are generally limited to a sum reasonably necessary for the support of the debtor and dependents. [Remember that these dollar amounts are for 2019 but are periodically adjusted for inflation.]

The 1978 Code did not bring national uniformity to bankruptcy exemptions for two reasons. First, it permitted debtors to choose either the federal exemption or those of the state where the debtor lived. Because many states' exemptions are more liberal than federal exemptions, debtors in those states naturally choose the state exemptions. Second, the Code allows state legislatures to prohibit debtors in their states from using the federal exemptions, and a majority of states did so.

Because Florida and Texas have particularly liberal homestead exemptions, formerly wealthy bankrupt individuals often moved to those states to shield assets from creditors. The law now has several provisions aimed at preventing debtors from simply picking the most liberal state exemption around. For example, debtors seeking to invoke a state exemption must choose the law of the place where their domicile was located in the two years before filing. They may no longer simply move to Florida a week before filing for bankruptcy and build a mansion to claim as their homestead. Also, the law now imposes an absolute federal cap of $170,350 (in 2019) for the state homestead exemption under certain circumstances. Those circumstances are that either (a) the court determines that the debtor has been convicted of a felony demonstrating that the filing of the bankruptcy petition was an abuse of the provisions of the Bankruptcy Code, or (b) the debtor owes a debt arising from a violation of federal or state securities laws, fiduciary fraud, racketeering, or crimes or intentional torts that caused serious bodily injury or death in the preceding five years. There is a loophole if more valuable homestead property is "reasonably necessary for the support of the debtor."

Voidable Transfers

In a number of circumstances, the trustee has the power to sue and restore to the debtor's estate property or funds which the debtor had transferred to some third party. People seeking to hide assets from creditors often transfer title to relatives, friends, or others for inadequate or even fake consideration. These situations, called *voidable transfers,* include:

1. The trustee generally may cancel any transfer of property of the debtor's estate which was made *after* the debtor became subject to the bankruptcy proceeding. The trustee must exercise this power within two years after the transfer was made, or before the bankruptcy case is concluded, whichever occurs first.
2. The trustee may cancel *any fraudulent transfer* (fraudulent conveyance) made by the debtor within two years prior to the filing of the bankruptcy petition. This power of the trustee applies to both *fraud in fact* and *fraud implied in law,* as discussed earlier in the chapter. It will be remembered that insolvency is an element of fraud implied in law. In determining the fair value of assets for this purpose under the bankruptcy law, exempt property and the property transferred in the particular transaction being challenged are not included.
3. The trustee has the power to cancel a property transfer on any ground that the debtor could have used, such as fraud, mistake, duress, undue influence, incapacity, or failure of consideration.
4. A trustee may avoid any transfer by a debtor to a self-settled trust (or similar device) within 10 years of filing of the petition, if the debtor had "actual intent to hinder, delay, or defraud any entity to which the debtor was or became, on or after the date that such transfer was made, indebted."

Voidable Preferences

A key objective of bankruptcy law is to insure equal treatment of most types of unsecured creditors. Equal treatment is important because a bankrupt debtor's assets are usually sufficient to pay only a fraction of creditors' total claims. Therefore, the law grants the trustee the power to cancel any transfer by the debtor to a creditor which amounted to a *preference*, which is essentially a transfer of property or money, in payment of an existing debt, which causes creditors to receive more of the debtor's estate than they would be entitled to receive in the bankruptcy proceeding had the transfer not occurred.

General Rules for Canceling Preferences

In the ordinary situation, a preferential transfer to a creditor can be canceled by the trustee, and the property or funds returned to the debtor's estate, if (1) it occurred within 90 days prior to the filing of the bankruptcy petition, and (2) the debtor was insolvent at the time of the transfer. In this situation, however, insolvency is *presumed*. So, if a creditor has received a preferential transfer within the 90 days prior to the filing of the bankruptcy petition, that creditor must prove that the debtor was not insolvent at the time.

Insiders. If the creditor receiving the preference was an *insider*, the trustee's power of cancellation extends to any such transfer made within one year before the bankruptcy petition was filed. In general, an insider is an individual or business firm which had a close relationship with the debtor at the time of the transfer. Examples would include a relative or partner of the debtor, a corporation of which the debtor was a director or officer, or a director or officer of a corporate debtor. In such a case, however, the presumption of insolvency only applies to the 90 days prior to the petition filing. Therefore, if the preference being challenged by the trustee had taken place more than 90 days but less than a year before the petition filing, the trustee must prove that the debtor was insolvent. Figure 21.1 illustrates these rules.

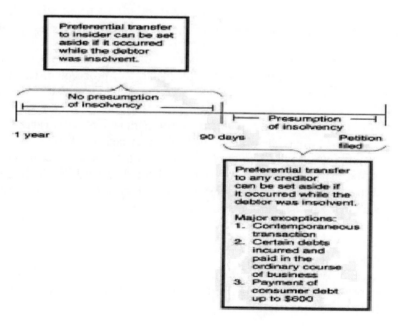

Figure 21.1 Trustee's Recovery of Voidable Preference

Exceptions. In certain circumstances, a payment or transfer to a creditor cannot be canceled even though it meets the basic requirements of a voidable preference. Three of the most important exceptions are:

1. A transaction which involved a "contemporaneous" (that is, within a very short period of time) exchange between debtor and creditor cannot be canceled by the trustee. For example, the debtor may have bought goods from the creditor and either paid for them immediately or within a few days. This type of transaction is treated differently than one in which the debtor was paying off a debt which had existed for some time. Such a contemporaneous exchange will be left standing even though it occurred during the 90-day period prior to the filing date.
2. Even though there is no contemporaneous exchange, a payment or transfer to a creditor within the 90-day period will not be canceled if (1) the particular debt had been incurred by the debtor in the ordinary course of business, (2) the payment was made in the ordinary course of the debtor's business, and (3) the payment was made according to ordinary business terms. An example would be the debtor's payment, during the 90-day period, of the previous month's utility bill.
3. A debtor's repayment of up to $600 in *consumer debt* is not treated as a voidable preference.

Voidable preferences can occur in an almost infinite variety of circumstances. The following case illustrates one such situation, and also shows one of the many reasons why it is so important for a creditor to obtain and perfect a security interest whenever possible.

PIERCE v. SKILLMAN'S AUTO SALES
2019 Bankr. LEXIS 3405 (U.S. Bankruptcy Court, W.D. Ky., 2019)

Sandra Pierce (plaintiff-debtor) bought a car from defendant Skillman's Auto Sales on February 24, 2017. After Pierce fell behind on the payments, Skillman's repossessed and resold the vehicle, incurred a deficiency balance, and acquired a default judgment against Pierce in January 2019. The state civil court awarded Skillman's a judgment of $4,275.81 and soon entered an Order for Wage Garnishment. In February and March of 2019, six wage garnishments took place and Pierce's employer's payroll processor sent six checks to Skillman's attorney. The six checks totaled $600.64, but only the first five were processed. Those were for a total of $497.66.

The sixth check was written on March 24, 2019, but Pierce filed for bankruptcy on that day. Skillman's attorney was notified of the bankruptcy filing before receiving the sixth check on March 26, 2019, and filed a Notice of Release of Garnishment on the 25th.

Pierce brought this lawsuit to recover alleged preferential transfers to Skillman's that were made in the 90 days before the bankruptcy petition was filed. Skillman's moved to dismiss on grounds that the small preference exception (less than $600) applied here.

U.S. Bankruptcy Judge Fulton:

The plaintiff bears the burden of proving each element of a preferential transfer under 11 U.S.C. § 547(b) by a preponderance of the evidence. For a transfer to constitute a voidable preference, the plaintiff must show: (1) benefit to a creditor; (2) on account of an antecedent debt; (3) made while the debtor was insolvent; (4) within ninety days before bankruptcy; and (5) which enabled the creditor to receive a larger share of the estate than if the transfer had not been made. But a transfer under this section may not be avoided if, in a case filed by an individual debtor whose debts primarily are consumer debts (such as the present case), the aggregate value of all property that constitutes or is affected by such transfer is less than $600. See § 547(c)(8).

Skillman's claims that the funds garnished, after deducting the sixth unprocessed check from the total received, total $497.66 and are therefore protected by the de minimis $600.00 exception. The Court agrees. Although Skillman's counsel did receive check #6 on March 26, 2019, neither party disputes that the sixth check was ultimately never processed, distributed, or presented for payment by Skillman's. On the contrary, check #6 was returned to ADP's counsel and, according to the parties' testimony, was eventually refunded to Pierce. Ultimately, Skillman's only ever received $497.66 in wages garnished from the debtor.

Courts generally find no avoidable preference under § 547(b) when the total amount of money actually transferred to the garnishee does not exceed $600, despite the fact that additional checks may have been sent and received but were never processed. The underlying facts are analogous to those of *In re Pierce*, a case in which the Eighth Circuit Bankruptcy Appellate Panel upheld the lower bankruptcy court's decision that, under § 547(c)(8), debtors were not allowed to recover $562.78 withheld from debtor's pay and paid to a judgment creditor, because the aggregate sum the creditor actually received was less than $600. 504 B.R. 506 (B.A.P. 8th Cir. 2013). Even though two additional payments totaling $296.20 were received by the creditor after debtors declared bankruptcy, the bankruptcy court excluded those payments when determining if the creditor received more than $600, because those payments were returned to debtor's employer and paid back to the debtor. The *Pierce* court found as follows:

> We agree with the Pierces that at one time all six wage garnishments, totaling $858.98, constituted preferences. We have previously held that for preference purposes, if the property transferred is the debtor's wages then the transfer occurs precisely when wages are earned. In this case, each garnishment was a preference at the time Pierce earned his wages. However, when the Pierces brought this preference action the garnishee had already returned $296.20 to them. As the Pierces recognized, the only remedy available to them was avoidance of the wages still in possession of Collection Associates. Accordingly, their requested relief was for the return of $562.78, an amount less than $600. Therefore, under any definition of the word transfer and regardless of the benefit Collection Associates received § 547(c)(8) applies as a defense to this preference action.

…Ultimately, Debtor can only seek to avoid preferential transfers of wages still in the garnishee's possession. But here, it remains undisputed that Skillman's processed just five of the six checks received and retained only $497.66 of the total aggregate $600.64 funds garnished from debtor's employer. Any remaining checks Skillman's received were returned and were never processed. … The Court will enter Judgment in favor of the Defendant.

Claims

As a general rule, any legal obligation of the debtor existing pre-petition gives rise to a claim against the debtor's estate in the bankruptcy proceeding. There are, however, several special situations we should mention.

1. If the claim is contingent on the happening or nonhappening of some future event or, if its amount is in dispute, the bankruptcy court has the power to make an estimate of the claim's

value.

2. If the claim against the debtor is for breach of contract, it will include any damages which accrued prior to the filing of the bankruptcy petition, and also those damages attributable to the debtor's failure to perform any future obligations under the contract. Of course, this is no different from an ordinary breach of contract claim when bankruptcy is not involved. However, under the bankruptcy law, if the claim arises out of an employment contract or a real estate lease, limits are placed on a claim for damages relating to future nonperformance. In the case of an employment contract, such damages are limited to a term of one year from the filing date or the date the contract was repudiated, whichever is earlier. In the case of a real estate lease, damages are limited to either one year or 15 percent of the remaining term of the lease, whichever is greater, up to a maximum of three years. The starting point for measuring this time is the same as for employment contracts. One reason for these limits is that contracts of these two types are frequently long-term ones, and the farther in the future we try to compute damages, the more speculative they get.

3. A creditor who has received a voidable transfer or preference may not assert a claim of any kind until the wrongfully received property or funds are returned to the debtor's estate.

Subject to the above limitations, any claim filed with the bankruptcy court is allowed unless it is contested by an interested party, such as the trustee, debtor, or another creditor. If challenged, the court will rule on the claim's validity after pertinent evidence is presented at a hearing held for that purpose. In this regard, claims against the debtor's estate will be subject to any defenses that the debtor could have asserted had there been no bankruptcy. The fact that a claim is allowed, of course, does not mean that the particular creditor will be paid in full; it just means that the creditor has the hope of receiving *something*.

Distribution of Debtor's Estate

A secured creditor—one having a security interest or lien in a specific item of property—can proceed directly against that property for satisfaction of his claim. This is true even though the debtor is or is about to become subject to a bankruptcy proceeding. In a sense, then, *secured creditors* have priority over all classes of unsecured creditors (usually referred to as *general creditors*). However, if a portion of a secured creditor's claim is not secured, that portion is treated like any other unsecured claim.

When the trustee has gathered all the assets of the debtor's estate and reduced them to cash, these proceeds will be distributed to unsecured creditors. There are certain unsecured claims which are given priority in this distribution. If there are sufficient proceeds, these claims are paid in full in the order of their priority. The following classes of debts are listed in order of priority. [Numbers are adjusted for inflation periodically.] Each class must be fully paid before the next is entitled to anything. If available funds are insufficient to satisfy all creditors within a class, they receive payments in proportion to the amounts of their claims.

1. Domestic support obligations. BAPCPA elevated such claims to top priority.
2. Costs and expenses of administration (trustees', auctioneers', and attorneys' fees, for example).
3. If the proceeding is an involuntary one, any expense incurred in the ordinary course of the debtor's business or financial affairs after commencement of the case but before appointment of the trustee.
4. Any claim for wages, salaries, or commissions, including vacation, severance, and sick leave pay earned by an individual within 180 days before the filing of the petition or the cessation

of the debtor's business, whichever occurs first, limited to $13,650 per individual.

5. Any claim for contributions to an employee benefit plan arising from services performed within 180 days before filing or business cessation, limited to $13,650 per individual. However, a particular individual cannot receive more than $13,650 under the fourth and fifth priorities combined.

6. Claims of grain producers or U.S. fishermen against a debtor who owns or operates a grain or fish storage facility for the produce or its proceeds, limited to $6,725 for each such individual.

7. Claims of individuals, up to $3,050 per person, for deposits made on consumer goods or services that were not received.

8. Claims of governmental units for various kinds of taxes, subject to time limits that differ depending on the type of tax.

If all priority claims are paid and funds still remain, general creditors are paid in proportion to the amounts of their claims. Any portion of a priority claim that was beyond the limits of the priority is treated as a general claim. [These are the dollar amounts for 2019; they are adjusted for inflation periodically.]

Discharge

After the debtor's estate has been liquidated and distributed to creditors, the bankruptcy court may conduct a hearing to determine whether the debtor should be discharged from liability for remaining obligations.

Grounds for Refusal of Discharge

Under certain circumstances the court will refuse to grant the debtor a discharge. Among these are the following:

1. Only an individual can receive a discharge in a liquidation proceeding. For a corporation to receive a discharge it must go through a reorganization proceeding (discussed later in the chapter), or be dissolved in accordance with state corporation statutes.

2. Debtors will be denied a discharge if they had previously received such a discharge within eight years before the present bankruptcy petition was filed.

3. Debtors will be denied a discharge if they have committed any of the following acts (a) intentionally concealed or transferred assets for the purpose of evading creditors, within one year before the filing of the petition or during the bankruptcy proceedings; (b) concealed, destroyed, falsified, or failed to keep business or financial records unless there was reasonable justification for such action or failure; (c) failed to adequately explain any loss of assets; (d) refused to obey a lawful court order or to answer a material court-approved question in connection with the bankruptcy case; or (e) made any fraudulent statement or claim in connection with the bankruptcy case.

4. If a discharge has been granted, the court may revoke it within one year if it is discovered that the debtor had not acted honestly in connection with the bankruptcy proceeding.

In *Norwest Bank Nebraska, N.A. v. Tveten*, 858 F.2d 871 (8th Cir. 1988) a physician debtor in financial difficulties liquidated all his nonexempt property (including land, pension funds, and other property) and converted it into $700,000 worth of life insurance and annuity benefits with the Lutheran Brotherhood, a fraternal benefit organization. Under Minnesota law, these benefits could not be attached by creditors. Because the debtor admitted to making these transactions for the sole purpose of shielding his property from creditors while knowing of many legitimate claims, the court held that he had acted fraudulently and denied him a discharge in bankruptcy proceedings. While state law governed the exemptions, federal law governed the debtor's entitlement to a bankruptcy discharge.

Non-dischargeable Debts

Even if debtors are granted a general discharge from obligations, there nevertheless are a few types of claims for which they will continue to be liable. These *non-dischargeable debts* include the following:

1. Obligations for payment of taxes are not discharged if (a) the particular tax was entitled to a priority in the distribution of the debtor's estate, but was not paid; or (b) a tax return had been required but was not properly filed; or (c) the debtor had willfully attempted to evade the particular tax.
2. Claims arising out of the debtor's false pretenses, false representation, or actual fraud.
3. The debtor is not excused from liability for a willful and malicious tort.
4. Claims for alimony and child support are not discharged.
5. Debtors are not discharged from a claim that they failed to list in the bankruptcy case if this failure caused the creditor not to assert the claim in time for it to be allowed.
6. A fine, penalty, or forfeiture payable to a governmental unit, which is neither compensation for actual pecuniary loss nor a tax penalty, is not discharged.
7. Obligations to repay student loans, scholarships, stipends or other educational benefits are not dischargeable unless to refuse discharge would impose an "undue hardship" on the debtor or the debtor's dependents. To show undue hardship, courts have required student loan borrowers to show that they could not maintain a minimal standard of living if they had to repay the student loans, that the situation would continue to exist, and that the borrower had made a good-faith attempt to pay the money back. Because it is hard to know the future, most courts made it very hard for borrowers to prove that their inability to maintain a minimal standard of living would "continue to exist." They often required borrowers to show that they would likely *never* be able to achieve that minimal standard of living. Recently, some courts have made it slightly easier for such borrowers to meet the standard by, for example, requiring borrowers to show only that they will have such difficulties during a significant portion of the repayment period, not forever. *Rosenberg v. N.Y. State Higher Ed. Services Corp.* (S.D.N.Y. Bkrtcy., Jan. 7, 2020).
8. Any judgments or awards of damages resulting from the debtor's operation of a motor vehicle while legally intoxicated are not dischargeable.
9. Primarily because of credit card abuse by debtors shortly before filing for bankruptcy, two types of consumer debts have been made non-dischargeable: (a) debts of more than $725 to a particular creditor for luxury goods or services, if incurred within 90 days of the order for relief (i.e., the petition); and (b) cash advances totaling more than $1,000 obtained by using a credit card or other open-ended consumer credit arrangement, if incurred within 70 days of the order for relief.

The following is a recent Supreme Court case defining "actual fraud" in this statute relating to non-dischargeable debts.

HUSKY INTERNATIONAL ELECTRONICS, INC. V. RITZ
136 S. Ct. 1581 (2016)

Between 2003 and 2007, Husky International Electronics, Inc. sold electronic components to Chrysalis Manufacturing Corp., which incurred a debt to Husky of

$163,999.38. During the same period, respondent Daniel Lee Ritz, Jr., served as a director of Chrysalis and owned at least 30% of Chrysalis' common stock.

Between 2006 and 2007, Ritz drained Chrysalis of assets it could have used to pay its debts to creditors like Husky by transferring large sums of Chrysalis' funds to other entities that he controlled. As just two of numerous examples, Ritz transferred $52,600 to CapNet Risk Management, Inc., a company he owned in full and $121,831 to CapNet Securities Corp., a company in which he owned an 85% interest.

In 2009, Husky sued Ritz seeking to hold him personally responsible for Chrysalis' $163,999.38 debt, arguing that Ritz' intercompany-transfer scheme was "actual fraud" for purposes of a Texas law that allows creditors to hold shareholders responsible for corporate debt. Later, Ritz filed for Chapter 7 bankruptcy in the United States Bankruptcy Court for the Southern District of Texas. Husky then initiated an adversarial proceeding in Ritz's bankruptcy case again seeking to hold Ritz personally liable for Chrysalis' debt. Husky also contended that Ritz could not discharge that debt in bankruptcy because the same intercompany-transfer scheme constituted "actual fraud" under 11 U.S.C. §523(a)(2)(A)'s exemption to discharge.

The District Court held that Ritz was personally liable for the debt under Texas law, but that the debt was not "obtained by . . . actual fraud" under §523(a)(2)(A) and could be discharged in his bankruptcy. Husky appealed, arguing that Ritz's asset-transfer scheme was effectuated through a series of fraudulent conveyances—or transfers intended to obstruct the collection of debt. And, Husky said, such transfers are a recognizable form of "actual fraud." The Fifth Circuit disagreed, holding that a necessary element of "actual fraud" is a misrepresentation from the debtor to the creditor, as when a person applying for credit adds an extra zero to her income or falsifies her employment history. In transferring Chrysalis' assets, Ritz may have hindered Husky's ability to recover its debt, but the Fifth Circuit found that he did not make any false representations to Husky regarding those assets or the transfers and therefore did not commit "actual fraud." Husky appealed to the Supreme Court.

Sotomayor, Justice:

The Bankruptcy Code prohibits debtors from discharging debts "obtained by . . . false pretenses, a false representation, or actual fraud." The Fifth Circuit held that a debt is "obtained by . . . actual fraud" only if the debtor's fraud involves a false representation to a creditor. That ruling deepened an existing split among the Circuits over whether "actual fraud" requires a false representation or whether it encompasses other traditional forms of fraud that can be accomplished without a false representation, such as a fraudulent conveyance of property made to evade payment to creditors. We granted certiorari to resolve that split and now reverse.

The term "actual fraud" in §523(a)(2)(A) encompasses forms of fraud, like fraudulent conveyance schemes, that can be effected without a false representation. Before 1978, the Bankruptcy Code prohibited debtors from discharging debts obtained by "false pretenses or false representations." In the Bankruptcy Reform Act of 1978, Congress added "actual fraud" to that list. The prohibition now reads: "A discharge under [Chapters 7, 11, 12, or 13] of this title does not discharge an individual debtor from any debt . . . for money, property, services, or an extension, renewal, or refinancing of credit, to the extent obtained by . . . false pretenses, a false representation, or actual fraud."

When "'Congress acts to amend a statute, we presume it intends its amendment to have real and substantial effect.'" *United States v. Quality Stores, Inc.*, 572 U.S. ___ (2014). It is therefore sensible to start with the presumption that Congress did not intend "actual fraud" to mean the same thing as "a false representation," as the Fifth Circuit's holding suggests. But the historical meaning of "actual fraud" provides even stronger evidence that the phrase has long encompassed the kind of conduct alleged to have occurred here: a transfer scheme designed to hinder the collection of debt.

This Court has historically construed the terms in §523(a)(2)(A) to contain the "elements that the common law has defined them to include." *Field v. Mans*, 516 U.S. 59 (1995). "Actual fraud" has two parts: actual and fraud. The word "actual" has a simple meaning in the context of common-law fraud: It denotes any fraud that "involv[es] moral turpitude or intentional wrong." Neal v. Clark, 95 U.S. 704 (1878). "Actual" fraud stands in contrast to "implied" fraud or fraud "in law," which describe acts of deception that "may exist without the imputation of bad faith or immorality." *Ibid.* Thus, anything that counts as "fraud" and is done with wrongful intent is "actual fraud."

Although "fraud" connotes deception or trickery generally, the term is difficult to define more precisely. See 1 J. Story, Commentaries on Equity Jurisprudence §189, p. 221 (6th ed. 1853) (Story) ("Fraud . . . being so various in its nature, and so extensive in its application to human concerns, it would be difficult to enumerate all the instances in which Courts of Equity will grant relief under this head"). There is no need to adopt a definition for all times and all circumstances here because, from the beginning of English bankruptcy practice, courts and legislatures have used the term "fraud" to describe a debtor's transfer of assets that, like Ritz' scheme, impairs a creditor's ability to collect the debt.

One of the first bankruptcy acts, the Statute of 13 Elizabeth, has long been relied upon as a restatement of the law of so-called fraudulent conveyances (also known as "fraudulent transfers" or "fraudulent alienations"). In modern terms, Parliament made it fraudulent to hide assets from creditors by giving them to one's family, friends, or associates. The principles of the Statute of 13 Elizabeth—and even some of its language—continue to be in wide use today. *BFP v. Resolution Trust Corporation*, 511 U.S. 531, 540 (1994) ("The modern law of fraudulent transfers had its origin in the Statute of 13 Elizabeth"). The degree to which this statute remains embedded in laws related to fraud today clarifies that the common-law term "actual fraud" is broad enough to incorporate a fraudulent conveyance.

Equally important, the common law also indicates that fraudulent conveyances, although a "fraud," do not require a misrepresentation from a debtor to a creditor. As a basic point, fraudulent conveyances are not an inducement-based fraud. Fraudulent conveyances typically involve "a transfer to a close relative, a secret transfer, a transfer of title without transfer of possession, or grossly inadequate consideration." In such cases, the fraudulent conduct is not in dishonestly inducing a creditor to extend a debt. It is in the acts of concealment and hindrance. In the fraudulent-conveyance context, therefore, the opportunities for a false representation from the debtor to the creditor are limited. The debtor may have the opportunity to put forward a false representation if the creditor inquires into the whereabouts of the debtor's assets, but that could hardly be considered a defining feature of this kind of fraud.

Relatedly, under the Statute of 13 Elizabeth and the laws that followed, both the debtor and the recipient of the conveyed assets were liable for fraud even though the recipient of a fraudulent conveyance of course made no representation, true or false, to the debtor's creditor. The famous *Twyne's Case*, which this Court relied upon in *BFP*, illustrates this point. *See Twyne's Case*, 76 Eng. Rep., at 823 (convicting Twyne of fraud under the Statute of 13 Elizabeth, even though he was the recipient of a debtor's conveyance). That principle underlies the now-common understanding that a "conveyance which hinders, delays or defrauds creditors shall be void as against [the recipient] unless . . . th[at] party . . . received it in good faith and for consideration." Glenn, Law of Fraudulent Conveyances §233, at 312. That principle also underscores the point that a false representation has never been a required element of "actual fraud," and we decline to adopt it as one today.

Because we must give the phrase "actual fraud" in §523(a)(2)(A) the meaning it has long held, we interpret "actual fraud" to encompass fraudulent conveyance schemes, even when those schemes do not involve a false representation. We therefore reverse the judgment of the Fifth Circuit and remand the case for further proceedings consistent with this opinion. So ordered.

BUSINESS REORGANIZATION

If it is felt that reorganization and continuance of a business is feasible and is preferable to liquidation, a petition for reorganization may be filed under Chapter 11 of the Bankruptcy Code. The reorganization procedure is intended for use by businesses, but it does not matter whether the owner of the business is an individual, partnership, or corporation.

A *reorganization case* can be either voluntary or involuntary, and the requirements for filing an involuntary case are the same as for a liquidation proceeding. In general, the types of debtors exempted from reorganization proceedings are the same as those exempted from liquidation proceedings. The most important aspects of a reorganization case are summarized below.

As soon as the petition is filed, an *automatic stay* is in operation just as in a liquidation proceeding. The automatic stay is even more important in a reorganization proceeding, because without such a stay the debtor often would find it impossible to continue operating its business.

There may or may not be a trustee in a reorganization case. If trustees are appointed, they will take over the business and will have basically the same duties and powers as in a liquidation case. Essentially, the court will appoint a trustee if requested by an interested party (such as a creditor) and if it appears that such an appointment would be in the best interests of all parties involved. Obviously, a court will appoint a trustee if the judge feels there is a possibility of the debtor's business being mismanaged or assets being wasted or concealed. If a trustee is not appointed, the debtor remains in possession and control of the business. In this situation, the debtor is called the *debtor in-possession*, and has all the powers of a trustee.

After commencement of the case, the U.S. Trustee must appoint a committee of unsecured creditors. If necessary, the court or the U.S. Trustee may appoint other creditors' committees to represent the special interests of particular types of creditors. A committee of shareholders may also be appointed to oversee the interests of that group, if the debtor is a corporation.

The creditors' and shareholders' committees, and the trustee (if one was appointed), will investigate the business and financial affairs of the debtor. A *reorganization plan* will then be prepared and filed with the bankruptcy court. This plan must divide creditors' claims and shareholders' interests into classes according to their type. For instance, claims of employees, secured creditors, bondholders, real estate mortgage holders, and government units might be segregated into different classes. The plan must indicate how claims within each class are going to be handled and to what extent each class will receive less than full payment, as well as provide adequate means for the plan's execution. Treatment of claims within each class must be equal.

The court will *confirm* (approve) the reorganization plan if (a) each class has approved the plan and (b) the court rules that the plan is "fair and equitable" to all classes. A plan is deemed to be accepted by a class of creditors if it received favorable votes from those representing at least two-thirds of the amounts of claims and more than half of the number of creditors within that class. If the parties are unable to produce an acceptable plan or if the plan subsequently does not work as expected, the court may either dismiss the case or convert it into a liquidation proceeding.

After a reorganization plan has been confirmed, the debtor is discharged from those claims not provided for in the plan. However, the types of claims that are not discharged in a liquidation case are also not discharged in a reorganization case.

Following is an important Supreme Court case interpreting and applying Chapter 11.

CZYZEWSKI v. JEVIC HOLDING CORP.
137 S. Ct. 973 (2017)

Jevic Holding Corp. wholly owned Jevic Transportation, a trucking company (cumulatively termed "Jevic"). In 2006, Sun Capital Partners led a leveraged buyout financed by CIT Group. The buyout provided Jevic with $85 million in revolving credit extended by CIT so long as Jevic maintained $5 million in capital. It did not, and on May 19, 2008, Jevic ceased operations and informed its employees of their termination. On the next day, Jevic filed a voluntary Chapter 11 petition, owing $53 million to Sun and CIT, which held first-priority liens on Jevic's assets. Jevic also owed $20 million to tax creditors and general unsecured creditors.

During the bankruptcy proceeding, a group of terminated truck drivers sued Jevic for a violation of the WARN Act (Worker Adjustment and Retraining Notification), which requires 60 days' notice prior to terminating employees. The bankruptcy court held that Jevic was liable for $12.4 million, $8.3 million of which was a claim for employee wages that was entitled to special priority. Also, the Official Committee of Unsecured Creditors ("the committee") which was appointed to represent unsecured creditors sued Sun and CIT alleging fraudulent conveyances.

Eventually, when Jevic's only remaining assets were $1.7 million in cash (subject to Sun's and CIT's priority claim) and the claim for fraudulent conveyance against Sun and CIT, the parties all met to negotiate a settlement. Sun, CIT, and the committee agreed to a "structured dismissal"—a dismissal of the Chapter 11 proceeding with conditions. The conditions were that Sun, CIT and the committee would release claims against each other (including dismissal of the fraudulent conveyance claim), CIT would pay $2 million into an account to pay Jevic's and the committee's legal fees, and Sun would assign its lien on Jevic's $1.7 million to a trust which would pay tax and administrative creditors first and then general unsecured creditors on a pro rata basis. The settlement gave nothing to the drivers and they objected to it, as did the U.S. Bankruptcy Trustee.

The bankruptcy court overruled the objections and approved the settlement. The drivers and the trustee appealed, but the district court and subsequently the Third Circuit affirmed the settlement, so they appealed on to the Supreme Court.

Breyer, Justice:

Bankruptcy Code Chapter 11 allows debtors and their creditors to negotiate a plan for dividing an estate's value. But sometimes the parties cannot agree on a plan. If so, the bankruptcy court may decide to dismiss the case. The Code then ordinarily provides for what is, in effect, a restoration of the prepetition financial status quo.

In the case before us, a Bankruptcy Court dismissed a Chapter 11 bankruptcy. But the court did not simply restore the prepetition status quo. Instead, the court ordered a distribution of estate assets that gave money to high-priority secured creditors and to low-priority general unsecured creditors but which skipped certain dissenting mid-priority creditors [the drivers]. The skipped creditors would have been entitled to payment ahead of the general unsecured creditors in a Chapter 11 plan (or in a Chapter 7 liquidation). The question before us is whether a bankruptcy court has the legal power to order this priority-skipping kind of distribution scheme in connection with a Chapter 11 dismissal.

In our view, a bankruptcy court does not have such a power. A distribution scheme ordered in connection with the dismissal of a Chapter 11 case cannot, without the consent of the affected parties, deviate from the basic priority rules that apply under the primary mechanisms the Code establishes for final distributions of estate value in business bankruptcies.

We begin with a few fundamentals: A business may file for bankruptcy under either Chapter 7 or Chapter 11. In Chapter 7, a trustee liquidates the debtor's assets and distributes them to creditors. In Chapter 11, debtor and creditors try to negotiate a plan that will govern the distribution of valuable assets from the debtor's estate and often keep the business operating as a going concern.

Filing for Chapter 11 bankruptcy has several relevant legal consequences. First, an estate is created comprising all property of the debtor. Second, a fiduciary is installed to manage the estate in the interest of the creditors. This fiduciary, often the debtor's existing management team, acts as "debtor in possession." It may operate the business and perform certain bankruptcy-related functions, such as seeking to recover for the estate preferential or fraudulent transfers made to other persons. Third, an "automatic stay" of all collection proceedings against the debtor takes effect.

It is important to keep in mind that Chapter 11 foresees three possible outcomes. The first is a bankruptcy-court-confirmed plan. Such a plan may keep the business operating but, at the same time, help creditors by providing for payments, perhaps over time. The second possible outcome is conversion of the case to a Chapter 7 proceeding for liquidation of the business and a distribution of its remaining assets. That conversion in effect confesses an inability to find a plan. The third possible outcome is dismissal of the Chapter 11 case. A dismissal typically "revests the property of the estate in the entity in which such property was vested immediately before the commencement of the case"—in other words, it aims to return to the prepetition financial status quo.

Nonetheless, recognizing that conditions may have changed in ways that make a perfect restoration of the status quo difficult or impossible, the Code permits the bankruptcy court, "for cause," to alter a Chapter 11 dismissal's ordinary restorative consequences. A dismissal that does so (or which has other special conditions attached) is often referred to as a "structured dismissal," defined by the American Bankruptcy Institute as a "hybrid dismissal and confirmation order . . . that . . . typically dismisses the case while, among other things, approving certain distributions to creditors, granting certain third-party releases, enjoining certain conduct by creditors, and not necessarily vacating orders or unwinding transactions undertaken during the case." Although the Bankruptcy Code does not expressly mention structured dismissals, they appear to be increasingly common.

The Code also sets forth a basic system of priority, which ordinarily determines the order in which the bankruptcy court will distribute assets of the estate. Secured creditors are highest on the priority list, for they must receive the proceeds of the collateral that secures their debts. Special classes of creditors, such as those who hold certain claims for taxes or wages, come next in a listed order. Then come low-priority creditors, including general unsecured creditors. The Code places equity holders at the bottom of the priority list. They receive nothing until all previously listed creditors have been paid in full.

The Code makes clear that distributions of assets in a Chapter 7 liquidation must follow this prescribed order. It provides somewhat more flexibility for distributions pursuant to Chapter 11 plans, which may impose a different ordering with the consent of the affected parties. But a bankruptcy court cannot confirm a plan that contains priority-violating distributions over the objection of an impaired creditor class (a class that will not be paid all that is owed its members).

The question here concerns the interplay between the Code's priority rules and a Chapter 11 dismissal. Can a bankruptcy court approve a structured dismissal that provides for distributions that do not follow ordinary priority rules without the affected creditors' consent? Our simple answer to this complicated question is "no." The Code's priority system constitutes a basic underpinning of business bankruptcy law. Distributions of estate assets at the termination of a business bankruptcy normally take place through a Chapter 7 liquidation or a Chapter 11 plan, and both are governed by priority. In Chapter 7 liquidations, priority is an absolute command—lower priority creditors cannot receive anything until higher priority creditors have been paid in full. Chapter 11 plans provide somewhat more flexibility, but a priority-violating plan still cannot be confirmed over the objection of an impaired class of creditors. The priority system applicable to those distributions has long been considered fundamental to the Bankruptcy Code's operation. …

[There are some cases that have] approved interim distributions that violate ordinary priority rules. But in such instances one can generally find significant Code-related objectives that the priority-violating distributions serve. Courts, for example, have approved "first-day" wage orders that allow payment of employees' prepetition wages, "critical vendor" orders that allow payment of essential suppliers' prepetition invoices, and "roll-ups" that allow lenders who continue financing the debtor to be paid first on their prepetition claims. In doing so, these courts have usually found that the distributions at issue would enable a successful reorganization and make even the disfavored creditors better off. By way of contrast, in a structured dismissal like the one ordered below, the priority-violating distribution is attached to a final disposition; it does not preserve the debtor as a going concern; it does not make the disfavored creditors better off; it does not promote the possibility of a confirmable plan; it does not help to restore the status quo ante; and it does not protect reliance interests. In short, we cannot find in the violation of ordinary priority rules that occurred here any significant offsetting bankruptcy-related justification.

The judgment of the Court of Appeals is reversed, and the case is remanded for further proceedings consistent with this opinion.

The Small Business Reorganization Act of 2019

Although some truly large companies (*e.g.*, Sears, Pacific Gas & Electric, American Airlines, Montgomery Ward), file for Chapter 11 bankruptcy, 95% of filers are small- and medium-sized businesses. Many believe that it has been too much of a struggle for small business debtors to reorganize under Chapter 11. In 1994, Congress established a "fast-track" Chapter 11 provision for small businesses. Under this provision, they can save time and expense over the normal Chapter 11 rules. For example, orders in small business cases do not require creditor committee consent. More changes were made with BAPCPA in 2005, but Congress believed that even more needed to be done for small debtors, so in 2019 it passed the Small Business Reorganization Act which creates a new subchapter V for Chapter 11 for use by "small business debtors"--generally, debtors with secured and unsecured debts totaling less than $2,725,625.

The SBRA alters Chapter 11 for these small debtors in these ways:
- A trustee will be appointed in every case to facilitate the reorganization
- Only the debtor may file a plan of organization, which must be done within 90 days after the order for relief
- An unsecured creditors committee will not generally be appointed
- Requirements for confirming the plan are altered to be more debtor-friendly, particularly when there is opposition by an impaired class of creditors
- Changes make it easier for individual debtors to retain their residences

ADJUSTMENT OF DEBTS

Of an Individual with Regular Income

Debtors who have a regular income can and generally should pay more to creditors than those without regular income. For debtors without regular income, Chapter 7 may be the only real choice. For others, Chapter 13 provides for "Adjustment of Debts of an Individual with Regular Income," known as a wage earner's plan. Individuals with regular income who owe fixed unsecured debts less than $419,275 or fixed secured debts less than $1,184,200 (in 2019) may choose this method, which has parallels to Chapter 11's reorganization plan for businesses, but is less complex and expensive. Sole proprietors, salaried employees, individuals living on fixed incomes, and others are eligible to use Chapter 13. It often enables them to save their homes from foreclosure.

As noted earlier, a major goal of the 2005 BAPCPA was to force individuals into Chapter 13 rather than allowing them to just write the slate clean in Chapter 7 liquidation. While the Bankruptcy Code has always allowed a bankruptcy court to dismiss a Chapter 7 proceeding, or to convert it to a Chapter 11 or Chapter 13 proceeding if it constituted an "abuse" of the bankruptcy process, the law now requires that a court must presume that abuse exists if debtors have a total disposable income over a certain level ($12,850 in 2019). These individuals are generally to be shifted to Chapter 13 and ordered to make payments on credit card and other bills. Debtors may also convert their reorganization plans into liquidation plans, although this can raise significant legal issues itself. To further discourage filing of bankruptcy petitions by consumers, BAPCPA requires that debtors must undergo credit counseling before being allowed to file.

The Petition

When an individual voluntarily files a Chapter 13 petition or a court converts a Chapter 7 proceeding to Chapter 13, a trustee will be appointed to make payments under the plan. Filing of the plan activates an automatic stay that applies to consumer debt but not the debtor's business debt. The stay prevents creditors from attempting to collect prepetition debts or seizing control of the debtor's assets through foreclosure, garnishment, or similar means. The stay helps preserve order in debt collection so that all creditors in the same class may be treated equally.

The Repayment Plan

The debtor must file a repayment plan, often called a "wage earner plan" under Chapter 13. It may provide for payment of all obligations, or a lesser percentage. Before BAPCPA, payment plans could not exceed three years without court approval. Today, plans will typically run for five years.

The plan must provide for turning over to the trustee the debtor's future earnings or income as needed to execute the plan. Priority claims must be respected, and all claims within a particular class must be treated equally.

The bankruptcy court will hold a confirmation hearing at which interested parties may lodge objections to the plan. Regarding claims of secured creditors, courts will confirm the plan if (a) the secured creditors have accepted it, (b) it provides that they retain their liens and receive property not less than the secured portion of their claims, or (c) the debtor surrenders the secured property to the creditors.

Unsecured creditors are not entitled to vote regarding the plan, but may object to it. The court can approve the plan over their objection if (a) the value of the property to be distributed is at least equal to the amount of the claims, or (b) when all the debtor's projected "disposable income" (all income minus amounts needed to support debtor and dependents and/or needed to meet ordinary expenses to continue operation of a business) will be paid to creditors.

A plan will not be confirmed if the debtor is not current in payments on any post-petition domestic support obligation. The provisions on redemption and reaffirmations under Section 7, discussed earlier, generally apply under Chapter 13 as well.

Discharge

In order to induce individual debtors to choose Chapter 13 rather than Chapter 7 so that creditors will likely gain a greater recovery, somewhat more liberal discharge has been accorded debtors under Chapter 13. However, the so-called "super-discharge" provision of Chapter 13 was pared down somewhat by BAPCPA. Chapter 13 had allowed discharge of virtually all debts except those arising from (a) alimony or child support obligations, (b) student loans, (c) judgments caused by driving while intoxicated, and (d) restitution orders or fines resulting from conviction of a crime.

BAPCPA restricts the Chapter 13 discharge to more closely resemble that of Chapter 7 by adding that obligations also cannot be discharged if they arise from: (a) unfiled, late-filed, and fraudulent tax returns, (b) fraud, including credit card misuse, (c) failure to notify creditors of the bankruptcy filing in order for them to file a timely claim, (d) embezzlement and breach of fiduciary duty, (e) willful or malicious injury to another or another's property.

No discharge will be granted if debtors do not certify that they are current on all domestic support obligations. As you may have noticed, several provisions of BAPCPA are aimed at ensuring that domestic support obligations are enforced.

INTERNATIONAL CONSIDERATIONS

In the age of large, multinational corporations owning assets and owing obligations in several countries, bankruptcy law has become an exceedingly complex matter. Most nations have traditionally operated under the "grab" rule. That is, creditors in Country X will be allowed by its courts to grab the debtor's assets in Country X. Outside creditors will be relegated to whatever crumbs, if any, are left when Country X's creditors are satisfied. Country Y's creditors will grab the debtor's assets located in Country Y, and so on. When Robert Maxwell's worldwide business empire collapsed in 1991 and the Bank of Credit and Commerce International (BCCI) went under a year later, it became exceedingly clear that some order needed to be brought to the field of international bankruptcy.

The United Nations Commission on International Trade Law (UNCITRAL) developed a model law by 1997. Its primary purpose is to reduce uncertainty and costs by establishing at the outset which country will have the responsibility to handle the bankruptcy proceedings involving a multinational enterprise. The United States adopted this model law in 2005 as Chapter 15 of the U.S. Bankruptcy Code. The UK adopted the provision as well. So, if a company with headquarters in the U.S. goes bankrupt, the U.S. liquidator will be able to go to the UK where the bankrupt firm has assets, and induce UK courts to freeze assets, sell assets, or otherwise assist in winding up the business. Before the new provision, the courts might have cooperated, but they might not have. Now they will.

A leading bankruptcy expert from the University of Texas has described the essence of the new approach:

> In general, universalism would treat a multinational bankruptcy ideally as a unified global proceeding administered by a single court assisted by courts in other countries, while territorialism is the traditional approach by which each court in a country in which assets are found seizes them (the "grab rule") and uses them to pay local creditors. Both approaches have become considerably more sophisticated in recent years. Universalism is now characterized as modified universalism, meaning a pragmatic approach that seeks to move steadily toward the ideal of universal proceedings while accepting the reality of step-by-step progress through cooperation. Territorialism has changed also, moving toward cooperative territorialism, which seeks to ameliorate some of the most wasteful features of the grab rule by a measure of judicial cooperation.

Jay Westbrook, *Chapter 15 at Last,* 79 AMERICAN BANKRUPTCY LAW JOURNAL 713 (2005).

Nearly 50 nations, including Canada, Mexico, Australian, and Japan have also signed on. The EU has similar rules, in that they also focus on the company's home country and place courts in that nation in charge of handling the international bankruptcy proceedings. However, there are enough differences between UNCITRAL's model law and the EU's Regulation on Insolvency to create some complications.

PART IV
AGENCY, PARTNERSHIPS, AND CORPORATIONS

CHAPTER 22

AGENCY: NATURE, CREATION, DUTIES, AND TERMINATION

- Nature of the Agency Relationship

- Creation of the Agency Relationship

- Duties of Principal and Agent

- Termination of the Agency Relationship

NATURE OF THE AGENCY RELATIONSHIP

In a legal context the term *agency* ordinarily describes a relationship in which two parties—the principal and the agent—agree that one will act as a representative of the other. The *principal* is the person who wishes to accomplish something, and the *agent* is the one employed to act in the principal's behalf to achieve it.

Agency relationships are ubiquitous. Anyone who has purchased merchandise at a retail store almost certainly has dealt with an agent—the sales clerk. Similarly, anyone who has ever held a job probably has served in some type of representative capacity for the employer.

The usefulness of the agency relationship in the business world is obvious. With few exceptions, no single individual is capable of performing every act required to run a business enterprise. Furthermore, many businesses are organized as corporations, which by definition can act only by employing agents. As a result, most business transactions throughout the world are handled by agents.

The term *agency* is often used to describe many different types of relationships in which one party acts in a representative capacity for another. *Principal* and *agent* are also sometimes used loosely to denote the parties to various types of arrangements. However, throughout our discussion these terms are used narrowly to describe a particular type of relationship. The *principal-agent relationship*, as we use it, means a relationship in which the parties have agreed that the agent is to represent the principal in negotiating and transacting business; that is, the agent is employed to make contracts or enter similar business transactions on behalf of the principal. The term will ordinarily be used in discussions of contractual liability.

Two similar relationships are the *employer-employee relationship* (which is still sometimes referred to by the older term *master-servant relationship),* and the employer-independent contractor relationship**.** The distinction between an employee and an independent contractor is important to many different kinds of legal questions. For example, state workers' compensation laws, federal antidiscrimination statutes, and many other laws regulating employment are applicable only to employees and not to independent contractors. Similarly, federal tax laws requiring the employer to withhold income and social security taxes and to contribute to the worker's social security account are applicable only to employees and not to independent contractors. In the law of agency, the distinction is important when a third party tries to hold the employer legally responsible for a tort committed by the employee. As we will see toward the end of the next chapter, an employer often can be held liable for the job-related torts of its employees, but usually cannot be held liable for such torts committed by those working for it as independent contractors.

It also is important to note that the same worker can be both an agent and an employee or both an agent and an independent contractor. Which relationship is relevant depends on the nature of the legal issues in the dispute. When the legal question involves either (1) the rights and duties between the superior and subordinate or (2) the superior's liability to third parties for contracts or other transactions executed by the subordinate, the relevant question is usually whether the subordinate was an agent who acted with authority. On the other hand, if the legal question involves the superior's liability for a tort committed by the subordinate, the relevant question is usually whether the subordinate was an employee who acted within the scope of employment.

Sometimes, however, it is appropriate to use the term agent and to discuss the agent's authority when the legal issue is the superior's tort liability. This happens mainly in two situations. First, it is appropriate to use agent and authority concepts when the superior has directly authorized the agent to engage in the wrongful conduct. In such a case, the superior is liable to the third party for the subordinate's tort regardless of whether the latter is an employee or an independent contractor. Second, courts sometimes use agent and authority concepts when the subordinate's tort was *nonphysical* in nature, such as fraud, defamation, and so on.

Most of our discussion in these two chapters involves the principal-agent relationship; the employer-employee and employer-independent contractor relationships are dealt with in the latter part of the next chapter.

CREATION OF THE AGENCY RELATIONSHIP

Necessary Elements

Consent

The agency relationship is consensual—that is, based on the agreement of the parties. Often it is created by a legally enforceable employment contract between the principal and the agent. A legally binding contract is not essential, however. An agency relationship that gives the agent authority to represent the principal and bind him or her by the agent's actions can generally be established by any words or actions that indicate the parties' consent to the arrangement. Consideration is not required.

In fact, no formalities are required for the creation of an agency relationship in most circumstances. For example, it is not usually necessary to spell out the agent's authority in writing; oral authority is ordinarily sufficient. Exceptions do exist, however. The most common one occurs when an agent is granted authority to sell real estate. In a majority of states an agent can make a contract for the sale of real estate that will bind the principal only if the agent's authority is stated in writing.

Even though formalities are usually not required for the creation of an agency, it is certainly wise to express the extent of an agent's authority and any other relevant matters in writing. This precaution often prevents misunderstandings between the principal and agent or between the agent and third parties with whom the agent is dealing. The formal written authorization given by a principal to an agent is frequently referred to as a *power of attorney*. When a formal power of attorney is used, the agent is sometimes referred to as an *attorney-in-fact*. This is simply another term for an agent, and should not be confused with attorney-at-law (a lawyer), although, of course, a power of attorney (POA) may be granted to an attorney.

A *general power of attorney* grants the agent broad powers to act on the principal's behalf. A *special power of attorney* grants the agent power to act only in narrow ways, such as to sell the principal's house. A *durable power of attorney* usually appoints a relative as agent and is limited in the kinds of powers that can be assigned. A durable POA usually continues after the principal's incompetency; other types of POA typically do not.

The general rule is that powers of attorney are interpreted very strictly, that grants of authority must be clearly stated, and that good intentions are no substitute for legal authority. For example, in *King v. Bankerd*, 492 A.2d 608 (Md. App. 1985), Bankerd signed a power of attorney granting his attorney the authority:

…to convey, grant, bargain and/or sell [my (Bankerd's) interest in a home that he owned in tenancy by the entirety with his wife] on such terms as to him may seem best, and in my name, to make, execute, acknowledge and deliver, good and sufficient deeds and conveyances for the same with or without covenants and warranties and generally to do and perform all things necessary pertaining to the future transfer of said property, and generally to do everything whatsoever necessary pertaining to the said property.

When Bankerd disappeared for several years, the attorney, apparently acting in good faith and believing that Bankerd might well be dead, *gave* Bankerd's 50% interest in a home to Bankerd's abandoned wife. Later Bankerd reappeared and successfully challenged the conveyance on grounds that although the POA was broadly written, it did not expressly authorize the attorney to give away the interest. The attorney, Bankerd's agent, was held liable to Bankerd for the value of his 50% interest.

The following case provides an additional application of these rules.

LIBERTY LIFE ASSURANCE CO. v. MILLER
2007 U.S. Dist. LEXIS 88729 (S.D.Fla. 2007)

Cynthia Miller ("Mrs. Miller") was married to Rennie Miller ("Decedent"). They had a child ("N.R.E.M") in 2000 and then divorced in 2003. Their settlement agreement required Rennie to maintain $100,000 in life insurance naming his child as the beneficiary until the child turned 18. Rennie bought such a policy from Liberty Life, though it had only $81,000 in coverage.

Cynthia and Rennie then remarried, but Rennie again filed for divorce on December 3, 2004. On December 7, Rennie made his friend Dale Thomas the primary beneficiary on the insurance policy, leaving N.R.E.M. as a contingent beneficiary.

On September 14, 2005, the second divorce was finalized. On October 20, 2005, Rennie removed $40,500 from the insurance policy as an accelerated death benefit, leaving $40,500 to be payable at death. Knowing he was sick, Rennie decided to execute a Durable Power of Attorney naming Cynthia as his attorney in fact. Invoking this power of attorney, Cynthia then changed the beneficiary on the insurance policy from Thomas to "Estate of Rennie Miller." Nine days later, Rennie died.   Liberty filed this suit asking the court to declare to whom it should pay $40,500. Cynthia filed for summary judgment.

Highsmith, Judge:

An attorney in fact has full authority to perform, without prior court approval, every act authorized and specifically enumerated in the durable power of attorney. An attorney-in-fact, however, may not amend or modify any document or other disposition effective at the principal's death unless expressly authorized by the power of attorney to do so. Therefore, an attorney in fact may not change the named beneficiary on an insurance policy unless expressly authorized to do so by the power of attorney. *Spoerr v. Manhattan Natl. Life Ins. Co.*, 2007 U.S. Dist. LEXIS 2752 (S.D. Fla. 2007). Therefore, in order for Mrs. Miller to have been authorized to change the named beneficiary on decedent's insurance policy, decedent would have had to authorize Mrs. Miller to do so through the power of attorney.

Construction of a durable power of attorney is a matter of law. In construing a power of attorney the court must look at the language of the instrument in order to ascertain its object and purpose. However, powers of attorney are strictly construed. And, only the principal's intent is considered when construing the power of attorney, not the agent's intent. *Kotsch v. Kotsch,* 608 So.2d 879 (Fla. App. 1992).

First, the Decedent intended to give broad powers to Mrs. Miller as his attorney-in-fact. Under paragraph 4 of the power of attorney, labeled "No Limitation on Attorney-In-Fact's Powers," the Decedent states that he "intend[s] to give [his] Attorney-in-Fact the fullest powers possible, including all powers set forth in Florida Statute Section 709.08 as now in effect or hereafter enacted, and [he] [does] not intend, by the enumeration of [his] Attorney-in-Fact's powers to limit or reduce them in any fashion." Here, the Decedent expressed his desire to relay to Mrs. Miller all the powers that he could possibly give her.

The Decedent specifically states that he intends to give her the full extent of powers available pursuant to §709.08. Among the powers available pursuant to §709.08, is the power to "amend or modify any document or other disposition effective at the principal's death." §709.08(7)(a). This power is only available if the decedent expressly authorized his attorney in fact, Mrs. Miller, to use that power. Therefore, the powers are available because he expressly states that he intends to give Mrs. Miller the full powers available under §709.08, and the power to change beneficiaries under his insurance policy is one of the powers available under §709.08.

Furthermore, under the section [of the Durable Power of Attorney] entitled "Management and Contracting Powers," the Decedent expressly authorizes Mrs. Miller to alter, insure, and in any manner deal with any real or personal property tangible or intangible and any interest therein. He further authorized Mrs. Miller under this same section to improve, manage and insure intangible property that he owns "upon such terms and conditions as the Attorney in Fact shall deem proper." And, under section P, "Special," the Decedent declares that he gives his attorney in fact the full power of substitution, in other words, the full power to do and perform every act necessary and convenient to be done as if he were still personally present.

The Decedent clearly intended to give his attorney-in-fact, Mrs. Miller, the full extent of the powers that he could give her. The Decedent granted Mrs. Miller the "fullest powers possible" pursuant to Florida Statute §709.08, which he did not intend to limit by enumerating further power. Therefore, his intent was clear, and strictly construing this contract, we must conclude that the Decedent intended to authorize Mrs. Miller to be able to change the named beneficiary on the insurance policy. Because there is no genuine issue of material fact and the law indicates that Mrs. Miller was authorized to change the named beneficiary on the Decedent's insurance policy, summary judgment shall be granted in favor of Mrs. Miller and the Estate of the Decedent is entitled to the proceeds of the Decedent's insurance policy.

Capacity

If an agent, acting on behalf of a principal, makes a properly authorized contract with a third party, the contract is viewed legally as being one between the principal and the third party; that is, it is the principal's contract, not the agent's. For this reason, the principal's capacity to make contracts may be important in determining the validity of the contract in question. The minority, insanity, or other incapacity of the principal has the same effect on contracts made through an agent as it does on contracts made personally.

On the other hand, the agent's capacity is usually immaterial. The reason is the same—the contract made by the agent for the principal is the principal's contract. Minors, for example, can serve as agents; their lack of contractual capacity ordinarily has no effect on a contract made in behalf of the principal. (Of course, the agent's lack of contractual capacity has an effect on her own contract of employment with the principal, and can also be important if for any reason the third party attempts to hold the agent personally responsible on a contract made with that party.)

DUTIES OF PRINCIPAL AND AGENT

The principal-agent relationship is a *fiduciary relationship*—one of trust. Each party owes the other a duty to act with the utmost good faith. Each should be entirely open with the other, not keeping any information from the other that has any bearing on their arrangement. Other duties, some of which are merely specific applications of the general fiduciary obligation, are discussed below and outlined in Figure 22.1.

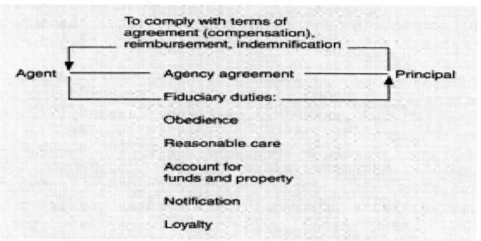

Figure 22.1 Duties of Agents and Principals to Each Other

Duties Owed by Principal to Agent

The primary duty owed by the principal to the agent is simply that of complying with the terms of their employment contract, if one exists. Failure of the principal to do so will render him or her liable to the agent for damages; if the breach is material, it will justify the agent in refusing to act for the principal any further. For example: Assume that P (principal) and A (agent) have agreed that A is to be paid a specified percentage of the sales she makes for P. If P refuses or fails to pay A, A can rightfully terminate their arrangement and hold P responsible for damages.

In addition, the principal is under a duty to reimburse the agent for any expenditures reasonably incurred by the agent in furthering the interests of the principal. For example, if P directs A to travel from Chicago to Los Angeles to transact business for P, but does not provide her with any funds for travel expenses, P will be under a duty when A returns to reimburse her for amounts she reasonably expended in making the trip, such as her round-trip air fare.

Similarly, the principal has an obligation to indemnify agents for liabilities or losses the latter suffer while acting lawfully and within the scope of their authority.

Duties Owed by Agent to Principal

Obedience

It is the duty of the agent to obey the clear instructions of the principal, so long as such instructions are legal. If the instructions are ambiguous, the agent cannot disregard them altogether, but the agent can fulfill the duty by acting in good faith and interpreting them in a manner that is reasonable under the circumstances.

Where the instructions are both legal and clear, the agent is justified in departing from them only on rare occasions. One such occasion is when an *emergency* occurs and following the principal's original instructions is not in the principal's best interests. The agent should, of course, consult with the principal and obtain new instructions if possible. But if there is no opportunity to consult, the agent is justified in taking reasonable steps to protect the principal, even if it means deviating from prior instructions. Indeed, the agent may even be under a duty to depart from instructions if following them in the emergency can be considered so unreasonable as to be negligent. (The agent's authority to act in emergencies is discussed more fully in the next chapter.)

Reasonable Care

Unless special provisions in the agreement say otherwise, an agent is normally expected to exercise the degree of care and skill that is reasonable under the circumstances. In other words, the agent has a duty not to be negligent. For example, suppose that B has funds which he wishes to lend to borrowers at current interest rates. He employs C to act on his behalf in locating the borrowers. C lends B's money to T without investigating T's credit rating and without obtaining from T any security for the loan. T turns out to be a notoriously bad credit risk and is actually insolvent at the time of the loan. If B is unable to collect from T later on, C will probably be liable to B because he failed to exercise reasonable care in making the loan.

Under some circumstances, an agent may be under a special duty to exercise more than an ordinary degree of care and skill. For example, if a person undertakes to serve in a capacity that necessarily involves the possession and exercise of a special skill such as that of a lawyer or stockbroker, that person is required to exercise the skill ordinarily possessed by competent persons pursuing that particular calling.

In any agency relationship, the principal and agent can by agreement change the agent's duty of care and skill, making it either stricter or more lenient.

Duty to Account

Unless principal and agent agree otherwise, it is the agent's duty to keep and make available to the principal an account of all the money or property received or paid out in behalf of the principal. In this regard, agents should never mix their own money or property with that of the principal. The agent should, for example, set up a separate bank account for the principal's money. If agents commingle (mix) their own money or property with the principal's in such a way that it cannot be separated or identified, the principal can legally claim all of it.

Duty to Notify

Another important duty of the agent is to notify the principal of all relevant facts—just about any information having a bearing on the interests of the principal—as soon as reasonably possible after learning of them. For example, if A (the agent) discovers that one of P's (the principal's) creditors is about to foreclose a lien on P's property, A should promptly notify P. Or, if A learns that one of P's important customers, who owes P a substantial amount of money, has just filed for bankruptcy, A should contact P as soon as possible.

Loyalty

Perhaps the most important duty owed by the agent to the principal is that of loyalty. Violation of this duty can occur in numerous ways. A few of the more significant actions constituting a breach of the duty are discussed below.

Quite obviously, the agent should not *compete* with the principal in the same type of business, unless the principal expressly gives consent. To illustrate: X, who owns a textile manufacturing business, employs Y to act as his sales agent. Y will be violating his duty of loyalty if, without X's consent, he acquires a personal interest in a textile manufacturing business that competes with X's.

The law presumes that a principal hires an agent to serve the principal's interests and not the personal interests of the agent. Thus, the agent should avoid any existing or potential conflict of interest. For example, if B is hired to sell goods for R, he should not sell to himself. Or if he is hired to buy goods for R, he should not buy them from himself. It is difficult, if not impossible, for agents to completely serve their principals' interests when their own personal interests become involved. Of course, such things can be done if the principal is fully informed and gives consent.

In a similar fashion, the agent should not further the interests of any third party in his dealings for the principal. The agent also should not work for two parties on opposite sides of a transaction unless both parties agree to it.

If agents, in working for the principal, acquire knowledge of any *confidential information,* they should not disclose this information to outsiders without the principal's consent. To illustrate: G hires H, a lawyer, to represent G in defending a lawsuit filed against G by T. T alleges that his factory was damaged in a fire caused by certain chemicals, purchased by T from G, that were highly flammable and not labeled with an adequate warning. In order to properly defend G, H must learn the secret formulas and processes for producing the chemicals. After learning them, he should not disclose them to anyone without G's consent, either at that time or at any time in the future.

The following case applies one jurisdiction's approach to a common situation where breach of the duty of loyalty is often claimed.

ABETTER TRUCKING CO. v. ARIZPE
Texas Court of Appeals, 113 S.W.3d 503 (2003)

For many years, Arizpe drove for Abetter as an independent contractor hauling sand and gravel. In 1995, Abetter hired Arizpe to run all field operations, including recruiting, hiring, and firing drivers, and handling any problems that arose with the drivers or clients. Abetter's principal client was Vulcan Materials. As part of his responsibilities, Arizpe maintained a close relationship with Scott Brady, Vulcan's manager, and with Abetter's truck drivers. Arizpe was an at-will employee and an independent contractor who could cease driving for Abetter at will, as could all of the drivers. Arizpe did not have a covenant not to compete with Abetter.

Arizpe and his brothers owned seven of the 30 trucks in Abetter's fleet. When Abetter's owner, Bessie Hastings, expressed her intent to retire and sell the business, Arizpe indicated he was interested in forming his own company. Hastings ultimately sold the business to a different employee, but did sell Arizpe a building he could use for his new venture. In the fall of 2000, Arizpe informed Brady that he intended to form his own trucking company and asked if Vulcan would be interested in hiring his trucks. After Brady expressed his interest, Arizpe took a number of steps in December 2000 to organize his own business, including incorporating Houston Haulers, applying for hauling permits from the Texas Department of Transportation, and obtaining insurance for approximately 25 trucks. The drivers were aware of Arizpe's plans; many of them contacted Arizpe to express an interest in driving for his company. Although Abetter was aware that Arizpe and his brothers were likely to leave and take their trucks, Abetter did not know this would occur very quickly, or that two dozen other truckers would leave Abetter and join Arizpe as part of his new hauling company. That is precisely what happened.

Arizpe resigned from Abetter on January 8, 2001, taking the family's seven trucks. The following day, 12 additional drivers began to haul for Arizpe instead of Abetter. The loss of so many trucks at one time was a very heavy blow to Abetter, which quickly sued Arizpe for breach of fiduciary duty, among other theories. The jury found for Arizpe, and Abetter appealed.

Keyes, Judge:

For Abetter to recover for breach of fiduciary duty, the jury was required to find the existence of a fiduciary duty, breach of the duty, causation, and damages. [Although the jury's verdict was somewhat confusing in this regard, the court ruled that the jury had found that Arizpe owed a fiduciary duty to Abetter.]

When a fiduciary relationship of agency exists between employee and employer, the employee has a duty to act primarily for the benefit of the employer in matters connected with his agency. Among the agent's fiduciary duties to his principal are the duty not to compete with the principal on his own account in matters relating to the subject matter of the agency and the duty to deal fairly with the principal in all transactions between them. The employee has a duty to deal openly with the employer and to fully disclose to the employer information about matters affecting the company's business. If an agent, while employed by his principal, uses his position to gain a business opportunity belonging to the employer, such conduct constitutes an actionable wrong. A fiduciary relationship, however, does not preclude the fiduciary from making preparations for a future competing business venture; nor do such preparations necessarily constitute a breach of fiduciary duties. An at-will employee may properly plan to compete with his employer, and may take active steps to do so while still employed. *Augat, Inc. v. Aegis, Inc.*, 565 N.E.2d 415 (Mass. 1991). The employee has no general duty to disclose his plans and may secretly join with other employees in the endeavor without violating any duty to the employer.

Absent special circumstances, once an employee resigns, he may actively compete with his former employer. In Texas, to resign from one's employment and go into business in competition with one's former employer is, under ordinary circumstances, a constitutional right. There is nothing legally wrong in engaging in such competition or in preparing to compete before the employment terminates. Moreover, the possibility of crippling, or even destroying, a competitor is inherent in a competitive market. An employer who wishes to restrict the post-employment competitive activities of a key employee may seek to accomplish that goal through a non-competition agreement.

Courts have been, and should be, careful in defining the scope of the fiduciary obligations an employee owes when acting as the employer's agent in the pursuit of business opportunities. This is because an employer's right to demand and receive loyalty must be tempered by society's legitimate interest in encouraging competition. The tension between the obligations of a fiduciary and his rights as a potential competitor reflects two conflicting public policies: one that seeks to protect a business from unfair competition, and the other that favors free competition in the economic sphere. *Metal Lubricants Co. v. Engineered Lubricants Co.*, 411 F.2d 426 (8th Cir. 1969). If the former is carried to its extreme, it deprives a person of the right to earn a living; conversely, the latter right, if unchecked, could make a mockery of the fiduciary concept, with its concomitants of loyalty and fair play.

Here, Arizpe informed Abetter that he planned to form his own company and would be taking seven trucks belonging to him and his brothers. However, he did not inform Abetter that he had incorporated his company (Houston Haulers), obtained permits, and obtained insurance; nor did he tell Abetter that a number of the company's drivers had expressed their intent to drive for Arizpe's company. Abetter did not learn of the formation of the new company, or that it was losing 20 trucks instead of only seven, until the day after Arizpe resigned

For the right of employees to agree among themselves to compete with an employer to be meaningful, it must be exercisable without the necessity of revealing the plans to the employer. *Metal Lubricants*, 411 F.2d at 429. Arizpe disclosed his intention to form a competing company, including taking his and his brothers' trucks, to Abetter. Despite his fiduciary obligations, Arizpe was not required to disclose even this much information. To form his own company, Arizpe had to incorporate or otherwise establish a business entity, obtain permits, and obtain insurance. These were permissible preparations to compete, not breaches of a fiduciary duty. Furthermore, the record shows that Abetter had sold Arizpe a building to use in this planned business.

The true surprise, and injury, to Abetter was the timing of Arizpe's resignation, the immediacy with which the competition ensued, and the number of Abetter's drivers who chose to immediately terminate their contracts with Abetter in favor of driving for Arizpe. The right to prepare to compete notwithstanding, if the nature of a party's preparation to compete is significant, it may give rise to a cause of action for breach of a fiduciary duty. This is particularly true if a supervisor-manager acts as a "corporate pied piper" and lures all of his employer's personnel away, thus destroying the business. An employee may use his general knowledge, skill, and experience acquired in the former employment to compete. However, there are recognized limitations on the conduct of an employee who plans to compete with his former employer. The employee may not (1) appropriate the company's trade secrets; (2) solicit his employer's customers while still working for his employer; (3) solicit the departure of other employees while still working for his employer, or (4) carry away confidential information, such as customer lists.

There were no trade secrets or confidential information for Arizpe to appropriate. The question, then, is whether he solicited customers or solicited the departure of other employees. Abetter contends that Arizpe breached his fiduciary duties by unfairly soliciting business from Vulcan and unfairly luring away Abetter's drivers. These actions, if proved, would constitute a breach of Arizpe's fiduciary duty to Abetter. However, the record contains contradictory testimony on both points.

Brady, Vulcan's manager, testified that Arizpe had told him about Bessie Hastings's upcoming retirement, mentioned that he would like to start his own company, and "just briefly broached the subject of hauling for Vulcan someday." There was no testimony that Arizpe sought or obtained a "commitment" from Brady. Brady also testified that there "was no question at all" that when Arizpe was at Vulcan on Abetter business, he was doing his best for Abetter. Brady described Arizpe as a good, faithful, and loyal Abetter employee.

Several of the defecting truck drivers testified that Arizpe did not approach them about working for his company; instead, they approached him. The drivers further testified that it was they, not Arizpe, who speculated about whether Abetter would still be in business after Arizpe left the company. Aside from Arizpe, the Abetter employees did not interact much with the drivers; e.g., they rarely attended social functions planned for the drivers and would not directly deal with the drivers to solve problems. Although most of the drivers spoke Spanish exclusively or predominantly, the only Abetter employee who spoke Spanish was Arizpe. Miguel Cardenas, the agent who replaced Arizpe at Abetter, testified that he understood the drivers left Abetter because Arizpe was offering a better rate. Cardenas also testified, however, that Abetter has been unsuccessful at regaining the drivers by offering them even better rates.

The jury could reasonably have concluded that Arizpe's acts did not rise to the level of solicitation, that he acted in Abetter's best interests while functioning as its agent, that the information he disclosed was sufficient, and that his acts were permissible preparation to compete. The jury could also have reasonably concluded that the drivers left Abetter simply because Arizpe offered better working conditions, a more personal relationship, and lower rates, not because Arizpe unfairly induced them to work for his company. We hold the evidence was legally and factually sufficient to support the jury's verdict. Affirmed.

TERMINATION OF THE AGENCY RELATIONSHIP

Like most private consensual arrangements, the agency relationship usually comes to an end at some point. Termination can occur because of something done by the parties themselves or by operation of law (something beyond their control). Our discussion focuses on the termination of the relationship between the principal and the agent, ignoring for the moment the effects of termination on third parties who might deal with the agent. (The circumstances under which third parties should be notified of the termination and the type of notice required are dealt with in the next chapter.)

Termination by Act of the Parties

Fulfillment of Purpose

Agents are often employed to accomplish a particular object, such as the sale of a tract of land belonging to the principal. When this object is accomplished and nothing else remains to be done, the agency relationship terminates.

Lapse of Time

If principal and agent have agreed originally that the arrangement will end at a certain time, the arrival of that time terminates their relationship. If nothing has been said as to the duration of the agency, and if nothing occurs to terminate it, the relationship is deemed to last for a period of time that is reasonable under the circumstances. This generally is a question of whether, after passage of a particular period of time, it is reasonable for the agent to believe that the principal still intends for him or her to act as earlier directed. Of course, if the principal knows that the agent is continuing to make efforts to perform, and if the principal does nothing about the situation, the agency relationship may remain alive for a period of time longer than would otherwise be held reasonable.

Occurrence of Specified Event

In a similar fashion, if the principal and agent have originally agreed that the agency, or some particular aspect of it, will continue until a specified event occurs, the occurrence of the event results in termination. For example: P authorizes A to attempt to sell P's farm, Blackacre, for him "only until P returns from New York." When P returns, A's authority to sell Blackacre as P's agent comes to an end. An analogous situation occurs when principal and agent have agreed that the agency, or some aspect of it, will remain in existence only during the continuance of a stated condition. If the condition ceases to exist, the agent's authority terminates. For instance: X directs Y, X's credit manager, to extend $10,000 in credit to T, so long as T's inventory of goods on hand and his accounts receivable amount to $50,000 and his accounts payable do not exceed $25,000. If T's combined inventory and accounts receivable drop below $50,000, the agency terminates insofar as it relates to Y's authority to grant credit to T.

Mutual Agreement

Regardless of what the principal and agent have agreed to originally, they can agree at any time to end their relationship. It makes no difference whether the relationship has been based on a binding employment contract or whether no enforceable employment contract exists; their mutual agreement terminates the agency in either case. It is a basic rule of contract law that the parties can rescind (cancel) the contract by mutual agreement.

Act of One Party

Since the agency relationship is consensual, it can usually be terminated by either the principal or the agent if that person no longer wants to be a party to the arrangement. In most circumstances, termination occurs simply by one party indicating to the other that she no longer desires to continue the relationship. This is true even if the parties had originally agreed that the agency was to be irrevocable.

If no binding employment contract exists between the two of them, the party terminating the agency normally does not incur any liability to the other by this action. If an enforceable employment contract does exist, one party may be justified in terminating it if the other has violated any of the duties owed under it. Of course, if there are no facts justifying termination, the party taking such action may be responsible to the other for any damages caused by the breach of contract. Nevertheless, the agency relationship is ended.

One major exception exists to the ability of either party to terminate the relationship. If the agency is not just a simple one but instead is an *agency coupled with an interest* (that is, the agent has an interest in the subject matter of the agency), the principal cannot terminate the agent's authority without the agent's consent. (Note, however, that agents are not considered to have an interest in the subject matter simply because they expect to make a commission or profit from the activities as agent.) To illustrate: P borrows $5,000 from A. To secure the loan, P grants a security interest (a property interest for the sole purpose of securing a debt) in P's inventory to A. As part of the agreement, P makes A his agent for the sale of the inventory in case P defaults on the loan. Since A has an interest in the subject matter of the agency (the inventory), the arrangement is an agency coupled with an interest, and P cannot terminate A's authority to sell without A's consent (unless, of course, P repays the loan, in which case A no longer has an interest in the subject matter).

The reason for the exception is that the agent is not really acting for the principal in this situation. By exercising this authority, the agent is acting in her own behalf to assert a personal interest.

Termination by Operation of Law

Death or Insanity

The death or insanity of the *agent* immediately terminates an agency relationship. The death or insanity of the *principal* also terminates an agency relationship. In most cases the termination of an agency by the principal's death or insanity occurs immediately, regardless of whether the agent knows what has happened.

Bankruptcy

The insolvency or bankruptcy of the *agent* does not always terminate the agency, but will do so in those circumstances where it impairs the agent's ability to act for the principal. To illustrate: B is authorized by I, an investment house, to act as its agent in advising I's local clients about investments. If B becomes bankrupt, he will no longer be authorized to act for I. The reason is simple; the agent in this situation should realize that the principal probably would not want him to act in its behalf any longer if it knew the facts.

Suppose, however, that the *principal* becomes insolvent or bankrupt, and the agent knows about it. In this case the agent might no longer have authority to act for the principal— but only under circumstances where the agent ought to realize that the principal would no longer want such transactions to be conducted in her behalf. For example: P has authorized A to buy an expensive fur coat on credit for P. If P becomes bankrupt, this will probably terminate the agency when A learns of it. A should reasonably infer that under the circumstances P will no longer want him to make such a purchase. However, if A is P's housekeeper and has been authorized to buy groceries for P's household, P's bankruptcy probably will not extinguish that authority. The inference that A should reasonably draw when learning the facts is that P will want her to continue buying necessities such as food until informed otherwise. It is simply a matter of reasonableness.

Change of Law

If a change in the law makes the agency or the performance of the authorized act *illegal*, the agent's authority is ordinarily extinguished when the agent learns of the change. To illustrate: S is a salesperson for T, a toy manufacturer. If a federal agency determines that certain of T's toys are dangerous and bans them, S's authority to sell them to retailers probably will be terminated when she learns of the government ban. That is, upon learning the facts, S should reasonably assume that T will no longer want her to sell the banned items.

Even if the change in the law does not make the agency or the authorized act illegal, termination can still occur if the agent learns of the change and should reasonably expect that the principal will no longer want him or her to act in the manner previously authorized. For instance: A is authorized to purchase fabricated aluminum from a foreign supplier. The federal government imposes a new tariff on imported aluminum that results in substantially higher prices. It is likely that A's authority to buy foreign aluminum will be terminated when he learns of the change.

Loss or Destruction of Subject Matter

The loss or destruction of the subject matter of an agency relationship will terminate the agent's authority. If, for example, X employs Y to sell grain belonging to X that is being stored in a particular storage elevator, the destruction by fire of the elevator and the grain will ordinarily extinguish Y's authority.

Whether the agent's authority terminates automatically or only when the agent learns of the facts depends on the nature and terms of the original agreement between principal and agent. In the instant case, if, instead of a fire, X himself sells the grain to a buyer (which actually amounts to X revoking Y's authority), Y's authority may or may not be automatically terminated. If X has given Y *exclusive authority* to sell, that authority ends only if X notifies Y that he has sold the grain himself. On the other hand, if the authority is not exclusive and Y should realize that X may try to sell the grain himself, Y's authority will terminate when X sells the grain even if Y does not know of the sale.

If the subject matter of the agency (such as the grain) is not lost or destroyed but is merely damaged, Y's authority is terminated if the circumstances are such that Y ought to realize that X would not want the transaction to be carried out.

Miscellaneous Changes of Conditions

The various occurrences we have discussed that terminate an agency by operation of law are by no means an exclusive list. For instance, in some circumstances the outbreak of war, a sudden change in the market value of the subject matter of the agency, or an unexpected loss of some required qualification by the principal or the agent (such as a license) may terminate the agency. Again, if all the circumstances known to the agent are such that the agent, as a reasonable person, ought to realize that the principal would no longer wish her to continue in the endeavor, the authority is ended. The agent simply must act in a reasonable fashion until there is an opportunity to consult with the principal.

CHAPTER 23

AGENCY: LIABILITY OF THE PARTIES

- Contractual Liability of the Principal
- Contractual Liability of the Agent
- Contractual Liability of the Third Party
- Nonexistent, Partially Disclosed, and Undisclosed Principals
- Tort Liability
- Criminal Liability

We have already discussed the formation and termination of the agency relationship and the duties existing between the parties. Now we will focus our attention on the legal consequences of this relationship, beginning with the *contractual liability* of those involved: principal, agent, and third parties. Then we will deal with a superior's liability for the *torts* and *crimes* of subordinates.

CONTRACTUAL LIABILITY OF THE PRINCIPAL

The principal (P) is, of course, liable to the agent (A) if the principal breaches a valid employment contract with the agent or violates any other duty owed to the agent. However, the most important questions in this area relate to the principal's liability to the third parties (T) with whom the agent has dealt. If A, acting on behalf of P, makes a contract with T, what is P's legal responsibility to T? If P does not perform as required in the contract, is P required by law to compensate T for T's losses resulting from P's breach?

The answers to these questions usually depend on the court's decision on another question: Were the agents acting within the scope of their *authority* in making this particular contract? We will now examine the approach taken by the courts in arriving at an answer.

The Agent's Authority to Act for the Principal

The fact that you have hired people to act as your agents does not mean that they can represent you in any way they see fit. An agent ordinarily can act for the principal in such a way as to make the principal legally responsible only when the agent has *authority* to act that way. The agent's authority can be divided into two basic types: actual and apparent. *Actual authority* is the authority that the agent does, in fact, have. For convenience it can be further divided into *express authority* and *implied authority*. On the other hand, *apparent authority* is something of a contradiction in terms. It describes a concept which, because of unusual circumstances giving rise to an appearance of authority, occasionally holds the principal responsible for certain actions of the agent that were not actually authorized.

Express Authority

Express authority is the most obvious and the most common type of authority—that which is directly granted by the principal to the agent. To illustrate: P authorizes A to sell P's farm for at least $250,000. If A sells the farm to T for $300,000, P is bound by the transaction and must honor it. The obvious reason is that A's actions are within the scope of his express authority. Conversely, under most circumstances, P will not be required to honor the transaction if A sells the farm for only $200,000.

Implied Authority

As is the case with most business transactions, the principal and agent rarely, if ever, contemplate and provide for every possible event that might occur during the existence of their relationship. The law seeks to allow for this fact through the concept of implied authority. *Implied authority* is primarily a matter of what is *customary*. In other words, where the principal has said nothing about a particular aspect of the agent's authority, whether the agent has such authority normally depends on what type of authority a person in a similar position customarily has. Of course, the principal has the final word as to what authority the agent possesses and can grant more or less authority than such an agent usually has. The concept of implied authority serves only to fill in gaps where the principal has not spoken specifically on the subject but where it is reasonable to assume that the principal would have granted such authority if she had thought about it.

An agent who has been given broad control over a complex undertaking, such as managing a store, office, or factory, will necessarily have more implied authority than an agent who has been given limited control of a relatively narrow task, such as selling a parcel of real estate or managing a specific financial account. The former is sometimes called a *general agent*, and the latter is sometimes called a *special agent*, although courts often apply these concepts without using that terminology.

Many examples of implied authority can be found. For instance, unless the principal has given indications to the contrary, a traveling salesperson ordinarily has authority to take orders but not to make a binding contract to sell the principal's goods. Such a salesperson often will be in possession of samples but there usually is no implied authority to sell them. If, however, the salesperson is one who possesses goods for *immediate sale* (such as a salesclerk in a retail store or a door-to-door sales agent who actually carries the principal's merchandise), she ordinarily has authority to sell them and collect payment. But this type of agent still does not have implied authority to grant credit or accept payment from the customer for prior credit purchases. Such authority usually exists only if expressly given by the principal, because it is simply not customary for a salesperson to do these things.

Another common application of the concept of implied authority enables an agent to perform those acts which are merely incidental to the main purpose of the agency. (Some legal writers, in fact, use the term *incidental authority*.) Again, the key is what is customary. The rule regarding such authority is: *Unless the principal has indicated otherwise, their agent has implied authority to do those things that are reasonably and customarily necessary to enable that person to accomplish the overall purpose of the agency.*

To illustrate: O, the owner of a retail clothing store, hires M to act as manager of the store and gives M express authority to act in certain ways. For instance, M probably will be expressly authorized to purchase inventory and make sales. In addition, M will have implied authority to handle matters that are incidental to the main purpose of the agency. Thus, if the plumbing in the store begins to leak, M can hire a plumber, and O is bound to pay for the services. Similarly, unless instructed otherwise, M can hire an electrician to repair a short in the wiring or a janitorial service to clean the floors. He can also hire a salesclerk or other necessary assistants.

Of course, if the transaction is out of the ordinary or involves a substantial expenditure, the agent should first consult with the principal, because the agent's implied authority may not extend to such matters. Thus, if the electrician hired by M to repair a shorted wire informs him that the wiring in the building is badly worn and does not comply with city building code requirements, M should not act on his own to contract for the rewiring at a substantial cost. Instead he should consult with O before taking further action.

Interesting questions regarding an agent's authority are sometimes raised by the occurrence of an *emergency*. Although it is often said that the scope of an agent's implied authority is "expanded" in emergency situations, this is only sometimes true. If an emergency occurs and there is no opportunity to consult with the principal, the agent has implied authority to take steps that are reasonable and prudent under the circumstances—including actions that may be contrary to prior instructions by the principal.

To illustrate: A has been ordered by P to purchase badly needed raw materials from country X and to ship them through country Y, which has the nearest port facility where the goods can be loaded on vessels. A makes the purchase but then learns from a usually reliable source that a revolution is imminent in country Y and will probably break out while the goods are en route. Fearing that transportation may be impaired or that the goods may be seized by the revolutionaries, A attempts to contact P but is unable to do so. Since he knows that P needs the goods quickly, A arranges for shipment to another port through country Z. Shipment over the other route will be slightly more expensive and time-consuming but also presumably safer, and P will still receive the goods in time to meet his needs.

In this case, A was impliedly authorized to act as he did—even if no revolution actually occurred. What is important is that two elements were present: (1) A, the agent, *was unable to consult with his principal*; and (2) he acted reasonably, in light of all the knowledge available to him, to protect the interests of his principal.

Apparent Authority

Thus far we have dealt with situations where the agent has actual authority, either express or implied. Now we will examine the peculiar concept of *apparent authority* (sometimes called *ostensible authority*). As we mentioned earlier, speaking of apparent authority as a specific type of authority is something of a contradiction, because the phrase describes a situation where the agent has no actual authority. If agents act outside the scope of their actual (express or implied) authority, the principal is normally not responsible on the unauthorized transaction. However, if principals, by *their own conduct,* have led reasonable third parties to believe that the agent actually has such authority, the principals may be responsible. In discussing implied authority, we were concerned with what appeared reasonable to the agent. But for apparent authority, our concern is with the viewpoint of reasonable *third parties*. Obviously, some situations can fall within the scope of either implied or apparent authority. In such cases we usually speak in terms of implied authority; apparent authority is used as a basis for holding the principal responsible only where no express or implied authority is present. The importance of apparent authority can be illustrated by two examples:

1. S, a salesman for R, has in his possession R's goods (not just samples). It is customary for an agent in S's position who is handling this type of goods to have authority to actually sell and collect payment for them. While making his rounds, S calls the home office. R tells him that he is afraid some of the items S has are defective and instructs him not to sell the goods in his possession but merely to take orders for a period of time. Contrary to instructions, S sells the goods. R is bound by the transactions and will be responsible to T, the buyer, if the goods actually are defective. It appears that R has acted in a reasonable fashion under the circumstances. However, by allowing S to have possession of the goods, he has led T to believe that S is authorized to sell—because it is customary. T has no way of knowing that S's actual authority has been expressly limited to something less than what is customary. The basis of R's liability is not S's implied authority, because S knew that he had no authority and was acting contrary to express instructions. Instead, the basis for R's liability is apparent authority—arising out of the fact that T has been misled by the *appearance of authority.*

2. When the agency is terminated, the agent's *actual authority* is also terminated. (Note that a few courts have held that where the agency is terminated by the principal's death, the estate can continue to be liable for the agent's actions, under the doctrine of apparent authority, until the third party learns of the death.) But this does not automatically dispose of the problem of *apparent authority*. It is sometimes necessary to notify third parties of the termination in order to keep the principal from being liable under the concept of apparent authority. As a general rule, where termination has

occurred *as a matter of law* (see Chapter 22 for details), all authority ceases automatically and the principal is not responsible for the agent's further actions regardless of whether the third party has been notified. Most problems involving termination and apparent authority arise when the agency has been ended *by act of the parties* (such as the principal firing the agent). Where termination is by act of the parties, the principal may still be bound by the agent's actions (because of apparent authority) unless and until the third party is notified of the termination. The principal must notify third parties with whom the agent has dealt in the past by letter, e-mail, text, telephone, or some other method of *direct communication* if their identities are reasonably easy to ascertain. Regarding all other third parties, the principal can protect himself simply by giving *public notice*. An advertisement in a local newspaper is the most common form of such notice, but other methods may be sufficient if they are reasonable under the circumstances.

Ratification of Unauthorized Transactions

If an agent's action is not within the scope of her actual (express or implied) authority, and if the facts are such that no apparent authority is present, the principal generally is not liable to the third party for that action. Even in the absence of actual or apparent authority, however, principals may become responsible if they *ratify* (or *affirm*) the agent's unauthorized actions. An unauthorized act ratified by the principal is treated by the courts in the same manner as if it had been actually authorized from the beginning. The two forms of *ratification*—express and implied—are discussed below.

Express Ratification. If, upon learning of the agent's unauthorized dealings, the principal decides to honor the transaction, the principal can simply inform the agent, the third party, or someone else of that intention. In this situation an *express ratification* has obviously occurred.

Implied Ratification. Even if the principal has not expressly communicated the intent to ratify, the person may nevertheless be deemed to have done so if his words or conduct reasonably indicate that intent. Inaction and silence may even amount to ratification if, under the circumstances, a reasonable person would have voiced an objection to what the agent had done. The following five examples will help clarify the concept of implied ratification. For each example, no actual authority exists, and there are no facts present to indicate apparent authority.

Example 1. A, who is a driver of a truck owned by P, enters into an unauthorized agreement with T, under which A is to haul T's goods on P's truck. Sometime later, while A is en route, T becomes concerned about the delay and calls P. Upon learning of the transaction, P does not repudiate it but instead assures T that "A is a good driver and the goods will be properly cared for." P has ratified the agreement.

Example 2. Same facts as Example 1. This time, however, T does not call P. The goods arrive safely at their destination, and T sends a check for the shipping charges to P. This is when P first learns of the transaction and its details. If P cashes or deposits the check and uses the money, he will be deemed to have ratified the agreement. Even if he simply retains the check for an appreciable period of time and says nothing, he will probably be held to have ratified.

Example 3. A makes an unauthorized contract to sell P's goods to T. Upon learning of the contract, P says nothing to A or T but assigns the right to receive payment for the goods to X. P has ratified the agreement.

Example 4. Same facts as Example 3. This time, however, P does not assign the right to receive payment. Instead he ships the goods to T. P has ratified the agreement.

Example 5. Same facts as Example 4, but the goods are shipped to T without P's knowledge. P then learns of the transaction, and when T does not make payment by the due date, P files suit against T to collect the purchase price. P has ratified the transaction (P would not have ratified if he had filed suit to rescind the sale and get his goods back.)

Requirements for Ratification. Certain requirements must be present for ratification to occur. Following are the most important of them:

1. The courts generally hold that a principal can ratify only if agents, in dealing with the third party, have indicated that they are acting *for a principal* and not in their own behalf.

2. At the time of ratification, the principal must have *known* or *had reason to know* of the essential facts about the transaction. What this means is that the principal must have had either actual knowledge of the relevant facts or sufficient knowledge so that it would have been easy to find out what the essential facts were. The requirement of knowledge is usually important when the third party tries to hold the principal liable by claiming that some words or actions of the principal had amounted to ratification.

3. Ratification must occur within a *reasonable time* after the principal learned of the transaction. What constitutes a reasonable time will, of course, depend on the facts of the particular case. However, a court will automatically rule that a reasonable time period has already expired, and thus that there can be no ratification, if there has been a fundamental change in the facts that had formed the basis of the transaction. An example would be damage to or destruction of the subject matter of the transaction. Similarly, the principal will not be permitted to ratify if the third party has already indicated a desire to withdraw from the transaction. The third party has the right to withdraw prior to ratification and, when she does so, any later attempt by the principal to ratify will be treated as being too late.

4. If the principal ratifies, she must ratify the *entire transaction* rather than ratifying that part which is to her advantage and repudiating that which is to her disadvantage. For example, a principal ratifying a contract for the sale of goods to a third party is obligated on any warranties that accompany the goods.

5. The transaction obviously must be *legal*, and the principal must have the *capacity* required to be a party to the transaction.

6. If any *formalities* (such as a writing) would have been required for an original authorization, the same formalities must be met in ratifying the transaction. Of course, if formalities are required, the ratification will have to be express—it cannot be implied. Since most authorizations do not require any special formalities, this usually poses no problem.

The following case deals with questions of an actual authority, apparent authority, and ratification in a setting where the facts and the conclusions to be drawn from them are hotly contested.

PARAGON INDUS. APPLCA'S, INC. v. STAN EXCAVATING, LLC
Court of Appeals of Texas, 432 S.W.3d 542 (2018)

Plaintiff Stan Excavating sued defendant Paragon Industrial Applications and its bonding company FLI Insurance Company for failure to pay for work Stan Excavating had performed as Paragon's subcontractor on a road construction project. Paragon moved to compel arbitration, arguing that the subcontract agreement between Stan Excavating and Paragon contained an arbitration clause. Stan Excavating argued that David Hagood, who signed the contract on Stan Excavating's behalf, had no authority to do so and therefore it was not bound by the arbitration clause. The trial court denied defendants' motion and they appealed, arguing that Stan Excavating was bound on grounds of actual authority, apparent authority, and ratification.

Moseley, Judge:

At first viewing, this appears to be a case that would be controlled by laws pertaining to arbitration. It is not. Rather, it is governed by the laws regarding agency. In their sworn pleadings, Stan Excavating, Paragon, and RLI attached a copy of the agreement, which purports to be an agreement between Paragon (the general contractor) and Stan Excavating (the subcontractor) regarding the Brinlee road project in Nash, Texas. The party signing on behalf of Stan Excavating was Hagood, this being the only place on the contract where his name appears; immediately below the line for his signature is the handwritten identification of Hagood as a "Co Owner" of Stan Excavating.

An "agent" is one who is authorized by a person or entity to transact business or manage some affair for the person or entity. An agent's authority to act on behalf of a principal depends on some communication by the principal, either to the agent, as the basis for actual or express authority, or to a third party, as the basis for apparent or implied authority. An agent cannot bind a principal unless the agent has either actual or apparent authority to do so.

The general rule is that a party dealing with an agent is bound, at his peril, to ascertain not only the fact of the agency, but the extent of the agent's power; if either is controverted, he bears the burden of establishing the existence of the agency or the extent of the agency. Thus, when the existence of an agency relation or the authority of an alleged agent is at issue, the party relying on the agency or asserting that a particular act was within the scope of the agent's authority has the burden of proving the allegation.

Actual Authority. Actual authority generally denotes the existence of authority that a principal (1) intentionally confers upon an agent, (2) intentionally allows the agent to believe that he possesses, or (3) allows the agent to believe, by want of due care, that he possesses the authority to act on behalf of the principal. Express authority is delegated to an agent by words that expressly and directly authorize the agent to do an act or series of acts on behalf of the principal.

The owners of Stan Excavating are James Naples and Patti Hamilton, with Naples being a minority owner and Hamilton the majority owner. Even though Hagood signed the agreement as co-owner, Naples testified that Hagood was not an owner but is, rather, "just an employee" and "that's all he's ever been." Naples testified that Hagood did not have the authority to enter into contracts on Stan Excavating's behalf and that by signing the contract as co-owner, Hagood misrepresented his capacity and, for all effects, forged the company's signature. Naples admitted that despite Hagood's actions, he is still employed by Stan Excavating.

According to Naples, any proposed agreement binding Stan Excavating would have been sent to Stan Excavating's corporate attorney, who would have negotiated the terms of the contract on Stan Excavating's behalf before it was signed by anyone. That vetting and negotiating did not happen in this case, as Naples denied that any member of Stan Excavating had seen the contract before this litigation began.

Even though there is evidence to the contrary, we find there is some evidence from which the trial court could have found that Hagood lacked the actual authority to bind Stan Excavating to the agreement. Therefore, we must defer to the trial court's implied finding.

Apparent Authority. An agent acting within the scope of apparent authority binds a principal as thoroughly as it would if the principal performed the action. Apparent authority is based on estoppel arising either from a principal knowingly permitting an agent to hold [himself] out as having authority or by a principal's actions which lack such ordinary care as to clothe an agent with the indicia of authority, thus leading a reasonably prudent person to believe that the agent has the authority [he] purports to exercise. _Baptist Mem'l Hosp. Sys. v. Sampson_, 969 S.W.2d 945, 949 (Tex. 1998). A principal's full knowledge of all material facts is essential to establish a claim of apparent authority based on estoppel. To determine an agent's apparent authority, we examine the conduct of the principal, reliance by the party alleging apparent authority, and the reasonableness of the third party's assumptions regarding the agent's authority. Declarations of the alleged agent, without more, are incompetent to establish either the existence of the agency or the scope of the alleged agent's authority. Even if an agent is not authorized to act on behalf of the principal, the agent's actions may nonetheless be binding on the principal if the principal later ratifies the agent's conduct.

Paragon's vice president, Aaron Stephens, testified that it was Hagood who approached Paragon on behalf of Stan Excavating about the Brinlee Road Project. Stephens said that Hagood told them he was one of the owners of Stan Excavating and that Paragon acted under that impression until this lawsuit was filed. Stephens stated that he knew Naples was one of Stan Excavating's owners, but he admitted that Paragon made no effort to ascertain either the veracity of Hagood's claims to part ownership of the entity or the extent of his authority to act for it. When the lawsuit was filed, Stephens checked the website for the Texas Secretary of State and discovered that Hagood was not listed as one of Stan Excavating's owners, whereas Naples and Hamilton were listed as owners.

Texarkana Construction was a subcontractor on the project. James Brower, the company's owner, testified that he worked on the project at Hagood's request. While he knew Hagood did not own Stan Excavating, he knew from his prior dealings with Hagood that if Hagood asked him to work on a project, "it would be fine." Naples denied that anyone at Stan Excavating had ever seen the contract with Paragon before this litigation began. He further testified that although he was fully aware that Stan Excavating was working on the Brinlee Road Project, he believed that Stan Excavating had been retained only as a subcontractor to perform a limited scope of work, mostly comprising excavation, drainage, and dirt work.

Hagood submitted invoices to Paragon regarding the project, and Paragon produced a couple of waivers relating to this project and one other, both signed by Hagood on Stan Excavating's behalf. Naples testified that Hagood submitted invoices because, as the representative of Stan Excavating who was physically at the project site, he was in the best position to warrant that the work being submitted for payment was actually completed. Naples admitted that when he and Hamilton are unavailable, Hagood would be given authority to sign waivers on behalf of Stan Excavating. If Naples alone were unavailable, Hagood would also occasionally sign documents on Stan Excavating's behalf because Hamilton, as a notary, could not notarize her own signature.

Taking into account that Hagood was apparently either the sole employee or the primary employee of Stan Excavating with whom the representatives of Paragon dealt, it is understandable that they may have held a good-faith belief that Hagood was the agent of Stan Excavating. However, even though one of the parties may be operating under a good-faith belief that the person with whom they are dealing is the agent of another, that fact alone is not enough to bind the purported principal.

Ratification by Stan Excavating. Without a great deal of elaboration, Paragon premises that the actions taken by Stan Excavating subsequent to the signing of the contract by Hagood amounted to a ratification of the contract by Stan Excavating. At first blush, this argument might appear to hold some merit. However, this Court has previously held that "[t]he critical factor in determining whether a principal has ratified an unauthorized act by his agent is the principal's knowledge of the facts of the prior transaction and his actions in light of such knowledge." *Old Republic Ins. Co. v. Fuller*, 919 S.W.2d 726 (Tex. App.1996). Ratification of an agreement by a party takes place only after that party (upon learning all of the material facts) confirms or adopts an earlier act that did not then legally bind it and that it could have repudiated. *Avary v. Bank of Am., N.A.*, 72 S.W.3d 779 (Tex. App. 2002). The testimony of Naples was that the principals of Stan Excavating were unaware of the existence of the contract urged by Paragon until *after* the lawsuit was filed. If the testimony of Naples is to be believed, the actions taken by Stan Excavating antedated its awareness of the existence of the alleged written contract.

From examining the principal's conduct, Paragon's reliance, and whether that reliance was reasonable, we find there is some evidence in the record to support the trial court's implied findings that Hagood lacked apparent authority to bind Stan Excavating to the agreement and that Stan Excavating did not subsequently ratify the written agreement by its actions. Even if we weighed the evidence differently, we must defer to the trial court's determination of the facts. [Affirmed.]

Importance of the Agent's Knowledge

In deciding the question of a principal's liability to a third party, sometimes a key issue is whether the principal has received notice of a particular fact. For example, assume P is obligated under a contract to make payment to T. T assigns her right to receive this payment to X, an assignee. Assuming that T's right is assignable, P is bound to honor the assignment and pay X instead of T only if he has received notice of the assignment. But what if P's agent, A, receives this notice rather than P himself? If A promptly relays the information to P, there is usually no problem. What happens, though, if A fails to do so and P, not knowing of the assignment, pays T instead of X? Is P liable to X because P's agent had received notice?

Ordinarily, in any case where notice to the principal is important, notice to the agent is treated as notice to the principal if the agent's receipt of the notice is within the scope of his actual or apparent authority. In other words, in such cases the law will treat the principals as if they had received notice even if the agent did not transmit it. Obviously, however, this does not apply where the third party who notifies the agent knows that the agent is acting adversely to the interests of the principal (as where the third party and the agent are conspiring to defraud the principal).

CONTRACTUAL LIABILITY OF THE AGENT

When the agent is acting for the principal, the agent ordinarily incurs no personal responsibility if acting in a proper fashion. However, circumstances do exist where the agent can become liable.

Breach of Duty

If agents violate any of the duties owed to the principal, they naturally are liable for the damages caused by the breach. Where the duty which has been violated is that of loyalty, the penalties may be even more severe. Disloyal agents are not only responsible to the principal for any resulting loss sustained by the latter but also usually forfeit their right to be compensated for services rendered. Furthermore, the agents must turn over to the principal any profits made from their disloyal activity.

Exceeding Authority

Agents who exceed their actual authority are personally responsible unless the principal ratifies the unauthorized actions. Whether this responsibility is to the principal or to the third party depends on the circumstances. If the agents exceed their actual authority, but the principal is liable to a third party on the ground of apparent authority, the agents' liability is to the *principal*. On the other hand, if the agents exceed their actual authority and the facts are such that the principal is not liable to a third party under apparent authority, then the agents' liability is to the *third party*.

Assuming Liability

If agents personally assume liability for a particular transaction, then they obviously are responsible. For instance: A is attempting to purchase goods for P on credit. T, the seller, is wary of P's credit rating and refuses to grant credit unless A also becomes obligated. A signs the agreement as P's agent *and* in his own individual capacity. A is in effect a *co-principal* and therefore personally liable to T if P defaults.

Nondisclosure of Principal

If agents, in dealing with a third party, fail to disclose that they are *acting for a principal* or fail to disclose the *principal's identity*, the agents are personally responsible to the third party. Additionally, agents will sometimes be liable if they act for a nonexistent principal or for one not having legal capacity. (These subjects are dealt with specifically later in the chapter.)

CONTRACTUAL LIABILITY OF THE THIRD PARTY

Relatively little need be said about the liability of the third party. Since that party is acting on her own behalf, she is personally responsible to the other party to the transaction. This ordinarily means that:

1. If the third party fails to live up to his part of the bargain, he will be liable to the principal.

2. The third party owes no responsibility to the agent unless the agent has personally become a party to the transaction.

NONEXISTENT, PARTIALLY DISCLOSED, AND UNDISCLOSED PRINCIPALS

In discussing the principal-agent relationship, we have thus far assumed that the principal exists when the agent executes the transaction in question and that both the existence and the identity of the principal are disclosed to the third party. This is usually, but not always, the case. The special problems that arise in connection with *nonexistent, partially disclosed,* and *undisclosed principals* are discussed below.

Nonexistent Principals

If an agent purports to act for a principal who does not exist at the time, the agent is usually liable to the third party. Of course, since there is no principal, the agent is not really an agent at all; the agent merely claims to be one.

While this situation does not occur frequently, it is by no means rare. A common instance of the *nonexistent principal* is that of a person attempting to act for an organization that is not legally recognized as a separate entity. (A *legal entity* is an organization—such as a corporation—that is recognized by the law as having the rights and duties of a person, although it is not flesh and blood. It can, for example, make contracts, sue, and be sued in its own name.) Thus, a member of an unincorporated association, such as a church, club, fraternity, or the like, may attempt to contract on behalf of the association. Since the "principal" is not legally recognized as one, the members who make the agreement are personally responsible. It is for this reason that many churches and other such organizations form corporations.

The contracts of *corporate promoters* (those who play a part in the initial organization of a corporation) have posed similar problems. Quite often, these people make various types of agreements before the proposed corporation is formed. They may, for example, enter contracts for the purpose of raising capital, purchasing a building site, or procuring the services of an attorney, an accountant, or other professionals.

A similar situation occurs when a principal has existed but is now dead or lacks contractual capacity when the agent contracts with the third party. Such an occurrence often terminates the agency, and the principal (or that person's estate) is not bound. If the agency is not terminated, the principal's status affects his own liability in the same way as if the principal had personally dealt with the third party.

Whether the *agent* is personally liable depends on the circumstances. If the principal is *dead* or has been *declared insane by a court* at the time of the transaction, the agent invariably is held personally liable to the third party. On the other hand, if, at the time the transaction is made, the principal is either a *minor* or *insane* (but not officially declared insane by a court), the agent is personally responsible to the third party in only two situations:

1. Agents are liable if they have has made representations to the effect that the principal has contractual capacity. This is true even if the agents are honestly mistaken.
2. Agents who have made no such representations are still liable to the third party if they *knew or had reason to know* of the principal's lack of capacity *and* the third party's ignorance of the facts.

Partially Disclosed Principals

As we indicated earlier, an agent usually is responsible to the third party if the agent discloses the fact that she is acting for a principal but does not *identify* that person. If the agent acts with authority, the principal is also responsible and may be held liable when the third party learns her identity. (There is conflict among the courts on whether third parties must make a choice (or *election*) between the agent and the principal in such a case or whether they can hold both of them responsible.) Since the third party knows that the agent is acting for someone else, the third party is, in turn, liable to the principal. In sum, the liability of the principal and the third party is the same as in the case of a completely disclosed principal. The only difference is that in the case of a *partially disclosed principal*, *the agent is also liable*, unless the agent and the third party agree otherwise.

Undisclosed Principals

Individuals and business organizations sometimes prefer not to have their connection with a transaction be known. If an agent acts in behalf of a principal but does not disclose to the third party the fact that she is representing another, it is said that the agent acts for an *undisclosed principal*. In other words, the third party, not knowing that a principal-agent relationship exists, believes that the agent is dealing solely for himself.

In a case such as this, the agent is personally liable to the third party. If and when the principal makes himself known, that person is also liable to the third party if the agent acted within the scope of his authority. In such an event, the third party must *elect* whether to hold the agent or the principal responsible.

Thus far we have focused on the liability of the undisclosed principal and the agent. But what about the liability of the *third party?* Since the agent is a party to the contract, the agent can enforce the agreement against the third party. Once revealed, the principal ordinarily can also enforce the agreement. In three situations, however, the third party can refuse to perform for the undisclosed principal and can continue to treat the agent as the sole party to whom she is obligated.

1. If the third party has already performed for the agent before the principal is revealed, the third party is not required to render a second performance.

2. If, prior to the transaction, third parties have indicated that they will not deal with the one who is the undisclosed principal, the third parties are not required to perform for that principal. Similarly, the third parties are not responsible to the undisclosed principal if the former has indicated beforehand or in the agreement that she will not deal with *anyone* other than the agent.

3. In all other situations, undisclosed principals are treated in much the same way as an *assignee* from the agent. They can demand performance from the third party only if the contract is of a type that can be assigned. Thus, if the contract calls for personal service by the agent or if the agent's personal credit standing, judgment, or skill played an important part in the third party's decision to deal with that individual, the third party cannot be forced to accept the undisclosed principal as a substitute.

TORT LIABILITY

Until now, our discussions of legal responsibility have focused almost exclusively on the parties' contractual liability. Now we will turn to their *tort liability*.

Circumstances in which the Superior Is Liable for the Subordinate's Torts

Obviously, if the superior, the subordinate, or the third party personally commits a tort, that person is liable to the one injured by the wrongful act. If the *subordinate* commits a tort, the additional question often arises as to whether her superior is also liable to the injured third party. This is often important because ordinarily the superior is insured or otherwise more financially capable of paying damages.

If the superior is personally at fault, then the superior obviously is liable for having committed a tort. This can be seen in the following situations:

1. If the superior *directs* the subordinate to commit the tort (or even if the superior merely intends

that the tort be committed), the superior is responsible.

2. If the superior carelessly allows the subordinate to operate potentially dangerous equipment (such as an automobile or truck), even though the superior knows or should know that the subordinate is unqualified or incapable of handling it safely, the superior is responsible for any resulting harm. The phrase *negligent entrustment* is often used to describe this situation.

3. Similarly, superiors are held liable if they are negligent in failing to properly *supervise a subordinate*.

Most often, however, the superior has not directed or intended the commission of a tort. Therefore, the third party usually seeks to impose *vicarious liability* (liability imposed not because of one's own wrong but solely because of the wrong of one's subordinate) on the superior. The imposition of liability on the superior for a tort committed by a subordinate is based on the doctrine of *respondeat superior* ("let the master answer").

The theoretical justification for holding superiors responsible is that they can treat the loss—or the premiums for liability insurance—as a cost of doing business. The cost is thus reflected in the price of the product, and the loss is ultimately spread over that segment of the population benefiting from that product.

When the superior is required to pay damages to a third party because of the tort of a subordinate, the superior usually has a legal right to recoup the loss from that subordinate. As a practical matter, this is an often and illusory right, because the subordinate is often unable to pay.

Of course, the superior is not always responsible for the torts of subordinates. In this regard, we must deal with two important questions. First, was the relationship employer-employee (*i.e.*, master-servant) or employer-independent contractor? And, second, if an employer-employee relationship did exist, was the employee acting within the scope of employment when committing the tort? If the subordinate was an employee acting within the scope of employment, the principal will typically be liable to the injured third party for the subordinate's tort.

Employer-Employee or Employer-Independent Contractor

Legal Significance of the Distinction

The imposition of vicarious liability often depends on the nature of the relationship involved. If it is found to be that of employer-employee, the employer is liable for a tort committed by the employee if it was committed in the scope of the employee's employment for the employer. On the other hand, if the relationship is found to be that of employer and independent contractor, the employer generally is not liable for a tort committed by the independent contractor. Those few instances in which the employer is liable for a tort are as follows.

1. If the task for which the independent contractor was hired is *inherently dangerous*, the employer will be responsible for harm to third parties caused by the dangerous character of the work. The employer's responsibility in such a case is based on the tort concept of *strict liability*. That is, the responsibility exists solely because of the nature of the activity, regardless of whether any negligence or other fault brought about the damage. Activities deemed to be inherently dangerous include blasting, using deadly chemicals, or working on buildings in populated areas where people must pass below the activity.

2. If employers owe a *nondelegable duty*, they cannot escape ultimate responsibility for performing

that duty by obtaining an independent contractor to perform it. Thus, if the independent contractor is negligent or commits some other tort in the performance of such a task, the employer is liable to the injured third party. Nondelegable duties are those duties owed to the public which legislatures or courts feel to be of such importance that responsibility cannot be delegated. Activities recognized as involving nondelegable duties vary widely from state to state, but may include (a) the statutory duty of a railroad to keep highway crossings in a safe condition; (b) the duty of a city to keep its streets in a safe condition; (c) the duty of a landlord who has assumed responsibility for making repairs to the premises to see that those repairs are done safely; and (d) the duty of a business establishment to maintain its public areas in a reasonably safe condition.

3. As is usually the case regardless of the exact nature of the relationship between the superior and subordinate, an employer is liable for the independent contractor's tort if the employer specifically directed, authorized, or intended the wrongful conduct.

Making the Distinction

The determination of whether a particular subordinate is an employee or an independent contractor most commonly turns on the issue of *control*. If the employer has hired the subordinate merely to do a job or achieve a particular result and has left decisions regarding the method and manner of achieving that result up to the subordinate, the latter is an independent contractor. On the other hand, if the superior actually controls or has the right to control the method and manner of achieving the result, then the subordinate is an employee. Thus, a construction contractor hired to erect a building is usually an independent contractor, while a receptionist in a dentist's office is usually an employee.

As is true of all distinctions, this one is easy to make at the extremes, but sometimes can present a close factual question. In recent years there have been many controversial decisions as companies such as Uber and Federal Express have attempted to exert as much control over their workers as possible without having them classified as employees. The following case takes a common approach and addresses multiple specific factors that can be helpful in deciding whether control is being exerted over workers such that they cannot be termed independent contractors. None of these factors is individually determinative; each is simply a factor to be weighed along with all the others. Although the following case involves employee benefits and does not involve an employer's tort liability, the approach used by the court to determine whether the hired party was an employee or an independent contractor is the same in both contexts.

MCGILLIS v. DEPARTMENT OF ECONOMIC OPPORTUNITY
210 So. 3d 220 (Fla. App. 2017)

Uber is a technology platform that connects drivers with paying customers seeking transportation services. McGillis served as an Uber driver until Uber revoked his access to the technology based on alleged violations of Uber's user privacy policy. McGillis then filed a claim for reemployment assistance against Uber's wholly-owned subsidiary. Under Florida law, employees are entitled to such assistance; independent contractors are not. After a substantial administrative hearing, the Department of Economic Opportunity held that McGillis was an independent contractor rather than an employee. McGillis appealed.

Logue, Judge:

At the hearing before the Department, witnesses explained in detail how Uber's transportation network software works. The software consists of two applications that are generally accessible on smartphones: a "user application," used by individuals seeking transportation services, and a "driver application," used by individuals willing to provide transportation services. Drivers receive a percentage of the fare charged to the passengers, and Uber processes payments to drivers weekly by direct deposit.

Uber supplies additional insurance coverage for commercial operation of a vehicle, but it does not provide other benefits such as medical insurance, vacation pay, or retirement pay. At the end of each year, Uber sends each driver a "Form 1099"—an Internal Revenue Service form used to report payments to independent contractors—setting out the amounts paid to the driver for the year.

A prospective Uber driver must agree to the terms and conditions of Uber's "Software Sublicense and Online Agreement." This contract specifies that the driver is an independent contractor and not an employee. It further explains that the driver, as an independent contractor, is not entitled to unemployment benefits:

> This Agreement is between two co-equal, independent business enterprises that are separately owned and operated. The Parties intend this Agreement to create the relationship of principal and independent contractor and not that of employer and employee. The Parties are not employees, agents, joint venturers or partners of each other for any purpose. As an independent contractor, you recognize that you are not entitled to unemployment benefits following termination of the Parties' relationship.

The contract further specifies that each trip request accepted is considered a "separate contractual engagement," that drivers are "entitled to accept, reject, and select" requests as they see fit, and that drivers have no obligation to accept any request. Uber may deactivate the driver's account if the driver's acceptance rate is persistently below a specified level or after 180 consecutive days of inactivity. But even if deactivated, the driver may request reactivation of the account and return to using the driver application. Drivers are free to set their own schedules and to determine what locations they will serve.

A prospective driver is subject to a background check and must provide Uber with information about the driver's vehicle, registration, license, and insurance. Drivers are responsible for supplying, maintaining, and fueling their own vehicles. Uber does not require drivers to display Uber signage in their vehicles, nor does Uber control the drivers' attire. Drivers are free to switch between using Uber's driver application and the application of a competitor, such as Lyft. Uber does not directly evaluate or supervise its drivers. Instead, passengers rate their drivers on a scale ranging from one to five stars. If a driver's overall rating falls below the level set by the region's general manager and no improvement is shown, Uber may deactivate the driver's account.

During his time as an Uber driver, McGillis experimented with when and where to use the driver application. He spent his own time and money investigating the most profitable times and locations. Uber did not reimburse him for any costs related to this market research, such as the cost of gas. And although McGillis left his previous job to use Uber's driver application, Uber did not require him to do so. Nor did Uber prohibit him from receiving ride requests from Lyft's driver application. In fact, McGillis switched between using Uber and Lyft at his discretion.

In this case, we must decide whether a multi-faceted product of new technology should be fixed into either the old square hole or the old round hole of existing legal categories, when neither is a perfect fit. The narrow issue on appeal is whether McGillis performed transportation services using Uber's software application as an "employee" within the meaning of Chapter 443. This determination is based on "the usual common-law rules applicable in determining the employer-employee relationship." § 443.1216(1)(a)(2). To determine whether an individual is an employee or independent contractor, Florida law requires courts to initially look to the parties' agreement. *Keith v. News & Sun Sentinel Co.*, 667 So. 2d 167, 171 (Fla. 1995). If a provision disclaims an employer-employee relationship in favor of independent contractor status, courts honor that provision "unless other provisions of the agreement, or the parties' actual practice, demonstrate that it is not a valid indicator of status." *Id.* If the parties' actual practice contradicts their written agreement, the actual practice controls.

Indeed, independent contractor or employee status "depends not on the statements of the parties but upon all the circumstances of their dealings with each other." *Cantor v. Cochran*, 184 So. 2d 173, 174 (Fla. 1966). So to determine whether the parties practice an independent contractor or employee-servant relationship, Florida courts consider several factors outlined in the Restatement (Second) of Agency § 220:

(a) the extent of control which, by the agreement, the master may exercise over the details of the work;

(b) whether or not the one employed is engaged in a distinct occupation or business;

(c) the kind of occupation, with reference to whether, in the locality, the work is usually done under the direction of the employer or by a specialist without supervision;

(d) the skill required in the particular occupation;

(e) whether the employer or the workman supplies the instrumentalities, tools, and the place of work for the person doing the work;

(f) the length of time for which the person is employed;

(g) the method of payment, whether by the time or by the job;

(h) whether or not the work is a part of the regular business of the employer;

(i) whether or not the parties believe they are creating the relation of master and servant; and

(j) whether the principal is or is not in business.

Among these ten factors, the "extent of control" is recognized by Florida courts as the most important factor in determining whether a person is an employee or independent contractor. "Control" refers to "the right to direct what shall be done and how and when it shall be done." *Herman v. Roche*, 533 So. 2d 824, 825 (Fla. 1st DCA 1988).

Of course, both employees and independent contractors "are subject to some control by the person or entity hiring them. The extent of control exercised over the details of the work turns on whether the control is focused on simply the result to be obtained or extends to the means to be employed." *Harper ex rel. Daley v. Toler*, 884 So. 2d 1124, 1131 (Fla. 2d DCA 2004) "[I]f control is confined to results only, there is generally an independent contractor relationship . . . ." *4139 Mgmt., Inc. v. DOL & Empl.*, 763 So. 2d 514, 517 (Fla. 5th DCA 2000). By contrast, "if control is extended to the means used to achieve the results, there is generally an employer-employee relationship." *Id.*

For example, in *A Nu Transfer, Inc. v. Department of Labor & Employment Security Division of Employment Security*, 427 So. 2d 305 (Fla. 3d DCA 1983), this court held that an owner-operator truck driver for an inland carrier was an independent contractor because drivers provided their own vehicles, were not required to work a specific number of hours, and were permitted to work for a competitor company. And in *Jean M. Light Interviewing*

Services, Inc. v. State Department of Commerce, 254 So. 2d 411 (Fla. 3d DCA 1971), this court held that interviewers for market research were independent contractors because they were "free" to refuse a job, to work for competitors, and to complete an assignment "at such time and in such matter, or fashion, as the interviewers might desire." *See also VIP Tours of Orlando, Inc. v. State Dep't of Labor & Emp't Sec.*, 449 So. 2d 1307, 1310 (Fla. 5th DCA 1984) (concluding tour guides were independent contractors because they were free to reject an assignment, free to determine the nature of each tour, and "free to work for other tour services"; the tour company "had no right of control over the tour guides other than to require them to show up at a particular place at a particular time wearing the [company] uniform and to travel in [company] transportation").

We agree with the Department's conclusion that Uber drivers like McGillis are not employees for purposes of reemployment assistance. Here, the parties' agreement unequivocally disclaims an employer-employee relationship. And the parties' actual practice reflects the written contract. As the Department here found, "the central issue is the act of being available to accept requests" and "[t]his control is entirely in the driver's hands." Drivers supply their own vehicles—the most essential equipment for the work—and control whether, when, where, with whom, and how to accept and perform trip requests. Drivers are permitted to work at their own discretion, and Uber provides no direct supervision. Further, Uber does not prohibit drivers from working for its direct competitors. Accordingly, we agree with the Department's assessment that,

[a]s a matter of common sense, it is hard to imagine many employers who would grant this level of autonomy to employees permitting work whenever the employee has a whim to work, demanding no particular work be done at all even if customers will go unserved, permitting just about any manner of customer interaction, permitting drivers to offer their own unfettered assessments of customers, engaging in no direct supervision, requiring only the most minimal conformity in the basic instrumentality of the job (the car), and permitting work for direct competitors.

In conclusion, Uber and McGillis contractually agreed that McGillis' work did not make him an employee. A review of the parties' working relationship confirms this understanding. Due in large part to the transformative nature of the internet and smartphones, Uber drivers like McGillis decide whether, when, where, with whom, and how to provide rides using Uber's computer programs. This level of free agency is incompatible with the control to which a traditional employee is subject. Affirmed.

As this case makes clear, the distinction between being an employee and being an independent contractor is vitally important, not only for vicarious liability purposes in tort cases, but also for various legal rights and protections that are accorded employees but not independent contractors. Some of these distinctions are discussed in the chapter on employment law. There are also important tax and other financial ramifications arising from the distinction. The new "gig economy," where companies like Uber and Lyft denominate their workers as independent contractors rather than employees, raises the stakes on this distinction.

In 2018, in *Dynamex Operations W. v. Superior Court,* 416 P.3d 1 (Cal. 2018), the California Supreme Court adopted *for some purposes* a different test for distinguishing between independent contractors and employees. Rejecting the common multi-factor test applied in *McGillis*, the court adopted the so-called "ABC test." As explained in the later case, *Garcia v. Border Transportation Group*, 28 Cal.App. 5th 558 (2018):

> Under the ABC test, a worker is presumed to be an employee, unless the hiring entity establishes each of the following: "(A) that the worker is free from the control and direction of the hiring entity in connection with the performance of the work, both under the contract for the performance of the work and in fact; and (B) that the worker performs work that is outside the usual course of the hiring entity's business; and (C) that the worker is customarily engaged in an independently established trade, occupation, or business of the same nature as the work performed." *Id.*
>
> Part A involves the common law "control" test, recognizing that "a business need not control the precise manner or details of the work in order to be found to have maintained the necessary control" for an employer-employee relationship. [question is "whether the business has retained 'necessary control' over the work"].
>
> Part B asks whether the worker can reasonably be viewed as working in the hiring entity's business. This inquiry turns on whether the worker is "reasonably viewed as providing services to the business in a role comparable to that of an employee, rather than in a role comparable to that of a traditional independent contractor." A plumber hired by a retail store would not be considered an employee; by contrast, a cake decorator servicing a bakery for custom cakes, or an at-home seamstress sewing dresses from patterns supplied by a clothing manufacturer, would.
>
> Part C asks whether the worker "independently has made the decision to go into business for himself or herself." This factor can be proven with evidence that the worker has "take[n] the usual steps to establish and promote his or her independent business—for example, through incorporation, licensure, advertisements, routine offerings to provide the services of the independent business to the public or to a number of potential customers, and the like." Critically, as we will discuss, this part requires that the worker *is* engaged in an independent business, not that the worker could have become so engaged.

Because the company has the burden of proof and must carry it as to all three parts of this test to prevent workers from being treated as "employees" even if the company has labeled them "independent contractors," commentators have suggested that widespread adoption of the ABC test could significantly damage development of the gig economy. Unsurprisingly, tech and other companies are, at this writing, furiously lobbying the California legislature to overturn *Dynamex*.

Scope of Employment

If subordinates are deemed to be an employee, the employer is liable to third parties for those torts committed by the employees in the *scope of their employment*. There exists no simple definition of the *scope of employment* (sometimes called course of employment) concept. Obviously, an employee is acting within the scope of employment while performing work that he has been expressly directed to do by the employer. To illustrate: X has directed Y to drive X's truck from Dallas to Houston via a certain route. While on that route, Y drives negligently and injures T. X is liable to T.

In the absence of a specific directive given by the employer, an act usually is in the scope of employment if it is *reasonably incidental to an activity that has been expressly directed.* Thus, in the above example, if Y had stopped to buy gasoline and had negligently struck a parked car belonging to T, X would have been liable to T.

Deviations

The employer sometimes can be held liable even though the employee has deviated from the authorized activity. The employer's liability in such cases depends on the *degree* and *foreseeability* of the deviation. If the deviation is great, the employer usually is not responsible. Suppose that Y, in driving X's truck from Dallas to Houston, decides to go a hundred miles off his authorized route to visit an old friend. On the way there, Y negligently collides with T. In this situation, X is not liable.

But what if Y has been to see his friend and was returning to his authorized route when the collision occurred? Three different viewpoints have been taken by various courts. Where there has been more than a slight deviation from the scope of employment, as in this case, some courts have held that the reentry into the scope of employment occurs only when the employee has *actually returned to the authorized route or activity*. Others have held that there is reentry the moment that the employee, with an intent to serve the employer's business, *begins to turn back toward the point of deviation*. However, a majority of courts have held that reentry occurs when the employee, with an intent to serve the employer's business, *has turned back toward and come reasonably close to the point of deviation*.

If the deviation from the authorized route or activity is only slight, many courts have held that the employee is still within the scope of employment if the type of deviation was *reasonably foreseeable* by the master. For example: While driving from Dallas to Houston, Y stops at a roadside establishment to get something to eat or buy a pack of cigarettes. While pulling off the road, he negligently strikes a parked car. In this situation X is liable. Although buying something to eat or smoke may not be necessary to drive a truck from Dallas to Houston (as is the purchase of gasoline) and although Y was not really serving his employer, the deviation was only slight and was of the type that any employer should reasonably expect.

Many examples of the scope of employment issue involve auto accidents (though certainly the issue is not limited to them).

ARBELAEZ v. JUST BRAKES CORP.
Texas Court of Appeals, 149 S.W.3d 717 (2018)

In January 2001, Brian Paul, a mechanic for defendant Just Brakes, arrived at work at approximately 6:45 a.m. and his manager soon gave Paul his "first assignment" of the day, which was to pick up breakfast for himself, his manager, and his other co-workers at a nearby McDonald's restaurant. This was a daily routine for Paul and at other Just Brakes locations. Just Brakes paid Paul $10 a week in gas money to run this errand and he was considered "on the clock" as he did so. While exiting the Just Brakes parking lot in his own vehicle, Paul collided with plaintiff Arbelaez, who later filed a negligence lawsuit against Paul and Just Brakes. Just Brakes moved for summary judgment, arguing that it was not vicariously liable for Paul's careless driving. The trial judge granted the motion and Arbelaez appealed.

Kidd, Justice:

An employer may be held liable for the tortious acts of an employee if the acts are within the course and scope of employment. To defeat Arbelaez's claim of vicarious liability,

Just Brakes was required to establish as a matter of law either that: (1) Paul was not an employee; (2) no negligent act occurred; or (3) Paul was not acting within the course and scope of his employment at the time of the collision. Only the third prong--course and scope of employment--is at issue here.

To ultimately prove that an employee acted within the course and scope of employment, however, Arbelaez must prove at trial that the act was (1) within the general authority given to the employee; (2) in furtherance of the employer's business; and (3) for the accomplishment of the object for which the employee was employed. We can only uphold the district court's summary judgment if Just Brakes disproved as a matter of law at least one of these essential elements. Because Paul's manager authorized Paul to obtain breakfast for the crew, Just Brakes does not dispute that Paul's actions were within the general authority given to him. We therefore address only the second two prongs.

In its attempt to prove as a matter of law that Paul was not within the course and scope of employment, Just Brakes advances several arguments. First, Just Brakes states: "It is well established that an employee is not acting in the furtherance of his employer's business when he deviates from that employer's business for a personal purpose." Just Brakes then asserts that Paul's manager possibly "condoned," "knew of, or allowed" Paul to make the breakfast run, but Paul was "not ordered" to go. Just Brakes concludes that Paul's personal errand did not benefit Just Brakes, "regardless of whether [Paul's] manager knew of, or condoned, the diversion."

Just Brakes' argument fails to prove that Paul was not within the course and scope of his employment for several reasons. First, Just Brakes' argument presupposes that Paul's manager merely acquiesced in allowing Paul to make the breakfast run. The summary-judgment evidence indicates, however, that Paul's manager affirmatively asked Paul to make the breakfast run for the shop. Under our standard of review, we cannot--as Just Brakes would have us do--assume that Paul requested permission to make the breakfast run; we must assume Paul's manager asked Paul to perform this errand.

Next, Just Brakes argues that Paul deviated from his employment because the breakfast run was for purely personal purposes. This argument is contradicted by the evidence that Paul made the breakfast run as his "first assignment" of the day after he was requested to do so by his manager. "If the purpose of serving the master's business actuates the servant to any appreciable extent his acts are within the scope of employment." *Howard v. American Paper Stock Co.*, 523 S.W.2d 744 (Tex. Civ. App. 1975). Even if Paul was personally benefitted to some degree by his breakfast run, his actions could still be within the course and scope of his employment. We therefore hold that Just Brakes failed to prove that Paul deviated from his employment by complying with his manager's request to make the breakfast run.

Finally, Just Brakes argues that Paul's "personal errand" was not in furtherance of Just Brakes' business. Evidence exists to indicate that Just Brakes was indeed benefitted by Paul's breakfast run. Just Brakes' corporate representative testified in a deposition that (1) Just Brakes can complete more work in a shorter time period with more mechanics present; (2) the practice of using one employee to obtain breakfast for the entire shop was common at various Just Brakes locations; (3) to get a day's work done, a store requires a minimal number of mechanics; (4) it is important to have a manager present at all times; and (5) a reasonable manager would try to reduce the number of mechanics missing at any given time. Because this routine practice benefitted Just Brakes, albeit indirectly, Just Brakes has failed to prove that Paul's conduct was a purely personal errand that was not in furtherance of Just Brakes' business.

We also address the numerous cases Just Brakes cites in support of its contentions laid out above. Each of these cases is easily distinguishable. *See Gant v. Dumas Glass & Mirror, Inc.*, 935 S.W.2d 202 (Tex. App.1996) (employee commuting from lunch break); *J&C Drilling Co. v. Salaiz*, 866 S.W.2d 632 (Tex. App. 1993) (employee commuting to work site following dinner). [These cases do not address] a situation where an employee complied with an employer's request to run an errand that benefited, even indirectly, the employer's business.

Finally, Just Brakes cites two cases for the proposition that an employer's reimbursement of gas money to an employee does not create a fact issue on course and scope of employment. These cases, too, are easily distinguishable in that they involve employees commuting to or from work, where the reimbursement of gas money was the only factor supporting a contention that the employee was within the course and scope of employment. … Here, the evidence indicates not only that Paul was reimbursed his gas money on a weekly basis, but also that Paul's manager asked Paul to perform this errand on a routine basis, and that the errand benefitted Just Brakes.

We hold that Just Brakes failed to prove as a matter of law that Paul was not acting within the course and scope of his employment. We therefore reverse the summary judgment of the district court and remand for further proceedings.

[A dissenting judge in *Arbelaez* stated "that the public policy choice here is pure and simple: employers should not be vicariously liable for the torts of their employees committed while engaged in personal errands, even while 'on the clock.'"]

Comment. The general rule is that employees are not within the scope of employment, and therefore their employers are not liable for their negligent driving, when they are commuting to and from work. This "coming and going" rule has a "special mission: exception that applies if employees, when going to or returning from their place of employment or place of residence undertake a special mission at the direction of their employer (e.g., picking up supplies or delivering goods to customers), or perform a service in furtherance of their employers' business with the express or implied approval of the employer.

Intentional Torts

Thus far we have assumed the tort to be that of *negligence* (simple carelessness). Most cases in fact are concerned with the employee's negligence. However, an employee's *intentional tort*, such as assault and battery, libel, slander, fraud, trespass, or the like, can also subject the employer to liability. The test is the same. The employer is liable if the employee was acting within the scope of employment at the time. It should be emphasized, though, that an employer is *less likely* to be responsible if the employee's tort was *intentional* rather than merely negligent. The reason is that when an employee intentionally commits a wrongful act, that employee is more likely to be motivated by personal reasons rather than by a desire to serve the employer. Those cases where the employer *has* been held liable for an employee's intentional torts usually fall within one of four broad categories.

1. *Where the tort occurs in a job in which force is a natural incident.* An example is a bouncer in a saloon, who is naturally expected to use force occasionally. But if excessive force is used, the employer may well be liable.

2. *Where the employee is actually attempting to promote the employer's business but does so in a wrongful manner.* For example, two competing tow truck drivers are attempting to beat each other to the scene of an accident to get the business for their respective employers. One intentionally runs the other off the road. The employer of the one committing the tort is liable.

3. *Where the tort results from friction naturally brought about by the employer's business.* For instance, the employee, who works for a building contractor, argues with an employee of a subcontractor about the method for laying a floor. They become angry, and the building contractor's employee strikes the other party. The building contractor, as employer, is probably liable.

4. *Where the tort was directly authorized or clearly intended by the employer.* This situation usually, but not always, involves a nonphysical tort such as fraud or defamation. As mentioned at the beginning of this discussion of the employer's tort liability, an employer who authorizes or intends the subordinate's wrongful act is usually held liable regardless of the kind of tort or the type of relationship between superior and subordinate.

There are different points of view regarding the appropriate test for determining when a principal should be liable for an agent's intentional tort. In *Patterson v. Blair*, 172 S.W.2d 361 (Ky. 2005), for example, Blair was attempting to repossess plaintiff Patterson's car on behalf of his employer, Courtesy Autoplex, when he shot out its tires. Blair was convicted of wanton endangerment, a first-degree felony, and Patterson sued Courtesy and Blair. The court held that a master should be held liable for any intentional tort committed by the servant where its purpose, however misguided, is wholly or in part to further the master's business. On the other hand, the master should not be liable if the servant acted solely from personal motives unconnected with the master's business. In this case, the agent was clearly acting to benefit the employer (although in a misguided way) when he shot out the tires, rendering Courtesy Autoplex liable to Patterson for Blair's wrongdoing.

Contrast the *Patterson* result with *Cantwell v. Franklin County Board of Commissioners,* 2012 WL 1852183 (Ohio App. 2012), where Cantwell, a jail guard, asked an inmate to place his penis on a bologna sandwich so that he could photograph it, and then gave the sandwich to another inmate, Copeland. After Copeland ate the sandwich, the guard showed him the photo and teased him. When Copeland sued Cantwell's employer, Cantwell argued that his actions were within the scope of his employment. The court naturally had no problem rejecting this argument. Also, the county subsequently fired both the jail guard and the coworker who took the photo.

CRIMINAL LIABILITY

As a general rule, a superior cannot be criminally prosecuted for a subordinate's wrongful act unless the superior expressly authorized it. Thus, if Y, a subordinate, while acting within the scope of her employment, injures T, and T dies, Y's superior can be held liable in a civil suit for damages but cannot be subjected to criminal liability. Any criminal responsibility rests on the shoulders of the subordinate. The rule exists because crimes ordinarily require intent, and the superior in this situation had no criminal intent. Exceptions to the rule usually involve either (1) the criminal statute specifically places criminal responsibility on the superior, or (2) A superior can sometimes be criminally prosecuted under statutes that do not require intent for a violation, such as for the the offense of selling adulterated food under the federal Food, Drug, and Cosmetic Act.

CHAPTER 24
PARTNERSHIPS AND OTHER
FORMS OF BUSINESS
ORGANIZATIONS

- The Nature of Partnerships
- Formation of a Partnership
- Partnership Property
- Other Forms of Business Organization

INTRODUCTION

This chapter will begin by focusing on one of the foundational forms of business organization—the general partnership—and certain of its important features. It will conclude with a brief discussion of some other non-corporate forms.

THE NATURE OF PARTNERSHIPS

Governing Law

Partnerships were governed by the common law until 1914, when the Uniform Partnership Act (UPA) was promulgated by the American Law Institute and the National Conference of Commissioners on Uniform State Laws. The UPA codified most of the common law rules and significantly altered some of them. It was updated by the Revised Uniform Partnership Act (RUPA) of 1994 (amended several times since). The UPA is still in effect in some states, while most (37 or so) have adopted some version of RUPA. The discussion in this chapter will focus on rules that the two uniform acts have in common, although some important differences will be noted.

Defining a Partnership

Both UPA and RUPA define a *partnership* as "an association of two or more persons to carry on as co-owners of a business for profit." This definition can be broken into elements as follows.

Association: The term *association* indicates that a partnership is a voluntary arrangement formed by agreement.

Person: The term *person* includes not only individuals but also corporations, other partnerships, and other types of associations. With regard to minors and insane persons, the same basic rules apply to partnership agreements as to other types of contracts. Thus, a minor may treat the partnership agreement with the other partners as voidable. Furthermore, minors may usually repudiate personal liabilities to creditors beyond the amount of their investment in the business. But this investment is subject to the claims of partnership creditors, although it is the maximum liability that the minor ordinarily can incur.

Co-owners: The partners are co-owners of the business, which distinguishes them from those who are merely agents, servants, or other subordinates. Courts often say that true partners share in three communities of interest: capital, management, and profits. Typically, partners will contribute money, property, or services to the enterprise's capital, have a voice in management, and enjoy a right to share in the profits.

To Carry on a Business: The term *business* includes "every trade, occupation, or profession."

For Profit: An association cannot be a partnership unless the purpose of forming it is to make profits directly through its business activities. Associations for other purposes (including religious, patriotic, or public improvement purposes, or furtherance of the *separate* economic interests of members) are not partnerships, even if they engage in business transactions. Thus, the local chapter of a fraternal lodge cannot be a partnership, and the rights and duties of partners cannot attach to its members. For example, individual members are not personally liable for debts incurred for the lodge by its officers unless an agency relationship has been expressly created.

The Entity Theory versus the Aggregate Theory

Drafters of the UPA could not agree as to whether a partnership should be treated (1) like a corporation, as an *entity*, separate and apart from its owners, or (2) as it traditionally had been at common law as a mere *aggregation* of its individual partners. The UPA ultimately treated a partnership as an entity for some purposes and an aggregation of individuals for others. The trend today is strong in favor of the entity approach, and Revised Uniform Partnership Act (RUPA) leans this way. Even the original UPA recognized the concept of property owned by the partnership as an entity, and the ability of that entity to buy and sell property. In addition, liability for acts of individual partners in conducting partnership business rests primarily on the partnership entity and the partnership property, and only secondarily on individual partners and their individual property.

Also, every partner is an agent *of the partnership* as an entity, capital contributions are made *to the partnership*, books are kept *for the partnership*, and every partner is accountable as a fiduciary *to the partnership*. Moreover, the partnership entity can survive the death of one of its partners.

Thus, under state law, a partnership is primarily viewed as a separate legal entity. Outside of state partnership law, however, the federal IRS pass-through taxation feature for partnerships is consistent with an aggregation theory.

FORMATION OF A PARTNERSHIP

The Partnership Agreement

Unlike corporations, which are created by statute and require filings with the state, partnerships are formed by the parties' express or implied agreements. Although no formal filing is requisite to the formation of a general partnership, under RUPA a "Statement of Partnership Authority" may be voluntarily filed with the Secretary of State's office. The primary purpose of this filing is to facilitate the sale of real property, because the statement must specify the partners required to sign a transfer of real property held in the partnership name. The statement may contain other information, including the authority (or limitations upon the authority) of various partners.

Because parties need not have any written (or even oral) agreement before becoming partners, UPA and RUPA serve as "form contracts" that provide the rules for partnerships in the absence of express agreement. By agreement, the partners may vary the form terms to suit their purposes, with some limitations. Under RUPA, for example, partners may not prejudice rights of third parties, waive the duties of loyalty or good faith and fair dealing that partners owe one another, unreasonably restrict partners' access to books and records, or unreasonably reduce the duty of care partners owe each other.

Despite the fact that a written partnership agreement is usually not required, it is highly desirable. Formation of a business is a substantial undertaking and for several reasons should not be left to the oral declarations of the parties. These reasons include:

1. There are many inherent problems in proving the exact terms of an oral agreement.

2. Numerous problems (such as those relating to taxation) can often be satisfactorily resolved only by a carefully drafted written instrument.

3. If the parties go through the process of drafting a formal document with the aid of an attorney, they are much more likely to foresee many problems they otherwise would not have thought about. For example, matters such as procedures for expulsion of a partner or for settlement of disputes between partners are easily overlooked because they seem so remote when the partnership is first formed.

Desirable Elements of a Partnership Agreement

Today's partnership law emphasizes the predominant role of the partners' agreement. The formal partnership agreement, often referred to as the articles of partnership, should clearly reflect the intent of the partners as to the rights and obligations they wish to assume in the business. What is contained in these articles will depend on the nature of the business and the desires of the partners, but ordinarily the written instrument should include, among many others, such items as the name of the firm, the nature and location of the business, the date of commencement and duration of the partnership, the amount of contributions in money or property each partner is to make, the salaries and drawing accounts of the partners (if any), how net profits are to be shared, and procedures for settling disputes among the partners.

Determining the Existence of a Partnership

When the parties have clearly expressed their intentions in a written instrument, there is ordinarily no difficulty in determining whether a partnership exists. But when the parties have not been explicit in declaring their intentions, problems frequently arise. The most fundamental, of course, is whether a partnership has even been *created.* This issue arises with surprising frequency, because of its importance in regard to the rights and obligations of the "partners," as well as third parties. For example, a creditor may seek to hold several persons liable for the transactions of one of them on the ground that they are partners. Or one party might claim that he and another are partners and that the other party has violated a resulting fiduciary duty by having a conflicting business interest.

When the existence of a partnership is disputed by an interested party, such existence becomes a question of fact to be decided on the basis of all the circumstances. The burden of proof is upon the party seeking to establish that a partnership exists. Typically, no single factor is controlling, and the court's ultimate decision is commonly based on several considerations. *Intent* of the parties is important, but not the labels that they use. If persons associated in business call themselves *partners,* that label is indicative, but not necessarily controlling. Similarly, the fact that persons believe and perhaps even explicitly state that they are not partners is irrelevant if the actual substance of the relationship they intend to create is what the law calls a *partnership.*

Substance controls over form. The most important substantive factors in determining the parties' intent are (1) sharing of profits and losses, (2) joint control of the business, and (3) joint ownership and control of capital or property.

Sharing of Profits and Losses

If there has been no sharing of profits or agreement to share them, a court is very likely to find that no partnership exists. On the other hand, the sharing of *net profits* (as opposed to mere *gross revenues*) usually gives rise to a rebuttable presumption that a partnership exists. That the presumption is rebuttable means that it may be overcome by the weight of contrary evidence, but profit sharing remains a potent aid to the party seeking to establish the existence of a partnership.

There are certain situations, however, where the sharing of profits does *not* give rise to a rebuttable presumption of partnership existence. These are situations where logical alternative explanations for the sharing of profits are present. To give just one example, no presumption of partnership exists where the profits are received by a creditor in payment of a debt. For example, O, the owner of a business in financial difficulty, owes a debt to X. In settlement of this debt, X agrees to accept a certain percentage of O's profits for a period of time. No inference of partnership is created by the sharing of profits, and no partnership exists between O and X (unless, perhaps, X takes title to a portion of the business property and takes an active role in managing the business).

Other situations where sharing of profits does not give rise to a presumption of partnership are where the profits are received as wages by an employee, as consideration for the sale of property, as rent by a landlord, as an annuity by a spouse or representative of a deceased partner, or as interest on a loan by a creditor.

Absence of an agreement to share losses does not necessarily weigh heavily against the existence of a partnership. Often partners will agree to share profits, but they may not even consider that they might suffer a loss, or they may believe it will bring bad luck to even think about the possibility. Hence, they will have no agreement as to losses even though they clearly intended to be partners. On the other hand, if there is an agreement to share losses, an extremely strong presumption of partnership arises. While there are many non-partnership explanations for why persons would agree to share profits, there are few non-partnership reasons that would explain an agreement to share losses.

Joint Control and Management

Although sharing of profits is a cardinal element of the partnership, another factor often felt to be important by the courts is whether the parties have *joint control* over the operation of the business. *Exercise of management powers* is obviously very strong evidence of control. But the fact that management powers have been expressly delegated to one or more of the partners or to one or more non-partner managers does not mean that those who do not manage are not true partners if the other facts indicate that they are. In a sense, agreeing to relinquish control is itself an exercise of the right of control.

Joint Ownership of Property

Another factor that frequently finds its way into court opinions is *joint ownership of assets.* Of the three basic tests for existence of a partnership, this is the least important, although courts consider it, along with all the other evidence. The UPA provides that co-ownership of property does not, of itself, establish a partnership. An inference of partnership is also not necessarily created by the fact that the co-owners share any profits made by the use of the property. This seems at first to be inconsistent with our earlier discussion of the presumption of partnership that is usually engendered by profit sharing. But there is no real inconsistency. In the case of co-owners of property, the sharing of profits made from the property is a basic part of co-ownership. In most cases the owner of property wishes to receive whatever income it generates; thus, it is reasonable to assume that co-owners will want to share the income from their jointly owned property. A partnership should not be presumed simply because the owners act in a way totally consistent with simple co-ownership. On the other hand, if the property and its use are only part of a larger enterprise, and the parties share profits from the whole enterprise, an inference of partnership is justified. The following case illustrates the type of evidence considered by courts in determining whether a partnership exists.

TUBB v. ASPECT INT'L, INC.
Court of Appeals of Texas, 2017 Tex. App. LEXIS 362 (2017)

In 2011, Superior Shooting Systems, Inc. (and its representative, Tubb) and Aspect International (and its representative, Sterling) began a venture to make and sell weapons. Both companies would participate in control of the business and split the profits equally. Superior agreed to fund the purchase of production equipment and materials, lend Tubb's name to the venture, and provide access to its distribution network. Aspect agreed to contribute the amount Superior owed it on invoices for certain information technology (IT) work Sterling had performed for Superior, convert Sterling's garage into a manufacturing facility, obtain retail packaging for the ammunition, and run the manufacturing operation.

The parties retained an engineering firm, FillPro, to design and construct an ammunition loading machine capable of producing high quality precision ammunition. Superior funded the purchase of the machine. Sterling devised and, with FillPro, created a hybrid computer-controlled loading system. Once construction was complete, FillPro installed the machine in Sterling's repurposed garage, trained Sterling, and certified the machine as production ready.

Sterling soon grew concerned over whether Tubb was willing to proceed with the parties' venture as he originally had agreed. The two discussed reducing their agreement to writing and both agreed that a written agreement was necessary. By January 2013, Sterling concluded that Tubb no longer intended to perform the venture as agreed. Litigation ensured and one issue that arose was whether a partnership existed between Superior and Aspect. The trial court held, among other things, that no partnership existed. Superior and Tubb ("Appellants") appealed on several issues; Aspect and Sterling cross-appealed on other issues. (The ruling that no partnership existed is the only issue addressed in the excerpted opinion below).

Hoyle, Judge:

In determining whether a partnership was created, we consider several factors, including (1) the parties' receipt or right to receive a share of profits of the business; (2) any expression of an intent to be partners in the business; (3) participation or right to participate in control of the business; (4) any agreement to share or sharing losses of the business or liability for claims by third parties against the business; and (5) any agreement to contribute or contributing money or property to the business.. But an agreement by the owners of a business to share losses is not necessary to create a partnership.

Agreement to Share Profits and/or Losses. The trial court's finding that the parties agreed to share profits equally is an uncontested fact. This factor weighs heavily in support of a finding that the nature of the venture was a partnership.

No Agreement Regarding the Nature of the Entity. The record is in accord with the trial court's finding that Tubb and Sterling had no agreement regarding the nature of the entity. But we cannot overlook the fact that the trial court made no finding concerning what type of entity the parties did, in fact, create. Superior and Tubb contend there is evidence that Sterling proposed written agreements concerning entities other than partnerships. But the record likewise supports that Tubb never accepted any of Sterling's proposed agreements. Appellants cite *Hoss v. Alardin,* 338 S.W.2d 635 (Tex.App. 2011), in support of their contention that there is no evidence that a tax return was filed on behalf of the entity. But in *Hoss,* the court's consideration of the fact that no tax return was filed for the entity was predicated by the statement that the alleged partnership had existed for "several years." In this case, the entity did not exist for much more than one year, and it is reasonable to conclude from the evidence that both parties had doubts about its future several months before Sterling formally repudiated the agreement. Ultimately, the trial court's finding and the parties' failure to agree on another form for the entity lends support to a conclusion that the entity was a partnership.

Participation or Right to Participate in Control of the Business. The trial court also found that Appellants held all the rights to control the business and right to make the executive decisions because they held the "checkbook." The right to "control" a business is the right to make executive decisions. The "checkbook," as referenced in the trial court's findings, was not the property of the entity. Indeed, the record reflects that the entity had no checking account or other entity-owned property. However, the record supports that, because of Tubb's shooting expertise and outlay of capital to purchase the loading machine, Appellants made many decisions concerning the finer details of the ammunition that would be manufactured and held responsibilities concerning the procurement of raw materials.

However, the trial court's finding concerning the terms of the agreement and the evidence of record nonetheless establishes that Appellees had the right to make, and made, many decisions. These decisions included helping to devise a hybrid computer-controlled loading system for the loading machine, the preparation of Sterling's garage to be used as a manufacturing location for the business, devising the "Absolute" branding for the ammunition, and the procurement of packaging for the ammunition.

The record further indicates that when Tubb suggested to Sterling that the manufacturing should be moved to Canadian, Texas, before manufacturing even had commenced, Sterling strongly objected, and Tubb relented on the issue. This evidence clearly indicates that Sterling and Aspect had the right to make an executive decision concerning the location of the business's manufacturing facility. The evidence conclusively supports that Appellees participated in the control of the business.

Contribution of Money or Property to the Business. The trial court further found that both Tubb and Sterling contributed property to the venture. Indeed, the evidence demonstrates that Tubb contributed approximately $250,000.00 to procure the machine while Sterling contributed value in the form of IT invoices for work he previously had done for Appellants in the amount of approximately $35,000.00. Thus, we conclude that both parties' contributions of property to the venture supports the creation of a partnership.

Expression of Intent to be Partners in the Business. Lastly, the trial court found that Superior and Aspect expressed the general intent to be "partners" in the business venture. *But see Ingram v. Deere,* 288 S.W.3d 886 (Tex. 2009) (merely referring to another person as "partner" in a situation where recipient of message would not expect declarant to make a statement of legal significance is not enough; courts should look to terminology used by putative partners, the context in which statements were made, and identity of speaker and listener). We are mindful that while intent is among the factors indicating that persons have created a partnership, a partnership may be created regardless of whether the persons intended to create it. Furthermore, apart from their self-serving testimonies, in their communications with one another both parties repeatedly referred to the ammunition project as a "joint venture." [We hold that the evidence does not support the trial court's finding that there is no partnership.]

Partnership by Estoppel

Under both RUPA and UPA, people may be deemed partners for liability purposes, even if they are not truly partners. Under RUPA they are called "purported partners," and under UPA they are called "partners by estoppel." Under both approaches, the essential notion is that people who holds themselves out as partners, or who allow themselves to be held out as partners, may be liable as partners to third parties who relied upon this appearance to their detriment. Thus, if the ABC Bank loans money to the XYZ partnership because wealthy Ms. Q holds herself out as an XYZ partner (or allows X, Y, and Z to do so), it is equitable to hold Ms. Q liable for the debt even if she did not meet the legal criteria of a partner and did not intend to be a partner.

These doctrines apply much more often to contract cases than tort cases because tort plaintiffs are seldom able to meet the reliance requirement. Obviously, Mrs. Q could not be held liable as a purported partner on the basis of fraudulent representations that were unknown to her.

PARTNERSHIP PROPERTY

A partnership commonly requires various types of property for the operation of its business, including, for example, real estate, equipment, inventory, or intangibles such as cash or securities. Under the UPA, a partnership is recognized as an entity insofar as property ownership is concerned and can own either real estate or other types of property. The UPA uses the phrase *tenants in partnership* to describe the status of individual partners with respect to the partnership property.

Although today a partnership can (and quite often does) own such property itself, it is not essential that it owns any property at all. The partners themselves may wish to individually own the property needed for the operation of the business.

One of RUPA's most important changes is elimination of the tenancy-in-partnership concept. RUPA eliminates any mention of a partner's rights in specific partnership property, making it clear that partners are not co-owners of partnership property and have no interest in it that can be transferred. The partnership entity owns partnership property under RUPA.

For a number of reasons, it is sometimes important to determine whether an item of property belongs to the partnership or to an individual partner. Among them:

1. In most states, creditors of the partnership must resort to partnership property for satisfaction of their claims before they can take property of individual partners.
2. The right of a partner to use partnership property is usually limited to purposes of advancing the partnership business.
3. The question of ownership can also be important with regard to taxation, distribution of assets upon dissolution of the partnership, and other matters.

Factors in Determining Ownership

Agreement

The ownership of property is determined by *agreement* of the partners. Sound business practices dictate that the partners should explicitly agree on the matter of property ownership and should keep accurate records of their dealings with property. Unfortunately, partners often fail to indicate clearly their intentions as to whether ownership of particular items of property rests with the partnership or with one or more individual partners. In such cases, the courts consider all pertinent facts in an attempt to discover the partners' *intent*.

Legal Title

In the absence of a clear agreement as to ownership, the strongest evidence of property ownership is the name in which the property is held, often referred to as the *legal title*. If an item of property is held in the name of the partnership, courts will hold it to be partnership property in almost every case. This principle most often plays a part where real estate is involved, because a deed has been executed in the name of some party and usually has been "recorded" (made part of official county records). Such formal evidence of ownership is frequently not available for property other than real estate, but if it is available, it will play the same important role. For example, this principle applies to motor vehicles, for which there is usually a state-issued certificate of title.

Problems regarding ownership seldom arise if title to the property in question is held in the partnership name. Those that do arise usually occur in either of two situations: (1) where the property is of a type for which there is no deed, certificate, or other formal evidence of ownership; or (2) where title is held in the name of one or more individual partners, but there is a claim that it is actually partnership property. In the first instance, evidence must be presented to establish just where ownership actually rests. In the second, evidence must be introduced to overcome the presumption of individual ownership and prove that the property actually belongs to the partnership. No single factor is controlling; the court's determination ordinarily is based on the cumulative weight of several factors.

Specific Factors

Property purchased with partnership funds is presumed to be partnership property. This presumption is rebuttable, but typically it is very difficult to overcome.

Evidence indicating that the property has been used in the business of the partnership also weighs in favor of the conclusion that it is partnership property. This factor, however, is not conclusive because courts realize that it is not uncommon for individual partners to allow their property to be used in the partnership business without intending to surrender ownership of it.

If property is carried in the partnership books as an asset of the firm, this strongly indicates that it is partnership property. The inference is even stronger if an unpaid balance on the property's purchase price is carried in the records as a partnership liability.

Among other factors that a court may consider in determining whether specific property belongs to the partnership or an individual partner are the following:

1. If property had been purchased with funds of an individual partner, the fact that partnership funds were later used to improve, repair, or maintain the property *tends* to show that it now belongs to the partnership. (But additional evidence usually is required, because most courts have been unwilling to infer that the property is owned by the partnership solely on the basis that partnership funds were later used to maintain it.)
2. The fact that *taxes* on the property have been paid by the partnership can be important.

3. The receipt by the partnership of *income* generated by the property is evidence that the partnership is the owner.

4. Any other conduct of those involved is considered if it tends to indicate their intent regarding property ownership.

This discussion is based on the UPA, but RUPA provisions are comparable. The following case illustrates the strong presumption that property acquired with partnership funds or labor is partnership property, as well as some of the problems that may sometimes result from having partnership property in the name of one of the partners instead of the partnership.

ACKERMAN v. HOJNOWSKI
804 A.2d 412 (Maine 2002)

Ackerman and Hojnowski were living together in Ackerman's Abington, PA home when, in 1992 they bought a residence in Castine, ME for $83,500, and Ackerman sold the Abington residence for $146,000. Ackerman paid the entire purchase price of the Castine property with the proceeds of the sale of the Abington residence. Title to the Castine property was held by Ackerman and Hojnowski as joint tenants.

As part of their decision to move to Castine, Hojnowski and Ackerman decided to start a pasta making business which would be operated out of their home. Ackerman spent $32,000 from the excess proceeds of the sale of the Abington property to purchase equipment for the business and an additional $15,000 to improve the Castine property. Ackerman and Hojnowski also borrowed $65,000 secured by a mortgage to finish the improvements as well as a $10,000 home equity loan. Mortgage payments were paid with funds generated from the pasta business. In addition, Ackerman and Hojnowski have other joint debts that total approximately $12,500.

On October 4, 2000, Ackerman filed a lawsuit requesting an equitable partition of the Castine property and an accounting and division of personal and business assets. Ackerman alleged that he obtained a temporary protection from abuse order against Hojnowski on December 2, 1999, that granted him exclusive possession of the Castine property, and he alleged that he had continued to operate the pasta business as a sole proprietorship. At trial, he testified that he had continued to make mortgage payments and that he had paid all other joint debts.

Following the trial, the court entered judgment ordering that the Castine property be sold and the proceeds distributed to the parties equally. The court also set aside the partnership assets and any liabilities to Ackerman. Following a request for findings of fact and conclusions of law and a motion to alter or amend the judgment, the court amended its order to provide that the sale price of the property be at least $96,000, that Ackerman "be responsible for all costs associated with mortgages, taxes, insurance, and minor repairs . . . in exchange for the right to possess the property exclusively," and that either party may purchase the property from the other if both so agreed. The amended order also provided that the partnership assets be set aside to Ackerman "in exchange for the partnership debts which he paid from his own personal funds." Ackerman then filed the present appeal.

One of the issues presented by Ackerman's appeal was whether the court erred by finding that the property was not a partnership asset.

Gonzalez, Judge:

The court made the following finding regarding the Castine property:

(4) The Court finds that the initial and continuing intent of the parties was to purchase the Castine property for retirement purposes. Its use as a place to conduct their business was only incidental. Therefore upon the de facto termination of their partnership, the property reverted to its intended use and is not deemed now by this Court to be partnership property.

Ackerman contends that this finding is clearly erroneous. He contends that rather than grant his "alternative count for partition of real estate" and divide the property equally, the court should have applied partnership law and divided the property unequally in accordance with the parties' relative contributions [to the partnership].

Partnership property is "all property originally brought into the partnership stock or subsequently acquired by purchase or otherwise, on account of the partnership." 31 M.R.S.A. Sec. 288(2) (1996). Title to real property of a partnership may be held either in the name of the partnership or in the individual name or names of one or more of the partners. *Id.* Generally, the intent of the partners governs whether property held in the partners' individual names is properly considered partnership property. The intent of the partners is a question of fact. *Eckert v. Eckert,* 425 N.W.2d 914 (N.D. 1988). We will uphold the trial court's factual findings unless they are clearly erroneous.

In the present case, there is competent evidence to support the trial court's determination that the parties' intended the Castine property to be their individual property and not the property of their business partnership. Their primary motivation for purchasing the Castine property was to move to Castine and reside in the residence, and only incidentally to conduct their business there. Hojnowski and Ackerman did not decide to start a pasta making business until after they were under contract to buy the residence. In addition, the residence was initially purchased with Ackerman's non-partnership funds, and the title to it was taken in Hojnowski and Ackerman's individual names. There was ample support for the conclusion that the parties did not intend to contribute their residence to their business partnership. Affirmed on this issue.

OTHER FORMS OF BUSINESS ORGANIZATION

In a general partnership, each partner is potentially personally liable for the obligations of the partnership. When employees and partners are acting on behalf of the partnership, agency law applies and both the partnership and the other partners are principals who may be liable. If a partnership suffers catastrophic losses because of a bad business deal or a tort committed by a partnership employee, partners might have to dig into their own pockets to satisfy a judgment against the partnership. They have "general liability." The purchase of insurance is the primary way that general partners can avoid individual liability for partnership losses. For these reasons, a general partnership is really not the best form of organization for most businesses. These days most general partnerships are formed accidentally by people who go into business together without paying any attention to the legalities of their relationship. If they talked to a lawyer, that lawyer would likely recommend to them some other form of business organization. There are several other forms.

Corporations. The corporate form provides substantial protection from liability for firm debts and is therefore often a very attractive form of business organization, and will be discussed in detail in the following three chapters.

Limited Partnerships. A limited partnership is a partnership that is composed of at least one general partner and at least one limited partner. Typically, there are one or a few general partners who actively run the business and many limited partners who are essentially passive investors comparable to shareholders in a public corporation. Under limited partnership law, limited partners enjoy the limited liability accorded to shareholders of a corporation rather than the general liability of partners in a general partnership. That is to say, if things go badly for the enterprise, they might lose their entire investment, but they will almost never have to reach into their own pocket to pay any additional sums when firm obligations go unpaid. On the other hand, general partners who run the limited partnership do have the same potentially unlimited liability for firm obligations as do all partners in a general partnership. However, in most jurisdictions, a corporation can be the sole general partner, which leaves all individuals involved in the firm (whether as limited partners or as shareholders of the corporate general partner) enjoying limited liability.

So long as limited partners remain relatively passive, they will enjoy the limited liability of corporate shareholders. But if they roll up their sleeves and start participating in the partnership's affairs, they may find themselves saddled with the general liability of a general partner.

Limited Liability Companies (LLCs). Limited liability companies are a fairly recent development designed to encourage the formation of businesses by providing a non-corporate structure that, unlike limited partnerships, provides limited liability to *all* owners of the business. If limited partners in a limited partnership take an active role in managing the firms, they risk being treated as general partners and saddled with unlimited liability for firm obligations. However, all LLC members can take an active role managing the firm's business without sacrificing their limited liability. Unlike corporate shareholders, they do not face double taxation. Rather, LLCs feature "pass-through" taxation just like general and limited partnership. The LLC pays no taxes; firm income is "passed through" to LLC members who pay individual income tax on it. It is usually quite desirable to enjoy both limited liability (unlike general partners of partnerships) and at the same time single, pass-through taxation (unlike shareholders of a corporation). For that reason, LLCs have become fabulously popular. Courts around the country are still trying to lay down clear guidelines for when they should draw from partnership law and when they should draw from corporate or other bodies of law in order to clarify application of LLC law. The Uniform Law Commission has promulgated a revised Uniform Limited Liability Company Act ("RULLCA") that by 2020 had been adopted in 20 states and the District of Columbia.

LLCs are usually either "member-managed" (where the LLC members themselves run the business as if it were a general partnership) or "manager-managed" (where the LLC members delegate management to one or more members or perhaps even a third party, much like a limited partnership is managed). LLC law generally grants members the power to shape the organization contractually to be whatever they wish it to be, so long as outside parties are not misled or unduly prejudiced. In Texas, for example, the law presumes that LLC managers and/or members owe a fiduciary duty to other members, but enables the LLC to "expand or restrict" these duties contractually. This freedom to contract can work both for and against a member's interests, as the following case demonstrates.

TOUCH OF ITALY SALUMERIA & PASTICCERIA, LLC v. BASCIO
2014 Del. Ch. LEXIS 2 (Del. Ch. 2014)

Glasscock, Vice Chancellor:

A lie can be an insidious thing. It can destroy friendships and business relationships. It can also be the basis for a successful lawsuit, where it is in aid of fraud or conceals actionable wrongdoing. But sometimes a lie, no matter how morally problematic, is just a lie. This case, as pled, involves such a lie.

In 2009, several individuals formed an LLC, Touch of Italy Salumeria & Pasticceria, LLC ("Touch of Italy") which operates a specialty Italian grocery in Rehoboth Beach. One member, Robert Ciprietti, provided cash in exchange for his membership; at least one other member, Louis Bascio, a defendant here, provided business goodwill and sweat equity. The business was successful, and an additional member entered, while others left. Eventually, Louis decided to leave the business. He gave notice, as specified in the LLC agreement, and withdrew as a member on December 15, 2012.

The lie alleged is this: Louis told the other members that he was moving to Pennsylvania, perhaps to open a business there. Although he told them he would not compete with Touch of Italy after his withdrawal, ten weeks later Louis and his brother, Frank Bascio, also a defendant here, formed their own LLC, Bascio Bros. Italy, LLC ("Bascio Bros."), which then opened a competing Italian grocery, doing business as Frank and Louie's Italian Store ("Frank and Louie's"). Frank and Louie's is located on the same block in Rehoboth Beach as Touch of Italy. Louis' former partners, understandably, feel betrayed. Those partners, however, chose to associate themselves with Louis under an LLC agreement. Delaware's law with respect to LLCs, as this Court has repeatedly noted, is explicitly contractarian; it allows those associating under this business format to structure their relationship in the way they believe best suits them and their business. This particular LLC agreement was written to allow members to readily withdraw, without triggering any obligation to forgo competition thereafter. Thus, Louis faced no legal impediment to withdrawing and opening Frank and Louie's as a competing grocery. Given this fact, had his fellow members known his true intentions—that is, had the lie as alleged never occurred—they would have been contractually powerless to change the course of events. The Plaintiffs can point to no acts or omissions of their own, taken in reliance on the lie. They allege that Louis breached fiduciary duties, but fail to allege a single act undertaken before his withdrawal, other than the lie, in furtherance of his competing business or in derogation of any duty to Touch of Italy. In reality, this complaint is an attempt to achieve a result—restraint on post-withdrawal competition—that the members could have but chose not to forestall by contract. Dismissed.

Limited Liability Partnerships (LLPs). Another recent and very popular form of business organization is the LLP, which is an organizational form aimed at making life better especially for professionals such as doctors, lawyers, accountants, and architects. LLPs provide limited liability protection for partners in general partnerships. Like LLCs, LLPs feature pass-through taxation and limited liability for partners. Typically, a partner in, say, an accounting firm formed as an LLP, will have limited liability regarding the *contractual* obligations of the firm, and limited liability regarding the *tort* obligations of the firm as well *except for those torts committed by particular partners or those under their supervision.*

This contrasts with a general partnership where all partners are potentially personally liable for the malpractice committed by any other partner or employee in the firm. In general, LLP law is much more flexible and favorable for professionals than the *professional corporation* form of organization that preexisted LLPs.

Limited Liability Limited Partnerships (LLLPs). LLLPs provide additional limited liability for all partners in limited partnerships. In limited partnerships, while limited partners enjoy limited liability and generally cannot lose more than they have invested in the venture, a limited partner's general partners are jointly and severally liable for the limited partnerships' debts and obligations. The impact of this liability can be limited by ensuring that the general partner is a corporation. However, the LLLP form goes even further, allowing a limited partnership to make an election under state law to afford limited liability to even the general partners of a limited partnership during the time covered by the election. This form really requires third parties such as creditors to actively protect their own interests and tips the balance of protection away from them and toward general partners.

CHAPTER 25

CORPORATIONS: NATURE, FORMATION, AND POWERS

- Introduction to the Corporation
- The Corporation as a Legal Entity
- Formation of the Corporation
- Financing the Corporation
- Corporate Powers
- Corporate Management
- Management of Close Corporations

INTRODUCTION TO THE CORPORATION

The Nature and History of the Corporation

Suppose for a moment that you have been given the authority to create a new organizational form for conducting a business enterprise. You probably would want to create an artificial being with a legally recognized identity of its own so that it could make contracts, own property, sue and be sued, and do all the other things necessary for running a business. This artificial being, having existence only on paper but nevertheless recognized by law as a "person," could have perpetual existence. It would be unfettered by the limitations of a flesh-and-blood existence. There would be no worries about death and its effect upon the continuing vitality of the business. True, it would have to act through human agents, but these agents could be replaced with no effect on the artificial being.

You probably would want the ownership of this new organizational form to rest in the hands of investors who would have no management responsibilities. In this way, an investor's interest in the business could be sold to another investor with no effect on the operation of the enterprise. And management would be centralized, thus improving the efficiency of the business.

Investors could be attracted by making their ownership interests freely transferable and by shielding them from liability for business debts. The possibilities for raising capital would be practically endless. New shares in the ownership of the business could be issued as needed for capital requirements, and if the business had been successful, investors would buy them.

But despite the worthiness of your creation, it possesses one flaw: it is not new. It has already been conceived of and put into practice. It is called a *corporation.*

Today there are many ways to organize a business enterprise—sole proprietorships, general partnerships, limited partnerships, limited liability companies, limited liability partnerships, limited liability limited partnerships, etc. But most of the *largest* business enterprises organize as corporations, making a basic understanding of corporate law essential for sophisticated businesspersons.

Governing Law

Corporations are creatures of statute. All 50 states and the District of Columbia have corporate codes that govern the internal affairs of corporations formed in their states and regulate all corporations' relationships with other businesses, individuals, and government entities. There is substantial variation in the states' corporate codes, although most are based generally upon either the Delaware Corporate Code or some version of the Revised Model Business Corporation Act (RMBCA). This text will focus on features that most state corporate codes have in common. It is important to note that under the *internal affairs doctrine,* the internal practices of corporations, including the rights of shareholders and the authority of the board of directors, are governed by the law of the state in which the firm is incorporated. However, when those firms do business in other states, the laws of those other states may well govern the firm's relationships with external parties.

Although corporation law is primarily state law, the legal practices of all corporations in the United States are heavily constrained by federal law, especially federal securities law. Indeed, the federal Sarbanes-Oxley Act of 2002 (SOX), passed in the wake of the Enron scandal, federalized aspects of corporate law that had traditionally been viewed as solely within the jurisdiction of the states. For example, SOX mandates that larger corporations' boards of directors must have an audit committee and that all three members must be independent and one must be a financial expert. Before SOX, composition of the board of directors of even the largest public companies was determined solely by individual state law.

Terminology

When a firm incorporates in Texas, for example, it is a *domestic corporation* in Texas. In other states where it does business, it is a *foreign corporation.*

Most corporations are *private corporations*, but sometimes government entities form corporations (such as the Tennessee Valley Authority and the United States Postal Service) and these are called *government corporations.*

In addition to the private/government distinction, there is a private/public distinction. A corporation that is owned by one or only a few shareholders is called a *private* or *closely-held* corporation, in contrast to a *publicly-held* corporation which has stock that is more broadly held. Google, Facebook, Microsoft, Boeing, General Motors and most other corporations you read or hear about in the media are public corporations, as are any corporations that are listed on a national stock exchange.

There are *professional corporations* which attempt to confer upon law firms, accounting firms and other professionals some of the benefits that go with the corporate form. With the creation of LLCs, LLPs, and LLLPs described in the previous chapter, the professional corporation is not nearly as popular as it once was.

Some corporations are *not-for-profit corporations* in contrast to for-profit or *business corporations.* Not-for-profits (or non-profits) may actually make a profit, but they do not distribute it to their owners or members. They may undertake any number of functions, often charitable or educational in nature.

In order to assist social entrepreneurs in raising capital from a much broader range of investors than is typical of the traditional non-profit corporation, many states have recently authorized what are variously called "flexible purpose corporations," "low-profit limited liability corporations," and "low-profit limited liability companies" ("L3Cs"). L3Cs enable entrepreneurs to tap into conventional capital markets as well as accept capital infusions from philanthropy (distinguishing them from pure non-profits), yet emphasize a social mission rather than making money (distinguishing them from pure for-profit corporations).

Many states have authorized creation of Benefit Corporations ("B-Corps"), which are generally required to operate under articles of incorporation that establish the B-Corp's purpose as creating a material positive impact on society and the environment. Whereas the Holy Grail for most for-profit companies is financial return for shareholders, the directors of a B-Corp. are authorized, and even required, to pursue social impact over return to investors. "The benefit corporation model puts some actual power behind the idea that corporations should be governed not simply for the best interests of stockholders, but also for the best interests of the corporation's employees, consumers, and communities, and society generally." (Leo Strine, *Making it Easier for Directors to 'Do the Right Thing'?* 4 HARVARD BUSINESS LAW REVIEW 235 (2014)).

THE CORPORATION AS LEGAL ENTITY

Perhaps the most important characteristic of the corporation is its recognition as a legal entity—an artificial being or person. Because the law recognizes the corporate entity, it may own property, make contracts, sue and be sued in court, and generally perform most of the legal functions that a natural person can perform. Recognition of corporate personhood means that individuals who own the corporation (known as shareholders or stockholders) are generally not liable for the corporation's debts unless they have contractually chosen to assume such liability. Shareholders of large, publicly-held corporations generally enjoy "limited liability" (in that the maximum amount they can lose is limited by the amount of their investment) for both the corporation's contractual and tort liabilities.

Another consequence of recognition of the corporate entity is "double taxation." Not only does the corporation pay taxes on its income, but when it distributes excess funds to shareholders in the form of dividends, they must pay an additional tax on this personal income. There are many ways of minimizing this double taxation, and one method involves the corporation organizing as a *Subchapter S* corporation. Firms that meet the requirements for Subchapter S status (no more than 100 shareholders who are all individuals [with some exceptions], no nonresident alien shareholders, and only one class of stock) do not pay federal corporate income taxes, although their income or losses are passed through to the shareholders who do pay individual income tax on such income. There are obviously enough loopholes built into the federal tax code that even huge *Subchapter C* corporations often pay little or no tax even on huge earnings.

Although corporations are generally viewed as legal "persons," the courts have held that they enjoy some, but not all, of the rights of natural citizens under the United States Constitution. Some of these notions are explained in more detail in the chapter on Constitutional law.

Piercing the Corporate Veil

Although the corporate entity is well-recognized in American law and limited liability is an important benefit for shareholders, in some situations policy considerations will dictate that courts *pierce the corporate veil* so that creditors of the corporation may recover from the personal pocketbooks of shareholders. The law regarding when the corporate veil may be disregarded is somewhat vague. Latty wrote in his book SUBSIDIARIES AND AFFILIATED CORPORATIONS (1936), that what the rule "comes down to once shorn of verbiage about control, instrumentality, agency, and corporate entity, is that liability is imposed [on individual shareholders] to reach an equitable result."

Over the years, courts have considered innumerable factors in deciding whether to pierce the corporate veil in various situations. Decisions are rendered on a case-by-case basis after weighing relevant factors. No single factor is determinative. Courts will not pierce the corporate veil of a public corporation with widely-held shares. Piercing of the veil is limited to closely-held corporations. Although the following case involves an attempt to pierce the veil of a limited liability company (LLC), the court used the same standards it would if the organization had been a closely held corporation.

UNDERWOOD v. MILLER
Court of Appeals of Tennessee, 2020 Tenn. App. LEXIS 64 (2020)

Plaintiffs Underwood and Stamps sued Defendant Miller, alleging that she had breached her contract to employ Plaintiffs and pay the debts of a previous interior design business Plaintiffs owned. Miller moved to dismiss on the grounds that she was not a party *to the contract. Rather, Plaintiffs contracted with Nashville Design Center, LLC (NDC) of which Miller was the sole member. Plaintiffs dismissed Miller, sued NDC instead, and ultimately won a $709,500 judgment against the LLC, which could not pay.*

Plaintiffs then filed this suit, seeking to satisfy the NDC judgment by piercing its corporate veil and reaching into Miller's personal pocket. The trial court refused to pierce, granting Defendant's motion. Plaintiffs appealed.

Clement, Judge:

"A corporation is presumptively treated as a distinct entity, separate from its shareholders, officers, and directors." *Oceanics Sch., Inc. v. Barbour*, 112 S.W.2d 135 (Tenn. App. 2003). In this way, the corporate form acts as a veil or shield, protecting its shareholder from personal liability for the debts of the corporation. "In appropriate circumstances, however, the corporate veil may be pierced and the acts of a corporation attributed to a shareholder." *Rogers v. Louisville Land Co.*, 367 S.W.2d 196 (Tenn. 2012). In order to pierce the corporate veil, the party seeking to do so must establish that "the separate corporate entity 'is a sham or a dummy' or that disregarding the separate corporate entity is 'necessary to accomplish justice.'" *CAO Holdings, Inc. v. Trost*, 333 S.W.3d. 73 (Tenn. 2010). "Despite the inapplicability of the remedy's name, the 'corporate veil' of a Tennessee limited liability company may also be pierced, [using] the same standards." *Edmunds v. Delta Partners, LLC*, 403 S.W.2d 812 (Tenn.App. 2012).

To determine whether piercing the corporate veil is appropriate, Tennessee courts apply the factors articulated in *FDIC v. Allen*, 584 F.Supp. 386 (E.D.Tenn. 1984). In *Allen*, the court stated:

> Factors to be considered in determining whether to disregard the corporate veil include not only whether the entity has been used to work a fraud or injustice in contravention of public policy, but also: (1) whether there was a failure to collect paid-in capital; (2) whether the corporation was grossly undercapitalized; (3) the nonissuance of stock certificates; (4) the sole ownership of stock by one individual; (5) the use of the same office or business location; (6) the employment of the same employees or attorneys; (7) the use of the corporation as an instrumentality or business conduit for an individual or another corporation; (8) the diversion of corporate assets by or to a stockholder or other entity to the detriment of creditors, or the manipulation of assets and liabilities in another; (9) the use of the corporation as a subterfuge in illegal transactions; (10) the formation and use of the corporation to transfer to it the existing liability of another person or entity; and (11) the failure to maintain arms-length relationships among related entities.

No single factor is dispositive, nor is it necessary that all factors support piercing the corporate veil. However, "the equities must 'substantially favor' the party requesting relief, and the presumption of the corporation's separate identity should be set aside only 'with great caution and not precipitately.'" *Id.*

Additionally, even if a plaintiff presents evidence sufficient to pierce the corporate veil under the *Allen* factors, Tennessee law also requires a showing of fraud or injustice. The parties agree that two factors are inapplicable: factor three, "non-issuance of stock certificates," and factor eleven, "the failure to maintain arms-length relationships among related entities." *Allen.* Accordingly, we will consider the other nine factors and whether

Plaintiffs' undisputed facts established that Defendant used the corporate form to commit fraud or to cause an injustice.

[1] *Failure to Collect Paid-in Capital.* [After NDC's bankruptcy, its assets were auctioned.] Defendant conceded that she deposited the auction proceeds from the sale of NDC's assets into her personal account instead of NDC's business account. She contended, however, that this was proper because NDC owed her more than $200,000, and as a creditor of NDC, she was entitled to the auction proceeds to partially satisfy NDC's debt to her. [Plaintiffs claim that this constituted a failure to collect paid-in capital.] The trial court held that according to NDC's 2008 financial statement, the auction proceeds were accounted for as income, and Plaintiffs proffered no authority suggesting that auction proceeds are paid-in capital and not income to the business. Accordingly, the trial court correctly held that "the auction proceeds were income to NDC. As such, NDC did not fail to collect paid-in capital." Therefore, this factor does not favor Plaintiffs.

[2] *Grossly Undercapitalized.* Plaintiffs argued that NDC was grossly undercapitalized as evidenced by NDC's inability to pay the debts incurred by Nashville Designer's Resource, which NDC acquired from Plaintiffs and agreed to assume as part of its obligation under NDC's contract with Plaintiffs. Plaintiffs supported their contention with the finding of the Bankruptcy Court that NDC failed to pay Plaintiffs' business debt totaling $146,193.79.

A corporation's "legitimacy is suspect" if, from the time of its formation, the "corporation [was] unable to pay its costs of doing business because of grossly inadequate capitalization." 18 Am.Jur.2d Corporations §56. Thus, gross undercapitalization means that, at its inception, the corporation did not have enough capital to operate. Plaintiffs, however, do not dispute Defendant's factual assertion that in NDC's first year of business, NDC obtained a line of credit from Prime Trust Bank in the amount of $364,000. Nor do Plaintiffs dispute Defendant's factual assertion that NDC subsequently obtained a line of credit from SunTrust Bank, and for four years, both banks made loans to NDC on an as-needed basis amounting to more than one million dollars.

The undisputed facts show that NDC had sufficient capital to operate, irrespective of whether it paid Plaintiffs' debts as agreed. Therefore, this factor does not favor Plaintiffs.

[3] *Inapplicable.*

[4] *Sole Ownership by One Individual.* It is undisputed that Defendant was the sole member/owner of NDC. "However, it is not uncommon for a corporation [or company] to be owned by one individual, and this fact standing alone does not weigh heavily either way on the question of whether the corporate veil should be pierced." *F&M Mktg. Servs., Inc. v. Christenberry Trucking & Farm,* 523 S.W.3d 663 (Tenn. App. 2017).

[5] *Same Office or Business Location.* Plaintiffs identified no evidence to dispute the fact that NDC leased its own showroom using funds from the company's bank accounts.

[6] *Employment of Same Employees.* It is undisputed that NDC hired its own employees and paid its employees' salaries and health insurance premiums from NDC's business accounts.

[7] *Use of the Entity as an Instrumentality or Business Conduit for an Individual.* It is undisputed that Defendant deposited the net proceeds of $114,617.56 from the auction into Defendant's personal banking account, and as the trial court correctly found, "[t]his is the only transaction Plaintiffs offer to show that NDC was used as an instrumentality of [Defendant]." It is also undisputed that NDC was in business for four years, was involved in

thousands of business transactions, and all of NDC's business and financial transactions, including its lines of credit, were in the company's name. Therefore, we agree with the trial court that Defendant did not use NDC as an instrumentality or business conduit for herself.

[8] *Diversion of Assets by or to an LLC Member to the Detriment of Creditors.* [In relation to Defendant depositing the proceeds of the auction into her bank account,] Defendant did not retain any surplus, and Plaintiffs do not cite to any authority supporting the proposition that Defendant violated the public policy of this state. Moreover, Defendant was paid less than what NDC owed her. Therefore, this factor does not favor Plaintiffs.

[9] *Use of the LLC as a Subterfuge in Illegal Transactions.* Plaintiffs argued that "[t]o the extent that the breach of contract was illegal, if not criminally then civilly, the use by [Defendant] of NDC was a subterfuge with respect to its contract with Plaintiffs." But Plaintiffs cited no authority to support the contention that a breach of contract is illegal in the context of this *Allen* factor, and we are not aware of any. Therefore, this factor does not favor Plaintiffs.

[10] *Use of the LLC to Transfer Existing Liability of Another.* Plaintiffs do not dispute the fact that Defendant personally guaranteed a loan to NDC from SunTrust Bank for over $995,000. In light of this undisputed fact, Plaintiffs' assertion that Defendant formed NDC with the purpose of transferring, and thus avoiding existing individual liabilities is unsupported by any competent evidence and is without merit.

[11] *Inapplicable.*

Not only have Plaintiffs failed to establish a single *Allen* factor that favors them, they also failed to identify any evidence to support a finding that the breach of contract at issue here was fraudulent. Plaintiffs' fraud or injustice claim is premised on the contention that NDC breached its contract with Plaintiffs. However, as the trial court noted, citing *Southeast Texas Inns, Inc.,* 462 F.3d at 673: "[t]he law requires that fraud or injustice be found in the defendants' use of the corporate form," which is not the type of "injustice" or harm that typically flows from a mere breach of contract. Moreover, Plaintiffs' argument that Defendant committed fraud by failing to defend NDC in the bankruptcy action is without merit for several reasons including the obvious fact that Defendant was not a party in the bankruptcy action. Affirmed.

FORMATION OF THE CORPORATION

Promoters

A **promoter** is the driving force behind formation of a corporation. Typically, a promoter recognizes a business opportunity, analyzes it to determine its economic feasibility, and brings together the necessary resources and personnel. In planning for the proposed corporation, the promoter often finds it necessary to employ the services of attorneys, accountants or other professionals. Promoters may also have to borrow money and lease or buy real estate, equipment, or patent rights. In other words, the promoter often acts as sort of an agent, albeit for a principal that does not yet exist. Because the principal does not yet exist and the law assumes that the third party will wish someone to be liable on the other side of the deal, promoters will be personally liable on the contracts they negotiate on behalf of the proposed corporation unless the other party has clearly agreed to look solely to the corporation once it is formed for performance.

If things work smoothly, the corporation will eventually come into existence and its board of directors will adopt the contracts entered into by the promoter. With such adoption, corporations become liable on the contracts as well as entitled to enforce them in order to gain the benefits negotiated on their behalf. Absent agreement by the third parties, the promoters will remain liable on the contracts along with the corporation. If the third parties agree to a *novation*, however, the corporation can be substituted for the promoter as a party to the contract and the promoter will have no further liability. Absent a novation, if the corporation does not adopt the contract or does adopt it but does not perform, the promoter will be on the hook absent clear agreement to the contrary.

For example, in *Coopers & Lybrand v. Fox*, 758 P.2d 683 (Colo.App. 1988), Fox, while acting on behalf of a corporation he was forming, hired Coopers & Lybrand as an accountant for the firm. A month later, the corporation was formed. Soon thereafter, Coopers billed "Mr. Garry R. Fox, Fox and Partners, Inc." in the amount of $10,827. When the bill went unpaid, Coopers sued Fox individually. Although Fox had not agreed to pay the bill in his personal capacity, he was a promoter and the law presumes that promoters are personally liable for the contracts they negotiate on behalf of their prospective firms. Fox could point to no evidence that Coopers had released him from this presumed liability, as by a novation, for example, so he was held liable

Promoters owe a fiduciary duty to the corporation, to other promoters, and to foreseeable investors in the corporation. It is fine for promoters to profit from their activities, but there must be full disclosure and approval by the board of directors or the shareholders. Secret profits are forbidden and must be disgorged, even if their amount is theoretically "fair."

If the corporation adopts the contract the promoter has entered into on its behalf either expressly via directors' resolution or impliedly by voluntary acceptance of the contract's benefits, it not only becomes liable on the contract but may also enforce its rights against the third party.

Process of Incorporation

The word *incorporation* refers to the process of forming a corporation. Although details vary from state to state, the general procedural mechanics are quite similar. Corporations are always creatures of the state that must comply with state legal requirements in order to come into existence and to remain viable.

Articles of Incorporation

The first step in the formative process is preparation of articles of incorporation, a legal document that should be prepared by an attorney and that must be signed by the incorporators (those individuals who technically apply to the state for incorporation). They are usually the persons actually forming the corporation, but may be completely disinterested parties. Many states require signatures by three incorporators.

Although many more subjects may be addressed in articles of incorporation, most states require at a minimum that the following matters be addressed.

1. The name of the corporation. This name cannot be the same as, or deceptively similar to, that of any other corporation legally doing business within the state.

2. The duration of the corporation. In most states this can be perpetual.

3. The purpose or purposes for which the corporation is organized. In most states, corporations may be organized for "any lawful purpose." However, in some states various forms of business such as banks, insurance companies, and railroads cannot be formed under general incorporation statutes because they are required to incorporate under other, specialized statutes.

4. The financial structure of the corporation. Detailed information must usually be included about the methods by which the corporation will raise capital needed for its operations.

5. Provisions for regulating the internal affairs of the corporation. Examples of such provisions include the location of shareholders' meetings, quorum and voting requirements for shareholders' and board of directors' meetings, and procedures for removing directors and filling board vacancies.

6. The address of the corporation's registered office and the name of its registered agent at this address. The registered office is simply the corporation's official office in the state, and the registered agent is its official representative. The purpose of this requirement is to ensure that there will be an easily identifiable place and person for the receipt by the corporation of summonses, subpoenas, and other legal documents.

7. The name and address of each incorporator.

Certificate of Incorporation

The articles of incorporation must be filed with the designated state official (usually the secretary of state). If they are in conformance with all legal requirements and if all required fees are paid, the state official will issue a *certificate of incorporation* (sometimes called a *charter*). This certificate represents the permission granted by the state to conduct business in the corporate form. The corporation comes into existence when the certificate of incorporation is issued.

Initial Organization

Under the laws of most states, the incorporators must hold an *organizational meeting* after issuance of the charter. In states where the initial board of directors is not named in the articles of incorporation, the incorporators elect the directors at this meeting. In all states, authorization will usually be given to the board of directors to issue shares of stock. Perhaps the most important purpose of the meeting, however, is to adopt bylaws.

Bylaws are the rules or "private laws" that regulate and govern the internal actions and affairs of the corporation. Although they ordinarily are not filed with a state official, the bylaws must not conflict with the provisions of the articles of incorporation. The relationship between the articles and the bylaws is analogous to the relationship between the constitution and the statutes of a state. A corporation's bylaws sometimes amount to only a brief statement of rules for internal management of the corporation. Often, however, the bylaws are extremely detailed, sometimes even including a restatement of applicable statutes as well as provisions from the articles of incorporation. As an example of the type of details frequently included in the bylaws, many provisions relate to the specifics of conducting directors' and shareholders' meetings.

The board of directors also holds an organizational meeting, at which time it transacts whatever business is necessary to launch the operations of the enterprise. In some states the incorporators do not hold organizational meetings, and in these states the board adopts bylaws and performs the other tasks described earlier as functions of the incorporators. In the states in which incorporators do meet, the directors at their initial meeting usually approve all actions taken by the incorporators. In addition, the agenda of the first directors' meeting includes such matters as selection of corporate officers, adoption of pre-incorporation contracts made by the promoters, selection of a bank for depositing corporate funds, and other pertinent items of business.

Doing Business in Other States

A corporation that has been incorporated in one state may wish to do business in other states as well. Before doing so, the corporation must apply for and receive a *certificate of authority* in each state where it plans to do business. The process of obtaining the certificate is largely a formality. However, the corporation is also usually required to maintain a registered office and registered agent in each state where it does business.

The penalties levied by various states against foreign corporations that have not obtained a certificate of authority include fines, denial of the privilege of filing lawsuits in the courts of that state, and placement of personal liability for corporate obligations incurred in that state on the directors, officers, or agents involved.

FINANCING THE CORPORATION

After incorporation, the corporation must obtain the funds necessary to launch and initially operate the business. When the business has been in operation for a substantial period of time, a wider range of financing alternatives are available, including retained earnings, short-term borrowing, and accounts receivable financing.

The principal method of initially financing a corporation is by issuance of *securities*, which are sold to investors. The board of directors usually authorizes their issuance during its initial organizational meeting. The most common types of securities are equity securities and debt securities.

Equity securities are usually referred to as *shares of capital stock*, or simply *shares*. Each share represents an interest in the ownership of the corporation. Therefore, the investors who purchase them (the *shareholders* or *stockholders*) are the owners of the corporation.

Debt securities are usually referred to as *bonds*. Corporate bonds do not represent ownership interests in the corporation, but are loans to the firm from the investors who purchase them. The relationship between bond owners and the corporation is that of creditor and debtor.

Registration of Securities

When a corporation issues securities to meet either its initial capital requirements or its later financial needs, it usually must comply with the securities laws (*"blue sky laws"*) of those states in which they are offered for sale. The laws of some states simply prohibit fraud in the sale of securities. In other states, however, the issuance of securities must be *registered* with the state agency empowered to administer the law, often a state securities board. To register, the corporation must supply detailed financial and other information about itself. Penalties for failing to register can be severe, although all state statutes contain at least some exemptions from registration that may apply.

Many issuances of securities must also be registered with the federal government's *Securities and Exchange Commission (SEC)*. This process is discussed in this text's chapter on securities regulation. Federal registration also entails significant disclosure, SEC oversight, and potential liability for registration errors and misstatements. Fortunately, the SEC has also created many exemptions from registration that a corporation may take advantage of. In recent years both regulatory and technological changes have worked together to make holding a public offering a less important form of capital raising than it once was. Raising capital through so-called private placements and other transactions that do not require registration is relatively more important today.

The purpose of both the state and federal securities laws is to ensure that investors are given sufficient information to make knowledgeable investment decisions and to protect them from fraud. Such laws may also benefit the corporations by increasing investor confidence and thereby encouraging capital formation. Corporations in countries with vigorous securities regulation are able to raise more funds faster and cheaper than corporations in countries that lack such investor protection. These issues are addressed in more detail in the chapter on securities regulation.

CORPORATE POWERS

As an artificial person, a corporation possesses the power to do most of the things an individual can do in the operation of a business enterprise, such as own property, make contracts, borrow money, and hire employees. Corporate powers derive from several sources, traditionally classified as statutory, express, and implied powers. State corporation laws ordinarily contain a list of *statutory powers*—those activities in which corporations are permitted to engage. Originally this was a fairly limited list, but over time it has vastly increased to cover most or all activities that are legal for any sort of business enterprise. *Express powers* are those set forth in the articles of incorporation. Although these may be restricted to prevent firms from venturing into business activities that its owners and directors would like to avoid, the articles typically provide that the corporation may engage in "any lawful activities." If there do happen to be gaps in the statutory or express powers, courts typically hold that corporations also have *implied powers* to do any other things reasonably necessary for carrying on their business.

When firms act outside their statutory, express, and implied powers they are said to be acting *ultra vires,* although only the state Attorney General or a shareholder of the corporation is legally empowered to challenge *ultra vires* act. Third-parties cannot do so.

CORPORATE MANAGEMENT

The structure of corporate control can be viewed as a pyramid. At the top are the officers who run the day-to-day affairs of the corporation. These officers are selected and monitored by the board of directors. Corporations operate under the supervision of the board of directors. At the bottom of the pyramid are the owners, the shareholders who have the right to elect the directors (but not the officers) and to vote regarding proposals to make major structural changes to the corporation (such as mergers with other corporations). Note that in large public corporations, these various roles are fairly distinct. However, in smaller closely-held corporations, many or all shareholders may also serve as officers and/or directors. Indeed, in most jurisdictions a single person may be the sole shareholder, director, and officer.

Shareholder Powers

Shareholders as shareholders have no authority to participate in the ordinary business and affairs of the corporation. Shareholders do not, for example, have authority to hire officers, pay dividends, or enter into contracts on the corporation's behalf. Of course, shareholders in a small firm may also serve as officers or directors and be authorized in those capacities to do more, but in their role as simple shareholders they enjoy no such authority. However, they are not completely without influence.

Right to Vote

The most important shareholder power is the right to vote. Shareholders have the right to vote in two situations. First, they have authority to vote to elect directors in the annual shareholder meetings that are mandated by state corporate statutes. In this way, shareholders enjoy indirect input into the day-to-day managing of the corporation. They elect the directors who select the officers who make the daily decisions. Second, shareholders vote to approve or disapprove proposed "extraordinary" transactions such as mergers, sales of most corporate assets, and corporate dissolution. In this way they may have a voice in decisions to dramatically change the nature of the firm in which they chose to invest.

Notice and Meetings. Annual shareholder meetings are held each year at a time and place specified in the bylaws. Written notice stating the place, day, and hour of the meeting are to be delivered to all legal shareholders. If the meeting is not an *annual meeting* to elect directors, but instead a *special meeting* regarding an extraordinary transaction, the notice shall state the purpose of the meeting.

A *quorum* is needed for effective action. A majority of outstanding shares constitutes a presumptive quorum, but many states allow the articles to establish a quorum as one-third of the shares or even lower. Usually courts will not order shareholders to attend shareholders' meetings even if their absence prevents attainment of a quorum. However, if a quorum is established, in most jurisdictions effective action cannot be thwarted by a subsequent walkout of some shareholders.

Proxies. Shareholders may vote in person or by a written authorization to another known as a *proxy*. The proxy holder acts as the agent of the shareholder. Proxies typically must be in writing and can be valid for no more than eleven months, forcing management to resolicit proxies every year so that theoretically it will be more responsive to shareholder concerns.

Proxies are particularly important for large, publicly-held corporations. Some have hundreds of thousands of shareholders and could never attain a quorum if shareholders were required to appear in person at the annual meeting. Therefore, to be reelected, directors must solicit proxies. This is a fairly routine practice, but larger corporations must comply with significant layers of *federal proxy regulation* that supplement state rules to ensure that shareholders are treated fairly and are adequately informed in the voting process. If some shareholders are disgruntled with current leadership, they may launch a *proxy contest* or *proxy fight* in an attempt to elect a dissident director or slate of directors in order to change the direction of the corporation. When a proxy fight occurs, competing factions will vie vigorously for the right to vote the proxies of shareholders just as political candidates vie for the votes of the American electorate. A proxy may be revoked orally, in writing, or simply by giving a later, inconsistent proxy.

Board of Directors

Shareholders choose directors and the corporation is operated under their guidance. The number of directors is typically established in the corporation's articles or by-laws. Many states allow corporations to have a single director. Many large corporations have many directors, perhaps nearly twenty. There are few legal qualifications for being a director, although some states have minimum age requirements and some require that directors be shareholders. Directors may also be employees or otherwise closely associated with the corporation (*inside directors*) or be otherwise unaffiliated with the corporation (*outside* or *independent directors*). The federal Sarbanes-Oxley Act of 2002 (SOX) requires that most public company boards have *audit committees* and that all members of the audit committee be independent. At least one member must be a "financial expert."

Directors are normally reelected annually, although most states allow *classified boards* where, for example, a nine-person board might be divided up into three groups of three directors serving rotating three-year terms. In any one year, only one-third of the board would be up for election.

Directors may always be removed *for cause* if they misbehave (criminal acts, breach of fiduciary duty, etc.), and most states allow removal *without cause*. However, shareholders may also amend the articles of incorporation to eliminate the power to remove directors without cause.

Functions

Even though the corporation generally is bound by the actions of the board, the directors are not agents of the corporation or of the shareholders who elect them for two reasons. First, their powers are conferred by the state rather than by the shareholders. Second, they do not have *individual* power to bind the corporation, as agents do. Instead, they can act *only as a body*.

With the exception of certain extraordinary matters mentioned earlier, the board of directors is empowered to manage all the affairs of the corporation. It not only has authority to determine corporate policies but also supervises their execution. The management powers of the board of directors usually include the following:

1. Setting the basic corporate policy in such areas as product lines, services, prices, wages, and labor-management relations.

2. Decisions relating to financing the corporation, such as issuance of shares or bonds.

3. Determination of whether (and how large) a dividend is to be paid to shareholders at a particular time.

4. Selection, supervision, and removal of corporate officers and other managerial employees.

5. Decisions relating to compensation of managerial employees, pension plans, and similar matters.

6. Proposing major changes in corporate structure (e.g., sale of major corporate assets, merger with another corporation, corporate dissolution) for shareholder vote.

Officers

Directors choose the officers who will execute corporate policy established by the board by making needed day-to-day decisions. There may be any number of officers with a large variety of titles, but it is typical to have a president, one or more vice-presidents, secretary, and treasurer. Other potential titles are chief executive officers (CEO), chief financial officers (CFO), chief information officers (CIO), general counsel (GC), comptroller, and the like.

In closely-held corporations, one person may usually hold more than one (or all) officer positions. Officers hold their positions at the pleasure of the board of directors who

611 © **2020 John R. Allison & Robert A. Prentice**

may remove them at any time. Of course, if officers have signed a long-term contract with the company and are removed before the end of the term without cause, they may well have a breach of contract lawsuit.

Officers, like lower level employees, are agents of the corporation, and all the rules of agency law (discussed in earlier chapters) apply to the relationships created. Thus, the corporation is bound by the actions of its officers and other employees if they are acting within the scope of their authority—whether it is express, implied, or apparent. The express authority of officers may come from state statutes or the articles of incorporation, but it most frequently emanates from corporate bylaws or from resolutions of the board of directors. A third party who is unsure of the authority of a corporate officer with whom she is dealing may require that officer to produce a board of directors' resolution granting the officer authority to act before proceeding.

MANAGEMENT OF CLOSE CORPORATIONS

A closely-held corporation typically has relatively few shareholders. They may all be family members, friends, or some combination thereof. Commonly all the shareholders are also officers and/or directors. Therefore, the management of a close corporation in practice frequently more nearly resembles a sole proprietorship or partnership than the management of a major public corporation.

Despite these practical differences, a close corporation is still a *corporation* and must comply with state corporate code requirements that do not apply to partnerships or sole proprietorships. On the other hand, most states recognize the special nature of closely held firms and have enacted special corporate codes just for them that reduce formalities and allow extra flexibility in organizing the corporation's management structure. A typical close corporation statute allows shareholders by unanimous agreement to alter the typical corporate management process in the following ways:

1. Eliminate the board of directors or restrict its discretion. In other words, shareholders may, for example, agree to run the corporation like a partnership where every shareholder has a vote in the decisions that in a larger corporation would be made by the board of directors.

2. Establish policy for corporate distributions, such as dividends.

3. Select directors or officers as well as their terms of employment and manner of removal.

4. Establish voting power. To keep control of the corporation in the hands of the founders, for example, the shareholders may agree to various "control devices" such as weighted voting, irrevocable proxies, and the like.

5. Establish terms and conditions of any contract transferring property between the corporation and shareholders, officers or directors. In other words, the shareholders may agree to vary the fiduciary duty that the law imposes upon officers and directors.

6. Establish means of breaking deadlocks when shareholders disagree. If shareholders envision that they might split evenly on an important vote, they may appoint one or more persons to make all important decisions or appoint a third-party to act as an arbitrator to break deadlocks.

7. Require corporate dissolution upon the occurrence of a specific contingency or the agreement of a certain percentage of the shareholders.

The bottom line is that states, sensibly, have given shareholders of small corporations roughly the same flexibility to establish the management structure of their firm that they would have if the firm were a partnership or a limited liability company.

Close Corporation Fiduciary Duty

In succeeding chapters, we will discuss the fiduciary obligation that officers and directors of corporations owe to the corporate owners, the shareholders. They exert substantial control over the operation of the company and have substantial opportunities to abuse that control to benefit themselves at the expense of the shareholders. This power is counterbalanced by imposition of the fiduciary responsibility.

In publicly held corporations, it would be rare for a shareholder to hold a majority position, but in closely held corporations, this is common. Abuse of that power is also common. Courts are divided as to whether to impose fiduciary obligations upon majority shareholders and, if so, under what circumstances. Views vary from state to state. In Illinois, for example, the fewer shareholders there are, the more likely courts are to impose a fiduciary duty upon shareholders. In *Hagshenas v. Gaylord*, 557 N.E.2d 316 (Ill.App. 1990), the court found a breach of the duty of loyalty when a 50% shareholder in a close corporation opened a new business that competed directly with the firm. The following case represents Utah's view.

McLAUGHLIN v. SCHENK
2009 UT 64 (Utah Supreme Court, 2009)

Cookietree, Inc. is a privately held Utah corporation that sells baked goods. It was formed in 1981 with appellee Greg Schenk as its president, a role he retains today. In 1992, Schenk recruited appellant McLaughlin to work for Cookietree. McLaughlin quickly was promoted to COO and slowly over the years purchased shares of Cookietree. McLaughlin's employment agreement provided him with the option of acquiring up to 200,000 shares of common stock in Cookietree and made him an at-will employee--either party could terminate the employment relationship at any time so long as six months' notice was given.

In 1993, Cookietree and McLaughlin entered into an Incentive Stock Option Agreement that allowed McLaughlin to purchase an additional 200,000 shares of the company's common stock. In 2003, Schenk, who owned approximately 65% of Cookietree's shares, indicated that he was interested in selling Cookietree. McLaughlin wanted to purchase the company, but never was able to raise the full amount of the purchase price.

Schenk began discussions with another cookie company, Otis Spunkmeyer. At this point, the relationship between McLaughlin and Schenk began to deteriorate. McLaughlin would not agree to various terms of the Otis Spunkmeyer transaction, including consent to a noncompete agreement. In 2004, Schenk confronted McLaughlin and fired him without cause. Pursuant to McLaughlin's employment agreement, the termination date was not effective for six months. Thus, McLaughlin continued to receive his salary and bonuses for six months, although this compensation was paid at his original contract rate rather than his current salary and bonus rate. McLaughlin was immediately relieved of all duties, blocked from company email, and excluded from the corporate premises. When McLaughlin refused to leave, police escorted him from the property. After McLaughlin's termination, Cookietree contacted McLaughlin's lawyer and indicated that "everything [was] negotiable; [they] were looking for a global resolution." Following his termination McLaughlin continued to receive dividends from his Cookietree holdings. This income, along with his wife's stock dividends, comprised half of their family's income. McLaughlin's wife Kim continued to work at Cookietree for some time after McLaughlin's termination.

McLaughlin sued Cookietree and Schenk for breach of fiduciary duty, among other claims. The trial court ruled against McLaughlin on this and other issues, and McLaughlin appealed.

Durham, Chief Justice:

In a public corporation, directors and officers owe the corporation and the shareholders collectively a duty to act in good faith and in the best interest of the corporation. In a partnership, each partner owes each of the other partners individually a duty to act with the utmost good faith. McLaughlin, a minority shareholder in a closely held corporation, asks this court to impose on shareholders in such corporations a duty to individual shareholders similar to the duty owed in a partnership. We hold that the appellee Schenk, as a close corporation shareholder, owed McLaughlin individually a duty to act in the utmost good faith, but that he did not violate this duty because his actions did not thwart McLaughlin's reasonable expectations.

This case presents the question of whether shareholders of closely held corporations--also commonly known as close corporations--should be treated differently than shareholders of publicly traded corporations. Directors and officers are required to carry out their corporate duties in good faith, with prudent care, and in the best interest of the corporation. These corporate duties have been interpreted to coincide with the common law understanding that officers and directors owe these duties to the corporation and shareholders collectively, not individually. In this case, however, McLaughlin urges us to apply a different standard--the partnership standard. In contrast to the general standard for corporate duties, the statutory partnership standard of care has been interpreted to require the utmost good faith between individual partners.

Whether to modify the fiduciary duty standard in closely held corporations is an issue of first impression for this court. Numerous other states have considered the question. McLaughlin urges us to follow the partnership-like duty standard originally articulated by Massachusetts courts and subsequently adopted by several other states. Beginning with *Donahue v. Rodd Electrotype Co. of New England*, 328 N.E.2d 505 (Mass. 1975), Massachusetts changed the landscape of duties owed by shareholders in close corporations.

Relying on (1) the resemblance between close corporations and partnerships, (2) the need for trust and confidence in such companies, and (3) the inherent risk of loss due to shareholders' inability to recoup their investments, the Massachusetts court imposed on close corporation shareholders the same duties owed by partners--utmost good faith and loyalty to all shareholders of the corporation. Compared to the fiduciary duty owed by directors and stockholders of public corporations, the court found this duty to be "more rigorous" than the "somewhat less stringent" corporate duty of "good faith and inherent fairness." The *Donahue* court explained, "stockholders in close corporations must discharge their management and stockholder responsibilities in conformity with this strict good faith standard. They may not act out of avarice, expediency or self-interest in derogation of their duty of loyalty to the other stockholders and to the corporation." The *Donahue* standard has been adopted by other jurisdictions.

The defendants, however, urge this court to follow the minority position, which has been adopted by Delaware and Texas. The minority position narrowly construes the duties of shareholders in a closely held corporation and differentiates between a person's status as employee and shareholder. [These jurisdictions] impose identical duties on shareholders of closely held corporations and public corporations.

Presented with two divergent approaches, we must assess which approach best suits Utah's corporate law scheme. Shareholders in close corporations lack a ready market for their shares. This means that closely held corporation shareholders have no liquidity in their shares, and have no avenue for price discovery other than the costly process of acquiring an independent valuation for the company. Without an available market in which to sell their interest in a company, minority shareholders who disagree with the direction or governance of the close corporation must rely on contractual or statutory remedies, which are often nonexistent, impractical, or inadequate. This, in effect, leaves the shareholder with no remedy for the abuses and oppression that may result due to the small number of shareholders, the frequency of familial and other personal relationships, and the likelihood that majority shareholders control the board in close corporations. Though the Utah Corporation Act provides for dissolution, this is often a drastic remedy that may not serve the interest of the complaining shareholder and certainly not the corporation of which he is a part owner.

Without a market remedy, shareholders in close corporations are easily subjected to freeze outs, squeeze outs, and other forms of oppression, which the Corporation Act aims to prevent. Thus, the Massachusetts approach of recognizing broader fiduciary duties in closely held corporations better achieves the goals of the Act by stemming shareholder oppression and is the appropriate standard for evaluating fiduciary relationships among shareholders in a closely held corporation. Our adoption of the Massachusetts standard is a logical extension of our existing case law regarding close corporations, which acknowledges the unique nature of such corporations and seeks to protect their shareholders by interpreting the Corporation Act with different corporate circumstances in mind. By adopting this broader fiduciary obligation for close corporation shareholders, alternative remedies exist for oppressed shareholders, such as an equitable claim for dissolution or a claim for breach of fiduciary duty.

Having concluded that shareholders in closely held corporations owe their co-shareholders fiduciary obligations, we now consider whether the Defendants breached these duties in this case. Breaches of the fiduciary duty owed by close corporation shareholders arise in several circumstances, the facts of which commonly overlap. These circumstances have been identified as unequal treatment, frustration of reasonable expectations of involvement, and a freezeout or squeeze-out. James M. Van Vliet, Jr. & Mark D. Snider, *The Evolving Fiduciary Duty Solution for Shareholders Caught in a Closely Held Corporation Trap*, 18 N. Ill. U. L. Rev. 239, 252 (1998). In all cases there is a common element—a shareholder's investment expectation in a close corporation is frustrated by another shareholder's actions.

Analyzing breach of fiduciary claims in this light, courts have narrowed the potentially broad duty espoused by *Donahue* to a more investment-based analysis. For example, beginning again with Massachusetts, in *Wilkes v. Springside Nursing Homes, Inc.*, the court described the termination of an officer from the close corporation as a squeeze-out that "effectively frustrate[d] the minority stockholder's purpose in entering on the corporate venture and also den[ied] him an equal return on his investment." Under this standard for fiduciary duty protection, the termination of an employee is not always a breach of fiduciary duty.

"Not every discharge of an at-will employee of a close corporation who happens to own stock in the corporation gives rise to a successful breach of fiduciary duty claim." *Merola v. Exergen Corp.*, 668 N.E.2d 351 (Mass. 1996). Instead, the court must consider the formal policies and practices of the close corporation, and how these policies and practices are interpreted by and impact all shareholders to determine whether or not a shareholder's reasonable expectations were thwarted. As the North Dakota Supreme Court has explained, when considering an allegation of oppressive conduct, a court should review "what the majority shareholders knew, or should have known, to be the petitioner's expectations in entering the particular enterprise. Majority conduct should not be deemed oppressive simply because the petitioner's subjective hopes and desires in joining the venture are not fulfilled. Disappointment alone should not necessarily be equated with oppression." *Balvik v. Sylvester*, 411 N.W.2d 383 (N.D. 1987). This close consideration of shareholders' expectations is necessary to ensure that corporations are not crippled and kept from efficiently operating their business; it is well accepted that corporate officers "must have a large measure of discretion . . . in declaring or withholding dividends, deciding whether to merge or consolidate, establishing the salaries of corporate officers, dismissing directors with or without cause, and hiring and firing corporate employees." *Wilkes*.

Applying the foregoing principles to this case, we conclude that Cookietree did not thwart McLaughlin's investment expectation. McLaughlin was not a founding member who created the company with the expectation of employment. Instead, after the corporation was well established, McLaughlin was recruited for his specialized experience in similar industries. His primary reason for joining Cookietree was employment. This employment allowed him to purchase stock in Cookietree, but he was not required to do so. And, while it is likely that his initial stock purchase allowance and the later stock purchase agreement were offered as an incentive or reward for McLaughlin's work performance, the purchase allowances were not inextricably tied to his employment; they were a separate investment in the company. In addition to his stock purchases, and unlike the plaintiff in *Wilkes*, McLaughlin was paid a competitive salary for his contributions to the company. His investment in the company was separately rewarded through the payment of dividends, which he continued to receive after his termination. Therefore, in terminating McLaughlin, Schenk did not thwart McLaughlin's investment expectations in the company and therefore did not violate any duty owed to McLaughlin. Affirmed.

Comment: This case is just one sign that some courts have treated smaller corporations much differently than large public corporations. As noted, some state legislatures have enacted special corporate codes just for closely-held corporations that allow them maximum flexibility for structuring their business enterprise. The need to do so is not as strong as it once was in light of the relatively recent creation of LLCs and LLPs (described in the previous chapter).

CHAPTER 26

CORPORATIONS: RIGHTS AND LIABILITIES OF SHAREHOLDERS AND MANAGERS

- Rights of Shareholders
- Liabilities of Shareholders
- Rights of Managers
- Liabilities of Managers

Successful operation of the corporate enterprise involves the concerted efforts of many people. Although success demands that their efforts be focused on essentially the same goals and objectives, their own individual interests inevitably come into play on some occasions. For this reason, we will now discuss the rights and liabilities of the parties to the corporate venture, with respect to one another, and with respect to the corporation as an entity.

RIGHTS OF SHAREHOLDERS

Right to Vote

The most important shareholder power is the right to vote. Unless otherwise provided in the articles of incorporation, a shareholder has one vote for each share. The right to vote does not have to be expressed in the articles; it is inherent in the ownership of shares. Of course, the articles can expressly exclude or limit the right to vote by, for example, providing for the issuance of a certain number of special shares without voting rights.

Treasury stock consists of shares that have been issued and later repurchased by the corporation. They carry no voting rights since a corporation cannot logically act as a shareholder of itself. If these shares are subsequently resold, however, they once again carry voting rights.

Right to Inspection and Information

In order to effectively exercise their franchise and otherwise protect their interests, shareholders must have access to sufficient relevant information. As noted earlier, federal statutes require substantial disclosure by public companies in the proxy solicitation process. However, especially for smaller corporations that are closely-held, the right of shareholders to inspect corporate records and otherwise gain access to important corporate information can be crucial.

Common Law Inspection Rights

Under the common law in most jurisdictions, shareholders enjoy a broad right to inspect corporate records and documents such as shareholder lists, minutes of directors' meetings, financial statements, and even contracts. The right must be exercised at proper times and in proper places and, most importantly, for *proper purposes.* The burden of proof to establish a common law proper purpose is upon the shareholder. Shareholders may not inspect records solely to harass management or to access sensitive corporate information that may be divulged to competitors. According to one court, proper purposes are those "reasonably related to the shareholder's interest in the corporation, [including], among others, efforts to ascertain the financial condition of the corporation, to learn the propriety of dividend distributions, to calculate the value of stock, to investigate management's conduct, and to obtain information in aid of legitimate litigation." *Tatko v. Tatko Bros. Slate Co., Inc.*, 569 N.Y.S.2d 783 (A.D. 1991).

Statutory Inspection Rights

States commonly provide statutory shareholder inspection rights that supplement, rather than replace, common-law inspection rights. Many states require corporations to keep as permanent records certain basic documents (*e.g.,* minutes of all meetings of shareholders and directors, records of all actions taken by shareholders and directors without a meeting or by a committee or directors on behalf of the entire board, appropriate accounting records, and a list of shareholders), and to maintain at their principal office certain other key documents (*e.g.,* articles of incorporation, bylaws, board resolutions, lists of directors and officers, most recent annual report).

The latest (2016) revision of the Model Business Corporation Act gives shareholders the right to inspect and copy, during regular business hours at a reasonable location, many of the corporate records listed in the previous paragraph if the shareholder makes a demand at least five days before inspection and (a) the demand is made in good faith and for a proper purpose, (b) the demand describes with reasonable particularity both the purpose of the inspection and the records desired to be inspected, and (c) the records are directly connected to the purpose.

Derivative Actions

Shareholders also enjoy the right to bring and defend lawsuits on the corporation's behalf. Suits brought on behalf of the corporation are called *derivative suits* because the shareholder's right to sue derives from wrongs done primarily to the corporation and not to the shareholder individually. The derivative suit was developed by the courts primarily as a mechanism to solve the dilemma created when those who have wronged the corporation are the very officers and directors who control the corporation and can typically refuse to authorize a suit against themselves. However, a derivative suit can also be brought against persons having no connection with the corporation.

The derivative suit has great potential as a device to protect the corporation and its shareholders. A single shareholder can institute the suit and take the wrongdoers to task. However, this potent weapon is also subject to great abuse. In the derivative context, that abuse often takes the form of a *strike suit*, a spurious suit brought not to benefit the corporation but to blackmail defendants into a settlement that will personally profit plaintiffs and their attorneys. Striking a proper balance that encourages meritorious suits without giving too much free rein to strike suits is a difficult task. The RMBCA requires shareholders wishing to bring a derivative suit to first demand that the board of directors acts in the matter. Only if the board refuses to act may the shareholder file the derivative suit.

Plaintiff Qualifications

Derivative lawsuits impose several procedural requirements aimed at ensuring that plaintiffs will adequately protect the interests of the other shareholders and of the corporation.

Most jurisdictions impose two types of ownership requirements. First, the *contemporaneous ownership* requirement demands plaintiffs must have owned shares of the corporation at the time of the challenged transaction (or have received the shares by operation of law, such as inheritance, from someone who was a shareholder at that time). This requirement prevents persons from learning of a transaction and then purchasing one or more shares in order to buy into litigation. Second, the *continuous ownership* requirement demands that plaintiff remain a shareholder continuously until judgment.

Courts often require derivative plaintiffs, upon the request of the defendant corporation's management, to post a bond as security for defendants' expenses should the suit fail. Courts in many states also require that the plaintiff in a derivative suit must "fairly and adequately" represent the corporation's interests. This requirement imposes upon a person who has volunteered himself or herself to represent the corporation a fiduciary duty akin to that owed by directors and officers. Among other things, the requirement prevents a shareholder from selling the corporation down the river by settling the claim in return for a large personal settlement.

Right to Receive Dividends

A person who purchases shares from a business corporation is making an investment and typically intending to receive a profit. Depending on the nature of the business and the type of shares purchased, the investor may expect such profit to arise either from increases in the market value of the shares (which may then be sold at a profit), or from dividends, or perhaps from both.

Dividends are simply payments made by the corporation to its shareholders, representing income or profit on their investment. The payment is usually in the form of money, but it can consist of some type of property, such as the securities of another company that the corporation has been holding as an asset.

Sometimes firms pay *stock dividends* by issuing to the shareholders additional shares of the corporation's own stock. Such a distribution is technically not a dividend, because it does not represent a transfer of any property from the corporation to its shareholders. Instead, each shareholder simply becomes the owner of a larger number of shares. Although shareholders may not benefit immediately from a stock dividend, because the value of the preexisting shares is diluted, they usually do benefit in the long run because of the tendency of such shares to later increase in value.

Because a corporation could harm creditors by taking corporate funds obligated to creditors and paying them to shareholders instead in the form of dividends, there are limits on the payment of dividends. Because creditors can be similarly disadvantaged when a corporation dips into its treasury to repurchase shares of existing shareholders, there are similar restrictions on share repurchases. It is improper for the board of directors to authorize the payment of dividends or other transfers from the corporate treasury to shareholders unless the corporation, after the payments, remains solvent in two senses. First, it must be able to continue to meet its obligations as they come due. Second, it must have more assets than liabilities on the books. If the corporation is insolvent in either sense after a dividend payment, stock repurchase, or similar transaction, the board is liable to creditors for having made an illegal transfer. Shareholders are also liable to repay the funds if they knew of the impropriety.

Shareholders have no absolute "right" to receive dividends. Whether a dividend is to be declared and paid (and how much) is within the discretion of the board of directors. Even if a firm has sufficient funds to legally pay a dividend, the board of directors may decide to retain the funds in order to save them for a rainy day or to invest them in a project to benefit the corporation. Shareholders may successfully challenge a board's decision not to pay dividends only by establishing that funds were legally available for distribution and that the board *abused its discretion* in not making the payments. Such challenges seldom succeed where public companies are involved. Disgruntled shareholders may simply sell their shares if they are not pleased with dividend payments. However, in closely-held corporations where there may not be a market for shares, majority factions may sometimes abuse minority factions and even attempt to freeze them out of corporate benefits by refusing to pay dividends. Therefore, courts may take a more active role in dividend disputes in closely-held corporations. The following case presents a relevant example of such a dispute.

ZIDDELL v. ZIDDELL, INC.
560 P.2d 1086 (Or. 1977)

The Zidell family business started as a partnership and was later incorporated. Eventually defendant Emery Zidell and plaintiff Arnold Zidell, sons of the founder, came to each own 37.5% of the stock of four closely related family corporations. They were directors. Emery was CEO. In 1972, Rosenfeld sold to Emery's son Jay enough of his stock in the corporation to give Jay and Emery voting control of the corporations.

There had previously been friction between Emery and Arnold and that friction increased after the sale, especially when Emery increased Jay's salary but not Arnold's. Emery was also apparently displeased with Arnold's lifestyle. Arnold demanded that his salary be raised from $30,000 to $50,000 a year, saying that he would resign if his request were not granted. It wasn't and he did. He resigned only his employment, not his directorships, but when his terms expired, he was not reelected.

Prior to Arnold's resignation, the companies had retained their earnings rather than paying dividends. Once he was no longer receiving a salary, Arnold objected to this practice. Thereafter, a small dividend was paid on 1973 earnings, but Arnold brought this suit, claiming that he was entitled to a larger return on his equity. He pointed out that at about the same time the small dividend was declared, employee salaries and bonuses were raised substantially. Although he did not claim these were excessive, he argued that they were evidence of concerted activity against him.

The trial judge declined to find that the defendants (the directors and the corporations) acted in bad faith, but did order payment of a larger dividend. Defendants appealed.

Howell, Justice:

We have recognized that those in control of corporate affairs have fiduciary duties of good faith and fair dealing toward the minority shareholders. Insofar as dividend policy is concerned, however, that duty is discharged if the decision is made in good faith and reflects legitimate business purposes rather than the private interests of those in control.

In *Gay v. Gay's Super Markets, Inc.*, 343 A.2d 577 (Me. 1975), the court analyzed both the duties of corporate directors and the proper role of the courts in overseeing corporate dividend policies in the following terms:

> To justify judicial intervention in cases of this nature, it must, as a general proposition, be shown that the decision not to declare a dividend amounted to fraud, bad faith or an abuse of discretion on the part of the corporate officials authorized to make the determination. …
>
> Furthermore, judicial review of corporate management decisions must be viewed in the light of this other rule that "it is not the province of the court to act as general manager of a private corporation or to assume the regulation of its internal affairs." *Bates Street Shirt Co. v. Waite*, 156 A. 293 (Me. 1931).
>
> *If there are plausible business reasons supportive of the decision of the board of directors, and such reasons can be given credence, a Court will not interfere with a corporate board's right to make that decision. It is not our function to referee every corporate squabble or disagreement.* It is our duty to redress wrongs, not to settle competitive business interests. Absent any bad faith, fraud, breach of fiduciary duty or abuse

of discretion, no wrong cognizable by or correctable in the Courts has occurred. *Id.* at 580 (Emphasis added).

Plaintiff had the burden of proving bad faith on the part of the directors in determining the amount of corporate dividends. In the present case, plaintiff has shown that the corporations could afford to pay additional dividends, that he has left the corporate payroll, that those stockholders who are working for the corporations are receiving generous salaries and bonuses, and that there is hostility between him and the other major stockholders. We agree with plaintiff that these factors are often present in cases of oppression or attempted squeeze-out by majority shareholders. *See generally* F. H. O'Neal, Oppression of Minority Stockholders 57-103, §§ 3.02-3.03 (1975). They are not, however, invariably signs of improper behavior by the majority. *See Gottfried v. Gottfried,* 73 N.Y.S.2d 692 (Sup. 1947):

> There are no infallible distinguishing earmarks of bad faith. The following facts are relevant to the issue of bad faith and are admissible in evidence: Intense hostility of the controlling faction against the minority; exclusion of the minority from employment by the corporation; high salaries, or bonuses or corporate loans made to the officers in control; the fact that the majority group may be subject to high personal income taxes if substantial dividends are paid; the existence of a desire by the controlling directors to acquire the minority stock interests as cheaply as possible. *But if they are not motivating causes they do not constitute 'bad faith' as a matter of law".* (Emphasis added.)

Defendants introduced a considerable amount of credible evidence to explain their conservative dividend policy. There was testimony that the directors took into consideration a future need for expensive physical improvements, and possibly even the relocation of a major plant; the need for cash to pay for large inventory orders; the need for renovation of a nearly obsolescent dock; and the need for continued short-term financing through bank loans which could be "called" if the corporations' financial position became insecure. There was also evidence that earnings for 1973 and 1974 were abnormally high because of unusual economic conditions that could not be expected to continue.

In rebuttal, plaintiff contends that the directors did not really make their decisions on the basis of these factors, pointing to testimony that they did not rely on any documented financial analysis to support their dividend declarations. This is a matter for consideration, but it is certainly not determinative. All of the directors of these corporations were active in the business on a day-to-day basis and had intimate first-hand knowledge of financial conditions and present and projected business needs. In order to substantiate their testimony that the above factors were taken into consideration, it was not necessary that they provide documentary evidence or show that formal studies were conducted. Their testimony is believable, and the burden of proof on this issue is on the plaintiff, not the defendants.

Nor are we convinced by plaintiff's arguments that we should approve the forced declaration of additional dividends in order to prevent a deliberate squeeze-out. Plaintiff left his corporate employment voluntarily. He was not forced out. Although the dividends he has since received are modest when viewed as a rate of return on his investment, they are not unreasonable in light of the corporations' projected financial needs. Moreover, having considered the evidence presented by both sides, we are not persuaded that the directors are employing starvation tactics to force the sale of plaintiff's stock at an unreasonably low price.

Since we have determined that plaintiff has not carried his burden of proving a lack of good faith, we must conclude that the trial court erred in decreeing the distribution of additional dividends. Reversed and remanded with directions to enter decrees of dismissal.

Right to Have Preferences Respected

Corporations often issue many different classes of stock carrying different rights. Most corporate stock is classified as common or preferred. *Common stock*, the most basic and frequently issued type, enjoys no special privilege or preferences. *Preferred stock*, on the other hand, guarantees its owner some type of special privilege or preference over the owners of common stock. Most commonly, holders of preferred stock are entitled to get in line ahead of common shareholders with respect to distributions of dividends or of other corporate funds (such as a distribution of assets upon liquidation).

For example, assume that Zeta Corp. has issued one class of common stock and one class of preferred stock (the preferred stock being "$3 preferred"). In any given year the owners of Zeta common stock cannot be paid a dividend until the owners of the preferred stock have received a dividend of $3 per share. The owners of the preferred shares have the right to have their preferences respected.

Shares that are preferred as to dividends may be cumulative or noncumulative. Assume the Zeta has a bad year and the board of directors decides the corporation cannot pay any dividends. If the preferred shares are *cumulative preferred*, the following year the board must pay the preferred shareholders $6 per share before paying any dividends to common shareholders. If the shares are *noncumulative*, however, in the following year the preferred shareholders are entitled to only $3 per share before dividends may be paid to the common shareholders.

Preemptive Rights

Assume that Jupiter Corp. has a capitalization of $100,000 consisting of 1,000 shares of $100 par value common stock. X owns 100 shares and therefore has 10% of the voting power in the company. Jupiter needs additional capital, so the shareholders authorize issuance of another 1,000 shares. If X is not given an opportunity to buy some of the new issuance, her proportionate voting and financial interest in the corporation will be reduced. And if the shares are issued for less than $100 per share, her equity position will be diluted.

To ensure fair treatment of X, the common law gave Jupiter's shareholders a *preemptive right* to buy their proportionate share of the new offering. In other words, X must be given the opportunity to purchase 10% of the new offering before outsiders can purchase in order to maintain her proportionate position in the corporation.

Preemptive rights are of vital importance in closely held corporations where majority factions could, in the absence of preemptive rights, issue new securities to themselves in order to greatly reduce the financial position and influence of a minority shareholder. While preemptive rights are generally zealously protected in closely-held corporations, they are not particularly useful to minority shareholders of public corporations and can present many bureaucratic headaches. Therefore, most publicly-held corporations are allowed to (and do) eliminate preemptive rights in their corporate charters.

Transferability of Shares

The right to sell, give, devise, or otherwise transfer shares is typically very important to shareholders. Joe might want to sell his shares because he needs to raise cash to pay his child's college tuition. Mary might want to sell her shares because she wishes to take the proceeds and invest in real estate instead. Shareholders have the right to transfer their shares *unless* a valid restriction has been placed on transferability.

There are few valid reasons to restrict transferability of the shares of public corporations. However, such restrictions are commonly employed by close corporations because the shareholders themselves, who are few in number, often actively manage the corporation and deal personally with one another on a daily basis. For example, assume that A, B, and C are the only shareholders of Prestige Corp. A and B will not want to wake up one morning and find that C has transferred his interest to D, a complete stranger with whom they will then have to share the management of the business. Therefore, the shareholders may well enter into an agreement that restricts the transfer of shares.

For example, the shareholders may agree that if any one of them wishes to sell their shares, they must first offer them to the other shareholders at a price to be determined by reference to the corporation's financial statements. The agreement serves the interests of the remaining shareholders by allowing them to prevent strangers from entering the business against their will. It also serves the interests of the departing shareholders by ensuring that they receive fair value for their shares.

A transferability restriction should always be indicated explicitly on the stock certificate.

LIABILITIES OF SHAREHOLDERS

Unless the corporate veil is pierced, shareholders typically are not personally liable for the corporation's obligations unless they have contractually guaranteed them. However, there are a few other situations where the personal liability of shareholders can become an issue.

Liability on Stock Subscriptions

A *stock subscription* is an offer by a prospective investor (a "subscriber") to buy shares of stock in a corporation. The ordinary rules of contract law apply to such offers and they thus can be revoked prior to acceptance—with two main exceptions.

First, stock subscriptions are frequently made by the promoters before formation of the corporation. It is not uncommon for several promoters to agree that their subscriptions cannot be revoked for some period of time. In such a case, the subscriptions are irrevocable for the agreed time.

Second, most state corporate codes provide that a subscription is irrevocable for a certain period of time (commonly six months), unless the subscription itself expressly provides that it can be revoked.

When the corporation comes into existence (in some states) or when the board of directors meets and votes to accept the subscriptions (in other states), acceptance occurs. A subscriber who refuses to pay thereafter is in breach of contract and may be sued for damages.

Liability for Watered Stock

Assume that ABC Corporation's board of directors authorizes issuance of 100 shares for $25/share. However, the directors issue 50 shares to Joe in exchange for only $15/share. This is termed *watered stock*, and both Joe (if he knows of the deficiency) and the directors who allowed the sale are personally liable in a lawsuit by corporate creditors or others who claim that ABC was shortchanged by $500.

Liability for Illegal Dividends

As noted earlier, if a board of directors authorizes payment of a dividend that is illegal because, for example, payment will render the corporation unable to pay its bills as they come due, the directors are personally liable for the illegal payment. Shareholders who receive the funds are also liable to pay them back *if* they knew the payment was unlawful.

RIGHTS OF CORPORATE MANAGERS

Directors

Duly-elected corporate directors have the right to receive notices of board meetings and to attend and participate in them.

Directors also have comprehensive *inspection* rights. Certainly, they have the right to inspect all corporate records as necessary to carry out their fiduciary responsibilities as directors. Most states provide that a director's right of inspection is *absolute and unqualified*, although a few cases have held that a director's inspection right can be denied where their motive is obviously hostile or otherwise improper. A more common approach is to allow the inspection and then hold the director liable if any corporate information is used in a wrongful manner.

Directors have the right to fair compensation for doing their jobs. Interestingly, directors generally set their own salary because there is no one else to do it. If they abuse this power and loot the corporation for their own gain, the shareholders may, of course, sue them for breach of fiduciary duty and vote them out of office.

Directors who are sued in the course of carrying out their corporate responsibilities are typically entitled to *indemnification*, that is, to be reimbursed by the corporation for judgments they must pay and legal expenses they incur. If the directors prevail, the indemnification is clearly proper. If directors are held liable for intentional wrongdoing, indemnification is usually not allowed. However, there is substantial state-to-state variation in handling such issues as (a) indemnification in cases where directors are held to be merely negligent, and (b) requests for advancement of attorneys' fees and other expenses while litigation is ongoing and determinations of liability have not yet been made. Delaware, for example, allows advancement of fees as necessary to induce qualified persons to serve as directors, but may well require repayment of those fees if it is later determined that they were not entitled to indemnification. Corporations typically pay premiums for liability policies ("D&O policies") to cover such liabilities and expenses.

Finally, courts have generally held that directors do *not* have authority to bring derivative actions in their capacity as directors, although of course they may bring such suits in their capacity as shareholders if they own shares.

Officers

In general, the rights of officers are established by contract and by agency law. They enjoy many of the same rights (to be paid, to be indemnified, etc.) as directors. Unlike directors, they do not set their own pay, of course.

LIABILITIES OF CORPORATE MANAGERS

Those who manage the corporate enterprise owe to the corporation and its shareholders a number of basic duties that can be classified under the headings of *obedience, due care,* and *loyalty.* A corporate manager incurs personal liability for the failure to fulfill any of these duties. In addition to these fundamental duties, certain special duties are imposed by federal securities laws. Our discussion will make no distinction between directors and officers, for their duties are roughly (though not completely) the same.

Obedience

Corporate managers have a duty to see that the corporation obeys the law and confines its operations to those activities that are within the limits of its corporate powers. If they knowingly or carelessly involve the corporation in either an illegal or an *ultra vires* act, they are personally liable for any resulting damage to the corporation. And, of course, any manager who participates in the commission of an illegal act also may be personally subject to fines or other penalties imposed by the particular law.

Duty of Attention

Years ago, courts were surprisingly reluctant to impose liability upon directors who regularly missed board meetings and otherwise did not pay much attention to corporate business. Today, however, directors must direct. And directors who are unable to fulfill designated responsibilities should resign or face liability.

In *Francis v. United Jersey Bank*, 432 A.2d 814 (N.J. 1982), for example, the court held a director personally liable for not paying attention to a corporation's business as the company's money was stolen right under her nose. From *Francis* and similar cases, it has become clear that directors have a duty to monitor the affairs of a corporation and must, at a minimum, gain a basic understanding of the corporation's business, obtain and read basic financial documents, and attend most board meetings. If something suspicious occurs, they must investigate. Should that inquiry disclose improper activity by the officers or other directors, a director should object, consult legal counsel, or even resign. A director "does not exempt himself from liability by failing to do more than passively rubberstamp the decisions of the active managers." *Barr v. Wackman,* 329 N.E.2d 180 (N.Y. 1975).

Due Care

Closely related to the duty of attention is the duty of care. Just as every driver has a duty of due care in operating an automobile, officers and directors have a duty of due care in running the affairs of a corporation. Perfection is not expected, but directors, for example, are to act "with the care an ordinarily prudent person would exercise under similar circumstances," according to a common formulation. A similar standard is expected of officers. Before making important decisions, officers and directors must do their homework. Often this requires consultation with experts, such as investment bankers, accountants, and attorneys.

Right to Rely

The duty of care has not been applied in a burdensome manner. For example, courts have reasonably held that officers and directors, particularly outside directors, are entitled to rely on information, reports, opinions, financial statements, and financial data prepared or provided by officers, employees, auditors, or others that are reasonably believed to be reliable. Absent suspicious circumstances ("red flags"), officers and directors may rely on the honesty and integrity of their colleagues and underlings.

However, red flags must be investigated. Furthermore, the Delaware Supreme Court held in *In re Caremark, Int'l,* 698 A.2d 959 (1996) that directors have a responsibility to implement and maintain adequate reporting systems designed to ensure that they are receiving reasonably reliable information so that they make informed decisions on the corporation's behalf. On the other hand, the court held that only an "utter failure" to maintain such a reporting system would create liability for breach of the duty of due care.

Ultimately, the Delaware courts were never very vigorous in their enforcement of the *Caremark* duty, which some observers think may have contributed to the Enron-era scandals. After Enron, Congress passed the Sarbanes-Oxley Act of 2002 (SOX) which required that most public corporations establish a system of internal financial controls designed to ensure that the information flowing into the corporation's financial statements that will be filed with the Securities Exchange Commission is reasonably reliable and accurate. CEOs and CFOs of these public companies must certify both that they believe in the accuracy of the information contained in financial statements filed with the SEC and that they have established adequate internal financial controls. The corporations' outside auditors must certify the reliability of the internal financial controls under the controversial Section 404 of SOX.

Business Judgment Rule

Officers and directors will make many decisions that succeed and, inevitably, some that fail. Shareholders who are unhappy with the results of managers' decisions may sue, but the courts have been reluctant to impose liability for honest mistakes, even "though the errors may be so great that they demonstrate the unfitness of the directors to manage the corporation's affairs." (*In re Caremark Int'l*).

This judicial reluctance to second-guess corporate directors and officers, known generally as the *business judgment rule,* manifests itself in two forms. First, it substantially insulates the directors' decisions from court review. Second, it shields the directors and officers from personal liability. Judges realize that they are not experts in business and therefore hold that:

> …[i]n the absence of a showing of bad faith on the part of the directors or of a gross abuse of discretion the business judgment of the directors will not be interfered with by the courts… The acts of directors are presumptively taken in good faith and inspired for the best interests of the corporation, and a minority shareholder who challenges their *bona fides* of purpose has the burden of proof. (*Warshaw v Calhoun*, 221 A.2d 487 (Del. 1966)).

If shareholders can establish self-dealing or other abuses of discretion, the business judgment rule will not protect investors. The protection of the rule is similarly limited in some other circumstances, including when there is a tender offer for control of the company and the directors are in an almost automatic conflict-of-interest situation due to the fact that they will likely lose their positions if the offer succeeds. A classic business judgment rule case follows.

SHLENSKY v. WRIGLEY
237 N.E.2d 776 (Ill.App.Ct. 1968)

Shlensky, the plaintiff, was a minority shareholder in Chicago National League Ball Club, Inc. The corporation owned and operated the major league professional baseball team known as the Chicago Cubs. The individual defendants were directors of the Cubs. Defendant Philip K. Wrigley was also president of the corporation and owner of approximately 80% of the corporation's shares.

Plaintiff Shlensky filed a derivative suit on behalf of the corporation, claiming that it had been damaged by the failure of the directors to have lights installed at Wrigley Field, the Cubs' home park, so that the Cubbies could play games at night. Shlensky pointed out that all other major league teams played night games, that the Cubs drew fewer fans to their home games than to away games that were played mostly at night, that the cross-town White Sox drew similar numbers of fans on weekend day games but more fans than the Cubs on weekday games when they played mostly at night, and that the Cubs lost money from 1961-1965 and would probably continue to do so absent a change. Plaintiff further alleged that the Cubs' failure to install lights was due to defendant Wrigley's personal belief that baseball should not be played at night and his concern that night baseball would have an adverse effect on the neighborhood surrounding Wrigley Field. Plaintiff also claimed that the other directors had allowed Wrigley to dominate the board.

The judge dismissed the complaint on grounds of the business judgment rule. Shlensky appealed.

Sullivan, Justice:

The question on appeal is whether plaintiff's amended complaint states a cause of action. It is plaintiff's position that fraud, illegality and conflict of interest are not the only bases for a stockholder's derivative action against the directors. Contrariwise, defendants argue that the courts will not step in and interfere with honest business judgment of the directors unless there is a showing of fraud, illegality or conflict of interest.

In *Davis v. Louisville Gas & Electric Co.*, 142 A. 654, a minority shareholder sought to have the directors enjoined from amending the certificate of incorporation. The court said:

> We have then a conflict in view between the responsible managers of a corporation and an overwhelming majority of its stockholders on the one hand and a dissenting minority on the other -- a conflict touching matters of business policy, such as has occasioned innumerable applications to courts to intervene and determine which of the two conflicting views should prevail. The response which courts make to such applications is that it is not their function to resolve for corporations questions of policy and business management. The directors are chosen to pass upon such questions and their judgment *unless shown to be tainted with fraud* is accepted as final. The judgment of the directors of corporations enjoys the benefit of a presumption that it was formed in good faith and was designed to promote the best interests of the corporation they serve." (Emphasis supplied.)

Similarly, the court in *Toebelman v. Missouri-Kansas Pipe Line Co.*, 41 F.Supp. 334, [said:] "In a purely business corporation . . . the authority of the directors in the conduct of the business of the corporation must be regarded as absolute when they act within the law, and the court is without authority to substitute its judgment for that of the directors."

Plaintiff argues that the allegations of his amended complaint are sufficient to set forth a cause of action under the principles set out in *Dodge v. Ford Motor Co.*, 170 N.W. 668 (Mich.). In that case plaintiff, owner of about 10% of the outstanding stock, brought suit against the directors seeking payment of additional dividends and the enjoining of further business expansion. In ruling on the request for dividends the court indicated that the motives of Ford in keeping so much money in the corporation for expansion and security were to benefit the public generally and spread the profits out by means of more jobs, etc. The court felt that these were not only far from related to the good of the stockholders, but amounted to a change in the ends of the corporation and that this was not a purpose contemplated or allowed by the corporate charter.

[Even in *Dodge*, however,] it is clear that the court felt that there must be fraud or a breach of that good faith which directors are bound to exercise toward the stockholders in order to justify the courts entering into the internal affairs of corporations. This is made clear when the court refused to interfere with the directors' decision to expand the business:

> We are not, however, persuaded that we should interfere with the proposed expansion of the business of the Ford Motor Company. In view of the fact that the selling price of products may be increased at any time, the ultimate results of the larger business cannot be certainly estimated. *The judges are not business experts.* It is recognized that plans must often be made for a long future, for expected competition, for a continuing as well as an immediately profitable venture. . . . We are not satisfied that the alleged motives of the directors, in so far as they are reflected in the conduct of the business, menace the interests of the shareholders. (Emphasis supplied.)

Plaintiff in the instant case argues that the directors are acting for reasons unrelated to the financial interest and welfare of the Cubs. However, we are not satisfied that the motives assigned to Philip K. Wrigley, and through him to the other directors, are contrary to the best interests of the corporation and the stockholders. For example, it appears to us that the effect on the surrounding neighborhood might well be considered by a director who was considering the patrons who would or would not attend the games if the park were in a poor neighborhood. Furthermore, the long run interest of the corporation in its property value at Wrigley Field might demand all efforts to keep the neighborhood from deteriorating. By these thoughts we do not mean to say that we have decided that the decision of the directors was a correct one. That is beyond our jurisdiction and ability. We are merely saying that the decision is one properly before directors and the motives alleged in the amended complaint showed no fraud, illegality or conflict of interest in their making of that decision.

Finally, we do not agree with plaintiff's contention that failure to follow the example of the other major league clubs in scheduling night games constituted negligence. Plaintiff made no allegation that these teams' night schedules were profitable or that the purpose for which night baseball had been undertaken was fulfilled. Furthermore, it cannot be said that directors, even those of corporations that are losing money, must follow the lead of the other corporations in the field. Directors are elected for their business capabilities and judgment and the courts cannot require them to forgo their judgment because of the decisions of directors of other companies. Courts may not decide these questions in the absence of a clear showing of dereliction of duty on the part of the specific directors and mere failure to "follow the crowd" is not such a dereliction. Affirmed.

Loyalty

Directors, officers, and other corporate managers are deemed to be *fiduciaries* of the corporation they serve. Their relationship to the corporation and its shareholders is one of trust. They must act in good faith and with the highest regard for the corporation's interests as opposed to their personal interests. Several problems that commonly arise in the context of the duty of loyalty are discussed below.

Use of Corporate Funds

Obviously, directors or other fiduciaries must not use corporate funds for their own purposes.

Confidential Information

A director or other manager sometimes possesses confidential information that is valuable to the corporation, such as secret formulas, product designs, marketing strategies, or customer lists. Managers are not allowed to appropriate such information for their own use.

Contracts with the Corporation

A corporate manager who enters into a contract with the corporation should realize that it is not an "arm's-length" transaction. That is, managers should make full disclosure of all material information they possess regarding the transaction. That does not mean that managers may never profit from a transaction with the corporation. For example, they may own real estate that the corporation truly needs to buy. Contracts between the corporation and its managers will generally be upheld if they are approved by a majority of disinterested, knowledgeable directors or a majority of knowledgeable shareholders. Even absent such approval, a contract will be upheld if it is shown to be fair to the corporation.

Corporate Opportunities

The *corporate opportunity rule* prohibits corporate managers from personally taking advantage of business opportunities that, in all fairness, should belong to the corporation. An obvious violation of this rule occurs when a manager has been authorized to purchase land or other property for the corporation but instead purchases it for themself.

Application of the corporate opportunity rule is sometimes not so clear-cut, however. A much more difficult problem is presented, for instance, when a director or other manager is confronted with a business opportunity arising from an *outside source* rather than from direct corporate authorization. For example: C is a director of Ace Air Freight, a corporation engaged in the business of transporting freight by air. C learns that M, a third party, has a used airplane in excellent condition that he is offering for sale at a low price. Can C purchase the airplane for himself? If the plane is of a type suitable for the corporation's freight business, the answer is probably no. He is obligated to inform the corporation of the opportunity. Only if the firm passes on the chance to buy the plane may C do so.

This example illustrates the so-called "line of business" test employed by many courts in resolving such questions. Under this approach, a corporate manager cannot take personal advantage of a business opportunity that is *closely associated with the corporation's line of business* without first calling it to the attention of the corporation. Furthermore, the rule includes opportunities not only in the area of current corporate business but also in areas where the corporation might naturally expand.

Vcom INT'L MULTI-MEDIA CORP. v. GLUCK
U.S. District Court, District of New Jersey, 2017 U.S. Dist. LEXIS 44425

Defendant Gluck managed Vcom's Alltec Division, which operates a number of websites that function "as an e-commerce center, enabling customers to register for an account, purchase various products through the online shopping cart merchant feature, and receive direct shipping from door-to-door." Through an Alltec website, known as projectorscreenstore.com ("ScreenStore.com"), Vcom sells a variety of projector screens, such as "home theater screens, portable screens, auditorium screens, business screens, and classroom screens."

In August, 2011, Gluck engaged in a Skype conversation with a third party where he stated that he might buy a website called projectorscreens.com. Gluck said that he might "use it as leverage in [his] company to get a piece of [his] division, or to go into business . . . against [ScreenStore.com]." Gluck told the third party that he had "all of the screen connections and all of the sales data, etc." and that he "could easily replicate [ScreenStore.com] for [himself]." Gluck said that "it's a matter of do i [sic] get it rollign [sic] while i [sic] keep my regular job until its all ofa [sic] sudden #1?"

In September 2011, Gluck suggested to Vcom's president, Sheldon Goldstein, that Vcom should consider purchasing other websites with similar names to ScreenStore.com. Gluck explained that purchasing those websites would "secure [ScreenStore.com's] spot on top of the search engines." In October 2011, Gluck informed Goldstein that he believed the two best options to purchase were projectorscreen.com ("Screen.com") and projectorscreens.com. Gluck told Goldstein that the price for each website was $15,000 and $19,000, respectively. Goldstein asked Gluck whether the prices of those websites were negotiable. Gluck responded that he had already been negotiating with the websites' owners and that he was "[n]ot sure if [Screen.com] will budge." The following day Gluck personally purchased Screen.com for $5,500; he bought it anonymously and never told Goldstein that it was available for $5,500. Gluck did not disclose to anyone at Vcom that he had purchased Screen.com.

In November 2011, Gluck began operating Screen.com as a website offering sales as an affiliate of Amazon.com. He functionally competed with plaintiff for more than a year. When confronted with this fact, he initially denied it, but then claimed that he was operating it as research. He admitted not turning the money that he made over to Vcom, but claimed that this was a mere innocent omission on his part. Vcom fired Gluck and sued him for a number of things, including usurpation of a corporate opportunity in violation of his duty of loyalty and fiduciary duty. Gluck filed a motion for summary judgment.

Vasquez, U.S. District Judge:

New Jersey considers four factors when determining whether an employee breached the duty of loyalty to his or her employer: "1) the existence of contractual provisions relevant to the employee's actions; 2) the employer's knowledge of, or agreement to, the employee's actions; 3) the status of the employee and his or her relationship to the employer, e.g., corporate officer or director versus production line worker; and 4) the nature of the employee's conduct and its effect on the employer." *Kaye v. Rosefielde,* 121 A.3d 862 (N.J. 2015). In essence, the Court "considers the parties' expectations of the services that the employee will perform in return for his or her compensation, as well as the 'egregiousness' of the misconduct that leads to the claim."

One way an employee may breach the duty of loyalty is by usurping a corporate opportunity from his or her employer. A claim under the corporate opportunity doctrine requires proof of the following five elements:

(1) that there is presented to a corporate officer a business opportunity; (2) that the corporation is financially able to undertake that opportunity; (3) that the opportunity is, by its nature, in the line of the corporation's business and is of practical advantage to it; (4) that the opportunity is one in which the corporation has an interest or a reasonable expectancy; and (5) that by embracing the opportunity, the self-interests of the officer will be brought into conflict with the interests of the corporation. *Torsiello v. Strobeck,* 955 F.Supp.2d 300 (D.N.J. 2013).

Here, the record indicates that in October 2011 Gluck presented Vcom with the opportunity to purchase Screen.com for $15,000. Goldstein asked Gluck whether the price was negotiable, and Gluck replied that he was "[n]ot sure if [Screen.com] will budge." The next day Gluck purchased Screen.com for $5,500 without disclosing the lower price to Vcom. In short, Vcom never rejected purchasing Screen.com for $5,500 because it was not presented with the opportunity to buy the website at that price. And Vcom specifically asked if a lower price could be had. Moreover, there is a genuine issue of material fact as to whether Vcom was interested in purchasing Screen.com. Goldstein's questions to Gluck regarding whether Screen.com's price of $15,000 was negotiable indicate that Vcom may have been interested in the website had it been available at a lower price. Therefore, Gluck's motion for summary judgment on Vcom's claim for usurping a corporate opportunity is denied.

Additionally, there is a genuine material issue of fact as to whether Gluck breached his fiduciary duty and duty of loyalty to Vcom. Gluck argues that he was not competing with Vcom during his employment and that his use of "affiliate links on an otherwise 'dead' site as research . . . was well within [his] discretion." Vcom counters that Gluck was engaging in "secret competition with Vcom during his employment" by operating Screen.com. The Court finds that there is a genuine material issue of fact regarding whether Gluck was competing against Vcom through Screen.com or whether he was operating the website as an experiment without any intention to make a profit. Gluck's summary judgment motion is denied.

Most states have provided procedures whereby an officer or director can present a business opportunity to its shareholders or other directors who may choose to pass on the opportunity on behalf of the corporation and authorize the person to exploit the opportunity as an individual.

CHAPTER 27

CORPORATIONS: MERGERS AND TERMINATIONS

- Mergers
- Sale of Assets
- Dissolution and Liquidation
- Tender Offers and Other Takeovers

In the preceding chapters we examined the nature and formation of the corporation, its basic operation, and the rights and liabilities of its individual participants. This final corporate law chapter focuses on more unusual aspects of corporate operation. Initially, we discuss changes in the fundamental structure of the corporation brought about by mergers. Then we deal with the various circumstances in which the corporate existence can be terminated.

MERGERS

The terms *merger* and *consolidation* are often used interchangeably to describe any situation in which two or more independent businesses are combined under a single ownership. Technically, however, there is a difference in meaning between the two terms. A *merger* is the absorption of one existing corporation by another; the absorbing corporation continues to exist while the absorbed firm ceases to exist. A *consolidation*, on the other hand, is a union resulting in the creation of an entirely new corporation and the termination of the existing ones. Symbolically, a merger can be illustrated by the equation $A + B = A$, while a consolidation is represented by $A + B = C$. Today, both types of transactions are typically termed "mergers," the terminology we will use here.

Reasons for Merging

Corporations may have any number of different reasons to merge. Perhaps two smaller firms believe that if they joined together they could better compete against a larger firm that dominates their industry. Perhaps A wishes to acquire its competitor B in order to reduce the competition it faces. Perhaps a large corporation wishes to acquire a smaller firm that owns intellectual property that the acquiring firm would like access to. Perhaps A wishes to diversify its business by acquiring B, which is in a completely different line of business. Maybe A has extra cash on hand and believes that buying B would be a good way to put that cash to use. These and many other possible motives can give rise to mergers. (In planning such transactions, of course, managers must consider antitrust laws.)

Procedures

Most states' corporate codes provide similar procedures for mergers. First, the board of directors of each corporation must adopt a resolution approving the merger. The resolution should set forth the names of the corporations, the terms and conditions of the proposed combination, the method and basis to be used in converting the securities of each corporation into the securities of the resulting corporation, and, in the case of a merger, any changes caused thereby in the articles of incorporation of the surviving corporation. In the case of what formerly was called a consolidation, the resolutions of the respective boards should include the entire articles of incorporation for the resulting new corporation.

Second, the plan must then usually be approved by the shareholders of each corporation, at either an annual or special meeting. The shareholders are entitled to notice and disclosure before they vote. The presumptive vote required for approval varies among the states from a simple majority to four-fifths of the outstanding shares. A two-thirds requirement is common, but corporations generally have the right to vary the number in their articles of incorporation. Shareholders have the right to vote regarding a merger because the transaction typically involves a major change in the corporation's business and structure. Note, however, that if a giant corporation like Google acquired a small software firm through a merger, the shareholders of the acquired firm would have a right to approve the deal because it means a big change for that corporation. However, Google shareholders would not have a right to vote on the merger because the acquisition would make no meaningful difference in Google's business or in their position as shareholders. If a merger increases the number of the Google's shares by no more than 20%, most state corporate codes would not require approval by Google shareholders.

Third, after approval, the plan for the combination must be submitted to the appropriate state official (usually the secretary of state) in a document referred to as the *articles of merger*. If all documents are in the proper form, the state official issues a *certificate of merger*.

Merger with a Subsidiary

State corporate codes simplify the merger procedures when a subsidiary corporation is merged into its parent corporation. In many situations, such mergers may be effected without shareholder approval.

If the parent owns *all* of the subsidiary's shares, the only requirements are that (1) the parent's board of directors adopt a resolution setting forth the plan for the merger, (2) articles of merger be filed, and (3) a certificate of merger be issued.

If some of the subsidiary's shares are owned by others (minority shareholders), there is an additional requirement that these minority shareholders be given notice of the merger; under the 2016 MBCA, that notice need not be given until *after* this "short-form" merger has been completed. These simplified procedures can be used, however, only if the parent owns a very large portion of the subsidiary's shares, typically 90%. If the parent owns a smaller share than that, typical merger procedures must be followed and the minority shareholders will have the right to vote regarding approval of the merger.

The Appraisal Right

At common law, a merger or other corporate combination once required *unanimous* shareholder approval. This allowed minority shareholders to "hold up" the majority and led to statutes that approved mergers with less than unanimous approval (say, two-thirds or 51%).

One result of this change, however, was that any shareholders who disapproved of a merger might find themselves unwilling investors in a corporation different from the one whose shares they originally had purchased. Out of concern for fairness to these shareholders, provisions were included in state corporate codes giving them the right to sell their shares back to the corporation for cash. This right has generally become known as the *dissenter's right* or the *appraisal right*.

A dissenting shareholder must strictly follow the required procedures, or this appraisal right will be lost. The most important requirement is that the dissenting shareholder object to the merger and demand payment within the designated time period. Generally, a dissenting shareholder must give the corporation written notice of objection to the proposed combination either prior to or at the meeting where the matter is voted upon. If the combination is approved at the meeting, the dissenting shareholder must soon make written demand for payment from the corporation, commonly within ten days.

The corporation must then quickly (again, commonly within ten days) make a written offer to all dissenting shareholders regarding purchase of their shares. This offer should be accompanied by the most recent balance sheet and income statement of the corporation whose stock is owned by the dissenting shareholder.

The overriding concern of dissenting shareholders is, of course, the price to be paid for their shares. The requirement found in most state statutes is that the corporation pay the *fair value* of the shares, computed as of the day of the combination. If the dissenting shareholder feels that the offer does not reflect the fair value of the shares and refuses to accept it, the corporation can institute a court action to have the value determined. The shareholder can personally file such a suit only if the corporation fails to do so within a specified period of time (often 60 days).

In the court proceeding, the judge sometimes appoints an official appraiser to hear evidence and recommend a fair value. The fair value should be computed as of the date of the combination and should *not* take into account any expected future impact (good or bad) of the combination. In Delaware, the courts have held that the burden of proof is upon both parties to convince the court that their approach to valuing the company is the proper one. If neither side succeeds, the judge must exercise independent judgment in order to value the shares.

SALE OF ASSETS

Obviously, corporations sell assets all the time. Often such sales are the entire point of their business. Therefore, corporate codes typically provide that corporations may, on terms and conditions established under the board of directors' supervision, sell, lease, exchange, or otherwise dispose of corporate property. They may also mortgage corporate property or transfer it to a corporate-owned subsidiary. None of this requires shareholder approval.

However, if a sale of assets dramatically changes a corporation's business, the alteration can be as significant as a merger and therefore may well require shareholder approval and the granting of appraisal rights to dissenters.

A common provision is that a corporation may sell, lease, or otherwise dispose of "all or substantially all" of its property *in the ordinary course of business* with no complications. For example, a small firm might buy real estate, develop it, and then sell almost all of it with the notion that it will take the proceeds in order to buy other real estate and repeat the process. In other words, selling substantially all its assets from time to time is the way the firm does business.

However, for most corporations, sale of "all or substantially all" of its assets would not be in the ordinary course of business. It would change the nature of the enterprise dramatically. In such cases, the RMBCA, for example, requires that the board recommend the transaction to the shareholders and that the shareholders (after due notice) approve the transaction by a majority vote. As noted, dissenters may exercise their appraisal rights.

DISSOLUTION AND LIQUIDATION

Although theoretically corporations may have perpetual legal existence, the realities of business do not allow for this. In practice, corporations sometimes are dissolved, often involuntarily.

Voluntary and Involuntary Dissolution

Under the RMBCA, for example, a corporation's dissolution is *voluntarily* authorized when its directors propose and its shareholders approve dissolution. The corporation then dissolves by filing articles of dissolution with the secretary of state. No appraisal rights attach, but shareholders will receive a distribution of the proceeds of the sale of corporate assets if there are any left over after corporate obligations are paid.

A corporation may be *administratively* dissolved by the secretary of state in most jurisdictions if it fails to meet certain statutory requirements, such as timely paying of franchise taxes, timely filing of annual reports, and proper establishment of a registered agent or office.

The RMBCA provides for *judicial dissolution* of a corporation in proceedings initiated (a) by the state attorney general (if the corporation obtained its articles of incorporation through fraud or has abused the authority conferred upon it by law); (b) by shareholders (if management is deadlocked, if those controlling the corporation are acting in an illegal or oppressive way, or if the shareholders are deadlocked and cannot elect directors); or (c) by creditors (if a judgment creditor's claim is unsatisfied and the corporation is insolvent or if the corporation admits in writing that the creditor's claim is due and owing and the corporation is insolvent.).

Effect of Dissolution

Dissolution does not terminate the corporation's existence. It continues to exist, but only for the purpose of winding up and liquidating its business. At this juncture, protection of creditors is paramount.

The RMBCA procedure, for example, looks like this. Section 14.06 addresses *known claims*, providing a procedure by which "[a] dissolved corporation may dispose of the known claims against it…" The procedure involves notifying known claimants of the dissolution in a writing that informs them of how they may assert their claims and informing them that their claims will be barred if not received within a stated deadline not fewer than 120 days from the effective date of the notice. If a claim is rejected by the corporation, that claimant must sue within 90 days or the claim is barred.

Assume that after a corporation dissolves, a product it had previously manufactured proves to be defective and injures a consumer. In other words, the claim arises only *after* the corporation dissolves and is therefore *unknown* at the time of dissolution. How do we balance the interests of the injured consumer with those of the dissolved corporation's shareholders who may well have spent all the funds that were distributed to them in liquidation? RMBCA § 14.07 addresses *unknown claims* against dissolved corporations, providing that a dissolving corporation should publish in a newspaper of general circulation or post conspicuously on its website for 30 days information about how a claim may be asserted and a statement that a claim against the corporation will be barred unless sued upon within three years of the publication.

Such publication will bar claims of the following claimants that are not brought within the specified period: (a) a claimant who did not receive written notice under Section 14.06, (b) a claimant whose claim was timely sent to the dissolved corporation but was not acted upon, and (c) a claimant whose claim is contingent or based on an event occurring after the effective date of dissolution.

Such a provision buys peace of mind for shareholders and directors of dissolved corporations. After the specified time period for filing suit, they are no longer vulnerable to claims they did not know about at the time of dissolution. This may seem unfair to the claimants who are not even injured until after their right to sue has expired, but the drafters of the RMBCA reasoned:

> It is recognized that a five-year cut-off [later reduced to three years in the RMBCA] is itself arbitrary, but it is believed that the great bulk of post dissolution claims will arise during this period. This provision is therefore believed to be a reasonable compromise between the competing considerations of providing a remedy to injured plaintiffs and providing a period of repose after which dissolved corporations may distribute remaining assets free of all claims and shareholders may receive them secure in the knowledge that they may not be reclaimed.

What about suits that *are* brought within the three-year period? According to RMBCA Sec. 14.07(d), these claims may be enforced:

> (1) against the dissolved corporation to the extent of its undistributed assets; and (2) if the assets have been distributed in litigation, against a shareholder of the dissolved corporation to the extent of his pro rata share of the claim or the corporate assets distributed to him in liquidation, whichever is less, but a shareholder's total liability for all claims under this section *may not exceed the total amount of assets distributed to him.* (emphasis added).

The following case applies the Michigan version of these provisions.

GILLIAM v. HI-TEMP PRODUCTS, INC.
677 N.W.2d 856 (Mich. Ct. App. 2003)

Hi-Temp sold asbestos products. Many individuals, claiming that their exposure to Hi-Temp's products caused asbestos-related diseases, sued Hi-Temp frequently and continuously after the mid-1980s. In 1992, Hi-Temp ceased active business operations. Its sole shareholder resolved on October 8, 1993, that Hi-Temp be dissolved and its assets distributed. On October 14, 1993, Hi-Temp filed a certificate of dissolution pursuant to MCL §450.831(b). The Bureau of Corporations and Securities stamped the certificate filed on October 25, 1993, thereby making the dissolution effective.

Hi-Temp then made a "complete distribution of its corporate assets" by selling its inventory and equipment, collecting its receivables, paying bills, and making provisions for the payment of its outstanding liabilities. It is undisputed that Hi-Temp made a final distribution of assets in the amount of $ 9,571.99.

Hi-Temp published a notice of dissolution in the Oakland Press on October 25, 1993, July 3, 1996, and October 20, 1998. Hi-Temp also gave notice of its dissolution through its counsel directly to plaintiffs' counsel on October 15, 1993, and October 21, 1998. MCL §450.842a(3), based generally upon the RMBCA, essentially provides that all claims against a dissolved corporation are barred unless "the claimant commences a proceeding to enforce the claim against the dissolved corporation within 1 year after the publication date . . . ." Plaintiffs' actions alleging personal injury or death as a consequence of the use of, or exposure to, asbestos in Hi-Temp's products were filed after October 21, 1999. In all cases, Hi-Temp moved for summary disposition, asserting the statutory bar to claims filed more than one year after publication of notice in accordance with §842a. Plaintiffs argued that they had shown good cause for not presenting their latent claims earlier and that Hi-Temp's insurance coverage was an undistributed asset within the meaning of §851(2), a statutory exception.

The trial court denied Hi-Temp's motion and Hi-Temp appealed, arguing that plaintiffs' asbestos-related personal injury claims are barred by §842a because they were filed beyond the one-year period allowed for the filing of claims after Hi-Temp published its notice of dissolution.

Markey, Judge:

We conclude that plaintiffs' claims are barred when the plain language of §842a is applied to the undisputed facts. Hi-Temp properly published notice of its dissolution. Plaintiffs' claims are "contingent" within the plain meaning of §843a(3)(c), but they were not filed within one year of publication of notice of dissolution as required by §842a(3). An insurance liability policy is not an asset that a corporation could distribute in the process of winding up its affairs after dissolution. Therefore, it is not an undistributed asset of a corporation that has dissolved and distributed all assets capable of distribution. Accordingly, §851(2) affords no relief from the bar even if plaintiffs have "good cause" for not timely filing their claims.

By its plain language, §842a generally bars claims against a dissolved corporation that has published notice of dissolution unless the suits are brought within one year of publication. This Court has acknowledged that the purpose of the statute is "'to compel all creditors who may reasonably be expected to file their claims to do so within the prescribed time and to . . . [bar] . . . the claim upon failure to do so'" *Dissolution of Esquire Products,* 377 N.W.2d 356 (Mich. 1985). We agree that Judge Colombo correctly read and applied §842a(3)(c) to conclude that plaintiffs' claims were contingent because they were dependent on a future event or they were "based on an event occurring after the effective date of dissolution." The contingency or the event was the manifestation of an asbestos-related illness.

Moreover, §842a is not a statute of limitations; it is part of a legislative scheme intended to avoid the consequences of corporate dissolution at common law. At common law, upon dissolution of a corporation, "there is no one to serve, because, in law, a dissolved corporation is a dead person, so much so that, in the absence of statute and revival, even pending actions by or against it would abate." *US Truck Co. v. Pennsylvania Surety Corp.,* 243 N.W. 311 (1932). Thus, an action brought against a corporation that then dissolves would, as a matter of law, be abated in the absence of §834(f), which provides, "An action brought against the corporation before its dissolution does not abate because of the dissolution." So-called "survival statutes" extend the life of a corporation after dissolution to permit actions by or against the dissolved corporation for a specified period. Or they may be statutes of repose that extinguish untimely causes of actions before they accrue.

Under the statute, … the Legislature has provided for the orderly winding up of corporate affairs, including the liquidation and distribution of assets, and which may include court supervision, particularly when the liabilities of the corporation exceed its assets. This Court has held that "the primary purpose of the provisions relating to dissolution is to protect the rights of all creditors by providing for the payment of debts 'ratably', and to prevent individual creditors from procuring a preferment by pursuing independent action to the detriment of other creditors." *Esquire Products.* A claim against the dissolved corporation, whether existing or contingent, is barred if not timely filed. The "Legislature has created a process whereby a dissolved corporation can bar future claims, thus cutting off the possibility that the corporation's potential liability could never be completely resolved." *Freeman v. HiTemp Products,* 580 N.W.2d 918 (Mich.App. 1998).

We also reject the reasoning that §842a is not intended to bar latent claims or claims that could not reasonably be brought within one year of notice of corporate dissolution. The unambiguous language of the statute rebuts such an interpretation. Section 842a(3)(c) plainly bars claims that are "contingent or based on an event occurring after the effective date of dissolution." Moreover, the intent of the Legislature to bar claims that are both unknown and that arise after the dissolution of the corporation is shown in §842(a)(3)(a) which bars a claim by a "claimant who did not receive written notice."

Furthermore, the argument that it is patently or inherently unfair to bar plaintiffs' claims must be rejected in light of the plain words of the statute. Neither this Court nor the circuit courts may interpret or apply the statute using a personal view of the fairness or wisdom of the Legislature's policy decision. Courts must enforce the statute as written. Reversed and remanded.

TENDER OFFERS AND OTHER TAKEOVERS

When A Corporation wishes to buy B Corporation, often friendly mergers are negotiated between the boards of the two companies and shareholder approval smoothly follows. The relevant legal procedures were discussed earlier in this chapter.

But what if A Corporation wishes to acquire B Corporation, and B Corporation's board resists the idea? A Corporation might launch a *hostile tender offer* which bypasses B Corporation's board and goes straight to B's shareholders and offers to buy their shares at a premium over market price. If enough of B's shareholders tender their shares for sale in response to the offer, A can buy control of B, replace its directors, and, likely, acquire the remainder of B's shares via a *freezeout merger*. Because A usually buys a majority interest in B's shares via the tender offer, it will control enough shares to ensure that a proposed merger with a wholly-owned subsidiary will go through. In that merger, the remainder of B's shareholders will be cashed out at a price established by A.

The federal rules regulating tender offers are discussed in this text's chapter on securities regulation. However, the fiduciary responsibilities of the target's (B Corporation, in this example) board are a matter of state law. Delaware, the leading corporate jurisdiction, has an extensive and complicated body of jurisprudence in this area.

Assume that B Corporation's board wishes that B remain independent. It opposes all proposed acquisitions. The potential target corporation's board may use a variety of defensive tactics that corporate lawyers have invented over the years, including perhaps a *poison pill*. A poison pill is a takeover defense, usually inserted in a corporation's articles of incorporation, that makes it virtually impossible for any third-party bidder to gain control of the corporation. They work in many different ways. For example, the target might place a provision in its articles giving current shareholders the right to purchase one share of company stock for each share they already own at 50% of market price with this right to come into existence only upon a "change of control." That is, if A buys 51% of B, B's shareholders suddenly have the right to purchase huge amounts of B's stock at a bargain price that would so dilute A's interest in B that it would be impossible for B to complete the deal unless the poison pill were dismantled.

These defensive tactics may make it essentially impossible for any hostile bid to prevail. But what if B's shareholders wish to tender? If bidder Corporation A or any of B's shareholders who wish to sell their shares at a premium to A challenge the validity of the poison pill and the propriety of B's board's decision not to dismantle it so that shareholders can successfully tender their shares, the target board's actions will be judged by the "proportionality test" enunciated by the Delaware Supreme Court in *Unocal Corp. v. Mesa Petroleum Co.*, 493 A.2d 946 (Del. 1985).

In *Unocal,* the court held that any defensive tactics must be "proportional" to the threat to shareholder interests posed by the acquiring corporation's bid. A coercive or obviously inadequate bid threatens shareholders' interests and may be vigorously opposed by management. However, an all-cash, all-shares offer without any coercive elements does not threaten shareholder interests and generally speaking management should not be allowed to prevent shareholders from considering such an offer. The *Unocal* test is applied in the following case.

AIR PRODUCTS AND CHEMICALS, INC. v. AIRGAS, INC.
16 A.3d 48 (Del.Ch. 2011)

In 2009, plaintiff Air Products began negotiations to buy Airgas. Airgas resisted and Air Products launched a hostile tender offer in 2010. Airgas's board vigorously defended the company's independence, even though Air Products' offer ultimately became a non-coercive all-cash, all-shares offer at a healthy premium. Both Air Products and various Airgas shareholders sued to force redemption of the poison pill as inconsistent with the board's Unocal *duties. The case went to the Delaware Supreme Court, which generally supported the defendant board and remanded the case to the chancery court for further proceedings. Air Products raised the offering price several times during the course of negotiations and litigation. Its "final offer" was $70/share. Airgas directors insisted that the firm was worth at least $78/share. The Airgas board moved to dismiss the lawsuit. The following is a brief introduction from the judge's 153-page opinion.*

Chandler, Chancellor:

This case poses the following fundamental question: Can a board of directors, acting in good faith and with a reasonable factual basis for its decision, when faced with a structurally non-coercive, all-cash, fully financed tender offer directed to the stockholders of the corporation, keep a poison pill in place so as to prevent the stockholders from making their own decision about whether they want to tender their shares—even after the incumbent board has lost one election contest, a full year has gone by since the offer was first made public, and the stockholders are fully informed as to the target board's views on the inadequacy of the offer? If so, does that effectively mean that a board can "just say never" to a hostile tender offer?

The answer to the latter question is "no." A board cannot "*just* say no" to a tender offer. Under Delaware law, it must first pass through two prongs of exacting judicial scrutiny by a judge who will evaluate the actions taken by, and the motives of, the board. Only a board of directors found to be acting in good faith, after reasonable investigation and reliance on the advice of outside advisors, which articulates and convinces the Court that a hostile tender offer poses a legitimate threat to the corporate enterprise, may address that perceived threat by blocking the tender offer and forcing the bidder to elect a board majority that supports its bid.

In essence, this case brings to the fore one of the most basic questions animating all of corporate law, which relates to the allocation of power between directors and stockholders. That is, "when, if ever, will a board's duty to 'the corporation and its shareholders' require [the board] to abandon concerns for 'long term' values (and other constituencies) and enter a current share value maximizing mode?" *TW Servs., Inc. v. SWT Acquisition Corp.*, 1989 Del.Ch.LEXIS 19 (Del. Ch. 1989). More to the point, in the context of a hostile tender offer, who gets to decide when and if the corporation is for sale?

Since the Shareholder Rights Plan (more commonly known as the "poison pill") was first conceived and throughout the development of Delaware corporate takeover jurisprudence during the twenty-five-plus years that followed, the debate over who ultimately decides whether a tender offer is adequate and should be accepted—the shareholders of the corporation or its board of directors—has raged on. Starting with *Moran v. Household International, Inc.*, 490 A.2d 1059 (Del. 1985), when the Delaware Supreme Court first upheld the adoption of the poison pill as a valid takeover defense, through the hostile takeover years of the 1980s, and in several recent decisions of the Court of Chancery and the Delaware Supreme Court, this fundamental question has engaged practitioners, academics, and members of the judiciary, but it has yet to be confronted head on.

For the reasons much more fully described in the remainder of this Opinion, I conclude that, as Delaware law currently stands, the answer must be that the power to defeat an inadequate hostile tender offer ultimately lies with the board of directors. As such, I find that the Airgas board has met its burden under *Unocal* to articulate a legally cognizable threat (the allegedly inadequate price of Air Products' offer, coupled with the fact that a majority of Airgas stockholders would likely tender into that inadequate offer) and has taken defensive measures that fall within a range of reasonable responses proportionate to that threat. I thus rule in favor of defendants. Air Products' and the Shareholder Plaintiffs' requests for relief are denied, and all claims asserted against defendants are dismissed with prejudice.

Trial judges are not free to ignore or rewrite appellate court decisions. Thus, for reasons explained in detail below, I am constrained by Delaware Supreme Court precedent to conclude that defendants have met their burden under *Unocal* to articulate a sufficient threat that justifies the continued maintenance of Airgas's poison pill. That is, assuming defendants have met their burden to articulate a legally cognizable threat (prong 1), Airgas's defenses have been recognized by Delaware law as reasonable responses to the threat posed by an inadequate offer—even an all-shares, all-cash offer (prong 2).

In my personal view, Airgas's poison pill has served its legitimate purpose. Although the "best and final" $70 offer has been on the table for just over two months (since December 9, 2010), Air Products' advances have been ongoing for over sixteen months, and Airgas's use of its poison pill—particularly in combination with its staggered board—has given the Airgas board over a full year to inform its stockholders about its view of Airgas's intrinsic value and Airgas's value in a sale transaction. It has also given the Airgas board a full year to express its views to its stockholders on the purported opportunistic timing of Air Products' repeated advances and to educate its stockholders on the inadequacy of Air Products' offer. It has given Airgas *more time than any litigated poison pill in Delaware history*—enough time to show stockholders four quarters of improving financial results, demonstrating that Airgas is on track to meet its projected goals. And it has helped the Airgas board push Air Products to raise its bid by $10 per share from when it was first publicly announced to what Air Products has now represented is its highest offer. The record at both the October trial and the January supplemental evidentiary hearing confirm that Airgas's stockholder base is sophisticated and well-informed, and that essentially all the information they would need to make an informed decision is available to them. In short, there seems to be no threat here—

the stockholders know what they need to know (about both the offer and the Airgas board's opinion of the offer) to make an informed decision.

That being said, however, as I understand binding Delaware precedent, I may not substitute my business judgment for that of the Airgas board. *Paramount Commc'ns, Inc. v. Time, Inc.*, 571 A.2d 1140 (Del. 1990). The Delaware Supreme Court has recognized inadequate price as a valid threat to corporate policy and effectiveness. *Unitrin, Inc. v. Am. Gen. Corp.*, 651 A.2d 1361 (Del. 1995). The Delaware Supreme Court has also made clear that the "selection of a time frame for achievement of corporate goals . . . may not be delegated to the stockholders." *Paramount.* Furthermore, in powerful dictum, the Supreme Court has stated that "[d]irectors are not obliged to abandon a deliberately conceived corporate plan for a short-term shareholder profit unless there is clearly no basis to sustain the corporate strategy." *Id.* Although I do not read that dictum as eliminating the applicability of heightened *Unocal* scrutiny to a board's decision to block a non-coercive bid as underpriced, I do read it, along with the actual holding in *Unitrin*, as indicating that a board that has a good faith, reasonable basis to believe a bid is inadequate may block that bid using a poison pill, irrespective of stockholders' desire to accept it.

Here, even using heightened scrutiny, the Airgas board has demonstrated that it has a reasonable basis for sustaining its long term corporate strategy—the Airgas board is independent, and has relied on the advice of three different outside independent financial advisors in concluding that Air Products' offer is inadequate. Air Products' *own three nominees* who were elected to the Airgas board in September 2010 have joined wholeheartedly in the Airgas board's determination, and when the Airgas board met to consider the $70 "best and final" offer in December 2010, it was one of those Air Products Nominees who said, "We have to protect the pill." Indeed, one of Air Products' *own directors* conceded at trial that the Airgas board members had acted within their fiduciary duties in their desire to "hold out for the proper price," and that "if an offer was made for Air Products that [he] considered to be unfair to the stockholders of Air Products . . . [he would likewise] use every legal mechanism available" to hold out for the proper price as well. Under Delaware law, the Airgas directors have complied with their fiduciary duties. Thus, as noted above, and for the reasons more fully described in the remainder of this Opinion, I am constrained to deny Air Products' and the Shareholder Plaintiffs' requests for relief.

After *Unocal*, the most popular defensive response quickly became a competing bid by a third party (often called a *white knight*) or by a managerial group in a *leveraged buy-out*. The Delaware Supreme Court then introduced new rules to cover a situation where a corporation has put itself up for sale. In *Revlon, Inc. v. MacAndrews & Forbes Holdings*, 506 A.2d 173 (Del. 1986), the court held that when a company's board of directors has decided to sell the company, its role shifts from "defender of the corporate bastion" to that of "auctioneer" and its primary job is to get the highest possible sale price for the company's shareholders. While there may be situations in which it is appropriate for a target company's board to consider the interests of other constituencies, such as employees, suppliers, or the communities in which the company operates, when a sale of the firm seems to be the proper course of action, the target's board of directors have a duty to maximize short-term sale price for shareholders. The law in this area has continued to evolve, as shown in the following case.

CORWIN v. KKR FINANCIAL HOLDINGS LLC
125 A.3d 304 (Del. Supreme Court 2015)

The plaintiffs filed a challenge in the Court of Chancery to a stock-for-stock merger between KKR & Co. L.P. ("KKR") and KKR Financial Holdings LLC ("Financial Holdings") in which KKR acquired each share of Financial Holdings' stock for 0.51 of a share of KKR stock, a 35% premium to the unaffected market price. Plaintiffs argued that the transaction was presumptively subject to the entire fairness standard of review because Financial Holdings' primary business was financing KKR's leveraged buyout activities, and instead of having employees manage the company's day-to-day operations, Financial Holdings was managed by KKR Financial Advisors, an affiliate of KKR, under a contractual management agreement that could only be terminated by Financial Holdings if it paid a termination fee. As a result, the plaintiffs alleged that KKR was a controlling stockholder of Financial Holdings, which was an LLC, not a corporation.

The defendants moved to dismiss. The Chancellor granted the motion, holding that because there was no real evidence that Financial Holdings was dominated by KKR, the entire fairness *standard of review did not apply for that reason. Further, the Chancellor held that because a disinterested majority of shareholders had approved the transaction, the business judgment rule applied in any event. Plaintiff appealed.*

Strine, Chief Justice:

The Chancellor found that the defendants were correct that the plaintiffs' complaint did not plead facts supporting an inference that KKR was Financial Holdings' controlling stockholder. Among other things, the Chancellor noted that KKR owned less than 1% of Financial Holdings' stock, had no right to appoint any directors, and had no contractual right to veto any board action. Although the Chancellor acknowledged the unusual existential circumstances the plaintiffs cited, he noted that those were known at all relevant times by investors, and that Financial Holdings had real assets its independent board controlled and had the option of pursuing any path its directors chose.

In addressing whether KKR was a controlling stockholder, the Chancellor was focused on the reality that in cases where a party that did not have majority control of the entity's voting stock was found to be a controlling stockholder, the Court of Chancery, consistent with the instructions of this Court, looked for a combination of potent voting power and management control such that the stockholder could be deemed to have effective control of the board without actually owning a majority of stock.

After carefully analyzing the pled facts and the relevant precedent, the Chancellor held:

> [T]here are no well-pled facts from which it is reasonable to infer that KKR could prevent the [Financial Holdings] board from freely exercising its independent judgment in considering the proposed merger or, put differently, that KKR had the power to exact retribution by removing the [Financial Holdings] directors from their offices if they did not bend to KKR's will in their consideration of the proposed merger.

Although the plaintiffs reiterate their position on appeal, the Chancellor correctly applied the law and we see no reason to repeat his lucid analysis of this question.

Plaintiffs further contend that, even if the Chancellor was correct in determining that KKR was not a controlling stockholder, he was wrong to dismiss the complaint because they contend that if the entire fairness standard did not apply, *Revlon* did, and the plaintiffs argue that they pled a *Revlon* claim against the defendant directors. But, as the defendants point out, the plaintiffs did not fairly argue in the court below that *Revlon* applied and even if they did, they ignore the reality that Financial Holdings had in place an exculpatory charter provision, and that the transaction was approved by an independent board majority and by a fully informed, uncoerced stockholder vote. Therefore, the defendants argue, the plaintiffs failed to state a non-exculpated claim for breach of fiduciary duty.

But we need not delve into whether the Court of Chancery's determination that *Revlon* did not apply to the merger is correct for a single reason: it does not matter. *Because the Chancellor was correct in determining that the entire fairness standard did not apply to the merger, the Chancellor's analysis of the effect of the uncoerced, informed stockholder vote is outcome-determinative, even if Revlon applied to the merger.*

As to this point, the Court of Chancery noted, and the defendants point out on appeal, that the plaintiffs did not contest the defendants' argument below that if the merger was not subject to the entire fairness standard, the business judgment standard of review was invoked because the merger was approved by a disinterested stockholder majority. The Chancellor agreed with that argument below, and adhered to precedent supporting the proposition that when a transaction not subject to the entire fairness standard is approved by a fully informed, uncoerced vote of the disinterested stockholders, the business judgment rule applies.

Although the plaintiffs argue that adhering to the proposition that a fully informed, uncoerced stockholder vote invokes the business judgment rule would impair the operation of *Unocal* and *Revlon*, or expose stockholders to unfair action by directors without protection, the plaintiffs ignore several factors. First, *Unocal* and *Revlon* are primarily designed to give stockholders and the Court of Chancery the tool of injunctive relief to address important M & A decisions in real time, before closing. They were not tools designed with post-closing money damages claims in mind, the standards they articulate do not match the gross negligence standard for director due care liability under *Smith v. Van Gorkom*, 488 A.2d 858 (Del. 1985), and with the prevalence of exculpatory charter provisions, due care liability is rarely even available.

Second and most important, the doctrine applies only to fully informed, uncoerced stockholder votes, and if troubling facts regarding director behavior were not disclosed that would have been material to a voting stockholder, then the business judgment rule is not invoked. Here, however, all of the objective facts regarding the board's interests, KKR's interests, and the negotiation process, were fully disclosed.

Finally, when a transaction is not subject to the entire fairness standard, the long-standing policy of our law has been to avoid the uncertainties and costs of judicial second-guessing when the disinterested stockholders have had the free and informed chance to decide on the economic merits of a transaction for themselves. There are sound reasons for this policy. When the real parties in interest—the disinterested equity owners—can easily protect themselves at the ballot box by simply voting no, the utility of a litigation-intrusive standard of review promises more costs to stockholders in the form of litigation rents and inhibitions on risk-taking than it promises in terms of benefits to them. The reason for that is tied to the core rationale of the business judgment rule, which is that judges are poorly positioned to evaluate the wisdom of business decisions and there is little utility to having them second-guess the determination of impartial decision-makers with more information (in the case of directors) or an actual economic stake in the outcome (in the case of informed, disinterested stockholders). In circumstances, therefore, where the stockholders have had the voluntary choice to accept or reject a transaction, the business judgment rule standard of review is the presumptively correct one and best facilitates wealth creation through the corporate form. Affirmed.

PART V

GOVERNMENT REGULATION OF BUSINESS

CHAPTER 28

SECURITIES REGULATION

Securities regulation is one of the most complicated areas of the law. It is also one of the fastest-changing due to changes in technology that are revolutionizing much of the securities industry, new forms of business transactions, and an increasingly global marketplace. Few persons in business can afford to remain ignorant of securities regulation's effects on the way business is done in this country and around the world.

Many aspects of securities regulation are highly visible. Most Americans are familiar with the hustle and bustle of the New York Stock Exchange. Because of the popularity of mutual funds, tens of millions of Americans own stock, at least indirectly, in major corporations such as Google and Facebook. Through securities regulation, the federal government, and to a lesser degree the states, regulate trading on the stock exchanges, protect the interests of shareholders, and attempt to protect the interests of investors and preserve the integrity of U.S. capital markets. In this chapter, we survey some of the more important aspects of the law of securities regulation.

INTRODUCTION TO SECURITIES REGULATION

A security such as a stock or a bond has no intrinsic value—its value lies in the ownership interest that it represents. The value of that ownership interest is often difficult to discover and easy to misrepresent. Once upon a time, securities could be produced in nearly limitless supply at virtually no cost by anyone with access to a printing press. Today, the printing press has been replaced by the computer. Fraud, manipulation, and deceit have been frequent companions of the security. Government regulation of securities dates back to at least 1285, when King Edward I of England attempted to gain some control over the capital markets by licensing brokers located in London.

Securities regulation in the United States was almost nonexistent until 1911, when Kansas enacted securities laws. Other states soon followed suit, but without federal laws, companies could evade regulation by operating across state lines.

The 1920s were an especially active time for the issuance and trading of securities. The securities business was then characterized by price manipulation, deceitful practices, buying on excessive credit, and the abuse of secret information by corporate insiders. Of the $50 billion of new securities offered for sale in the United States in the 1920s, about one-half were worthless. The public and the national economy were devastated when stock market prices fell 89 percent between 1929 and 1933, a situation that finally produced federal securities legislation.

Federal Legislation

The first federal securities law was the *Securities Act of 1933* (the 1933 Act), which regulated the initial issuance of securities by companies. Fraudulent and deceptive practices were outlawed, and registration was required before a new security could be offered or sold, unless that security was entitled to an exemption from registration.

A year later, Congress passed the *Securities Exchange Act of 1934* (the 1934 Act), which extended federal regulation to trading in securities already issued, required registration of securities brokers and dealers, and created the Securities and Exchange Commission (SEC), the federal agency that enforces the federal securities laws through its extensive powers.

During the next decade, Congress passed several other laws, including (a) the Investment Company Act of 1940, which regulates mutual funds; and (c) the Investment

Advisers Act of 1940, which requires persons or firms who engage in the business of advising others about investments for compensation to register with the SEC, as brokers and dealers are required to register under the 1934 Act. The Securities Investor Protection Act of 1970 (SIPA) amended the 1934 Act in response to a rash of failures in the late 1960s in the broker-dealer business. SIPA created the Securities Investor Protection Corporation (SIPC), which manages a fund to protect investors from the failure of broker-dealers in the same manner as the Federal Deposit Insurance Corporation protects the customers of banks.

Courts have interpreted the 1934 Securities Exchange Act to allow injured investors to sue companies for securities fraud under Section 10(b) and Rule 10b-5. Each year many large class action lawsuits are filed, claiming huge amounts of damages. Lobbying by Silicon Valley high-tech firms and large accounting firms convinced Congress that many of these lawsuits were without merit and motivated primarily by the interests of plaintiffs' attorneys. Therefore, in 1995 Congress passed the Private Securities Litigation Reform Act (PSLRA) with the main goal of making it harder for plaintiffs to win these class action fraud suits and more difficult for plaintiffs' attorneys to profit from them. Recent Supreme Court cases have also made bringing these suits a much less appealing proposition for investors who have lost money through alleged frauds.

Perhaps coincidentally, just a few years after the PSLRA provided protection for potential defendants in securities fraud suits, the Enron-era scandals occurred, prompting Congress to pass the Sarbanes-Oxley Act (SOX) of 2002. SOX made many important changes in the other direction, including (a) stiffening penalties for securities fraud, (b) creating a new entity to regulate audit firms, the Public Company Accounting Oversight Board (PCAOB), (c) requiring CEOs and CFOs to swear to the accuracy of their companies' major financial disclosure, upon penalty of prosecution, (d) restricting the types of non-audit services that accounting firms may provide to public company audit clients, (e) requiring that public companies have audit committees that are composed entirely of independent directors, (f) reducing investment banker influence over financial analysts in order to reduce conflicts of interest, and (g) requiring more and prompter disclosure of important corporate developments and of insider trading activity.

SOX was not completely successful, as its enactment was quickly followed by the subprime mortgage crisis and financial meltdown circa 2008. Congress reacted by passing the Dodd-Frank Act in 2010. Dodd-Frank was an enormous law (2000+ pages) that broadly sought to strengthen financial market performance by (a) improving financial institutions' accountability and transparency, (b) protecting taxpayers from being saddled with future bailouts, and (c) protecting consumers from a plethora of abusive practices.

More specifically, Dodd-Frank sought to, among other things: (a) limit "too big to fail" risk by creating the Financial Stability Oversight Council (FSOC), (b) reduce the risk posed by federally-insured depository institutions engaged in risky trading via the "Volcker Rule", (c) increase transparency in the trading of derivative instruments like credit default swaps, (d) require SEC registration of hedge funds, (e) protect consumers from a broad range of fraudulent and predatory practices by creation of the Consumer Financial Protection Bureau (CFPB), and (f) reform the practices of credit rating agencies, such as Standard & Poor's. Several years after Dodd-Frank's enactment, many of its complicated provisions still had not been fully implemented by the SEC. At this writing, the Trump Administration is taking aim at several of these Dodd-Frank provisions to advance the cause of deregulation. Without question, many of the Dodd-Frank provisions were expensive for companies to implement.

What Is a Security?

Securities are commonly thought of as the stock issued by corporations. The shares of common and preferred stock issued by corporations constitute a major type of security. These are *equity securities* which evidence an ownership interest in the corporation. Holders of equity securities are normally entitled to vote on important corporate matters and to receive dividends as their share of the corporate profits. The other major type of security is the debt security, such as the bond, note, or debenture. Holders of *debt securities* are creditors rather than owners. They have no voice in corporate affairs but are entitled to receive regular interest payments according to the terms of the bond or note.

Because the inventive human mind has devised an inordinate variety of investment interests, securities regulation goes beyond items that are clearly labeled *stocks or bonds*. Sec. 2(1) of the 1933 Act broadly defines security to include

> Any note, stock, treasury stock, bond, debenture, evidence of indebtedness, certificate of interest or participation in any profit-sharing agreement, . . . investment contract, voting-trust certificate, fractional undivided interest in oil, gas or other mineral rights, or, in general, any interest or instrument commonly known as a "security."

This broad definition has, of necessity, been liberally construed by the courts. Interests in limited partnerships, condominiums, farm animals with accompanying agreements for their care, franchises, whiskey warehouse receipts, and many other varied items have been deemed to be securities. The term *investment contract* in the 1933 Act's definition of security has been broadly construed, as the following case illustrates.

BALESTRA v. ATBCOIN LLC
U.S. District Court, 380 F. Supp. 3d 340 (S.D.N.Y. 2019)

Defendants Ng and Hoover co-founded and operated defendant ATBCOIN LLC ("ATB"), a technology start-up company aimed at facilitating rapid, low-cost digital financial transactions through revolutionary blockchain technology. In 2017, ATB conducted an initial coin offering ("ICO"), through which ATB offered digital "ATB Coins" to the general public in exchange for other digital assets. Defendants promoted the ATB Coin as "an innovative decentralized cryptocurrency incorporating the advanced technologies that tailor the needs of primary market players—users, investors, and business owners." The ATB Coin was "designed to overcome well-known inefficiencies within government central banks and other crypto currencies and to induce transactions that are fully secure, private and anonymous."

Defendants held the ICO in order to raise capital to fund creation and launch of a new blockchain (the "ATB Blockchain") on which the ATB Coins would operate. Defendants made elaborate claims for the potential of their product. When the ATB ICO launched, Defendants offered one ATB Coin for $1, payable in the cryptocurrencies Bitcoin, Ether (ETH), or Litecoin.

When the ATB Blockchain was not able to perform as defendants had promised, investors filed this class action lawsuit claiming, among other things, that defendants had violated §12(a) of the 1933 Securities Act by selling unregistered securities in the form of

ATB Coins. Defendants moved to dismiss the lawsuit, claiming that the ATB coins were not "securities" under the meaning of the 1933 Act and therefore did not have to be registered.

Broderick, U.S. District Judge:

Section 12(a)(1) of the Securities Act of 1933 provides a private right of action against any person who "offers or sells a security" in violation of §5 of the Act, which in turn prohibits the offer or sale of unregistered securities. Accordingly, the item that is offered or sold must constitute a "security" within the meaning of the Act. Under §2(a)(1), the definition of a "security" includes an "investment contract." "[T]he 'touchstone' of an investment contract [is] the presence of an investment in a common venture premised on a reasonable expectation of profits to be derived from the entrepreneurial or managerial efforts of others." *SEC v. Edwards*, 540 U.S. 389 (2004).

The determination of whether a particular offering qualifies as an investment contract—and, in turn, a security—is governed by the three-prong test set forth in *S.E.C. v. W.J. Howey Co.* ("Howey"), 328 U.S. 293 (1946). Under *Howey*, an offering is an investment contract security where there is "(i) an investment of money; (ii) in a common enterprise; (iii) with the expectation of profits to be derived solely from the efforts of others." The *Howey* test is a "flexible rather than a static principle, one that is capable of adaptation to meet the countless and variable schemes devised by those who seek the use of the money of others on the promise of profits."

Defendants do not dispute that the first prong of the test—an investment of money—is satisfied, where Plaintiff exchanged 2.1 ETH for 388.5 ATB Coins. Defendants contend, however, that the complaint fails to plead facts satisfying the second and third prongs of the *Howey* test.

1. Common Enterprise

A plaintiff may demonstrate a common enterprise by pleading the existence of "horizontal commonality." *Revak v. SEC Realty Corp.*, 18 F.3d 81, 87 (2d Cir. 1994). In an enterprise marked by horizontal commonality, "the fortunes of each investor in a pool of investors" are tied to one another and to the "success of the overall venture." "In fact, a finding of horizontal commonality requires a sharing or pooling of funds." *In re J.P. Jeanneret Assocs., Inc.*, 769 F. Supp. 2d 340 (S.D.N.Y. 2011).

Plaintiff alleges that the fortunes of all ATB Coin purchasers were tied to one another because "the ATB ICO investments were pooled under the control of Defendant ATB." The Complaint also alleges that the primary goal of the ATB ICO "was to raise capital to create and launch a new blockchain that would 'deliver blazing fast, secure and near-zero cost payments to anyone in the world.'" Thus, the funds raised through the ICO were pooled together to facilitate the launch of the ATB Blockchain, the success of which, in turn, would increase the value of Plaintiff's ATB Coins.

Although Defendants insist that purchasers of the ATB Coin "gained no share in a common enterprise, but rather exercised individual control over the ATB Coin asset," Plaintiff plausibly alleges that the "potential profits stemming from the future valuation of the ATB Coins [] w[ere] entirely reliant" on the success of Defendants' new blockchain. (see also *Rensel v. Central Tech, Inc.*, 2018 U.S. Dist. LEXIS 106642 (S.D. Fla. June 25, 2018) (finding a common enterprise where "the fortunes of individual investors in [Defendants'] ICO were directly tied to the failure or success of the products the Defendants purported to develop"). Indeed, that is—at least in part—the way Defendants marketed ATB Coins.

Essentially, Defendants encouraged investors to purchase ATB Coins based on the claim that the speed and efficiency of the ATB Blockchain would result in an increase in the coins' value…. [T]he value of ATB Coins was dictated by the success of the ATB enterprise as a whole, thereby establishing horizontal commonality.

2. Profits Derived Solely from the Efforts of Others

The third prong of the *Howey* test is satisfied where investors have been "led to expect profits solely from the efforts of the promoter." *U.S. v. Leonard*, 529 F.3d 83, 88 (2d Cir. 2008). The Second Circuit has established that "the word 'solely' should not be construed as a literal limitation; rather [courts] consider whether under all the circumstances, the scheme was being promoted primarily as an investment." I find that Plaintiff's allegations establish that purchasers of ATB Coins reasonably believed that those coins would increase in value based primarily on Defendants' entrepreneurial and managerial efforts.

First, Defendants launched a marketing campaign for ATB Coins that highlighted the potential profits that would result simply from holding those coins. In a July 9, 2017 press release, ATB stated: "ATB investors are serious people from many prosperous countries, they are interested in the development of the company, the growth of the rate, and of course, the profit, which as is known, will soon come to those who are 100% sure of the possibilities of cryptocurrency." That same press release described the ATB ICO as "the realization of a crowdfunding model, where participants finance the development of the company now in order to get revenue from it in the future." Similarly, the Frequently Asked Questions section of ATB's website states: "the first users of ATB Coin cryptocurrency can be compared to investors in a start-up, which can later acquire value, due to its usefulness and popularity. Thus, the acquisition of the first ATB Coin becomes a kind of investment with a long-term perspective." All of these advertisements "promoted" ATB Coins "as an investment" that would generate profits for investors without any effort on their part.

Furthermore, the Complaint satisfactorily pleads that the success of ATB Coins was entirely dependent on Defendants' following through on their promise to launch and improve the ATB Blockchain. As the Complaint alleges, "the value of ATB Coins was expected to rise from the speed of transactions on the ATB Blockchain that was promoted as 'the fastest blockchain-based cryptographic network in the Milky Way galaxy.'" When the ATB Blockchain failed to deliver the groundbreaking technology that Defendants touted, users did not adopt it and the value of the ATB Coins plummeted. Purchasers had no control over whether the new ATB Blockchain technology worked. [Motion to dismiss is denied.]

The creation of many complicated forms of derivative securities, swaps, exchange-traded funds (ETFs), digital currency and the like has meant that eighty years after enactment of the first federal securities law, the courts and administrative agencies are still often embroiled in the task of determining which instruments are "securities" and which are not. These decisions help demarcate the limits of federal regulation.

1933 ACT: REGULATING THE ISSUANCE OF SECURITIES

A major portion of federal securities regulation concerns the issuance of securities by companies. Congressional investigations after the 1929 stock market crash disclosed that enthusiasm for investment opportunities in the 1920s was often so great that large offerings of stock would be bought up by an investing public that knew nothing about the selling company.

The 1933 Securities Act was passed to protect the investing public. It is a disclosure statute, frequently called the "Truth in Securities" law, that requires full disclosure by companies wishing to issue and sell securities to the public. By requiring such companies to file a registration statement with the SEC and to use an offering document called a *prospectus* when attempting to sell securities, the law attempts to enable the investor to make an informed decision when considering public offerings. The SEC, which is charged with enforcement of the law, neither attempts to judge the value of the securities offered nor to advise investors to purchase or not purchase the securities of particular companies. Rather, the Commission primarily devises and enforces disclosure requirements and punishes fraud and deceit in the distribution of shares that are registered. Section 10(b) and Rule 10b-5 of the 1934 Act also punish such fraud, as well as fraud in the distribution of shares that the law does not require to be registered.

These rules generally cover *initial* public offerings, when firms sell to the general public for the first time, as Saudi Aramco, Uber, Lyft, and Pinterest did in 2019. They also cover *seasoned* public offerings, where firms that have previously "IPO'd" dip back into the market to raise additional capital.

Registration Process

Elements of the Process

Traditionally, securities have been distributed much like any product. The corporation selling securities to raise capital, the issuer, is analogous to the manufacturer of goods. *Underwriters* act as wholesalers, *dealers* act as retailers, and the *investor* is a consumer. By regulating the activities of the issuer, underwriter, and dealer, the 1933 Act seeks to ensure that the investor has access to adequate information before purchasing a particular security.

The keystones to the disclosure process are the registration statement and the prospectus, the contents of which are discussed presently. From 1933 until 2006, it was fair to say that: (i) §5(a) of the 1933 Act made it unlawful to sell or deliver any security without first filing with the SEC a registration statement that had become effective; (ii) §5(b)(1) made it unlawful to sell a security by means of a prospectus that did not meet statutory standards; (iii) §5(b)(2) made it unlawful to sell securities that were not accompanied or preceded by a prospectus; and (iv) §5(c) made it illegal even to *offer* to sell or buy securities before a registration statement was filed. In December 2005, major changes became effective that will be discussed presently.

SEC Approval. Except for those prepared by certain well-established firms known as WKSIs (well-known, seasoned issuers), registration statements filed with the SEC are not automatically effective. Rather, the staff of the SEC may review the statement for omissions and inaccuracies. Some reviews may be more thorough than others. Because of budgetary cutbacks and staff reductions, the SEC in recent years has had to give cursory reviews to many registration statements, reserving the full review process primarily for statements filed by new issuers selling to the public for the first time. Indeed, today most registration statements are not reviewed at all.

The 1933 Act further provides that if the SEC is silent, the registration statement automatically becomes effective on the twentieth day after its filing. The registration process may be analyzed in terms of its three major time periods. The first stage of the process is the period before the registration statement is filed (the *pre-filing period)*. The second stage lasts from the filing of the statement until it becomes effective (the *waiting period)*. The final stage is, of course, after the statement becomes effective (the *post-effective period*).

Pre-filing Period. To prevent circumvention of the provisions of §5, issuers have traditionally been strictly limited during the pre-filing period. The issuer could not sell or even offer to sell a security before the registration statement was filed. The term "offer" was broadly construed and encompassed not only formal sales campaigns, but any type of activity meant to "precondition" the market. A simple speech by a corporate executive or a press release about how well the company was doing could be a violation of this "quiet period" if it just happened to be soon followed by the filing of a registration statement.

The only activities permitted during the pre-filing period, other than normal advertising and communications with shareholders by an issuer, were preliminary negotiations between the issuer and underwriters that were necessary to assemble a syndicate of underwriters to manage a large distribution of securities. Any other communications were viewed as "gun-jumping" and could lead to liability under §12 of the '33 Act.

Before a firm spends much time and money preparing to hold a public offering, it will obviously be helpful for the firm to know whether the market will be receptive to that offering. But to communicate with potential investors about a contemplated offering almost certain would constitute gun-jumping under the traditional rules. Then, in 2012, Congress authorized the SEC to change the rules to allow certain small, growing companies ("Emerging Growth Companies"—EGCs) to "test the waters" by communicating with certain institutional investors before filing for an IPO without being accused of illicit "gun-jumping." This experiment worked so well that in 2019, the SEC authorized *all issuers* to test the waters by communicating with qualified institutional buyers ("QIBs") and institutional accredited investors ("IAIs") without being deemed to violate '33 Act communications restrictions.

Waiting Period. The purpose of the waiting period is to slow the distribution process so that the dealers and the public have time to familiarize themselves with the information disclosed in the registration process. Although traditionally no sales could be consummated during this period, certain types of offers were allowed, and underwriters could arrange with dealers for their assistance in distribution.

In addition to oral offers, certain types of written offers were permissible during the waiting period. For example, an issuer could place in *The Wall Street Journal* a short announcement known as a *tombstone ad* because it is usually surrounded by a black border. It could contain only minimal information about the offering.

The other primary goal of the waiting period, besides to slow down the process, was to ensure that the type of information that Congress thought investors needed would be widely distributed. Therefore, offers could also be made by use of a *preliminary prospectus* that contains information from the registration statement then under review. These are also called *red herring prospectuses,* because SEC Rule 430 requires that a special legend be printed in red ink on each one labeling it a preliminary prospectus, stating that a registration statement has been filed but is not yet effective, that no final sale can be made during the waiting period, and that it does not constitute an offer to sell.

Post-Effective Period. Traditionally, once the registration statement became effective, sales of securities could be completed. However, the law still imposed requirements aimed at encouraging dissemination of information. With some exceptions, the issuer, underwriter, and dealer had to provide a copy of the final prospectus with every written offer, supplemental sales literature (called "free writing"), written confirmation of sale, or delivery of securities.

Thus, from 1933 to 2006, it is fair to say that the basic rule, simplistically put, was that (a) before the registration statement was filed, neither sales nor offers could occur; (b) during the waiting period, no sales could occur but oral offers and certain written offers (primarily those made via a red herring prospectus) could be made; and (c) after the effective date, both offers and sales were permitted. This is still the case for many issuers, but the rules, especially for the largest corporations, have changed.

Shelf Registration

Originally, an insurer was required to file a new registration statement every time it sought to initiate a new distribution of stock. However, in 1980 the SEC promulgated Rule 415 which established a system known as *shelf registration.* Under this system, the largest 2,000 or so companies in the nation were allowed to file one registration statement announcing their plans for sales of securities during the following two years. Then, whenever the company believed market conditions and its own financial needs required the sale of securities, it could issue the additional securities without going through the registration process described above to achieve SEC approval because it already had a registration statement and a prospectus "on the shelf." The shelf registration statement was periodically updated as the company filed its annual, quarterly, and interim reports with the SEC and they were incorporated by reference. Rule 415 enhanced the ability of large corporations to raise capital on short notice with a minimum of fuss.

The Securities Offering Reform Program and WKSIs

Shelf registration worked so well and its theory seemed so sound that eventually the SEC got around to promulgating what might be called limited "company registration." The basic theory is that certain companies reveal so much about themselves through their periodic filings with the SEC (quarterly reports, annual reports and the like that we are about to discuss) and are so closely followed in the market that it makes little sense to require them to file registration statements every time they want to have a public offering of securities. Indeed, the restrictive rules regarding the types of offers that can be made in the pre-filing and waiting periods seem rather silly when applied to these companies.

So, in 2005 the SEC issued rules, sometimes called the Securities Offering Reform Program (SORP), that tailored the requirements we have just described for different types of issuers. For example, the most freedom was granted to Wiksees (noted earlier and pronounced "wick-sees"). These are the largest 30% of companies that are publicly traded in the U.S. They own approximately 90% of the assets controlled by public companies.

Under the new rules, WKSIs should file a registration statement every three years indicating roughly what securities they intend to issue during the following three-year period. After that, they need not worry about quiet periods or waiting periods. When they wish to sell securities, they may file a registration statement supplement with the SEC that is immediately effective.

Furthermore, WKSIs are entitled to use "free writing prospectuses" (FWPs) at all times. FWPs are written communications used to sell the companies' stock (other than the preliminary and final prospectuses). They may be used before or after the WKSI starts selling. The old rule of "no offer and no sale" before the registration statement is filed no longer applies to WKSIs. WKSIs need not worry about traditional waiting period restrictions. However, FWPs usually must be filed with the SEC and any misleading statements in them are punishable.

The new rules create a second category of issuer known as seasoned issuers. These firms meet the general requirements for being WKSIs in that they file regular reports with the SEC and have not suffered any major reporting problems or financial complications recently, but they are smaller than the WKSIs. Under the new rules, seasoned issuers can use FWPs after they file a registration statement, but not before. The new rules increase seasoned issuers' freedom to distribute information, but did not grant them the leeway that WKSIs enjoy.

Other new categories of issuers include unseasoned issuers, non-reporting issuers, and ineligible issuers. They also have more freedom from traditional restraints than existed before 2005, but they do not have all the flexibility of WKSIs and seasoned issuers. Firms holding their initial public offerings (IPOs), for example, must generally follow the pre-2005 rules, although all firms may now "test the waters" before filing a registration statement.

Periodic Disclosure Requirements

The information disclosure requirements of the 1933 Act and the 1934 Act were for a long time separate, often overlapping and sometimes conflicting. In 1980, with the shelf registration rules and then in 2005 with the new WKSI rules, the SEC has obviously attempted to harmonize and coordinate disclosure under the two acts.

Registration and Reporting

Section 12 of the 1934 Act requires certain companies to register their shares with the SEC. For example, all companies with shares traded on national exchanges such as the New York Stock Exchange (NYSE). Until 2012, a second category was companies with more than $10 million in assets and more than 500 shareholders. The JOBS Act changed the second category to any company with either (1) 2,000 shareholders or (2) 500 shareholders who are not *accredited investors* (sophisticated investors who can protect themselves).

These companies are referred to as registered or reporting companies. The required registration statement must contain extensive information about such areas as the organization, financial structure, and nature of the business; the structure of present classes of stock; the directors and officers and their remuneration; important contracts; balance sheets; and profit-and-loss statements for the three preceding fiscal years.

Sec. 13 requires that the registration statement be continually updated with annual reports (called 10-Ks) and quarterly reports (10-Qs). In addition, if important facts change between quarterly reports, the company should amend the registration statement by use of an 8-K report. It is the contents of these reports that keep the investing public up to date regarding reporting companies' affairs and convinced the SEC to allow WKSIs to dispense with filing traditional registration statements.

Materiality

Exactly which details must be included in the registration statement and prospectus is a matter governed not only by statutes and rules but also by the concept of *materiality*. The most important element in the disclosure provisions of both the 1933 and 1934 Acts is that all matters that are important or material to an investor's decision should be disclosed. Materiality is an elusive concept, but the Supreme Court has described information as material "if there is a substantial likelihood that a reasonable shareholder would consider it important" in making an investment decision. This is usually limited to matters having a significant bearing on the economic and financial performance of the company.

Examples of material facts include an erratic pattern of earnings, an intention to enter into a new line of business, adverse competitive conditions, litigation with the government that might lead to imposition of a financially damaging fine, and a substantial disparity between the price at which the shares are being offered to the public and the cost of the shares owned by officers, directors, and promoters.

Exemptions

In certain situations where there is less need for regulation, §§3 and 4 of the 1933 Act provide exemptions from §5's registration requirements (although not from the anti-fraud provisions of the 1933 and 1934 Acts). Firms other than WKSIs must be vitally interested in these exemptions.

Perhaps the most important exemption is that for "transactions by any person other than an issuer, underwriter, or dealer" provided by §4(1). This simply means that once the issue is sold to the investing public, the public may trade, and the dealers may handle most transactions, without any worry about registration or prospectus delivery requirements. Thus, the 1933 Act does not generally apply to so-called secondary market trading, which is regulated by the 1934 Act.

Sec. 3(a) exempts from registration the securities of governments (state and federal), charitable organizations, banks, savings and loans, and common carriers, which are regulated under other federal laws. These are *exempt securities*. There are also three major categories of *exempt transactions* in nonexempt securities: private placement exemptions, small offering exemptions, and the intrastate offering exemption.

Private Placements

Sec. 4(2) of the 1933 Act exempts from registration "transactions by an issuer not involving any public offering," an exemption used primarily in connection with so-called *private placements*—privately negotiated sales of securities to large institutional investors and the promotion of business ventures by a few closely related persons. Because sophisticated investors with access to the same information that is normally available in a registration statement can protect themselves without SEC assistance, private placements are exempt from registration. Section 4(2)'s requirements are fleshed out in a "safe harbor" provision, Rule 506 of Regulation D. Regulatory and technological developments have made the private placement market, probably for the first time in decades, more important to American capital markets than the public offering market.

Rule 506 has two subparts. Under Rule 506(b), sellers may not engage in general advertising, but may raise as much money as they can from an unlimited number of *accredited investors* and no more than 35 unaccredited investors (all of whom the issuer must reasonably believe to be either "sophisticated" or acting through a "purchaser representative"—a financial adviser acting in the investor's best interest). Rule 506(c) does allow general advertising, but issuers may sell *only* to accredited investors or investors acting through purchaser representatives. "Accredited investors" are institutional investors of a certain size or individual investors who through their own sophistication or ability to hire advisers can look out for themselves and do not need SEC protection. At this writing in May 2020, the SEC is strongly considering expanding the current definition of "accredited investor." If the Rule 506 requirements are met, companies may raise a large amount of money without filing a registration statement with the SEC. They need file only a Form D within 15 days of commencing the offering; this is a one-page form that informs the SEC that the issuer is claiming this exemption.

Small Offerings

Sec. 3(b) authorizes the SEC to exempt securities if it finds that registration "is not necessary in the public interest and for the protection of investors by reason of the small amount involved or the limited character of the public offering."

Rule 504 of Regulation D allows issuers to raise up to $5 million in a 12-month period without filing a registration statement. This exemption is aimed at smaller businesses and is not available to 1934 Act reporting companies. Investors need not be accredited or sophisticated, nor need they act through a purchaser representative.

Regulation A allows small companies to engage in general solicitation and still raise lots of money from a broad range of investors. Under Tier 1, there are no investor qualifications and issuers may raise up to $20 million in a 12-month period. Under Tier 2, an issuer may raise up to $50 million in a 12-month period, but unaccredited investors may not buy stock constituting more than 10% of their annual income or net worth. Reg A is often called the "mini-IPO" provisions, because issuers do have to file with the SEC, but it is a stripped-down version of a registration statement and not very onerous at all.

Regulation Crowdfunding allows small companies to raise up to $1 million in a 12-month period without filing a registration statement. General solicitation is allowed (although issuers must sell through registered brokers or "funding portals"). Issuers may sell to anyone, but to protect investors from fraud and excessive enthusiasm, the amount any single investor can invest in all crowdfunded investments (not just in a single company) in any 12-month period is limited to an amount not to exceed: (a) the greater of $2,000 or 5% of the investor's annual income or net worth if both of these are less than $100,000, and (b) 10% of the lesser of the investor's annual income or net worth not to exceed $100,000, if the investor's annual income or net worth is $100,000 or more. (Note that these limitations are adjusted upward for inflation from time to time).

Intrastate Offerings

A final important exemption is Rule 147A, which since its creation in 2017 has become much more important than Rule 147. The notion here is that if a company from a particular state sells securities only in that state, then the state should worry about it and the SEC can keeps its federal hands off. Using Texas as an example, an issuer will be viewed as a Texas resident if its principal place of business (where it's corporate "nerve center" is located) is in Texas and it is "doing business" in Texas. A firm is "doing business" in Texas if 80% of its revenue is derived from Texas, 80% of its assets are located there, it uses 80% of the proceeds of the offering in Texas, *or* a majority of its employees are located in Texas. The Texas issuer may use general advertising to raise an unlimited amount of money from Texas residents without filing with the SEC or providing any information to investors. However, it must reasonably believe that every sale it makes is to a Texas resident.

Enforcement and Civil Liabilities

Government Action

The SEC has numerous powers to enforce compliance with the provisions of the 1933 Act. For example, if the SEC believes that a registration statement is incomplete or inaccurate, §8(b) authorizes issuance of a "refusal order," which prevents the statement from becoming effective until SEC objections are satisfied. If inaccuracies are discovered after the effective date, the SEC may issue a *stop order* pursuant to §8(d), as was done in the *Doman Helicopters* case, to suspend the effectiveness of the statement. §8(e) authorizes the SEC to conduct an "examination" to investigate fully whether a stop order should issue. Additionally, the SEC has substantial formal and informal authority to investigate violations of these rules.

The 1933 Act even contains criminal provisions. Section 24 provides that any person who willfully violates any provision of the Act or any SEC rule or any person who willfully makes an untrue statement or omits a material fact in a registration statement is subject to fine and imprisonment. The Department of Justice enforces these criminal provisions.

Private Suit

The 1933 Act provides remedies for violation of its provisions in the form of lawsuits that may be brought by injured investors.

Sec. 11. An investor who is injured after buying securities with reliance on a rosy picture falsely painted in a prospectus will probably not be satisfied with the SEC's injunction remedy or even criminal prosecution. The investor will desire to recoup losses through a civil action for damages, and the 1933 Act has express provision for such lawsuits. §11 states that if "any part of the registration statement, when such part became effective, contained an untrue statement of a material fact or omitted to state a material fact required to be stated therein or necessary to make the statements therein not misleading, any person acquiring such security" may file a civil action. Potential defendants in such an action include every person who signed the registration statement (which includes the issuer, its principal executive officers, chief financial officer, principal accounting officers, and most of the board of directors), every person who was a director or identified as about to become a director, every accountant, every appraiser or other expert who is named as having helped prepare it, and every underwriter.

The §11 cause of action is loosely patterned after a common-law fraud action but is modified to greatly ease a plaintiff's burdens in seeking recovery in many ways. For example, plaintiffs need not prove the common-law fraud elements of privity of contract and reliance. If the plaintiff proves the registration statement contained misstatements or omissions of material facts, the law presumes that these caused the plaintiff's damages, and the burden of proof shifts to the defendants to prove that other factors were the true cause of the plaintiff's losses.

Furthermore, §11 does not require proof of fraudulent intent. Proof of misstatement or omission shifts the burden of proof to the defendants to establish that they were guilty of neither fraudulent intent nor negligence in preparing the registration statement. Individual defendants must establish that they used "due diligence" in preparing the registration statement. The amount of diligence that is due from defendants depends on their position as an insider (with full access to key information) or an outsider, and a defendant is generally allowed to rely on "expertised" portions of the statement—those portions prepared by experts such as independent auditors. The due diligence defense is not available to the issuing company, which is strictly liable for inaccuracies in the registration statement.

One aspect of the §11 cause of action that is very pro-defendant, however, is the requirement that plaintiffs be able to "trace" their shares to a defective registration statement and to establish conclusively that the shares they purchased were not shares that had been previously issued. In practice, this makes it exceedingly difficult for most investors to recover under §11 except in the case of an initial public offering (IPO).

Sec. 12. Complementing §11 are §12(a)(1), which allows an investor to recover when offers or sales are made in violation of §5 (that is, without the filing of a required registration statement, by use of a defective prospectus, or where securities are delivered without an accompanying prospectus), and §12(a)(2), which allows recovery by investors injured by misrepresentations made outside a prospectus (such as in an oral sales pitch or in literature ["free writing"] accompanying a registered offering). The Supreme Court held that §12(a)(2) does not apply to shares purchased in the secondary market or in a private placement. The elements of recovery and defenses in §12 suits are roughly the same as under §11, although the range of potential defendants is limited to ''sellers'' of securities—those who actually pass title or those who "solicit" transactions, such as brokers and dealers. Audit firms face much greater liability under §11, because they certify the accuracy of the financial statements contained in registration statements and are listed as potential defendants in the statute, than they do under §12 where they seldom act as "sellers."

1934 SECURITIES EXCHANGE ACT: REGULATING THE TRADING OF SECURITIES

While the 1933 Act regulates primarily the initial issuance of securities, the 1934 Act regulates the trading of those securities. An array of complex problems comes within the purview of the 1934 Act. The general registration and reporting requirements of the 1934 Act have already been discussed. Attention is now turned to several other major concerns of the act.

Insider Trading

Knowledge of the inner workings of a corporation can be very valuable in making investment decisions. For example, if a corporate vice-president learned that her company had just been granted an important patent that will open up new markets, she would have a distinct and arguably unfair trading advantage over most investors who could not learn of that information no matter how vigilant and intelligent they might be. Insider trading was a widespread phenomenon in the 1920s, yet the common law provided little protection from such abusive practices.

Sec. 10(b)/Rule 10b-5

Another provision of the 1934 Act that regulates insider trading, as well as many other facets of securities trading, is §10(b). This provision makes it unlawful to "use or employ, in connection with the purchase or sale of any security, ... any manipulative or deceptive device or contrivance in contravention of such rules and regulations as the Commission may prescribe. ..."

Pursuant to §10(b), the SEC has issued the most famous of all its rules, Rule 10b-5, quoted in full:

It shall be unlawful for any person, directly or indirectly, by the use of any means or instrumentality of interstate commerce, or of the mails, or of any facility of any national securities exchange,

(a) to employ any device, scheme or artifice to defraud,

(b) to make any untrue statement of a material fact or to omit to state a material fact necessary in order to make the statements made, in the light of the circumstances under which they were made, not misleading, or

(c) to engage in any act, practice, or course of business which operates or would operate as a fraud or deceit upon any person, in connection with the purchase or sale of any security.

General Provisions. One important category of rule 10b-5 cases involves insider trading. The broad purpose of §10(b) and Rule 10b-5 is to protect the investing public by preventing fraud and equalizing access to material information. Sec. 10(b) applies to any purchase or sale by any person of any security—there are no exceptions. Thus, small, closely-held corporations (the shares of which are not offered to the public for sale but are typically held by just a few, perhaps members of a single family) are covered as well as the largest public corporations. Transactions covered include those occurring on the stock exchanges, in over-the-counter sales through stockbrokers, or even in privately-negotiated sales. Any person connected with the transaction is regulated, not only company insiders.

The SEC in a civil case or DOJ in a criminal case must prove actual use of material, nonpublic information to establish a violation.

Enforcement. A willful violation of any provision of the antifraud provisions of 1934 Act, including those banning insider trading, subjects the violator to the criminal provisions of §32, which carry penalties of imprisonment up to 20 years, and/or a fine of up to $10 million for individuals. Corporations can be fined up to $25 million.

The SEC refers criminal cases to the Department of Justice (DOJ) for prosecution. Recently, some inside traders have been punished by multimillion-dollar criminal fines and jail terms of over a decade. The SEC itself can take steps against inside traders. It can hold disciplinary proceedings if a regulated broker, dealer, or underwriter is involved. It can go to federal district court to obtain an injunction to halt illegal practices and perhaps an order rescinding the fraudulent sale. In 1988, the SEC was authorized to seek civil fines against securities firms that "knowingly and recklessly" fail properly to supervise their employees who engage in insider trading. Additionally, the SEC is authorized in civil insider trading cases to seek relief in the form of disgorgement of illicit profits and assessment of a civil penalty of up to three times the profit gained or loss avoided. The SEC also has broad civil powers to impose fines, seek injunctions, bar bad actors from serving as officers and directors of public companies, seek disgorgement of ill-gotten gains, and the like. Although all developed nations have adopted rather vigorous insider trading rules in recent years, most do not enforce their rules as aggressively as does the SEC.

Potential Defendants. The key to insider trading liability is the "disclose or abstain rule" which requires that certain persons either disclose material nonpublic information that they possess or abstain from trading in the relevant company's stock until that information becomes public. The "disclose or abstain" rule promotes fairness in securities trading by equalizing access to important information affecting the value of securities. Equal information is not the goal, only equal access. Although the goal cannot be perfectly achieved, small investors will likely be more willing to enter the market if they know the SEC and DOJ are actively promoting equal access.

Four major categories of persons owe a duty to disclose or abstain. The first category consists of *corporate insiders*, a term that includes any corporate employee with access to material inside information, not just officers and directors. Secretaries and custodians may be corporate insiders. Corporate employees owe a fiduciary duty to the corporation and its owners not to take material, nonpublic information that belongs to the firm and convert it to their own use by trading on it illicitly.

Temporary insiders make up a second category of potential insider trading defendants. These are persons who receive confidential corporate information for a corporate purpose and with the expectation that it will be kept confidential, but then use it in insider trading. Examples are attorneys, accountants, consultants, and investment bankers hired temporarily by a corporation. If Corporation A plans to merge with Corporation B and hires a law firm to help it with the transaction, an attorney (let's call her "Jane") in that law firm working on the engagement would be a temporary insider of Corporation A. If she learns during her work that the deal is going to be very favorable to Corporation A and buys its stock based on nonpublic information, selling it at a profit after public announcement of the deal, Jane will liable as a temporary insider. She has misappropriated her client's information and used it for her own purposes. Not all courts recognize temporary insiders as a separate category. Most people who would qualify as temporary insiders also qualify as misappropriators, the next category.

Misappropriators are noninsiders who misappropriate confidential inside information for their own purposes. Their "disclose or abstain" obligation rests on a fiduciary duty owed to the *source* of their information. If in the previous example, Jane had traded in the shares of B Corporation, she would have been liable as a misappropriator. She stole information from her client, A Corporation, and used it to trade in B. She was neither a company insider nor a temporary insider of B Corporation, but she will be liable as a misappropriator. The misappropriation category of insider trading (sometimes called "outsider trading") is the most controversial and is illustrated in the following opinion that adopted a "fraud on the source" approach to discerning who is a misappropriator.

UNITED STATES v. O'HAGAN
U.S. Supreme Court, 521 U.S. 642 (1997)

James O'Hagan was a partner in the law firm of Dorsey & Whitney. After Grand Metropolitan PLC (Grand Met) retained the law firm of Dorsey & Whitney to represent it regarding a potential tender offer for the Pillsbury Company's common stock, respondent O'Hagan, who did no work on the representation, began purchasing call options for Pillsbury stock, as well as shares of the stock. Dorsey & Whitney withdrew from representing Grand Met. Grand Met publicly announced its tender offer, the price of Pillsbury stock rose dramatically, and O'Hagan sold his call options and stock at a profit of more than $4.3 million.

A Securities and Exchange Commission (SEC) investigation culminated in a 57-count criminal indictment alleging that O'Hagan defrauded his law firm and its client, Grand Met, by misappropriating for his own trading purposes material, nonpublic information regarding the tender offer. O'Hagan was charged and convicted of several counts of violating §10(b and Rule 10b-5.

The Eighth Circuit reversed all of the convictions, holding that §10(b)/ Rule 10b-5 liability may not be grounded on the "misappropriation theory." The government appealed.

Ginsburg, Justice:

Is a person who trades in securities for personal profit, using confidential information misappropriated in breach of a fiduciary duty to the source of the information, guilty of violating §10(b) and Rule 10b-5? Our answer is yes.

The "misappropriation theory" holds that a person commits fraud "in connection with" a securities transaction, and thereby violates §10(b) and Rule 10b-5, when he misappropriates confidential information for securities trading purposes, in breach of a duty owed to the source of the information. Under this theory, a fiduciary's undisclosed, self-serving use of a principal's information to purchase or sell securities, in breach of a duty of loyalty and confidentiality, defrauds the principal of the exclusive use of that information. In lieu of premising liability on a fiduciary relationship between company insider and purchaser or seller of the company's stock, the misappropriation theory premises liability on a fiduciary-turned-trader's deception of those who entrusted him with access to confidential information.

The misappropriation theory outlaws trading on the basis of nonpublic information by a corporate "outsider" in breach of a duty owed not to a trading party, but to the source of the information. The misappropriation theory is thus designed to "protect the integrity of the securities markets against abuses by 'outsiders' to a corporation who have access to confidential information that will affect the corporation's security price when revealed, but who owe no fiduciary or other duty to that corporation's shareholders."

In this case, the indictment alleged that O'Hagan in breach of a duty of trust and confidence he owed to his law firm, Dorsey & Whitney, and to its client, Grand Met, traded on the basis of nonpublic information regarding Grand Met's planned tender offer for Pillsbury common stock. This conduct, the Government charged, constituted a fraudulent device in connection with the purchase and sale of securities.

We agree with the Government that misappropriation, as just defined, satisfies §10(b)'s requirement that chargeable conduct involve a "deceptive device or contrivance" used "in connection with" the purchase or sale of securities. We observe, first, that misappropriators, as the Government describes them, deal in deception. A fiduciary who "[pretends] loyalty to the principal while secretly converting the principal's information for personal gain," Brief for United States 17, "dupes" or defrauds the principal.

Deception through nondisclosure is central to the theory of liability for which the Government seeks recognition. Under the misappropriation theory urged in this case, the disclosure obligation runs to the source of the information, Dorsey & Whitney and Grand Met.

Full disclosure forecloses liability under the misappropriation theory: Because the deception essential to the misappropriation theory involves feigning fidelity to the source of information, if the fiduciary discloses to the source that he plans to trade on the nonpublic information, there is no "deceptive device" and thus no §10(b) violation—although the fiduciary-turned-trader may remain liable under state [breach of loyalty law]. Reversed.

Bill Tsai was president of the student body at NYU's Stern School of Business. After graduating in 2018, he took a job as an analyst at investment bank RBC Capital Markets where he learned that client Siris Capital Group was preparing to buy EFI. Tsai bought EFI call options based on this material, nonpublic information and profited by exercising them after the deal was publicly announced. He was a misappropriator who breached his duty of loyalty to his client, Siris. He pled guilty to criminal insider trading in late 2019.

The fourth category of person who owes a duty to "disclose or abstain" under Rule 10b-5 includes any *tippee* of any of the first three categories. Unless tippees are covered, insiders could tip their spouses and then enjoy the fruits of the spouse's trading. The Supreme Court has held that a tippee's liability is derivative of the tipper's liability, and therefore that tippees cannot be liable for insider trading unless they know or should know that the tipper breached a duty in passing along the information. Such a breach occurs if the information is passed for personal benefit, whether monetary or reputational.

The SEC enjoys special authority to issue rules regulating tender offers and pursuant to that authority has issued Rule 14e-3 which punishes inside traders who are trading on inside information that relates to a *tender offer*, and not any other type of material, nonpublic information. Liability may be imposed on the trader if someone has taken substantial steps toward beginning the tender offer and the trader knows or has reason to know that the inside information came from the acquiring corporation, the target corporation, or any of their insiders. Unlike under § 10(b)/Rule 10b-5 that punish insider trading based on other types of material nonpublic information, a trader punished under Rule 14e-3 for having traded on tender offer information need not be categorized as a company insider, temporary insider, misappropriator or tippee in order to be punished.

False or Inadequate Corporate Disclosures

A second major category of §10(b) cases relates to disclosures of information about corporations. Already noted are the registration and reporting requirements of the 1934 Act. The periodic reporting forms (the 10-Ks, 10-Qs, and 8-Ks) are all designed to promote full disclosure of information important to the investing public. When a corporation or some person fraudulently misstates or fails to disclose material information, a §10(b) violation may occur.

Investors who are injured because they bought or sold shares on the basis of inaccurate or incomplete corporate information may bring a private cause of action under the antifraud provisions of §10(b). Whereas private lawsuits by investors are seldom brought to remedy insider trading violations, they are often brought to remedy disclosure fraud that violates §10(b). The requirements of a valid claim in such a lawsuit are patterned after those of common law fraud: (1) a misrepresentation of material fact, (2) made by defendant with knowledge of the falsity, (3) an intent to induce the plaintiff to rely, (4) actual reliance by the plaintiff, (5) privity of contract between the plaintiff and the defendant, and (6) damage sustained. Modification of some of these common-law elements has been a source of controversy in this type of §10(b) case.

Privity

Privity of contract has been largely eliminated as a requirement of a §10(b) cause of action in the corporate disclosure setting. An injured shareholder is normally allowed to sue those persons responsible for false statements whether or not the stockholder purchased shares from or sold shares to the defendants. The Supreme Court has in recent years narrowly defined the parties responsible for a communication.

Intent

Actual intent to defraud arising from knowledge of the falsity of a statement is a traditional element of common-law fraud. It is also an element of §10(b), as the Supreme Court has held that 10(b) defendants are not liable "in the absence of any allegation of scienter—intent to deceive, manipulate, or defraud."

The PSLRA of 1995 raised the pleading requirement regarding scienter. Plaintiffs must now plead very specific facts about what false statement was made, when it was made, by whom it was made, why it is false, and why the source of the statement knew it was false. This pleading requirement has caused plaintiffs' attorneys to be much more careful about the lawsuits they file and has led to a big increase in the number of such suits that are dismissed at an early stage.

Reliance

In a common-law fraud case, the plaintiff must normally prove that he or she relied upon the defendant's fraudulent statement in making the sale or purchase. To advance the broadly remedial purposes of the 1934 Act, some adjustments have been made to the traditional reliance requirement.

A misleading corporate disclosure can occur either when a material fact is concealed or when it is misrepresented. Because it is impractical to require an investor to prove reliance on a fact that was concealed from him or her, the Supreme Court has eliminated the reliance requirement in concealment cases. In *Affiliated Ute Citizens v. United States,* 406 U.S. 128 (1972), the plaintiffs, mixed-blood Ute Indians, sold shares in the Ute Development Corporation through the defendants, bank officials. The defendants failed to disclose to the plaintiffs their own interest in the transactions or the fact that shares were trading at higher prices among whites. The Court held:

> Under the circumstances of this case, involving primarily a failure to disclose, positive proof of reliance is not a prerequisite to recovery. All that is necessary is that the facts withheld be material in the sense that a reasonable investor might have considered them important in the making of this decision. This obligation to disclose and this withholding of a material fact establish the requisite element of causation in fact.

In cases of active misrepresentation, proof of reliance is practicable; nonetheless, there have been some important modifications of the reliance requirements even in misrepresentation cases, partly because of the impersonal nature of transactions that occur through the stock exchanges. The leading case for what is called the "fraud on the market" theory of reliance follows.

Although the outer limit of permissible rule 10b-5 actions is not completely settled, the Supreme Court has attempted to confine the actions to situations involving deceit and manipulation. Simple corporate mismanagement or breaches of fiduciary duty by corporate officials, not involving deceit, are not actionable under rule 10b-5.

BASIC, INC. v. LEVINSON
U.S. Supreme Court, 485 U.S. 224 (1988)

In 1965, Combustion Engineering, Inc. expressed an interest in acquiring Basic, Inc. That interest was reawakened by regulatory developments in late 1976. Beginning in September 1976, Combustion representatives had meetings and phone calls with Basic officers and directors about a possible merger. During 1977 and 1978, Basic made three public statements denying that it was engaged in merger negotiations. On December 18, 1978, Basic was asked by the New York Stock Exchange to suspend trading in its shares. It issued a press release stating that it had been "approached" about a merger. On December 19, Basic's board accepted Combustion's offer, and this was publicly announced on December 20.

Former Basic shareholders (respondents), who sold their stock after Basic's first denial that it was engaged in merger talks (October 21, 1977) and before the suspension of trading, sued Basic and its directors (petitioners). The respondents claimed that petitioners' misleading statements caused them to miss the opportunity to sell at the higher merger price, in violation of § 10(b) of the 1934 Securities Act.

The district court (1) granted class action status to the respondents adopting a presumption that they had relied on petitioners' public statements, thereby satisfying the "common question of fact or law" requirement of the Federal Rules of Civil Procedure; and (2) granted summary judgment to petitioners on the merits, holding that petitioners had no obligation to disclose the ongoing merger negotiations. The circuit court affirmed on the class action issue, adopting the district court's "fraud on the market" theory, but reversed on the merits, finding that a duty to disclose the merger talks might have existed. Petitioners appealed.

Blackmun, Justice:

[The Supreme Court first rejected the circuit court's resolution of the merits of the case. Unlike the circuit court, which held that almost any misleading statement about merger negotiations could be material, the Supreme Court held that materiality must depend on a balancing of (1) the indicated probability that the merger will occur, and (2) the anticipated magnitude of the merger in light of the totality of the company's activities. It then catalogued various factors, such as board resolutions and instructions to investment bankers (which might show probability that the merger would occur) and the size of the corporations involved and of the premium over market price being discussed (which might show magnitude of the event), for lower courts to consider in applying its subjective, fact specific approach.] [Regarding the fraud-on-the-market theory:]

> The fraud-on-the-market theory is based on the hypothesis that, in an open and developed securities market, the price of a company's stock is determined by the available material information regarding the company and its business.... Misleading statements will therefore defraud purchasers of stock even if the purchasers do not directly rely on the misstatements.... The causal connection between the defendants' fraud and the plaintiffs' purchase of stock in such a case is no less significant than in a case of direct reliance on misrepresentations.

Peil v. Speiser, 806 F.2d 1154 (CA3 1986). We agree that reliance is an element of a rule 10b-5 cause of action. *See Ernst & Ernst v. Hochfelder*, 425 U.S. 185 (1976). Reliance provides the requisite causal connection between a defendant's misrepresentation and a plaintiff's injury.... There is, however, more than one way to demonstrate the causal connection....

The modern securities markets, literally involving millions of shares changing hands daily, differ from the face-to-face transactions contemplated by early fraud cases [that required a showing of privity], and our understanding of Rule 10b-5's reliance requirement must encompass these differences.

In face-to-face transactions, the inquiry into an investor's reliance upon information is into the subjective pricing of that information by that investor. With the presence of a market, the market is interposed between the seller and buyer and, ideally, transmits information to the investor in the processed form of a market price. Thus the market is performing a substantial part of the valuation process performed by the investor in a face-to-face transaction. The market is acting as the unpaid agent of the investor, informing him that given all the information available to it, the value of the stock is worth the market price.

Requiring a plaintiff to show a speculative state of facts, i.e., how he would have acted if omitted material information had been disclosed, . . . or if the misrepresentation had not been made . . . would place an unnecessarily unrealistic evidentiary burden on the Rule 10b-5 plaintiff who has traded on an impersonal market.

The presumption of reliance employed in this case is consistent with, and, by facilitating Rule 10b-5 litigation, supports the congressional policy embodied in the 1934 Act. In drafting that Act, Congress expressly relied on the premise that securities markets are affected by information, and enacted legislation to facilitate an investor's reliance on the integrity of those markets....

The presumption is also supported by common sense and probability. Recent empirical studies have tended to confirm Congress' premise that the market price of shares traded on well developed markets reflect all publicly available information, and, hence, any material misrepresentation. It has been noted that "it is hard to imagine that there ever is a buyer or seller who does not rely on market integrity. Who would knowingly roll the dice in a crooked crap game?" *Schlanger v. Four Phase Systems,* Inc., 555 F.Supp. 535, 538 (S.D.N.Y. 1982).

Any showing that severs the link between the alleged misrepresentation and either the price received (or paid) by the plaintiff, or his decision to trade at a fair market price, will be sufficient to rebut the presumption of reliance. [The Court of Appeals' judgment is vacated and remanded.]

In 2018, Elizabeth Holmes, the infamous founder of Theranos, a company that falsely claimed to have reinvented blood testing and garnered nearly a billion dollars in capital from investors it deceived, settled SEC civil charges of securities fraud by paying a $500,000 fine. Her criminal trial is, at this writing, set for summer 2020. DOJ could have charged her with intentionally violating §10(b), but instead focused on wire fraud, which is easier to prove.

STATE REGULATION

Because every state has its own system of securities regulation, corporations must always be cognizant of these rules also. The Commissioners on Uniform State Laws have produced the Uniform Securities Act, which has been used as a pattern for many states' laws. Still, because many large states have not followed this act and many have amended it to varying degrees, there is a lack of uniformity that complicates the marketing of securities.

Recent changes in federal law aimed primarily at reducing duplicative state and federal regulations have reduced, but scarcely eliminated, the importance of state securities laws. New York, for example, has a securities fraud provision called the Miller Act that state prosecutors often invoke because of its similarity to §10(b). In 2019, a state trial judge ruled that the New York Attorney General had failed to prove beyond a reasonable doubt that Exxon Mobil had defrauded its investors by deliberately lying about the likely adverse impact of climate change on the company's share price.

INTERNATIONAL IMPLICATIONS

Each year, Americans buy billions of dollars' worth of foreign securities, and foreign investors purchase similarly large amounts of U.S. securities. Many American investors watch the London and Tokyo stock markets almost as closely as they monitor the New York Stock Exchange. Because our economy increasingly intersects with those of other nations, international concerns affect virtually every sphere of U.S. securities law.

Registration Exemptions

Earlier we listed the important domestic exemptions to the registration requirements of the 1933 Act. To encourage foreign issuers to raise equity in American markets, in 1990 the SEC added a foreign exemption—Regulation S. Generally speaking, Regulation S provides that §5's registration requirement does not apply to sales or resales of securities if two requirements are met. First, the sale must be an off-shore transaction, defined as one in which no offer is made to a person in the United States, and either (1) at the time the buy order is originated the buyer is outside the United States or (2) the transaction is executed through the facilities of a designated offshore securities market. Second, there can be no "directed selling efforts" in the United States. Issuers must take additional precautions to assure that the shares, once purchased outside the United States, are not quickly resold in the United States as a means of circumventing the registration requirements.

Regulation S provides an exemption only from registration, not from antifraud rules. Therefore, §10(b)/Rule 10b-5 fraud lawsuits are often filed in U.S. courts by American investors against foreign defendants, by foreign investors against American defendants, and sometimes even by foreign investors against foreign defendants. The courts were generally receptive to such holdings until recently. In *Morrison v. National Australia Bank*, 561 U.S. 247 (2010), the Supreme Court limited the jurisdiction of U.S. courts to hear such lawsuits, holding that "Section 10(b) reaches the use of a manipulative or deceptive device or contrivance only in connection with the purchase or sale of a security listed on an American stock exchange, and the purchase or sale of any other security in the United States."

Insider Trading Internationally

Many of the insider trading schemes occurring in the United States in the 1980s were aided by the bank secrecy laws of Switzerland and other countries. In recent years, with pressure from the United States, many of these nations have become more cooperative in divulging information, thereby allowing the SEC to prosecute more successfully foreign citizens who are inside traders as well as U.S. citizens who attempt to cover their tracks with use of foreign bank accounts. Over the past 25 years, often because of American urging, most developed nations have outlawed insider trading, though, none prosecute it as vigorously as the United States.

CHAPTER 29

ANTITRUST LAW

- Introduction
- Objectives of Antitrust Law
- The Antitrust Statutes
- Coverage, Exemptions, & Enforcement
- Horizontal Restraints of Trade
- Vertical Restraints of Trade
- Monopolization
- Mergers
- International Considerations

INTRODUCTION

Competitors must be very careful in their dealings with each other so as to avoid acting together in a way that limits competition. And a corporation with a monopolistic share of a particular market must avoid conduct tending to prove that it is abusing its economic power. Or, a company that is not quite a monopolist but nevertheless has a very large market share has to be careful not to engage in conduct that is aimed at harming smaller competitors in ways that do not represent legitimate competition, such as doing things that are clearly aimed at raising the costs of its smaller rivals. And, when a proposed corporate merger involves two competitors each having large enough market shares that the resulting combination will leave seriously inadequate competition in their market, the Federal Trade Commission (FTC) or the antitrust division of the U.S. Department of Justice is likely to take action, up to and including a civil lawsuit, that requires either or both of the companies to sell off assets in areas of the country where they are in direct competition.

In 1998, for example, the U.S. Department of Justice and twenty state attorneys general filed a civil action against Microsoft, alleging that the company had acquired and abused monopoly power in the market for operating system software for personal computers. After the federal district court in the District of Columbia concluded that Microsoft was indeed a monopolist and had abused that power in various ways, the U.S. Court of Appeals for the D.C. Circuit reversed the district court's holding that Microsoft should be broken into two separate companies, one that would make and sell operating system software, and another that would make and sell all of the company's other software products. After four years of extremely expensive litigation that cast great uncertainty on the future of the company, the plaintiffs and Microsoft reached a settlement agreement in which the company would not be broken into parts, but that did require the company to change a number of business practices that allegedly harmed both consumers and Microsoft's smaller competitors.

The case, chronicled in popular books such as John Heileman's *Pride Before the Fall*, demonstrates that companies are wise to avoid antitrust entanglements in the first place. In addition to the massively expensive U.S. litigation just outlined, Microsoft was ordered by European Union antitrust enforcers to make specific changes in how it marketed its software as well as to pay a $648 million fine. Over the past fifteen years or so, antitrust problems have cost Microsoft several *billion* dollars. Microsoft's experience, plus the later $1.05 *billion* judgment in an antitrust case involving U.S. Smokeless Tobacco, and the $650 million in fines that Samsung and its competitors in the American market for dynamic random access memory chips paid in a price-fixing case in 2005, indicates that the strategic manager should most definitely have a solid grounding in the essentials of antitrust law.

There are more recent examples, as well. In 2017 a federal district judge in California refused to dismiss a civil case brought by the FTC against Qualcomm alleging that the company had engaged in anticompetitive tactics to maintain a monopoly on the chips that let cell phones connect to mobile data networks. Qualcomm thus had to defend against the FTC complaint at the same time it was a defendant in a $1 billion antitrust lawsuit brought by one of its customers, Apple Computers.

There also can be criminal charges for violations of the Sherman Act by the Justice Dept. Although Sherman Act criminal prosecutions are far less common than civil actions, such prosecutions of both companies and their managers do occasionally take place. In 2015, the Justice Dept. began investigating price fixing in the market for canned tuna among StarKist Co., Bumble Bee Foods, and Chicken of the Sea for the purpose of raising worldwide prices. In May 2017, industry giant Bumble Bee Foods agreed to pay a $25 million fine after pleading guilty to price fixing, and two of its executives also pleaded guilty for their participation in the conspiracy. Two months later, Stephen Hodge, a former senior vice president for sales at StarKist, pleaded guilty to the criminal charge that he had participated in a price-fixing scheme with the other tuna producers.

Later in 2017, it was revealed that Thai Union Group, the parent company of one of the major world producers of tuna, Chicken of the Sea, had been the whistleblower that reported the global price-fixing scheme to the U.S. Department of Justice. Thai Union and its subsidiary Chicken of the Sea were given conditional leniency status, which meant that neither Tri-Union nor any of its cooperating executives or employees would face criminal fines or jail time. At the time of this writing, these executives were awaiting sentencing. In 2019, Starkist was fined $100 million, and also settled a private antitrust suit brought by one of its buyers, Walmart, for a reported $20.5 million. Also in 2019, Bumble Bee paid a fine of $25 million, and went into Chapter 11 bankruptcy. Bumble Bee's fired former CEO, Chris Lischewski, was convicted of a felony violation of Section 1 of the Sherman Act after two of his former subordinates cooperated with the government and testified against him. In late May 2020, a federal judge in San Francisco was conducting online discussions with attorneys about whether an in-person sentencing hearing for Lischewski would be feasible, or whether the coronavirus pandemic required that it would have to be done through video conferencing. Lischewski is facing up to 10 years in prison.

First it was tuna, then it was chicken, or so it seems. In June 2020, a federal grand jury in Colorado issued felony indictments alleging that Pilgrim's Pride Corp. and Claxton Poultry Farms, two of the largest poultry producers in the U.S, as well as several of their executives, had engaged in a conspiracy to rig bids and fix prices or several years in their sales to restaurant chains, wholesale food distributors, and large retailers such as Walmart, Kroger, and Albertson's. Pilgrim Pride's CEO Jayson Penn was personally indicted, as was a former Pilgrim's vice president, Roger Austin. The president of Georgia-based Claxton, Mikell Fries, and a vice president, Scott Brady, were both indicted. The indictments followed private price-fixing lawsuits brought since 2017 all of the country's major chicken producers by large purchasers of chicken products.

It is not just in the U.S. that managers must pay attention to antitrust law. For example, during the late 1990s and early 2000s when vitamin manufacturers from Switzerland, Germany, France, and Japan were caught agreeing to fix prices at a top secret meeting in the Black Forest in Germany, high ranking officers at two of the companies went to prison. In addition, the five companies paid $862 million in U.S. fines, €855 million in EU fines, $1.4 billion to settle private class action lawsuits by direct and indirect purchasers of vitamins.

In June 2017, the European Union antitrust enforcement agency levied a fine of €2.4 billion Euros ($2.7 billion US dollars) against Google for abusing its monopoly power in the online search market in Europe. Google maintains a 90% share of that market in the EU, and was found to have abused this monopoly power by favoring its own offerings of goods and services in what was claimed by the company to be an objective comparison shopping function. The market price of Google's shares of stock declined significantly after announcement of the fine. Then, in 2019, German price-comparison portal Idealo became the first major company to sue Google based on the 2017 European antitrust decision to fine Google for abusing its dominant position in search. If it succeeds, the litigation could spark similar actions in Europe by other tech firms that have so far hesitated to take on Google. Idealo alleges that Google made it harder for users of its search engine to find links to Idealo after it started promoting its own price-comparison offering, now called Google Shopping.

In November 2019, Google announced a deal to buy Fitbit for $2.1 billion. The EU has much stronger privacy and data protection laws than the U.S., and the EU privacy regulatory authority has questioned whether Google would improperly use personal fitness data collected by Fitbit devices. Based on assurances from Google, the EU has not intervened, but almost certainly will keep a watch on the situation.

European Union antitrust enforcers continue to investigate the activities of Google and other very large companies like Amazon for possible violations. Regarding Amazon, EU regulators have recently begun to look into the company's treatment of its resellers as Amazon increasingly competes with them in the sale of products and services; often, Amazon today operates as both a critical point of entry into markets for tens of thousands of other online sellers, and simultaneously competes with them. This is not illegal in itself, but EU regulators are showing interest in whether Amazon squeezes these smaller companies in ways that give Amazon a competitive advantage, because Amazon has far greater market power than these other companies that depend on it. For online selling by tens of thousands of smaller companies, Amazon has almost become an "essential facility" such as a shipping terminal at a major port or an airport. U.S. antitrust authorities, and perhaps those in China, may also show increasing attention to how Amazon operates.

The Objectives of Antitrust Law

An economy such as that of the United States, which depends primarily on the operation of market forces, cannot function properly without competition. Although the word "competition" is subject to various shades of meaning, it most often refers to a condition of economic rivalry among firms. That is, firms should be engaged in a contest for customers, the outcome of that contest depending on each firm's ability to satisfy customer needs and wants. The primary purpose of antitrust law is to promote competition.

In the various types of markets, competition can take somewhat different forms. In the case of many kinds of products, for example, price is a very important factor in customers' buying decisions (that is, "price elasticity" is high), and much of the competitive rivalry among sellers may focus on price. On the other hand, in some markets price may not be quite as important to most customers as good service, availability of many product options, convenience, or other factors. In such markets, competition among sellers is likely to emphasize these non-price attributes to a greater extent.

Not only does the form of competition vary somewhat among markets, but the intensity of competition also is less in some markets than in others. The job of antitrust law is to encourage competition in its various forms and to preserve it to the extent feasible in a given market. Most economists feel that a competitive, market-based economy produces a number of beneficial results such as efficient allocation of scarce resources, lower prices, higher quality, greater innovation, and economic freedom. In the view of some authorities, there is another reason for having a strong antitrust policy in the United States—more competition in an economic sense may diminish the amount of power that large firms have over the political process and over the lives of large numbers of people.

Has antitrust law achieved its goals? This question cannot be answered with certainty because it is practically impossible to measure the effects of antitrust law on the American economy. There are many markets (so-called *oligopolies*) in which most of the sales are made by a few large companies. Many of these firms are very efficient; some are not. Some do not abuse their power, but some do. In some of these markets, competition appears to be quite vigorous, but in others it is rather stagnant.

Moreover, in many of these markets concentration of power in a few firms is an inevitable result of extremely large capital requirements and economies of scale. On the other hand, the *degree* of economic concentration is clearly not always inevitable. Thus, it is not surprising to find substantial disagreement among authorities concerning the wisdom and effect of antitrust law. Some say the law has not been enforced aggressively enough, while others say that it has been applied too aggressively to the wrong things. Many points of criticism and support have been raised over the years. Only two conclusions are relatively certain: (1) although the interpretation of some of the antitrust rules will vary over time, the fundamental principles will remain with us; and (2) antitrust law will always be important.

The Federal Antitrust Statutes

The first, and still the most important, of the federal antitrust laws is the Sherman Act, passed by Congress in 1890. Section 1 of the Act prohibits "contracts, combinations, and conspiracies in restraint of trade." The focus of Section 1 is collusion among firms that are supposed to be acting independently when making basic business decisions. Section 2 prohibits "monopolization, attempts to monopolize, and conspiracies to monopolize." The prohibition of monopolization, which is the most important part of Section 2, focuses on single-firm domination of a market.

In 1914, Congress enacted the Clayton Act with two main purposes in mind: (1) to make the prohibitions against certain anticompetitive practices more specific, and (2) to make it easier to challenge certain practices, such as mergers, when the evidence shows only probable future anticompetitive effects and not actual present effects. Section 2 of the Act prohibits price discrimination; Section 3 prohibits some tying and exclusive dealing agreements; and Section 7 forbids anticompetitive mergers. In any of these cases, the law is violated only if the evidence demonstrates an actual or highly probable anticompetitive effect of a substantial nature.

In 1936, Congress passed the Robinson-Patman Act, which amended Section 2 of the Clayton Act in an effort to make the law against price discrimination more rigorous. This law is no longer relevant to business because questions about the legitimacy of protecting only individual companies rather than protecting competition itself caused the Justice Department to refuse to enforce it from the beginning, and the Federal Trade Commission to cease its enforcement after the 1960s. Courts also made private enforcement almost impossible. As a result, this chapter will not discuss the Robinson-Patman Act any further.

Also in 1914, Congress passed the Federal Trade Commission Act (FTC Act). In addition to creating the Federal Trade Commission (FTC) as an enforcement agency, the Act also prohibited "unfair methods of competition" in Section 5. Any conduct that violates one of the other antitrust laws, plus a few other types of conduct, constitutes an unfair method of competition. In 1938, Congress added another phrase to Section 5 prohibiting "unfair or deceptive acts or practices." Thus the first part of the statute deals with antitrust matters, and the second part deals with various forms of consumer deception such as false advertising.

Our attention in this chapter is focused only on *federal* antitrust law. Most states have their own antitrust laws, which usually apply to the same basic practices as federal law.

Coverage and Exemptions

Like many other federal statutes that are based on the Commerce Clause of the U.S. Constitution, the federal antitrust laws apply to business activities that either directly involve or substantially affect interstate commerce. Business activities occurring in foreign commerce, such as imports and exports, are also covered by U.S. antitrust law if there is a substantial effect on an American market.

Exemptions

The actions of the federal government are exempt from the antitrust laws, as are most actions of state governments so long as they are acting pursuant to legitimate and clearly expressed state regulatory interests. In this regard, actions of cities and other local governments are treated as state action if the local government is essentially just carrying out some aspect of state regulatory policy. Actions by foreign governments also are not within the scope of the antitrust laws.

If particular activities of a firm are subject to special regulation by a federal agency, such as the Securities Exchange Commission or the Commodity Futures Trading Commission, any possible anticompetitive consequences of those activities will usually not be scrutinized under the antitrust laws if the responsible agency has approved the activities after carefully considering the impact on competition.

In addition, the formation and ordinary activities (collective bargaining and strikes, for instance) of labor unions are exempt because of special federal legislation. Similarly, the actions of employers are exempt to the extent that they form a legitimate part of the union-company collective bargaining agreement and do not affect parties outside the union-company relationship. Finally, the joint activities of two kinds of selling cooperatives are exempt from the antitrust laws: (1) those formed by agricultural or livestock producers and (2) export groups so long as the limitation on export competition among members of the group does not adversely affect a domestic U.S. market.

Use of Litigation and Administrative Proceedings to Suppress Competition

When two or more competitors acting together seek to limit competition among them, or when a single firm attempts to obtain or abuse monopoly power in a market, the most effective way to do so may sometimes involve the use of governmental processes as part of the scheme. It has been relatively common over the years for such parties to seek passage of legislation, file lawsuits, or petition state or federal administrative agencies as part of an effort to suppress competition. Such actions could very well violate the Sherman Antitrust Act if not for the fact that "petitioning the government for redress of grievances," that is, asking a court or other government entity to take action, is treated by the law as constitutionally protected by the First Amendment to the U.S. Constitution. Thus, under the so-called "Noerr-Pennington doctrine," attempts by companies to influence the passage or enforcement of laws cannot violate the federal antitrust laws, even if the laws they advocate for would have anticompetitive effects. The doctrine takes its name from two U.S. Supreme Court cases, *Eastern Railroad Presidents Conference v. Noerr Motor Freight, Inc.*, 365 U.S. 127 (1961), and *United Mine Workers v. Pennington*, 381 U.S. 657 (1965). In addition to First Amendment protection for attempts to influence government, the Supreme Court stated in *Noerr* that the doctrine is based "upon a recognition that the antitrust laws, tailored as they are for the business world, are not at all appropriate for application in the political arena."

The Supreme Court has held on multiple occasions that this immunity from being held civilly or criminally liable for a violation of the Sherman Act does not exist when an attempt to influence government action is a "sham." Called the "sham litigation exception," this exception to the Noerr-Pennington doctrine applies both to lawsuits and attempts to influence other kinds of government action. The sham exception applies when the allegations made when seeking to influence government action are "objectively baseless," such that no reasonable party could realistically expect success. In addition, the evidence must show that those instituting the request for government action had no actual intent to obtain substantive action by the court or other government entity, instead having the sole aim to harm competitors. One of many examples is found in *California Motor Transport v. Trucking Unlimited*, 404 U.S. 508 (1972), where the United States Supreme Court held that the *Noerr–Pennington* doctrine did not protect members of a group of trucking companies that had intervened in a state agency proceeding involving the licensing of a competitor, because the intervention was not based on a good-faith effort to enforce the law, but was solely for the purpose of harassing those competitors and driving up their costs of doing business. When the competitor whose state trucking license had been at issue in the administrative proceeding sued the companies that had intervened for a violation of Sherman Act § 1, the Supreme Court held that the antitrust lawsuit could proceed because of the sham litigation exception to Noerr-Pennington.

Enforcement

Enforcement of the federal antitrust laws can take one or more of several different forms. The Antitrust Division of the U.S. Department of Justice, which operates under the Attorney General as part of the executive branch, can institute civil lawsuits and criminal prosecutions in federal district court. In a civil suit, if the Justice Department proves a violation of the Sherman or Clayton Acts, the remedy it normally obtains from the court is an injunction. The injunction will order the cessation of particular illegal actions, and may even require substantial modification of a firm's everyday business practices so as to lessen the likelihood of future violations. Many times the terms of an injunction are the result of an agreed settlement between the Justice Department and the defendant.

If the case falls under the Sherman Act and involves a flagrant violation, such as price fixing among competitors, the Justice Department may file a criminal prosecution in federal court. Upon conviction (which is a felony), the maximum penalty in a criminal case is a $10 million fine for corporations, and a $350,000 fine and three years' imprisonment for individuals.

The FTC also has authority to enforce the Clayton and FTC Acts. Even though it technically has no power to enforce the Sherman Act, any conduct that would violate the Sherman Act will also constitute an "unfair method of competition" under Section 5 of the FTC Act. FTC enforcement, which is always civil in nature because the agency has no power to institute criminal prosecutions, consists of a hearing before an administrative law judge of the agency, with subsequent review by the five-member FTC. If a violation is found, the FTC will issue a "cease and desist order," which is essentially the same as an injunction. Violation of an FTC order is punishable by a penalty of up to $10,000 for each day of noncompliance.

A private party can file a civil lawsuit in federal court claiming a violation of the Sherman or Clayton Acts. The plaintiff sometimes can obtain an injunction in such a suit, but the remedy normally sought is *treble* damage, or three times the plaintiff's actual loss.

We first examine the antitrust laws as they focus on particular kinds of conduct in our discussion of *horizontal restraints of trade and vertical restraints of trade.*

HORIZONTAL RESTRAINTS OF TRADE

Our first inquiry into the behavioral side of antitrust is horizontal restraints of trade—arrangements between two or more competitors that suppress or limit competition. The applicable statute is Section 1 of the Sherman Act which, as stated earlier, prohibits "contracts, combinations, or conspiracies in restraint of trade."

The Requirement of Collusion

Section 1 of the Sherman Act can be applied only if there was collusion between two or more independent entities. Many different terms are used to describe the concept: joint action, concerted action, agreement, combination, conspiracy, and others. As is true of all things that must be proved in the law, the collusion requirement is sometimes obvious and sometimes not. An example of a case in which the requirement obviously was present is *National Society of Professional Engineers v. United States*, 435 U.S. 679 (1978), in which the Court held illegal an ethical rule of the society that prohibited competitive bidding by its 69,000 members. The collusion requirement was so obviously satisfied that it was not even an issue. In such a case, even if the association has been incorporated and thus is a single independent entity, its rules and other actions are in reality the collective actions of its members who explicitly or implicitly granted their approval.

If collusion is not obvious, or admitted by defendants, courts normally have to rely on circumstantial evidence to decide the question. Evidence of any or admi *communications* among the parties can be very important, but such evidence may or may not be strong enough to permit the fact finder to conclude that collusion has taken place. If there is no such evidence, or if it is not sufficient to prove collusion, there must at least be evidence demonstrating that the parties had an *opportunity to conspire*. To establish a circumstantial case of collusion, it usually is also necessary to prove *uniformity of action* among the defendants. Thus, a court is quite unlikely to find that collusion occurred unless the defendants acted in a very similar fashion in pricing, in refusing to deal with another party such as a customer or supplier, or in other important matters.

However, because there can be many legitimate reasons for competing firms to act similarly, it is not enough merely to prove that they did so. This is especially true in a market with a relatively small number of firms. In an oligopoly, for example, it sometimes is inevitable that several companies will make similar pricing moves within a relatively short time span, primarily because they all know what the others are doing and the actions of each one are quite important. In other situations, there also may be reasonable explanations for uniformity; for instance, the same external factors, such as a supply shortage, may have affected all firms simultaneously. If there is substantial uniformity, however, without any legitimate explanation, the situation is suspicious and the firms' parallel conduct is fairly strong evidence of collusion. Also, the greater the degree of uniformity, the more strongly this evidence points toward collusion.

In 1986, the United States Supreme Court made it more difficult for either the government or a private party to prove unlawful collusion. In *Matsushita Electric Industrial Co., Ltd. v. Zenith Radio Corp.*, 475 U.S. 574 (1986), the Court held that there must be *unambiguous* evidence that *tends to exclude the possibility* that the defendant-competitors were acting independently rather than together. Thus, the mere fact that competitors have done the same thing with respect to prices or other factors affecting competition is not enough evidence from which to infer a conspiracy.

The Rule of Reason

Assuming that collusion has been proved, the defendants' action violates Section 1 only if it "restrains trade." What this means is that their conduct must have suppressed or limited competition. Relatively early in the history of the Sherman Act, in *Standard Oil Co. v. United States*, 221 U.S. 1 (1911), the Supreme Court held that Section 1 does not forbid all arrangements that limit competition. If the statute had been interpreted in a literal, all-inclusive fashion, it could have produced strange and inefficient results such as prohibiting the formation of partnerships, corporations, and other business organizations because they involve the combination of individuals who might otherwise be competitors. Instead, the Court adopted the so-called *rule of reason*, under which arrangements are illegal only if they "unreasonably" restrict competition.

The next question, of course, is how do the courts decide whether a particular arrangement is reasonable or unreasonable? In essence, the rule of reason involves an examination of the *purpose* and the *effect* of the conduct being challenged.

Purpose

The firms will always claim that their purpose was legitimate—i.e., not anticompetitive. They may insist, for example, that their motive was to promote ethical conduct in their industry, prevent fraudulent practices by their suppliers or customers, encourage product standardization or safety, or any one of many other lawful purposes. The court will examine all pertinent evidence before deciding whether the defendants are to be believed, or whether their predominant motive was to restrict competition. If the court concludes that their primary motive was to limit competition, a court will not require as much evidence of actual anticompetitive effect as it would if the defendants' motive was apparently benign. If, on the other hand, the court decides that their primary motive was a legitimate one, the court will find a violation of Section 1 only if the evidence indicates that competition will be diminished in a substantial way. There is actually something of a rough sliding scale. The greater the apparent bad effect on competition, the less weight the court will give to any legitimate motive.

Effect on Competition

Perhaps the most important factor in the analysis of an arrangement's effect on competition is the collective *market power* of the group. Market power is evaluated in the same way here as in the more structurally oriented situations of monopoly and merger. A group's aggregate market power does not have to be huge for an arrangement to violate the rule of reason, but if the group's purpose was apparently all right, its power must be substantial enough to convince a court that serious anticompetitive effects are likely to result.

Another factor that often plays a part in the court's analysis is the existence of a *less restrictive alternative*. Thus, if the evidence establishes that the firms could have achieved their claimed objectives by using some other arrangement that would have posed less danger to competition, a court is somewhat more likely to find a violation of Section 1. The existence of a less restrictive alternative does not automatically cause their arrangement to be illegal, but it does tip the scales a bit in that direction, for two reasons. First, it demonstrates that the firms caused a greater negative effect on competition than they really had to. Second, such evidence may even cause a court to view their alleged motive with more suspicion.

If evidence of market power and other relevant factors indicates that a substantial negative effect on competition is possible, the legality of the arrangement sometimes can be saved by clear evidence that it also will have offsetting procompetitive effects. These effects are just positives to offset the negatives, and usually involve some aspect of the arrangement that will improve the efficiency of the market. The court will engage in a rough balancing of these procompetitive effects against the anticompetitive ones to determine which seem to predominate. Examples of procompetitive effects include creating a new kind of market that otherwise would not exist, stimulating competition by bringing more transactions into the market, improving the quality or quantity of information available to buyers and sellers, and so on.

Joint Ventures

Although the term *joint venture* has no precise meaning, it has been likened to a partnership for a limited purpose. For example, a joint research lab is a type of joint venture. When two or more firms collaborate for some reason, their joint undertaking may or may not be a joint venture. The basic characteristics of a legitimate joint venture are (1) a partial pooling of resources by two or more firms, (2) a limited degree of integration of some aspect of the firms' operations, and (3) an intent to accomplish a defined business objective that could not be accomplished as efficiently (or at all) by a single firm. Situations in which joint ventures are commonly accepted as legitimate include those in which extremely large economies of scale, very high risks, or unusually extended long-term payoffs are involved, or where the nature of the product is such that it cannot be produced or marketed efficiently without collaboration between two or more firms.

Joint ventures usually do not violate the antitrust laws, but they can do so on occasion. Section 1 of the Sherman Act is the primarily applicable statute, and joint ventures are normally judged under the rule of reason. If formation of the joint venture involves an asset or stock acquisition, Section 7 of the Clayton Act also can be applied, although the legal standards for joint ventures are basically the same under both statutes.

The risk of illegality obviously is greater when actual or potential competitors are involved. In addition, certain kinds of activities are more likely to limit competition than those involving other kinds of activities. A joint venture might involve matters ranging along a continuum from basic research to applied research, product development, production, promotion and other marketing activities, selling, and finally, distribution. The risk of harm to competition, and thus the degree of scrutiny under the antitrust laws, increases as the activity moves along the continuum away from research. Joint ventures involving activities farther along the continuum, such as production, can be valid, but their justification must be stronger.

Assuming that the basic objectives of the joint venture are legitimate, three basic types of antitrust questions can still be raised. First, the formation of a joint venture occasionally may create dangers to competition that probably will not be outweighed by increased efficiency or other positive effects. This may happen if the venture is just too big—that is, if it is larger than really necessary to accomplish its legitimate objectives. Second, even if the venture is not too large, it may include some *ancillary restriction* that limits competition among the participants more than necessary.

For example, participants might agree to exchange certain kinds of information which, if misused, could make it fairly easy to engage in horizontal price fixing. This restriction would require a very strong justification. Third, the joint venture may harm outsiders who are excluded from participation. This situation is analyzed as described earlier in the discussion of various group activities that tend to exclude others. A Sherman Act section 1 complaint against a true joint venture that arguably has some positive effects on competition will be analyzed under the Rule of Reason.

The following landmark Supreme Court case illustrates most of these aspects of rule-of-reason analysis. In this case, the Court examines (1) motives; (2) market power (although it does not use this term); (3) the fact that the scope of the arrangement seemed to be limited so that it was not any more restrictive than it had to be; and (4) what the judges viewed as offsetting procompetitive effects brought about by taking quite a few transactions from a few large dealers and bringing them into the organized market where information was more accurate and up-to-date and trading more open and competitive.

CHICAGO BOARD OF TRADE v. UNITED STATES
U.S. Supreme Court, 246 U.S. 231 (1918)

In the late 1800s and early 1900s Chicago was the leading grain market in the world, and the Board of Trade was the commercial center through which most of the trading in grain was done. Its 1,600 members included brokers, commission merchants, dealers, millers, manufacturers of corn products, and grain elevator owners. Grain transactions usually took one of three forms: (1) spot sales—sales of grain already in Chicago in railroad cars or elevators ready for immediate delivery; (2) future sales—agreements for delivery of grain at a later time; (3) sales "to arrive"—agreements for delivery of grain which was already in transit to Chicago or which was to be shipped almost immediately from other parts of the Midwest.

On each business day, sessions of the Board of Trade were held at which all bids and sales were publicly made. Spot sales and future sales were made during the regular session between 9:30 a.m. and 1:15 p.m. Special sessions, referred to as the "Call," were held immediately after the close of the regular session. During the Call, which usually lasted about 30 minutes, members of the Board of Trade engaged only in "to arrive" transactions. These transactions usually involved purchases from farmers or small dealers in one of the Midwestern states. Participation in the Call session was limited to members, but they could trade on behalf of nonmembers if they wished. Members also could make any of the three types of transaction privately with each other at any place, either during or after board sessions. Members could engage privately in any type of transaction at any time with nonmembers, but not on the board's premises.

With respect to "to arrive" transactions, a particular market price would be established by the public trading during the short Call session. Until 1906, however, members were not bound by that price during the remainder of the day. In that year the Board of Trade adopted what was known as the "Call rule." The rule, which applied only to "to arrive" transactions, required members to use the market price established at the public Call session when they bought grain in private transactions between the end of that session and 9:30 the next morning.

The government filed suit in federal district court, claiming that the Call rule violated Section 1 of the Sherman Act. The board contended that the purpose and effect of the rule was to bring more of the "to arrive" transactions into the public market at the Call session. By bringing more of these transactions into the public market, the board felt that four or five large grain warehouse owners in Chicago would no longer have such a controlling grip over "to arrive" transactions. The district court, however, ruled that evidence relating to the history and purpose of the rule was irrelevant and issued an injunction against the operation of the rule. The Board of Trade then appealed to the U.S. Supreme Court.

Brandeis, Justice:

Every agreement concerning trade, every regulation of trade, restrains. To bind, to restrain, is of their very essence. The true test of legality is whether the restraint imposed is such as merely regulates and perhaps thereby promotes competition or whether it is such as may suppress or even destroy competition. To determine that question the court must ordinarily consider the facts peculiar to the business to which the restraint is applied; its condition before and after the restraint was imposed; the nature of the restraint and its effect, actual or probable. The history of the restraint, the evil believed to exist, the reason for adopting the particular remedy, the purpose or end sought to be attained, are all relevant facts. This is not because a good intention will save an otherwise objectionable regulation or the reverse; but because knowledge of intent may help the court to interpret facts and to predict consequences. The District Court erred, therefore, in striking from the [Board's] answer allegations concerning evidence on that subject. But the evidence admitted makes it clear that the rule was a reasonable regulation of business consistent with the provisions of the Antitrust Law.

First: The nature of the rule: The restriction was upon the period of price-making. It required members to desist from further price-making after the close of the Call until 9:30 a.m. the next business day: but there was no restriction upon the sending out of bids after close of the Call. Thus, it required members who desired to buy grain "to arrive" to make up their minds before the close of the Call how much they were willing to pay during the interval before the next session of the Board. The rule made it to their interest to attend the Call; and if they did not fill their wants by purchases there, to make the final bid high enough to enable them to purchase from country dealers.

Second: The scope of the rule: It is restricted in operation to grain "to arrive." It applies only to a small part of the grain shipped from day to day to Chicago, and to an even smaller part of the day's sales members were left free to purchase grain already in Chicago from anyone at any price throughout the day. It applies only during a small part of the business day; members were left free to purchase during the sessions of the Board grain "to arrive," at any price, from members anywhere and from nonmembers anywhere except on the premises of the Board. It applied only to grain shipped to Chicago: members were left free to purchase at any price throughout the day from either members or nonmembers, grain "to arrive" at any other market. Country dealers and farmers had available in practically every part of the territory called tributary to Chicago some other market for grain "to arrive."

Thus Missouri, Kansas, Nebraska, and parts of Illinois are also tributary to St. Louis; Nebraska and Iowa, to Omaha; Minnesota, Iowa, South and North Dakota, to Minneapolis or Duluth; Wisconsin and parts of Iowa and of Illinois, to Milwaukee; Ohio, Indiana and parts of Illinois, to Cincinnati; Indiana and parts of Illinois, to Louisville.

Third: The effects of the rule: As it applies to only a small part of the grain shipped to Chicago and to that only during a part of the business day and does not apply at all to grain shipped to other markets, the rule had no appreciable effect on general market prices; nor did it materially affect the total volume of grain coming to Chicago. But within the narrow limits of its operation the rule helped to improve market conditions thus:

(a) It created a public market for grain "to arrive." Before its adoption, bids were made privately. Men had to buy and sell without adequate knowledge of actual market conditions. This was advantageous to all concerned, but particularly so to country dealers and farmers.

(b) It brought into the regular market hours of the Board sessions more of the trading in grain "to arrive."

(c) It brought buyers and sellers into more direct relations; because on the Call they gathered together for a free and open interchange of bids and offers. (d) It distributed the business in grain "to arrive" among a far larger number of Chicago receivers and commission merchants than had been the case there before.

(d) It increased the number of country dealers engaging in this branch of the business; supplied them more regularly with bids from Chicago; and also increased the number of bids received by them from competing markets.

(f) It eliminated risks necessarily incident to a private market, and thus enabled country dealers to do business on a smaller margin. In that way the rule made it possible for them to pay more to farmers without raising the price to consumers.

(g) It enabled country dealers to sell some grain "to arrive" which they would otherwise have been obliged either to ship to Chicago commission merchants or to sell for "future delivery."

(h) It enabled those grain merchants of Chicago who sell to millers and exporters to trade on a smaller margin and, by paying more for grain or selling it for less, to make the Chicago market more attractive for both shippers and buyers of grain....

The decree of the District Court is reversed with directions to dismiss the [complaint].

The Per Se Rule

Also relatively early in the history of the Sherman Act, the Supreme Court recognized that certain types of practices are obviously anticompetitive and do not really have any redeeming social virtues. In such a case, the *per se rule* applies. This means that once a particular type of activity is identified as one that falls within a per se category, it is automatically illegal and the inquiry ends. Of the various horizontal restraints of trade, price fixing, market division, and boycotts are per se illegal. It is very important to understand, however, that the per se rule has its greatest impact in situations where the challenged activity can be easily labeled as price fixing, market division, or a boycott. If there is a close question whether the arrangement should be characterized in this way, the court must analyze its purpose and effect in order to decide how to label it. This analysis is basically the same as in a rule-of-reason case.

Horizontal Price Fixing

Price fixing among competitors is per se illegal. This activity occurs when two or more competitors agree explicitly to charge a specific price, or to set a price floor, but many other arrangements can also constitute price fixing because they substantially interfere with the price-setting function of the market. Some examples include agreements or understandings among competitors to (1) not submit competitive bids; (2) rotate the privilege of being low bidder on contracts; (3) artificially manipulate supply or demand in a way that affects price substantially; (4) not advertise prices; (5) not grant certain discounts; (6) maintain uniformity on a particular term that constitutes a component of price, such as shipping or credit charges; (7) keep prices within a particular range; and even (8) maintain a *ceiling* on prices because this cripples the ability of the free market to set prices and can provide a good disguise for what ends up as an effort to stabilize or even raise prices.

Many other joint arrangements may have an arguable effect on the market's pricing mechanism. If the court is convinced that the parties' main purpose is to suppress price competition, it will probably call the arrangement price fixing and find it per se illegal. As mentioned earlier, however, if there is significant doubt about the question, a court will probably engage in a rule-of-reason type analysis, regardless of whether it uses that phrase. In *Texaco v. Dagher,* 547 U.S. 1 (2006), Texaco and Shell had collaborated in a joint venture, Equilon Enterprises, to refine and sell gasoline in the western United States under the two companies' original brand names. Texaco and Shell service station owners sued under Sherman Section 1 for price fixing after Equilon set a single price for both brands. However, the Supreme Court held that because Texaco and Shell were integrated joint venturers rather than competitors in this very specific situation, the *per se* rule did not apply and the arrangement had to be evaluated under the *rule of reason.*

Horizontal Market Division

Market division among competitors is also per se illegal, assuming that such division is found to be the primary objective of a particular arrangement. The same rule can be applied to market division agreements involving potential competitors making decisions about entering new markets. Market division arrangements can take at least three forms: (1) in a *territorial* market division, the firms agree to refrain from competing with each other in designated geographic areas; (2) in a *customer allocation* arrangement, the firms assign particular customers or classes of customers to each seller and agree not to solicit customers of another seller; and (3) in a *product line* division, the firms agree to limit their activities to particular types of products or services so as to avoid competing with each other.

Group Boycotts

A firm ordinarily has freedom to choose those with whom it will transact business. However, when two or more parties agree not to deal with some other party, antitrust problems arise. When the agreeing parties are competitors and their primary purpose apparently is to curtail competition, the resulting *boycott* is per se illegal. Two or more firms will violate Section 1, for example, if they agree to quit selling to a customer because the latter is trying to integrate upstream and become their competitor. Likewise, a group of firms would be engaged in an illegal boycott if they agreed to stop selling to certain customers unless those customers quit buying from a competitor of those in the agreeing group. A similar violation would occur if the group agreed not to buy from a supplier unless that supplier refrained from selling to a competitor or potential competitor of the group. Boycotts are sometimes used to drive a firm out of a market, keep it from entering in the first place, or discipline a firm by "showing it who's boss" and thus convincing it to stop competing so aggressively.

Although labeling problems occur with respect to all of the per se categories, they seem to be especially troublesome in the case of boycotts. The reason is that there are many group activities that have legitimate reasons for existing, but that also may have the tendency to exclude other firms. Suppose for example, that many of the automotive repair businesses in Missouri, Kansas, and Oklahoma form an organization called the Midwest Auto Repair Association (MARA). The stated purposes of the group are to promote the auto repair business in various ways and encourage high ethical standards in the industry. Like any organization, MARA establishes rules for membership that might require such things as full-time participation in the auto repair business, a fee to cover the organization's costs, fewer than a specified number of verified customer complaints during a given period of time, and so on. Jones does not meet one of the requirements and is either denied membership initially or is forced out later. He may claim to be the victim of a boycott.

Similar problems can arise if a group of firms in the same industry tries to establish uniform product standards for the purpose of either safety or reducing customer confusion and dissatisfaction. One firm's product does not meet the standard and thus does not receive the approval of the group. The firm may complain of an illegal boycott.

Yet another example arises where a group of firms pool their resources to develop a facility such as a research lab. This can be legitimate where the great cost, risk, and uncertainty of constructing a major facility or engaging in a particular undertaking is too much for a single firm. (This last example describes a "joint venture," which will be discussed shortly.) A competitor that is not permitted to join the venture may claim a boycott.

When confronted with such claims, courts first look at the group's apparent purpose. If the primary purpose was to exclude others and achieve some restriction on competition, it will be per se illegal as a boycott. If the main purpose appears to have been a legitimate one, the court engages in a rule-of-reason type of analysis. The court will try to determine just how important it is for a firm to participate. (This is just another kind of inquiry into a group's collective market power.) If exclusion really does not harm a firm's ability to compete in the relevant market, the arrangement is legal. On the other hand, if participation is very important to a firm's ability to compete, the rules or restrictions that have the result of excluding others must be *reasonable*. To be reasonable, they must (1) have a logical relationship to the group's legitimate objectives, and (2) not exclude others any more than is necessary to accomplish those objectives.

Following is a 2018 decision by the U.S. Court of Appeals for the Ninth Circuit in a case involving an alleged bid-rigging scheme in connection with foreclosed real estate in California. Bid-rigging is sometimes spoken of as a separate type of antitrust violation, but in actuality, it is simply one form of horizontal price fixing.

United States v. Joyce
United States Court of Appeals, Ninth Circuit, 895 F.3d 673 (2018)

Defendant Thomas Joyce was charged by indictment with conspiring to suppress and restrain competition by rigging bids, in violation of the Sherman Act. Joyce brought a pretrial motion, arguing that the matter should be adjudicated under a rule of reason analysis rather than the per se analysis advocated by the government. The district court ruled against Joyce, concluding the bid-rigging scheme alleged in the indictment was illegal per se under Section 1 of the Sherman Act. Joyce proceeded to trial and was convicted. He challenges his conviction, arguing the district court erred by refusing to apply the rule of reason analysis to the bid-rigging charge.

The felony indictment in this matter alleged that Joyce participated in a bid-rigging scheme involving foreclosed real property in Contra Costa County, California. Specifically, the indictment charged that Joyce and his coconspirators agreed to suppress competition by refraining from bidding against each other at public auctions. The means and methods alleged included: agreeing not to compete to purchase selected properties at public auctions; designating which conspirators would win selected properties at public auctions; refraining from bidding for selected properties at public auctions; purchasing selected properties at public auctions at artificially suppressed prices; negotiating, making, and receiving payoffs for agreeing not to compete with coconspirators; and holding second, private auctions, to determine the payoff amounts and choose the conspirator who would be awarded the selected property.

Prior to trial, Joyce filed a "Motion to Adjudicate Government's Sherman Act Allegations Pursuant to the Rule of Reason." In the motion, Joyce asked the district court to decide that the per se rule is inapplicable to the bid-rigging charges. Under the per se rule, arguments and evidence relating to, inter alia, the procompetitive nature of the conduct at issue are not admissible. The district court denied the motion, concluding that bid rigging "falls squarely within the per se category." Joyce was convicted at trial and sentenced to federal prison for twelve months and one day. He appealed, asserting that the district court erred by denying his motion and refusing to admit evidence that allegedly shows the procompetitive benefits of his conduct.

MURPHY, Circuit Judge:

Section 1 of the Sherman Act prohibits "Every contract, combination in the form of trust or otherwise, or conspiracy, in restraint of trade or commerce." Despite the broad language used in the statute, the Supreme Court has held that Section 1 prohibits only agreements that *unreasonably* restrain trade. *Standard Oil Co. of N.J. v. United States*, 221 U.S. 1 (1911); Board of Trade of Chicago. v. United States, 246 U.S. 231 (1918). Typically, the determination of whether a particular agreement in restraint of trade is unreasonable involves a factual inquiry commonly known as the "rule of reason." The rule of reason weighs legitimate justifications for a restraint against any anticompetitive effects.

The rule of reason inquiry, however, is inapplicable if "the restraint falls into a category of agreements which have been determined to be per se illegal." *United States v. Brown*, 936 F.2d 1042 (9th Cir. 1991). The per se rule is applied when the practice appears on its face to be one that would always or almost always tend to restrict competition and decrease output. *NCAA v. Bd. of Regents of Univ. of Okla.*, 468 U.S. 85 (1984). Such agreements or practices are conclusively presumed to be unreasonable because of their pernicious effect on competition and lack of any redeeming virtue. If a business arrangement is a type conclusively presumed to be unreasonable, the government is relieved of any obligation to prove the unreasonableness of the specific scheme at issue and any business justification for the defendant's conduct is neither relevant nor admissible. In a criminal antitrust prosecution, the government need not prove specific intent to produce anticompetitive effects where a per se violation is alleged. [The same is true of a civil lawsuit by a private party where the defendant's conduct is per se illegal.]

The Supreme Court has held that horizontal price fixing is a per se violation of the Sherman Act. *United States v. McKesson & Robbins, Inc.*, 351 U.S. 305 (1956). It has been held too often to require elaboration that price fixing is contrary to the policy of competition underlying the Sherman Act. Horizontal price fixing, division of markets, group boycotts, tying arrangements, and output limitations are restraints of trade the Supreme Court has held to be within the per se category. Although this court has never expressly held that bid rigging is a per se violation of Section 1 of the Sherman Act, bid rigging is a form of horizontal price fixing. In *United States v. Fenzl*, 670 F.3d 778, 780 (7th Cir. 2012), the Court of Appeals for the Seventh Circuit described bid rigging as "a form of price fixing in which bidders agree to eliminate competition among them, as by taking turns being the low bidder." The Eighth Circuit has held likewise. *See United States v. Bensinger Co.*, 430 F.2d 584 (8th Cir. 1970) (holding that bid rigging is "a price-fixing agreement of the simplest kind, and price-fixing agreements are per se violations of the Sherman Act"). Bid rigging is, therefore, a per se violation of the Sherman Act.

Joyce does not contest that the conduct described in the indictment was classic bid rigging or that the evidence presented at trial was insufficient to establish he engaged in bid rigging. Instead, he argues the per se rule should not apply to the scheme in which he participated because that scheme, which he says involved "a few participants in a narrow set of public foreclosure auctions," did not have any "demonstrable effect on the pricing or quantity of the real estate sold." When a defendant's conduct falls squarely into a category of economic restraint necessarily prohibited by Section 1 of the Sherman Act, however, the per se rule applies and the need to study the reasonableness of an individual restraint on trade is eliminated. A case-by-case analysis is unnecessary when the restraint on trade falls into a category of agreements which have been determined to be per se illegal. Accordingly, Joyce's assertion that the district court erred by not allowing him to present evidence to the jury regarding the actual effect his conduct had on the market for foreclosed properties is misplaced. The per se rule eliminates the need to inquire into the specific effects of certain restraints of trade. The very purpose of the per se rule is to avoid the necessity for an incredibly complicated and prolonged economic investigation into the entire history of the industry involved, as well as related industries, in an effort to determine at large whether a particular restraint has been unreasonable.

Joyce's related argument that the courts are not sufficiently familiar with non-judicial public foreclosure auctions was rejected by the Supreme Court decades ago. In 1982, the Court held that the per se rule is applicable to price-fixing agreements, of which bid rigging is a form, regardless of the industry in which the conduct occurred. *Maricopa County. Medical Society*, 457 U.S. at 349–51 (applying the per se rule to a price-fixing agreement among health care providers). Rejecting two arguments identical to the ones Joyce makes here, the Court stated:

We are equally unpersuaded by the argument that we should not apply the *per se* rule in this case because the judiciary has little antitrust experience in the health care industry. The argument quite obviously is inconsistent with [our cases holding that horizontal price fixing is per se illegal]. In unequivocal terms, we have stated that, whatever may be its peculiar problems and characteristics, the Sherman Act, so far as price-fixing agreements are concerned, establishes one uniform rule applicable to all industries alike. We also stated that the elimination of so-called competitive evils in an industry is no legal justification for price-fixing agreements. Finally, the argument that the *per se* rule must be re-justified for every industry that has not been subject to significant antitrust litigation ignores the rationale for *per se* rules, which in part is to avoid the necessity for an incredibly complicated and prolonged economic investigation into the entire history of the industry involved, as well as related industries, in an effort to determine at large whether a particular restraint has been unreasonable—an inquiry so often wholly fruitless when undertaken.

The respondents' principal argument is that the *per se* rule is inapplicable because their agreements are alleged to have procompetitive justifications. The argument indicates a misunderstanding of the *per se* concept. The anticompetitive potential inherent in all price-fixing agreements justifies their facial invalidation even if procompetitive justifications are offered for some. Those claims of enhanced competition are so unlikely to prove significant in any particular case that we adhere to the rule of law that is justified in its general application.

The Court's holding in *Maricopa County* makes it clear that for purposes of the per se rule, it is irrelevant that Joyce's bid rigging activities took place in any particular industry or during a downturn in the broader economy.

Because Joyce's appellate arguments fail as a matter of law, his attempt to persuade this court that his conduct was procompetitive is unavailing. The government is not required to prove specific intent to produce anticompetitive effects where a per se violation is alleged. Because bid rigging is per se illegal under Section 1 of the Sherman Act, the district court did not err by refusing to permit Joyce to introduce evidence of the alleged ameliorative effects of his conduct. Accordingly, the judgment of the district court is affirmed.

Competition between Patented and Generic Pharmaceutical Drugs

Pharmaceutical companies invest years and many millions of dollars in the development of new drugs. Many times they are able to patent the resulting medications and produce what are sometimes called "brand-name" drugs. Patents on drugs are perhaps the most valuable kinds of patents in existence. Although the availability of patent protection and the large profits it can produce because of the absence of competition attract much more investment to research and development in the search for new drugs, some of these patents are not valid. In such a situation, consumers suffer from paying unnecessarily high profits.

Generic drug manufacturers produce pharmaceuticals that are essentially the same as the patented ones. They cannot do so legally, of course, while the corresponding brand-name drug is still protected by a valid patent, and making the huge investment required to manufacture and sell the drug is too risky without some way to test the patent's validity.

In 1984, Congress enacted the Hatch-Waxman Act that set up a procedure to allow generic manufacturers to test a drug patent's validity with less cost and risk. Patented drugs that have been approved for marketing by the Food and Drug Administration (FDA) are listed in the so-called "Green Book." The law permits a generic manufacturer to file a petition called an "Abbreviated New Drug Application (ANDA)," which, if ultimately successful, will not only allow the generic maker to make and sell the drug in competition with the currently patented one, but also to make use of all of the clinical test data that the patent owner submitted to the FDA as part of the approval process. This saves the generic maker from having to duplicate the large investment already made by the drug's original developer (patent owner) in conducting expensive clinical trials.

The procedure is only fair, of course, and only legal, if the generic drug maker proves that the drug's patent is invalid. When the generic company files the ANDA, this action is treated legally as an act of patent infringement even though that firm has not yet made or sold the drug. The patent owner will always follow this with the filing of a patent infringement lawsuit in federal district court. In most cases, infringement is clear and not even an issue, the only issue for the court being validity. The generic maker tries to prove patent invalidity in the same way any other company would do in other circumstances. If the challenger is successful, it may then legally make and sell the drug, which normally reduces the drug's price dramatically.

A lot of money is needed to pay attorneys, expert witnesses, and other legal expense on the part of the generic drug company to challenge the validity of the brand-name drug company's patent. Recognizing that the public would be served by having generic makers institute these challenges for the purpose of weeding out drug patents that should not have been granted, Congress provided an additional incentive for the generic to do so. Thus, the Hatch-Waxman Act gives the successful generic challenger a 180-day exclusive during which it is the only company other than the drug's originator that can market the drug. During this period, no other generic manufacturer is permitted to sell the drug, thus enabling the challenger to not only recoup its investment in taking on the patent owner, but also earn greater-than-competitive profits from not having to compete with other generics. After other generic makers are allowed to enter the market, prices to consumers often fall even more than they did when the first generic began marketing the drug.

In this situation, one can observe that a genuine temptation is likely to exist for the originator (owner of the now-invalid patent) to make a deal in which the originator and the now-successful generic challenger agree on a "pay-for-delay" arrangement. Such an agreement will involve a payment of money or other consideration from the originator to the generic that is larger than the profit the challenger would probably earn during its 180-day exclusive (with two companies selling the drug), but smaller than the profit to be made by the originator during that time with no competition at all. The U.S. Supreme Court, *in FTC v. Actavis*, Inc., 570 U.S. 136 (2013), held that when such a pay-for-delay agreement can be proved, it will usually be an antitrust law violation under Section 1 of the Sherman Act as an illegal contract, combination, or conspiracy in restraint of trade.

VERTICAL RESTRAINTS OF TRADE

When firms operating at different levels of the distribution chain enter some arrangement that may harm competition, we call it a *vertical restraint of trade.*

Resale Price Maintenance

Nature and Effects

Resale price maintenance (RPM), which is also called vertical price fixing, occurs when a seller and buyer agree on the price at which the buyer will resell to its own customers. RPM usually is a method by which a manufacturer or other supplier limits price competition among its dealers or distributors in the market for resale of the product. Competition among such dealers for sales of the manufacturer's product is called *intrabrand competition,* in contrast with the *interbrand competition* that occurs between different manufacturers' brands.

RPM has always been controversial. Many economists and legal scholars believe that RPM and other forms of restriction on intrabrand competition are usually employed to increase efficiency. They claim that these limits on intrabrand competition can be used by a manufacturer to make sure that its dealers invest in the facilities, trained personnel, and promotional activities necessary to stimulate sales and properly serve customers. If one dealer makes such an investment and thereby stimulates demand for the manufacturer's product, but another dealer does not, the latter has lower costs and can underprice the former. The first dealer will then be discouraged and will stop making such investments. Because of some dealers' *free riding,* the argument goes, many (or most) of the manufacturer's dealers will not do those things necessary to compete vigorously with other brands. If the manufacturer uses RPM to put a floor below its dealers' resale prices, however, some argue that this will solve the problem by reducing dealers' incentives to take a free ride on the investment of other dealers. The incentive is gone because they cannot use their lower costs to underprice and take customers from another dealer. Those arguing that the law should treat RPM very leniently also claim that, because any potential harm to competition is only intrabrand, customers are protected so long as competition among different brands remains active.

Other experts have serious doubts about the "free rider" justification for RPM. They argue that free rider problems are really not that common, and that many cases of resale price maintenance have involved products like toothpaste or blue jeans, for which there is not much need for the kinds of costly facilities or services that are susceptible to free riding. They also claim that, even if free rider problems are common, other means are available for solving them that do not cause similar harm to price competition. Such means include contractual commitments from dealers to provide the necessary facilities, personnel, promotion, and services. Opponents of RPM claim that the true reason for the practice often may be the manufacturer's desire to keep dealers' prices up and relieve them from intrabrand competition so that they do not pressure the manufacturer to lower its prices to them. They also sometimes argue that RPM can be used as a device to carry out a horizontal price-fixing conspiracy among dealers.

Legal Standards

The statute applicable to RPM is Section 1 of the Sherman Act. From the early days of the Sherman Act, RPM was viewed as per se illegal. This rule was applied to situations in which the seller imposed either maximum *or* minimum resale prices on the dealers or distributors to which it sold. In 1997, in *State Oil Co. v. Khan*, 522 U.S. 3 (1997), the U.S. Supreme Court changed the per se rule to the rule of reason for *maximum* RPM. Ten years later, in the case below, the Supreme Court changed from the per se rule to the rule of reason for *minimum* RPM.

LEEGIN CREATIVE LEATHER PRODUCTS, INC. v. PSKS, INC.
127 S.Ct. 2705 (2007)

Petitioner, Leegin Creative Leather Products, Inc. (Leegin), designs, manufactures, and distributes leather goods and accessories. In 1991, Leegin began to sell belts under the brand name "Brighton." The Brighton brand has now expanded into a variety of women's fashion accessories. It is sold across the United States in over 5,000 retail establishments, for the most part independent, small boutiques and specialty stores. Leegin's president, Jerry Kohl, also has an interest in about 70 stores that sell Brighton products. Leegin asserts that, at least for its products, small retailers treat customers better, provide customers more services, and make their shopping experience more satisfactory than do larger, often impersonal retailers. Kohl explained: "[W]e want the consumers to get a different experience than they get in Sam's Club or in Wal-Mart. And you can't get that kind of experience or support or customer service from a store like Wal-Mart."

Respondent, PSKS, Inc. (PSKS), operates Kay's Kloset, a women's apparel store in Lewisville, Texas. Kay's Kloset buys from about 75 different manufacturers and at one time sold the Brighton brand. It first started purchasing Brighton goods from Leegin in 1995. Once it began selling the brand, the store promoted Brighton. For example, it ran Brighton advertisements and had Brighton days in the store. Kay's Kloset became the destination retailer in the area to buy Brighton products. Brighton was the store's most important brand and once accounted for 40 to 50 percent of its profits.

In 1997, Leegin instituted the "Brighton Retail Pricing and Promotion Policy." Following the policy, Leegin refused to sell to retailers that discounted Brighton goods below suggested prices. The policy contained an exception for products not selling well that the retailer did not plan on reordering. In the letter to retailers establishing the policy, Leegin stated:

> In this age of mega stores like Macy's, Bloomingdales, May Co. and others, consumers are perplexed by promises of product quality and support of product which we believe is lacking in these large stores. Consumers are further confused by the ever popular sale, sale, sale, etc. We, at Leegin, choose to break away from the pack by selling [at] specialty stores; specialty stores that can offer the customer great quality merchandise, superb service, and support the Brighton product 365 days a year on a consistent basis. We realize that half the equation is Leegin producing great Brighton product and the other half is you, our retailer, creating great looking stores selling our products in a quality manner.

Leegin adopted the policy to give its retailers sufficient margins to provide customers the service central to its distribution strategy. It also expressed concern that discounting harmed Brighton's brand image and reputation.

A year after instituting the pricing policy, Leegin introduced a marketing strategy known as the "Heart Store Program." ... In December 2002, Leegin discovered Kay's Kloset had been marking down Brighton's entire line by 20 percent. Kay's Kloset contended it placed Brighton products on sale to compete with nearby retailers who also were undercutting Leegin's suggested prices. Leegin, nonetheless, requested that Kay's Kloset cease discounting. Its request refused, Leegin stopped selling to the store. The loss of the Brighton brand had a considerable negative impact on the store's revenue from sales.

PSKS sued Leegin, alleging that Leegin had violated the antitrust laws by entering into agreements with retailers to charge only those prices fixed by Leegin. Leegin planned to introduce expert testimony describing the procompetitive effects of its pricing policy. The district Court excluded the testimony, relying on the rule established by the Supreme Court in Dr. Miles Medical Co. v. John D. Park & Sons Co., 220 U. S. 373 (1911), that it is per se illegal under §1 of the Sherman Act for a manufacturer to agree with its distributor to set the minimum price the distributor can charge for the manufacturer's goods. At trial PSKS *argued that the Heart Store program, among other things, demonstrated Leegin and its retailers had agreed to fix prices. The jury agreed with PSKS and awarded it $1.2 million. Pursuant to §1 of the Sherman Act, the district court trebled the damages and reimbursed PSKS for its attorney's fees and costs. It entered judgment against Leegin in the amount of $3,975,000.80. The Court of Appeals for the Fifth Circuit affirmed, and Leegin appealed.*

Kennedy, Justice:

Section 1 of the Sherman Act prohibits "[e]very contract, combination in the form of trust or otherwise, or conspiracy, in restraint of trade or commerce among the several States." The rule of reason is the accepted standard for testing whether a practice restrains trade in violation of §1. Under this rule, the fact finder weighs all of the circumstances of a case in deciding whether a restrictive practice should be prohibited as imposing an unreasonable restraint on competition. Appropriate factors to take into account include specific information about the relevant business" and the restraint's history, nature, and effect. Whether the businesses involved have market power is a further, significant consideration. In its design and function the rule distinguishes between restraints with anticompetitive effect that are harmful to the consumer and restraints stimulating competition that are in the consumer's best interest.

The rule of reason does not govern all restraints. Some types are deemed unlawful *per se*. The *per se* rule, treating categories of restraints as necessarily illegal, eliminates the need to study the reasonableness of an individual restraint in light of the real market forces at work. Restraints that are *per se* unlawful include horizontal agreements among competitors to fix prices or to divide markets. Resort to *per se* rules is confined to restraints, like those mentioned, that would always or almost always tend to restrict competition and decrease output. As a consequence, the *per se* rule is appropriate only after courts have had considerable experience with the type of restraint at issue, and only if courts can predict with confidence that it would be invalidated in all or almost all instances under the rule of reason . It should come as no surprise, then, that "we have expressed reluctance to adopt *per se* rules with regard to restraints imposed in the context of business relationships where the economic impact of certain practices is not immediately obvious.

The Court has interpreted *Dr. Miles Medical Co.* v. *John D. Park & Sons Co.*, 220 U. S. 373 (1911) , as establishing a *per se* rule against a vertical agreement between a manufacturer and its distributor to set minimum resale prices. ... *Dr. Miles* treated vertical agreements a manufacturer makes with its distributors as analogous to a horizontal combination among competing distributors. ... Though each side of the debate can find sources to support its position, it suffices to say here that economics literature is replete with procompetitive justifications for a manufacturer's use of resale price maintenance. In the theoretical literature, it is essentially undisputed that minimum resale price maintenance can have procompetitive effects and that under a variety of market conditions it is unlikely to have anticompetitive effects. There is a widespread consensus [among economists] that permitting a manufacturer to control the price at which its goods are sold may promote *inter*brand competition and consumer welfare in a variety of ways. Even those more skeptical of resale price maintenance acknowledge it can have procompetitive effects, [some stating that] "the overall balance between benefits and costs of resale price maintenance is probably close."

Absent vertical price restraints, the retail services that enhance interbrand competition might be underprovided. This is because discounting retailers can free ride on retailers who furnish services and then capture some of the increased demand those services generate. Consumers might learn, for example, about the benefits of a manufacturer's product from a retailer that invests in fine showrooms, offers product demonstrations, or hires and trains knowledgeable employees. Or consumers might decide to buy the product because they see it in a retail establishment that has a reputation for selling high-quality merchandise. If the consumer can then buy the product from a retailer that discounts because it has not spent capital providing services or developing a quality reputation, the high-service retailer will lose sales to the discounter, forcing it to cut back its services to a level lower than consumers would otherwise prefer. Minimum resale price maintenance alleviates the problem because it prevents the discounter from undercutting the service provider. With price competition decreased, the manufacturer's retailers compete among themselves over services.

Resale price maintenance, in addition, can increase interbrand competition by facilitating market entry for new firms and brands. New manufacturers and manufacturers entering new markets can use the restrictions in order to induce competent and aggressive retailers to make the kind of investment of capital and labor that is often required in the distribution of products unknown to the consumer. New products and new brands are essential to a dynamic economy, and if markets can be penetrated by using resale price maintenance there is a procompetitive effect. Resale price maintenance can also increase interbrand competition by encouraging retailer services that would not be provided even absent free riding. It may be difficult and inefficient for a manufacturer to make and enforce a contract with a retailer specifying the different services the retailer must perform. Offering the retailer a guaranteed margin and threatening termination if it does not live up to expectations may be the most efficient way to expand the manufacturer's market share by inducing the retailer's performance and allowing it to use its own initiative and experience in providing valuable services….

While vertical agreements setting minimum resale prices can have procompetitive justifications, they may have anticompetitive effects in other cases; and unlawful price fixing, designed solely to obtain monopoly profits, is an ever present temptation. Resale price maintenance may, for example, facilitate a manufacturer cartel. An unlawful cartel will seek to discover if some manufacturers are undercutting the cartel's fixed prices. Resale price maintenance could assist the cartel in identifying price-cutting manufacturers who benefit from the lower prices they offer. Resale price maintenance, furthermore, could discourage a manufacturer from cutting prices to retailers with the concomitant benefit of cheaper prices to consumers.

Vertical price restraints also might be used to organize cartels at the retailer level. A group of retailers might collude to fix prices to consumers and then compel a manufacturer to aid the unlawful arrangement with resale price maintenance. In that instance the manufacturer does not establish the practice to stimulate services or to promote its brand but to give inefficient retailers higher profits. Retailers with better distribution systems and lower cost structures would be prevented from charging lower prices by the agreement.

A horizontal cartel among competing manufacturers or competing retailers that decreases output or reduces competition in order to increase price is, and ought to be, *per se* unlawful. To the extent a vertical agreement setting minimum resale prices is entered upon to facilitate either type of cartel, it, too, would need to be held unlawful under the rule of reason. This type of agreement may also be useful evidence for a plaintiff attempting to prove the existence of a horizontal cartel.

Resale price maintenance, furthermore, can be abused by a powerful manufacturer or retailer. A dominant retailer, for example, might request resale price maintenance to forestall innovation in distribution that decreases costs. A manufacturer might consider it has little choice but to accommodate the retailer's demands for vertical price restraints if the manufacturer believes it needs access to the retailer's distribution network. A manufacturer with market power, by comparison, might use resale price maintenance to give retailers an incentive not to sell the products of smaller rivals or new entrants. As should be evident, the potential anticompetitive consequences of vertical price restraints must not be ignored or underestimated.

Notwithstanding the risks of unlawful conduct, it cannot be stated with any degree of confidence that resale price maintenance always or almost always tends to restrict competition and decrease output.… Resale price maintenance, it is true, does have economic dangers. If the rule of reason were to apply to vertical price restraints, courts would have to be diligent in eliminating their anticompetitive uses from the market. This is a realistic objective, and certain factors are relevant to the inquiry. For example, the number of manufacturers that make use of the practice in a given industry can provide important instruction. When only a few manufacturers lacking market power adopt the practice, there is little likelihood it is facilitating a manufacturer cartel, for a cartel then can be undercut by rival manufacturers. Likewise, a retailer cartel is unlikely when only a single manufacturer in a competitive market uses resale price maintenance. Interbrand competition would divert consumers to lower priced substitutes and eliminate any gains to retailers from their price-fixing agreement over a single brand. Resale price maintenance should be subject to more careful scrutiny, by contrast, if many competing manufacturers adopt the practice. …

The rule of reason is designed and used to eliminate anticompetitive transactions from the market. This standard principle applies to vertical price restraints. A party alleging injury from a vertical agreement setting minimum resale prices will have, as a general matter, the information and resources available to show the existence of the agreement and its scope of operation. As courts gain experience considering the effects of these restraints by applying the rule of reason over the course of decisions, they can establish the litigation structure to ensure the rule operates to eliminate anticompetitive restraints from the market and to provide more guidance to businesses. Courts can, for example, devise rules over time for offering proof, or even presumptions where justified, to make the rule of reason a fair and efficient way to prohibit anticompetitive restraints and to promote procompetitive ones.…

For these reasons the Court's decision in *Dr. Miles Medical Co.* is now overruled. Vertical price restraints are to be judged according to the rule of reason.

Proving a Vertical Agreement

"Suggested" resale prices at the retail level are quite common. They do not constitute RPM unless there is evidence that there really has been an agreement (either voluntary or coerced) that gives the manufacturer or other supplier effective control over the dealer's resale prices. Although the law recognized that a RPM agreement could be implicit, i.e., inferred from circumstances, today there must be clear evidence of an explicit agreement.

Historically, one of the most difficult issues in this area involves the extent to which a seller lawfully may use a *refusal to deal* in an attempt to control buyers' resale prices. In *United States v. Colgate & Co.,* 250 U.S. 300 (1919), the Supreme Court stated that a "unilateral refusal to deal" cannot violate Section 1 of the Sherman Act even if controlling resale prices is the seller's ultimate goal. In other words, so long as a seller acts entirely on its own ("unilaterally") it can refuse to sell to anyone it chooses, regardless of the motive. For many years, courts struggled to distinguish between unilateral action by the seller and action that is part of an RPM arrangement between the seller and buyer. Today, a refusal to deal must clearly be an effort by the seller to enforce a definite RPM agreement for there to be any possibility of illegality.

Vertical Nonprice Restrictions

Nature and Effects

Vertical restrictions may relate to matters other than price. The vertical nonprice restrictions (VNRs) that can cause some concern under Section 1 of the Sherman Act generally are those involving some type of market division. VNRs take many forms, depending on several factors. These factors include the relative bargaining power of the manufacturer and its dealers or distributors, and the nature of the product and the markets in which it sells.

One type of VNR is the *territorial exclusive,* in which M, the manufacturer, guarantees its dealers that they will have the exclusive right to market M's product in their respective geographic areas. In order to honor this arrangement with each dealer, M obviously must keep all dealers from reselling outside their own areas. Because this restriction places a contractual limitation on M's freedom, M will not use exclusive territories in its distribution system unless it has relatively less bargaining power than its dealers. More often, M will use *territorial and customer restrictions,* without any promise of exclusive territories. Such an arrangement requires dealers or distributors to resell only within their respective territories or only to particular customers, but does not guarantee them exclusive rights to sell in those areas or to those customers. A similar provision that restricts dealers somewhat less is the *area of primary responsibility,* which does not absolutely prohibit a dealer from reselling outside its designated territory but requires only that the territory be thoroughly served before sales can be made outside the area. Another fairly common provision is the *location requirement,* which requires a dealer to sell only from a specified location. In most cases, a location requirement has the same effect as a territorial restriction.

Like RPM, all forms of VNRs have the common characteristic of limiting intrabrand competition. Also like RPM, there is a longstanding debate about the competitive benefits and dangers of VNRs. Today, and commonly during the past, the prevailing attitude toward these restrictions has been more favorable than the attitude toward RPM. Generally, the feeling has been that VNRs are more likely than RPM (1) to be based on legitimate motives and (2) to help intrabrand competition more than they hurt intrabrand competition. A significant number of authorities think, however, that the law should not treat VNRs and RPM any differently because they are usually employed for the same purposes, have basically the same effects, and can be difficult to distinguish in practice.

Legal Standards

The legal status of VNRs has varied over the years. Until 1967, they were analyzed under the rule of reason. In that year, a decision of the U.S. Supreme Court caused some kinds of nonprice restriction on dealers to be per se illegal. This decision was overruled by the Court in 1977, and since then the rule of reason has been applied to all forms of VNRs.

In the case of VNRs, the question of motive is usually not as important as it can be when the rule of reason is applied to horizontal restrictions. Courts generally accept as legitimate M's objective of using a VNR to limit intrabrand competition, so long as there apparently is some business justification for the limitation. Under the rule of reason, M's market share will be the most important factor. If it is below approximately 10 percent, the restriction usually will be legal without further inquiry. If the share is at or above this level, courts normally will look at other factors. Other factors that could increase the chances of illegality in a close case include (1) evidence that *interbrand competition* in this particular market is not very strong, and that intrabrand competition is especially important; (2) evidence that most other manufacturers in this market also use such restrictions to limit *intrabrand competition* among their dealers; and (3) evidence that M selected a form of VNR that limits intrabrand competition much more than is really necessary under the circumstances.

In the following case, the U.S. Supreme Court switched from the per se rule back to the rule of reason for judging VNRs. The Court's discussion outlines and adopts some of the arguments made by those who feel that VNRs usually produce more economic benefits than harms.

Tying Agreements

Nature and Effects

When one party agrees to supply (sell, lease, etc.) a product or service only on the condition that the customer also take another product or service, a *tying agreement* has been made. The desired item is the *tying* product, and the item the customer is required to take is the tied product. Tying agreements are scrutinized under both Section 1 of the Sherman Act and Section 3 of the Clayton Act.

An early landmark case provides a clear example of tying. In *IBM v. United States,* 298 U.S. 131 (1936), IBM was found guilty of illegal tying by requiring all customers leasing its tabulating machines to also purchase their tabulating cards from IBM. In 2003, Visa and MasterCard settled a lawsuit brought by Wal-Mart (and claiming $3 billion in damages) that alleged defendants had illegally tied use of debit cards to credit card purchases. And in 2004, the EU fined Microsoft $600 million for, among other things, incorporating a media player into its Windows computer operating system and thereby "tying" the two products together.

The main concern about tying is that a supplier may use power in one market (the market for the *tying* product) to distort competition in another market (the market for the *tied* product). Such distortion can occur, it is argued, because the supplier's sales of the tied product are not based on the independent competitive merits of that product.

Several different motivations may lead a supplier to use tying arrangements. In some cases, the supplier may be trying to use the power it has in the tying market to expand its power in the tied market. Such a practice is sometimes referred to as leveraging. There is quite a bit of debate among experts as to the extent to which power actually can be leveraged from one market to another.

A supplier also might use tying in an attempt to *protect its goodwill.* This could be the motive, for example, where the supplier sells or leases product X, and where product Y must be used in conjunction with X. The supplier may be concerned that some customers might use inferior versions of Y that will cause X to perform poorly, and thus hurt the reputation of X. In such a case, the supplier might require buyers to buy the supplier's own version of Y along with X. The general feeling under the antitrust laws, however, has been that the supplier should accomplish its objective by requiring the customer to use any version of Y that meets specifications set by the supplier, unless the use of specifications is very difficult.

Another possible motive for tying is to *discriminate among customers* according to the intensity with which they use the supplier's product. Suppose that M manufactures a machine used by food processing companies to inject salt into foods during processing. If M feels that customers who use the machine more may be willing to pay more for it, M may try to charge them based on intensity of use so as to maximize its total revenues. Direct metering may be very difficult. Sometimes, however, intensity of use is directly proportional to the amount of a second product the customer uses in connection with M's product. In the case of the salt-dispensing machine, intensity of use can be measured by the amount of salt used by the customer. Thus, M may try to measure intensity by requiring customers of its machines also to buy its salt. Through the salt sales, M's total revenue will be greater in transactions with high-intensity users.

Legal Standards

Tying can occur only if two separate products are involved. Often this is obvious, but sometimes it is not, as for example in the case of various options on new automobiles. Generally, a transaction will be viewed as including two separate products if the evidence demonstrates that there really are two separate markets in which the different items are commonly demanded. However, even if there are two separate markets, courts usually will treat a transaction as involving only one product if packaging two items is significantly more efficient than selling them separately.

If there are two separate products, tying is illegal only if the supplier has *substantial power in the market for the tying product.* The reason for this requirement is the generally accepted proposition that tying cannot cause any substantial harm in the tied market unless the supplier has quite a bit of power in the tying market. Market power is measured in the same way here as in other cases. Today, a supplier probably has to have at least a 30 percent share of the tying market to be viewed as having substantial power in that market. Until recently, the Supreme Court assumed that if the defendant had a patent in the high-demand product, that it had market power. In *Illinois Tool Works, Inc. v. Independent Ink, Inc.*, 547 U.S. 28 (2006), however, the Court removed that presumption which will require plaintiffs to undertake the difficult task of establishing defendant's market power in the tying product.

Other factors, such as entry barriers, are also very important. According to the courts, there is a second requirement for tying to be illegal, namely, that the supplier's tying arrangements must generate a substantial amount of business in the tied market. This requirement is so easy to establish, however, that it is practically always present.

In recent years, courts have moved slowly from applying a per se illegality approach to tying when the defendant had market power for the high-demand product, to a rule of reason approach. Although the U.S. Supreme Court in *Jefferson Parish Hospital Dist. v. Hyde*, 466 U.S. 2 (1984), seemingly applied a per se approach, clearly many justices on the court were more comfortable with a rule of reason approach. Because tying is so ubiquitous in commerce and often has economic benefits (consider the hotel that provides soaps and shampoos to customers and wraps those costs up into the overall room charge), several courts have reconsidered the legal tests in the area. For example, in *U.S. v. Microsoft Corp.,* 253 F.3d 34 (D.C. Cir. 2001), the government charged that Microsoft was illegally tying its not-so-popular Web browser to its highly popular operating system by bundling the software all together. The court held, consistent with a rule of reason approach, that the government bore the burden of proving that the harm to competition from this integration of features outweighed efficiency benefits.

Exclusive Dealing

The most common form of *exclusive dealing* agreement is one in which the customer makes a commitment that it will purchase a particular product or service only from the supplier (and, implicitly or explicitly, *not* from the supplier's competitors). Many times these arrangements are called "requirements contracts" because the parties often speak in terms of the buyer's commitment to purchase its "requirements" of a product from the seller. The primary concern caused by this type of arrangement is that there may be fewer and less frequent opportunities for the seller's competitors to compete for those customers who are parties to the exclusive dealing. Widespread use of such agreements in a market may also increase entry barriers for potential competitors.

Today, exclusive dealing is likely to be illegal under Sections 1 or 2 of the Sherman Act or Section 3 of the Clayton Act only if a dominant share—probably more than 30 percent—of the relevant market is locked away from competitors. Thus, the practice creates a real legal risk only when a leading or dominant firm in a market makes widespread use of it.

In *U.S. v. Dentsply Int'l,* 399 F.3d 181 (3d Cir. 2005), the court held that the nation's largest false teeth manufacturer had illegally monopolized sales of false teeth to dental laboratories and dealers by prohibiting its distributors from carrying competing lines of false teeth. Although exclusive dealing arrangements can in proper circumstances create market efficiencies, this arrangement was held illegal under Section 2 of the Sherman Act because defendant's dominant market position meant that the exclusive dealing foreclosed others from competing by wrapping up vital outlets to the marketplace. Similarly, in *U.S. v. Visa U.S.A., Inc.,* 344 F.3d 229 (2d Cir. 2003), exclusionary rules imposed by MasterCard and Visa that preventing their issuing banks from also issuing Discover or American Express cards were invalidated under Section 1 of the Sherman Act.

In the following sections, we look first at that portion of the law concerned primarily with industry structure--the law of monopolization and mergers.

MONOPOLIES

In trying to formulate a working definition of *monopoly* under Section 2 of the Sherman Act, as a practical matter the courts could not simply adopt the classical economic model of monopoly: one seller, very high entry barriers to the market, and no close substitutes for the product. Instead, they defined a monopoly in more pragmatic terms as "a firm having such an overwhelming degree of market power that it is able to control prices or exclude competition."

The center of this definition is market power. Essentially, market power is the ability of a firm to behave differently than it could behave in a perfectly competitive market. Stated differently, market power is a firm's ability to exercise *some* degree of control over the price of its product, that is, to raise its price without losing most of its customers. In virtually every market, there will be firms with some control over the price they charge, although the degree of control varies greatly from case to case.

The concept of market power is critical to any examination of competition under the antitrust laws, because competition usually cannot be harmed unless one firm, or a group of firms acting together, possesses some degree of market power. With respect to other issues in antitrust law, degrees of market power that are less than monopolistic can be very important. However, in deciding whether there is a monopoly under Section 2 of the Sherman Act, courts look for an *overwhelming degree* of market power. This exists when one firm dominates a market to such an extent that it does not have to worry much about the response of competitors.

Measuring Market Power

Traditionally, the enforcement agencies and courts have looked primarily at the structure of a market when trying to draw inferences about degrees of market power. The most important structural factor is usually the firm's *market share*. In other words, what percentage share of the relevant market does the firm have? The courts have not developed hard and fast rules as to what market share definitely does or does not demonstrate overwhelming market power. However, the cases indicate that a market share of less than 50 percent will never be enough, and a share of 75 percent will frequently (but not always) be enough. Although other indicators of market power are always important, they become critical when the share is below or above this range.

Other structural factors include the following:

1. The *relative size of other firms* in the market can be important. If M has, for example, 60 percent of the market, M generally will have less market power if there are at least one or two other very large firms with perhaps 20 or 30 percent shares than if the remainder of the market is occupied by a large number of very small firms. The reason is that if the other firms are themselves quite large, albeit smaller than M, they are more likely to have economies of scale and costs similar to M. Thus, although oligopoly may not be the most desirable market structure, it is usually much better than monopoly.

2. The *size and power of customers* is also relevant. Even monopolistic sellers may be unable to exert significant market control if they sell primarily to large, powerful buyers that can exert counter pressure.

3. The market's *entry barriers* are quite important. Entry barriers are conditions that make entry into the market by a new competitor significantly more costly and risky. If a market has low entry barriers, and a powerful firm in the market earns very high returns by using its power to charge high prices, the high returns will attract new competition to the market that will diminish the dominant firm's power. High entry barriers, on the other hand, provide substantial insulation for the powerful firm so that it can fully exploit its market power.

Examples of entry barriers include excess production capacity in the market, higher costs of capital for potential competitors than for the dominant firm, strong customer preferences for brands produced by the dominant firm, important technology or know-how that is protected by patents or by trade secret law, complex distribution channels, and so forth. Entry barriers are not necessarily good or bad; they are just conditions that may be relevant. It also should be noted that some entry barriers are inevitable, whereas some can be intentionally erected by a dominant firm. Although the importance of entry barriers has long been recognized, in recent years some authorities have come to view them as even more important to the question of market power than the internal composition of the market.

4. In addition to market share and other structural factors, the *dynamics* of the market can also be relevant to the question of how much power a firm has. For instance, if the market is characterized by rapidly developing technology, or if total market demand is expanding rapidly, it will be much harder for a firm to hold on to its dominant position for very long.

Defining the Relevant Market

Before seeking to determine whether a firm has overwhelming power, it is necessary to define the relevant market. Essentially, the process of market definition involves an attempt to identify a category of business transactions that accurately reflects the operation of competitive forces. A market can be thought of as the context within which competitive forces can be measured with reasonable accuracy. Any market must be defined in terms of two elements: (1) a particular product or service, or some grouping of products or services, and (2) a geographic area.

Product Market

Suppose that M Company is charged with monopolizing the market for the sale of zippers in the United States. Most of M's zippers are sold to clothing manufacturers, but some are sold to fabric stores and other retail outlets for resale to consumers. M produces 90 percent of the zippers sold in the United States. If "zippers" is the proper market definition, M's market share almost certainly demonstrates overwhelming market power. M argues, however, that zippers actually face stiff competition from buttons, snaps, hooks, and Velcro, and that the 90 percent figure does not accurately portray M's power. If buttons, snaps, hooks, and Velcro are included in the market definition, let us suppose that M's share of this larger "clothing fastener" market will be only 23 percent, a figure that certainly does not indicate overwhelming power.

The approach that most courts have taken to such a problem is to look first at the *cross elasticity of demand* among the products in question. The term describes the concept of interchangeability. If there is a substantial degree of cross elasticity of demand between two or more products, they usually will be treated as occupying the same product market. In other words, if the evidence indicates that a substantial portion of customers view two products as being reasonable substitutes for one another, a court is likely to treat the products as being part of a single market.

The evidence in such a case, like so many others, will usually not be very "neat." It probably will show that zippers are preferred by most customers for particular uses, and that these customers are willing to pay significantly more for zippers than other fasteners for these uses. Buttons are probably preferred for certain other uses, snaps for others, and Velcro for still others. For some uses, two or more types of fasteners may be viewed as basically equivalent, and customers may choose solely on the basis of price. Courts necessarily must employ some fairly rough approximations in such cases. Thus, if the evidence convinces a court that a substantial body of customers views two or more products as reasonably interchangeable for a substantial number of important uses, they probably will be included in a single product market. It is also possible, of course, that the evidence will justify a conclusion that fasteners for one particular use constitute a separate market, and that one or more other markets exist for other uses. This conclusion is likely only if the use is quite distinctive from other uses and the volume of business for this use is very substantial.

Another factor that sometimes is relevant to the process of product market definition is *cross elasticity of supply*. This refers to the relative ease or difficulty with which producers of related products may respond to increases in demand. Suppose, for example, that many customers view buttons and zippers as basically interchangeable for certain important uses. Thus, there may be a high degree of cross elasticity of demand. However, all button manufacturers are operating at close to their production capacity, and the building of additional button-making facilities is very costly and time-consuming. Therefore, if M raises the price of zippers substantially and many customers would consider switching to buttons, button manufacturers cannot absorb the additional demand. These zipper customers will have to keep buying zippers at a higher cost. Button makers will not build additional capacity unless they think that zipper prices will remain high for the foreseeable future, so they could count on the additional demand for buttons for a long enough time to justify the investment in new button-making capacity.

Thus, even though *demand* cross elasticity may be relatively high, there is low *supply* cross elasticity, and courts will probably treat zippers and buttons as two separate markets. It is also true that high cross elasticity of supply can support a conclusion that two products should be in the same market even though there is currently a low degree of demand cross elasticity. Suppose, for example, that most customers view zippers and Velcro as not being interchangeable for a particular use. However, if a price increase for zippers causes many customers to look for a substitute, and if Velcro manufacturers could modify their product easily and inexpensively so that it would be a reasonable zipper substitute for this particular use, zippers and Velcro may be treated as one market.

Geographic Market

Depending on the situation, the relevant geographic market can be local, regional, national, or international. It represents the area within which buyers can reasonably be expected to seek alternative sources of supply. Retail geographic markets tend to be smaller than wholesale markets, which tend to be smaller than manufacturing markets, although there are many exceptions to this generalization. The factor that usually determines the size of a geographic market is the relative cost of searching for and shipping products from more distant geographic locations. When we speak of relative cost, we mean relative to the cost of the product itself. Buyers obviously will spend more time and money searching for better deals and shipping from more distant places when the desired purchase is 100 million computer chips than when it is a loaf of bread.

Intent to Monopolize

If a firm has overwhelming market power and thus is a monopolist, is there automatically a violation of Section 2 of the Sherman Act? Or must something else be proved? The answer is that the evidence must also demonstrate that the dominant firm had the intent to monopolize, that is, that it willfully acquired or maintained its monopoly power. This obviously means that there can be legal monopolies. For example, a monopoly is legal if it exists solely because of lawful patents or trade secrets, or because economies of scale are so large that the market will support only one profitable firm.

As in other areas of law, intent is inferred from conduct. In the case of monopolization, courts usually will infer intent to monopolize only if the dominant firm has engaged in *predatory* conduct, that is, conduct which is aimed at inflicting economic harm on one or more other firms for reasons that are not related to greater efficiency or better performance. There are two very general categories of predatory behavior: predatory pricing and non-price predation.

Predatory pricing is usually found where the dominant firm has persistently sold at prices below its average variable cost. Such pricing is viewed as predatory because it cannot be justified by a legitimate profit motive; while these prices are being charged, it is a money-losing proposition for the dominant firm. Instead, predatory pricing can only pay off for the dominant firm if it permits that firm to maintain its monopoly position so that it can later recover its losses by charging very high prices and earning monopoly profits. Thus, the Supreme Court has held that plaintiffs can establish predatory pricing by showing (a) the prices complained of are below cost, and (b) defendant had a "dangerous probability" of recouping its investment in below-cost pricing. *Brooke Group Ltd. v. Brown & Williamson Tobacco Corp.*, 509 U.S. 209 (1993). Predatory pricing may be used to drive another firm out of the market, although this is so costly for the dominant firm and has such uncertain long-term payoffs that it may not happen very often. Strategic predatory pricing can also be used on a periodic basic to discourage other firms from entering the market, or to send a clear signal to smaller firms in the market that they had better not engage in aggressive price competition. Predatory pricing for these purposes is probably more common than for the purpose of actually driving a competitor out.

In *Weyerhaeuser Co. v. Ross-Simmons Hardwood Lumber Co.*, 127 S.Ct. 1069 (2007), the Supreme Court held that when *buyers* engage in *predatory bidding* by bidding up the price of inputs so as to make it impossible for competitors to be profitable, a mirror-version of the *Brooke Group* test should apply. Plaintiffs should have to prove that defendant's bidding caused the cost of the relevant output to rise above the revenues generated by sale of those outputs and that there is a "dangerous probability" that defendant will be able to recoup those losses through the exercise of monopsony (monopoly buyer) power.

Nonprice predation is certainly more common than any kind of predatory pricing because it does not cost the dominant firm as much. Most forms of non-price predation are aimed at increasing competitors' costs or increasing entry barriers for potential competitors. A few examples are (1) tying up customers with long-term contracts that are not justified by cost savings, so that it is much more difficult for existing and potential competitors to engage in a fair contest for those customers; (2) taking away key employees from a smaller competitor; (3) falsely disparaging the products of smaller competitors; (4) forcing smaller firms into completely unjustified lawsuits and administrative proceedings because the costs of such proceedings hurt the smaller firms more than the dominant firm; and (5) various forms of sabotage. Some kinds of nonprice predation may violate other laws as well, but many kinds do not.

LEPAGE'S INC. v. 3M
U.S. Court of Appeals, Third Circuit, 324 F.3d 141 (2003)

With its Scotch brand tape, 3M enjoyed a monopoly in the transparent tape home and office use market, with around 90% of market share. LePage's made "second brand" and private label transparent tape. This tape sold at a lower price than branded tape. With the rise of office superstores and large retailers, the demand for private label tapes rose. 3M therefore entered that business, selling its own second brand under the name "Highland."

LePage's claimed that 3M engaged in a series of related, anticompetitive acts aimed at restricting the availability of lower-priced transparent tape to consumers, and that 3M devised programs that prevented LePage's and the other domestic company in the business, Tesa Tuck, Inc., from gaining or maintaining large volume sales. LePage further claimed that 3M maintained its monopoly by stifling growth of private label tape and by coordinating efforts aimed at large distributors to keep retail prices for Scotch-brand tape high.

LePage's brought this antitrust action asserting that 3M used its monopoly over its Scotch tape brand to gain a competitive advantage in the private label tape portion of the transparent tape market in the United States through the use of 3M's multi-tiered "bundled rebate" structure, which offered higher rebates when customers purchased products in a number of 3M's different product lines. LePage's also alleges that 3M offered to some of LePage's customers large lump-sum cash payments, promotional allowances and other cash incentives to encourage them to enter into exclusive dealing arrangements with 3M.

LePage's asserted several antitrust claims, including monopolization and attempted monopolization under Sec. 2 of the Sherman Act. A jury rendered a verdict for LePage's on all counts and awarded LePage's $68,486,697 after it was trebled. The district judge entered a judgment enforcing the jury's verdict, and 3M appealed, claiming that bundled rebates were legal as long as prices were not below cost. LePage's argued that the below-cost standard was irrelevant in a case that did not involve predatory pricing. An appellate court panel first reversed the judgment, but then decided to rehear the case en banc.

Sloviter, Circuit Judge:

In this case, the parties agreed that the relevant product market is transparent tape and the relevant geographic market is the United States. Moreover, 3M concedes it possesses monopoly power, with a 90% market share. Therefore we need not dwell on the oft-contested issue of market power.

The sole remaining issue is whether 3M took steps to maintain that power in a manner that violated Sec. 2 of the Sherman Act. A monopolist willfully acquires or maintains monopoly power when it competes on some basis other than the merits. LePage's argues that 3M willfully maintained its monopoly in the transparent tape market through exclusionary conduct, primarily by bundling its rebates and entering into contracts that expressly or effectively required dealing virtually exclusively with 3M, which LePage's characterizes as de facto exclusive. 3M does not argue that it did not engage in this conduct. Instead, 3M argues that its conduct was legal as a matter of law because it never priced its transparent tape below its cost.

In its brief, 3M states "above-cost pricing cannot give rise to an antitrust offense as a matter of law, since it is the very conduct that the antitrust laws wish to promote in the interest of making consumers better off." For this proposition it relies on *Brooke Group Ltd. v. Brown & Williamson Tobacco Corp.*, 509 U.S. 209 (1993).

Before turning to consider LePage's allegation that 3M engaged in exclusionary or anticompetitive conduct and the evidence it produced, we consider the type of conduct Sec. 2 encompasses. As one court of appeals has stated: "'Anti-competitive conduct' can come in too many different forms, and is too dependent upon context, for any court or commentator ever to have enumerated all the varieties." *Caribbean Broad. Sys. Ltd. v. Cable & Wireless PLC,* 148 F.3d 1080 (D.C. Cir. 1998). Numerous cases hold that the enforcement of the legal monopoly provided by a patent procured through fraud may violate Sec. 2. A monopolist's denial to competitors of access to its "essential" goods, services or resources has been held to violate Sec. 2. Even unfair tortious conduct [such as disparaging advertising about a competitor] unrelated to a monopolist's pricing policies has been held to violate Sec. 2.

A recent decision of the United States Court of Appeals for the Sixth Circuit, *Conwood LP v. U.S. Tobacco Co.,* 290 F.3d 768 (6th Cir. 2002), presents a good illustration of the type of exclusionary conduct that will support a Sec. 2 violation. That court upheld the jury's award to plaintiff Conwood of $350 million, which trebled was $ 1.05 billion, against United States Tobacco Company ("USTC") because of USTC's monopolization. USTC was the sole manufacturer of moist snuff until the 1970's when Conwood, Swisher, and Swedish Match, other moist snuff manufacturers, entered the moist snuff market. Not unexpectedly, USTC's 100% market share declined and it took the action that formed the basis of Conwood's complaint against USTC alleging unlawful monopolization in violation of Sec. 2.

The evidence that the court of appeals held proved that USTC systematically tried to exclude competition from the moist snuff market included the following: USTC (1) removed and destroyed or discarded racks that displayed moist snuff products in the stores while placing Conwood products in USTC racks in an attempt to bury Conwood's products; (2) trained its "operatives to take advantage of inattentive store clerks with various 'ruses' such as obtaining nominal permission to reorganize or neaten the moist snuff section" in an effort to destroy Conwood racks; (3) misused its position as category manager (manages product groups and business units and customizes them on a store by store basis) by providing misleading information to retailers in an effort to dupe them into carrying USTC products and to discontinue carrying Conwood products; and (4) entered into exclusive agreements with retailers in an effort to exclude rivals' products.

On appeal, USTC contended that Conwood had failed to establish that USTC's power was acquired or maintained by exclusionary practices rather than by its legitimate business practices and superior product. The court of appeals rejected USTC's argument, finding that there was sufficient evidence for a jury to find willful maintenance by USTC of monopoly power by engaging in exclusionary practices.

[Here, LePage's argues that 3M attempted to monopolize the market by use of two exclusionary practices, bundled rebates and exclusive dealing contracts.]

Bundled Rebates. 3M offered many of LePage's major customers substantial rebates to induce them to eliminate or reduce their purchases of tape from LePage's. Rather than competing by offering volume discounts which are concededly legal and often reflect cost savings, 3M's rebate programs offered discounts to certain customers conditioned on purchases spanning six of 3M's diverse product lines. The rebates were considerable, not "modest" as 3M states. Just as significant as the amounts received is the powerful incentive they provided to customers to purchase 3M tape rather than LePage's in order not to forgo the maximum rebate 3M offered. The penalty would have been $264,000 for Sam's Club, $450,000 for Kmart, and $200,000 to $310,000 for American Stores.

One of the leading treatises discussing the inherent anticompetitive effect of bundled rebates, even if they are priced above cost, notes that "the great majority of bundled rebate programs yield aggregate prices above cost. Rather than analogizing them to predatory pricing, they are best compared with tying, whose foreclosure effects are similar. Indeed, the 'package discount' is often a close analogy." Phillip E. Areeda & Herbert Hovenkamp,

ANTITRUST LAW, at 83 (Supp. 2002).

The principal anticompetitive effect of bundled rebates as offered by 3M is that when offered by a monopolist they may foreclose portions of the market to a potential competitor who does not manufacture an equally diverse group of products and who therefore cannot make a comparable offer. The jury could reasonably find that 3M used its monopoly in transparent tape, backed by its considerable catalog of products, to squeeze out LePage's.

Exclusive Dealing. The second prong of LePage's claim of exclusionary conduct by 3M was its actions in entering into exclusive dealing contracts with large customers. 3M acknowledges only the expressly exclusive dealing contracts with Venture and Pamida which conditioned discounts on exclusivity. It minimizes these because they represent only a small portion of the market. However, LePage's claims that 3M made payments to many of the larger customers that were designed to achieve sole-source supplier status.

Even though exclusivity arrangements are often analyzed under Sec. 1, such exclusionary conduct may also be an element in a Sec. 2 claim. [And agreements which effectively foreclose the business of competitors can be illegal even if not expressly exclusive.] LePage's introduced powerful evidence that could have led the jury to believe that rebates and discounts to Kmart, Staples, Sam's Club, [and others] were designed to induce them to award business to 3M to the exclusion of LePage's. Many of LePage's former customers refused even to meet with LePage's sales representatives. A buyer for Kmart, LePage's largest customer which accounted for 10% of its business, told LePage's: "I can't talk to you about tape products for the next three years" and "don't bring me anything 3M makes." Kmart switched to 3M following 3M's offer of a $1 million "growth" reward which the jury could have understood to require that 3M be its sole supplier. The purpose and effect of 3M's payments to the retailers were issues for the jury which, by its verdict, rejected 3M's.

The Court of Appeals for the District of Columbia relied on the evidence of foreclosure of markets in reaching its decision on liability in *U.S. v. Microsoft Corp.*, 253 F.3d 34 (D.C. Cir. 2001). In that case, the court of appeals concluded that Microsoft, a monopolist in the operating system market, foreclosed rivals in the browser market from a "substantial percentage of the available opportunities for browser distribution" through the use of exclusive contracts with key distributors. Microsoft kept usage of its competitor's browser below "the critical level necessary for [its rival] to pose a real threat to Microsoft's monopoly." The Microsoft opinion does not specify what percentage of the browser market Microsoft locked up--merely that, in one of the two primary distribution channels for browsers, Microsoft had exclusive arrangements with most of the top distributors. Significantly, the Microsoft court observed that Microsoft's exclusionary conduct violated Sec. 2 "even though the contracts foreclose less than the roughly 40% or 50% share usually required in order to establish a Sec. 1 violation."

Section 2, the provision of the antitrust laws designed to curb the excesses of monopolists and near-monopolists, is the equivalent in our economic sphere of the guarantees of free and unhampered elections in the political sphere. Just as democracy can thrive only in a free political system unhindered by outside forces, so also can market capitalism survive only if those with market power are kept in check. That is the goal of the antitrust laws.

The jury heard the evidence and the contentions of the parties, accepting some and rejecting others. There was ample evidence that 3M used its market power over transparent tape, backed by its considerable catalog of products, to entrench its monopoly to the detriment of LePage's, its only serious competitor, in violation of Sec. 2. Affirmed.

MERGERS

A *merger* between two companies is clearly a "combination" that could be scrutinized under Section 1 of the Sherman Act, which prohibits "contracts, combinations, and conspiracies in restraint of trade." In the early years after Congress passed the Sherman Act, however, the Supreme Court interpreted Section 1 in such a narrow way, at least as applied to mergers, that a merger could be illegal only if it occurred between two direct competitors with very large market shares. Because Congress intended antitrust law to reach some other mergers as well, in 1914 it enacted Section 7 of the Clayton Act. The statute was amended substantially by the Cellar-Kefauver Act of 1950, further demonstrating congressional intent to prevent mergers when the evidence indicates either actual harm to competition or a substantial probability of such harm in the future. Another amendment in 1976 requires the participants in most mergers of any significant size to give both the Justice Department and the FTC advance notice of a merger so that these agencies can assess its possible effects before it occurs.

Section 7 prohibits one company from acquiring the stock or assets of another company if the acquisition is likely to diminish competition in a substantial way. Total or partial acquisitions are covered. Obviously, however, a stock acquisition cannot raise any concerns about harming competition unless the acquiring company obtains a large enough stake in the acquired company either to control it or at least to have substantial influence over its board of directors. Similarly, an acquisition of assets cannot harm competition unless the assets are very important to competition in the particular market, such as major manufacturing facilities, airline routes, critical patented technology, and so on.

In attempting to assess a merger's actual or probable effects on competition, a court will first define the relevant market or markets. This is done in exactly the same way as in a monopoly case. As we will see in our discussion of the different types of mergers, the question of market power is also very important in merger cases. Although substantial market power is necessary for substantial anticompetitive effects, that power does not have to be overwhelming for such effects to occur.

Another important point about the law in this area is that periodic political changes in Washington affect the enforcement and interpretation of Section 7 to a greater extent than the other antitrust laws. Although such changes affect antitrust law in general, private lawsuits are much less important as an enforcement tool in the case of mergers than in other areas of antitrust. Most challenges to mergers are made by either the Justice Department or the FTC, rather than by private plaintiffs. Thus, when the current political climate is relatively conservative and pro-business, the enforcement attitude toward mergers is likely to be quite lenient. On the other hand, when an administration is in power that distrusts large concentrations of economic power and does not really believe that most mergers contribute to economic efficiency, more mergers are usually challenged under Section 7. In recent times, the attitude toward mergers has generally been stricter during Democratic administrations and more lenient during Republican administrations.

Horizontal Mergers

A merger between competitors poses the greatest danger to competition because the market has one less competitor. In assessing the impact of a *horizontal merger*, the courts usually emphasize the same general kinds of evidence that are important in measuring market power in a monopoly case.

Market Share. The *combined market* share of the merging firms is often the first thing the courts look at. During earlier periods when the attitude toward mergers was very strict, a number of them were challenged and ruled illegal when the combined market share was above 10 percent and other evidence indicated a definite trend toward concentration of economic power in the relevant market. Today, however, a horizontal merger is not likely to get much attention under Section 7 unless the combined market share exceeds 30 percent.

Market Concentration. The *overall concentration of the market* is also important. In general, the more concentrated the market is at the time of the merger, the more likely it is that a questionable merger will be held illegal. Suppose, for example, that a merger occurs between two firms having market shares of 20 percent and 15 percent, and the remainder of the market consists of three other firms with shares of 25 percent, 20 percent, and 20 percent. This merger would be somewhat more likely to violate Section 7 than it would if the remainder of the market consisted of, say, six other firms with shares of approximately 11 percent each.

Acquisition by Leading Firm. In addition, if a single firm already dominates a market rather completely and there are no other firms that can come close to its resources and scale economies, any acquisition of a competitor by the dominant firm runs a great risk of being held illegal.

Entry Barriers. If the market is characterized by high entry barriers, a borderline merger is much more likely to be ruled illegal, and vice versa. Indeed, as we mentioned in the discussion of monopoly, an increasing number of authorities have begun to view a market's entry barriers as being at least as important to the market power question as the market's internal composition. One practical difficulty with this view, however, is that entry barriers usually are much more difficult to measure with any kind of precision than the market's internal structure.

Increased Risk of Collusion. Another relevant factor could be the existence of evidence indicating that collusion among competitors had been a problem in this market in the past, and that by further reducing the number of competitors this merger could make collusion even easier in the future. In general, the lower the number of competitors, the easier it is for them to put together and maintain a price-fixing conspiracy or other collusive anticompetitive arrangement.

Other Factors. Other factors can also be important to the evaluation of horizontal mergers. For example, a firm with 15 or 20 percent of a market ordinarily could acquire a firm with a 2 or 3 percent share without much fear of legal challenge. Suppose, however, that the smaller firm had recently developed patented technology of major significance to future competition in the market, or that it had traditionally been a very efficient "maverick" and frequently had led the way in vigorous price competition. In such a case, the acquisition would run a significantly higher risk of being challenged successfully under Section 7.

Vertical Mergers

Although a *vertical merger* is much less likely to harm competition than a horizontal one, it is possible for such a merger to diminish competition. Essentially, a vertical merger creates *vertical integration*, which occurs when one firm operates at more than one level of the distribution chain for a product. (Obviously, a firm can also become vertically integrated, without a merger, by creating new facilities to operate at another level.) Suppose that S Company is an important producer of a key component or ingredient used by B Company in manufacturing an end product, and that S acquires B. S would be using the merger to vertically integrate "downstream." If B had acquired S, B would be vertically integrating "upstream."

There has been a long-standing debate about the merits of vertical integration. Currently, the prevailing attitude among a majority of economists and enforcement officials toward vertical integration is a favorable one. Not everyone shares that view, however, and the pendulum of expert opinion could swing in the other direction at some point in the future.

Vertical integration can create *economic efficiencies*, primarily by *saving transaction costs*. If the vertically integrated firm ("S-B") is managed properly, it usually should be able to transfer goods and services from one level to another more cheaply than if it were two separate firms operating at the two levels. Being part of one company ideally should permit better coordination and planning. Having an assured source of supply for B and an assured market for S should permit better inventory control. This, in turn, should produce lower carrying costs by avoiding excess inventory and lower delay-related costs by reducing instances of shortage. Vertical integration also can reduce the various kinds of selling costs between S and B, such as those associated with promotion, sales personnel, and contract drafting and monitoring. Opponents of vertical integration also argue that, even if efficiencies are created, many of the same efficiencies can be achieved through relatively long-term contracts without creating the same degree of risk for competition. Also, vertical mergers can lead to various inefficiencies caused by the lack of innovation and slower decision making that one often sees as organizations become ever larger.

Some observers argue that vertical integration can increase *entry barriers* and thus insulate firms in the market from new competition. The reason, they say, is that a firm thinking about entering a market in which the major competitors are vertically integrated will have to come into the market at two levels simultaneously, which is more costly and difficult. Those favoring vertical integration, however, reply that new entry into such a market is more difficult simply because the vertically integrated firms in the market are more efficient, and that it is more difficult to compete against efficient firms with low costs.

Some critics of vertical integration also claim that it can *make collusion easier* for the vertically integrated firms, especially those at the "upstream" level (in our example, S's level). This can happen, they claim, because removing the layer of independent buyers from the downstream level does away with an important set of "watchdogs" on the upstream firms. Those with a favorable view of vertical integration often admit that this is a possibility, but point out that it is likely to happen only if there are very few firms at both levels and if most of these large firms are already vertically integrated. Besides, they say, antitrust enforcers can just watch out for the collusion and take action if they find it.

Because of today's generally favorable attitude toward vertical integration, a vertical merger will usually be legal. A successful challenge to such a merger is likely only if most of the firms in the market are already vertically integrated, this vertically combined market is a highly concentrated oligopoly, and both S and B have large market shares. It is mainly the fear of collusion being made easier in this kind of situation that creates the risk of a successful legal challenge.

Conglomerate Merger

Mergers without horizontal or vertical characteristics are usually called *conglomerate mergers*. Although several grounds for striking down conglomerate mergers have been employed by courts in past years, such a merger creates almost no legal risk today.

Merger Guidelines

The Justice Department's Antitrust Division has issued Merger Guidelines that are not binding law, but do provide business with a valuable planning tool by specifying the circumstances in which the two agencies can ordinarily be expected to challenge a merger. One of the key innovations of the current guidelines is the use of the Herfindahl-Hirschman Index (HHI) for measuring the relative level of economic concentration in a market. This index involves squaring the market share of each firm in the market and then adding the squares. Thus, a market with 10 firms of equal size would have an HHI of 1,000. The greater the level of concentration in the relevant market, the more likely it is that a merger will be challenged and that it will be ruled illegal. The specification in the guidelines of what degree of concentration triggers a greater likelihood of challenge by the government has been revised several times over the years, and today an HHI in the market of 1800 or more is viewed as highly concentrated, and a merger that will increase that HHI by several hundred points is quite vulnerable to challenge and possible illegality in court. The Merger Guidelines also indicate that factors other than concentration can be taken into account, such as the barriers to entry into the particular market, or evidence that the merging firms had been engaged in vigorous competition between themselves.

The following decision is from a case involving a horizontal merger between two relatively large competitors. It is an important decision because, among other things, it illustrates how evidence of surrounding economic circumstances may convince a court that such a merger is legal.

UNITED STATES v. ORACLE CORP.
U.S. District Court, Northern District of California, 331 F. Supp. 2d 1098 (2004)

Oracle sought to acquire Peoplesoft, a rival maker of software. The Department of Justice's antitrust division, in conjunction with various state attorneys general (plaintiffs), sought to invoke Section 7 of the Clayton Act to prevent the acquisition, arguing that the relevant product market was providers of large-scale applications software for HRM (human resources management) and FMS (financial management systems), and that the relevant geographic market was the United States. Plaintiffs argued that if Oracle and Peoplesoft merged, the only remaining competitor would be Germany's SAP, creating a highly concentrated duopoly.

Oracle argued, to the contrary, that HRM and FMS products are just part of a broad range of ERP (enterprise resource planning) applications software, that many firms compete to provide such products, that price competition comes additionally from firms providing outsourcing of data processing, that the geographic area of competition was worldwide or at least the U.S. and Europe, that many purchasers of ERP software are large, knowledgeable and sophisticated and would therefore impede any exercise of market power by a merged Oracle/Peoplesoft, and that potential competitors were poised to enter the market to counter any anticompetitive effects of the merger. After a lengthy trial, the judge ruled for defendant.

Walker, District Judge:

Section 7 of the Clayton Act prohibits a person "engaged in commerce or in any activity affecting commerce" from acquiring "the whole or any part" of a business' stock or assets if the effect of the acquisition "may be substantially to lessen competition, or to tend to create a monopoly." To establish a section 7 violation, plaintiffs must show that a pending acquisition is reasonably likely to cause anticompetitive effects. "Section 7 does not require proof that a merger or other acquisition [will] cause higher prices in the affected market. All that is necessary is that the merger create an appreciable danger of such consequences in the future." *Hospital Corp. of Am. v. FTC,* 807 F.2d 1381 (7th Cir. 1986). Substantial competitive harm is likely to result if a merger creates or enhances "market power," a term that has specific meaning in antitrust law.

Market Definition. In determining whether a transaction will create or enhance market power, courts historically have first defined the relevant product and geographic markets within which the competitive effects of the transaction are to be assessed. This is a "necessary predicate" to finding anticompetitive effects. Market definition under the case law proceeds by determining the market shares of the firms involved in the proposed transaction, *Philadelphia Nat'l Bank,* 374 U.S. 321 (1963), the overall concentration level in the industry and the trends in the level of concentration. A significant trend toward concentration creates a presumption that the transaction violates section 7. In other words, plaintiffs establish a prima facie case of a section 7 violation by showing that the merger would produce "a firm controlling an undue percentage share of the relevant market, and [would] result in a significant increase in the concentration of firms in that market." *Id.* Under *Philadelphia Nat'l Bank,* a post-merger market share of 30 percent or higher unquestionably gives rise to the presumption of illegality.

To rebut this presumption, defendant may show that the market-share statistics give an inaccurate account of the merger's probable effects on competition in the relevant market. Arguments related to efficiencies resulting from the merger may also be relevant in opposing plaintiffs' case. If the defendant successfully rebuts the presumption [of illegality], the burden of producing additional evidence of anticompetitive effects shifts to [plaintiffs], and merges with the ultimate burden of persuasion, which remains with the government at all times.

An application of the burden-shifting approach requires the court to determine (1) the "line of commerce" or product market in which to assess the transaction; (2) the "section of the country" or geographic market in which to assess the transaction; and (3) the transaction's probable effect on competition in the product and geographic markets. Both the Supreme Court and appellate courts acknowledge the need to adopt a flexible approach in determining whether anticompetitive effects are likely to result from a merger. Reflecting their "generality and adaptability," application of the antitrust laws to mergers during the past half-century has been anything but static.

Accordingly, determining the existence or threat of anticompetitive effects has not stopped at calculation of market shares. In *Hospital Corp. of Am.* the court upheld the FTC's challenge to the acquisition of two hospital chains, but noted that "the economic concept of competition, rather than any desire to preserve rivals as such, is the lodestar that shall guide the contemporary application of the antitrust laws, not excluding the Clayton Act." Hence, the court held that it was appropriate for the FTC to eschew reliance solely on market percentages and the "very strict merger decisions of the 1960s." In addition to market concentration, probability of consumer harm in that case was established by factors such as legal barriers to new entry, low elasticity of consumer demand, inability of consumers to move to distant hospitals in emergencies, a history of collusion and cost pressures creating an incentive to collude.

The trend in [recent] cases away from the "very strict merger decisions of the 1960s," is also reflected in the FTC Horizontal Merger Guidelines. The Guidelines view statistical and non-statistical factors as an integrated whole, avoiding the burden shifting presumptions of the case law. The Guidelines define market power as "the ability profitably to maintain prices above competitive levels for a significant period of time." Five factors are relevant to the finding of market power: (1) whether the merger would significantly increase concentration and would result in a concentrated market, properly defined; (2) whether the merger raises concerns about potential adverse competitive effects; (3) whether timely and likely entry would deter or counteract anticompetitive effects; (4) whether the merger would realize efficiency gains that cannot otherwise be achieved; and (5) whether either party would likely fail in the absence of the merger.

Once the market has been properly defined, the Guidelines set about to identify the firms competing in the market and those likely to enter the market within one year. Following these steps, the Guidelines calculate the market share of each participant, followed by the Herfindahl-Hirschman Index (HHI) concentration measurement for the market as a whole. The HHI is calculated by squaring the market share of each participant, and summing the resulting figures. The Guidelines specify safe harbors for mergers in already concentrated markets that do not increase concentration very much. Notwithstanding these statistical data, the Guidelines next focus on the likely competitive effects of the merger. [Applying these standards after listening to expert testimony from both parties and additional evidence from a myriad of witnesses, the court ruled against plaintiffs because they had not established, among other points:]

1. that the product market they allege, high function HRM and FMS, exists as a separate and distinct line of commerce;
2. that the geographic market for the products of the merging parties is, as they allege, confined to the United States alone;
3. that a post-merger Oracle would have sufficient market shares in the product and geographic markets, properly defined, to apply the burden shifting presumptions of *Philadelphia Nat'l Bank;*
4. that the post-merger level of concentration (HHI) in the product and geographic markets, properly defined, falls outside the safe harbor of the Horizontal Merger Guidelines (Guidelines);
5. that the ERP products of numerous other vendors, including Lawson, AMS and Microsoft, do not compete with the ERP products of Oracle, PeopleSoft and SAP and that these other vendors would not constrain a small but significant non-transitory increase in price by a post-merger Oracle;
6. that outsourcing firms, such as Fidelity and ADP, would not constrain a small but significant non-transitory increase in price by a post-merger Oracle; and
7. that the ability of systems integrators to adapt, configure and customize competing ERP vendors' products to the needs of the group of customers that plaintiffs contend constitute a separate and

distinct product market would not constrain a small but significant non-transitory increase in price by a post-merger Oracle. Judgment is entered in favor of defendant Oracle.

Hart-Scott-Rodino Act

In most large takeovers the acquirer must be cognizant of its filing responsibilities under the *Hart-Scott-Rodino (HSR) Antitrust Improvements Act of 1976*. This amendment to the Clayton Antitrust Act requires acquirers to give the Federal Trade Commission and the Department of Justice premerger notice so that the government can analyze the anticompetitive effects of a takeover before it occurs. After the filing, the parties may have to wait up to 30 days to consummate the deal. Filing fees can run well into six figures, so companies would rather not file. However, the consequences of ignoring the rule are even worse. Companies have been fined as much as $4 million and individual CEOs as much as $500,000 for failing to timely file under HSR.

The triggering threshold for requiring filing under HSR is periodically adjusted to account for growth in GNP. In 2020, FTC rules state that the size-of-transaction threshold for reporting proposed mergers and acquisitions under Section 7A of the Clayton Act increased from $90 million to $94 million. The law is complicated in that a filing is required only if the parties meet both "size of person" and "size of transaction" thresholds. "Size of person" refers to the size of the firm.

In recent years, the government has been increasingly aggressive in enforcing HSR in the case of horizontal mergers. In fiscal year 2015, 1,801 transactions were reported under HSR. As a result of these required filings, in 2015 the FTC challenged 22 mergers and succeeded in blocking several, such as Sysco Corporation's proposed merger with U.S. Foods; both are very large competitors in the broad-line food distribution business. The FTC also successfully blocked Dollar Tree, Inc.'s proposed $9.2 billion acquisition of rival discount store Family Dollar Stores, Inc. Dollar Tree and Family Dollar both sell deeply discounted general merchandise items, such as food, home products, apparel and accessories, generally at prices below $10.

The Antitrust Division of the Department of Justice (DOJ) also challenged 20 proposed mergers based on HSR filings in 2015, including NCM's proposed acquisition of Screenvision; the two companies are the only two major cinema advertising networks in the United States. The merger was blocked. The DOJ also successfully challenged Electrolux's proposed acquisition of General Electric's appliance business, a merger that would have combined two of the leading manufacturers of ranges, cooktops, and wall ovens sold in the United States. After four weeks of trial in a federal district court, the two firms abandoned the deal.

Other countries, including China, also require that large mergers affecting the country's economy significantly to report and seek advance approval. In 2018, for example, Qualcomm had to seek approval in China for its planned $44 billion acquisition of Netherlands-based NXP Semiconductors because both companies do business in the country. China ultimately approved the merger after the eight other major antitrust regulators had already approved it after studying its possible effects in their countries.

CHAPTER 30

EMPLOYMENT LAW

- Labor Relations Law
- Employment Discrimination Law
- Protection of Safety and Welfare
- Employer's Right to Discharge Employees
- Protection of Employee Privacy

For much of our nation's history, the legal relationship between employer and employee was governed by general traditional principles of common law, which in practice typically tilted in the direction of the employer's authority. For example, employers lawfully could discharge their workers for any (or no) reason, including the individual employee's race, union membership, or job-related injury.

The growth of unions was the working person's first response to this legal regime, which seemingly favored employers to an inordinate degree. Unionization was frustrated at first by a series of judicial decisions, but once Congress provided statutory protection in the 1930s, the new labor organizations were able to thrive and provided considerable benefits to member workers.

Notwithstanding the advantages provided to the majority of employees, unions had some serious shortcomings, especially when it came to protecting small groups of employees and dealing with noneconomic issues. In the 1960s Congress once again intervened to expand the protection of workers in areas where unions had contributed little. A number of antidiscrimination laws were enacted, the most significant being the Civil Rights Act of 1964. The Occupational Safety and Health Act of 1968 established a new agency and granted it considerable power to guard against workplace hazards. Legislation expanded worker rights in other areas as well. Perhaps prodded by this congressional activity, the courts also began to reexamine old precedents and initiate new common-law protections for employees. This chapter explores these developments in the law of employment relations and the complications the changes create for employers.

LABOR RELATIONS LAW

In the early nineteenth century, attempts to unionize were stymied by the view that they represented unlawful criminal conspiracies at common law. This theory gradually fell into disfavor and by 1900 unions began to achieve some success, especially with the advent of industrialization and a rise in perceived employer abuse of power. Even in the early twentieth century, however, the courts continued to frustrate union development by enjoining critical functions of such organizations, such as striking and picketing. This was an era of much labor strife and periodic outbreaks of violence associated with labor/management disputes.

Recognizing the existence of a serious national problem, Congress passed several laws in an attempt to resolve labor/management difficulties, including the Railway Labor Act and the Norris-La Guardia Act, which prohibited, among other provisions, the use of injunctions against many union activities. Although these statutes eased the situation somewhat, it soon became clear that more extensive legislation was necessary if unions were to thrive. In 1935 Congress created a comprehensive framework for labor relations law by passing the National Labor Relations Act (NLRA). While this act has been amended, the basic rules established by the original NLRA survive today as the foundation of current law.

The NLRA unambiguously recognized an employee's right to organize by forming unions and authorized these labor organizations to bargain collectively with employers. Certain practices were declared to be unfair labor practices, and these were prohibited. Unfair labor practices were defined to include employer domination of unions, interference with employee organizing, discrimination against union members, and refusal to bargain collectively.

In order to enforce these requirements, the NLRA established an independent federal agency, the National Labor Relations Board (NLRB). The NLRB consists of the General Counsel and the Board itself. The General Counsel investigates charges of unfair labor practices and, if they are found meritorious, initiates an action against the responsible party. These actions are heard by an administrative law judge and may be appealed to the entire Board. If the Board finds a violation, it can seek enforcement of a number of sanctions, including cease-and-desist orders and back pay awards. Board decisions may be appealed to the U.S. Courts of Appeals.

Coverage

The NLRA protects employees, however, and does not cover independent contractors. In addition, some categories of employees are specifically excluded from the act's coverage. Government employees, as well as workers for railways and airlines (protected under a different statute) are outside the NLRA's coverage. Significantly, managerial and supervisory employees are not covered by the act, as they are considered to be part of "management" rather than "labor."

Right to Organize

Central to the NLRA is its guarantee of a right to form unions. Once a group of employees determines that it desires to form an organization for collective bargaining, the group seeks out other workers for support. Once 30 percent of the eligible employees in an appropriate job category sign authorization cards, the employee group may petition for an election to certify a union as the employees' bargaining representative. Conduct of such elections is carefully scrutinized by the NLRB to ensure "laboratory conditions" of fairness. Employers opposing unionization must take special care in their actions and statements lest they be found to have committed an unfair labor practice, in which case the union may be automatically certified by the Board, regardless of the election's outcome. In addition to such an election, employees may convince their employer to voluntarily recognize a union by showing that a majority of them have signed authorization cards or in some other way demonstrated their approval of the union.

Collective Bargaining

Collective bargaining is the term for negotiations between an employer and the union representative. Once a union has been certified as an official bargaining representative of a category of employees, the NLRA imposes a duty to bargain in good faith on both employer and union. Mandatory subjects of bargaining include wages and most working conditions. The good faith provision requires the parties to make a sincere effort to reach agreement. Approaches such as "take it or leave it" proposals may support an inference of bad faith and hence an unfair labor practice finding. An employer also must be willing to furnish certain information to the union and cannot delay unduly in doing so.

Strikes

The most powerful device possessed by unions under the NLRA is the right to strike. This right is available when collective bargaining has reached an impasse. For a strike to be legal it must be supported by a majority of members and cannot be a "wildcat" strike by a disgruntled minority. The NLRA also restricts strikes to those against the primary employer and prohibits strikes against third parties in an attempt to coerce that third party to pressure the primary employer. For example, Company A's union may not picket its biggest customers in an attempt to coerce Company A to accede to the union's demands. Even primary strikes are unlawful if they are violent or designed to compel "featherbedding" (the hiring of unnecessary employees) or other illegal contract terms.

The NLRA imposes other conditions on the conduct of strikes. For example, if workers are on strike against one employer at a multi-employer location (such as a construction site), the employees may not picket the entire site, as this applies unlawful secondary pressure against the other employers. Workers may picket a portion of the site that is used largely by their primary employer. If a strike is legal, the employer may be restricted in dealing with its striking employees. If the workers are engaged in an authorized strike protesting the employer's unfair labor practices, the strikers are automatically entitled to reinstatement after the strike is resolved. In the more traditional economic wage strike, the employer need not necessarily rehire strikers but never can discriminate against strikers, who have a right to seek reemployment on terms equal to those offered other prospective employees.

Nonunion Employees

Although the NLRA was designed primarily to protect unionization, it extends certain rights to nonunion workers as well. Where nonunion employees engage in "concerted action," when *two or more employees acting together* protest against or take action regarding *wages, hours, or working conditions*, they are protected much like strikers who are union members. Otherwise, however, employers have a relatively free hand in dealing with nonunion workers. This situation gives rise to one potentially serious pitfall, however. If an employer sets up "employee committees" or other groups to address grievances in the absence of a union, the committee's independence from management must be carefully ensured. Otherwise, the employer may be found to have created a company-dominated labor organization, which is an unfair labor practice under the NLRA.

The above discussion represents an exceedingly brief review of labor relations law. There is a huge body of precedent under the NLRA elaborating on the above principles. Many of the legal rules in this field have become quite picayune. Consequently, employers must take special care in any controversy involving an organization of employees, especially because NLRB interpretations of rules often change back and forth as Republican (generally pro-employer) and Democratic (generally pro-union) majority membership on the NLRB switches back and forth over the years with changing political winds. Anti-union forces have generally gotten the best of the battle as union membership has declined from around 35% of all U.S. workers in 1945 to 10.3% in 2019 (33.6% in the public sector and 6.2% in the private sector).

EMPLOYMENT DISCRIMINATION LAW

For much of America's history, employers had the legal right to discriminate among employees on any basis other than union membership. However, antidiscrimination laws have now been enacted that affect all phases of the employment process and that prohibit discrimination based on race, color, religion, sex, age, national origin, or perceived handicap.

Title VII of the 1964 Civil Rights Act Coverage

The Civil Rights Act of 1964 is a comprehensive federal enactment prohibiting discrimination in various settings, including housing, public accommodations, and education. Title VII of the Act deals specifically with discrimination in employment. Title VII prohibits workplace discrimination against individuals because of their race, color, religion, sex, or national origin. Although Title VII was one of the earliest laws prohibiting employment discrimination, it remains the most significant.

The provisions of Title VII apply to employers, employment agencies, and labor unions. An employer is subject to Title VII if it (1) has 15 or more employees and (2) is engaged in business that affects interstate or foreign commerce. State and local governments are also within the definition of employer, and their employment practices are covered by Title VII. In most instances, the federal government's employment practices are also covered.

Scope of Protection

Title VII's prohibition against discrimination on the basis of *race or color* is very broad. It obviously protects African Americans, but it also protects many other classes from unequal treatment, including Hispanics, American Indians, and Asian Americans. Even whites are protected against racial discrimination.

The prohibition against *national origin* discrimination is violated if an employer discriminates on the basis of a person's country of origin. It is not illegal, however, for an employer to require employees to be U.S. citizens. (However, a government employer must have a very good reason for requiring its employees to be U.S. citizens, or the requirement will violate the equal protection clause of the U.S. Constitution.) Title VII also protects individuals against discrimination based on the race, color, or national origin of their family members or friends.

Title VII's prohibition against *sex* discrimination is aimed primarily at discrimination against females, but also protects males against gender-based discrimination. Courts have interpreted the law to prohibit sexual harassment of both genders. In a landmark decision in 2020, *Bostock v. Clayton County,* 2020 U.S. LEXIS 3252, the U.S. Supreme Court held that the statute also made it illegal to discriminate in employment against individuals because of their homosexuality or transgender status. Also, Title VII, as amended by the Pregnancy Discrimination Act of 1978, protects women from discrimination because of pregnancy or childbirth, as well.

Under President Obama, the EEOC and DOJ both took the position that gender discrimination includes discrimination based on gender preference and gender identity, thus expanding Title VII protection to LGBTQ individuals. The Trump administration disagreed. Courts have also disagreed and the matter is, at this writing, far from settled though the Supreme Court may soon weigh in on this significant issue.

Although *religious* organizations may lawfully hire some employees based on their religious beliefs, other employers cannot make distinctions for religious reasons. The term religion includes not only well-recognized religious faiths, but also unorthodox ones. For Title VII purposes, the courts use the same broad definition of religion that they use in freedom of religion cases under the First Amendment to the Constitution: "a sincere and meaningful belief occupying in the life of its possessor a place parallel to that filled by the God of those admittedly qualified" for protection. In addition to forbidding discrimination based on religion, the law also requires an employer to make "reasonable accommodation" for employees' religious beliefs and practices, which means that equal treatment is not always the lodestar in religious discrimination cases as it is in cases involving other forms of discrimination.

However, employers do not have to go to great lengths or incur significant expense in order to make reasonable accommodations. For example, in *Patterson v. Walgreen Co.*, 727 Fed.Appx. 581 (11th Cir. 2018), Patterson was a customer care representative at a Walgreen's call center that operated seven days a week. Patterson was a Seventh Day Adventist and demanded that he never be required to work on any Saturday, his sabbath. The court held that Walgreen need not guarantee that Patterson never had to work on Saturdays. It fulfilled its "reasonable accommodation" obligation by allowing Patterson to arrange a schedule swap with other employees when they were willing to do so, and by offering to move him to different jobs where there would be more employees available to ask for a swap. In 2020, the Supreme Court refused to hear Patterson's appeal.

Procedures and Remedies

Title VII establishes special procedures for enforcing its dictates. Individual who believe themselves to be the victim of unlawful discrimination cannot simply take an employer to court. Rather, the Civil Rights Act created the Equal Employment Opportunity Commission (EEOC) to receive complaints of violations. The EEOC investigates these complaints and, when they are adequately supported by facts, the Commission attempts conciliation measures between the employer and employees. If conciliation efforts fail, the EEOC may file suit in federal district court. Individuals may sue to enforce Title VII only after EEOC and the relevant state's equal employment opportunity agency have had the opportunity to act.

Once a court finds that Title VII has been violated, the court is empowered to grant an injunction prohibiting future violations and correcting past actions. Retroactive back pay or seniority may be ordered for employees who have suffered from unlawful discrimination. In addition, a court may compel an offending company to implement an "affirmative action" program to recruit and retain minority employees.

What Constitutes Discrimination Under Title VII?

Plaintiffs may establish illegal discrimination in either of two ways. First, the plaintiff may show that the defendant had engaged in intentional discrimination—sometimes referred to as "disparate treatment." Second, the plaintiff may show that some employment practice or policy of the defendant has had a discriminatory effect, or impact—sometimes referred to as "disparate impact." The following discussion explains the use of these terms.

Intentional Discrimination—"Disparate Treatment"

In general, any employment decision or practice that treats individuals unequally because of race, color, religion, sex, or national origin violates Title VII. Illegal discrimination might occur, for example, in connection with firing, refusing to hire, refusing to train or promote, granting unequal compensation or fringe benefits, or practicing any type of segregation or classification of employees or applicants that tends to deprive them of employment opportunities.

A violation of Title VII may be proved by showing that an employer intended to discriminate for a prohibited reason. Intentional discrimination is often referred to as *disparate treatment.* When there is a claim that the employer violated Title VII by committing disparate treatment, the employer's unlawful motivation can be proved in several ways.

Explicit Exclusionary Policy. If a company has a policy of excluding those of a particular gender, race, color, national origin, or religion, there is no question about whether there was intentional discrimination. This is clearly illegal unless it is one of the really unusual cases in which the employer can prove the so-called BFOQ defense (i.e., that being of a particular gender or national origin is a *bona fide occupational qualification*—a genuine necessity for doing the job). As discussed later, however, race cannot be a BFOQ. Also, a special provision in Title VII allows religious organizations to restrict hiring to those having particular religious beliefs.

Evidence of Intentional Discrimination. Even if there is not an explicit exclusionary policy, sometimes there is direct evidence of intentional discrimination that makes it obvious that an adverse employment action was intentionally based on a person's gender, race, color, national origin, or religion, so that there is no need for a court to carefully sift through many bits of circumstantial evidence. Suppose that Guy is hired to drive a delivery truck by Julie's Fashion Furniture, Inc. On one occasion, Julie is driving to lunch and observes one of her company's delivery trucks rolling through a stop sign without stopping. She saw the license number on the truck but not the identity of the driver. When she returns to work after lunch, she asks an assistant to ascertain who was driving the truck with that license number. Upon hearing that it was Guy, Julie says, "Oh, that doesn't surprise me. Stupid men drivers. They're too aggressive, and they let their testosterone drive for them. Or, when they're not being aggressive, they don't pay attention. He was probably reading his Penthouse while driving. Get the paperwork ready so that I can fire that Neanderthal!" Although these words would not have been illegal by themselves, when she follows up on them by firing Guy, evidence of her words clearly shows that she was motivated in large measure by Guy's gender. Many courts would call this direct evidence of a gender-based motivation. The fact that he was male does not have to be Julie's only reason for firing him, but just a *substantial contributing factor* to the employment decision.

Circumstantial Evidence. In most cases in which there is an allegation of disparate treatment, the evidence is not clear-cut. In such cases, the plaintiff asks the court to draw an inference that there was an underlying discriminatory motivation from an aggregation of circumstantial evidence. The ultimate questions are the same as in other types of cases: First, has the plaintiff presented enough evidence to create a genuine fact issue regarding the employer's discriminatory motivation? An affirmative answer prevents the plaintiff from losing at the summary judgment or directed verdict stage. If so, the next question is whether the plaintiff has proved disparate treatment by a preponderance of the evidence-in other words, does this evidence show that it is more likely than not that the employer's adverse employment decision was based on the plaintiff's race, gender, national origin, or religion. Unlike cases in other areas of law, however, courts in these kinds of Title VII cases have used a three-stage process for analyzing circumstantial evidence. It accomplishes the same results that are accomplished in non-Title VII cases involving circumstantial evidence, but simply goes about it in a somewhat different way.

Prima Facie Case. A court in a Title VII disparate treatment case first seeks to determine whether the plaintiff has established a so-called prima facie case. If not, the plaintiff has not even created a genuine issue of fact on the question and the case will end at a preliminary stage. If the plaintiff does so, however, the case goes forward. In general, a *prima facie case* is established when the EEOC or an individual plaintiff proves facts that permit (but do not compel) an inference that intentional discrimination on the basis of race, color, national origin, gender, or religion was the employer's motivation. More specifically, however, the courts have identified particular facts that must be proved in particular situations to establish a prima facie case.

Suppose, for example, that an individual job applicant is rejected and has reason to believe that the employer's refusal to hire was motivated by unlawful discrimination. In a hiring situation such as this, a prima facie violation of Title VII can be established by showing that (1) the applicant is within a protected class (e.g., a racial minority); (2) the applicant applied for a job for which the employer was seeking applicants; (3) the applicant was qualified to perform the job; (4) the applicant was not hired for the job; and (5) the employer either filled the position with a nonminority person or continued trying to fill it. If the claim of discrimination is based on a discharge rather than a refusal to hire, a prima facie case can be established by showing that (1) the plaintiff is within a protected class; (2) the plaintiff was performing the job satisfactorily; (3) the plaintiff was discharged; and (4) the plaintiff's work was then assigned to someone who was not within a protected class. In other employment decisions, the requirements of a prima facie case would similarly have to be modified to fit the circumstances.

Employer's Rebuttal. When the plaintiff in such a case introduces evidence sufficient to create a prima facie case, the burden then shifts to the employer to bring forth evidence of a *legitimate, nondiscriminatory reason* for its decision. To overcome plaintiff's prima facie case, the employer can introduce evidence relating to matters such as the applicant's past experience and work record, letters of recommendation, or the superior qualifications of the person actually hired. An example is found in *Peters v. Jefferson Chemical Co.,* 516 F.2d 447 (5th Cir. 1975), in which the employer successfully rebutted the female plaintiff's prima facie case by showing that she had not been hired as a laboratory chemist because she had not done laboratory work for several years. The court did not require the employer to prove that her skills were actually inadequate, but accepted the employer's assumption that laboratory skills diminish from nonuse over a substantial period of time. In another case, *Boyd v. Madison County Mutual Insurance Co.,* 653 F.2d 1173 (7th Cir. 1981), a male employee established a prima facie case of sex discrimination against the employer by showing that the employer had a policy of awarding attendance bonuses only to clerical employees, all of whom were women. The employer was able to rebut the prima facie case successfully by demonstrating that there had been a serious absenteeism problem with clerical staff and that the bonus policy was aimed at correcting that problem.

In a case based on an allegedly discriminatory discharge, the employer might overcome the plaintiff's prima facie case by showing evidence of the plaintiff's poor performance, absenteeism, insubordination, and so on.

Pretext. If the plaintiff establishes a prima facie Title VII violation and the employer fails to come forth with acceptable evidence of a legitimate, nondiscriminatory reason, the plaintiff wins. If the employer does produce such evidence, plaintiffs will lose unless they can then convince the court that the employer's asserted reason was really just a *pretext*— that is, a cover-up for intentional discrimination. Plaintiffs might be able to show, for example, that the employer offered shifting and inconsistent rationales for its action. Or plaintiffs might demonstrate that the employer's "legitimate reason" was applied discriminatorily. In *Corley v. Jackson Police Dept.,* 566 F.2d 994 (5th Cir. 1978), the employer proved that the plaintiffs, black police officers, had been fired for accepting bribes. Although this clearly was a legitimate reason for firing them, the plaintiffs proved that white officers who also had been accused of the same conduct by an informant were not investigated as thoroughly and were not fired. The court held that the employer's reason was a pretext for racial discrimination and that Title VII had been violated.

Harassment as a Special Case of Disparate Treatment

Harassment of an employee because of that employee's race, sex, religion, or national origin is a particular form of disparate treatment discrimination under Title VII. The same basic principles apply to all types of harassment, but there can be some differences when sexual demands or requests are made. Because of the special nature of harassment cases, the courts often do not follow the prima facie-rebuttal-pretext decision model.

Sexual Harassment

Harassment or intimidation of an employee violates Title VII when it is based on that person's sex just as it does when based on race, color, religion, or national origin. Sexual harassment may take the same form that other illegal harassment normally takes, namely, slurs, taunts, epithets, or other abuses that create a hostile, intimidating, or offensive working environment. In some situations, however, sexual harassment may be quite different from harassment for racial or other reasons. Sexual harassment may take the form of unwelcome requests for sexual favors. Sexual harassment is a form of intentional sex discrimination because the harasser would not treat the victim this way if the victim were of the other gender.

The courts and the EEOC have recognized two general kinds of situations in which such unwelcome requests constitute illegal sexual harassment. These two varieties, which may sometimes overlap, are referred to as "quid pro quo" and "hostile environment" sexual harassment.

Quid Pro Quo Harassment. The Latin term *quid pro quo* means "something for something," and refers to the situation in which continued employment, a favorable review, promotion, or some other tangible job benefit is explicitly or implicitly conditioned upon an employee's positive response to a requested sexual favor. Although there is no rule that only supervisors can commit quid pro quo harassment, as a practical matter it is only one with supervisory or managerial authority who has control over job benefits and who is thus capable of committing this form of sexual harassment. The evidence must convince a court that the sexual advances were unwelcome. When the unwelcome request or demand for sexual activities causes the target to believe that a negative response will lead to adverse job-related consequences, and when the evidence shows that a reasonable person would also believe this, there is quid pro quo harassment.

Hostile Environment Sexual Harassment. So-called "hostile environment" sexual harassment occurs when a supervisor, manager, or co-worker engages in sexually-oriented language or conduct that is unwelcome and that is sufficiently "severe or pervasive" to alter the terms and conditions of employment for an employee who has been targeted. Repeated sexual advances can constitute hostile environment sexual harassment, as can language and conduct that manifest gender-based hostility. Sometimes, hostile environment cases involve a mixture of unwelcome sexual advances and gender-based hostility.

The question whether the harassment is severe or pervasive is analyzed in the same way in sexual harassment cases as in other forms of impermissible harassment. The court first determines whether the unwelcome language and conduct is aimed at the victims because of their gender. Then, the court ascertains whether the language and conduct were sufficiently severe or pervasive to alter the work environment, both subjectively from the victim's perspective and objectively from the perspective of a reasonable person in the victim's position. In other words, when the victim is female, the objective determination is made from the perspective of a reasonable woman. The decision whether the harassment was severe or pervasive takes account of several factors, including the severity of particular instances, the frequency and duration of occurrences, and the overall workplace ambience.

Most victims of sexual harassment are females, but occasionally females victimize males. The Supreme Court also has ruled that same-sex sexual harassment is actionable under Title VII, as long as the evidence shows that the victims were harassed because of their gender. Some courts have held, however, that if the evidence shows that the harassment based solely on the employee's homosexuality, it is not a violation because Title VII does not prohibit discrimination based on homosexuality.

Employer Liability for Sexual Harassment. For most alleged violations of Title VII, the only question is whether the evidence shows that there was such a violation. If there is a violation, the employer is liable. In the case of harassment, however, the rules for employer liability are somewhat different. The main reason for the difference is that illegal harassment can be committed by co-workers and not just by managers. The question of employer liability is especially important in Title VII cases because only the employer can be held monetarily liable; individuals cannot be liable for damages in their personal capacity as they can in tort law. A court can issue an injunction against both the employer and particular individuals in a Title VII case, however. In harassment cases involving particularly egregious conduct, the victim frequently asserts tort law claims such as intentional infliction of emotional distress, assault and battery, or false imprisonment against the individual wrongdoers, who can indeed be personally subjected to tort liability.

As with other types of harassment, the employer can be held strictly liable if the harassment is committed by a supervisor. Employees are "supervisors" in this setting only if they are empowered by the employer to take tangible employment actions against the plaintiff. If the harassment is committed by a co-worker, the employer can be liable only if a supervisor knows or should know about the harassment and fails to take prompt action to stop the harassment and prevent it from recurring. In sexual harassment cases, however, the Supreme Court has created a special defense (often known as the *Faragher/Ellerth* defense) for employers even when the requisite degree of supervisory involvement exists. The defense strongly encourages employers to have anti-harassment policies in the workplace. For this defense to be applicable, the following must be proved:

1. The employee did not suffer a tangible job detriment, such as discharge, demotion, undesirable reassignment, and so forth. If there was such a detriment to the employee, the defense does not exist.
2. The employer had a stated company policy condemning sexual harassment that provided a clear procedure for employees to make complaints. The policy must have been well publicized in the

workplace, such as being prominently displayed in signs or prominently included in an employee handbook. The complaint procedure must provide a means for the employee to go over the head of a supervisor when the supervisor is the alleged harasser.

3. If the employee did not suffer a tangible job detriment, and the employer had a clear and well publicized policy against sexual harassment with adequate complaint procedures, the employer is not liable for the Title VII violation if the employee failed to use these complaint procedures. The courts have held, however, that an employee does not have to immediately report the harassment. In other words, the employee will be deemed to have used the available complaint procedures, thus removing the employer's defense, even when the employee waits a substantial period of time before complaining.

With regard to the first element of the employer defense, there are, of course, many situations in which the fact of a tangible job detriment is obvious, such as those in which the employee's resistance to sexual harassment leads to being fired, demoted, or denied benefits. There also are situations in which the courts will have no difficulty in concluding that the employee did not suffer a tangible job detriment. For example, suppose that a supervisor commits quid pro quo harassment by making unwelcome sexual overtures to an employee and indicating that there will be negative consequences if the employee resists. But then nothing else happens—the supervisor does not carry out his threats and doesn't continue the behavior. In such a case, the employer is not liable if an adequate policy and complaint procedures were in place, and the employee failed to use them.

One question that several courts have had to face is whether employees suffer a tangible job detriment when they submit to sexual demands because of a fear of losing their job. As long as it is clear that the sexual demands were unwelcome and the submission was coerced, courts have treated the submission as a tangible job detriment, thus depriving the employer of any defense to the Title VII violation. The Supreme Court has held that a constructive discharge, which occurs when an employee voluntarily quits because working conditions are so bad that a reasonable person would find them to be intolerable, is by itself not a tangible job detriment. The Court held that, if an employer has a well-designed anti-harassment policy with good complaint procedures and the harassed employees prove only that they quit because the sexually hostile environment created working conditions that would be intolerable to a reasonable victim, the employer is not liable. The employees must additionally prove that the employer did something concrete such as demoting, decreasing compensation or benefits, or giving an undesirable reassignment.

The following is a recent sexual harassment case that discusses both types of sexual harassment claim (quid pro quo and hostile environment) as well as a retaliation claim that will soon be discussed in more detail in this text.

OKOLI v. CITY OF BALTIMORE
648 F.3d 216 (4ᵗʰ Cir. 2011)

Stewart was director of a city agency in Baltimore. In June of 2004, he hired plaintiff/appellant Okoli, an African-American woman, to serve as his executive assistant. Things went smoothly at first, but in September 2004 Stewart began propositioning Okoli to have sex with him in a Jacuzzi as part of his sexual fantasy. He first did so on September 13, 2004. During a September 24, 2004 work meeting, Stewart then asked Okoli whether she was wearing any underwear, what color it was, and whether she would come to work the next day without underwear. On October 4, 2004, Stewart told Okoli about a sexual experience he had with an African-American woman and her daughter. Okoli reacted with shock and disgust, which Stewart noticed. Another time, Stewart again mentioned this sexual experience with a mother and daughter. Okoli reiterated that the daughter would despise and regret having such a lewd sexual encounter with her mother.

Stewart continued to proposition Okoli about his Jacuzzi fantasy, and on November 10, 2004, asked her to sit on his lap and to join him in a Jacuzzi in Las Vegas. Whenever Stewart traveled, he continued to request Okoli to join him in his Jacuzzi, and became angry when she rejected his advances. Furthermore, Stewart touched Okoli's legs under the conference table "two or three times" during their morning meetings. Whenever this occurred, Okoli would move away from Stewart and tell him "don't do that."

On January 10, 2005, Stewart asked Okoli to come back in a conference room, then forcibly grabbed and kissed her. Okoli pushed him away and ran out the door. She was so distraught that she went home and remained there for the day. When she returned to work the next day, Okoli stressed to Stewart that she still wanted to have only a professional relationship. While he initially said "O.K.," Stewart repeated his Jacuzzi fantasy again that same day.

Okoli then began reaching out to Stewart's superiors for help in various ways, to no avail. When her complaints to superiors were forwarded to Stewart, he fired Okoli. Following proper procedures, Okoli sued for a violation of Title VII (quid pro quo harassment, hostile environment harassment, and retaliation) and the case ultimately came before a federal district judge who ruled, among other things, that the actions alleged did not constitute a case of hostile environment sexual harassment because there were "[j]ust three or four incidents [of physical contact] over a five-month period," and no physical threat to Okoli. Okoli appealed.

Gregory, Circuit Judge:

First, Okoli alleges she was subject to a hostile work environment. "To demonstrate sexual harassment and/or a racially hostile work environment, a plaintiff must show that there is (1) unwelcome conduct; (2) that is based on the plaintiff's sex [and/or race]; (3) which is sufficiently severe or pervasive to alter the plaintiff's conditions of employment and to create an abusive work environment; and (4) which is imputable to the employer." *Mosby-Grant v. City of Hagerstown,* 630 F.3d 326 (4th Cir. 2010).

The third factor is dispositive here: whether Stewart's treatment was severe or pervasive enough. The City contends it was not, characterizes Stewart's conduct as sporadic and infrequent, depicts Stewart as promptly stopping this conduct once Okoli objected, and questions whether some of Stewart's comments and gifts were sexual at all.

We conclude that Okoli presents a strong claim for hostile work environment. Here, we look to the totality of the circumstances, including the "'frequency of the discriminatory conduct; its severity; whether it is physically threatening or humiliating, or a mere offensive utterance; and whether it unreasonably interferes with an employee's work performance.'" *Faragher v. City of Boca Raton,* 524 U.S. 775 (1998). Viewing the facts in the light most favorable to Okoli, she suffered upwards of twelve (12) incidents in just four months: (1) disparaging jokes about gays and lesbians; (2) comments about Okoli and Jacuzzi fantasy; (3) comments about Okoli and group sex fantasy; (4) questions about Okoli's underwear; (5) comments about sexual relations with another African-American woman; (6) additional inquiries about Okoli sitting on lap and Jacuzzi fantasy; (7-10) three incidents of fondling her leg under a table; (11) forcible kissing; (12) more propositions to join in a Jacuzzi fantasy. These events took place from September 8 through January 11. Functionally, these incidents span fondling, kissing, propositioning, describing sexual activities, and asking intimate questions. Some of the incidents may have been severe enough to be actionable in and of themselves.

Collectively, Okoli was subject to repeated propositioning and physical touching. By any objective and reasonable standard, the allegations here are far beyond "simple teasing [and] offhand comments." *Faragher,* at 778. Moreover, Stewart's alleged conduct is much more than "'generalized' statements that pollute the work environment"—they clearly constitute "'personal gender-based remarks' that single out individuals for ridicule." *EEOC v. Fairbrook Med. Clinic,* 609 .3d 320 (4th Cir. 2010). Here too, there is a significant "disparity in power," *Jennings v. UNC,* 482 F.3d 686 (4th Cir. 2007). Stewart is a political appointee who sits in the Mayor's cabinet and heads an agency with more than a hundred employees. Okoli was a new secretary whose job required her to have a lot of one-on-one contact with her boss.

Furthermore, the sexual advances here were more numerous and explicit than in *Beardsley v. Webb,* [30 F.3d 524 (4th Cir. 1994), where we found a hostile work environment when, over six months, a supervisor massaged an employee's shoulders, stated he wanted to "make out" and "have his way" with her, falsely accused her of having an affair, and asked her about her underwear, birth control, and the bodily effects of taking maternity leave.

Second, Okoli claims she experienced quid pro quo discrimination. This requires an employee prove five elements:

1. The employee belongs to a protected group.

2. The employee was subject to unwelcome sexual harassment.

3. The harassment complained of was based upon sex.

4. The employee's reaction to the harassment affected tangible aspects of the employee's compensation, terms, conditions, or privileges of employment. The acceptance or rejection of the harassment must be an express or implied condition to the receipt of a job benefit or cause of a tangible job detriment to create liability. Further, as in typical disparate treatment cases, the employee must prove that she was deprived of a job benefit which she was otherwise qualified to receive because of the employer's use of a prohibited criterion in making the employment decision.

5. The employer, as defined by Title VII, 42 U.S.C. § 2000e(b), knew or should have known of the harassment and took no effective remedial action.

Brown v. Perry, 184 F.3d 388 (4th Cir. 1999).

With the fourth element, "[a] tangible employment action constitutes a significant change in employment status, such as hiring, firing, failing to promote, reassignment with significantly different responsibilities, or a decision causing a significant change in benefits." *Burlington Indus. v. Ellerth,* 524 U.S. 742 (1998). The fifth element is "automatically met" when the harassment was alleged to have been perpetrated by a supervisor. If the plaintiff makes a prima facie showing, the burden shifts to the employer to articulate a legitimate, non-retaliatory reason for the adverse action. Then, if the employer satisfies its burden, the burden returns to the plaintiff to establish that the employer's proffered reason is a pretext for discrimination.

In this case, the inquiry turns on the fourth factor: whether Okoli's reaction to Stewart's advances affected "tangible aspects" of her employment. The parties focus mostly on whether Stewart's decision to conduct an informal performance feedback—as opposed to a formal, periodic performance review—was "tangible" enough. Performance reviews are clearly related to employment and promotion. But the record contains no details about what reviews are standard or required by office policy. The more "tangible" employment action taken by Stewart was Okoli's allegation that Stewart fired her for rejecting his advances and complaining about his conduct.

The City also maintains it had a legitimate non-discriminatory reason for terminating Okoli that has not been shown to be pretextual. Okoli must then show that the proffered reason is false: "In appropriate circumstances, the trier of fact can reasonably infer from the falsity of the explanation that the employer is dissembling to cover up a discriminatory purpose." *Washington v. City of Charlotte,* 219 Fed. Appx. 273 (4th Cir. 2007). In this case, there is some evidence that Okoli occasionally had scheduling conflicts and made typographical errors. But it appears deeply suspicious that Stewart fired Okoli only hours after she culminated her rejection of him by complaining to the Mayor. There is little in the record to suggest Okoli would have been fired for the occasional typo, notwithstanding her "at-will" employment status. "[W]hen all legitimate reasons for rejecting an applicant have been eliminated as possible reasons for the employer's actions, it is more likely than not the employer, who we generally assume acts with some reason, based his decision on an impermissible consideration . . . ." *Furnco Const. Corp. v. Waters,* 487 U.S. 567 (1978).

Third, Okoli maintains that Stewart retaliated against her. "To state a prima facie case of retaliation, a plaintiff must show that (1) the plaintiff engaged in a protected activity, such as filing a complaint with the EEOC; (2) the employer acted adversely against the plaintiff; and (3) the protected activity was causally connected to the employer's adverse action." *Beall v. Abbott Labs,* 130 F.3d 614 (4th Cir. 1997).

The parties disagree centrally about whether Okoli's April 1 letter to the Mayor constituted protected activity because it did not explicitly mention sexual harassment. … Here, it was enough for Okoli to twice complain of "harassment," even if it might have been more ideal for her to detail the sexual incidents she later relayed. Okoli's April 1 memo to the Mayor described "unethical and unprofessional business characteristics, e.g., harassment, degrading and dehumanizing yelling and demanding, disrespect, mocking and gossiping about other colleagues (anyone in the City government) and lack or disregard for integrity." The City surely should have known that Okoli's complaints of "harassment" likely encompassed sexual harassment. Viewing the evidence in the light most favorable to Okoli, we can infer that Stewart did not intend to fire her before April 1—and therefore a genuine dispute of material fact still exists on this front.

We remand this case for a jury to resolve Okoli's three claims.

Discriminatory Impact ("Disparate Impact")

Another way to prove that an employer has violated Title VII is to show that a particular employment rule or practice, although apparently neutral on its face, actually has an unequal impact on a protected group. Examples include height and weight requirements having the effect of excluding a disproportionate number of females, or a standardized test or educational requirement having the effect of excluding a disproportionate number of persons from a particular ethnic group. In such a case, the plaintiff is not required to show that the defendant had an intent to discriminate.

Prima Facie Case. The individual plaintiff, or the EEOC acting in the individual's behalf, must initially prove that the employment practice in question has an adverse impact on the protected group of which the individual is a member. This can be accomplished by the use of several different types of evidence. It could be shown, for example, that the employment practice has caused the employer to hire 40 percent of the whites who had applied, but only 20 percent of black applicants. Or, in another situation, discriminatory impact might be proved by showing that some action of the employer had the effect of eliminating 75 percent of all women from possible consideration, even though women comprise approximately one-half of the total population. Another method for proving discriminatory impact is to do a statistical comparison of the composition of the employer's work force with the composition of the relevant labor pool. For example, if the plaintiff alleges that a job criterion or selection method has a discriminatory impact on blacks, the plaintiff might attempt to show that the percentage of blacks working for the employer is much smaller than the percentage of qualified blacks in the available labor market. When a statistical disparity is used to prove discriminatory impact, the plaintiff must produce evidence linking the particular practice being challenged to the statistical imbalance in the employer's work force. If several employment practices are being challenged on the grounds that they have an aggregate discriminatory impact, the plaintiff will be permitted to lump them together if it is not feasible to single out a specific practice and show its impact alone.

It is important to realize, however, that the method used to prove discriminatory impact must be tailored to fit the particular employment practice being challenged and the particular group allegedly being affected. Thus, a court usually would not accept a comparison of the employer's minority hiring rate with general population statistics where the job in question required special qualifications.

Employer's Rebuttal. As we have seen, an employer may rebut a prima facie case of discriminatory intent merely by producing some plausible evidence of a nondiscriminatory reason for the employer's action. When the plaintiff has established a prima facie case by proving discriminatory impact, however, the employer's task of rebuttal is somewhat more difficult. In an impact case, the employer has to prove (not just introduce some plausible evidence) "business necessity." To meet this burden, the employer must prove that (1) the challenged employment practice was necessary to achieve an important business objective, and (2) the practice actually achieves this objective.

Employee's Proof of Alternatives. If the employer has proved business necessity, the plaintiffs lose unless they can then prove that the employer had some other feasible alternative for achieving its important business objective, that the alternative would have accomplished the objective without having a discriminatory effect, and that the employer failed to use this non-discriminatory alternative.

Disparate Impact in Recent Years. Proving a Title VII violation by showing disparate impact once was a fairly commonly used alternative to proving a violation by showing disparate treatment. In recent years, however, the federal courts have made it far more difficult to prove disparate impact. In most cases, a plaintiff has to make a rather sophisticated statistical demonstration of disparate impact, and the courts have substantially raised the standards for doing this. Disparate impact can still be proved in some cases, such as height requirements that obviously have the effect of excluding a much larger portion of women than men. In most other situations, however, proving disparate impact has become much more difficult. This fact, coupled with the fact that Congress made *disparate treatment* cases much more attractive for plaintiffs by providing for jury trials and increasing the amount of damages that can be recovered, has led to the result that very few disparate impact cases are filed anymore.

The following case addresses the difference between disparate treatment and disparate impact cases and talks about the important issue of causation in a religious discrimination case.

EEOC v. ABERCROMBIE & FITCH STORES, INC.
575 U.S. 768 (Supreme Court 2015)

Consistent with the image Abercrombie & Fitch (respondent) seeks to project for its clothing stores, the company imposes a Look Policy that governs its employees' dress. The Look Policy prohibits "caps" as too informal for Abercrombie's desired image. Samantha Elauf, a practicing Muslim, wears a headscarf as she believes is required by her religion. Elauf applied for a position in an Abercrombie store, and was interviewed by Heather Cooke, the store's assistant manager. Cooke rated Elauf as qualified to be hired, but her supreriors concluded that Elauf's headscarf would violate the Look Policy, as would all other headwear, religious or otherwise, and directed Cooke not to hire Elauf.

The EEOC sued Abercrombie on Elauf's behalf, claiming that its refusal to hire Elauf violated Title VII. The trial court held a trial and ruled for the EEOC, but on appeal the Tenth Circuit Court of Appeals granted Abercrombie summary judgment, concluding that ordinarily an employer cannot be liable under Title VII for failing to accommodate a religious practice until the applicant (or employee) provides the employer with actual knowledge of his need for an accommodation. The EEOC appealed.

Scalia, Justice:

Title VII of the Civil Rights Act of 1964 prohibits two categories of employment practices. It is unlawful for an employer:

> (1) to fail or refuse to hire or to discharge any individual, or otherwise to discriminate against any individual with respect to his compensation, terms, conditions, or privileges of employment, because of such individual's race, color, religion, sex, or national origin; or
> (2) to limit, segregate, or classify his employees or applicants for employment in any way which would deprive or tend to deprive any individual of employment opportunities or otherwise adversely affect his status as an employee, because of such individual's race, color, religion, sex, or national origin.

These two proscriptions, often referred to as the "disparate treatment" (or "intentional discrimination") provision and the "disparate impact" provision, are the only causes of action under Title VII. The word "religion" is defined to "includ[e] all aspects of religious observance and practice, as well as belief, unless an employer demonstrates that he is unable to reasonably accommodate to" a "religious observance or practice without undue hardship on the conduct of the employer's business."

Abercrombie's primary argument is that an applicant cannot show disparate treatment without first showing that an employer has "actual knowledge" of the applicant's need for an accommodation. We disagree. Instead, an applicant need only show that his need for an accommodation was a motivating factor in the employer's decision.

The disparate-treatment provision forbids employers to: (1) "fail . . . to hire" an applicant (2) "because of" (3) "such individual's . . . religion" (which includes his religious practice). Here, of course, Abercrombie (1) failed to hire Elauf. The parties concede that (if Elauf sincerely believes that her religion so requires) Elauf's wearing of a headscarf is (3) a "religious practice." All that remains is whether she was not hired (2) "because of" her religious practice.

The term "because of" appears frequently in antidiscrimination laws. It typically imports, at a minimum, the traditional standard of but-for causation. *University of Tex. Southwestern Medical Center v. Nassar*, 133 S. Ct. 2517 (2013). Title VII relaxes this standard, however, to prohibit even making a protected characteristic a "motivating factor" in an employment decision. 42 U. S. C. §2000e-2(m). "Because of" in §2000e-2(a)(1) links the forbidden consideration to each of the verbs preceding it; an individual's actual religious practice may not be a motivating factor in failing to hire, in refusing to hire, and so on.

It is significant that §2000e-2(a)(1) does not impose a knowledge requirement. As Abercrombie acknowledges, some antidiscrimination statutes do. For example, the Americans with Disabilities Act of 1990 defines discrimination to include an employer's failure to make "reasonable accommodations to the known physical or mental limitations" of an applicant. Title VII contains no such limitation.

Instead, the intentional discrimination provision prohibits certain motives, regardless of the state of the actor's knowledge. Motive and knowledge are separate concepts. An employer who has actual knowledge of the need for an accommodation does not violate Title VII by refusing to hire an applicant if avoiding that accommodation is not his motive. Conversely, an employer who acts with the motive of avoiding accommodation may violate Title VII even if he has no more than an unsubstantiated suspicion that accommodation would be needed.

Thus, the rule for disparate-treatment claims based on a failure to accommodate a religious practice is straightforward: An employer may not make an applicant's religious practice, confirmed or otherwise, a factor in employment decisions. For example, suppose that an employer thinks (though he does not know for certain) that a job applicant may be an orthodox Jew who will observe the Sabbath, and thus be unable to work on Saturdays. If the applicant actually requires an accommodation of that religious practice, and the employer's desire to avoid the prospective accommodation is a motivating factor in his decision, the employer violates Title VII.

Abercrombie urges this Court to adopt the Tenth Circuit's rule "allocat[ing] the burden of raising a religious conflict." This would require the employer to have actual knowledge of a conflict between an applicant's religious practice and a work rule. The problem with this approach is the one that inheres in most incorrect interpretations of statutes: It asks us to add words to the law to produce what is thought to be a desirable result. That is Congress's province. We construe Title VII's silence as exactly that: silence. Its disparate-treatment provision prohibits actions taken with the motive of avoiding the need for accommodating a religious practice. A request for accommodation, or the employer's certainty that the practice exists, may make it easier to infer motive, but is not a necessary condition of liability.

Abercrombie argues in the alternative that a claim based on a failure to accommodate an applicant's religious practice must be raised as a disparate-impact claim, not a disparate-treatment claim. We think not. That might have been true if Congress had limited the meaning of "religion" in Title VII to religious belief—so that discriminating against a particular religious practice would not be disparate treatment though it might have disparate impact. In fact, however, Congress defined "religion," for Title VII's purposes, as "includ[ing] all aspects of religious observance and practice, as well as belief." 42 U. S. C. §2000e(j). Thus, religious practice is one of the protected characteristics that cannot be accorded disparate treatment and must be accommodated.

Nor does the statute limit disparate-treatment claims to only those employer policies that treat religious practices less favorably than similar secular practices. Abercrombie's argument that a neutral policy cannot constitute "intentional discrimination" may make sense in other contexts. But Title VII does not demand mere neutrality with regard to religious practices—that they be treated no worse than other practices. Rather, it gives them favored treatment, affirmatively obligating employers not "to fail or refuse to hire or discharge any individual . . . because of such individual's" "religious observance and practice." An employer is surely entitled to have, for example, a no-headwear policy as an ordinary matter. But when an applicant requires an accommodation as an "aspec[t] of religious . . . practice," it is no response that the subsequent "fail[ure] . . . to hire" was due to an otherwise-neutral policy. Title VII requires otherwise-neutral policies to give way to the need for an accommodation. Reversed and remanded.

Bona Fide Occupational Qualification Defense

Once discrimination has been proved, the employer has few defenses. One such defense in Title VII provides that it is not illegal to discriminate on the basis of religion, sex, or national origin in situations where religion, sex, or national origin is a bona fide occupational qualification (BFOQ). The law states that race or color cannot be a BFOQ, although the First Amendment would likely be construed to ensure that it is legal to cast an actor of a particular race to portray a historical figure of that race, Lin-Manuel Miranda's "Hamilton" notwithstanding. Congress intended the BFOQ defense to be a very limited exception that would apply only to rare situations. The EEOC and the courts have indeed recognized this defense only infrequently.

Most of the situations in which the BFOQ defense has been an issue have involved sex discrimination, and most of those have involved employer policies that clearly excluded women from certain jobs. Stereotypes or traditional assumptions about which jobs are appropriate for males or females do not establish the BFOQ exception. A basic principle of Title VII is that the individual should decide whether the job is appropriate, assuming that person is qualified to perform it. Thus, males cannot be barred from jobs such as airline flight attendant or secretary, and females cannot automatically be barred from mining, construction, or other jobs requiring lifting, night work, and so forth. Even the fact that the employer's customers strongly prefer employees to be of one sex or the other does not give rise to a BFOQ exception.

In a few circumstances, however, gender is an essential element of the job. For example, the BFOQ defense has been permitted where one sex or the other is necessary for authenticity, as in the case of models or actors. In addition, being a woman has been held to be a BFOQ for employment as a salesperson in the ladies' undergarments department of a department store, and as a nurse in the labor and delivery section of an obstetrical hospital. Being a man has been held to be a BFOQ for employment as a security guard, where the job involved searching male employees, and also as an attendant in a men's restroom.

EVERTS v. SUSHI BROKERS LLC
247 F.Supp.3d 1075 (D. Arizona 2017)

Beginning in early 2011, Plaintiff Everts worked as a sushi server at Defendant's restaurant. Later that year, she became pregnant, and her pregnancy began to show. On September 18, 2011, Randon L. Miller, Defendant's managing member and thus owner of the restaurant, left a voicemail for Plaintiff's shift manager, Ms. Morton, stating the following:

"[W]e got Baby Momma. We got—oh, I can't leave these messages because obviously we'd get in trouble—but it's just ridiculous. It's all the same stuff. We can't have a big fat pregnant woman working in my restaurant. I'm sorry it doesn't fly. I will not hire them when they walk in. I will not eat them with eggs. I will not eat them with ham. No green eggs; no ham; no nothing . . . I don't know how I have—who I have to deal with to get people off my schedule. So please call me tomorrow and we'll work it out."

On September 20, 2011, Ms. Morton fired Plaintiff without citing her pregnancy as the reason for the termination. Plaintiff claimed that Defendant terminated her after she refused to accept a reassignment to the hostess position because of her pregnancy. Defendant concedes that one of the reasons it fired Plaintiff was because she refused to accept reassignment to the hostess position as a reasonable accommodation designed to protect her health and safety during her pregnancy. Plaintiff timely filed a charge of discrimination with the EEOC, which issued to her a Notice of Right to Sue. Plaintiff filed this suit claiming pregnancy discrimination in violation of Title VII. Plaintiff moved for summary judgment.

Tuchi, District Judge:

Under Title VII, an employer cannot discharge or discriminate against an individual based on sex. As amended by the Pregnancy Discrimination Act (PDA), sex discrimination under Title VII includes discrimination on the basis of pregnancy. … To prove disparate treatment under Title VII using direct evidence, a plaintiff must show that the employer had a facially discriminatory policy—one which on its face applies less favorably to a protected group. When an employer openly and explicitly uses gender as a basis for disparate treatment, the employer in effect admits systematic discrimination and the case turns on whether such disparate treatment is justified under Title VII. Once a policy is shown to be facially discriminatory, the court simply asks whether sex was a "bona fide occupational qualification" ("BFOQ"). The BFOQ defense is read narrowly and can be established only by "objective, verifiable requirement[s] . . . [that] concern job-related skills and aptitudes." *UAW v. Johnson Controls, Inc.*, 499 U.S. 187 (1991). To prove that sex is a BFOQ, an employer must prove by a preponderance of the evidence that "1) the job qualification justifying the discrimination is reasonably necessary to the essence of its business; and 2) that [sex] is a legitimate proxy for the qualification because (a) it has a 'substantial basis for believing that all or nearly all [pregnant women] lack the qualification,' or . . . (b) it is impossible or 'highly impractical . . . to insure by individual testing that its employees will have the necessary qualifications for the job." *EEOC v. Boeing Co.*, 843 F.2d 1213 (9th Cir. 1988).

[After examining the testimony in the case, the Court held that] Defendant indisputably tried to reassign Plaintiff to a hostess position, in part, out of fear for the safety of her fetus and subsequently fired Plaintiff when she refused to accept this reassignment.

Having concluded that no dispute of material fact remains that Defendant overtly discriminated against Plaintiff based on her pregnancy, the Court next addresses if such disparate treatment is justified under Title VII. Defendant argues that reassigning Plaintiff to a hostess position was necessary because non-pregnancy "is a [BFOQ] reasonably necessary to the normal operation of that particular business or enterprise." To qualify for the BFOQ defense, Defendant must prove that 1) specific job qualifications of a server justifying the discrimination are necessary to the essence of its business, and 2) sex is a legitimate proxy for the qualification because nearly all visibly pregnant servers lack the qualification or it is highly impractical to individually test servers to insure that they have the necessary qualification.

Regarding the first prong of the BFOQ test, Defendant asserts that a prerequisite for the sushi server position is the ability to carry heavy plates in close proximity to sharp sushi knives in a crowded area where a server may get bumped or fall. Defendant cites to specific testimony in the record that could lead a factfinder to agree. Therefore, the Court finds that Defendant has raised a triable issue of fact that ability to work under certain conditions at the restaurant is reasonably necessary to the essence of its business.

However, regarding the second prong, the Court finds that Defendant has not shown any evidence that nearly all visibly pregnant women lack the ability to work in the conditions required by the server position or that it is impracticable to insure employees are qualified through individual testing. Defendant cites broad, scientific studies regarding trauma during pregnancy to argue that all pregnant women must be reassigned because it is impracticable to test on a case-by-case basis whether Plaintiff could handle trauma to her stomach. This argument and the supporting evidence are unpersuasive because Defendant presumes that servers are likely to experience trauma to the stomach that is severe enough to harm a fetus or a pregnant employee. Defendant proffers no evidence to support this presumption, such as expert testimony regarding the risk of fetal injury at the restaurant or evidence of previous injuries to servers. Defendant's argument is solely based on a barebones speculation of danger. Even if Defendant had supported this argument with evidence, Defendant's reasoning is explicitly rejected by the Ninth Circuit Court of Appeals and the United States Supreme Court.

Concerns for the safety of an unborn fetus, even if such concerns are well-founded and altruistic, are not sufficient to establish sex as a BFOQ. For example, in *Johnson Controls*, a battery manufacturer barred all women, except those whose infertility was medically documented, from jobs involving actual or potential lead exposure exceeding the Occupational Safety and Health Administration ("OSHA") standard. The Supreme Court held that the company's fetal-protection policy is sex discrimination forbidden under Title VII and that sex was not a BFOQ in that case. The Court reasoned that "moral and ethical concerns about the welfare of the next generation do not suffice to establish a BFOQ." Instead, the PDA mandates that decisions about the welfare of future children be left to parents, not employers.

Sex can be a BFOQ in very limited situations. The Supreme Court held that an employer's concerns for the physical safety of its clientele may qualify sex as a BFOQ. *See Dothard v. Rawlinson*, 433 U.S. 321 (1977) (reasoning that employing women as prison guards—in a maximum-security prison where an estimated 20% of the male prisoners were sex offenders scattered throughout the prison's dormitory facility—could pose a threat to the basic control of the penitentiary and the protection of the inmates and other security personnel). However, courts can only consider the safety of third parties in the BFOQ analysis if those third parties are indispensable to the "essence of the business." *Western Air Lines v. Criswell*, 472 U.S. 400 (1985); *see also Johnson Controls* (rejecting the company's BFOQ defense in regards to a policy that excludes pregnant workers, in part, because fetuses are not customers or third parties whose safety is essential to the company's business).

Additionally, arbitrary stereotypes about the physical capabilities of women generally attributable to the group cannot be used to establish sex as a BFOQ. *See EEOC v. Spokane Concrete Products, Inc.*, 534 F.Supp. 518 (E.D.Wash. 1982) (holding that sex was not a BFOQ for a truck driver position because the employer's decision to exclude women relied solely on myths and purely habitual assumptions about the physical differences between men and women).

The Court agrees with Plaintiff that it is undisputed that non-pregnancy in this case is not a BFOQ. First, there is no evidence that Plaintiff's pregnancy created a risk to customers. Second, the only third-party whose safety Defendant is concerned about is Plaintiff's fetus, which is not an indispensable party to the essence of Defendant's business. Third, Defendant's reason for reassigning Plaintiff—concerns about the safety of her fetus—is explicitly rejected by *Johnson Controls*. Fourth, Defendant's statements about the weight of plates, sharp knives, and other conditions in the restaurant that Defendant sees as inappropriate for a pregnant server are arbitrary stereotypes about the physical capabilities of pregnant women that are insufficient to establish a BFOQ. Defendant can only exclude upon a showing of individual incapacity instead of based on habitual assumptions about all pregnant workers.

Overall, Plaintiff has indisputably established through direct evidence that Defendant has a workplace policy that discriminates against pregnant women, a protected class under Title VII as modified by the PDA, and the discriminatory policy is not excused by a BFOQ. Accordingly, the Court will grant plaintiff's motion for summary judgment.

Seniority Systems

Seniority refers to the length of time an employee has worked for a company, or perhaps the time worked within a particular department or other division of the company. Many companies, especially those having collective bargaining agreements with unions, have seniority systems. These systems provide that many kinds of employment rights and privileges are to be determined on the basis of seniority. For example, the right to bid for another job or another shift within the company, or the right to be protected from layoff, may be determined by seniority. Although far from perfect, seniority systems are generally recognized as one of the few truly objective means for making many kinds of employment decisions. Because of their positive aspects, seniority systems are partially exempted from Title VII. A ''bona fide'' (good faith) seniority system does not violate Title VII just because it has a discriminatory impact; the system is illegal only if it is intentionally used to discriminate.

Affirmative Action in Employment

The primary strategy in the legal battle against employment discrimination has been simply to prohibit discriminatory practices and to strike them down when they are discovered. Another important weapon, however, has been affirmative action—actually giving preferences to minorities and women in the hiring process. In many cases, affirmative action programs include goals and timetables for increasing the percentage of minorities and women in the employer's work force. The purpose of affirmative action is to rectify the effects of previous discrimination.

Affirmative action has been used by some courts as a remedy in specific cases of discrimination. In other words, after concluding that an employer had practiced discrimination, some courts have both ordered the cessation of the practice and required the employer to implement an affirmative action program. In addition, some employers, either on their own or in connection with union collective bargaining agreements, have instituted voluntary affirmative action programs.

Since their inception, affirmative action programs have raised difficult legal questions. By granting preferences to minorities and women, these programs discriminate in some degree against white males. White males are protected against race and sex discrimination by Title VII; does so-called reverse discrimination, brought about by affirmative action programs, violate Title VII or other discrimination laws? Supreme Court precedent indicates that a voluntary affirmative action plan is permissible under Title VII if:

1. It is intended to break down old patterns of segregation and hierarchy and to open employment opportunities for minorities in occupations that have traditionally been closed to them;

2. It does not unnecessarily hinder the interests of non-minority employees and does not require them to be fired and replaced with new minority hires;

3. It does not create an absolute bar to the advancement of non-minority employees

4. It is temporary and designed to end as soon as the percentage of non-minority employees in the position at issue approximates the percentage of non-minority employees in the local labor force;

5. It is aspirational in nature and is not used in making any specific employment decisions;

6. Minority employees are concentrated in traditionally minority jobs;

7. Race or gender is one of many factors considered in employment decisions;

8. The plan is limited to attaining and not maintaining a balanced workforce; and

9. The plan is remedial—that is, designed to correct a manifest racial imbalance in traditionally segregated job categories.

Equal Pay Act

The first antidiscrimination in employment act, predating even Title VII, is the Equal Pay Act of 1963. This statute prohibits an employer from paying an employee of one sex less than an employee of the opposite sex, when the two are performing jobs that require "equal skill, effort, and responsibility" and "under similar working conditions." Proof that the pay differential is due to the workers' varying merit or pursuant to a legitimate seniority system are available defenses under the Act. The Equal Pay Act is limited to sex discrimination in the form of wages and overlaps considerably with Title VII. There are slight differences in employers covered by the two Acts, however, and the Equal Pay Act may be a worker's only recourse for wage discrimination in some companies with fewer than 15 employees.

Age Discrimination in Employment Act

Title VII expanded the scope of employment discrimination protection in 1967, when it passed the Age Discrimination in Employment Act (ADEA). The coverage of this Act is quite similar to Title VII, except that it applies only to situations where there is a minimum of 20 employees. The ADEA prohibits discrimination based on age against anyone age 40 and over. Almost all age discrimination cases involve alleged disparate treatment of individual workers. Such cases are analyzed in the same manner as under Title VII. The U.S. Supreme Court held that an employee had to prove that age was not just a contributing factor to the employer's adverse employment action (such as firing or demoting), but instead had to be the *deciding* factor. However, Congress amended the ADEA to overturn this ruling and require that the employee only must prove that the employee's age was a motivating factor in its decision; that is, the employer commits age discrimination if the employee's age is at least one significant reason for the adverse employment action even if there might also have been one or more other reasons.

Although the U.S. Supreme Court held that the disparate impact theory can be used in age discrimination cases, it is unlikely that we will see many such cases because, as in Title VII, disparate impact has come to be very difficult to prove in recent years.

Only the age of the victim of discrimination is relevant. Thus, an employer favoring a 45-year-old over a 60-year-old because of the age of the latter has violated the ADEA just as surely as if the employer had favored a 25-year-old. In such a situation, the "favored" employee just has to be sufficiently younger than the "disfavored" employee so that an inference of age discrimination is logical. The evidence must convince the court, however, that the plaintiff's age was the main reason for the disparate treatment.

The ADEA provides several statutory defenses for employers. An employee may always be discharged or otherwise penalized for good cause other than age. A bona fide occupational qualification defense also exists and closely resembles that under Title VII. Bona fide seniority systems or employee benefit plans are also exempted from ADEA violation. Courts have interpreted these defenses somewhat more expansively, in the employer's favor, than in most cases decided under Title VII.

Discrimination Against Persons with Disabilities

In the Rehabilitation Act of 1973, Congress prohibited discrimination in employment against handicapped persons. That law, however, applied only to the employment practices of federal government agencies, businesses having contracts with the federal government, and organizations or programs receiving federal funding (e.g., universities receiving federal research funds). The Rehabilitation Act still applies to these three groups of employers.

In 1990, Congress passed the Americans with Disabilities Act (ADA), which provides comprehensive protection against discrimination to persons with disabilities. The ADA includes provisions dealing not only with discrimination in employment, but also with problems of discrimination and access in public transportation, public accommodations (such as restaurants, hotels, and office buildings), and communications. Title I of the ADA, dealing with employment, is the only part relevant to our discussion in this chapter. The employment portions of the ADA cover the same employers as Title VII of the 1964 Civil Rights Act; in addition, the new law adopts most of the procedures and methods of proving discrimination from Title VII.

The ADA borrows most of its basic concepts and definitions, however, from Rehabilitation Act. Instead of speaking of "handicapped persons," as did the Rehabilitation Act, the ADA speaks of "persons with disabilities." Under the ADA, people have a disability if they have a "physical or mental impairment that substantially affects one or more of the major life activities." Major life activities include functions such as caring for one's self, performing manual tasks, walking, seeing, hearing, speaking, breathing, learning, and participating in social relationships and activities. The law does not attempt to include an exhaustive list of disabilities. However, conditions that obviously would constitute disabilities include orthopedic, visual, speech, and hearing impairments; cerebral palsy; muscular dystrophy; multiple sclerosis; HIV infection; cancer; diseases of the heart or other major organs; diabetes; seizure disorders (epilepsy); mental retardation; emotional illness; serious learning disabilities; drug addiction; and alcoholism. Although alcoholism and drug addiction constitute disabilities, the ADA expressly provides that a current user of alcohol or illegal drugs is not protected by the law. Finally, the ADA also contains a list of conditions referred to as ''behavioral'' that are expressly excluded from the definition of disability, including homosexuality, bisexuality, gender identity disorders, exhibitionism, voyeurism, compulsive gambling, kleptomania, pyromania, and several others.

In addition to prohibiting discrimination in employment against a person actually having a "physical or mental impairment substantially affecting a major life activity," the ADA also prohibits discrimination against a person who either has a record of such an impairment or is regarded as having such an impairment. That part of the law dealing with having a record of an impairment is intended to protect those victimized by mistaken records (which are often difficult to correct) or by the stigma of a past affliction that no longer constitutes an impairment. Although that part of the law dealing with one who is "regarded" as having an impairment will sometimes overlap with the "record of" provision, its main purpose is to protect those who are victimized by stereotypes. In other words, there are some conditions that may cause no impairment at all, or at least no impairment for a certain kind of job, but because of stereotypes those with the condition are often treated as if they are impaired.

Even if a person is protected by the ADA, an employer is under no obligation to hire unless the person is qualified to do the job. If the person can do the job without any special accommodation, the employer should not even bring up the subject of changing the job, changing the working environment, or similar subjects. However, if an individual is not qualified as the job now exists, but would be qualified if the employer makes a "reasonable accommodation" for the person's impairment, then the person is viewed by the law as being qualified. The question of reasonable accommodation should not be dealt with, however, unless the disabled person brings it up or unless the need to make some adjustment in the job becomes obvious after the individual has been performing it for a time. An adjustment of the work environment or schedules may be reasonable, or perhaps rearranging a job into different parts if such a change does not significantly affect efficiency. To meet the burden of making a reasonable accommodation for a person's disability, however, the employer is not required to incur an "undue hardship."

When statistics indicated that employers were winning 90% of filed ADA cases and the Supreme Court held that people are not disabled if their condition can be remedied by medicine or devices, Congress tilted the scales back toward employees just a bit by enacting the ADA Amendments Act of 2008 (ADAAA). EEOC rules issued pursuant to that law presume that certain conditions will generally be treated as giving rise to a disability, including blindness, mobility impairments requiring the use of a wheelchair, diabetes, cancer, HIV infection and a variety of mental disorders, among others. Also, impairments may now constitute "substantial limitation" on a major life activity if the individual is substantially impaired relative to the general population.

Many ADA cases are controversial. One court held that obesity is not a "disability" within the meaning of the act, though its causes or consequences could be. *Morriss v. BNSF Ry. Co.*, 817 F.3d 1104 (8th Cir. 2016). Another court held that a person with a cantankerous personality who was fired because he could not get along with co-workers was not protected by the ADA. According to some commentators, this means that being a jerk is not a protected disability under the Act. *Weaving v. City of Hillsboro*, 763 F.3d 1106 (9th Cir. 2014). And in 2019, the Supreme Court refused to review an appellate court ruling (*Robles v. Domino's Pizza*, 913 F.3d 898 (9th Cir. 2019)) that a blind plaintiff had stated a claim that Domino's Pizza was violating the ADA because its website and mobile application were not fully accessible to visually-impaired persons.

Retaliation

The protections from discrimination provided by Title VII, the ADEA, and the ADA would be greatly reduced if employees could be fired or otherwise punished for asserting those rights. Therefore, all these laws provide protection from retaliation, and discrimination lawsuits often include retaliation claims. Indeed, a retaliation claim could succeed even if the underlying discrimination case failed. The *Okoli* case from earlier in the chapter discussed the elements of a retaliation claim. Note that to win a status-based discrimination case, a plaintiff need prove only that the motive to discriminate was *one* of the employer's motives, even if the employer also had other, lawful motives that played a causal role in the employer's decision. *Price Waterhouse v. Hopkins,* 490 U.S. 228 (1989). However, to prove a retaliation claim, the causation requirement is stricter. A retaliation plaintiff must show that the adverse employment action would not have occurred "but for" the motive to retaliate.

PROTECTION OF EMPLOYEE SAFETY AND WELFARE

Numerous laws have been passed to protect workers from on-the-job injuries and the financial consequences of such injuries. Congress also has legislated to preserve the financial welfare of workers, especially in the context of pension and other employee benefit plans.

Workers' Compensation

In the 19th century, workers were frequently injured on the job and often had no effective legal recourse to compensate them for their injuries. In response, state legislatures passed workers' compensation statutes. All fifty states have such laws and while they vary somewhat, the laws all share certain common features. Workers' compensation is paid without regard to employer negligence and workers receive a predetermined amount, based on the injury suffered. Benefits payable include medical costs, income replacement, death benefits, and rehabilitation costs. Levels of compensation are typically lower than a worker might receive in a lawsuit, but the system avoids much of the attorney fees and other costs of litigation, while eliminating most employer defenses to payment of the lesser sum.

The main restriction on recovery under workers' compensation statutes is the requirement that the injury must have arisen "out of and in the course of employment." Although the majority of injuries are clearly job-related, a large number of cases lie on the disputed borderline of work. For example, an employee whose job requires travel will ordinarily be able to receive benefits for injuries incurred in the course of such travel. By contrast, a mere commuter will not be compensated if injured on the way to work.

Employees typically are also covered while engaging in activities reasonably incidental to job duties. Thus, an employee on a lunch break who slips and falls in the employer's cafeteria would be covered. State laws also cover diseases arising out of employment, but proof of the source of disease is much more complicated to obtain than is proof of work injuries, and such cases are more often disputed. Independent contractors are not covered by workers' compensation benefits.

Occupational Safety and Health Act

In 1970, Congress passed the Occupational Safety and Health Act to help prevent workplace disease and injuries. The Act created the Occupational Safety and Health Administration (OSHA), part of the U.S. Department of Labor, to administer its provisions. This statute applies to virtually every United States employer.

Central to OSHA's powers is its standard-setting authority. The agency promulgates regulations compelling employers to make their workplaces safer in a variety of ways. Most of the early standards were intended to prevent job injuries, and OSHA was ridiculed because of the highly detailed nature of its rules. For example, the agency devoted considerable effort to regulating the number of toilets to be available and the allowable design of such facilities. As the agency has gained experience, its standards have allowed more flexibility for employers, and the regulatory focus has shifted toward prevention of occupational diseases.

OSHA's rules have given rise to litigation that has helped define the extent of the agency's powers. In an attempt to prevent a cancer associated with the inhalation of benzene, a petroleum byproduct, OSHA promulgated a stringent standard without attempting to specify the magnitude of the harm created by existing levels. The agency believed that it was simply fulfilling its mandate to create the healthiest workplace feasible, but the Supreme Court overturned the regulation in *Industrial Union Department v. American Petroleum Institute*, 448 U.S. 607(1980). The Court held that OSHA could regulate only "significant risks" and generally should quantitatively measure a risk before promulgating rules. Shortly after this decision, industry challenged an OSHA regulation limiting exposure to cotton dust, which causes several lung diseases. Industry contended that OSHA had to base regulation on a cost/benefit analysis, but the Supreme Court upheld the agency's regulation in *American Textile Manufacturers Inst. v. Donovan*, 452 U.S. 490 (1981), holding that OSHA possessed authority to require any health protection "feasible" for industry and was not required to weigh the costs of a rule against its benefits before acting.

While OSHA has broad standard-setting authority, the task of establishing rules against all workplace hazards is beyond the capabilities of any agency. In recognition of this limit, Congress created a "general duty clause" in the Safety Act. This provision requires all employers to provide a place of employment free from recognized hazards of death or serious harm. As an example of the application of this clause, one employer was found in violation for permitting untrained employees to attempt electrical repairs on a wet floor without any protective equipment. OSHA's General Duty Clause does not apply when there is a specific safety standard covering the situation.

Beyond standards development, OSHA is also responsible for enforcing the Act, and considerable controversy has circulated around these enforcement powers. The agency's compliance officers make unannounced inspections. While search warrants are required for the inspections, they are liberally granted. When violations are found, OSHA may issue citations and impose fines. An employer may contest these penalties before a separate, independent organization known as the Occupational Safety and Health Review Commission.

Fair Labor Standards Act

The Fair Labor Standards Act (FLSA) was among the federal government's first employment law statutes. Passed in response to the Great Depression, the FLSA regulates the hours that employees may be required to work and the wages they must be paid. FLSA coverage is extremely broad. An employer involved in any way in interstate commerce falls under the Act's purview. An exception is made for managerial and supervisory employees, as well as those employed in the professions, such as lawyers and accountants.

Among the most controversial provisions of FLSA immediately after its passage was the Act's prohibition of certain forms of child labor. Employees under 18 years of age are excluded from occupations designated as hazardous, such as mining, logging, and excavation work. Hours are strictly regulated for employees who are less than 16 years old.

The FLSA is also the source of the federal overtime and minimum wage requirements. Any work in excess of 40 hours per week (a 7-day period that may begin or end on any day if the period is a regular one) must be paid at a "time-and-a-half" rate—50 percent greater than the employee's normal wage. If employees are not paid on an hourly basis, the FLSA requires at least as much compensation as a per hour minimum wage rate would require for the hours they actually worked. Employers must maintain complete employment and payroll records for review by the Department of Labor. Substantial penalties are imposed for violations. With the exception of the above provisions, the Act imposes no other requirements on the employment relationship, such as mandatory vacations or rest periods.

In recent years employees have filed many class action lawsuits claiming "wage theft" in that their employers had violated minimum wage and overtime requirements.

EMPLOYER'S RIGHT TO DISCHARGE EMPLOYEES

An employer must have considerable freedom to discipline or fire employees in order to manage its work force effectively and efficiently. If an employer is unable to discharge disgruntled or shirking workers, we all pay. On the other hand, many feel that employees deserve protection from unjustified dismissals. (Incidentally, when we speak of an employee being fired or discharged, we are referring not only to actual firing but also to *constructive discharges*, where the employer creates such an intolerable situation for the employees that they are forced to quit.)

An employee who has a legally enforceable employment contract obviously has whatever job security the contract specifies. Most employees, however, do not have such a contract. An employee who is covered by a labor-management collective bargaining agreement usually enjoys considerable protection from improper discharge. Most such contracts provide that employees can be fired or otherwise disciplined only for "good cause." Approximately 13% of the total public and private workforce is covered by collective bargaining agreements, but only about 6% of the private sector American work force is covered by such agreements. Public employees, i.e., those who work for a federal, state, or local government agency, also enjoy significant job security under federal and state civil service laws even when they are not unionized. In general, after a designated probationary period, these employees can be fired only for good cause and only after specified procedures have been followed. Public employees account for about 15% of the American work force. With regard to public employees at the state and local government level, the extent to which they are protected by civil service systems varies greatly from state to state. In general, more state and local government employees have civil service protection in the northeastern and upper mid-western U.S. where laws traditionally have been more favorable to employees in many ways than in other parts of the country.

Employment at Will

Most other employees are subject to the so-called employment-at-will doctrine. This traditional common-law rule provides that, in the absence of a contract providing to the contrary, either the employer or employee can terminate the relationship at any time, for any reason or no reason. In recent years, however, many people have come to view this rule as overly harsh toward employees and, consequently, a number of exceptions have been created.

Statutory Exceptions

A few federal and state statutes provide protection for employees in specific situations. For example, federal employment laws like Title VII, FLSA, and OSHA include provisions making it illegal for an employer to punish an employee for filing a complaint or cooperating with an investigation or proceeding under the particular law. Such retaliation furnishes the grounds for litigation.

In some states, employees are protected from being penalized for filing a workers' compensation claim or taking time off to serve on a jury. Also, several states have statutes giving an employee a right to sue an employer for damages if the employer fired the employee for *whistle-blowing*. So do the Sarbanes-Oxley Act of 2002 and the Dodd-Frank Act of 2010 in a variety of situations. Whistle-blowing occurs when a worker objects to or reports the employer's suspected illegal activities. Even if the employee turned out to be wrong, and the employer was not actually doing anything illegal, these statutes apply so long as the employee was sincere and had a solid factual basis for believing that illegal practices were occurring.

The Public Policy Exception

In addition to statutes such as these, courts in a majority of states have carved out additional exceptions to employment at will. The most notable of these exceptions can be grouped together under the idea of "public policy." In other words, these courts have ruled that an employee should be able to recover damages for the tort of *wrongful discharge* (or "retaliatory discharge") when the employer's conduct is contrary to a clearly established public policy. The public policy exception to the employment-at-will doctrine has been recognized to varying degrees by the courts in most states. Defining public policy is not always an easy task, however. Most courts are fully aware that a vague, expansive public policy concept will provide very little guidance to employers or employees. Without reasonable guidance, employers will find it very difficult to maintain an effective personnel management system because of the fear that every discharge might lead to an expensive lawsuit.

As a result, most courts have concluded that the public policy claimed to have been violated by the employer must be clearly stated in a federal or state statute, or widely recognized and accepted judicial decision. In those states permitting an employee to assert a claim for wrongful discharge based on public policy, a fired employee is likely to have a good claim in the following situations:

1. The employer may not discharge a worker for refusing to commit an act that is illegal under a federal or state statute. For example, courts have found employers liable for firing employees who refused to participate in an illegal price-fixing scheme, commit perjury, mislabel food products, falsify a pollution control test, perform a medical procedure for which the nurse-employee was not licensed, or pump a ship's bilges containing sewage and toxic waste into the water. Most of these states also recognize the public policy exception when a company has fired an employee for refusing to commit a tort, such as refusing to sign a false defamatory statement about a co-worker.

2. Generally, employees have a good wrongful discharge claim if they have been fired for exercising a statutory right. For example, an employer has been held liable for damages to an employee who was fired for exercising the right to sign a union authorization card. Similarly, employers have been held liable for discharging employees because they filed workers' compensation claims or served on juries, even if there was no specific anti-retaliation statute in that state covering the situation.

3. An employer often will be held liable to an employee who was fired for whistle blowing—objecting to or disclosing the employer's violations of the law, even if there is not a state statute providing protection to whistleblowers. Employees normally have a valid claim if they (a) acted in good faith and (b) had reasonable cause to believe that the employer was violating the law, even if later investigation reveals that the employer actually did not act illegally. On the question of whether an employee must first give company management an opportunity to correct the problem before complaining to the authorities, the courts are split. A majority of them, however, recognize the wrongful discharge claim regardless of where the employee first lodged an objection. Although most of the states recognizing the public policy exception do so in the case of whistle blowing, not all of them do. But, as noted, the federal Sarbanes-Oxley Act often fills this state law void.

Courts usually have stressed that employees are not protected from discharge just because they acted out of strong, and even admirable, convictions if a purely private matter is involved that does not affect the public interest. For example, one court concluded that there was no wrongful discharge claim where the employee was fired for refusing to follow a particular research program. As a matter of personal conscience, the employee felt that the research was not proper, but there was nothing illegal, immoral, or hazardous about it. Two Illinois cases also provide an illustrative contrast. In one, the court found that no violation of public policy had occurred when a company's chief financial officer was fired for a continuing disagreement with the company's president about accounting methods. There was no plausible claim that the president's methods were deceptive or violated securities or tax laws or generally accepted accounting principles. In the other case, the court held that the employee did have a claim for wrongful discharge where he had been fired for complaining about the company's use of accounting methods that substantially overstated income and assets in a way that very likely would violate tax laws and the disclosure provisions of federal securities laws. The following case illustrates an unfortunate situation that led one state supreme court to adopt the public policy exception to employment at will.

WAGENSELLER v. SCOTTSDALE MEMORIAL HOSPITAL
Arizona Supreme Court, 710 P.2d 1025 (1985)

Catherine Wagenseller worked as an emergency room nurse for the Scottsdale

Memorial Hospital. She had originally been recruited personally by the emergency department's manager, Kay Smith, and for four years maintained a superior work record and enjoyed excellent professional and personal relationships with Smith and others in the department. She was an "at will" employee, with no contractual or other job guarantees.

Wagenseller, Smith, and a group of others from the emergency department, as well as a number of employees from other area hospitals, went on an eight-day camping and rafting trip down the Colorado River. While on the trip, Wagenseller became very uncomfortable because of the behavior of Smith and a few others. This behavior included heavy drinking, group nude bathing and other public nudity, and a lot of unnecessary closeness while rafting. In addition, Smith and others staged a parody of the song "Moon River," which ended with members of the group "mooning" the audience. Wagenseller declined to participate in any of these activities. Smith and others also performed the "Moon River" skit twice at the hospital after the group's return from the river, but Wagenseller declined to participate there as well.

After the trip, relations between Wagenseller and Smith deteriorated. Smith began harassing Wagenseller, using abusive language and embarrassing her in the presence of other staff. These problems continued, and Wagenseller was fired about five months after the camping trip. Wagenseller appealed her dismissal to the hospital's administrative and personnel department, but the dismissal was upheld. She then filed suit for damages against Smith, the hospital, and several of its personnel administrators. In the suit, she alleged that her termination violated public policy and therefore constituted the tort of wrongful discharge. Although Wagenseller's claims had been substantiated by the pretrial statements of several others, the trial court refused to recognize any exception to the employment-at-will doctrine and granted the defendants' motions for summary judgment. The appeals court reversed part of the judgment, but still did not grant Wagenseller the relief she sought, so she appealed to the Arizona Supreme Court.

Feldman, Justice:

Under the traditional employment-at-will doctrine, an employee without an employment contract for a definite term can be fired for cause, without cause, or for "bad" cause.... In recent years there has been apparent dissatisfaction with the absolutist formulation of the common law at-will rule.... The trend has been to modify the at-will rule by creating exceptions to its operation.... The most widely accepted approach is the "public policy" exception, which permits recovery upon a finding that the employer's conduct undermined some important public policy.... A majority of the states have now either recognized a cause of action based on the public policy exception or have indicated their willingness to consider it, given appropriate facts. The key to an employee's claim in all of these cases is the proper definition of a public policy that has been violated by [their] actions.

Before deciding whether to adopt the public policy exception, we first consider what kind of discharge would violate the rule. The majority of courts required, as a threshold showing, a "clear mandate" of public policy. The leading case recognizing a public policy exception to the at-will doctrine is *Palmateer v. International Harvester Co.*, 421 N.E.2d 876 (Ill. 1981), which holds that an employee stated a cause of action for wrongful discharge when he claimed he was fired for supplying information to police investigating alleged criminal violations by a co-employee. Addressing the issue of what constitutes "clearly mandated public policy, the court stated:

There is no precise definition of the term. In general, it can be said that public policy concerns what is right and just and what affects the citizens of the State collectively. It is to be found in the State's constitution and statutes and, when they are silent, in its judicial decisions. Although there is no precise line of demarcation dividing matters that are the subject of public policies from matters purely personal, a survey of cases in other States involving retaliatory discharges shows that a matter must strike at the heart of a citizen's social rights, duties, and responsibilities before the tort will be allowed. It is difficult to justify this court's further adherence to a rule which permits an employer to fire someone for a cause that is morally wrong.... Certainly, a court would be hard-pressed to find a rationale to hold that an employer could with impunity fire an employee who refused to commit perjury.... We therefore adopt the public policy exception to the at-will termination rule. We hold that an employer may fire for good cause or for no cause. He may not fire for bad cause—that which violates public policy....

In the case before us, Wagenseller refused to participate in activities which arguably would have violated our indecent exposure statute. This statute provides that a person commits indecent exposure by exposing certain described parts of the body when someone else is present and when the defendant is "reckless about whether such other person, as a reasonable person, would be offended or alarmed by the act." ... While this statute may not embody a policy which "strikes at the heart of a citizen's social rights, duties, and responsibilities" as clearly and forcefully as some other statutes, such as a statute prohibiting perjury, we believe that it was enacted to preserve and protect the commonly recognized right of public privacy and decency. The law does, therefore, recognize bodily privacy as a "citizen's social right." ... We are compelled to conclude that termination of employment for refusal to participate in the public exposure of one's buttocks is a termination contrary to the policy of this state.... [The trial court's action granting summary judgment against Wagenseller was in error. The decision is reversed and remanded to the trial court for a trial where Wagenseller will have a full opportunity to prove her allegations.]

PROTECTION OF EMPLOYEE PRIVACY

Lie Detector Testing

Employers have extremely important interests in learning certain kinds of background information about people who are applying for jobs. Incompetent, dishonest, or violent employees can cause untold harm to an employer. A company may need to know about a job applicant's past work record, criminal record, and general character when legitimately attempting to protect itself against lawsuits and against a damaged reputation, as well as to protect its customers and its other employees from physical harm. Employers also have a valid interest in obtaining information from existing employees when theft or other wrongdoing has occurred at the workplace.

During the past several decades, more and more employers used the lie detector (polygraph) examination in an effort to get accurate information from employees and job applicants. Because of mounting evidence that these examinations are not very reliable, and that thousands of employees and applicants were being harmed each year by erroneous results, Congress passed the *Employee Polygraph Protection Act of 1988*. This law prohibits most uses of the polygraph by private employers, subject to only a few limited exceptions. The most important exception permits a private employer to require an employee to take a lie detector test as part of an ongoing investigation of theft, sabotage, trade secret misappropriation, or other property loss, if this employee had custody of the property and if there is other independent evidence creating a reasonable suspicion that this employee was involved in the incident. The law also does not prohibit federal, state, or local government agencies from requiring their employees and job applicants to take lie detector tests, mainly because the Constitution applies to government employers. The constitutional right of privacy protects against many unreasonable uses of the polygraph by government employers, but clearly does not protect employees to the extent that the federal polygraph statute does.

Employee Drug Testing

Employees who are impaired by drugs or alcohol endanger the public and their fellow workers, and cost their employers millions of dollars annually as a result of accidents, absenteeism, higher health insurance claims, low productivity, and poor workmanship. Employers have legitimate interests in minimizing these costs; maintaining a safe, secure, and productive workplace; and protecting themselves against liability to those injured by the actions of impaired employees. Both co-workers and members of the public have a legitimate claim to protection against the unsafe conduct or defective products resulting from employees' drug or alcohol use.

Employees subjected to drug testing, on the other hand, have important interests in preventing harm to their reputations and economic security resulting from inaccurate test results and avoiding unwarranted intrusions into their personal lives. Drug tests are not always accurate, and the analysis of urine, blood, or hair specimens often reveals a lot of private information about the subject that has nothing to do with the use of illicit drugs. It is certainly true that alcohol use causes the same kinds of workplace problems as drug use, but alcohol-impaired employees often can be identified more easily without the risk of erroneous test results or the disclosure of irrelevant private information that may be revealed in drug testing. Most of the difficult legal issues, therefore, have involved employers testing for controlled substances other than alcohol.

Most employers take some kind of action against an employee who refuses a test or who tests positive for illicit drugs. This action can range from required enrollment in a rehabilitation program to immediate discharge. Similarly, job applicants who refuse testing or test positive are virtually assured of not getting the job. As a result, legal action by employees challenging drug-testing programs is becoming increasingly common. The legal system has not yet had sufficient time, however, to develop a coherent, uniform set of principles to balance the various interests that are involved. Although the law pertaining to employee drug testing is still in a formative stage, it is possible to make some generalizations.

If the employer is a federal, state, or local government agency, the Constitution provides a measure of protection for the legitimate privacy interests of employees. The Constitution also applies if the government requires a private employer to do drug testing.

The most obviously applicable constitutional provision is the Fourth Amendment prohibition of unreasonable searches and seizures. The taking of a urine, blood, or hair specimen is a "search and seizure." Generally, people and their belongings can be searched only if there is "probable cause" to believe that they possess evidence of a violation of the law. In *National Treasury Employees Union v. Von Raub*, 489 U.S. 656 (1989) (involving testing by a government agency), and *Skinner v. Railway Labor Executives Ass'n*, 489 U.S. 602 (1989) (involving government-required testing by private employers), the U.S. Supreme

Court held that drug testing sometimes is constitutionally permissible even without any evidence that a particular employee is a drug user. The Court said that, in the case of employees whose work creates significant safety, health, or security risks, testing may be done on a random or mass basis so long as the testing program is conducted in a reasonable manner overall. To be reasonable, the program must include ample safeguards to ensure accuracy and privacy.

The Constitution does not apply to drug testing by private employers unless the testing is required by the government. Both federal law and state law provide few limitations on the right of private employees to adopt drug and alcohol testing policies for their workers. Tort law does apply, however, if an employer conducts a test or uses the results in such a way that a tort is committed. If the employer intentionally reveals private information from the test to others who have no legitimate interest in receiving it, the employer may be liable to the employee for the tort of invasion of privacy. If the test produces a false positive result, and the employer reveals it to others without a legitimate interest in knowing it, the employer may be liable for defamation. In some cases, carelessness in the administration of the test or use of the results may cause the employer to be liable for the tort of negligence.

A few states have passed statutes specifically regulating the design and implementation of drug testing programs by private employers. The objective of these statutes is to increase the likelihood that results will be accurate and that employee privacy will be protected to the fullest extent possible.

In the case of unionized workers, the implementation of a drug testing program is a so-called "mandatory subject of collective bargaining." This means that the employer cannot make such a decision on its own, but must submit the question to the process of collective bargaining with the union. If the company and the union cannot agree, either or both may use economic weapons such as lockouts or strikes to put pressure on the other side.

Genetic Testing

In April 2001, the EEOC successfully settled a case charging an employer with violating the Americans with Disabilities Act (ADA) by its practice of genetically testing its employees. In addition, more than 30 states have restricted genetic testing in the workplace. These developments prompted Congress to pass the 2008 Genetic Information Non-Discrimination Act (GINA), which specifically prohibits employers, employment agencies, and labor unions, as well as insurance companies, from discriminating against people because they have a genetically higher risk of later developing a disease. It also restricts the collection of such "genetic information," which includes information about an individual's (or their family members') (a) genetic tests, and (b) manifestation of a disease or disorder in family members. Like most other employment discrimination acts, GINA includes an anti-retaliation provision. GINA does not preempt more restrictive statutes passed by individual states. As with the ADA and ADEA, GINA requires plaintiffs to file discrimination charges with the EEOC or with a state's fair employment practices agency before they can file a private lawsuit in federal court.

In one case, an employer took cheek cell samples from two employees in attempting to locate someone who was mysteriously defecating around the company's warehouse. This was an obvious violation of GINA and a $2.2 million jury verdict resulted. (*Lowe v. Atlas Logistics,* 102 F.Supp.3d 1360 (N.D.Ga. 2015).

Criminal Record

Because members of certain ethnic minority groups have historically been arrested more than have members of other racial or national origin groups, it is a violation of Title VII of the 1964 Civil Rights Act to refuse to hire candidates because of their arrest record alone. But what about refusing to hire someone because she has an actual criminal *conviction*, not just an arrest? It is not a violation of Title VII for a company to refuse to hire a convict. However, it is clearly in the best interest of society as a whole for those who have been convicted of crimes to be able to find a job after they have completed their sentences. The ability to support themselves and their families reduces the chance that they will again commit a crime. The odds of such people reoffending are clearly higher if no one hires them.

Historically, it has been the practice of many companies to ask job applicants to state whether they have ever been convicted of a crime on the application for employment. Moreover, many employers have systematically refused to consider a job seeker who has "checked the box" beside a question about previous convictions. In recent years, a "ban the box" movement has developed across the country to prohibit most employers from asking questions about or considering an applicant's criminal history *until after they make a conditional offer of employment*. Absent such restrictions in this "Fair Chance Hiring Ordinance," many believe that ex-convicts have no realistic chance to obtain gainful employment. More than 30 states and 150 cities have enacted some version of such provisions, which typically exclude, among other categories, jobs for which a statute disqualifies an individual based on criminal history.

FAMILY MEDICAL LEAVE ACT (FMLA)

In 1993 Congress passed the Family Medical Leave Act (FMLA) to help balance employees' workplace demands with their familial responsibilities. The Act provides eligible employees with 12 weeks of *unpaid* leave in most cases (there being special provisions for military caregivers). The employer need not pay the employees during this time, but must preserve their jobs for them when they return. To be eligible, an employee must have worked for the employer for at least 12 months *and* at least 1,250 hours during the preceding year. The FMLA covers employers with over 50 employees within 75 miles, as well as state and local government agencies.

Employees must request this leave; employers need not volunteer it. What situations does the act cover? The FMLA provides: (A) *12 work weeks* of leave in a 12-month period for: (1) the birth of a child and to care for the newborn child within one year of birth; (2) the placement with the employee of a child for adoption or foster care and to care for the newly placed child within one year of placement; (3) to care for the employee's spouse, child, or parent who has a serious health condition; (4) a serious health condition that makes the employee unable/ to perform the essential functions of the job; and (5) any qualifying exigency arising out of the fact that the employee's spouse, son, daughter, or parent is a covered military member on "covered active duty"; or (B) *26 work weeks* of leave during a single 12-month period to care for a covered service member with a serious injury or illness if the eligible employee is the servicemember's spouse, son, daughter, parent, or next of kin.

CHAPTER 31
ENVIRONMENTAL LAW

- Common Law and Pollution
- National Environmental Policy Act
- Water Pollution Control
- Air Pollution Control
- Solid Waste and Its Disposal
- Regulation of Toxic Substances
- Noise Pollution
- Indoor Pollution
- Endangered Species
- The Environment, Industry, and Society
- International Considerations

As Americans have gradually become more aware of the adverse impact that human consumption of resources and human technology can have on the land, sea, and air, their support for more comprehensive governmental regulation of environmental matters has grown. Well-known incidents include the accident at the Three Mile Island nuclear facility, the contamination by dioxins of Times Beach, Missouri, the indiscriminate dumping of hazardous wastes in Love Canal, New York, and the Alaskan oil spill caused by the Exxon *Valdez*.

In 2010, the British Petroleum (BP) *Deepwater Horizon* drilling rig exploded and the oil well blew out 5,000 feet deep in the Gulf of Mexico. The well was not capped for 87 days, and vast quantities of crude oil destroyed fishing grounds and countless fish and other marine animal species, ultimately producing oily muck that sank to the ocean floor, emulsified, and has been ingested by marine life. The BP disaster put much more oil into the sea than any previous accidental oil spill, including Exxon *Valdez* and the huge *Ixtoc 1* spill in the Bay of Campeche off the coast of Mexico. Much more about the *Deepwater Horizon* disaster is found later in the *In re Deepwater Horizon* case from 2014. It is important to remember, however, that even though this represents the worst accidental oil spill thus far in our history, it is only one of many large spills and leakages over the years in all of our seas, oceans, rivers and on land. Several different oil spills in the Gulf of Mexico have, for example, pushed Atlantic Bluefin Tuna and the Dwarf Seahorse close to extinction.

Problems such as acid rain transcend national boundaries and cause international concern, as does the phenomenon of global climate change. Though scientists knew of and tried to warn about climate change in the 1980s, it has only recently become a matter of major concern to people around the world, as indicated by the Obama administration's initiatives regarding automobile mileage requirements and "cap and trade" plan for carbon emissions. Some are calling the American Recovery and Reinvestment Act of 2009 one of the most far-reaching pieces of environmental legislation in decades as it provides over $70 billion for investment in renewable energy, increasing energy efficiency, encouraging telework and distance learning to reduce commuter pollution, and also provides funds for environmental cleanup.

Since 2016, though, the Trump administration has continually called global warming a "hoax" despite the continual rising of average global temperatures, the retreat of most glaciers around the world, the rising levels of the seas, gigantic ice melts in the Arctic and in other places like Greenland, and the melting of the permafrost in spots around the world that are near or above the Arctic Circle. Melting permafrost in Alaska, northern Canada, Siberia, and many other places releases tens of millions of tons of trapped methane, which puts vast amounts of carbon into the atmosphere. The Trump administration also withdrew the U.S. from the Paris Accord, an international agreement entered into during the Obama Administration for the purpose of collectively reducing the release of carbon into the atmosphere.

Over the years environmental problems have led to a strengthening of state and local regulation of pollution, to the creation of a mammoth array of federal pollution regulations, and to some initial efforts at international cooperation in pollution control. For businesses, these rules and regulations are decidedly a mixed blessing. On the one hand, the owners, officers, and employees of businesses are individuals who need a clean, safe environment for themselves and their employees as much as anyone else. On the other hand, many of these laws impose additional burdens on what many consider to be an already overregulated economy.

The Environmental Protection Agency (EPA) is the largest nonmilitary federal agency, and its thousands of rules and regulations have become a part of the legal environment of business with which companies must become familiar. Many small firms have gone out of business because they could not meet various antipollution requirements imposed by the EPA. Others, both large and small, have found that compliance has become an extremely costly budget item. As we shall see in this chapter, two obvious manifestations of the heightened level of environmental regulation *until 2016* lay in (1) the increasing use of *criminal* sanctions against environmental offenders and (2) regulations requiring that persons who did not actually pollute pay for the cleanup of pollution caused by others (for example, landowners may be liable for millions of dollars to clean up pollution caused entirely by previous owners of the land).

Since 2016, however, the Trump Administration has downsized the EPA and, through the EPA's presidentially appointed Administrator, has repealed and replaced the Obama-era emissions rules for power plants and vehicles; weakened protections for more than half the nation's wetlands; and withdrawn the legal justification for restricting mercury emissions from power plants. In the same vein, the Interior Department under this administration has worked to open up more publicly-owned land for oil and gas leasing by cutting back protected areas and limiting wildlife protections. A lengthy but non-exhaustive list of environment protection measures rolled back by the Trump administration compiled primarily by academic researchers was reported by the New York Times in mid-2020, and can be found at
https://www.nytimes.com/interactive/2020/climate/trump-environment-rollbacks.html

Nothing could be more important than saving our environment—our planet. However, the many governmental regulations outlined in this chapter do place a substantial financial burden on industry, much of which is passed on to the consuming public. Many businesses do see the need for environmental protection laws, but some of them seem to agree with the substantial loosening of many environmental protections under the Trump Administration. Environmentalists view this attitude as manifesting short-term thinking that will bring greater economic and personal harm in the future. During the coming years the debate will continue as to the proper balancing of environmental versus economic interests both domestically and internationally. The coronavirus pandemic, still raging at the time this is being written, has devastated economies all over the world and cost tens of millions of jobs, making it impossible to predict what resources will be available in the near- and intermediate-term for continuing to protect our planet.

In this chapter we examine several of the known causes of pollution and the major remedial measures designed to prevent further deterioration of the environment. We also briefly address the matter of *indoor* air pollution. In many instances, we simply describe these laws and their application, but occasionally make further reference to the Trump administration's major efforts to weaken them on the federal level, and to not enforce the ones that remain. And we will explore the fledgling international efforts to preserve the global environment by multinational cooperation. Initially, however, we will look at common-law remedies that have long been available at the state level to remedy certain types of pollution.

COMMON LAW AND POLLUTION

Common law remedies founded on the law of torts are totally inadequate to provide a comprehensive method of regulating air, land, and water pollution in the United States. However, as a remedial or loss-shifting device, common law torts may be useful to individual plaintiffs who may have suffered some environmental harm. A farmer's water supply may be contaminated by industrial discharge of pollutants into a stream. Homeowners near a sanitary landfill may be exposed to noxious fumes from the constant trash fires used by the landfill to dispose of burnable refuse. Or homeowners may suffer property damage when caustic fumes from a chemical plant blanket their property, killing vegetation and causing house paint to peel and crack. In each case the individual plaintiff may seek injunctions to prohibit further damage from the pollutants and, in appropriate cases, recover money damages. The common-law tort remedies available include nuisance, negligence, trespass, and strict liability.

Nuisance

When property is used in such a manner that it inflicts harm on others, there may be a cause of action in tort for *nuisance* against the owner. If the harm is widespread, affecting the common rights of a substantial segment of a community, it is considered a public nuisance. Because fishing rights belong to the public, a discharge of pollutants into a navigable stream that killed fish would be a public nuisance. If an individual's right to quiet enjoyment of his or her land is disturbed by unreasonable and unwarranted use of property by another property owner, a private nuisance has occurred. Most public nuisances are abated through action by public officials charged with controlling the facility that is causing the harm. An action to abate a private nuisance is usually brought by the party affected against the party whose conduct gives rise to the nuisance.

In the case of either public or private nuisances, courts are often called on to balance the interests of plaintiffs and defendants. No court would eagerly close an offending industrial plant that employs an entire community. Similarly, residents near a large airport may be expected to endure some inconvenience caused by noise and vibration. A homeowner who buys near an existing airport or industrial facility may not find the courts sympathetic when a complaint is registered, but this is not invariably the case. To balance the interests of the community properly, courts often cannot simply rule in favor of the party who arrived first.

For example, in *Spur Industries, Inc. v. Del E. Webb Development Co.*, 494 P.2d 700 (Ariz. 1972), a major developer bought 20,000 acres of farm land near Phoenix to develop Sun City, a retirement village. Nearby were cattle feedlots, later purchased and expanded by Spur Industries. As the developer completed houses and Spur expanded, only 500 feet separated the two operations. Prevailing winds blew flies and odors from the cattle pens over the home sites, thus making it difficult to sell the sites most affected. The developer filed a nuisance suit against Spur, asking that Spur be enjoined from operating its cattle feedlots in the vicinity of the housing development. In an attempt to balance the parties' competing interests reasonably, the court permanently enjoined Spur from operating the feedlots but further held that Spur should be awarded damages, a reasonable amount of the cost of moving or shutting down, because the developer had brought people to the nuisance, thus causing Spur damage.

Numerous nuisance lawsuits were filed early in this century in attempts to change practices contributing to climate change. For example, several states and some land trusts sued five coal-burning utilities claiming that they had created a public nuisance by contributing to climate change and its effects. A lower court held that the plaintiffs had stated a claim under the *federal* common law of nuisance, but the U.S. Supreme Court in *American Power Co. v. Connecticut,* 131 S.Ct. 2527 (2011) ruled that Congress's decision to delegate to the EPA, via the Clean Air Act, the authority to set emission limits necessarily displaced the federal common law. The Court noted that "…Congress designated an expert agency, here, EPA, as best suited to serve as primary regulator of greenhouse gas emissions. The expert agency is surely better equipped to do the job than individual district judges issuing ad hoc, case-by-case injunctions. Federal judges lack the scientific, economic, and technological resources an agency can utilize…." The Supreme Court did not decide whether *state* common law nuisance claims were preempted and some courts have held that they are not.

Negligence, Trespass, and Strict Liability

The tort of negligence involves a breach by the defendant of a duty owed to the plaintiff to use reasonable care to avoid injury to the plaintiff's person or property. If the operator of a plant negligently maintained its equipment so that harmful pollutants were discharged into a waterway, neighbors injured by the pollution would probably have a valid negligence claim against the careless plant operator.

An intentional entering onto another's land without permission is a trespass. So too, causing particles to be borne onto another's land may be a trespass if the owner of the source of the particles has reason to believe that the activity would cause damaging deposits. For example, a physical and obvious trespass occurs when cement dust from a plant is deposited, layer on layer, on the property of nearby residents. Of course, if the particles deposited are undetectable by human senses and not harmful to health, although real, a court, in balancing the societal interests, will likely dismiss a trespass action.

In certain cases in which the threat or damage is caused by abnormally or inherently dangerous activities, the theory of strict liability may be used to recover damages or to halt the activity. The spraying of crops with toxic chemicals and the storage of explosive or other hazardous materials are examples of activities that may result in a defendant being held strictly liable. In such cases, a defendant's reasonable care is no defense. The inherent danger of the activity and resulting damages are sufficient to justify the plaintiff's recovery.

These common law theories are of ancient origin but have been adapted to the environmental context in "toxic tort" litigation in recent years. A toxic tort situation involving Erin Brockovich was made into a movie starring Julia Roberts and Albert Finney. In addressing the enhanced risk doctrine and the medical monitoring doctrine, the following case illustrates the modern evolution of the doctrine of negligence made necessary by the peculiar problems caused by exposure to environmental hazards.

IN RE PAOLI RAILROAD YARD PCB LITIGATION
U.S. Court of Appeals, 3d Circuit, 916 F.2d 829 (1990)

The plaintiffs are 38 persons who have either worked in or lived adjacent to the Paoli rail yard, an electric railcar maintenance facility in Philadelphia. Their primary claim is that they have contracted a variety of illnesses as the result of exposure to polychlorinated biphenyls (PCBs). PCBs are toxic substances that, as the result of decades of PCB use in the

Paoli railcar transformers, can be found in extremely high concentration at the rail yard and in the surrounding air and soil. Defendants include Monsanto (maker of PCBs), General Electric (maker of transformers), Amtrak (owner of the site since 1976), and Conrail (operator of the site).

The district court excluded much of the plaintiffs' proffered testimony and thereafter granted summary judgment to the defendants. The trial court also rejected as a matter of law the plaintiffs' claim based on the medical monitoring doctrine. The plaintiffs appealed.

Becker, Circuit Judge:

[The court held that the trial judge had improperly excluded plaintiffs' expert testimony and therefore concluded that summary judgment had been inappropriately granted. In the following excerpt, the court addressed the plaintiffs' medical monitoring theory.] We turn . . . to the viability of certain plaintiffs' "medical monitoring" claims by which plaintiffs sought to recover the costs of periodic medical examinations that they contend are medically necessary to protect against the exacerbation of latent diseases brought about by exposure to PCBs. [Pennsylvania state courts have not] decided whether a demonstrated need for medical monitoring creates a valid cause of action.

Therefore, sitting in diversity, we must predict whether the Pennsylvania Supreme Court would recognize a claim for medical monitoring under the substantive law of Pennsylvania and, if so, what its elements are.

Medical monitoring is one of a growing number of non-traditional torts that have developed in the common law to compensate plaintiffs who have been exposed to various toxic substances. Often, the diseases or injuries caused by this exposure are latent. This latency leads to problems when the claims are analyzed under traditional common law tort doctrine because, traditionally, injury needed to be manifest before it could be compensable.

Nonetheless, in an effort to accommodate a society with an increasing awareness of the danger and potential injury caused by the widespread use of toxic substances, courts have begun to recognize claims like medical monitoring, which can allow plaintiffs some relief even absent present manifestations of physical injury. More specifically, in the toxic tort context, courts have allowed plaintiffs to recover for emotional distress suffered because of the fear of contracting a toxic exposure disease, the increased risk of future harm, and the reasonable costs of medical monitoring or surveillance....

It is easy to confuse the distinctions between these various non-traditional torts. However, the torts just mentioned involve fundamentally different kinds of injury and compensation. Thus, an action for medical monitoring seeks to recover only the quantifiable costs of periodic medical examinations necessary to detect the onset of physical harm, whereas an enhanced risk claim seeks compensation for the anticipated harm itself, proportionately reduced to reflect the chance that it will not occur. We think that this distinction is particularly important because . . . in *Martin v. Johns-Manville Corp.*, 494 A.2d 1088 (Pa. 1985), the [Pennsylvania Supreme Court] made clear that a plaintiff in an enhanced risk suit must prove that future consequences of an injury are reasonably probable, not just possible.

Martin does not lead us to believe that Pennsylvania would not recognize a claim for medical monitoring, however. First, the injury that the court was worried about finding with reasonable probability in Martin is different from the injury involved here. The injury in an enhanced risk claim is the anticipated harm itself. The injury in a medical monitoring claim is the cost of the medical care that will, one hopes, detect that injury. The former is inherently speculative because courts are forced to anticipate the probability of future injury. The latter is much less speculative because the issue for the jury is the less conjectural question of whether the plaintiff needs medical surveillance. Second, the Pennsylvania Supreme Court's concerns about the degree of certainty required can easily be accommodated by requiring that a jury be able reasonably to determine that medical monitoring is probably, not just possibly, necessary.

[We predict] that the Supreme Court of Pennsylvania would recognize a cause of action for medical monitoring established by proving that:

Plaintiff was significantly exposed to a proven hazardous substance through the negligent actions of the defendant.

As a proximate result of exposure, plaintiff suffers a significantly increased risk of contracting a serious latent disease.

That increased risk makes periodic diagnostic medical examinations reasonably necessary. Monitoring and testing procedures exist which make the early detection and treatment of the disease possible and beneficial.

The policy reasons for recognizing this tort are obvious. Medical monitoring claims acknowledge that, in a toxic age significant harm can be done to an individual by a tortfeasor, notwithstanding latent manifestation of that harm. Moreover, as we have explained, recognizing this tort does not require courts to speculate about the probability of future injury. It merely requires courts to ascertain the probability that the far less costly remedy of medical supervision is appropriate. Allowing plaintiffs to recover the cost of this care deters irresponsible discharge of toxic chemicals by defendants and encourages plaintiffs to detect and treat their injuries as soon as possible. These are conventional goals of the tort system as it has long existed in Pennsylvania. [Reversed.]

Regulation by State Legislatures

In addition to the common-law role played by the courts, all state governments (and many subordinate governmental units) have passed laws dealing with the quality of the environment. These laws deal with all types of pollution—water, air, solid waste, noise, and others. Often state laws are patterned after federal laws. For example, several states have "mini-Superfunds" for hazardous waste site cleanup patterned after the federal Superfund law discussed later in this chapter. One popular type of state statute is the "bottle bill," designed to regulate the dumping of cans and bottles. Additionally, many federal laws presently provide a substantial state role in the establishing and enforcing of pollution standards. Even cities often get into the act, as with recent urban bans on plastic bags in retail stores.

NATIONAL ENVIRONMENTAL POLICY ACT

Although all states and many localities have significant environmental rules and regulations, federal regulations clearly dominate the regulatory landscape. Recognizing that a national environmental policy was needed, Congress enacted the National Environmental Policy Act (NEPA) in 1969 to "encourage productive and enjoyable harmony between man and his environment and biosphere and stimulate the health and welfare of man; to enrich the understanding of the ecological systems and natural resources important to the Nation; and to establish a Council on Environmental Quality." NEPA is a major step toward making each generation responsible to succeeding ones for the quality of the environment.

Environmental Impact Statements

NEPA requires that an environmental impact statement (EIS) be prepared by the appropriate agency whenever proposed major federal action will significantly affect the quality of the human environment. This requirement affects private enterprise as well because an EIS will be required if federal funds have been committed to a particular private venture. For example, a contractor building a federal highway or a naval base may have to help provide a detailed statement describing the environmental impact of the proposed action, unavoidable adverse effects, acceptable alternatives to the proposed project, and any irreversible and irretrievable commitments of resources involved.

Preparation of an EIS can be a costly and time-consuming task, even though regulations now limit the length to 150 pages (except in unusual circumstances.) NEPA requires that the statement be clear, to the point, and in simple English. It also requires that all key points and conclusions be set forth in a summary of no more than 15 pages. No matter how well prepared, an EIS is merely a prediction as to future environmental consequences of a proposed federal action. The proposed agency action, evaluated in light of the EIS, can be successfully challenged in court only if it can be shown to be "arbitrary and capricious."

Litigation over EISs often substantially delays and increases the costs of federal projects. Although very few federal projects have ever been halted by court actions based on NEPA, it is likely that many environmentally unsound projects have been abandoned or never begun because of EIS requirements. The EIS requirement remains controversial because it is impossible to quantify whether the environmental benefits of this process outweigh the additional time and expense incurred.

Environmental Protection Agency

In 1970 the EPA was created, consolidating into one agency the power to regulate various aspects of the environment that previously had been scattered across several federal agencies and departments. The EPA establishes and enforces environmental protection standards, conducts research on pollution, provides assistance to state and local antipollution programs through grants and technical advice, and generally assists the Council on Environmental Quality (CEQ). The CEQ was established to facilitate implementation of NEPA by issuing guidelines for the preparation of impact statements and generally to assist and advise the President on environmental matters. In its guidelines, CEQ has required that EISs be prepared as early in the decision-making process as possible and that other agencies and the public be given a chance to comment and criticize before any final decision is made to go ahead with major federal action.

Consolidation of diverse functions under the EPA has provided a center of control for the continuing war on pollution. How it works can be illustrated by studying the major areas of concern.

WATER POLLUTION CONTROL

As in other areas of environmental concern, federal regulation of water pollution is based on a series of measures passed over the years. For example, the Rivers and Harbors Act of 1890 prohibited the dumping of refuse into all navigable waters, and the 1899 Rivers and Harbors Appropriations Act made it unlawful for ships and manufacturing establishments to discharge refuse into any navigable waterway of the United States or into any tributary of a navigable waterway. Efforts to clean up the nation's waterways began in earnest with passage of the Federal Water Pollution Control Act in 1948, which has been repeatedly amended over the years.

Clean Water Act

The Clean Water Act (passed in 1971 and subsequently amended) is the major federal law governing water pollution. It provided a comprehensive plan to eliminate water pollution, setting standards and guidelines on an industry-by-industry basis for controlling water pollution from industrial sources. The types of discharges with which the law is concerned are as varied as the industries to be controlled. Thermal pollution from heat-generating plants and particulates and toxic wastes from manufacturing activities are subject to regulation and continual monitoring to assure that prescribed standards are being met. In general, industry is expected to control and eliminate its discharge of pollutants as soon as possible through the "best available technology (BAT) economically achievable."

The law placed primary responsibility on the states but provided for federal aid to local governments and small businesses to help them in their efforts to comply with the law's requirements. It also provided a licensing and permit system, at both state and federal levels, for discharging into waterways and a more workable enforcement program.

Citizen Suits

The government can enforce the Clean Water Act, but the law also allows citizens or organizations whose interests are affected by water pollution to sue violators of standards established under the law. Similar provisions are contained in several other environmental laws. Groups such as the National Resources Defense Fund, the Sierra Club Legal Defense Fund, and the Friends of the Earth often file notices of intent to sue under the Clean Water Act. Only a tiny percentage of such suits are preempted by governmental enforcement action, and most lead to negotiations and court-approved settlements and consent decrees. Such citizen suits have become quite controversial. Supporters believe that they are a beneficial supplement to actions brought by overworked agencies such as the EPA and its state counterparts. Critics believe that the suits have become so numerous (and arguably driven by provisions allowing for recovery of attorneys' fees) that they do not bring about cost-effective results and subvert consistency and fairness in national enforcement. The Supreme Court's decision to deny the right of environmental groups to sue in *Lujan v. Defenders of Wildlife*, 504 U.S. 555 (1992), a citizens' suit brought under the Endangered Species Act, reflects a hostility to such suits that may foreshadow additional imposition of restrictive procedural requirements.

Water Quality Act of 1987

In the Water Quality Act of 1987, Congress amended the Clean Water Act by emphasizing a state-federal program to control non-point source pollution. Whereas point sources such as municipal or industrial discharge pipes account for much water pollution, Congress determined that non-point source pollution such as oil and grease runoff from city streets, pesticide runoff from farmland, and runoff from mining areas must be addressed. The states were charged with developing programs to improve water quality by combating this pollution, which is very difficult to track.

The 1987 Act also clamped down on toxic water pollution and empowered the EPA to assess administrative penalties for water pollution. The penalties were placed on a sliding scale. For more serious offenses (considering the nature, circumstances, extent, and gravity of the violation, and the violator's ability to pay, history of violations, degree of culpability, and savings resulting from the violation), the EPA must provide relatively formal hearings but can assess larger penalties. Smaller penalties are assessed for minor violations after less formal procedures.

Responding to concerns about abuses of citizen suits, the 1987 Act also gave the EPA more supervision of settlement agreements in such cases, and a greater ability to preclude such suits administratively.

Oil Spills

All too frequently, vessels from small coastal barges to huge supertankers accidentally (or otherwise) discharge their cargos into the sea near the coast. The ecologic effect on fish, shellfish, and waterfowl and on the public and private shorelines and beaches can be immense. Consequently, the Clean Water Act imposes severe sanctions on those responsible for such pollution. The owner or operator of a grounded oil-carrying vessel can be liable for substantial amounts of the cost of cleaning up its spilled oil; if the oil spill is the result of willful negligence or misconduct, the owner or operator of the vessel can be held liable to the U.S. government for the full cost of cleaning up the shore. Operators of onshore and offshore facilities are also held liable for spillage and pollution, under ordinary conditions, to the extent of $50 million and, where willful negligence and misconduct are involved, to the full extent of the cost of cleanup and removal, including the restoration or replacement of natural resources damaged or destroyed by the discharge of oil or hazardous substances.

After the Exxon *Valdez* oil spill in Alaska, Exxon was charged with a variety of criminal offenses and sued by all manner of private and governmental officials. A wide variety of laws and regulations dealing with water pollution and wildlife were allegedly violated. Exxon settled state and federal litigation by agreeing to pay $900 million over 11 years (in civil penalties), plus $100 million for restoration of the injured area to be split between the United States and Alaska and $25 million in criminal fines. The settlement did not affect about $59 billion in private civil suits then pending against Exxon. The following Clean Water Act case arose out of a more recent environmental debacle.

IN RE DEEPWATER HORIZON
753 F.3d 570 (5th Cir. 2014)

The Macondo Well was the source of the 2010 Deepwater Horizon oil spill in the Gulf of Mexico. Defendants Anadarko and BP were co-owners of the well and co-lessees of the continental shelf block where it was located. The well itself was drilled by the Deepwater Horizon, a mobile offshore drilling vessel owned and operated by several entities. The Deepwater Horizon was connected to the well by a riser. At the junction of the well and the riser was a blowout preventer that could be used automatically or manually to interrupt an impending blowout. Both the blowout preventer and riser were appurtenances of the Deepwater Horizon.

The blowout occurred on April 20, 2010 while the Deepwater Horizon was preparing to depart from the site in anticipation of the permanent extraction operation. As part of this preparation, the well had been lined and sealed with cement. Before the Deepwater Horizon departed, this cement failed, resulting in the high-pressure release of gas, oil, and other fluids. The blowout preventer also failed, thus allowing these fluids to burst from the well, flowing up through the riser and onto the deck of the Deepwater Horizon. The oil and gas subsequently caught fire, and the ensuing blaze capsized the Deepwater Horizon, which was still connected to the well via the riser. The strain from the sinking vessel severed the riser, and for nearly three months oil flowed continuously through the broken riser and into the Gulf of Mexico. Authorities eventually installed a cap over what remained of the riser, and oil continued to leak for two days, with the well finally sealed on July 15, 2010.

The federal government filed this suit seeking civil penalties under Sec. 311 of the Clean Water Act, which mandates the assessment of fines on the owners or operators of any vessel or facility "from which oil or a hazardous substance is discharged." It is undisputed that defendants Anadarko and BP owned the Macondo Well which was the source of the oil spill. The trial judge granted the federal government's motion for summary judgment. Defendants appealed.

Benavides, Circuit Judge:

The Clean Water Act is "not a model of clarity." In its current form, the Act is the result of over a century of successive statutory schemes and amendments. Yet it is, in some respects, not overly complex. The legislation attempts to eliminate the introduction of any kind of pollutant—everything from paint and pesticides to rocks and dirt—into the waters of the United States. The Act does so by creating a regulatory framework and then prohibiting any discharge in violation of the regulations. Because of the heightened potential for "environmental disaster" resulting from the release of oil or hazardous waste, 33 U.S.C. § 1321 establishes increased fines for the discharge of these pollutants.

Specifically, the section prohibits the "discharge of oil or hazardous substances (i) into or upon the navigable waters of the United States, adjoining shorelines, or into or upon the waters of the contiguous zone . . . in such quantities as may be harmful," except under circumstances not [relevant here]. 33 U.S.C. § 1321(b)(3). The section further provides that: "Any person who is the owner, operator, or person in charge of any vessel, onshore facility, or offshore facility from which oil or a hazardous substance is discharged in violation of [the statute] shall be subject to a civil penalty in an amount up to $25,000 per day of violation or an amount up to $1,000 per barrel of oil or unit of reportable quantity of hazardous substances discharged."

In the instant case, no one denies that there has been a discharge of harmful quantities of oil into navigable waters. Anadarko and BP further stipulate that the well is an offshore facility, and that they are the owners of that facility. The only question, then, is whether it is beyond factual dispute that the well is a facility "from which" the harmful quantity of oil was discharged. We find no dispute as to the question.

Discharge is not defined for the purposes of this section, but is instead illustrated by a list of examples. Discharge "includes, but is not limited to, any spilling, leaking, pumping, pouring, emitting, emptying or dumping[.]" 33 U.S.C. § 1321(a)(2). Each of these statutory examples denotes the loss of controlled confinement. Similarly, the ordinary use of "discharge" refers to a fluid "flow[ing] out from where it has been confined." Accordingly, a vessel or facility is a point "from which oil or a hazardous substance is discharged" if it is a point at which controlled confinement is lost. Turning to the facts, we find no dispute as to whether the well is such a facility. The parties stipulate that cement had been deposited at the well. There is no genuine dispute that controlled confinement was lost when this cement failed—the defendants do not contest the cement's failure, and they concede that oil then "escaped" and "flowed freely" from the well and ultimately into navigable waters. And although the defendants argue that the blowout preventer should have engaged and prevented the progression of the blowout, the need for this intervention only underscores the extent to which the oil was already unconfined and flowing freely. Accordingly, we find that the well is a facility from which oil was discharged in violation of 33 U.S.C. § 1321(b)(3).

It is immaterial that the oil flowed through parts of the vessel before entering the Gulf of Mexico. Anadarko argues that discharge is the point at which oil "enters the marine environment." Yet Anadarko provides no relevant legal authority in support of the proffered interpretation. Nor does our research reveal any. On the contrary, it seems well settled that the section proscribes any discharge of oil that ultimately flows "into or upon . . . navigable waters," irrespective of the path traversed by the discharged oil. For example, a discharge of oil violates the section even where the oil flows over a rail yard or hillside before reaching water. *Union Petroleum Corp. v. United States*, 651 F.2d 734 (Ct. Cl. 1981). Similarly, the Environmental Protection Agency fined a factory owner for oil that spilled from a boiler gasket, into an industrial drain, through a conduit, and eventually into a creek. *Pepperell Assocs. v. United States EPA*, 246 F.3d 15 (1st Cir. 2001). So oil need not flow from a facility directly into navigable waters to give rise to civil-penalty liability under 33 U.S.C. § 1321.

Nor is liability precluded by the fact that the property traversed by the oil was owned by a third party. The Pepperell factory owner was held liable for his facility's discharge even though the oil had traveled through a third party's conduit before reaching water. Likewise, when spilled oil subsequently traverses municipal sewers or ditches, liability is imposed upon the owner of the facility where the oil was first discharged, and not on the owner of the municipal facilities. In one recent incident, EPA authorities discovered that oil and brine were being released from an oil exploration site. *In re D&L Energy, Inc.*, V-W-13 C-006 (EPA ALJ Feb. 27, 2013). Authorities found that a nearby river was polluted with oil and that a tributary was "impacted with oil at least a foot deep." Upon further investigation, they realized that fluids from the drilling site were flowing through a municipal sewer, into a creek, and eventually to the Mahoning River. The agency found the drilling site's owner liable, notwithstanding the fact that the oil flowed through third-party facilities before reaching water. Indeed, we are aware of no case in which a court or administrative agency exempted a defendant from liability on account of the path traversed by discharged oil. The well owners' liability is thus unaffected by the fact that the oil traversed part of Transocean's vessel before entering the Gulf of Mexico.

Civil-penalty liability under 33 U.S.C. § 1321 arises irrespective of knowledge, intent, or fault. In fact, courts have consistently rejected attempts to shift liability on the basis of shared fault, instead choosing to consider any contributing cause as a mitigating factor at penalty calculation. This Court, in particular, recognizes the section as "an absolute liability system with limited exceptions, which are to be narrowly construed." *U.S. v. W. of Eng. Ship Owner's Mut.*, , 872 F.2d 1192, 1196 (5th Cir. 1989). And although 33 U.S.C. § 1321 includes a third-party-fault exception for removal-cost liability, it includes no such exception for civil-penalty liability. That being the case, any culpability on the part of the Deepwater Horizon's operators does not exempt the well owners from the liability at issue here.

Affirmed.

Additional Regulations

Of related concern are the Marine Protection, Research, and Sanctuaries Act, which regulates the discharge and introduction of pollutants into coastal waterways and marine areas, and the Safe Drinking Water Act of 1974, which gave primary responsibility for enforcing national standards for drinking water to the states. Under the act, the EPA has set maximum drinking water contaminant levels of certain chemicals, pesticides, and microbiologic pollutants.

AIR POLLUTION CONTROL

Clean Air Act

The Clean Air Act of 1970 empowered the EPA to set standards to attain certain primary ambient (outside) air quality standards designed by Congress to protect public health. Because achieving the standards is costly, the EPA's role is to balance the economic, technological, and social factors that must be considered in attaining the clean air goals that have been set.

Several programs formed the essential elements of the Clean Air Act. Foremost was the setting of primary (health) and secondary (welfare) ambient air quality standards. Because the Clean Air Act's approach involved a federal-state partnership, another program required the states to draft State Implementation Plans (SIPs) for achieving ambient air quality standards. When approved by the EPA, such plans permitted the states to enforce air quality standards within their borders. Operators of air pollution sources could be required to monitor, sample, and keep appropriate records, all of which were subject to on-premises inspection by the EPA. When a proper SIP was not prepared, the EPA had to adopt a Federal Implementation Plan (FIP).

To reduce emissions in accordance with prescribed schedules, the Act also set new source performance standards (NSPSs)—emission standards for various categories of large industrial facilities. Major polluters must use the best acceptable control devices, those with proven capabilities to reduce emissions. To ease the burden on industry, the EPA adopted the bubble concept, under which a large plant with multiple emission points (stacks) does not have to meet standards for each one. The plant instead is under a ''bubble'' with a single allowable emission level. Plant management can manage each point source within the bubble to meet the sum total of emission limits by the most economical means.

Finally, the Act addressed automobile pollution by developing emission standards and fuel additive regulations. Use of unleaded gasoline and catalytic converters has resulted in substantial progress. However, industry continues to complain that the standards are too burdensome, and environmentalists still claim that the rules are too lax and are ineffectually enforced.

1990 Amendments

Although measurable progress was made in many areas pursuant to the 1970 Clean Air Act, it is undeniable that serious air pollution problems remain. Therefore, in 1990, Congress enacted significant amendments to the Act that emphasized four critical areas: (1) ozone, carbon monoxide, and particulate matter, (2) air toxins, (3) acid rain, and (4) automobile pollution (by prohibiting the sale of leaded gasoline).

The amendments created increased expenses and record-keeping for giant corporations and many small businesses as well. As many as 50,000 points of pollution may be required to obtain permits under the amendments. Those who fail to comply face the stiffest penalties yet. For example, previously violations were generally misdemeanors, but now they are felonies with criminal penalties that may run up to $1 million per violation. Additionally, the EPA Administrator may assess civil administrative penalties up to $25,000 a day per violation, and the role of litigation by citizens and private organizations in the enforcement process has been expanded. For example in *Gwaltney of Smithfield Ltd. v. Chesapeake Bay Foundation*, 484 U.S. 49 (1987), the Supreme Court held that citizens could sue only for ongoing violations of the Clean Water Act, a holding applied to the Clean Air Act as well. The 1990 amendments specifically permit citizens to file complaints over past violations that have been repeated.

Another form of citizen input comes in the permit process. All large pollution sources (except vehicles) must obtain permits from state pollution authorities specifying that their emissions do not violate Clean Air Act limits. Those permits are subject to EPA review, and if the EPA does not object to a permit, citizens may petition the agency to do so and may comment on permits and request public hearings during the approval process. Tens of thousands of facilities are covered by the permit program.

Proponents stress that the long-term benefits to the environment and public health may well outweigh the burdens that the act places on industry and on consumers who purchase products. The 1990 Amendments are viewed as having been substantially successful, because American power plants have significantly reduced their output of sulfur dioxide under the EPA's Acid Rain Guidelines established by the Amendments.

In the area of air pollution, as well as most others, major environmental programs have been established in a sequential fashion. That is, instead of having a master comprehensive plan, major initiatives have been amended and then amended again to address new problems or old problems that have proved to be intractable.

The following case addresses the latitude the Supreme Court will (or will not) give the EPA in regulating (or not regulating) pollution.

MASSACHUSETTS ET AL. v. ENVIRONMENTAL PROTECTION AGENCY
U.S. Supreme Court, 549 U.S. 497 (2007)

Calling global warming "the most pressing environmental challenge of our time," a group of States, local governments, and private organizations filed this suit alleging that the Environmental Protection Agency (EPA) has abdicated its responsibility under the Clean Air Act to regulate the emissions of four greenhouse gases, including carbon dioxide. Petitioners raised two issues concerning the meaning of Sec. 202(a)(1) of the Act: whether EPA has the statutory authority to regulate greenhouse gas emissions from new motor vehicles; and if so, whether its stated reasons for refusing to do so are consistent with the statute. The D.C. Circuit Court of Appeals ruled for the EPA; petitioners brought the case to the Supreme Court.

Stevens, Justice:

A well-documented rise in global temperatures has coincided with a significant increase in the concentration of carbon dioxide in the atmosphere. Respected scientists believe the two trends are related. For when carbon dioxide is released into the atmosphere, it acts like the ceiling of a greenhouse, trapping solar energy and retarding the escape of reflected heat. It is therefore a species -- the most important species -- of a "greenhouse gas."

In response, EPA correctly argued that we may not address the two questions unless at least one petitioner has standing to invoke our jurisdiction under Article III of the Constitution. [The Court then held that petitioners, at least the State of Massachusetts, had "standing" to bring this lawsuit. The EPA argued: (1) that the damage caused by global warming is so widespread that petitioners suffered no "particularized" injury; (2) that the EPA's actions didn't *cause* petitioners' alleged injuries; and (3) that the EPA could not prevent petitioners' injuries simply by issuing rules regarding auto emissions. The Court rejected these arguments. First, it would be perverse to hold that when injuries are particularly widespread no single party has standing to sue over them. Parties who are injured in a "concrete and personal" way have standing to challenge the action that injured them. Massachusetts has provided substantial evidence that its coastline will be damaged by rising ocean waters if global warming is not stemmed. Second, that auto emissions are not the *only* cause of global warming does not mean that the EPA is justified in doing nothing about them. That regulating emissions of new automobiles is only an incremental step toward addressing global warming does not mean that a wrongful failure to so regulate cannot be redressed in federal court. Furthermore, American autos contribute huge amounts of carbon pollution to the atmosphere, so this is hardly an insignificant matter. Third, that the EPA cannot completely solve the global warming problem by itself does not mean that it may sit by and do nothing. Petitioners need not prove that EPA action could solve their every injury in order to establish standing.]

Section 202(a)(1) of the Clean Air Act provides:

The [EPA] Administrator shall by regulation prescribe (and from time to time revise) in accordance with the provisions of this section, standards applicable to the emission of any air pollutant from any class or classes of new motor vehicles or new motor vehicle engines, which in his judgment cause, or contribute to, air pollution which may reasonably be anticipated to endanger public health or welfare

The Act defines "air pollutant" to include "any air pollution agent or combination of such agents, including any physical, chemical, biological, radioactive . . . substance or matter which is emitted into or otherwise enters the ambient air." Sec. 7602(g). "Welfare" is also defined broadly: among other things, it includes "effects on . . . weather . . . and climate." Sec. 7602(h).

[The Court then recounted the history of the issue, citing federal legislation in 1978 and 1987 that addressed manmade contributions to atmospheric pollution in a general way. The Court also recounted the evolution of scientific understanding about the significance of greenhouse gases' contribution to global warming, noting that the first President Bush attended the "Earth Summit" in Rio de Janeiro in 1992 and signed the resulting United Nations Framework Convention on Climate Change (UNFCCC), a nonbinding agreement among 154 nations to reduce atmospheric concentrations of carbon dioxide and other greenhouse gases for the purpose of "preventing dangerous anthropogenic [i.e., human-induced] interference with the [Earth's] climate system." The court also noted the 1999 Kyoto Protocol that assigned mandatory targets for industrialized nations to reduce greenhouse gas emissions. The U.S. did not ratify that agreement because those targets did not apply to developing and heavily polluting nations such as China and India.

Although the EPA had indicated in 1998 that it had authority to regulate CO[2] emissions, the current administration claims claimed that it lacks authority to act. The EPA now claims that the issue is so important that unless Congress spoke with exacting specificity, it could not have meant the agency to address it. The EPA further argues that if Congress did not wish it to address global warming, then greenhouse gases cannot be "air pollutants" within the meaning of the CAA. Finally, the EPA argues that even if it had authority over greenhouse gases it would refuse to exercise that authority because the link between human activities and an increase in global surface air temperatures "cannot be unequivocally established" and, furthermore, regulation of motor-vehicle emissions would constitute a "piecemeal approach" to climate change that would conflict with President Bush's "comprehensive approach" to the problem.]

The scope of our review of the merits of the statutory issues is narrow. As we have repeated time and again, an agency has broad discretion to choose how best to marshal its limited resources and personnel to carry out its delegated responsibilities. *See Chevron U.S.A. Inc. v. NRDC,* 467 U.S. 837 (1984). We therefore "may reverse any such action found to be . . . arbitrary, capricious, an abuse of discretion, or otherwise not in accordance with law." Sec. 7607(d)(9).

On the merits, the first question is whether Sec. 202(a)(1) of the Clean Air Act authorizes EPA to regulate greenhouse gas emissions from new motor vehicles in the event that it forms a "judgment" that such emissions contribute to climate change. We have little trouble concluding that it does. In relevant part, Sec. 202(a)(1) provides that EPA "shall by regulation prescribe . . . standards applicable to the emission of any air pollutant from any class or classes of new motor vehicles or new motor vehicle engines, which in [the Administrator's] judgment cause, or contribute to, air pollution which may reasonably be anticipated to endanger public health or welfare." Because EPA believes that Congress did not intend it to regulate substances that contribute to climate change, the agency maintains that carbon dioxide is not an "air pollutant" within the meaning of the provision.

The statutory text forecloses EPA's reading. The Clean Air Act's sweeping definition of "air pollutant" includes "*any* air pollution agent or combination of such agents, including *any* physical, chemical. . . substance or matter which is emitted into or otherwise enters the ambient air . . . ." Sec. 7602(g). On its face, the definition embraces all airborne compounds of whatever stripe, and underscores that intent through the repeated use of the word "any." Carbon dioxide, methane, nitrous oxide, and hydrofluorocarbons are without a doubt "physical [and] chemical . . . substances which [are] emitted into . . . the ambient air." The statute is unambiguous.

Rather than relying on statutory text, EPA invokes postenactment congressional actions and deliberations it views as tantamount to a congressional command to refrain from regulating greenhouse gas emissions. Even if such post-enactment legislative history could shed light on the meaning of an otherwise-unambiguous statute, EPA never identifies any action remotely suggesting that Congress meant to curtail its power to treat greenhouse gases as air pollutants. That subsequent Congresses have eschewed enacting binding emissions limitations to combat global warming tells us nothing about what Congress meant when it amended Sec. 202(a)(1) in 1970 and 1971. And unlike EPA, we have no difficulty reconciling Congress' various efforts to promote interagency collaboration and research to better understand climate change with the agency's pre-existing mandate to regulate "any air pollutant" that may endanger the public welfare. Collaboration and research do not conflict with any thoughtful [regulation]; they complement it.

EPA has not identified any congressional action that conflicts in any way with the regulation of greenhouse gases from new motor vehicles. Even if it had, Congress could not have acted against a regulatory "backdrop" of disclaimers of regulatory authority. Prior to the order that provoked this litigation, EPA had never disavowed the authority to regulate greenhouse gases, and in 1998 it in fact affirmed that it *had* such authority. There is no reason, much less a compelling reason, to accept EPA's invitation to read ambiguity into a clear statute.

EPA finally argues that it cannot regulate carbon dioxide emissions from motor vehicles because doing so would require it to tighten mileage standards, a job (according to EPA) that Congress has assigned to DOT. But that DOT sets mileage standards in no way licenses EPA to shirk its environmental responsibilities. EPA has been charged with protecting the public's "health" and "welfare," a statutory obligation wholly independent of DOT's mandate to promote energy efficiency. The two obligations may overlap, but there is no reason to think the two agencies cannot both administer their obligations and yet avoid inconsistency.

While the Congresses that drafted Sec. 202(a)(1) might not have appreciated the possibility that burning fossil fuels could lead to global warming, they did understand that without regulatory flexibility, changing circumstances and scientific developments would soon render the Clean Air Act obsolete. The broad language of Sec. 202(a)(1) reflects an intentional effort to confer the flexibility necessary to forestall such obsolescence. Because greenhouse gases fit well within the Clean Air Act's capacious definition of "air pollutant," we hold that EPA has the statutory authority to regulate the emission of such gases from new motor vehicles.

The alternative basis for EPA's decision -- that even if it does have statutory authority to regulate greenhouse gases, it would be unwise to do so at this time -- rests on reasoning divorced from the statutory text. While the statute does condition the exercise of EPA's authority on its formation of a "judgment," 42 U.S.C. Sec. 7521(a)(1), that judgment must relate to whether an air pollutant "causes, or contributes to, air pollution which may reasonably be anticipated to endanger public health or welfare." Put another way, the use of the word "judgment" is not a roving license to ignore the statutory text. It is but a direction to exercise discretion within defined statutory limits.

If EPA makes a finding of endangerment, the Clean Air Act requires the agency to regulate emissions of the deleterious pollutant from new motor vehicles. [The Act states that "[EPA] shall by regulation prescribe . . . standards applicable to the emission of any air pollutant from any class of new motor vehicles"). EPA no doubt has significant latitude as to the manner, timing, content, and coordination of its regulations with those of other agencies. But once EPA has responded to a petition for rulemaking, its reasons for action or inaction must conform to the authorizing statute. Under the clear terms of the Clean Air Act, EPA can avoid taking further action only if it determines that greenhouse gases do not contribute to climate change or if it provides some reasonable explanation as to why it cannot or will not exercise its discretion to determine whether they do. To the extent that this constrains agency discretion to pursue other priorities of the Administrator or the President, this is the congressional design.

EPA has refused to comply with this clear statutory command. Instead, it has offered a laundry list of reasons not to regulate. For example, EPA said that a number of voluntary executive branch programs already provide an effective response to the threat of global warming, that regulating greenhouse gases might impair the President's ability to negotiate with "key developing nations" to reduce emissions, and that curtailing motor-vehicle emissions would reflect "an inefficient, piecemeal approach to address the climate change issue."

Although we have neither the expertise nor the authority to evaluate these policy judgments, it is evident they have nothing to do with whether greenhouse gas emissions contribute to climate change. Still less do they amount to a reasoned justification for declining to form a scientific judgment. In particular, while the President has broad authority in foreign affairs, that authority does not extend to the refusal to execute domestic laws. In the Global Climate Protection Act of 1987, Congress authorized the State Department -- not EPA -- to formulate United States foreign policy with reference to environmental matters relating to climate. EPA has made no showing that it issued the ruling in question here after consultation with the State Department.

Nor can EPA avoid its statutory obligation by noting the uncertainty surrounding various features of climate change and concluding that it would therefore be better not to regulate at this time. If the scientific uncertainty is so profound that it precludes EPA from making a reasoned judgment as to whether greenhouse gases contribute to global warming, EPA must say so. That EPA would prefer not to regulate greenhouse gases because of some residual uncertainty -- which, is in fact all that it said ("We do not believe . . . that it would be either effective or appropriate for EPA *to establish [greenhouse gas] standards for motor vehicles* at this time" (emphasis added))—is irrelevant. The statutory question is whether sufficient information exists to make an endangerment finding.

In short, EPA has offered no reasoned explanation for its refusal to decide whether greenhouse gases cause or contribute to climate change. Its action was therefore "arbitrary, capricious, . . . or otherwise not in accordance with law." We need not and do not reach the question whether on remand EPA must make an endangerment finding, or whether policy concerns can inform EPA's actions in the event that it makes such a finding. We hold only that EPA must ground its reasons for action or inaction in the statute. Reversed.

[Author's note: Despite cases like this one from the U.S. Supreme Court, as this is being written in 2020, the Trump administration is doing everything it can to interfere with efforts to slow down the effects of global warming.]

International Cooperation

International cooperation can be important for combating many forms of pollution, but it is obviously especially important regarding air pollution. For example, the world recognizes with increasing alarm that climate change is a phenomenon that must be dealt with. Many multilateral approaches have been tried. The United States ratified the *United Nations Framework Convention on Climate Change (UNFCCC)*, committing itself to cooperate with other nations in seeking to develop multilateral solutions to global climate change. While the U.S. helped to negotiate the *Kyoto Protocol* to this Convention, as noted in the previous case, it later withdrew from the Protocol on grounds that it called for disproportionate reductions in greenhouse gas emissions from developed nations but relatively little sacrifice by developing nations. Many nations, including the United States, continue to work on refining the UNFCCC, but easy advances have proved elusive. It seems imperative that the nations of the world find an alternative means of getting global cooperation back on track.

In April 2016, the U.S. joined a large number of other countries in the *Paris Climate Accord,* an agreement within the United Nations Framework Convention on Climate Change dealing with greenhouse gas emissions mitigation. In 2017, however, President Donald Trump unilaterally withdrew the U.S. from the Paris Accord, in the process incurring the enmity of many other nations. In the aftermath of this withdrawal, many U.S. states and cities have pledged to intensify their own local efforts to reduce carbon emissions and other greenhouse gasses.

SOLID WASTE AND ITS DISPOSAL

The disposal of millions of tons of solid waste produced annually in this country presents a problem of staggering proportions. Periodic garbage pickups at residences or small businesses or weekly trips to the county or municipal sanitary landfill solve the problem for most people. However, less than 10 percent of solid waste is classified as residential, commercial, or institutional. The greater portion is classified as agricultural or mineral. Agriculture alone contributes more than 50 percent. Undisposed of, the waste creates enormous health and pollution problems; inadequate disposal methods often create greater hazards. If burned, solid waste pollutes the air. If dumped into waterways, lakes, or streams, the Clean Water Act is violated. Consequently, federal statutes have been enacted to combat the problem.

Solid Waste Disposal Act/Resource Conservation Recovery Act

The primary goal of the Solid Waste Disposal Act of 1965 and the 1976 amendment known as the Resource Conservation and Recovery Act (RCRA) is more efficient management of waste and its disposal through financial and technical assistance to state and local agencies in the development and implementation of new methods of waste disposal. RCRA defined hazardous waste as a solid waste, or combination of solid wastes, that because of its quantity, concentration, physical, chemical, or infectious characteristics may

A. cause, or significantly contribute to an increase in mortality or an increase in serious irreversible, or incapacitating reversible, illness, or

B. pose a substantial present or potential hazard to human health or the environment when improperly treated, stored, transported, disposed of, or otherwise managed.

RCRA also established an Office of Solid Waste within the EPA to regulate the generation and transportation of solid waste (both toxic and nontoxic), as well as its disposal, thus providing "cradle-to-grave" regulation. Although RCRA focuses primarily on the regulation and granting of permits for ongoing hazardous waste activities, it does have a corrective action program for site cleanup. The EPA is authorized to sue to force the cleanup of existing waste disposal sites presenting imminent hazards to the public health.

These acts generally treat toxic wastes more harshly than nontoxic wastes. But where is the line drawn? The Hazardous and Solid Waste Amendments (to RCRA) of 1984 required the EPA to expand the list of constituents characterized as toxic. In 1990, the EPA issued its rules, adding 25 organic chemicals to a preexisting list of eight metals and six pesticides regulated for toxicity. Many thousands of small (and large) businesses generating solid waste containing these substances must now comply with rules regarding hazardous waste, and a substantial number of landfills must now be treated as hazardous waste facilities, greatly expanding the costs of required disposal and cleanup. The 1984 amendments also created a comprehensive program for regulating underground storage tanks, such as gasoline tanks at service stations.

Comprehensive Environmental Response, Compensation, and Liability Act of 1980 (CERCLA or "Superfund")

Although RCRA provides cradle-to-grave regulation of active hazardous waste sites, in the wake of the Love Canal incident referred to earlier, Congress passed the Comprehensive Environmental Response, Compensation, and Liability Act of 1980 (CERCLA), better known as the "Superfund" legislation, to clean up abandoned or inactive sites. CERCLA initially established a $1.6 billion Hazardous Substance Response Trust Fund to cover the cost of "timely government responses to releases of hazardous substances into the environment."

Addressing a much broader range of hazardous substances than RCRA, CERCLA holds the polluter, rather than society, responsible for the costs of cleaning up designated hazardous waste sites, instructing the EPA to list the nation's worst toxic waste sites, identify responsible parties, and sue them for cleanup costs, if necessary. The following potentially responsible parties (PRPs) were initially enumerated: (1) present owners and operators of facilities; (2) any person who, at the time of disposal, owned or operated such a facility; (3) generators of hazardous substances who arrange for disposal or treatment at another's facility; or (4) transporters of hazardous substances. These parties are strictly liable for cost of removal and remediation, response costs incurred by others, and damages to natural resources owned or controlled by any government. Due care and compliance with existing laws are no defense. Once determined to be responsible, a PRP may have to bear the entire cost of cleanup because liability can be joint and several. In other words, if the government proves that owner A, prior owner B, and transporter C are all PRPs, and B and C are insolvent, A may have to pay for the entire cleanup. Furthermore, CERCLA is retroactive, covering both disposal acts committed and response costs incurred before the law was passed. Thus, potential CERCLA liability can be staggering.

The act also allows a category of exceptions, including owners of property incident to a security interest (*security interest exception*) and owners of land contaminated by the acts or omissions of third parties who are not contractually related to the owner (*third-party defense*). CERCLA also allows a PRP to avoid liability when pollution is caused by a natural disaster or war. The third-party defense is unavailable if the polluter is an employee or agent of the responsible party or one in a direct or indirect contractual relationship with that party.

Under the original version of CERCLA, completely innocent current owners of hazardous dumps faced liability for cleanup. In 1986, Congress passed the Superfund Amendments and Reauthorization Act (SARA), which provided an *innocent landowner defense* for those who could not only establish the third-party defense but also show (1) they had no reason to know of the contamination of the property when they purchased it and (2) they had made all appropriate inquiry into the previous ownership and uses of the property consistent with good commercial and customary practice. SARA also replaced the original CERCLA trust fund with the $8.5 billion Hazardous Substance Superfund (Superfund) financed by general revenue appropriations, certain environmental taxes, and monies recovered under CERCLA on behalf of the Superfund, and CERCLA-authorized penalties and punitive damages. SARA authorized civil penalties of up to $25,000 per day for willful failure to comply with EPA regulations.

Although in the earlier years, the costs of Superfund fell primarily on large corporations, in recent years, those corporations have spread the pain by suing small businesses and even municipalities for contributions specifically authorized by CERCLA. For example, two large corporations, who had settled an EPA action by agreeing to pay for a $9 million cleanup of a landfill, sued a tiny pizzeria (among several other small businesses), surmising that it might have included cleanser, insecticide cans, or other items containing traces of toxins in its garbage sent to the landfill. Small companies often settle such cases out of court because the cost of defending would be so high.

The financial threat that CERCLA poses to industries that generate toxic wastes and companies that dispose of them is obvious. Additionally, CERCLA poses substantial hidden liabilities for a wide range of entities, including the pizzeria mentioned above; real estate buyers, lessees, and landlords; purchasers of corporations with unknown environmental liabilities; and indirect owners and operators such as lenders or parent corporations. For example, a lender might under certain circumstances be liable to clean up a borrower's waste site at an expense far in excess of the amount of the loan. The follow case discusses both potential liability as a PRP and allocation of liability among various defendants.

BURLINGTON NORTHERN & SANTA FE RY. v. U.S.
556 U.S. 559 (2009)

In 1960, B&B began operating an agricultural chemical distribution business, purchasing pesticides and other chemicals from Shell Oil and others. B&B started on a 3.8 acre parcel of land in Arvin, California, and in 1975, expanded operations onto an adjacent .9 acre parcel owned jointly by Burlington Northern Co. and Union Pacific Railroad Company (Railroads). Both parcels were graded to drain toward a sump and drainage pond which were not lined until 1979 and therefore allowed waste water and chemical runoff to seep into the ground water below.

B&B stored and distributed various hazardous chemicals, including the herbicide dinoseb, sold by Dow Chemicals, and the pesticides D-D and Nemagon, both sold by Shell. Dinoseb was stored in 55-gallon drums and 5-gallon containers on a concrete slab outside B&B's warehouse. Nemagon was stored in 30-gallon drums and 5-gallon containers inside the warehouse. In the mid-1960's, Shell began requiring its distributors to maintain bulk storage facilities for D-D.

When B&B purchased D-D, Shell would arrange for delivery by common carrier. When the product arrived, it was transferred from tanker trucks to a bulk storage tank located on B&B's primary parcel. From there, the chemical was transferred to various types of trucks. During each of these transfers leaks and spills often occurred.

Shell encouraged the safe handling of its products by providing B&B with detailed safety manuals and requiring B&B to obtain an inspection by a qualified engineer and to certify its compliance with applicable regulations. B&B's Arvin facility was inspected twice, and in 1981, B&B certified to Shell that it had made a number of recommended improvements to its facilities. Despite these improvements, B&B remained a "sloppy operator." During B&B's 28 years of operation, delivery spills, equipment failures, and the rinsing of tanks and trucks allowed Nemagon, D-D and dinoseb to seep into the soil. In 1983, the California Department of Toxic Substances Control (DTSC) began investigating B&B's violation of hazardous waste laws, and the United States Environmental Protection Agency (EPA) soon followed suit, discovering significant contamination of soil and ground water.

By 1989, B&B had become insolvent and ceased all operations. That same year, the Arvin facility was added to the National Priority List, and subsequently, DTSC and EPA (Governments) exercised their authority under 42 U.S.C. §9604 to undertake cleanup efforts at the site. By 1998, the Governments had spent more than $8 million and their costs have continued to accrue.

In 1991, EPA issued an administrative order to the Railroads directing them, as owners of a portion of the property on which the Arvin facility was located, to perform certain remedial tasks in connection with the site. The Railroads did so, spending more than $3 million. Seeking to recover at least a portion of their response costs, in 1992 the Railroads brought suit against B&B. In 1996, that lawsuit was consolidated with two recovery actions brought by DTSC and EPA against Shell and the Railroads.

The District Court held that both the Railroads and Shell were potentially responsible parties (PRPs) under CERCLA; however, it did not impose joint and several liability upon them for the entire response cost incurred by the Governments. The court found that the site contamination created a single harm but concluded that the harm was divisible and therefore capable of apportionment. Based on three figures -- the percentage of the total area of the facility that was owned by the Railroads, the duration of B&B's business divided by the term of the Railroads' lease, and the Court's determination that only two of three polluting chemicals spilled on the leased parcel required remediation and that those two chemicals were responsible for roughly two-thirds of the overall site contamination requiring remediation -- the court apportioned the Railroads' liability as 9% of the Governments' total response cost. Based on estimations of chemicals spills of Shell products, the court held Shell liable for 6% of the total site response cost.

The Court of Appeals also held the defendants liable, but reversed the District Court finding that the record established a reasonable basis for apportionment. Because the burden of proof on the question of apportionment rested with Shell and the Railroads, the Court of Appeals reversed the District Court's apportionment of liability and held Shell and the Railroads jointly and severally liable for the Governments' cost. Shell and the Railroads appealed.

Stevens, Justice:

[I. Is Shell a PRP?] In 1980, Congress enacted the Comprehensive Environmental Response, Compensation, and Liability Act (CERCLA) in response to the serious environmental and health risks posed by industrial pollution. The Act was designed to promote the "'timely cleanup of hazardous waste sites'" and to ensure that the costs of such cleanup efforts were borne by those responsible for the contamination. These cases raise the questions whether and to what extent a party associated with a contaminated site may be held responsible for the full costs of remediation.

CERCLA imposes strict liability for environmental contamination upon four broad classes of PRPs:

(1) the owner and operator of a vessel or a facility,

(2) any person who at the time of disposal of any hazardous substance owned or operated any facility

at which such hazardous substances were disposed of,

(3) any person who by contract, agreement, or otherwise arranged for disposal or treatment, or **arranged** with a transporter for transport for disposal or treatment, of hazardous substances owned or possessed by such person, by any other party or entity, at any facility or incineration vessel owned or operated by another party or entity and containing such hazardous substances, and

(4) any person who accepts or accepted any hazardous substances for transport to disposal or treatment facilities, incineration vessels or sites selected by such person, from which there is a release, or a threatened release which causes the incurrence of response costs, of a hazardous substance . . . . 42 U.S.C. §9607(a).

Once an entity is identified as a PRP, it may be compelled to clean up a contaminated area or reimburse the Government for its past and future response costs. It is undisputed that the Railroads qualify as PRPs under both §§ 9607(a)(1) and 9607(a)(2) because they owned the land leased by B&B at the time of the contamination and continue to own it now. The more difficult question is whether Shell also qualifies as a PRP under §9607(a)(3) by virtue of the circumstances surrounding its sales to B&B.

To determine whether Shell may be held liable as an arranger, we begin with the language of the statute. Section 9607(a)(3) applies to an entity that "arrange[s] for disposal . . . of hazardous substances." It is plain from the language of the statute that CERCLA liability would attach if an entity were to enter into a transaction for the sole purpose of discarding a used and no longer useful hazardous substance. It is similarly clear that an entity could not be held liable as an arranger merely for selling a new and useful product if the purchaser of that product later, and unbeknownst to the seller, disposed of the product in a way that led to contamination. Less clear is the liability attaching to the many permutations of "arrangements" that fall between these two extremes -- cases in which the seller has some knowledge of the buyers' planned disposal or whose motives for the "sale" of a hazardous substance are less than clear. In such cases, courts have concluded that the determination whether an entity is an arranger requires a fact-intensive inquiry that looks beyond the parties' characterization of the transaction as a "disposal" or a "sale" and seeks to discern whether the arrangement was one Congress intended to fall within the scope of CERCLA's strict-liability provisions.

Liability may not extend beyond the limits of the statute itself. In common parlance, the word "arrange" implies action directed to a specific purpose. *See* MERRIAM-WEBSTER'S COLLEGIATE DICTIONARY 64 (10th ed. 1993) (defining "arrange" as "to make preparations for; plan . . . to bring about an agreement or understanding concerning"). Consequently, under the plain language of the statute, an entity may qualify as an arranger when it takes intentional steps to dispose of a hazardous substance

The Governments do not deny that the statute requires an entity to "arrang[e] for" disposal; however, they interpret that phrase by reference to the statutory term "disposal," which the Act broadly defines as "the discharge, deposit, injection, dumping, spilling, leaking, or placing of any solid waste or hazardous waste into or on any land or water." The Governments assert that by including unintentional acts such as "spilling" and "leaking" in the definition of disposal, Congress intended to impose liability on entities not only when they directly dispose of waste products but also when they engage in legitimate sales of hazardous substances knowing that some disposal may occur as a collateral consequence of the sale itself. Applying that reading of the statute, the Governments contend that Shell arranged for the disposal of D-D within the meaning of §9607(a)(3) by shipping D-D to

B&B under conditions it knew would result in the spilling of a portion of the hazardous substance by the purchaser or common carrier. Because these spills resulted in wasted D-D, a result Shell anticipated, the Governments insist that Shell was properly found to have arranged for the disposal of D-D.

While it is true that in some instances an entity's knowledge that its product will be leaked, spilled, dumped, or otherwise discarded may provide evidence of the entity's intent to dispose of its hazardous wastes, knowledge alone is insufficient to prove that an entity "planned for" the disposal, particularly when the disposal occurs as a peripheral result of the legitimate sale of an unused, useful product. In order to qualify as an arranger, Shell must have entered into the sale of D-D with the intention that at least a portion of the product be disposed of during the transfer process by one or more of the methods described in §6903(3). Here, the facts found by the District Court do not support such a conclusion.

Although the evidence showed that Shell was aware that minor, accidental spills occurred during the transfer of D-D from the common carrier to B&B's bulk storage tanks after the product had arrived at the Arvin facility and had come under B&B's stewardship, the evidence does not support an inference that Shell intended such spills to occur. To the contrary, the evidence revealed that Shell took numerous steps to encourage its distributors to *reduce* the likelihood of such spills, providing them with detailed safety manuals, requiring them to maintain adequate storage facilities, and providing discounts for those that took safety precautions. Although Shell's efforts were less than wholly successful, given these facts, Shell's mere knowledge that spills and leaks continued to occur is insufficient grounds for concluding that Shell "arranged for" the disposal of D-D within the meaning of §9607(a)(3). Accordingly, we conclude that Shell was not liable as an arranger for the contamination that occurred at B&B's Arvin facility.

[II. How Should Liability Be Apportioned to the Railroads?]

Next, we must determine whether the Railroads were properly held jointly and severally liable for the full cost of the Governments' response efforts. In *U.S. v. Chem-Dyne Corp.* (S.D. Ohio 1983), Judge Rubin concluded that although CERCLA imposed a "strict liability standard," it did not mandate "joint and several" liability in every case. Rather, Congress intended the scope of liability to "be determined from traditional and evolving principles of common law …."

Following *Chem-Dyne*, the courts of appeals have acknowledged that "[t]he universal starting point for divisibility of harm analyses in CERCLA cases" is §433A of the Restatement Second of Torts. "When two or more persons acting independently caus[e] a distinct or single harm for which there is a reasonable basis for division according to the contribution of each, each is subject to liability only for the portion of the total harm that he has himself caused. But where two or more persons cause a single and indivisible harm, each is subject to liability for the entire harm. *Chem-Dyne,* at 810. In other words, apportionment is proper when "there is a reasonable basis for determining the contribution of each cause to a single harm." §433A

Not all harms are capable of apportionment, however, and CERCLA defendants seeking to avoid joint and several liability bear the burden of proving that a reasonable basis for apportionment exists. When two or more causes produce a single, indivisible harm, "courts have refused to make an arbitrary apportionment for its own sake, and each of the causes is charged with responsibility for the entire harm." §433A

Both lower courts agreed that the Arvin site was theoretically capable of apportionment. The question then is whether the record provided a reasonable basis for the District Court's conclusion that the Railroads were liable for only 9% of the harm caused by contamination at the Arvin facility.

The District Court criticized the Railroads for taking a "'scorched earth,' all-or-nothing approach to liability," failing to acknowledge any responsibility for the release of hazardous substances that occurred on their parcel throughout the 13-year period of B&B's lease. According to the District Court, the Railroads' position on liability, combined with the Governments' refusal to acknowledge the potential divisibility of the harm, complicated the apportioning of liability. Yet despite the parties' failure to assist the court in linking the evidence supporting apportionment to the proper allocation of liability, the District Court ultimately concluded that this was "a classic 'divisible in terms of degree' case, both as to the time period in which defendants' conduct occurred, and ownership existed, and as to the estimated maximum contribution of each party's activities that released hazardous substances that caused Site contamination." Consequently, the District Court apportioned liability, assigning the Railroads 9% of the total remediation costs.

The District Court calculated the Railroads' liability based on three figures. First, the court noted that the Railroad parcel constituted only 19% of the surface area of the Arvin site. Second, the court observed that the Railroads had leased their parcel to B&B for 13 years, which was only 45% of the time B&B operated the Arvin facility. Finally, the court found that the volume of hazardous-substance-releasing activities on the B&B property was at least 10 times greater than the releases that occurred on the Railroad parcel, and it concluded that only spills of two chemicals, Nemagon and dinoseb (not D-D), substantially contributed to the contamination that had originated on the Railroad parcel and that those two chemicals had contributed to two-thirds of the overall site contamination requiring remediation. The court then multiplied .19 by .45 by .66 (two-thirds) and rounded up to determine that the Railroads were responsible for approximately 6% of the remediation costs. "Allowing for calculation errors up to 50%," the court concluded that the Railroads could be held responsible for 9% of the total CERCLA response cost for the Arvin site.

The Court of Appeals criticized the evidence on which the District Court's conclusions rested, finding a lack of sufficient data to establish the precise proportion of contamination that occurred on the relative portions of the Arvin facility and the rate of contamination in the years prior to B&B's addition of the Railroad parcel. The court noted that neither the duration of the lease nor the size of the leased area alone was a reliable measure of the harm caused by activities on the property owned by the Railroads, and -- as the court's upward adjustment confirmed -- the court had relied on estimates rather than specific and detailed records as a basis for its conclusions.

Despite these criticisms, we conclude that the facts contained in the record reasonably supported the apportionment of liability. The District Court's detailed findings make it abundantly clear that the primary pollution at the Arvin facility was contained in an unlined sump and an unlined pond in the southeastern portion of the facility most distant from the Railroads' parcel and that the spills of hazardous chemicals that occurred on the Railroad parcel contributed to no more than 10% of the total site contamination, some of which did not require remediation. With those background facts in mind, we are persuaded that it was reasonable for the court to use the size of the leased parcel and the duration of the lease as the starting point for its analysis. Although the Court of Appeals faulted the District Court for relying on the "simplest of considerations: percentages of land area, time of ownership, and types of hazardous products," these were the same factors the court had earlier acknowledged were *relevant* to the apportionment analysis.

The Court of Appeals also criticized the District Court's assumption that spills of Nemagon and dinoseb were responsible for only two-thirds of the chemical spills requiring remediation, observing that each PRP's share of the total harm was not necessarily equal to the quantity of pollutants that were deposited on its portion of the total facility. Although the evidence adduced by the parties did not allow the court to calculate precisely the amount of hazardous chemicals contributed by the Railroad parcel to the total site contamination or the exact percentage of harm caused by each chemical, the evidence did show that fewer spills occurred on the Railroad parcel and that of those spills that occurred, not all were carried across the Railroad parcel to the B&B sump and pond from which most of the contamination originated. The fact that no D-D spills on the Railroad parcel required remediation lends strength to the District Court's conclusion that the Railroad parcel contributed only Nemagon and dinoseb in quantities requiring remediation.

The District Court's conclusion that those two chemicals accounted for only two-thirds of the contamination requiring remediation finds less support in the record; however, any miscalculation on that point is harmless in light of the District Court's ultimate allocation of liability, which included a 50% margin of error equal to the 3% reduction in liability the District Court provided based on its assessment of the effect of the Nemagon and dinoseb spills. We conclude that the Court of Appeals erred by holding Shell liable as an arranger. And we conclude that the District Court reasonably apportioned the Railroads' share of the site remediation costs at 9%. Reversed.

The potentially crushing liability that CERCLA imposes created "brownfields" that no one wanted to touch. To encourage development of these areas, in 2000 Congress reduced CERCLA liability by passing the Small Business Liability Relief and Brownfields Revitalization Act, which:

1. Clarified the "innocent purchaser" defense which had not protected landowners because Congress had not defined the ''all appropriate inquiry'' that purchasers of land were supposed to take before buying land. The defense is now available to purchasers who (a) inquired as to the previous ownership and uses of the facility, and (b) took reasonable steps to prevent future releases of hazardous substances.

2. Created a "bona fide prospective purchaser" defense for those who knowingly buy contaminated properties, but can establish that all disposals of hazardous substances occurred before they brought the property and that they have exercised appropriate care to prevent releases of hazardous material, cooperated with clean-up authorities, and provided all necessary information.

3. Created a "contiguous property exemption" for innocent owners of down gradient property.

4. Created a "small business" exemption. The broad language of CERCLA meant that virtually all waste, including ordinary household waste or restaurant waste, contains hazardous substances. So, small business owners could find themselves liable as PRPs. The Brownfields amendments created exceptions for very small amounts of waste and for "municipal solid waste."

An important related issue that has been repeatedly litigated is the responsibility of corporate parents for the CERCLA liability of their subsidiaries. In *United States v. Bestfoods*, 524 U.S. 1 (1998), the Supreme Court held that state corporate law principles of corporate veil piercing should be applied and that CERCLA did nothing to broaden the liability of corporate parents in Superfund cases specifically. The Court did hold that under corporation law principles, parents are liable not only when the corporate form would otherwise be misused to accomplish wrongful purposes, but also where they directly participate in the operation of the offending facility that is owned by the subsidiary. The Court concluded that the parent in *Bestfoods* could potentially be liable because of evidence that its governmental and environmental affairs director actively participated in and exerted control over a variety of the subsidiary's environmental matters.

REGULATION OF TOXIC SUBSTANCES

In addition to the identifiable pollutants that are controlled at the source by the EPA, a more serious threat may be posed by the thousands of chemicals and compounds that are manufactured for commercial and generally beneficial use. These include herbicides, pesticides, and fertilizers, some of which may be highly toxic as single elements or may become toxic when combined with other elements. It is now apparent that toxic substances, initially applied to serve some useful purpose, are working their way into the environment, often with potentially dangerous results to humans exposed to those substances. An infamous example occurred at Times Beach, Missouri, where deadly dioxins deposited years before may have caused severe health problems for local residents.

Toxic Substances Control Act

In 1976 Congress enacted the Toxic Substances Control Act (TSCA) to create a review and control mechanism for the process of bringing chemical substances into the marketplace. The EPA is required to develop a comprehensive inventory of existing chemicals by calling on manufacturers to report the amount of each chemical substance they produce. TSCA imposes testing requirements on manufacturers and requires notice to the EPA when a new substance is being considered for development and production. The main purpose of the act is to prohibit the introduction of substances that would present an uncontrollable risk. Additionally, TSCA provides for testing, warnings, and instructions leading to the safe use of toxic chemicals with minimal effects on humans and the environment. Enforcement procedures permit the EPA to issue an order to prohibit the manufacture of high-risk substances. Pursuant to TSCA, the EPA has developed specific standards for PCBs, asbestos, chlorofluorocarbons, dioxins, and other substances.

Unlike some other environmental laws (the Clean Air Act, for example), TSCA orders the EPA to consider the economic and social impact of its decisions as well as the environmental effects. Therefore, more than some environmental regulations, TSCA seeks to avoid unnecessary burdens on the economy.

Pesticide Regulation

Obviously pests such as insects and mice cause significant crop damage and health problems. For that reason, chemicals that can kill or inhibit the reproduction of such pests are quite valuable for the health and economic welfare of Americans. Unfortunately, the widespread and long-term use of such substances can itself endanger the environment, injuring wildlife and human health. For that reason, Congress passed the Federal Environmental Pesticide Control Act in 1972, amending an earlier 1947 law, the Federal Insecticide, Fungicide, and Rodenticide Act (FIFRA). These acts together require that pesticides be registered with the EPA before they can be sold. Applicants for registration must provide comprehensive safety testing information to the EPA, which will approve the application only if the pesticide is properly labeled, lives up to its claims, and does not cause "unreasonable adverse effects on the environment." Such substances, when applied to crops that provide food for animals or people, may be used only within established limits. It is under this legislation that the EPA substantially banned the well-known insecticide DDT.

Food Quality Protection Act

FIFRA was altered with passage of the controversial Food Quality Protection Act (FQPA) of 1996 that mandated a cataloging of the nation's overall pesticide use to determine all the routes by which humans are exposed to pesticides and provided a single health-based safety standard for pesticide residues in all raw and processed food (replacing multiple standards for various residues). The law was supported by environmentalists and opposed by farmers who worried that it would put them out of business by unduly limiting their use of pesticides. Its goal was to protect America's children.

The FQPA required the EPA to determine that there is a "reasonable certainty of no harm" from exposure to the residue. The law required an additional safety factor of up to 10 times to account for uncertain data and ordered the EPA to consider children's special sensitivity and exposure to pesticides. The FQPA also limited consideration of economic benefits when setting pesticide tolerances, required the EPA to review all pesticide registrations every 15 years, and, required the distribution of brochures at food stores to provide consumers with more information about the health effects of pesticides. The Act has led to a phasing out of many pesticides previously used in producing foods, prompting agricultural producers to look for biopesticide replacements.

NOISE POLLUTION

The Noise Control Act of 1972, the first major federal assault on excessive noise emanating from sources to which the public is exposed on a continual basis, empowers the EPA to establish noise emission standards for specific products in cooperation with agencies otherwise concerned with them and to limit noise emissions from those products that can be categorized as noise producers. The act specifically targets transportation vehicles and equipment, machinery, appliances, and other commercial products. The act subjects federal facilities to state and local noise standards and expressly reserves the right to control environmental noise in the state through licensing and regulation or restriction of excessively noisy products.

The thrust of the Noise Control Act is to reduce environmental noise in an effort to prevent what are recognized as long-range effects (hearing problems) on public health and welfare. Violations of the prohibitions of the act are punishable by fines, imprisonment, or both. Many states and localities have their own noise pollution rules and regulations.

ENDANGERED SPECIES

The 1973 Endangered Species Act (ESA) has been called the world's most stringent environmental law because of its unstinting protection of plant and animal species endangered or threatened with extinction. Aside from the moral principles underlying preservation of endangered species, there is the simple utilitarian consideration that an extinct species can no longer provide food, medicine, and other benefits to mankind. In past years, animals and plants, such as the yew tree, were discovered to contain substances leading to the production of drugs that are life-saving or used to treat other debilitating or painful conditions even if not life-threatening.

Today, there are over 100 active ingredients derived from plants for use as drugs and medicines. *See* Veeresham, Ciddi. "Natural Products Derived From Plants as a Source of Drugs." *Journal of Advanced Pharmaceutical Technology & Research*, vol. 3, no. 4, Oct. 2012, doi:10.4103/2231-4040.104709. A non-exhaustive list of these plants and drugs can be found at https://www.thoughtco.com/drugs-and-medicine-made-from-plants-608413#citation-1.

On the other hand, a tiny fish (the snail darter) interrupted the construction of a $100 million dam project, a bird (the northern spotted owl) arguably has endangered thousands of jobs in the lumber industry in the Northwest, and millions of acres of land have been subject to land use restrictions under the ESA. As with all environmental laws and regulations, there is sometimes an inevitable tradeoff between negative economic effects and longer-term goals of protecting our planet's diversity of animal and plant species. Moreover, many environmental protection advocates have observed that the choice between economic concerns and environmental ones is a false dichotomy, because there are typically ways to balance the two with far less economic harm. Often, they say, environmental regulations motivate companies and researchers to adopt or even invent new technologies that achieve environmental goals much more economically.

More than two-thirds of the plants and animal populations on the ESA's protected list have become more stable or even increased in number since becoming protected, such as the bald eagle. Nonetheless, the ESA remains deeply unpopular in many quarters and many conservatives are working to repeal or heavily amend it.

INTERNATIONAL CONSIDERATIONS

The various forms of pollution do not respect national borders. Therefore, pollution has a critical international dimension that cannot be overlooked. Domestic laws, such as the proposed U.S. Climate Change Bill, can have a significant impact on the behavior of foreign companies, particularly when they apply import levies or other restrictions for those products that are not manufactured to domestic environmental standards. Additionally, international law and international organization now play an increasingly important role in solving important environmental problems. Unfortunately, as in non-environmental areas, their weaknesses prevent truly effective action. Nonetheless, important strides have been made.

International Organizations

Naturally, a look at international organizations must begin with the United Nations. Unfortunately, the United Nations has no executive environmental agency. Its strongest arm is UNEP (United National Environment Programme), which has helped formulate international treaties on pollution but has a limited budget and therefore can neither fund major projects nor comprehensively enforce international law.

The International Court of Justice plays at least a minor role in enforcing customary international law on transnational pollution. For example, in the *Corfu Channel Case (Greece v. Italy,* 1949 I.C.J. 18), that body ruled that countries have an obligation not to allow their territory to be used for acts (including polluting acts) contrary to the rights of other states. An International Joint Commission established a similar ''good neighbor'' principle in a pollution dispute between the United States and Canada in the *Trail Smelter Arbitration (United States v. Canada,* 3 R. Int'l. Arb. Awards 1907 (1949)), which involved claims by citizens of the state of Washington against smelters located in the British Columbia province, ruling that "under the principles of international law, . . . no state has the right to use or permit the use of its territory in such a manner as to cause injury by fumes in or to the territory of another or the properties or persons therein, when the case is of serious consequence and the injury is established by clear and convincing evidence."

International Conventions

The international community has in recent years attacked various aspects of the pollution problem through conventions and conferences. For example, as a starting point, Principle 21 of the Stockholm Conference (1972) provides that States have, in accordance with the Charter of the United Nations and the principles of international law, the sovereign right to exploit their own resources pursuant to their own environmental policies, and the responsibility to ensure that activities within their own jurisdiction or control cause no damage to the environment of other states or of areas beyond the limits of national jurisdiction.

Pursuant to that principle, several important conventions have been formulated. To attack the problem of "garbage imperialism" (the exporting of waste by developed countries for disposal in underdeveloped countries), the Basel Convention (1989) sought to prohibit transboundary movement of hazardous wastes absent written consent by all countries involved. Another requirement is that the receiving country have an environmentally sound way to dispose of the waste.

Water pollution in the form of oil spills by tankers has been addressed several times, including through the Protocol of 1984 to Amend the International Convention of Civil Liability for Oil Pollution Damage and the Protocol of 1984 to Amend the International Fund for Compensation for Oil Pollution Damage. The goal of these conventions was to create international standards of liability and an internationally enforced insurance scheme.

The endangering of species has been addressed in the 1973 Convention on International Trade in Endangered Species and Wild Fauna and Flora and the 1979 Convention on Conservation of Migratory Species of Wild Animals. These conventions address such matters as the illicit international trade in ivory, exotic birds, and rhinoceros horns.

The matter of ozone depletion is of primary importance in the international legal community because of the potential for worldwide adverse effects. The Montreal Protocol called for industrialized nations to completely phase out the use of ozone-depleting chlorofluorocarbons (CFCs) by the year 2000. It also provided a $100 million "financial mechanism" trust fund to enable developing countries to reduce their reliance of CFCs and to fund the attempt to find nonpolluting substitutes.

The June 1992 U.N. Conference on the Environment and Development ("Earth Summit") in Brazil led to several potential advances in international cooperation, including two treaties—the U.N. Framework Convention on Climate Change (UNFCCC) and the Convention on Biological Diversity. These two treaties bind all countries that ratify them; 153 nations signed the Biological Diversity treaty. *Only the United States refused.*

Limitations

Unfortunately, although most of these conventions look good on paper and all are important symbolic steps, most suffer in varying degrees from limitations that are common to all international legal measures. Most of the conventions were signed by substantially more nations than ultimately ratified them. Most do not apply to nations that did not ratify. Most lack methods of enforcement and suffer from vagueness in terminology. Many point to the United States' withdrawing support for the Kyoto Protocol relative to global warming as a classic example of the limitations of international approaches to environmental problems.

Still, international cooperation seems essential to saving the planet, and every effective step in the right direction should be appreciated and supported. Many people across the political spectrum view recent actions taken by the Trump administration in America to backtrack on or terminate U.S. cooperation with other nations on the resolution of environmental degradation as major steps backward that will have serious and possibly irreparable effects on the ability of Earth to sustain human life long-term.

CHAPTER 32

THE LEGAL ENVIRONMENT OF INTERNATIONAL BUSINESS

As early as 1816 in *The Schooner Exchange v. McFadden,* 11 U.S. 116 (1812), Chief Justice Marshall wrote: "The world [is] composed of distinct sovereignties . . . whose mutual benefit is promoted by intercourse with each other, and by an exchange of those good offices which humanity dictates and its wants require." As long as nations have existed, there has been commercial activity among them. That activity is generally beneficial to all the parties involved, and in our modern world the amount of international commercial activity is exploding.

The Covid-19 pandemic of 2020 demonstrated clearly how interconnected the world is. It also showed that this interconnectedness has both advantages and disadvantages. It may cause some nations to reassess how much they wish to rely upon goods and services provided by other nations, especially in a time of peril. Some countries, encouraged by nationalist movements within their borders, had already been taking fresh stock of these issues.

Nonetheless, it seems likely that capital, labor, and trade will continue to cross national borders in huge amounts. In 2019, before the coronoavirus began negatively impacting world trade, the United States total trade with foreign countries was $5.6 *trillion* dollars--$2.5 trillion in exports of goods and services and $3.1 trillion in imports. Many of the largest U.S. corporations derive more than half their profits from sales outside the country. On the flip side of the coin, most U.S. manufacturers face direct foreign competition for sales in the United States.

Foreign direct investment (FDI) occurs when firms invest in other countries by buying companies, building new plants, hiring more workers, investing in R&D, and the like. In 2018, global FDI was approximately $1.3 trillion and the U.S. was the biggest recipient of FDI. Many millions of Americans are employed by companies directly owned by foreign investors. More than half of all products made in the U.S. have foreign components and more than half of all imports and exports are between companies and their foreign parents or affiliates. The United States was not one of the major providers of FDI because its companies were busy bringing capital they'd stashed abroad back to the U.S. in response to U.S. tax law changes, highlighting the direct connection between domestic political actions and foreign trade and investment activity.

Foreign entities also own trillions of dollars of U.S. securities and total cross-border securities trading has skyrocketed in recent years. Thousands of traders watching computer screens around the globe constitute an international financial market that sends a stream of capital 50 times the value of international trade flowing across international borders. In 2018, foreign entities owned 48% of outstanding Treasury debt, 25% of American corporate bonds, and 15% of American stocks.

All in all, an already small world is growing smaller. Every day investors around the world watch the American stock markets, for what happens here will affect markets everywhere. Similarly, happenings in the European and Asian stock markets will have a direct impact on U.S. markets. Crop failures in Russia affect commodity prices in the U.S. Epidemics in China can dramatically disrupt the supply chains of many U.S. companies.

Just as each company or investor hoping to do business abroad must be concerned with the events occurring in other countries, so must they be concerned with legal aspects of international transactions. The laws of the countries in which they intend to do business, as well as international law, must be considered in each and every transaction.

Legal problems are pervasive and inescapable. Can a U.S. company selling its goods in South Korea expect protection from trademark infringement by local companies? Must a Japanese company operating its plant on American soil comply with U.S. laws when making its employment decisions? Does a European company wishing to purchase an American company face any barriers that a potential U.S. purchaser would not face? An endless variety of such legal questions shape international commerce.

This chapter introduces readers to the basic aspects of international legal rules as they bear most directly on persons and business organizations engaged in commercial transactions across national borders. It does not discuss in detail other important fields such as public international law, which regulates legal and political relationships among nations.

Classifying International Trade

Today we classify within the term international trade any movement of goods, services, or capital across national boundaries. In its normal use, the term includes three major components:

1. *Export* of goods, services, or commodities from one country to another.
2. *Import* of goods, services, or commodities into one country from another.
3. *Foreign direct investment*, such as the acquisition of interests in capital facilities in one country by investors from another.

Each of these components of international trade is distinct from the other; each raises particular legal and business issues; and each has been met with a distinct legal response intended to facilitate, harmonize, and regulate this aspect of global commercial and economic relations. With the growth in complexity of modern trade, the competition among nations as expressed in trade policy, and the shrinking presence of centrally planned economies in socialist bloc and Third World countries, the three main facets of international trade noted above have come to demonstrate, to varying degrees, three different sources of regulations:

1. Procedures developed by the *international trading community,* intended to ease trading relations and foster the resolution of disputes.
2. Regulations developed by *national governments* designed to protect national trading interests and to make them more competitive in international markets.
3. Laws and standards for international trade relations established by *international governmental organizations* such as the United Nations (UN) and the Organization for Economic Cooperation and Development (OECD), intended to harmonize trading community and national principles, to eliminate trade abuses, and to develop a greater participation in world trade, especially on the part of those nations that form the developing world.

This chapter looks at some of the major features of each of these components of the international trade framework.

INTERNATIONAL SALES CONTRACTS

Although foreign direct investment and foreign portfolio investment have become increasingly significant factors in world commerce in recent years, the transfer of goods across national frontiers remains extremely important. This type of transaction—an export from the seller's perspective and an import from the buyer's point of view—is fundamentally a contract of sale, much like its domestic cousin in its essential features. However, special factors such as the great distances involved, accompanying insurance considerations, and differences in legal systems present special problems. An overriding factor in the formation

781 © 2020 John R. Allison & Robert A. Prentice

of the international sales contract is that the parties do not, in many cases, know each other well; this ignorance can lead to uneasiness over the creditworthiness of the buyer and the dependability of the seller, and anxiety about the enforcement of the obligations of the parties if there should be a breach of contract.

In response to these and other concerns, international private sector merchants have over time devised a series of specialized but fairly standard techniques and legal devices that take the form of a series of "side" contracts that supplement the basic sales contract.

Financing the Transaction: The Letter of Credit

Because of the presumed lack of knowledge on the part of the seller as to the creditworthiness of the buyer, the export trade has developed a reliance on the *letter of credit* financing device. In the United States, Article 5 of the Uniform Commercial Code regulates letters of credit. However, in practice most letters of credit incorporate the provisions of the International Chamber of Commerce's Uniform Customs and Practice for Documentary Credits (UCP), creating some level of international uniformity in practice.

Basically, the letter of credit is an irrevocable assurance by the bank of the importer/buyer that funds for the payment of goods sold by the exporter/seller are available beyond the control of the buyer and that these can be obtained by the seller on provision of documentary proof that the goods have been shipped and that other contractual obligations of the seller have been fulfilled and are thus beyond the arbitrary control of the seller.

The documents that the seller must produce to be paid can include (1) inland and ocean *bills of lading* to establish receipt of the goods by the shipper and to serve as *documents of title* for the merchandise; (2) commercial invoices and packing lists to attest to the contents of bulk and packaged materials; (3) an *export license* and shipper's export declaration to show compliance with any applicable export controls; and (4) any *import licenses*, consular invoices, or *certificates of origin* necessary to comply with the import laws of the receiving country.

Because the buyer's bank is typically a foreign bank, the seller may have no more confidence in it than in the buyer itself. It is not unusual, then, for the seller to involve its own bank in the transactions to transmit the funds or to confirm or guarantee the performance of the buyer's bank that is issuing the letter of credit. In these circumstances, the seller's bank may undertake only to accept the transfer of funds from the buyer's bank and to credit these to the account of the seller (an advising bank); it may go further, however, and contract to guarantee this payment to the seller (a standby or confirming bank). In either event, an additional layer of contractual obligation will appear, this time between the seller and its bank and, further, between the seller's bank and the buyer's bank.

The letter of credit is essentially a means to make the seller comfortable that the goods will be paid for and to assure the buyer that the purchase money will not be released to the seller until proper, conforming goods are suitably shipped. In a high percentage of cases, there are discrepancies between the documents produced and the letter of credit. In almost all cases, the buyers waive these discrepancies; absent such waivers, the issuing bank may avoid its payment obligation. The following case shows how important compliance with technicalities can be.

MAGO INT'L v. LHB AG
U.S.Court of Appeals for the Second Circuit, 833 F.3d 270 (2016)

In 2011, Mago (a New York company) contracted to sell chicken, beef, and other meat products to NTP Genita (based in Kosovo). As is common in international transactions, in order to ensure it received payment, Mago required Genita to obtain a stand-by letter of credit (an SLOC), issued by Bank for Business, a Kosovar bank, and confirmed by LHB. Under the terms of the letter, if Genita failed to pay Mago within 45 days after the date of an invoice, Mago could present a defined set of documents to LHB and obtain payment on the SLOC. Among the documents LHB required was a "photocopy of B/L evidencing shipment of the goods to the applicant."

Mago shipped twelve containers of products to Genita under four invoices, designated 199(1-5), 199(6-7), 208(1-2), and 208(3-5), respectively. Genita defaulted on all four invoices. Mago tendered its first set of documents to LHB on September 19, 2012, including two unsigned bills of lading for each of the two 199 invoices. LHB rejected this tender for, inter alia, not containing signed bills of lading. Mago's second tender cured other deficiencies identified by LHB but contained the same unsigned bills of lading for the two 199 invoices. LHB again rejected the tender, emailing Mago's managing director that the unsigned bills of lading were not in conformity with the terms of the letter. Mago's third tender occurred on October 8, 2012, the last day possible to submit a demand for payment. As all previous tenders had done, this one contained signed bills of lading for the 208 invoices—but instead of unsigned bills of lading for the 199 invoices, Mago provided two telexes from the shipping company, Mediterranean Shipping Company ("MSC"). These telexes announced that MSC had retained the original, signed bills of lading in its files and authorized release of the shipments to Genita without the latter presenting the original bill of lading. LHB rejected this tender as well. Finally, on October 11, 2012, Mago tendered a set of documents containing signed bills of lading for each invoice. LHB rejected this tender as untimely.

Mago then sued in the Southern District of New York, alleging wrongful dishonor of the SLOC and naming both LHB and Bank for Business as defendants. The district court granted summary judgment to LHB and Mago appealed.

Wesley, Circuit Judge:

An SLOC is an agreement by a bank to pay a beneficiary on behalf of a customer who obtains the letter, if the customer defaults on an obligation to the beneficiary. "Originally devised to function in international trade, a letter of credit reduced the risk of nonpayment in cases where credit was extended to strangers in distant places." *Voest-Alpine Int'l Corp. v. Chase Manhattan Bank, N.A.*, 707 F.2d 680 (2d Cir. 1983). "The issuing bank, or a bank that acts as confirming bank for the issuer, takes on an absolute duty to pay the amount of the credit to the beneficiary, so long as the beneficiary complies with the terms of the letter." *Beyene v. Irving Tr. Co.*, 762 F.2d 4 (2d Cir. 1985). However, "[i]n order to protect the issuing or confirming bank, this absolute duty does not arise unless the terms of the letter have been complied with strictly." *Id.* "Adherence to this rule ensures that banks, dealing only in documents, will be able to act quickly, enhancing the letter of credit's fluidity. Literal compliance with the credit therefore is also essential so as not to impose an obligation upon the bank that it did not undertake and so as not to jeopardize the bank's right to indemnity from its customer." *Voest-Alpine*, at 762-63. Therefore, "[i]n determining whether to pay, the bank looks solely at the letter and the documentation the beneficiary presents to determine whether the documentation meets the requirements in the letter." *Marino Indus. Corp. v. Chase Manhattan Bank, N.A.*, 686 F.2d 112 (2d Cir. 1982). "The corollary to the rule of strict compliance is that the requirements in letters of credit must be explicit and that all ambiguities are construed against the bank. Since the beneficiary must comply strictly with the requirements of the letter, it must know precisely and unequivocally what those requirements are." *Id.*

As the District Court noted, resolution of this case turns on whether Mago strictly complied with the terms of the SLOC—specifically, whether presentation of unsigned copies of bills of lading satisfy the credit's requirement that Mago submit a "photocopy of B/L evidencing shipment of the goods to the applicant." Mago argues principally that, under the Uniform Customs and Practice for Documentary Credits (the "UCP") and interpretive guidance issued by the International Chamber of Commerce Banking Commission, where a letter of credit requires "copies" of transport documents like bills of lading, those copies do not need to be signed. Although the letter does explicitly incorporate the UCP and even assuming Mago interprets the UCP correctly, Mago's argument fails for the simple reason that LHB's letter did not simply require a copy of a bill of lading, but required one that "evidenc[ed] shipment of the goods to the applicant." Thus, whatever general guidelines are applicable, the copies here were required to evidence shipment. Because the bill of lading at issue required a signature to evidence shipment, the presentation of those documents did not strictly comply with the terms of the letter.

Even though the unsigned copies of the bills of lading here reflect the name of a ship and purported date of shipment, absent the carrier's signature, there is no evidence that the shipping information on the bill of lading reflects the actual shipment of the goods—precisely the information that the SLOC requires. Notably, the signature block on the bills where the carrier would have signed is immediately preceded by language to that effect:

> RECEIVED by the Carrier in apparent good order and condition (unless otherwise stated herein) the total number or quantity of Containers or other packages or units indicated in the box entitled Carrier's Receipt for carriage subject to all the terms and conditions thereof from the Place of Receipt or Port of Loading to the Port of Discharge or Place of Delivery, whichever is applicable.

Without the carrier's signature, the presented copy of the bill of lading does not appear to fulfill the terms of the SLOC. While copies of bills of lading may not generally require signatures, see INTERNATIONAL STANDARD BANKING PRACTICE FOR THE EXAMINATION OF DOCUMENTS UNDER DOCUMENTARY CREDITS SUBJECT TO UCP 600 ("ISBP") ¶ 20, the copies of the bill of lading here appear to require such a signature to satisfy the SLOC's requirement that the document "evidenc[e] shipment of the goods to the applicant." *See also* UCP 600, Art. XIV ("[B]anks will accept the document as presented if its content appears to fulfill the function of the required document." Although Mago presented telexes that it claimed also evidenced shipment, those telexes cannot satisfy the letter's requirement that such evidence be contained in a bill of lading. For the same reason, Mago's argument that the SLOC did not explicitly require a signature is unavailing; it explicitly required evidence of shipment in the bill of lading, and the bill of lading at issue required a signature for confirmation of shipment. Accordingly, neither the unsigned bills of lading nor the telexes tendered by Mago in its presentations to LHB satisfied the requirement of strict compliance, and LHB was entitled to reject the presentations. [Affirmed.]

The complexity of these multilayered arrangements is greatly reduced by the frequency with which they are used and their corresponding familiarity in the international trading community. It may help to chart the usual financing techniques of a typical international sales transaction in goods (see Figure 32.1).

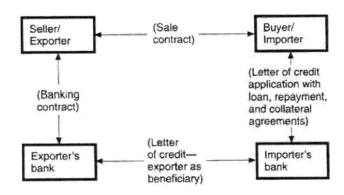

Figure 32.1
Financing Techniques of Typical International Sales Transaction

Trade Terms

Financing is, of course, only a means to an end, and a myriad of other factors—almost all of them bearing directly on the ultimate price paid for the goods—will be resolved in the terms of the international sales contract. The parties may wish to provide for a fixed rate of currency exchange or to specify the currency of payment for the contract; they may elect to identify the "official" language of the sales contract or to provide that two or more languages each represent the agreed terms of the transaction; they may choose the applicable law and identify the court that will have jurisdiction in the event of a subsequent disagreement; or they may decide to refer any contract disputes to binding or nonbinding arbitration. Clauses such as these, although very important, may or may not appear in the final contract, depending on a host of subtle factors, including the current economic and political climate, the degree of mutual trust and familiarity between the parties, and the extent to which they share common linguistic, cultural, business, or legal tradition. For instance, an American exporter will have, in most cases, fewer questions about the conditions of commerce with a long-time Canadian business associate than, for instance, with a first-time trading partner in Sri Lanka or Uzbekistan.

Various commonly accepted *trade terms*, addressing matters of universal concern such as factors of distance, language barriers, and general unfamiliarity between the parties, have evolved over time within the international trading community. These terms are often used to allocate responsibility between the parties. For example, *CIF* stands for "cost, insurance, and freight," meaning that the seller's quoted price is inclusive of the cost of goods, shipping charges, and marine insurance policy providing at least minimum coverage. This implies that the seller will bear the risk of loss during transit from the factory to the port of shipment; thereafter the risk shifts to the buyer who pays for the marine insurance policy that is usually arranged by the seller.

The term *FAS* (Free Alongside) implies that the risk of loss will pass from the seller/exporter when the goods are delivered alongside a vessel, usually designated by the buyer. Risk of damage in the onloading operation rests on the buyer. *FOB* (Free on Board) contemplates delivery of the goods by the seller, usually on a designated vessel where shipment has been arranged by the buyer; risk of loss passes at the ship's rail. *CAF* (Cost and Freight) is similar to *CIF* but the buyer arranges for insurance during carriage. *Ex* terms (ex factory) can be used to designate a place of delivery from seller to buyer that is other than the location of the carrier—for instance, at the factory, or perhaps at the ultimate destination of the goods.

Convention on International Sale of Goods Contracts

In an attempt to add uniformity and certainty to the terms of international sales of goods contracts, several countries have ratified the 1980 United Nations Convention on Contracts for the International Sale of Goods (CISG). The CISG became part of American law on January 1, 1988, and has been ratified by more than 90 nations, including most of America's major trading partners, except the United Kingdom and India.

Assume that Country A and Country B have both ratified the CISG. If a purchaser with a place of business in A makes a contract to buy goods from a company with a place of business in B, the CISG's provisions will automatically govern the contract unless the parties opt out of its coverage.

The CISG does not apply to consumer sales and has no provisions governing the validity of contracts, ownership claims of third parties, or liability claims for death or personal injury. However, it does have provisions governing most other issues that could arise in a contractual setting. The parties may provide their own variations, but the CISG augments contractual terms and provides the rules for situations the parties did not contemplate or address in their agreement.

The CISG could be loosely termed an international Uniform Commercial Code. It addresses most of the same subjects as Article 2 of the UCC, such as definiteness and revocability of offers, timeliness of acceptances, risk of loss, excuse from performance, and remedies. However, the CISG differs from the UCC in several respects. For example, Article 11 of the Convention largely abolishes the statute of frauds requirement of a written contract. Article 16 states that an offer cannot be revoked if it was reasonable for the offeree to rely on it as being irrevocable and the offeree has acted in reliance thereon. Article 35 alters the UCC's "perfect tender" rule. A seller must deliver goods fit for ordinary use of the buyer's particular purpose that is known to the seller. A buyer may reject goods only if there is a "fundamental breach." Article 50 addresses buyers' remedies, providing that a buyer may require a seller to perform in accordance with the promise or fix an additional time for the seller to perform. This latter option is not contained in the UCC but is derived from German law. A complete discussion of the CISG's provisions is beyond the scope of this chapter, but these differences and others (for example, the CISG contains no obligation to act in good faith, as does the UCC's Article 2), many American lawyers advise their clients to opt out of the CISG where possible. This is not always easy.

In *Asante Technologies v. PMC-Sierra, Inc.,* 164 F.Supp.2d 1142 (N.D.Cal. 2001), a Canadian company bought electronic products from a California firm. The parties did not have a single contract with a clear choice-of-law provision, but four of five purchase orders specified that California law should apply. Nonetheless, the buyer argued that because both Canada and the U.S. are signatories of the CISG, it should govern. The court concluded that the purchase order provisions did not evidence a clear enough intent to opt out of the CISG. Furthermore, even if the law of California did apply, under the Supremacy Clause of the

U.S. Constitution California law is subordinate to U.S. treaties. In the absence of clearer "opt out" language, the court held that the CISG applied even under California law. Had the choice of law provision stated "This contract is governed by the laws of the State of California, *not* including the 1980 United Nations Convention on Contracts for the International Sale of Goods," a successful opt out likely would have been recognized. Lawyers have learned their lessons and most U.S. companies routinely opt out of the CISG in most of their international contracts.

Other Commercial Conventions

The CISG's attempt to add uniformity to international sales law is representative of the work of the United Nations Commission on International Trade Law (UNCITRAL), which actively promotes conventions, including the Convention on the Limitations Period in the International Sale of Goods; on the Carriage of Goods by Sea; on International Bills of Exchange and Promissory Notes; and on Recognition and Enforcement of Foreign Arbitral Awards. UNCITRAL also promotes model laws, including the Model Law on International Awards; on International Credit Transfers; on Procurement of Goods, Construction and Services; and on Electronic Commerce.

RESOLVING INTERNATIONAL TRADE DISPUTES

No contract—including one for an international business transaction—can be so tightly drawn that it is totally impervious to later disagreement. Similarly, unforeseen changes in circumstances may make performance of the contract impossible or, perhaps, more difficult or expensive than originally contemplated by the parties. An international trader should, therefore, have a clear understanding of the means available to resolve such disputes if they should arise.

Judicial litigation is rarely the best means to resolve any business dispute: The costs associated with it (attorneys' fees, court costs, and general expenses) will often offset any profit expected from the transaction. These difficulties are exacerbated in transnational litigation.

Difficulties often arise in identifying a court with proper jurisdiction over the subject matter of the action or the parties to the transaction. In many types of litigation, the question will arise as to which nation has authority to assert its law over the transaction and the parties.

Domestic Court Jurisdiction

In business litigation, and in other types of litigation touching the international sphere, the rules of jurisdiction are evolving but are as yet unclear. The American Law Institute's *Restatement (Third) of the Foreign Relations Law of the United States* may be a good indicator of the direction in which the law is heading. Rather than use the traditional categories of subject matter jurisdiction and personal jurisdiction, the Restatement (Third) establishes three categories: (1) *jurisdiction to prescribe,* that is, the authority of a state to make its law applicable to persons or activities; (2) *jurisdiction to adjudicate,* that is, the authority of a state to subject particular persons or things to its judicial process; and (3) *jurisdiction to enforce,* that is, the authority to use the resources of government to induce or compel compliance with its law.

Attempts by the United States to impose its legal regulations on activities occurring abroad have caused substantial resentment in foes and allies alike over the years. The

Restatement (Third)'s §402 recognizes a nation's *jurisdiction to prescribe* with respect to

1. (a) conduct, a substantial part of which takes place within its territory; (b) the status of persons, or interests in things, present within its territory; (c) conduct outside its territory which has or is intended to have substantial effect within its territory;
2. the activities, status, interests or relations of its nationals outside as well as within its territory; or
3. certain conduct outside its territory by persons not its nationals which is directed against the security of the state [example: terrorism] or a limited class of other state interests.

Thus, links of territoriality and nationality are ordinarily necessary to the power to prescribe law, although they are not sufficient in all cases. Furthermore, these criteria are expressly limited by §403, which states that even when they are present, jurisdiction to prescribe should not be exercised when it would be "unreasonable" as determined by an evaluation of all relevant factors, including (1) the extent to which the activity takes place in the regulating state and has a substantial, direct, and foreseeable effect there; (2) the connections, such as nationality, residence, or economic activity, between the regulating state and the persons responsible for the activity to be regulated or between the state and those whom the law is designed to protect; (3) the character of the activity to be regulated, the extent to which other states regulate it, and its general acceptability; (4) the existence of justified expectations that might be injured; (5) the importance of the regulation to the international political, legal, or economic system; (6) the extent to which such regulation is consistent with the traditions of the international system; (7) the extent to which another state may have an interest in regulating the activity; and (8) the likelihood of conflict with regulation by other states. A state should defer to another state whose interest in regulating the same conduct is clearly greater.

Reasonableness also is the hallmark of the Restatement (Third)'s approach to *jurisdiction to adjudicate.* According to §421, personal jurisdiction is to be exercised only if reasonable. Such exercise will generally be deemed reasonable if an individual defendant is present (other than transitorily) in the territory of the state; or is a domiciliary, resident, or national of the state; or regularly carries on business there; or has consented to the exercise of jurisdiction. Additionally, exercise of jurisdiction to adjudicate will be reasonable if the person has carried on activity in the state that created the liability in question or has carried on outside the state an activity having substantial, direct, or foreseeable effect within the state that created the liability in question.

Finally, under §431 of the Restatement, *jurisdiction to enforce* will be present only where a state had the power to prescribe, in accordance with §§402 and 403, and the power to adjudicate as to the particular defendant. Enforcement measures must be proportional to the gravity of the violation and may be used against persons located outside the territory of the enforcing state only if such persons are given fair notice and an opportunity to be heard.

The case below illustrates the struggles legislatures and courts go through in attempting to set reasonable boundaries upon international application of primarily domestic laws.

F. HOFFMAN-LA ROUCHE, LTD. v. EMPAGRAN, S.A.
542 U.S. 155 (2004)

Plaintiffs filed a class-action suit on behalf of foreign and domestic purchasers of vitamins under the Sherman Antitrust Act (among other provisions), alleging that defendant/petitioners, foreign and domestic vitamin manufacturers and distributors, had engaged in a price-fixing conspiracy, raising the price of vitamin products to customers in the United States and to customers in foreign countries. Petitioners moved to dismiss the suit as to the foreign purchasers (the respondents here), five foreign vitamin distributors located in Ukraine, Australia, Ecuador, and Panama, each of which bought vitamins from petitioners for delivery outside the United States. The District Court dismissed the claims under the Foreign Trade Antitrust Improvements Act of 1982 (FTAIA). The D.C. Court of Appeals reversed and defendants appealed.

Breyer, Justice:

The FTAIA excludes from the Sherman Act's reach much anticompetitive conduct that causes only foreign injury. It does so by setting forth a general rule stating that the Sherman Act "shall not apply to conduct involving trade or commerce . . . with foreign nations." It then creates exceptions to the general rule, applicable where (roughly speaking) that conduct significantly harms imports, domestic commerce, or American exporters.

We here focus upon anticompetitive price-fixing activity that is in significant part foreign, that causes some domestic antitrust injury, and that independently causes separate foreign injury. We ask two questions about the price-fixing conduct and the foreign injury that it causes. First, does that conduct fall within the FTAIA's general rule excluding the Sherman Act's application? That is to say, does the price-fixing activity constitute "conduct involving trade or commerce . . . with foreign nations"? We conclude that it does.

Second, we ask whether the conduct nonetheless falls within a domestic-injury exception to the general rule, an exception that applies (and makes the Sherman Act nonetheless applicable) where the conduct (1) has a "direct, substantial, and reasonably foreseeable effect" on domestic commerce, and (2) "such effect gives rise to a [Sherman Act] claim." We conclude that the exception does not apply where the plaintiff's claim rests solely on the independent foreign harm.

To clarify: The issue before us concerns (1) significant foreign anticompetitive conduct with (2) an adverse domestic effect and (3) an independent foreign effect giving rise to the claim. In more concrete terms, this case involves vitamin sellers around the world that agreed to fix prices, leading to higher vitamin prices in the United States and independently leading to higher vitamin prices in other countries such as Ecuador. We conclude that, in this scenario, a purchaser in the United States could bring a Sherman Act claim under the FTAIA based on domestic injury, but a purchaser in Ecuador could not bring a Sherman Act claim based on foreign harm.

The FTAIA seeks to make clear to American exporters (and to firms doing business abroad) that the Sherman Act does not prevent them from entering into business arrangements (say, joint-selling arrangements), however anticompetitive, as long as those arrangements adversely affect only foreign markets. It does so by removing from the Sherman Act's reach, (1) export activities and (2) other commercial activities taking place abroad, unless those activities adversely affect domestic commerce, imports to the United States, or exporting activities of one engaged in such activities within the United States.

The FTAIA says:

Sections 1 to 7 of this title [the Sherman Act] shall not apply to conduct involving trade or commerce (other than import trade or import commerce) with foreign nations unless—

(1) such conduct has a direct, substantial, and reasonably foreseeable effect—

    (A) on trade or commerce which is not trade or commerce with foreign nations [i.e., domestic trade or commerce], or on import trade or import commerce with foreign nations; or

    (B) on export trade or export commerce with foreign nations, of a person engaged in such trade or commerce in the United States [i.e., on an American export competitor]; and

(2) such effect gives rise to a claim under the provisions of sections 1 to 7 of this title, other than this section.

If sections 1 to 7 of this title apply to such conduct only because of the operation of paragraph (1)(B), then sections 1 to 7 of this title shall apply to such conduct only for injury to export business in the United States.

This technical language initially lays down a general rule placing all (nonimport) activity involving foreign commerce outside the Sherman Act's reach. It then brings such conduct back within the Sherman Act's reach provided that the conduct both (1) sufficiently affects American commerce, i.e., it has a "direct, substantial, and reasonably foreseeable effect" on American domestic, import, or (certain) export commerce, and (2) has an effect of a kind that antitrust law considers harmful, i.e., the "effect" must "giv[e] rise to a [Sherman Act] claim."

We ask here how this language applies to price-fixing activity that is in significant part foreign, that has the requisite domestic effect, and that also has independent foreign effects giving rise to the plaintiff's claim.

Because the underlying antitrust action is complex, potentially raising questions not directly at issue here, we reemphasize that we base our decision upon the following: The price-fixing conduct significantly and adversely affects both customers outside the United States and customers within the United States, but the adverse foreign effect is independent of any adverse domestic effect. In these circumstances, we find that the FTAIA exception does not apply (and thus the Sherman Act does not apply) for two main reasons.

First, this Court ordinarily construes ambiguous statutes to avoid unreasonable interference with the sovereign authority of other nations. This rule of construction reflects principles of customary international law--law that (we must assume) Congress ordinarily seeks to follow. See Restatement (Third) of Foreign Relations Law of the United States §§ 403(1), 403(2) (1986) (hereinafter Restatement) (limiting the unreasonable exercise of prescriptive jurisdiction with respect to a person or activity having connections with another State); *Murray v. Schooner Charming Betsy*, 6 U.S. 64 (1804) ("[A]n act of Congress ought never to be construed to violate the law of nations if any other possible construction remains").

This rule of statutory construction cautions courts to assume that legislators take account of the legitimate sovereign interests of other nations when they write American laws. It thereby helps the potentially conflicting laws of different nations work together in harmony--a harmony particularly needed in today's interdependent commercial world.

No one denies that America's antitrust laws, when applied to foreign conduct, can interfere with a foreign nation's ability independently to regulate its own commercial affairs. But our courts have long held that application of our antitrust laws to foreign anticompetitive conduct is nonetheless reasonable, and hence consistent with principles of prescriptive comity, insofar as they reflect a legislative effort to redress domestic antitrust injury that foreign anticompetitive conduct has caused.

But why is it reasonable to apply those laws to foreign conduct insofar as that conduct causes independent foreign harm and that foreign harm alone gives rise to the plaintiff's claim? Like the former case, application of those laws creates a serious risk of interference with a foreign nation's ability independently to regulate its own commercial affairs. But, unlike the former case, the justification for that interference seems insubstantial. See Restatement § 403(2) (determining reasonableness on basis of such factors as connections with regulating nation, harm to that nation's interests, extent to which other nations regulate, and the potential for conflict). Why should American law supplant, for example, Canada's or Great Britain's or Japan's own determination about how best to protect Canadian or British or Japanese customers from anticompetitive conduct engaged in significant part by Canadian or British or Japanese or other foreign companies?

We recognize that principles of comity provide Congress greater leeway when it seeks to control through legislation the actions of American companies, see Restatement § 402; and some of the anticompetitive price-fixing conduct alleged here took place in America. But the higher foreign prices of which the foreign plaintiffs here complain are not the consequence of any domestic anticompetitive conduct that Congress sought to forbid, for Congress did not seek to forbid any such conduct insofar as it is here relevant, i.e., insofar as it is intertwined with foreign conduct that causes independent foreign harm. Rather Congress sought to release domestic (and foreign) anticompetitive conduct from Sherman Act constraints when that conduct causes foreign harm. Congress, of course, did make an exception where that conduct also causes domestic harm. See House Report 13 (concerns about American firms' participation in international cartels addressed through "domestic injury" exception). But any independent domestic harm the foreign conduct causes here has, by definition, little or nothing to do with the matter.

We thus repeat the basic question: Why is it reasonable to apply this law to conduct that is significantly foreign insofar as that conduct causes independent foreign harm and that foreign harm alone gives rise to the plaintiff's claim? We can find no good answer to the question.

The Areeda and Hovenkamp treatise notes that under the Court of Appeals' interpretation of the statute

> a Malaysian customer could . . . maintain an action under United States law in a United States court against its own Malaysian supplier, another cartel member, simply by noting that unnamed third parties injured [in the United States] by the American [cartel member's] conduct would also have a cause of action. Effectively, the United States courts would provide worldwide subject matter jurisdiction to any foreign suitor wishing to sue its own local supplier, but unhappy with its own sovereign's provisions for private antitrust enforcement, provided that a different plaintiff had a cause of action against a different firm for injuries that were within U. S. [other-than-import] commerce. It does not seem excessively rigid to infer that Congress would not have intended that result. P. Areeda & H. Hovenkamp, Antitrust Law P 273, pp 51-52 (Supp 2003).

We agree with the comment. We can find no convincing justification for the extension of the Sherman Act's scope that it describes. Second, the FTAIA's language and history suggest that Congress designed the FTAIA to clarify, perhaps to limit, but not to expand in any significant way, the Sherman Act's scope as applied to foreign commerce. And we have found no significant indication that at the time Congress wrote this statute courts would have thought the Sherman Act applicable in these circumstances. [The respondents cite several cases, but they are all distinguishable.]

The upshot is that no pre-1982 case provides significant authority for application of the Sherman Act in the circumstances we here assume. Indeed, a leading contemporaneous lower court case contains language suggesting the contrary. See *Timberlane Lumber Co. v. Bank of America,* 549 F.2d 597 (9th Cir. 1976) (insisting that the foreign conduct's domestic effect be "sufficiently large to present a cognizable injury to the plaintiffs.")

Taken together, these two sets of considerations, the one derived from comity and the other reflecting history, convince us that Congress would not have intended the FTAIA's exception to bring independently caused foreign injury within the Sherman Act's reach. [The appellate court's decision is vacated.]

Foreign Sovereign Immunities Act

Even in circumstances in which the court should be willing to assert its jurisdiction over the defendant under the effects or reasonableness tests, it may be barred from doing so because of a personal immunity of the defendant. This bar is most often encountered when the defendant is a foreign state or state agency, a circumstance more frequently present today when many nations—especially those with centrally planned economies—are engaging directly in trading activities. The Foreign Sovereign Immunities Act (FSIA), passed by Congress in 1976, modifies the absolute sovereign immunity that the common law had recognized but continues to limit a plaintiff's ability to recover a judgment from a foreign state or state agency.

Under the FSIA, U.S. courts have jurisdiction over foreign sovereigns primarily in cases arising out of the latter's *commercial activities,* as illustrated in the following case.

OBB PERSONENVERKEHR AG v. SACHS
Supreme Court, 136 S.Ct. 390 (2015)

Plaintiff Sachs lives in Berkeley, CA, and bought a Eurail pass in the U.S. for rail travel in Europe. Unfortunately, she was seriously injured when she fell onto the tracks in Innsbruck, Austria while boarding a train operated by the defendant OBB, the Austrian state-owned railway. Sachs sued OBB in federal court in the U.S. on negligence, breach of warranty, and other theories. OBB moved to dismiss on sovereign immunity grounds, among others. Sachs argued that her claim was not barred by sovereign immunity because it is "based upon" the railway's sale of the pass to her in the U.S. The trial court dismissed the suit, but the Ninth Circuit reversed. OBB appealed.

Roberts, Chief Justice:

The Foreign Sovereign Immunities Act "provides the sole basis for obtaining jurisdiction over a foreign state in the courts of this country." *Argentine Republic v. Amerada Hess Shipping Corp.,* 488 U.S. 428 (1989). The Act defines "foreign state" to include a state "agency or instrumentality," and both parties agree that OBB qualifies as a "foreign state" for purposes of the Act. OBB is therefore "presumptively immune from the jurisdiction of United States courts" unless one of the Act's express exceptions to sovereign immunity applies. *Saudi Arabia v. Nelson,* 507 U.S. 349 (1993). Sachs argues that her suit falls within the Act's commercial activity exception, which provides in part that a foreign state does not enjoy immunity when "the action is based upon a commercial activity carried on in the United States by the foreign state." §1605(a)(2).

[The Ninth Circuit] asked whether Sachs's claims were "based upon" the sale of the Eurail pass within the meaning of §1605(a)(2). The "based upon" determination, the court explained, requires that the commercial activity within the United States be "connected with the conduct that gives rise to the plaintiff's cause of action." But, the court continued, "it is not necessary that the entire claim be based upon the commercial activity of OBB." Rather, in the court's view, Sachs would satisfy the "based upon" requirement for a particular claim "if an element of [that] claim consists in conduct that occurred in commercial activity carried on in the United States."

Applying California law, the court analyzed Sachs's causes of action individually and concluded that the sale of the Eurail pass established a necessary element of each of her claims. Turning first to the negligence claim, the court found that Sachs was required to show that OBB owed her a duty of care as a passenger as one element of that claim. The court concluded that such a duty arose from the sale of the Eurail pass. Turning next to the other claims, the court determined that the existence of a "transaction between a seller and a consumer" was a necessary element of Sachs's strict liability and breach of implied warranty claims. The sale of the Eurail pass, the court noted, provided proof of such a transaction. Having found that "the sale of the Eurail pass in the United States forms an essential element of each of Sachs's claims," the court concluded that each claim was "based upon a commercial activity carried on in the United States" by OBB.

OBB contends that Sachs's suit is not "based upon" the sale of the Eurail pass for purposes of §1605(a)(2). We agree. The Act itself does not elaborate on the phrase "based upon." Our decision in *Nelson*, however, provides sufficient guidance to resolve this case. In *Nelson*, a husband and wife brought suit against Saudi Arabia and its state-owned hospital, seeking damages for intentional and negligent torts stemming from the husband's allegedly wrongful arrest, imprisonment, and torture by Saudi police while he was employed at a hospital in Saudi Arabia. The Saudi defendants claimed sovereign immunity under the Act, arguing, inter alia, that §1605(a)(2) was inapplicable because the suit was "based upon" sovereign acts—the exercise of Saudi police authority—and not upon commercial activity. The Nelsons countered that their suit was "based upon" the defendants' commercial activities in "recruit[ing] Scott Nelson for work at the hospital, sign[ing] an employment contract with him, and subsequently employ[ing] him." We rejected the Nelsons' arguments.

The Act's "based upon" inquiry, we reasoned, first requires a court to "identify[] the particular conduct on which the [plaintiff's] action is 'based.'" *Nelson*. Considering dictionary definitions and lower court decisions, we explained that a court should identify that "particular conduct" by looking to the "basis" or "foundation" for a claim, "those elements . . . that, if proven, would entitle a plaintiff to relief," ibid., and "the 'gravamen of the complaint,'" (quoting *Callejo v. Bancomer, S.A.*, 764 F.2d 1101 (5th Cir. 1985)). Under that analysis, we found that the commercial activities, while they "led to the conduct that eventually injured the Nelsons," were not the particular conduct upon which their suit was based. The suit was instead based upon the Saudi sovereign acts that actually injured them. The Nelsons' suit therefore did not fit within §1605(a)(2).

The Ninth Circuit held that Sachs's claims were "based upon" the sale of the Eurail pass because the sale of the pass provided "an element" of each of her claims. Under *Nelson*, however, the mere fact that the sale of the Eurail pass would establish a single element of a claim is insufficient to demonstrate that the claim is "based upon" that sale for purposes of §1605(a)(2).

The Ninth Circuit apparently derived its one-element test from an overreading of one part of one sentence in *Nelson*, in which we observed that "the phrase ['based upon'] is read most naturally to mean those elements of a claim that, if proven, would entitle a plaintiff to relief under his theory of the case." We do not see how that mention of elements—plural—could be considered an endorsement of a one-element test, nor how the particular element the Ninth Circuit singled out for each of Sachs's claims could be construed to entitle her to relief.

Be that as it may, our analysis in *Nelson* is flatly incompatible with a one-element approach. A one-element test necessarily requires a court to identify all the elements of each claim in a complaint before that court may reject those claims for falling outside §1605(a)(2). But we did not undertake such an exhaustive claim-by-claim, element-by-element analysis of the Nelsons' 16 causes of action, nor did we engage in the choice-of-law analysis that would have been a necessary prelude to such an undertaking.

Nelson instead teaches that an action is "based upon" the "particular conduct" that constitutes the "gravamen" of the suit. Rather than individually analyzing each of the Nelsons' causes of action, we zeroed in on the core of their suit: the Saudi sovereign acts that actually injured them. As the Court explained:

> "Even taking each of the Nelsons' allegations about Scott Nelson's recruitment and employment as true, those facts alone entitle the Nelsons to nothing under their theory of the case. The Nelsons have . . . alleged . . . personal injuries caused by [the defendants'] intentional wrongs and by [the defendants'] negligent failure to warn Scott Nelson that they might commit those wrongs. Those torts, and not the arguably commercial activities that preceded their commission, form the basis for the Nelsons' suit."

Under this analysis, the conduct constituting the gravamen of Sachs's suit plainly occurred abroad. All of her claims turn on the same tragic episode in Austria, allegedly caused by wrongful conduct and dangerous conditions in Austria, which led to injuries suffered in Austria.

We therefore conclude that Sachs has failed to demonstrate that her suit falls within the commercial activity exception in §1605(a)(2). OBB has sovereign immunity under the Act, and accordingly the courts of the United States lack jurisdiction over the suit. Reversed.

Act of State Doctrine

Closely related in effect to the doctrine of sovereign immunity is the *act of state doctrine*. This doctrine is based on the concept that it is beyond the sensible exercise of judicial powers for a court in this country to sit in judgment on the actions of another sovereign nation taken in its own territory. Any redress of grievances caused by such actions should be obtained by the United States government dealing directly with the other sovereign. Unlike the sovereign immunity defense, which raises a jurisdictional issue, the act of state doctrine provides a substantive defense on the merits. Thus, in *Banco Nacional de Cuba v. Sabbatino,* 376 U.S. 398 (1964), involving a challenge to Cuba's expropriation of the property of a Cuban corporation that was largely owned by U.S. residents, the Supreme Court held:

> [T]he Judicial Branch will not examine the validity of a taking of property within its own

territory by a foreign sovereign government, extant and recognized by this country at the time of the suit, in the absence of treaty or other unambiguous agreement regarding controlling legal principles, even if the complaint alleges that the taking violates customary international law.

Also related to sovereign immunity is the doctrine of *sovereign compulsion*, under which American courts will refuse to hold a defendant liable for actions that it was compelled to take under the law of a recognized foreign sovereign.

The following case illustrates some of the difficult questions that can arise in application of the act of state doctrine.

SEA BREEZE SALT, INC. v. MITSUBISHI CORP.
U.S. District Court, Central District of California, 2016 U.S. Dist. LEXIS 139342

ESSA produces solar sea salt products and is owned 49% by Mitsubishi and 51% by the Mexican Government. Mitsubishi holds 100% of the distribution rights for ESSA-produced salt, but ESSA's board of directors has authorized "excess salt" (that not purchased by Mitsubishi) to be sold to other entities. In 2014, ESSA contracted to sell 250,000 tons of excess solar sea salt a year to Innofood. ESSA breached the contract, failing to deliver any salt to plaintiff Innofood, which was then unable to fulfill its contractual obligations to sell salt to plaintiff Sea Breeze Salt, which in turn was forced to breach contracts with its customers. Plaintiffs filed suit in the U.S. against Mitsubishi and ESSA, claiming, among other things, that granting exclusive rights to Mitsubishi violated the federal Clayton and Sherman antitrust laws and California's Cartright Act. Mitsubishi moved to dismiss, in part based upon the Act of State doctrine.

Gee, District Judge:

"Every sovereign State is bound to respect the independence of every other sovereign State, and the courts of one country will not sit in judgment on the acts of the government of another done within its own territory. Redress of grievances by reason of such acts must be obtained through the means open to be availed of by sovereign powers as between themselves." *Yahoo! Inc. v. La Ligue Contre Le Racisme Et L'Antisemitisme*, 433 F.3d 1199 (9th Cir. 2006). The Act of State Doctrine therefore prohibits a lawsuit where "(1) there is an official act of a foreign sovereign performed within its own territory; and (2) the relief sought or the defense interposed in the action would require a court in the United States to declare invalid the foreign sovereign's official act." *Credit Suisse v. United States District Court*, 130 F.3d 1342 (9th Cir. 1997). "The doctrine reflects the concern that the judiciary, by questioning the validity of sovereign acts taken by foreign states, may interfere with the executive's conduct of American foreign policy." *Sarei v. Rio Tinto, PLC*, 487 F.3d 1193 (9th Cir. 2007).

In this case, the first prong of the Act of State Doctrine has been met insofar as Plaintiffs challenge an official act of a foreign sovereign performed within its own territory. First, as discussed above, ESSA is a "foreign sovereign" for the purposes of the Act of State Doctrine because the Mexican government holds a 51% stake in it.

Second, the conduct which serves as the basis for Plaintiffs' complaint consists of "official acts." Plaintiffs' Sherman, Clayton, and Cartwright Act claims depend upon the assertions that ESSA and Mitsubishi entered into exclusive contracts making Mitsubishi the lone distributor of ESSA produced salt, ESSA underprices salt sold to Mitsubishi, and ESSA "engaged in vertical restraints on trade by means of price discrimination against non-Mitsubishi distributors." *See In re Fresh & Process Potatoes Antitrust Litig.,* 834 F.Supp.2d 1141 (D. Idaho 2011) (holding that the Act of State Doctrine required dismissal of an antitrust suit against defendant United Potato Growers of Canada, which had the sovereign "power to dictate price, supply, quality, quantity, and exports of Canadian potatoes."). It is undisputed that these official acts were performed within Mexico.

The Ninth Circuit and the Supreme Court have consistently held that the second prong of the Act of State Doctrine bars inquiries which "impugn or question the nobility of a foreign nation's motivation." *See Von Saher v. Norton Simon Museum of Art,* 754 F.3d 712 (9th Cir. 2014); *W.S. Kirkpatrick & Co., v. Environmental Tectonics Corp., Int'l,* 493 U.S. (1990). In this case, resolution of Plaintiffs' claims would require the Court to do precisely that, as Plaintiffs' suit turns upon the validity of and motivation behind ESSA's decisions to grant exclusive rights to Mitsubishi, offer Mitsubishi below-market pricing for its products, and renege on a contract it had reached with Innofood, all of which Plaintiffs attribute to Mitsubishi's having "taken advantage of the neglect of some Mexican government officials while actively corrupting or subverting others." For example, for Plaintiffs' antitrust claims to succeed, Plaintiffs must prove the participation of ESSA, a joint-venture majority controlled by the Mexican government, in a conspiracy to restrain trade. All of Plaintiffs' other claims similarly require scrutiny of actions taken by ESSA.

The remedies sought by Plaintiffs include a declaration from the Court that Defendants (including an instrumentality of the Mexican government) have violated our nation's antitrust laws, damages in excess of $600 million subject to trebling, and injunctive relief restraining Defendants from continuing to engage in the sort of conduct that is the subject of this suit. Indeed, "the granting of any relief would in effect amount to an order from a domestic court instructing a foreign sovereign to alter its chosen means of allocating and profiting from its own valuable natural resources."

Further, as the Ninth Circuit has noted, "the government of Mexico is the only entity that may own and exploit the country's natural resources[.] . . . The Constitution permits the federal government to create organizations that manage and distribute these resources." *Corporacion Mexicana de Servicios Maritimos, S.A. de C.V. v. M/T Respect,* 89 F.3d 650 (9th Cir. 1996). The Court finds that the Act of State Doctrine is applicable to this case and, therefore, barring an applicable exception, this case cannot proceed.

Plaintiffs contend that the Act of State Doctrine does not apply here because "ESSA, despite being a (partially) state-owned enterprise, is not functioning as the Mexican state, but rather a private commercial company. This is important because, much like cases concerning the application of the Foreign Sovereign Immunities Act, act of state doctrine cases look to whether the purported act of state was commercial or non-commercial." The commercial activities exception, however, is a statutory provision of the FSIA expressly applicable only to the limitations on a court's jurisdiction. The Act of State Doctrine, in contrast, is a prudential, not jurisdictional, limitation, and there is no statutory support for a commercial activity exception to this doctrine. Mitsubishi's motion to dismiss is granted. [This decision was later affirmed on appeal in *Sea Breeze Salt, Inc. v. Mitsubishi Corp.,* 899 F.3d 1064 (9th Cir. 2018).]

International Litigation: Other Concerns

In the domestic setting, it can be quite troublesome to obtain service of summons over a proper defendant; obtain evidence to support the claim through oral depositions, written interrogatories, and document production; and ultimately enforce the judgment against a recalcitrant defendant. In the international context, such tasks can be overwhelming. To reduce these barriers to the civil prosecution of a valid claim, several international agreements have been reached that are intended generally to increase international cooperation in these respects.

The Hague Convention on Service Abroad of Judicial and Extrajudicial Documents in Civil or Commercial Matters provides that each signatory state will maintain a Central Authority to process judicial documents, such as complaints, and expedite their transmission. The Hague Convention on the Taking of Evidence Abroad in Civil or Commercial Matters of 1970 seeks to reduce the barriers raised by national laws to obtaining evidence for use in court and to streamline the discovery process in international litigation. The Convention creates Central Authorities in each signatory nation through which discovery requests ("Letters of Request") are channeled; it permits consuls to conduct some discovery procedures regarding their own nationals; and, finally, it allows the use of court-appointed commissioners for discovery purposes in limited circumstances. The United States is a signatory of both Conventions.

What happens if an American company, for example, receives a judgment against a foreign defendant in a foreign country's court and wishes to enforce that judgment against the defendant's property located in the United States? Will U.S. courts recognize such foreign judgments? Enforcement of foreign judgments is a matter of state law, which varies somewhat from jurisdiction to jurisdiction. Guidance is provided by the Restatement (Third) of the Foreign Relations Law of the United States, which provides that final money judgments of the courts of a foreign state will generally be enforced in the United States. However, a U. S. court is prohibited from enforcing a judgment that (1) was rendered by a judicial system that does not provide impartial tribunals or due process of law or (2) was rendered by a court lacking personal jurisdiction over the defendant under its own law or international law. Furthermore, an American court has discretion to refrain from enforcing a foreign judgment on several grounds, including that the rendering court did not have subject matter jurisdiction, that the defendant did not receive notice of the proceedings in time to defend, that the judgment was obtained by fraud, or that the judgment is based on a cause of action repugnant to American public policy.

The following case involves a very practical issue faced by many litigants.

ANOVA APPLIED ELECS., INC. v. HONG KING GRP., LTD.
U.S. District Court, District of Massachusetts, 2020 U.S. Dist. LEXIS 13063

Plaintiff Anova Applied Electronics, Inc. is a Delaware corporation that manufactures and sells kitchen appliances. Defendants are several companies located in China that Anova claims have infringed on the trademark and trade dress of its product, the Sous Vide Precision Cooker. Anova filed this lawsuit on November 20, 2017 and has repeatedly attempted to serve process on defendants through the Ministry of Justice in China, the primary means of service set forth by the Hague Convention on the Service Abroad of Judicial and Extrajudicial Documents. But after nearly two years, the Ministry has yet to serve defendants or even provide an estimate as to when it expects to do so. Anova moved for an order by this Court that authorizes it under Federal Rule of Civil Procedure 4(f)(3) to serve defendants by e-mail.

Saylor, District Judge:

The question presented here is not whether service by e-mail is an expedient and cost-effective method of providing actual notice to a defendant of the existence of a lawsuit. Obviously, it is. Rather, it is whether such service is permitted under the relevant federal rule (Fed. R. Civ. P. 4(f)(3)) and international treaty (the Hague Convention). [Under Rule 4(f), defendants]

> may be served at a place not within any judicial district of the United States:
> (1) by any internationally agreed means of service that is reasonably calculated to give notice, such as those authorized by the Hague Convention on the Service Abroad of Judicial and Extrajudicial Documents;
> (2) if there is no internationally agreed means, or if an international agreement allows but does not specify other means, by a method that is reasonably calculated to give notice . . .
> (3) by other means not prohibited by international agreement, as the court orders.

A threshold question is whether a plaintiff must attempt service under Rule 4(f)(1) before it resorts to court-ordered service under Rule 4(f)(3). [Federal courts have disagreed on this issue, but i]n any event, here plaintiff has attempted service under Rule 4(f)(1). Rule 4(f)(1) permits service "by any internationally agreed means of service that is reasonably calculated to give notice," including the Hague Convention on the Service Abroad of Judicial and Extrajudicial Documents. "Article 2 of the Hague Convention requires all judicial documents in civil matters to be served through a Central Authority." Plaintiff first attempted service through the Chinese Ministry of Justice in February 2018. Nearly two years later, and after plaintiff re-submitted its service request to comply with changes in policy at the Ministry, the Ministry has yet to complete service on defendants—or even provide a time estimate for the completion of service. Accordingly, because plaintiff has attempted service under Rule 4(f)(1), it may seek court-ordered service under Rule 4(f)(3).

Rule 4(f)(3) permits courts to order any means of service if it is "not prohibited by international agreement [and comports with constitutional notions of due process]" *Rio Props., Inc. v. Rio. Int'l Interlink,* 284 F.3 1007 (9th Cir. 2002).

Generally, whether a means of service is prohibited by international agreement depends on the terms of the Hague Convention. "The 'primary innovation' of the Hague Service Convention, set out in Articles 2-7, is that it 'requires each state to establish a central authority to receive requests for service of documents from other countries.'" *Water Splash, Inc. v. Menon,* 137 S.Ct. 1504 (2017), *quoting Volkswagenwerk Aktiengesellschaft v. Schlunk,* 486 U.S. 694 (1988). "Submitting a request to a central authority is not, however, the only method of service approved by the Convention." *Id.* The Convention provides several other means of service, such as service by diplomatic and consular agents.

The Convention does not explicitly prohibit e-mail service. It "does not speak in specific terms of service by email, fax, or other means of delivery unknown in the 1960's." *Luxottica Grp. S.p.A. v. Partnerships & Unincorporated Ass'ns,* 391 F.Supp.3d 816 (N.D.Ill. 2019). Still, the question remains "whether the Convention's textual silence on a method of service leaves this court free to authorize service by that method." *Id.*

This is a difficult question on which many courts have disagreed. It appears to have two parts. The first is whether a country's objection to Article 10(a) of the Convention precludes e-mail service. The second is whether (if the answer to the first question is negative) the Convention nevertheless prohibits service by e-mail because it is inconsistent with the methods of service authorized by the convention.

"Courts generally approach the problem of email service through the prism of Article 10(a) [of the Hague Convention], which states that "[p]rovided the State of destination does not object, the present Convention shall not interfere with . . . the freedom to send judicial documents, by postal channels, directly to persons abroad." China has objected to that provision.

[Courts have split on whether e-mail is sufficiently different from service through "postal channels" that objections to Article 10(a) should be construed to include objections to e-mail. The court decided that it did not have to resolve that issue.]

Even if China's objection to Article 10(a) does not by itself preclude e-mail service, it is a separate question whether the Hague Convention nonetheless prohibits a means of service that is not explicitly addressed by its terms. Two decisions by the Supreme Court indicate that the Convention bars methods of service that, while not explicitly prohibited, are inconsistent with its enumerated methods. In *Water Splash, Inc.*, the Court held that the Convention "specifies certain approved methods of service and 'pre-empts inconsistent methods of service' wherever it applies." Similarly, the Court's analysis in *Schlunk* also implies that the Convention's specified methods of service preempt other, inconsistent methods. In *Schlunk*, the Court held that the Convention's drafters "wanted to eliminate" a method of service called "notification au parquet." As evidence, the Court looked at the history of the Convention, but it also found that Articles 15 and 16 are incompatible with notification au parquet, although they do not say so explicitly. Like the Court's decision in *Water Splash*, this analysis implies that methods not explicitly addressed by the Convention may nevertheless be prohibited if they are inconsistent with its terms.

E-mail service is one such method. To permit service by e-mail would bypass the means of service set forth in the Convention. If the Convention left parties free to serve each other by e-mail, it is hard to see why they would ever choose slower, more costly methods. The parties to the Convention could hardly have intended that result; it is unlikely that they desired that the enumerated methods of service they agreed to could be superseded as soon as any new means of service became available. Thus, service by e-mail is inconsistent with the Convention's terms, and is not permitted. Accordingly, the Court concludes that Rule 4(f)(3) does not permit e-mail service on defendants, and plaintiff's motion will therefore be denied.

Arbitration

In view of the special difficulties encountered in international court litigation, it is not surprising that the international business community has actively sought alternative methods of commercial dispute resolution. Quite popular is *arbitration*, a process whereby parties to a transaction agree (either within the terms of their basic agreement or subsequently) to submit any future (or existing) disputes to an impartial third party (or panel) for nonjudicial resolution. The decision of the arbitrator—termed an award—may, depending on the agreement of the parties, be binding or nonbinding.

Binding arbitration within the international trading context has a long and colorful history and today is the preferred alternative to litigation in international commercial circles. The advantages of arbitration are many, including: (1) it is usually less expensive and faster than court procedures; (2) it is more private than litigation; and (3) the parties may choose knowledgeable experts (rather that generalist judges and untrained juries) to decide the matter based on commercial realities.

Arbitration is not, however, without its disadvantages. Arbitral panels generally do not have the power to compel the attendance of witnesses or the production of other information relevant to the case. The informality of the procedure can lead to an undesired degree of "looseness" in the process; and, because arbitrators are generally not bound by the strict letter of the law, final outcomes may be difficult to forecast.

Several organizations have sought to facilitate this means of dispute resolution by providing standard arbitral rules and procedures. Chief among these organizations are the International Chamber of Commerce (headquartered in Paris), the U.N. Commission on International Trade Law (UNCITRAL), the American Arbitration Association, the International Centre for Settlement of Investment Disputes (ICSID), the Inter-American Commercial Arbitration Commission, and the London Court of Arbitration.

So well accepted is the use of arbitration in international commercial disputes that most nations readily enforce such awards. In the United States, such enforcement is a matter of federal law. As with foreign court judgments, guidance is provided by the Restatement (Third) of Foreign Relations, which provides that awards pursuant to valid written arbitral agreements will generally be enforced, although a court may deny recognition on such grounds as: (1) the agreement to arbitrate was not valid under applicable law; (2) the losing party was not given an opportunity to present its case; (3) the award deals with matters outside the terms of the agreement to arbitrate; or (4) recognition of the award would be contrary to public policy. The Restatement's rules are based on the U.N. Convention on the Recognition and Enforcement of Foreign Arbitral Awards (known as the *New York Convention*). More than 150 nations are parties to this Convention, reflecting the widespread acceptance of arbitration in the international sphere.

NATIONAL REGULATION OF THE IMPORT/EXPORT PROCESS

The impact of export trade transcends, of course, the private interests of the parties to the international sales contract. Concerns at the national level touch on defense and security matters (especially in the export of high technology with military applications) and the depletion of national stocks of critical materials. Moreover, the volumes and direction of flow of export sales are inextricably bound up in the general economic posture of a nation and thus bear directly on its overall pattern of foreign relations. Not surprisingly, almost all nations have responded to these factors by adopting broad regulatory schemes to control exports. The implementation of these programs will directly affect international traders and the methods used in trade.

Export Controls

All nations wish to export their goods, but this desire must be weighed against national security concerns. If military weapons, nuclear materials, advanced technology, or the like are in the mix, concerns for national security may outweigh companies' desire to sell to foreign nations or companies.

In the United States, the power to regulate international trade is vested in the Congress under the provisions of the commerce clause of the U.S. Constitution. Congress has used this power repeatedly since the early days of the Republic and the trail of congressional legislation dealing with import and export matters continues into the present day. For many years, the Export Administration Act of 1979 was perhaps the most important piece of federal legislation affecting American export traders. It contained a comprehensive scheme to regulate exports from the United States and, together with the regulations adopted pursuant to it, extended its controls in some instances to the re-export of certain American goods to third countries. The Act granted discretionary authority to the Office of Export Administration (OEA) of the Department of Commerce to impose export controls for three basic reasons: (1) national security (to prevent "dual use" products that might have military applications from reaching our enemies), (2) foreign policy (for example, to prevent goods from reaching countries that practice terrorism or apartheid), and (3) short supply of goods in the United States.

In 2001, the Export Administration Act was not renewed by Congress. Since that time, presidents have maintained export controls pursuant to the International Emergency Economic Powers Act, as implemented by executive order. Court challenges claiming that the IEEPA delegated too much authority to the Executive Branch have been rejected.

Since the tragic events of September 11, 2001, export controls have naturally evolved to focus in part on securities threats posed by non-nation entities.

Export Incentives

U.S. export policy and legislation are not, however, totally negative. Important legislation has long been on the books to encourage increased export trade by manufacturers and suppliers in this country.

As early as 1918, Congress adopted the Webb-Pomerene Act to promote American export trade by granting limited exemptions to exporters from the application of U.S. antitrust laws, principally the Sherman and Clayton acts. Congress acted in the belief that American traders could better compete in foreign markets if they were permitted to form associations capturing the benefits of economies of scale and greater efficiency. Such associations, however, involved a danger of criminal or civil liability under American antitrust laws. The Webb-Pomerene Act, therefore, relieved export associations of this risk but conditioned the exemption in important respects. Principally, such an association is prohibited from entering into any agreement that "artificially or intentionally" depresses commodity prices within the United States or that "substantially lessens competition within the United States, or otherwise restrains trade therein." Further, the benefits of the act (obtained by registration of the association with the Federal Trade Commission) are limited to associations formed for the export of commodities; transactions for services or technology are not protected. As a result of these limitations and lingering anxiety about possible antitrust liability, comparatively few Webb-Pomerene associations are registered with the FTC.

To further encourage increased exports from this country, especially by small and medium-sized companies historically underrepresented in international trade transactions, Congress passed the Export Trading Company Act of 1982. The ETCA made changes in both antitrust laws and banking laws. Significantly, it allowed bank holding companies to own commercial business ventures—international export trading companies and provided substantial exemptions from antitrust laws.

The Act's scope is comprehensive. It extended antitrust protection to activities related to the export of goods and merchandise and (going beyond the reach of the Webb-Pomerene Act) to services. This latter category is defined to include services that are the subject of the transaction (as in trans-border management agreements) and includes accounting, architectural, data processing, business, communications, consulting, and legal services. Also eligible for exemption from possible antitrust liabilities are "export trade services," that is, international market research, product research and design, transportation, warehousing, insurance, and the like.

Regulating Imports

Compared with the elaborate nature of export controls and incentives, the regulation of imports into the United States is relatively straightforward. The application of these import control laws can, however, be quite complex.

Under the import export clause of the federal Constitution, the power to levy import customs and duties rests exclusively with the federal government. Using federal power in this regard, the government has established a comprehensive system of tariff schedules that apply to goods entering the United States—the Harmonized Tariff Schedules of the United States (HTSUS). Tariffs vary from nation to nation and product to product. The HTSUS will be applied by federal customs officials first to classify the entering goods and then to determine the applicable tariff rate to the goods so classified.

Because tariffs vary from nation to nation and product to product, fierce disputes can arise during the categorization process. The federal government sets the tariff rate, but does so subject to bilateral or multilateral restraints that it has assumed. For example, a treaty with another nation may stipulate the tariff level or, more generally, the applicable tariff may have been negotiated within the framework of a multinational commitment, for example, the General Agreement on Tariffs and Trade (GATT). In either event, the tariff generally must be paid before the goods are admitted into this country.

An important exception to this principle is the use of a foreign trade zone (FTZ). Established by federal law, these zones are fenced-off, policed warehouses and industrial parks usually located near American ports of entry. Goods entering the port from abroad may be taken into the FTZ and stored there without paying any applicable tariff and with a minimum of formality and procedure. As long as the goods are warehoused within the FTZ, no duty is payable and the goods may be further processed, assembled, or finished. Only when the merchandise leaves the confines of the FTZ will the duty be imposed, frequently at a reduced rate. In 2017, $87.1 billion in merchandise was exported through U.S. FTZs and in 2018 $794 billion in foreign merchandise was received into FTZs. Texas has more FTZ import and export activity than any other U.S. state, although all 50 states have at least one zone.

Whereas import licenses are generally not required for imports into the United States, certain goods may be denied entry altogether. Bans may be applied against undesirable imports such as narcotics, pornographic material, or printed materials advocating the violent overthrow of the United States. Import bans may be applied to prevent entry of automobiles that do not meet vehicle safety regulations or other products not meeting standards established to protect public health and safety. Products violating the patent, trademark, and copyright laws of the United States may also be excluded. Moreover, certain goods may be subjected to tariff increases to offset foreign government subsidies that unfairly reduce their U.S. market price or to counteract a foreign producer's deliberate attempt to destabilize or destroy the product's domestic production in the United States. These countervailing and *antidumping* measures are considered again in this chapter with regard to the GATT.

Trade and Tariff Act

One method of increasing the access of U.S. companies to foreign markets is retaliation against countries that treat U.S. companies unfairly. A series of laws over the years have authorized and encouraged the President to take such retaliatory action. In recent years Congress has been specifically concerned with the difficulty U.S. companies have had gaining access to markets in Asia, especially Japan. At various times Congress has authorized, and even mandated, the President to respond to unfair trade practices by use of higher tariffs, import quotas, or withdrawal from existing trade agreements with offending parties. Prying open new markets for U.S. companies without unduly antagonizing existing trading partners requires the striking of a delicate balance.

Protection from Unfair Competition

Various provisions of federal law protect U.S. companies from unfair practices by foreign competitors selling in this country. The primary protective provision is Sec. 337 of the Tariff Act of 1930, which protects "domestic industries" from "substantial injury" stemming from "unfair methods of competition and unfair acts in the importation of articles into the United States, or in their sale. . .." In the 10 years preceding 2005, 158 complaints in Section 337 investigations were filed. Ninety percent of such proceedings involve cases of alleged patent infringement, but it also protects U.S. businesses from copyright and trademark infringement, false advertising, trade secret misappropriation, computer hacking, palming off (misleading consumers into thinking they are buying another company's goods), and even "dumping."

Sec. 337 is activated by a domestic company's complaint to the U.S. International Trade Commission (ITC), an independent federal regulatory commission. The commission follows the Administrative Procedure Act in investigating the complaint and determining whether there has been a violation. The President has 60 days to review the commission's decision. Damages are not available under Sec. 337, but remedies can include cease-and-desist orders, temporary exclusion orders, and even permanent exclusion orders that will keep the infringing goods from entering the U.S. market. Note that any company that imports products can be named as a respondent in a Sec. 337 proceeding, including a domestic U.S. firm.

ORGANIZING FOR INTERNATIONAL TRADE

The massive devastation of the Second World War had among its many casualties the international trade infrastructure, which had been growing slowly but perceptibly since the middle of the nineteenth century. One of the major tasks of reconstruction following 1945 was the recreation of a framework for international trade. Negotiations focusing on trade, money, and finance led to establishment of the current international economic institutions, including the GATT, the International Monetary Fund, and the International Bank for Reconstruction and Development. More recently, regional trade agreements have become a prominent means of facilitating international trade.

The GATT

The United Nations Conference on Trade and Employment met in Havana in late 1947 and was attended by more than 50 countries. Although the conference was unsuccessful in creating a proposed International Trade Organization, it led almost two dozen countries to conclude the GATT (General Agreement on Tariffs and Trade), the essential purpose of which was to achieve a significant reduction of the general level of national tariffs and, further, to provide an institutional framework within which future tariff conflicts could be resolved. The GATT has, since its creation, shown itself to be of enduring significance in international economic and trade relations. According to its supporters, the GATT trading system has achieved unprecedented trade expansion and world prosperity. (Its detractors note that GATT provisions are often breached by participating countries.)

The GATT achieves its overall objective of liberalized international trade by addressing a series of key issues regarding important restrictions. It requires that each signatory state extend ''most favored nation'' tariff rates to goods from other signatory nations and, further, obligates participating nations to afford "national treatment" to the imported goods from other signatory countries. Article III of the agreement provides:

> The products of the territory of any contracting party imported into the territory of any other contracting party shall be accorded treatment no less favorable than that accorded to like products of national origin in respect of all laws, regulations and requirements affecting their internal sale, offering for sale, purchase, transportation, distribution or use.

The GATT prohibits discrimination by participating states through quantitative trade restrictions by providing that import quotas, if adopted at all by a state, shall be applied equally to all nations that are parties to the agreement. An even more ambitious objective of the GATT is the elimination of all prohibitions or restrictions (other than duties, taxes, or other charges) on imports and exports among the member nations.

In large measure, the GATT implements its goals of free trade through a series of published tariff schedules that are developed through an intricate negotiation process within the framework of the organization and that, once published, are binding on each of the participating states. In recognition of inevitable trade anomalies and to secure the willing participation and cooperation of member states in its tariff reduction program, the GATT provides special circumstances when unilateral exceptions to the schedules of tariffs may be made. The most well-known of these circumstances relate to antidumping duties and countervailing subsidies.

If the products of one country are "dumped" into another at prices below their fair market value in the exporting country in an effort to disrupt or destroy the domestic production of those goods in the receiving nation, the GATT contemplates that the government of the receiving country may impose an "antidumping duty" in an effort to equalize the domestic price in those goods with the prevailing fair market price in the exporting country. Similarly, when the production of certain goods in the exporting state is heavily subsidized by the government of that nation (leading to a reduced export price for that product), the GATT permits the receiving state to impose a "countervailing duty" to bring the market price up to a competitive level.

In its formative years, the GATT concentrated almost exclusively on measures to reduce tariff barriers in order to increase international trade. More recently, it has turned its attention to the reduction of nontariff barriers, such as unreasonably restrictive local standards and inaccessible national distribution systems, to further increase the volume of trade among nations.

During the rounds of negotiation, nations bargain to advance their positions. The United States, for example, seeks to induce Europe and Japan to lower subsidies for their farmers who compete with American agriculture and to induce developing nations to refrain from pirating U.S. trademarks, copyrights, and patents. Many nations seek to induce Japan to open its economy to foreign sellers and urge the United States to reduce its protection for textiles. For their part, developing nations seek freer access to advanced technology and markets for their agricultural products.

One of the most important GATT developments was the Uruguay Round of GATT negotiations that were completed in 1994. The Uruguay Round resulted in applying GATT to reduce tariff and non-tariff barriers on *services*, not just on goods as had previously been the case. In addition, the Uruguay Round produced an agreement on environmental protection, and an agreement on Trade-Related Aspects of Intellectual Property Rights (TRIPS). Under TRIPS, all members of the newly-created WTO committed themselves to enacting and enforcing modern copyright, patent, trade secret, and trademark laws. Parties committed themselves to punishing intellectual property pirates. Compliance with TRIPS has been spotty in many nations and several disputes have arisen.

The World Trade Organization

The World Trade Organization (WTO) was created by the Uruguay Round GATT in 1994 to resolve trade disputes, such as those arising under TRIPS. The WTO can resolve tariff and non-tariff barrier disputes among signatory nations. It may order compliance with GATT agreements and impose trade sanctions. Several nations were uncomfortable granting this much power to an international body. The WTO, an institution, essentially replaced GATT's simple body of rules. The WTO's meetings have become very controversial as protestors who worry that WTO agreements exploit lesser-developed nations and endanger the environment often protest vigorously.

Although negotiations seem to become more and more contentious, the WTO has had some success in encouraging free trade through the gradual abolition of trade barriers like import duties, subsidies, and quotas. The Doha Round, which is the ninth round of negotiations since the 1940s, began in 2001 and was still ongoing in 2020. These negotiations have brought the average import duty down to less than 4%. This number does not reflect any effects caused by the ad hoc raising of tariffs on goods from China and even many U.S. allies initiated by the White House since 2016.

The IMF and the IBRD

The International Monetary Fund (IMF), like the GATT, is intended to coordinate the activities of governments regarding international trade functions and does not primarily address the individual international trader. Growing out of discussions held at Bretton Woods, New Hampshire, late in the Second World War, the IMF was designed to speed international financial and economic reconstruction by providing an institutional structure within which intergovernmental loans would be used to stabilize currency exchange rates and, through a system of credits (termed Special Drawing Rights or SDRs), to enable member countries to borrow from the fund or from each other as a means of stabilizing their national currencies with the international monetary system.

Affiliated with the International Monetary Fund is the International Bank for Reconstruction and Development (IBRD), which was founded to "assist in the reconstruction and development of territories of members by facilitating the investment of capital for productive purposes'' and to ''promote private foreign investment by means of guarantees or participations in loans and other investments made by private investors.'' The IBRD, located in Washington, D.C., is permitted under its charter to guarantee, participate in, or make loans to member states and to any business, industrial, or agricultural enterprise in the territories of a member state. The availability through IMF and IBRD of massive amounts of financial credit was particularly significant in Western Europe during the immediate postwar years and has had, in addition, a very significant role in the industrial development of Asia and Africa in the past several decades.

Regional Trade Agreements

The creation of cooperative organizations to break down trade barriers in regions of the world is a feature of international economic relations. For example, the Association of South-East Asian Nations (ASEAN) seeks to reduce tariffs and duties among its ten members—Brunei, Indonesia, Laos, Malaysia, Myanmar, the Philippines, Singapore, Thailand, Vietnam, and Cambodia. And Mercosur hopes to do the same in trade among South American countries.

The U.S. has also been party to various trade agreements. ASEAN's agreements have been more stable than many in the world. After his election in 2016, President Trump initiated a renegotiation of the North American Free Trade Agreement (NAFTA) with Mexico and Canada. In Europe, the UK withdrew from the European Union in "Brexit." All in all, it is fair to say that the 2020s will be a time of transition in the use of regional trade agreements, but it is unlikely that they will go away. They will increasingly be shaped by political trends, however.

OTHER WAYS OF DOING BUSINESS

Thus far, we have spoken of international trade mainly in terms of direct sales from a seller in one country to a buyer in another. However, there are many other forms of international transactions. Take the case of an American corporation wishing to export its goods. Rather than send its own employees to the foreign markets to drum up business at the retail or wholesale level, it might hire an agent in that foreign country to act on its behalf. Such agents would typically have authority to contract on behalf of the American sellers. Complications would likely arise from the differences between agency law and customs in the United States and those of the foreign country.

Or the American company might choose to do business through a *licensee* in the foreign country. That licensee would pay a fee to the American company for the right to sell the company's goods. Such licensees, of course, will want exclusive rights to sell the American company's products, if possible. Legal problems here may result from antitrust laws of the United States and the foreign country. An increasingly popular form of such licensing arrangement is the franchising of trademarks, trade names, and copyrights. Many American service industries, such as fast food chains and convenience store chains, are expanding to foreign markets through use of this device.

Or an American seller may wish to have a foreign subsidiary corporation formed in the foreign nations in which it seeks to do business. This process is complicated by the many restrictions that most countries, especially in the underdeveloped world, place on such corporations. Such restrictions may take the form of *currency controls*, which make it difficult to take profits out of the country. Or the host country may require a certain percentage of host country ownership of the American company's subsidiary or require that the company enter into a joint venture with the host government or a local company.

India, for example has endeavored to "Indianize" foreign companies operating there. In the wake of the terrible 1984 Bhopal, India, gas leak that killed 2700 and injured perhaps 200,000, the Union Carbide Corporation has claimed that its subsidiary—Union Carbide India Ltd.—was so "Indianized" that Union Carbide could not have shut the plant down out of safety concerns had it wanted to. All 9000 employees of the company were Indian, and quasi-governmental Indian financial institutions owned 25 percent of its stock. Union Carbide itself retained only 50.9 percent of the subsidiary's stock. In many lesser developed countries, foreign corporations are limited to 49 percent ownership; local entities must retain control.

REGULATING THE TRANSNATIONAL CORPORATION

The rise of huge and powerful *multinational enterprises* (MNEs) is one of the defining elements of the post-World War II global economic environment. MNEs such as IBM, Exxon, and Toyota can have tremendous impact on the economy, culture, and environment of developing host countries. In the early 1970s, a series of economic, political, and legal factors focused international attention on the role and impact of these MNEs in global economic relationships.

MNEs are naturally interested in gaining free entry to foreign economies and protecting the investments they make there. For their part, developing countries are concerned with avoiding repetition of the consequences of earlier colonialism. They wish to have their local laws and autonomy respected and to protect their resources, culture, environment, and workers. They wish to be fairly treated and assisted to develop and not merely exploited.

For the past several decades efforts at balancing these competing interests have been ongoing in a number of spheres. Several bilateral treaties have been signed between developed and developing nations, wherein the former promised certain concessions to obtain the latter's protection of MNE investments. Some regional pacts have also have been signed. Perhaps most importantly, the United Nations has played a major role. Fifteen years in the making, a draft U.N. Code of Conduct on Transnational Corporations was never adopted by the U.N. The code specified that treatment of MNEs by host countries should be fair and equitable. Specific standards on matters of nationalization and compensation, national regulation, transfer of payments, and settlements of disputes were all set forth.

Absent an overarching code of conduct, some guidance stems from such sources as an International Code of Marketing of Breast-Milk Substitutes (under the jurisdiction of the World Health Organization), Guidelines for Consumer Protection (adopted by the U.N. General Assembly), and Criteria for Sustainable Development (aimed at discouraging over-exploitation by MNEs).

Foreign Corrupt Practices Act

MNEs and other companies doing business abroad must be aware of the Foreign Corrupt Practices Act (FCPA) of 1977, which originally barred American companies from paying bribes to obtain or retain business from foreign governments. More specifically, the FCPA bans these companies (and their officers and agents) from offering money or "anything of value" to foreign officials, foreign political candidates, or foreign political parties if the purpose is to induce that entity to assist the American company in obtaining or retaining business. In addition to antibribery provisions, the FCPA also has accounting ("books and records") provisions designed to prevent large corporations from maintaining "off-the book accounts" or "slush funds" from which such payments might be made without alerting auditors or senior corporate officials.

There are both criminal and civil penalties for violation for the FCPA, and they can be severe. For criminal violations, an American company may be fined the greater of up to $2 million or twice their gross gain for violations of the FCPA's anti-bribery provisions. Individual agents of these companies may be fined up to $250,000, imprisoned for up to five years (per violation), or both. Lesser penalties may be imposed in civil actions brought by the Securities and Exchange Commission.

The antibribery provisions carry several exceptions, including (1) facilitating or "grease" payments made to officials in order to obtain routine government actions, such as the issuing of permits or licenses, the processing of government papers such as visas, the providing of police protection or mail delivery, and the providing of telephone, electrical power, or water service; (2) any payments lawful under the written laws and regulations of the recipient's home country; (3) bona fide expenses, such as for travel and lodging, directly related to promoting or demonstrating a product; and (4) payments made to a government itself.

Congress assumed other nations would join the U.S. in banning bribery, but not until 1997 did the Organization for Economic Cooperation and Development (OECD) promulgate the Convention on Combating the Bribery of Foreign Public Officials in International Business Transactions. More than 40 nations have signed the Convention. Because of differences between the Convention and the FCPA, Congress had to amend the FCPA in several particulars via the International Anti-Bribery and Fair Competition Act of 1998. Most importantly, it (a) expanded the scope of prohibited activities to include paying bribes to secure "any improper advantage," (b) expanded the scope of prohibited payees to include officials of public international organizations such as the World Bank and the International Red Cross, and (c) eliminated the jurisdictional requirement that there be an act in the U.S. that utilized the mails or some other instrumentality of interstate commerce to further an improper payment. U.S. firms may be liable for bribes paid by their foreign subsidiaries.

The FCPA has become quite a headache for U.S. companies doing business abroad, as Wal-Mart found out when it paid $282 million in 2018 to settle criminal and civil charges arising out of a scandal involving bribery in Mexico. There has been a significant recent increase in government attention to corruption, both here and abroad. Foreign nations, especially the UK and Germany, have also been actively enforcing their versions of the FCPA and penalties have become more and more severe. Halliburton paid $579 million to settle FCPA charges. Petrobras (Brazil) paid $1.78 billion, Ericsson (Sweden) paid $1.06 billion, and Siemens (Germany) paid a total of $1.6 billion to settle bribery charges in both the U.S. and Germany. Perhaps even more significantly, highly-ranked corporate officials now face meaningful odds of going to jail if they are involved in foreign bribery. A 15-year sentence was recently meted out to an executive who participated in bribery of telecommunications officials in Haiti.

The following criminal case addresses a couple of common issues in FCPA cases.

UNITED STATES v. SENG
934 F.3d 110 (2d Cir. 2018)

Defendant Ng Lap Seng paid two United Nations ambassadors, Lorenzo (the Dominican Republic's Deputy Ambassador to the U.N.) and Ashe (the U.N. Ambassador for Antigua and Barbuda and for a time President of the General Assembly), more than $1 million to secure a U.N. commitment to use Ng's Macau real estate development as the site for an annual U.N. conference (the "Pro Bono agreement"). Ng's convention center was to be part of a larger complex owned by Ng that would become more valuable if the U.N. conferences were held there. Ng was indicted for, among other things, violating the Foreign Corrupt Practices Act (FCPA). He was convicted and sentenced to 48 months in prison and various fines. Ng appealed.

Raggi, Circuit Judge

The "Corruptly" Challenge. When a statute uses the word "corruptly," the government must prove more than the general intent necessary for most crimes. It must prove that a defendant acted "with the bad purpose of accomplishing either an unlawful end or result, or a lawful end or result by some unlawful method or means." *U.S. v. McElroy*, 910 F.2d 1016 (2d Cir. 1990). Ng argues that to find him to have acted "corruptly" in violation of the FCPA, the jury was required to find something more, specifically, his intent to have Lorenzo or Ashe breach an "official duty" owed to the U.N. Ng faults the district court for failing to instruct the jury as to this component of the "corruptly" element of these statutes. Further, he maintains that the record evidence was insufficient, as a matter of law, to permit a reasonable jury to find that he acted corruptly because the government never proved a particular duty owed by Lorenzo or Ashe to the U.N.

Ng's arguments are defeated by precedent. In *U.S. v. Kozeny,* 667 F.3d 122 (2d Cir. 2011), this court upheld an instruction on the "corruptly" element of an FCPA crime that made no mention of breach of duty. The instruction charged simply as follows:

> A person acts corruptly if he acts voluntarily and intentionally, with an improper motive of accomplishing either an unlawful result or a lawful result by some unlawful method or means. The term "corruptly" is intended to connote that the offer, payment, and promise was intended to influence an official to misuse his official position.

Nor was the evidence insufficient to allow a reasonable jury to find that Ng acted corruptly. Ng argues that the government "did not introduce any evidence at trial describing any duties that Ashe and Lorenzo may have owed to the UN or the public, let alone any evidence that Ng sought to induce them to breach any such duty." The second part of this argument fails for reasons just explained: the "corruptly" element of the crimes of conviction does not require proof of a breach of duty. As for Ng's sufficiency challenge to evidence of duty, we need not here decide what, if any, duties ambassadors accredited to the U.N. owe to that organization because the evidence here showed that, at times pertinent to the charged crimes, Ashe served not only as an ambassador to the U.N., but also as an official of that organization, indeed, its second highest official, the President of the General Assembly. Viewing the evidence in the light most favorable to the government, a reasonable jury could find that, at least in that role, Ashe was an agent of the U.N. and, as such, owed a duty to that organization not to sell his ability to influence subordinate U.N. employees in entering into transactions or business arrangements for the U.N. Thus, a reasonable jury could find that Ashe misused his position as President of the General Assembly when he accepted hundreds of thousands of dollars from Ng in return for being influenced—in turn—to use his influence with [U.N. officials to hold meetings at Ng's conference center].

The "Obtaining or Retaining Business" Challenge. The FCPA prohibits bribing foreign officials for the purpose of "obtaining or retaining business for or with, or directing business to, any person." Although the district court tracked this statutory language in charging the jury, Ng argues that it erred in rejecting his request to define "business" as "commercial" business. According to Ng, the given instruction was erroneous because the jury had "no way to know whether 'business' referred to commercial business or more broadly to any transaction." Moreover, Ng argues that the trial evidence was insufficient for the jury to find this "business" element because he intended to build the convention center and to make it available for UNOSSC use at no cost to the U.N.

These arguments merit little discussion. Assuming arguendo that Congress intended to limit the FCPA to "commercial bribery," *U.S. v. Kay,* 359 F.3d 738 (5th Cir. 2004), a reasonable jury would so understand from the statutory text. While "business" can refer to any productive activity, a reasonable jury, instructed as here to consider the word in the context in which it is used in the FCPA, i.e., "obtaining or retaining business for, or with, or directing business to, any person," would need no further instruction to understand it to bear the common meaning of "commercial or mercantile activity," Webster's Third New Int'l Dictionary (2002).

Moreover, the record evidence would allow a reasonable jury to find that Ng paid the two U.N. ambassadors intending for them to obtain a commercial business deal with the U.N., specifically, a contract for his Macau Conference Center to serve as the official host site for the U.N.'s UNOSSC Expo. Ng does not dispute that contracts are a routine tool in obtaining, maintaining, and directing commercial business. *See U.S. v. Kay* (referencing corporate payments to assist in obtaining government contracts as one abuse informing FCPA). Indeed, at his request, the district court charged the jury that "business" includes "the execution or performance of contracts." Nevertheless, Ng argues that a contract, such as the Pro Bono Agreement, which imposed no monetary obligations on the U.N., cannot be deemed to have obtained "commercial" business for him.

Ng's argument fails because the FCPA prohibits commercial bribery without regard to whether the briber himself profits directly from the business obtained. Indeed, it prohibits bribery designed to obtain, retain, or direct business not only for or to the briber, but for or to "any person." Here, "any person" could refer to the U.N. A reasonable jury could find Ng guilty under the FCPA for bribing Lorenzo and Ashe in return for them using their influence to direct Ng's business to the U.N., specifically, his willingness contractually to obligate himself to provide the U.N. with the cost-free use of his Macau convention center as its permanent UNOSSC Expo site. While such a contract, on its face, might appear to give all commercial benefits to the U.N., the jury could find that by thus using bribery to direct his own business obligation to the U.N., Ng thought he would best be able to obtain greater business for and, thus, to maximize profits from, the larger commercial complex of which the convention center was a part. Thus, his sufficiency challenge to the business purpose component of the FCPA crimes also fails. The conviction is affirmed.

PART VI

PROPERTY AND WILLS, TRUSTS, & ESTATES

CHAPTER 33

REAL PROPERTY

- The Nature of Real Property

- Interests in Real Property

- Concurrent Ownership

- Sales of Real Property

- Adverse Possession

- Regulation of Real Property Ownership, Use, and Sale

In this chapter we survey the principles of law relating to the ownership and control of real property. After exploring the fundamental nature of real property, we examine the various types of ownership interests and the process of transferring those interests.

Issues pertaining to real property law arise constantly in many different contexts, including land transfers, wills leaving a deceased person's property to her heirs, the creation of trusts, divorce proceedings when real property ownership is an issue, bankruptcy proceedings, mortgage foreclosure actions by lenders, foreclosure actions for nonpayment of property taxes, and foreclosures of other types of liens. Other lien foreclosure actions include, for example, those occurring when the owner of a condominium does not pay homeowner association dues and the association places a lien on the condo, or when someone has made improvements to a home or office building forecloses on a *mechanic's or materialman's* lien because they have not been paid what is owed to them.

THE NATURE OF REAL PROPERTY

Land and most things attached to the land are called *real property*, often referred to in common usage as *real estate*. The most important element of real property is, of course, the land itself. Things affixed to the land take the form of either vegetation or fixtures, such as buildings.

Land

The definition of *land* includes not only the surface of the earth but also everything above and beneath it. Thus, the ownership of a tract of land theoretically includes both the air space above it and the soil from its surface to the center of the earth.

Air Rights

A landowner's rights with respect to the air space above the surface are called *air rights*. In recent years, air rights have become an important part of land ownership in some areas. In densely populated metropolitan areas, for instance, air space is often quite valuable. The owner of an office building might sell a portion of its air space to a party who wishes to build and operate a restaurant or group of apartments atop the building. And railroad companies with tracks running through a downtown area have been known to sell the space above their tracks for building construction.

For practical reasons, courts now hold that a landowner's air rights are not violated by airplanes flying at reasonable heights. If, however, a flight is low enough to actually interfere with the owner's use of the land (such as when the plane is taking off or landing), there may well be a violation of these air rights.

Many cases involving air rights are filed and either settled or litigated on a regular basis, involving issues such as trespass, eminent domain, interpretation of real property deeds and contracts, and in other contexts. Almost all of these cases, however, involve fact situations that are simply too complex to be usable for teaching and learning. The following case, however, presents a somewhat simpler situation in which the modern importance of air rights is showcased. Here, except for the failure of plaintiffs to present any evidence of the value of their rights, a substantial damage award would have been given.

Grey v. Coastal States Holding Co.

578 A.2d 1080 (Conn. App. 1990)

The plaintiffs Betty H. Grey and Louis D. Grey own one unit (4E) in a five-unit residential condominium, composed of four separate buildings, and known as Hawkins Landing. The plaintiff Peter Kingsbury owns one unit (4D) in the same building as the unit belonging to the other two plaintiffs. The defendants Coastal States Holding Company (Coastal States) and Alvin Farans, a partner in Coastal States, own unit 1A, and the defendant Ronald Kellogg owns units 2B and 3C. Each of the three units owned by the defendants is a separate structure. The defendant association is a non-stock corporation that manages and controls the condominium through its executive board. At the time of this litigation, Betty Grey, Kingsbury, Farans, and Kellogg comprised the executive board.

At the time the condominium declaration was adopted, units 1A and 2B were one-story cottages. Farans, acting for Coastal States, was issued a building permit by the local government to build an addition and add a second story to unit 1A.

At an executive board meeting, Betty Grey expressed concern about Kellogg's plans to renovate unit 2B to add second and third levels. At the meeting, Farans described his plan for a second floor addition to unit 1A. The plaintiffs were unaware that Coastal States had already been issued a building permit to construct a second story....

Soon thereafter, Coastal States began construction, allegedly "acting under the belief that an agreement had been reached," although the parties had all refused to sign the proposed agreement because of concern over some of the terms. Farans believed he had the right, pursuant to article VIII, § 8.1, of the declaration, to add a second story.

Kellogg then obtained a building permit for an addition and a second floor to be added to the other unit—2B—and began construction.

As a result of the additions, unit 1A was increased by 986 square feet of living space, representing an increase in appraised value of $182,410, and unit 2B was increased by 751 square feet of living space, for an increase in value of $138,935. The expanded footprint of unit 1A took fifty square feet of common area [in the air space above the units], and that of 2B took twenty eight square feet of this common area, the air rights above the two improved units.

Mr. and Mrs. Grey and Kingsbury sued Coastal States, alleging that the air space above the two defendant's two units was a common element in which each condominium unit owner owned a proportionate interest, and that the defendant had taken their combined 40% of the air rights above the two units expanded by Coastal States. The trial court agreed with the plaintiffs in all respects, except that it held that the defendant had not committed a willful violation of the condominium declaration and Connecticut state condominium law because it was somewhat justified in believing that there had been agreement by all condominium owners to allow it to build the expansions above its two units. The trial court also concluded that, because plaintiffs had presented no evidence at all of the market value of the air rights, it could not receive compensatory damages, thus entitling it to only nominal damages and attorney fees.

DUPONT, Chief Judge.

The defendants' expansions resulted in a benefit to them and a loss to the plaintiffs of their property interests. The expansion of the units took square footage of common areas and represented changes in the boundaries of those units requiring unanimous consent of the unit owners pursuant to the declaration. Because the expansions were not done with unanimous consent of the unit owners, the condominium agreement was violated. The expansions, however, were accomplished in the belief that an agreement among the unit owners had been reached, [because of ambiguous previous communications among the condominium unit owners and other factors], and the trial court therefore concluded that the defendants had not *willfully* failed to comply with the declaration and that the requested remedy of restoration was too harsh. On the basis of these findings and conclusions, the trial court denied the relief of restoring 1A and 2B to their original condition, and declined to award punitive damages ….

The plaintiffs also requested compensatory damages. They sought 40 percent of the increase in the value of units 1A and 2B. Evidence had been presented from which the court could assess the increase in the value of those units because of the additions to them.…

Because the plaintiffs, by the terms of the condominium documents, have an interest in any common elements, we must determine whether the land and air space taken were common elements. Common elements are defined as "all portions of the common interest community other than the units [themselves]." It is elementary to say that what is not a unit is a common element.… "Real property" includes spaces that may be filled with air. In addition to land itself, the right to use the air above that land is a property interest, capable of ownership, that may be conveyed or taken in condemnation. Air rights have value and may be assessed or taxed by a municipality. Implicitly, therefore, they have a fair market value. We, therefore, hold that the air space above the condominium units in this case is a common element, as are portions of the land owned by the association on which no unit was to have been built.

Under article IX of the declaration, the plaintiffs are entitled to a 20 percent interest in common elements for each unit of the condominium they own. The plaintiffs together, therefore, held a 40 percent interest in the air space above the original condominiums as well as in the land on which no unit was to be built. Pursuant to article XI, § 11.1, and article XIII, § 13.4, of the [condominium] declaration, the unanimous consent of the unit owners was required to change the boundaries of a unit and permission of the executive board was required to change the outward appearance of a unit.

If the defendants had abided by the declaration, they would not have been able to build the second stories or to change the ground boundaries of their units. The defendants essentially appropriated air space as well as square footage of land that did not belong to them individually, but belonged to them in common with the other unit owners. The plaintiffs are, therefore, entitled to compensatory damages for the property taken from them, [including damages for the loss of their portion of the value of the air rights above other the defendants' condominium units, which are part of the common elements owned proportionately by all condo owners. However, we agree with the trial court that the defendants did not knowingly and willfully violate the condominium declaration, and that they are therefore not liable for punitive damages.]

There are several possible ways of measuring the plaintiffs' damages in order to put them in the position they would have been in but for the breach. The plaintiffs would have been entitled to compensation for the additional square footage of land constituting common area that the defendants converted to their exclusive use by expanding their units outward, had the plaintiffs sought such damages and introduced sufficient evidence of valuation. They would also have been entitled to compensation for the air space directly above the defendants' original units as a part of the wrongfully appropriated common elements. The plaintiffs, however, failed to introduce evidence of the value of either the air space or the square footage of land appropriated by the defendants. They [were] able, therefore, to collect only nominal damages for the appropriation of those elements in this case.

Another means of placing the plaintiffs in the position they would have been in had the defendants not appropriated common elements would be to award them an amount equal to any decline in the value of their own units as a result of the unwarranted changes to their neighbors' units. As the trial court properly found, however, they introduced no such evidence, and therefore cannot recover anything other than nominal damages for such a decline in value.

In summary, we hold that, because the trial court found that the condominium agreement was not willfully violated and because that finding has not been attacked on appeal, the plaintiffs here were not entitled to punitive damages. They were, however, entitled to actual damages. Their actual damages could have been based upon the value of their proportionate shares of the air space and land taken by the defendants or upon any diminution in the value of the plaintiffs' own units as a result of the defendants' expansions. They proved neither. Even though no actual damages were proved, the plaintiffs were entitled to nominal damages because of the defendants' violation of the condominium agreement by appropriating to their private use, elements of land and air in which all unit owners had an interest. The trial court's judgment is affirmed. [Thus, the only reason why the plaintiffs were not awarded compensatory damages for the loss of their portion of the market value of the air rights above the defendants' condominium units is that they simply did not produce any evidence of the value of those air rights. The trial court's award of $27,000 in attorney fees to the plaintiffs was also affirmed.]

Subsurface Rights

The most practical result of the rule extending a landowner's property rights to the center of the earth is that they own the *minerals* beneath the surface. When the land is sold, the buyer acquires any existing minerals, such as coal, even if they are not expressly mentioned in the deed. These minerals in the ground can also be owned separately. Thus, a landowner might sell only the mineral rights, or sell the rest of the land and expressly retain the mineral rights. One who sells land cannot sell more than what they own, of course. Thus, if a seller has already sold all or part of the underlying mineral rights to someone else, a later buyer does not receive ownership of these rights when buying the surface. Or, if the seller had previously sold some other interest in the land, such as a lease or easement, a later buyer purchases the property subject to those earlier rights.

In some states, oil and natural gas are treated like other minerals with respect to ownership. That is, they can be owned while they are still in the ground ("ownership in place"). Courts in a minority of states, on the other hand, hold that oil and gas are not owned by anyone until pumped out of the ground. Regardless of the type of mineral or the particular jurisdiction, an owner who first removes the minerals and then sells them is making a sale of personal property ("goods"), not real property.

Vegetation

Both natural vegetation (such as trees) and cultivated vegetation (such as a growing wheat crop planted by a farmer) are considered to be real property. Thus, in a sale of land, the vegetation passes to the buyer of the land unless expressly excluded from the sale.

When growing vegetation is sold by itself, and not with the land, the general rule is that the transaction is a sale of personal property (goods). This rule holds true almost universally for growing crops under UCC 2-107. The same rule is followed for growing timber in most states, but several states treat a sale of growing timber as a sale of real property.

Fixtures

A *fixture* is an item that was originally personal property but that has been attached to the land (or to another fixture) in a relatively permanent fashion. Fixtures are viewed by the law as real property. Thus, title to them passes to the buyer of real property unless the seller expressly excludes them from the transaction. In other words, even if the documents employed in the transaction describe only the land and are silent with respect to fixtures, title to them nevertheless passes to the buyer. Items that are not fixtures, however, do not pass along with a sale of land unless they are expressly included in the terms of the transaction.

To illustrate: Jones contracts to sell his farm to Williams, and the contract describes only the boundaries of the land. Located on the farm are a house and a barn. These buildings are fixtures and will pass to Williams as part of the real property, as will the fence around the land. Inside the house, Jones's clothing and furniture are not fixtures, but the built-in cabinets and plumbing are. The hay stored in the barn is not a fixture, but the built-in feeding troughs are.

As is true of minerals, when a landowner removes a fixture from the soil or from the building to which it was attached and then sells the item *by itself*, it is considered a sale of *personal property* rather than real property. In fact, if a landowner removes a fixture (such as a kitchen cabinet) with the intention that removal will be permanent, the item reverts back to its original status as personal property regardless of whether it is sold.

Determining Whether an Item Is a Fixture

Although the decision as to whether a particular article is a fixture is often obvious, many items are difficult to classify. In general, a court will hold that an item is a fixture if there was an intent that it become a permanent part of the real property. When the owner or occupier of land has not clearly expressed his or her intent, it must be determined from all the circumstances of the case. Following are three factors that are often considered in determining whether an item was intended to be a fixture.

Attachment. An item is usually classified as a fixture if it is attached to a building in such a manner that it cannot be removed without damage to the building. Examples include shingles on the roof, built-in cabinets or appliances, a floor furnace, or a floor covering that is cemented in place.

Specialized Use. An item is usually considered a fixture if it was specially made or altered for installation in a particular building. Examples include specially fitted windows screens, drapes custom-made for an odd-sized window, and a neon sign created for particular business premises.

Custom. Sometimes local custom dictates whether an item is a fixture. For example, in some parts of the country it is customary for houses to be sold with refrigerators. Where this custom exists, a landowner's intent when installing the refrigerator is probably that it be a permanent addition. Thus, it is a fixture.

INTERESTS IN REAL PROPERTY

Ownership of real property is not an "all or nothing" proposition. The total group of legal rights constituting complete ownership can be divided among several individuals. The particular set of rights owned in a given situation is referred to as an *estate* or an *interest* in real property. The common law developed a complex system of classifying and defining these various interests, a system which is described here in simplified form. Much of the terminology used to classify real property interests is of ancient origin. At the outset, the law distinguishes those interests that include the right of possession from those that do not. The so-called *possessory interests* are further subdivided into *freehold estates* and *nonfreehold estates*. The following discussion examines these types of possessory interests, and then outlines the different *nonpossessory interests*. It concludes by describing another classification, the so-called future interests in real property.

Freehold Estates

A freehold estate is one that can legally exist for an indefinite period of time.

Fee Simple

When a person has complete ownership of real property, his or her interest is described as a *fee simple estate*. It is said that the estate is owned "in fee simple" or "in fee simple absolute." This is the most important type of freehold estate. In everyday usage, when someone is spoken of as the "owner" or as "having title," it generally means that the individual owns a fee simple interest. The characteristics of a fee simple interest are: (1) ownership is of unlimited duration and (2) the owner is free to do whatever they choose with the property so long as the owner abides by the law and does not interfere with the rights of adjoining landowners.

If O, the owner of a fee simple interest in real property, conveys (transfers) the property to B, it is presumed that the entire fee simple is being conveyed. B will acquire a lesser interest only if the terms of the conveyance clearly so indicate. Thus, a conveyance of the property "from O to B," with nothing said about the type of interest being conveyed, is deemed to transfer the entire fee simple interest to B.

Fee Simple Defeasible

Some interests in real property are classified as fee simple interests despite the fact that ownership is not absolute. Suppose, for example, that O conveys a fee simple interest to B, subject to the limitation that B's interest will cease upon the occurrence of a specified event. B's interest is a *fee simple defeasible*. It is a fee simple in every respect except that it is subject to the possibility of termination.

One of the most common limitations of this type relates to the *use* that is to be made of the land. For instance, the terms of the conveyance from O to B may state that B's ownership will continue only if the land is used for recreational purposes. The person entitled to the property if and when B's interest terminates is said to own a *future interest*. Future interests are discussed later in the chapter.

Life Estate

A *life estate* is an interest in real property, the duration of which is measured by the life of some designated person. For example, O, the fee simple owner, might convey the property to B "for B's lifetime." During his lifetime, B would own a life estate. Similarly, if O's conveyance to B was "for the life of X," B would still own a life estate. The person entitled to ownership after termination of a life estate owns a future interest.

Owning a life estate is not the equivalent of owning a fee simple for one's lifetime. It is true that the owner of the life estate (called the "life tenant") has the right to *normal use* of the property. For example, the life tenant can use it as a residence, farm it, conduct a business on it, allow another to use it in return for the payment of rent, or make any other reasonable use of it. However, the life tenant cannot do anything that will permanently damage the property and thus harm the owner of the future interest.

As an example of the limitations on a life tenant's use of the property, the right to cut timber on the land is restricted. The timber can be cut if it is required for fuel, fencing, or agricultural operations. But it cannot be cut for the purpose of *sale* unless (1) the life estate was conveyed to the life tenant specifically for that purpose, or (2) selling timber is the only profitable use that can be made of the land, or (3) the land was used for that purpose at the time the person became a life tenant, or (4) the owner of the future interest expressly permits the cutting.

Similarly, a life tenant can take oil and gas from existing wells and other minerals from existing mines if subsurface rights were not expressly excluded from the life estate. But this party cannot drill *new* wells or open *new* mines without authorization either in the document creating the life estate or at a later time from the owner of the future interest.

Although a life tenant is responsible to the owner of the future interest for any permanent damage they personally cause to the land, there is no such responsibility for damage caused by accidents, by third parties, or otherwise without the life tenant's fault.

A life tenant is also under a duty to pay taxes on the property. If this duty is neglected and the land is taken by the taxing authorities, the life tenant is liable to the owner of the future interest.

Nonfreehold Estates

The nonfreehold estates, sometimes called *leasehold estates*, are created by a *lease* of real property in which the owner grants to another the temporary right to possess the property in return for the payment of rent. In such a case, the owner is called the *lessor*, or *landlord*, and the occupier is called the *lessee,* or *tenant*. Several different types of nonfreehold, or leasehold, estates may be created, depending on the terms of the lease agreement.

Nonpossessory Interests

Easements

Essentially, an *easement* is the right to make some limited use of another's real property without taking possession of it. Stated another way, it is the right to do a specific thing on another's land. Sometimes an easement is referred to informally as a *right-of-way*. Examples of easements include the right to run a driveway or road across another's land, to run a power or telephone line above it, or to run a pipeline under it.

Types of Easements. Easements are either *appurtenant* or *in gross*. An *easement appurtenant* is one created specifically for use in connection with another tract of land. For example: A and B own adjoining tracts. A grants to B an easement to cross A's land to get to and from a highway. Here the easement on A's land is appurtenant, because it was created for use in connection with B's land. A's land is called the *servient estate* and B's the *dominant estate*.

An *easement in gross*, on the other hand, is one *not* used in connection with another tract of land. For example, a telephone company has an easement in gross when it acquires the right to run poles and wires across A's land.

Whenever a tract of land subject to either type of easement is sold, the purchaser must continue to recognize the easement if they knew or should have known of its existence at the time of purchase. Even without such knowledge, the purchaser's ownership is subject to the easement if a document creating the interest was *recorded* (filed with the appropriate county official) prior to the purchase.

An *easement appurtenant* is said to "run with the land." This means that if the land being benefited by the easement (the dominant estate) is sold, the easement goes with it. However, the owner of an easement appurtenant cannot sell or otherwise transfer it *by itself*, apart from the dominant estate. On the other hand, the owner of an easement in gross is generally allowed to transfer it to another party.

Creation of Easements. An easement can be created in several ways. Creation of an *easement by express grant or reservation* is the most common method. An express grant occurs when a landowner expresses an intent to convey an easement to another party. An express reservation occurs when a landowner sells the land itself but expressly reserves, or keeps, an easement on the land being sold. Because an easement is an interest in real property, the expression of an intent to grant or reserve such an interest may be made in a written document containing a legally sufficient description of both the land and the scope of the easement. The document also must contain the names of the parties, the duration of the interest, and the signature of at least the party making the grant or reservation. The document could be either a deed or a will.

An *easement by implication* also can be created where surrounding circumstances reasonably indicate that the parties probably intended to create such an interest. An easement exists by implication only if the following facts are proved:

1. An easement will be implied only when land is subdivided into two or more segments. This would occur, for example, when A, who owns twenty acres of land, sells ten acres out of the tract to B.

2. Prior to the subdivision, the owner of the entire tract must have been making a particular use of the property, and continuance of this use after the subdivision would require recognition of an easement. Thus, suppose that prior to A's sale of ten acres to B, A had constructed and used a ditch to improve the drainage on one part of the property. The ditch went through the portion that A kept, but it benefited the part sold to B by improving the drainage of that portion.

3. The use that A was making of the property before the subdivision must have been apparent; in other words, it must have been observable to anyone conducting a reasonable inspection of the property.

4. Continuation of the use must be reasonably necessary to B's use of his ten acres. In this case, because the drainage improvement benefited the land purchased by B, the ditch across A's ten acres probably would be viewed as reasonably necessary.

In the circumstances just described, B would have an easement across A's land giving B the

 © **2020 John R. Allison & Robert A. Prentice**

right to continue using the ditch to drain water from B's land.

An *easement by necessity* also can be created in some circumstances. In contrast with an easement by implication, neither a subdivision of land nor a particular prior use is a prerequisite for the existence of an easement by necessity. However, the easement must be an absolute necessity, not just a reasonably necessary use. For example, a person leasing space in an office building has an easement by necessity that permits use of the stairs, elevators, hallways, and other common areas. Another example can be found in a situation similar to the one in which A sold a portion of his land to B. If B's ten acres had been at the back of the original tract, with no means of access to a public road other than by crossing A's ten acres, B would have an easement by necessity to cross A's land when going to and from his or her own land.

An *easement by prescription* (or *prescriptive easement*) may be created when someone actually does something on another's land for a period of time. Creation of an easement by prescription is similar to the acquisition of title by *adverse possession*, which is discussed later in this chapter. Such an easement is created if one party has actually exercised an easement (such as a driveway) on someone else's land continuously for a period of time specified by state statute, the use was made without the express consent of the landowner, and the use was an apparent one. The required period of time for creation of a prescriptive easement in a particular state is usually the same as for acquisition of title by adverse possession.

Profits

A *profit*, technically, called a *profit a pendre*, is the right to go upon land and take something from it. Examples include the right to mine minerals, drill for oil, or take wild game or fish. A *right to take* minerals, which is a profit, must be distinguished from an actual sale of the fee simple interest in the minerals in the ground. The legal principles applicable to the creation, classification, transfer, and enforceability of profits are exactly the same as in the case of easements.

Licenses

In essence, a *license* is simply the landowner's permission for someone else to come upon his or her land. It does not create an interest in real property, because the landowner can revoke it at any time. But even though the grantee of the license does not have a legally enforceable *right* to go upon the land, the license, (prior to its revocation) does keep the grantee from being considered a trespasser. Two examples of situations where licenses exist are:

1. The purchaser of a ticket to a movie or other amusement or sporting event has a license to enter the premises.

2. Sometimes a license is created when there is an ineffective attempt to create an easement or a profit. For example, since these are required to be in writing, an oral easement or profit is merely a license.

Mortgages and Liens

A person who borrows money frequently has to grant the lender an interest in some item of property to secure payment of the debt. When the property to be used as security is real property, the landowner grants the lender an interest by executing a *mortgage*. The landowner-debtor is called the *mortgagor*, and the lender is called the *mortgagee*. In most states, the interest created by the mortgage is a *lien*. (Note that in some states a mortgage actually transfers *legal title* to the property so that the mortgagor does not actually own the property until the debt is paid and the mortgage released.) If the mortgagor defaults on the obligation, the mortgagee has a right to *foreclose* the mortgage. This means that the real property can be seized and sold, usually at a public sale (auction), and the proceeds used to pay off the debt. The most common situation in which a mortgage is executed occurs when a buyer of real property borrows a portion of the purchase price and signs a mortgage giving the lender an interest in the property being purchased. Because a mortgage conveys an interest in real property, it must be expressed in a written document that is sufficient to satisfy the statute of frauds.

In some situations, real property may be subjected to a creditor's interest without the landowner's consent. Such an interest is referred to very generally as an *involuntary lien*, in contrast to the voluntary lien created by a mortgage. Statutes or constitutional provisions in most states provide for the involuntary creation of a *mechanic's lien* to secure payment for work done on or materials added to real property. For example, the contractor who builds a house on the land or adds a new room to an existing house usually has a mechanic's lien on the real estate that can be foreclosed if payment is not made. Many states require that, before any work is done or materials provided, the person claiming the lien give the landowner written notice that a mechanic's lien will be asserted. In addition, most states require that a written document in which the mechanic's lien is claimed be filed with the county clerk, recorder of deeds, or other designated county official.

Other types of involuntary liens also exist. When a plaintiff in a civil lawsuit receives a judgment for money damages against the defendant, and the defendant does not pay, in some states the plaintiff may create a *judgment lien* against the defendant's real property by filing a copy of the judgment with the appropriate county official.

It is important to note that, in the case of mechanic's liens, judgment liens, and other involuntary liens, the act of filing the written document with a public official actually *creates* the lien. As we will discuss later in the chapter, deeds, mortgages, and other documents creating *voluntary* interests in real property can be recorded to give greater protection to the person holding the interest, but the act of recording does not create the interest in such situations.

Future Interests

A final category of real property interest is the *future interest*, which consists of the residue remaining when the owner of a fee simple estate transfers less than a fee simple interest to someone else. Despite its name, a future interest does have a present existence and can be transferred, mortgaged, and so on. It is the actual use and enjoyment of the interest that is unavailable until a future time.

The subject of future interests is quite complex, with its own system of classification. Very generally, there are two basic types of future interest. First, a *reversion* exists when the owner of a fee simple transfers a lesser interest and retains the residence. For example, suppose that O, the owner of a fee simple estate, conveys a fee simple defeasible or life estate to B. If no provision is made for ownership of the future interest, it is owned by O and is called a reversion. O can separately transfer the reversion to someone else, or let it pass to his or her heirs. On the other hand, a *remainder* exists when the owner of a fee simple transfers a lesser interest and expressly provides that ownership will pass to a third person upon expiration of the lesser interest. Suppose that when O conveys the fee simple defeasible or life estate to B, O expressly provides that ownership will pass to C upon expiration of B's interest. In this case, C's future interest is called a remainder. C can separately transfer the future interest or let it pass to his or her heirs. When B's interest terminates, the remainder becomes a fee simple estate.

CONCURRENT OWNERSHIP

Any interest in real property that can be owned by one person can also be owned jointly by two or more persons. We will now examine some of the more important types of concurrent ownership.

Tenancy in Common and Joint Tenancy

Characteristics

The most common types of concurrent ownership are the *tenancy in common* and the *joint tenancy*. In a tenancy in common, the co-owners are called *tenants in common* or *cotenants*. In a joint tenancy, they are called *joint tenants*. Here, obviously, the word *tenant* is not used in the same sense as it is in the case of a person who or business that leases a premises from its owner.

The most important distinction between these two types of concurrent ownership has to do with disposition of a co-owner's interest when they die. The interest of a tenant in common passes to that person's heirs according to his or her will, or according to state intestacy statute if there is no will. The heirs and the surviving co-owner(s) then become tenants in common. The joint tenancy, on the other hand, is characterized by a *right of survivorship*, which means that the interest of a deceased joint tenant passes to the surviving joint tenant(s).

Creation

A tenancy in common can be created in several ways. For example, if O conveys a fee simple estate "to A and B," the real property will be owned by A and B as tenants in common. Similarly, if O dies and his land passes to his heirs, A and B, the property will be owned by A and B as tenants in common. Or if O conveys a fractional interest (such as one-half or one-third) to A, the property will be owned by O and A as tenants in common.

A joint tenancy is more difficult to create and, consequently, is not as frequently used as a tenancy in common. In most states, concurrent ownership of real property is presumed to be a tenancy in common, and will be a joint tenancy only if explicitly created. Even the use of the terms "joint tenancy" or "joint tenants" is not a clear enough expression to create a joint tenancy in most states, because people often use such terms in a non-technical sense to refer to a tenancy in common. Thus, if O wishes to create a joint tenancy between A and B, in most states O would have to refer expressly to the *right of survivorship* in addition to using the terms joint tenancy or joint tenants. Moreover, a joint tenancy traditionally could be created only if the joint tenants received their interests at the same time and in the same document, and only if their fractional interests were *equal*. Today, statutes in some states have removed the requirement that a joint tenancy must be created at the same time by a single document. These requirements have never existed for the creation of a tenancy in common.

Partition

In either a tenancy in common or a joint tenancy, none of the co-owners owns any segregated portion of the land. Instead, each owns an undivided fractional interest in the entire tract of land. The tenants in common or joint tenants can agree in writing to *partition* the land; but if they do so, their relationship as co-owners ends, and each becomes the owner of a specifically designated section of the property. If one or more of the co-owners wants to partition the land but the parties are unable to reach unanimous agreement on the division, any one of them can initiate a lawsuit to have the land partitioned. In their decisions, courts commonly express a preference for a partition *in kind*, which is a physical division of the property into sections of equal value. As a practical matter, however, it is extremely difficult for a court to accomplish a physical division that gives each former co-owner a portion of clearly equal value. Consequently, most court-ordered partitions ultimately involve a sale of the property and an equal division of the proceeds.

Condominiums and Cooperatives

Most buildings subject to *condominium* ownership today are physically similar to apartments, and may contain only a few units or as many as several hundred. Ordinarily, a person owns a fee simple estate in the living space of a particular unit, but not in the land on which the unit rests. The fee simple interest in the living space may be owned solely by an individual, or it may be subject to any of the various forms of concurrent ownership such as the tenancy in common. In addition, each owner of an individual living space—a unit—owns a proportionate (percentage) interest in the land on which the condominium building(s) sits, and the so-called "common areas," or "common elements," such as common roofs and walls, parking lots, trees, lawns and flower beds, and recreation areas.

Although a building subject to *cooperative* ownership may physically resemble an apartment building, this form of ownership is quite different than a condominium. A *cooperative corporation* is formed under special state statutory provisions, and the corporation owns the building. Each occupier of a living unit owns shares of stock in the nonprofit corporation and leases the unit from that corporation. Because the corporate entity itself owns the real property, a cooperative is not technically a form of concurrent ownership.

Marital Property

Tenancy by the Entireties

Under English common law, a conveyance of real property to husband and wife created a *tenancy by the entireties*. A tenancy by the entireties is essentially the same as a joint tenancy with right of survivorship, the surviving spouse taking complete ownership on the death of the other. Unlike a joint tenancy, a tenancy by the entireties cannot be severed by one party. A tenancy by the entireties also cannot be transferred by one spouse without the consent of the other, and the creditors of one spouse cannot reach the property without the consent of the other.

The tenancy by the entireties has been abolished in several states and modified in others. Today, in those states abolishing this form of ownership, a conveyance of real property to husband and wife will create either a joint tenancy or tenancy in common, depending on the language of the conveyance.

Traditionally, the husband had the exclusive right to control and possession of property held in a tenancy by the entireties. Today, in those states still recognizing the tenancy by the entireties, statutory changes have given the spouses equal rights of control and possession.

Community Property

Another system of marital property ownership in this country is referred to as *community property*. Nine American states now use the community property system. Five of them (Arizona, California, Louisiana, New Mexico, and Texas) simply continued the Spanish system that had been in effect before statehood, while four others (Idaho, Nevada, Washington, and Wisconsin) adopted the system by legislation.

The community property system recognizes two types of property: *community property* and *separate property*. Each spouse owns an undivided one-half interest in all community property, an interest which passes to his or her heirs upon death. Each has complete ownership of his or her separate property.

Because the community property system is based on the concept that the marital relationship itself is an entity, and that this entity benefits materially from the time and effort of both spouses, most property acquired by the husband or wife during marriage is community property. This includes the salary, wages, or other income earned by either spouse, income earned from community property, and property bought with the proceeds or income from community property. Money or property is the separate property of one of the spouses only if it was acquired by that person before marriage, or acquired after marriage by gift or inheritance. The income generated by one spouse's separate property is his or her separate property in a majority of the community property states. In any situation in which there is a question whether an item of property is community or separate, there is a strong legal presumption that it is community. The various community property states have their own specific rules for determining which spouse has management rights over particular types of community property.

Other Marital Property Rights

Various other property rights are created by marriage. The English common law gave the wife a right called *dower*, consisting of a life estate in one-third of her husband's real property after his death. The husband had a right called *curtesy*, consisting of a life estate in all of his wife's real property after her death. All states have abolished or greatly altered these common-law rights in recent years. States do, however, provide a surviving spouse with some type of interest after the death of the other spouse to insure that the survivor will at least be able to continue living in the shared residence (i.e., the *homestead*).

SALES OF REAL PROPERTY

Next to leases, sales are the most common real estate transaction. Whether such sales involve a residential house and lot, a farm, a ranch, or other real property, they are the most monetarily significant transactions most people ever undertake.

Most real estate sales involve the transfer of a fee simple interest in the surface, minerals, or both. Transfer of other types of interests may be accomplished in much the same way, but the procedures are often modified to fit the particular circumstances. Leasehold interests are usually created simply by the signing of a lease contract. Throughout the following discussion, we will assume that the transaction is of the most common type—sale of a fee simple interest.

Brokers and Agents

When a landowner wishes to sell property, the first step usually is to contact and employ a real estate broker or agent ("realtor"). Although this is not required (the landowner can, of course, sell the land without help), it is often desirable to do so because there are many traps for the unwary in real estate transactions and a realtor can often assist in avoiding such traps. Here we refer to both brokers and agents as realtors because they can and do perform the same functions. In most states, however, a broker has to meet additional licensing requirements that agents do not have to meet, and the broker typically owns the real estate agency, with agents working for the broker.

The function of the realtor is to find a buyer. This is usually the extent of the realtor's authority; they ordinarily are not given authority to actually sell or even to make a contract to sell. In return for finding a buyer the realtor is entitled to be compensated, typically be receiving an agreed-upon *commission*, which is usually a percentage of the selling price. A formal employment contract setting out the terms of the arrangement should be made with the realtor. Indeed, in many states a realtor has no legally enforceable right to a commission unless the agreement to pay is in writing.

The arrangement with the realtor can be of several types, including an open listing, exclusive agency, or exclusive right to sell. In an *open listing*, the realtor is entitled to a commission only if they are the *first one* to procure a buyer who is "ready, willing, and able" to buy at the stated selling price. The owner is free to sell the land personally or through another realtor without incurring liability to the employed broker. Open listings are not especially common.

The *exclusive agency* arises when the owner gives assurance that no other realtor will be hired during the term of the agreement. If the owner does employ another realtor who procures a buyer, the sale is valid but the original realtor is still entitled to the agreed commission. However, the owner is entitled to sell the land *personally*, without the aid of the employed realtor or any other realtor. If the owner makes the sale without assistance, the employed broker is not entitled to a commission.

In an *exclusive right to sell* arrangement, the employed realtor is entitled to the agreed commission if the property is sold during the agreement's duration by *anyone* (even the owner acting without assistance).

Multiple Listing Services

In most localities, realtors have formed multiple listing services. A *multiple listing service* (MLS) is an arrangement whereby realtors in the area pool their listings, each member having access to the pool. A participating realtor ordinarily obtains either an exclusive agency or exclusive right to sell agreement from the landowner, and then places that listing in the local MLS. If another realtor finds a buyer for the property, the commission is split between the listing and selling realtors according to their agreement. The MLS is typically operated by a private, nonprofit entity supported by dues paid by member real estate agents (i.e., realtors) and brokers in the area, often called a board of realtors.

In recent years MLS systems have naturally moved from paper to the internet. In addition, the Internet has become a very important tool for realtors, sellers, and buyers even if an MLS is not used.

The Contract

When a buyer is found, a contract for sale will ordinarily be made. When making an offer to buy, or when entering the contract itself, the buyer often makes a deposit referred to as *earnest money*. The real estate sale contract sometimes is called an *earnest money contract*, and normally provides that the buyer will forfeit the earnest money if they breach the contract.

To be enforceable, a contract for the sale of land has to be in writing in almost all circumstances. Although the contract usually is evidenced by a detailed formal document signed by both seller and buyer, the requirement of written documentation can be satisfied by informal instruments such as letters or telegrams. The writing, whether formal or not, must contain all the essential terms of the agreement and must be signed by the party against whom enforcement is sought (or his or her duly-authorized agent). If essential terms are missing, the writing is considered insufficient; oral testimony will not be allowed to fill the gaps, and the contract is unenforceable.

Specifically, the terms that must be included in the writing contract for sale are (1) the *names* of the seller and buyer and an indication of their intent to be bound, (2) a *description* of the property sufficient to identify it, and (3) the *price*.

Title Examination, Insurance, and Survey

One of the main reasons for initially making a sale contract rather than immediately transferring ownership is to give the buyer an opportunity to investigate the seller's title (often called a *title examination*). This essentially involves an examination of all officially recorded documents concerning the property. The examination is usually made by an attorney employed either by the purchaser, by the lending institution from which the purchase price is being borrowed, or by a title insurance company.

The attorney may personally search the public records and on the basis of this investigation issue a "certificate of title" giving his or her opinion as to the validity of the seller's title. Or the attorney may examine an *abstract*, which is a compilation of the official records relating to a particular parcel of land. Privately-owned abstract companies produce such abstracts and keep them current.

The sale contract often requires the seller to provide evidence of good title. The certificate of title is used as such evidence in some parts of the country, while in others the abstract and the attorney's opinion based thereon provide the required evidence. It is also becoming more frequent for the contract to require the seller to provide the buyer with "title insurance." This may be used as the sole evidence of title, or it may be required in addition to other evidence. Title insurance, which is purchased from a company engaged in the business of selling such insurance (often called a *title company*), simply provides that the issuing company will compensate the buyer for any loss if the title ultimately proves defective. Of course, the title company will issue such a policy only if its own attorneys feel, after making a title examination, that the title is good.

Unless a survey has been made very recently, the seller is often required under the contract to have a new survey made. A licensed surveyor will be employed to make sure that the described boundaries are correct and that no buildings or other encroachments lie on the boundary line.

Financing and Closing the Sale

Many times the buyer does not have sufficient funds available to pay the agreed price. In such cases, after the contract is made but before the transfer of title, the buyer must obtain the necessary financing. As noted earlier, the buyer (mortgagor) normally executes a mortgage to the lender (mortgagee) as security for the loan. Sometimes the seller provides the financing by permitting the buyer to pay the purchase price in installments. In such a case, the seller may immediately transfer title to the buyer and take a mortgage to secure payment, or the seller and buyer may agree that title will not be transferred to the buyer until the purchase price is completely paid. The latter type of arrangement is often called a *contract for deed.*

The actual transfer of ownership usually takes place at the *closing* (or settlement)—the meeting attended by the seller and buyer as well as other interested parties such as their attorneys, the broker, and a representative of the mortgagee. At the meeting, the seller signs and delivers to the buyer a *deed* that transfers the ownership, and the buyer pays the purchase price. (As a practical matter, however, the representative of the mortgagee may actually pay the seller.) It is also common for the mortgage to be executed at the closing and for other incidental financial matters to be settled (such as apportionment of property taxes and insurance that the seller may have prepaid).

Sometimes a closing occurs in a different manner, by the use of an *escrow agent*, who is a disinterested third party to whom the seller has delivered the deed and to whom the buyer has made payment. It is fairly common for an institution such as a title insurance company to serve as escrow agent. This party's instructions generally are to close the deal by delivering the deed to the buyer and the payment to the seller on receipt of the required evidence of good title.

The Deed

Types of Deeds

As stated earlier, title to real property is conveyed by means of a written deed. Several types of deeds exist, each involving particular legal consequences.

General Warranty Deed. From the buyer's point of view, the *general warranty deed* is by far the most desirable kind to obtain, because it carries certain warranties, or covenants, that the title is good. These warranties may be expressed in the deed, but even if not expressed they are *implied* if the document is actually a general warranty deed. Whether a particular deed is one of general warranty depends on the language used in it. The wording necessary to create such a deed varies from state to state. In some states, the verb phrase "convey and warranty" makes it a general warranty deed. The warranties, which overlap somewhat, usually consist of the following: (1) *Covenant of seisin.* The seller (called *grantor* in the deed) guarantees that they have good title to the land conveyed. (2) *Covenant against encumbrances.* The grantor guarantees that there are no encumbrances on the land except as stated in the deed. An *encumbrance* includes any type of lien or easement held by a third party. The existence of such an encumbrance causes a breach of this warranty by the grantor, even if the grantee (the buyer) knows about it when receiving the deed, unless the deed states that the title is subject to the particular encumbrance. (3) *Covenant for quiet enjoyment.* The grantor guarantees that the grantee (or those to whom the grantee later conveys the property) will not be evicted or disturbed by a person having a better title or a lien.

Special Warranty Deed. In a *special warranty deed,* there is a warranty only that the title has not been diminished in any way by a personal act of the grantor. For example, suppose the grantor had previously executed a mortgage on the land that the deed does not mention. If the grantee later has to pay off the mortgage or if it is foreclosed and the grantee loses the property, the grantor will be liable to the grantee for damages. On the other hand, if the grantor has not personally encumbered the title but an outstanding title or interest in the land is later asserted by some third person, the grantor incurs no liability. This situation might arise, for instance, if the land is encumbered by a valid lien created by someone who owned the land prior to the grantor. The special warranty deed is a sufficient performance of the seller's obligations under the sale contract unless that contract specifically required a general warranty deed.

Quitclaim Deed. In a *quitclaim deed,* the grantor does not really purport to convey any title at all to the grantee. The deed says, in essence, "If I have any present interest in this land, I hereby convey it to you." This deed is not a sufficient performance of the grantor's obligations under the sale contract unless the contract so provides. Quitclaim deeds are often used as a form for *release.* For example, A owns the land, but X arguably has some type of interest in it, and A negotiates with X for a release of X's claim. One way of accomplishing the release is for A to obtain a quitclaim deed from X.

Deed of Bargain and Sale. The *deed of bargain and sale* purports to convey title but does not contain any warranties. Even though differing in form, this deed conveys the same type of title as a quitclaim deed. It also is not a sufficient performance of the grantor's obligations under the sale contract unless the contract so provides.

Requirements of a Valid Deed

Because an owner may give away property, a deed does not require *consideration.* Of course, a *sale contract* must be supported by consideration, as must any other executory contract. A promise to make a gift of land or anything else is generally not enforceable; but a completed gift by delivery of a deed is perfectly valid, assuming that there is no intent to defraud the grantor's creditors. Even though there is no requirement that a grantee give consideration for a deed or that consideration be stated in the deed, it is customary for the deed to contain a *recital of consideration*—a statement of what consideration is being given by the grantee. It is also customary for the recital to state merely a nominal consideration (such as $10) rather than the price actually paid.

There are several requirements that a deed must meet in order to transfer a real property interest. Although these requirements vary slightly among the states, they may be summarized as follows.

Grantor and Grantee. The deed must name a grantor and grantee. The grantor must have legal capacity. If the grantor is married, it is generally desirable to have the grantor's spouse named as a grantor as well, for several reasons. In most states, if the property is occupied by husband and wife as their residence (homestead), both must join in a conveyance of the property even if only one of them owns it. And as previously mentioned, the laws of many states give one spouse certain types of rights with respect to the property of the other regardless of whether the property is their homestead, and these rights are extinguished only if the grantor's spouse joins in the deed.

Words of Conveyance. The deed must contain words of conveyance—words indicating a present intent to transfer ownership to the grantee, such as "I, Alice B. Toklas, do hereby grant, sell, and convey...."

Description. The deed must contain a description of the land being conveyed that is clear and precise enough so that someone who knows nothing about the parties, the transaction, or the land could find the property described, perhaps with expert assistance from someone like a surveyor.

Signature. The deed must be signed by the grantor. For the reasons already discussed, it is also usually desirable to obtain the signature of a married grantor's spouse.

Delivery. The deed must be delivered to the grantee.

Methods of Describing Land

As stated, a valid deed must contain an adequate description of the property being conveyed. Although this description should be (and usually is) stated in the deed, it is permissible for the deed to refer to a sufficient description contained in another document.

Land can be adequately described in several ways, but regardless of the method employed, the property must be identified in such a way that there can be no mistake about exactly which parcel of land is being conveyed. There is a general tendency for the courts to require a greater degree of precision in a deed than in a sale contract. For example, in the case of residential property, a sale contract usually is enforceable if the description is merely a street name and number in a particular city and state. In many states, however, such a description is not sufficient for a deed to be a valid conveyance of title to the property.

Government Survey. In many states west of the Mississippi River (except Texas) and in another half dozen or so states east of the Mississippi, land can be described by reference to the United States Government Survey. This survey was adopted by Congress in 1785 for the purpose of describing government-owned land that was to be transferred to states, railroads, and settlers. It uses meridians and parallels to divide the surveyed areas into quadrangles that are approximately 24 miles on each side. Each quadrangle is further divided into 16 tracts called *townships* that are approximately 6 miles on each side.

Metes and Bounds. In those states not using the U.S. Government Survey, it is common for land outside the limits of an incorporated city to be described by *metes and bounds*. *Metes* means measures of length; *bounds* refers to the boundaries of the property. A metes and bounds description essentially just delineates the exterior lines of the land being conveyed. It may make use of a *monument* (a natural or artificial landmark such as a river or street) to constitute a boundary or to mark a corner of the tract. A metes and bounds description begins at a well-identified point and runs stated distances at stated angles, tracing the boundary until it returns to the starting point.

Plat. The two methods just discussed are normally used to describe land in rural and semi-rural areas that have not been formally subdivided and platted. Most land in urban areas has been surveyed by private developers and subdivided into numbered blocks and lots on a *plat* (map) that is recorded with a designated county official. In almost all parts of the country, it is common to describe urban land by reference to the name of a local region such as the name of a residential subdivision, and the lot and block number in the recorded plat.

In the following case, we will see how problems can arise from "homemade" deeds. The case also illustrates that a court will, where it is possible to do so, attempt to make sense out of an imprecisely drafted deed.

Incorporation by Reference. Real property can be described adequately by a specific incorporation of a sufficient description contained in another document, if the document referred to is publicly available. The most common example of describing land this way is the adoption of a description from a previous deed, mortgage, or similar legal instrument that was itself recorded in the public deed records. The reference in such a case must, naturally, clearly specify where the deed record is (state, county), and refer to it by volume and page number or other means by which it can be readily located. Usually, though, it is a better practice to simply include the exact description in the later deed by copying it in, although one must take care to ensure that the earlier description is correct and adequate, and to avoid mistakes in copying it.

The following case shows how courts will find an imperfect deed to be valid if they can find evidence within the deed itself to assist in making a property description adequate.

Garlock v. Roland
830 S.E.2d 700 (N.C. App. 2019)

Raleigh Brisco Roland and Betty Ann Roland acquired real property described in a warranty deed they recorded in 1970 in Deed Book 1017 at page 399 in the Office of the Register of Deeds for Buncombe County, North Carolina. Betty Roland died before her husband, and he inherited her share of their joint property, including the property at issue in this case. On April 10, 2007, one of the Roland's two sons, defendant Eric Roland, recorded a quit claim deed in the Buncombe County Register of Deeds in which the father, Raleigh B. Roland, stated that he "hereby quitclaims and transfers all right, title, and interest" in real estate located at 153 Gashes Creek Rd. in Asheville. On January 29, 2013, Raleigh Roland died. The heirs entitled to share in the estate of Raleigh Roland were his sons, Daniel Roland and defendant Eric Roland. As part of the probate of Raleigh Roland's estate, Eric Roland verified that the Gashes Creek Rd. property was part of the deceased father's estate. The judge of the probate court appointed Victor Garlock as the administrator of Raleigh Roland's estate.

The administrator, Garlock, filed a complaint in Buncombe County District Court against Eric Roland to "quiet title" and set aside the deed to Eric as void. Because of doubts about the validity of the 2007 quit claim deed, the administrator of the estate needed to have a court sort out the title to the property. Clearing up the title would also be of benefit to the heirs, brothers Daniel and Eric. With what is often called a "cloud on the title," no one would ever be able to sell or mortgage the property. In the complaint, the plaintiff Garlock also asserted that the quit claim deed recorded by Eric on April 10, 2007 failed to refer to anything extrinsic by which the land could be identified with certainty. Therefore, he alleged, the quit-claim deed was void and never divested Raleigh Brisco Roland of title to the Gashes Creek Rd. property. The trial judge granted summary judgment in favor of plaintiff, and defendant appealed.

Bryant, Judge:

Defendant argues that listing a street address as a description of real property is a legally sufficient description to support the conveyance of marketable title. Defendant contends that the trial court erred by concluding the description of real property by the street address 153 Gashes Creek Rd, Asheville, in a quit claim deed was not a legally sufficient description, rendering the quit claim deed void.

It is a general rule that the deed must be upheld, if possible, and the terms and phraseology of description will be interpreted with that view, and to that end, if this can reasonably be done. To constitute color of title [i.e., evidence of good title], a deed must contain a description identifying the land or referring to something that will identify it with certainty. A deed purporting to convey an interest in land is void unless it contains a description of the land sufficient to identify it or refers to something extrinsic by which the land may be identified with certainty.

Where property . . . has a known and commonly used and recognized name [within a local area], the use of this name to describe and identify the property sold is [not sufficient by itself, but] is sufficient to permit the introduction of other evidence to show that the property claimed is in fact the property named.

[However,] when it is apparent upon the face of the deed itself that there is uncertainty as to the land intended to be conveyed and the deed refers to nothing extrinsic by which such uncertainty can be resolved, the description is patently ambiguous. As Justice Barnhill, later Chief Justice, speaking for the [North Carolina Supreme] Court, said in *Thompson v. Umberger*, 19 S.E.2d 484, "[A] patent ambiguity is such an uncertainty appearing on the face of the instrument that the court, reading the language in the light of all the facts and circumstances *referred to in the instrument*, is unable to derive *therefrom* the intention of the parties as to what land was to be conveyed." (Emphasis added.) Parol evidence may *not* be introduced to remove a patent ambiguity since to do so would not be a use of such evidence to fit the description to the land but a use of such evidence to create a description by adding to the words of the instrument.

[But,] when the terms used in the deed leave it uncertain what property is intended [but the deed also refers to other, extrinsic evidence by which the uncertainty can be resolved], parol evidence is admissible to fit the description to the land. The deed itself must point to the source from which evidence *aliunde* ["from elsewhere"] to make the description complete is to be sought.

In support of his argument, defendant cites *Bank of Am., N.A. v. Charlotte Prop. Investments, LLC*, 2014 WL 2795915 (N.C. App. 2014), an appeal of a summary judgment order in an action to quiet title. "The physical address for the property was designated in the Warranty Deed as 2816 Oasis Lane, Charlotte, North Carolina 28214, the brief description for the real estate index listing was 'Lot 39 of Belmeade Green,' and the parcel ID number was '053–074–33.'" This court reasoned as follows: [T]he record indicates that the Deed of Trust contained the correct physical address and parcel ID number, thereby referring to extrinsic sources from which the land could be identified with certainty. ... For this reason, we conclude the Deed of Trust, by referring to the correct physical address *and* parcel ID number, was sufficient to identify the parcel with certainty. ... [Note: a "deed of trust" serves a purpose similar to that of a mortgage by conveying a debtor's title to a trustee, who holds title until the debt is paid; when the debt is paid, the deed of trust is released, but if the debtor ultimately defaults, the trustee transfers title to the creditor.]

Here, the record on appeal contains the quit claim deed filed with the Buncombe County Register of Deeds. The quit claim deed states as follows:

Property Tax Parcel/Account Number: 5294600
QUITCLAIM DEED

This Quitclaim Deed is made on Apr. 16, 2007, between Raleigh B. Roland, Grantor of 153 Gashes Ck. Rd. City of Asheville, State of North Carolina, and Eric D. Roland, Grantee of 153 Gashes Ck. Rd., City of Asheville, State of North Carolina.

For valuable consideration, the Grantor hereby quitclaims and transfers all right, title, and interest held by the Grantor to the following described real estate and improvements to the Grantee, and his or her heirs and assigns, to have and hold forever, located at 153 Gashes Creek Rd., City of Asheville, State of North Carolina.

In its summary judgment order, the trial court made the following findings of fact:

14. On or about April 10, 2007, Defendant ERIC DALE ROLAND caused to be created and recorded that Quit Claim Deed recorded in Consolidated Book 4392 at page 538 in the Office of the Register of Deeds for Buncombe County, North Carolina.... 16. The Quit Claim deed referenced fails to contain a description of the land sufficient to identify it or to refer to something extrinsic by which the land may be identified with certainty.

But we note that the quit claim deed in the record describes the land by a street address and a property tax parcel/account number. ...Our courts have held that a street address, standing alone, is not a description of real property legally sufficient to support the conveyance of record marketable title, and we do not do so now. We hold that the face of the deed leaves uncertain what tract of real property was intended to be embraced by the quit claim deed, but refers to extrinsic evidence [the property's ID number in the county tax records] by which such uncertainty may be resolved. As such, parol evidence is admissible to fit the description to the land. Accordingly, the trial court's judgment is vacated, and the case is remanded to the trial court for a factual determination of whether the extrinsic evidence makes the deed's description sufficiently definite.]

Acknowledgment

An acknowledgment is a formal declaration before a designated public official, such as a notary public, by a person who has signed a document, that they executed the document as a voluntary act. The public official places his or her signature and seal after the declaration and the declarant's signature. The resulting instrument, referred to as a *certificate of acknowledgment*, is attached to the document to which it relates. In most states an acknowledgment is not required for a deed to be valid, but it is required as a prerequisite to "recording."

Recording

Recording is the act of filing the deed with a public official, referred to in different states as the "recorder of deeds," "register of deeds," or any of several other titles. The official copies the deed into the record books, indexes it, and returns the original to the person who filed it.

As between the grantor and grantee, an otherwise valid deed is perfectly good even if it is not recorded. The purpose of recording procedures, which exist in every state, is to give notice to the world at large that the transfer of title has taken place. Frequently referred to as "constructive notice," this means that third parties are treated as having notice regardless of whether they actually do.

State recording statutes generally provide that an unrecorded deed, though valid between grantor and grantee, is void with respect to any subsequent bona fide purchaser. A *bona fide purchaser* (BFP) is a good faith purchaser for value. For example, suppose that O sells a tract of land to B, and B does not record her deed. O then sells the same land to C by executing another deed. If C pays for the land rather than receiving it as a gift, he is giving *value*. If C does not know of the earlier conveyance to B when he purchases, he is acting in *good faith*. Thus, C qualifies as a BFP and has good title. In this situation B has no title. But if B has recorded her deed prior to C's purchase, B would have title even if C later gave value and acted in good faith. The reasoning is that C could have discovered B's interest if he had checked the records.

Although there is some conflict on the point, courts in a majority of states hold that C qualifies as a BFP even if he does not record his own deed. (Of course, if he does not do so, he runs the risk of having the same thing happen to him that happened to B. If there was a "C," there could later be a "D.")

Regarding the status of C as a BFP, another point must be made. If B, the first grantee from O, is actually *in possession of the land* when C acquires his interest, this possession serves as notice to C. Thus, even if B did not record and C did not have actual knowledge of B's interest, C nevertheless is not a BFP.

Recording statutes apply not only to the sale of a fee simple interest but also to the conveyance of any other type of interest in land. For example, if O executes a mortgage to B, giving her a lien on the property, B should record her mortgage. If she does not, she risks losing her interest to a subsequent BFP.

Furthermore, the word *purchaser* actually means a grantee of any type of interest in the land, even such interests as liens or easements. Suppose, for instance, that O sells to B, who does not record her deed. O later borrows money from C and executes a mortgage purporting to give C a lien on the land. By making the loan to O, C is giving value. If C receives the mortgage without knowledge of the earlier conveyance to B, he is acting in good faith and is treated as a BFP. Thus, C's mortgage is valid, and B's ownership is subject to it. If B had been a mortgagee herself instead of an actual grantee of the title, the same rules would apply to the conflict between B and C, the two mortgagees.

Mortgage-Backed Securities, MERS, and a Big Mess

The reasonably straight-forward system for transferring title to real estate and foreclosing upon those who do not pay on their mortgages described in the past few pages has become a convoluted nightmare. This treatment will not be lengthy enough to do the problem justice, but a brief sketch may be useful.

In order to encourage more financing for the housing market and to diversify their risk, banks that formerly simply loaned money to Homeowner A and held A's mortgage began packaging many mortgages into bundles, securitizing them, and then selling the securities around the globe. This made it very difficult to know who held A's mortgage and who could foreclose on it.

To facilitate the trading of mortgage on the secondary mortgage market as well as to save lenders the cost of filing assignments, lending institutions created the Mortgage Electronic Registry System (MERS). Today, roughly half of the mortgages in the United States, some sixty million, are held in MERS name. MERS was created to eliminate the need to prepare and record assignments when mortgages are transferred. Recorded transfers in county offices have been replaced by electronic transfers, often inaccurate and incomplete, in MERS computer system.

MERS undermines a practice that is as old (or older) than the country wherein any potential seller of land could, with some diligence, construct a chain of title that could go back hundreds of years and would clarify with precision who had what rights in the land. So, if Bank X wished to foreclose on Homeowner A's house, traditionally Bank A would be able to easily demonstrate that it held the mortgage on A's house and that A had fallen behind on payments. When the subprime crisis hit in the 2006-2008 timeframe, MERS began foreclosing on homes in its own name. But did it really have the right to do so? Some courts have had their doubts. *See U.S. Bank Nat'l Ass'n v. Ibanez*, 941 N.E.2d 40 (Mass. 2011). Such doubts can create an awful mess. The following case addresses the issue and takes a different point of view.

BANK OF N.Y. MELLON v. ARGO
2015 Ohio App. LEXIS 212 (Ohio App. 2015)

On February 1, 2012, appellee Bank of New York Mellon, as Trustee for the Certificate holders CWALT, Inc., Alternative Loan Trust 2005-85CB, Mortgage-Pass Through Certificates, Series 2005-85CB, sued appellants Barry and Lynn Argo. Appellee alleged that it is a person entitled to enforce the mortgage note, and attached a copy of the note, mortgage, and assignment of mortgage to the complaint. The note, dated November 7, 2005, designates the Lender as Residential Finance Corporation. The mortgage dated November 7, 2005, secures the property located at 56 Grand Blvd., Shelby, Ohio. The Lender is listed on the mortgage as Residential Finance with Mortgage Electronic Registration Systems ("MERS") listed as the mortgagee and nominee for Lender and Lender's successor and assigns. The mortgage assignment recorded on October 26, 2011, assigns the mortgage dated November 7, 2005 to appellee. The original lender is listed on the assignment as Residential Finance and the assignment is signed by MERS.

Appellee moved for summary judgment, including an affidavit by Mayoh, a Document Control Officer for Select Portfolio Servicing, Inc., the servicer for appellee. Mayoh attached copies of the note, mortgage, and assignment of mortgage to her affidavit. The copy of the note that Mayoh attached differed from the note attached to the complaint, as it contained an extra page entitled "allonge," from Residential Finance to Countrywide Bank, N.A. The allonge was endorsed from Countywide Bank, N.A. to Countrywide Home Loans, Inc., and then endorsed by Countrywide Home Loans, Inc. in blank.

Appellee's motion for summary judgment was granted and the Argos appealed.

Gwin, Appellate Judge:
Appellants argue summary judgment is not appropriate in this case because appellee

was not the holder of the note and mortgage when the foreclosure was filed. We disagree.

To have standing to pursue a foreclosure action, a plaintiff "must establish an interest in the note or mortgage at the time it filed suit." *Home Loan Mtge. Corp. v. Schwartzwald*, 979 N.E.2d 1214 (Ohio 2012). The current holder of the note and mortgage is the real party in interest in a foreclosure action. *U.S. Bank Nat'l Assn. v. Marcio*, 908 N.E.2d 1032 (Ohio App. 2009). [Ohio Code] 1303.31 provides:

> (A) Person entitled to enforce an instrument means any of the following persons:
> (1) The holder of the instrument;
> (2) A nonholder in possession of the instrument who has the rights of a holder;
> (3) A person not in possession of the instrument who is entitled to enforce the instrument pursuant to Section 1303.38 or division (D) of section 1303.58 of the Revised Code.
> (B) A person may be a "person entitled to enforce" the instrument even though the person is not the owner of the instrument or is in wrongful possession of the instrument.

Appellants argue that the assignment of the mortgage is not sufficient for appellee to be the holder of the note and mortgage without an assignment of the note. Further, that the assignment of the mortgage is not sufficient for appellee to enforce the note and mortgage as the holder of the note and mortgage because MERS never had any interest in the note and appellee failed to submit any evidence that MERS is a nominee of Residential Finance.

Pursuant to the decisions of this Court, the assignment of the mortgage, without the express transfer of the note, is sufficient to transfer both the note and mortgage if the record indicates that the parties intended to transfer both the note and mortgage. *Bank of New York v. Dobbs*, 2009-Ohio-4742; *Freedom Mtge. Corp v. Vitale*, 2014-Ohio-1549. This case is analogous to *Dobbs* and *Vitale* as the record indicates the parties intended to transfer both the note and the mortgage. The note dated November 7, 2005 provides that, "in addition to the protections given to the Note Holder under this Note, a Mortgage * * * (the "Security Instrument"), dated the same date as this Note, protects the Note Holder from possible losses which might result if I do not keep the promises which I make in this Note." Further, that the Security Instrument "describes how and under what conditions I may be required to make immediate payment in full of all amounts I owe under this Note * * *."

The November 7, 2005 mortgage was notarized on November 7, 2005 and recorded at the Richland County Recorder on November 15, 2005. This mortgage, in which MERS is the mortgagee and nominee for lender Residential Finance, defines "Note" as "the promissory note signed by Borrower and dated November 7, 2005. The Note states that Borrower owes Lender two hundred seven thousand and 00/100 Dollars * * *." Further, that the mortgage secures to Lender "(i) the repayment of the Loan, and all renewals, extensions and modifications of the Note, and (ii) the performance of Borrower's covenants and agreements under this Security Instrument and Note." Finally, the mortgage provides that the Borrower and Lender covenant and agree that "Borrower shall pay when due the principal of, and interest on, the debt evidenced by the Note and any prepayment charges and late charges due under the Note." The note refers to the mortgage and the mortgage refers to the note. Thus, we find a clear intent by the parties to keep the note and mortgage together rather than transferring the mortgage alone. The assignment of the mortgage was sufficient to transfer both the mortgage and the note.

In addition, the mortgage assignment refers to the note as it provides that the assignor transfers to appellee "all beneficial interest under that certain Mortgage described below together with the note and obligations therein described * * *." The mortgage assignment was notarized on October 18, 2011 and recorded in the Richland County Recorder's office on October 26, 2011. Since the mortgage assignment was recorded on October 26, 2011, prior to the complaint being filed in this case on February 1, 2012, the note was effectively transferred on that date. Accordingly, there are no genuine issues of material fact as to whether appellee is the real party in interest with standing to pursue this foreclosure action.

Appellants argue the assignment of mortgage is not sufficient to transfer the note because MERS, who assigned the mortgage, had no interest in the note. This Court has repeatedly upheld the right and authority of MERS, when designated as a nominee and mortgagee, to transfer interests in notes and mortgages. *Vitale, supra; Wells Fargo v. Elliott,* 2013-Ohio-3690 (2013). In this case, the mortgage provides that "Borrower does hereby mortgage, grant, and convey to MERS (solely as nominee for Lender and Lender's successors and assigns) and to the successors and assigns of MERS * * * the following described property * * *." The Lender is listed in the mortgage as Residential Finance. The assignment filed by appellee and attached to its complaint and motion for summary judgment was recorded on October 26, 2011 and states that MERS, as the holder of the mortgage and nominee for Residential Finance, assigns and transfers the mortgage to appellee. Accordingly, MERS had the authority to assign the mortgage to appellee and MERS properly executed the assignment as nominee for Residential Finance prior to the filing of the complaint in this case. Further, the mortgage signed by appellants provides that they "understand and agree that MERS (as nominee for Lender and Lender's successors and assigns) has the right: to exercise any or all of those interests, including, but not limited to, the right to foreclose and sell the Property; and to take any action required of Lender * * *."

Appellants also argue that appellee did not provide evidence that MERS was a nominee of the originating lender and thus the assignment of mortgage is not valid. As noted above, appellants specifically signed the mortgage stating they understood MERS, as nominee for Lender, had the right to exercise any or all interests of the Lender. Further, as noted by this Court in *U.S. Bank v. Lawson,* 2014-Ohio-463 (Ohio 2014), because a debtor is not a party to the assignment of a mortgage, the debtor lacks standing to challenge its validity when there is no dispute between the original mortgagee and the entity subsequently named as an assignee of the mortgage as to the assignment's validity and there was no dispute that the borrower had defaulted on his loan and was subject to foreclosure. There is no dispute between MERS and appellee as to whether the mortgage was properly assigned. There is also no dispute appellants defaulted on their mortgage loan. Accordingly, the assignment of mortgage is not invalid. Affirmed.

ADVERSE POSSESSION

Under some circumstances, a party can acquire ownership of land by taking possession of it and staying in possession for a certain number of years. The required time period is established by statute and varies from state to state, ranging from five years in California to thirty years in Louisiana.

Ownership acquired in this manner is frequently referred to as *title by adverse possession* or *title by limitation*. Since it is not acquired by deed, there is nothing to record. Thus, the recording statutes do not apply, and title by adverse possession, once acquired, cannot be lost to a subsequent BFP. Of course, even though such title is not *acquired* by deed, it can be *conveyed* by deed to someone else. Such a deed would be subject to all of the rules applicable to deeds in general, including recording statutes.

Requirements for Title by Adverse Possession

Not all types of possession will ripen into ownership. The possession must be "adverse," which means, in effect, that it must be actual, hostile, open and notorious, and continuous.

Actual Possession

The requirement that possession be *actual* simply means that the possessor must have exercised some type of *physical control* over the land that indicates a claim of ownership. The person need not actually live on the property, although this certainly constitutes actual possession. What is required is that the possessor act toward the land as an average owner probably would act, taking into account the nature of the land. For example, if it is farmland, the farming of it constitutes actual possession. Erecting buildings or other improvements may also be sufficient.

Construction of a fence or building that extends over the true boundary line and onto the land of an adjoining property owner generally constitutes actual possession of that part of the land encompassed by the fence or located under the building. Thus, if the other requirements of adverse possession are met, the party erecting the fence or building will become the owner of the area in question after the prescribed period of time.

Hostile Possession

The requirement that the possession be *hostile* does not mean that it must be accompanied by ill feelings. What it means is that possession must be *nonconsensual*; it is not adverse if it occurs with the consent of the true owner. Thus, a tenant's possession of a landlord's property under a lease agreement is not hostile unless the tenant clearly communicated to the landlord that the tenant was claiming ownership.

Similarly, if two parties are co-owners of a tract of land, each of them has a right to possession. Therefore, possession by one co-owner is not hostile as to the other unless the possessor notifies the other that they are claiming sole ownership.

Continuous Possession

In order for adverse possession to ultimately ripen into ownership, it must be *reasonably continuous* for the required period of time. The possessor does not have to be in possession every single day of the period. For instance, they could leave temporarily with an intent to return, and the law would treat the possession as not having been interrupted.

In answering the question of whether possession has been continuous, a court will take into account the nature of the land and the type of use being made of it. Thus, farming the land only during the growing season each year constitutes continuous possession.

Also, the uninterrupted possession by two or more successive possessors can sometimes be added together, or "tacked," to satisfy the statutory time requirement. For "tacking" to be permitted, there must have been *privity* between the successive possessors. This simply means that the possessions by different persons must not have been independent of each other; rather, there must have been a transaction between them which purported to transfer the property. To illustrate: In State X the required period for adverse possession is ten years. O is the true owner. B meets all the requirements for adverse possession except that he stays on the land only six years. B then purports to sell or otherwise transfer the land to C. If C stays in possession for four more years, continuing to meet all the requirements for obtaining title by adverse possession, C becomes the owner of the land.

The following case illustrates the applicability of the adverse possession doctrine to a common problem—a boundary dispute between "unneighborly" neighbors.

SEXTON v. WAGNON
Alabama Court of Civil Appeals, 958 So.2d 892 (2006)

Sexton and the Lowes (plaintiffs) are the holders of record title to tract 10 of a subdivision in Etowah County. Wagnon (defendant) is the holder of record title to tract 9, which lies adjacent to and <u>west</u> of tract 10. Wagnon's father was deeded tract 9 in 1973. He then hired a surveyor to mark the boundary line between tract 9 and tract 10 with stakes. Later, Wagnon's father drove a portion of an old metal bed rail into the ground beside one of the stakes the surveyor had used to mark the boundary line between tract 9 and tract 10, and drove a galvanized pipe into the ground beside another stake the surveyor had used. Over the years, the surveyor's stakes disappeared, but the bed rail and the galvanized pipe remained, and Wagnon's father treated them as landmarks marking the boundary line between tract 9 and tract 10.

In 1980 or 1981, Wagnon's father placed a mobile home a short distance southwest of the bed rail. In 1982 or 1983, he marked the straight line running from the southern terminus of the boundary line to the bed rail by planting three poplar trees along that line. Soon after Wagnon's father planted the three poplar trees, defendant Wagnon married, and she and her husband began living in the mobile home. From that time on, either Wagnon or her father mowed the grass in the triangular piece of land that is the subject of dispute (the "gore") all the way up to the possession line every one or two weeks. No one other than Wagnon, her husband, and her father has used the gore since 1973. In 1996, Wagnon's father conveyed tract 9 to her. The deed did not purport to convey to her any part of tract 10 that her father may have possessed adversely.

The owners of tract 10 never gave their permission for Wagnon's father or Wagnon and her husband to use the gore. In 2005, a surveyor prepared a survey of tract 10 for plaintiffs, finding that the gore was located <u>east</u> of the survey line. Plaintiffs then demanded that Wagnon cease using the gore and recognize the survey line as the boundary line between the parties' properties. Wagnon ceased some of her use of the gore but refused to cease using it altogether, and she insisted that the possession line, rather than the survey line, is the boundary line between the parties' properties. Plaintiffs sued, and the trial judge found that Wagnon had acquired title to the gore by adverse possession and, therefore, that the possession line is the true boundary line between the parties' properties. Plaintiffs appealed.

Bryan, Judge:

Plaintiffs argue that the trial court erred in finding that Wagnon owned the gore by virtue of adverse possession because: (1) Wagnon did not hold title to tract 9 for 10 years, the period required to establish **adverse possession** of a coterminous landowner's property [in Alabama]; and (2) Wagnon was not entitled to **tack** her father's **adverse possession** of the gore because the deed by which her father conveyed tract 9 to her did not purport to convey the gore to her. Wagnon concedes that she did not hold title to tract 9 for 10 years before plaintiffs filed this action; however, she argues that she is entitled to **tack** her father's **adverse possession** of the gore despite the fact that her deed does not purport to convey the gore to her. We agree.

In *Watson v. Price*, 356 So.2d 625 (Ala. 1978), the Alabama Supreme Court stated:

> For the purpose of effecting title by **adverse possession,** where all the traditional elements are present, **tacking** of periods of possession by successive possessors is permitted against the coterminous owner seeking to defeat such title, unless there is a finding, supported by the evidence, that the claimant's predecessor in title did not intend to convey the disputed strip. We hold that this rule should apply even though the conveying instrument contains no legal description of the property in question, and irrespective of the period for which the property was possessed by the present claimant's predecessor in title.

In the case at bar, Wagnon introduced clear and convincing evidence establishing that her father exercised possession of the gore under a claim of right for more than 10 years; that his possession of the gore was actual, exclusive, open, notorious, and hostile; and that, in addition to conveying tract 9 to Wagnon, he delivered possession of the gore to her. Under *Watson,* that evidence established a rebuttable presumption that Wagnon was entitled to tack the period her father adversely possessed the gore despite the absence from her deed of language purporting to convey the gore to her. [Plaintiffs] did not introduce any evidence to rebut that presumption. Therefore, the trial court did not err in finding that Wagnon had adversely possessed the gore.

Although plaintiffs argue that Wagnon's father did not adversely possess the gore because he did not erect a fence or post signs to mark where the possession line deviated from the survey line, they cite no legal authority for the proposition that the erection of a fence or the posting of signs was a sine qua non of adverse possession by Wagnon's father. AFFIRMED.

REGULATION OF REAL PROPERTY OWNERSHIP, USE, AND SALE

Eminent Domain

The power of the government to take private property for public purposes (such as a highway) is referred to as the power of *eminent domain*. The federal government derives the power of eminent domain from the Fifth Amendment to the U.S. Constitution. Individual states draw the power from their own constitutions. In addition, states have delegated the power of eminent domain to local governments (such as countries, cities, and school districts) and to railroads and public utilities.

The power can be exercised without the owner's consent, but the government must pay *just compensation* (i.e., the fair value of the property) to the owner. In many cases, a governmental body seeking to acquire property for a public purpose will negotiate a purchase from the owner. If the owner does not consent, or if there is disagreement as to the fair value of the property, the government exercises the power of eminent domain by instituting a court action called *condemnation*. In a condemnation proceeding, the court will set a fair value for the property based on the evidence of that valu/e.

In some situations, a property owner may claim that an activity by a government body has so deprived the owner of the use of the property that a "taking" of the property has actually occurred. The property owner can institute a legal action known as *inverse condemnation*, in which a court will determine whether there has been a taking of the property and, if so, the fair value to be paid to the owner. The mere fact that a governmental activity has diminished the use or value of property does not establish that there has been a "taking"; the evidence must demonstrate that the owner has been effectively deprived of any reasonable use of the land. For example, the taking off and landing of airplanes at a city-owned airport could constitute a taking of an adjoining property's land if the land was so close to the airport that the planes flew over it at extremely low altitudes.

Constitutional limitations on the government's eminent domain power were discussed in Chapter 5.

Land Use Control

Restrictive Covenants

A deed may contain significant restrictions on the use of the property. For example, it might provide that only a single-family dwelling can be built on the land. Such *restrictive covenants* are usually valid and can be enforced by surrounding landowners. It also is common for a real estate developer to place restrictive covenants on all the residential lots in a subdivision and to specify those restrictions in the recorded plat. These restrictions, such as those relating to the type and appearance of structures that can be built on the lots, are intended to preserve property values, and can also be enforced by surrounding landowners in the subdivision.

Zoning

Pursuant to their constitutional police power, all states have passed legislation giving cities the power to enact zoning ordinances. In some states, similar powers have been given to counties. A *zoning ordinance* is essentially a law specifying the permissible uses of land in designated areas. Such an ordinance might specify zones for single-family dwellings, several categories of multiple-family dwellings, office buildings, various classifications or commercial structures, industrial facilities, and so on. Moreover, a zoning ordinance may impose even more detailed restrictions on use, such as minimum distances of structures from streets, lot sizes, and minimum parking accommodations for commercial buildings. The purposes of zoning laws are to permit the orderly planning of growth, protect against deterioration of surrounding property values from obnoxious uses, maintain the residential character of neighborhoods, and further other public purposes such as the prevention of overcrowding.

To prevent zoning from constituting a "taking" of property, zoning ordinances usually permit the continuance of a preexisting use even though it does not conform to the zoning restrictions for that area. In addition, a landowner may obtain a *variance*—permission from the city to make a use of the property that does not conform to the zoning ordinance— if they prove the following: (1) the zoning ordinance makes it impossible for the owner to receive a reasonable return on his or her investment in the land; (2) the negative effect of the zoning ordinance is unique to this owner's property and not an effect common to all landowners in the area; and (3) granting the variance will not substantially alter the basic character of the surrounding neighborhood.

The Implied Warranty of Habitability

Courts in most states have recognized an *implied warranty of habitability* in the sale of new residential housing. The warranty exists separately from, and in addition to, any express warranties made by the seller. The warranty of habitability does not apply to minor defects, but only to major defects that substantially interfere with the buyer's use of the property as a residence. Examples of defects that probably would be a breach of the warranty include a defective foundation, leaking roof, malfunctioning heating or cooling system, and unsafe electrical wiring. Breach of the warranty entitles the buyer to receive damages from the seller based on the cost of repairing defects that are reasonably correctable, or the amount by which the home's market value has been reduced in the case of non-correctable defects.

The implied warranty of habitability generally has been applied only to sales by a builder or other seller who is in the housing business. Real estate brokers and agents normally have not been held responsible under this warranty. Although some courts have extended the builder's liability under the implied warranty of habitability to the subsequent sale of used homes, a majority of courts have restricted it to the first sale of new homes. Most states have also imposed an implied warranty of habitability on landlords who *lease* residential properties.

CHAPTER 34

PERSONAL PROPERTY AND BAILMENTS

- Ownership of Personal Property

- Gifts of Personal Property

- Other Methods of Acquiring Ownership

- Bailments of Personal Property

- Special Bailments

OWNERSHIP OF PERSONAL PROPERTY

All property is classified as either real or personal property. In some ways, the legal framework for personal property ownership is similar to that for real property. For example, personal property can be subject to many of the same categories of concurrent ownership as real property, including tenancy in common and joint tenancy, as well as marital co-ownership categories such as tenancy by the entireties and community property. The rules for creating and regulating these types of co-ownership are essentially the same for personal property as for real property.

In addition, a creditor can acquire a voluntary security in an item of personal property that is similar to the interest created by a real property mortgage. The debtor retains title to the property, but the creditor with such a security interest owns an interest that serves as security until the debt is paid. The creation, protection, and enforcement of security interests in personal property are governed by Article 9 of the Uniform Commercial Code (covering "secured transactions"), but will not be discussed in this chapter.

In many ways, however, ownership of personal property is legally quite different than ownership of real property. Ownership of personal property is usually a simpler matter, primarily because the law does not formally recognize the numerous types of interests that it does for real property. Ordinarily, a person either is the owner of an item of personal property or is not. There sometimes can be a difficult question regarding *who* is the owner of an item of personal property, but once that question is resolved ownership usually is an all-or-nothing proposition. One example of this fact is found in the use of leases. A lease of real property actually creates another type of ownership interest. A lease of personal property, however, merely creates a *bailment*; the lessee has temporary possession but no ownership interest in the item of personal property.

This chapter deals with several basic topics concerning the ownership, possession, and use of personal property. It first discusses gifts of personal property, and then examines several other methods by which ownership of personal property can change. The chapter then provides a detailed discussion of bailments, an important form of personal property transaction in which possession, but not ownership, is transferred. It should be pointed out that several other topics related to personal property are sufficiently specialized and complex that they are dealt with in separate chapters. The subject of *sales of goods*, for instance, is explored in Chapters 19 and 20. And transfers of both real and personal property by will are discussed in Chapter 35 on wills and trusts.

GIFTS OF PERSONAL PROPERTY

A gift occurs when an owner of property (the *donor*) voluntarily transfers ownership of the property to another (the *donee*) without receiving any consideration in return. In order for the donor to accomplish a transfer of ownership by gift, two fundamental requirements must be met: (1) the donor must have a *present intent* to transfer ownership, and (2) the donor must *deliver possession* to the donee.

Present Intent to Transfer Ownership

The language and conduct of the donor, considered in the light of all the surrounding circumstances, must indicate a *present intent* to transfer ownership, similar in concept to that in a real property deed. The idea is captured by the phrase "I hereby give." A promise or expression of intent to transfer ownership in the future is not sufficient. A promise to make a gift is not the same thing as an actual gift. By its very nature, such a promise is not made in return for consideration, as required by contract law. Accordingly, it usually confers no rights on the promisee and cannot be enforced.

It also is critical that the expression of present intent relate to *ownership*. If the evidence indicates that the current owner merely intends to transfer present custody or the right to use the property, there is no gift.

Delivery of Possession

The donor also must actually carry out the expression of intent by delivering possession of the property to the donee. Once there has been an expression of present intent to transfer ownership coupled with actual delivery, the absence of consideration from the donee becomes irrelevant. Title to the property has passed. Many of the disputes involving gifts of personal property have centered on the question of whether there was delivery of possession to the donee. The most common problems relating to the question of delivery are outlined below.

Retention of Control

If the donor attempts to retain a degree of control over the property, there usually is not a legally effective gift. There must be a "complete stripping of the donor of dominion or control over the thing given." To illustrate: X indicates he wants to give a diamond ring to Y. If X then places the ring in a safe-deposit box to which both X and Y have access, there is not a sufficient delivery. In *Lee v. Lee*, 5 F.2d 767 (D.C. Cir. 1925), the widow of a grandson of General Robert E. Lee prepared a written document stating that she was giving to her two sons a trunk containing several items which had belonged to the general. She deposited the trunk with a storage company, with instructions to the company obligating it to deliver the trunk to either her or her sons. In holding that there had not been an adequate delivery, the court said, "[T]here was not that quality of completeness present in the transaction which distinguishes a mere intention to give from the completed act, and where this element is lacking the gift fails."

Delivery to an Agent

If delivery of the property is made to the donor's *own agent*, with instructions to deliver to the donee, there is not a completed gift until the donee actually receives the gift. The reason, again, is that the donor does not part with sufficient control until the donee takes possession. If the donor delivers possession to the *donee's* agent, however, a valid gift has been made.

Property Already in Possession of the Donee

If the donee already possesses the property when the donor indicates an intent to presently make a gift, the gift is immediately effective. There is no need to make a formal delivery in this situation.

Constructive Delivery

In most cases, delivery of actual physical possession is required. However, in two types of situations, *constructive delivery* (or *symbolic delivery*) will suffice:

Impracticality. If it is impractical or inconvenient to deliver actual physical possession because the item is too large or because it is located at too great a distance from the parties, constructive delivery is allowed. In such cases it ordinarily takes the form of a delivery of something that gives the donee control over the property. For example, if the item being given is a car, delivery to the donee of the car's key is sufficient.

Intangibles. Constructive delivery is permissible for a gift of *intangible* personal property, for the obvious reason that there is nothing physical to deliver. Some types of intangible property rights are evidenced by written documents that either by law or business custom are accepted as representing the intangible right itself. Examples are bonds, promissory notes, corporate stock certificates, and insurance policies. For these types of property rights, delivery of the written instrument evidencing the right is treated as delivery of the right itself. If the property right is an ordinary contract right not represented by any commercially recognized document, most courts allow constructive delivery of it by delivery of a writing setting forth the *present intent* to assign the right to the donee. In modern times, when the use of paper documents to represent ownership of these kinds of intangible property, delivery of something else that gives the donee access to and control over the item of property will be sufficient.

The following case illustrates how courts in modern times can be flexible and even creative in deciding whether there is sufficient evidence to show delivery of a gift of intangible property.

Algren v. Algren
916 N.E.2d 491 (Ohio App. 2009)

In 2005, Debora Algren filed for a divorce from her husband, Thomas W. Algren, in a domestic relations court. Mark, their adult son, told them that he would claim part ownership of potential marital property—the interest that Thomas owns in Dayton Capscrew Company. Mark claimed that over several years, Thomas gave him shares of Dayton Capscrew as gifts.

Dayton Capscrew is a family business. In the beginning, Thomas and Debora jointly owned Dayton Capscrew as a partnership. Thomas ran the day-to-day operations, and Debora fulfilled the role of bookkeeper. In 1990, Dayton Capscrew was incorporated as an Ohio corporation. The articles of incorporation authorized the company to issue 750 shares of common stock. It issued 400 such shares to Thomas, and he became the corporation's sole officer and shareholder.

Mark started working in the family business in 1989 as an outside sales representative. In 1998, however, Mark established Industrial Fastener Supply, L.L.C. Mark left Dayton Capscrew and began operating Industrial Fastener in early 2000. Mark's company sells products similar to those sold by Dayton Capscrew, so he became a competitor to his father's company. Mark said that he made the move because he believed that Thomas was not going to give him control of Dayton Capscrew as he had promised.

The interest that Thomas owns in the company is, at least in part, marital property, which is subject to division between Thomas and Debora. For this reason, in September 2006, Debora filed a complaint against Mark seeking a declaratory judgment on what interest, if any, Mark has in Dayton Capscrew. In his answer, Mark claimed to own 108 shares. In April 2007, Debora filed a motion for summary judgment, claiming that Mark has no ownership interest in Dayton Capscrew. Two months later, Mark filed his own motion for summary judgment that asked the court to find him the lawful owner of 136 shares of Dayton Capscrew. Mark further asked the court to find that the terms and provisions of a stock-sale agreement, signed by him, Thomas, and Dayton Capscrew, are valid and enforceable.

On September 14, 2007, the domestic relations court entered judgment on the declaratory judgment complaint. The court found that the existence and delivery of stock certificates are, as a matter of law, essential elements of Mark's claim. Because he could not produce this evidence, his ownership claim failed. Accordingly, the court sustained Debora's motion for summary judgment and overruled Mark's. The court also expressly resolved the complaint by declaring that Mark has no ownership interest in Dayton Capscrew. Mark appealed.

BROGAN, Judge:

The central dispute is over the ownership of 136 shares of Dayton Capscrew's stock. When recent ownership of personal property has been established, ownership is presumed to continue until divestiture is proved. No one disputes that immediately after incorporation, Thomas owned all 400 issued shares. No evidence suggests that Thomas transferred any of those shares to anyone other than Mark, and none of the 350 unissued shares were ever issued. Thus, if Mark owns any shares, he must have acquired them directly from Thomas. Mark contends that Thomas gave the shares to him as gifts. Debora contends that the gifts were uncompleted. She appears to concede that the evidence shows Thomas had donative intent, but she argues that he never carried out his intentions and delivered stock certificates to Mark. While the ultimate question is Mark's ownership interest, the strength of his claim to ownership depends in large part on his ability to prove that Thomas completed the gifts that he intended to make.

The trial court concluded that Mark owns no interest in Dayton Capscrew because Thomas made no gift to Mark of his shares because he never delivered stock certificates. The question that we must first address, then, is whether a transfer of certificates is necessary to make a gift of corporate stock.

A "gift" in the eyes of the law—one that effects a transfer of title—requires two things. (Technically, acceptance of the gift is also required, but acceptance of a thing of value is generally presumed.) First, there must be an intention on the part of the giver to part with his property, but there must be something more than an intention. The intention to give to be made effective must be carried out by the donor, relinquishing dominion over the property and delivering it to the donee.

The delivery requirement is fundamentally about relinquishing ownership and control. Delivery is important because it manifests a transfer of legal title. Perhaps the best evidence (the most specific and definite) of delivery is actual physical delivery of the thing given (e.g., handing over a book, given as a gift). While such evidence alone is not dispositive, it strongly suggests that a gift was made. Of course, not all things that one might wish to give are amenable to this sort of manual delivery.

For things whose nature precludes actual physical delivery, the requirement can be satisfied in constructive or symbolic form. Constructive delivery means delivery imputed by law, in other words, delivery in the eyes of the law, though not necessarily in fact. Symbolic delivery refers to delivery of some "thing" that symbolizes the property. So, for example, one can make a gift of land by giving a deed that names the recipient as grantee.

But one can also make the same gift without manual delivery of a deed. One who instead records a deed that names the recipient as grantee also satisfies the delivery requirement. The record takes the place of a manual delivery. Each situation features a different means of relinquishing ownership and control over the land, satisfying the delivery requirement. The key to delivery, and thus a completed gift, is for the one making the gift to do something that shows he gave up ownership and control in favor of the recipient.

A share of corporate stock is personal property that, like land, one cannot deliver in an actual and physical way. Unlike land, though, corporate shares are intangible. A share of stock merely represents or is a fractional part of some other property. The owner of a share of stock cannot hold it in her hand; rather, to own stock is to be entitled to a bundle of rights flowing from the corporation. ... Corporate shares are sometimes represented by paper certificates. It is important, however, not to confuse the intangible share—what is actually owned—with the tangible piece of paper, which merely represents the thing owned.

Because a certificate only represents a share, one does not need a certificate in hand to prove ownership. As the Ohio Supreme Court recognized early on, "It is a well-settled principle, so far as Ohio jurisprudence is concerned, that the shares of stock are property, but that the certificates are only the evidence of the ownership of those shares, and that they amount to no more than the title deeds of real estate. The certificates are a great convenience, and of great value as evidence, but they are certainly no more than evidence." *Cassidy v. Ellerhorst*, 144 N.E. 252 (Ohio 1924). Possession of certificates generally creates only a presumption that the holder is the owner of the represented shares. The accepted rule in Ohio then is that share certificates are not essential to ownership. (Rarely, however, stock certificates are held in "bearer" form, which means that physical possession of the certificate does bestow rights. But most certificates are in "registered" form. This means that the paper certificate is simply evidence of title, and the list of actual owners is maintained elsewhere.)

Thus it appears that the trial court misunderstood the law that it applied to the evidence. The existence and transfer of certificates may be the clearest evidence—the best evidence—of a completed gift of corporate stock, but such evidence is not required as a matter of law. Rather, what is required for a completed gift is clear and convincing evidence that the one who intended to make a gift of corporate stock in fact relinquished ownership and control.

Neither Debora nor Mark proved that they are entitled to summary judgment, because there is a genuine issue of fact regarding the number of shares that Thomas gave to Mark as gifts. Upon reviewing the evidence, we think that reasonable minds can find that the number of shares was more than zero but less [sic, should be "fewer"] than 136.

First, Thomas filed federal gift tax returns indicating that he made gifts of shares to Mark. One return, for calendar year 1994, tells the Internal Revenue Service ("IRS") that on June 1, 1994, Thomas, with Debora consenting, made a gift to Mark of 40 shares of Dayton Capscrew stock. This return was prepared and signed by John E. Cashdollar, C.P.A., and is dated March 31, 1995. A second return, also for calendar year 1994, tells the IRS that on June 1, 1994, Thomas, with Debora's consent, made a gift to Mark of 30 shares. The return was also prepared by Cashdollar, but remains unsigned and undated. A third return, for calendar year 1997, states that on December 29, 1997, Thomas, again with Debora consenting, made another gift to Mark of 28 shares of stock. This return too was prepared and signed by Cashdollar and is dated March 30, 1998. The return also states that gift tax returns had been filed for tax years 1994, 1995, and 1996. Further, there is a letter to Thomas from the IRS regarding this return—evidence that the return was actually filed. With these returns, Thomas essentially told the IRS, under penalty of perjury, that he in fact made gifts of corporate stock to Mark.

Second, there are several corporate documents that support Mark's ownership claim. In May 1994, Thomas, Mark, and Dayton Capscrew (represented by Thomas) signed a Corporate Restricted Stock Sale Agreement. Debora signed the agreement as a witness. The agreement begins with several recitals, the first of which reads, "Thomas W. Algren and Mark T. Algren are the sole shareholders of the corporation, owning respectively 360 and 40 shares."

Also, according to the minutes of Dayton Capscrew's fifth annual meeting of the board of directors, held in January 1994, the board agreed that "a transfer of forth [sic] shares, (40 shares) will be transferred [sic] to Mark T. Algren, and each year thereafter, as determined by the Board of Directors." And at the following year's meeting of the board of directors, the board agreed that "a transfer of thirty six shares, (36 shares) will be transferred, to Mark T. Algren, and each year thereafter, as determined by the Board of Directors." January 6, 1995 Minutes of the Sixth Annual Meeting of the Board of Directors. Moreover, Dayton Capscrew's corporate income tax returns indicate that Thomas relinquished ownership and control over part of his interest. The returns in the record show a decrease in the percentage of corporate stock owned by Thomas: from 1991 to 1993 Thomas owned 100 percent of the stock (400 shares); in 1995 his ownership decreased to 81 percent (324 shares); and from 1997–2004 Thomas owned 66 percent of the stock (264 shares). In 2005 his ownership inexplicably increased back to 100 percent.

Finally, in 1996, Thomas's attorney sent him a letter that reads, "Enclosed please find the new stock certificates for you and your son for 292 and 108 shares, respectively. It is my understanding that you will update the share ledger in your minute book." There is a copy of a Dayton Capscrew stock certificate in the record that presumably accompanied the letter. The certificate is in Thomas's name and is signed by him in his individual capacity and in his capacity as an officer of Dayton Capscrew. It contains the following:

> Certificate Number: 6 For 292 shares
> Number Original Certificate: 4 Number Original Shares: 324
> Number of Shares Transferred: 32
> Received Certificate No. 4 For 324.

This certificate, in particular, provides considerable support to Mark's claim of ownership. Based on this evidence, we think that reasonable minds can find that Thomas made a gift of at least some of the shares that Mark claims to own. Accordingly, because the evidence does not compel one to conclude either that Mark owns no shares or that he owns 136 shares, summary judgment is inappropriate. Thus, the trial court erred by sustaining Debora's motion for summary judgment.

The trial court's incorrect view of the law caused it to regard a single fact as dispositive. For this reason, the court did not weigh and consider carefully all the evidence that Mark presented before declaring him void of interest. We will remand to give the court the opportunity to do so.

Grounds for Invalidating Gifts

Of course, a gift will not be valid if the donor's action was induced by fraud, duress, mistake, or undue influence. In addition, the courts always examine very carefully any gift occurring between persons in a *fiduciary* relationship (a relationship of trust and confidence). Thus, if X owes a higher degree of trust to Y because of a fiduciary relationship, and X receives a gift from Y, the law places the burden upon X to prove that all was fair.

GORDON v. BIALYSTOKER CENTER & BIKUR CHOLIM, INC.
Court of Appeals of New York, 385 N.E.2d 285 (1978)

Ida Gorodetsky was 85 years old when she suffered a stroke and was admitted to Brookland-Cumberland Hospital in August 1972. Her closest relatives, two brothers and a niece, had not seen her for several years, and she had lived alone since 1962. From the time of her stroke until her death four months later, Ida remained partially paralyzed, confused, and sometimes semi-comatose.

At the suggestion of one of Ida's acquaintances, the Bialystoker nursing home sent one of its social workers to visit Gorodetsky in the hospital in October 1972. After learning that Ida had funds of her own, the director of the nursing home sent the social worker back to visit Ida on November 3 for the purpose of having her sign a withdrawal slip. A request had already been made for her admittance to the home, and the purpose of the withdrawal slip was to obtain funds for her care at the home. Using her withdrawal slip, the home obtained a $15,000 check from Ida's account payable to the home "for the benefit of Ida Gorodetsky."

On November 13, Ida was moved to the infirmary of the nursing home. That same day, within an hour and a half of admission, she was visited by a group consisting of the home's executive director, its fund raiser, one of its social worker, and a notary public. She was presented with several instruments on each of which she places her mark. These instruments included an application for admission to the home, an admission agreement, a withdrawal slip for the $12,864.46 remaining in her bank account, an assignment of that amount to the home, and a letter making a donation to the home of any part of the $27,864.46 remaining after paying expenses for her lifetime care.

Ida died on December 5 while still a resident of the nursing home. Her brother, Sam Gordon, administrator of her estate, filed suit against the nursing home to recover these funds, less the amount necessary to pay her expenses. The trial court ruled for the defendant nursing home on the ground that a valid gift had been made. The intermediate level appellate court reversed, ruling in favor of plaintiff administrator, and defendant appealed to New York's highest court.

Jones, Justice:

It is indisputable that on November 13, 1972, when the gift on which defendant predicates its claim to the funds in dispute was made, there existed between the donor and donee a fiduciary relationship arising from the nursing home's assumption of complete control, care and responsibility of and for its resident. As the executive director of that institution testified at some length, the residents of the nursing home are dependent on the home "to take care in effect of their very livelihood, their existence"; they "rely upon the people in the home to take care of them * * * They have no means of taking care of themselves", and ask and receive help from the staff of the home. According to the witness, "every one of [the residents'] particular needs * * * is administered to them by the help, the nurses or the doctors" of the home and in many instances -- as was the case with the decedent

-- "they have no other source of getting that kind of help and don't get any help other than from the institution". The acceptance of such responsibility with respect to the aged and infirm who, for substantial consideration availed themselves of the custodial care offered by the institution, resulted in the creation of a fiduciary relationship and the applicability of the law of constructive fraud. Under that doctrine, where a fiduciary relationship exists between parties,

> …transactions between them are scrutinized with extreme vigilance, and clear evidence is required that the transaction was understood, and that there was no fraud, mistake or undue influence. Where those relations exist there must be clear proof of the integrity and fairness of the transaction, or any instrument thus obtained will be set aside or held as invalid between the parties (*Ten Eyck v. Whitbeck*, 156 N.Y. 341).

So here, the Appellate Division properly concluded that defendant, rather than plaintiff (as the trial judge had held), bore the burden of proof on the issue whether Ida's gift of funds was freely, voluntarily and understandingly made. Examination of the record demonstrates without cavil the correctness of the Appellate Division's determination that that burden had not been met.

Both the Trial Justice and defendant focus on the absence of any fiduciary relationship between Ida and the nursing home on November 3, 1972 (the date on which she executed withdrawal slips for defendant's social worker while still a patient in Brooklyn-Cumberland Hospital) and from that fact have moved to the conclusion that the burden of proof had not shifted to the nursing home. To this there are two responses. What is overlooked is the circumstance that in legal contemplation the gift of funds was not effected at that time but was completed on November 13, after the donor had become a resident at the home, when the instrument of donation was executed. Defendant's executive director testified repeatedly that when she sent the social worker to see Ida in the hospital on November 3 to have a withdrawal slip executed it was "to get funds for the woman to stay at the home." That the nursing home itself regarded the gift as made on November 13 is evident from the letter which the director and others presented to Ida for execution when she was admitted to the home on that date, the first paragraph of which states, "I do hereby make a donation of the sum of $15,000 to the Bialystoker Center and Bikur Cholim, Inc., also known as Bialystoker Home and Infirmary for the Aged," and which recites the fact of her previously having executed a withdrawal slip for such sum for the issuance of a check to the home. It is therefore the relationship which existed on November 13, and not the absence of a relationship on November 3, which fixes the burden of proof in the present action.

The home was aware of the patient's mental and physical infirmities and weakness. Nothing to that point had remotely suggested that the patient might be disposed to make a gift to the home, or indeed that she even knew of its existence. The parties were brought together only in contemplation of the patient's transfer to the home; the transaction between them had no other meaning. That the patient was inescapably reposing confidence in the home from the moment of their first encounter was implicit in the circumstances.

We reject out of hand defendant's contention that, as a charitable organization, it should not be made subject to the same evidentiary burden that would be imposed on a profit-making institution. However worthy may be the objectives to which its funds are dedicated, no justification exists for relieving it of the obligation, when circumstances suggest a substantial risk of overreaching, of affirmatively demonstrating that assets it has acquired have come to it from a willing and informed donor, untainted by impermissible initiative on the part of the donee.

…The testimony offered, in conjunction with the other evidence in the case was insufficient as a matter of law to sustain the burden of proof resting on the nursing home. [Affirmed; defendant nursing home must return to Ida's estate all funds beyond what was necessary to pay her expenses.]

Special Treatment of Joint Bank Accounts

It is rather common for a bank account to be in the names of two persons, such as husband and wife. The phrase *joint account* is often used in a nontechnical sense to describe any bank account in the names of two people. These accounts are either a tenancy in common or a joint tenancy with survivorship rights, depending on the terms of the agreement with the bank.

In connection with the law of gifts, the requirement that the donor part with all control over the property is frequently an issue in cases involving a bank account jointly owned by the donor and the donee. For example, suppose that X deposits money belonging to him in a bank account that is in the name of X and Y. Both X and Y have the right to withdraw funds from the account. Obviously, there is a completed gift with X to Y of all money actually taken from the account by Y. But because of the retention of control by X, money that is not withdrawn from the account by Y is not considered a gift.

Suppose, however, that the agreement between X and the bank provides that on the death of X or Y, the funds remaining in the account will go to the *survivor* (that is, a "joint tenancy with a right of survivorship" is created). If X dies first, the question will arise whether a valid gift of the remaining funds has been made by X to Y. A few courts have held that in such a situation there is not a sufficient relinquishment of control by X to create a gift. However, they also have usually held that Y is nevertheless entitled to the money as a *third party beneficiary* of an enforceable contract between X and the bank. On the other hand, a majority of courts have simply relaxed the delivery requirement in this type of case and have held that there is a valid gift to Y despite the retention of some control by X.

Of course, as is true of any other gift, X must have *intended* to make a gift to Y. In the case of a joint tenancy bank account (one with a right of survivorship), there is a *presumption* of intent on the part of X to make a gift to Y, and this presumption can be rebutted only by evidence clearly showing that X did *not* intend to make a gift. For instance, the evidence might show that the joint account was established solely to give Y access to X's funds so as to enable Y to help X handle his financial affairs.

Gifts *Inter Vivos* and *Causa Mortis*

Gifts are classified as either *inter vivos* or *causa mortis*. A *gift inter vivos* is simply an ordinary gift between two living persons. A *gift causa mortis* is also between living persons, but it is made by the donor in contemplation of his or her death from some existing affliction or impending peril.

Although a gift *cause mortis* resembles a *will*, because both involve gifts in contemplation of death, it is important to emphasize their differences. A will must meet several formal statutory requirements such as written documentation, a signed attestation before a notary, and a specified number of witnesses. A gift *causa mortis*, on the other hand, must meet only the requirements as a regular gift: intent and delivery. Execution of a formal will is the only way to make a gift conditional on the donor's death without an immediate transfer of possession.

Two special rules apply to the gift *cause mortis*, distinguishing it slightly from a regular gift: (1) the gift is revoked automatically if the donee dies before the donor, with the result that ownership reverts back to the donor; and (2) the gift is also revoked automatically if the donor does not die from the current illness or peril.

OTHER METHODS OF ACQUIRING OWNERSHIP

Ownership of Wild Game

As a general rule, the law views wild animals, fish, and birds as being *unowned* property. The first person who takes possession with an intent to become an owner usually acquires legal ownership. The technical name for such acquisition is *occupation*. The one taking possession does not become the owner, however, if that person is a *trespasser* or is acting in violation of state or federal fish and game laws. A trespasser is one who is on land without the express or implied consent of the owner or tenant who has legal control of the land. Wild game taken by a trespasser belongs to the owner or the tenant of the land. In addition, no title is acquired to wild game taken in violation of state or federal laws.

Abandoned, Lost, and Mislaid Property

The common law made a distinction between abandoned, lost, and mislaid property. An item was deemed to be *abandoned property* if found under circumstances indicating either that it was left by someone who did not want it any more, or was left so long ago that the former owner almost certainly was no longer living. The nature of the property, its location, and other relevant factors can be taken into account in determining whether the property should be classified as abandoned. The common law characterized an item as *lost property* if it was discovered under circumstances indicating that it was *not* placed there voluntarily by the owner (such as a purse, billfold, or ring found on a street or sidewalk or on the floor of a hotel or theater lobby). *Mislaid property*, on the other hand, was property discovered under circumstances indicating that it was placed there voluntarily by the owner and then forgotten (such as a suitcase under the seat of an airplane or bus or a purse on a table in a restaurant).

The common law treated abandoned property in the same manner as wild game, the first person taking possession becoming the owner. If the acquirer was a trespasser on the land where the game was taken, however, the landowner or tenant became the owner. The finding of lost or mislaid property, on the other hand, did not change ownership of the item. Either the finder or the landowner (or tenant, if leased) acquired only a right to possession that was superior to the rights of everyone but the true owner. The finder or landowner taking possession was required to take reasonable steps to preserve the property and locate its owner. If the owner appeared to claim the property, they were obligated to pay the reasonable costs of storing and preserving it, but was not legally required to pay a reward. All of this assumes, of course, that the identity of the true owner was unknown. If the true owner's identity was known, the finder or landowner voluntarily taking possession had an absolute duty to deliver the property to its owner and was guilty of a crime for not doing so.

The distinction between lost and mislaid property was used to determine who was entitled to possession in the situation where the item was found by someone who did not own or control the premises. The owner or tenant of the land was entitled to possession if the item was characterized as mislaid property, because of the possibility that the true owner might remember where it was left and return to reclaim it. In the case of lost property, however, the finder was entitled to possession unless they were a trespasser, in which case the landowner or tenant had the possessory right.

Finding Statutes

In modern times, almost all jurisdictions have enacted legislation regulating the possession and ownership of found property. These laws are referred to as *finding statutes* (or *estray statutes*), and vary substantially from state to state. Several of these statutes, as interpreted by the courts, have retained the common-law distinctions between abandoned, lost, and mislaid property. Some of them apply only to lost property, not to mislaid or abandoned property. However, courts in some of these states have applied a strong presumption that found property is lost and therefore subject to the statute. In other states, the finding statutes have completely preempted the common-law rules and apply to any found property regardless of its characterization as abandoned, mislaid, or lost.

State finding statutes typically require that the finder of an item of personal property turn it over to a designated governmental authority within a certain period of time, such as ten days. Some statutes designate a local authority for receipt and custody of the item, such as the city police, county sheriff, or county clerk. Others designate a state authority such as the state police. Depending on the provisions of the statute, either the finder or the custodial authority must then take specified steps to locate the true owner, such as by publishing newspaper notices a certain number of times during a particular time period. If the prior owner does not appear and establish ownership within a stated period of time, such as one year, most statutes provide that the finder acquires ownership (not just possession) of the property. A finder who does not comply with the finding statute in a particular state does not acquire ownership or a right to possession, and usually is guilty of a crime. Finding statutes normally place obligations and give rights to the *finder*, regardless of who owns or controls the land where the property is found. Some of these statutes, however, have been interpreted as incorporating the common-law rule that a finder who is a willful trespasser acquires no rights in found property; in such a case, the owner or tenant of the land where the item was found acquires the rights granted by the statute.

STATE OF TEXAS v. $281,420.00
312 S.W.3d 547 (Tex. 2010)

Mercado asked Huerta, owner of Greg's Towing, to tow a disabled Freightliner truck-tractor from Alvin, TX to Mercedes, TX for approximately $2,800. Huerta agreed. Law enforcement officers seized the truck while it was being towed. Huerta gave them permission to search the truck and, indeed, helped them. They discovered a large amount of cash ($281,420) hidden in an axle. Neither the person who hired Huerta to tow the truck (Mercado) nor the owner of the truck (Pulido) made any claim regarding the money.

The Hidalgo County District Attorney's Office filed separate forfeiture proceedings against the truck and the currency pursuant to Chapter 59 of the Code of Criminal Procedure. Mercado and Pulido were served with citation, but neither answered nor appeared in the suit. Huerta then filed a petition, seeking to intervene as the last person in possession of the currency at the time it was seized. According to Huerta, the currency was not contraband, Mercado and Pulido had abandoned any claims they held to the currency by failing to answer or appear, and Huerta's interest in the currency was superior to that of the State.

The jury found that the currency was not contraband, that Huerta was in actual or joint possession of the currency at the time of seizure, and that Huerta should be awarded $70,000 (roughly 25%) of the currency found in the hub housing. The trial judge set the verdict aside and ordered forfeiture of all the money to Hildalgo County. The court of appeals held that the state had not established that the money was contraband and that Huerta was entitled to the entire amount. The State appealed.

O'Neill, Justice:

Huerta asserts two theories to support his claim. First, he argues that he is entitled to the currency as a bailee because the property was abandoned while in his possession. Alternatively, he argues that he is entitled to possession as the finder of the currency.

Abandonment.

One who seeks to acquire abandoned property must take possession of the property with an intent to acquire title. Huerta contends he had possession of the currency before it was seized by law enforcement officers because he was the first to remove it from the axle and the first to discover that the bundles contained currency. We disagree. Huerta removed the hub housing while assisting law enforcement and customs officials. By the time the currency was discovered, Huerta had already turned the vehicle over to law enforcement, and it had been subjected to a roadside search, an x-ray, and a sniff search by dogs. The fact that Huerta was the first to remove the currency bundles from the axle does not establish that he was in legal possession of them. Moreover, Huerta never expressed an intent to acquire title to the currency; when Huerta inquired further about the money after it had been seized, he merely sought a reward for finding it, not the return of money that had been abandoned while in his possession. Huerta's theory of legal entitlement based upon simple abandonment is unavailing.

Mislaid/Lost Property. Huerta also claims a right to possession of the currency under a common law "treasure trove" or "finders keepers" doctrine. The treasure-trove doctrine applies to "[v]aluables found hidden in the ground or other private place, the owner of which is unknown." BLACK'S LAW DICTIONARY 1539 (8th ed. 2004); *see also Schley v. Couch*, 284 S.W.2d 333 (Tex. 1953) (stating that such valuables generally consist of "money or coin, gold, silver, plate, or bullion"). However, we have previously declined to recognize the treasure-trove doctrine as part of Texas law. *Schley.* Instead, we apply the common law distinctions of "lost" and "mislaid" property. Accordingly, we examine Huerta's claim to the currency as either lost or mislaid property.

Mislaid property includes "property which the owner intentionally places where he can again resort to it, and then forgets." *Id.* It is presumed that the owner or occupier of the premises on which the mislaid property is found has custody of the property. The owner or occupier's possession of the property is superior to all except the true owner. For example, in *Martin v. Johnson*, money that was found under a rug in a garage was found to be mislaid property. 365 S.W.2d 429. As the owner of the premises on which the money was found, Johnson was determined to have a right to its possession as against an individual who claimed he had found the money, and as against the former occupants of the home. In this case, by contrast, it is undisputed that Huerta did not own the "premises"--the Freightliner--

on which the currency was found. Accordingly, Huerta cannot establish possession to the currency by characterizing it as mislaid property.

Neither can Huerta establish a right to possess the currency as lost property. In contrast to mislaid property, "lost" property includes "that which the owner has involuntarily parted with through neglect, carelessness or inadvertence." *Schley*. Unlike mislaid property, the owner or occupier of the premises on which lost property is found does not acquire title to the property. Instead, the finder of lost property retains possession as against the owner of the premises on which the property is found, but not against the lost property's true owner. In *Schley*, we held that money that had been placed in a jar and then buried was not lost property. The circumstances surrounding the money in *Schley* "repell[ed] the idea that it ha[d] been lost." Where the owner does not part with property as a result of carelessness or neglect, but instead demonstrates "a deliberate, conscious and voluntary [desire] to hide his [property] in a place where he thought it was safe and secure, and with the intention of returning to claim it at some future date," it is mislaid property._ The property in this case-- $281,420 in various denominations found in tightly--wrapped bundles in the axle of a truck-- was clearly deliberately hidden. As in *Schley*, the manner in which the money was placed in the axle forecloses any argument that it was lost rather than mislaid.

Because Huerta failed to establish a valid legal claim to possession of the currency, we reverse the judgment of the court of appeals awarding the money to him, and remand the case to the trial court for further proceedings consistent with this opinion.

Escheat Statutes

All states also have enacted *escheat statutes*, which normally provide that intangible property such as money, corporate stock, or bonds is presumed abandoned if it has remained in the possession of a custodian, such as a bank or securities dealer, for a specified time period without any deposits, withdrawals, or other contact by the owner. The time period provided by these statutes is usually lengthy, seven years being a common term. After passage of this time period, a state governmental authority ordinarily is required to publish notices identifying the property; if the property still remains unclaimed for a shorter period, such as six months, the state becomes the owner. Escheat statutes generally apply also to unclaimed stolen property recovered by police, and to the unclaimed property of a person who dies without heirs or a will. Some escheat statutes include other abandoned property as well.

Accession

An *accession* is a change in or an addition to an item of personal property. If the change or addition occurs with the owner's knowledge or consent, there is no effect on ownership of the item or property, and the question of compensation to the one making the addition or change depends entirely on the express or implied contract between the parties.

If the change or addition occurs without the owner's knowledge or consent, however, then it is possible for ownership to be affected. The person causing the change or addition might have acted with knowledge that the action was wrongful (in bad faith), or with the honestly mistaken belief that they owned the item or otherwise had the right to make the change or addition (in good faith). Good faith accessions frequently occur when someone buys an item such as a boat or automobile, makes substantial changes or additions, and then finds out that the title to the purchased item was void because the seller had stolen it. The rules regarding accession are outlined below.

Change in Personal Property by Labor

If a change in an item of personal property is brought about entirely or almost entirely by a nonowner's *labor*, ownership passes to the person performing the labor only if (1) the *identity* of the property has been changed, or (2) the value of the property is *many times greater* than it was prior to the change. An example of a change in identity: A makes B's grapes into wine without B's consent. An example of a sufficiently great increase in value: A takes a piece of stone belonging to B and carves a statue from it without B's consent. There is a definite tendency on the part of courts to deal more harshly with someone who caused the accession while knowing that it was wrong. A greater magnitude of change is often required to pass title to such a party than to someone who acted in good faith.

Addition of Other Property

When one person permanently attaches something to another's personal property without the other's consent, ownership of the resulting product goes to the owner of the "principal" item. For example, if A puts a new engine in a car owned by B, the car and the new engine belong to B. On the other hand, if A puts an engine owned by B in A's car, the car and engine are owned by A.

Compensation to Owner

In either of these situations, where an item is changed by a nonowner's labor or where other property has been added to the item, the party who caused the accession (the improver) is responsible for any loss to the other party. Thus, if the circumstances are such that the improver acquired title to the item as a result of the accession, that person must compensate the original owner. If the improver acted in good faith, they are required to pay the original owner only for the value of the property in its original condition. But if the improver acted in bad faith, they are required to pay to the original owner the value of the property in its improved state.

Where the accession itself does not cause title to pass to the improver, but the original owner simply chooses not to reclaim the property, the situation is treated the same as if the accession *had* caused title to pass. Where the accession does not cause title to pass to the improver, and the original owner *reclaims* the improved property, the improver usually is not entitled to any compensation at all, regardless of whether they acted in good faith.

Confusion of Goods

A *confusion of goods* occurs where there has been an intermingling of the goods of different persons. It usually occurs in connection with fungible goods (i.e., each unit is identical), such as the same grade of grain, oil, or chemicals. It can, however, occur with nonfungible goods, such as cattle or quantities of packaged merchandise.

If the goods of A and B have been confused (1) by agreement between A and B, (2) by an honest mistake or accident, or (3) by the act of some third party, a tenancy in common is created. Here, A and B each owns an undivided interest in the mass according to the particular proportions they contributed to it.

Suppose, however, that A caused the confusion by deliberately wrongful or negligent conduct. In this case, if the goods of A and B are fungible, A can get his portion back if he proves with reasonable certainty how much that portion is. On the other hand, if the goods are not fungible, A must prove which specific items are his or else he gets nothing.

BAILMENTS OF PERSONAL PROPERTY

Examples of *bailments* include the taking of a dress to a dry cleaner, the lending of a car to a friend, and the delivering of goods to a railroad for shipment. A *bailment* can be defined as the delivery of possession of personal property from one person to another under an agreement by which the latter is obligated to return the property to the former or to deliver it to a third party. The person transferring possession is the *bailor* and the one receiving it is the *bailee*.

The common law provides most rules for bailment relationships. Certain kinds of bailments, however, are subject to statutory enactments. As we will see later in this chapter, Article 7 of the Uniform Commercial Code governs many aspects of the bailment relationships created when one ships goods by common carrier or stores goods with a warehouseman. Also discussed later is the fact that special state statutes regulate some of the obligations of innkeepers regarding the property of guests.

Article 2A of the Uniform Commercial Code covers *leases* of personal property, which are a form of bailment that occurs when one pays rent to the owner of an item such as a car, equipment, home appliances, etc., for the right to use the item for a designated time. Article 2A leaves most of the traditional common-law rules intact for this kind of bailment. Importantly, Article 2A applies the same basic warranty obligations to lessors in lease transactions that Article 2 applies to sellers in sales transactions. One example of a bailment is found in the *Gonzalez v. A-1 Self Storage* case on unconscionability in Chapter 14.

Elements of a Bailment

By definition, the creation of a bailment requires that (1) one party must deliver possession (but not title) to the other, (2) the property delivered must be classified as personal property, and (3) the parties must agree that the recipient of the property will later return it, deliver it to a third party, or otherwise dispose of it in some specified manner.

Delivery of Possession

The requirement that possession of the property be delivered normally means that (1) the property must be transferred to the bailee, (2) the bailee must acquire control over the item, and (3) the bailee must knowingly accept the property.

Although actual physical possession of the bailed property is almost always transferred to the bailee, it is possible for a bailment to be created by delivery of something that gives the bailee effective control over the item, such as the keys or certificate of title to a boat or car.

In addition to a transfer of the property, the circumstances must indicate that the recipient acquired control over it. For example, when a customer hangs his or her coat on a coat rack at a restaurant, and can get it back without notifying the restaurant's management or employees, there is no bailment because the restaurant did not acquire control over it. Similarly, if a waiter or other restaurant employee takes the coat and hangs it on a rack that is freely accessible to the customer, who may retrieve it without notice or assistance, there still is no bailment. On the other hand, if the coat is left with a coatroom attendant or other restaurant employee, who puts it in a place that is not accessible to the customer without assistance, a bailment has been created because the restaurant has control over the coat.

For the same reason, leaving a car at a parking lot or parking garage is generally held to constitute a bailment only if the car owner is required to leave the keys with an attendant. Otherwise, the parking lot company does not have sufficient control over the car. In a situation in which the car owner is permitted to lock the car and keep the keys, the transaction usually is not a bailment, but is merely a *license*—a contractual permission to use the parking space. The owner of the parking lot is a *licensor* and the car owner is a *licensee*. Sometimes this relationship is characterized as lessor-lessee rather than licensor-licensee. The owner of the car is viewed as leasing the parking space.

Although the bailor normally is the owner of the bailed property, this is not always the case. What is required is that the bailor have a "superior right of possession" with regard to the bailee. Thus, if Jose lends his lawn mower to Robert for the summer and Robert takes it to a repair shop in September before returning it to Jose, a bailment exists between Robert and the repair shop while the mower is being repaired.

As we have seen, a physical delivery of property by one person to another does not create a bailment unless the recipient knowingly accepts the property. For example, suppose that Joan has several packages of merchandise in the trunk of her car when she leaves it at a parking lot under circumstances in which a bailment exists as to the car. There is no bailment of the packages unless Joan notifies the parking lot attendant of their presence.

MEAUX v. SISTERS OF CHARITY OF THE INCARNATE WORD
Texas Court of Appeals, 122 S.W.3d 428 (2003)

Plaintiff/Appellee Meaux's Rolex watch, money clip and $400 in cash was stolen after the locker he was using at defendant/appellant's "Wellness Center" was pried open on January 19, 2000. Appellant furnished a lock and key for use on the locker and retained a master key for use if appellee lost the key loaned to him or if appellee inadvertently left the premises with the key and the locker locked. The appellant's rules provided, "All personal belongings should be stored in your locker. The Health & Wellness Center is not responsible for lost or stolen items. . . . The Wellness Center cannot assure the safety of your valuables and we suggest that you do not bring items of high personal or monetary value to the center." Appellee did not give appellant notice he was storing his Rolex watch and $400 cash, and admitted he knew and relied on the rules of the "Wellness Center" before he stored such property. Appellee also admitted appellant did not guarantee that appellee's property would not be stolen and that he had read and relied on the Center's rule that it was not responsible for lost or stolen items of members or guests. A sign stating "We cannot assure the safety of your valuables" was posted at the Center's sign-in desk. Appellant sued, alleging causes of action for negligence and breach of a bailment contract and warranty.

A jury found appellant was not negligent, but that appellant failed to comply with a bailment agreement and a warranty, and awarded $19,500 damages to appellee for the loss of his property. Appellant appealed.

Amidei, Judge:

This case decides the question of whether the loss of valuables by theft from a locker being used by a member or guest of a gym, health club, wellness center, swimming pool, or similar facility creates a bailment, a landlord-tenant relationship and/or a warranty, express or implied.

Appellant argues there was no evidence to prove the essential bailment elements of knowledge and delivery, [citing] several cases decided by out-of-state courts where the controlling issue was whether a bailment or a lease is created between the user of a locker or storage area and the owner of the premises, and claims a lease relationship, not a bailor/bailee relationship, existed between appellant and appellee.

The basic elements of a bailment are: (1) the delivery of personal property by one person to another in trust for a specific purpose; (2) acceptance of such delivery; (3) an express or implied contract that the trust will be carried out; and (4) an understanding under the terms of the contract that the property will be returned to the transferor or dealt with as the transferor directs. A bailee has the duty to exercise ordinary care over the goods and is therefore "responsible" for the bailor's goods. In contrast, a lease is "a transfer of interest in and possession of property for a prescribed period of time in exchange for an agreed consideration called 'rent'." *Marine Indem. Ins. Co. v. Lockwood Warehouse & Storage*, 115 F.3d 282 (5th Cir. 1997). The lessor has the duty of ordinary care in maintaining the premises it controls, but does not have a duty to exercise care regarding the lessee's property stored on the premises. The lessor is therefore not "responsible" for the property of the lessee.

As between the owner of premises and the owner of personal property left in a locker on the premises when exclusive possession thereof has not been delivered and control and dominion of the property is dependent in no degree upon the co-operation of the owner of the premises, a landlord and tenant relationship is created, not a bailment. *See Marsh v. American Locker Co.*, 72 A.2d 343 (N.J.Super. 1950) (held that the deposit of a package in a locker in a railroad station did not create a common law bailment upon which an action could be based without any affirmative showing of negligence or other proof of contractual relationship between the parties).

In *Theobald v. Satterthwaite*, 190 P.2d 714 (Wash. 1948), a beauty shop customer left her expensive fur coat on a hook in the defendant's reception room from where it was stolen. The court held there was no bailment because of defendant's lack of knowledge of the plaintiff's fur coat, and "there was no change of possession or delivery" of the property and the defendant had "not knowingly received the exclusive possession and dominion over it" and was "unaware that a valuable fur coat had been left in the reception room."

There was no evidence of delivery and acceptance of appellee's property by appellant. Appellant had no knowledge of what appellee placed in the locker but had the right to expect no belongings of a high monetary value would be placed in the locker contrary to its rules, and that it would not be liable for the loss of appellee's property by theft. We conclude there was no bailment agreement between appellant and appellee, and the use of the locker by appellee created a landlord-tenant relationship between the parties. The parties' respective responsibilities and liability are governed by the rules of the Wellness Center and there is no presumption of negligence as ordinarily used in bailment cases. The appellant had no knowledge, and no semblance of custody, possession or control, and where there is no such delivery and relinquishment of exclusive possession, and its control and dominion over the appellee's property is dependent in no degree upon the co-operation of appellant, and its access thereto is in no wise subject to its control, the appellee is a tenant or lessee of the locker upon the premises where appellee's property was left. There was no evidence from which an informal, constructive or implied bailment could have been established or inferred. Reversed.

Personal Property

By definition, bailments involve only transfers of personal property. Although owners of real property frequently transfer possession of it to others for limited periods of time, such transactions are not bailments. Most bailments involve items of tangible personal property, such as automobiles or jewelry. It is possible, however, for intangible personal property to be the subject of a bailment. This occurs, for example, when a stock certificate representing ownership of corporate stock is delivered by a debtor to a creditor as security for the debt.

The Agreement to Return

A bailment necessarily involves an agreement that the property ultimately is to be returned by the bailee to the bailor or delivered to a designated third party. The bailment contract can be either express or implied, and in most cases is not legally required to be in writing. Obviously, however, it is advisable to have the bailment contract in writing if the value of the bailed property is substantial and particularly if a commercial bailor or bailee is involved. Most commercial bailors, such as car rental agencies, and commercial bailees, such as a company that is in the business of storing the property of others, customarily use detailed written contracts.

As a general rule, the bailee is required to return or deliver the *identical* goods at the end of the bailment. Thus, if a Buick dealer delivers a car to Joyce under a contract providing that in return she will deliver her used motor home to the dealer within a month, the transaction is a sale rather than a bailment. The arrangement also would be a sale if the contract gives Joyce the option of returning the car or delivering the motor home in a month.

The rule requiring delivery of the identical property is subject to two well-established exceptions, which are outlined below.

Fungible Goods. If the subject of the transaction is *fungible goods*, each unit of which is interchangeable, with the contract obligating the recipient merely to later redeliver the same quantity of goods of the same description to the owner or to a third party, the transaction is still a bailment. This rule is especially important in grain storage situations, with the result that grain elevators taking in grain for storage are bailees even though the grain they later return to their customers or deliver to third parties is probably not the same grain they originally received from those customers.

Options to Purchase. The second exception arises in a situation where the one receiving possession of the property has a specified period of time within which to decide whether to purchase or return it. This type of transaction, sometimes called a *bailment with the option to purchase*, is a bailment despite the fact that the bailee has the choice of turning it into a sale by giving the bailor the agreed price rather than returning the property itself. Bailments of this type can take several forms, including a *lease with the option to purchase*.

Constructive Bailments

There are a few cases in which the courts treat transactions as if they are bailments even though one of the usual requirements is missing. One example of such a *constructive bailment* is found in the use of a bank safe-deposit box. When a customer places property in a safe-deposit box, the bank does not acquire *exclusive* control because access to the box requires both the customer's and the bank's key. In addition, the bank usually does not have actual knowledge of the contents of the box. Despite these differences from a traditional bailment, a majority of courts treat the arrangement as a bailment and hold the bank to the responsibilities of a bailee. In a few states, however, legislation has been passed declaring the use of a safe-deposit box to be only a rental of the space—that is, a *license* rather than a bailment.

The courts also usually treat a finder of personal property as a bailee even though the owner did not deliver the item to the finder. The bailment continues until the finder surrenders possession to a governmental authority or becomes the owner of the property by complying with a state finding statute.

Types of Bailments

Bailments can be broadly classified as *ordinary bailments* and *special bailments*. As the name implies, ordinary bailments comprise the vast majority of bailment transactions. Special bailments are discussed briefly at the end of the chapter. Ordinary bailments may be further divided into 1) bailments for the sole benefit of the bailee, (2) bailments for the sole benefit of the bailor, and (3) mutual benefit bailments.

Sole Benefit of the Bailee

A bailment for the sole benefit of the bailee exists when the owner of an item permits another to use it without compensation or any other benefit. Examples include the loan of a car to a friend or a lawn mower to a neighbor.

Sole Benefit of the Bailor

A bailment for the sole benefit of the bailor exists when a person stores or takes care of someone else's property as a favor, without receiving any compensation or other benefit. Such a bailment would arise, for example, where Ruth permits George to store his furniture in her garage while he is away for the summer, with no benefit at all to Ruth.

Mutual Benefit Bailments

Because people ordinarily do not enter into bailments unless they receive some sort of gain from the transaction, mutual benefit bailments are by far the most common kind. Most mutual benefit bailments involve a bailor or bailee who received direct compensation, as in the case of an equipment rental firm or a company that is in the business of storing the property of others.

It is possible, however, for the benefit to be an indirect one. Suppose, for example, that an employer prohibits its employees from keeping their coats or other personal belongings in the immediate working area, and maintains a separate coatroom or other area where such items are left under the control of an attendant. Even though no direct compensation is paid, there is a mutual benefit bailment. The employees benefit by having a secure place to keep their property during working hours. The employer, on the other hand, benefits in several ways, including having an uncluttered working area with fewer distractions for employees and less potential for theft among employees.

The example of the restaurant's providing a coatroom and taking control of customers' coats and hats, presented earlier in the discussion of bailments, also illustrates a mutual benefit bailment involving indirect compensation.

Rights of the Bailee

The bailee's rights in a bailment transaction depend almost entirely on the express or implied terms of the parties' contract. These rights normally involve *possession, use,* and *compensation.*

If the contract provides that the bailee is to have possession for a specified period of time and if the bailor is receiving consideration in return, the bailee ordinarily has the right to retain possession for the entire time. And if the bailor wrongfully retakes possession before the agreed time has expired, the bailee is entitled to damages for breach of contract. The bailee also can enforce this possessor right against a third party who wrongly interferes with it. Thus, if the bailed property is stolen, destroyed, or damaged by a third party, the bailee has the right to initiate legal action to recover the property or receive monetary damages from the third party.

Whether the bailee has the right to use the bailed property depends on the express terms of the contract or, if there are no such terms, on the general purposes of the bailment. If the contract is for *storage*, for example, the bailee usually has no right to use the property while it is in their possession. On the other hand, if the bailee is *renting* the property, they obviously have the right to use it in a normal manner.

Except for bailments in which the bailee is renting property for the purpose of using it, or in situations where there is a clear understanding that they are not to receive any payment, the bailee normally has the right to some form of compensation for the safekeeping of the property. In the case of a bailee who is in the business of storing the property of others, the compensation is almost always spelled out in the contract. Where the amount of the compensation is not expressly agreed upon, the bailee is entitled to the reasonable value of his or her services. If the purpose of the bailment is to have the bailee perform a service, such an automobile repairs, the amount of the compensation again depends on the express or implied terms of the contract.

Duties of the Bailee

Use and Return

If the bailee uses the property in a way that is beyond the consent granted in the agreement, such use constitutes a breach of contract and the bailee is liable for any damages resulting from the unauthorized use regardless of whether they committed negligence or any other tort. For instance, Vance, a resident of Dallas, borrows a pickup truck from his neighbor, Perez, to move some furniture from Topeka to Dallas. After Vance reaches Topeka and loads the furniture, he decides to go to Kansas City, about 45 miles farther, to visit his brother. If the truck is damaged in an accident while Vance is in Kansas City, he is fully liable to Perez for the damage even if the accident was not his fault in any respect.

A bailee who *intentionally* does not return the bailed property at the end of the bailment commits both a breach of contract and the intentional tort of conversion, and is liable to the bailor for the value of the property. The bailee in such a situation also probably commits the crime of theft. Some states have a statutory criminal offense called "theft by a bailee."

Due Care and the Presumption of Negligence

When the bailed property is damaged, lost, stolen, or destroyed because the bailee has failed to exercise reasonable care in handling the item, the bailee is guilty of the torts of negligence and conversion and is responsible to the bailor for the amount of the damage or loss.

A variety of circumstances are taken into account to determine whether the bailee exercised due care, including the value of the bailed property, the susceptibility of this particular type of bailed property to damage or theft, and the amount of experience the bailee has had in dealing with similar types of property in the past. Thus, a bailee is expected to exercise greater care in handling a $2,000 diamond ring than a $200 chair. A bailee also would be expected to exercise more care in handling a thoroughbred horse than a truckload of bricks.

Until recent years, most courts applied different degrees of care to the different categories of bailment. The bailee was required to exercise great care in a bailment for the sole benefit of the bailee, and only slight care in a bailment for the sole benefit of the bailor. In a mutual benefit bailment, the bailee was required to exercise reasonable care, which was defined as the amount of care a reasonable person would exercise in protecting his or her own property. Although the courts in some states still make this rigid distinction, many of them have abandoned it as a strict basis for determining the bailee's required degree of care. These courts apply the general standard of reasonable care to all types of bailments and simply treat the amount of benefit the bailee was receiving from the bailment as another one of the factors relevant to the question of whether they used such care. An example of this is found in *Gonzalez v. A-1 Self-Storage* in Chapter 14.

Unlike almost all other negligence cases, when a bailee fails to return the property in its former condition, there is a *presumption of negligence*. In other words, when the bailor proves that the property was not returned at all, or was returned in a damaged condition, the burden then shifts to the bailee to explain exactly what happened and to demonstrate how the loss occurred without negligence. This rule makes it very difficult for a bailee to avoid liability once it is established that a bailment existed and the property was damaged or not returned. Therefore, the question of whether a bailment existed frequently determines the outcome of such a case.

Exculpatory Clauses

Bailees frequently attempt to contractually excuse themselves from liability for harm to the bailed property. It is common, for example, for parking lots, automotive repair shops, or dry cleaners to post signs or give tickets or documents to bailors containing statements such as: "The owner assumes all risk for damage to or loss of the property, and the proprietor is not responsible for such damage or loss resulting from fire, theft, flood, or negligence." Statements of this nature are referred to as *exculpatory clauses*. These clauses were discussed in Chapter 13.

Exculpatory clauses usually are not effective to free the bailee from liability, for two reasons. First, courts normally hold that such provisions are *not legally communicated* to the bailor unless specifically called to the bailor's attention. Second, even if the exculpatory clause is legally communicated and thus becomes part of the bailment contract, courts often conclude that the clause *violates public policy* and is unenforceable on the grounds of illegality. This conclusion is almost always reached when the bailee is in the business of handling the property of others and the terms of the bailment contract are presented by the bailee to the bailor on a non-negotiated, "take it or leave it" basis. (In other words, the agreement is a *contract of adhesion*, a concept that was discussed at several points in the chapters on contracts.)

Rights of the Bailor

Essentially, the rights of the bailor arise from the duties of the bailee. Thus, the bailor's most important rights are to have the bailed property returned at the end of the bailment period, to have the bailee use due care in protecting the property, and to have the bailee use the property (if use is contemplated at all) in conformity with the express or implied terms of the bailment contract. Additionally, if the bailor is having work performed on the property by the bailee, the bailor is entitled to have it done in a workmanlike fashion. If the purpose of the bailment is use of the property by the bailee, the bailor has the right to compensation under the express or implied terms of the contract.

Duties of the Bailor

Liability for Defects in the Bailed Property

Obviously, the bailor has duties corresponding to the rights of the bailee discussed previously. In addition, the bailor has certain basic duties with respect to the condition of the bailed property.

Negligence. The bailor must not knowingly delivery property containing a hidden defect that is likely to cause injury. In either a mutual benefit bailment or one of the sole benefit of the bailee, the bailor is legally required to notify the bailee of any dangerous defect about which the bailor has *actual knowledge*. In a mutual benefit bailment, the bailor's duty regarding the condition of the bailed property is somewhat greater, and they can be held responsible for injury caused by hidden defects about which the bailor *either knew or should have known*. Thus, in a mutual benefit bailment, the bailor's duty includes reasonably inspecting the property and maintaining it in a safe condition before delivery to a bailee.

In either of these situations, a violation of the bailor's duty constitutes negligence, and the bailor is liable for resulting harm to the bailee and to others coming into contact with the defective property in a reasonably foreseeable manner. For example, a bailor's liability for delivering a defective automobile to the bailee would include injuries to the bailee and his or her immediate family, as well as to innocent third parties such as the driver of another automobile involved in an accident because of the defect.

Warranty and Strict Liability. In addition to imposing liability for the bailor's negligence, most courts in recent years have placed additional liability on commercial bailors. In the case of bailors who are in the business of renting property, such as automobiles, construction equipment, and so on, a majority of courts have held the bailor responsible for dangerous defects in the bailed property on the basis of the *implied warranty* and *strict products liability* theories. These courts have drawn an analogy from the liability imposed on merchants in *sales* transactions. The importance, as we saw in the chapter on products liability, is that the supplier of a defective item can be held liable without any proof that the supplier knew or should have known of the defect. Moreover, the supplier's defenses are much more limited under the warranty and strict liability theories.

As mentioned earlier, Article 2A of the UCC formally adopts the same basic warranty obligations for lessors of personal property as exist under Article 2 for sellers of personal property.

Bailor's Disclaimers

We saw previously that commercial *bailees* frequently attempt to limit their liability contractually. It also is very common for commercial *bailors* to make similar attempts. This type of provision, whether it is called an exculpatory clause, disclaimer, or liability limitation, is given essentially the same treatment by the courts as bailees' exculpatory clauses. In fact, in the majority of states that have drawn an analogy between the bailor who is in the business of renting personal property and the merchant who is in the business of selling goods, a disclaimer by the bailor is given even harsher treatment by the courts. Such a provision violates public policy and thus is not allowed to shield a commercial bailor from liability for negligence, breach of warranty, or strict liability when a defect in the bailed property causes personal injury or property damage to either the bailee or someone else whose contract with the item was reasonably foreseeable.

SPECIAL BAILMENTS

Special bailments are those involving common carriers, warehouse companies, and innkeepers. Although bailments involving these types of bailees have most of the characteristics of ordinary bailments and are subject to most of the same rules, they are singled out because of certain unique aspects.

Common Carriers

A *common carrier* is a company that is licensed by the state or federal government to provide transportation services to the general public. Most airlines, trucking companies, and railroad companies are common carriers. A company doing business as a common carrier must do business with the public on a nondiscriminatory basis. A common carrier can be contrasted with a *contract carrier*, which does not hold itself out as providing transportation services to the public and is not licensed to do so. A contract carrier provides service under contract to only a few selected customers.

Suppose that a furniture manufacturer in Pittsburgh, Pennsylvania, delivers a large quantity of furniture to a railroad company for shipment to a wholesale furniture distributor in St. Louis, Missouri. When the manufacturer (the *shipper*) turns over possession of the furniture to the railroad company (the *carrier*) a type of mutual benefit bailment has been created.

Bailments of this type are different from ordinary bailments in several important respects.

Obligation to Transport

Unlike most bailees, the carrier has a contractual obligation to transport the bailed property.

Bills of Lading

Also unlike other bailees, the carrier issues a *bill of lading* to the shipper. The bill of lading, the rules for which are set out in Article 7 of the Uniform Commercial Code, serves as both a *contract of bailment* and a *document of title*. In other words, it sets forth the terms of the agreement between shipper and carrier and also serves as evidence of title to the goods.

A bill of lading or other document of title can be either *negotiable* or *nonnegotiable*.

A bill of lading ordering the carrier to "deliver to X" is a nonnegotiable document of title. The carrier's obligation in such a case is to deliver the goods only to X, and the nonnegotiable document does not confer the right to receive the goods to anyone else who might come into possession of the document.

On the other hand, a bill of lading ordering the carrier to "deliver to the order of X," or to "deliver to bearer," is a negotiable document of title. Lawful possession of a negotiable document is tantamount to ownership of the goods, and the carrier is obligated to deliver them to anyone having such possession. In the case of a bill of lading ordering the carrier to "deliver to the order of X," the carrier is required to surrender the goods to Y if X has endorsed and delivered the document to Y and Y presents it to the carrier. In the case of a bill of lading ordering the carrier to "deliver to bearer," the carrier is required to surrender the goods to anyone to whom the document has been delivered, even without the presence of an endorsement.

Bills of lading, especially negotiable ones, are often used to facilitate sales transactions by providing the seller (shipper) a document that can be sent to the buyer and then used by the buyer to take possession of the goods when they reach their destination. This document may be sent directly from the seller to the buyer, or it may be sent through banking channels with the seller's and buyer's banks acting as agents for delivery of the document and receipt of payment.

Strict Liability

Contrary to ordinary bailments, the carrier is absolutely liable to the shipper for damage to or loss of the goods. In other words, usually the carrier's liability is not based upon negligence or other fault. There are, however, several narrow categories of circumstances in which the carrier is not liable. If the goods are damaged, stolen, lost, or destroyed during shipment, the carrier has the burden of proving that the situation falls within one of these categories. The categories are as follows.

Natural Disasters. The carrier is not liable if it can show that the loss was caused by an unexpected force of nature that was of such magnitude that damage to the goods could not have been prevented. The ancient term "act of god" is sometimes still used out of habit, and simply refers to an unforeseeable occurrence of nature. The term is interpreted very strictly; evidence that the goods were damaged or destroyed by a flood, for example, will not suffice to excuse the carrier unless the flood was of such an unforeseeable nature that no reasonable precautions could have forestalled the loss.

Act of a Public Enemy. This term is also interpreted very narrowly, and is usually applied only to a situation in which the goods were damaged, destroyed, or seized by a foreign nation at war with the United States.

Act of a Public Authority. The term public authority is much broader, and applies to actions by various local, state, or federal government officials. Examples would include the seizure of an illegal drug shipment by law enforcement officers, or the seizure of goods by a sheriff acting under a *writ of execution*. A writ of execution is a court order requiring an officer to seize property and sell it for the purpose of paying off a judgment against the owner.

Act of the Shipper. The carrier is not responsible if the shipper's own actions are shown to have caused the loss. For example, the carrier is not liable for the death of the shipper's chickens if the shipper's improperly ventilated crates caused those deaths.

The Inherent Nature of the Goods. The carrier is not liable if the loss is caused by an inherent characteristic of the goods themselves that the carrier had no control over. This category also is construed very strictly. For example, it would not be sufficient for the carrier to show that a shipment of fruit spoiled and that fruit is prone to spoilage. To escape liability, the carrier would have to prove that the fruit spoiled for a very specific reason, such as the fact that it was overripe at the time of shipment, and that the carrier could not have prevented the spoilage.

Liability Limitations

Despite the fact that carriers are liable for harm to the bailed property even without being at fault, they are permitted to limit their liability contractually to a greater extent than ordinary bailees. Under federal and state regulations, common carriers may obtain the shipper's agreement to place a dollar limit on the carrier's liability, and the limitation is valid if the shipper was given a choice of paying a higher transportation fee for a higher dollar limitation.

CHAPTER 35
WILLS, TRUSTS, AND ESTATE PLANNING

- Wills

- Intestacy—Statutes of Descent and Distribution

- Administration of the Estate

- Trusts

- Estate Planning

Although few people amass large fortunes in their lifetimes, most will not die penniless. Many people are surprised at the actual value of their holdings. Real estate acquired early in life may appreciate dramatically; life insurance, both individual and group, may be owned in substantial amounts, and investment in the stock market through mutual funds is commonplace. One's personal property, slowly acquired over a period of years, may constitute a sizable asset. Some knowledge of wills, trusts, and other estate planning devices is essential to make informed decisions about one's personal financial situation.

The case of Pablo Picasso is a good example of what can happen when a person with a substantial estate fails to provide for its orderly disposition. When the famous artist died in 1973, he left a tremendous fortune—millions of dollars in assets. To whom did he leave it? As a matter of fact, Picasso died *intestate*; that is, at the time of his death he had not prepared a document—a will—to provide specific and detailed instructions about what to do with his property. A properly planned, drafted, and executed will might have eliminated most of the bitter controversy that arose among those close to him over the disposition of his wealth.

Picasso apparently felt that making a will was an act in contemplation of death and therefore an unpleasant subject to be avoided. He resisted all efforts by those who anticipated protracted legal proceedings to persuade him to make a will to provide for an orderly disposition of his property. When any person of considerable means refuses to provide for their estate's distribution on death, controversy is almost as certain as death itself. Picasso is scarcely the only example: Michael Jackson, Prince, Jimi Hendrix, Bob Marley, and Stieg Larsson all died without wills, creating massive problems for their loved ones.

WILLS

A *will* transforms a person's wishes about the disposition of their property into a valid, legal instrument. This section covers formal, written wills in detail and mentions other types briefly. Following are some commonly used terms with which the student may be unfamiliar. A man who makes a will is a *testator* and a woman who makes a will is a *testatrix*. A person who dies is a *decedent*. A decedent leaving a valid will is said to die *testate*. It is customary for a testator to designate a personal representative to carry out the provisions of the will. This person is an *executor* if male and an *executrix* if female. If there is no will or the will does not designate a personal representative, the court will appoint an *administrator* or *administratrix* to handle the decedent's estate. With regard to the testator's property, disposition of real estate is properly called a devise, money passing under a will is a *legacy*, and other property is disposed of by *bequest*. The Uniform Probate Code, which has been largely adopted in only about 15 states and partially in some others, uses the term *devise* to refer to any sort of testamentary gift, whether of land, money, or personal property. In any event, today, lawyers tend to use these terms interchangeably. In 2019, a Revised Uniform Probate Code was promulgated, but at this writing no states have adopted it so we do not address it further.

(Note that the term *testatrix* is now considered obsolete and *administratrix* and *executrix* should be. Therefore, we will use the terms testator, administrator, and executor to cover people who fill that role regardless of gender.)

Testamentary Capacity

A will is valid only if the testator had *testamentary capacity* at the time of its making.

In most states the testator must have attained a specific minimum age, usually 18. In all states the testator must possess the mental capacity to dispose of the property intelligently. Testamentary capacity is not identical to capacity to contract. In general, testators have the capacity to make wills if they have attained the statutory age, if they know what property they own, and if they reasonably understand how and to whom they want to leave their property.

Undue Influence

Even if a testator has the legal capacity to make a will, that will should not be admitted to probate if it is the product of fraud, duress, or, more typically, *undue influence*, which has been defined as "influence which deprives [the] person influenced of free agency and destroys freedom of his will and renders it more the will of another than his own." *Conner v. Brown*, 3 A.2d 64 (Del. 1938). Often courts find both lack of testamentary capacity and undue influence in the same case. The following case contains an allegation of undue influence.

YOST v. FAILS
Court of Appeals of Texas, 534 S.W.3d 517 (2017)

Sara McGowan was in her nineties and lived alone when she fell and had to be hospitalized. In January 2011, after her discharge and brief convalescence at a rehabilitation center, she moved in with her nephew, Fails. McGowan, who was very ill and unable to take care of her own physical needs, granted Fails power of attorney, and he began managing her finances and transferred several hundred thousand dollars from her accounts to his own. Ten months later, in November 2011, McGowan signed a new will naming Fails her primary beneficiary. McGowan died in hospice care shortly thereafter, in March 2012.

Fails applied to probate McGowan's 2011 will, but McGowan's niece, Bernice Yost, opposed the application on behalf of her mother, Georgia Cox, who is McGowan's sister. As special conservator for Cox, Yost alleged that the 2011 will was invalid because McGowan signed it as a result of Fails's undue influence. A jury found undue influence, but the trial judge entered a judgment notwithstanding the verdict, finding the jury's conclusion unsupported by the evidence. Yost appealed.

Huddle, Judge:

A will contest based on a claim that the will was procured by undue influence has three elements: (1) an influence existed and was exerted, (2) the exertion of the influence subverted or overpowered the mind of the testator at the time she signed the will, and (3) the testator would not have made the will but for the influence. *Rothermel v. Duncan*, 369 S.W.2d 917 (Tex. 1963); *Guthrie v. Suiter*, 934 S.W.2d 820 (Tex.App. 1996). To satisfy the first element, the party contesting a will must show that an influence existed and was exerted. The focus is on the opportunities for the exertion of the alleged influence, the circumstances of the drafting and execution of the will, the existence of a fraudulent motive, and whether the testator was habitually under the control of another. The exertion of influence, however, cannot be inferred from opportunity alone, such as might result from taking care of the testator or seeing to her needs. There must be proof showing both that the influence existed and that it was exerted.

To satisfy the second element, the contesting party must show that the exertion of the influence subverted or overpowered the mind of the testator at the time she signed the will. The focus of this element is on the testator's state of mind and evidence relating to her ability to resist or susceptibility to the influence of another, such as mental or physical infirmity. But evidence that a testator was susceptible to influence or incapable of resisting it does not prove that her free will was in fact overcome when the will was made. Likewise, close relations or the provision of care standing alone do not suffice to show undue influence. Influence is undue only if the volition of the testator is destroyed and the resulting will expresses the wishes of the one exerting the influence. Such undue influence may include force, intimidation, duress, importunate requests or demands, or deceit.

To meet the third element, the contesting party must show that the testator would not have made the challenged will but for the influence. In general, this element focuses on whether the will is unnatural in its disposition of property. A disposition may be unnatural, for example, if it excludes a testator's natural heirs or favors one heir at the expense of others who ordinarily would receive equal treatment. *Long v. Long,* 125 S.W.2d 1034 (Tex. 1939). Whether a particular disposition is unnatural, however, usually is for the factfinder to decide based on the circumstances. The disinheritance of close relatives or loved ones is not necessarily an unnatural disposition. *See Guthrie,* 934 S.W.2d at 832 (exclusion of testator's only living son from will not unnatural given strained and distant relationship between him and his mother). But a testator's preference for one heir over others of an equal or similar degree of kinship may be unnatural if the record does not disclose a reasonable basis for the preference or contains proof that calls the preference into question or discredits it.

Fails concedes that there is legally sufficient evidence that he had the opportunity to influence McGowan but argues that there is insufficient evidence of two elements of undue influence: that he exerted his influence on McGowan to such an extent that he subverted or overpowered McGowan's mind and thereby procured a will she otherwise would not have made.

The jury heard evidence that, in the months preceding the execution of the challenged will, McGowan was frail and in poor physical health, lived with Fails in his home, and was totally dependent on him for all of her basic needs. There was also evidence that McGowan's cell phone was disconnected and that she became less communicative during this time. Darlene Hardin testified that McGowan was afraid to speak openly, testifying that McGowan seemed afraid to talk on the telephone.

It is undisputed that Fails assumed management of McGowan's finances and used a power of attorney to transfer funds from McGowan's accounts into his personal checking account. Hardin and Elizabeth Moore, McGowan's cousin, testified that Fails insisted on this power of attorney, making it a condition of McGowan living with him. And Hardin testified that McGowan did not want to give Fails this power and was upset when she learned how Fails was spending her money. There was also evidence that Fails cut off McGowan's access to her financial information by placing it "under lock and key" and that he "cussed" at McGowan when she complained about Fails's use of her money.

With respect to the preparation and execution of the 2011 will itself, there was evidence that Fails steered McGowan to attorney Lipman, who prepared the 2011 will and whose firm previously represented Fails. Lipman testified that she did not recall telling McGowan about any potential conflict of interest, notwithstanding that Fails was a preexisting client and the 2011 will made him McGowan's primary beneficiary. Indeed,

Lipman did not recall telling McGowan that Fails was a preexisting client of the firm. Nor is there any evidence that Lipman advised McGowan that she could or should consult her own conflict-free attorney.

There was evidence that Fails paid the firm for the preparation of the will and that he assisted in the planning of the will by, among other things, supplying his own will as a template for McGowan's and drafting a handwritten list of McGowan's bequests. Further, he acted as an intermediary between the firm and McGowan; the firm sent a draft of the will to McGowan, care of Fails, and he went over its terms with her. And Fails drove McGowan to Lipman's office to execute the will. There was conflicting testimony regarding whether Fails was in the room when McGowan signed it, and the jury was free to credit the version adverse to Fails. Likewise, the jury heard evidence to support a finding that the disposition under the 2011 will, under which Fails became the new primary beneficiary and Cox, McGowan's previous beneficiary, was disinherited, was unnatural given the nature of McGowan's relationships with her family members.

In short, considering the cumulative effect of the evidence concerning McGowan's susceptibility and dependence on Fails, Fails's misuse of McGowan's finances and the power of attorney, and the details surrounding the planning and preparation of the 2011 will, we hold that reasonable jurors could conclude that Fails exerted his influence and subverted or overpowered the mind of McGowan at the time she signed the will.

Fails further argues that no evidence shows that he overbore McGowan's free will at the time McGowan executed the 2011 will. We disagree. Fails and Lipman had a prior attorney-client relationship, and Lipman knew of Fails's active involvement in planning the 2011 will, yet Lipman prepared—and Fails paid for—a will that named Fails the primary beneficiary of McGowan's estate without counseling McGowan about the potential conflict. It is undisputed that Fails handwrote the bequests that were incorporated into the will and discussed the terms of the draft with McGowan, and the jury could have credited the conflicting evidence that Fails was in the room when the frail McGowan signed the 2011 will. Cumulatively, this is some evidence contemporaneous with the making of the will from which the jury reasonably could have concluded that the will reflected Fails's wishes rather than McGowan's. We hold that the record contains legally sufficient proof from which the jury could have found undue influence. Reversed.

Tortious Interference with Inheritance Rights

In another portion of the *Fails* opinion, the court of appeals recognized the right of potential beneficiaries to sue for tortious interference with inheritance rights, which is vaguely analogous to the tort of intentional interference with contract rights discussed in Chapter 8.

According to the Restatement (Third) of Torts, a defendant is potentially liable for interfering with an inheritance or gift if:

(a) the plaintiff had a reasonable expectation of receiving an inheritance or gift;
(b) the defendant committed an intentional and independent legal wrong;
(c) the defendant's purpose was to interfere with the plaintiff's expectancy;
(d) the defendant's conduct caused the expectancy to fail; and
(e) the plaintiff suffered injury as a result.

Although about half the states recognize this cause of action, the Texas Supreme

Court later rejected the *Fails* opinion on this issue. In *Archer v. Anderson*, 556 S.W.3d 228 (Tex. 2018), attorney Anderson allegedly unfairly convinced his elderly client Archer, who was not in full possession of his faculties, to disinherit his closest relatives and give everything in his multi-million dollar-estate to Christian charities. The Texas Supreme Court refused to recognize the existence of this tort, believing that there are already sufficient remedies in the law to protect beneficiaries such as the Archers.

The Formal Will

The term *formal* indicates that the will has been prepared and executed in compliance with the state's law of wills—the state's *probate code*. Although the right to make a will generally exists independent of statute, the procedures for drafting, executing, and witnessing the formal written document are governed by statute. Such statutory requirements, although basically similar, vary from state to state. Therefore, the drafter must be thoroughly acquainted with the law of the state in which the testator's will is to be effective and must be sure to comply with its provisions. Noncompliance usually means that the will is declared invalid. If this happens, the decedent's property passes in accordance with the state's law of descent and distribution. (Such statutes and their application are discussed later in another section.)

General Requirements

A will must be written. It must be signed by the testator or at her direction. In most states, the signing must be witnessed by two competent persons who themselves must sign as witnesses in the presence of each other and of the testator. A few states require three witnesses. Most states require an *attestation clause*, a paragraph beneath the testator's signature to the effect that the will was *published*—that is, declared by the testator to be the last will and testament, and signed in the presence of the witnesses, who themselves signed as attesting witnesses. These are the formalities required by statute, and they must be strictly observed. The witnesses do not need to read or know the contents of the will. The testators simply announce to the witnesses that the document is the will and that they are going to sign it. The function of the attestation clause is to serve as a self-proving affidavit to relieve the witnesses of the burden of testifying when the will is submitted for admission to probate after the death of the testator.

Specific Provisions

The main function of a will is to provide for the disposal of property. However, it can appoint an executor and cancel all previous wills if it so states. It can also provide for an alternative disposition of property in the event the primary beneficiary predeceases the testator. If the testator is married, the surviving spouse is usually appointed as the executor; if unmarried, a close relative or friend may be designated.

A will can also cover the disposition of property in the event that husband and wife die nearly simultaneously. It is essential for the will to state that it revokes any and all prior wills. The existence of two or more wills can create insurmountable problems. Sometimes none are admitted to probate (the court proceedings whereby a will is proved and the estate of the decedent is disposed of), in which event the state's statutory provisions for the division of an estate are followed.

The will can also name a guardian for minor children. If both husband and wife die, the guardian they have appointed in their wills can be confirmed by the court if qualified and willing to serve in that capacity. This will obviate the necessity for a court-appointed guardian and a possible controversy between the two competing, though well-meaning, sides of the family.

Modification

While it is possible in some states to change one's will by erasure, by striking out portions, or by interlineation, such procedures are risky undertakings at best. The proper method is to modify by means of a *codicil*. This is an addition to the will and must be executed with the same formalities as the original document. Consequently, if extensive modification is necessary, the testator would be well-advised to consider making a new will. Moreover, since the advent of word processing software, creating a new will is typically as easy as making a codicil, and codicils are not commonly used today when the testator uses an attorney.

Revocation

A will becomes effective only at the death of the testator. The testator can revoke or amend the will at any time until death. Revocation can be accomplished in several ways, but usually must be done in strict compliance with statute by means evincing a clear intent to revoke. Executing a new will with a clause expressly revoking all prior wills and codicils is a customary method of revoking a will.

The necessity for strict statutory compliance is illustrated in *In re Estate of Haugk,* 280 N.W.2d 684 (Wis. 1979). Marie Haugk wished to revoke her will. Her husband, Horst, took it down into the basement and burned it. Because of a heart condition, Marie was unable to descend the stairs and stayed up in the kitchen. Marie died before she could meet with her lawyer to execute a new will and the question arose regarding whether the will had been effectively revoked. Wisconsin law provided that "[a] will is revoked in whole or in part by … (b) Burning, tearing, canceling, or obliterating the will or part, with the intent to revoke, by the testator or by some person *in the testator's presence* and by his direction." Because Horst had not been in Marie's presence when he burned the will, the revocation was held ineffective. Despite the inconsistency with Marie's obvious intent, the court held that the law had to be strictly construed, which is fairly common in cases involving wills. Only a few states allow a will to be revoked by the testator's direction alone.

Revocation can also be caused by operation of law. Marriage, divorce, or the birth of a child subsequent to making a will may affect its validity by revoking it completely or partially. State laws on wills are not uniform—the birth of a child may revoke a will completely in one state but only partially in another. Marriage and divorce also affect wills differently from state to state.

Limitations

There are a few limitations on a person's right to dispose of property through a will. For example, if a married person's will leaves no provision for inheritance by the spouse, many states allow the spouse to claim a share of the estate, typically one-third, under what is called a "forced share," "widow's share," or "elective share." If the spouse is left less than the statutory "forced share," the spouse has the right to renounce the actual devise and take the larger "forced share." In addition, many states provide the spouse a "homestead right" to a specific amount of land (for example, 1 acre in town or 160 acres in the country).

In community property states, each spouse owns one-half of the community property. In most of these states, the surviving spouse receives title to half the community property and the deceased spouse's share passes by will, if one exists, or by intestacy if no will exists. In no event can either spouse dispose of more than one-half the community property by will.

Holographic Wills

Many states allow testators to execute their own wills without formal attestation. These *holographic wills* must be entirely in the testator's own handwriting, including the signature. These wills differ from formal wills in that no attestation clause or witnesses are required. However, most states allowing holographic wills require that the testator's handwriting and signature be proved by two witnesses familiar with them during probate of the will. Competent witnesses would include persons who had received correspondence from the testator. A holographic will is purely statutory—that is, it must be made in accordance with the appropriate state's law and is subject to prescribed conditions and limitations. The principal requirement is that it be entirely in the testator's own handwriting. In *Estate of Thorn,* 192 P. 19 (Cal. 1920), the testator of a holographic will used a rubber stamp to insert "Cragthorn" in the phrase "my country place Crag-thorn." The will was held to be invalid since it was not entirely in the testator's handwriting. In some jurisdictions the holographic will must be dated in the testator's handwriting. The requirements of testamentary capacity and intent are the same as those for formal wills, but a holographic will is otherwise informal and may even take the form of a letter if it conveys "testamentary intent" (the mental determination or intention of the testator that the document constitute the person's will).

Nuncupative Wills

Some states permit *nuncupative wills,* or *oral wills.* These are also known as *soldiers' and sailors' wills.* In general, statutes impose strict limitations on the disposal of property through a nuncupative will. Most states require that it be made during the testator's "last sickness"; that it be written down within a short period afterwards; that it be proved by two witnesses who were present at its oral making; and that the value of the estate bequeathed not exceed a certain amount, usually quite small. Some states also require that the decedent have been a soldier in the field or a sailor at sea in actual contemplation or fear of death. Nuncupative wills, where recognized, usually effect distribution of personal property only, not real property.

Nuncupative wills are difficult to establish, and the restrictions placed on them are intended to discourage their use. There is always the possibility of mistake or fraud and, except on rare occasions, a testator can easily plan sufficiently ahead to use the more traditional and acceptable type of will.

INTESTACY—STATUTES OF DESCENT AND DISTRIBUTION

State laws govern the disposition of a decedent's estate when the decedent has died without a will—intestate. Such laws are called statutes of descent and distribution. They provide for disposition of the decedent's property, both real and personal, in accordance with a prescribed statutory scheme. Real property descends; personal property is distributed. Consequently, the law of the state where the decedent's real estate is located will determine the heirs, by class, to whom it will descend. The decedent's personal property will be distributed in accordance with the law of the state in which the decedent is domiciled. In addition to prescribing the persons who will inherit a decedent's property, statutes of descent and distribution also prescribe the order and proportions in which they will take.

The Surviving Spouse

Without exception, statutes of descent and distribution specify the portion of a decedent's estate that will be taken by their lawful, surviving spouse. Variation in this area is significant from state to state. Formerly, under common law, the surviving spouse was entitled only to a life estate (ownership for life) or *dower* (to the widow) or *curtesy* (to the widower) in the real property owned by the decedent. Personal property was divided among the surviving spouse and any children of the marriage. Today, the law of dower and curtesy has been either abolished or altered significantly by statute in all jurisdictions. Typically, if a husband or wife dies intestate, the statutes provide that the surviving spouse takes one-half or one-third of the estate if there are children or grandchildren. If there are no children or grandchildren, in most jurisdictions the surviving spouse takes the entire estate. However, the states vary considerably in their treatment of this matter. In general, if there are children the surviving spouse must share the estate with them. The number of children or grandchildren will determine the share which is to pass to the surviving spouse. If there are no children or grandchildren, or none have survived the decedent, the surviving spouse takes everything.

As noted earlier, in a community property state, the surviving spouse owns one-half of the community property. The remaining half is subject to intestacy rules if no will exists.

Descendants of the Decedent

There is little disparity in the statutes that govern the shares of an intestate's children or other lineal descendants (those in a direct line from the decedent—children and grandchildren). It is generally the case that, subject to the statutory share of a surviving spouse, children of the decedent share and share alike, with the children of a deceased child taking that child's share. This latter provision is known as a *per stirpes* distribution. For example, assume that a decedent dies after his spouse, leaving two children, a son and a daughter, who have two and three children of their own, respectively. If both son and daughter survive the decedent, each will take half the estate. However, if the son predeceases the decedent, his two children will take his share, each of them taking one-fourth of the estate with the daughter taking the other half. (If the decedent's spouse were still alive, the fractions described here would still apply, but only to that portion of the estate remaining after the spouse took her share.)

Adopted children are generally treated the same as natural children; non-marital ("illegitimate") children generally inherit only from their mother unless their father's paternity has been either acknowledged or established through legal proceedings.

If the descendants are all of one class, that is, children or grandchildren, they will take *per capita*, each getting an equal share. Thus, if the intestate had a son and daughter who predeceased him, but those children left behind five living grandchildren, each grandchild would take one-fifth of what is left after the surviving spouse's share has been provided for. Figure 35.1 illustrates these differences.

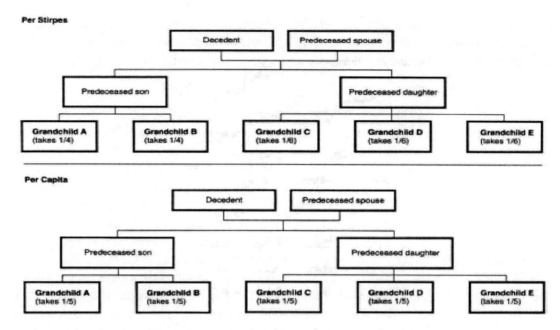

Figure 35.1 Per Stirpes and Per Capita

The Surviving Ascendants

There is general agreement that children of the decedent and subsequent generations of lineal descendants will take to the exclusion of other blood relatives such as parents or brothers and sisters. With regard to the ascendants of the intestate (parents and grandparents), there is much less uniformity in state law. In most states, where decedents leave no descendants, their parents will take the estate, with brothers and sisters (known as collaterals) taking if the parents are not living. In other jurisdictions, brothers and sisters share with the parents. Nephews and nieces may take the share of a predeceased parent if other brothers and sisters of the decedent are still living. If not, the nephews and nieces, as sole survivors, share and share alike in a per capita distribution. In any event, a distribution to ascendants and collaterals is made only if there are no surviving descendants or spouse.

Other than the surviving spouse, relatives by marriage have no claim on the decedent's estate. If the intestate has died leaving no heirs or next-of-kin whatsoever—no spouse, children, grandchildren, ascendants, or collaterals —the estate will pass to the state by a process known as escheat. This rarely happens, but it is provided for by law.

Administration of the Estate

Administration of decedents' estates is accomplished by a proceeding in *probate* if they die leaving a will. The word derives from the Latin *probatio*, proof. In the law of wills, it means the proof or establishment of a document as the valid last will and testament of the deceased. In most states, the court having jurisdiction is called the probate court, and the principal question to be decided by judicial determination is the validity or invalidity of the will. Once the will has been admitted to probate—that is, determined to be valid—the probate court insures efficient distribution of the estate. Funeral expenses, debts to creditors and taxes are paid first. Then homestead rights and forced shares must be taken into account. Finally, the remaining assets are distributed impartially to heirs, devisees, legatees, and others, in accordance with the testator's wishes.

The *personal representative* of the decedent (called the executor if appointed by will and the administrator if appointed by the court) administers the estate under the supervision of the court—to collect decedent's assets, to pay or settle any lawful claims against the estate, and to distribute the remainder to those who will take under the will. If there is no will, the state's law of descent and distribution will determine how the estate is to be distributed.

Probate and the administration of decedents' estates are strictly regulated by statute and can be complex procedures when the estate is substantial and the interest in property of the deceased is not clear. Many parties may be affected by the administration process, so attention to detail and compliance with the state's probate law or code are essential. A personal representative who has effectively handled the estate and wound up its affairs may petition the court and be discharged from any further responsibilities.

Avoiding Administration

Quite frequently, the formal administration of decedents' estates can be wholly or partially avoided. In fact, it is safe to say that fewer than half the deaths in this country result in administration proceedings. Obviously, if the decedent died with no assets or a very small estate, there is no need for an involved administration. Most jurisdictions permit the handling of decedents' affairs without official administration in such cases.

There are several other specific situations in which probate or formal administration can be avoided, at least for a portion of the decedent's assets. For example, if some or all of the property was co-owned with others as a "joint tenancy" with a right of survivorship, it passes to the surviving owners and not to the estate. Joint tenancy bank accounts or securities or a residence owned as a joint tenancy or as a tenancy by the entirety all pass to the surviving owner. This method of owning property is sometimes referred to as the "poor man's will." It should be noted, however, that even though the decedent's interest in such property bypasses the estate, it can still be subject to an estate or inheritance tax.

If the decedent owned one or more life insurance policies, they will not be subject to administration if a beneficiary has been named. The proceeds go straight to the beneficiary and need not pass through the estate. If a beneficiary has not been named or if the one named has predeceased the decedent, however, the proceeds pass to the estate.

TRUSTS

The trust is a versatile legal concept that is typically used to conserve family wealth from generation to generation, to provide for the support and education of children, and to minimize the tax burden on substantial estates. Trust law recognizes two types of property ownership, legal and equitable. One person can hold legal title to property while another can have the equitable title.

To establish a trust, the party intending to create a trust, called a *settlor* or *trustor*, transfers legal ownership of property to a *trustee* for the benefit of a third party, the *beneficiary*. The trustee is the legal owner of the property, called the *res* or *corpus*, but it is owned in trust to be used and managed solely for the benefit of others, who own the equitable title. A trust established and effective during the life of the settlor is known as an *inter vivos* or "living" *trust*. If it is created by the settlor's will, to be effective on that person's death, it is a *testamentary trust*. Trusts are also classified as *express, implied, private,* or *charitable,* depending on the purpose they serve and how they are created.

The Express Private Trust

An express private trust is created when a settlor, with clear intent to do so, and observing certain formalities, sets up a fiduciary relationship involving a trustee, the beneficiaries, and management of the trust res for a lawful purpose. There is little uniformity in the statutes that govern trusts and their creation. It is a general requirement, however, that trusts be established by a writing or, if oral, subsequently proved by a writing. The writing need not be formal so long as it clearly identifies the trust property and the beneficiary and states the purpose for which the trust is created. The intent of the settlor to create a trust must be clear from the circumstances and the action taken. No particular language is required, but the settlor's instructions should be direct and unambiguous. If the purpose of the trust is to put children through college, this should be stated clearly. Language that "requests," or "hopes," or "desires" that the trustee do certain things is considered to be *precatory* in nature (a mere request and not an order or command) and may not be binding on the trustee. Further, words or phrases that fall short of appointing a trustee or imposing positive responsibilities should be avoided. For example, in *Comford v. Cantrell*, 151 S.W. 1076 (Tenn. 1941), a husband left his estate to his wife, stating in the will that it was his "request" that upon her death his wife "shall give my interest to each of my brothers." The court viewed the language as purely *precatory*. The brothers had no legal right to object when the wife gave the land to her nephew instead.

The Trust Property

The subject matter of a trust may be any property of value. For example, money, interests in real estate, securities, and insurance are commonly used. However, settlors must own the property at the time they create the trust. They cannot transfer in trust property they expect to acquire and own at a later date. When the property is transferred to the trustee it becomes the trustee's to manage for the benefit of the beneficiaries and in accordance with the terms of the trust. If the essential elements of a valid trust are missing or if the trust fails, the property will revert to the settlor, if living, or to that person's estate, if deceased.

The Trustee

A *trustee* is, of course, essential; a trust without one cannot be effective. However, the courts will not let an otherwise valid trust fail for want of a trustee. If the named trustee dies or declines to serve or is removed for cause, the court will appoint a replacement. The court will also appoint a trustee when the settlor fails to name one in the trust. No special qualifications are necessary. Since trustees take title to property and manage it, they must be capable of owning property. Minors and incompetents can own property, but they are under a disability in regard to contractual capacity. Consequently, since their contracts are voidable, they cannot function as trustees. Settlors can appoint themselves trustees and, in fact, designate themselves as beneficiaries. The settlor cannot, however, be the sole trustee and the sole beneficiary of a single trust. This relationship would merge both legal and equitable titles to the trust property in the trustee who would hold it free of any trust.

If a corporation (an artificial person) is not prohibited by its charter from doing so it can act as a trustee. Trust companies and banks, for example, frequently serve as trustees for both large and small trusts. They typically charge fees amounting to 1 percent of the value of the *res* per year.

Beneficiaries

The express private trust is ordinarily created for the benefit of identified, or identifiable, beneficiaries. A father can establish a trust for the care and education of his minor children, and can name them in the trust instrument. However, a settlor can also simply specify as the beneficiaries a class of persons, such as "my minor children" or "my brothers and sisters." In either case, the persons who are to benefit are readily identifiable. Trusts have also been held to be valid when established for domestic animals, household pets, and even inanimate objects. Such trusts present problems though, since nonhuman and inanimate beneficiaries are incapable of holding title to property. Additionally, there will be no beneficiary with the capacity to enforce the provisions of the trust against the trustee. This is not to say that a charitable trust for animals in general or a trust for humane purposes will fail. (The charitable trust is discussed in a following section.)

The beneficiary does not have to agree to accept the benefits of the trust. It is presumed that beneficiaries accept the trust unless they make a specific rejection. Their interest in the trust can, in general, be reached by creditors, and they can sell or otherwise dispose of their interests. However, beneficiaries can transfer only the interests they hold—the equitable title. If a beneficiary holds more than a life estate, and the trust does not make other provisions, this interest can be disposed of in a will or can pass to the beneficiary's estate after death.

Managing the Trust

The administration of a trust is highly regulated by statute. Trustees must know the law of their jurisdictions. In general, they must make every effort to carry out the purpose of the trust. They must act with care and prudence and use their best judgment, and at all times they must exercise an extraordinary degree of loyalty to the beneficiary—the degree of loyalty required of those in a fiduciary position.

In carrying out the purposes of a trust, the trustees ordinarily have broad powers that are usually described in the trust instrument. In addition, they may have implied powers that are necessary to carry out their express duties. For example, trustees can have express authority to invest the trust property and pay the beneficiary the income from such investments. They can also have the implied power to incur reasonable expenses in administering the trust.

Trustees should exercise the care and skill of a *prudent person* in managing the trust. A reasonable goal for a trustee is to exercise the diligence necessary to preserve the corpus and realize a reasonable return on income from "prudent" investments at the same time. State laws often specify the types of investments a trustee can make. In one state, for example, trust law authorizes investment in bonds or securities issued by the state and by the U.S. government and certain of its agencies and in certain banks or trust companies insured by the Federal Deposit Insurance Corporation. With certain exceptions, any other investment of trust funds must be under an order of the superior court or at the risk of the trustee. If the trust instrument gives the trustee wide discretion to invest in "other" securities, many jurisdictions allow this. Statutes often indicate that prudent persons should diversify their investments. However, the trustee can still be held accountable for a failure to exercise proper care. In other words, the law discourages bad investments.

The relationship between the trustee and the beneficiary is fiduciary in nature. Consequently, in managing trusts, trustees must act solely for the benefit of the beneficiaries.

For example, trustees cannot borrow any portion of the trust funds or sell their own property to the trust. Neither can they purchase trust property for themselves. Even though the trustee's personal dealings with the trust may prove to be advantageous to the beneficiary, the duty of loyalty is breached and the trustee can be charged with such breach. If there are multiple trustees, an innocent trustee may well be held liable for not preventing a co-trustee's breach of fiduciary duty. The duties of a trustee are highlighted in the following case.

WITMER v. BLAIR
Missouri Court of Appeals, 588 S.W.2d 222 (1979)

At his death in 1960, Henry Nussbaum's will created a trust for the education of his grandchildren. Defendant Jane Ann Blair, Nussbaum's niece, was named trustee. Nussbaum's daughter, Dorothy Janice Witmer (defendant's cousin) was given a reversionary interest in the residue of the trust should none of the grandchildren survive to inherit the estate. Marguerite Janice Witmer (Dorothy's daughter) became the only beneficiary of the trust.

Defendant Blair received the trust estate in 1961. It consisted of $1,905 in checking and savings accounts, $5,700 in certificates of deposit, and a house valued at $6,000. The house was sold in 1962, netting $4,467 to the trust estate, which amount was deposited in a trust checking account. For the next several years, the trustee kept funds in checking and savings accounts and in certificates of deposit. As of December 31, 1975, the trust assets consisted of $2,741 checking account, $5,474 savings, and $8,200 certificates of deposit.

Marguerite was 23 years old at the time of trial. She had not attended college, but various sums of money had been expended from the trust for her benefit, including a typewriter, clothes, glasses, modeling school tuition and expenses, and a tonsillectomy, all totaling some $1,250. The trust also spent $350 for dentures for Dorothy.

Marguerite and Dorothy brought this suit against Blair for breach of trust for failure to properly invest the funds of the trust. The trial judge removed the trustee and surcharged her account for $309 in unexplained expenditures, but refused to assess actual or punitive damages for breach of trust. Plaintiffs appealed.

Welborn, Special Judge:

The trust was handled by appellant rather informally. She kept no books for the trust. The expenditures were in most cases advanced by her from her personal account and she reimbursed herself from the trust income. In 1965, the bank erroneously credited the trust account with $560 which should have gone to the trustee's personal account. The mistake was not corrected and that amount remained in the trust account. The trustee received no compensation for her services. Asked at the trial whether she had ever been a trustee before, she responded negatively, adding "And never again." She explained the large checking account balances in the trust account by the fact that college for Janice "was talked about all the way through high school.... [I]n my opinion, it was the sensible way to keep the money where I could get it to her without any problems at all in case she needed it quickly."

An accountant testified that had $500 been kept in the checking and savings accounts (the $800 was based upon the maximum disbursement in any year) and the balance of the trust placed in one-year certificates of deposit, $9,138 more interest would have been earned as of September 30, 1976.

A concise summary of the law applicable to the situation appears in 76 Am. Jur.2d

Trusts §379 (1975):

> It is a general power and duty of a trustee, implied if not expressed, at least in the case of an ordinary trust, to keep trust funds properly invested. Having uninvested funds in his hands, it is his duty to make investments of them, where at least they are not soon to be applied to the purposes and objects or turned over to the beneficiaries of the trust. Generally, he cannot permit trust funds to lie dormant or on deposit for a prolonged period, but he may keep on hand a fund sufficient to meet expenses, including contingent expenses, and he need not invest a sum too small to be prudently invested. A trustee ordinarily may not say in excuse of a failure to invest that he kept the funds on hand to pay the beneficiaries on demand.

The trustee is under a duty to the beneficiary to use reasonable care and skill to make the trust property productive. Restatement (Second) of Trusts §181(1959).

A breach of trust is a violation by the trustee of any duty which as trustee he owes to the beneficiary. Restatement (Second) of Trusts §201(1959). Comment b to this section states:

> Mistake of law as to existence of duties and powers. A trustee commits a breach of trust not only where he violates a duty in bad faith, or intentionally although in good faith, or negligently, but also where he violates a duty because of a mistake as to the extent of his duties and powers. This is true not only where his mistake is in regard to a rule of law, whether a statutory or common-law rule, but also where he interprets the trust instrument as authorizing him to do acts which the court determines he is not authorized by the instrument to do. In such a case, he is not protected from liability merely because he acts in good faith, nor is he protected merely because he relies upon the advice of counsel.

Under the above rules, there has been a breach of trust by the trustee in this case and her good faith is not a defense to appellants' claim. In 1962, appellant Marguerite was some nine years of age. Obviously there was no prospect of the beneficiary's attending college for a number of years. However, when Marguerite became of college age [around 1971] and was considering a college education, the respondent should not be faulted for keeping readily available a sum of money which would permit the use of the trust fund for such purpose.

Reversed, and remanded with directions to enter judgment for plaintiffs for $2,840.

The *Uniform Prudent Investor Act*, adopted in most states, requires trustees to consider modern portfolio theory in making investments on behalf of beneficiaries, providing that "[a] trustee's investment and management decisions respecting individual assets must be evaluated not in isolation but in the context of the trust portfolio as a whole and as part of an overall investment strategy having risk and return objectives reasonably suited to the trust." Among the factors that trustees are directed to consider are (a) general economic conditions, (b) possible effects of inflation or deflation, (c) expected tax consequences of investment decisions, (d) the role that each investment plays within the overall trust portfolio, (e) expected total return from income and appreciation of capital, (f) the beneficiaries' other resources, (g) needs for liquidity, regularity of income, and preservation of capital, and (h) an asset's special relationship or special value, if any, to the purposes of the trust or to the beneficiary.

The Directed Trust

The common trusts that we have been discussing make the trustee responsible for both the administration of the trust's property and how it is invested. This is a lot of responsibility and sometimes results in problems, as the *Witmer* case indicates. **Directed trusts** enable the grantor of the trust to choose a trustee to administer the trust and a separate advisor or manager to invest the trust's assets. Although the investment manager remains subject to trustee supervision, most of the trustee's liability for poor investment decisions is eliminated absent "willful misconduct." Several states have adopted the Uniform Directed Trust Act.

The Spendthrift Trust

Settlors may be concerned that beneficiaries may be incapable of managing their own affairs either because of inexperience and immaturity or simply because they are "spendthrifts." Settlors can therefore determine that beneficiaries will not sell, mortgage, or otherwise transfer their rights to receive principal and income and that the beneficiaries' creditors will not reach the income or principal while it is in the hands of the trustee. Such a provision no longer applies after the income or principal has been paid over to the beneficiary. Further, some modern statutes limit the *spendthrift trust*. They either limit the income that is protected from creditors or they permit creditors to reach amounts in excess of what the beneficiary is considered to need.

Because most states have traditionally had little statutory law relating to trusts, courts created most of the law of trusts, often relying upon the persuasive authority of various versions of the Restatement of Trusts. However, in 2000 the *Uniform Trust Code (UTC)* was promulgated. It has now been adopted by more than 30 states, though not by Texas. The UTC is largely patterned after the Restatement and does not significantly alter the preexisting law of trusts in the states in which it is adopted. The following case applies the UTC in a case that raises a common question: how can beneficiaries of spendthrift trusts get their hands on the trust's assets?

ESTATE OF SOMERS
Kansas Supreme Court, 89 P.3d 898 (2004)

Eula Somers died in 1956, leaving a testamentary trust of $120,000 for her two grandchildren. By January 2001, the value of the Trust had increased to approximately $ 3,500,000. The trust provided for $100 monthly payments to the grandchildren, with the remainder of the trust after their deaths to be paid to the Shriners Hospital for Crippled Children. Firstar Bank is currently the trustee of the trust.

The Shriners Hospitals for Children (Shriners) and the Grandchildren reached an agreement to terminate the Trust. They agreed that the Grandchildren would each receive a distribution of $150,000 from the Trust and that the remainder of the Trust assets would immediately be distributed to Shriners. Shriners agreed to continue the $100 monthly payments to the Grandchildren. Firstar opposed the termination of the Trust. Shriners and the Grandchildren then filed a joint petition in district court asking that the Trust be terminated immediately. Each side filed a motion for summary judgment. The district court denied the petition to terminate the Trust and the Grandchildren's request for individual distributions of $150,000. However, the district court concluded that it had equity jurisdiction and ordered an immediate, partial distribution of the corpus of the Trust to Shriners, but required that $500,000 remain in the Trust to fund the annuity payments to the Grandchildren. The court further ordered that the attorney fees and expenses of the Grandchildren's attorneys be paid from the Shriners' distribution. All the parties appealed.

Gernon, Justice:

This appeal requires us to determine whether the trial court ruled properly when it partially distributed funds from a spendthrift trust at the request of each of the beneficiaries. The beneficiaries acted in concert, and none were or are under any incapacity.

A spendthrift trust is defined in *Estate of Sowers*, 574 P.2d 224 (Kan. 1977), as "a trust created to provide a fund for the maintenance of a beneficiary and at the same time to secure the fund against his improvidence or incapacity. Provisions against alienation of the trust fund by the voluntary act of the beneficiary or by his creditors are its usual incidents."

The parties do not dispute that this Trust is a spendthrift trust. Thus, the question is whether a court can terminate a spendthrift trust at the request of the beneficiaries, who are all in agreement and competent to consent, if the settlor is not available to consent to the termination. This is an issue of first impression in Kansas, requiring the application and interpretation of the Kansas Uniform Trust Code (KUTC). Section 410(a) of the KUTC provides: "A trust terminates to the extent the trust is revoked or expires pursuant to its terms, no purpose of the trust remains to be achieved, or the purposes of the trust have become unlawful, contrary to public policy, or impossible to achieve." And Section 411 provides:

> a) A noncharitable irrevocable trust may be modified or terminated upon consent of the settlor and all qualified beneficiaries, even if the modification or termination is inconsistent with a material purpose of the trust. A settlor's power to consent to a trust's termination may be exercised by an agent under a power of attorney only to the extent expressly authorized by the power of attorney or the terms of the trust; by the settlor's conservator with the approval of the court supervising the conservatorship if an agent is not so authorized; or by the settlor's guardian with the approval of the court supervising the guardianship if an agent is not so authorized and a conservator has not been appointed.
> b) A noncharitable irrevocable trust may be terminated upon consent of all of the qualified beneficiaries if the court concludes that continuance of the trust is not necessary to achieve any material purpose of the trust. . . .
> c) A spendthrift provision in the terms of the trust is presumed to constitute a material purpose of the trust.

The Grandchildren claim that the district court had the power to terminate the Trust with all of the beneficiaries' consent because the spendthrift provision is not a material purpose of the trust. They appear to raise two arguments in this regard. First, the Grandchildren argue that the spendthrift provision is not a material purpose because it is a small fraction of the entire trust. The Grandchildren cite no authority for their proposition that a spendthrift provision must apply to a substantial portion of the trust to be considered a material purpose. The material purposes of a trust are subject to the settlor's discretion, which is limited "only to the extent its purposes are lawful, not contrary to public policy, and possible to achieve." (KUTC Sec. 404) Accordingly, we find no merit in this argument.

Second, the Grandchildren claim that an annuity could continue their lifetime payments, thereby continuing the material purpose of the trust after its termination. This argument overlooks the purpose of a spendthrift provision, which "restrains either voluntary or involuntary transfer of a beneficiary's interest." An annuity purchased by Shriners outside the confines of the trust is not protected from alienation or attachment by the annuitant's creditors. The only way to ensure the protection of the spendthrift provision is for sufficient funds to remain in the Trust. Thus, Eula Somers' purpose to protect the trust assets from her grandchildren's creditors cannot be accomplished by terminating the Trust and purchasing an annuity that would merely maintain the beneficiaries' lifetime payments.

It should be noted that KUTC Sec. 411, by its express terms, applies to the modification or termination of a noncharitable trust. Clearly, this is a charitable trust. Thus, we must consider whether, under these facts, a charitable trust with a spendthrift provision for certain beneficiaries for their lives may be modified, terminated, or partially terminated. When there is no law directly on point, Kansas courts turn to the Restatement of Trusts, which does not distinguish between charitable and noncharitable trusts, and provides in Sec. 337:

> (1) Except as stated in Subsection (2), if all of the beneficiaries of the trust consent and none of them is under an incapacity, they can compel the termination of the trust.
> (2) If the continuance of the trust is necessary to carry out a material purpose of the trust, the beneficiaries cannot compel its termination.

The Restatement's comment l to Sec. 337 specifically proscribes the termination of spendthrift trusts, stating: "If by the terms of the trust or by statute the interest of one or more of the beneficiaries is made inalienable by him, the trust will not be terminated while such inalienable interest still exists, although all of the beneficiaries desire to terminate it or one beneficiary acquires the whole beneficial interest and desires to terminate it."

[Existing authorities] support a conclusion that the tenet from KUTC Sec. 411 may be applied equally to charitable and noncharitable trusts. Thus, the beneficiaries are precluded from terminating the Trust while continuation of the Trust is necessary to achieve a material purpose of the Trust. Section 411(c) does not make a spendthrift provision a material purpose under all circumstances. Rather, it raises a rebuttable presumption that the spendthrift provision is a material purpose. The Grandchildren, however, offer no evidence to rebut the presumption that the spendthrift provision is a material purpose of the trust. As a result, we find the spendthrift provision of the Trust to be a material purpose of the Trust. The Grandchildren's proposal that Shriners would purchase an annuity to continue their monthly payments does not satisfy the protections required by the spendthrift provision. Thus, termination of the trust would frustrate a material purpose of the Trust. The trial court did not err when it reached the same conclusion and refused to terminate the Trust.

[The appellate court then held that the trial court acted properly in ordering the $3,000,000 distribution to Shriners before the death of both grandchildren, especially in light of the fact that the reserved $500,000 would easily fund the continuing $100 monthly payments to the grandchildren. The payment to Shriners advanced an important purpose of the Trust and was proper because the accumulation of so much money in the Trust was unforeseen to the testator. The lower court also properly refused to order the Shriners to make the $300,000 distribution to the grandchildren, because Eula Somers' will and the Trust did not provide for any cash distributions to the grandchildren beyond the specified monthly payments. Affirmed.

Trust Termination

In most states, settlors can revoke a trust at any time if they have reserved that power. However, most trusts are terminated when the stated period has elapsed or when the trust purpose has been served. In a trust for the care of minor children, it logically ends when the beneficiaries have reached their majority. In a trust for the college education of the beneficiary, it will terminate when that goal has been attained. In any event, upon termination of a trust, any balance of funds remaining reverts to the settlor or is disposed of in accordance with the instructions contained in the trust.

Charitable Trusts

The purpose of a charitable trust is the general benefit of humanity. Its beneficiaries can be education, science, religion, hospitals, homes for the aged or handicapped, and a host of other charitable or public entities. Charitable trusts are much like private trusts.

Furthermore, the courts of most jurisdictions will find another suitable purpose for a charitable trust when the settlor's stated purpose is impossible or difficult to achieve. The courts do so under the doctrine of *cy pres,* meaning so near or as near. The doctrine is used to prevent a charitable trust from failing for want of a beneficiary. To illustrate: a testator establishes a testamentary trust for the support and maintenance of orphans in a specified orphanage. If the specified orphanage ceased to exist after the settlor's death, the court could use the *cy pres* doctrine, find that the settlor's intent was to benefit orphans generally, and apply the trust to some other orphanage in the area. The *cy pres* doctrine applies only where there is definite charitable intent, never to private trusts.

Implied Trusts

An implied trust, constructive or resulting, is created by law. While the distinction is not always clear, a *constructive trust* is usually imposed upon property by the courts to correct or rectify fraud or to prevent one party from being unjustly enriched at the expense of another. In reality, it is a fiction or remedy to which a court of equity will resort to prevent injustice. Suppose that A and B have agreed to purchase a tract of land jointly with the deed to list both of them as grantees. If, despite the agreement, A secretly buys the land alone, and the deed fails to list B as grantee, the court will impose a constructive trust on the property to the extent of the half interest B should have. This procedure assumes that B is ready and willing to pay half the purchase price. In another case, directors of corporations who take advantage of their positions to make secret profits from corporate opportunities will be constructive trustees for the corporations to the extent of the profits they make. Constructive trusts commonly arise out of the breach of a fiduciary relationship where no trust intent is present or required.

The *resulting trust* arises out of, or is created by, the conduct of the parties. It is imposed in order to carry out the apparent intentions of the parties at the time they entered into the transaction that gave rise to the trust. The most frequent use of the resulting trust occurs when one party purchases property but records the title in the name of another. For example, A wants to purchase a tract of real estate but does not want it subjected to the hazards of his business ventures. He therefore buys the land but has the deed made out in the name of a friend, B. There is no problem if B conveys the real estate to A on demand in accordance with their understanding of the nature of the transaction. However, if B refuses to convey the land, the courts can impose a resulting trust on B for A's benefit. Some difficulty can arise if, in the situation above, A has title taken in the name of his wife or a close relative, because it could be valid to presume that A intended the land as a gift. And if A had purchased in the name of another to defraud his creditors, it is likely that the courts would refuse to impose the resulting trust, being reluctant to afford relief to a wrongdoer.

Uniform Fiduciary Access to Digital Assets Act

Technological advances mean that many people now own digital assets that are stored as data on computer servers and accessed via the Internet. Because many traditional laws in both the area of wills and of trusts and estates were written before such forms of property were even dreamed of, the Uniform Law Commission recently promulgated the Uniform Fiduciary Access to Digital Assets Act (UFADAA) to give executors or administrators of deceased persons' estates, trustees of trusts, and similar guardians and agents limited power to access and manage such assets. According to the Commission, "UFADAA gives people the power to plan for the management and disposition of their digital assets in the same way they can make plans for their tangible property: by providing instructions in a will, trust, or power of attorney." The vast majority of states have enacted the UFADAA.

In New York's version of the Act, if a will does not mention digital assets, the Act tries to balance the fiduciary's need to access and administer the decedent's digital assets with the decedent's right to privacy. To give a representative example, in *Matter of White* (Suffolk County, NY, 2017), a fiduciary went to court to gain access to the decedent's Google e-mail account. The fiduciary argued that the deceased may have owned a business and that such access would help her to identify assets and otherwise aid in administration of the estate. Although there were no other authorized users to the account, Google refused to grant access without a court order. However, because the decedent's will did not mention digital assets, the judge denied the fiduciary's request to the extent it asked for more than the contact information stored and associated with the account, writing:

> Although no one has appeared in opposition to the request for relief, in this evolving area the undersigned is concerned that unfettered access to a decedent's digital assets may result in an unanticipated intrusion into the personal affairs of the decedent or disclosure of sensitive or confidential data, for example, information unrelated to his business or corporation. Thus, the court must balance the fiduciary's duty to properly administer this estate, while avoiding the possibility of unintended consequences.

ESTATE PLANNING

"*Estate Planning* is applying the law of property, trusts, wills, future interests, insurance, and taxation to the ordering of one's affairs, keeping in mind the possibility of retirement and the certainty of death." (R. J. Lynn, AN INTRODUCTION TO ESTATE PLANNING, 1 (1975)). Wills and trusts are the most commonly used estate planning devices. When they are not used, there often follow dire consequences for the surviving heirs. Many people tend to equate estate planning with death, but lifetime planning is more important than death planning. The aim of wise estate planning is not merely to dispose of one's estate at death but to organize resources during life in order to provide for the present and future well-being of one's family.

Perhaps the major consideration in preserving estate integrity is the impact taxes may have, if little thought is given to methods for reducing estate shrinkage. The decedent's survivors may find on settling the estate that the principal heir is the government. It is, of course, unlawful to evade taxes, but there is nothing illegal about doing everything possible to avoid paying unnecessary taxes. Various planning devices can keep unwanted heirs, in the form of estate and inheritance taxes, and the expense of probate and administration to a minimum.

As presently (2017) structured, the federal estate tax law excludes the first $5.49 million from estate taxes and carries a maximum tax rate of 40%. The law further provides that estates of decedents survived by a spouse may elect to pass any of the decedent's unused exemption to the surviving spouse. However, many members of Congress are committed to completely eliminating the federal estate tax ("the death tax").

Gifts

One of the keys to cutting estate taxes is to give away some assets before death. The gifts shift income to children or perhaps retired parents who may be in lower tax brackets. Giving, as an estate planning device, may be hard to accept for the donor who has spent a lifetime slowly accumulating an estate. Nevertheless, it is something to consider, keeping in mind one's personal situation. Amateur philanthropy, however, can be dangerous. Property given outright to a poor manager can be wasted away; a gift with too many strings attached can be something less than useful to the donee. Gift taxes must also be considered. Under current (2017) tax law, each person may transfer $14,000 each year to any recipient, including children, without any gift tax liability.

Life Insurance

Life insurance, in its various forms, can serve many purposes in estate planning. Ownership can be so arranged that the proceeds will not become part of the insured's estate to be taxed. It is a good means of providing liquid funds so that forced sales of other property to pay estate charges or debts can be avoided. In general, life insurance is not subject to probate and administration expenses and is a good way to make *inter vivos* (during lifetime) gifts to children, to grandchildren, or, if the donor is so inclined, to charity. Many kinds of policies are available—term, whole life, and endowment, for example—and there may be a place for one or more types in an estate plan. For the average wage earner life insurance is the major, perhaps the only, means of providing security for the family. Indeed, it may be all that is necessary, other than a valid will. With regard to business ventures, the members of a partnership often enter into buy and sell agreements with a view to continuing the partnership after the death of a partner. The partnership agreement sometimes provides that the estates of deceased partners will sell their interests to surviving partners and that the partners will buy such interests. Insurance is frequently used by the partnership to fund the agreement.

The Marital Deduction

For federal estate tax purposes, the *marital deduction* is a useful device in estate planning involving substantial assets. It reflects the social concept that property accumulated during marriage should be treated as community property, disregarding the fact that the husband and wife could have contributed differing amounts. The marital deduction was designed to more nearly equate tax treatment between residents of states that have community property laws and those of states which do not. No matter what amount a decedent spouse passes to a surviving spouse, that amount will not be taxed in the decedent spouse's estate. This allows surviving spouses to continue to have the use of up to all of the "community" assets for the rest of their lives. The amount passing to surviving spouses is included in their estates and will be taxed at the surviving spouse's death. The amount passing to the surviving spouse under the marital deduction must be determined through careful planning to maximize tax savings and meet the objectives of a particular family.

Expert legal counsel and financial advice, preferably from specialists, should be sought early in the estate planning process.

PART VII

BUSINESS ETHICS

CHAPTER 36

BUSINESS ETHICS AND THE LAW

- The Importance of Business Ethics

- The Value of Teaching Business Ethics

- What is Ethics?

- The Relationship Between Law and Ethics

- Evolution of a Moral Sense

- Philosophical Approaches to Ethical Reasoning

- Moral Reasoning and Decision Making

- Moral Relativism Versus Moral Pluralism

"The most important human endeavor is the striving for morality in our actions. Our inner balance and even our existence depend on it. Only morality in our actions can give beauty and dignity to life." –Albert Einstein[1]

Jill is a regional sales manager for a nationwide chain of retail consumer electronics stores. She and her assistants at company headquarters design promotional programs for stores in the region, supervise store managers' implementation of company marketing strategies, and conduct sales seminars for salespeople at these stores. Questions continually arise about how far promotional materials and the statements of individual salespeople can go in pushing their products. These questions relate not only to what is legal, but also to what is "appropriate" or "ethical." If particular statements are legal, is there any reason at all to be concerned about them? Are there any other standards that must be followed to support good business practices (or promote efficient exchanges or maintain one's standing in the community)? Jill and her associates know that it is usually illegal to brazenly lie about the quality of a product. But they also know that it is often very difficult for a buyer to prove that a seller made intentionally deceptive statements, so the legal risk is small even in such a case. Jill understands that a company's reputation, and ultimately its sales, may suffer if it gains a reputation for dealing dishonestly. She also knows, however, that if some forms of subtle deception are practiced with skill, most customers will never know. Although a few customers may ultimately discover the deception, the company does not depend on repeat business in most of its product lines. For Jill, the legal risks and risks to her reputation seem small.

Even if the legal or financial risks are not great, Jill feels that it is "wrong" to lie to a customer. When she receives a lot of pressure from her superiors to increase sales, however, she begins challenge her feelings and finds herself pondering various questions: "Why is it wrong, really?" "Who, after all, defines what is wrong if it isn't illegal?" "We're selling to adults; aren't they supposed to look after themselves?" "Isn't this just the free market at work, and doesn't the market operate impersonally on the assumption that all sellers and buyers pursue their own economic self-interests?" "Isn't it okay to do it if I feel okay about it?" "But what if I feel good about it only after some strained rationalizing?" "And . . . let's face it—I don't always feel good about what happens."

When Jill tries to define what is "wrong," she finds it difficult to come up with any clear rationale or any systematic way to develop standards. Not only that but she cannot even decide whether there is a rational way to analyze problems of this nature.

Assuming, again, that there are no significant legal risks, Jill wonders how much latitude salespeople should have in extolling the virtues of their product. Must every shortcoming of the item be revealed? Surely not. But why not? May the sales pitch be couched in vague, laudatory terms or must all responses be absolutely factual, precise, and to-the-point? Should the salesperson be concerned about the customer's real need for the product, or is the customer's apparent willingness to purchase the only thing that matters? Should there be any regard for the customer's particular susceptibilities to advertising? What if the advertising campaign that brought the customer into the store was full of "subliminal" messages that subconsciously persuaded him that this product would improve his love life? Jill finally decides that she does not have the time or energy to worry about such things.

[1] WALTER ISAACSON, EINSTEIN 393 (2007).

896 © 2020 John R. Allison & Robert A. Prentice

Rather, she will just be guided by the opinion of the company's attorneys about the legal risks of particular strategies and statements. Over a period of time, however, she is increasingly bothered by some of the promotional strategies that she initiates or approves. After doing some reading, she realizes that she has been grappling with age-old questions and that there is an entire field of study concerned with questions of this nature. Jill has discovered "business ethics."

THE IMPORTANCE OF BUSINESS ETHICS

In the wake of the many ethical lapses that contributed so substantially to the Enron-era scandals and to the subprime mortgage crisis, few businesspeople today are unaware of the importance of business ethics. Indeed, it is possible that for commercial actors today, the topic has never been more important.

There Has Never Been a Better Time for Individuals to Act Ethically

While acting ethically should be its own reward, it remains true that there has never been a better time for individuals and businesses to act ethically. Certainly, there are today, and will always be, situations where a particular individual or business can profit by acting unethically. There will always be chances to lie, cheat or steal and get away with it. However, in the long-run it usually pays to act ethically.

Regarding individuals, consider initially that a recent survey of recruiters indicated that the three most valued traits of potential employees among a list of 12 were: (1) communication and interpersonal skills, (2) team skills, and (3) ethics. And in another recent survey performed by IBM, 65% of 1,709 CEOs worldwide cited "ethics and values" as the most important "organizational attribute" they would like to stimulate in their employees.

Second, it has been pointed out by others that the best way to advance through an organization is to have your boss think that you are the kind of person who would return a missing billfold full of money to its rightful owner rather than to pocket the cash. And the best way to persuade your boss that you are that kind of person is *to be that kind of person.*

Third, note that the emerging literature in hedonic psychology indicates that people who strive primarily for achievement and wealth are less happy, on average, than those whose strivings focus on three other categories: (1) relationships and intimacy, (2) religion and spirituality, and (3) generativity (leaving a legacy and contributing something to society).[2] Other studies indicate that people who act ethically tend to be happier than those who do not. This is not surprising, for there is evidence that we are evolutionarily shaped to derive pleasure from receiving the approval of others and from doing the "right" (societally-accepted) thing.[3] Brain scans indicate that when we act consistently with social norms, the same primary reward centers in the brain are affected as when we eat our favorite foods.[4] People with a strong moral sense even tend to be more prosperous than others.[5] Perhaps doing the right thing is its own reward in more ways than one.

Fourth, we need a hero! Society often honors and rewards those who act the hero. Consider *Time* magazine's honoring of whistleblowers Sherron Watkins (Enron), Cynthia

---

[2] JONATHAN HAIDT, THE HAPPINESS HYPOTHESIS 143 (2006).

[3] RICHARD LAYARD, HAPPINESS: LESSONS FROM A NEW SCIENCE 100-01 (2005).

[4] Nina Mazar et al., *The Dishonesty of Honest People: A Theory of Self-Concept Maintenance*, 45 JOURNAL OF MARKETING RESEARCH 633 (2008).

[5] RICHARD LAYARD, HAPPINESS: LESSONS FROM A NEW SCIENCE 102 (2005).

Collins (WorldCom), and Colleen Rowley (FBI) as "Persons of the Year" in 2002. Of course, heroes often pay dearly for their honors.

Most of us would rather live in an honest society than a dishonest one because honest ones are more efficient, more pleasant, and more secure. When we act ethically, we add to the overall trust level of society which facilitates all manner of positive outcomes. Francis Fukuyama observed that "a nation's well-being … is conditioned by a single, pervasive cultural characteristic: the level of trust inherent in the society."[6] When we act as free riders, leaving it to our fellow citizens to act responsibly while we attempt to lie, cheat, steal and otherwise shirk our responsibilities, we tear at the social fabric in a way that will tend to create exactly the kind of society that we do *not* wish to live in. When we act in a trustworthy fashion, we add to the social capital that enables the conditions of safety and prosperity that we would all like to enjoy.

There Has Never Been a Worse Time for Individuals to Act Unethically

Many people wish to do the right thing because it is the right thing, not merely because it survives a cost-benefit analysis. However, those who do wish to perform a cost-benefit analysis before deciding whether to choose the ethical or the unethical path, would be well-served to remember that perhaps at no time in history has acting unethically been potentially costlier.

Employees who act like jerks cost firms money in hiring new co-workers, providing sensitivity training, fending off lawsuits, and the like. Therefore, many firms have adopted "No Jerks Need Apply" rules. For example, a law firm reported that it refused to hire an otherwise qualified attorney because he had been inexcusably rude to a receptionist before his job interview.[7]

For those who go beyond just being a jerk to being a criminal, the penalties have never been stiffer. For example, the Sarbanes-Oxley Act of 2002, passed in the wake of the Enron-era scandals, not only created new crimes and increased the penalties for a host of old ones but also made the federal government's sentencing guidelines stiffer than ever before. Never before have white collar criminals gone to jail for more crimes or for longer periods of time. For example, a Dynegy executive was recently sentenced to 24 years in jail in a securities fraud case. In several recent insider trading cases and Foreign Corrupt Practice Act cases, defendants were sentenced to a decade or so in jail.

Not only are the penalties stiffer than ever before, but technical advances have improved surveillance and investigation, increasing the chance that wrongdoers will be caught committing crimes (or just being a jerk). For example, people seem willing to put all manner of incriminating items into e-mails that they would not otherwise place in written form. Powerful Wall Street banker Frank Quattrone was indicted for allegedly sending e-mails to his employees asking them to destroy potentially incriminating e-mails. An accountant was convicted of telling his employees in an e-mail to alter documents so that they would not be second-guessed "by some smart-ass lawyer." Indeed, the SEC has won several cases based on evidence contained in incriminating e-mails. Furthermore, bad actors are often busted based on e-mails or text messages that they (incorrectly) that that they had deleted.

---

[6] FRANCIS FUKUYAMA, TRUST: THE SOCIAL VIRTUES AND THE CREATION OF PROSPERITY 7 (1995).
[7] ROBERT I SUTTON, THE NO ASSHOLE RULE (2007).

Cell phone cameras are ubiquitous, so it is increasingly difficult to commit a crime, be a jerk, or just act inappropriately without being detected. Thus, embarrassing (ask Matt Leinhart, Arizona Cardinals quarterback who was photographed in a hot tub acting indiscreetly with a number of nubile young women or ESPN reporter Britt McHenry who was videoed while insulting in the most mean-spirited way a towing company's clerk) and incriminating (ask the burglar in the UK who got trapped breaking into an apartment through a window and was photographed by a number of neighbors with cell phones) photographs are often taken. And nearly as often these photos end up on Facebook, YouTube, or some other form of social media for the entire world to peruse. Twitter has also been the undoing of the indiscreet.[8] "In the Twitter world it's far harder to keep a lid on"[9] wrongdoing.

Perhaps more importantly, we have all evolved to feel guilt when we act unethically. This is not a pleasant emotion, and it is experienced by almost everyone, except psychopaths, who tend not to "get" moral rules.[10] Some brain scientists believe that this may well be due to the fact that psychopaths don't have the emotional equipment necessary to experience guilt. If we act immorally and others find out, we also will tend to suffer embarrassment and shame, two more unpleasant emotions. If acting ethically is not its own reward, acting unethically is its own punishment for all but psychopaths.

THE VALUE OF TEACHING BUSINESS ETHICS

The Enron/Arthur Andersen debacle put business ethics on the radar screen for many people. The subprime mortgage debacle refreshed the screen. More recently the headlines have been filled with the Deepwater Horizon debacle, Wells Fargo fake accounts scandal, the LIBOR manipulation scandal, the Volkswagen emissions scandal, the Theranos health fraud scandal, the sexual harassment scandals that gave rise to the "#MeToo" movement, and too many others to recount. The factors that make it the best time in history to act ethically and the worst time to act unethically have additionally emphasized business ethics' importance. Therefore, there has never been more pressure for business schools (where 59% of college students recently admitted to cheating on exams) to teach business ethics. In part this is because business schools have been accused of having an adverse effect on students' ethical practices. Professor Ghoshal of the London Business School recently asserted that "by propagating ideologically inspired amoral theories, business schools have actively freed their students from any sense of moral responsibility."[11] This may be a little strong, but Robert Shiller, a professor of economics at Yale, also noted that business school "courses often encourage a view of human nature that does not inspire high-mindedness."[12]

Many, including the authors of this text, suspect that by the time students are old

---

[8] Helen A.S. Popkin, *Twitter Gets You Fired in 140 Characters or Less,* MSNBC (Mar. 26, 2009), *available at* http://today.msnbc.msn.com/id/29796962/print/1/displaymode/1098/.

[9] Rhymer Rigby, *Under Ever Closer Scrutiny,* FINANCIAL TIMES, June 5, 2012, at 10 (quoting Philippa Foster Back, director of the Institute of Business Ethics).

[10] PAUL BABIAK & ROBERT D. HARE, SNAKES IN SUITS: WHEN PSYCHOPATHS GO TO WORK (2007).

[11] Sumantra Ghoshal, *Bad Management Theories Are Destroying Good Management Practices,* 4 ACADEMY OF MANAGEMENT LEARNING & EDUCATION 75 (2005).

[12] Robert J. Shiller, *How Wall Street Learns to Look the Other Way; Teaching Ethics,* N.Y. TIMES, Feb. 9, 2005, at 6.

© 2020 John R. Allison & Robert A. Prentice

enough to take a college business law course their moral standards are largely set.[13] If parents, teachers, and religious leaders have not already influenced them to wish to act ethically, a college course emphasizing business ethics is unlikely to have a huge impact. That said, there is a difference between having a good moral compass and the ability to navigate the intricacies of modern ethical dilemmas. Consequently, there are several reasons to emphasize business ethics in a business school curriculum.

First, those who believe that acting ethically is unimportant and seek only to advance their own self-interest may learn in a business ethics class that one of the best ways to advance one's self-interest is to act ethically, as this chapter has already indicated.

Second, the large majority of students who are already inclined to act ethically can gain the tools to do so more effectively. There is at least some evidence that wrestling with ethical dilemmas in a classroom setting can improve students' ability to reason through such dilemmas when they confront them in the real world. Moral reasoning is a skill that can be honed. There is empirical evidence that ethics training can sensitize students to moral issues and affect their behavior.[14] Some studies indicate that people in their twenties and thirties can, with proper training, advance further in moral reasoning than teens and other younger people.[15]

Third, most professors and administrators in business schools believe that acting ethically is important in life and will be important to students when they enter the business world. Given that, it makes little sense to just ignore the issue. To emphasize business ethics in a business school curriculum serves to signal to the students that their schools' leaders believe that acting ethically is not optional, while ignoring the topic projects a lack of importance.

Fourth, if we are aware of, and consider in advance the implications of moral challenges, we can anticipate ethical dilemmas before we find ourselves enmeshed in them. We can thereby lessen the likelihood that we will make inadvertent ethical mistakes.

For all these reasons, there is a strong trend across both graduate and undergraduate business education throughout the world to emphasize business ethics education.[16]

This text's explicit ethics discussion consists of three chapters. This chapter contains a lengthy and detailed introduction to the topic of business ethics, asking questions such as: (a) What is ethics? (b) What is the relationship between law and ethics? (c) Do humans have an evolved moral sense? (d) What philosophical approaches exist for resolving ethical dilemmas? (e) Is there a duty to "do good"?

The next chapter helps individual businesspeople who wish to think and act ethically

---

[13] In a related vein, several recent studies indicate that the political leanings of college professors do not significantly impact the political view of college students. Patricia Cohen, *Professors' Liberalism Contagious? Maybe Not,* N.Y. TIMES, Nov. 3, 2008, at C1.

[14] Craig V. VanSandt et al., *An Examination of the Relationship Between Ethical Work Climate and Moral Awareness,* 68 JOURNAL OF BUSINESS ETHICS 409 (2006).

[15] J.R. Rest, "Moral Judgment: An Interesting Variable for Higher Education Research," (1987).

[16] Dana Middleton & Joe Light, *Harvard Changes Course,* WALL STREET JOURNAL, Feb. 3, 2011 (reporting on HBS's change in curriculum to focus on cultivating judgment rather than basic analytical tools "with a stated effort to create more ethical leaders"); Bettina Von Stamm, *Traditional MBA Skills Are No Longer Enough*" FINANCIAL TIMES, December 19, 2011, p. 13 (founder of the Innovation Leadership Forum arguing that traditional MBA programs produce managers who are excessively analytical and detached and that softer skills are needed, focusing on "integrative, systemic thinking, emotional intelligence, self-awareness and a deep commitment to a bedrock of business ethics.")

do so successfully. And the third chapter focuses on corporations and other business entities, discussing both whether they should act as moral agents and, if so, how they can successfully do so.

WHAT IS ETHICS?

In a formal sense, the term *ethics* refers to the study of *morality* by systematically exploring moral values, moral standards and obligations, moral reasoning, and moral judgments. The terms morality and morals refer to the appropriate treatment of our fellow human beings. Although some people observe a technical distinction between "ethics" and "morals," these terms are often used interchangeably. When someone says, for example, that "Joe did not act ethically in that situation," the word "ethically" means the same thing as "morally." In this text, we are not very fussy about the use of these terms. The context will make the meaning clear.[17]

There are innumerable definitions of ethics and morals. Berreby points out that "moral codes are almost entirely about restraining that impulse to maximize your fitness, as the Darwinians put it. Ethical behavior restrains the individual's desires for the sake of fairness, kindness, and the rights of others."[18]

Is Business Ethics Different?

Should a study of "business ethics" differ from a more general study of ethical concepts? Questions about how we ought to interact with and treat others arise in all aspects of life. Moral issues arise not only in business but in the realm of the family, social groups, neighborhoods, politics and government, interactions between nations, professional associations, and other relationships. The basic questions, arguments, and problem-solving methods remain the same for all these domains. The factual contexts will vary, of course, depending on the nature of the relationship. In studying *business* ethics, we focus on business relationships and use examples of business problems that raise ethical questions. In other words, business ethics consists of the application of moral principles to people in a business setting.

Unfortunately, some people believe that while it is appropriate to act ethically in their personal lives, to succeed in the business world they must act unethically. This is decidedly *not* the case. In virtually every field of endeavor, people who act ethically—who are "long-run" greedy rather than "short-run" greedy—can succeed.

THE RELATIONSHIP BETWEEN LAW AND ETHICS

Even assuming that business schools should teach ethics, one might legitimately ask whether they should attempt to do so in a business law course. There are, however, a number of ways in which ethics and law fit together very naturally. Indeed, in many ways law and business ethics are the most complementary subjects imaginable.

Differences between Legal and Moral Standards

As we will see shortly, legal standards often have their counterparts in the ethical

---

[17] For brief video definitions of "ethics," "morals," and other relevant terms, see http://ethicsunwrapped.utexas.edu/glossary .

[18] DAVID BERREBY, US AND THEM: UNDERSTANDING YOUR TRIBAL MIND 302 (2005).

domain, and vice-versa. For example, lying may not only violate a fundamental moral standard but also constitute fraud under the law of torts and under various criminal statutes. It may constitute sufficient legal justification for rescinding a contract or putting someone in jail for perjury. Similarly, breaking a promise may not only be unethical but also may constitute a legally impermissible breach of contract in some circumstances. There are, however, several basic differences between legal and moral standards.

First, legal standards have a different source than moral ones. Whether found in a constitution, statute, judicial decision, or administrative agency regulation, legal standards are defined and applied by governmental processes. It takes governmental power to adopt and enforce laws. Actions are illegal only when the government explicitly says so.

Moral standards, however, may not have the backing of official government machinery. Much of what the law does is put the power of the state behind accepted moral standards, but not all such standards receive this support. The law comes from government. Where do moral standards come from? There is strong evidence that our tendency to judge others on moral dimensions is instinctive (intuitive), likely the product of evolution. People live successfully in groups because they relentlessly judge others (and are judged by others) regarding compliance with the community's moral standards. As Jonathan Haidt notes, "the human mind is designed to 'do' morality, just as it's designed to do language..."[19]

The content of the moral standards that are applied is significantly shaped by cultural factors that vary from society to society.[20] Although there appear to be a few moral universals (e.g., be fair, and do not harm others in your in-group), there is substantial variation from culture to culture, religion to religion, and country to country.

Second, the consequences of violating legal and moral standards are different. Violations of the law, if detected, often result in concrete sanctions. When lying violates the law against fraud, for example, the guilty person may have to pay damages to the victim in a civil lawsuit, and may even be prosecuted in a criminal action and forced to pay a fine or serve a jail term. There are no clearly defined, externally imposed sanctions for violating moral standards, however. Although lying is considered unethical in most situations, even if it does not meet the legal definition of fraud, the violation of ethical norms by itself is not subject to any definite penalties. It is true that unethical conduct often results in tangible consequences such as lost business because of a damaged reputation; however, the consequences sometimes are like the standards themselves, internal and difficult to define.

Third, legal and ethical standards clearly influence one another, but are not the same. Laws are often enacted to put the power of government behind people's most important cultural and moral standards. If an action is illegal, it is usually unethical. If an action is legal, it is usually ethical. However, there are exceptions. Disobedience to fugitive slave laws in the 1860s, to segregation laws in the 1960s, and to anti-Jewish proclamations of Hitler's Nazi regime would have been ethical, though illegal. And while it is illegal to drive 37 miles per hour in a zone marked with a 35-mph speed limit, it is not intrinsically immoral to do so.

Just as legal standards may be more demanding than ethical standards, as in the case of speed limits and other regulatory provisions, legal standards may also be less demanding

---

[19] JONATHAN HAIDT, THE RIGHTEOUS MIND: WHY GOOD PEOPLE ARE DIVIDED BY POLITICS AND RELIGION xii (2012).

[20] MARK PAGEL, WIRED FOR CULTURE: ORIGINS OF THE HUMAN SOCIAL MIND (2012).

for a variety of reasons, many of them practical. Consider *Soldano v. O'Daniels*,[21] a case involving the question of whether to impose a legal obligation to be a Good Samaritan upon a tavern owner. One person had pulled a gun on another in an establishment across the street. A would-be Good Samaritan ran to defendant's bar and asked the bartender to either call the police or to allow the Good Samaritan to do so. The bartender refused, and the fellow with the gun later shot the man in the other establishment. The shooting victim's family sued the bartender and the bar's owner for refusing to help.

Should the ethical and legal standards applicable to the bar tender and bar owner be identical? All major religions espouse a moral obligation to help others in need. Think of the Christian parable of the Good Samaritan. However, judges and legislators establishing laws must consider a variety of extra-ethical factors. While the law should and generally does reflect society's ethical standards, there are times that the two must part company. Sometimes ethical standards cannot be practically enforced. Enforcement in some settings may carry impractical implications for other situations. The judges in *Soldano* held that the defendants could be legally liable not because they refused to be Good Samaritans themselves, but because they interfered with another's attempt to be a Good Samaritan. By creating a modest exception to the general American rule that there is no general "duty to rescue," the judges in *Soldano* attempted to align the legal rule a little more closely to society's ethical beliefs. But how far they could go was clearly constrained by practical considerations as illustrated by the *Clockwork Orange* scenario that the court's opinion discussed wherein thugs invaded the home of innocent citizens on the pretense of needing assistance. Because defendant's tavern was a public place, the judges felt comfortable imposing a duty that they would not have imposed on homeowners.

Lying is another area where legal and ethical rules diverge. Lying is usually considered immoral, but for a variety of very practical reasons, the legal system does not attempt to punish all lies that people tell. Assume that Sam tells Molly that he can't make their date on Saturday night because he has come down with the flu. Molly later finds out that Sam felt fine, and he just decided to go out with Sarah instead. Sam acted unethically, but the law would not allow Molly to win a case for breach of contract or any other theory.

The Legal/Ethical Overlap

Despite their differences, law and ethics have much in common. For example, they serve the same general purpose. Remember the Tom Hanks movie *Cast Away* where he was stranded on a desert island with his volleyball "Wilson"? Did he need law? Was ethics a concern for him? Probably not. Rules of law and ethical principles are important for the same reason—both make it possible for humans to live in social groups. Morality evolved to facilitate such living.

> Why do we have moral values? The obvious answer is that morality emerges as a system of rules for getting people to function collectively in stable and productive ways. We have morality to build a coherent social group. Moral values lead us to cooperate and prevent us from harming members of our communities... Robinson Crusoe would have no need for [them].[22]

---

[21] 190 Cal. Rptr. 310 (Cal.App. 1983). This case should be familiar from Chapter One of this text.

[22] JESSE PRINZ, THE EMOTIONAL CONSTRUCTION OF MORALS 185 (2007). Joshua Greene and colleagues have demonstrated that different parts of the brain activate when people consider throwing the switch (Denise) versus pushing the big guy (Frank) in the trolley problem, leading Prinz to surmise that the

Law and ethics both represent society's expression of its most basic values. Questions of fairness and avoiding harm to others are at the bottom of many if not most legal *and* moral issues. "Whether legal norms [such as proximate cause, side effects, and mental states] are built into the very fabric of the human mind is one of cognitive science's deepest and most persistent questions."[23] The same is true regarding moral standards, as we shall see in the next section.

Because law and ethics serve the same purpose (enabling people to live together in groups), they largely (though not completely) overlap. As noted earlier, breaking the law is in and of itself generally (though not universally) considered to be unethical.[24] In constructing a decision tree for the ethical manager, Yale School of Management's Constance Bagley recently noted that the first question the ethical decision maker must always ask is: "Is it legal?"[25]

Not only is this the first question that the ethical decision maker must ask, often it is the last question that need be asked. A corporate ethics officer for a Fortune 500 company once said that employees often asked her: "Is this action ethical?" She found that 90% of the time that question was answered by simply asking: "Is it legal?" Our society's ethical and legal standards are sufficiently conflated that it is rare that an illegal action will be ethical. That is one reason that a course in business law is so important for students who wish to not only avoid adverse legal consequences but also to "do the right thing" in their business careers.

Importantly, law not only reflects society's ethical values, it can shape them as well. After laws were passed outlawing racial discrimination in employment and insider trading, studies showed that a much higher percentage of people viewed those activities as improper than had held that view before the laws were passed. When people engage in ethical reasoning, often they use the law, perhaps unconsciously, as an ethical referent. "Even at more sophisticated levels of moral reasoning, law is often considered the embodiment of universal principles, to be followed unless one's own principled reasoning conflicts with the law."[26] Ethical principles thus shape our laws and vice versa.

Also, as we shall soon see, sound moral reasoning is quite similar in methodology to sound legal reasoning. The methods that businesspeople can use to identify and analyze ethical issues are very much the same as methods for dealing with legal issues.

EVOLUTION OF A MORAL SENSE

The history of how our legal systems have evolved is an interesting story. Most business law textbooks explain how in jolly old England courts of equity were created to

---

more direct act of pushing the person has a greater emotional impact on the potential actor than does the more removed act of simply throwing a switch. Joshua D. Greene, et al., *An fMRI Investigation of Emotional Engagement in Moral Judgment,* 293 SCIENCE 2105 (2001).

[23] John Mikhail, *Moral Grammar and Intuitive Jurisprudence: A Formal Model of Unconscious Moral and Legal Knowledge,* in 50 THE PSYCHOLOGY OF LEARNING AND MOTIVATION: MORAL COGNITION AND DECISION MAKING (2009).

[24] N. Craig Smith et al., *Why Managers Fail to Do the Right Thing: An Empirical Test of Unethical and Illegal Conduct,* 17 BUSINESS ETHICS QUARTERLY 633 (2007).

[25] Constance Bagley, *Forethought: The Ethical Leader's Decision Tree,* 81 HARVARD BUSINESS REVIEW 18 (Feb. 2003).

[26] Sandra L. Christensen, *The Role of Law in Models of Ethical Behavior,* 77 JOURNAL OF BUSINESS ETHICS 451 (2008).

supplement courts of law, in part to more closely align the results of the legal system with societal notions of fairness and equity. The formalism of the courts of law often prevented justice from being done. In the United States, we originally honored the sharp distinction between courts of law and courts of equity, but over time that distinction has largely disappeared. Just as law evolves over time, many believe that the universal human capacity for moral thought has evolved.

Among many pieces of evidence supporting this conclusion is the concept of "moral dumbfounding." There are many snap moral judgments that humans around the world tend to make that they cannot explain intellectually. Consider a hypothetical scenario in which a brother and sister decide to have sexual relations with one another in order to make their relationship more "special." Most people around the world react with revulsion to this scenario. This reaction helps prevent the inbreeding that could cause adverse genetic consequences. If the brother is sterile or the sister infertile or if they have used multiple levels of birth control (she's on the pill and he uses a condom), the rational reasons for condemning the practice go away. But most people still say "ewww!" because we have evolved to avoid incest and the genetic disadvantages that go with it. Because of this innate moral instinct, we react with revulsion to the siblings' decision, but have difficulty explaining the logic of our moral judgment if the possibility of pregnancy is removed from the equation. A similarly strong emotional (not logical) reaction is expressed by most people asked to judge a pathologist who while performing an autopsy late at night in a lab, nibbles a bit of discarded human flesh because she is hungry.

And consider these two scenarios that derive from philosopher Philippa Foot:

1. Denise is standing near a track when she spots an out-of-control trolley. The conductor has fainted and the trolley is headed toward five people walking on the track; the banks are so steep that they will not be able to get off the track in time. The track has a side track leading off to the left, and Denise just happens to be standing near a switch that she can flip to turn the trolley onto the side track. There is, however, one person on the left-hand track. Denise can turn the trolley, killing the one; or she can refrain from flipping the switch, letting the five die. *Is it morally permissible for Denise to flip the switch, turning the trolley onto the side track?*

2. Frank is on a footbridge over the trolley tracks. He knows trolleys and can see that the one approaching the bridge is out of control, with its conductor passed out. On the track under the bridge there are five people; the banks are so steep that they will not be able to get off the track in time. Frank knows that the only way to stop an out-of-control trolley is to drop a very heavy weight into its path. But the only available, sufficiently heavy weight is a large person also watching the trolley from the footbridge. Frank can shove the large person onto the track in the path of the trolley, resulting in his death; or he can refrain from doing this, letting the five die. *Is it morally permissible for Frank to push the large person onto the tracks?*

In each scenario, a person has an opportunity to take an action that will save five lives at the cost of one. When asked, most people quickly conclude that it is morally permissible for Denise to flip the switch. Conversely, when asked most people say that it is *not* morally permissible for Frank to push the large person onto the track. Importantly, most people seem unable to rationally explain their differing answers. Why is it morally permissible to kill one person in order to save five in one setting, but not in the other? Humans' inability to rationally explain their strong reactions to the sibling sex and cannibalism scenarios, as well as their inability to rationally justify their differing reactions to the Denise and Frank hypothetical examples, illustrates what is often called "moral dumfounding," which some people believe provides evidence that our brain's reasoning power plays a less significant role in human moral decision making than might appear on the surface to be the case.

In addition, evidence from brain scans indicates that the emotional part of the brain is often activated to condemn an action before the cognitive portion of the brain is activated. Hence, our moral decisions may be decided largely outside our consciousness. Even young children can tell the difference between rules that represent mere conventions and rules that represent moral principles. For example, they know that in school both talking in class and hitting another child are prohibited. They also know that if the teacher permits talking in class it is okay to do so, but it is not okay to hit another child even if the teacher has no rules against it. Amish teenagers believe that it would be okay to work on Sunday if God did not forbid it, but that it would not be okay to hurt other people, even if God had no rule against it, again indicating an understanding of the difference between social conventions and moral rules.[27] The two factors that children seem to use to distinguish moral principles from simple conventions are fairness and harm to others.

Finally, note that some animals seem to have evolved a moral sense as well, and for similar reasons. Both humans and chimpanzees, for example, will sacrifice what is in their best individual interest in order to punish cheaters in cooperative settings (which benefits the social group). It has been argued that for evolutionary reasons some animals have developed a "moral sense" in much the same way that humans have.[28]

Thus, there is substantial evidence that many of our most basic moral beliefs are a product of evolution, like so much of our physical and mental makeup. Our automatic responses are pervasive and important. Every day we have hundreds of opportunities to violate ethical rules by hitting people we don't like, stealing from others when they are not looking, cheating at school or at work, etc. Most of us most of the time follow accepted moral practices without calling to mind Aristotle or Kant and consciously reasoning through the situation. In short, recent studies suggest "that many decision processes that were previously thought to be the product of logical inference and rational deliberation are instead more accurately described as being the product of relatively automatic emotional intuitions and perceptions."[29]

Self-focused emotions such as shame, embarrassment, regret, and guilt often lead people to act consistently with perceived moral principles, even when it might not be in their clear self-interest to do so. Other-focused sentiments such as contempt, anger, disgust, and *schadenfreude* are often emotions we feel when evaluating the ethical nature of the conduct of others.[30] The impact that these emotions have upon our own decision making and our evaluations of others' actions are obvious and significant. Empirical studies show that people with stronger feelings of guilt and shame, for example, will make decisions that more strongly take into account the interests of others than will people with weaker feelings of these emotions.[31]

---

[27] SHAUN NICHOLS, SENTIMENTAL RULES: ON THE NATURAL FOUNDATIONS OF MORAL JUDGMENT 5-6 (2004).

[28] DALE PETERSON, THE MORAL LIVES OF ANIMALS (2011).

[29] Timothy Ketelaar, *The Role of Moral Sentiments in Economic Decision Making,* in SOCIAL PSYCHOLOGY AND ECONOMICS 97 (De Cremer et al., eds. 2006).

[30] *Id.* at 102.

[31] *Id.*

However, although the evidence for evolutionary morality is interesting and vivid, the field is very new and the views of the best scientists are currently inconclusive. Most of us feel guilty when we have cheated others and contempt when others violate normative rules regarding community standards and customs. These are strong candidates for relatively universal, culturally shared emotional reactions,[32] yet not all persons experience them and certainly not to the same degree.

Even if the essence of the notion is true, many ethical dilemmas we face in the modern world do not generate automatic responses, leaving much room for rational examination of the issues involved. Mark Johnson has argued strongly that people should endeavor to use what he calls "imaginative moral deliberation" to ensure that their cognitive processes can intervene when their emotional reactions lead to suboptimal moral judgments.[33]

Nonetheless, in determining what is ethical in a particular situation, we would be unwise to completely disregard our inherited emotional responses. When our "gut" tells us that a course of action we are contemplating is wrong, it probably is. Strong emotional reactions to ethical situations cannot be safely ignored.[34] Furthermore, in attempting to persuade others as to what is ethical and in attempting to influence people's behavior via legal rules,[35] we cannot safely ignore the considerations described in this section.

All this said, we humans have the power to put our cognitive processes to work to reevaluate and perhaps override our more immediate intuitive responses to moral questions. We do not do so nearly as often as we should. But if we realize the imperfections of our emotional-response system, perhaps we can resolve to do better in this regard.[36]

PHILOSOPHICAL APPROACHES TO ETHICAL REASONING

For much of recorded history, philosophers and regular people alike have struggled to develop legitimate, consistent and fair approaches to determining what is "right" and "wrong" in the ethical sphere. Most of our modern ethical dilemmas involve issues (e.g., insider trading) that were not prevalent on the savannah ten thousand years ago when our basic moral superstructure may have evolved. Therefore, being able to reason ethically may be helpful, just as thinking quantitatively can be important in many contexts. For instance, the core moral value of fairness is not new to this era, but the situations where we encounter fairness concerns differ, requiring us to develop our moral reasoning so that we can continually reevaluate how we will apply our moral belief in fairness to novel factual situations.

---

[32] P. Rozin et al., *The CAD Triad Hypothesis: A Mapping Between Three Moral Emotions (Contempt, Anger, Disgust) and Three Moral Codes (Community, Autonomy, Divinity)*, 76 JOURNAL OF PERSONALITY AND SOCIAL PSYCHOLOGY 574 (1999).

[33] MARK JOHNSON, MORALITY FOR HUMANS: ETHICAL UNDERSTANDING FROM THE PERSPECTIVE OF COGNITIVE SCIENCE (2014).

[34] *See* Rommel Salvador & Robert G. Folger, *Business Ethics and the Brain,* 19 BUSINESS ETHICS QUARTERLY 1 (Jan. 2009) (noting that "[a] number of neuroethics scholars have argued that moral judgment is, for the most part, an unconscious (and therefore reflexive) process.").

[35] Haidt argues that "[w]e do moral reasoning not to reconstruct the actual reasons why *we ourselves* came to a judgment; we reason to find the best possible reasons why *somebody else ought to join us* in our judgment." JONATHAN HAIDT, THE RIGHTEOUS MIND 44 (2012).

[36] JOSHUA MAY, REGARD FOR REASON IN THE MORAL MIND (2018); HANNO SAUER, MORAL THINKING, FAST AND SLOW (2019).

Some argue that, although there are no overarching specific moral "rules" that can be applied to all human behavior, the general standard of *utilitarianism* can serve as a guide for moral behavior. Advanced by noted philosophers such as Jeremy Bentham and John Stuart Mill, utilitarianism is an ethical theory that is committed solely to the purpose of promoting "the greatest good for the greatest number." Utilitarianism has many forms, but essentially permits all conduct that will serve the objective of maximizing the social utility (i.e., the social "benefit" or "good"). As an abstract theory, utilitarianism makes a lot of sense. What could be wrong with seeking to create the greatest good for the greatest number? Utilitarianism and other approaches that concentrate on the consequences of moral choices are termed, naturally enough, *consequentialist* theories.

In actual practice, it can be all but impossible to calculate, even roughly, which specific actions are likely to provide the greatest benefit to society. Moreover, even deciding how to define "benefit to society" can be an exercise in futility because of the many possible value judgments involved. What one person reasonably views as a benefit to society may be quite different from the reasonable view of another person. Additionally, killing an innocent healthy person and harvesting his organs might save the lives of several other individuals who need organ transplants to survive, thus creating a net gain in lives preserved. However, few would argue that saving the lives of the several justifies taking the life of the involuntary donor. In large part because of these and similar difficulties, many ethicists view utilitarianism as being just one component in a rational process of ethical reasoning.

Some well-known philosophers do feel that we can identify and apply certain threshold standards of moral behavior to real problems across various circumstances and cultures. This *deontological* view is a rule-based or Ten Commandments ("Thou Shalt Not Kill") sort of analysis, often identified with German philosopher Immanuel Kant, who wrote that every person's actions should be judged morally by asking the question: "Can this action be justified by reasons that are uniformly applicable to all other persons?" In other words, he suggested as an overarching standard of moral behavior the rule that people cannot make exceptions of themselves; one's behavior is morally defensible only if everyone else could do the same thing without interfering with the optimal functioning of an organized society. Each person should be treated as an end in himself, not as a means to an end. This means, among other things, that we should all treat others as we would wish to be treated, a wisdom embodied in the so-called Golden Rule. Virtually every major religion in the world has some version of this treat-others-as-you-would-wish-to-be-treated standard.

A third basic approach is that of Aristotelian *virtue ethics* that concentrates more on the actor attempting to become a virtuous person in all aspects, rather than on the resolution of specific ethical issues. The focus is not on deciding individual moral dilemmas in the correct way. Instead, the notion is that each person should focus on developing and practicing important virtues such as honesty, integrity, truthfulness, reliability and so on. If people embody these virtues, the ethical decisions they make will likely be good ones.

For fans of the Batman movie *The Dark Knight*, an obvious issue with which the Batman struggles is whether to kill the Joker, who seems to exist only to cause chaos and carnage. Ethicists Mark White and Robert Arp write:

> Utilitarianism…would probably endorse killing the Joker, based on comparing the many lives saved against the one life lost.
> Deontology… would focus on the act of murder itself, rather than the consequences….While it may be preferable for the Joker to be dead, it may not be morally

right for any person (such as Batman) to kill him. If the Joker is to be punished, it should be through official procedures, not vigilante justice. More generally, while the Joker is evil, he is still a human being, and is thus deserving of at least a minimal level of respect and humanity.

Finally, virtue ethics … would highlight the character of the person who kills the Joker. Does Batman want to be the kind of person that takes his enemies' lives? If he killed the Joker, would he be able to stop there, or would every two-bit thug get the same treatment?

Mark D. White & Robert Arp, *Should Batman Kill the Joker?* INTERNATIONAL HERALD TRIBUNE, July 26-27, 2008, at 5.

These three approaches often lead to the same conclusions regarding what course of action would be the ethical one. The Batman-Joker dilemma indicates that they do not always do so. Nonetheless, there is certainly merit in all of these approaches. The best approach to being an ethical person and making ethical decisions may well include elements of each. Process is also extremely important. It is often helpful to employ a rational process for analyzing these kinds of questions. (We will present such a process later in this chapter.)

MORAL REASONING AND DECISION MAKING

To the extent that moral questions are subject to rational analysis, it would pay to develop an ability to invoke that analysis effectively. The following process of analyzing moral questions is essentially the same as rational problem-solving in other situations, including analysis of legal questions.

Identifying Issues

Any time your potential actions may injure others, violate basic rules of ethicality (*e.g.,* involve lying, cheating, stealing, etc.), or would cause you do the sort of thing that virtuous people do not do, an ethical issue is likely presenting itself.

The necessary first step in problem solving is to figure out exactly what the problems are. In other words, one must identify the issues. If one is confronted with legal, financial, or marketing issues, for example, they first should be recognized and spelled out as clearly as possible. The same is true of ethical issues. Problems have to be defined narrowly enough so that we have the ability both to analyze them adequately *and* exercise some degree of influence over the outcome.

Consider the following scenario. Assume that Alexis works in the tax division of a large public accounting firm. One of the firm's major clients is Leviathan Corp. While working on one part of Leviathan's tax return, Alexis discovers that some expense items appear to have been overstated. No single item has been grossly inflated, and the total amount of expense overstatement is significant but not huge. Thus, the risk of detection by the Internal Revenue Service probably is relatively small. Also, Alexis cannot determine with certainty whether the overstatements are intentional or simply resulted from honest mistakes or incompetence. She speaks with her immediate supervisor about the matter, but the supervisor dismisses the evidence as a "nonproblem." When Alexis presses the issue a little harder, the supervisor says: "Just do your job and don't stick your nose in too far." Should Alexis take up the matter with a higher-level manager, perhaps even with the firm's top management? Suppose that she does so and receives the same kind of response at that level. What then?

The issue Alexis must cope with immediately is not (1) whether it is wrong in general to cheat on one's taxes; (2) whether her superiors are bad people; (3) whether her accounting firm or Leviathan Corp. has developed an organizational structure that is insufficient to establish lines of individual accountability for wrongdoing; or (4) whether she can sue her employer for the tort of wrongful discharge if she is fired for objecting to the expense overstatements or reporting them to the IRS. The issue that Alexis must confront at the present time is whether her most morally defensible course of action is to keep quiet, and go along with her firm's possibly inappropriate behavior, or to resist it by "blowing the whistle." Other issues will arise later, but right now this issue is all she needs to deal with from an ethical perspective.

Identifying the Governing Principles

For every kind of issue there are governing principles or rules that guide or limit our decision. The source of these principles will vary, depending on the nature of the issue. There are legal rules, generally accepted accounting principles, generally accepted courses of medical treatment for particular illnesses, formulas for computing stress in the construction of bridges, and so on. In ethics there are also foundational moral obligations.

In some cases, the principles will be relatively *specific* but in others they may be quite *general*. Whether they are specific or general, different principles may be characterized by varying degrees of *certainty or acceptance*. In the case of some legal principles, it can be difficult to determine precisely what the rule is. This uncertainty can result from conflicting court decisions, ambiguous statutory language, or other factors. In addition, some principles are more generally accepted than others, whether the relevant field is law, medicine, accounting, engineering, ethics, or another discipline. These qualifying remarks do not diminish the importance of guiding principles. They represent the collective knowledge gained from experience and rational thought, and should serve as the foundation for rational problem solving.

In ethics, the principles are fairly general. As indicated earlier, one approach is utilitarian—to attempt to calculate which course of action will lead to the best result for the most people. Another approach is deontological—to treat individuals as ends in themselves and avoid lying, cheating, stealing, and other wrongful behaviors. A third approach is to focus on being a virtuous person and try to decide how such a person would act in the face of this ethical issue.

When analyzing ethical issues, it is important to identify the pertinent moral obligations as precisely as possible. What is the *nature* of the obligation? Honesty? Loyalty? Keeping commitments? Doing no harm? After identifying the nature of each moral obligation, we must make sure we understand exactly *who* owes which obligation to whom. In Alexis's case we have already done a pretty good job of identifying the obligations that she owes to various parties. If we are doing a complete ethical analysis of the entire situation, we also would find it necessary to identify the moral obligations owed to Alexis by her superiors. One can argue persuasively that they are violating their duty of doing no harm by intentionally, recklessly, or negligently engaging in conduct that may cause reasonably foreseeable harm to Alexis. Acting on behalf of the firm, essentially what they have done is ask her to participate in conduct that may be dishonest and possibly even illegal. Even if she does not get into any legal trouble, emotional trauma also can be viewed as "harm" when it is a reasonably foreseeable result of their actions.

Collecting, Verifying, and Drawing Inferences from Information

Issues of any kind always arise in a factual context—they do not exist in a vacuum. In our hypothetical case, the relevant information (i.e., "evidence" or "data") that initially caused Alexis to perceive a problem was the apparent inconsistency between entries in Leviathan's general ledgers used to prepare its tax return and the figures in supporting documentation. When information raises potential ethical, legal, or other issues, we should first do what we can to verify the accuracy, reliability, and completeness of that information. If the issues are sensitive, we obviously must exercise great care in doing this. Caution and thoroughness are essential. The best and most well-intentioned reasoning in the world is for naught if based on inaccurate facts. Fact-gathering, then, is critically important to ethical decision making.

We may find that the true facts are very different than we initially suspected, and that there is no problem at all. Of course, we may find that things are much worse than we thought. Frequently we may conclude after an initial inquiry that our information is incomplete and that we need additional evidence to understand the situation. Again, in the subsequent search for more evidence, caution is the watchword. It is usually impossible to acquire information that is so complete and so clearly accurate and reliable as to resolve all doubt. Decisions usually have to be made on the basis of information that is less than perfect. When analyzing important issues and preparing to make important decisions, however, it is essential that our information be as complete and accurate as circumstances will allow.

As with any fact-finding process that serves as a foundation for problem solving, in ethical analysis we infer relevant facts from the evidence. In other words, we infer that certain things have happened. In addition to inferring facts, we use the evidence as a basis for making predictions about likely future events. Thus, from the evidence she has at her disposal, Alexis might infer that her firm condones or possibly even assists in tax cheating by clients, although more information is needed to support this inference. Alexis also may have enough information to predict that any further objection to superiors within the firm is likely to be fruitless, and that she may even be penalized in some way for making a fuss.

Applying the Facts to the Principles and Balancing Competing Obligations

The remainder of the ethical problem-solving, or moral reasoning, process involves further application of the guiding principles to the facts that we have inferred from the evidence. In other words, we must determine how the identified moral obligations should apply to these particular facts. This determination should be relatively straightforward, of course, if there are no excusing conditions or moral dilemmas. Such complicating factors are present in many cases, however, and must be incorporated into the analysis.

In our hypothetical scenario, we already have identified the moral dilemmas created by several conflicting duties. The next step is to weigh and balance these obligations against one another. In doing so, we must keep in mind that this is not algebra. Despite being a rational analytical process, it is highly qualitative and involves a degree of subjectivity. The process of balancing conflicting obligations should incorporate at least the following factors.

Excusing Conditions

Are there any excusing conditions that might lessen the strength of one obligation relative to another? Moral accountability can be diminished or eliminated by genuine lack of knowledge or of freedom to act. In Alexis's case, one can argue that her status as an employee who is acting under orders from her superiors causes her freedom of action to be considerably less than if she were in charge. No doubt this is true; the degree of her moral responsibility surely is not as great as it would be if she had more power over the firm's decisions. Is her freedom of action curtailed so much, however, that she has no moral duty at all? Certainly not—otherwise a person in a subordinate position could be morally answerable for his conduct only if he initiated and controlled the situation. In such a case, of course, either he would be acting outside his authority or else he really would not be acting as a subordinate at all. Completely relieving all subordinates of moral responsibility for their actions within the organization's chain of command has the potential to lower substantially the level of moral behavior within organizations and throughout society. Thus, Alexis should continue to have a moral duty of honesty with respect to her complicity in the firm's possible wrongdoing, although the strength of her obligation may be somewhat less than in other situations where she is not playing a subordinate role.

Conflict Reduction

Are there ways to minimize conflicts? As in this case, a *prima facie* moral duty usually is not eliminated by an excusing condition. Most of the time there either is no such condition or else the condition merely curtails the strength of a duty rather than doing away with it entirely. Thus, any moral dilemma that we previously identified still exists. Before getting to the point of having to make an all-or-nothing choice between conflicting duties, however, we should search for creative solutions that may diminish or remove the conflict.

Alexis might consider requesting reassignment within the firm, perhaps to another geographic location, so as to remove her from any direct role in the questionable activity. Reassignment may not be feasible, and even if it is feasible it may damage her future opportunities in the firm. Moreover, if the attitude of her current superiors is found throughout the organization, she may encounter similar problems in her new position. Assuming that she finds a higher level of ethical standards at her new location, Alexis still *knows* about the possible dishonesty at her previous one. If she remains silent about it, is she guilty of complicity in the questionable behavior even though she is no longer a participant? Many people would say yes. If we take the view that the duty of loyalty to her employer continues to exist, Alexis still owes the same basic duty because she has remained in the same organization. One can see that removing ourselves from direct involvement does not always eliminate a moral dilemma, although this course of action may reduce the acuteness of the conflict. There remain other options for Alexis, which we will not pursue here.

In other situations, creative ideas for minimizing the degree of conflict between obligations will take other forms. For example, in some cases a person caught in a moral dilemma might be able to work out agreements with one or more of the parties to whom duties are owed so that the duties no longer conflict and all can be fulfilled. If we cannot make agreements that enable us to fulfill all moral duties, it may be possible to work out compromises that permit us to comply fully with one and partially with another. Such opportunities will not always exist, but it is important to carefully consider the possibilities.

Prioritizing

When we cannot eliminate a moral dilemma, we must choose between the obligations that we will attempt to satisfy. The choice should be made only after carefully weighing the strength and importance of the conflicting duties. In other words, we must prioritize the obligations. We already may have gone a long way toward weighing and prioritizing our duties as we considered whether excusing conditions were present and sought creative ways to minimize the conflict. We may have found that excusing conditions reduce the significance of one moral duty with respect to another. Similarly, we may have worked out agreements or discovered alternative courses of action that strengthen or weaken different obligations and, consequently, make our choice easier.

If the relative importance of particular obligations, and thus their proper place on our list of priorities, still remains unclear, we should next attempt to evaluate the *harm* that may result from violating the various moral duties. A careful evaluation of harm will take into account both *degree* and *probability*. Other factors being equal, the relative importance of a moral obligation increases proportionately with increases in (1) the degree of harm (e.g., injury to people is more harmful than injury to property, risk of death is more serious than risk of injury) that is likely to be caused by violating the obligation and (2) the probability (or likelihood) that the harm actually will occur.

In the case of Alexis, for instance, the harm done to taxpayers by this instance of expense overstatement, or even by all similar actions by her employer's clients, is probably pretty small in relative terms. On the other hand, we should also consider cumulative effects. When one tax cheater is reported and gets caught, other cheaters may change their behavior. Thus, the harm to taxpayers caused by her firm's conduct, and the harm that may be prevented by her reporting it, could be a lot greater than one might think. With regard to probability, the harm caused by even a single instance of cheating is certain to occur even if it is very small.

If Alexis reports the expense overstatements to the IRS, there is no doubt that short-term harm will be caused to both her employer and Leviathan, especially if the overstatements are found to have been intentional. They will incur penalties, and perhaps substantial legal fees and court costs. These harms appear to be high in both degree and probability. In addition, the accounting firm and Leviathan may suffer long-term harm in the form of damaged company reputations and the various costs associated with an increased level of future oversight by the IRS. This kind of harm probably is somewhat less certain to occur, but if it does occur it could be even more substantial than the short-term damage. At the same time, we must not overlook the possibility that, if Alexis's firm and Leviathan are reported and get into legal trouble now, this event could lead them to clean up their general level of ethical behavior. Arguably, more ethical behavior in the future will reduce their chances of encountering costly legal problems.

Finally, we need much more information before evaluating the degree or probability of harm that might be caused to others if Alexis loses her job after "blowing the whistle." How likely is it that she will actually lose her job? If she gets fired, how likely is it that she will be able to recover damages from her former employer in a lawsuit claiming the tort of wrongful discharge? Will she have a difficult time finding comparable employment? Do others depend on her for support?

Making a Moral Decision

Ultimately, Alexis must make a decision that reflects a choice. Even inaction is a choice. There may be no choice that is totally satisfactory, and there almost certainly will not be one that is completely free of doubt or negative consequences. Whatever course she takes, her choice should be the conscious result of a rational process similar to the one we have described.

It is true that quick decisions sometimes have to be made. They are often made intuitively with little rational input. In those cases, we may not have the luxury to gather as much information or reflect on our choices as much as we would like. There is often, and this is true of Alexis's situation, time for reflection and rational thinking. When emotionally-charged ethical questions arise, we are far more likely to work them out through a rational analytical process if we have already anticipated and carefully thought about general problems of this nature. This is especially true when decisions have to be made under pressure and in relatively short periods of time. If we have not already practiced rational thinking about ethical issues in our actual experiences, we should at least take the time to examine our own values and to think about how we would deal with particular moral questions should they arise. Without some preparation, we run a much greater risk of making rash responses under pressure.

It is true that decisions, moral or otherwise, may turn out all right even if not preceded by sound analytical reasoning. Perhaps innate moral sense is responsible, or maybe just simple good fortune. In any event, it is also true that rational thinking does not guarantee optimal results. Although carrying no guarantees, such a process can have the following benefits:

1. It increases our chances of having better and more complete information on which to base a decision.
2. It lowers the risk of completely overlooking an important issue.
3. It improves our chances of making a decision that best balances the various conflicting interests that may be present.
4. If we are later called upon to defend our decision, we will be better prepared to do so.

Difficult decisions that affect others are often challenged, and a decision resulting from the type of process described here is more defensible. We have our facts straighter, and our reasons for making particular choices can be presented more clearly and forcefully because they have been thought through carefully. In addition, we are able to demonstrate a good faith effort to do the right thing. Evidence of good faith is no small matter, and often can make the difference when close judgment calls are at issue.

MORAL RELATIVISM VERSUS MORAL PLURALISM

Across individuals in a given culture and often across individuals in different cultures around the world "there is a remarkable degree of consensus in judgments regarding the degree of blameworthiness of various moral transgressions."[37] Rape is bad. Murder is bad. Theft is bad. Fairness is good. These are near universals. That said, there are enough differences that Haidt probably has it right when he says that "…morality can be innate (as a set of evolved intuitions) and learned (as children learn to apply those intuitions within a particular culture). We're born to be righteous, but we have to learn what, exactly, people like us should be righteous about."[38].

---

[37] Paul H. Robinson & John M. Darley, *Intuitions of Justice: Implications for Criminal Law and Justice Policy,* 81 SOUTHERN CALIFORNIA LAW REVIEW 1 (2007).

[38] JONATHAN HAIDT, THE RIGHTEOUS MIND 26 (2012).

914 © 2020 John R. Allison & Robert A. Prentice

Different cultures can and do reach different answers as to the best ways to resolve the issues that make it difficult for people to live together. Contrast the individualistic orientation of most Western cultures with the more communitarian or sociocentric orientation of most Asian cultures or the stark differences between Christian and Muslim cultures on many important issues. How does a thoughtful person reconcile things? Decide that anything goes and become a relativist? Or become an absolutist and reject any departures from one's own moral code?

There is definitely no easy answer to this question. Jonathan Haidt notes that:

The philosopher Isaiah Berlin wrestled throughout his career with the problems of the world's moral diversity and what to make of it. He firmly rejected moral relativism:

"I am not a relativist; I do not say 'I like my coffee with milk and you like it without; I am in favor of kindness and you prefer concentration camps'—each of us with his own values, which cannot be overcome or integrated. This I believe to be false."

He endorsed pluralism instead, and justified it this way:

"I came to the conclusion that there is a plurality of ideals, as there is a plurality of cultures and of temperaments….There is not an infinity of [values]: the number of human values, of values which I can pursue while maintaining my human semblance, my human character, is finite—let us say 74, or perhaps 122, or 27, but finite, whatever it may be. And the difference this makes is that if a man pursues one of these values, *I who do not, am able to understand why he pursues it* or what it would be like, in his circumstances, for me to be induced to pursue it. Hence, the possibility of human understanding."[39]

A defensible way to evaluate which course of action is the most moral would be to ask: "Which choice would most help sentient beings flourish?"[40] There are right and wrong answers to that question. We should do our best to learn what those answers are, and then stand up for them as vigorously as possible. "Whatever!" is not a solid moral philosophy. However, we should also remember that these are often devilishly difficult questions and easy answers are hard to come by. Therefore, while searching insistently for right answers, we should be very open to taking into consideration the ideas of others from different religions, different cultures, different generations, different philosophies, and different countries.

---

[39] JONATHAN HAIDT, THE RIGHTEOUS MIND 316 (2012) (quoting Berlin).
[40] SAM HARRIS, THE MORAL LANDSCAPE (2010).

CHAPTER 37

BUSINESS ETHICS AND INDIVIDUAL DECISION MAKING

- Introduction

- Social and Organizational Pressures and Ethical Decision Making

- Cognitive Heuristics and Biases and Ethical Decision Making

- Situational Factors and Ethical Decision Making

- Being a Better Person

INTRODUCTION

In 1999, Daniel H. Bayly, known as "Eagle Scout Bayly" for his straight-arrow image, was the 52-year-old head of investment banking at Merrill Lynch. He was part of a 5-minute phone call in which he approved Merrill's purchase of three Nigerian barges owned by Enron Corporation. It seemed like a win-win deal. Merrill's $7 million investment would allow Enron to book $12 million in revenue right before the end of the year. Merrill would cultivate a relationship with Enron that could lead to substantial investment banking revenue in the future. And the risk was minimal—Enron's CFO Andy Fastow promised to find a third-party buyer for the barges or, failing that, to repurchase the barges in six months at a 15% profit to Merrill. Because the transaction enabled Enron to disguise a loan as a revenue-producing transaction, that 5-minute phone call led to a 30-month prison term for Bayly.[41]

Betty Vinson was a senior manager in WorldCom's corporate accounting division in 2000 when her superiors instructed her to dip into a reserve account set up to pay certain expenses. They wanted her to fish out $828 million and use it to pay different expenses in order to boost earnings for the quarter so that WorldCom could meet its earnings projections. The maneuver was clearly wrong under accounting conventions and the sum involved was huge. Mrs. Vinson noted this, but her supervisor said that although he, too, knew that it was improper, his supervisor had assured him that it would never happen again. Reluctantly, Mrs. Vinson went along. Later, when she threatened to resign, her superiors told her to think of the company as an aircraft carrier with airplanes in the air. Once the airplanes had been landed, once the company's fiscal ship had been righted, then she could resign. Until then she should stay on board, they insisted. And she did, assisting in the scheme that ultimately evolved into an $11 billion fraud.[42] Betty Vinson soon found herself facing both federal and state criminal securities fraud charges.[43]

What can we learn from the experiences of Daniel Bayly and Betty Vinson? The bulk of most business law textbooks focus on legal rules that that enable, guide, and constrain companies and individuals operating in our capitalist system. Many of these rules comport with simple common sense. Others are more complex and occasionally seem counterintuitive. All in all, however, they give substantial guidance to individuals and firms wishing to act legally and ethically. Gray areas and borderline questions will certainly arise, but there is also substantial concrete guidance as to what types of actions will be considered legal and ethical, and which will not. Few people go to jail because they were insufficiently schooled in Kantian philosophy or the details of John Stuart Mill's version of consequentialist ethics.

To stay within ethical and legal boundaries, one must learn and follow both the law and the spirit behind it. As Jennings pointed out in the wake of the Enron-era scandals, "[n]o one within the field looks at Jack Grubman [the scandal-ridden former lead telecom industry stock analyst]…, the fees structures, the compensation systems, and the conflicts [of interest] and frets, 'These were very nuanced ethical issues. I never would have seen those

---

[41] Landon Thomas, Jr., *Deals and Consequences: A 5-Minute Phone Conversation, a 30-Month Prison Term,* N.Y. TIMES, Nov. 20, 2005, at BU1.

[42] Susan Pulliam, *Ordered to Commit Fraud, A Staffer Balked, Then Caved,* WALL STREET JOURNAL (2003).

[43] For general information on this scandal, *see* CYNTHIA COOPER, EXTRAORDINARY CIRCUMSTANCES (2008).

coming.'"[44] Most of the wrongdoing in more recent scandals—those of Bernard Madoff (Ponzi scheme), Raj Rajaratnam (insider trading), Volkswagen (environmental fraud), Purdue Pharma (opioid crisis), Wells Fargo (customer fraud), Lori Laughlin and Felicity Huffman (Varsity Blues college admissions scandal), Harvey Weinstein, Bill O'Reilly, and Roger Ailes (sexual harassment)--also did not result from anyone's inability to logically analyze subtle ethical questions.[45]

This chapter makes an important point: even when the law and ethics of a situation are relatively clear, more may yet be needed to ensure ethical conduct. It is one thing to be able to analyze and understand ethical and legal rules; it is another thing to live them.[46] Empirical research indicates "that the strength of the association between moral reasoning and moral action is small or moderate, meaning that other mechanisms must be involved in moral functioning."[47] Walking the walk can be much more difficult than talking the talk.

The Psychology Literature

It is not always easy to do the right thing, especially where temptations are great. Virtually every endeavor in the business world creates some temptations to stray from the straight-and-narrow. In marketing, sales representatives are often compensated based on how much they sell and they know they can often sell more by using unethical sales pitches. Auditors in the 1990s were often compensated not by how well they audited, but by how many dollars' worth of consulting services they could induce their audit clients to purchase. This situation contributed to the Enron-era scandals. And many of the factors leading to the subprime meltdown and credit crunch of 2007-2008 illustrate that "[f]inance provides extraordinary temptation. [Its heady reward structure] not only turns people into scoundrels but also attracts to the profession those already scoundrels. Although most people derive noneconomic satisfaction from ethical behavior, in finance, the warm glow simply costs too much."[48]

Despite the many temptations of the work-a-day world, this chapter makes two assumptions. First, it assumes that most people want to do the right thing most of the time, Bernie Madoff notwithstanding. The Enron and subprime scandals have combined to create an atmosphere in which a higher percentage of people seemingly wish to act ethically than has been the case for quite a while. Second, this chapter assumes that in most situations economic actors can determine the proper ethical path when they put their minds to it. Certainly, situations will occasionally arise where the correct ethical approach is not clear and a good argument can be made for more than one course of action, even among people with good intentions. A good faith effort to do the right thing may be all that we can reasonably expect in such a case. But most of the folks we see doing the "perp walk" in the

---

[44] Marianne M. Jennings, *Ethics and Investment Management: True Reform,* 61 FINANCIAL ANALYSTS JOURNAL 45 (June 2005).

[45] The same is true of the acts that led to the credit crisis and Great Recession of 2007-2008. *See* CHARLES R. MORRIS, THE TWO TRILLION DOLLAR MELTDOWN (2009).

[46] Note that an adapted version of this chapter was recently published in Robert A. Prentice, *Ethical Decision Making: More Needed Than Good Intentions,* 63 FINANCIAL ANALYSTS JOURNAL 17 (Nov./Dec. 2007).

[47] Ruodan Shao et al., *Beyond Moral Reasoning: A Review of Moral Identity Research and Its Implications for Business Ethics,* 18 BUSINESS ETHICS QUARTERLY 513 (2008).

[48] William J. Bernstein, *Corporate Finance and Original Sin,* 62 FINANCIAL ANALYSTS JOURNAL 20 (May-June 2006).

newspapers and on our screens committed acts that, in hindsight, were obviously unethical as well as illegal.

Traditional approaches to business ethics education assume that when students enter the real world they will (a) recognize ethical dilemmas, and (b) be able to rationally consider those dilemmas. Although economists often model decision makers as rational actors, the *heuristics and biases literature* that springs from the psychology research of Nobel Prize winner Daniel Kahneman and his late colleague Amos Tversky demonstrates that people make decisions that depart from the optimal model in systematic ways. In particular, social and organizational pressures, cognitive heuristics and biases, and even seemingly innocuous situational factors often lead people to act unethically.[49] Readers have likely been introduced to the basics of this literature in classes on behavioral finance and organizational behavior. But readers most likely have not fully considered this literature's implications for *ethical decision making*. Businesspeople must learn not only how to rationally recognize and resolve ethical dilemmas but also to recognize limitations in their own decision making and judgment processes that might lead them to make unethical decisions without full realization. If officers, directors, brokers, bankers, lawyers, auditors, and others are on guard against errors in their own decision-making processes, perhaps they can avoid some of the ethical pitfalls that often place business figures so painfully in the spotlight and, often, in the dock.

Ethics and Actors

Over the years business-related scandals have seemed to involve a wide range of miscreants. First, at the egregious end of the scale, are the active, knowing wrongdoers. These people not only know that they are doing wrong, they are the active proponents of the fraud. If the control fraud is a play, they are Woody Allen—scripting, directing, and playing a lead role. Inside trader Raj Rajaratnam would be a prototype, as would control fraud genius Charles Keating of the savings & loan debacle.[50] CFO Andy Fastow who surreptitiously pocketed tens of millions of dollars at his company's expense is the most obvious example from the Enron fiasco. At HealthSouth, CEO Richard Scrushy, in response to entreaties from accounting personnel to end earnings manipulation, allegedly responded: "Not until I sell my stock." In the Enron era it is clear that many CEOs, CFOs, hedge fund managers, stockbrokers, and others embezzled, falsified documents, insider traded, and committed other acts embodying a clear intent to violate ethical and legal principles for profit. In the subprime debacle, blatant fraud was often committed by many parties in the mortgage loan business in order to keep the loans (and compensation from granting those loans) flowing, even if the borrowers had no realistic hope of paying the mortgages. Many highly risky mortgages were knowingly foisted off on those who did not adequately understand the risks they faced with their adjustable rate mortgages. These were people who were disadvantaged and more vulnerable because of extreme age, poverty, or lack of education,

Second, in the middle of the spectrum, are those who are passive, but knowing wrongdoers. They realize at some level that they are involved in wrongdoing but persist, often because of pressure from their superiors or their peers. They are not the initiators of the fraudulent scheme, but cannot summon the courage to blow the whistle on a crooked

---

[49] This chapter is based upon an article by the author. Robert A. Prentice, *Teaching Ethics, Heuristics, and Biases,* 1 JOURNAL OF BUSINESS ETHICS EDUCATION 57 (2004).

[50] *See generally* WILLIAM K. BLACK, THE BEST WAY TO ROB A BANK IS TO OWN ONE (2005).

client, to stand up to a superior who wants to look the other way, or to go against the flow when all their colleagues are on board. In most major corporate wrongs, there are employees working for the CFO, such as mid-level accountant Betty Vinson at WorldCom, who know what is going on and occasionally play an important role in the scheme. Often there are outside auditors, such as David Duncan who headed Arthur Andersen's Enron account, who are very well informed as to their clients' shady dealings. In the Volkswagen pollution scandal, it is clear that scores of employees knowingly and intentionally played key roles in creating "defeat devices" to fool environmental regulators.[51] Hundreds of employees at Wells Fargo signed customers up for fake accounts in furtherance of an overall scheme that they didn't start and probably didn't approve of. The long-running sexual harassment activity of Roger Ailes and Harvey Weinstein was made possible by what scholars Minette Drumwright and colleagues call "networks of complicity."[52] Frequently there are investment bankers who seem to know that their clients are committing frauds and often actively assist them, but still manage to conclude that they themselves have not done anything materially wrong. For example, the head of JPMorgan Chase stressed in relation to WorldCom that "[t]here's a big difference between committing a fraud and knowing the committer of a fraud."[53]

Finally, many schemes seem to involve actors who are important to the fraud but seemingly unaware of the wrongdoing they are involved in. They often focus on being loyal to their firm and/or their client. Loyalty is generally a good quality, but can serve improper ends. Although the illicit nature of their conduct would be obvious to objective third parties and although they themselves can usually see it with hindsight, at the time of their actions these people do not seem to appreciate the "big picture" ethics-wise.

As noted in the previous chapter, courses in business law or business ethics are unlikely to be helpful in changing the direction of the moral compass of those in the first category—the intentional wrongdoers. Somewhere between one and four percent of Americans are psychopaths and some of them end up in business. They are unlikely to act in an ethically admirable fashion. For everyone else, personal ethical codes are largely shaped before people become undergraduate or MBA students and well before they enter the business world. At least some subset of economic actors (the active, knowing wrongdoers) will make a calculated decision to advance what they perceive to be their best interests--perhaps using a client's confidential information to engage in insider trading or winking at a client's fraud in order to preserve a lucrative investment banking relationship. It is unlikely that urging these people to ethical action will have much impact when they are determined to aggressively serve their own perceived self-interest. However, reminding them that there are laws against such action and that the laws carry severe consequences might change the outcome of their rational weighing of self-interest and thereby reduce the amount of unethical and illegal activity. It was no coincidence that HealthSouth's CFO stepped aside in August of 2002 saying that he no longer wanted to be a part of the filing of false financial statements, for it was in that month that Sarbanes-Oxley (passed by Congress in July 2002) first explicitly required CEOs and CFOs to vouch for the accuracy of their company's financial statements and made it a felony to lie. Studies by ethicists provide

---

[51] *See* JACK EWING, FASTER, HIGHER, FARTHER: THE VOLKSWAGEN SCANDAL (2017).

[52] Minette Drumwright, Peggy Cunningham & K.W. Foster, *Networks of Complicity: Social Networks and Sex Harassment*, EQUALITY, DIVERSITY, AND INCLUSION (Dec. 2019).

[53] John Kay, *The Changing Character of Doing Deals,* FINANCIAL TIMES, Feb. 1, 2005, at 15.

evidence that fear of consequences does move some actors to muster the "courage" to do the right thing.

Our basic moral code is so engrained that even knowing crooks, who so facilely lie to others, must find ways to live with themselves. Their every day is filled with huge doses of rationalization. "Everybody does it." "It's not really hurting anyone." "The firm really owes it to me because of all the 80-hour weeks I've been working." In the 1990s, these rationalizations often seemed plausible because earnings management and similar accounting shenanigans were so widespread, as insider trading had been in the 1980s. Similarly, in the early 2000s, chicanery was rampant in the mortgage industry, making "everybody does it" a common excuse. But laws Congress passed in the 1980s made it clear that insider trading was not legally acceptable, and many people's attitudes toward the moral acceptability of that practice changed as well. Sarbanes-Oxley made it clear that fraudulent earnings management is not acceptable either and that CEOs, CFOs, and auditors will be held to account. Earnings management is much more difficult to rationalize after Enron and Sarbanes-Oxley, both for managers and auditors.

Congressional passage of the Dodd-Frank Act should similarly make the unacceptability of certain mortgage practices clearer than ever before. It is important that people know the law, because the law helps shape people's views as to what is right and wrong. It sends signals regarding what society will and will not tolerate. Hopefully, explications of the black and white letter of the law, such as those contained in business law textbooks, advance that goal.

Although economists have modeled criminal activity as rational decision making involving the weighing of potential benefits of the crime against the potential punishments multiplied by the chance of detection, this model is questionable. Most people who break the law and/or breach generally accepted ethical standards do not fit the knowing crook mold. They do not engage in such rational calculations. As Lerner observed:

> Throughout our lives, below the level of our consciousness, each of us develops values, intuitions, expectations, and needs that powerfully affect both our perceptions and our judgments. Placed in situations in which we feel threatened, or which implicate our values, our brains, relying on those implicitly learned, emotionally weighted, memories, may react automatically, without reflection or the opportunity for reflective interdiction. We can "downshift" to primitive, self-protective problem-solving techniques. Because these processes operate below the radar of our consciousness, automatic "emotional" reaction, rather than thoughtful, reasoned analysis may drive our responses to stressful questions of ethics and professional responsibility.[54]

Most of the principals in recent corporate scandals were plagued more by bad decision making than by an inability to recognize or analyze ethical dilemmas. Indeed, as Della Costa has noted, "[t]here are truly sinister businesspeople with sinister intentions, but, for the most part, ethical and legal lapses are the stuff of average people who know better."[55]

How can people avoid unethical actions in situations where they "know better"? How can good people avoid doing bad things? One helpful approach entails an appreciation

---

[54] Alan M. Lerner, *Using Our Brains: What Cognitive Science and Social Psychology Teach Us About Teaching Law Students to Make Ethical, Professionally Responsible, Choices,* 23 QUARTERLY LAW REVIEW 643 (2004).
[55] JOHN D. COSTA, THE ETHICAL IMPERATIVE: WHY MORAL LEADERSHIP IS GOOD BUSINESS (1998).

of the research being generated by the new field of *behavioral ethics* that examines scientifically human decision making. Building on the heuristics and biases literature, this research has produced overwhelming evidence that people do not always make decisions in a rationally optimal manner. Indeed, various social and organizational pressures, cognitive biases and decisional heuristics, and even subtle situational factors often lead people to systematically diverge from optimal decision making. Less often studied is the fact that many of these factors can render even the best-intentioned people susceptible to committing unethical and even illegal acts.

In the next three sections of this chapter, we will study the organizational and social pressures, the cognitive heuristics and biases, and the situational factors that can make it difficult for people to live up to their own ethical standards.

SOCIAL AND ORGANIZATIONAL PRESSURES AND ETHICAL DECISION MAKING

People are social animals, as David Brooks pointed out in his popular book.[56] In their attempt to get along with others, people's decision making is often affected, including in the realm of moral decisions. If people focus so much on getting along with others that they fail to activate and follow their own moral compass, problems can result.

Obedience to Authority

Some of the major actors in the Enron-era scandals pleaded that they were "just following orders." People instinctively reject the "Good Nazi" defense, yet this gut reaction produces a huge disconnect in our everyday lives because all of us tend to defer to authority. In an attempt to understand the Holocaust, psychologist Stanley Milgram undertook his famous experiments on obedience to authority. Although people to whom his experiment was described predicted that less than 1% of participants would obey the experimenter's instructions to administer apparently injurious shocks to an innocent, protesting victim, fully 65% did so.[57] As the inaccurate prediction illustrates, most people simply do not understand the great extent to which others, and especially they themselves, are susceptible to blindly following the instructions of people in apparent positions of authority. A much more recent study found quite similar results.[58] The mistreatment of prisoners at the Abu Ghraib prison in Iraq may well have resulted from the same obedience to authority.[59] Milgram himself suggested:

> The most common adjustment of thought in the obedient subject is for him to see himself as not responsible for his own actions. He divests himself of responsibility by attributing all the initiative to the experimenter, a legitimate authority. He sees himself not as a person acting in a morally accountable way, but as the agent of external authority.[60]

Eric Fair, a U.S. interrogator who tortured prisoners at Abu Ghraib in Iraq described

---

[56] DAVID BROOKS, THE SOCIAL ANIMAL (2011).

[57] Stanley Milgram, *Behavioral Study of Obedience,* 57 JOURNAL OF ABNORMAL & SOCIAL PSYCHOLOGY (1963).

[58] Jerry M. Burger, *Replicating Milgram: Would People Still Obey Today?,* 64 AMERICAN PSYCHOLOGIST 1 (Jan. 2009).

[59] PHILIP ZIMBARDO, THE LUCIFER EFFECT (2007).

[60] STANLEY MILGRAM, OBEDIENCE TO AUTHORITY (1974).

his thought process: "I think about following [my superior's] instructions. It's not my interrogation. It's not my sin."

There is substantial evidence that when people make decisions they are often much more concerned about the acceptability of the decision to the people to whom they are accountable than they are about the content of the decision itself. Pursuant to this *acceptability heuristic,* people often judge whether their decision is right not in terms of content or philosophical ethicality, but whether it will be acceptable to their superiors. Because of this inclination, people are much more likely to undertake an unethical action in the workplace when urged to do so by a superior than to choose that unethical course of their own volition. A subordinate who is pressured by a CFO to cook the books is much more likely to act improperly than an employee who is not so pressured. And studies show that CFOs themselves are more likely to cook the books to benefit their CEOs financially than to benefit themselves.[61] The Enron scandal has been traced in part to

> ...the "cult-like" atmosphere at Enron. Specifically, Enron employees reported being "fanatically loyal" to the CEOs... One Enron employee asserted: "[E]very time [CEO Jeff] Skilling spoke, I'd believe everything he'd say."[62]

Private emails by stock analysts during the dot.com boom often indicated that they wished they had the courage to stand up to their superiors and "call them like they saw them," but many times they failed to do so. Instead, they continued to knuckle under to supervisory pressure to hype questionable stocks so their firms could gain investment banking business. As the subprime mess unfolded, employees of ratings agencies that gave cover to sellers of extraordinarily risky mortgages complained in internal e-mails that "[w]e rate every deal....It could be structured by cows and we would rate it," but kept on doing so under pressure from superiors.

These stories of a lack of courage in the face of a superior's pressure are discouraging. Even more disturbing, however, is the fact that employees can become so focused on pleasing the boss that they do not even see the ethical dimensions of an action they are asked to take. Former Nixon White House employee Egil "Bud" Krogh has written of his overwhelming desire to please his superiors who were, after all, among the most powerful people on the planet. When Assistant to the President for Domestic Affairs John Ehrlichman asked Krogh to head a unit that became known as the "Plumbers" in order to break into Daniel Ellsberg's psychiatrist's office to hopefully obtain records to discredit Ellsberg (who had embarrassed the White House by leaking the "Pentagon Papers" to the *New York Times*), Krogh focused on pleasing his superiors by complying with their admonition— "Don't get caught." He did not until much later attempt to use his own personal judgment to determine whether he was engaged in an ethical or unethical activity. When he did do so, he was deeply disappointed in himself. As with many white-collar criminals, he found himself asking: "What was I thinking?"[63]

All business actors must keep in mind this very human tendency to defer to authority,

---

[61] Mei Feng et al., *Why Do CFOs Become Involved in Material Accounting Manipulations* (2010), *available at* http://papers.ssrn.com/sol3/papers.cfm?abstract_id=1260368.

[62] M. A. O'Connor, *The Enron Board: The Perils of Groupthink,* 71 UNIVERSITY OF CINCINNATI LAW REVIEW 1233 (2003).

[63] EGIL KROGH, INTEGRITY: GOOD PEOPLE, BAD CHOICES, AND LIFE LESSONS FROM THE WHITE HOUSE (2007).

so that they can guard against its potentially corrosive influence.

Conformity Bias

Parents are typically ill-disposed to accept a child's plea of "everyone else is doing it." "If everybody else jumped off a cliff, would you jump, too?" is the standard witty riposte. However, the *conformity bias*, (also known as the theory of *social proof*) tells us that those same parents, and everyone else, tend to take their cues as to proper behavior in most social contexts from the actions of others. In our decision making, we have a bias toward conforming to the actions and standards that we perceive to be accepted by our peers. In his famous experiments, psychologist Solomon Asch found that when asked to tell which of three lines was the same length as a fourth line, subjects had no difficulty whatsoever unless they were placed in an experimental condition in the presence of six of the experimenter's confederates who gave obviously wrong answers. Almost all subjects then found it very painful to give the obviously correct answer in contradiction of these strangers' erroneous answers. Most participants gave an obviously incorrect answer at least once. Consider how much greater is the pressure to conform when the others in the group are co-employees and/or friends or when the right answer is not obvious, but is instead a subjective ethical choice.

Some believe that the most important finding of social psychology since World War II may be just how much people's behavior is caused externally by pressures and situations rather than internally by their own disposition. Obedience to authority and susceptibility to peer pressure are two significant illustrations of these external influences. A reading of tell-all books by Enron insiders indicates that many Enron employees readily bought into Enron's fast-and-loose corporate culture without fully recognizing the ethical implications of company practices. For example, one employee in a risk-management position at Enron said: "If your boss was [fudging], and you never worked anywhere else, you just assume that everybody fudges earnings....Once you get there and you realize how it was, do you stand up and lose your job? It was scary. It was easy to get into 'Well, everybody else is doing it, so maybe it isn't so bad.'"[64] A student who engaged in illegal downloading of music rationalized: "I don't think me [sic] alone is making that much of a difference by downloading. When you think about it, everyone downloads."[65]

The conformity bias induces executives in one company to decide that obscenely high compensation is ethically justified because executives at competing companies are receiving similarly outrageous compensation. The bias also leads managers and auditors to conclude that earnings management, capacity swaps, and other forms of accounting aggression are defensible because industry innovators such as Enron and WorldCom are using them. It convinces officers and lower level employees of mortgage firms that it is okay to shovel mortgages out the door to borrowers who have little hope of repaying them, because competitors are doing exactly the same thing to borrowers who are even worse off.

The desire to fit into an organization, to be a team player, to get along with co-employees, it has been argued, accounts for Ford employees selling the Pinto despite awareness of its gas tank dangers, A. H. Robins employees continuing to sell the Dalkon Shield contraceptive device despite knowledge of its ghastly medical consequences, and

---

[64] John A. Byrne, *The Environment was Ripe for Abuse,* BUSINESS WEEK, Feb. 25, 2002, at 118.
[65] CARRIE JAMES, DISCONNECTED YOUTH (2014).

Morton Thiokol employees remaining silent about known O-ring dangers that caused the Challenger space shuttle disaster. The conformity bias certainly had an impact on Betty Vinson at WorldCom.

An Australian who had been caught up in a huge scandal at the options desk of the National Australia Bank (NAB) later wrote:

> With the benefit of hindsight, it was quite clear that during my time in the currency options business at the NAB, the situational forces at play made certain individuals (including myself) behave in ways which those closest to us would have considered to be totally out of character. We all, some of us more than others, adopted the immoral social norms that emerged in the business. ... It is this backdrop that provides groups with a cult-like appearance—dysfunctional social norms and an insular group dynamic that gives group members little choice but to embrace the prevailing norm.[66]

Thus, people are more likely to undertake unethical actions in the workplace and elsewhere if peers are engaging in similar behavior.[67] And they certainly are less likely to blow the whistle on unethical activity when peers seem to accept it, just as a bystander to a crime is less likely to help the victim when others nearby are not helping. Sherron Watkins at Enron and Cynthia Cooper at WorldCom, simply did what was clearly the ethical thing—blew the whistle on blatant frauds in their firms. Most of us are told from our earliest years that we should not stand idly by when we see wrongdoing. The fact that these women are widely considered to be heroines demonstrates that people intuitively realize how difficult (and rare) it truly is to act in accordance with ethical standards that are not aligned with the expectations of superiors and the practices of peers.

Groupthink

The impairment of individual decision making known as "groupthink" can also play a role here as people attempt to merge into their social collective. "Groupthink" causes collections of people to make much different decisions than the same people would make individually. Group decisions are often much more extreme than the median decision that members of the group would make individually. Groupthink has been associated with the Enron catastrophe. Although the Enron board of directors was composed of many outstanding individuals, they shared common backgrounds and many were long-time associates. Board meetings, therefore, tended to involve little critical discussion and decisions almost never involved dissenting votes. Many believe that groupthink also played a major role in the 1961 Bay of Pigs foreign policy debacle and the 1986 space shuttle Challenger disaster.[68]

COGNITIVE HEURISTICS AND BIASES AND ETHICAL DECISION MAKING

---

[66] DENNIS GENTILIN THE ORIGINS OF ETHICAL FAILURES (2016).

[67] People naturally tend to divide the world into in-group members (people like us) and out-group members (those not like us). The actions of in-group members are naturally more influential than actions of out-group members. In one experiment, a confederate of the experimenter obviously cheated in completing a task. The subjects' level of unethical behavior in completing the same task increased if they viewed the confederate as an in-group member, but actually decreased if they viewed him as an out-group member. Francesca Gino et al., *Contagion and Differentiation in Unethical Behavior: The Effect of One Bad Apple on the Barrel,* 20 PSYCHOLOGICAL SCIENCE 393 (2009).

[68] SCOTT PLOUS, THE PSYCHOLOGY OF JUDGMENT AND DECISION MAKING 203 (1993).

In many settings people are subject to cognitive biases and utilize various decisional heuristics that systematically prevent their decision making from being objectively optimal. As Hastie and Dawes note, "[n]ot only do the choices of individuals and social decision making groups tend to violate the principle of maximizing expected utility, they are often patently irrational."[69] As in all other areas of decision making, when confronted with ethical dilemmas, most people use "moral heuristics—moral short-cuts, or rules of thumb, that work well most of the time, but that also systematically misfire."[70]

Overoptimism

Humans are an optimistic lot--so much so that they often entertain irrational beliefs. For example, studies show that although they know that the national divorce rate is around 50%, newlyweds tend to rate their own chance of ever divorcing at 0%. In general, people tend to think that good things are more likely to happen to them than to others and that bad things are less likely to be inflicted upon them than upon others.[71]

Some scientists have suggested that *overoptimism* is evolutionarily beneficial, but it can lead to systematic errors in decision making and, in some circumstances, it can induce conduct that appears unethical. For example, Langevoort suggests that it is quite possible that in many cases of corporate disclosure fraud, the offending officers and directors are not consciously lying but instead are expressing honestly-held, but irrationally optimistic views of their firms' conditions and prospects.[72] In fact, a recent empirical study supports that view.[73]

Many stock analysts who touted sky-high target prices for technology stocks in the dot.com boom may not have been blatantly lying (although some were), but instead may have been caught up in the euphoria of the moment. Academic studies indicate that irrational optimism can also play a role in plaintiffs' (and attorneys') decisions to file frivolous lawsuits.[74] Auditors can also be overly optimistic regarding their clients' practices and conditions, as Arthur Andersen proved in its handling of client Enron.

Overconfidence

Overoptimism is often exacerbated by *overconfidence*. Psychological studies indicate that in many settings (though not all) people are not just confident, but irrationally overconfident. A substantial majority of people believe erroneously that they are better than average drivers, more likely to be able to afford to own a house than their peers, and more accurate eyewitnesses than most others. Entrepreneurs like Bernie Ebbers of WorldCom and

---

[69] REID HASTIE & ROBYN DAWES, RATIONAL CHOICE IN AN UNCERTAIN WORLD: THE PSYCHOLOGY OF JUDGMENT AND DECISION MAKING (2001).

[70] Cass R. Sunstein, *Moral Heuristics and Moral Framing*, 88 MINNESOTA LAW REVIEW 1556 (2004).

[71] *See* Tim Smits & Vera Hoorens, *How Probable is* Probably*? It Depends on Whom You're Talking About*, 18 JOURNAL OF BEHAVIORAL DECISION MAKING 83 (2005).

[72] Donald Langevoort, *Organized Illusions: A Behavioral Theory of Why Corporations Mislead Stock Market Investors (And Cause Other Social Harms)*, 146 UNIVERSITY OF PENNSYLVANIA LAW REVIEW 101 (1997).

[73] Robert Libby & Kristina M. Rennekamp, *Self-Serving Attribution Bias, Overconfidence, and the Issuance of Management Forecasts*, 50 JOURNAL OF ACCOUNTING RESEARCH 197 (2012).

[74] Chris Guthrie, *Framing Frivolous Litigation: A Psychological Theory*, 67 UNIVERSITY OF CHICAGO LAW REVIEW 163 (2000).

HealthSouth's Richard Scrushy, who have had a series of successes in building small, obscure companies into economic powerhouses, may gain a sense of invulnerability. Their minds underplay or ignore altogether the role that good fortune served in their success. Overconfident executives with unrealistic beliefs about their future performance are more likely to commit financial reporting fraud than other executives. Essentially, they are more likely to get themselves into predicaments where committing fraud seems the only way to deliver on their promised or previously reported performance.[75]

People's overconfidence in themselves can translate into overconfidence in the ethical correctness of their acts and judgments. People tend to rate themselves as well above average in most traits, including honesty. In one survey more people thought that they themselves would more assuredly go to heaven than would Princess Diana, Michael Jordan, *or even Mother Teresa*![76] Studies indicate that businesspeople tend to believe that they are more ethical than their competitors,[77] and that most auditors believe that they will act more ethically than their peers.[78] A recent survey indicated that 61% of physicians believed that the freebies they receive from drug companies do not affect their judgments, but only 16% believed the freebies do not affect the judgments of other physicians. Jennings notes:

> Recent studies indicate that 74 percent of us believe our ethics are higher than those of our peers and 83 percent of us say that at least one-half of the people we know would list us as one of the most ethical people they know. An amazing 92 percent of us are satisfied with our ethics and character.[79]

Overconfidence in one's own ethical compass can lead people to accept their own decisions without any serious moral reflection. For example, studies show that overconfidence in one's ability to perform an accurate audit can lead to taking short-cuts that might look unethical in retrospect.[80] And Enron employees' overweening confidence in the competence and strategies of their company, often named the "most innovative" in America, caused them to express surprise that anyone would question the morality, let alone legality, of many of the firm's activities that in retrospect seem so nefarious. Outsiders who questioned Enron's tactics or numbers were told that they "just didn't get it."

Harvard Law School professor Eugene Soltes interviewed many of the executives who went to jail in the Enron-era frauds. He often saw indications of overconfidence:

> "What we all think is, when the big moral challenge comes, I will rise to the occasion," argued Steven Garfinkel, the former chief financial officer of DVI. Garfinkel believed that he would successfully handle difficult and complex situations when they came his way as an executive. But now, with the benefit of hindsight, he sees how this confidence was misplaced. "There's not actually that many of us that will actually rise to the occasion," lamented Garfinkel. "I

---

[75] Cathern M. Schrand & Sara L.C. Zechman, "Executive Overconfidence and the Slippery Slope to Fraud," (Aug. 2008), *available at* http://ssrn.com/abstract=1265631.

[76] *See generally* MICHAEL SHERMER, THE SCIENCE OF GOOD & EVIL (2004).

[77] David Messick & Max Bazerman, *Ethical Leadership and the Psychology of Decision Making*, 9 SLOAN MANAGEMENT REVIEW 9 (1996).

[78] J. Cohen et al., *An Exploratory Examination of International Differences in Auditors' Ethical Perceptions*, 7 JOURNAL OF ACCOUNTING RESEARCH 37 (1996).

[79] Marianne M. Jennings, *Ethics and Investment Management: True Reform*, FINANCIAL ANALYSTS JOURNAL, May/June 2005, at 45.

[80] Jane Kennedy & Mark Peecher (1997), *Judging Auditors' Technical Knowledge*, 35 JOURNAL OF ACCOUNTING RESEARCH 279 (1997).

didn't realize I would be a felon."[81]

Self-Serving Bias

Perhaps the most influential of the heuristics and biases discussed in this chapter is the *self-serving bias*, the tendency we have to gather information, process information, and even remember information in such a manner as to advance our self-interest and support our pre-existing views. Bazerman and colleagues observe that teaching ethics in the traditional way in business schools will not have an impact on this bias.[82] It is imperative that students be educated about the self-serving bias because even when people try their hardest to be fair and impartial, their judgments are inevitably shaded by it. For example, when A, B, and C are each asked how much credit they each deserve for a joint project that they successfully completed at work, their allocations will typically add up to around 140% rather than just 100% because in each of their minds they were more responsible for the success than an objective observer would likely have concluded.

Is it possible that Andy Fastow believed that he deserved the millions of dollars he took out of the Enron special purpose entities (SPEs) in exchange for his "creative" efforts in taking debt off Enron's books? Is it possible that Bernie Ebbers thought he was really worth the hundreds of millions of dollars that he took (much of it secretly) out of WorldCom? Is it possible that Arthur Andersen's auditors believed that Enron's financial statements truly represented Enron's financial condition? Research on the self-serving bias suggests that these things are possible.

Consider Enron, for example. Enron was extraordinarily entrepreneurial. It sought to reward success. Indeed, so eager was the firm to incentivize its employees that it often generously rewarded perceived successes long before the success of the transaction could be manifested:

> When Enron employees valued proposed deals, which affected the numbers Enron could put on its books, which in turn determined whether or not employees met their bonus targets, which in turn determined whether millions of dollars in bonuses were paid to the very people who were deciding what the numbers should be, even assuming good faith (and at least some of the Enron officers must have been acting in good faith), the self-serving bias must have had an impact. This is especially so because Enron employees were often not choosing between legitimate Option A and legitimate Option B; rather 'the prices were pulled from [someone's ass]…because there was nowhere else to get them!'[83]

Or think of Arthur Andersen's David Duncan, the auditor in charge of the Enron account. Enron was one of Andersen's largest clients and Duncan's career essentially hung on the success of Enron. Andersen was making a healthy $25 million a year auditing Enron and another $27 million by providing non-audit services. Andersen expected that its Enron related revenue would soon double to $100 million a year. In other words, Andersen, Duncan, and Duncan's subordinates all had a strong self-interest in concluding that Enron was in good financial shape and that its various financial machinations were consistent with

---

[81] EUGENE SOLTES, WHY THEY DO IT: INSIDE THE MIND OF THE WHITE COLLAR CRIMINAL (2016).

[82] Max Bazerman et al., *Why Good Accountants Do Bad Audits* 80 HARVARD BUSINESS REVIEW 97 (Nov. 2002).

[83] Robert A. Prentice, *Enron: A Brief Behavioral Autopsy,* 40 AMERICAN BUSINESS LAW JOURNAL 417 (2003), *quoting* BRIAN CRUVER, ANATOMY OF GREED: THE UNSHREDDED TRUTH FROM AN ENRON INSIDER (2002).

good accounting practices. In the shadow of such a strong self-interest, it would have been very difficult for even an auditor with the best of intentions to make close and complicated judgments in an objective manner.[84]

In valuing their deals, Enron employees would have been prone, the psychological studies show, to seek out information that would support the higher valuations that were consistent with their self-interest. Similarly, in auditing Enron's books, the auditors would be prone to search for information that supported the conclusion that the financial statements accurately represented Enron's financial condition and to ignore evidence that contradicted that conclusion. This is called the *confirmation bias*. Psychologists are well aware of this tendency, and studies show that even auditors and research scientists who are supposedly trained to be skeptical are as prone to it as anyone else.[85] Related is the notion of *belief persistence*--the fact that people tend to persist in beliefs they hold long after the basis for those beliefs is substantially discredited.

The self-serving bias and its closely related phenomena of confirmation bias and belief persistence unconsciously affect the information that people seek out. They also cause them not only to search for confirming rather than disconfirming evidence and to hold on to beliefs even if the face of conflicting evidence, they also affect how people process the information that they do access. Thus, when psychologists give a relatively ambiguous document to two groups of people holding opposing views, members of each side tend to interpret the document as supporting their point of view. When scientists review articles, they will tend to conclude that those supporting their preexisting point of view are of higher quality than those opposing that view. When scientific studies of drug efficacy are funded by the drug company they are 5.3 times more likely to conclude that this is the treatment of choice than studies independently funded.[86] A British civil servant in charge of helping his government make the case for invading Iraq wrote eloquently of the impact of this bias:

> The speeches I drafted for the Security Council and my telegrams back to London were composed of facts filtered from the stacks of reports and intelligence that daily hit my desk. As I read these reports, facts and judgments that contradicted the British version of events would almost literally fade into nothingness. Facts that reinforced our narrative would stand out to me almost as if highlighted, to be later deployed by me, my ambassador and my ministers like hand grenades in the diplomatic trench warfare. Details in otherwise complex reports would be extracted to be telegraphed back to London, where they would be inserted into ministerial briefings or press articles. A complicated picture was reduced to a selection of facts that became "factoids", such as the suggestion that Hussein imported huge quantities of whisky or built a dozen palaces, validated by constant repetition: true, but not the whole truth.[87]

Because of the self-serving bias, documents that a disinterested person might view as not supporting Enron's desired position or not of high quality, might be viewed much differently by a self-interested Enron employee or Arthur Andersen auditor. Likewise, makers of asbestos, tobacco and other harmful products who initially believed them to be

---

[84] Robert A. Prentice, *The Case of the Irrational Auditor: A Behavioral Insight into Securities Fraud Litigation*, 95 NORTHWESTERN UNIVERSITY LAW REVIEW 133 (2000).

[85] E. Michael Bamber, *An Examination of the Descriptive Validity of the Belief-Adjustment Model and Alternative Attitudes to Evidence in Auditing*, 22 ACCOUNTING, ORGANIZATION & SOCIETY 249 (1997).

[86] *Zyprexa Products Liability Litigation*, 253 F.R.D. 69 (E.D.N.Y. 2008).

[87] Carne Ross, *Believing is Seeing,* FIN. TIMES, Jan. 29-Jan. 30, 2005, at W1.

beneficial products had difficulty processing new information regarding their carcinogenic effects, thus creating an ethical minefield.[88]

The self-serving bias even affects how people remember information. Studies show that people are more likely to recall evidence that supports their point of view than evidence that opposes it. People involved in negotiations tend to remember information that supports their bargaining position more than information that undermines it.

Inevitably, subjective judgments of fairness are also affected by the self-serving bias. People naturally tend to conflate what is "good for me" with what is "good." Obviously, the more subjective the judgment and the less certain the facts, the more influential the self-serving bias is likely to be, but the bias is pervasive and unrelenting. Banaji and colleagues note:

> Research done with brokerage house analysts demonstrates how conflict of interest can unconsciously distort decision making. A survey of analysts conducted by the financial research service First Call showed that during a period in 2000 when the Nasdaq dropped 60%, fully 99% of brokerage analysts' client recommendations remained "strong buy," "buy," or "hold." What accounts for this discrepancy between what was happening and what was recommended? The answer may lie in a system that fosters conflicts of interest. A portion of analysts' pay is based on brokerage firm revenues. Some firms even tie analysts' compensation to the amount of business the analysts bring in from clients, giving analysts an obvious incentive to prolong and extend their relationships with clients. But to assume that during this Nasdaq free fall all brokerage house analysts were consciously corrupt, milking their clients to exploit this incentive system, defies common sense. Surely there were some bad apples, but how much more likely is it that most of these analysts believed their recommendations were sound and in their clients' best interests? What many didn't appreciate was that the built-in conflict of interest in their compensation incentives made it impossible for them to see the implicit bias in their own flawed recommendations.[89]

People have a psychological need to see themselves as "good and reasonable" and the self-serving bias subconsciously distorts evidence, allowing them to do so. Inevitably, self-interest clouds moral judgment, even that of well-intentioned people. David Solomon has written that "nobody is ever the villain in their own narrative. So if someone takes actions that threaten to paint them as a bad person, they are more likely to change their opinion of what's right and wrong, rather than change their opinion of themselves."[90] Therefore, even well-intentioned people "have a tendency to credit themselves for their ethical decisions but to blame situational forces imposed by the environment for their unethical decisions."[91]

Framing

If there is one overriding lesson of the heuristics and biases literature, it is that in decision making, context counts. A simple reframing of a question can produce a totally

---

[88] Joshua Klayman, *Ethics as Hypothesis Testing, and Vice Versa*" in CODES OF CONDUCT: BEHAVIORAL RESEARCH INTO BUSINESS ETHICS 243 (1996). Obviously, the self-serving bias can play a role in "belief persistence" that was mentioned earlier.

[89] Mahzarin R. Banaji et al., *How (Un)Ethical Are You?*, HARVARD BUSINESS REVIEW, Dec. 2003, at 56.

[90] SOLTES, *supra* (quoting Solomon).

[91] THOMAS OBERLECHNER, THE PSYCHOLOGY OF ETHICS IN THE FINANCE AND INVESTMENT INDUSTRY 29 (2007).

different answer from the same respondent. People's risk preferences change dramatically depending on whether an option is framed in terms of potential loss or potential gain. As a simple example of the impact of framing, people would rather buy potato chips labeled 90% fat free than identical chips labeled 10% fat.[92] This framing effect has many implications for ethical decision making.

Decisions made by business managers, accountants, lawyers and others often occur in a context where subjective factors predominate. The self-serving bias may lead an actor to frame decisions in such a way as to lead to untoward conclusions. In Enron's declining days, the company actually attempted to save some money by encouraging employees to minimize travel expenses. An Enron employee later wrote that he intentionally flouted the new policy. This might seem like a clear violation of company policy and an ethical lapse, but in the employee's mind, he deserved to stay in the most expensive hotels and to eat at the best restaurants because of how very hard he was working.[93] Had he framed the issue in terms of the broader picture of helping the company remain viable rather than his narrow self-serving interests, he might have acted differently. But then, maybe not, because he noted that other employees were also ignoring the new policy (conformity bias).

The Tyco case presents another example of framing. Director Frank Walsh proposed, advocated, and voted for a particular acquisition in which he expected to receive a secret $20 million "finder's fee." Other board members felt betrayed when they learned of the fee, which would have been flagrantly improper even had it been disclosed. But Walsh's frame of reference was not the proper code of conduct for directors. His self-serving frame of reference was comparative compensation; he maintained that the amount he got was low compared with what the investment bankers got in fees.

It seems obvious that CFOs and accounting personnel at Enron, WorldCom, HealthSouth, and other scandal-ridden companies probably did not need a philosophy course to help them figure out that their manipulation of financial statements was unethical. One of their problems was that at the time of their actions, their frame of reference was loyalty to the company (colored by self-interest) and to the company's goal of maximizing stock price. Had they been able to think in terms of the bigger ethical picture, they might have acted differently.

Too many stock analysts during the dot.com boom had as their key metric the amount of investment banking revenue they drummed up for their Wall Street firms. Accuracy of their calls was often sacrificed and occasionally not even considered. Too many bank employees during the subprime boom had as their key metric the volume of loan business they were doing. The accuracy of the paperwork they ran regarding their borrowers was often sacrificed to the stronger goal of increasing revenue.

In November 2003, the *Wall St. Journal* reported that in 1998 KPMG decided to promote tax shelters without registering them with the IRS. The firm did so after calculating that the "rewards of a successful marketing of the...product [and the competitive disadvantages that may result from registration] far exceed the ... penalties that may arise." In other words, if KPMG did not register and "got caught," it faced potential IRS penalties of only $31,000 in contrast to potential profits of $360,000 per tax shelter. Conceivably, this

---

[92] WRAY HERBERT, ON SECOND THOUGHT: OUTSMARTING YOUR MIND'S HARD-WIRED HABITS 94 (2010).

[93] BRIAN CRUVER, ANATOMY OF GREED: THE UNSHREDDED TRUTH FROM AN ENRON INSIDER (2002).

decision was a naked determination to flout the rules to gain profit with an "ethics be damned" attitude. But the *Wall St. Journal* also quoted KPMG employees' descriptions of a business "culture that has focused on revenue growth."[94] When revenue growth becomes the only metric by which a firm evaluates itself and it ignores the bigger picture, including ethical factors, such decisions cannot be surprising.

Some evidence indicates that the *Challenger* spacecraft disaster illustrates this point. When the safety of a cold weather launch was discussed the evening before the launch, engineers who raised safety concerns were asked to put on their "management hats." In other words, they were asked to minimize safety considerations and emphasize monetary and other practical considerations. When asked to reframe the decision as one of timing and expense, the engineers assented to a launch they had objected to when focusing on safety factors.[95]

Unfortunately, even when we keep the law in our frame of reference, as we always should when making decisions, we tend to "miss the big picture of industry practices that clearly cross ethical lines but continue because current regulations have not yet found them to be legally problematic."[96]

Incrementalism

Incrementalism ("the slippery slope") is often called the "boiling frog" syndrome after the folk wisdom that if you drop a frog in a pot of boiling water it will jump out but if you put it in a pot of cool water and gradually turn up the heat the frog will eventually cook to death because of an inability to detect the gradual increase in water temperature. Some psychologists believe that, similarly, much "unethical behavior occurs when people unconsciously 'lower the bar' over time through small changes in the ethicality of behavior."[97]

Research indicates that German doctors who participated in euthanasia of "undesirables" in the Nazi era were generally introduced to the process slowly. They were not initially asked to perform the deed themselves. Rather, they were first brought to the place where the work was done. Then they were asked to sign a relevant document. Then they were to supervise a "mercy killing." Only later were they asked to do themselves what they likely would have refused to do had they been asked in the beginning. One such doctor said: "In the beginning it was impossible. Afterward it became almost routine. That's the only way to put it."[98]

And so it is that rather than making a significant, conscious decision to violate ethical precepts, people more often slide down a slippery slope in tandem with their peers in an organization. People who would not have signed off on bogus special purpose entities (SPEs) or engaged in roundtrip energy trades on the day they began working for Enron, all-too-quickly adapted to a corporate culture that encouraged and rewarded aggressive actions that

---

[94] Cassell Bryan-Low, *KPMG Didn't Register Strategy,* WALL ST. JOURNAL, Nov. 17, 2003, at C1.

[95] RICHARD BOOKSTABER, A DEMON OF OUR OWN DESIGN: MARKETS, HEDGE FUNDS, AND THE PERILS OF FINANCIAL INNOVATION 160 (2007).

[96] Marianne M. Jennings, *Ethics and Investment Management: True Reform,* FINANCIAL ANALYSTS JOURNAL, May/June 2005, at 45.

[97] Francesca Gino & Max H. Bazerman, *Slippery Slopes and Misconduct: The Effect of Gradual Degradation on the Failure to Notice Unethical Behavior* (Harvard NOM Research Paper No. 06-01), http://ssrn.com/abstract=785987 (2005).

[98] ROBERT JAY LIFTON, THE NAZI DOCTORS (1986).

increasingly crossed the line into the unethical and the illegal.[99] One C-suite executive convicted of financial fraud explained from jail:

> I call it increment…incrementalization, whether that's even a word. You…you get to here so it must be okay to go to here. And if you're here, it surely is okay to go here. It's really fuzzy where you cross the line […] At what point do you cross the line where the act becomes illegal? I don't know. I don't know.[100]

Role Morality

One reason that people may look at ethical issues through different frames is the notion of "role morality," which is the concept that people may adopt different moralities for different roles they play in society. Adopting role morality, people might do things at work that they would never view as acceptable at home. In his book *Moral Mazes,* sociologist Robert Jackall quoted a corporate executive who said: "What is right in the corporation is not what is right in a man's home or in his church. *What is right in the corporation is what the guy above you wants from you.* That's what morality is in the corporation."[101]

While there are different circumstances at home and at work, to check one's personal moral code at the door when entering the workplace simply cannot be a good idea. It easily becomes simply an excuse for exercising no ethical judgment at all. In one case, a doctor examined a plaintiff on behalf of a defendant in a lawsuit. The doctor discovered that the plaintiff had a dangerous aneurysm, but *did not tell the plaintiff,* who did not find out for more than two years. As a physician who had taken the Hippocratic oath, the doctor should have informed the plaintiff. Instead, the doctor viewed himself as playing the role of a representative of a company in a lawsuit and focused on the company's financial interests rather than the plaintiff's life-and-death situation.[102]

In an interesting study, experimenters asked engineers about the propriety of U.S. firms engaging in "gifting" to help their firms enter new markets, even if it violated federal law. A group of engineers primed to think of themselves as playing the role of engineers mostly (87.5%) said that such activity should never occur. In a similar group of engineers who were primed to think of themselves working primarily as managers, only 46.7% said

---

[99] Business law professor Constance Bagley recently noted in this connection:

> It starts small. Perhaps there is a shortfall in orders that will cause the company to miss analysts' quarterly earnings estimates. The stock price will get hammered and the company may lose its best engineers if their stock options are underwater. So the VP of marketing persuades a customer to accept an early shipment of goods not needed until the next quarter. The manager robs Peter to pay Paul, assuming that he or she can make up the shortfall the next quarter. But the economy takes a downturn and orders are down again. So this time the manager ships a product to an independent warehouse and invoices a nonexistent customer. Before you know it, the company is doing what computer disk drive maker Miniscribe did: shipping boxes filled with bricks instead of disk drives to nonexistent customers.

CONSTANCE E. BAGLEY: WINNING LEGALLY 65 (2005).

[100] Ikseon Suh, et al., *Boiling the Frog Slowly: The Immersion of C-Suite Financial Executives into Fraud,* 162 JOURNAL OF BUSINESS ETHICS 645 (2018).

[101] ROBERT JACKALL, MORAL MAZES 6 (1988).

[102] Spaulding v. Zimmerman, 116 N.W.2d 704 (Minn. 1962).

that gifting should never occur, indicating that the role these subjects thought of themselves playing significantly impacted their moral judgments.[103]

Consider the following extreme example of role morality where an engineer checked his morality and his humanity at the door:

> At Auschwitz, an order from the commandant for two four-retort ovens was bid on by several firms and the winner was I.A. Topf and Sons. Engineers designed ovens to burn 1500 bodies a day. In 1943, Topf technicians even sought a way to make burning more efficient. They experimented with different kinds of coke and corpses, measuring their combustibility. One of the Topf engineers, Fritz Sander, testified after the war that he had gone so far as to take the initiative in late 1942 to build a better high-capacity crematorium for mass incineration. He had even put in for a patent. [When asked about his actions in light of his knowledge regarding what the furnaces were used for,] Sander replied, "I was a German engineer and key member of the Topf works, and I saw it as my duty to apply my specialist knowledge in this way to help Germany win the war, just as an aircraft construction engineer builds airplanes in wartime, which are also connected with the destruction of human beings."[104]

Cognitive Dissonance

In 1954, a doomsday cult leader in Chicago predicted that aliens from the planet Clarion were about to invade earth and everyone on the planet would die, except the cult members. In preparing for the impending doomsday, most of the cult members gave away all of their possessions. Spoiler alert: the world didn't end. And when the announced doomsday came and went without incident, you might think that the cult's members would lose faith in the leader, but instead they seemed to believe in her more than ever.[105] What accounts for that? A psychological process called *cognitive dissonance*.[106] The notion here is that to avoid uncomfortable psychological inconsistency, once people have made decisions or taken positions, they will cognitively screen information and tend to reject that which undermines their decisions or contradicts their positions.

Cognitive dissonance can have moral implications. Langevoort has explained how cognitive dissonance can delay lawyers from realizing that their clients are crooks.[107] The same point has been made regarding auditors.[108] Once a person has taken a particular position—such as "My client is innocent." "My employer is innovative." "My client's financial statements are accurate."—the process of cognitive dissonance makes it difficult for the person to process accurately new, contradictory information. Once a cigarette company has taken the public position that second-hand smoke does not cause cancer, its employees will have difficultly departing from that position, even in the face of substantial

---

[103] Keith Leavitt, Scott J. Reynolds, Christopher M. Barnes, Pauline Schilpzand & Sean T. Hannah, *Different Hats, Different Obligation: Plural Occupational Identities and Situated Moral Judgments*, 55 ACADEMY OF MANAGEMENT JOURNAL 1316 (2012)

[104] RONALD A. HOWARD & CLINTON D. KORVER, ETHICS FOR THE REAL WORLD: CREATING A PERSONAL CODE TO GUIDE DECISIONS IN WORK AND LIFE 27 (2008).

[105] Whet Moser, *Apocalypse Oak Park: Dorothy Martin, The Chicagoan Who Predicted the End of the World and Inspired the Theory of Cognitive Dissonance*, CHICAGO MAGAZINE (May 20, 2011).

[106] LEON FESTINGER, ET AL., WHEN PROPHECY FAILS: A SOCIAL AND PSYCHOLOGICAL STUDY OF A MODERN GROUP THAT PREDICTED THE DESTRUCTION OF THE WORLD (1956).

[107] Donald C. Langevoort, *Where Were the Lawyers? A Behavioral Inquiry Into Lawyers' Responsibility for Clients' Fraud*, 46 VANDERBILT LAW REVIEW 75 (1993).

[108] Robert A. Prentice, *The Case of the Irrational Auditor: A Behavioral Insight into Securities Fraud Litigation*, 95 NORTHWESTERN UNIVERSITY LAW REVIEW 133 (2000).

new evidence. In retrospect, what appears to have been dishonesty and foolhardy loyalty to an employer or client, may have been cognitive dissonance at work.[109]

The Tangible and the Abstract

Decision making is naturally impacted more by vivid, tangible, contemporaneous factors than by factors that are removed in time and space. People are more moved by relatively minor injuries to their family, friends, neighbors and even pets than to the starvation of millions of people abroad. This perspective on decision making can cause problems that have ethical dimensions.

Consider a corporate CFO who realizes that if she does not sign false financial statements, the company's stock price will immediately plummet. Her firm's reputation will be seriously damaged today. Employees whom she knows and likes may well lose their jobs tomorrow. Those losses are vivid and immediate. On the other hand, to fudge the numbers will visit a loss, if at all, mostly upon a mass of nameless, faceless investors sometime far off in the future.[110] This puts substantial pressure on the CFO to go ahead and fudge. After interviewing numerous white-collar criminals, Eugene Soltes saw the presence of this tangible & abstract phenomenon:

> [F]or most white-collar crimes, the harm created by a dab of a pen or an adjustment on a spreadsheet does not require getting close to individuals. The victims are physically and psychologically distant. In some cases, like insider trading, the victims might not even be identifiable. As a result, perpetrators of white collar offenses do not experience the same gut feelings of doing harm that kept my interviewees from reaching for my wallet.[111]

Similarly, designers and marketers of products with safety concerns have found it tremendously difficult to decide to pull the plug on a product (even a Ford Pinto or a Dalkon Shield), lay off employees working on the product, and damage the company's profits in the short-term when the potential injuries are hypothetical and the victims merely impersonal future statistics.

---

[109] Regarding cognitive dissonance, note the following:

> After making decisions, one way people reduce dissonance is to reassure themselves that they made the right choice by focusing on information that will lead them to that conclusion. Once a dependent gatekeeper has agreed to an engagement, he has committed himself to the client's ends and is more likely to focus on positive aspects of the choice and downplay negative ones.
>
> This commitment has important consequences. After executing an underwriting agreement, which generally occurs immediately before the offering closes, an underwriter must continually assess whether the prospectus should be updated or revised so as to not be materially misleading. But since directional goals predominate over accuracy goals, an underwriter committed to the transaction has an incentive to filter information to avoid amending the registration statement with negative information which would impede selling efforts. This was the context of the famous case of *SEC v. Manor Nursing Centers, Inc.* [458 F.2d 1082 (2d Cir. 1972)]. The court held that the appellants, including the underwriters, were under a duty to amend the prospectus to reflect developments that occur after the SEC declares the registration statement effective, and the failure to do so was a violation not only of the registration provisions, but also the anti-fraud provisions.

Arthur B. Laby, *Differentiating Gatekeepers,* 1 Brooklyn Journal of Corporate Finance and Commercial Law 119 (2006).

[110] George Loewenstein, *Behavioral Decision Theory and Business Ethics: Skewed Trade-Offs Between Self and Others*, in Codes of Conduct: Behavioral Research into Business Ethics 214 (1996).

[111] Eugene Soltes, Why They Do It: Inside the Mind of the White Collar Criminal (2016).

Related to the "tangible and abstract" concept is the notion of *moral distance*. It is often pointed out that it weighs less on one's conscience to kill by pressing a button in an airplane 30,000 feet in the sky to drop bombs, than to pull a trigger on a rifle to kill a clearly visible human being not far away. The farther people are located from the impact of the consequences of their actions, the easier it is for them to act immorally. Because capital markets supposedly are so efficient that individual players can have little direct impact, they often feel very distant from the potential victims of their misdeeds.[112]

Time-Delay Traps

Temporal factors can play a role in some considerations seeming tangible and others seeming abstract, leading to the time-delay trap. Unfortunately, when an action has both short-term and long-term consequences, the former are much easier for people to consider. People subject to this time-delay trap in decision making often prefer immediate to delayed gratification. Some studies indicate that our prisons are populated largely by people who have an inability to defer gratification and a tendency to underestimate the pain of long-term consequences.

The long-term adverse consequences in terms of legal liability and reputational damage that may be caused by allowing an audit client to push the envelope may be underappreciated by auditors worried about the immediate loss of revenue and even of friendships that would occur if harder choices were made.

In the long-run, most investment bankers, stockbrokers, and other Wall Street professionals and corporate executives presumably wish to follow the rules, to act in such a way as to enhance their reputations, and to avoid the costs that can follow the cutting of ethical corners. However, in the short-run they often face temptations that are difficult to resist:

> [People] want to be relatively patient in future periods, but they become increasingly impatient the closer that they get to incurring an immediate cost or receiving an immediate reward. From a long-term point of view, people tend to have the best intentions for their long-run selves: they make plans to start diets, stop smoking, finish writing papers, and so on. However, when the time to act arrives, the chocolate cake trumps the diet, the Camel prevails, and finishing the paper gives way to going to the movies. In the end, our best intentions are always up for reconsideration, particularly when they stand in the way of immediate gratification.[113]

One must suspect that the short-term gratification that Bernard Ebbers at WorldCom and Andy Fastow at Enron enjoyed in the form of their fabulous (if illicit) remuneration outweighed in their minds the long-term risks of being caught (which may have been underappreciated due to overconfidence and overoptimism biases). Almost every day the financial newspapers report about more top corporate officials who have, to their ultimate regret, succumbed to a time-delay trap. Many highly-respected lawyers at high profile firms have been disciplined for billing fraud in recent years, one suspects for the same reason.

Many officers at Enron found it easy to value deals they entered into for future streams of revenue in an optimistic fashion. In the short term, they reaped millions of dollars of performance bonuses. In the long run, many of those deals lost huge amounts of money;

---

[112] Jean-Michel Bonvin & Paul H. Dembinski, *Ethical Issues in Financial Activities*, 37 J. BUS. ETHICS 187 (2002).

[113] Manuel A. Utset, *Time-Inconsistent Management & the Sarbanes-Oxley Act*, 31 OHIO NORTHERN LAW REVIEW 417 (2005).

but in the long run we're all dead. At least Enron and Arthur Andersen are.

Loss Aversion

People detest losses more than they enjoy gains, about twice as much (several studies show). This *loss aversion* is probably related to the *endowment effect*, the notion that we easily attach ourselves to things and then value them much more than we valued them before we identified with them. A simple coffee mug becomes much more valuable to us once we view it as part of our endowment. Wide-ranging studies show that people typically demand up to seven times as much to part with something as they would have paid to obtain it in the first place.

One implication of the endowment effect and loss aversion is that people will make decisions in order to protect their endowment that they would never have made in the first place to accumulate that endowment. Consider a famous accounting case, *U.S. v. Simon*, 425 F.2d 796 (2d Cir. 1969). Auditors discovered that they had not detected a fraud that their client had been committing. It is unlikely that these auditors would have consciously cast their lot with a fraudster in the first place. But once they learned of the fraud, of their own negligence, and of their potential liability, they did knowingly decide to help cover up the fraud so as to avoid loss of their jobs and professional reputations. This is consistent with studies that have found that the worst lies people tell tend to be to cover up other misbehavior that was often not intentional.[114]

Darley has argued that it is at the cover-up stage that many people who have almost inadvertently acted unethically first cross over to conscious wrongdoing.[115] Thus, employees of manufacturers often find themselves covering up errors in design or testing. Lawyers may begin by defending the tobacco industry in product liability suits and end by fraudulently concealing research showing links between tobacco and cancer.[116] Martin Grass, CEO of Rite-Aid Corporation, who was sentenced to eight years in prison for accounting fraud, had a similar story: "In early 1999, when things started to go wrong financially, I did some things to try to hide that fact. Those things were wrong. They were illegal. I did not do it to line my own pockets."[117]

Martha Stewart was not convicted of insider trading, but of obstructing justice to prevent financial, reputational, and other losses that would come from an insider trading conviction. Frank Quattrone was not convicted of securities fraud but of inducing subordinates to destroy e-mails that would have created the loss that follows such a conviction.[118] Stewart was perhaps the most high-profile female entrepreneur in America and Quattrone was likely the most influential investment banker on Wall Street. Neither would have wished to lose their positions and it seems likely that both acted atypically in the face of grave potential losses.

It seems unlikely that former Baylor University basketball coach Dave Bliss would

---

[114] Scott Rick & George Loewenstein, *Commentaries and Rejoinder to "The Dishonesty of Honest People,"* 45 JOURNAL OF MARKETING RESEARCH 645 (2008).

[115] George Loewenstein, "*Behavioral Decision Theory and Business Ethics: Skewed Trade-Offs Between Self and Others*, in CODES OF CONDUCT: BEHAVIORAL RESEARCH INTO BUSINESS ETHICS 214 (1996).

[116] DAN ZEGART, CIVIL WARRIORS: THE LEGAL SIEGE ON THE TOBACCO INDUSTRY (2000).

[117] Mark Maremont, *Rite Aid's Ex-CEO Sentenced to 8 Years for Accounting Fraud,* WALL STREET JOURNAL, May 28, 2004, at A3.

[118] Note that Quattrone's conviction was later overturned on appeal due to a technicality.

have stooped so low as to try to pin a drug dealing rap on a former player who had been murdered in order to get his coaching job in the first place. But in order to avoid the loss of that same job, it appears that Bliss was willing to do so.[119] Consistent with this surmise, one set of experiments found that subjects were more likely to be in favor of gathering "insider information" and more likely to lie in a negotiation if facing a loss rather than a potential gain.[120]

Loss aversion interacts with framing to create a volatile mix. A recent study found that *even in the absence of a direct economic incentive*, people are more willing to manage earnings when to do so would avoid reporting a loss, an earnings decrease, or a negative earnings surprise. Even people who thought that earnings management was highly unethical were more likely to play that game in order to avoid a perceived loss.[121] In other words, most managers who commit fraud do not do so to raise their companies' stock price beyond those of peers. Rather, they find themselves in situations where they expect large stock price declines if they do not commit fraud.[122] To avoid the loss, they begin the fraud. Managers are thus less likely to commit fraud in order to raise their firm's stock price from $50 to $70 than they are to keep it from slipping from $70 to $50.

Sunk Costs

Another factor that may keep an actor on a self-destructive course that in retrospect will appear unethical is the notion of *sunk costs* and the related phenomenon, *escalation of commitment*. While economists model hypothetical rational economic actors who do not consider sunk costs in deciding future courses of action, most people in real life do so. Thus, people will attend a play that they have decided they don't really want to see just because they have already bought the tickets. Worse yet, sunk costs can lead to an escalating commitment where people throw good money after bad in a deteriorating situation. The Pentagon's behavior in the Vietnam War has been so characterized.

Because of these phenomena, managers of an audit firm that has low-balled an audit bid in order to get a foot in the door in order to sell a client non-audit services will have great difficulty discharging that client when evidence begins to come to light that it is engaged in shady operations. Studies show, comparably, that managers of companies that have poured huge amounts of resources into development of a new product will have great difficulty scrapping that product when evidence of safety problems surface. Investment banks that have invested substantial resources in developing a relationship with an Enron or a WorldCom or a promising new start-up will have difficulty cutting the cord even when they learn that their client is a fraudster.

SITUATIONAL FACTORS AFFECTING ETHICAL DECISION MAKING

People often do not realize how situational factors can influence their ethical judgments and actions. For example, numerous studies show that people will generally judge

---

[119] Mike Wise, *College Basketball: Death and Deception,* NEW YORK TIMES, Aug. 28, 2003, at D1.

[120] Mary C. Kern & Dolly Chugh, *Bounded Ethicality: The Perils of Loss Framing,* 20 PSYCHOLOGICAL SCIENCE 378 (2009).

[121] Arianna S. Pinello & Richard Dusenbury, *The Role of Cognition and Ethical Conviction in Earnings Management Behavior* (2005).

[122] Shane A. Johnson et al., *Managerial Incentives and Corporate Fraud: The Sources of Incentives Matter,* 13 REV. FIN. 115 (2009).

the ethicality of another's actions more harshly if asked to do so in a room that is dirty and disgusting, because the unclean conditions will trigger the disgust emotion that will influence judgments.[123] In a clean room, people tend to be less judgmental. And people are more likely to cheat in a dimly lit room, because they subconsciously feel it less likely that others can observe their actions.[124] In this section, we discuss just a couple of those situational factors which often affect people's ethical decision making without their even being aware of it.

Time Pressure

In a famous study,[125] seminary students were asked to walk across campus and give a talk on the Good Samaritan to some waiting visitors. As each student walked across campus to give the talk, the experimenters arranged for them to come upon a person lying by the sidewalk in obvious distress...in need of a Good Samaritan. If the students were not in a hurry, almost all stopped to help the person. But students who had been placed in a moderate "hurry up" frame of mind by the experimenters stopped to help only 63% of the time, and other students who had been strongly urged to hurry stopped only 10% of the time. It is highly unlikely that the students realized how time pressure affected their decision making, but the results of this study certainly indicate to business people--such as tax accountants in the days before April 15—that they should monitor themselves because when they face extreme time pressure they are more likely to make ethical missteps than otherwise.

Money

Wall Street often appears to be a bit of an ethical cesspool, and part of the reason is the impact that thinking about money has on people. Numerous studies have been done where people have been prompted to think about money and then their decisions and actions are compared to similar people who have not been so prompted. According to some experts, morality is rooted in social relationships and thinking about money weakens those relationships and has an adverse effect on ethical decision making.

Thus, as compared to their peers, people in one study[126] who were prompted to think about money before judging or acting tended to:

- Choose solitary activities over social activities.
- Be less helpful when others asked for assistance.
- Be more reluctant to ask for assistance themselves.
- Donate less to charity.
- Maintain greater social distance when meeting someone new.
- Choose more often to work alone rather than with a peer.

---

[123] PAUL BLOOM, JUST BABIES: THE ORIGINS OF GOOD AND EVIL 150 (2013).

[124] FRANCESCA GINO, SIDETRACKED: HOW OUR DECISIONS GET DERAILED AND HOW WE CAN STICK TO THE PLAN 121 (2013)

[125] John M. Darley & C. Daniel Batson, *"From Jerusalem to Jericho": A Study of Situational and Dispositional Variables in Helping Behavior,* 27 JOURNAL OF PERSONALITY AND SOCIAL PSYCHOLOGY 100 (1963).

[126] Kathleen Vohs et al., *The Psychological Consequences of Money,* 314 SCIENCE 1154 (2006).

In another study,[127] people prompted to think about money:

- More frequently indicated that they would do unethical acts if given the chance.
- Lied more often to other subjects in a deception game where they could profit by lying.
- Lied more often to the experimenters to gain money rewards.
- Were more likely to say that they would hire a candidate who promised that if hired he would bring a competitor's confidential information to the job.

Many people in business find themselves in jobs where they are surrounded all day by money considerations. The success of all of their actions is judged by a monetary metric. They must be wary that such a narrow focus on money does not cause them to act unethically.

Conclusion

Psychologists speak of the *fundamental attribution error,* which is people's tendency to underestimate how situational factors affect others' decisions and to overestimate how much they affect their own. In other words, we tend to assume that other people do bad things because they are bad people, but believe that we do bad things because we had to. The other guy fudged the numbers because he's a crook, but I fudged the numbers because my boss made me. The other guy cheated on his wife because he is a slime ball, but I cheated on my wife because I accidentally got drunk. The other guy cheated customers to get a big commission because he is greedy; I did the same thing because I have a family to feed. This chapter should make it clear that social and organizational factors, cognitive heuristics and biases, and situational factors affect everyone's ethical decision making. But when the headlines hit the newspapers or the cops arrive on your doorstep, these situational factors, which definitely do impact everyone's actions, are not going to be an excuse for unethical behavior. They are an *explanation* for bad decision making, but not an *excuse* for it.

Although this introduction to behavioral psychology's relevance to ethical decision making constitutes the bulk of this chapter, the discussion closes with some suggestions on how individuals who wish to act ethically in the business context can improve their chances of doing so.

[Many of the topics discussed in this section are further explained in free ethics videos located at the Ethicsunwrapped.utexas.edu website, and freely accessible on YouTube.]

BEING THE PERSON YOU WANT TO BE

Dr. Laura Schlessinger's admonition—"Now go do the right thing"—is easier said than done, even for those who are well meaning. As psychologist John Darley notes, "most harmful actions are not committed by palpably evil actors carrying out solitary actions … [but] by individuals acting within an organizational context."[128] It is therefore important that well-meaning individuals be aware of their susceptibility to authority, peer pressure, and other organizational influences, as well as to the various heuristics, biases, and organizational pressures discussed in this chapter. People who wish to act ethically in their financial, managerial, marketing, law, and accounting careers must have more than good

---

[127] Maryam Kouchaki et al, *Seeing Green: Mere Exposure to Money Triggers a Business Decision Frame and Unethical Outcomes,* 121 ORGANIZATIONAL BEHAVIOR & HUMAN DECISION PROCESSES 53 (2013).

[128] John Darley, *How Organizations Socialize Individuals into Evildoing*, CODES OF CONDUCT: BEHAVIORAL RESEARCH INTO BUSINESS ETHICS 13 (1996).

intentions, although good intentions are always a nice start. What else might be helpful?

Develop a Moral Identity

A high school student who views herself as too cool to care is going to act differently than a high school student who views herself as an Ivy-Leaguer-to-be. A young man who views himself as a ladies' man is going to act differently than a young man who views himself as a pillar of his conservative church. An adult who views himself as way smarter than those 40-hour-a-week chumps who wear "monkey suits" to work is going to make different decisions than an adult who views himself primarily as a responsible breadwinner for his family. Mother Teresa's self-image was different than Lindsay Lohan's and led to different choices.

If you wish to be a moral person, you need to think of yourself as one. Ethical activity needs to be part of your personal identity. Research on moral identity theory is not well-developed, but one approach highlights the "Self Model," which contains three components. First, the model notes that people not only decide what is the "right" way to act in a given situation by making a moral judgment, but they also make a decision regarding their own responsibility for acting on the judgment. Second, the criteria for making these judgments arises from a person's *moral identity,* which reflects the degree to which being moral is an essential characteristic of the person's sense of self. Third, the model emphasizes the human tendency to strive for self-consistency. "This tendency provides the motivational impetus for moral action, so that a person whose self-definition is centered on moral concerns will feel compelled to act in a manner that is consistent with his or her moral self-construal."[129]

Simply put, if you think of yourself as a moral person and if being a moral person is an important part of your concept of yourself, you are more likely to act as a moral person would act. Now this is far from a guarantee of perfection. Everyone errs. Everyone is affected by the social and organizational pressures and the psychological limitations discussed in the first half of this chapter, such as the self-serving bias and especially overconfidence. Even a person who wishes to be a moral person and who makes that an important part of her self-definition will sometimes make patently unethical choices and rationalize them away. Nonetheless, it seems obvious that as a general rule, someone who views herself as a moral person will make different choices than someone who views herself as just too clever to be reined in by the conventions of society. And there is empirical evidence that people with a strong moral identity, if they can stay humble, are more likely to engage in pro-social behaviors like charitable giving and community service, are less likely to engage in antisocial behavior such as trying to injure an opponent during an athletic contest or lying during negotiations, are less likely to engage in moral disengagement (whereby they suspend moral evaluations of their own actions), and are more likely to be viewed as ethical leaders by others.[130]

Dennis Gioia was intimately involved in the famous Ford Pinto debacle. He had opportunities to stop production of the Pinto and did not do so—decisions he later greatly regretted. Later he became an academic and studied ethical decision making. Among his bits of advice for people entering into the business world is this:

---

[129] Ruodan Shao et al., *Beyond Moral Reasoning: A Review of Moral Identity Research and Its Implications for Business Ethics,* 18 BUSINESS ETHICS QUARTERLY 513 (2008).

[130] *Id.*

[D]evelop your ethical base now! Too many people do not give serious attention to assessing and articulating their own values. People simply do not know what they stand for because they haven't thought about it seriously. Even the ethical scenarios presented in classes or executive programs are treated as interesting little games without apparent implications for deciding how you intend to think or act. These exercises should be used to develop a principled, personal code that you will try to live by. Consciously decide your values. If you don't decide your values now, you are easy prey for others who will gladly decide them for you or influence you implicitly to accept theirs.[131]

Obviously, you cannot make yourself an ethical person just by thinking of yourself as ethical. Wishing it so does not make it so. But strengthening your moral identity can improve your chances of acting morally.

Keep Your Ethical Antennae Up

Although some people knowingly and affirmatively choose to act unethically, more ethical lapses stem from inattention and inadvertence. Many people stumble into ethical minefields unaware of the dangerous position in which they have put themselves. To avoid such errors, you should always keep your ethical antennae fully extended. Think to yourself every day that you want to be a good person (*i.e.*, strengthen that moral identity) and remind yourself that the next ethical trap could be just around the corner. If you do not constantly remind yourself of your desire to act ethically, then you could become a victim of "ethical fading." If you become too caught up in pleasing the boss, in fitting in with the team, in production goals, in earnings targets, in promotions and bonuses, then the ethical dimension of decisions you face can fade into the background and you may miss them altogether.

Studies show that if people are reminded of the Ten Commandments or of their school's honor code right before they take an exam, they will tend to cheat less. Being prompted to think through an ethical lens alters their behavior for the better. It is your job to strive to constantly keep ethics in your decisional framework, no matter the context of the decision, in case no one else prompts you.

Monitor Your Own Overconfidence

One of the authors recently polled his students and 75% responded that they were "more ethical" than their classmates. While mathematically unlikely, this is not at all an unusual result. As indicated earlier in the chapter, most people do tend to be overconfident regarding their own ethical standards. Yet, it is people just like these students who make the mistakes that lead to the losses, arrests, and scandals that we read about in the newspaper every day.

If you are confident that you are a good person, you can actually feel less pressure to act ethically. Moral psychologist Bernard Monin says: "The choices we make are influenced by how confident we are that we're a good person. If you're confident in your self-worth, you're not as sensitive to [ethical] threats." Think of all the religious figures and "family values" politicians who have been embroiled in sordid moral scandals over the years. In matters of ethics, a little dose of humility is almost always a good idea, particularly if it causes one to be more deliberate and reflective in making ethically-tinged decisions.

---

[131] Dennis A. Gioia, *Reflections on the Pinto Fires Case,* in LINDA K. TREVINO & KATHERINE NELSON, MANAGING BUSINESS ETHICS 138 (2007).

Monitor Your Own Rationalizations

A key factor in "good" people doing bad things is the near universal ability of human beings to rationalize. As noted earlier, we tend to view ourselves as good people. When we are tempted to do something unethical for personal gain, we tend to either refrain from the unethical act so that we can act consistently with our values, or to resort to "moral disengagement," which is "the process of making detrimental conduct personally acceptable by persuading oneself that the questionable behavior is actually morally permissible."[132] We can use various cognitive mechanisms to deactivate our moral self-regulation.[133] This process may involve various "psychological tricks" that allow us to act unethically yet reduce our cognitive dissonance:

> For example, a salesperson at an investment company who is using dishonest sales tactics with his customers may remind himself of an instance when he felt tricked by a customer and think, I want to make sure I do not get cheated again. Or he may think of his family and explain his behavior to himself as a sign of a good father who makes sure his children can afford college tuition. Another way to reduce cognitive dissonance is to change one's self-image from somebody who is innocent and naive to somebody who simply understands how to "play the game" successfully.[134]

As another example, studies show that if we know a product was manufactured with sweat shop labor, we may be willing to boycott it on ethical grounds....unless we really, really want the product in which case we are likely to ethically disengage to square our actions with our self-image.[135]

Because they are able to use mechanisms such as rationalization to induce moral disengagement, most white-collar criminals, surveys show, do not view themselves as corrupt, as bad people, or as criminals. Rather, they rationalize and compartmentalize so that in their minds they remain normal businessmen and businesswomen.

According to one formulation, "rationalizations" are:

- self serving explanations;
- that assist in making behavior appear more acceptable to both self and others;
- involve a degree of self deception;
- often occur outside the realm of the conscious mind;
- can reduce feelings of responsibility and/or anxiety for the negative aspects of behavior; and
- can neutralize the impact of legal or ethical issues involved in a decision.[136]

In the process of squaring our image of ourselves as good people and our less-than-completely-honest actions, we often resort to these rationalizations:

---

[132] ALBERT BANDURA, SOCIAL FOUNDATIONS OF THOUGHT AND ACTION (1986). See also ALBERT BANDURA, MORAL DISENGAGEMENT: HOW PEOPLE DO HARM AND LIVE WITH THEMSELVES (2016).

[133] Lisa L. Shu et al., "Dishonest Deed, Clear Conscience: Self-Preservation through Moral Disengagement and Motivated Forgetting," (2009), *available at* http://ssrn.com/abstract=1323803.

[134] THOMAS OBERLECHNER, THE PSYCHOLOGY OF ETHICS IN THE FINANCE AND INVESTMENT INDUSTRY 35 (2007).

[135] Neeru Paharia & Rohit Deshpande, "Sweatshop Labor is Wrong Unless the Jeans are Cute: Motivated Moral Disengagement," (2009), *available at* http://ssrn.com/abstract=1325423.

[136] Kath Hall & Vivien Holmes, "The Power of Rationalization to Influence Lawyers' Decisions to Act Unethically," 11 LEGAL ETHICS 137 (2009).

In the process of creating a self-narrative, the role of rationalization is crucial. It is at the heart of how we consciously and unconsciously create consistency between our version of events and reality. Because life often provides information and experiences that contradict our self-narrative, rationalizing these contradictions helps us to "patch up" the holes in our story and maintain a sense of self. It also allows us to reinterpret our view of events, particularly when events challenge our notion of ourselves as "good people."[137]

Anand, Ashforth, and Joshi[138] recently suggested the following table summarizing rationalization strategies.

Strategy	Description	Examples
Denial of Responsibility	The actors engaged in corrupt behaviors perceive that they have no other choice than to participate in such activities	"What can I do? My arm is being twisted." "It is none of my business what the corporation does in overseas bribery."
Denial of Injury	The actors are convinced that no one is harmed by their actions; hence the actions are not really corrupt	"No one was really harmed." "It could have been worse."
Denial of Victim	The actors counter any blame for their actions by arguing that the violated party deserved whatever happened.	"They deserved it." "They chose to participate."
Social weighting	The actors assume two practices that moderate the salience of corrupt behaviors: 1. Condemn the condemnor, 2. Selective social comparison	"You have no right to criticize us." "Others are worse than we are."
Appeal to higher loyalties	The actors argue that their violation is due to their attempt to realize a higher-order value."	"We answered to a more important cause." "I would not report it because of my loyalty to my boss.
Metaphor of the ledger	The actors rationalize that they are entitled to indulge in deviant behaviors because of their accrued credits (time and effort) in their jobs.	"We've earned the right." "It's all right for me to use the Internet for personal reasons at work. After all, I do work overtime."

A recent survey indicated that many business school faculty worry that students are being taught these rationalizations in business school.[139] Rationalizations that are commonly heard but are unlikely to move regulators or jurors include:

- "Sure, I exaggerate, but customers are smart. You can't really fool them."
- "If customers are dumb enough to believe some of this stuff, they deserve to lose money."
- "If it's legal, it must be moral."
- "Everybody does it."

Ashforth and Anand point out that corruption can only continue if newcomers are socialized into their corrupt environment.[140] Three prominent methods of accomplishing this are:

- **Co-optation**, where rewards are used to induce attitude change toward unethical behavior.

---

[137] Hall & Holmes, *supra* at 6.

[138] Vikas Anand, et al., *Business as Usual: The Acceptance and Perpetuation of Corruption in Organizations,* 18 ACADEMY OF MANAGEMENT EXECUTIVE 39 (2004).

[139] Mary C. Gentile, *Giving Voice to Values, or Is There Free Will in Business?* (2005).

[140] Blake E. Ashforth & Vikas Anand, *The Normalization of Corruption in Organizations,* 25 RESEARCH IN ORGANIZATIONAL BEHAVIOR 1 (2003).

Sufficient compensation can, in conjunction with the self-serving bias, convince people that they truly are not really doing anything unethical.

- **Compromise,** where individuals essentially back into corruption in an attempt to resolve a pressing problem. In order to procure good quality products for customers in a time of shortage, merchants may begin to pay bribes to suppliers. Because one member of an audit team has serious health issues and another is dealing with the death of a parent, other members of the team that is falling well behind in an audit may pretend that certain (hopefully less important) audit procedures have been performed when really they have not.

If you find yourself in an organization that starts cutting ethical corners, even a little bit, you should be worried. The slippery slope can accelerate before you know it. No one can be perfect all the time, but it probably pays to try. One of the Harvard Business School's most influential professors, Clayton Christensen, tells the story of how while at Oxford he refused to play in the national championship basketball game, resisting the pleas of his coach and teammates, because it was scheduled on Sunday and to play would violate his religious convictions. He realized that if he compromised this time, he would have no standing to refuse the next time he was asked to make an exception. The lesson he learned was that it is easier to do the right thing 100% of the time than it is to do it 98% of the time.[141]

Acting Courageously[142]

For even the most prosaic business decision, it requires courage and inner strength to disagree with peers and superiors regarding a course of action. It requires even more courage and persuasive ability to advocate for an ethical course of action than a mere strategic action with no ethical overtones, for in this setting managers are telling their colleagues not only that they are making an erroneous decision, but also that they are acting unethically as well. In the immortal words of Albus Dumbledore, "It takes a great deal of bravery to stand up to our enemies, but just as much to stand up to our friends"[143]

We all wish to be team players. We all wish to please the boss. But companies hire managers to formulate and express their independent viewpoints. Managers who are simple "yes men" or "yes women" add nothing to the company's decision-making process. Charles Keating at Lincoln Savings & Loan (the most disastrous of all the 1980s savings & loan frauds) and Charles Scrushy at HealthSouth were famous for hiring and promoting only those who would tell them what they wanted to hear, and things did not end well for those firms.

In his memoir, a member of President Kennedy's cabinet recalled the debate over whether to go forward with the Bay of Pigs invasion of Cuba. He believed that the idea was a terrible one, but thought that everyone else in the room felt it was a good idea. Not wishing to appear to lack the courage to make this militarily aggressive decision, the cabinet member held his tongue. Only later did he learn that many other people in the room felt as he did and

---

[141] Larissa MacFarquhar, *When Giants Fail: What Business Has Learned from Clayton Christensen,* NEW YORKER, May 14, 2012, at p. 95.

[142] The last portion of this chapter draws from materials created by Mary Gentile (formerly of Harvard University), Steven Tomlinson (University of Texas), and Minette Drumwright (University of Texas) for an MBA mini-course on business ethics that one of the authors helped present at the McCombs School of Business, University of Texas at Austin in October 2003. These ideas come largely from Mary Gentile's Giving Voice to Values ethical program and free videos depicting her seven-step plan are available on the Ethics Unwrapped website—ethicsunwrapped.utexas.edu.

[143] J.K. ROWLING, HARRY POTTER AND THE SORCERER'S STONE 306 (1997).

kept quiet for the same reason.[144] Had just one person in the room had the courage to speak up and point out that the emperor had no clothes, this debacle of American foreign policy likely would not have happened.

Remember Solomon Asch's experiments with the lines? When just one confederate of the experimenter gave the right answer, errors by the subject were reduced by 75%. And in one variation of Stanley Milgram's experiments, he had two confederates refuse to administer shocks when the dial was turned into the dangerous range. When that happened, 92.5% of the subjects defied the experimenter's orders. In other words, it just takes one or two people with a little courage to save organizations from terrible mistakes. Public companies, investment banks, law, and accounting firms need employees with the courage to raise their hands and speak their minds when ethical errors are about to me made. Just one person can have a major impact.

Pre-Scripting

As indicated earlier, many people back into ethical mistakes. They do not consider the ethical dimensions of a decision before acting and only later realize that had their "ethical antennae" been activated, they likely would have considered different factors in making their decisions and would have come to different conclusions. The best evidence shows that people are more likely to make ethical errors when they are barely aware that a decision has an ethical aspect…when "moral intensity" is low.[145] On the other hand, when moral intensity is high….when the decision makers clearly perceive the ethical dimensions of a decision and wish to do the right thing, it is much more likely that they will act ethically.

Consistent with this notion, some research on people who have acted heroically— for example, European civilians who helped shelter Jews from the Nazis during World War II--indicates that they had *pre-scripted* themselves to act in such a way. In other words, they explain that they had thought in advance about how they would act in such a circumstance and, when the situation arose, merely acted in accordance with the course of action they had scripted for themselves. People who wish to act ethically must work to create that moral intensity that can help them avoid making inadvertently unethical choices.[146]

Therefore, it makes sense for people who wish to act ethically during their professional careers to spend time envisioning ethical problems that they may confront in their careers and to anticipate how they will react when faced with such dilemmas. Business law textbooks present many examples of legal and ethical mistakes made by commercial actors. Many are simply technical mistakes, but many have an ethical dimension. Hopefully, readers of these cases will resolve that they will do better should they face a similar problem. Simply thinking about such ethical pitfalls in advance and considering a proper course of action should dramatically improve the odds that people will "do the right thing" when faced with a difficult ethical choice.

Advocating Effectively

All companies need managers who can determine when a particular financial,

---

[144] ARTHUR SCHELSINGER, JR., A THOUSAND DAYS 255 (1965).

[145] Bruno F. Frey, *The Impact of Moral Intensity on Decision Making in a Business Context*, 26 JOURNAL OF BUSINESS ETHICS 181 (2000).

[146] For an excellent discussion of moral intensity, *see* THOMAS OBERLECHNER, THE PSYCHOLOGY OF ETHICS IN THE FINANCE AND INVESTMENT INDUSTRY 17-19 (2007).

managerial, or marketing strategy is likely to be ineffective. These companies also need managers who can advocate effectively inside the corporate bureaucracy in order to derail inefficient or ineffective operational or strategic decisions. A bright manager who does not have the courage to stand up against an ineffective financial, managerial or marketing strategy and the ability to convince others to avoid making a self-defeating decision is not a very useful employee. Similarly, companies need managers with the ability and the courage to identify and advocate against unethical courses of action. Decisions that lead to unethical actions can be just as expensive, if not more so, than decisions that simply lead to ineffective strategies. If Enron still existed, you could ask it.

A person who not only resolves to follow an ethical course but can also persuade colleagues and superiors to follow that course is a truly valuable employee. Changing other people's minds is, of course, a formidable task. Harvard professor of cognition Howard Gardner notes that "[i]t is never easy to bring about a change of mind."[147] This is especially true when the others' perceived self-interest would be served by unethical choices. This chapter closes with three simple suggestions that can be useful.

First, help others see the "big picture" through a long-term lens. The framing literature discussed above makes it clear that many unethical decisions are made because decision makers are focusing only upon a single metric—gross revenue, net profits, stock price, Christmas bonuses, etc. They are not considering the bigger picture, which may include ethical dimensions. Even more commonly, decision makers fail to plan for the long-term; their focus regarding earnings is simply upon making this quarter's numbers. They fail to consider how reporting earnings in this quarter that will not truly be earned until next quarter can lead to an even greater problem next quarter than can soon spiral out of control. Managers who can help their colleagues see the big picture and the long-term implications of unethical decisions can often convince decision makers that the right thing to do will also prove to be the profitable thing to do.

Second, don't be a "goody two-shoes." Employees who try to appear morally superior to their colleagues are not going to be effective advocates for their position. Instead, they will be perceived as pains in the posterior. Therefore, they should avoid saying "no," "no," "no," and "no." Instead, they should be a source of workable alternatives. Rather than take the blanket position: "No, we can't do that; it would be unethical," effective advocates should formulate and present workable (and ethical) alternatives.

Finally, be pragmatic. People should realize that their colleagues, firms, and clients will often have identifiable benefits flowing from the arguably unethical course of action being debated. They cannot be expected to be excited to give up those benefits at the drop of a naysayer's hat. This means that the effective advocate for a more ethical course must identify alternatives that will be palatable to these other decision makers…alternatives that will minimize their losses or be appealing for some other reason. The effective advocate will generate and forcefully present alternatives that make it feasible and reasonable for others to select the ethical course of action.

---

[147] HOWARD GARDNER, CHANGING MINDS: THE ART AND SCIENCE OF CHANGING OUR OWN AND OTHER PEOPLE'S MINDS 92 (2004).

CHAPTER 38

ETHICS, ORGANIZATIONS, AND CORPORATE
SOCIAL RESPONSIVENESS

- Introduction

- Are Corporations Moral Agents?

- Corporate Social Responsiveness

- How to Encourage Employees to Act Ethically

- Ethics on the Global Stage

INTRODUCTION

In the previous chapter, we discussed the decision-making errors that individuals often make that can lead to unethical actions. We also warned about, among other things, the organizational pressures that can induce individuals to make unethical decisions. In this chapter, we move beyond the individual, to focus on business organizations. Corporations, for example, are extremely powerful actors in today's global business environment. Can corporations be held to an ethical standard? Is the standard the same for companies as for individuals? Can corporations act ethically? Should their owners and agents worry about whether they do? If the answer to these questions is in the affirmative, how can we set up structures to ensure that firms act as ethically as possible?

This chapter addresses these and other questions in light of the general consensus that business leaders should be responsible not only for their own individual actions, but also for those of their firms. "Leadership is responsible not only for setting the company's strategic direction, but also for its ethical tone."[148] As the authors of *Freakonomics* note, the role of leaders is "not simply financial and administrative, but social, political, and moral."[149] For these reasons, a Carnegie Foundation book on undergraduate business education reform recommends that more liberal arts–type learning, such as business law and business ethics, be introduced into the undergraduate business curriculum so that students can prepare to be civic leaders within the business domain by more fully understanding the effects that business has on society and the implications that other social institutions hold for business activity.[150]

When a corporation's ethical culture goes off the rails, the impact can be significant, both on the firm itself and on the victims of its wrongdoing. The Volkswagen emission scandal is an example. For most of the 21st Century, Volkswagen, until it was definitively caught in 2016, installed "defeat devices" on its diesel engines to fool emission detectors. The picture inside VW was a familiar one to those who study corporate scandals. Top officers set impossibly high expectations for employees, desiring powerful, low-cost, and nearly emission-free engines that went beyond any technology that VW's engineers possessed. Asked to do the impossible, employees cheated. Top managers countenanced the cheating. Whistleblowing was strongly discouraged. This combination of factors led to a multi-year fraud. Although the company initially tried to place the blame on a few "rogue employees," it ultimately became clear that the fraud involved scores, if not hundreds, of employees. Because of the cheating, scores of people in the U.S. alone will die prematurely. The environmental impact in Europe will be far worse because VW sold more cars there. All the lawsuits are not over, but several VW employees are facing criminal charges and the costs to the firm in fines and other losses exceed $30 billion.

On the other hand, the Covid-19 crisis provided many firms the opportunity to go above and beyond in helping customers, employees, and society in a time of need. Many donated money or equipment to hospitals and other charities. Many dipped into reserves to keep paying employees' salaries or providing sick leave protection well beyond contractual

---

[148] Chester Barnard, 1938.

[149] Stephen J. Dubner & Steven D. Levitt, *What the Bagel Man Saw*, NEW YORK TIMES MAGAZINE, June 6, 2004, at 62.

[150] ANNE COLBY ET AL., RETHINKING UNDERGRADUATE BUSINESS EDUCATION: LIBERAL LEARNING FOR THE PROFESSION (2011).

obligations. Others retooled their manufacturing processes to begin making masks, ventilators, and other equipment needed in the crisis. Few committed money and resources in a more proactive and thoughtful way than the HEB grocery chain in Texas.[151]

There Has Never Been a Better Time for Businesses to Act Ethically

As indicated in a previous chapter, there has never been a better time for individuals to act ethically. The same is true for firms which can, as never before, benefit by acting ethically and thereby building reputational capital.[152] Talking about the firms that did the right thing in the early stages of the Covid-19 pandemic, ethicist Alison Taylor noted that "[f]or businesses that can afford it, this is a long-term play on building (or rebuilding) public trust and brand loyalty, which they hope will last when the situation turns. Also, acting quickly and proactively has a lot of benefit, as it is the first movers that will be remembered."[153]

Investors are looking for good corporate citizens. One in every nine dollars under professional management in the U.S. today is targeted at socially responsible investing (SRI) and such funds are growing six times faster than non-SRI funds. A 2014 study found that in the U.S. funds that apply various environmental, social, and governance criteria to their investment analysis and portfolio selection held $6.2 *trillion* in assets.[154] In late 2008, proxy voting research firm Glass Lewis announced that it would include environmental and social data in its research service for the first time in response to client demand.[155] In a recent letter to corporate leaders, Larry Fink, Chair and CEO of BlackRock noted the perils of climate change and the needs for increasingly sustainable practices and opined that corporations that do not pay serious attention to these matters will have increasing difficulty accessing capital.[156] To act ethically and responsibly can, therefore, attract capital.

More and more prospective employees want to work for "family friendly," "gay friendly," "Hispanic friendly," "eco-friendly" companies and the like, and magazines are filled with polls listing who is "friendly" and who is not. Never before has it been easier for potential employees to find companies that will treat them fairly and responsibly. Importantly, employees will work for less for good corporate citizens, giving those companies a competitive advantage. People identify with their employers and want to be proud of them. Therefore, businesses that have reputations as good citizens can attract higher quality employees as well as employees who are willing to work for less.[157]

Psychologists' studies find a strong correlation between the ethical perception of a company and its employees' job satisfaction. Consider that:

---

[151] Dan Solomon & Paula Forbes, *Inside the Story of How H-E-B Planned for the Pandemic*, TEXAS MONTHLY, March 26, 2020.

[152] KEVIN T. JACKSON, BUILDING REPUTATIONAL CAPITAL (2004).

[153] Aaron Nicodemus, *For Some Companies in the Age of Coronavirus, Ethics Pays,* COMPLIANCE WEEK, Mar. 17, 2020 (quoting Taylor).

[154] Forum for Sustainable and Responsible Investing, Report on US Sustainable, Responsible, and Impact Investing Trends (2014), p. 12.

[155] Sophia Greene, *Investors Sign Up to a Better World,* FINANCIAL TIMES, Nov. 3, 2008, Sec. FTfm, p. 1.

[156] Larry Fink, "A Fundamental Reshaping of Finance," at https://www.blackrock.com/corporate/investor-relations/larry-fink-ceo-letter.

[157] ROBERT H. FRANK, WHAT PRICE THE MORAL HIGH GROUND? (2004). Much of the information in this section comes from studies described by Frank.

- Employees rate "give me an opportunity to be helpful to others" as a more important job feature than salary.
- Employers have reported that their firm's ethical posture affected their ability to recruit in the labor market.
- For-profits must pay 59% higher wages, on average, than non-profits. Even controlling for grades, law school quality, and the like, New York City law firms must pay much more in the way of salary than organizations such as the ACLU must pay for similarly qualified attorneys.
- In the tobacco litigation cases, plaintiffs' expert witnesses believed in what they were doing and often testified for free, whereas defendants' expert witnesses charged very large fees to testify.
- People indicate that if both jobs paid $30,000 they'd rather be an accountant for a large art museum than for a large petrochemical firm, and it would take a salary boost of $14,000 to get them to switch.[158]

Employees will not only work for less at an ethical employer, they will also work harder. "People who know that they are working for something larger with a more noble purpose can be expected to be loyal and dependable, and, at a minimum, more inspired."[159] One study found that 55% of the employees at firms with good ethics can be rated as "truly loyal," in that they are willing to "go the extra mile." At firms rated "neutral" in ethics that percentage dropped to 24%. At firms rated as having poor ethics, the proportion of "truly loyal" employees was only 9%. The bottom line is that employees will work harder for good corporate citizens.

Investors and employees are not the only people concerned with business ethics. Increasingly *customers* are concerned with the ethics of the companies they purchase from. While there are obviously limits, many people are willing to boycott a company that they view as unethical and to pay more for similar goods they buy from companies they believe do act ethically. For example, when Sunkist slapped a "dolphin friendly" label on its cans of tuna, its sales went up despite the fact that it had also raised prices. In a poll, 51% of consumers said that they had either rewarded or punished companies in the past year based on their social performance, which is why companies such as Ben & Jerry's and the Body Shop did very well while striving mightily to act as good corporate citizens.

More prosaically, customers want to do business with companies that have treated them ethically. Most firms can make money in the short-term by ripping people off. However, any firm taking the long-view realizes that reputation matters. Return business is important in most lines of commerce, and treating customers fairly is an important prerequisite to developing customer loyalty. Suppliers, employees, and other constituencies also will prefer to associate with companies that act ethically. "A reputation for honest dealing can be a powerful competitive advantage."[160]

Putting all this together, it makes sense that firms that act ethically should prosper in comparison with those that do not. Many empirical studies have addressed the issue of whether it pays to be ethical. Although results are not definitive, one meta-analysis of those studies indicated that corporations that act more ethically tend to be more profitable. Of 95 studies, 55 found a positive relationship between social performance and financial performance. Only four found a negative relationship. The rest showed a mixed

---

[158] *Id.*

[159] Jim Channon, *Creating Esprit de Corps*, in NEW TRADITIONS IN BUSINESS 53 (J. Renesch, ed. 1992).

[160] ROBERT F. HARTLEY, BUSINESS ETHICS: MISTAKES AND SUCCESSES 4 (2005).

relationship.[161]

Finally, note that there appear to be tremendous profit opportunities in sustainability, being eco-friendly, etc—ask Wal-Mart, which has been a leader in the sustainability movement, believing that such initiatives would increase innovation, cut costs, and create new markets. Indeed, Robert Reich has argued that the CSR movement is overhyped and that a primary reason that firms engage in socially-responsible activities is that they are profit-generating over the long run.[162]

There Has Never Been a Worse Time for Businesses to Act Unethically

These are "bet the company" times. Ask Drexel Burnham Lambert, Arthur Andersen, Enron, Bear Stearns, AIG, Lehman Brothers, Washington Mutual, and Takata. Firms that violate the rules may not only suffer tremendous financial losses; they may blink out of existence. It seems obvious that "[a] firm that violates the public trust today is vulnerable to competitors more eager to develop good relationships."[163]

As with individuals, companies that act illegally or unethically are more likely than ever to be caught. Companies have always had to deal with television investigative reporting shows like "60 Minutes," but new technology (e-mails, text messages, cell phone cameras, etc.) have greatly increased the chances of people and companies being caught when they are committing wrongdoing. A Lockheed whistleblower placed a video on YouTube when he could not otherwise draw attention to his information. Passengers took videos of a fellow passenger being dragged off a United Airlines flight. It has never been easier for firms to be embarrassed and their reputation to be sullied.

Sarbanes-Oxley's requirements for internal controls have made it easier to detect financial wrongdoing (e.g., bribery payments in violation of the Foreign Corrupt Practices Act) and have encouraged and (at least somewhat) protected whistleblowers. "In a world of instant communications, whistleblowers, inquisitive media, and googling, citizens and communities routinely put firms under the microscope."[164]

As with individuals, penalties for corporations that are caught acting illegally or unethically are also higher than ever. Potential fines and liability for judgments in civil cases are higher than ever, partly because of mandates of Sarbanes-Oxley.

Worse is the reputational penalty multiplier. Conviction of wrongdoing often leads to loss of licenses and of the ability to bid for government contracts. Just the bad publicity from wrongdoing often leads to reputational damage. Customers may boycott. Suppliers may sever ties. Potential employees may refuse to apply. Investors may sell stock and/or refuse to buy stock. A study of 132 cases of corporate fraud found that the average firm was punished by a $60 million drop in its market capitalization. Only a small percentage of that amount could be accounted for by potential civil and criminal penalties; the rest was reputational damage. Other studies indicate that fines and damages account for only 6% of

---

[161] Lynn Sharp Paine, Value Shift 53 (2003).

[162] Robert Reich, "The Case Against Corporate Social Responsibility," (2009), *available at* http://ssrn.com.abstract=1213129. Reich argues strongly that the CSR movement has been over-hyped in that it is based on a false premise regarding how much discretion modern corporations have to sacrifice profits for the sake of social goals and that the entire movement misleads the public into believe that more is being done by the private sector to meet public goals than is in fact the case.

[163] Robert F. Hartley, Business Ethics: Mistakes and Successes 1 (2005).

[164] Don Tapscott & David Ticoll, The Naked Corporation (2003).

the stock price drop loss that companies sustain when they are involved in scandals. The remaining 94% derives from the market's anticipation of future adverse impacts from investors, employees, and customers. Given all this, it is unsurprising that a review of 27 studies covering 2,000 incidents of socially irresponsible behavior found these wrongdoing firms took substantial stock price hits, destroying shareholder wealth.[165]

Finally, acting badly invites cumbersome and expensive government regulation, such as the Foreign Corrupt Practices Act (FCPA), the Racketeering Influenced Corrupt Organizations Act (RICO), and the Sarbanes-Oxley Act (SOX). As Harvard ethicist Lynn Sharp-Paine noted: "Antitrust laws, food and safety laws, advertising regulations, securities regulations, consumer protection, environmental protection, anticorruption laws, equal employment laws, and workplace-safety standards are just a few examples of legislation triggered by corporate indifference to social concerns."[166] In the midst of the subprime mess, bad acting even invited government co-ownership of banks and other commercial enterprises.

It has been reported that in a visit to the Harvard Business School, former Enron CEO Jeff Skilling was asked what he would do if his company was producing a product that caused death to its users. He responded: "I'd keep making and selling the product. My job as a businessman is to be a profit center and to maximize returns to the shareholders. It's the government's job to step in if a product is dangerous."[167] Pursuant to his job as a profit center, Skilling was, of course, also doing everything he could through lobbying and campaign contributions to influence government not to step in. Some believe that Enron ultimately reaped what it sowed. Such excesses, many argue, are capitalism's Achilles heel.

ARE CORPORATIONS MORAL AGENTS?

There is nearly unanimous agreement that individuals are morally responsible for their actions within business organizations. Managers and employees in corporations, like other individuals in other settings, have moral obligations. These obligations can never be erased by joining anything, be it a club, fraternity, political party, or business organization. We do not, or at least should not, leave our values at the door when we enter the workplace. There is less consensus, however, about whether a corporation itself can owe moral obligations independent of the individuals within the organization.

While it seems clear that employees, customers, and investors believe that corporations are moral actors, the matter is less settled among philosophers and economists. A corporation is recognized as a *legal entity* that is capable of owning property, making contracts, being a party to legal proceedings, and so on. On the other hand, it can act only through human beings. Does it therefore make sense to speak of a corporation (or other business organization) as being a *moral agent* in addition to being a legal entity?

The View That Corporations are Not Moral Agents

The most widely advanced view that corporations cannot have moral obligations is that of philosopher John Ladd, who regards corporations as purely formal organizations analogous to programmable robots or machines. Machines have neither a will nor any

---

[165] Jeff Frooman, *Socially Irresponsible and Illegal Behavior and Shareholder Wealth: A Meta-Analysis of Event Studies,* 36 BUSINESS AND SOCIETY 221 (1997).
[166] LYNN SHARP PAINE, VALUE SHIFT 161 (2003).
[167] John Plender, *Inside Track: Morals Pay Dividends,* FINANCIAL TIMES, Sept. 18, 2002.

freedom of action. Similarly, according to Ladd, a corporation is merely an aggregation of legally binding documents such as a state charter and the corporate bylaws, organizational charts, operating procedures, and customs. The human cogs in this machine are role-players. Moreover, they are replaceable and often virtually interchangeable. Rule-governed activities and impersonal operating procedures prevent the application, or even the hint, of moral responsibility. Support for Ladd's view may be found, among other places, in Chief Justice John Marshall's description of a corporation as

> ...an artificial being, invisible, intangible, and existing only in contemplation of law. Being the mere creature of law, it possesses only those properties which the charter of creation confers upon it, either expressly, or as incidental to its very existence. These are such as are supposed best calculated to effect the object for which it was created.[168]

The fact that corporations are mere "artificial being(s)," or "creature(s) of law," does seem to support the argument that corporations cannot be moral agents with separate moral obligations. The lifeless pieces of paper that bring the corporation into existence and provide governing rules for its operation do not provide it with autonomy or reason. Therefore, we must look elsewhere for support if we are to argue that corporations are moral agents.

The View That Corporations Do Have Moral Responsibilities

We mentioned that violations of moral obligations frequently cannot be traced to a particular individual within a corporation. As a rule, most actions and inactions of relatively large corporations cannot be tallied as the sum of individual actions—the whole is truly greater than the sum of its parts. As a result, individuals tend to escape moral accountability, leaving the practical question of how to align responsibility with damage caused by unethical activity within a firm. This fact, in itself, provides considerable support for the argument that corporations should be viewed as separate moral agents so that accountability is not avoided altogether.

Organization theory's concept of *group dynamics* indicates that groups of employees often behave very differently than any single employee would have behaved in isolation, because the dynamics of the group transcend individual reason and autonomy. People sometimes just get "caught up in the spirit of things." Examples range all the way from the lynch mob to a corporate board that makes an ethically questionable decision despite the fact that each of its individual members may have high personal moral standards. We find the phenomenon not only in groups of co-equal members, but also in chains of command. For example, managers at the top may set policies and give orders but deny any responsibility for conduct by their subordinates that they did not intend. Similarly, we often find those at the bottom denying responsibility because they did not make the policy and they themselves intended no harm; they were "just carrying out orders." Several complex factors seem to be responsible for the peculiarities of group dynamics in corporations and other large organizations.

First, because the action is motivated by corporate purposes rather than personal reasons, participating individuals may not view their conduct as really their own. If they do not associate the action with themselves as human beings, they are less likely to apply their own personal moral standards to it.

Second, a member of a group may feel that there is "safety in numbers." As the

---

[168] *Dartmouth College*, 17 U.S. 518 (1819).

number of individual participants in group action increases, each member's feeling of anonymity may also increase. Even if a person does recognize and feel somewhat responsible for the moral consequences of his group's proposed action, he nevertheless may go along with a plan because he doubts that he personally will ever be called upon to defend it. *Moral diffusion* occurs.

Third, formal lines of authority and accountability within the organization may be fuzzy, thus increasing the chances that no single person really feels responsible. When people do not feel responsible, they are less likely to act responsibly.

Fourth, communication among individuals within the decision-making group may be less than perfect, and thus different individuals or subgroups may be acting on the basis of somewhat different facts and assumptions. One individual or subgroup within the organization may not be completely aware of the total picture, leading to the classic situation of the "right hand not knowing what the left hand is doing."

Ultimately, some argue that it makes sense to visit responsibility and accountability upon corporations and other artificial business actors because that will increase the likelihood that their owners and controllers will take actions to prevent individual employees or groups of employees from making unethical decisions. The organizational form tends to disperse responsibility in such a way that individual employees do not feel personally to blame for illicit conduct. To counteract that effect, society can visit moral responsibility (and perhaps legal liability) upon the firm, hoping that its managers will act to minimize wrongdoing that could injure it.

CORPORATE SOCIAL RESPONSIVENESS

If we accept the notion that corporations are moral agents and thus owe moral obligations separate and apart from those of its employees, another question arises. Is it appropriate for a corporation to not only not do wrong things, but do good things? Should a corporation expend corporate resources "doing good" by meeting societal needs? Such actions are sometimes described by the phrase "corporate social responsibility" (CSR), but "responsiveness" may describe the idea better than "responsibility." Going further, if it is *appropriate* for a corporation to do these kinds of things, is there actually an *obligation* to do them?

We first must recognize that questions about corporate social responsiveness do not necessarily arise every time a corporation's management considers spending corporate funds for a socially worthwhile cause such as helping a local elementary school offer enrichment programs for gifted students. Voluntarily responding to community needs often can be justified solely on economic grounds. Such actions can provide excellent promotional opportunities for the company and enhance its reputation and goodwill in a variety of ways. Also improving the local community may improve the company's workforce and even its property values. Essentially, social responsiveness can provide some of the same economic benefits to a corporation that we mentioned earlier in our discussion of whether complying with the moral minimum can produce such benefits. There is substantial evidence that many firms that have earned much reputational capital by being good corporate citizens can benefit in all sorts of ways from having that capital in the bank, especially in times of distress. It is at least arguable that we should not put any less value on a corporation's voluntary contributions to society, just because management was motivated by the company's self-interest. Indeed, the motives of managers may have been very complex and indeterminate.

Our main question here, though, is how to deal with the issue on moral grounds. Is socially responsive conduct appropriate regardless of whether it pays? And are there any circumstances in which it is morally required? The answers to these questions depend on your view of the relationship of corporations to investors and society.

The Agents of Capital View

One of the most well-known proponents of the view that corporations do not owe a moral duty to be socially responsive is Milton Friedman, a Nobel laureate in economics and an influential spokesman on the role of corporations in society. To begin with, Friedman does not view corporations as moral agents; only managers and employees as individuals have moral status. In addition, he contends that there is no obligation to spend corporate resources correcting problems the company did not cause and, going even further, he asserts that it is not even appropriate for the company's managers to do so. They are *agents of capital*, that is, agents of the shareholders who own the corporation and provide its capital. As such, their only duty is to earn as much money as possible for the shareholders, within the limits of the law and customary ethical practices.

Unless specially approved by shareholder resolution, decisions concerning the use of corporate resources to do good necessarily are made by individual managers. According to Friedman, it is completely inappropriate for them to do so. Corporate managers are free to devote their own time and money to whatever pursuits they deem morally or socially appropriate, but when they divert corporate resources to such projects they breach their duty of loyalty to shareholders. Friedman finds the social responsiveness movement to be a "fundamentally subversive doctrine" that resembles theft—managers are using "someone else's money." The proper function of government is to attend to matters of the common good and social welfare. Corporate managers are not, by training or otherwise, equipped to do that, and even if they were, it would be intolerable in a democracy for unelected, unaccountable "civil servants" to be charged with the responsibility of improving general societal welfare. While government might be slow and unresponsive in addressing current social problems, the insistence that this gap be filled by corporate action is just an acknowledgment of defeat by proponents of corporate social responsiveness who "have failed to persuade a majority of their fellow citizens to be of like mind and [who] are seeking to attain by undemocratic procedures what they cannot attain by democratic procedures."[169]

Another argument along the same lines is that when a social or religious organization or a government agency attempts to meet the needs of society, it usually does so with resources that were placed under the organization's control because of the merits of its social objectives. For example, grants from the American Cancer Society to researchers seeking a cure for cancer are made from funds that were donated to the Society because of the knowledge that the money would be used to fight the disease. Because of scarce resources, there is a "competition among good causes." Although it is unfortunate that all such needs cannot be fully met, this competition provides a method for roughly measuring the relative importance and value to the public of particular social needs. This prioritizing of needs by the marketplace is a very imperfect process that will always leave worthy needs unsatisfied. It does, however, introduce some necessary utilitarianism into the allocation of resources by

---

[169] Milton Friedman, A Friedman Doctrine—The Social Responsibility of Business Is to Increase Its Profits, NEW YORK TIMES MAGAZINE, Sept. 13, 1970, 6, 13.

reducing the chances that too much will go to causes that benefit too few. On the other hand, resources come into a corporation solely because of its business success, unless shareholders invest with the explicit understanding that certain corporate moneys will be spent on identified good causes. Thus, when managers use corporate funds to do good, the needs they meet have not withstood the test of this "market for donated funds." Hence, under the Agents of Capital view, corporations do not owe a moral obligation to society. They owe a legal obligation to follow the law, but no more.

The Agents of Society View

There are those who argue that it is both appropriate and morally obligatory for corporations to contribute to the correction of problems they did not cause. They place this duty on the corporation as a moral agent, as well as on managers whose individual and group decisions energize the company. In a speech to the Harvard Business School in 1969, Henry Ford II stated: "The terms of the contract between industry and society are changing. . . . Now we are being asked to serve a wider range of human values and to accept an obligation to members of the public with whom we have no commercial transactions."[170] His words were foreshadowed by those of his grandfather some two generations earlier. "For a long time people believed that the only purpose of industry is to make a profit. They were wrong. Its purpose is to serve the general welfare."[171]

This notion of a "social contract" forms the foundation for many of the arguments that corporate social responsiveness is morally required. Under this view, a corporation is the result of a contract between those forming the corporation and the society that permits its creation. Thus, the corporation has a contract-like obligation to contribute positively to society, and the corporation's managers are not just agents of the shareholders but are also agents of society. One noted proponent of this view, philosopher Thomas Donaldson, hypothesized the existence of a society in which individuals always work and produce alone, and never in corporate form. A society such as this, composed of rational persons, would permit the legal creation of corporations only if the benefits to the public are great enough to justify the privileges granted to corporations and to outweigh the potential drawbacks. The privileges include limited liability—only the corporate entity and its assets are liable for corporate debts, not the individual shareholders or managers. This limited liability can come at a cost to other members of society. One potential drawback is that permitting corporations to exist generally leads to much larger aggregations of resources being under the effective control of a smaller number of people. Large resource accumulations in corporations can bring both economic and political power that few, if any, individuals could ever match. Such power can create risks for society and must therefore be held responsible for the injuries caused by exercise of that power.

Supporters of the agents of society view also use the same basic line of reasoning as those who argue that individuals have a moral obligation to do good. These arguments were discussed earlier. Similarly, for those wishing to build a rational argument in favor of morally required corporate social responsiveness, the same limits that were applied to the individual's obligation to do good would apply to the corporation's duty to be socially responsive. So, proponents of the Agents of Society view would answer that corporations do

---

[170] RICHARD C. CHEWNING ET AL., BUSINESS THROUGH THE EYES OF FAITH 207 (1990).
[171] THOMAS DONALDSON, CORPORATIONS AND MORALITY (1982).

have a duty to engage in socially responsive conduct.

As this debate continues among academics, it is interesting to note that in a major survey of 15,000 managers worldwide, in no country did a majority of managers believe that the only legitimate purpose of a company is to make a profit.[172] Although late to the party, in August 2019, the Business Roundtable, in a statement signed by 181 CEOs across America, issued a statement renouncing shareholder primacy as the guiding star for companies:

> Americans deserve an economy that allows each person to succeed through hard work and creativity and to lead a life of meaning and dignity. We believe the free-market system is the best means of generating good jobs, a strong and sustainable economy, innovation, a healthy environment and economic opportunity for all.
>
> Businesses play a vital role in the economy by creating jobs, fostering innovation and providing essential goods and services. Businesses make and sell consumer products; manufacture equipment and vehicles; support the national defense; grow and produce food; provide health care; generate and deliver energy; and offer financial, communications and other services that underpin economic growth.
>
> While each of our individual companies serves its own corporate purpose, we share a fundamental commitment to all of our stakeholders. We commit to:

- Delivering value to our customers. We will further the tradition of American companies leading the way in meeting or exceeding customer expectations.
- Investing in our employees. This starts with compensating them fairly and providing important benefits. It also includes supporting them through training and education that help develop new skills for a rapidly changing world. We foster diversity and inclusion, dignity and respect.
- Dealing fairly and ethically with our suppliers. We are dedicated to serving as good partners to the other companies, large and small, that help us meet our missions.
- Supporting the communities in which we work. We respect the people in our communities and protect the environment by embracing sustainable practices across our businesses.
- Generating long-term value for shareholders, who provide the capital that allows companies to invest, grow and innovate. We are committed to transparency and effective engagement with shareholders.

> Each of our stakeholders is essential. We commit to deliver value to all of them, for the future success of our companies, our communities and our country.

Much of the movement toward CSR in the U.S. has been driven by activists. For example, the GAP stores faced fierce criticism and consumer boycotts regarding the sourcing of their products. GAP responded by deploying more than 80 employees whose sole responsibility was to ensure that factories around the world that produce clothing for GAP complied with ethical sourcing criteria when buying supplies. NIKE, facing similar criticism and boycotts arising from labor conditions in its third-world factors, quadrupled the number of employees dealing with labor practices. Because their customers expect them to act responsibly, both GAP and NIKE found it worth the expense to try to ensure that their labor practices were not inconsistent with their customers' values.

Sustainability

Sustainability has been called "CSR's cousin." A 1987 United Nations commission

---

[172] CHARLES HAMPDEN-TURNER & ALFONS TROMPENAARS, THE SEVEN CULTURES OF CAPITALISM (1993).

defined "sustainable development" as "development that meets the needs of the present without compromising the ability of future generations to meet its needs." In a world of finite resources, keeping an eye on sustainability just makes sense. As with the broader concept of CSR, many firms believe that they owe a moral obligation to act in a sustainable way; other firms might disagree but still believe that they and their shareholders can do well by incorporating sustainability into their long-term strategies.

Wal-Mart "got religion" in this area many years ago. Wal-Mart has not only made a commitment to doing business in more sustainable ways itself, but has demanded more sustainable practices from its suppliers who, given the size of Wal-Mart as a customer, are typically disposed toward meeting Wal-Mart's demands. In its 2010 progress report on sustainability, Wal-Mart reported, among other developments:

- Its carbon emissions per $1 million in sales had declined by 16% since 2005
- Its truck fleet efficiency had improved by 60% since 2005, resulting in 145,000 fewer metric tons of CO_2 emissions
- 127 million pounds of food that previously would have been discarded was donated to food banks
- Wal-Mart had reused or recycled 64% of its garbage
- All personal computers sold in U.S. stores met the EU's stringent hazardous substance rules
- All TVs sold by Wal-Mart in the U.S. were 67% more energy efficient than in 2008[173]

Wal-Mart is a flawed company with many imperfect practices, but its efforts in the sustainability arena are applauded by most observers and are emblematic of "how sustainability moved to the top of the global business agenda."[174] In many areas, companies have gone well beyond governments in promoting environmentally-friendly developments. From 2010-2012, Google invested nearly a billion dollars in renewable energy projects, such as wind farms. The Danish toy maker LEGO has spent half a billion doing the same. Ditto IKEA. These companies hope to serve themselves as they serve the planet:

> …many companies undoubtedly feel more immediate pressure to overhaul their business models amid forecasts that the world's population will jump from 7 b[illion] to 9 b[illion] in 2050, largely driven by emerging economies. The consequent strains on water, food and energy resources have encouraged many executives to imagine how their business might cope with—or exploit—a world of $150-a-barrel water, let alone oil.[175]

Paul Polman, who runs the Unilever conglomerate, has told investors that if they disagree with his aggressive green policies, they should keep their money and not put it into Unilever stock.[176]

Social Enterprise/Social Entrepreneurship/Social Investing

While many people in business are primarily concerned with reforming the practices of for-profit companies in order to get them to act in a socially-responsive and sustainable way, others are becoming more and more interested in social enterprise, social entrepreneurship, and social investing. They want to put their business skills to use helping

---

[173] EDWARD HUMES, FORCE OF NATURE: THE UNLIKELY STORY OF WAL-MART'S GREEN REVOLUTION 230-232 (2011).

[174] ARON CRAMER & ZACHARY KARABELL, SUSTAINABLE EXCELLENCE: THE FUTURE OF BUSINESS IN A FAST-CHANGING WORLD 15 (2010).

[175] Pilita Clark, *Capitalist Conservationists,* FINANCIAL TIMES, June 5, 2012, at 7.

[176] *Id.*

nonprofit firms and solving society's ills, rather than focusing simply on making profits.

A priority in many business schools these days is creation of courses, programs, and case competitions in these areas.[177] Increasing numbers of people want the focus of their careers to be making a difference in communities they care about rather than making money doing jobs they find meaningless or worse. Many for-profit companies are finding that they can attract better employees by offering them opportunities to improve the world while doing their jobs.

HOW TO ENCOURAGE EMPLOYEES TO ACT ETHICALLY

As we saw from the prior discussion, one's opinion as to whether corporations owe an ethical duty to society tends to depend on one's political orientation. Consequently, business leaders must first decide how their organization will act regarding the ethical issues it faces as a firm. The executives must set the ethical tone for the company and, in turn, provides guidance for employees to follow. Shall it exist only to maximize shareholder return? Are the interests of employees and other stakeholders important? Should the firm give to charity, sacrifice bottom line profits to save employee jobs, or otherwise act to advance broader interests of society? The answers to these questions originate with management, but then permeate throughout the corporation. The Covid-19 pandemic forced many firms across the world to face these questions.

The other side of the coin for business leaders relates to employees. A corporation, for example, will typically fare better if its employees act ethically and (especially) legally. This involves more than wishing. After Citibank suffered a series of embarrassing scandals, its new CEO, Chuck Prince—a lawyer no less—was utterly exasperated. "I never thought before that you had to say to people, 'You've got to make your numbers, and, by the way, don't forget not to violate the law.'"[178] Ethical compliance inside organizations does not happen automatically. How does a firm improve employees' ethical performance? This section offers some hints.

Developing an Ethical Corporate Culture

Just as individuals who wish to act ethically should develop their own moral identity, organizations that wish their employees to act ethically should develop their own ethics-friendly corporate culture. Before we focus on various important steps in creating an ethical organization, such as hiring ethical people, training them, incentivizing them and the like, note the following summary of the literature regarding how to create an ethical firm culture:

> Leadership is often mentioned as one of the most important elements of an organization's ethical culture. Leaders who are perceived as being able to create and support an ethical culture in their organizations are those who represent, communicate, and role model high ethical standards, emphasize attention to goals other than economic, engage in "ethics talk," and maintain a long-term view of relationships within and outside the organization. These top managers create and maintain an ethical culture by consistently behaving in an ethical fashion and encouraging others to behave in such a manner as well.
>
> An ethical culture is associated with a structure that provides for equally distributed

---

[177] Anjli Raval, *Students Take on the Social Innovation Challenge,* FINANCIAL TIMES, April 23, 2012, at 10.

[178] RICHARD BOOKSTABER, A DEMON OF OUR OWN DESIGN: MARKETS, HEDGE FUNDS, AND THE PERILS OF FINANCIAL INNOVATION 133 (2007).

authority and shared accountability. It also has policies such as an ethical code of conduct that is clear, well communicated, is specific about expected procedures and practices, thoroughly understood, and enforced. In addition, incentive systems are deliberately and clearly tied to behaving in concert with the code of ethics and accomplishment of non-economic goals in addition to economic outcomes. The socialization process of an organization with an ethical culture reinforces the practice of the values in a mission statement on a daily basis; so behavior is focused on issues of health and safety of employees, customer and community responsiveness, and fairness. In fact, employee perceptions of fairness or justice in an organization have been found to have central importance in creating an ethical culture. ...

The informal elements of a cultural system ... include norms for behavior that are consistent with the ethical standards or the code of conduct, mission, and decision-making processes. ... Other elements of the informal culture include the communication and belief in heroes and role models, along with myths and stories about how ethical standards of the organization have been upheld and revered by members. Such heroes and stories transcend the formal organizational culture and inspire others to behave in an ethical fashion. ... Finally, the language used by organizational members plays a crucial role in shaping behavior in the informal ethical culture. Use of moral or ethics "talk" to address problem-solving and decision-making situations creates an awareness of the ethical dimension of such processes. Ethical cultures have leaders and members who engage in ethics talk regularly in pursuit of organizational activities.[179]

Hiring Ethical People

Lamar Pierce of the Olin Business School at Washington University in St. Louis, who studies motivation and corruption in organizations, stresses that the best way to ensure that you have an honest firm is to hire honest people. While hiring people who are skilled, intelligent and hard-working is great, it is even better if they are honest, kind, and well-intentioned. Warren Buffett has said that "in looking for people to hire, you look for three qualities: integrity, intelligence, and energy. And if you don't have the first, the other two will kill you." This is particularly true of leaders, for studies also show that, unfortunately, employees tend to more readily mirror a leader's unethical actions than ethical actions.[180]

Clearly what are sometimes called "internal control factors" (such as skills, abilities, emotions, and compulsions) can definitely have an impact on whether people will make ethical decisions and take ethical actions. But evidence indicates that "unethical behavior in organizations is a function of both individual characteristics and contextual factors."[181] Indeed, these contextual or "external control factors," primarily arising from the nature of the organizational setting in which individuals find themselves, are likely the more influential factors,[182] so the rest of the chapter focuses on them.

As noted earlier, people tend to try to please authority figures. If authority figures demand ethical actions, employees are much more likely to follow the rules than if they do

[179] Alexandre Ardichvili et al., *Characteristics of Ethical Business Cultures,* 85 JOURNAL OF BUSINESS ETHICS 445 (2008).

[180] David De Cremer, *On the Psychology of Preventing and Dealing with Ethical Failures: A Behavioral Ethics Approach, in* MANAGERIAL ETHICS: MANAGING THE PSYCHOLOGY OF MORALITY 111 (Marshall Schminke, ed., 2010).

[181] Alexandre Ardichvili et al., *Characteristics of Ethical Business Cultures,* 85 JOURNAL OF BUSINESS ETHICS 445 (2008).

[182] Brenda L. Flannery & Douglas R. May, *Environmental Ethical Decision Making in the U.S. Metal-Finishing Industry,* 43 ACADEMY OF MANAGEMENT JOURNAL 642 (2000).

not. People also tend to attempt to fit in with their peer group. Therefore, if the office culture is one of honesty, people will tend to act differently (and better) than if the corporate culture is one of dishonesty.[183] Establishing an ethics-friendly organizational culture is critically important for firms that wish to avoid the substantial costs that can be incurred when employees act unethically.

Treating Employees Well

When employees are treated well, they tend to view their employers' authority over them as legitimate. This is important because much evidence indicates that employees are more likely to comply with employers' rules when they view the firm as legitimate. When companies empower their employees by treating them with respect and cooperation, they have a much better chance of fostering ethical values in those employees that will result in rule-following.[184] The evidence is clear that not only do employees value a just result; they also value fair procedures. Almost everyone is more willing to accept a result with which they disagree if they believe in the inherent fairness of the process that led to the result. Process matters.

One reason it is particularly important for firms to treat employees fairly and for managers to act ethically is the concept of "moral spillover." Lawrence Friedman asked: "If a person sees unfairness, or illegitimacy, or unworthiness of trust in one instance, how far does his disillusionment extend? How much of his attitude spills over into other areas and into his actual behavior?"[185] It turns out that the answer is: "quite a lot." Psychologists found that experimental subjects who read about a legal trial where outcomes opposed their moral convictions were more angry, were less willing to accept the outcome, *and were more likely to take a borrowed pen* than similar subjects who read about a trial where the outcome was consistent with their moral convictions. In another experiment, participants who recalled another person's moral violation were more likely to cheat on an experimental task. The authors surmised that the 1992 Los Angeles riots following acquittal of four officers accused of beating Rodney King might have been a manifestation of such moral spillover.[186] Substantial evidence indicates that employees who work in unfair and otherwise dysfunctional organizations can become disaffected and therefore more likely to commit ethical and legal violations.

Codes of Ethics

Even employees with strong moral values who are inclined to act ethically will have a better chance of doing so if their employer sends a message that ethical conduct is expected and will be rewarded. Therefore, corporate leaders who wish to improve the ethical performance of employees should definitely adopt a corporate code of ethics or code of conduct. Having a code of ethics is not the only element of an ethics-friendly corporate culture, and certainly is not a cure-all, but it can be an important step. Such a code ensures

---

[183] Tom R. Tyler, *Cooperation in Groups,* in SOCIAL PSYCHOLOGY AND ECONOMICS 155 (De Cremer et al., eds. 2006).

[184] Tom R. Tyler, *Cooperation in Groups,* in SOCIAL PSYCHOLOGY AND ECONOMICS 155 (De Cremer et al., eds. 2006).

[185] LAWRENCE FRIEDMAN, THE LEGAL SYSTEM: A SOCIAL SCIENCE PERSPECTIVE 118 (1975).

[186] Elizabeth Mullen & Janice Nadler, "Moral Spillovers: The Effect of Moral Violations on Deviant Behavior" (2008), *available at* http://ssrn.com/abstract=1129806.

that the firm's leaders think about how important acting ethically actually is. Its adoption signals to employees, investors, customers and others that the firm is serious about its desire to act ethically. The code's provisions not only inform employees regarding their employer's values, but can also guide them to proper resolution of ethical dilemmas they face. Empirical evidence indicates that codes of ethics can influence the work climate positively, increase the moral awareness of employees, and ultimately result in more ethical behavior.[187] Experiments show that bringing ethical principles to people's minds by having them read or sign an honor code significantly reduced or eliminated unethical behavior,[188] just as reminding subjects of the basic principles of right and wrong before they have an opportunity to cheat for financial gain dramatically reduces the cheating compared to that by subjects not so reminded.[189]

Of course, adopting a code of ethics is not ever a panacea. Such codes are often just pieces of paper with no meaningful impact at all. An example would be Enron's RICE code of ethics that emphasized Respect, Integrity, Communication, and Excellence. Its provisions were waived by the directors in a tragic mistake and observed mainly in the breach by many top officers. Academic research in the area indicates that in order to improve the chances that a code of ethics will have an efficacious impact, companies should consider the following suggestions.[190]

- Engage employees in writing and revising the code. Active engagement can lead to more employee "buy-in" and more serious attempts to comply with the letter and spirit of the code.
- Word the code in a straight-forward fashion and pervasively communicate it.
- Reward employees who behave consistently with the code, and punish employees who violate its provisions.
- Actually use the code to resolve ethical issues. The code should be invoked in corporate strategy meetings. Lower level employees are much more likely to view the code as an important document if they see it actually utilized by managers.
- Remember that strengthening the structures, processes, and values that reinforce ethical behavior is a never-ending process. It must ever and always be a priority.

In every way possible, including some just suggested, the firm should actively and explicitly demonstrate "buy-in" by top brass. More than symbolic activity is needed, but symbolism is important also. There is substantial evidence that when leaders act ethically (for example, by giving generously to charities), subordinates will tend to follow suit (by giving more generously themselves than they typically do). On the other hand, when CEOs and other top officers cross ethical lines, then other employees "think it's okay to go over the line themselves."[191]

---

[187] Craig V. Van Sandt et al., *An Examination of the Relationship Between Ethical Work Climate and Moral Awareness,* 68 JOURNAL OF BUSINESS ETHICS 409 (2006).

[188] Lisa L. Shu et al., "Dishonest Deed, Clear Conscience: Self-Preservation through Moral Disengagement and Motivated Forgetting," (2009), *available at* http://ssrn.com/abstract=1323803.

[189] Nina Mazar et al., *The Dishonesty of Honest People: A Theory of Self-Concept Maintenance,* 45 JOURNAL OF MARKETING RESEARCH 633 (2008).

[190] Betsy Stevens, *Corporate Ethical Codes: Effective Instruments for Influencing Behavior,* 78 JOURNAL OF BUSINESS ETHICS 601, 614 (2008).

[191] Simon Gachter, *Conditional Cooperation: Behavioral Regularities from the Lab and the Field and Their Policy Implications, in* ECONOMICS AND PSYCHOLOGY 20, 41 (Bruno Frey & Alois Stutzer, eds., 2007) (quoting Unisys CEO Lawrence Weinstein).

We saw in an earlier chapter how much influence environment has over the decision making of individuals. It should not be surprising, then, that there is substantial evidence that employees will be more "morally aware" (able to spot the ethical dimensions of business issues) if they work in an "ethical work climate" wherein the organization prompts employees to think of the impact of their actions on more than just the firm's profits and the employee's paycheck.[192]

Ethics Training

Corporate America spends tens of millions of dollars a year on ethics training. The best suggestion for making that expenditure worthwhile is to make the training as "real" as possible. It should be specific. It should relate to the employees' real ethical concerns. It should be vivid, if possible. One corporate officer gave employees the "opportunity" to speak directly to consumers who had been injured by their careless and arguably unethical decisions. Another took his subordinates on a nature hike in the ecosystem surrounding the firm's manufacturing plant so they could see first-hand what damage environmental pollution might cause.[193]

Ethics training should inform employees in no uncertain terms that acting ethically is part of their job. Trevino and Nelson point out that employees enter work organizations in a state of "role readiness." They are prepared to do the job that is expected of them. If acting ethically, even in the form of whistleblowing, is clearly part of their job description, they will be more likely to act in that way.[194]

Ethics training also teaches employees to "talk the talk," which may not be as important as "walking the walk," but can help:

> The use of ethical language may be related to decision-making behavior. In one study, individuals who discussed their decision-making process using the language of ethics were more likely to be the ones who made an ethical decision. These people talked about ethics, morals, honesty, integrity, values, and good character. Those who had made the unethical decision were more likely to recount the decision in the more traditional business language of costs and benefits.[195]

Whistleblowers

Whistle-blowers present a dilemma for even well-meaning corporations. Whistle-blowers can be misinformed. They can make mistakes in judgment. They can overreact to minor matters. They can be vindictive. They can be delusional.

On the other hand, they can also be courageously correct. They can serve as conscience of the firm. They can prevent or short-circuit egregious and expensive ethical lapses.

Sarbanes-Oxley takes the point of view that the good whistleblowers can do outweighs the bad. It requires the audit committee of public corporations to set up a mechanism for whistle-blowers to communicate to the board. There is some evidence that

---

[192] Craig V. VanSandt et al., *An Examination of the Relationship Between Ethical Work Climate and Moral Awareness,* 68 JOURNAL OF BUSINESS ETHICS 409 (2006).

[193] For additional suggestions on how to provide effective ethical training, *see* THOMAS OBERLECHNER, THE PSYCHOLOGY OF ETHICS IN THE FINANCE AND INVESTMENT INDUSTRY 67-71 (2007).

[194] LINDA K. TREVINO & KATHERINE NELSON, MANAGING BUSINESS ETHICS 195-99 (2007).

[195] *Id.* at 291.

SOX's drafters made the right call in resolving this dilemma. Most firms suffer employee frauds at one time or another, but one study found that firms that had installed anonymous whistle-blower hot-lines caught frauds, on average, at half the size of frauds that bloomed at firms without such hot-lines. The Dodd-Frank Act of 2010 added further protections for whistleblowers.

Structuring Compensation

Although social motives, such as the desire to please superiors and to fit in with other group members, play a strong role in motivating people in the workplace (and elsewhere), more instrumental motivations, such as rewards and punishments, can also have an impact. Compensation can incentivize hard work, creative work, and, if poorly structured, dishonest work. Structuring incentives to encourage employees to work hard, but still obey the law and the firm's ethical principles, is very difficult business. Experts recommend several considerations to keep in mind.

First, be reasonable. "Aggressive goal setting within an organization will foster an organizational climate ripe for unethical behavior."[196] Many dot.com boom companies proved that outrageous compensation can create incentives for outrageous conduct. The Enron story is particularly illustrative. When executives can earn hundreds of millions of dollars by fudging the numbers, they are likely to do so. The Wells Fargo scandal is similarly instructive—employees were given aggressive sales goals that were impossible to meet without cheating. So they cheated.[197] Volkswagen set sales goals that were dependent on its diesel engines meeting emissions standards that VW's engineers did not have the technology to meet without cheating. So they cheated.[198]

Second, do not overemphasize performance measures that can be manipulated. Enron remains the poster child for this error. Top Enron managers were able to garner tens of millions of dollars in performance bonuses that were based on little more than their own estimates of how well a deal would perform over a lengthy future period. Wells Fargo employees were given the job of selling impossibly high numbers of products to customers, so they just made the sales up, creating millions of accounts that the customers had not ordered.[199] In the early 1990s, Sears, Roebuck & Co. imposed a sales quota on its auto repair staff of $147/hour. This aggressive goal caused Sears employees to widely overcharge for work and to perform unnecessary repairs. Ultimately, Sears took the repair staff off commission, but their wrongdoing caused Sears to enter into multimillion dollar settlements with many states that had brought consumer deception and fraud suits. During the height of the subprime mortgage excess, Washington Mutual (WaMu) mortgage brokers could make $40,000 on a single loan, which gave them a strong incentive to approve loans whether or not there was much hope of the borrower repaying it. This is part of the reason WaMu is no longer with us.[200]

---

[196] Lisa Ordonez et al., *Goals Gone Wild: The Systematic Side Effects of Over-Prescribing Goal-Setting* (2009), *available at* http://ssrn.com/abstract=1332071.

[197] Bethany McLean, *How Wells Fargo's Cutthroat Corporate Culture Allegedly Drove Bankers to Fraud,* VANITY FAIR, May 31, 2017.

[198] JACK INGRAM, FASTER, HIGHER, FARTHER: THE INSIDE STORY OF THE VOLKSWAGEN SCANDAL (2017).

[199] Adam Davidson, *How Regulation Failed with Wells Fargo,* THE NEW YORKER, Sept. 12, 2016.

[200] Gretchen Morgenson, *Was There A Loan It Didn't Like?,* N.Y. TIMES, Nov. 2, 2008, at BU1.

Third, as noted above, reward and promote those who do the right thing, just as you punish those who do the wrong thing. Not only did WaMu reward mortgage brokers for making loans, pretty much regardless of the borrower's ability to repay, it also punished brokers who tried to apply some reasonable standards to the loan applications they were presented.[201]

Fourth, remember that a firm must walk the walk, not just talk the talk. A two-hour lecture from an ethics officer sends a message. A five-minute performance review can either add substantial credibility to the ethics officer's message or completely cancel it out, depending on what happens during the performance review. If ethical acts are rewarded and unethical acts punished, that sends a clearer message than an army of ethics consultants can transmit.

In addition to rewarding ethical behavior, firms must also punish unethical behavior, which often involves creating credible surveillance systems that create reasonable risks of detection of employee rule-breaking.[202]

In a paper on goal-setting, four experts emphasized that errors in goal-setting can cause all sorts of problems, including unethical behavior:

> Goals narrow focus, such that employees may be less likely to recognize ethical issues. Goals also induce employees to rationalize their unethical behavior and can corrupt organizational cultures. *Multiple* safeguards may be necessary to ensure ethical behavior while attaining goals (e.g., leaders as exemplars of ethical behavior, making the costs of cheating far greater than the benefit, strong oversight).[203]

Vigilance

Acting ethically must be a corporate priority every day. A firm's managers and other employees cannot let down their guard. Minor changes in product quality controls, in the rigor of financial controls, in the content of sales brochures can begin a downward spiral in corporate moral culture. In November 2008, Lee Scott, CEO at Wal-Mart, told suppliers in China that he "firmly believe[d] that a company that cheats on overtime and on the age of its labor, that dumps its scraps and chemicals in our rivers, that does not pay its taxes and honor its contracts—will ultimately cheat on the quality of its products."[204] Perhaps Aristotle's virtue ethics has lessons to teach corporations as well as individuals.

Even in retrospect, it is difficult to tell the exact point at which Enron went from being a creative company with an admirable code of ethics to a firm where impressions were everything and the cold hard truth meant little.[205] But the lesson is clear: if firms do not pay attention to acting ethically every single day, minor departures from fair and honest practices can hit a slippery slope and quickly snowball into ethical disaster. Gino and Bazerman have

---

[201] *Id.*

[202] Tom R. Tyler, *Cooperation in Groups,* in SOCIAL PSYCHOLOGY AND ECONOMICS 155 (De Cremer et al., eds. 2006).

[203] Lisa Ordonez et al., *Goals Gone Wild: The Systematic Side Effects of Over-Prescribing Goal-Setting* (2009), *available at* http://ssrn.com/abstract=1332071.

[204] *Wal-Mart Announces Global Responsible Sourcing Initiative at China Summit,* ASIA PULSE, Oct. 22, 2008.

[205] Many have said that an entire course in business ethics could be taught based solely on the Enron scandal, and Stephen Arbogast has undertaken to demonstrate the truth of that statement. STEPHEN V. ARBOGAST, RESISTING CORPORATE CORRUPTION: LESSONS IN PRACTICAL ETHICS FROM THE ENRON WRECKAGE (2008).

observed that "[m]anagers involved in business scandals often fail to notice the gradual change in their own internal standards until it is too late."[206]

Top managers set the ethical tone for corporations and they must monitor their own behavior with particular care. There is scholarly evidence, however, that top managers are particularly prone to exempting themselves from ethical guidelines. They have, after all, performed exceptionally well during their entire careers. Like everyone else, they tend to view themselves as more ethical than the average person and certainly more ethical than their competitors. It is often shocking how top corporate officials (like WorldCom's Bernie Ebbers) and high government officials (like New York's Eliot Spitzer) come to the view that the rules that apply to everyone else do not apply to them. Often, they do outrageous things with little or no effort to hide their wrongdoing because they become so convinced of their importance to their firm's mission,[207] which somehow justifies their exempting themselves from legal and ethical standards that apply to others.

ETHICS ON THE GLOBAL STAGE

Is it ethical to take a product banned as dangerous in the U.S. and sell it in foreign countries where it is not illegal? Is it ethical to treat female employees of foreign subsidiaries in ways that are consistent with the local culture but would be considered gender discrimination in the U.S.? Is it ethical to make a payment to a local police officer in a foreign nation in order to get police protection for a plant where such payments are technically illegal but universally paid in that nation?

When firms do business internationally, ethical complications can easily multiply. Simply being in unfamiliar terrain, geographically and culturally, can throw employees off their game. Clear thinking is harder. Confidence may be lacking. Due to cultural differences, it may be more difficult to even spot ethical issues, let alone resolve them effectively.

There can be little doubt that cultural issues vastly complicate the ethical world of global firms and their employees. For a U.S. firm, for example, to ignore local ethical norms and simply follow its own ethical standards without exception would exhibit ethical imperialism and likely invite many unnecessary conflicts with local employees, customers, governments, and others. To simply adopt local standards, on the other hand, could be similarly disastrous. Extreme ethical relativism ("Whatever works for the foreign nation works for us") can lead to application of foreign standards that are in striking conflict with a firm's core values. Finding principled ways to reach compromises on touchy ethical issues in the global economy can be famously difficult.

Some firms "go native," following local ethical customs as much as possible, but drawing the line at actions that would be illegal or in direct violation of the firm's core values. Other firms apply their own core values as much as possible, even at the risk of creating substantial friction with local employees, customers, and regulators. In matters of safety, some firms apply whichever standard is higher—their own internal standard or the local standards.

Because legal, ethical, and cultural differences can be so stark, difficult conflicts are inevitable. In the U.S. for example, hiring relatives is generally viewed as improper

---

[206] Francesca Gino & Max H. Bazerman, *Slippery Slopes and Misconduct: The Effect of Gradual Degradation on the Failure to Notice Unethical Behavior* (Harvard NOM Research Paper No. 06-01), http://ssrn.com/abstract=785987 (2005), at 6.

[207] TERRY L. PRICE, ETHICAL FAILURES IN LEADERSHIP (2005).

nepotism. It is typically prohibited in corporate codes of ethics as constituting a significant conflict of interest. However, in many other nations hiring relatives is viewed as sensible and even desirable as a demonstration of the importance of family ties.

Similarly, in the U.S. making payments to attract business is typically labeled illegal bribery, which is also clearly immoral. In many other nations, such payments are ubiquitous. In many nations it often seems nearly impossible to do many forms of business without paying bribes, yet those bribes would often violate the United States' Foreign Corrupt Practices Act of 1977[208] and the OECD (Organization for Economic Cooperation and Development) Convention on Combating Bribery of Foreign Public Officials. What are managers to do when they have been charged with launching a business in a foreign country and then learn that without making payments in violation of the FCPA it will be nearly impossible to gain any customers or to obtain necessary government licenses?

These are hugely important issues, both ethically and practically, for global ethical scandals can seriously damage even the strongest firms. America's Halliburton and Germany's Siemens paid fines of $559 million and $1.3 billion, respectively, to settle recent bribery charges. Shell's attempt to sink the Brent Spar oil rig in the North Sea attracted the attention of environmental activists that bought it a decade's worth of bad publicity. It had even worse luck in Nigeria when the government jailed and executed many environmental protestors who were upset about the environmental impact of a Shell gas production project. Reebok, Nike, Levi Strauss and other U.S. shoe and apparel manufacturers have faced consumer boycotts and other adverse actions over child labor practices. And, of course, Union Carbide's Bhopal, India disaster (an industrial gas leak that killed thousands and injured half a million) ranks high on the list of disastrous corporate actions in the international arena.

A thoughtful, if not necessarily easy to apply, approach was suggested by ethicists Donaldson and Dunfee.[209] Their approach, which they call "integrated social contract theory" (ISCT), is worth describing if for no other reason than to provoke thought regarding these complicated issues. Donaldson and Dunfee suggest that domestic ethical values cannot be completely absolute. Some account must be taken of local cultural standards. Giving gifts, for example, may in some nations be viewed as a completely proper method for building a commercial relationship between strangers. Those same gifts might be viewed as illegitimate bribes by commercial actors in other nations. How does a company from one of the latter nations make its way in one of the former nations?

Although the following description oversimplifies Donaldson and Dunfee's full concept, imagine a series of concentric circles.[210] In the middle is a circle labeled "Hypernorms." Hypernorms represent values that would be fully accepted in almost all cultures and organizations. They would include fundamental human rights and basic prescriptions common to most religions. Opposition to slavery, torture, piracy, and genocide would be examples of hypernorms. Indeed, Donaldson and Dunfee make an argument that prohibitions of bribery are hypernorms, although this is perhaps questionable. Companies and individual businesspeople should observe hypernorms no matter where in the world they are operating.

---

[208] The FCPA is discussed in the chapter on international law.

[209] THOMAS DONALDSON & THOMAS W. DUNFEE, TIES THAT BIND: A SOCIAL CONTRACTS APPROACH TO BUSINESS ETHICS (1999).

[210] *See* DONALDSON & DUNFEE, at 222.

Moving out from the center, the next concentric circle is labeled "Consistent Norms." Consistent norms represent values that are less universal and more culturally specific than hypernorms. Nonetheless, they are consistent with both with hypernorms and with other legitimate norms, including those from other economic cultures. Donaldson and Dunfee believe that most corporate credos (e.g., "We exist to serve to customer," "Our goal is to advance the health of individuals") would be examples of consistent norms. Again, most companies operating around the world should follow these consistent norms.

Donaldson and Dunfee label the next concentric circle out from the center as "Moral Free Space." In this area, companies find norms that are inconsistent with at least some other legitimate norms existing in other economic cultures, and may even be in mild tension with hypernorms (though not in direct conflict with them). These norms often express unique, but strongly held, cultural beliefs. They often require creativity to accommodate. Donaldson and Dunfee give as an example a company that insisted on using exactly the same sexual harassment exercises and lessons with Muslim managers in the Middle East that they used in their normal U.S. training. The clashing norms meant that the training did not go well at all. A little cultural adaptation was warranted.

Outside the third concentric circle are "Illegitimate Norms." These norms are incompatible with hypernorms, such as norms allowing torture, genocide, and mass rape. When values or practices infringe upon fundamental human rights, they fall into the "incompatible" zone of illegitimate norms. Donaldson and Dunfee give exposing workers to unreasonable levels of carcinogens as an example.

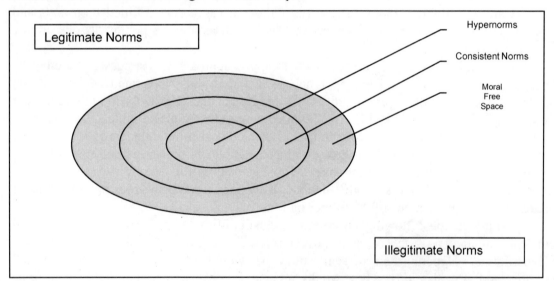

In an ideal world, global businesses would attend thoughtfully to ethical issues. If firms gave credence to hypernorms and recognized, where possible, the validity of cultural variations in norms, they would help to build toward a global consensus on the most important norms, which could add immeasurably to reducing world conflict.[211]

---

[211] *See* Jacob D. Rendtorff, "Towards Ethical Guidelines for International Business Corporations: Aspects of Global Corporate Citizenship," *available at* http://www.google.com/search?hl=en&rlz=1T4GGIH_enUS232US233&q=jacob+rendtorff+towards+ethical+guidelines